D1568732

University Casebook Series

December, 1991

ACCOUNTING AND THE LAW, Fourth Edition (1978), with Problems Pamphlet (Successor to Dohr, Phillips, Thompson & Warren)

George C. Thompson, Professor, Columbia University Graduate School of Business.
Robert Whitman, Professor of Law, University of Connecticut.
Ellis L. Phillips, Jr., Member of the New York Bar.
William C. Warren, Professor of Law Emeritus, Columbia University.

ACCOUNTING FOR LAWYERS, MATERIALS ON (1980)

David R. Herwitz, Professor of Law, Harvard University.

ADMINISTRATIVE LAW, Eighth Edition (1987), with 1989 Case Supplement and 1983 Problems Supplement (Supplement edited in association with Paul R. Verkuil, Dean and Professor of Law, Tulane University)

Walter Gellhorn, University Professor Emeritus, Columbia University.
Clark Byse, Professor of Law, Harvard University.
Peter L. Strauss, Professor of Law, Columbia University.
Todd D. Rakoff, Professor of Law, Harvard University.
Roy A. Schotland, Professor of Law, Georgetown University.

ADMIRALTY, Third Edition (1987), with 1991 Statute and Rule Supplement

Jo Desha Lucas, Professor of Law, University of Chicago.

ADVOCACY, see also Lawyering Process

AGENCY, see also Enterprise Organization

AGENCY—PARTNERSHIPS, Fourth Edition (1987)

Abridgement from Conard, Knauss & Siegel's Enterprise Organization, Fourth Edition.

AGENCY AND PARTNERSHIPS (1987)

Melvin A. Eisenberg, Professor of Law, University of California, Berkeley.

ANTITRUST: FREE ENTERPRISE AND ECONOMIC ORGANIZATION, Sixth Edition (1983), with 1983 Problems in Antitrust Supplement and 1991 Case Supplement

Louis B. Schwartz, Professor of Law, University of Pennsylvania.
John J. Flynn, Professor of Law, University of Utah.
Harry First, Professor of Law, New York University.

BANKRUPTCY, Second Edition (1989), with 1991 Case Supplement

Robert L. Jordan, Professor of Law, University of California, Los Angeles.
William D. Warren, Professor of Law, University of California, Los Angeles.

BANKRUPTCY AND DEBTOR–CREDITOR LAW, Second Edition (1988)

Theodore Eisenberg, Professor of Law, Cornell University.

UNIVERSITY CASEBOOK SERIES—Continued

BUSINESS ASSOCIATIONS, AGENCY, PARTNERSHIPS, AND CORPORATIONS (1991)

William A. Klein, Professor of Law, University of California, Los Angeles.
Mark Ramseyer, Professor of Law, University of California, Los Angeles.

BUSINESS CRIME (1990), with 1991 Case Supplement

Harry First, Professor of Law, New York University.

BUSINESS ORGANIZATION, see also Enterprise Organization

BUSINESS PLANNING (1991)

Franklin Gevurtz, Professor of Law, McGeorge School of Law.

BUSINESS PLANNING, Temporary Second Edition (1984)

David R. Herwitz, Professor of Law, Harvard University.

BUSINESS TORTS (1972)

Milton Handler, Professor of Law Emeritus, Columbia University.

CHILDREN IN THE LEGAL SYSTEM (1983), with 1990 Supplement (Supplement edited in association with Elizabeth S. Scott, Professor of Law, University of Virginia)

Walter Wadlington, Professor of Law, University of Virginia.
Charles H. Whitebread, Professor of Law, University of Southern California.
Samuel Davis, Professor of Law, University of Georgia.

CIVIL PROCEDURE, see Procedure

CIVIL RIGHTS ACTIONS (1988), with 1991 Supplement

Peter W. Low, Professor of Law, University of Virginia.
John C. Jeffries, Jr., Professor of Law, University of Virginia.

CLINIC, see also Lawyering Process

COMMERCIAL AND DEBTOR–CREDITOR LAW: SELECTED STATUTES, 1991 EDITION

COMMERCIAL LAW, Second Edition (1987)

Robert L. Jordan, Professor of Law, University of California, Los Angeles.
William D. Warren, Professor of Law, University of California, Los Angeles.

COMMERCIAL LAW, Fourth Edition (1985), with 1991 Case Supplement

E. Allan Farnsworth, Professor of Law, Columbia University.
John Honnold, Professor of Law, University of Pennsylvania.

COMMERCIAL PAPER, Third Edition (1984), with 1991 Case Supplement

E. Allan Farnsworth, Professor of Law, Columbia University.

COMMERCIAL PAPER, Second Edition (1987) (Reprinted from COMMERCIAL LAW, Second Edition (1987))

Robert L. Jordan, Professor of Law, University of California, Los Angeles.
William D. Warren, Professor of Law, University of California, Los Angeles.

COMMERCIAL PAPER AND BANK DEPOSITS AND COLLECTIONS (1967), with Statutory Supplement

William D. Hawkland, Professor of Law, University of Illinois.

UNIVERSITY CASEBOOK SERIES—Continued

COMMERCIAL TRANSACTIONS—Principles and Policies, Second Edition (1991)

Alan Schwartz, Professor of Law, Yale University.
Robert E. Scott, Professor of Law, University of Virginia.

COMPARATIVE LAW, Fifth Edition (1988)

Rudolf B. Schlesinger, Professor of Law, Hastings College of the Law.
Hans W. Baade, Professor of Law, University of Texas.
Mirjan P. Damaska, Professor of Law, Yale Law School.
Peter E. Herzog, Professor of Law, Syracuse University.

COMPETITIVE PROCESS, LEGAL REGULATION OF THE, Revised Fourth Edition (1991), with 1991 Selected Statutes Supplement

Edmund W. Kitch, Professor of Law, University of Virginia.
Harvey S. Perlman, Dean of the Law School, University of Nebraska.

CONFLICT OF LAWS, Ninth Edition (1990)

Willis L. M. Reese, Professor of Law, Columbia University.
Maurice Rosenberg, Professor of Law, Columbia University.
Peter Hay, Professor of Law, University of Illinois.

CONSTITUTIONAL LAW, Eighth Edition (1989), with 1991 Case Supplement

Edward L. Barrett, Jr., Professor of Law, University of California, Davis.
William Cohen, Professor of Law, Stanford University.
Jonathan D. Varat, Professor of Law, University of California, Los Angeles.

CONSTITUTIONAL LAW, CIVIL LIBERTY AND INDIVIDUAL RIGHTS, Second Edition (1982), with 1991 Supplement

William Cohen, Professor of Law, Stanford University.
John Kaplan, Professor of Law, Stanford University.

CONSTITUTIONAL LAW, Twelfth Edition (1991), with 1991 Supplement (Supplement edited in association with Frederick F. Schauer, Professor, Harvard University)

Gerald Gunther, Professor of Law, Stanford University.

CONSTITUTIONAL LAW, INDIVIDUAL RIGHTS IN, Fifth Edition (1992), (Reprinted from CONSTITUTIONAL LAW, Twelfth Edition), with 1991 Supplement (Supplement edited in association with Frederick F. Schauer, Professor, Harvard University)

Gerald Gunther, Professor of Law, Stanford University.

CONSUMER TRANSACTIONS, Second Edition (1991), with Selected Statutes and Regulations Supplement

Michael M. Greenfield, Professor of Law, Washington University.

CONTRACT LAW AND ITS APPLICATION, Fourth Edition (1988)

Arthur Rosett, Professor of Law, University of California, Los Angeles.

CONTRACT LAW, STUDIES IN, Fourth Edition (1991)

Edward J. Murphy, Professor of Law, University of Notre Dame.
Richard E. Speidel, Professor of Law, Northwestern University.

CONTRACTS, Fifth Edition (1987)

John P. Dawson, late Professor of Law, Harvard University.
William Burnett Harvey, Professor of Law and Political Science, Boston University.
Stanley D. Henderson, Professor of Law, University of Virginia.

UNIVERSITY CASEBOOK SERIES—Continued

CONTRACTS, Fourth Edition (1988)

E. Allan Farnsworth, Professor of Law, Columbia University.
William F. Young, Professor of Law, Columbia University.

CONTRACTS, Selections on (statutory materials) (1988)

CONTRACTS, Second Edition (1978), with Statutory and Administrative Law Supplement (1978)

Ian R. Macneil, Professor of Law, Cornell University.

COPYRIGHT, PATENTS AND TRADEMARKS, see also Competitive Process; see also Selected Statutes and International Agreements

COPYRIGHT, PATENT, TRADEMARK AND RELATED STATE DOCTRINES, Third Edition (1990), with 1991 Selected Statutes Supplement and 1981 Problem Supplement

Paul Goldstein, Professor of Law, Stanford University.

COPYRIGHT, Unfair Competition, and Other Topics Bearing on the Protection of Literary, Musical, and Artistic Works, Fifth Edition (1990), with 1991 Statutory and Case Supplement

Ralph S. Brown, Jr., Professor of Law, Yale University.
Robert C. Denicola, Professor of Law, University of Nebraska.

CORPORATE ACQUISITIONS, The Law and Finance of (1986), with 1991 Supplement

Ronald J. Gilson, Professor of Law, Stanford University.

CORPORATE FINANCE, Third Edition (1987)

Victor Brudney, Professor of Law, Harvard University.
Marvin A. Chirelstein, Professor of Law, Columbia University.

CORPORATION LAW, BASIC, Third Edition (1989), with Documentary Supplement

Detlev F. Vagts, Professor of Law, Harvard University.

CORPORATIONS, see also Enterprise Organization and Business Organization

CORPORATIONS, Sixth Edition—Concise (1988), with 1991 Case Supplement and 1991 Statutory Supplement

William L. Cary, late Professor of Law, Columbia University.
Melvin Aron Eisenberg, Professor of Law, University of California, Berkeley.

CORPORATIONS, Sixth Edition—Unabridged (1988), with 1991 Case Supplement and 1991 Statutory Supplement

William L. Cary, late Professor of Law, Columbia University.
Melvin Aron Eisenberg, Professor of Law, University of California, Berkeley.

CORPORATIONS AND BUSINESS ASSOCIATIONS—STATUTES, RULES, AND FORMS (1991)

CORRECTIONS, SEE SENTENCING

CREDITORS' RIGHTS, see also Debtor-Creditor Law

UNIVERSITY CASEBOOK SERIES—Continued

CRIMINAL JUSTICE ADMINISTRATION, Fourth Edition (1991), with 1991 Supplement

Frank W. Miller, Professor of Law, Washington University.
Robert O. Dawson, Professor of Law, University of Texas.
George E. Dix, Professor of Law, University of Texas.
Raymond I. Parnas, Professor of Law, University of California, Davis.

CRIMINAL LAW, Fifth Edition (1992)

Andre A. Moenssens, Professor of Law, University of Richmond.
Fred E. Inbau, Professor of Law Emeritus, Northwestern University.
Ronald J. Bacigal, Professor of Law, University of Richmond.

CRIMINAL LAW AND APPROACHES TO THE STUDY OF LAW, Second Edition (1991)

John M. Brumbaugh, Professor of Law, University of Maryland.

CRIMINAL LAW, Second Edition (1986)

Peter W. Low, Professor of Law, University of Virginia.
John C. Jeffries, Jr., Professor of Law, University of Virginia.
Richard C. Bonnie, Professor of Law, University of Virginia.

CRIMINAL LAW, Fourth Edition (1986)

Lloyd L. Weinreb, Professor of Law, Harvard University.

CRIMINAL LAW AND PROCEDURE, Seventh Edition (1989)

Ronald N. Boyce, Professor of Law, University of Utah.
Rollin M. Perkins, Professor of Law Emeritus, University of California, Hastings College of the Law.

CRIMINAL PROCEDURE, Third Edition (1987), with 1991 Supplement

James B. Haddad, Professor of Law, Northwestern University.
James B. Zagel, Chief, Criminal Justice Division, Office of Attorney General of Illinois.
Gary L. Starkman, Assistant U. S. Attorney, Northern District of Illinois.
William J. Bauer, Chief Judge of the U.S. Court of Appeals, Seventh Circuit.

CRIMINAL PROCESS, Fourth Edition (1987), with 1991 Supplement

Lloyd L. Weinreb, Professor of Law, Harvard University.

DAMAGES, Second Edition (1952)

Charles T. McCormick, late Professor of Law, University of Texas.
William F. Fritz, late Professor of Law, University of Texas.

DECEDENTS' ESTATES AND TRUSTS, See also Family Property Law

DECEDENTS' ESTATES AND TRUSTS, Seventh Edition (1988)

John Ritchie, late Professor of Law, University of Virginia.
Neill H. Alford, Jr., Professor of Law, University of Virginia.
Richard W. Effland, late Professor of Law, Arizona State University.

DISPUTE RESOLUTION, Processes of (1989)

John S. Murray, President and Executive Director of The Conflict Clinic, Inc., George Mason University.
Alan Scott Rau, Professor of Law, University of Texas.
Edward F. Sherman, Professor of Law, University of Texas.

DOMESTIC RELATIONS, see also Family Law

DOMESTIC RELATIONS, Second Edition (1990), with 1992 Supplement

Walter Wadlington, Professor of Law, University of Virginia.

EMPLOYMENT DISCRIMINATION, Second Edition (1987), with 1990 Supplement

Joel W. Friedman, Professor of Law, Tulane University.
George M. Strickler, Professor of Law, Tulane University.

EMPLOYMENT LAW, Second Edition (1991), with Statutory Supplement and 1991 Case Supplement

Mark A. Rothstein, Professor of Law, University of Houston.
Andria S. Knapp, Visiting Professor of Law, Golden Gate University.
Lance Liebman, Professor of Law, Harvard University.

ENERGY LAW (1983), with 1991 Case Supplement

Donald N. Zillman, Professor of Law, University of Utah.
Laurence Lattman, Dean of Mines and Engineering, University of Utah.

ENTERPRISE ORGANIZATION, Fourth Edition (1987), with 1987 Corporation and Partnership Statutes, Rules and Forms Supplement

Alfred F. Conard, Professor of Law, University of Michigan.
Robert L. Knauss, Dean of the Law School, University of Houston.
Stanley Siegel, Professor of Law, University of California, Los Angeles.

ENVIRONMENTAL POLICY LAW, Second Edition (1991)

Thomas J. Schoenbaum, Professor of Law, University of Georgia.
Ronald H. Rosenberg, Professor of Law, College of William and Mary.

EQUITY, see also Remedies

EQUITY, RESTITUTION AND DAMAGES, Second Edition (1974)

Robert Childres, late Professor of Law, Northwestern University.
William F. Johnson, Jr., Professor of Law, New York University.

ESTATE PLANNING, Second Edition (1982), with 1985 Case, Text and Documentary Supplement

David Westfall, Professor of Law, Harvard University.

ETHICS, see Legal Ethics, Legal Profession, Professional Responsibility, and Social Responsibilities

ETHICS OF LAWYERING, THE LAW AND (1990)

Geoffrey C. Hazard, Jr., Professor of Law, Yale University.
Susan P. Koniak, Professor of Law, University of Pittsburgh.

ETHICS AND PROFESSIONAL RESPONSIBILITY (1981) (Reprinted from THE LAWYERING PROCESS)

Gary Bellow, Professor of Law, Harvard University.
Bea Moulton, Legal Services Corporation.

EVIDENCE, Seventh Edition (1992)

John Kaplan, Late Professor of Law, Stanford University.
Jon R. Waltz, Professor of Law, Northwestern University.
Roger C. Park, Professor of Law, University of Minnesota.

EVIDENCE, Eighth Edition (1988), with Rules, Statute and Case Supplement (1990)

Jack B. Weinstein, Chief Judge, United States District Court.
John H. Mansfield, Professor of Law, Harvard University.
Norman Abrams, Professor of Law, University of California, Los Angeles.
Margaret Berger, Professor of Law, Brooklyn Law School.

FAMILY LAW, see also Domestic Relations

FAMILY LAW Second Edition (1985), with 1991 Supplement

Judith C. Areen, Professor of Law, Georgetown University.

FAMILY LAW AND CHILDREN IN THE LEGAL SYSTEM, STATUTORY MATERIALS (1981)

Walter Wadlington, Professor of Law, University of Virginia.

FAMILY PROPERTY LAW, Cases and Materials on Wills, Trusts and Future Interests (1991)

Lawrence W. Waggoner, Professor of Law, University of Michigan.
Richard V. Wellman, Professor of Law, University of Georgia.
Gregory Alexander, Professor of Law, Cornell Law School.
Mary L. Fellows, Professor of Law, University of Minnesota.

FEDERAL COURTS, Eighth Edition (1988), with 1991 Supplement

Charles T. McCormick, late Professor of Law, University of Texas.
James H. Chadbourn, late Professor of Law, Harvard University.
Charles Alan Wright, Professor of Law, University of Texas, Austin.

FEDERAL COURTS AND THE FEDERAL SYSTEM, Hart and Wechsler's Third Edition (1988), with 1992 Case Supplement, and the Judicial Code and Rules of Procedure in the Federal Courts (1991)

Paul M. Bator, Professor of Law, University of Chicago.
Daniel J. Meltzer, Professor of Law, Harvard University.
Paul J. Mishkin, Professor of Law, University of California, Berkeley.
David L. Shapiro, Professor of Law, Harvard University.

FEDERAL COURTS AND THE LAW OF FEDERAL–STATE RELATIONS, Second Edition (1989), with 1991 Supplement

Peter W. Low, Professor of Law, University of Virginia.
John C. Jeffries, Jr., Professor of Law, University of Virginia.

FEDERAL PUBLIC LAND AND RESOURCES LAW, Second Edition (1987), with 1990 Case Supplement and 1990 Statutory Supplement

George C. Coggins, Professor of Law, University of Kansas.
Charles F. Wilkinson, Professor of Law, University of Oregon.

FEDERAL RULES OF CIVIL PROCEDURE and Selected Other Procedural Provisions, 1991 Edition

FEDERAL TAXATION, see Taxation

FIRST AMENDMENT (1991)

William W. Van Alstyne, Professor of Law, Duke University.

FOOD AND DRUG LAW, Second Edition (1991), with Statutory Supplement

Peter Barton Hutt, Esq.
Richard A. Merrill, Professor of Law, University of Virginia.

FUTURE INTERESTS (1970)

Howard R. Williams, Professor of Law, Stanford University.

FUTURE INTERESTS AND ESTATE PLANNING (1961), with 1962 Supplement

W. Barton Leach, late Professor of Law, Harvard University.
James K. Logan, formerly Dean of the Law School, University of Kansas.

GOVERNMENT CONTRACTS, FEDERAL, Successor Edition (1985), with 1989 Supplement

John W. Whelan, Professor of Law, Hastings College of the Law.

UNIVERSITY CASEBOOK SERIES—Continued

GOVERNMENT REGULATION: FREE ENTERPRISE AND ECONOMIC ORGANI-ZATION, Sixth Edition (1985)

Louis B. Schwartz, Professor of Law, Hastings College of the Law.
John J. Flynn, Professor of Law, University of Utah.
Harry First, Professor of Law, New York University.

HEALTH CARE LAW AND POLICY (1988)

Clark C. Havighurst, Professor of Law, Duke University.

HINCKLEY, JOHN W., JR., TRIAL OF: A Case Study of the Insanity Defense (1986)

Peter W. Low, Professor of Law, University of Virginia.
John C. Jeffries, Jr., Professor of Law, University of Virginia.
Richard C. Bonnie, Professor of Law, University of Virginia.

IMMIGRATION LAW AND POLICY (1992)

Stephen H. Legomsky, Professor of Law, Washington University.

INJUNCTIONS, Second Edition (1984)

Owen M. Fiss, Professor of Law, Yale University.
Doug Rendleman, Professor of Law, College of William and Mary.

INSTITUTIONAL INVESTORS (1978)

David L. Ratner, Professor of Law, Cornell University.

INSURANCE, Second Edition (1985)

William F. Young, Professor of Law, Columbia University.
Eric M. Holmes, Professor of Law, University of Georgia.

INSURANCE LAW AND REGULATION (1990)

Kenneth S. Abraham, University of Virginia.

INTERNATIONAL LAW, see also Transnational Legal Problems, Transnational Business Problems, and United Nations Law

INTERNATIONAL LAW IN CONTEMPORARY PERSPECTIVE (1981), with Essay Supplement

Myres S. McDougal, Professor of Law, Yale University.
W. Michael Reisman, Professor of Law, Yale University.

INTERNATIONAL LEGAL SYSTEM, Third Edition (1988), with Documentary Supplement

Joseph Modeste Sweeney, Professor of Law, University of California, Hastings.
Covey T. Oliver, Professor of Law, University of Pennsylvania.
Noyes E. Leech, Professor of Law Emeritus, University of Pennsylvania.

INTRODUCTION TO LAW, see also Legal Method, On Law in Courts, and Dynamics of American Law

INTRODUCTION TO THE STUDY OF LAW (1970)

E. Wayne Thode, late Professor of Law, University of Utah.
Leon Lebowitz, Professor of Law, University of Texas.
Lester J. Mazor, Professor of Law, University of Utah.

JUDICIAL CODE and Rules of Procedure in the Federal Courts, Students' Edition, 1991 Revision

Daniel J. Meltzer, Professor of Law, Harvard University.
David L. Shapiro, Professor of Law, Harvard University.

JURISPRUDENCE (Temporary Edition Hardbound) (1949)

Lon L. Fuller, late Professor of Law, Harvard University.

JUVENILE, see also Children

JUVENILE JUSTICE PROCESS, Third Edition (1985)

Frank W. Miller, Professor of Law, Washington University.
Robert O. Dawson, Professor of Law, University of Texas.
George E. Dix, Professor of Law, University of Texas.
Raymond I. Parnas, Professor of Law, University of California, Davis.

LABOR LAW, Eleventh Edition (1991), with 1991 Statutory Supplement

Archibald Cox, Professor of Law, Harvard University.
Derek C. Bok, President, Harvard University.
Robert A. Gorman, Professor of Law, University of Pennsylvania.
Matthew W. Finkin, Professor of Law, University of Illinois.

LABOR LAW, Second Edition (1982), with Statutory Supplement

Clyde W. Summers, Professor of Law, University of Pennsylvania.
Harry H. Wellington, Dean of the Law School, Yale University.
Alan Hyde, Professor of Law, Rutgers University.

LAND FINANCING, Third Edition (1985)

The late Norman Penney, Professor of Law, Cornell University.
Richard F. Broude, Member of the California Bar.
Roger Cunningham, Professor of Law, University of Michigan.

LAW AND MEDICINE (1980)

Walter Wadlington, Professor of Law and Professor of Legal Medicine, University of Virginia.
Jon R. Waltz, Professor of Law, Northwestern University.
Roger B. Dworkin, Professor of Law, Indiana University, and Professor of Biomedical History, University of Washington.

LAW, LANGUAGE AND ETHICS (1972)

William R. Bishin, Professor of Law, University of Southern California.
Christopher D. Stone, Professor of Law, University of Southern California.

LAW, SCIENCE AND MEDICINE (1984), with 1989 Supplement

Judith C. Areen, Professor of Law, Georgetown University.
Patricia A. King, Professor of Law, Georgetown University.
Steven P. Goldberg, Professor of Law, Georgetown University.
Alexander M. Capron, Professor of Law, University of Southern California.

LAWYERING PROCESS (1978), with Civil Problem Supplement and Criminal Problem Supplement

Gary Bellow, Professor of Law, Harvard University.
Bea Moulton, Professor of Law, Arizona State University.

LEGAL ETHICS (1992)

Deborah Rhode, Professor of Law, Stanford University.
David Luban, Professor of Law, University of Maryland.

LEGAL METHOD (1980)

Harry W. Jones, Professor of Law Emeritus, Columbia University.
John M. Kernochan, Professor of Law, Columbia University.
Arthur W. Murphy, Professor of Law, Columbia University.

UNIVERSITY CASEBOOK SERIES—Continued

LEGAL METHODS (1969)

Robert N. Covington, Professor of Law, Vanderbilt University.
E. Blythe Stason, late Professor of Law, Vanderbilt University.
John W. Wade, Professor of Law, Vanderbilt University.
Elliott E. Cheatham, late Professor of Law, Vanderbilt University.
Theodore A. Smedley, Professor of Law, Vanderbilt University.

LEGAL PROFESSION, THE, Responsibility and Regulation, Second Edition (1988)

Geoffrey C. Hazard, Jr., Professor of Law, Yale University.
Deborah L. Rhode, Professor of Law, Stanford University.

LEGISLATION, Fourth Edition (1982) (by Fordham)

Horace E. Read, late Vice President, Dalhousie University.
John W. MacDonald, Professor of Law Emeritus, Cornell Law School.
Jefferson B. Fordham, Professor of Law, University of Utah.
William J. Pierce, Professor of Law, University of Michigan.

LEGISLATIVE AND ADMINISTRATIVE PROCESSES, Second Edition (1981)

Hans A. Linde, Judge, Supreme Court of Oregon.
George Bunn, Professor of Law, University of Wisconsin.
Fredericka Paff, Professor of Law, University of Wisconsin.
W. Lawrence Church, Professor of Law, University of Wisconsin.

LOCAL GOVERNMENT LAW, Second Revised Edition (1986)

Jefferson B. Fordham, Professor of Law, University of Utah.

MASS MEDIA LAW, Fourth Edition (1990)

Marc A. Franklin, Professor of Law, Stanford University.
David A. Anderson, Professor of Law, University of Texas.

MUNICIPAL CORPORATIONS, see Local Government Law

NEGOTIABLE INSTRUMENTS, see Commercial Paper

NEGOTIATION (1981) (Reprinted from THE LAWYERING PROCESS)

Gary Bellow, Professor of Law, Harvard Law School.
Bea Moulton, Legal Services Corporation.

NEW YORK PRACTICE, Fourth Edition (1978)

Herbert Peterfreund, Professor of Law, New York University.
Joseph M. McLaughlin, Dean of the Law School, Fordham University.

OIL AND GAS, Fifth Edition (1987)

Howard R. Williams, Professor of Law, Stanford University.
Richard C. Maxwell, Professor of Law, University of California, Los Angeles.
Charles J. Meyers, late Dean of the Law School, Stanford University.
Stephen F. Williams, Judge of the United States Court of Appeals.

ON LAW IN COURTS (1965)

Paul J. Mishkin, Professor of Law, University of California, Berkeley.
Clarence Morris, Professor of Law Emeritus, University of Pennsylvania.

PENSION AND EMPLOYEE BENEFIT LAW (1990), with 1991 Supplement

John H. Langbein, Professor of Law, University of Chicago.
Bruce A. Wolk, Professor of Law, University of California, Davis.

PLEADING AND PROCEDURE, see Procedure, Civil

UNIVERSITY CASEBOOK SERIES—Continued

POLICE FUNCTION, Fifth Edition (1991), with 1991 Supplement

Reprint of Chapters 1–10 of Miller, Dawson, Dix and Parnas's CRIMINAL JUSTICE ADMINISTRATION, Fourth Edition.

PREPARING AND PRESENTING THE CASE (1981) (Reprinted from THE LAWYERING PROCESS)

Gary Bellow, Professor of Law, Harvard Law School.
Bea Moulton, Legal Services Corporation.

PROCEDURE (1988), with Procedure Supplement (1991)

Robert M. Cover, late Professor of Law, Yale Law School.
Owen M. Fiss, Professor of Law, Yale Law School.
Judith Resnik, Professor of Law, University of Southern California Law Center.

PROCEDURE—CIVIL PROCEDURE, Sixth Edition (1990), with 1991 Supplement

Richard H. Field, late Professor of Law, Harvard University.
Benjamin Kaplan, Professor of Law Emeritus, Harvard University.
Kevin M. Clermont, Professor of Law, Cornell University.

PROCEDURE—CIVIL PROCEDURE, Successor Edition (1992)

A. Leo Levin, Professor of Law Emeritus, University of Pennsylvania.
Philip Shuchman, Professor of Law, Rutgers University.
Charles M. Yablon, Professor of Law, Yeshiva University.

PROCEDURE—CIVIL PROCEDURE, Fifth Edition (1990), with 1991 Supplement

Maurice Rosenberg, Professor of Law, Columbia University.
Hans Smit, Professor of Law, Columbia University.
Rochelle C. Dreyfuss, Professor of Law, New York University.

PROCEDURE—PLEADING AND PROCEDURE: State and Federal, Sixth Edition (1989), with 1991 Case Supplement

David W. Louisell, late Professor of Law, University of California, Berkeley.
Geoffrey C. Hazard, Jr., Professor of Law, Yale University.
Colin C. Tait, Professor of Law, University of Connecticut.

PROCEDURE—FEDERAL RULES OF CIVIL PROCEDURE, 1991 Edition

PRODUCTS LIABILITY AND SAFETY, Second Edition (1989), with 1989 Statutory Supplement

W. Page Keeton, Professor of Law, University of Texas.
David G. Owen, Professor of Law, University of South Carolina.
John E. Montgomery, Professor of Law, University of South Carolina.
Michael D. Green, Professor of Law, University of Iowa

PROFESSIONAL RESPONSIBILITY, Fifth Edition (1991), with 1992 Selected Standards on Professional Responsibility Supplement

Thomas D. Morgan, Professor of Law, George Washington University.
Ronald D. Rotunda, Professor of Law, University of Illinois.

PROPERTY, Sixth Edition (1990)

John E. Cribbet, Professor of Law, University of Illinois.
Corwin W. Johnson, Professor of Law, University of Texas.
Roger W. Findley, Professor of Law, University of Illinois.
Ernest E. Smith, Professor of Law, University of Texas.

PROPERTY—PERSONAL (1953)

S. Kenneth Skolfield, late Professor of Law Emeritus, Boston University.

UNIVERSITY CASEBOOK SERIES—Continued

SECURED TRANSACTIONS IN PERSONAL PROPERTY, Second Edition (1987) (Reprinted from COMMERCIAL LAW, Second Edition (1987))

Robert L. Jordan, Professor of Law, University of California, Los Angeles.
William D. Warren, Professor of Law, University of California, Los Angeles.

SECURITIES REGULATION, Sixth Edition (1987), with 1991 Selected Statutes, Rules and Forms Supplement and 1991 Cases and Releases Supplement

Richard W. Jennings, Professor of Law, University of California, Berkeley.
Harold Marsh, Jr., Member of California Bar.

SECURITIES REGULATION, Second Edition (1988), with Statute, Rule and Form Supplement (1991)

Larry D. Soderquist, Professor of Law, Vanderbilt University.

SECURITY INTERESTS IN PERSONAL PROPERTY, Second Edition (1987)

Douglas G. Baird, Professor of Law, University of Chicago.
Thomas H. Jackson, Dean of the Law School, University of Virginia.

SECURITY INTERESTS IN PERSONAL PROPERTY (1985) (Reprinted from Sales and Sales Financing, Fifth Edition)

John Honnold, Professor of Law, University of Pennsylvania.

SELECTED STANDARDS ON PROFESSIONAL RESPONSIBILITY, 1992 Edition

SELECTED STATUTES AND INTERNATIONAL AGREEMENTS ON UNFAIR COMPETITION, TRADEMARK, COPYRIGHT AND PATENT, 1991 Edition

SELECTED STATUTES ON TRUSTS AND ESTATES, 1992 Edition

SOCIAL RESPONSIBILITIES OF LAWYERS, Case Studies (1988)

Philip B. Heymann, Professor of Law, Harvard University.
Lance Liebman, Professor of Law, Harvard University.

SOCIAL SCIENCE IN LAW, Second Edition (1990)

John Monahan, Professor of Law, University of Virginia.
Laurens Walker, Professor of Law, University of Virginia.

TAXATION, FEDERAL INCOME (1989)

Stephen B. Cohen, Professor of Law, Georgetown University

TAXATION, FEDERAL INCOME, Second Edition (1988), with 1991 Supplement (Supplement edited in association with Deborah H. Schenk, Professor of Law, New York University)

Michael J. Graetz, Professor of Law, Yale University.

TAXATION, FEDERAL INCOME, Seventh Edition (1991)

James J. Freeland, Professor of Law, University of Florida.
Stephen A. Lind, Professor of Law, University of Florida and University of California, Hastings.
Richard B. Stephens, late Professor of Law Emeritus, University of Florida.

TAXATION, FEDERAL INCOME, Successor Edition (1986), with 1991 Legislative Supplement

Stanley S. Surrey, late Professor of Law, Harvard University.
Paul R. McDaniel, Professor of Law, Boston College.
Hugh J. Ault, Professor of Law, Boston College.
Stanley A. Koppelman, Professor of Law, Boston University.

UNIVERSITY CASEBOOK SERIES—Continued

TAXATION, FEDERAL INCOME, OF BUSINESS ORGANIZATIONS (1991), with 1991 Supplement

Paul R. McDaniel, Professor of Law, Boston College.
Hugh J. Ault, Professor of Law, Boston College.
Martin J. McMahon, Jr., Professor of Law, University of Kentucky.
Daniel L. Simmons, Professor of Law, University of California, Davis.

TAXATION, FEDERAL INCOME, OF PARTNERSHIPS AND S CORPORATIONS (1991), with 1991 Supplement

Paul R. McDaniel, Professor of Law, Boston College.
Hugh J. Ault, Professor of Law, Boston College.
Martin J. McMahon, Jr., Professor of Law, University of Kentucky.
Daniel L. Simmons, Professor of Law, University of California, Davis.

TAXATION, FEDERAL INCOME, OIL AND GAS, NATURAL RESOURCES TRANSACTIONS (1990)

Peter C. Maxfield, Professor of Law, University of Wyoming.
James L. Houghton, CPA, Partner, Ernst and Young.
James R. Gaar, CPA, Partner, Ernst and Young.

TAXATION, FEDERAL WEALTH TRANSFER, Successor Edition (1987)

Stanley S. Surrey, late Professor of Law, Harvard University.
Paul R. McDaniel, Professor of Law, Boston College.
Harry L. Gutman, Professor of Law, University of Pennsylvania.

TAXATION, FUNDAMENTALS OF CORPORATE, Third Edition (1991)

Stephen A. Lind, Professor of Law, University of Florida and University of California, Hastings.
Stephen Schwarz, Professor of Law, University of California, Hastings.
Daniel J. Lathrope, Professor of Law, University of California, Hastings.
Joshua Rosenberg, Professor of Law, University of San Francisco.

TAXATION, FUNDAMENTALS OF PARTNERSHIP, Third Edition (1992)

Stephen A. Lind, Professor of Law, University of Florida and University of California, Hastings.
Stephen Schwarz, Professor of Law, University of California, Hastings.
Daniel J. Lathrope, Professor of Law, University of California, Hastings.
Joshua Rosenberg, Professor of Law, University of San Francisco.

TAXATION OF CORPORATIONS AND THEIR SHAREHOLDERS (1991)

David J. Shakow, Professor of Law, University of Pennsylvania.

TAXATION, PROBLEMS IN THE FEDERAL INCOME TAXATION OF PARTNERSHIPS AND CORPORATIONS, Second Edition (1986)

Norton L. Steuben, Professor of Law, University of Colorado.
William J. Turnier, Professor of Law, University of North Carolina.

TAXATION, PROBLEMS IN THE FUNDAMENTALS OF FEDERAL INCOME, Second Edition (1985)

Norton L. Steuben, Professor of Law, University of Colorado.
William J. Turnier, Professor of Law, University of North Carolina.

TORT LAW AND ALTERNATIVES, Fourth Edition (1987)

Marc A. Franklin, Professor of Law, Stanford University.
Robert L. Rabin, Professor of Law, Stanford University.

TORTS, Eighth Edition (1988)

William L. Prosser, late Professor of Law, University of California, Hastings.
John W. Wade, Professor of Law, Vanderbilt University.
Victor E. Schwartz, Adjunct Professor of Law, Georgetown University.

UNIVERSITY CASEBOOK SERIES—Continued

TORTS, Third Edition (1976)

Harry Shulman, late Dean of the Law School, Yale University.
Fleming James, Jr., Professor of Law Emeritus, Yale University.
Oscar S. Gray, Professor of Law, University of Maryland.

TRADE REGULATION, Third Edition (1990)

Milton Handler, Professor of Law Emeritus, Columbia University.
Harlan M. Blake, Professor of Law, Columbia University.
Robert Pitofsky, Professor of Law, Georgetown University.
Harvey J. Goldschmid, Professor of Law, Columbia University.

TRADE REGULATION, see Antitrust

TRANSNATIONAL BUSINESS PROBLEMS (1986)

Detlev F. Vagts, Professor of Law, Harvard University.

TRANSNATIONAL LEGAL PROBLEMS, Third Edition (1986), with 1991 Revised Edition of Documentary Supplement

Henry J. Steiner, Professor of Law, Harvard University.
Detlev F. Vagts, Professor of Law, Harvard University.

TRIAL, see also Evidence, Making the Record, Lawyering Process and Preparing and Presenting the Case

TRUSTS, Sixth Edition (1991)

George G. Bogert, late Professor of Law Emeritus, University of Chicago.
Dallin H. Oaks, President, Brigham Young University.
H. Reese Hansen, Dean and Professor of Law, Brigham Young University.
Claralyn Martin Hill, J.D. Brigham Young University.

TRUSTS AND ESTATES, SELECTED STATUTES ON, 1992 Edition

TRUSTS AND WILLS, See also Decedents' Estates and Trusts, and Family Property Law

UNFAIR COMPETITION, see Competitive Process and Business Torts

WATER RESOURCE MANAGEMENT, Third Edition (1988), with 1992 Supplement

The late Charles J. Meyers, formerly Dean, Stanford University Law School.
A. Dan Tarlock, Professor of Law, IIT Chicago-Kent College of Law.
James N. Corbridge, Jr., Chancellor, University of Colorado at Boulder, and Professor of Law, University of Colorado.
David H. Getches, Professor of Law, University of Colorado.

WILLS AND ADMINISTRATION, Fifth Edition (1961)

Philip Mechem, late Professor of Law, University of Pennsylvania.
Thomas E. Atkinson, late Professor of Law, New York University.

WRITING AND ANALYSIS IN THE LAW, Second Edition (1991)

Helene S. Shapo, Professor of Law, Northwestern University.
Marilyn R. Walter, Professor of Law, Brooklyn Law School.
Elizabeth Fajans, Writing Specialist, Brooklyn Law School.

University Casebook Series

COMPARATIVE LAW

CASES — TEXT — MATERIALS

FIFTH EDITION

By

RUDOLF B. SCHLESINGER
Professor of Law, University of California
Hastings College of Law
William Nelson Cromwell Professor of
International and Comparative Law Emeritus, Cornell University

HANS W. BAADE
Hugh Lamar Stone Professor of Civil Law, University of Texas

MIRJAN R. DAMASKA
Ford Foundation Professor of Comparative and Foreign Law,
Yale Law School

and

PETER E. HERZOG
Crandall Melvin Professor of Law,
Syracuse University College of Law

Mineola, New York
THE FOUNDATION PRESS, INC.
1988

Library of Congress Cataloging in Publication Data

Comparative law.

  (University casebook series)
  Rev. ed. of: Comparative law / by Rudolf B. Schlesinger. 4th ed.
  Includes index.
  1. Comparative law—Cases. I. Schlesinger, Rudolf B. II. Schlesinger, Rudolf B. Comparative law.
III. Series.

K558.C66 1988   340'.2   87–30219
ISBN 0–88277–615–0

Schlesinger et al. Comp.Law 5th Ed. UCB
2nd Reprint—1992

To the Memory of June Schlesinger Katz

*

PREFACE

The first edition of this book, which appeared in 1950, was offered as a pioneering experiment. The years that have elapsed since then have brought general recognition of the view that a course in Comparative Law is a central and indispensable part of any well-designed program of international legal studies. Such a program must serve the non-specialist and the future specialist alike. The Comparative Law course thus should be responsive to the needs (a) of those students who upon completion of the course will not seek any further opportunities for studying foreign legal phenomena *and* (b) of those for whom the Comparative Law course merely serves as a necessary introduction to the more intensive study of specific, geographically or functionally selected aspects of foreign law or of transnational legal problems.

Variety characterizes not only the needs of students taking a Comparative Law course, but also the objectives which their teachers seek to attain in such a course. For this reason, an attempt has been made—even more deliberately in this edition than in its predecessors—to avoid rigidity in the objectives and methods of the projected course, and to design the course materials with maximum flexibility. In this context, "flexibility" means that each instructor should be able to use these materials in accordion-like fashion, compressing and expanding them so as to attune the course to his own preferences. The following devices, among others, have been used to this end:

(1) The manifold purposes which may be served by the comparative method are surveyed in the introductory chapter (infra pp. 1–43). This will make it easier for the instructor consciously to determine his own principal objective or objectives in teaching the course. The materials permit a considerable range of choice and of varying emphasis in this regard.

(2) The aggregate size of the book has been moderately increased, as compared to earlier editions. Thus an instructor will create no difficulty for himself by omitting certain chapters which are relatively less important in the light of his particular objectives; the remaining materials will still be ample for a 45-hour course. If it is sought, for example, primarily to widen the students' perspective in dealing with socio-legal problems arising in their own society, and correspondingly to de-emphasize the use of the comparative method in international litigation and international transactions, much of the material on pleading and proof of foreign law (pp. 43–146, 188–228) may be omitted.

(3) Those instructors who feel that a particular subject or a given legal system or group of systems should receive more intensive

v

coverage, and that accordingly the materials in the book should be expanded, may find the following features helpful:

(a) At every step, there are footnote references which, designed primarily for the instructor's use, should go a long way to facilitate the search for amplifying materials and illustrations.

(b) Many of the illustrative materials in the book are consciously designed to serve as points of contact at which an instructor, if he is so inclined, can introduce supplementary materials of his own choosing. To mention but two examples: (i) In the past, some instructors using previous editions of this book have prepared supplementary materials on Roman law; such materials can be conveniently introduced at one of several points of contact in the historical discussion (infra pp. 245 ff.) dealing with the pre-code evolution of the civil law. (ii) Law teachers who would like to draw supplementary illustrative topics from the field of torts will find connecting links in the materials on traffic accidents and products liability (pp. 552–67), on recovery of damages for non-pecuniary harm (pp. 627–42) and on the offensive use of the doctrine of abuse of rights (p. 740ff.).

Although there are differences of opinion among individual instructors as to the ultimate objectives of a course of this kind, there is also an area of agreement. As his immediate pedagogic aim, virtually every teacher of Comparative Law seeks to acquaint his students with the *technique* of using foreign materials (for whatever ultimate purpose), and to de-provincialize their minds by increasing their *knowledge* of legal institutions outside their own habitat. This two-fold aim cannot be attained without providing a relatively large amount of explanation and plain information, concerning (a) the use and pitfalls of the comparative method as such, and (b) the basic outlines of the foreign legal institutions selected for study.

Such informational material should not be limited to a single foreign country. This is particularly important in studying "civil law". Information limited to a single civil-law jurisdiction does not enlighten the student as to which of the features studied by him are typical of all or most of the civil-law systems, and which are just local peculiarities of the one country under direct observation. Therefore, while concentrating primarily on France, Germany and Switzerland as the seminal civil-law systems, these materials also attempt at every step to illustrate the world-wide radiation effect of the legal precepts, concepts and techniques first developed in the seminal countries. Thus Western institutions are very frequently compared with their counterparts in socialist systems, and in every section of the book it is shown how legal ideas and institutions originating in the seminal systems have fared in Japan or in the developing countries of Latin America, Asia and Africa.[1]

To achieve such breadth of geographic coverage, and for the sake of continuity, we have preserved and intensified the previous edition's pervasive use of textual presentation. Original text, including text-notes and explanatory footnotes, now constitutes considerably more than one-half of the book.[2] This, it is hoped, will make it possible for the instructor to spend relatively little time on purely informational lecturing; the time thus saved can be used for discussion of the most interesting points raised by the cases, especially those involving comparison with domestic institutions.

Some European reviewers of the earlier editions suggested that the format of a "casebook" be given up altogether and that a textbook or treatise would be a more appropriate tool for the teaching of Comparative Law. It may be possible to adduce some arguments in support of this suggestion; but in the opinion of most American law teachers it overshoots the mark. It has been demonstrated by experience, and especially by the comparative experience of those who have taught and studied law on both sides of the Atlantic, that student participation and liveliness of class sessions are best assured by a discussion focused on concrete fact situations.

In teaching Comparative Law, the need for a factual focus of presentation is particularly marked, more so than in other courses. The reason for this is obvious. In dealing with the legal problems of his domestic community, the student may be able sometimes to derive real benefit from a purely abstract exposition of legal precepts; but this is so only because, having lived in the community, he is already familiar with many of the social and human situations to which those precepts can be applied. In studying the law of foreign lands, the student lacks this experiential background. Thus, the burden of acquainting him with the relevant folkways, with the context and flavor of the "facts" to which foreign legal rules are addressed, necessarily falls upon the teaching materials. Clearly, this burden can be met only if systematic exposition is constantly supplemented by cases and other concrete illustrations based on live situations.

An exclusively expository and "systematic" discussion of foreign law, moreover, would be bound to stress surface differences in system and terminology; only an inquiry into actual results reached in response to concrete fact situations will show that those surface differences hide an amazingly large area of agreement among various legal systems, certainly among those belonging to the civil and common law orbits.

---

1. Illustrations of the seminal systems' radiation effect will be found throughout the book; in studying and coordinating those illustrations, the reader will derive assistance from the concise survey of legal systems that appears on pp. 310–337.

2. At the same time, we reduced to a minimum the borrowed textual excerpts which were included in the earliest editions.

Where, on the other hand, a comparison of actual results reached in different legal systems reveals real divergencies,[3] a factual focus will prove helpful for yet another reason: it will make it possible for the teacher of Comparative Law to go beyond comparison, and to alert his students to the *interaction* of legal systems which accounts for so many important legal phenomena in the world of today.[4]

Regarding the methods by which a factual focus of class discussion can be established, we have attempted to be flexible and realistic. It is true that ordinarily more time will be consumed in discussing a foreign case than a domestic one. For this reason, the number of foreign principal cases has been increased only moderately; but an intensified attempt has been made to indicate how each of these cases can be employed to illustrate several points. In addition, much use has been made of note cases and hypothetical Examples and Illustrations—usually much simpler vehicles for class discussion. Occasionally, moreover, a domestic case will serve incidentally to highlight a foreign institution or principle.

The principal illustrative topics continue to be drawn from the fields of substantive private law and of civil procedure. No apology is required for this basically *"civiliste"* orientation of the course. Private law is the most highly developed and systematized part of the civil-law systems. It exerts the greatest influence in forming the minds of civil lawyers, and "no other branch sheds so much light on the entire system." [5]

At the same time, it seems clear that the spirit and over-all direction of a foreign legal system cannot be grasped without taking note of the basic elements of its criminal process and of some of its public law institutions. For this reason, an attempt has been made in this new edition to strengthen the materials on criminal procedure in civil-law countries, and on the important subject of the interaction between the criminal process and private remedies. In addition, more attention has been devoted to selected topics of constitutional law and administrative law, in order: (a) to alert the student to the constant interaction between public law and private law, and to show how the private law sector is affected by changes in the constitution or the governmental system of a given country; (b) to explain the enormous jurisdictional significance of the civilians' dichotomy between public law and private law, and to point

---

3. Throughout the book, the reader will find references to the common-law counterparts of the civil-law institutions under discussion.

4. Among the many types of such interaction one can observe, for instance: measures designed to unify or harmonize conflicting national laws; reciprocity requirements; various kinds of extraterritorial legislation; and outright counter-legislation, intended to counter the effects of specified laws of another nation. Examples will be found in every chapter of this book. A particularly dramatic recent example of "interaction" (between national laws reflecting divergent attitudes toward discovery in civil litigation) is provided by the U.S. Supreme Court's June 1987 decision in the *Societe Aerospatiale* case, discussed infra pp. 446–48.

5. Amos and Walton's Introduction to French Law 2–3 (3rd ed. by F.H. Lawson, A. E. Anton and L. N. Brown, 1967).

to the difficulties bound to arise when it becomes necessary to stake out the precise line of demarcation between the two areas.

A word, finally, concerning the authorship of the present edition. Professor Schlesinger, who was the originator of this work and the sole author of the first four editions, asked the other undersigned to join him in preparing the fifth edition. Knowing that the book's value as a teaching tool had stood the test of time, we preserved its basic structure and contents; but some new materials were added in the Comparovich Dialogue and elsewhere; and of course every part of the book was updated and revised. This was done as a largely cooperative effort; but each of us assumes primary responsibility for additions and changes appearing in specified sections of the new edition, as indicated in the footnote.[6]

We acknowledge our debt of gratitude to Kevin P. Jewell, Esq., for his assistance in the preparation of the Index.

Like its predecessors, this edition has greatly benefited from helpful comments offered by the many users of the book. With our sincere thanks to them we couple an expression of our hope that in the future the flow of such comments will continue unabated.

December 1987

RUDOLF B. SCHLESINGER
HANS W. BAADE
MIRJAN R. DAMASKA
PETER E. HERZOG

---

6. Schlesinger: Pp. 1–43; 337–473; 597–657; 868–890. Baade: Pp. 43–146; 158–310; 684–696. Damaska: Pp. 310–337; 473–530; 657–684; 696–740. Herzog: Pp. 147–158; 530–596; 740–867; 891–898.

*

EXPLANATIONS AND ABBREVIATIONS

Translations. All translations of cases, code provisions, and other materials are by the editors, except where otherwise indicated.

Editorial Comments. Wherever editorial comments have been inserted into materials not written by the editors, i.e., into cases, code provisions or reprinted text materials, such comments appear in brackets.

Footnotes. Numbered footnotes are footnotes belonging to the original of the text. In other words, a numbered footnote appended to an opinion is one appearing in the original opinion; a numbered footnote appended to other reprinted materials appears in the original of such materials. In some instances such footnotes have been renumbered. Needless to say, all footnotes appended to original text and text-notes are the editors' own. Where editorial footnotes are appended to cases, code provisions, or text materials written by other authors, such footnotes are marked by asterisks or small letters.

Abbreviations. Abbreviations of foreign terms usually are explained in the text or the footnotes. The following, however, are used so frequently that a general explanation may be preferable: *

BGBl .... Bundesgesetzblatt (Official Gazette of the Federal Republic of Germany)

BGE .... Bundesgerichts–Entscheidungen (reports of decisions of the Federal Tribunal, the highest court of the Swiss Confederation; ATF = Arrêts du Tribunal Fédéral in French)

BGH .... Bundesgerichtshof (see following entry)

BGHZ .... Entscheidungen des Bundesgerichtshofs in Zivilsachen (reports of decisions of the civil divisions of the highest ordinary court of the Federal Republic of Germany)

Cass.Civ. .... Decision of a Chambre Civile (civil division) of the French Cour de Cassation

Cass.Rêq. .... Decision of the former Chambre des Requêtes of the French Cour de Cassation

D.J. .... Dalloz–Sirey Jurisprudence (French periodical)

D.L. .... Dalloz–Sirey Législation (French periodical)

IPRax .... Praxis des Internationalen Privat–und Verfahrensrechts

---

* For a more extensive listing of abbreviations used in France, Germany and Switzerland, see C. Szladits, Guide to Foreign Legal Materials—French, German, Swiss 113–16, 305–30, 501–07 (1959). See also C. Szladits & C.M. Germain, Guide to Foreign Legal Materials: French 171–182 (2d ed., 1985).

JuS................Juristische Schulung (a German periodical published primarily for the use of law students and Referendars)

JZ.................Juristenzeitung

NJW..............Neue Juristische Wochenschrift

OLG ....Oberlandesgericht (intermediate appellate court in the Federal Republic of Germany)

RGBl ....Reichsgesetzblatt (Official Gazette of the German Reich until 1945)

RGZ.............Entscheidungen des Reichsgerichts in Zivilsachen (reports of decisions of the civil divisions of the former German Supreme Court)

It should be noted at the outset (although the point will be taken up in our discussion of judicial decisions in civil-law countries) that in some countries of the civil-law orbit the names of the parties normally are deleted from judicial opinions, and replaced by mere initials, before such opinions are reported. Nor is the usual form of reference to volume and page of a law report the same as in common-law countries. If we refer to page 100 of volume 55 of the reports of the New York Court of Appeals, we use the form 55 N.Y. 100. A civilian, in referring to page 100 of volume 55 of the decisions of the civil divisions of the German Bundesgerichtshof, will cite BGHZ 55, 100.

TABLE OF CONTENTS

[handwritten annotations:]
does law operate in its own country
18
Look to Conflict of law / Judicial Notice Statutes of State where action is brought or Follow 44.1
-P951 — only general statement of foreign law required in pleading
see 61 123
104-107 Flexibility 106, 111
Doctrine-is-Based 54
Judicial notice -108
60, 61 New rule on court taking notice of foreign law. 75, 79, 80
62 Germany truly treats foreign law as "foreign"
71 Tx law on judicial notice
What law applies: 89, 94, 96, 99 choice of law

TABLE OF CONTENTS

TABLE OF CONTENTS

714 - standardized contracts _740 = Abuse of rights_
725 - Torts

C. A TOPICAL APPROACH TO THE CIVIL LAW: SOME ILLUSTRATIVE SUBJECTS

xv

Handwritten margin notes:
- _p 138 can Administrative J unwritten Hen sources_
- _641 - Precedent by two cases_
- _69 130 of Civil code is al act child is x bonos mores void._
- _520 - Case of Or. losing license Claim against German Cts_
- _France 555 542-552 Codes products liability_
- _560 - products liability_
- _627 case_
- _668 660 671 - Penalty Clause_
- _684 - LAND REGISTRY_
- _180-187 supra - See pg 279_
- _statutory analogy pg 164 supp_
- _740 Abuse of Right_

TABLE OF CONTENTS

TABLE OF CASES

Principal cases are in italic type. Cases cited or discussed are in roman type. References are to Pages. Foreign cases, which often do not reveal the names of the parties, generally are not listed in this Table.

AUTHOR INDEX

AUTHOR INDEX

AUTHOR INDEX

Page

AUTHOR INDEX

1

*

COMPARATIVE LAW

CASES — TEXT — MATERIALS

*

A. THE NATURE OF A FOREIGN LAW PROBLEM

I. INTRODUCTION: THE COMPARATIVE METHOD—ITS PURPOSE AND PROMISE

Unlike most of the other subjects in the law school curriculum, Comparative Law is not a body of rules and principles. Primarily, it is a *method*, a way of looking at legal problems, legal institutions, and entire legal systems. By the use of that method it becomes possible to make observations, and to gain insights, which would be denied to one who limits his study to the law of a single country.[1]

Neither the comparative method, nor the insights gained through its use, can be said to constitute a body of binding norms, i.e. of "law" in the sense in which we speak of "the law" of Torts or "the law" of Decedents' Estates. Strictly speaking, therefore, the term Comparative Law is a misnomer. It would be more appropriate to speak of Comparison of Laws and Legal Systems.[2] Yet by the force of tradition the term Comparative Law has become accepted as the title of our subject.[3]

The resources of Comparative Law can be used for a wide variety of practical or scholarly purposes. The introductory materials which follow are intended to show the range of these purposes,[4] and at the same time to provide initial illustrations of some of the problems and techniques which later on will be taken up in more detail.

1. For a more extensive discussion of the "concept" of comparative law, with further references, see 1 K. Zweigert and H. Kötz, An Introduction to Comparative Law 1–4 (transl. by T. Weir, 1977). See also 1 L.-J. Constantinesco, Rechtsvergleichung 204–73 (1971); M. Rheinstein, Einführung in die Rechtsvergleichung 11–15 (1974).

2. The word "comparison", it would seem, refers both to the process or method of comparing and to the insights gained by that process.

3. The French call our subject *droit comparé* (law compared). The German term *Rechtsvergleichung* has been criticized as too exclusively method-oriented. See M. Rheinstein, supra n. 1. But cf. supra n. 2.

4. For a discussion which supplements these introductory materials, and furnishes a wealth of further references, see G. Winterton, Comparative Law Teaching, 23 Am.J.Comp.L. 69 (1975). The views of a number of authors are presented (partly in English) in the collection of essays entitled Rechtsvergleichung (K. Zweigert & H.-J. Puttfarken, Eds., 1978).

1. THE COMPARATIVE METHOD APPLIED TO DOMESTIC PROBLEMS

A. THE FOREIGN SOLUTION AS A MODEL—FOREIGN ELEMENTS IN DOMESTIC LAW

GREENSPAN v. SLATE

Supreme Court of New Jersey, 1953.
12 N.J. 426, 97 A.2d 390.

VANDERBILT, C. J. Barbara Slate, the 17-year old daughter of the defendants, injured a foot while playing basketball at high school. Within two or three days it became exceedingly swollen and conspicuously discolored so that she could walk on it only with the greatest difficulty and pain. Her parents, thinking it nothing more than a sprain, declined to provide her with medical aid. The plaintiff, Garfield, a member of the bar of this State, discovered her plight by chance, when she was on a visit to his home in company with Berkley Badgett, his housekeeper's son, who was courting her.

Mr. Garfield promptly sent young Badgett, his mother and Barbara to the nearby office of the plaintiff, Dr. Sidney Greenspan, who discovered from X-ray plates he made that a bone of Barbara's foot had been fractured. He applied a cast which Barbara wore for about a month until it was removed by Dr. Greenspan. Meantime she used crutches. Barbara lived at home with her parents and the presence of the cast and her use of crutches were thus known to them. Clearly the broken bone that was causing much swelling, high discoloration and great pain necessitating the taking of X-ray plates, the application of a cast for a month and the use of crutches did present an emergency. The testimony of Dr. Greenspan that permanent injury would have ensued if there had not been proper medical care and attention at the time is uncontradicted.

On the completion of his services Dr. Greenspan rendered a bill to the parents of $45, which they have refused to pay. . . . At the end of the plaintiff's case the trial court granted the defendants' motion to dismiss on the ground that Dr. Greenspan had acted without any express authorization from the defendants [the parents Slate] and that the proofs were insufficient in the circumstances to establish an implied authorization by them. On appeal the Appellate Division of the Superior Court, considering itself bound by earlier decisions in our courts, reluctantly affirmed the judgment below. Because of the public importance of the question presented, we granted certification. 11 N.J. 410, 94 A.2d 699 (1953).

The question before us is whether or not the parents of an infant child are liable, in the absence of a contract, express or implied in fact, for necessaries furnished their child in an emergency.

[The Court refers to Freeman v. Robinson, 38 N.J.L. 383, 20 Am. Rep. 399 (1876), and to other New Jersey cases in which it was held, in accordance with Blackstone, that a parent's duty to support an infant child is "a mere moral obligation", not enforceable at law. From this, it was thought to follow that no quasi-contractual action could be brought by a plaintiff who unofficiously had furnished necessaries to the infant. Where, however, a court of equity had jurisdiction by virtue of the fact that the child had an estate of his own and that the parents petitioned the Chancellor for permission to use such estate for the infant's support, the rule was otherwise. At least indirectly, by disallowing such permission so long as the parents had sufficient means, a court of equity would enforce the parents' obligation to furnish support, education and medical care. See Alling v. Alling, 52 N.J.Eq. 92, 27 A. 655 (1893). Thus, there are divergent views at law and in equity as to the fundamental nature of a parent's obligation to maintain an infant child, and these divergent views have never been reconciled by a court of last resort.]

. . . As we have seen, there are no precedents in our courts of last resort so we are free to choose between the common law rule and the Chancery principle in deciding the instant case. Normal instincts of humanity and plain common honesty as well as the substantial weight of judicial decisions in this country, the uniform rule of the civil law in European countries, and the unanimous views of the text writers and the Restatement of the Law all combine to demonstrate the superiority of the equitable rule. Whatever objections may be raised thereto have been based either on fancied fears as to its effect in operation, which long experience with it in many jurisdictions have shown to be altogether groundless, or on procedural misconceptions which should long since have been discarded. . . .

[The court cites several collections of American authorities on the subject, and Sections 112 to 114 of the Restatement of the Law of Restitution (1937).]

The course of the Roman law and the modern civil law of Western Europe, which is based on it,* suggests that the common law rule, which we are now discarding in favor of the equitable doctrine, may be merely an instance of early undeveloped law. In the Roman law the duty of a father to support his child was enforced only by criminal proceedings, Radin, Handbook of Roman Law 108 (1927), but in the modern civil law the obligation of the parents is direct:

"The duty of taking care of children's support until such time as they are capable of supporting themselves is primarily incumbent on the father. Their physical care is primarily

---

* At this early stage of the course, the student would do well to suspend judgment on the question whether and to what extent the modern civil law of Western Europe is "based on" Roman Law. During its classical period, Roman Law was uncodified. To trace the path that led from the law of that period to the Codes of the modern civil-law world, is a matter of considerable complexity, which will be touched upon later in this book. See especially pp. 245–310, infra.

incumbent on the mother. In the event that the father is indigent the duty to take care of the children's support and in the event of the father's death [the duty to take care of] the children's education in general, is primarily incumbent on the mother. In the event that the mother shall not survive [the father] or is indigent, such duty is incumbent upon the paternal grandparents or, subordinately, on the maternal grandparents." *Austrian Civil Law, sec. 143.*

"Spouses are jointly obligated, by reason of the sole fact of contracting marriage, to feed, support and educate their children." *French Civil Code, Art. 203.*

"Relatives in the line of direct descendants are under the obligation of supporting each other." *German Civil Code, sec. 1601.* "Only the one who is incapable of supporting himself is entitled to support. An infant unmarried child may require his parents to support him although he own property, to the extent to which the income from his property and from his own work are not sufficient for his support." Ibid., *sec. 1602.*

"*Duties towards the Children.*—Marriage imposes upon both spouses the duty to support and to give an education and instruction to the issue. Education and instruction must conform to moral principles." *Italian Civil Code, Art. 147. "Contribution to the Burdens.*—The duty of supporting and of giving an education and instruction to the issue is borne by the father and by the mother in proportion to their property, including in the mother's contribution income from her dowry. If the parents do not have sufficient means, such duty falls on the other ascendants according to their order of proximity to the infants." Ibid., *Art. 148.*

"The father and the mother and the child owe each other the care and assistance which are required in the interest of the family." *Swiss Civil Code, Art. 271.* "The father and the mother shall bear the expenses for the support and education of the child [and they shall share in them] according to their matrimonial regime. If they are in need or if the child causes extraordinary expenses or under other exceptional circumstances, the supervising [judicial] authority may allow the father and the mother to subject the property of the infant child to contribution for his support and education to the extent fixed by it." Ibid., *Art. 272.*

. . . The judgment below is reversed. Judgment will be entered here in favor of the plaintiff, Dr. Sidney Greenspan, for $45.

For reversal—Chief Justice VANDERBILT, and Justices OLIPHANT, BURLING, JACOBS and BRENNAN—5.

For affirmance—Justices HEHER and WACHENFELD—2.*

---

* See Note, 39 Cornell L.Q. 337 (1954),   civil-law influence is evident, also, in statutes where it is pointed out (at 341-2), that the

Quasi-contractual right recognized in most countries [handwritten annotation]

NOTES AND QUESTIONS

(1) *A Brief Comment on the Principal Case*

(a) It will be noted that the code provisions quoted by the Court deal with the parents' duty to support their child, but not with the further question whether a third person who has provided such support has a quasi-contractual right of recovery against the neglectful parents. Actually, however, there is a quasi-contractual doctrine recognized in most civil-law countries which gives the third person such a right of recovery.[1] This doctrine, derived from Roman law and still widely known by its Latin label (*negotiorum gestio*), has been incorporated into many of the 19th and 20th century codes enacted throughout the civil-law world.[2] The following sections of the German Civil Code may be regarded as fairly typical of some of the *negotiorum gestio* rules thus embodied in the codes:[3]

> Sec. 677: A person who takes charge of an affair for another without having received a mandate from him . . . ., shall manage the affair in such manner as the interest of the principal requires, having regard to his actual or presumptive wishes.

> Sec. 679: The fact that the management of the affair is opposed to the wishes of the principal is not taken into consideration if, without the management of the affair, a duty of the principal the fulfilment of which is of public interest or a statutory duty [of the principal] to furnish maintenance to others . . . would not be fulfilled in due time.

> Sec. 683: If the undertaking of the management of the affair is in accordance with the interest and the actual or presumptive wishes of the principal, the agent may demand reimbursement of his outlay as a mandatary [i.e., in the same way as an agent]. In the cases provided for by Section 679 this claim belongs to the agent even if the undertaking of the management of the affair is opposed to the wishes of the principal.

On the basis of these or similar provisions, in conjunction with those quoted by Vanderbilt, C.J., the courts of Germany and of other civil-law countries are bound to hold for the plaintiff in fact situations such as that of the principal case.[4]

(b) Vanderbilt, C.J., thus was correct in feeling that most, if not all, of the civil-law systems would support the position taken by him and by the majority of the other judges in the principal case. A problem of

on the subject which have been passed in several states.

1. For illuminating comparative discussions of the doctrine see S. J. Stoljar, Negotiorum Gestio, in International Encyclopedia of Comparative Law, Vol. X, Ch. 17 (1984); Dawson, Negotiorum Gestio: The Altruistic Intermeddler, 74 Harv.L.Rev. 817, 1073 (1961); Lorenzen, The Negotiorum Gestio in Roman and Modern Civil Law, 13 Cornell L.Q. 190 (1928).

2. The articles by Dawson and Lorenzen, supra n. 1, contain translations of the

pertinent provisions in the principal codes. See 74 Harv.L.Rev. at 864–65; 13 Cornell L.Q. at 199–201.

3. The translation which follows is taken from the article by Lorenzen, supra nn. 1 and 2.

4. See Palandt, Bürgerliches Gesetzbuch, § 679, Anno. 2(c) (43rd ed., 1984); Berner Kommentar zum Schweizerischen Privatrecht, Vol. II Part 1 (by Hegnauer), Art. 272, Annos. 97–99 (1964).

theory may suggest itself at this point. Plainly, the civil codes of European countries are not "the law" of New Jersey. On what theory, then, did the majority opinion refer to those codes? What are the possible theories on which an American court might let itself be influenced by statutory, decisional or other authorities stemming from a different legal system?[5]

(2) *The Immediate Context: Civil Law Elements in American Case Law*

(a) The principal case is not unique. There are many other English and American decisions, especially in cases involving novel problems, in which the court's opinion reflects successful resort by counsel to civil-law authorities. The laws in effect "in foreign countries with problems and backgrounds comparable to our own are highly persuasive" in an American court that is faced with a problem not previously encountered here. "Where Congress has left . . . a large void to be filled entirely by the courts, it is appropriate for us to consider what other jurisdictions have done either by way of legislation or judicial decision." Williams & Wilkins Co. v. United States, 203 Ct.Cl. 74, 487 F.2d 1345, 1362 (1973).[6]

For further examples see Wolff, The Utility of Foreign Law to the Practicing Lawyer, 27 A.B.A.J. 253 (1941); Schlesinger, Research on the General Principles of Law Recognized by Civilized Nations—Outline of a New Project, 51 Am.J.Int.L. 734 (1957). Cf. Kisch, Statutory Construction in a New Key—"Harmonizing Interpretation".[7]

(b) Counsel, seeking to uphold the *constitutionality of a statute* which is attacked as allegedly violating due process, often have made effective use of the fact that a number of other civilized countries have statutes similar to the one under attack. The famous, almost legendary brief by which Mr. Brandeis, as counsel for the State of Oregon, won the landmark case of Muller v. State of Oregon, 208 U.S. 412, 28 S.Ct. 324 (1908), contained many references to foreign legislation concerning the working hours of women. In its opinion (at 419–20), the Court repeated some of these references and intimated that a statute which has counterparts in most countries of the civilized world, cannot easily be struck down as unreasonable, arbitrary and capricious.[7a]

---

5. The articles cited in the text below (preceding n. 7) may suggest some of the possible answers. See also Schlesinger, The Nature of General Principles of Law, in Rapports Généraux au VIe Congrès international de droit comparé (publ. 1964 by the Centre Interuniversitaire de Droit Comparé under the direction of Professor Limpens) pp. 235 ff.

6. Aff'd by an equally divided court, 420 U.S. 376, 95 S.Ct. 1344 (1975).

In maritime cases, the impact of authorities originating in continental Europe is even more direct and powerful. See, e.g., Peninsular & Oriental Steam Navigation Co. v. Overseas Oil Carriers, Inc., 553 F.2d 830, 834 (2d Cir. 1977). For further discussion of this point, and additional examples, see G. A. Zaphiriou, Use of Comparative Law by the Legislator, 30 Am.J.Comp.L. (Supplement) 71, 78–80 (1982).

7. Professor Kisch's article appears in the volume entitled XXth Century Comparative and Conflicts Law—Legal Essays in Honor of Hessel E. Yntema, at 262 ff. (1961). See also B. Aubin, Die rechtsvergleichende Interpretation autonom-internen Rechts in der deutschen Rechtsprechung, 34 Rabels Z. 458 (1970) (citing numerous decisions of the highest German court in which the court used the comparative method when dealing with novel problems of internal German law).

7a. More recently, the same kind of reasoning was employed by Judge Sneed in upholding the constitutionality of the California Resale Royalties Act (Cal.C.C. § 986) against a Due Process attack. Morseburg v. Balyon, 621 F.2d 972, 979 (9th Cir. 1980).

Similarly, in Palko v. Connecticut, 302 U.S. 319, 58 S.Ct. 149 (1937), upholding the constitutionality of a statute permitting appeals by the State in criminal cases, Mr. Justice Cardozo called attention to the practice of civil-law countries where the prosecutor generally has the right to appeal from an acquittal, or even from a judgment of conviction if he regards the sentence as too mild.[8] Insofar as the *Double Jeopardy* Clause of the United States Constitution is concerned, Palko has been overruled by a subsequent case which made that Clause binding on the states,[8a] thus severely limiting prosecutorial appeals in state as well as federal criminal proceedings.[9] But Palko's fundamental holding—that to permit prosecution appeals in criminal proceedings is not necessarily a shocking violation of *Due Process*—is still intact and continues to be of practical importance both in domestic cases [10] and in situations involving U.S. recognition of foreign criminal judgments.[11] In any event, whatever the present status of the Palko holding may be, it would seem that *the method* used in that case—i.e., the method of looking beyond national borders to gain perspective in deciding whether a given procedure is civilized—is still a viable one.[12]

The view that a rule traditionally followed in a number of civilized legal systems should not easily be struck down as being fundamentally unfair and hence violative of due process, has been adopted also by the Federal Constitutional Court of the German Federal Republic.[13]

Not only in seeking to uphold but also in attacking the constitutionality of a statute, counsel can make effective use of foreign laws and of the experience gained under them. Comparison with foreign laws may show, for instance, that a domestic statute providing for a certain type of punishment falls below "standards of decency more or less universally accepted." [14] As a further example, one might think of a case where a constitutional attack is launched against an old statute which for a long time has made entry into a given line of business dependent on a license, and where the statute is defended on the ground that certain evils would arise if access to that type of business

---

8. See Kepner v. United States, 195 U.S. 100, 120–21, 24 S.Ct. 797, 800–01 (1904) (discussion of Spanish law).

For a survey of state statutes similar to that upheld in Palko, see Note, 35 U.Cin.L. Rev. 501 (1966). Concerning the question of the continuing validity of those statutes, see infra nn. 9 and 10.

8a. Benton v. Maryland, 395 U.S. 784, 89 S.Ct. 2056 (1969).

9. The limits which the Double Jeopardy Clause, as construed in ever-shifting Supreme Court opinions, imposes on prosecutorial appeals, have been staked out in United States v. Scott, 437 U.S. 82, 98 S.Ct. 2187 (1978), where the prior authorities are reviewed.

10. See, e.g., Swisher v. Brady, 438 U.S. 204, 98 S.Ct. 2699 (1978).

11. See United States ex rel. Bloomfield v. Gengler, 507 F.2d 925, 929 (2d Cir. 1974). See also infra pp. 889–890.

12. There are some cases, however, which indicate that in the area of criminal

procedure the Supreme Court has shifted to a more provincial due process criterion; it now examines the fairness of a given practice within the framework of "the *American* scheme of justice" (emphasis supplied). See Duncan v. Louisiana, 391 U.S. 145, 149, 88 S.Ct. 1444, 1447–8 (1968). For comments on this shift from a "civilized" to an "American" standard, see Judge Wisdom's opinion in Melancon v. McKeithen, 345 F.Supp. 1025, at 1038–39 (E.D.La. 1972) (3-judge Court), aff'd mem. sub nom. Hill v. McKeithen, 409 U.S. 943, 93 S.Ct. 290 (1972).

13. Bundesverfassungsgericht, June 13, 1952, 1 BVerfGE 332 (1952). See Schlesinger, Western Germany: Recognition and Enforcement of Soviet Zone Criminal Judgments, 2 Am.J.Comp.L. 392 (1953).

14. See Francis v. Resweber, 329 U.S. 459, 469, 67 S.Ct. 374 (1947) (Frankfurter, J., concurring).

were free. This defense of the statute would be greatly weakened if counsel attacking it could show that in foreign countries having a basically similar social structure no such evils have appeared although in those countries there is no restriction upon a person's right to open such a business.[15]

(c) Students of American legal history have observed that, during the early 19th century, a "strong inclination towards French law had grown out of the political situation after the revolution. . . . It was chiefly in the form of comparative law, in the hands of Kent and Story, that French and Dutch authorities could be used to enrich our commercial law and to reinforce a point of common law doctrine, on a theory that [the foreign materials thus found were] declaratory of the law of nature." Pound, The Influence of the Civil Law in America, 1 La.L. Rev. 1, 9 (1938). As a result, we find *massive references to civil law authorities in many of the earlier American cases.*[16]

For reasons explained in Dean Pound's above-mentioned article, the courts' reliance on European codes and other civil-law authorities declined during the second half of the 19th century.[17] More recently, however, the trend again seems to be in the direction of a more cosmopolitan spirit.[18] This may be due to the country's growing involvement in world affairs, to the rapidly increasing availability of foreign-law materials presented and expounded in the English language, and perhaps also to the influence of European-bred legal scholars who came to this country as refugees from totalitarian oppression.

(3) *The Wider Context: Migration of Legal Ideas*

(a) A court is not always free to use foreign materials for the solution of domestic legal problems. Such freedom exists only in cases, such as those discussed above, which are not plainly governed by local statute or binding domestic precedent. For *legislative draftsmen*, on the other hand, resort to comparative materials is not thus restricted.[19]

15. See Baade, Social Science Evidence and the Federal Constitutional Court of West Germany, 23 Journal of Politics 421, 451–3, 460 (1961), referring to the so-called *Pharmacy* case, 7 BVerfGE 377, at 415–16 (1958), where the German Court, in striking down such a licensing requirement as unnecessary, referred to the expert testimony of a high Swiss official; the latter had testified before the German Court that in Switzerland, in spite of the absence of a comparable license statute, no "evils" had been encountered.

16. See O. Schroeder, Comparative Law: A Subject for American Lawyers, 41 A.B.A.J. 928, 929 (1955). One of the most famous examples of such early cases influenced by the civil law is Pierson v. Post, 3 Caines 175, 2 Am.Dec. 264 (N.Y.1805), which has found its way into many first-year Property casebooks.

For an illuminating discussion of civil-law influence on legal education and legal literature in the United States, up to the time of the Civil War, see P. Stein, The Attraction of the Civil Law in Post-Revolutionary America, 52 Va.L.Rev. 403 (1966).

17. Even during the late 19th and the early 20th century, when direct civil-law influence upon our law was in decline, jurisprudential ideas coming from Europe and especially from Germany remained highly influential among the intellectual leaders of this country's legal establishment—men such as Holmes, Pound and Llewellyn.

18. For an example, see text at n. 6 supra.

19. On the importance of comparative law as an aid to the legislator see, e.g., Schmitthoff, The Science of Comparative Law, 7 Camb.L.J. 94, 103–4 (1939). The point was well put by Lepaulle, The Function of Comparative Law, 35 Harv.L.Rev. 838, 858 (1922): "When one is immersed in his own law, in his own country, unable to see things from without, he has a psychologically unavoidable tendency to consider as natural, as necessary, as given by God, things which are simply due to historical accident or temporary social situation. . . . To see things in their true light, we must see them from a certain distance, as strangers, which is impossible

The desire of legislators to learn from foreign experience seems to have been the motive behind the very first comparative legal studies recorded in history. Both the Babylonian Code of Hammurabi (17th century B.C.) and the Old Testament contain legal rules which—as to formulation as well as substance—can be traced to earlier legislation elsewhere.[20] The laws of Solon were influenced by critical examination of the codes of other Greek or Greek-dominated city-states; and similar studies are said to have preceded the enactment of the Twelve Tables which marked the earliest period of Roman law.[21]

Turning to modern times,[21a] we find that in the most advanced countries of continental Europe it is standard practice to survey pertinent foreign legislation before an important and innovative bill is submitted to parliament.[22] In those countries it has long been recognized that in the legislative development of the law the public interest is not adequately represented by pressure groups. Therefore, the responsibility for undertaking, or at least co-ordinating, the necessary preparatory research and for formulating a draft proposal is assumed by an arm of the government, usually the Ministry of Justice.[23] Calling on the services of expert staff members or consultants, these permanent and well-organized government agencies tend, as part of their work in preparing important bills, routinely to resort to comparative research.[23a]

Note

Great Britain and most of the other common-law countries have not developed the institution of a Ministry of Justice.[24] But even the part-time and ad hoc committees which until 1965 were chiefly responsible for law reform in the United Kingdom, often undertook or sponsored comparative studies.[25] The Law Commissions Act of 1965, which has created permanent Law Commissions for England and Scotland,

when we study . . . phenomena of our own country. That is why cmparative law should be one of the necessary elements in the training of all those who are to shape the law for societies. . . ."

20. See A. Watson, Legal Transplants—An Approach to Comparative Law 22–23 (1974).

21. See Zepos, Die Bewegung zur Rechtsvereinheitlichung und das Schicksal der geltenden Zivilgesetzbücher, 19 Rev.Hell. Dr.Int. 14, at 17 (1966).

21a. Perhaps the most massive (though by now almost forgotten) comparative studies in preparation of legislative reform were those engaged in by Russian Tsarist drafting commissions charged with overhauling the procedural system. The reform included the transplantation of the jury system and its creative adaptation to Russian conditions. See S. Kucherov, Courts, Lawyers and Trials Under the Last Three Tsars 23–24, 51 ff. (1953).

22. See, e.g., Dölle, Der Beitrag der Rechtsvergleichung zum deutschen Recht, in Vol. 2 of "Hundert Jahre deutsches Rechtsleben—Festschrift zum hundertjährigen Bestehen des deutschen Juristentages" 19 ff. (1960); Escarra, The Aims of Comparative Law, 7 Temple L.Q. 296 (1933).

On the use of the comparative method by legislators on the Continent and in Great Britain, and on the relative paucity of similar efforts in the United States, see E. Stein, Uses, Misuses—and Nonuses of Comparative Law, 72 N.W.U.L.Rev. 198, 210–12 (1977).

23. Concerning the influence which the existence or absence of such a government agency is bound to have on the development of statutory law, and on its interpretation, see infra pp. 293–94, 585.

23a. Many examples and further references can be found in B. Grossfeld, Macht und Ohnmacht der Rechtsvergleichung 37–44 (1984).

24. A continental-type Ministry of Justice exists in New Zealand. Headed by a member of the Government, the New Zealand Department of Justice is responsible for law reform and acts as secretariat for a Law Revision Commission. See J. H. Farrar, Law Reform and the Law Commission 80–89 (1974), where further references can be found.

25. See, e.g., Report of the Royal Commission on Capital Punishment 1949–1953,

contains an express provision making it the duty of both Commissions "to obtain such information as to the legal systems of other countries as appears to the Commissioners likely to facilitate the performance of any of their functions." [26] Many of the Commissions' Working Papers and Reports show that in accordance with this legislative mandate they have indeed made substantial use of the comparative method.[27]

In the United States, where examination of the laws of 53 American jurisdictions imposes a heavy load on the legislative draftsman even if he neglects the study of foreign materials, it has not yet become the routine practice of legislators and of those assisting them to study the comparable laws of foreign countries; [28] but in recent years such studies have become more frequent,[28a] and leading agencies of law reform, such as the New York Law Revision Commission, very often study and utilize the experience of other countries.[29] This is borne out by the example presented on pp. 17–22 below.[29a]

In other parts of the world, legislators sometimes did not confine themselves to the study and occasional adoption of foreign legal institutions, but resorted to *wholesale importation*.[30] Most of the codes which are presently in force in Latin America are the result of extensive comparative study and of eclectic choice among European solutions. Many other examples of wholesale *reception* [31] of foreign laws could be given, such as the adoption of the Swiss Civil Code and of a modified version of the German Commercial Code in Turkey, of the German Civil Code in Japan, and of Soviet law in other communist legal

pp. 2–3, 411–13, 414–16, 420–28, 432–66, 475–85 (1953).

The English tradition of borrowing legislative ideas from the continent is an ancient one. It has been surmised that Edward I of England, the creator of the Statutes of Westminster, De Donis and Quia Emptores, may have become acquainted with the great medieval Spanish Code called *Las Siete Partidas* (1256–1265) when he visited his cousin and brother-in-law, Alfonso X of Castile and Leon, known as the "Wise". See Radin, Introduction to Nichols, Las Siete Partidas, 20 Calif.L.Rev. 260, 261 (1932). On firmer historical grounds, we know that the English Statute of Frauds was largely copied from the French Ordonnance de Moulins of 1566. See Rabel, The Statute of Frauds and Comparative Legal History, 63 L.Q.Rev. 174 (1947).

26. Law Commissions Act of 1965, Section 3(1)(f).

27. See N. S. Marsh, Law Reform in the United Kingdom: A New Institutional Approach, 13 William & Mary L.Rev. 263 (1971); L. Scarman, Inside the English Law Commission, 57 A.B.A.J. 867 (1971); L. N. Brown, A Century of Comparative Law in England, 19 Am.J.Comp.L. 233, 247–49 (1971); J. H. Farrar, supra n. 24, at 34; B. S. Markesinis, The Not So Dissimilar Tort and Delict, 93 L.Q.Rev. 78, 80 (1977).

28. See E. Stein, supra n. 22.

28a. See the instructive article by G. A. Zaphiriou, supra n. 6.

29. See J. W. MacDonald, The New York Law Revision Commission, 28 Mod.L. Rev. 1, at 13 (1965).

29a. Following that example, the discussion of the point touched upon in the text, supra, will be continued.

30. The method has the advantage of utilization of foreign achievements and of foreign experience. It involves the danger, however, that some foreign institutions may be copied without sufficient adaptation to local conditions. See, e.g., Hamson, The Istanbul Conference of 1955, 5 Int. and Comp.L.Q. 26 (1956); P. H. Sand, Die Reform des aethiopischen Erbrechts— Problematik einer synthetischen Rezeption, 33 Rabels Z. 413 (1969).

31. For an interesting general discussion of the phenomenon of reception, see Zajtay, Die Rezeption fremder Rechte und die Rechtsvergleichung, 156 Archiv fuer die Civilistische Praxis 361 (1957); Zajtay, La réception des droits étrangers et le droit comparé, 9 Rev.Int.Dr.Comp. 686 (1957).

Concerning the "reception" of a resurrected and somewhat transformed Roman law in Germany and other European countries (which forms an important part of the legal history of the Continent), see infra pp. 245–310, especially p. 255ff.

systems.[32] Developing countries, in particular, sometimes depend not only on foreign models but also on foreign personnel for the preparation, the drafting, and the educational and administrative implementation of their new laws.[33]

Reception may be voluntary, as in the above-mentioned examples of Turkey and of Japan's original adoption of western laws.[34] It may, on the other hand, be the result of conquest or colonization,[34a] or of other forms of military or political pressure. The subjection of the French settlers of Louisiana to Spanish law after the 1769 victory of the Spaniards under General O'Reilly, the extension of German law into Austria after the Anschluss of 1938, and the Sovietization of law in parts of Eastern Europe during the period from the end of World War II to the death of Stalin, may be cited as instances of the latter type of "reception". It should be noted, however, that foreign laws involuntarily received are not always abrogated when the pressure ends. Several of the European countries to which the French code system originally was brought by Napoleon's armies, retained that system for a long time after Napoleon had been crushed and they had regained their independence; some of them essentially adhere to the French system even today. Japan, likewise, voluntarily retained most of the legal institutions which had been imported from the United States during the occupation period following World War II.[35] Another example is pre-

32. For further examples see 1 Schnitzer, Vergleichende Rechtslehre 58 ff. (2d ed. 1961); Lobingier, The Modern Expansion of Roman Law, 6 U. of Cin.L.Rev. 152 (1932).

Reception of laws of European origin (i.e., of common law, civil law or socialist law), often superimposed on remnants of an indigenous system, is the earmark of most legal systems in Asia and Africa. The resulting crazy-quilt of legal systems will be described later when we discuss the legal map of those areas. See infra pp. 315–327.

33. For example: Working in close cooperation with the Government of Liberia, the Liberian Codification Project at Cornell, headed by Professor Milton Konvitz, compiled and subsequently revised that country's Code of Laws, and attended to the publication of the Liberian Law Reports. See P. Copeland, Konvitz Directs Liberian Codification Project, 25 Cornell Law Forum, No. 1, p. 5 (Winter 1973).

For further examples see E. D. Re, Legal Exchanges and American Foreign Policy, 21 J.Legal Ed. 419 (1969); Hardberger, The Men of the Peace Corps: "Founding Fathers" of a New Order, 52 A.B.A.J. 131 (1966); J. A. Hoskins, United States Technical Assistance for Legal Modernization, 56 A.B.A.J. 1160 (1970); L. E. Trakman, The Need for Legal Training in International, Comparative and Foreign Law: Foreign Lawyers at American Law Schools, 27 J.Legal Ed. 509, 518–19 (1976).

34. Since its adoption of a German-influenced civil code two generations ago, Japan has experienced a second reception of foreign legal institutions, this time of the common-law type. Concerning this second reception, which received its initial impulse from military occupation following World War II, and hence was not wholly voluntary, see infra pp. 319–322.

34a. The effects of conquest or colonization upon the legal system of the subdued group are interestingly discussed by R. Rodière, Introduction au droit comparé 12–14 (1979).

35. Though limited to a single area of law, a similar development can be observed in West Germany where antitrust legislation of distinctly American flavor was first introduced by the occupation authorities. See Loevinger, Antitrust Law in the Modern World, 6 Int. & Comp.L.Bull. No. 2 (pub. May 1962 by ABA Section of International and Comparative Law) 20, 26–27. Upon regaining full sovereignty, the German Federal Republic passed a Law Against Restrictive Competitive Practices (BGB1 1957 I 1081 ff.) which, although granting broad discretionary powers to the newly created Federal Cartel Authority, in principle adopted most of the prohibitions of restrictive trade practices which had made their first appearance in the German legal system under the auspices of occupying powers. See D. J. Gerber, The Extraterritorial Application of the German Antitrust Laws, 77 Am.J.Int.L. 756, at 757–58 (1983), where further references can be

sented by India, which upon gaining independence chose to preserve
and indeed to strengthen the common law features of its legal system.

Legal institutions may be transferred from one geographic location
to another not only by reception (voluntary or otherwise) but also by
migration of entire tribes or nations, or of smaller groups of conquerors
or colonists.[36] There is no part of the world that has remained
unaffected by such waves of migration; and in many countries, especially some of the former colonial ones, the elements of the legal system
originally brought in by the invading group may still be regarded as
foreign.

The whole subject of the present-day significance of migration and
reception of foreign laws will be taken up in more detail when we study
the legal map of the world (see infra pp. 310–337). Suffice it to sum up,
at this point, by saying that *every highly developed legal system,
including our own, contains some imported elements.* In some countries, a legal rule or institution imported from abroad may be an oddity.
In others, the entire legal system is of foreign origin. Allowing for
these considerable differences of degree, it is fair to say that lawyers
everywhere sometimes have to engage in comparative studies in order
to understand and intelligently to apply the foreign-derived elements in
their own domestic legal system.[37]

(b) In the United States, we no longer think of the English common
law as a foreign or "imported" element.[38] But we must remember that,
quite apart from the occasional civil-law influences mentioned above,
large sections of the United States have a *heritage of Spanish and
French law* derived from early settlers and conquerors.[39] Some of the

found. For a fascinating argument to the
effect that the German version of antitrust
has been more successful than its American model, see J. Maxeiner, Policy and
Methods in German and American Antitrust Law (1986).

36. In theory, the distinction between
reception and migration is reasonably
clear; but in applying these concepts it is
not always easy to keep them apart, especially in reference to colonial countries.
For example, the involuntary "reception"
of the common law in colonial India may
be called a "migration" to the extent that
British legal institutions were introduced
for the benefit of British interests and residents in India, and actually administered
by British judges and officials.

37. Those who transfer or "transplant"
legal rules and institutions from one
habitat to another, and those who subsequently have to live with such transplants,
of course should be aware of cultural, economic or political obstacles that may ob-
struct the healthy growth of the transferred institution in its new soil. See
supra n. 30. Attempts to list and systema-
tize these obstacles, and to arrive at generalizations concerning their strength under
various sets of historical conditions, have
led to lively and fascinating controversy.
Compare O. Kahn-Freund, On Uses and

Misuses of Comparative Law, 37 Mod.L.
Rev. 1 (1974), with A. Watson, Legal Transplants and Law Reform, 92 L.Q.Rev. 79
(1976). For a dispassionate view, see the
article by E. Stein cited supra n. 22.

38. In the development of English law
itself, from Lanfranc and Bracton to Lord
Mansfield, Roman and other continental
influences played an important part. See
infra pp. 263–265.

39. "There are many parts of Texas law
today that came from the Spanish law,
notably those relating to . . . marital and
community rights, and the lack of distinction between law and equity." Markham,
The Reception of the Common Law of England in Texas and the Judicial Attitude
Toward that Reception, 1840–59, 29 Tex.L.
Rev. 904, 909 (1951).

For comprehensive discussions of the
subject mentioned in the text, supra, see H.
W. Baade, The Form of Marriage in Spanish North America, 61 Cornell L.Rev. 1,
especially at 1–5 (1975); H. W. Baade, The
Formalities of Private Real Estate Transactions in Spanish North America, 38 La.L.
Rev. 655 (1978); G. A. Zaphiriou, supra n.
6; H. W. Baade, Book Review, 26 Am.J.
Comp.L. 647 (1978). The instructive symposium by M. Tarnawsky, K. Wallach, J.
Stepan and F. J. Figuerado, Bicentennial

early session laws of a number of states were published in Spanish, French or German, in addition to the English version.[40]

True, these remnants of the civil law often are hidden under a thick layer of common law;[41] but a lawyer who practices in Florida, Texas, New Mexico, Arizona or California, or in any of the states which were included in the Louisiana Purchase, cannot afford to overlook these remnants when dealing with problems of land titles,[42] mining law,[43] water rights[44] or matrimonial property.[45]

In no other part of the United States are civil-law influences as strong as in Louisiana and Puerto Rico. The French settlers of Louisiana originally lived under French law; but from 1769 to 1803, Spanish law was imposed upon them as a result of treaties concluded among European powers, followed by military conquest.[46] In 1803, French

Survey of Civil Law Influences on American Legal Development, 69 L.Lib.J. 610 (1976), contains a very useful bibliography. See also K. Knaup, The Transition from Spanish Civil Law to English Common Law in Missouri, 16 St. Louis U.L.J. 218 (1971).

40. See J. Fedynskyj, State Session Laws in Non-English Languages, 46 Ind. L.J. 473 (1971).

41. See R. R. Powell, Compromises of Conflicting Claims: A Century of California Law 1760–1860, especially at 127–32 (1977), and the authorities listed supra n. 39.

42. See Ainsa v. New Mexico & Arizona R.R., 175 U.S. 76, 79, 20 S.Ct. 28, 29 (1899). For massive references to further authorities see the articles cited supra n. 39, and H. W. Baade, Proving Foreign Law and International Law in Domestic Tribunals, 18 Va.J.Int.L. 619, 620–23 (1978).

In Humble Oil & Refining Co. v. Sun Oil Co., 190 F.2d 191, 194–95 (5th Cir. 1951), a question of title to Texas land was decided on the authority of a provision of the Siete Partidas (see infra p. 236). The court relied, also, on quotations from the Corpus Juris (see infra, p. 248.

43. See Swenson, Civil and Common Law Precedents to American Mining Law, in 1 The American Law of Mining, Section 1.1 (Looseleaf ed.); 1 Snyder, Mines and Mining 38 ff. (1902). Cf. Moore v. Smaw, 17 Cal. 199 (1861).

44. See City of Los Angeles v. San Fernando, 14 Cal.3d 199, 123 Cal.Rptr. 1, 537 P.2d 1250 (1975). In this case seventy trial days were devoted to the presentation of expert testimony and other evidence on the issue whether plaintiff had a *pueblo* water right under Spanish-Mexican law.

See also McCurdy v. Morgan, 265 S.W.2d 269 (Tex.Civ.App.1954) (holding that the civil-law doctrine of sovereign ownership of the beds of watercourses was limited to

perennial streams, and did not apply to dry creeks. The briefs in that case, written with the assistance of Spanish and Mexican scholars, traced the civil law distinction between perennial and torrential streams to Seneca, Ulpian, and Justinian's *Corpus Juris*); In re Adjudication of Water Rights in Medina River Watershed of San Antonio River Basin, 670 S.W.2d 250 (Tex. 1984); Maricopa County Municipal Water Conservation District No. 1 v. Southwest Cotton Co., 39 Ariz. 65, 4 P.2d 369 (1931). A thorough discussion and many further references can be found in H. W. Baade, The Historical Background of Texas Water Law, 18 St. Mary's L.J. 1 (1986).

45. See, e.g., McDonald v. Senn, 53 N.M. 198, 212, 204 P.2d 990, 998 (1949) ("It is the rule in this state that we should look to the Spanish-Mexican law for definitions and interpretations affecting our community property statutes"); Clark, Community Property and the Family in New Mexico 6–7 (1956). For comprehensive information concerning the civil law origin and civil law nature of community property, see Charmatz and Daggett, Comparative Studies in Community Property Law (1955); De Funiak and Vaughn, Principles of Community Property 39–108 (1971).

46. See Batiza, The Influence of Spanish Law in Louisiana, 33 Tul.L.Rev. 29 (1958); id., The Unity of Private Law in Louisiana Under the Spanish Rule, 4 Inter-American L.Rev. 139 (1962).

Concerning the nature and sources of the body of Spanish law introduced in Louisiana and other parts of the New World, see the articles by Baade cited supra n. 39.

Regarding the situation in Louisiana, it should be noted that while from 1769 to 1803 the official law was predominantly Spanish, the law in action, i.e., the legal practices of the inhabitants, largely continued to reflect French traditions. See H. W. Baade, Marriage Contracts in French

authorities again took possession of New Orleans, but only for three weeks, and merely for the purpose of handing over control to the United States under the terms of the Louisiana Purchase treaties. Shortly thereafter, in 1808, Louisiana's substantive private law was codified; this codification is of great present-day significance because large portions of the Civil Code of 1808 were subsequently incorporated into the Civil Codes of 1825 and of 1870, the latter being in effect today.[47]

The draftsmen of the 1808 Code utilized Spanish as well as French sources; the latter included not only the works of famous 17th and 18th century scholars such as Domat and Pothier, but also a draft and the final version of the Code Napoleon, which had been promulgated in 1804. The question whether the draftsmen relied predominantly on these French texts (as is generally believed), or on the Spanish ones, is hotly controverted and has given rise to a fascinating scholarly debate.[48] Certain it is, however, that the Louisiana Civil Code has its roots in the civil law.[48a]

In areas of the law not covered by the Civil Code, especially those of procedure, commercial law and public law, Louisiana experienced the intrusion of many common-law institutions. Even in the interpretation and application of the Civil Code itself, the impact of common-law methods was felt, and a few decades ago it was a matter of some controversy whether Louisiana had not, in essence, become a common law jurisdiction.[49] Since then, however, the Louisiana State Law Institute, pursuant to legislative mandate,[50] has sponsored and published English translations of leading French treatises on private law, and in preparation of the ongoing and future revision of the Civil Code has embarked on a program of encouraging the publication of other legal materials of a distinctly civilian bent.[51] Thus the present trend is

and Spanish Louisiana: A Study in "Notarial" Jurisprudence, 53 Tul.L.Rev. 3, especially at 73 ff. (1978).

47. The concordances among the Codes of 1808, 1825 and 1870 are listed in West's Louisiana Statutes Annotated, Civil Code, Vols. 16 and 17, 1972 Compiled Edition of the Civil Codes of Louisiana (J. Dainow, Ed., 1973 and annual pocket parts). In Vol. 17, ibid., at 803 ff., a helpful bibliography can be found.

For additions to the substantive private law of Louisiana which were enacted after 1870, see Louisiana Revised Statutes of 1950, Title 9 (Civil Code—Ancillaries), in West's Louisiana Statutes Annotated, Revised Statutes, Vols. 3, 3A and 4.

48. See Batiza, The Louisiana Civil Code of 1808: Its Actual Sources and Present Relevance, 46 Tul.L.Rev. 4 (1971); Pascal, Sources of the Digest of 1808: A Reply to Professor Batiza, 46 Tul.L.Rev. 603 (1972); Batiza, Sources of the Civil Code of 1808—Facts and Speculation: A Rejoinder, 46 Tul.L.Rev. 628 (1972); Batiza, The Actual Sources of the Louisiana Projet of 1823: A General Analytical Survey, 47 Tul.L. Rev. 1 (1972).

For a concise, detached and plausible summing up of the controversy, see A. N. Yiannopoulos, The Early Sources of Louisiana Law: Critical Appraisal of a Controversy, in E. F. Haas (Ed.), Louisiana's Legal Heritage 87 (1983).

48a. For excellent guides to the sources of Louisiana law, including the Roman, Spanish and French antecedents, see Yiannopoulos, ibid.; Wallach, Research in Louisiana Law (1958).

49. For conflicting answers to this question, see, on the one hand, Ireland, Louisiana's Legal System Reappraised, 11 Tulane L.Rev. 585, 591-2 (1937) and Comment, 7 Tulane L.Rev. 100 (1932); but see, on the other hand, Daggett, Dainow, Hebert and McMahon, A Reappraisal Appraised: A Brief for the Civil Law of Louisiana, 12 Tulane L.Rev. 12, 17-24 (1937) and Note, 17 Geo.Wash.L.Rev. 186, 192-3 (1949).

50. See Tucker, The Civil Law Objectives of the Louisiana State Law Institute, in Yiannopoulos (Ed.), Civil Law in the Modern World, at XI-XVI (1965).

51. See A. N. Yiannopoulos, Louisiana Civil Law Treatise: Property 15-18 (2d Ed., 1980). See also the other volumes in the

toward revitalization of the State's civil-law tradition. In any event, it is clear that few questions of substantive private law can be answered by a Louisiana lawyer without resort to the provisions of a Code of civil-law ancestry. The system, the terminology and the unarticulated assumptions of such a Code cannot be understood by one whose training is limited to the common law.[51a]

The Civil Code of Puerto Rico derives from Spain.[52] In interpreting its provisions, the courts of Puerto Rico have felt bound by Spanish decisions rendered prior to October 18, 1898.[53] Other Spanish authorities have persuasive force.[54] By virtue of a 1961 congressional enactment,[54a] it is no longer possible to appeal to any federal court from decisions of the Supreme Court of Puerto Rico interpreting the Civil Code or any other local laws. Even before 1961, the federal courts were not permitted to inject common law notions into the application of local laws derived from the civil law;[55] and the same rule still applies whenever federal courts, in the exercise of their ordinary jurisdiction (especially in diversity cases), are called upon to apply Puerto Rican law.[56] It is true that through other channels some elements of "continental law"[57] have been imported;[58] but at least in the area of substantive private law[59] the legal system of the Commonwealth has preserved its predominantly civilian character. Future revision of the Spanish-derived Civil Code, if and when it occurs,[59a] is unlikely to change the Code's civilian bent.[60]

(4) *The Treatment of [Imported Elements] Within a Legal System*

As the foregoing survey has shown, the problem of imported law has a double aspect. It can be viewed prospectively, through the eyes of a lawgiver who *in creating new statutory or decisional law* consults foreign solutions, and perhaps will adopt them as models or guides. On

---

important series Louisiana Civil Law Treatise.

51a. See the instructive article by A. N. Yiannopoulos, Louisiana Civil Law: A Lost Cause?, 54 Tul.L.Rev. 830 (1980).

52. See 31 Laws of Puerto Rico Ann. Sec. 1, Note "History of Civil Code" (1968).

53. Olivieri v. Biaggi, 17 P.R.R. 676 (1911); Marchan v. Eguen, 44 P.R.R. 396 (1933) (construing the term "professor" as used in the Code). See also infra p. 599.

54. Ibid. See also Geigel v. Mariani, 85 P.R.R. 43 (1962), where the court relied not only on a post-1898 decision of the Supreme Court of Spain, but also on a wide range of other civil-law authorities uncovered by comparative research.

54a. 75 Stat. 417, repealing former 28 U.S.C.A. § 1293.

55. Bonet v. Texas Co., 308 U.S. 463, 60 S.Ct. 349 (1940); Diaz v. Gonzalez, 261 U.S. 102, 43 S.Ct. 286 (1923), quoted infra p. 54.

56. See De Castro v. Board of Commissioners, 322 U.S. 451, at 459, 64 S.Ct. 1121 (1944); First National City Bank v. Gonzalez, 293 F.2d 919 (1st Cir. 1961). Cf. Fornaris v. Ridge Tool Co., 400 U.S. 41, 91

S.Ct. 156 (1970); Gual Morales v. Hernandez Vega, 579 F.2d 677, 682 (1st Cir. 1978).

57. When Puerto Rican lawyers speak of "continental" law, they refer to the legal system of the continental United States. This, of course, differs from ordinary, Webster-approved usage which associates continental law, like continental cuisine, with the continent of Europe.

58. For comments on the attempts of Puerto Rican courts to integrate the civil-law and common-law elements of their system, see J. J. Santa-Pinter, Law and Law Teaching in Puerto Rico, 8 Foreign Exchange Bull., No. 2 (Fall 1966) 5. See also infra p. 663.

59. For a highly interesting illustration see Infante v. Leith, 85 P.R.R. 24 (1962).

59a. For a discussion of the planned Code revision, see Symposium, Reforma del Codigo Civil de Puerto Rico, 52 Revista Juridica de la Universidad de Puerto Rico 141–380 (1983).

60. For further materials on the expansion of the civil law, especially in the Western Hemisphere, see infra pp. 310–337.

the other hand, the problem presents itself retrospectively to the lawyer or judge who *in applying existing law* discovers that the pertinent rule is an imported one, and who thus is faced with the question whether he should undertake comparative research in order to ascertain how the rule operates in the country of its origin.

Where local authorities are scanty, and the necessary foreign materials are easily accessible, it is likely that such research will be undertaken. Suppose, for instance, that Ruritania has adopted an essentially French-oriented legal system. So long as Ruritania has not yet developed a strong legal tradition of its own, and provided French legal materials are available, it is likely that Ruritanian lawyers and law students will make ample use of these imported materials.[61]

Where, on the other hand, the borrowing country itself has a highly developed legal culture, and the imported ideas relate only to an isolated problem or a limited segment of the legal order, the foreign antecedents of the borrowed elements may soon be forgotten. In the United States, for instance, not many persons remember today that the Workers' Compensation Acts which since 1910 have been adopted in every state, were largely based on a German model.[62]

It may even happen that a legislative draftsman, although in fact borrowing from foreign sources, consciously seeks to keep the future application of his statute free from any continuing alien influences.[63] An attempt of this kind has been made by the sponsors of the Uniform Commercial Code. The principal architect of the Code, the late Professor Karl N. Llewellyn, had spent considerable time in Germany; and there can be no doubt that some of the Code's important features were inspired by his study of German law. An example which readily comes to mind is the separation of the contract aspects of a sales transaction from the title aspects—probably the fundamental innovative idea embodied in Article 2. Equally "German" in style is the famous provision of § 2–302, by which unconscionable contracts and contract clauses are rendered unenforceable. The draftsmen, however, clearly sought to discourage any future tendency on the part of courts or commentators to look to German authorities in applying these and other German-inspired provisions. They did so by two devices, namely (a) by not flaunting the foreign model,[64] and (b) by an express provision emphasiz-

61. As time goes on, and local court decisions and other local materials become available, there is some danger that the courts and practitioners of Ruritania (which might be located in Latin America) will cease to pay attention to the foreign antecedents, while Ruritanian legal scholars and law teachers continue to rely on French or other imported textbooks almost to the exclusion of local authorities. This may lead to an estrangement between academic law and law in action, a situation of which the outsider studying Ruritanian law must be constantly aware if he is to avoid gross errors and misunderstandings.

62. See M. L. Perlin, The German and British Roots of American Workers' Compensation Systems, 15 Seton Hall L.Rev. 849, 860 (1985). This migration of the German compensation scheme has been called

"a triumph of comparative law". P. W. Schroth, Products Liability, in J. N. Hazard & W. J. Wagner (Eds.), Law in the United States in the Bicentennial Era 67, 68 (1978; Supplement to Vol. 26 of the Am. J.Comp.L.).

63. Some of the policy considerations which—even in a society not given to blind nationalism—may be cited in support of such "insularity", are pointed out by Summers, American and European Labor Law: The Use and Usefulness of Foreign Experience, 16 Buff.L.Rev. 210 (Lenhoff Festschrift 1966).

64. Concerning the lack of any published preparatory studies of a comparative nature, see Schlesinger, The Uniform Commercial Code in the Light of Comparative

ing that the Code must be read against a common-law background.[65] The first of these devices, by itself, would hardly be effective, because legal scholars have been quick to perceive some of the pertinent civil-law models and counterparts.[66] In combination, however, the two devices seem, at least thus far, to have accomplished the draftsmen's objective of minimizing reliance on foreign authorities.[67]

B. THE FOREIGN SOLUTION AS A CONTRAST OR A MEANS OF GAINING PERSPECTIVE

Illustration

At common law, a promise not supported by sufficient consideration could be made binding by the use of a seal. This ancient rule was invoked by the New York Court of Appeals, as late as 1937, to enforce an option, gratuitously granted and open for 120 days, to buy certain real and personal property for $115,000.[1] This decision reinforced the feeling, already widespread among New York lawyers, that the obsolete institution of the seal should be abolished. The legal profession remembered the words of Judge Cardozo:

> "In our day, when the perfunctory initials 'L.S.' have replaced the heraldic devices, the law is conscious of its own absurdity when it preserves the rubric of a vanished era. Judges have made worthy, if shamefaced efforts, while giving lip service to the rule, to riddle it with exceptions and by distinctions reduce it to a shadow. . . . The law will have cause for gratitude to the deliverer who will strike the fatal blow." [2]

In 1941, the New York Law Revision Commission [3] recommended, and the Legislature adopted, a statute reading as follows:

> "Except as otherwise expressly provided by statute, the presence or absence of a seal upon a written instrument hereafter executed shall be without legal effect." [4]

Law, 1 Inter-American L.Rev. 11, 27–28 (1959).

For a general (and most enlightening) description of the genesis of the Code, see W. Twining, Karl Llewellyn and the Realist Movement 270 ff. (1973).

65. § 1–103. See also § 1–102.

66. See, e.g., Note, Unconscionable Contract Provisions: A History of Unenforceability from Roman Law to the UCC, 42 Tul.L.Rev. 193 (1967), where further references can be found.

67. See T. B. Smith, The Preservation of the Civilian Tradition in "Mixed Jurisdictions", in Yiannopoulos (Ed.), Civil Law in the Modern World 3, at 8 (1965): "The Uniform Commercial Code . . . has drawn extensively on German solutions, though, perhaps surprisingly, leading commentators upon it do not seem much interested in comparative material." This seems to remain true today. Of course,

there is a growing number of studies comparing the Code's solutions with those of other legal systems; but little is done to utilize its civil-law antecedents in the interpretation and application of the Code itself.

1. Cochran v. Taylor, 273 N.Y. 172, 7 N.E.2d 89 (1937).

2. Cardozo, The Nature of the Judicial Process 155–56 (1921).

3. Acts, Recommendation and Study Relating to the Seal and to the Enforcement of Certain Written Contracts, 1941 Report of the New York Law Revision Commission 345 ff. The Study supporting the Recommendation of the Commission was prepared by Professor Paul R. Hays.

4. § 342 of the former New York Civil Practice Act. The substance of this provision appears now in § 44–a of N.Y.Gen. Construction Law.

In making this recommendation, the Law Revision Commission naturally examined the broader problem "whether and to what extent a person should be able to bind himself by a promise without consideration." More specifically, the Commission inquired whether it would be possible to substitute for the seal a more modern, *formal* device assuring deliberation and recognition by the parties of the legal consequences of their transaction. The consultant [5] called attention to the rule prevailing in most civil-law countries. There, the requirement of consideration is unknown; [6] but promises to make a gift, i.e., promises prompted by an *animus donandi*, are void unless made before a *notary*.

At first blush, this civil-law rule seemed to provide a feasible substitute for the seal. Closer examination,[7] however, revealed that a "notary" in a civil law country is an important official whose legal education, tested by difficult examinations, has been as thorough as that of an attorney or a judge.[8] Ordinarily, the office of notary is a full-time occupation in civil-law countries, and the official conduct of the incumbent is subject to intensive supervision by the Presiding Judge of the local court, by the Department of Justice and by the Chamber of Notaries. Normally, the notary is not salaried, but his clients have to pay him substantial fees fixed by a statutory tariff. Thus he is a professional practitioner as well as a public official. Within his district, he may or may not have a monopoly; but ordinarily there is not much competition among notaries, because the number of notarial offices (notariats) is severely limited in most civil-law countries.[9] As a result, many notaries achieve considerable affluence, and the Herr Notar or Monsieur le Notaire invariably is a man of high standing in his community.[9a]

Civil-law countries ordinarily require notarial form not only for gratuitous contracts but, inter alia, for nearly all transactions involving real estate, for marriage settlements and for many corporate acts such as the formation of a corporation and any amendment of its charter.[10]

5. See n. 3 supra.

6. See Lorenzen, Causa and Consideration in the Law of Contracts, 28 Yale L.J. 621 (1919). For a penetrating comparative study of the methods by which the actionability of promises is determined in the common law and the civil law, see Gorla, Il Contratto (2 vols. 1954), reviewed by Rheinstein, 4 Am.J.Comp.L. 452 (1955).

7. The examination took the form of a Study, prepared by Professor Schlesinger, on "The Notary and the Formal Contract in Civil Law", which was published as an Appendix to the consultant's Study, supra n. 3, 1941 Report of the New York Law Revision Commission 345, at 403 ff.

8. See infra pp. 147–188.

9. See G. F. Margadant, The Mexican Notariate, 6 Cal.West.L.Rev. 218, 224 (1970).

9a. Further details, and references covering several civil-law countries, are given in the Study cited supra n. 7. For a description of French practice, and a comparison of the French notary with the Eng-

lish solicitor, see L. N. Brown, The Office of the Notary in France, 2 Int. & Comp.L.Q. 60 (1953).

For surveys tracing the history of the notarial institution from Roman to modern days see Del Russo, The Notary Public in the Civil Law of Italy, 20 Geo.Wash.L.Rev. 524 (1952), and (with emphasis on Spain and Latin America) Margadant, supra n. 9.

10. For further examples, especially in connection with powers of attorney, see infra p. 779. Generally, a notarial instrument is necessary in the frequent cases in which the document is to serve as the basis for an entry in one of the public registers which are of such great importance in civil-law countries, e.g., the land register, the commercial register, or the matrimonial property register. See infra, pp. 684–702.

The functions of notaries in civil-law countries are not confined to the recording of transactions. As was said in Makofsky v. Cunningham, 576 F.2d 1223, 1228 (5 Cir. 1978): "Among the duties the notary public may perform in civilian legal systems

Frequently, this form requirement is not satisfied by mere authentication of the signatures of the parties; but the document must be executed in the form of a protocol the original of which is preserved forever, and protected against any insertion or alteration, by being kept in the office of the notary.[11] The parties can obtain certified copies of the document from the notary or his successor in office.

The civil-law notary is under a duty to use the utmost care in examining the legality, and generally the validity, of the transaction; this includes, of course, diligent inquiry into the identity and legal capacity of the parties.[12] If the transaction requires approval by a third party or by a public authority, he must so inform the parties. Generally, he is bound to advise the parties as to the legal significance of the contemplated act, including the tax liabilities arising therefrom. If one of the parties to the transaction appears to be of insufficient experience, he must try to avoid overreaching. Intentional or negligent violation of any of these duties may subject the notary to disciplinary proceedings and to civil liability for damages.[13]

When this comparative information concerning the status and functions of notaries had been submitted to the New York Law Revision Commission and its consultant, it became clear that in a civil-law country the requirement of a "notarial" document truly assures informed deliberation on the part of those who enter into the transaction. In addition, the parties are prevented from acting without legal advice, and are compelled to have the document embodying their transaction drawn up by a properly qualified person. At the same time, the requirement of notarial form protects the public, by making it more

are conveyancing of title, drafting of land title documents, holding of family meetings, making of inventories, appraisements and partitions. . . ."

Notaries in civil-law countries also perform functions which we would classify as judicial. In some of those countries, they conduct judicial sales of real property. In other civil-law (and socialist) jurisdictions one finds that letters testamentary and letters of administration can be issued by a notary, and that the notary likewise performs other official acts necessary for the processing of a decedent's estate. The result is that—in countries adhering to that system—probate matters "reach the courts only if one of the parties is dissatisfied with the notary's ruling." Estate of Chichernea, 66 Cal.2d 83, at 99, 57 Cal. Rptr. 135, 146, 424 P.2d 687, 698 (1967).

11. In France, for example, the original is kept in the office of the notary for 125 years; thereafter it may be delivered to the national or district archives.

A notarial protocol constitutes a so-called *acte authentique* or *oeffentliche Urkunde*, and as such has special probative force. See French Civil Code, Articles 1317–1319, and German Code of Civil Procedure, Sections 415, 417, 418; see also infra pp. 136–138.

12. If the notary is not satisfied concerning any of these points, he must refuse his services. See, e.g., the German Beurkundungsgesetz of August 28, 1969 (BGBl I 1513), Section 4. See generally Schlesinger, supra n. 7, at 411.

13. For details, see Schlesinger, ibid.

Whenever necessary, the notary performs the function of an escrow agent. Sometimes, moreover, he is responsible for collecting stamp taxes and for assisting in the collection of other taxes which become payable in connection with the transaction recorded by him. In addition to his other functions, he may thus serve as an auxiliary fiscal officer.

Under a totalitarian regime, the requirement of notarial form means in effect that the government must be informed of the transaction. See Guins, Soviet Law and Soviet Society 110, 116, 126 (1954). See also § 3 of the Notaries Law of the German Democratic Republic (Law of Feb. 5, 1976, Gesetzblatt p. 93), which makes it clear that a Notary must co-operate with other representatives of State and Party, and that "whenever in the exercise of notarial functions he notices violations of law, he must take measures to have such violations undone."

difficult for agents without proper authority and for persons lacking legal capacity to create the semblance of a valid legal transaction.[14]

The Commission concluded that in New York the adoption of a requirement of notarization would produce none of these beneficial effects. Except for the name, a "notary public" in New York, and generally in the United States, has little in common with the civil-law notary.[15] The *institution* of the notary, as developed in the civil-law world in the course of many centuries, was found by the Commission to have no counterpart in this country.[15a] Without such an institution, which cannot be created by a mere stroke of the legislative pen, it is very difficult, if not impossible, to subject the execution of certain types of instruments to formal requirements more effective and more solemn than a simple signed writing. From this it followed, in the Commission's view, that it would be impracticable for the New York legislator to fashion a satisfactory *formal* requirement as a substitute for the seal.[16]

Having reached this negative conclusion, and thus seeing the problem in its true perspective, the commission decided *of NY*

". . . that a sounder policy would be to make the requirement of consideration applicable to promises generally, making no distinction between sealed and unsealed promises, with express statutory provision that in specified cases a promise, in writing, shall not be unenforceable because of the absence of consideration. This method of dealing with the problem is the one already employed by the Legislature in the cases of releases and modification agreements.[17]

14. See supra, text at n. 12.

15. Concerning the qualifications and functions of notaries in the United States, see W. Gilmer, Anderson's Manual for Notaries Public (5th ed. 1976, and Cum. Supps.).

The instructive article by Leyser, Notaries in Australia, 37 Australian L.J. 308 (1964), traces the history of notaries in England and other Commonwealth countries, and compares their status with that of civil-law notaries. For a brief discussion of the historical reasons which account for the relatively low status of notaries in common-law countries, see 5 Holdsworth, History of English Law 114–5 (1945).

In Louisiana and Quebec, the status of notaries seems to be somewhere between the civil-law and common-law models. See D. B. Burke & J. K. Fox, The Notaire in North America: A Short Study of the Adaptation of a Civil Law Institution, 50 Tul. L.Rev. 318, 325–32 (1976).

15a. Many foreign-born residents of the United States, brought up in Mexico or other civil-law countries, erroneously believe that any person carrying the title of "Notary" is competent to render legal advice. American notaries sometimes have

fraudulently exploited this belief. See, e.g. Lawscope, Unscrupulous Notaries Spur Chicago Probe, 68 A.B.A.J. 1357 (1982). For a statute seeking to counteract such fraudulent practices—and thus taking cognizance of the essential difference between civil-law notaries and their common-law namesakes—, see Cal.Govt.Code Section 8219.5, as added in 1974 and amended in 1976.

16. The Commission pointed out that the Uniform Written Obligations Act, which was adopted only in Pennsylvania (and temporarily in Utah), cannot be regarded as providing a satisfactory modern substitute for the seal.

Concerning this question of a modern substitute for the seal (or of a functional equivalent of civil-law notarization) see also infra, Notes and Questions following this Illustration.

17. The Commission referred to § 33 subd. 2 of the New York Personal Property Law and § 279 subd. 1 of the Real Property Law. The substance of these provisions, which had been enacted prior to 1941, has meanwhile been transferred to N.Y.Gen. Obligations Law § 5–1103.

The Commission is now prepared to recommend that the requirement of consideration be dispensed with in the case of promises, in writing, expressly based upon a past consideration; in the case of assignments, in writing, of a chose in action; and in the case of an offer, in writing, which expressly states that it shall be irrevocable for a specified time. As experience demonstrates the desirability of further additions to the list of exceptions, they may be made without the necessity of revising the entire law of consideration." [18]

In following these recommendations, the New York Legislature not only deprived the seal of its ancient effect,[19] but at the same time modernized an important segment of the law of contracts.[20]

NOTES AND QUESTIONS

(1) In what way did the Law Revision Commission use the comparative method? By way of imitation? By way of simple contrast, i.e., pointing to a horrible example which should not be followed? [1] As a starting point for critical analysis of an existing rule (e.g., by showing available alternative solutions)? [2] As a means of discovering possible flaws in a proposal for reform? As an aid in understanding the social function of the rules in question and a vehicle for clarifying the historical and institutional context in which these rules must be developed and applied as part of our legal system? [3]

(2) It will hardly be denied that the New York Law Revision Commission, having taken a look at the functionally comparable civil law solution of the problem at hand, was able to view that problem in better perspective. It should be recognized, however, that here as in other instances the lessons derived from a comparative study were of a subtle and perhaps debatable character.

Surely the Commission was on solid ground when it concluded that New York, like most common-law jurisdictions, did not have a class of

18. See Recommendation to the Legislature, 1941 Report of the New York Law Revision Commission, supra n. 3, at 360.

19. See supra n. 4.

20. The statutory provisions adopted by the legislature pursuant to this recommendation of the Law Revision Commission originally were inserted into the Personal Property Law and the Real Property Law. More recently they have been transferred to, and they now appear in, N.Y.Gen.Obligations Law § 5–1105 (written promise expressing past consideration), § 5–1107 (written assignment), and § 5–1109 (written irrevocable offer).

1. Cf. Eder, A Comparative Survey of Anglo-American and Latin-American Law 157 (1950): "The most valuable contribution that comparative studies can make is perhaps a negative one", in that "comparative law teaches us, by the light of costly experience in other countries, what to avoid." One might add that the costliest experience, in terms of human suffering, is that of countries living under a totalitarian

regime. From that experience, we have much to learn. See People v. Barber, 289 N.Y. 378, 386, 46 N.E.2d 329, 332 (1943), and infra pp. 725, 752, 882.

2. See Frank, Civil Law Influences on the Common Law—Some Reflections on "Comparative" and "Contrastive" Law, 104 U. of Pa.L.Rev. 887, 914–5 (1956).

3. Cf. Rheinstein, Trends in Marriage and Divorce Law of Western Countries, 18 Law & Contemp.Probl. 3 (1953); Patterson and Schlesinger, Problems of Codification of Commercial Law, N.Y.Leg.Doc. (1955) No. 65A, 1955 Report of the New York Law Revision Commission, pp. 86 ff. (116 ff.); H. J. Ault & M. A. Glendon, The Importance of Comparative Law in Legal Education: United States—Goals and Methods of Legal Comparison, in J. N. Hazard & W. J. Wagner, Law in the United States of America in Social and Technological Revolution (U.S. Reports to the IX Congress of the International Academy of Comparative Law) 67 ff. (1974).

officials similar to the civil-law notary, and that it would be difficult for the New York Legislature to create, at a single stroke, a profession as efficient and as universally respected as that of the civil-law notary whose high standing is due, at least in part, to an uninterrupted professional tradition of more than two thousand years.[4] One might, however, question the Commission's further assumption that for a legal system which lacks the institution of a notary in the civil-law sense, it is wholly impossible to create *a fair equivalent* of a civil-law-style notarial document.[5] Under our system, it is normally the attorney who drafts legal documents and thus performs the most important of the traditional functions of the civil-law notary. Thus the question might be posed whether, e.g., a "written agreement concluded upon the advice of counsel to both parties as evidenced by counsels' signatures thereto"[6] and filed in a public office perhaps would constitute the fair equivalent of a document prepared by a civil-law notary. Reasonable men may differ concerning the answer to this question. Even if the answer is in the affirmative, it is not entirely clear what role such a novel type of form requirement could and should play in replacing the ancient seal. The point is raised here only in order to show that when a problem is viewed in the deeper perspective made possible by the comparative method, a number of alternative solutions may come into sight.

(3) Although the Law Revision Commission may have failed to consider all of the possible alternatives, there is agreement among most observers that the solution adopted by it was a sound and progressive one.[7] On other occasions, too, the Commission made significant and

---

4. This tradition pervades the whole civil-law world and indeed constitutes an element of cohesion among civil-law systems. In spite of differences of detail, the age-old essential elements of the notarial institution have remained common to all civil-law countries, so much so that the notaries of the countries in question have been able to form an international professional organization, for the joint study of problems shared by the notaries of all civil-law countries. See H.H. and H. Schippel, Lateinisches Notariat, 5 Juristen-Jahrbuch 78 (1964/65).

The essential uniformity, throughout the civil-law world, of the notarial institution and of the elements and requirements of a notarial document has made it possible for a number of civil-law countries to conclude the Hague Treaty of May 10, 1961, under which a notarial document issued in one signatory country is recognized as fully effective in any other signatory country, without the necessity of diplomatic legalization. See infra p. 137.

5. The statement in the text refers to a document prepared for domestic use. Where the document is to be used in a civil-law country, a New York notary, under existing law, has the powers of a civil-law notary. See infra p. 780.

6. This type of form requirement is not a product of the author's fancy. It has been used, for instance, in a Texas statute dealing with arbitration agreements. 1A Vernon's Ann.Rev.Civ.Stat., Art. 224 (1973). For a brief discussion of this statute, with further references, see J. M. Perillo, The Statute of Frauds in the Light of the Functions and Dysfunctions of Form, 43 Ford.L.Rev. 39, 53 (1974). (Note that a 1979 amendment changed the statutory language quoted in the text, supra; but a similar form requirement remains in force for certain types of arbitration agreements).

Cf. Cal.Code Civ.Pro., § 1132, subd. (b) (attorney's certificate required for cognovit note).

7. It will be recalled that one of the fruits of the Commission's recommendation was a New York statute (N.Y.Gen.Obligations Law § 5–1109) making certain written offers irrevocable in spite of the absence of consideration. More recently, the essential features (though not all of the details) of this innovation have been taken over into the famous "firm offer" provision of § 2–205 of the Uniform Commercial Code. It is possible that the latter provision has been inspired, also, by § 145 of the German Civil Code. See supra p. 16.

successful recommendations in the light of foreign experience brought home to it by comparative studies.[8]

One wonders, therefore, why other agencies of law reform throughout the United States so often fail to avail themselves of the advantages of the comparative method.[9] If a list of missed opportunities of this kind were to be compiled, it would be boringly long. The provincialism of our reformers is particularly flagrant in the area of criminal procedure [10]—an area of special concern at a time when the very fabric of our society is threatened by crime. There is no dearth of useful descriptions, in the English language, of the laws and practices that guide the criminal process in foreign countries.[11] But our criminal-law reformers (and this includes the U.S. Supreme Court, which has usurped such a prominent reformer's role in this area) invariably refuse to benefit from the experience of other countries.[12]

8. The most momentous task ever undertaken by the Commission was its study of the 1951–52 draft of the Uniform Commercial Code, with a view to advising the Legislature whether the Code should be adopted in New York. It was known at the time that New York's adoption or rejection of the Code might well determine its success or failure on a national scale. Thus the Commission's recommendation to the Legislature was a matter of nationwide significance. When the Commission made its historic recommendation—that after revision of the 1951–52 draft the Code be adopted in New York—, it relied heavily on arguments derived, inter alia, from "the experience of foreign countries as well as American states." See 1956 Report of the New York Law Revision Commission, Leg. Doc. (1956) No. 65(A), at p. 57(67).

One of the authors of this book, as the Commission's consultant, previously had prepared a report on "The Uniform Commercial Code in the Light of Comparative Law" (as part of the joint report by Patterson and Schlesinger, cited supra n. 3). In that report he had suggested, on the basis of the experience of code countries in the civil-law world, that adequate machinery be set up for "constant revision" of the Code in order to keep it modern and uniform. See Schlesinger, The Uniform Commercial Code in the Light of Comparative Law (a revised version of the report just mentioned), 1 Inter-American L.Rev. 11, at 33–35 (1959). This suggestion was adopted by the Commission. See its 1956 Report, at 58(68). Ultimately, the suggestion led to the establishment, by the American Law Institute and the National Conference of Commissioners on Uniform State Laws, of the Permanent Editorial Board for the Uniform Commercial Code. See R. E. Speidel, R. S. Summers and J. J. White, Teaching Materials on Commercial and Consumer Law 19 (3d ed., 1981). The creation of

this Board, which today is the most important American law reform agency in the field of commercial law, thus has been the direct result of a comparative study undertaken on behalf of the New York Law Revision Commission.

9. See E. Stein, Uses, Misuses—and Nonuses of Comparative Law, 72 N.W.U.L. Rev. 198, 210–12 (1977); with specific reference to the area of labor law see also C. W. Summers, Book Review, 72 Colum.L.Rev. 1119, 1125–26 (1972).

10. The attachment of lawyers and law reformers to the traditions of their own legal system seems to be particularly strong in the area of procedure, i.e., of the rules which have the most obvious impact on lawyering activities. In the area of substantive law, including substantive criminal law, there appears to be less reluctance to learn from foreign experience. See, e.g., H.-H. Jescheck, The Significance of Comparative Law for Criminal Law Reform, 5 Hastings Int. & Comp.L.Rev. 1, 18 (1981).

11. For materials and references on the law of criminal procedure in civil-law countries, see infra pp. 473–497.

12. See E. M. Wise, Legal Tradition as a Limitation on Law Reform, in J. N. Hazard & W. J. Wagner (eds.), Law in the U.S.A. in the Bicentennial Era, 26 Am.J.Comp.L. (Supplement) 1, at 14–15 (1973): "The National Commission on Reform of Federal Criminal Laws, besides having a director familiar with foreign criminal law, specially solicited outside comparative comments [dealing with substantive law] on its initial study draft; the Senate Subcommittee on Criminal Laws and Procedure also collected comparisons between the proposed federal criminal code and foreign law. Yet the immediate effect of these studies on successive modifications of the reform bill was practically nil."

2. THE COMPARATIVE METHOD APPLIED TO TRANSACTIONS ACROSS INTERNATIONAL BOUNDARIES

A. PROBLEMS ARISING FROM DIFFERENCES AMONG LEGAL SYSTEMS

(AA) COMPARATIVE LAW, CONFLICT OF LAWS AND INTERNATIONAL LAW

In the close-knit world of today, the practicing lawyer finds that to an ever-increasing extent his foreign and local clients, whether they be individuals or corporations, or governmental or international bodies, are faced with problems cutting across the territories and the legal systems of more than one nation. In metropolitan centers, matters of this kind have long been "part of the daily legal fare." [1]   What is perhaps less generally appreciated is the fact that through the American operations of foreign concerns, and the foreign operations and foreign subsidiaries of American manufacturers and distributors located in every part of the country, outlandish problems are carried into the offices of countless practitioners far from the big cities.   Similarly, in dealing with estates and domestic relations of millions of foreign-born individuals, and of approximately a million United States citizens permanently residing abroad, practitioners in every type of community encounter problems of foreign and international law. [2]   International travel by millions of Americans, for business and pleasure as well as for military and other governmental purposes, further adds to the growing volume of such transnational legal problems. [3]

To help in solving these problems, a lawyer must, first of all, know the internal law of his own state or country.   In addition, he will have to have some familiarity with the more specialized, internationally oriented subjects.   Traditionally, these subjects are grouped under three headings: International Law, Conflict of Laws [4] and Comparative Law. [5]   From a functional point of view, it might well be argued that all

---

1. Arthur H. Dean, The Role of International Law in a Metropolitan Practice, 103 U. of Pa.L.Rev. 886, 888 (1955).

2. See Schlesinger, Book Review, 41 Cornell L.Q. 527 (1956).

3. Formerly, the American Journal of Comparative Law used to publish in each issue a Digest of Foreign Law Cases. Even before the recent increase in transnational litigation, the Digest annually listed more than 500 reported opinions which, though handed down by American courts, involved and discussed points of foreign law. If it is considered that reported cases reflect only a minute fraction of the total volume of actual and threatened litigation, and if it is further considered that lawyers, especially

in international practice, devote much less time to litigation than to counseling and negotiation, this figure will indicate the magnitude of the international involvement and responsibility of the legal profession.

4. In the present context, the emphasis is on international rather than interstate conflicts. The term Conflict of Laws thus is used in the sense in which the civilians speak of Private International Law and International Law of Procedure.

5. From the standpoint of an American practitioner who is faced with legal problems arising from international transactions, the term Comparative Law, as used in the text supra, may be defined as the

of these subjects should be considered together.[6] But by merging them, one would create a unit much too large to be convenient for the teacher and the textbook writer; hence, as a rule, they continue to be presented separately.[7] In order to understand the organization of law school curricula, of library catalogues, and of the pertinent literature, it becomes necessary, therefore, to know approximately where the lines of demarcation are drawn between International Law, Conflict of Laws, and Comparative Law. The Illustration which follows will, it is hoped, be of some help in this regard.

Illustration

X, a resident and national of Ruritania, who had been Ruritanian sales-manager for Y Inc., a New York corporation, died recently. His holographic testament, valid under the Civil Code of Ruritania (a civil-law country), gives all of his property to his daughter Z, who has reached majority and, like the decedent, is a resident and national of Ruritania. Asserting that at the time of X's death Y still owed him a certain amount of salary and commissions, Z sues Y in a New York court.

Y moves to dismiss the action on the ground that Z lacks legal capacity to sue on behalf of X's estate, and that the complaint fails to state facts constituting a cause of action. Y points to the well-known common-law rule [8] that a foreign executor, administrator or other personal representative of a decedent's estate cannot bring an action in New York without having obtained ancillary letters from a New York Surrogates Court.[9] For Z, who has not taken out ancillary letters, things look grim at first blush. It seems that her complaint will be dismissed, and that she will have to go to the trouble and expense of having a properly qualified person [10] appointed as ancillary executor.[11]

---

body of knowledge and techniques which he must assimilate in order to deal successfully with the actual *foreign law* elements of such problems.

For some purposes it may be proper and indeed necessary to distinguish between comparative law and foreign law. But from the viewpoint of one who seeks to prepare himself, or to prepare his students, for the handling of legal problems presenting foreign aspects, the distinction has little utility. Comparative law, or the comparative method, can be learned and practiced only in dealing with foreign legal materials. Foreign law, on the other hand, can be understood only through the comparative method.

6. The term International Legal Studies has become accepted as pointing to integrated programs of research and instruction which cover or cut across all three of the traditional subjects. See J. B. Howard, International Legal Studies, 26 U. of Chi.L. Rev. 577 (1959).

7. Needless to say, each of the three traditional subjects mentioned in the text can be subdivided in various ways. Moreover, books and courses intended to perform more specialized functions increasingly tend to combine selected elements of all three subjects in exploring such areas as international and regional organizations, international business transactions, or the legal aspects of development. See, e.g., M. Katz, The International Education Act of 1966: The Place of Law and the Law Schools, 20 J.Leg.Ed. 201, 204–5 (1967).

8. See Ehrenzweig, Conflict of Laws § 14 (1962); E. F. Scoles & P. Hay, Conflict of Laws § 22.14 (1982, and 1986 Supp.); Restatement, Second, Conflict of Laws § 354, Reporter's Note (1971).

9. McKinney's New York Estates, Powers and Trusts Law § 13–3.5 (formerly Decedent Estate Law § 160, added in 1951) modifies this rule; but the section applies only to personal representatives appointed by a "state, territory or other jurisdiction of the United States", and not to representatives appointed in foreign countries. Gibb v. Chisholm, 204 Misc. 892, 126 N.Y.S.2d 150 (Sup.Ct. 1953).

10. Plaintiff herself, being a non-domiciliary alien, is not eligible to serve as the sole estate representative in New York. McKinney's N.Y.S.C.P.A. § 707.

Thereafter, the person so appointed will have to commence a new action against Y, subject to the additional risk that in the meantime the statute of limitations may have run out.

If, however, effective use is made by Z's lawyer of the law of Ruritania, this time-consuming and expensive detour can be avoided. The idea that upon a person's death his personal property passes to his "personal representative", is a common-law idea. In civil-law countries, title and right to possession of decedent's assets automatically vest, at the moment of death, in the testamentary or legal heirs as "universal successors" of the deceased.[12] It follows that upon X's death the plaintiff Z became the *owner* of the claim asserted in the action. She sues, not on behalf of the estate, but in her own right. Defendant's motion, attempting to defeat the action on technical grounds, thus will be denied.[13]

Note the interplay between "Conflict of Laws" and "Comparative Law". The rule that a foreign personal representative cannot sue in New York, is a rule of conflict of laws.[14] The provisions of Ruritanian

11. McKinney's N.Y.S.C.P.A. Art. 16. In the event that there have been no proceedings concerning the estate of X in Ruritania, an "ancillary" administration in New York would not be possible, and Z would have to go to the even greater trouble of seeking original probate of the testament in New York in order to have an estate representative appointed. See Powers, Practice Commentary on § 1601, in McKinney's N.Y.S.C.P.A.

12. In Anglo California Nat. Bank v. Lazard, 106 F.2d 693, 699 (9 Cir., 1939) the court said:

"Under the laws of the Republic of France, . . . the estates of decedents . . . are not administered by probate proceedings with an executor or administrator. Under the said laws all testamentary instruments of the decedent are filed with a Notary. The persons entitled to succeed to the estate of the decedent and the portion to which each is entitled are established by a written instrument executed by the Notary, known as "acte de notoriete". Title to the real and personal property of the decedent vests in the heirs or successors of a decedent at the moment of death of the decedent. The decedent's heirs and next of kin, or residuary devisees and legatees, as the case may be, take the proportion of the estate to which they are entitled, subject to a like proportion of the debts of the decedent, for which they remain personally liable. The Courts of France do not intervene in the administration of the estates of decedents, except for the purpose of directing the filing of holographic wills with the Notaries."

For a more elaborate description of the French system see Bell-Macdonald, French

Laws of Succession, 2 Int. & Comp.L.Q. 415, 422 (1953).

The Spanish doctrine, which is similar in its essentials, is explained in Estate of De Los Salmones, 203 Misc. 1068, 119 N.Y.S.2d 76 (Surr.Ct. 1953).

For comparative discussions of the pertinent common-law and civil-law concepts see J. Puig Brutau, An Introduction to the Law of Succession Mortis Causa, 1 Inter-American L.Rev. 291 (1959); Beinart, Heir and Executor, 1960 Acta Juridica 223; Rheinstein, European Methods for the Liquidation of the Debts of Deceased Persons, 20 Iowa L.Rev. 431 (1935); Rheinstein, Judicial and Administrative Control of the Liquidation of Decedents' Estates, in Rapports Généraux au Cinquième Congrès international de droit comparé 229 (1960); G. A. Pelletier & M. R. Sonnenreich, A Comparative Analysis of Civil Law Succession, 11 Villanova L.Rev. 323 (1966).

13. Du Roure v. Alvord, 120 F.Supp. 166 (S.D.N.Y. 1954); Roques v. Grosjean, 66 N.Y.S.2d 348 (Sup.Ct. 1946); Berney v. Drexel, 33 Hun 34 (1884). Cf. Emmerich v. May, 130 F.Supp. 426 (S.D.N.Y. 1955). For further authorities see Ehrenzweig, supra n. 8; Yiannopoulos, Wills of Movables in American International Conflicts Laws, 46 Calif.L.Rev. 185, at 199 (1958).

14. See the authorities cited supra n. 8. Of course, there may be a difference between the conflict of laws rule of New York and that of Ruritania. Normally the conflict of laws rule *of the forum* prevails. Hence, in speaking of conflict of laws rules in the present context, we mean the *New York* rules of conflict of laws.

law concerning succession to the assets of deceased persons, however, are a matter of foreign law, which must be made clear to a New York court by way of the comparative method.[15] Once these Ruritanian rules are explained, it becomes apparent that plaintiff is not "a personal representative" within the meaning of the conflict of laws rule.

How did Z's attorney win this victory? Familiarity with the New York conflict of laws rule alone would not have enabled him to see the crucial point. That he, as a New York attorney, had exact knowledge of the Ruritanian rule of succession, is quite improbable. But as a student of comparative law he *did not take it for granted* that the common-law concept of the "personal representative" prevails in Ruritania. Once a hunch, a creative doubt had arisen in the mind of Z's attorney, the battle was largely won; what remained to be done was merely to have the hunch confirmed, and to have the actual Ruritanian rule established by further research, if necessary with the help of an expert on Ruritanian law.

Suppose the attorney appearing for Z has not been retained by Z, but by the Ruritanian Consul in New York. Is the appearance authorized? This is a question of International Law. The answer must be found either in a treaty, or in the well-known rule of customary international law to the effect that consuls, in any court of the host country, may assert property rights of those of their nationals who are absent and not otherwise represented.[16] Again, however, this rule of international law becomes operative only in conjunction with rules of conflict of laws, and of the internal law of Ruritania, which establish Z (a Ruritanian national) as the owner of the cause of action.[17]

(BB) FOREIGN LAW PROBLEMS IN DOMESTIC LEGAL PRACTICE

"When counsel who are admitted to the Bar of this State are retained in a matter involving foreign law, they are responsible to the client for the proper conduct of the matter, and may not claim that they are not required to know the law of the foreign State."[18] This judicial pronouncement makes it clear that whenever an American lawyer encounters a foreign-law problem in litigation or in counseling, he is duty-bound either to familiarize himself with the relevant aspects of the foreign law, or to obtain proper advice from a person who has the requisite expertise.

There are various ways in which foreign law can become an important element in (actual or potential) domestic litigation. As we have seen, foreign law may govern the case at hand for the reason that

15. These substantive provisions of Ruritanian law govern the case at hand because of a second conflict of laws rule: that testamentary as well as intestate succession with respect to a decedent's personal estate normally is controlled by the law of his domicil. See E. F. Scoles & P. Hay, supra n. 8, §§ 20.3, 20.4 and 20.9.

16. Cf. Matter of Zalewski, 292 N.Y. 332, 55 N.E.2d 184 (1944). For an extensive discussion of the role which consular officials play in the administration of decedents' estates, see W. L. Boyd, The Administration in the United States of Alien Connected Decedents' Estates, 2 International Lawyer 601 (1968), where many further references can be found.

17. An interplay of foreign law, conflict of laws and international law may arise, also, from the fact that the applicable conflict of laws rule, pointing to the foreign law, is found in a treaty. See Bayitch, Conflict Law in United States Treaties (1955).

18. In re Roel, 3 N.Y.2d 224, 232, 165 N.Y.S.2d 31, 37, 144 N.E.2d 24, 28 (1957).

the conflict of laws rule of the domestic forum points to the internal law of a foreign country. Contracts made or performable (or otherwise having their center of gravity) abroad, marriages entered into abroad, torts committed abroad, estates of foreign domiciliaries leaving assets in this country—all these are examples of the countless matters arising in domestic legal practice which, according to our own conflict of laws rules, may be wholly or partly governed by foreign law.

Foreign law may have to be consulted, moreover, even in cases which are wholly "governed" by domestic law. Numerous examples are furnished by situations in which a foreign law, although not controlling in a conflict of laws sense, is invoked as a *de facto* excuse for non-performance of a contract [19] or for non-compliance with the discovery order of an American court.[20] The relevance of foreign law in domestic litigation is similarly illustrated by a case in which it was held that a witness in an American court can invoke the privilege against self-incrimination if he is able to show that his answer to a particular question might expose him to a substantial risk of prosecution under the law of a foreign country.[21]

Or suppose P, a citizen and domiciliary of Ruritania, has furnished goods to the United States Government under a contract which expressly stipulates that it shall be governed exclusively by the law of the United States. A dispute arises, and P sues the United States in the Court of Claims. Clearly, all substantive issues in this case are "governed" by our law. Nevertheless, the outcome of the litigation may be crucially affected by the law of Ruritania because citizens or subjects of a foreign government can bring such an action against the United States only if their government "accords to citizens of the United States the right to prosecute claims against [such] government in its courts." [22] A similar reciprocity rule applies in cases in which an alien sues the United States for damages caused by a public vessel, or for compensation for towage or salvage services.[23] These examples of reciprocity statutes (which can be found in state as well as federal legislation) could be multiplied without difficulty.[24] They provide a point of entry through which massive doses of foreign law penetrate into domestic legal practice.

Other domestic statutes, without referring to foreign law as such, may be predicated on foreign institutions which in turn must be viewed in the light of a foreign legal system. For instance, an individual or corporate citizen of the United States may, for purposes of the federal income tax, be entitled to a credit for "income taxes" paid abroad. What is meant by the term "income tax" in this context, is a matter of construction of our own statute; but can the term, however clearly we

---

19. See 18 Williston on Contracts § 1938 (3rd ed. by Jaeger, 1978 and 1986 Cum. Supp.).

20. See infra pp. 445–48.

21. In re Cardassi, 351 F.Supp. 1080 (D.Conn. 1972). For further authorities see McCormick on Evidence § 122 (3d ed. by E. W. Cleary et al., 1984).

22. See 28 U.S.C.A. § 2502(a). Reciprocal treatment sometimes is accorded by a bilateral Treaty of Friendship, Commerce and Navigation. See Zalcmanis v. United States, 146 Ct.Cl. 254, 173 F.Supp. 355

(1959), cert. denied 362 U.S. 917, 80 S.Ct. 668 (1960).

23. See 46 U.S.C.A. § 785.

24. See Lenhoff, Reciprocity in Function: A Problem of Conflict of Laws, Constitutional Law and International Law, 15 U. of Pittsburgh L.Rev. 44 (1953); id., Reciprocity: The Legal Aspect of a Perennial Idea, 49 N.W.U.L.Rev. 619, 752 (1954–55); id., Reciprocity and the Law of Foreign Judgments: A Historical—Critical Analysis, 16 La.L.Rev. 465 (1956).

understand its statutory meaning, be applied to a foreign tax unless we know (a) the position which the particular foreign tax occupies in the tax system of the country involved, and (b) the basis on which it is levied and computed? [25]

Many examples of statutory references to foreign institutions and conditions are provided by the immigration laws. The admission of a would-be immigrant may depend on whether under the law of his country of origin he is the "legitimate" child of a United States citizen or a resident alien. Thus that country's law must be consulted on its definition of legitimacy.[26] An otherwise deportable alien may not be deported to a particular country if the Attorney General determines "that such alien's life or freedom would be threatened in such country on account of race, religion, nationality, membership in a particular social group, or political opinion." [27] In discharging his duty under this provision, the Attorney General has to consider whether in fact as well as in form the legal system of the country in question protects the individual's life and freedom against such persecution.[28] Similarly, an understanding of foreign legal processes is needed if an event which occurred abroad is to be classified as a "conviction" or an "offense" within the meaning of exclusionary provisions of the immigration laws.[29]

Or suppose a criminal defendant, found guilty by a jury and due to be sentenced, is shown to have a record of previous "convictions" in a foreign country. Should he, for this reason, be treated as a multiple offender? Many of the pertinent recidivist statutes in terms provide that all previous judgments of conviction should be counted, regardless of whether they were rendered at the forum or in another state or country.[30] As a matter of due process, however, it is clear that a foreign conviction, though proved by proper documentary evidence, may not be used as a basis for multiple offender treatment if it resulted from proceedings which failed to meet certain minimum standards of fairness.[31] Thus it becomes unavoidable for the sentencing court to inquire into the standards which as a matter of law and of actual practice were observed in the previous foreign proceedings.

25. This question will be taken up in some detail infra, p. 875ff.

26. See Lau v. Kiley, 563 F.2d 543 (2d Cir. 1977) (involving the law of the People's Republic of China).

27. See 8 U.S.C.A. § 1253(h), as last amended in 1981.

28. See Berdo v. Immigration & Naturalization Service, 432 F.2d 824 (6th Cir. 1970); Coriolan v. Immigration & Naturalization Service, 559 F.2d 993 (5th Cir. 1977). See also infra p. 885.

29. 8 U.S.C.A. § 1182(a)(9) and (10), commented on by Professor Schlesinger in 2 Am.J.Comp.L. 392, 397–8 (1953). See also infra p. 889.

The fact that the foreign court's procedure was different from ours, is irrelevant, provided that no uncivilized methods were used to obtain the conviction. See Brice v. Pickett, 515 F.2d 153 (9th Cir. 1975); Pasquini v. United States Immigration & Naturalization Serv., 557 F.2d 536 (5th Cir. 1977). But U.S. authorities and U.S. courts cannot invoke a foreign "conviction" if it was procured by procedures "repugnant to the moral sense" of our community. Cf. Cooley v. Weinberger, 518 F.2d 1151, 1155 (10th Cir. 1975).

30. For references and an interesting discussion, see Pye, The Effect of Foreign Criminal Judgments in the United States, 32 U.M.K.C.L.Rev. 114, 127–30 (1964).

31. See, e.g., United States ex rel. Dennis v. Murphy, 265 F.2d 57 (2d Cir. 1959), upon remand 184 F.Supp. 384 (N.D.N.Y. 1959); United States ex rel. Foreman v. Fay, 184 F.Supp. 535 (S.D.N.Y. 1960). For further references, and a fine analysis of this and related problems, see Note, 90 Harv.L.Rev. 1500, especially at 1504–10 (1977). See also I. P. Stotzky & A. C. Swan, Due Process Methodology and Prisoner Exchange Treaties: Confronting an Uncertain Calculus, 62 Minn.L.Rev. 733 (1978).

The Foreign Corrupt Practices Act of 1977 [32] criminalizes certain "corrupt" payments to foreign public officials performing discretionary functions. The questions whether a given recipient is a public official and whether his functions are discretionary, clearly are determined by foreign law. Moreover, the issue whether the payment was "corrupt", quite often cannot be answered intelligently without some knowledge of the laws and the culture of the country involved.

In these and countless other instances our laws must deal with conditions and events shaped by foreign institutions.[32a] The world having become as small and close-knit as it is today, it should not surprise anyone that in myriad and often complex ways our own legal system interacts with the legal systems of other nations.[32b] A large body of our "domestic" laws reflects such interaction. To promote comprehension and proper application of this important part of our own laws, is one of the tasks of comparative law.[33]

(cc) Foreign Operations and Foreign Litigation

As a result of the accelerated transnational mobility of persons and goods which characterizes our age, it occurs more and more frequently that American corporations and individuals become parties to legal actions brought in the courts of other nations; [33a] every day, as a matter of large-scale routine, they enter into transactions which *in case* of a dispute *may* lead to litigation abroad, and which, therefore, must be negotiated and concluded with that possibility in mind.

A party faced with the prospect of litigation in Ruritania, or entering into an agreement which in case of a breach may have to be enforced in the courts of that country, will require the assistance of

---

32. 91 Stat. 1494.

32a. Recognizing that they have to deal with conditions and events shaped by foreign institutions, our legislators sometimes explicitly direct that a comparative study of those institutions be undertaken. An example is provided by Section 6 of the Federal Water Pollution Act of 1972, 86 Stat. 898, 33 U.S.C.A. § 1251 Note, which ordered the Secretary of Commerce to study the pollution laws of foreign countries in order to determine whether by virtue of differing standards of pollution control U.S. manufacturers are unduly disadvantaged vis-à-vis their foreign competitors.

32b. When extraterritorial application of the laws of country A affects individuals and business concerns in country B, it often happens that the latter country will enact countermeasures; such countermeasures, in turn, may have an impact felt by citizens and residents of country A. For a dramatic example see infra pp. 445–448. See also C. Olmstead (Ed.), Extraterritorial Application of Laws and Responses Thereto (1984), reviewed by B. Zagaris in 20 Int. Lawyer 1105 (1986).

33. When the applicable law is embodied in a Treaty, comparative studies may become necessary for the additional reason that the Treaty employs technical terms deriving their meaning from the legal systems of other signatories. For instance, some of the crucial terms of the Warsaw Convention (the official text of which is in French) can be correctly understood only in the light of their civil-law background. See Air France v. Saks, 470 U.S. 392, 105 S.Ct. 1338, 1342–43 (1985); Palagonia v. T.W.A., 110 Misc.2d 478, 442 N.Y.S.2d 670 (Sup. Ct. 1978).

33a. The overwhelming majority of such actions are civil proceedings; but the additional danger of criminal prosecutions (often used to reinforce civil claims) is far from negligible for those venturing into foreign markets and cultural environments. "In 1983, the last year for which we have complete statistics, more than 5,000 Americans were reported to have been arrested or detained abroad." R. D. Atkins & R. L. Pisani, How to Get Arrested Doing Business Abroad, 22 Across the Board (The Conference Board Magazine) No. 6, pp. 57, 58 (June 1985).

Ruritanian counsel.[34] To select such counsel, to make the proper arrangements concerning his compensation, and to instruct him in terms which can be understood by a lawyer brought up in the civil law, is a task which ordinarily will fall upon the client's American counsel. Since the Ruritanian agreement (or the Ruritanian lawsuit) probably will have effects in this country as well as in Ruritania, it may be necessary, at the same time, to familiarize Ruritanian counsel with certain points of our law, and to establish with him the kind of give-and-take communication which is necessary for a truly cooperative handling of the matter. Such cooperation, at its best, can yield highly gratifying results; but it requires, on the part of each of the participants, a measure of familiarity with the sources, the classificatory system, the procedure and the basic substantive concepts to which the mind of his foreign colleague is attuned.

B. BRIDGING THE DIFFERENCES AMONG LEGAL SYSTEMS

Up to this point the emphasis has been on the study of differences among legal systems. To compare, however, means to note similarities as well as differences.

Similarities among legal systems may be due (aa) to conscious, organized efforts, sponsored by international bodies or groups and aimed at unification or harmonization of diverse national laws, or (bb) to the play of more complex and less easily pinpointed forces. Similarities of the latter kind sometimes are called "accidental"; but this is a misnomer. Upon closer inspection, such "accidental" similarities will be found to result either from the migration of legal ideas, the various forms of which have been discussed above (pp. 8–17), or from the fact that—in resolving a pervasive or perhaps universal problem—several legal systems, independently of each other, have reacted in similar fashion and have given legal recognition to the same human needs and aspirations.

(AA) UNIFICATION AND HARMONIZATION [1]

At the beginning of this century, perhaps as a reaction against excessive nationalism, there arose a strong movement favoring massive comparative studies and postulating, as the ultimate aim of such studies, the total or at least substantial unification of all civilized legal systems.[2] Since then, this unbounded enthusiasm for universal unifica-

---

34. The consequences of a failure to make timely inquiry concerning Ruritanian law can be drastic. For some excellent examples, see J. Wolff, Trademark Protection of American Firms in Argentina, 16 Geo.Wash.L.Rev. 342 (1948).

1. The literature on the subject is vast. For extensive discussions, containing a wealth of further references, see R. David, The International Unification of Private Law (Vol. II, Ch. 5 of the International Encyclopedia of Comparative Law, 1971); O. Lando, The Contribution of Comparative Law to Law Reform by International Organizations, 25 Am.J.Comp.L. 641 (1977);

symposium (edited by Baade) on Unification of Law, 30 Law & Contemp.Prob. 231 ff. (1965); symposium (edited by Hay) on International Unification of Law, 16 Am.J. Comp.L. 1 ff. (1968). A brief description and critical appraisal of some of the most important regional and super-regional unification projects of modern times can be found in the excellent article by Ferid, Methoden, Möglichkeiten und Grenzen der Privatrechtsvereinheitlichung, 3 Zeitschrift für Rechtsvergleichung 193 (1962). For further references see infra nn. 2–12.

2. See Zepos, Die Bewegung zur Rechtsvereinheitlichung und das Schicksal der

tion has yielded to second thoughts. It has come to be recognized that legal systems reflect the values of diverse cultures; that cultural diversity should not be turned into monotony unless there are very strong reasons for doing so; and that there is no strong reason for world-wide, across-the-board unification of all law.

There may be good reasons, on the other hand, for unifying the law with respect to certain selected subjects, either on a regional or even on a world-wide scale.

The prime example of a successful regional unification effort is to be found in Scandinavia, where four independent nations (Denmark, Finland, Norway and Sweden) have unified relatively large segments of their legal systems.[3] Similar endeavors by the three Benelux countries, on the other hand, have yielded only meager results.[4]

For the whole continent of Europe (excluding the socialist bloc), the unification efforts of the Council of Europe are of rapidly growing importance. These efforts have resulted in a large number of proposed European Conventions, several of which have been widely adopted.[5] The European Convention on Compulsory Insurance Against Civil Liability Arising out of Motor Accidents, which has been ratified by a substantial number of nations, may be cited as an example.

example of successful Int'l. law

A bit out

Within the European Economic Community, certain areas of inter-member economic activity, and transactions relating thereto, are governed by Community law, i.e., by a system of supra-national law. This system, however, is of limited scope. With respect to the bulk of every-day legal matters, the legal systems of the member countries retain their national character; but the founding fathers of the Community correctly foresaw that some measure of unification, or at least of harmonization or coordination, of the members' national laws in certain fields would be necessary if serious distortions of the competitive process within the Community were to be avoided. Accordingly, they inserted into the Treaty of Rome a number of special provisions for the approximation of members' legislation in certain fields (e.g., corporation law, indirect taxes, transportation, and social security); in addition, the more general provision of Art. 3(h) of the Treaty announces, as one of the Community's objectives, "the approximation of [the members'] municipal laws to the extent necessary for the orderly functioning of the Common Market".[6] The process of harmonizing or "approximating" the legislation of member states in complex areas of the law has proven to be difficult and slow.[7] Nevertheless, this process has produced, and will continue to produce, significant changes in some

geltenden Zivilgesetzbücher, 19 Revue Hellénique de Droit International 14, at 17–18 (1966), where attention is called to the proceedings of the First International Congress of Comparative Law held in Paris in 1900.

3. See R. David, supra n. 1, at 180–88, where further references can be found. See also infra p. 327.

4. Id., at 188–91.

5. The Conventions are open for ratification or accession by the members of the Council of Europe. Other nations can be invited to accede, and such invitations (e.g., to the United States) have occasionally

been extended. For an example, see infra p. 136.

6. See also Arts. 100–102 of the Treaty of Rome. The literature on the harmonization efforts within the European Economic Community is vast. For references see the writings cited supra n. 1, and E. Stein, P. Hay & M. Waelbroeck, European Community Law and Institutions in Perspective, passim (1976 and 1985 Supp.).

7. This was true even during the initial period, when the Community consisted of only six nations, all of whom shared the civil-law tradition. Now that common-law countries have joined as members, the dif-

parts of the member nations' legal systems.[8]   Some examples of such changes, which in many instances affect large numbers of individuals and corporations, will be encountered later on in this course.

On an intercontinental or potentially world-wide scale, a modicum of unification or effective coordination of national laws has been accomplished only with respect to a few limited subjects, principally in the areas of transportation, communications and arbitration as well as protection of patents, trademarks and copyrights.[9]

[handwritten marginal note: modicum of unification on a world scale]

Whether the aimed-for harmonization be regional or intercontinental, it often turns out that the participating nations cannot agree upon complete unification [10] or even approximation of the legal rules and principles relating to a given subject.   Difficulties arising from existing differences among national laws must then be overcome by subtler and more modest techniques, such as unification of applicable conflict-of-laws rules.[11]   Sometimes the draftsmen limit themselves to unifying the law of *international* transactions of a particular kind, while leaving local transactions of the same nature to remain governed by diverse national laws.   The latter method is exemplified by some of the provisions of the Warsaw Convention [12] as well as by the United Nations Convention on Contracts for the International Sale of Goods which becomes effective on January 1, 1988.[13]   It is clear that this method does not reduce the number of discordant voices announcing the law; it merely adds one further voice—the one controlling "international" transactions as defined by the draftsmen—to the chorus of independent national legislators.   Such a limited "unification" hardly facilitates the task of a scholar engaged in comparative legal studies.   Nevertheless, it may well be useful from a practical standpoint.

[handwritten marginal note: ratified by 50 countries]

ficulties mentioned in the text, supra, have been vastly increased. See J. A. Jolowicz, New Perspectives of a Common Law of Europe: Some Practical Aspects and the Case for Applied Comparative Law, in M. Cappelletti (Ed.), New Perspectives for a Common Law of Europe 237 ff. (1978).

8. See Symposium, Rechtsvereinheit-lichung und Rechtsvergleichung (with summaries in English), 50 Rabels Z. 1–250 (1986); F. K. Juenger, The Role of Comparative Law in Regional Organizations, in J. N. Hazard & W. J. Wagner (Eds.), Law in the U.S. in Social and Technological Revolution (U.S. Reports for the IXth Congress of the International Academy of Comparative Law) 49 (1974).

Until recently, Art. 100 of the Treaty required unanimity for the adoption of harmonization directives. But under new Art. 100A (the "Single European Act" that became effective July 1, 1987), it will be possible in some cases to adopt such directives by a qualified majority, and this may accelerate the process of harmonization.

9. See Ferid, supra n. 1, at 202.

10. Moreover, even a successful effort to unify *the text* of the applicable law in the participating countries does not assure uniformity *of interpretation* of that text.

A striking example of nonuniform interpretation of a uniform text is discussed by B. H. Greene, Personal Defenses Under the Geneva Uniform Law on Bills of Exchange and Promissory Notes: A Comparison, 46 Marquette L.Rev. 281 (1962–63).

11. This technique is used in most of the international conventions proposed by the Hague Conference on Private International Law. See infra, text at n. 15. Many of those conventions have been widely adopted.

12. 137 League of Nations Treaty Series 11 (1929), 49 Stat. 3000 (1934). The Convention contains (a) a number of uniform rules of tort law applicable to international flights, plus (b) uniform rules relating to jurisdiction and (c) some uniform rules of choice of law relating to subjects as to which it proved impossible to unify the substance of the applicable law. Several methods of unification and harmonization thus are illustrated in a single treaty.

13. The United States, France, Italy and the People's Republic of China are among the 11 nations that had ratified the Convention by the end of 1986. For the text of the Convention, and an authoritative commentary, see J. Honnold, Uniform Law for International Sales (1982).

[handwritten note: Now over 50 countries]

International law w/ some success

Until fairly recently, the United States stood aloof from most of the organized international unification efforts.[14] At the end of 1963, however, Congress passed a statute authorizing U.S. participation in the work of the Hague Conference on Private International Law and the International (Rome) Institute for the Unification of Private Law.[15] Since then, U.S. delegates have participated in the work of these bodies.[16]

In the area of commercial law, where some of the divergencies of national laws have proved particularly irksome, special techniques have been developed to bring about a measure of international uniformity even in the absence of concerted action on the part of national legislators.[17] Under the sponsorship of private or public international organizations, many standard forms and agreed formulations of commercial usages have been drawn up.[18] In countless international transactions of a commercial nature, the terms of such uniform usages or forms become "the law" as between the parties, for the reason that these terms have been contractually adopted.

Whether prepared for governmental imposition or for contractual adoption by the parties, the terms of any instrument aiming at international unification or harmonization of legal rules must be fitted into the substantive and procedural law of the participating countries. Thus it is clear that the draftsmen of such instruments can do their work only on the basis of the most painstaking comparative studies; and experience has shown that unifying or harmonizing efforts, whenever and wherever undertaken, are accompanied by, and indeed wholly dependent on, extensive studies of this kind.

(BB) THE COMMON CORE OF LEGAL SYSTEMS

We have seen that organized attempts to make national laws more uniform have been successful only in relatively few, specialized areas. In nearly all fields of law, however, we observe that—even in the absence of organized unification efforts—there exists a common core of legal concepts and precepts shared by some, or even by a multitude, of the world's legal systems. To explain this phenomenon in terms of the underlying historical and social causes, is a task of considerable com-

---

14. See E. M. Wise, Legal Tradition As a Limitation on Law Reform, in J. N. Hazard & W. J. Wagner (Eds.), Law in the U.S.A. in the Bicentennial Era, 26 Am.J. Comp.L. (Supplement) 1, 4–7 (1978).

15. 22 U.S.C.A. § 269g, as amended in 1972.

16. For informative reports on the methods and results of U.S. participation in the work of the Hague Conference and the Rome Institute, see R. D. Kearney, The United States and International Cooperation to Unify Private Law, 5 Cornell Int'l L.J. 1 (1972); P. H. Pfund, United States Participation in International Unification of Private Law, 19 Int'l Lawyer 505 (1985).

17. See David, supra n. 1, at 56–61; Schmitthoff, The Law of International Trade—Its Growth, Formulation and Operation, in The Sources of the Law of Inter-

national Trade (Schmitthoff, Ed., 1964), at 3 ff.

18. Among the examples mentioned by Schmitthoff, id. at 18–19, are two documents sponsored by the International Chamber of Commerce and widely accepted in international trade: Incoterms (defining terms such as "f.o.b." and "c.i.f.") and Uniform Customs and Practice for Commercial Documentary Credits. The latter document is expressly referred to in § 5–102(4) of the Uniform Commercial Code as adopted in New York and some other states. Even in the absence of such a statutory reference, the Uniform Customs are of enormous importance, because bank forms relating to letters of credit ordinarily incorporate them into the parties' contract. See R. Braucher & R. A. Riegert, Introduction to Commercial Transactions 361–65 (1977).

plexity; the explanations will differ from subject to subject and from continent to continent.[1] In spite of the difficulty of establishing its etiology, however, the existence and vast extent of this common core of legal systems cannot be doubted.[2]

Shared principles and rules often furnish the only body of law available for the resolution of disputes which cut across national boundaries. It is for this reason that treaties and other instruments of public international law as well as private contracts (especially arbitration agreements) among parties in different countries more and more frequently provide for the application of principles and rules common to legal systems of more than one nation. What follows is an illustration of this technique of utilizing the common core.

Statute of the International Court of Justice *

Article 38.—1. The Court, whose function is to decide in accordance with international law such disputes as are submitted to it, shall apply:

    a. international conventions, whether general or particular, establishing rules expressly recognized by the contesting states;

    b. international custom, as evidence of a general practice accepted as law;

    c. *the general principles of law recognized by civilized nations*;

    d. subject to the provisions of Article 59,** judicial decisions and the teachings of the most highly qualified publicists of the various nations, as subsidiary means for the determination of rules of law.

2. This provision shall not prejudice the power of the Court to decide a case ex aequo et bono, if the parties agree thereto. (emphasis added)

NOTES

(1) "The Court" to which Art. 38 refers, is the International Court of Justice which in 1945 succeeded the former Permanent Court of International Justice. The significance of Art. 38, however, is not limited to the relatively infrequent cases submitted to that Court. Art. 38 defines the sources of international law. These sources must be consulted whenever a dispute involving a question of international law is adjudicated by any international or municipal tribunal. Resort must

1. See, e.g., 1 Schlesinger (Gen.Ed.), Formation of Contracts—A Study of the Common Core of Legal Systems 41 (1968); Sarfatti, Roman Law and Common Law: Forerunners of a General Unification of Law, 3 Int. & Comp.L.Q. 102 (1954).

2. In addition to the writings cited supra n. 1, see M. Gluckman, African Traditional Law in Historical Perspective, 60 Proceedings of the British Academy 295 ff. (1974).

Many of the components of a legal system are apt to be of a local or regional nature. See E. Wahl, Influences climatiques sur l'évolution du droit en orient et en occident—contribution au régionalisme en droit comparé, 25 Rev.Int. de Droit Comparé 261 (1973). This, however, does not preclude the existence of other components which respond to basic human needs and traits, and thus are bound—at least in their core—to be universal.

* Annexed to the Charter of the United Nations, San Francisco, June 26, 1945; entered into force October 24, 1945.

** Article 59 provides: "The decision of the Court has no binding force except between the parties and in respect of that particular case."

be had to the same sources in the many instances in which the settlement of such a dispute is sought by negotiation and conciliation rather than by formal adjudication.

The phrase *"general principles of law recognized by civilized nations"* refers to principles which find expression in the *municipal laws* of various nations. These principles, therefore, can be ascertained only by the comparative method.[1]

Example: During the second World War the Government of Uruguay requisitioned and used two Italian ships. After the war the owners of one of those ships, the *Fausto*, submitted a claim to the Uruguayan courts asking for just compensation. The Government of Uruguay, as defendant, relied on a provision in the Italian Peace Treaty of 1947, expressly waiving claims of this nature "against any of the United Nations which broke off diplomatic relations with Italy, and which took action in cooperation with the Allied and Associated Powers." Uruguay had broken off diplomatic relations with Italy during the war, and the seizure of the *Fausto* had been a measure taken in cooperation with the Allied and Associated Powers. The Government of Uruguay, however, had not declared war on Italy. Therefore, Uruguay was not a party to the Peace Treaty. The Italian claimants argued that for this reason Uruguay could not rely on the waiver stipulated in the Treaty. The Government of Uruguay, on the other hand, contended that it was a third-party-beneficiary of the waiver stipulation, and that the right of a third-party-beneficiary to enforce a stipulation made in his favor is established by "general principles of law" within the meaning of Art. 38. In support of this contention, counsel for the defendant Government proved that many nations, both in the civil-law and the common-law orbit, *in their law of contracts* recognize the right of a third-party-beneficiary to bring a direct action against the promisor.[2]

The claimants countered by pointing to Art. 1119 of the French Civil Code which provides that "As a general rule,[3] a party to a contract cannot . . . ., stipulate in his own name, except for himself." Claimants' counsel argued that the principle of stipulations for the benefit of a third party, although accepted in many countries, cannot be said to be "recognized by civilized nations", since it is rejected by a codification as important and as influential as the Code Napoleon. Counsel for the Government of Uruguay rebutted this argument by demonstrating, on the basis of thorough comparative research,

---

1. See 1 Schlesinger (Gen.Ed.), Formation of Contracts—A Study of the Common Core of Legal Systems (1968), especially at pp. 7–16 of the Introduction. For further references see id. at 62–63, and the interesting article by H.-V. von Hülsen, Sinn und Methode der Rechtsvergleichung, insbesondere bei der Ermittlung übernationalen Zivilrechts, 22 J.Z. 629 (1967). See also M. Bothe & G. Ress, The Comparative Method and Public International Law, in W. E. Butler, (Ed.), International Law in Comparative Perspective 49 (1980).

2. See E. Jiménez de Aréchaga, Treaty Stipulations in Favor of Third States, 50 Am.J.Int.L. 338, especially 346–8, 351–7 (1956), referring to the pertinent code provisions of a number of civil-law countries, and also to common-law (especially American) authorities. For a comparative discussion of more recent date see Millner, Ius Quaesitum Tertio: Comparison and Synthesis, 16 Int. & Comp.L.Q. 446 (1967).

3. This general rule is subject to somewhat vaguely formulated exceptions. French Civil Code Art. 1121.

that the enforceability of the rights of a third-party-beneficiary is judicially recognized even in those countries, such as France, in which old code provisions on their face seem to indicate a different result.[4] It follows that today, whatever may have been the situation in Napoleon's time, there *is* a "general principle" to the effect that the third-party-beneficiary of a consensual stipulation has the right to bring an action for its enforcement.[5] Uruguay, therefore, although not a signatory of the Peace Treaty, may avail itself of Italy's waiver.[6]

The resolution of international disputes, and the formulation of rules of international law, thus may depend on whether court and counsel can find a sufficient core of agreement, concerning the point at issue, among the legal systems of "civilized nations". As is shown by the efforts of counsel in the *Fausto* case, the requisite core of agreement can be proved or disproved only by the comparative method.[6a]

(2) Art. 38(1)(c) of the Statute of the International Court of Justice is by no means the only example of a provision pointing to the common core of legal systems as the source of applicable principles and rules.

Anyone drafting a legal instrument of a transnational nature, whether the prospective signatories be private or governmental parties, must provide some machinery for the settlement of possible disputes.

---

4. French case law on the subject has developed since the middle of the last century, especially in connection with life insurance policies. It permits the third-party-beneficiary, if he is sufficiently identified, to recover from the promisor. Theoretically, it is required that the beneficiary "accept" the benefit provided in the contract between the *promettant* and the *stipulant*; but such acceptance can be tacit, and it is implied in any attempt on the part of the beneficiary to enforce the contract. See 2 Planiol-Ripert, Traité élémentaire de droit civil, English Translation by the Louisiana State Law Institute, §§ 1234, 1251 (1959); 2 Julliot de la Morandière, Précis de droit civil 291 (1966); 1 Bonassies, Cours de droit civil 119–29 (1967); 1 M. Ferid, Das franzoesische Zivilrecht, par. 2E19 ff. (1971); Jiménez de Aréchaga, supra n. 2.

5. See Millner, supra n. 2, where the reader will find, also, a discussion of the somewhat unique position of English law. For a recent discussion of the problem from the standpoint of English law, see A. G. Guest, Anson's Law of Contract 363–381 (26th ed., 1984).

6. The claimants in the *Fausto* case had instituted their action in a court not having admiralty jurisdiction. Holding that the claims were within the exclusive admiralty jurisdiction which the Uruguayan constitution vests in another court, the court of first instance dismissed the case. See 1963 Revista de la Facultad de Derecho y Ciencias Sociales de Montevideo (No. 2, April/June) 395 ff. There was no appeal, and apparently no new action was brought in the proper court.

The statement in the text, supra, thus reflects the authors' opinion rather than a judicial decision, as the merits of the dispute were never reached by the Uruguayan courts.

6a. Note that in the *Fausto* case the defendant Government sought to prove, and the claimants sought to disprove, such a core of agreement. *Quaere* whether the claimants' lawyers supported their position in the best possible way. They pointed to France as the odd-man-out; but that argument was untenable. See supra n. 4. A better argument would have been to point to English law as the dissenting voice. See supra n. 5. In the end, however, even this better argument would not have helped the claimants, because Art. 38(1)(c) does not require complete unanimity among the world's legal systems concerning the point at issue. See R. B. Schlesinger & P. Bonassies, Le fonds commun des systèmes juridiques, 15 Rev.Int. de Droit Comparé 501, 514–16 (1963). A strong majority suffices, and there can be little doubt that the "general principle" invoked by the Government in the *Fausto* case is supported today by a strong, and indeed overwhelming, majority of the leading legal systems. See Millner, supra n. 2; 2 K. Zweigert & H. Kötz, An Introduction to Comparative Law 124–38 (Transl. by T. Weir, 1977).

In this context, the draftsman must face the further question what body of substantive law will be applied by those called upon to determine such a dispute. Very frequently, it turns out that the only body of law that is acceptable to the parties, is the core of norms common to the domestic legal systems of the parties, or to an even larger group of legal systems. Thus the draftsman will have to resort to a choice-of-law clause which expressly or by implication refers to that common core.[6b]

The disputes which in this way are to be resolved by reference to a multi-national common core of principles and rules, can be of many kinds. They may be intergovernmental disputes arising under treaties or executive agreements; they may involve the operational or housekeeping transactions of an international organization; they may relate to concession agreements, development contracts or other transactions between a private party in a highly industrialized country and the government of a developing nation; or they may, and frequently do, result from everyday transactions in international trade. Treaties, contracts, and other legal instruments often provide, in varying language, that such disputes be resolved by reference to legal principles and rules shared by more than one legal system.[7]

(3) There are additional reasons why it is important to ascertain and to formulate the common core of legal systems. As their professional tasks increasingly transcend the realm of local affairs, it becomes indispensable for lawyers (and future lawyers) to study at least some elements of the law of several legal systems. Until now it has been thought sufficient, even for an international practitioner, to acquire "that modicum of understanding and of familiarity with concept and language [of the foreign law] which will make it possible for him really to grasp an opinion of local counsel".[8] Past and current efforts to teach Comparative Law, including those based on the present casebook, as a rule have not sought to reach very far beyond this relatively modest objective. In the more integrated world of the future, however, "mere ability to communicate with colleagues in other lands will no longer be enough. At least in certain fields, the lawyers of the future will have to be truly familiar with a broad spectrum of legal systems".[9] The curricula and teaching tools responding to these future needs will have to offer a *synoptic* view of the guiding precepts and the most important institutions to be found in the various legal systems. The preparation of such teaching tools will require, and indeed will have to be preceded by, a great deal of common core research.[10]

(4) Even when not engaged in extensive comparative research, a lawyer encountering foreign law problems should always remember that to compare means to look for similarities as well as differences.

6b. For an example of such a choice-of-law clause, see Art. 46 of the 1954 Agreement between the Iranian Oil Consortium and the Government of Iran, quoted in Noto v. Cia. Secula di Armanento, 310 F.Supp. 639, at 646, footn. 17 (S.D.N.Y., 1970).

7. The subject is treated more extensively by Schlesinger, op. cit. supra n. 1, at 7–16.

8. Jessup, Foreword to Aglion's Dictionnaire Juridique Anglo-Français, p. 14 (1947).

9. Schlesinger, op. cit. supra n. 1, at p. 6.

10. The pilot project dealing with Formation of Contracts, cited supra n. 1, proved the feasibility of such research. On a larger scale, and by somewhat different methods, the International Encyclopedia of Comparative Law (as yet incomplete) is presenting comparative treatises which may help to lay the foundation for some of the synoptic future teaching tools envisaged in the text, supra.

In a course on Comparative Law it may be necessary constantly to warn the student against taking it for granted that the basic concepts and precepts of his own law will be duplicated in other systems. To combat an unperceptive and uncritical attitude toward one's own law is indeed one of the main objectives of teaching Comparative Law, and in pursuing this objective the instructor or casebook author may spend more time dwelling on differences than on similarities. But this should not becloud the fact that in comparing the solutions provided for a given problem under various legal systems, we encounter similarities more often than differences. At least in terms of actual results—as distinguished from the semantics used in reaching and stating such results—the areas of agreement among legal systems are larger than those of disagreement.[11]

Studying the civil-law materials in this book, the reader should as often as possible ask himself: How would the problem at hand be solved in the legal system with which I am familiar? He will find, time and again, that his own law, while employing different concepts and techniques, ordinarily reaches a similar practical result. In thus discovering that the law of other nations is not really as "foreign" as he had anticipated, a student of comparative law may have created, at least within himself, one of the pre-conditions of international understanding.

3. THE COMPARATIVE METHOD AS A SCIENTIFIC APPROACH

Basic Research. Some scholars distinguish between pure comparison of law (*Reine Rechtsvergleichung*) and the subsequent utilization of the results.[1] The distinction is analogous to that which natural scientists draw between basic and applied research. "Pure comparison", like basic research, does not connote efforts without practical utility. It means, rather, that at the time of the comparative studies in question it may be undetermined, or perhaps unpredictable, what use or uses will be made of the results in the future.[2]

Comparative Law and the Social Sciences. The reformer who strives to improve the law may resort to social science methods in order to gather empirical data demonstrating the unsatisfactory effects of an existing rule; but when he seeks to explore the probable effects of proposed alternative solutions, the methods of social science have to be supplemented by those of comparative law. In the social sciences, unlike the natural sciences, it is often impossible to subject alternative solutions to empirical testing. "Full-fledged experiments are seldom permitted in the field of law: scientists are not ordinarily able to have a law passed merely to permit them to study its effect. One of the best ways for the research scholar to learn how a rule of law is likely to

---

11. See Schlesinger, op. cit. supra n. 1, at 41. The experience of international practitioners appears to bear out the statement in the text. See, e.g., Doub, Experiences of the United States in Foreign Courts, 48 A.B.A.J. 63, 66 (1962).

1. See Schmitthoff, The Science of Comparative Law, 7 Camb.L.J. 94, 96 (1939),

referring especially to suggestions made by the late Prof. Ernst Rabel.

2. The great variety of possible uses has been the subject of our discussion on the preceding pages.

function in his society is for him to study the ways such a rule has functioned in a similar society." [2a]

Moreover, comparison of legal systems separated from each other by space or time may serve significant ends even if the results are not put to immediate professional use by lawyers, judges and legislators. The sociologist, anthropologist or historian who seeks to comprehend law as a product and as a cause of other societal phenomena,[3] depends on comparison to give meaning to his observed data.[4] This holds true not only for the anthropologist who studies primitive cultures,[5] but equally for the social scientist who seeks to explore the complex relations between law and social behavior in a highly developed civilization.[6] Comparative law thus becomes an important auxiliary method for the social scientist, just as the latter's findings in turn are used as indispensable tools by those shaping law and policy in our society.[6a]

Comparative Law and Jurisprudence. Efforts to arrive at generalizations about law, including those having a sociological, psychological, historical, analytical or metaphysical point of departure, are collectively referred to under the heading of Jurisprudence.[7] There is a close relationship between jurisprudence and comparative law.

An individual's jurisprudential outlook is bound to have a strong influence on the direction and intensity of his interest in comparative law. For instance, a disciple of the sociological school of jurisprudence, who regards law as a "specialized instrument of social control",[8] almost

---

2a. R. A. Riegert, Emprical Research About Law: The German Picture, 2 Dickinson Int.L. Annual 1, at 63 (1983).

3. See Schmitthoff, op. cit. supra n. 1, at 97.

4. See Lepaulle, The Function of Comparative Law, 35 Harv.L.Rev. 838, 852–5 (1922). For a comprehensive discussion of this subject see Hall, Comparative Law and Social Theory (1963), reviewed by Wagner, 64 ColumL.Rev. 985 (1964), and by Schlesinger, 50 Cornell L.Q. 570 (1965).

5. See Carlston, Social Theory and African Tribal Organization, especially at 88–93, 381–423 (1968). For an excellent example of the contribution which comparative law can make to our understanding of tribal cultures, see Gluckman, The Judicial Process Among the Barotse of Northern Rhodesia (2nd ed. 1967). The attempt made by Gluckman and other anthropologists to describe the legal processes of tribal societies in modern and often sophisticated terms, and to compare these processes with our own, has given rise to a lively methodological controversy. See Gluckman, id. at 375–408 (with bibliography at 448–54); L. Nader (Ed.), The Ethnography of Law (1965) (a special publication forming part of Vol. 67 of American Anthropologist); Carlston, op. cit. at 88–90.

6. The classical work on the subject is Max Weber, Wirtschaft und Gesellschaft (2nd ed. 1925), the most important parts of

which are available in English (translated by Shils and Rheinstein, and edited and annotated by Rheinstein) under the title Max Weber on Law in Economy and Society (Vol. VI of the 20th Century Legal Philosophy Series, 1954).

6a. For a discussion of the interaction of comparative legal research and social science research, with emphasis on the contrasting ways in which such research undertakings are organized in Germany and in the United States, see R. A. Riegert, The Max Planck Association's Institutes for Research and Advanced Training in Foreign Law, 25 J.Legal Ed. 312, especially at 323 ff. (1973); id., op. cit. supra n. 2a. See also K. Siehr, Book Review, 35 Rabels Z. 160 (1971).

7. In French, and in other Romance languages, the word *jurisprudence* has a different meaning. See infra pp. 622–623. In communicating with non-English-speaking persons, it may be preferable, therefore, to use such terms as "general theory of law" or "legal theory" rather than our "jurisprudence". The narrower terms indicating special branches of jurisprudence, such as philosophy of law or sociology of law, usually have exact counterparts in the languages of the civil-law orbit.

8. See Pound, Comparative Law in Space and Time, 4 Am.J.Comp.L. 70, 72 (1955).

automatically thinks in comparative terms.[8a] He looks at the different approaches to the same problem which are observable in several legal systems, with a mental attitude similar to that of a natural scientist who sets up a series of related experiments in his laboratory.[9]

The chief representatives of analytical jurisprudence have always stressed the close link between a jurisprudential and a comparative approach. In listing the uses of analysis, Bentham pointed out that it provides a common frame for comparing different legal systems, allowing a legislator to learn from his neighbors.[10] Similar views were expressed by Austin, who thought that without a proper analytical framework there could be no comparison of the laws of different countries, and that "without some familiarity with foreign systems no lawyer can or will appreciate accurately the defects or merits of his own." [11]

Legal philosophers postulating a natural or ideal law similarly emphasize (though for different reasons) the importance of comparative studies. To them, the ultimate source of law lies in Divine commands, or in Reason, or in the spirit and inner conscience of men. Followers of such a philosophy are apt to regard identities and resemblances which are discovered in the positive law of all nations, as evidence of the universality of moral and legal absolutes.[12]

The teachings of the historical school, on the other hand, based on Savigny's notion of a national *Volksgeist*, and suggesting that "law like language is peculiar to every nation",[13] are not conducive to attempts at

---

8a. Much interest in comparative law has been shown, also, by the leading representatives of the "realist" school. Both Jerome Frank and Karl Llewellyn drew heavily on the resources of comparative law. As an example, one might mention Judge Frank's renowned dissenting opinion in United States v. Grunewald, 233 F.2d 556, 587–92 (2d Cir. 1956), majority decision reversed 353 U.S. 391, 77 S.Ct. 963 (1957); and see W. Twining, Karl Llewellyn and the Realist Movement 309 (1973).

Both the "realist" and the sociological schools of jurisprudence were deeply influenced by Jhering (1818–1892), who regarded comparative law as an indispensable tool for a proper understanding of legal phenomena. See K. Zweigert & K. Siehr, Jhering's Influence on the Development of Comparative Legal Method, 19 Am.J. Comp.L. 215 (1971).

9. See Lepaulle, supra n. 4. See also supra, text at n. 2a.

10. See Stone, Legal System and Lawyers' Reasonings 53 (1964). Cf. Aufricht, Der Rechtssatz als Gegenstand der vergleichenden Rechtswissenschaft, 2 ZfRV 157, 164 (1961).

Perhaps the converse of Bentham's proposition is equally true: that comparative research, and especially common core research (see supra pp. 37–39), can help to enhance the quality and usefulness of analytical constructs.

11. Quoted by Stone, supra n. 10.

12. See Escarra, The Aims of Comparative Law, 7 Temple L.Q. 296, 307–8 (1933); Schmitthoff, op. cit. supra n. 1, at 101.

It is, of course, possible to study such identities and resemblances without looking for absolutes. There are valid pragmatic reasons for attempting to establish a common core of agreement among the legal systems of the world. See Schlesinger, The Nature of General Principles of Law, in Rapports Généraux au VIe Congrès International de droit comparé (Limpens, ed., 1964) 235, at 257–60, 269. A deep interest in the identities and similarities mentioned in the text thus may be found among pragmatists as well as idealists and natural law philosophers.

13. Schmitthoff, ibid., thus paraphrases Savigny's own words. The complete passage is quoted by Friedmann, Legal Theory 210 (1967).

In a trenchant passage that has become quite famous in the German-speaking world, Jhering ridiculed Savigny's views on this point. For an English translation of that passage, see Zweigert & Siehr, supra n. 8a.

international unification of law,[14] and will lead to skepticism concerning the ability of a lawgiver to profit from the legislative and judicial experience of other nations.[15]

Virtually all schools of jurisprudence, including the historical school, resort to comparative studies as part of their own jurisprudential efforts, in order (a) to determine the importance and universality of the problems to be explored, (b) to find concrete illustrations of abstract theories, and (c) to test the validity of general hypotheses against the realities of more than one legal system.[15a] The term Comparative Jurisprudence, sometimes employed to denote the use of comparative data for jurisprudential purposes, is almost a tautology. In the sense just indicated, all schools of jurisprudence, even those imbued with a strong dose of deductive speculation,[16] must in some measure depend on materials furnished by comparative law.[17]

In addition, comparative law supplies indispensable tools for those who seek to survey and appraise jurisprudential schools of thought. Most of the theorists, from antiquity to this day, have been in the habit of discussing legal institutions in terms of general abstractions, and sometimes of universal truths; but each theorist's own knowledge of such institutions is inevitably drawn from a limited reservoir of obser-

14. The nationalistic and isolationist implications of Savigny's theories were obscured by the fact that Savigny himself was a scholar of tremendous comparative learning; but in the words and deeds of his less brilliant intellectual offspring, the narrowing and ossifying effects of his philosophy became painfully apparent.

15. There is no school of jurisprudence, however, which denies the importance of comparative law in international legal practice. The followers of the historical school, emphasizing as they do the necessary and (in their opinion) unalterable diversity of the legal systems of various nations, usually recommend comparative studies as the only means to reduce the practical difficulties engendered by such diversity.

15a. Cf. F. H. Lawson, The Comparison (Vol. 2 of Selected Essays) 75 (1977): "The jurist who approaches legal theory by way of comparative law not only becomes sceptical of facile generalizations about law, but refuses to be exclusively interested in definitions or theories which squeeze out of the law of any country the peculiarities that give it life."

16. It has been suggested that purely deductive efforts to arrive at general statements about law are not "scientific." See Lepaulle, supra n. 4, as well as the two articles by Yntema, Comparative Legal Research, 54 Mich.L.Rev. 899, 902–3 (1956), and The Implications of Legal Science, 10 N.Y.U.L.Q.Rev. 279 (1933). This is, of course, controversial; there is no universal agreement on the meaning of the words

"science" and "scientific". It is safe to assume, however, that a scholar working in the field of jurisprudence, even if he purports to disdain the inductive method, always succumbs, consciously or not, to the impact of reality (i.e., of the real world of the various legal systems as they are and as they develop) when he chooses his subject, and when he tries to illustrate and to test his theories.

17. The dependence of jurisprudence on comparative legal studies was emphasized, 150 years ago, by the great German legal philosopher Anselm Feuerbach, who was also a practitioner of the law. As quoted by H. J. Berman, The Comparison of Soviet and American Law, 34 Ind.L.J. 559 (1959), Feuerbach wrote: "Why does the legal scholar not yet have a comparative jurisprudence? The richest source of all discoveries in every empirical science is comparison and combination. Only by manifold contrasts the contrary becomes completely clear; only by the observation of similarities and differences and the reasons for both may the peculiarity and inner nature of each thing be thoroughly established. Just as from the comparison of languages the philosophy of language, the science of linguistics itself, is produced; so from the comparison of the laws and legal customs of nations of all times and places, both the most nearly related and the most remote, is produced universal jurisprudence, the pure science of laws, which alone can infuse real and vigorous life into the specific legal science of any particular country."

vation and learning. It follows that the task of critically surveying jurisprudential schools of thought can be successfully undertaken only by a scholar who is able to relate the various schools to their founders' and followers' backgrounds of experience.[18]

II. FOREIGN LAW IN OUR COURTS: PLEADING AND PROOF OF FOREIGN LAW

1. THE BASIC DOCTRINES

A. THE COMMON LAW DOCTRINE: FOREIGN LAW AS A "FACT"

FITZPATRICK v. INTERNATIONAL RAILWAY CO.

Court of Appeals of New York, 1929.
252 N.Y. 127, 169 N.E. 112.

Appeal, by permission, from a judgment of the Appellate Division of the Supreme Court in the fourth judicial department, entered March 22, 1929, unanimously affirming a judgment in favor of plaintiff entered upon a verdict.

CRANE, J. The International Railway Company is a domestic corporation owning, maintaining and operating an electric street surface railroad in various parts of the United States and Canada, and at the time here in question owned and maintained a line of tracks upon the westerly side of the Niagara Gorge at Niagara Falls, Ont. Under an agreement with the Niagara Gorge Railroad Company these tracks were used by this latter company for the operation of its own cars in running a scenic road around the Niagara Gorge. The duty of maintaining the tracks and roadbed rested upon the International Railway Company, a duty regulated by the public authorities, as will hereafter appear. In the operation of its scenic route, the Niagara Gorge Railroad Company, at times, ran two cars hitched together, in charge of a conductor and an assistant, besides the motorman. The first car contained the power machinery, the second car was a trailer, partially controlled by the assistant who sat in the first seat of the car to operate the brakes. These were open cars with side steps which could be raised and lowered. For about a mile of this railway on the west side the cars

---

18. Authors having this ability can produce truly illuminating critical surveys of past and present jurisprudential thought. See, e.g., Bodenheimer, Jurisprudence (Rev.Ed., 1974); Friedmann, Legal Theory (5th ed. 1967); and Stone's trilogy entitled Legal System and Lawyers' Reasonings (1964), Human Law and Human Justice (1965), Social Dimensions of Law and Justice (1966).

ran very near to the edge of the gorge so that the passengers had an opportunity of seeing the wonders of nature below. The poles maintained by the defendant for its overhead wires were also on the gorge side of the railroad for this mile, that is, they were between the tracks and the edge of the gorge, at some places so near to the cars as they passed that the steps were raised and the guard rail lowered to protect the passengers from getting out on that side or from falling out.

The plaintiff was a young man, twenty-three years of age, attending college at the University of Pennsylvania, who, in the summer time, obtained employment with the Shredded Wheat Company of Niagara Falls to obtain money to pay his college expenses. Saturdays and Sundays, the rush days, he got a job with the Niagara Gorge Railroad Company to act as assistant to the conductor in charge of the brake on the trailer or rear car of the two that made the trip around the gorge. On August 23d, 1925, as the cars were running through this narrow belt of a mile or more near the edge of the gorge on the westerly side, the conductor in charge of the cars, a man named Culp, was standing on the rear platform of the forward car near the right-hand edge trying to adjust the trolley pole or hold it in place as the cars speeded round a curve. He was bending out backwards toward the side of the car when his head came in contact with a pole of the defendant company sweeping him off the car. The plaintiff, sitting almost directly behind him in the front seat of the trailer near the brake handle, immediately sprang up and instinctively grabbed for the conductor to save him, if possible, with the result that both Culp and Fitzpatrick were carried off and beneath the cars, Fitzpatrick being mutilated for life.

We need not dwell at length upon the negligence of the defendant as it became a question of fact not reviewable in this court. The points which we must touch upon do not involve the defendant's negligence. The International Railway Company maintained the pole causing the damage as one of its overhead line poles within a distance of about twelve inches from the step of the trolley cars as they went by. This was unnecessary as there was a distance of about sixteen and one-half feet between the outside of the rail and the edge of the gorge, in any portion of which the pole might have been placed. By section 104, chapter 185 of the Revised Statutes of Ontario, 1914, the Railway and Municipal Board of the Province of Ontario was given power to make orders and regulations regarding the maintenance and operation of these lines of railway. By order of May 26th, 1916, the Board made the following order:

. . .

"(15) Where the trolley wire is carried on span wires, the trolley poles supporting the span wires shall be erected and maintained at a minimum distance of seven feet from the centre line of the nearest track, such distance to be measured to the face of the trolley pole nearest the track; provided that where this is impracticable owing to the proximity of the railway to the cliff the Board may permit a trolley pole or poles to be erected nearer the centre line of the nearest track."

The legal experts called to testify as to the foreign law differed in their views as to the application of these rules and ordinances under the Ontario law, to which reference will be made later. The fact that the International Railway Company was bound to obey these rules, and could have placed its pole further back from the railway, was without doubt, the chief element of the defendant's negligence.

With this brief statement of the nature of this case, we will pass to the consideration of the two main points raised by this appeal.

. . .

[The first point raised by defendant-appellant related to the choice-of-law question whether the burden of proof with respect to plaintiff's own negligence was governed by New York law or Ontario law.[a] The Court of Appeals held that the trial court had committed no error regarding this point.]

. . .

Another point raised by the appellant relates to the charge of the court regarding the law of Ontario.[b] The court apparently left it to the jury to determine the law of Ontario, including the construction of the statutes and the court decisions as explained by the experts. Section 15 of the Board's order of May 26th, 1916, provided that the trolley poles supporting span wires shall be erected and maintained at a minimum distance of seven feet from the center line of the nearest track. The pole which Culp, the conductor, struck was nearer to the track than seven feet. It was within twelve inches of the step of the car. The pole, however, had been erected long before May 26th, 1916, the date of the order. Experts attempted to explain the meaning of section 15. Mr. Proudfoot, a barrister of Toronto, in behalf of the plaintiff, testified that this order of the Railway Board applied to equipment and to railways theretofore existing as well as to railroads constructed and poles erected thereafter. Mr. Grant, another barrister of Toronto, in behalf of the defendant, said that the International Railway Company had a vested or property right which could not be affected by the order.

Mr. Proudfoot, also in behalf of the plaintiff, testified that the law of rescue as applied to negligence cases in Canada was similar to that of New York State as stated in Wagner v. International Ry. Co., 232 N.Y. 176, 133 N.E. 437, expressing it as follows: "As I read the law of Ontario the question is whether the man under the circumstances acted as a reasonable man would do . . ." taking "into consideration the fact that the man acted in an emergency, acted on impulse and would

a. This part of the *Fitzpatrick* opinion is reproduced, or at least discussed, in most of the casebooks on Conflict of Laws; but it is not important for our present purpose.

b. In the *Fitzpatrick* litigation it was undisputed—and indeed indisputable un-der the choice-of-law rule prevailing at that time—that all substantive issues in the case were governed by the law of the place of the accident, i.e., by the law of Ontario.

naturally not exercise the same amount of care as if he had time to reflect upon what he was doing." [c] Fitzpatrick, we will recall, jumped for Culp, the conductor. The questions arising in the case were whether Fitzpatrick was guilty of contributory neglect in trying to rescue Culp and whether he was chargeable under such circumstances with Culp's negligence, if any.[d] We need not specify all the instances in which these experts on the foreign law testified. The point raised by appellant is that the court should not have submitted all these questions to the jury. With this we agree. The difficulty with the appellant's position is, however, that the trial counsel did not attempt to separate the questions of law for the court and the questions of fact for the jury by any proper request.

When it becomes necessary to establish the law of a foreign country it must be proved as facts are proven, but when, after such proof is given, the questions involved depend upon the construction and effect of a statute or judicial opinion, those questions generally are for the court and not questions of fact at all. Bank of China, etc. v. Morse, 168 N.Y. 458, 61 N.E. 774. In Hanna v. Lichtenhein, 225 N.Y. 579, 122 N.E. 625, this court said: "On a trial of an issue of fact when the evidence furnished is conflicting or inconclusive the law of a foreign State may be a question for the jury although ordinarily when the evidence is all furnished it is the function of the judge to decide as to the law of a foreign State." These rules, however, like many others, are easier stated than applied. Events test our theories and tax our philosophy. A look at the cases indicates that it is not always easy to separate the functions of the court and the functions of the jury in this particular. . . . Greenleaf on Evidence (§ 486) says: "The better opinion seems to be, that this proof [of foreign laws] must be made to the Court, rather than to the Jury," and he quotes from Mr. Justice Story's Conflict of Laws the following: "For all matters of law are properly referable to the Court and the object of the proof of foreign laws is to enable the Court to instruct the Jury what, in point of law, is the result of the foreign law to be applied to the matters in controversy before them. The Court are, therefore, to decide what is the proper evidence of the laws of a foreign country; and when evidence is given of those laws, the Court are to judge of that applicability, when proved, to the case in hand." Charlotte v. Chouteau (25 Mo. 465, at p. 474; S.C., 33 Mo. 194), went quite far in extending the duty of the court, while a more conservative rule has been stated in such cases as Electric

c. This view as to Ontario law was later confirmed in Moddejonge v. Huron County Bd. of Education, [1972] 2 O.R. 437, 444. As to liability for violation of statutory duty, see Henzel v. Brussels Motors Ltd., [1973] 1 O.R. 339, 345 (Co. Ct. 1972).

d. The trial judge had instructed the jury in accordance with the comparative negligence statute of Ontario, which provided that the jury should find "the degree in which each party was in fault", and that the amount of damages should be apportioned accordingly. But the trial judge left it to the jury to determine the Ontario "law of rescue" and its impact on the apportionment of fault and damages. The jury found that the plaintiff's negligence had contributed to the accident to the extent of ten per cent. The trial court's judgment thus awarded the plaintiff 90% of the damages suffered by him.

Welding Co., Ltd. v. Prince, 200 Mass. 386, at p. 390, 86 N.E. 947, and Hite v. Keene, 149 Wis. 207, at p. 215, 134 N.W. 383. In the former case we have the rule stated as follows: "The proof of the law of a foreign country may be by the introduction in evidence of its statutes and judicial decisions, or by the testimony of experts learned in the law, or by both. If the law is found in a single statute or in a single decision, the construction of it, like that of any other writing, is a question of law for the court. . . . 'Where the law is to be determined by considering numerous decisions which may be more or less conflicting, or which bear upon the subject only collaterally, or by way of analogy, and where inference may be drawn from them, the question to be determined is one of fact, and not of law.'" In the Wisconsin case the court said: "Where the only proof of a foreign law is some statute which has been offered in evidence, a number of courts hold that its construction is for the court. But where . . . oral testimony is taken in which there is a sharp conflict and where the case must practically be decided upon this oral testimony, the authorities are well nigh harmonious to the effect that the disputed question of fact presents a jury question in a case triable by a jury, and not one that can be taken from the jury and be decided by the court." This case also calls attention to the authorities which hold that judicial opinions, like statutes, are to be construed by the court.

All of the authorities agree that the construction of foreign statutes is a matter for the court and that their meaning should not be left to the jury as a question of fact. Such, no doubt, would also be the rule regarding orders of official bodies, having the force of law, that is, having the force of statute law. But how about court decisions? When these state the unwritten law of the foreign jurisdiction with reasonable certainty and clearness, their application should not be left to the speculation of twelve men. If instances should arise, which will be rare, where the decisions are so perplexing or doubtful that experts disagree on the law we shall have to determine whether the question of the foreign law must then be solved by the jury.[e] How the jury can do this as well as the judge, experienced in the law, I cannot quite appreciate. Personally, I am quite in sympathy with the expressions found in O'Rourke v. Cunard Steamship Co., Ltd., 169 App.Div. 943, 154 N.Y.S. 29,[f] and with Professor Wigmore's statement in section 2558 of

---

e. The authorities cited and quoted in the opinion seem to hold that a question of foreign decisional law is sometimes for the court and sometimes for the jury. What is the criterion? Is it predicated on (a) the number of the foreign decisions to be considered; or (b) their complexity; or (c) conflict among the decisions; or (d) conflict among the experts; or (e) a distinction drawn between foreign judicial opinions which, being actually before the court, may constitute documentary evidence, and those which were merely referred to in the oral testimony of the experts? In support of the last of these criteria, see Schweitzer v. Hamburg-Amerikanische Packetfahrt Actien Gesellschaft, 149 App.Div. 900, 903–4, 134 N.Y.S. 812, 814–5 (2d Dept., 1912). Should a similar criterion be used in deciding whether the effect of a foreign statute is to be determined by the court or by the jury?

f. These expressions are found in the dissenting opinion in the O'Rourke case; but it would seem that, on the question of proof of foreign law, the dissenting opinion was concurred in by the majority. The

Rule

his work on Evidence, to the effect that "the only sound view, either on principle or on policy, is that it [foreign law] should be proved to the judge, who is decidedly the more appropriate person to determine it."

Judge should interpret law but this case still stands

However, applying the law as we find it in the decisions, the judge in this case should have told the jury the meaning and application of the order of the Railway and Municipal Board. If there was no substantial dispute or question as to the unwritten law as found in the decisions of the Ontario courts introduced in evidence he should also have given this law to the jury and told them to apply it. The appellant we find is not in a position to raise these questions or to complain of the result reached by the jury. The jury's finding is in accordance, at least, with what the court should have charged as a matter of law regarding the Ontario statutes and regulations. Moreover, while the counsel took an exception to the charge of the court he made no requests embodying what he considered to be questions of law for the court and questions of fact for the jury. It is a fair procedure to require counsel to specify the objections to a charge by making a request calling attention to the alleged error so that it may be corrected then and there. And again, when the jury returned, late in the afternoon, and made a request for a further charge as to the application and meaning of the Ontario law and the orders of the Railway Board, counsel acquiesced in the charge which was a repetition of that previously given and took no exception to it.[g] . . .

The judgment below should be affirmed, with costs.[h]

CARDOZO, Ch. J., POUND, LEHMAN, KELLOGG, O'BRIEN and HUBBS, JJ., concur.

Spent significant time on this case, particularly the contract formation. Perhaps some relevance by analogy to ppr on general of Intl.

———

MILWAUKEE CHEESE CO. v. OLAFSSON

Supreme Court of Wisconsin, 1968.
40 Wis.2d 575, 162 N.W.2d 609.

This is an appeal from an order overruling a demurrer by the plaintiff to the answer of the intervening impleaded defendant in a garnishment action.

O'Rourke case, although it never came before the Court of Appeals, acquired some notoriety because of the poignancy of its facts.

g. See McKinney's N.Y.C.P.L.R. §§ 4017, 4110–b and 5501(a)(3) (similar to § 446 of the old C.P.A., which was in force at the time of the principal case). Cf. Fed. R.Civ.Pro. Rule 51; Anno, 35 A.L.R.Fed. 727 (1977).

h. Note that this case was decided prior to the enactment of McKinney's N.Y.C.P. L.R. § 4511, set forth infra p. 57, and of its predecessors (C.P.A. §§ 391 and 344–a, by which a judicial notice rule was first introduced in 1933 and strengthened in 1943). At the time of the principal case, there was no New York statute authorizing judicial notice of foreign law. If the case arose today, would you expect the decision of the Court, or its reasoning, to be different?

In early December of 1966, the principal defendant, Icelandic Seafood Company of Reykjavik, Iceland, invoiced a shipment of fish to the plaintiff, Milwaukee Cheese Co., for a purchase price of $9,611.[a]

A sight draft was drawn by the principal defendant, Icelandic Seafood Company, upon the plaintiff and delivered to the impleaded defendant, Fisheries Bank of Iceland, who endorsed it and forwarded it to the garnishee defendant, Marshall & Ilsley Bank, in Milwaukee, together with other documents of title for the fish.

On December 23, 1966, the plaintiff delivered its certified check in the amount of $9,621 to the Marshall & Ilsley Bank in payment of the sight draft. The bank delivered the draft and documents of title to the fish to the plaintiff.

On the same day, December 23, 1966, the plaintiff commenced this garnishment action wherein it alleged that the principal defendant, Icelandic Seafood Company, was indebted to the plaintiff in the amount of $12,267.47 because of other claims, and garnisheed the Marshall & Ilsley Bank for property in its possession belonging to Icelandic Seafood Company.[b]

The bank, as garnishee defendant, answered admitting it had $9,611 in its possession but alleged . . . upon information and belief that the Fisheries Bank of Iceland claims to have an interest in the funds.

After notice and motion, Fisheries Bank of Iceland was made an impleaded defendant by order of the court pursuant to sec. 267.17, Stats.

The answer and claim of Fisheries Bank of Iceland alleged that the owner and producer of the fish invoiced to plaintiff was an Icelandic corporation known as Fiskidjan, Ltd., and that Icelandic Seafood Company was merely an export agent for Fiskidjan; that Fiskidjan, Ltd., hypothecated and pledged to Fisheries Bank as a first mortgage and, as security for a loan of about 5,000,000 kronur (about $135,000), all future catch and seafood products existing and after-acquired during 1966, and the right to any kind of price allowances and foreign exchange emoluments on the catch and product; and that, by reason of the foregoing, Fisheries Bank has a recorded first mortgage on the catch and a lien on all proceeds, including the money paid to the Marshall & Ilsley Bank by the plaintiff.

Plaintiff demurred to the answer of the impleaded defendant on the grounds that the pleading did not state facts sufficient to constitute a cause of action. From an order overruling the demurrer the plaintiff appeals.

a. Note that this falls barely short of the amount-in-controversy prerequisite for the diversity jurisdiction of federal courts, 28 U.S.C. § 1332.

b. Could jurisdiction over a foreign-country defendant be obtained in this manner today? See *Shaffer v. Heitner*, 433 U.S. 186 (1977).

BEILFUSS, Justice.

The issue is whether the answer and the claim of the respondent, the impleaded defendant, Fisheries Bank of Iceland, allege facts sufficient to constitute a cause of action.

The plaintiff contends and the impleaded defendant does not dispute that under the substantive law of Wisconsin the answer and claim do not state facts sufficient to constitute a cause of action for the reason that the security instruments held by the impleaded defendant are imperfect security interests because there is no allegation that the security instruments were signed by the debtor as required by sec. 409.402(1), Stats.[c] Sec. 409.301(1)(b) provides that ". . . an unperfected security interest is subordinate to the rights of: . . . A person who becomes a lien creditor without knowledge of the security interest and before it is perfected."

The impleaded defendant argues that the law of Iceland applies and that under that law it has a good lien and that this lien is superior to any subsequent lien for a period of four months.[1]

The impleaded defendant contends that it was not required to plead the applicable law of Iceland and cites the Wisconsin Uniform Judicial Notice of Foreign Law Act as its authority. Sec. 891.01, Stats., states:

> "*Judicial Notice of Foreign Laws.* (1) Courts Take Notice. Every court of this state shall take judicial notice of the common law and statutes of every state, territory and other jurisdiction of the United States.

c. This admission by the impleaded defendant perhaps was unnecessary. *Quaere* whether under the Uniform Commercial Code, as incorporated into Wisconsin law, the impleaded defendant did not acquire a perfected security interest *in the documents of title* by obtaining possession thereof. See U.C.C. § 9–305.

1. "409.103(3). If personal property other than that governed by subs. (1) and (2) is already subject to a security interest when it is brought into this state, the validity of the security interest in this state is to be determined by the law (including the conflict of laws rules) of the jurisdiction where the property was when the security interest attached. However, if the parties to the transaction understood at the time that the security interest attached that the property would be kept in this state and it was brought into this state within 30 days after the security interest attached for purposes other than transportation through this state, then the validity of the security interest in this state is to be determined by the law of this state. If the security interest was already perfected under the law of the jurisdiction where the property was

when the security interest attached and before being brought into this state, the security interest continues perfected in this state for 4 months and also thereafter if within the 4-month period it is perfected in this state. The security interest may also be perfected in this state after the expiration of the 4-month period; in such case perfection dates from the time of perfection in this state. If the security interest was not perfected under the law of the jurisdiction where the property was when the security interest attached and before being brought into this state, it may be perfected in this state; in such case perfection dates from the time of perfection in this state."

[Needless to say, this provision, as quoted by the Court, reflects § 9–103 of the U.C.C. prior to the 1972 and 1977 amendments. Insofar as the principal case is concerned, however, it makes no difference whether one applies the old or the new version of § 9–103. Under either version, it can be argued that the rights asserted by the impleaded defendant depend on the law of Iceland. Ed.]

"(2) Information of the court. The court may inform itself of such laws in such manner as it may deem proper, and the court may call upon counsel to aid it in obtaining such information.

"(3) Determined by court; Ruling Reviewable. The determination of such laws shall be made by the court and not by the jury, and shall be reviewable.

"(4) Evidence of foreign laws. Any party may also present to the trial court any admissible evidence of such laws, but, to enable a party to offer evidence of the law in another jurisdiction or to ask that judicial notice be taken thereof, reasonable notice shall be given to the adverse parties either in the pleadings or otherwise.

"(5) Foreign country The law of a jurisdiction other than those referred to in sub. (1) shall be an issue for the court, but shall not be subject to the foregoing provisions concerning judicial notice.

"(6) Interpretation. This section shall be so interpreted as to make uniform the law of those states which enact it."

The impleaded defendant argues that the section must be read as a whole, and that sub. (5) restricts the court from only taking judicial notice of the laws of foreign countries but does not prevent a party from offering evidence of the laws of foreign countries when the party has given reasonable notice to the adverse parties, either in the pleading or otherwise under sub. (4).

We do not agree. Sub. (4) applies solely to the common law and statutes of every state, territory and other jurisdiction of the United States. Prior to the enactment of the statute it was settled that one relying on the law of a foreign state had to plead it and that evidence as to the foreign law was not admissible if not pleaded. [Citations]. With the addition of sec. 891.01, Stats., judicial notice can be taken not only of the statutes but the common law of this country, states, and territories; if there is reasonable notice, evidence of those laws is admissible even though the laws were not pleaded.

It is clear from a reading of the statute that the changes in the established law affect only the laws and statutes referred to sub. (1). Subs. (2), (3) and (4) all refer to "such laws" and do not include laws of foreign countries. Thus, the laws of foreign countries must be pleaded and proved as any other fact. [Citations].

We do not deem it necessary for the one relying on the foreign law to thoroughly quote the law in his pleadings. In the interest of fair notice, it is sufficient if he alleges the foreign law is relied upon and includes in general a statement of what that law is. Even those states which statutorily allow judicial notice of the laws of foreign countries require a plain and concise statement of the material facts sufficient to allow the other party to controvert them. Greiner v. Freund (1955),

286 App.Div. 996, 144 N.Y.S.2d 766. This affords the adverse party a basis from which he can intelligently respond, either by pleading or demand for greater specificity. In addition, it will aid the trial court in informing itself of the laws.

There are more practical aspects of a case such as this than clear-cut legal ones. It is relatively easy to gain access to the laws of the states. Access to the laws of foreign countries is far more difficult. Even if the laws were readily available, language barriers, problems of interpretation, and unfamiliar legal systems compound the difficulties involved in a search of the law.

In view of the above, the impleaded defendant's final contention that its pleadings, claim, affidavit, and hypothec, read as a whole, allege the law of Iceland is without merit.

Order reversed and remanded with leave to impleaded defendant to amend its answer within 15 days after remittitur.[d]

pleadings

NOTES AND QUESTIONS

(1) *What Is "Foreign" Law?* Under the common-law rule illustrated by the preceding cases, a state court treats both sister state law and foreign country law as "foreign law", and hence as "fact". In this book, however, in the context of a study of comparative law, emphasis will be placed on the procedural treatment accorded by our courts to the law of foreign nations.

Whether a given territory and its law must be treated as that of a foreign nation, depends on the status of the territory under international law, and not on the nature of its legal system. The common law of our neighbors in Ontario is "foreign" law for any court in the United States. But the law of the Commonwealth of Puerto Rico, or of United States "territories and insular possessions" (as authoritatively defined in Title 48 of the U.S.C.A.)[1] is not "foreign" in that sense, even though it may contain elements that appear alien to a lawyer brought up in the common law. The Spanish-derived law of Puerto Rico, or the Danish law governing pre-1921 land titles in the Virgin Islands,[2] is domestic law in a federal court sitting there; this remains true if an appeal is taken from that court to the U.S. Court of Appeals or the U.S. Supreme Court, with the result that those courts must of their own motion inform themselves of such law as best they can. See Ponce v. Roman Catholic Apostolic Church, 210 U.S. 296, 309, 28 S.Ct. 737, 741–2 (1908); Callwood v. Kean, 189 F.2d 565, 573–4 (3 Cir., 1951); Summa Corp. v. Calif. ex rel. Lands Comm'n, 466 U.S. 198, 202 n. 1, 104 S.Ct. 1751, 1753–54 n. 1 (1984).

d. In effect, the Court sustains the plaintiff's demurrer to the answer of the impleaded defendant, with leave to amend. Would the demurrer have been overruled if the Court had concluded that the answer (although silent on the law of Iceland, which was applicable pursuant to the forum's choice-of-law rule) stated a valid claim under the internal law of Wisconsin? See infra pp. 88–120.

1. See also FRCP Rule 44(a).

2. Danish tradition also affects the law of divorce in the Virgin Islands. See Burch v. Burch, 195 F.2d 799, 805 ff. (3d Cir. 1952); Shearer v. Shearer, 356 F.2d 391 (3d Cir. 1965), cert. denied 384 U.S. 940, 86 S.Ct. 1463 (1966).

Although the law of the former sovereign is in theory domestic law, it can nevertheless be proved by expert testimony. Fremont v. United States, 58 U.S. (17 How.) 542, 557 (1854); State v. Valmont Plantations, 346 S.W.2d 853 (Tex.Civ.App.—San Antonio 1961), decision adopted, 163 Tex. 381, 355 S.W.2d 502 (1962). International law, too, "is part of our law," The Paquete Habana, 175 U.S. 677, 700, 20 S.Ct. 290, 299 (1900); Banco Nacional De Cuba v. Sabbatino, 376 U.S. 398, 423, 84 S.Ct. 923, 937 (1964); but it, too, can be proved by expert testimony. See, *e.g.*, Palagonia v. TWA, 110 Misc.2d 478, 442 N.Y.S.2d 670 (1978), and generally H. W. Baade, Proving International Law in Domestic Tribunals, 18 Va.J.Int.L. 619 (1978).

The law of Cuba, Japan and Germany was "foreign law" even during the periods when these countries were wholly or partly occupied by United States military forces. See Goodyear Tire & Rubber Co. v. Rubber Tire Wheel Co., 164 F. 869 (C.C.S.D.Ohio, 1908; Lurton, J.); cf. Cobb v. United States, 191 F.2d 604 (3 Cir., 1951), cert. den. 342 U.S. 913, 72 S.Ct. 360.[3] Decrees and regulations issued by American occupation authorities in Germany, however, were held to constitute domestic law for a court in the United States. Estate of Muller, 199 Misc. 745, 104 N.Y.S.2d 133 (Surr.Ct.Kings Co., 1951); Kent Jewelry Corp. v. Kiefer, 119 N.Y.S.2d 242 (S.Ct.N.Y.Co., 1952). Such regulations, it must be remembered, are easily accessible. They were published, in English, in the Code of Federal Regulations and in the Federal Register.[3a]

The Pacific Islands Trust Territory was held to be a "foreign country" for purposes of the Federal Torts Claims Act.[3b] It may, therefore, be arguable that the law of that Territory is foreign law.[3c]

(2) *History and Rationale of the "Fact" Doctrine.* The common law rule, that foreign law should be treated as a fact (or like a fact), had its origin in the 18th century.[4] It was first announced by Lord Mansfield, who thought that in the context of a trial a proposition of foreign law should be treated like a matter of commercial custom; the element that is common to foreign law and commercial customs is that ordinarily both are unknown to judge and jury.

The essence of Lord Mansfield's rationale is that for practical courtroom purposes a question of foreign law is basically different from a question of domestic law. In this connection, two factors must be considered:

(a) When a question of domestic law arises in a court, the judge is expected to know the applicable rule, or at least to be sufficiently familiar with legal methods and sources so that he can arrive at a

---

3. Comparable problems arise under the Federal Tort Claims Act which specifically excludes from its operation "any claim arising in a foreign country." 28 U.S.C.A. § 2680(k). See Bell v. United States, 31 F.R.D. 32, 34 (D.Kan. 1962). Further authorities are collected in Annos., 63 A.L.R.2d 997 (1959) and 6 L.Ed.2d 1422, at 1476–81 (1962).

3a. Concerning the constitutional basis and the legal nature of American military government in a foreign country, see the interesting study by S. W. Wurfel, Military Government—The Supreme Court Speaks, 40 N.Car.L.Rev. 717 (1962).

3b. See Callas v. United States, 253 F.2d 838 (2d Cir. 1958), cert. denied 357 U.S. 936, 78 S.Ct. 1384 (1958). See also supra n. 3.

3c. Cf. People of Saipan v. United States Dept. of Interior, 502 F.2d 90 (9th Cir. 1974), cert. denied 420 U.S. 1003 (1975); World Communications Corp. v. Micronesian Telecommunications Corp., 456 F.Supp. 1122 (D.Hawaii 1978).

4. The interesting history of the rule is discussed by S. L. Sass, Foreign Law in Civil Litigation: A Comparative Survey, 16 Am.J.Comp.L. 332, at 335–39 (1968), where further references can be found.

sound conclusion after he has listened to the arguments of counsel and has conducted his own research.[4a] No such expectation can exist in a case governed by rules of foreign law, especially if they are rules expressed in a foreign tongue and in terms of a strange legal system. Speaking of a civil law system, Mr. Justice Holmes observed:

> "When we contemplate such a system from the outside it seems like a wall of stone, every part even with all the others, except so far as our own local education may lead us to see subordinations to which we are accustomed. But to one brought up within it, varying emphasis, tacit assumptions, unwritten practices, a thousand influences gained only from life, may give to the different parts wholly new values that logic and grammar never could have gotten from the books."[5]

It follows that the background knowledge necessary to pierce the "wall of stone", must be supplied in the course of the lawsuit itself.[5a] Once this is recognized, it is logically possible to go a step further and to say that the foreign law should not be treated like law, presumed to be known to the court, but rather like a fact, which must be brought into court by way of pleading and evidence.

Lord Mansfield

(b) It is frequently pointed out that a domestic court, even if it had the requisite background knowledge, may not have access to library facilities which would make it possible to find and to verify the applicable rules of foreign law. If the judge cannot find the foreign law by the usual process of "looking it up", then such law must be brought to his attention by other methods.

(3) *Criticism of the Rule.* The law of sister states is not so strange as to defy our understanding; and today, whatever may have been the situation in bygone times, library facilities in most communities are quite sufficient to look up the statutory and decisional law of other states. There is, therefore, virtual agreement among practicing as well as academic lawyers that the old rule equating foreign law with "facts", as applied to sister state law, is an obsolete relic.[5b] That rule, incidentally, has never prevailed in federal courts, which have routinely taken judicial notice not only of the laws of the states in which they were sitting, but of the laws of all component states and territories of the United States. Bowen v. Johnston, 306 U.S. 19, 23, 59 S.Ct. 442, 444 (1939); Hanley v. Donoghue, 116 U.S. 1, 6, 6 S.Ct. 242, 245 (1885); Lamar v. Micou, 114 U.S. 218, 223, 6 S.Ct. 242, 245 (1885); Owings v. Hull, 34 U.S. (9 Pet.) 607 (1835).

4a. See E. M. Morgan, Judicial Notice, 57 Harv.L.Rev. 269, 270–71 (1944). Judicial notice statutes, such as Cal.Ev.Code § 451, often reflect the same view.

5. Diaz v. Gonzalez, 261 U.S. 102, 105–6, 43 S.Ct. 286, 287 (1923). See also General Box Co. v. United States, 351 U.S. 159, 168, 76 S.Ct. 728, 734 (1956) (dissenting opinion by Douglas, J.).

5a. The "wall of stone" also may produce collateral effects. The fact that important issues in a case are governed by alien law, sometimes is invoked as a factor militating in favor of a *forum non con-* *veniens* dismissal. Unless aided by other factors, however, the mere need to delve into foreign law is not, by itself, a sufficient justification for such dismissal. "The interpretation of the law of a foreign country is a task from which federal courts do not shrink." D'Angelo v. Petroleos Mexicanos, 398 F.Supp. 72, 85 (D.Del. 1975).

5b. In the overwhelming majority of states, statutes now direct, or at least authorize, the courts to take judicial notice of sister state law. For references see infra pp. 78–81.

With respect to foreign country law, the matter is more doubtful. It is true that there are now a few libraries in this country which have impressive collections of foreign law materials.[6] Whether these libraries, most of which are situated in metropolitan centers, can be used conveniently by judges and lawyers in more remote localities, may be open to some question.[7] Even where library facilities are ample, it is not easy for one trained exclusively in the common law to find and to understand a civil-law rule without the guidance of an expert.

Most observers agree that the law of foreign countries, especially of civil-law countries, should not be presumed to be known to the court. But does it follow that in presenting such law to the court the parties should be restricted by all the formalities which surround the pleading and proving of facts? Is it axiomatic that what is treated as a "fact" for one purpose, must with inexorable logic be so treated for every purpose? Is it sound policy to have questions of foreign law determined by a jury? Should the judge, in cases in which he decides such questions, be prohibited from conducting any research of his own even if he is willing and competent to do so?

Although for some time there was controversy concerning the answers to most of these questions,[8] a reformist view ultimately prevailed in the majority of jurisdictions.[8a] The reforms thus engendered came in the shape of various types of statutory enactments. We now turn our attention to these statutes.

B. STATUTORY MODIFICATIONS AND INNOVATIONS

INTRODUCTORY NOTE

(1) The rules which today govern the procedural treatment of foreign law in American courts, usually result from an interplay between the traditional common law doctrine and some modern stat-

---

6. E.g., the Library of Congress, the library maintained by the Association of the Bar of the City of New York, the Los Angeles County Law Library, and several law school libraries.

7. There are certain difficulties even in the metropolitan centers. See Report of the Committee on Foreign and Comparative Law of the Association of the Bar of the City of New York, 22 The Record (Supplement—Committee Reports 1966–67) 31, 32 (1967): "The Committee concluded that while New York City is rich in foreign law materials, they are so scattered among various institutions as to make research difficult. . . . ." A similar complaint was voiced by a metropolitan court in Telesphore Couture v. Watkins, 162 F.Supp. 727, 730–31 (E.D.N.Y. 1958). Note, however, that British and European Communities materials are increasingly becoming available through commercial electronic retrieval systems.

8. For many years, Professor Arthur Nussbaum of Columbia University was the principal spokesman for the reformist view. See his articles, The Problem of Proving Foreign Law, 50 Yale L.J. 1018 (1941); Proving the Law of Foreign Countries, 3 Am.J.Comp.L. 60 (1954); Proof of Foreign Law in New York: A Proposed Amendment, 57 Col.L.Rev. 348 (1957). See also, as reflecting liberal views, Keeffe, Landis and Shaad, Sense and Nonsense About Judicial Notice, 2 Stan.L.Rev. 664 (1950). There were others, however, who emphasized the merits rather than the defects of the traditional approach. See, e.g., O. C. Sommerich and B. Busch, Foreign Law—A Guide to Pleading and Proof 119–23 (1959); W. B. Stern, Foreign Law in the Courts: Judicial Notice and Proof, 45 Cal. L.Rev. 23 (1957).

8a. Significantly, this majority now includes New York, California, Texas, and the federal courts, i.e., those jurisdictions that are faced with the greatest volume of transnational litigation. See the materials on the next-following pages.

utes.[8b] For counsel planning or conducting litigation involving foreign law, it becomes necessary, therefore, in almost every case to separate, and to consider the interaction of, the following questions: (a) How would the case be analyzed and decided in the absence of a statute? (b) Does the forum state have a statute dealing with the procedural and evidentiary treatment of foreign law? (c) Does the statute, assuming it is constitutional, apply to the particular kind of foreign law which is involved in the case? (d) Is the statute mandatory or permissive, or partly mandatory and partly permissive? (e) To the extent that the statute is permissive, what are the factors influencing the exercise of judicial discretion?

(2) As the common law rules concerning pleading and proof of foreign law are fairly complex, and the superimposed statutes are variegated and not always clear, the subject is one of some intricacy. It is hoped that the materials which follow will acquaint the reader with the more important problems arising in this area. Those who wish to pursue the study of the subject beyond the limits necessarily imposed on a coursebook, may derive some assistance from the references collected in the footnote.[9]

8b. In England, the impact of statutes on the common-law rules concerning the procedural treatment of foreign law has been far less drastic than in the majority of American jurisdictions. An English statute of 1925 provides that the judge, and not the jury, determines issues of foreign law; but inasmuch as civil jury trials have become a rarity in England, this statute is of limited practical importance today. A few rules of evidence, as applied to proof of foreign law, have been modified in § 4 of the Civil Evidence Act 1972, eff. June 1, 1974, see infra p. 145. In general, however, English law still adheres to the rule that foreign law must be pleaded and proved as a "fact". J. H. C. Morris, The Conflict of Laws 37–41 (3d ed. 1984); Cheshire & North, Private International Law 124–30 (10th ed. P. M. North 1979). A different rule prevails as to the law of the European Communities. Pursuant to § 3 of the European Communities Act 1972, questions of European Communities law are treated as "questions of law," and "judicial notice" is taken of the Treaties, the Official Journal, and the decisions of the European Court.

9. In addition to the writings referred to in nn. 4 and 8, supra, see Symposium, Pleading and Proof of Foreign Law, 19 Stan.J.Int.L. 1–206 (1983); M. Pollack, Proof of Foreign Law, 26 Am.J.Comp.L.

470 (1978); Anno., Pleading and Proof of Law of Foreign Country, 75 A.L.R.3d 177 (1977); Comment, Determination of Foreign Law Under Rule 44.1, 10 Tex.Int.L.J. 67 (1975); G. S. Alexander, The Application and Avoidance of Foreign Law in the Law of Conflicts, 70 N.W.U.L.Rev. 602 (1975); R. B. Schlesinger, A Recurrent Problem in Transnational Litigation: The Effect of Failure to Invoke or Prove the Applicable Foreign Law, 59 Cornell L.Rev. 1 (1973); A. R. Miller, Federal Rule 44.1 and The "Fact" Approach to Determining Foreign Law, 65 Mich.L.Rev. 613 (1967); S. L. Cohn, The New Federal Rules of Civil Procedure, 54 Geo.L.J. 1204, 1241–47 (1966); R. A. Jefferies, Recognition of Foreign Law by American Courts, 35 U.Cin.L. Rev. 578 (1966); W. A. Rafalko, Pleading, Proving and Obtaining Information on Foreign Law, 43 U.Det.L.J. 95 (1965); P. Hay, Vereinigte Staaten von Amerika, in the volume Die Anwendung ausländischen Rechts im internationalen Privatrecht (publ. by Max Planck-Institut für ausländisches und internationales Privatrecht 1968), at 102ff.; R. B. Schlesinger, Die Behandlung des Fremdrechts im amerikanischen Zivilprozess, 27 Rabels Z. 54 (1962). In these articles the reader will find further references, not only to a wealth of cases and statutes, but also to numerous other scholarly discussions.

NEW YORK CIVIL PRACTICE LAW AND RULES

R 3016. Particularity [of pleading] in specific actions

. . .

(e) Law of foreign country. Where a cause of action or defense is based upon the law of a foreign country or its political subdivision, the substance of the foreign law relied upon shall be stated.

R 4511. Judicial notice of law

(a) *When Judicial Notice Shall Be Taken Without Request.* Every court shall take judicial notice without request of the common law, constitutions and public statutes of the United States and of every state, territory and jurisdiction of the United States and of the official compilation of codes, rules and regulations of the state except those that relate solely to the organization or internal management of an agency of the state and of all local laws and county acts.

(b) *When Judicial Notice May Be Taken Without Request; When It Shall Be Taken on Request.* Every court may take judicial notice without request of private acts and resolutions of the congress of the United States and of the legislature of the state; ordinances and regulations of officers, agencies or government subdivisions of the state or of the United States; and the laws of foreign countries or their political subdivisions. Judicial notice shall be taken of matters specified in this subdivision if a party requests it, furnishes the court sufficient information to enable it to comply with the request, and has given each adverse party notice of his intention to request it. Notice shall be given in the pleadings or prior to the presentation of any evidence at the trial, but a court may require or permit other notice.

(c) *Determination by Court; Review as Matter of Law.* Whether a matter is judicially noticed or proof is taken, every matter specified in this section shall be determined by the judge or referee, and included in his findings or charged to the jury. Such findings or charge shall be subject to review on appeal as a finding or charge on a matter of law.

(d) *Evidence to Be Received on Matter to Be Judicially Noticed.* In considering whether a matter of law should be judicially noticed and in determining the matter of law to be judicially noticed, the court may consider any testimony, document, information or argument on the subject, whether offered by a party or discovered through its own research. Whether or not judicial notice is taken, a printed copy of a statute or other written law or a proclamation, edict, decree or ordinance by an executive contained in a book or publication, purporting to have been published by a government or commonly admitted as evidence of the existing law in the judicial tribunals of the jurisdiction where it is in force, is prima facie evidence of such law and the unwritten or common law of a jurisdiction may be proved by witnesses or printed reports of cases of the courts of the jurisdiction.*

NOTES

(1) The reader will note that to some extent these provisions diminish the differences in procedural treatment that used to exist between "domestic" and "foreign" law.

Under traditional common-law notions, a question of domestic law must always be resolved by the court on the basis of its own knowledge or research, regardless of whether the court has been aided by arguments of counsel. Questions of foreign law, on the other hand, at common law had to be tried like ordinary issues of fact.

In analyzing the provisions of Rule 4511, one readily observes that most matters of domestic law are covered in subd. (a), while foreign law comes under subd. (b). It should be noted, however, that the important procedural provisions of subds. (c) and (d) apply to all matters that are judicially noticed, regardless of whether the authority for such judicial notice flows from subd. (a) or subd. (b). It follows that under subd. (c) all matters of law, whether domestic or foreign, are to be determined by the court, and not by the jury, and are subject to unrestricted review on appeal. Likewise, the flexible and informal methods by which matters of law can be ascertained under subd. (d), are available regardless of whether the court deals with domestic or with foreign law.

Subd. (d), in speaking of "testimony," seems to confer discretionary power upon the court, as one of several alternative procedures, to hold a hearing at which experts can testify. But since subd. (d) refers to subd. (a) as well as subd. (b), it is clear that such a hearing may be held even where the law to be applied is technically "domestic" law. Normally, the court will not need the help of experts when dealing with questions of domestic law.[1] Suppose, however, that a treaty ratified by the United States, which as the supreme law of the land (U.S. Constitution, Art. VI, cl. 2) certainly constitutes domestic law, is written in a foreign language and contains technical expressions that are understandable only in terms of a foreign legal system. In such a case, where the meaning of the official foreign-language text of a treaty is in dispute, "a CPLR 4511 hearing is appropriate to enable the court to arrive at an accurate translation," even though a treaty cannot be regarded as "foreign law."[2]

* These provisions have been in effect since Sept. 1, 1963. For a reference to the New York statutes which governed judicial notice of foreign law prior to that date, see the footnote appearing at the end of the *Fitzpatrick* case, supra.

1. Expert evidence has been commonly employed to ascertain the law of former territorial sovereigns (*e.g.*, Spanish and Mexican law) although it is technically domestic law, see supra, p. 53. More recently, expert legal testimony has been used in purely domestic settings to establish commercial usage, standards for business judgment, the intent of a Restatement or even of an amendment to the Louisiana Civil Code. See Aluminum Co. of America v. Essex Group, Inc., 499 F.Supp. 53, 62–63 (W.D.Pa. 1980), Equibank v. United States I.R.S., 749 F.2d 1176, 1178 (5th Cir. 1985), and generally Comment, Expert Legal Testimony, 97 Harv.L.Rev. 797 (1984).

2. Rosman v. T.W.A., 34 N.Y.2d 385, 392–93, 358 N.Y.S.2d 97, 103, 314 N.E.2d 848, 852 (1974); Palagonia v. TWA, 110 Misc.2d 478, 442 N.Y.S.2d 670 (1978).

For a more general discussion of the propriety of expert testimony on the interpretation of treaties and other matters of international law, see H. W. Baade, Proving Foreign and International Law in Domestic Tribunals, 18 Va.J.Int.L. 619 (1978).

(2) To the point just made, there is an important counter-point. It is true that Rule 4511 treats questions of "domestic law" and of "foreign law" alike; but this is so only if, and to the extent that, the court in dealing with questions of foreign law actually utilizes the provisions of the Rule. While judicial notice of domestic law is mandatory under the traditional maxim of jura novit curia and under the provisions of Rule 4511, subd. (a), a fair reading of subd. (b) makes it plain that in deciding whether to take judicial notice of foreign law, the court normally has broad discretion.[3] If in the exercise of such discretion the court declines to take judicial notice of the foreign law, then Rule 4511 becomes inoperative, and in that event the common-law rules enshrining the "fact" doctrine necessarily reassert themselves. Thus it would be quite erroneous to think that modern judicial notice statutes, where they exist, have *completely* assimilated the procedural treatment of foreign law to that of domestic law.

(3) The exercise of the important discretionary powers which the court possesses under provisions such as Rule 4511, subd. (b), will be influenced principally by two factors: (a) the nature of the foreign legal system involved in the case, and (b) the extent to which the parties, by furnishing relevant materials, have aided the court in ascertaining the foreign law.

Where (as in the Frummer case, infra) the applicable foreign law belongs to the common-law family, a judge may be willing to ascertain it, even though he has received no help from the parties. But when the foreign legal system is alien in language and structure—as is normally the case with a civil-law system—, courts are reluctant to dig up the foreign law on their own.[4] In a civil-law case, therefore, the court will tend to limit its "judicial notice" to appraising, and occasionally supplementing, the foreign-law materials submitted to it by the litigants.

(4) It follows from the foregoing that even in jurisdictions where judicial notice statutes such as Rule 4511 are in existence, the burden of invoking and presenting the foreign law continues to rest very largely on the shoulders of counsel (rather than the court). Such judicial notice statutes have, nevertheless, turned out to be of enormous importance in practice, because they enable the litigants to present foreign-law information to the court without regard to technical, exclusionary rules of evidence. Statements and declarations by officials of a foreign country, extracts from books which are not physically in the courtroom, opinions by scholars not available for cross-examination—all of these may be submitted or referred to, or may be woven into the examination and cross-examination of those experts who do testify in open court.[5] Technical objections become quite useless under a modern

---

3. Even that portion of subd. (b) which seemingly is cast in mandatory terms, leaves it to the court to determine whether a party has furnished "sufficient" information. See, e.g., Petition of Petrol Shipping Corp., 37 F.R.D. 437 (S.D.N.Y. 1965) (declining to take judicial notice under N.Y. CPLR Rule 4511(b)).

4. See M. Pollack, Proof of Foreign Law, 26 Am.J.Comp.L. 470, 471 (1978).

5. In a case where the decisive point of foreign law is not really controversial, properly prepared affidavits or written opinions may be quite sufficient to supply the necessary information. For an example, see Matter of Gyfteas, 59 Misc.2d 977, 300 N.Y.S.2d 913 (Surr.Ct. 1968). In this way the parties can (with or without a formal stipulation not to call expert witnesses at the trial) save the heavy expense of having the experts appear in court.

On the other hand, when the pertinent doctrines of foreign law are complex, or their application to the facts of the case is genuinely debatable, a party producing an expert in open court may sometimes have

judicial notice statute because the presiding judge can always overrule the objection by saying: "Whether or not this particular item of information be admissible as evidence, I shall in any event informally receive and use it to increase my knowledge concerning the foreign law." Some of the materials which thus go into the record, may be of questionable reliability; but this affects weight rather than admissibility. Questions of foreign law being for the court, it is no longer necessary, by exclusionary rules, to protect a jury from being misled.

Unnecessary, purely technical obstacles to the presentation of foreign-law materials thus are greatly reduced, with the result that speed and efficiency are enhanced, and that—at least in some cases— [6] a considerable saving of needless expense is achieved.

CONFLICT OF LAW QUESTION

FEDERAL RULES OF CIVIL PROCEDURE

Rule 44.1 Determination of foreign law *

A party who intends to raise an issue concerning the law of a foreign country shall give notice in his pleadings or other reasonable written notice. The court, in determining foreign law, may consider any relevant material or source, including testimony, whether or not submitted by a party or admissible under the Federal Rules of Evidence. The court's determination shall be treated as a ruling on a question of law.

see NY law pages?

may not raise foreign law on appeal

Advisory Committee's Note **

Rule 44.1 is added by amendment to furnish Federal courts with a uniform and effective procedure for raising and determining an issue concerning the law of a foreign country.

To avoid unfair surprise, the *first sentence* of the new rule requires that a party who intends to raise an issue of foreign law shall give notice thereof. The uncertainty under Rule 8(a) about whether foreign law must be pleaded—compare Siegelman v. Cunard White Star, Ltd., 221 F.2d 189 (2d Cir. 1955), and Pedersen v. United States, 191 F.Supp. 95 (D.Guam 1961), with Harrison v. United Fruit Co., 143 F.Supp. 598 (S.D.N.Y. 1956)—is eliminated by the provision that the notice shall be "written" and "reasonable." It may, but need not be, incorporated in the pleadings. In some situations the pertinence of foreign law is apparent from the outset; accordingly the necessary investigation of

an advantage over his opponent who submits only written materials.

6. See supra n. 5.

* This Rule went into effect July 1, 1966. Prior to that date, the FRCP did not contain any provision directly addressing itself to the procedural treatment of foreign-law issues. The Rule was slightly amended in 1972, eff. July 1, 1975. See 88 Stat. 1926.

Civil Rule 44.1 has been reenacted in the Rules of the United States Claims Court (Rule 44.1), the United States Court of International Trade (Rule 44.1), and the

United States Tax Court (Rule 146), and in the Military Rules of Evidence (Rule 201A(b)). It has been incorporated by reference into the Bankruptcy Rules (Rule 917).

Rule 26.1 of the Federal Rules of Criminal Procedure, also effective July 1, 1966, is substantially the same as Civil Rule 44.1.

** This Advisory Committee Note, which presumably was consulted by the Supreme Court before it adopted the Rule, appeared in 39 F.R.D. 73, at 117–19 (1966).

Pittway Corp 1996 : (7th cir): Ct looked to state of incorporation (France). Ct must determine what French law provides. Ct displeased w/ parties b/c they failed to provide the French code provisions. Ct warned "parties must be prepared is inform ct fully on ?s of foreign law when pertinent to the case. submit agreed translation

FOREIGN LAW IN OUR COURTS 61

that law will have been accomplished by the party at the pleading stage, and the notice can be given conveniently in the pleadings. In other situations the pertinence of foreign law may remain doubtful until the case is further developed. A requirement that notice of foreign law be given only through the medium of the pleadings would tend in the latter instances to force the party to engage in a peculiarly burdensome type of investigation which might turn out to be unnecessary; and correspondingly the adversary would be forced into a possibly wasteful investigation. The liberal provisions for amendment of the pleadings afford help if the pleadings are used as the medium of giving notice of the foreign law; but it seems best to permit a written notice to be given outside of and later than the pleadings, provided the notice is reasonable. *notice requirement*

The new rule does not attempt to set any definite limit on the party's time for giving the notice of an issue of foreign law; in some cases the issue may not become apparent until the trial, and notice then given may still be reasonable. The stage which the case has reached at the time of the notice, the reason proffered by the party for his failure to give earlier notice, and the importance to the case as a whole of the issue of foreign law sought to be raised, are among the factors which the court should consider in deciding a question of the reasonableness of a notice. If notice is given by one party it need not be repeated by any other and serves as a basis for presentation of material on the foreign law by all parties. *No time* *Test*

. . . *does the silence of the parties = acquiescence*

In further recognition of the peculiar nature of the issue of foreign law, the new rule provides that in determining this law the court is not limited by material presented by the parties; it may engage in its own research and consider any relevant material thus found. The court may have at its disposal better foreign law materials than counsel have presented, or may wish to reexamine and amplify material that has been presented by counsel in partisan fashion or in insufficient detail. On the other hand, the court is free to insist on a complete presentation by counsel. *court may conduct independent research*

There is no requirement that the court give formal notice to the parties of its intention to engage in its own research on an issue of foreign law which has been raised by them, or of its intention to raise and determine independently an issue not raised by them. Ordinarily the court should inform the parties of material it has found diverging substantially from the material which they have presented; and in general the court should give the parties an opportunity to analyze and counter new points upon which it proposes to rely. See Schlesinger, Comparative Law 142 (2d ed. 1959); Wyzanski, A Trial Judge's Freedom and Responsibility, 65 Harv.L.Rev. 1281, 1296 (1952); *cf.* Siegelman v. Cunard White Star, Ltd., supra, 221 F.2d at 197. To require, however, that the court give formal notice from time to time as it proceeds with its study of the foreign law would add an element of undesirable rigidity to the procedure for determining issues of foreign law.

The new rule refrains from imposing an obligation on the court to take "judicial notice" of foreign law because this would put an extreme burden on the court in many cases; and it avoids use of the concept of "judicial notice" in any form because of the uncertain meaning of that concept as applied to foreign law. See, e.g., Stern, Foreign Law in the *noted in class*

Pleadings = 121

Supp 15

See page 224 for a German comparison

but see Cal. pg 79, 80, 85, 101, 103, 111

93 = disadvantage of fact doctrine

Courts: Judicial Notice and Proof, 45 Calif.L.Rev. 23, 43 (1957). Rather the rule provides flexible procedures for presenting and utilizing material on issues of foreign law by which a sound result can be achieved with fairness to the parties.

Under the *third sentence*, the court's determination of an issue of foreign law is to be treated as a ruling on a question of "law," not "fact," so that appellate review will not be narrowly confined by the "clearly erroneous" standard of Rule 52(a). . . .

The new rule parallels Article IV of the Uniform Interstate and International Procedure Act, approved by the Commissioners on Uniform State Laws in 1962, except that section 4.03 of Article IV states that "[t]he court, not the jury" shall determine foreign law. The new rule does not address itself to this problem, since the rules refrain from allocating functions as between the court and the jury. See Rule 38(a). It has long been thought, however, that the jury is not the appropriate body to determine issues of foreign law. See, e.g., Story, Conflict of Laws § 638 (1st ed. 1834, 8th ed. 1883); 1 Greenleaf, Evidence § 486 (1st ed. 1842, 16th ed. 1899); 4 Wigmore, Evidence § 2558 (1st ed. 1905); 9 id. § 2558 (3d ed. 1940). The majority of the States have committed such issues to determination by the court. See Article 5 of the Uniform Judicial Notice of Foreign Law Act, adopted by twenty-six states, 9A U.L.A. 318 (1957) (Supp. 1961, at 134); N.Y.Civ.Prac.Law & Rules, R. 4511 (effective Sept. 1, 1963); Wigmore, *loc. cit.* And Federal courts that have considered the problem in recent years have reached the same conclusion without reliance on statute. See Jansson v. Swedish American Line, 185 F.2d 212, 216 (1st Cir. 1950); Bank of Nova Scotia v. San Miguel, 196 F.2d 950, 957 n. 6 (1st Cir. 1952); Liechti v. Roche, 198 F.2d 174 (5th Cir. 1952); Daniel Lumber Co. v. Empresas Hondurenas, S.A., 215 F.2d 465 (5th Cir. 1954).

NOTES AND QUESTIONS

(1) Some writers have claimed that the promulgation of Rule 44.1 sounded the death-knell of the old "fact" approach to determining foreign law, and that the Rule permits and indeed requires us to treat foreign law as "law." That this is an exaggerated view of the significance of Rule 44.1, will become evident a little later (see infra pp. 224–227) when we consider the German rule concerning procedural treatment of foreign law. In Germany, foreign law is truly treated as law, with the consequence that the responsibility for its ascertainment is thrust upon the court rather than the litigants. When faced with an issue governed by foreign law, a German judge *must* ascertain the tenor of such foreign law, even if he receives no help whatsoever from the parties. The most cursory glance at Rule 44.1 reveals the stark contrast between its provisions and the German rule. Under Rule 44.1, it is wholly left to the discretion of the judge whether he should engage in independent research concerning the foreign law, and we have it on the authority of a well-known federal trial judge that he and his brethren, in dealing with a civil-law point on which the parties have not submitted sufficient materials, normally will not conduct such independent research.[1] Thus, our approach remains very different from the German one, under which foreign law is clearly regarded as "law."[2]

1. See M. Pollack, Proof of Foreign Law, 26 Am.J.Comp.L. 470, 471 (1978).

2. D. R. Tueller, Reaching and Applying Foreign Law in West Germany: A Sys-

It is true that for certain purposes—especially for the purpose of determining the scope of appellate review—Rule 44.1 treats a foreign-law issue as one of law. This is made clear by the last sentence of the Rule. But it does not follow that a foreign-law issue must be treated as one of law for all purposes. In the all-important context of determining whether the principal responsibility for invoking and ascertaining the foreign law is borne by the court or by the litigants, it is clear that we (in contrast to the Germans) do not regard foreign law as "law." If we did, we would have to thrust that responsibility upon the court; but that is precisely what we do *not* do, neither under the traditional doctrine *nor under Rule 44.1.*

That Rule 44.1 has merely modified, and not completely abrogated, our traditional "fact" approach,[3] is highlighted also by the recent Fifth Circuit case discussed in the next-following Note.

(2) In United States v. McClain,[4] the defendants were charged with having received, concealed and/or sold stolen goods in interstate or foreign commerce, in violation of the National Stolen Property Act (NSPA).[5] They were also charged with conspiracy to commit similar acts in the future. The goods in which they had dealt were pre-Columbian artifacts imported into this country from Mexico. There was no evidence that the defendants or anyone else had taken these artifacts from the personal possession of another. The legal theory under which the case was tried was that by laws protecting its cultural heritage, the Government of Mexico had made itself the *owner* of the artifacts, even though possession may have remained in the hands of private individuals. It followed, so the prosecution argued, that (in the absence of permission granted by the Mexican Government) any act seeking to dispose of the artifacts while they were still in Mexico, or to export them from Mexico, constituted theft under Mexican law.

The prosecution further argued, and the court agreed, that such theft, although committed in Mexico and criminalized by Mexican law, would make it possible to treat the artifacts as "stolen" within the meaning of the NSPA. The prosecution, however, apparently had difficulty in proving that the acts by which the Mexican Government had been deprived of the artifacts, and by which the artifacts were said to have acquired the character of "stolen" goods, had occurred after

tematic Study, 19 Stan.J.Int.L. 99, 115–17 (1983). It is interesting to note that the German Code of Civil Procedure, although in general treating foreign law as "law", does not authorize the court of last resort to review a question of foreign law. See id. at 155, note 66; Baumbach, Zivilprozessordnung, § 549, Anno. 2B (33rd ed. 1975); and generally K. D. Kerameus, Revisibilität ausländischen Rechts, ein rechtsvergleichender Überblick, 99 Zeitschrift für Zivilprozess 166 (1986). This stands in sharp contrast to Rule 44.1, which on the contrary treats an issue of foreign law as one of "law" for purposes of appellate review, but not for other purposes. See also infra n. 3.

3. "The soundest approach would be to give up all attempts to characterize foreign law as either 'fact' or 'law' and to start writing a new theory on a clean slate. But in the United States, at least, this seems almost impossible. American common-law doctrines, and in large part the pertinent statutes, are so clearly based on the fact theory that in dealing with existing law we cannot afford completely to dismiss that unsound theory from our minds." R. B. Schlesinger, A Recurrent Problem in Transnational Litigation: The Effect of Failure to Invoke or Prove the Applicable Foreign Law, 59 Cornell L.Rev. 1, at 3–4 (1973).

4. 545 F.2d 988 (5th Cir. 1977), rehearing denied 551 F.2d 52 (5th Cir. 1977); second appeal after retrial 593 F.2d 658 (5th Cir. 1979).

5. 18 U.S.C.A. §§ 2314, 2315.

May 1972. That date was important for the following reason: Beginning in 1897, Mexico had enacted a number of successive statutes for the protection of its pre-Hispanic cultural heritage. Most of these statutes, however, were poorly drafted, and it was at least doubtful whether the pre-1972 statutes vested *title* to the artifacts in the Mexican Government. A statute passed in May 1972, on the other hand, unequivocally made the Mexican Government the *owner* of all artifacts of the kind involved in this case.

At the first trial, the district judge instructed the jury that the Mexican Government had been the owner of the artifacts in question since 1897. The jury found the defendants guilty. On appeal, the Court of Appeals thoroughly reviewed the course of the Mexican legislation from 1897 to 1972, and concluded that the Mexican Government had acquired title to artifacts in or on immovable archeological monuments in 1934, but title to other pre-Columbian artifacts only in 1972. The Court held, therefore, that the district judge's instruction concerning Mexican law had been erroneous,[6] and that under a correct view of the Mexican law the defendants could be convicted only if it were shown beyond a reasonable doubt that the artifacts were "stolen" from the Mexican Government after the effective date of the May 1972 statute, or of the 1934 statute if applicable. 545 F.2d at 1003. The result was a reversal and remand for a new trial.

Upon the new trial, there was again much conflicting evidence concerning the Mexican law, and especially concerning the question whether the Mexican Government could be said to have become the owner of the artifacts prior to 1972. This time the trial judge left it to the jury to decide whether and when Mexico validly acquired national ownership of the artifacts involved. The jury again brought in a verdict of guilty. The defendants appealed for the second time, arguing (among other points) that the district court had erred in leaving determination of the Mexican law to the jury. The Court of Appeals dealt with this argument as follows (593 F.2d, at 669–670):

> Rule 26.1 of the Federal Rules of Criminal Procedure provides in part that "[t]he court, in determining foreign law, may consider any relevant material or source, including testimony, whether or not submitted by a party or admissible under [the Federal Rules of Evidence]. The court's determination shall be treated as a ruling on a question of law." Despite appellants' fond hopes, Rule 26.1 does not itself mandate that the judge rather than the jury decide all questions of foreign law. Rather, it provides that any determination a judge does make shall be treated as a ruling on a question of law. This "functional approach," carefully sidestepping the issue of who is to decide the question, was deliberate on the part of the draftsmen.[7]

6. The appellate court's power to review the foreign-law issue was derived from Federal Rules of Criminal Procedure, Rule 26.1 (quoted infra), which is identical in this respect with Civil Rule 44.1.

7. The Advisory Committee Notes on the Fed.R.Civ.P. 44.1 to which we are referred by the draftsmen of the Rules of Criminal Procedure observe that Rule 44.1, to which Rule 26.1 is substantially identical, does not address itself to this problem because the rules generally refrain from allocating functions between judge and jury. The committee adds, "It has long been thought, however, that the jury is not the appropriate body to determine issues of foreign law," citing, among other authorities, our pre-Federal Rules cases, Daniel Lumber Co. v. Empresas Hondurenas, S.A., 215 F.2d 465 (5th Cir. 1954), cert. denied

Our pre-Rule cases make clear that the proper procedure is for the judge rather than the jury to determine questions of foreign law. [Citations] To close the gap left in the Federal Rules of Criminal Procedure, we reaffirm that division of functions now, as we have done in the corresponding civil context. First Nat. City Bank v. Compania de Aguaceros, S.A., 398 F.2d 779, 782 (5th Cir. 1968). But it does not necessarily follow that putting the matter to the jury is reversible error. There is no automatic prejudice to the substantial rights of a defendant inherent in letting the jury decide the question on the basis of expert testimony. Indeed, the question whether the right to a jury trial in criminal matters requires submission of a question of foreign law to the jury, because it can be found as a matter of fact, has never been definitively laid to rest.[8] In the absence of compelling evidence of prejudice, we would be loath to reverse a conviction such as this where the evidence of guilt and of intent to violate both foreign and domestic law is near overwhelming. We believe, nevertheless, that reversal of at least the substantive count is required here because the most likely jury construction of Mexican law upon the evidence at trial is that Mexico declared itself owner of all artifacts at least as early as 1897. And under this view of Mexican law, we believe the defendants may have suffered the prejudice of being convicted pursuant to laws that were too vague to be a predicate for criminal liability under our jurisprudential standards.

The Court, however, affirmed the defendants' conviction on the conspiracy count, holding that with respect to that count the trial judge's error was harmless,[9] because the conspiracy clearly aimed at illegally dealing with artifacts exported (and to be exported) from Mexico after the effective date of the 1972 statute.[10]

(3) As is frequent in foreign-law litigation, the McClain case, supra, bristles with questions of procedure and procedural tactics.

Could the prosecutor, as appellee, have avoided the reversal of the conviction on the substantive count if he had argued that, as a matter of constitutional law, the issues concerning Mexican law *had* to be submitted to the jury, and that, consequently, the trial judge committed no error?

Neither party objected to the instruction by which the trial judge left the issues of Mexican law to the jury. Did their failure to raise a timely objection preclude the defendants from attacking that instruction on appeal?[11] Had this been a civil case, FRCP Rule 51 arguably would have mandated such preclusion. In a criminal case, however,

---

348 U.S. 927, 75 S.Ct. 340, 99 L.Ed. 727 (1955), and Liechti v. Roche, 198 F.2d 174 (5th Cir. 1952). Advisory Committee Note to Rule 44.1, Fed.R.Civ.P., Title 28, U.S.C.A. [Footnote by the Court, renumbered.]

8. See, e.g., Kaplan, "Continuing Work of the Civil Committee: 1966 Amendments of the Federal Rules of Civil Procedure (II)," 81 Harv.L.Rev. 591, 617 (1968). Because no one argues the point here, we express no opinion on the issue. [Footnote by the Court, renumbered.]

9. Shades of Fitzpatrick! See supra p. 48.

10. A reader who is an aficionado of pre-Columbian art, of art law, or of thrilling crime stories, will find it rewarding to peruse the full text of the three opinions written in this case. They are cited supra n. 4.

11. Remember what happened to the appellant in the *Fitzpatrick* case? See supra p. 48.

one must note the interplay between Rule 30 and Rule 52(b) of the Federal Rules of Criminal Procedure. Criminal Rule 30 is similar to Civil Rule 51; but Criminal Rule 52(b) provides that "Plain errors . . . affecting substantial rights may be noticed although they were not brought to the attention of the court."

(4) In the Fifth Circuit, the proper construction of a legal term describing an essential element of a federal offense is itself an essential element of that offense, and has to be submitted to the jury. United States v. Johnson, 718 F.2d 1317, 1322–23 (5th Cir. 1983) ("security" as used in federal securities legislation). Under this approach, it is reversible error to keep expert evidence on the meaning even of domestic-law terms from the jury. United States v. Garber, 607 F.2d 92 (5th Cir. 1979) (remuneration for taxpayer's blood as "income" for federal income tax purposes). In United States v. McLean, Cr. H–82–224 (S.D.Tex. 1985), both the prosecution and the defense presented expert testimony to the jury on the question whether Pemex (Petroleos Mexicanos) was an "instrumentality" of the Mexican state for purposes of the Foreign Corrupt Practices Act, 15 U.S.C.A. § 78dd–2. As the defendant was acquitted, there was no appellate sequel. For background, see United States v. McLean, 738 F.2d 655 (5th Cir. 1984).

FRUMMER v. HILTON HOTELS INTERNATIONAL, INC.

New York Supreme Court (Trial Term, Kings County, 1969).
60 Misc.2d 840, 304 N.Y.S.2d 335.

MANGANO, J. In this negligence action the jury has returned a verdict in favor of the defendant, and the court has been asked by the plaintiff to set aside that determination and grant a new trial.

[The opinion then outlines the evidence received at the trial, which showed that plaintiff, while a registered guest at defendant's hotel in London, England, was the victim of an accident. As he was taking a shower, plaintiff slipped and fell in the bathtub, and as a result suffered serious injuries. Plaintiff contends that the accident was due to defendant's failure to provide a rubber shower mat (although plaintiff had asked for such a mat), and to certain defects in the facilities provided by the defendant.]

. . . A serious question of this court's jurisdiction over this defendant was raised and ultimately resolved in favor of jurisdiction by the Court of Appeals (19 N.Y.2d 533, 281 N.Y.S.2d 41, 227 N.E.2d 851).

. . . The motion to set aside the judgment entered upon the jury's verdict is based upon two grounds. The first is that the court failed to charge properly the relevant provisions of English law, particularly the Occupiers' Liability Act of 1957 (5 and 6 Eliz. 2, c. 31), and second, that certain photographic evidence was improperly excluded.

[The court found both of these arguments to be without merit.]

During the course of the court's research on the Occupiers' Liability Act, the court became aware of an issue not raised by plaintiff's counsel. It is that contributory negligence is not a defense to this action under English law. That country has adopted a comparative negligence statute which reduces a plaintiff's damages to the extent that plaintiff can be said to be responsible for his own injuries. The statute—entitled the Law Reform (Contributory Negligence) Act (8 and 9 Geo. VI., c. 28)—became law in 1945, and provides in pertinent part (S.1) as follows:

> "(I) where any person suffers damage as the result partly of his own fault and partly of the fault of any other person or persons, a claim in respect of that damage shall not be defeated by reason of the fault of the person suffering the damage, but the damages recoverable in respect thereof shall be reduced to such extent as the court thinks just and equitable having regard to the claimant's share in the responsibility for the damage."

[handwritten margin note: The court this located this English stat oh Plaintiff behalf.]

Here the jury was charged in accordance with established New York law, that any negligence on the part of the plaintiff contributing to the accident required a verdict for the defendant.* Three questions are thus raised: (1) Assuming that the English statute applies, was the failure to charge the provisions of that statute prejudicial? (2) If the answer to the first question is affirmative, then is the English law the proper controlling rule? (3) Again, if the answer to the latter question be in the affirmative, does plaintiff's failure to bring the matter to the court's attention preclude relief?

[handwritten margin note: NP law different from English law]

[handwritten note inline: It could, but here it would be against the interests of justice, so decided by NYSC]

Reviewing the record as a whole, it cannot be gainsaid that the issue of contributory fault was important. It may well have been the decisive consideration in the jury's deliberations. This is so despite the fact that the court charged the jury that momentary forgetfulness by the plaintiff of the risk of slipping did not require a finding of contributory negligence. The defendant strenuously argued to the jury—and now in opposition to the present motion again urges—that the plaintiff, by proceeding to shower without the mat he claims he asked for, was guilty of contributory negligence as a matter of law. In light of plaintiff's fairly substantial evidence of negligence, it is reasonable to assume that this argument of the defendant carried much if not conclusive weight with the jury. There is, therefore, a strong probability that had England's comparative negligence doctrine been applied, the jury would have returned a verdict in plaintiff's favor—albeit in an amount reduced by the jury's assessment of the respective responsibilities of the plaintiff and the defendant for the accident.

[handwritten margin note: ct found]

As the use of New York's contributory negligence rule rather than England's comparative negligence law was in all likelihood the determining factor, it must be decided which rule properly applies here.

[handwritten margin note: Issue]

---

* At the time of this case, New York had not yet adopted the comparative negligence rule.

[The court then proceeds to examine whether in the present case the issue of the effect of the plaintiff's own negligence is governed by English law or New York law. After an extended discussion of the choice of law principles recently developed by the New York Court of Appeals, the court concludes that in the present case that issue is governed by English law.]

Finally, we deal with plaintiff's failure to bring the Law Reform Act to the court's attention which should normally bar any consideration of the statute's application at this point. In James v. Powell, 19 N.Y.2d 249, 279 N.Y.S.2d 10, 225 N.E.2d 741, the Court of Appeals, sua sponte, raised a conflict of law question which neither side had briefed or argued; but *James* involved the laws of a jurisdiction of the United States, of whose laws our courts are required to take judicial notice (CPLR 4511[a]). We are here dealing with the law of a foreign country where the court is authorized to take judicial notice but is not required to do so unless the party seeking to have the court invoke foreign law presents the necessary data to the court (CPLR 4511[b]). On the other hand this court has the power—which the Court of Appeals does not—to order a new trial in the interest of justice (CPLR 4404[a]), and the court is quite convinced that this is such a case. The action has been in litigation many years. A costly appeal to the Court of Appeals on the question of jurisdiction has taken place. The court elects, therefore, to take judicial notice of England's Law Reform Act of 1945.

In the court's opinion, to allow the judgment to stand would not conform with the interests of justice. Accordingly, motion for a new trial is granted.*

NOTES AND QUESTIONS

(1) As the court noted in the principal case, *plaintiff's* counsel failed to bring the English comparative negligence statute to the attention of the court. In this connection, consider the following statement of the New York Court of Appeals in In re Roel, 3 N.Y.2d 224, at 232, 165 N.Y.S.2d 31, 37, 144 N.E.2d 24, 28 (1957):

> "When counsel who are admitted to the Bar of this State are retained in a matter involving foreign law, they are responsible to the client for the proper conduct of the matter, and may not claim that they are not required to know the law of the foreign State." [1]

In Degen v. Steinbrink, 202 App.Div. 477, 195 N.Y.S. 810 (1922), aff'd mem. 236 N.Y. 669, 142 N.E. 328 (1923), New York lawyers were held liable for preparing security instruments which turned out to be invalid at the out-of-state situs of the chattels. This case was cited with approval in *Roel*, supra, and in Rekeweg v. Federal Mutual Insurance

---

* In other cases arising under similar statutes, the courts sometimes have undertaken independent research concerning the law of foreign *common law* countries, and sometimes have declined to do so. Compare Siegelman v. Cunard White Star Ltd., 221 F.2d 189, 196–97 (2 Cir. 1955) with Tsacoyeanes v. Canadian Pacific Ry. Co., 339 Mass. 726, 162 N.E.2d 23 (1959).

1. The context of the *Roel* case makes it clear that when speaking of a "foreign State", the Court referred to foreign countries as well as sister states.

Co., 27 F.R.D. 431, 436 (N.D. Ind. 1961). Fenaille & Despeaux v. Coudert, 44 N.J.L. 286 (1882), contains a quaint alternative ruling to the contrary which—although not formally overruled—is not likely to be accepted as authoritative today. See D. F. Vagts, Transnational Business Problems 152 (1986).

(2) The defendant in the principal case was Hilton Hotels (U.K.) Ltd., a British corporation then operating a hotel in London. *Defendant's* counsel, too, failed to bring the English comparative negligence statute to the attention of the court. The American Bar Association's Model Code of Professional Responsibility requires a lawyer, in *presenting a matter to a tribunal*, to disclose "legal authority in the controlling jurisdiction known to him to be directly adverse to the position of his client and which is not disclosed by opposing counsel." A.B.A. Model Code DR 7–106. The Model Rules of Professional Responsibility adopted by the ABA House of Delegates in 1983 impose an *affirmative obligation of candor* in this respect, stating without qualification that a lawyer "shall not knowingly . . . fail to disclose" such matter. A.B.A. Model Rules, Rule 3.3(a)(3). Note, however, that in the principal case, New York was the original "controlling jurisdiction," and English law became "controlling" only through the application of New York choice-of-law rules which had to be invoked by one of the parties or raised by the court sua sponte. Cf. B. Currie, On the Displacement of the Law of the Forum, 58 Colum.L.Rev. 964 (1958), and generally infra, pp. 88–120.

(3) Would the court have reached a different result in the principal case if there had been no pertinent judicial notice statute in New York?

(4) Note that in the principal case the court discovered the crucial English statute only after the jury had rendered a verdict. In order to grant relief to the plaintiff at this late stage, the court had to rely not only on the judicial notice statute, but also on another statutory provision authorizing a New York trial court to grant a new trial "in the interest of justice." In many other jurisdictions, the provisions concerning the granting of new trials are less liberal; the court may be able to grant a new trial only on specific grounds,[2] and these specific grounds perhaps do not include the accidental discovery, by the court, of an uninvoked provision of foreign law. Suppose the situation presented by the principal case had occurred in a jurisdiction thus restricting the court's power to grant a new trial. The court then might have been in a position where it had power to take judicial notice of the English statute, but still could not make any use of its discovery. Again, as so frequently in foreign-law cases, we observe the great importance of procedural considerations.

(5) Suppose that in the principal case the trial judge had not discovered the English comparative negligence statute. In that event, he would have denied the motion for a new trial, and a judgment would have been entered upon the jury's verdict for the defendant. If the plaintiff had then appealed from that judgment, and the *appellate court* had stumbled upon the English statute, could it have reversed and ordered a new trial?[3] Consider, in this connection, that plaintiff's

2. See, e.g., Cal.Code Civ.Proc. § 657.

3. For a spectacular illustration, see Oppenheimer v. Cattermole, [1976] A.C. 249 (H.L. 1973 & 1975): After hearing oral argument, the House of Lords determined by independent research that a point of German law had been decided below on the basis of inadequate materials, and remanded for a new determination in the light of F. A. Mann, The Present Validity of Nazi Nationality Laws, 89 L.Q.Rev. 194 (1973), which had appeared in the interim.

counsel apparently took no exception when the trial court instructed the jury in accordance with the contributory negligence rule which at that time still prevailed in New York. Consider also that, the English comparative negligence statute not having been invoked by either party, the trial judge perhaps committed *no error* when he instructed the jury in accordance with New York law.[4] If they find no error committed by the trial court, the appellate judges cannot reverse.

(6) If a situation exactly like that in the principal case arose in a federal District Court, would the outcome be the same? Or would the first sentence of Rule 44.1 prevent the trial judge from noticing and utilizing the English statute discovered by him? Assuming that Rule 44.1 does not permit the judge to notice the uninvoked English statute, could he suggest to the parties that it would be a good idea to invoke that statute by way of a written notice complying with the first sentence of Rule 44.1?

(7) In California and in Texas, the statutes authorizing judicial notice of foreign law have been revised more recently than the New York provisions quoted above. In essence, California has adopted a scheme similar to that embodied in New York's Rule 4511. See West's Ann.Cal.Evid.Code, §§ 310–11, 450–60, eff. Jan. 1, 1967. The California legislator, however, has laid down detailed, specific provisions concerning some matters which in New York, and a fortiorari under FRCP Rule 44.1, would be left to (more or less discretionary) judicial determination. Among these specific provisions of the California statute are the following:

§ 455. Opportunity to present information to court

With respect to any matter specified in Section 452 [which inter alia refers to the law of foreign nations] . . . that is of substantial consequence to the determination of the action:

(a) If the trial court has been requested to take or has taken or proposes to take judicial notice of such matter, the court shall afford each party reasonable opportunity, before the jury is instructed or before the cause is submitted for decision by the court, to present to the court information relevant to (1) the propriety of taking judicial notice of the matter and (2) the tenor of the matter to be noticed.

(b) If the trial court resorts to any source of information not received in open court, including the advice of persons learned in the subject matter, such information and its source shall be made a part of the record in the action and the court shall afford each party reasonable opportunity to meet such information before judicial notice of the matter may be taken.

§ 459. Judicial notice by reviewing court
. . .

(c) When taking judicial notice under this section of a matter specified in Section 452 . . . that is of substantial consequence to the determination of the action, the review-

---

4. For a fuller treatment of this point see infra pp. 88–120.

ing court shall comply with the provisions of subdivision (a) of Section 455 if the matter was not theretofore judicially noticed in the action.

(d) In determining the propriety of taking judicial notice of a matter specified in Section 452 . . . that is of substantial consequence to the determination of the action, or the tenor thereof, if the reviewing court resorts to any source of information not received in open court or not included in the record of the action, including the advice of persons learned in the subject matter, the reviewing court shall afford each party reasonable opportunity to meet such information before judicial notice of the matter may be taken.

The Texas rule governing proof of foreign-country law is of even more recent origin. Texas Rules of Evidence, Rule 203 (effective in its present version as of November 1, 1984) reads as follows:

Rule 203. Determination of the Laws of Foreign Countries

A party who intends to raise an issue concerning the law of a foreign country shall give notice in his pleadings or other reasonable written notice, and at least 30 days prior to the date of trial such party shall furnish all parties copies of any written materials or sources that he intends to use as proof of the foreign law. If the materials or sources were originally written in a language other than English, the party intending to rely upon them shall furnish all parties both a copy of the foreign language text and an English translation. The court, in determining the law of a foreign nation, may consider any material or source, whether or not submitted by a party or admissible under the rules of evidence, including but not limited to affidavits, testimony, briefs, and treatises. If the court considers sources other than those submitted by a party, it shall give all parties notice and a reasonable opportunity to comment on the sources and to submit further materials for review by the court. The court, and not a jury, shall determine the laws of foreign countries. The court's determination shall be subject to review as a ruling on a question of law.

If either the California provisions or the Texas provisions quoted above had been in effect in New York, would they have affected the procedure or the result in Frummer v. Hilton Hotels International, supra? Does the New York, California or Texas approach seem preferable in the the context of that case?

(8) Where a judge has acquired knowledge of pertinent foreign-law provisions by his own research, the above-quoted California statute and the Texas rule require him to give the parties an opportunity to discuss such provisions before he utilizes them. As explicitly noted by the Advisory Committee (see supra p. 61), FRCP Rule 44.1 contains no such requirement. It is arguable, however, that the requirement spelled out in the California statute and in the Texas rule is one of due process, and that as a matter of fundamental procedural fairness a court may

not base its decision on surprise use of foreign-law information which the parties have had no opportunity to meet.[5]

[handwritten note: §. Re Disciplinary Action of cure : 1956 : Curl admonished for misinterpreting a foreign judgment b/f the ct. the case not done his homework]

FIRST NATIONAL CITY BANK v. COMPANIA DE AGUACEROS S. A.

United States Court of Appeals, Fifth Circuit, 1968.
398 F.2d 779.

[Some of Court's footnotes omitted; others renumbered.]

Before RIVES, GOLDBERG and AINSWORTH, Circuit Judges.

GOLDBERG, Circuit Judge.   This case concerns the liability vel non of the First National City Bank of New York (Bank) for having cashed forged checks of the Compania de Aguaceros, S.A., (Depositor). The villainous artful forger, Carlos Echeverria, has clouded the equities between the two protagonists not only by his consummate calligraphic talents but also by his position as the Depositor's agent and auditor in Panama.   The district court below discarded a relevant Panamanian statute as being vague and inconclusive, found the proximate cause of Echeverria's success to be the Bank's negligence, and ruled for the Depositor.   Compania de Aguaceros, S.A. v. First National City Bank, D.C.C.Z.1966, 256 F.Supp. 658.   We find unequivocal and controlling sustance [sic] in said statute and reverse.

The Depositor was a Panamanian corporation engaged in the sale of various airlines and aircraft throughout Latin America.   Although the Depositor maintained a checking account with the Bank's Panamanian branch, Joseph M. Silverthorne, who was the Depositor's organizer and treasurer, and who was the only executive authorized to sign checks on the Panamanian Bank, resided in Tegucigalpa, Honduras. Panamanian law required the Depositor to maintain a resident agent in Panama, and Silverthorne engaged the auditing firm of Farca, S.A. (Farcasa).   In 1962 Echeverria bought out the owner of Farcasa and thus placed himself in the position of trust from which he later gamed his gains.

[handwritten margin note: Utilized Panamanian Law]

The nine forged checks on the Depositor's account totaled $44,000 and covered the period from October 11, 1963, to February 25, 1964. Each check was returned by the Bank, with the statement for the month in which it was paid, on or about the first of the following month.   However, because Farcasa received the canceled checks and

---

5. See Arams v. Arams, 182 Misc. 328, 45 N.Y.S.2d 251 (Sup.Ct., N.Y. County, 1943). Cf. Saunders v. Shaw, 244 U.S. 317, 37 S.Ct. 638 (1917).

West Germany's Bundesgerichtshof (the highest court in civil and criminal matters) has held that a lower court violates a party's constitutionally guaranteed right to be heard if it decides a case on the basis of foreign-law information dug up by the court and not brought to the attention of the litigants. The lower court's decision based on such information was called a "surprise decision" and was, of course, reversed. BGH decision of December 19, 1975, NJW 1976, p. 474. See also the interesting discussion by J. Einmahl, Book Review, 34 Rabels Z. 756, at 765 (1970). The point will be taken up again infra pp. 420–422.

statement, Silverthorne remained an innocent abroad and no protest was made prior to March 20, 1964.

On March 19, 1964, Silverthorne returned to Panama, having been absent since October 29, 1963. He went to the Bank to establish a letter of credit and, while there, discovered that the balance in his company's account was substantially lower than it should have been. Because Echeverria's forgeries were skillfully done, Silverthorne was unable to determine immediately which checks he himself had not signed. With the Bank's help, however, he did trace the forged checks to Echeverria. According to the Bank, Echeverria was less artful at the casino than he was in the auditor's office, and so the two victims of the fraud must contest the ultimate loss.

At trial both parties stipulated the existence of the following three Panamanian statutes:

Article 989 of the Panama Commercial Code:

whether preclusion clause applies to forgery

"Article 989.—Banks are required to furnish their customers their accounts current at least eight days after the end of each quarter or liquidation period agreed upon, requesting their written conformity thereof, and the latter, or any comments that may be in order with respect thereto, must be presented within five days.

"Should a customer fail to reply within said period, his account will be held as admitted and the debit or credit balance shall be definitive as of the date of such account."

Article 23 of the Negotiable Instruments Law of Panama:

"Article 23.—When a signature is forged or made without the authority of the person whose signature it purports to be, it is wholly inoperative, and no right to retain the instrument, or to give a discharge therefor, or to enforce payment thereof against any party thereto, can be acquired through or under such signature, unless the party, against whom it is sought to enforce such right, is precluded from setting up the forgery or want of authority."

Article 9 of the Civil Code of Panama:

"Article 9.—When the meaning of the law is clear, its literal content shall not be discarded under pretext of questioning its true spirit or intention. However, for the purpose of interpreting any obscure expression of law it is permissible to have recourse to the intention or spirit clearly manifested in the law itself or in the trustworthy history of its institution." *

Noted compare to 536

---

* Civilian codes typically contain provisions giving directions to the courts as to how the code is to be interpreted, and how gaps in the written law are to be filled. See infra pp. 651–653. Article 9 of the Panamanian Civil Code constitutes such a directory provision.

The first sentence of Art. 9 reads as follows in the Spanish original: "Cuando el sentido de la ley es claro, no se desatenderá su tenor literal a pretexto de consultar su espíritu." "Consultar" is better translated into "considering" or simply, "consulting." This sentence, thus read, invites compari-

The trial judge, in his conclusions of law, found: "5. Article 989 is ambiguous and needs interpretation for its exact meaning cannot be determined from its language." 256 F.Supp. at 663.

[Among the trial court's other conclusions of law is the following (256 F.Supp. 663):

> 6. The experts are divided on the effect that is given in Panama to the provisions of Article 989 but it seems that the proper interpretation is that it is not peremptory and establishes only a prima facie situation which is subject to rebuttal. The eminent Dr. Ricardo J. Alfaro, former member of the World Court and a man of more than 50 years of experience in the practice of law which involved a close relationship with banking and mercantile law, in testifying for the defendant that he thought the terms were peremptory, nevertheless admitted that proof could be introduced to establish that there had been no receipt of the balance sheet by the depositor. Dr. Erasmo de la Guardia, former member of the Supreme Court of Panama and author of a treatise entitled "Law of Negotiable Instruments", was of the opinion that the effect of the statute is "to place the depositor in a state of alert" and "it does have the effect also of placing the depositor at a disadvantage in the sense that he has the burden of proving afterward, if he makes a claim, that there was error or fraud or duress".]

In the remainder of his opinion the trial judge exculpated Silverthorne and placed the determinative blame on the Bank. He awarded to the Depositor the sum of $44,000 plus interest from March 20, 1964.

We will not review the trial court's finding of negligence because we find that Panamanian Article 989 clearly precludes the Depositor's recovery.

I.   Panamanian Law, Question of Law or Question of Fact?

This first issue, a procedural one, is brought to light by the Depositor's brief. The first sentence of that brief begins, "This case involves several questions, all of them only of fact . . ." and concludes by quoting the "clearly erroneous" rule of Fed.R.Civ.P. 52(a).* Further in the brief the following conclusion is reached:

> "We, therefore, submit that the trial court found as a fact the proper interpretation of foreign law—and, of course, it is a

son with our own "plain meaning" rule. As to the latter, see A. W. Murphy, Old Maxims Never Die: The "Plain-Meaning Rule" and Statutory Interpretation in the "Modern" Federal Courts, 75 Colum.L.Rev. 1299 (1975).

* FRCP Rule 52(a) provides: ". . . Findings of fact, whether based on oral or documentary evidence, shall not be set aside unless clearly erroneous, and due regard shall be given to the opportunity of the trial court to judge of the credibility of the witnesses. . . ."

fundamental proposition that foreign law is a question of fact in the trial court."

Although we find no direct attack on this "fundamental proposition" in the Bank's brief, we refer both parties to Rule 44.1 of the Federal Rules of Civil Procedure.

[The court quotes Rule 44.1, italicizing the last sentence, and also quotes the next-to-the-last paragraph of the Advisory Committee Note (supra p. 62).]

Prior to July 1, 1966, although our Court had accepted the common law classification of foreign law as an issue of fact [Citations], we had consistently recognized the hybrid nature of such a classification. Thus, the "clearly erroneous" rule was often ignored on review especially when the relevant foreign statutes were available in English. [Citations] Moreover, the responsibility of interpreting foreign statutes at trial was given to the judge rather than to the jury. [Citations] Further reconciliation of the "fact" label with the predominantly "law" application has been made unnecessary by the functional approach of Rule 44.1. Regardless of the special procedures of proof listed in Rule 44.1, without doubt one purpose of the Rule is the relief of foreign law schizophrenia by the recognition of such law *as law*. . . . **

[The court holds that Rule 44.1 should be applied in this case, although the litigation began in November, 1964. The decision of the District Court was rendered on August 11, 1966, i.e., after the effective date of Rule 44.1. The order of the Supreme Court of February 28, 1966, which promulgated certain amendments of the FRCP including new Rule 44.1, provided that the new Rules should govern all further proceedings and actions pending on July 1, 1966, except to the extent that in the opinion of the court their application in a particular action then pending "would not be feasible or would work injustice."]

Under the facts of this case, we can hardly see how our acceptance of Rule 44.1 on appeal would work an injustice to either side; . . . .

II. Article 989 of the Panama Commercial Code

Article 989 imposes obligations on two parties. First, it requires a bank to furnish accounts current to depositors "at least eight days after the end of each quarter or liquidation period agreed upon, requesting their written conformity thereof." There is no contention that the Bank failed to meet this responsibility. Second, Article 989 requires each depositor to present any comments concerning the accounts cur-

---

** The same view—that under Rule 44.1 the "clearly erroneous" standard no longer applies to findings of foreign law—is again expressed in Gillies v. Aeronaves de Mexico, 468 F.2d 281, 286 (5 Cir., 1972). This is a correct reading of the Rule. In Kaho v. Ilchert, 765 F.2d 877, 881 (9th Cir. 1985), the de novo standard for review under Rule 44.1 was extended to foreign-law determinations of the Immigration and Naturalization Service. Similarly, it is now clear that under Rule 26.1 of the Federal Rules of Criminal Procedure a ruling of the District Court on a point of foreign law can be reviewed by the Court of Appeals as a ruling on the law. See United States v. McClain, 545 F.2d 988, 1000 (5 Cir., 1977).

rent "within five days." The next paragraph provides the only express sanction of the Article:

> "Should a customer fail to reply within said period, his account will be held as admitted and the debit or credit balance shall be definitive as of the date of such account."

Our analysis focuses initially on the sanction. Without doubt the sanction is directed against only the depositor. The substance of the sanction is nearly as obvious; if activated, it prevents any contest of the accounts current presented to the depositor. The only indefinite item in the sentence [1] is the time of activation, and we cannot agree with the trial court that this lack of chronological precision renders the statute a nudum statutum.

The trial court discarded the sanction to Article 989 because the eight-day time limit on a bank and the five-day time limit on a depositor were ambiguous.* This analysis seeks to prove too much—for example, whether "*at least* eight days after . . ." means "*within* eight days after . . ." and whether "within five days" refers to the mailing or to the receipt of the bank's statement. The words of Article 989 may be awkward, inelegant, or maladroit; but a common sense interpretation grants eight days within which to mail and five days after receipt to object. Moreover, the specifics of the limitations periods are not vital to this case. No combination or permutation of days before us in this case and no rational or logical addition or subtraction from or to eight and five could yield any answer except the barring of the Depositor's relief. When a case arises in which time limits are in issue, we can and perhaps will reconsider the specifics. But we will not

---

1. Because the facts of this case do not raise any question of fraud by the bank or justifiable impossibility of performance, we do not need to consider here whether any such considerations may limit or modify the express sanction.

* To bolster his position, the trial judge cited numerous American authorities. He did not explain, however, on what theory he believed these authorities to be helpful in interpreting one of the codes of a civil-law country.

The trial court was the U.S. District Court for the Canal Zone. There is some support for the proposition that when dealing with a doubtful or unprovided-for point of Canal Zone law, a court may look to other American authorities. The instant case, however, was not governed by the law of the Canal Zone. The plaintiff was a corporation incorporated under the laws of the Republic of Panama. The defendant Bank is authorized to do business under the laws of the United States and has qualified to do business both in the Canal Zone and in the Republic of Panama.

Plaintiff's bank account, which was the subject of the dispute, was maintained at defendant's branch in Panama City, Republic of Panama. Plaintiff's office, to which the bank statements were sent, also was located in the Republic of Panama. The trial court's Conclusion of Law No. 2 (256 F.Supp. 662) reads as follows: "The events in this case occurred in the country of Panama; therefore, the rights and duties of the parties toward each other are governed by the law of that country. Counsel for both parties agree with the court on this principle of law." Thus, there is no doubt that the substantive law to be applied in this case is that of the Republic of Panama, a foreign country which, at least with respect to its private law, belongs to the civil law orbit.

It should be noted, however, that although the trial judge's reliance on American authorities may have been misplaced, his ultimate conclusion was supported also by the testimony of Judge de la Guardia, an expert of eminent qualifications.

discard the plain substance of a statute because of theoretical and irrelevant ambiguities.

Most jurisdictions have a bank-protection statute such as Article 989. . . . The Depositor denies neither the existence of such statutes nor that a few states compel notice within thirty days. He contends, however, that the five-day period is unduly harsh, that the Uniform Commercial Code provides a one-year period,[2] and that even the Bank's statement specified ten days for reply. Thus, he concludes, the five-day period cannot be peremptory. We will not penalize the Bank for granting a period more liberal than that specified by statute. Moreover, we cannot ignore statutes merely because they are harsh. Harshness does not in itself constitute ambiguity.

Courts have consistently denied recovery to depositors who had failed to report discrepancies within the statutory period. Moreover, they have labeled such reporting requirements as substantive conditions precedent to recovery.

[The court points out that in the United States such statutory reporting requirements have been applied quite literally, regardless of whether the period allowed by the particular statute was long or short.]

We are construing a solemn statute with a discernible intention to limit the period of bank liability. Although we may question the equities in a five-day notice requirement, we cannot assume a legislative role and deny the statute's vitality. Cf. West Side Bank v. Marine Nat. Exchange Bank, Wisc., January 30, 1968, 37 Wis.2d 661, 155 N.W.2d 587 (requirements of posting under U.C.C. § 4–109). To do so would be to violate Article 9 of the Civil Code of Panama, quoted supra, as well as to ignore prior court decisions. [Citations]

We have examined the trial testimony of the experts on Panamanian law and have found no effective refutation of our determination. We conclude that the District Court's interpretation of Panamanian law was erroneous.

The judgment is reversed.

QUESTIONS

If the preceding case had come up in a jurisdiction strictly adhering to the "fact" doctrine, what would have been the scope of review in the appellate court? Would the outcome have differed from that in the actual case?

Assuming that the essence of the experts' testimony is fully and fairly stated in the trial court's Conclusion of Law No. 6, does it seem that the experts were effectively examined and cross-examined? Even if no relevant Panamanian cases throwing light on the specific question arising under Art. 989 of the Commercial Code could be found, should counsel not have asked the experts to cite cases and other pertinent authorities indicating the use which *a Panamanian court* would make

---

2. U.C.C. § 4–406(4). Note that the one-year period is a maximum and that the depositor's negligence can preclude recovery even if he reports the disparity within one year. U.C.C. § 4.406.

of the general principles of interpretation stated in Art. 9 of the Civil
Code? *

A BRIEF SURVEY OF PERTINENT STATUTES

Under the common law rule, sister state law as well as foreign-
country law is treated as "foreign law." Modern statutes, however,
tend more and more to differentiate between the two.

For purposes of a course on Comparative Law, the statutes dealing
with the procedural treatment of sister state law are of merely tangen-
tial interest, except insofar as (in some states) the same statute may
deal with proof of sister-state and of foreign-country law. By way of
background information, however, a student of Comparative Law
should know that statutes either directing or authorizing the courts to
take judicial notice of sister-state law have been enacted virtually in all
states,[1] and that common law proof of sister-state law today is required
only in a very small and dwindling number of jurisdictions.

With respect to the treatment of foreign-country law,[2] several types
of statutes can be distinguished:

* Judging by the testimony of the experts, one must conclude that the principal
case confronted an American court with a
question of Panamanian law which probably was *novel* in Panama. In situations of
this kind, which are not infrequent, our
courts have developed two conflicting lines
of approach. Some courts recognize only
those propositions of foreign law that are
directly supported by authority, and refuse
to perform a creative (essentially law-making) function, even though the courts of the
foreign country in question, if they were
dealing with the same case, might well use
it as a vehicle for boldly developing their
decisional law. See, e.g., McClure v. United States Lines Co., 247 F.Supp. 272 (E.D.
Va. 1964), vacated and remanded largely
on other grounds 368 F.2d 197 (4th Cir.
1966). Other courts, however, have felt
that in such a situation they should exercise all of the powers—including broad
powers of interpretation which in effect
may amount to law-making powers—conferred upon the courts by the foreign law.
For an outstanding example of this bolder
approach, see Bamberger v. Clark, 390 F.2d
485 (D.C.Cir. 1968).

An analogous problem often faces federal courts, when in diversity cases they
have to apply state law, and the point at
issue turns out to be novel or unsettled
under the law of the state in question. Cf.
Smith v. Sturm, Ruger & Co., Inc., 524 F.2d
776 (9th Cir. 1975). As to federal appellate
review in such cases, see Note, The Law/
Fact Distinction and Unsettled State Law
in the Federal Courts, 64 Tex.L.Rev. 157
(1985).

1. Twenty-eight jurisdictions adopted
the Uniform Judicial Notice of Foreign
Law Act, 9A U.L.A. 550 (1965), which mandates judicial notice of sister-state law.
See B. H. Greene, The Uniform Acts and
Their New York Statutory Counterparts; 7
Syracuse L.Rev. 38, 65 (1955). Although in
1966 the Commissioners on Uniform State
Laws withdrew their recommendation of
this Act, it remains in force in many
states. With respect to foreign-country
law, the Act merely provides that such law
is to be determined by the court rather
than the jury (see supra pp. 50–51); the
other provisions of the Act refer only to
sister-state law.

Other statutes, providing for mandatory
or permissive judicial notice of sister-state
law but not cast in the form of the old
Uniform Act, are in force in a substantial
number of additional states.

Occasionally (though infrequently),
courts have ruled that even in the absence
of a statute they had power to take judicial
notice of sister-state law. See, e.g.,
Saloshin v. Houle, 85 N.H. 126, 155 A. 47
(1931).

2. To avoid confusion and frustration in
research, the reader should realize that in
some states the provisions dealing with
judicial notice of foreign-country law are
separate from, and not always to be found
in the immediate vicinity of, the statute
mandating or authorizing judicial notice of
sister-state law. The reason for this probably is that the statutes (and, more commonly, the rules of procedure and of evidence) concerning judicial notice of foreign-

(i) *Statutes Patterned After FRCP Rule 44.1.* At least twenty states,[3] and the District of Columbia, have adopted provisions substantially identical with Federal Rule 44.1. Texas has adopted the substance of Rule 44.1, but with some significant additions, see supra p. 71. Moreover, Art. IV of the Uniform Interstate and International Procedure Act[4] is very similar to Federal Rule 44.1. That provision is in force in the Virgin Islands, but it has been displaced elsewhere by more recent enactments on proof of foreign law.[5]

(ii) *Judicial Notice Statutes of the New York-California Type.* These statutes, though differing among each other in important details (see supra pp. 57–71 share one characteristic feature: judicial notice of foreign-country law is (a) mandated if the court is furnished sufficient information, and if proper notice is given to the opponents, but (b) left to the discretion of the court when these conditions are not met. In addition to California and New York, seven other states have adopted bifurcated judicial notice statutes of this type.[6] Most of these enactments are contained in local variants of the Federal Rules of Evidence.[7]

(iii) *Simpler Judicial Notice Statutes.* Judicial notice statutes not fitting into either of the above-mentioned patterns have been enacted in six states. In one of these,[8] the relevant provision is permissive, while in the five remaining states[9] the statutes are phrased in mandatory language.[10] It should be noted, however, that in a case involving foreign-country law, and especially the law of a civil-law country, there may not always be much difference in practice between a mandatory and a permissive statute. Even a mandatory judicial notice statute must be read together with other, more general procedural requirements. Thus, a party who has not even invoked the foreign law in the trial court, ordinarily will not be permitted to raise the foreign-law

country law often are of more recent vintage than those relating to sister-state law. When the more recent statute was enacted, its systematic connection with the earlier one was not always recognized by the legislators, rule-making authorities, and editors of statutory compilations.

3. Alabama, Arizona, Arkansas, Colorado, Delaware, Indiana, Maine, Massachusetts, Minnesota, Montana, Nevada, New Mexico, North Dakota, Ohio, Pennsylvania, South Dakota, Vermont, Washington, West Virginia, and Wyoming.

4. 13 U.L.A. 281, 309–313 (1975). The only important difference between this Uniform Act and Rule 44.1 is that the Act expressly provides for court (rather than jury) determination of foreign-law issues.

5. Pennsylvania and Michigan, where Article IV appears to remain unrepealed, have more recently adopted, respectively, the equivalent of Rule 44.1, see supra note 3, or the bifurcated judicial notice model, see infra note 6.

6. Alaska, Florida, Hawaii, Kansas, Michigan, New Jersey, and Oregon.

7. For texts and comment, see J. B. Weinstein & M. A. Berger, 1 Weinstein's Evidence #201[09] (1986 Supp.). Note that at least one state (Montana) has adopted both the equivalent of Rule 44.1 in its Rules of Procedure and the optional-mandatory bifurcation as part of its Rules of Evidence. The Federal Rules of Evidence do not contain a provision on judicial notice of foreign law because in the judgment of the Advisory Committee, "the manner in which law is fed into the judicial process is never a concern of the rules of evidence but rather of the rules of procedure." 56 F.R.D. 183, 207 (1973).

8. Utah.

9. Connecticut, Mississippi, North Carolina, Virginia, and West Virginia. In Connecticut, however, judicial notice of foreign law is mandatory only with respect to statutes; as to decisional law it is discretionary.

10. A seventh state, Maryland, provides for (mandatory) judicial notice of "the common law and statutes of every state, territory and other jurisdiction of the United States, and of every other jurisdiction having a system of law based on the common law of England."

point for the first time on his appeal.[11] Some courts have gone further and have held—in the teeth of the unqualified terms of a mandatory judicial notice statute—that neither trial nor appellate judges, if unaided by the parties, are required to plunge into an independent exploration of a strange legal system.[12]

Summary. Thirty-six states, the District of Columbia, and the Virgin Islands have enacted statutes or Rules either providing for "judicial notice" of foreign-country law or in other ways authorizing the court, in determining foreign law, to consider any relevant material or source, regardless of admissibility under technical rules of evidence, and regardless also of whether or not such material was submitted by a party. Although they differ considerably among each other, all of the statutes and rules in this majority group have the effect of greatly liberalizing the approach to the procedural treatment of foreign-country law.

A small number of the states, on the other hand, have not yet enacted legislation of the kind mentioned in the preceding paragraph, and have limited their reforming efforts to piecemeal modifications of some of the most extreme consequences of the "fact" doctrine. Seemingly all of the states in this minority group have enacted legislation to the effect that foreign-country law, while not a proper subject of judicial notice, shall be an issue for the court rather than the jury.[13] A number of these states have also adopted provisions making it possible to prove foreign statutes or other written sources of foreign law without the necessity of putting an expert witness on the stand.[14] Subject to these modifications, however, a small minority of jurisdictions appear to require even at this late date that foreign-country law be pleaded and proved as a "fact." — The Anomaly

This number does not necessarily correspond to that of states without judicial-notice statutes or Rules encompassing foreign-country law, for at least one such state takes judicial notice of foreign law in the absence of legislative authority,[15] and two others take judicial notice of the law of foreign "states," which might include foreign countries.[16] More importantly, however, with the baffling exception of Illinois,[17] the minority states are the ones in which litigation cutting across national

---

11. See Donahue v. Dal, Inc., 314 Mass. 460, 463, 50 N.E.2d 207, 209 (1943). This case was decided under the former Massachusetts statute, which purported to be mandatory. The decision is simply an application of the general rule against appellants' raising of new issues on appeal.

On the other hand, judicial notice of foreign law may be taken by the appellate court where the trial court, without decision, has reported the case to the Supreme Judicial Court. Dicker v. Klein, 360 Mass. 735, 277 N.E.2d 514 (1972).

12. See Cannistraro v. Cannistraro, 352 Mass. 65, 223 N.E.2d 692, 695 (1967); (concurring opinion by Cutter, J.); Strout v. Burgess, 144 Me. 263, 274–76, 68 A.2d 241, 249–50 (1949), and cases there cited. Cf. Heating Acceptance Corp. v. Patterson, 152 Conn. 467, 208 A.2d 341 (1965).

13. E.g., Illinois, Kentucky, Louisiana, and Nebraska. Many of these statutes are based on § 5 of the Uniform Judicial Notice of Foreign Law Act, supra n. 1. Sec. 5 is the only provision of that Act dealing with foreign-country law.

14. E.g., Illinois, Iowa, and Louisiana.

15. New Hampshire; see supra n. 1.

16. Idaho and Missouri.

17. Criticism of the "schizophrenic fact approach" and of the "archaic" rules then prevailing earned a young Illinois lawyer a state bar association prize in 1970, but seemingly produced no other results. Ader, Foreign Law in Illinois Courts, 58 Ill. B.J. 420, 436 (1970). One explanation might be that a Gresham's-Law-in-Reverse drives Illinois cases posing complicated foreign-law questions into the federal courts. For statistics, see note following.

boundaries has not yet become a matter of daily routine. The vast bulk of litigation involving issues of foreign-country law is centered in majority jurisdictions such as New York, Texas, California, and Florida, i.e., in state and federal courts operating under liberalized statutes and Rules.[18]

Twenty years after the enactment of Rule 44.1, it has been absorbed into federal jurisprudence through some 140 reported decisions, and its main features have been adopted throughout the specialized federal judiciaries and copied or emulated in all but a few states. As illustrated by the recent case of Mitsubishi Motors Corp. v. Soler Chrysler-Plymouth, 473 U.S. 614, 105 S.Ct. 3346 (1985), seasoned judges have come to assume that yesteryear's difficulties in proving foreign-country law have now been solved by Rule 44.1 and its progeny. In that case, the court appealed from had expressed concern that foreign arbitrators sitting in Japan "would lack 'experience with or exposure to our law and values.'" 105 S.Ct. 3358 note 18. The Supreme Court disposed of this argument in the same footnote, saying: "The obstacles confronted by the arbitration panel in this case, however, should be no greater than those confronted by any judicial or arbitral tribunal required to determine foreign law. See, e.g., Fed. Rule Civ. Proc. 44.1."

What is cited *exempli gratia* by the Supreme Court is obviously taken to be the rule, not the exception. Yet as Maitland observed in another but related context: "The forms of action we have buried, but they still rule us from their graves."[19] For some time to come, the statutes and Rules summarized above will continue to be viewed against the common-law background from which they have emerged.

C. RAMIFICATIONS OF THE "FACT" DOCTRINE

As the foregoing survey has shown, a minority of American jurisdictions still treat foreign-country law as "fact" for most purposes. Even in the majority jurisdictions which have adopted modern statutes or Rules concerning the ascertainment of foreign-country law, we have observed (see supra pp. 57–72) the survival of remnants of the "fact" approach. What follows is a checklist, not purporting to be exhaustive, of the important practical purposes for which the "fact" doctrine has been invoked:

(1) *Pleadings, Bills of Particulars and Discovery.* The traditional rule is that foreign law, being a "fact", must be pleaded, and that such "fact" may have to be detailed in a bill of particulars and may be a

---

18. Reported federal cases citing Rule 44.1 (through June, 1986) are distributed as follows: New York, 54; Texas, 11; California and Florida, 9 each; Illinois, 7; District of Columbia and Pennsylvania, 6 each; Georgia, Louisiana, New Jersey, and the Canal Zone, 3 each; Connecticut, Maryland, Minnesota, New Mexico, Ohio, Washington, and Virginia, 2 each; and one citation from Alaska, Alabama, Delaware, Hawaii, Massachusetts, Mississippi, Nebraska, Oklahoma, Rhode Island, Utah, West Virginia, and Wyoming. Another indicator for the geographic distribution of foreign-law concerns in the United States is the location of law firms with branches in foreign countries. Almost 50 of the 250 largest United States law firms had offices abroad in 1986. More than half of these (26) were located in New York, five in California, four each in Illinois and Texas, two each in Massachusetts and Minnesota, and one each in the District of Columbia, Georgia, and Missouri. (Compiled from "The NLJ 250, 9th Annual Survey of the Nation's Largest Law Firms," 9 Nat'l L.J. No. 2, pp. S1–S24 (Sept. 22, 1986)).

19. F. W. Maitland, The Forms of Action at Common Law 2 (A. H. Chaytor & W. J. Whittaker, eds. 1941).

proper subject of discovery. This rule, and its recent modifications and ramifications, will be discussed in a separate sub-chapter (infra pp. 120–127).

(2) *Admissions and Stipulations.* Specific propositions of foreign law often have been held to be a proper subject of admissions and stipulations.[1] Even stipulations of considerable breadth (e.g., "that Liberia had adopted the non-statutory general maritime law of the United States") have been treated as controlling.[2]

Under Rule 36 of the Federal Rules of Civil Procedure, and under similar provisions existing in many states, it is possible to compel an opponent, by a notice to admit, either to admit a certain allegation, or to file a specific denial. This procedure can be used effectively to compel admissions of foreign law, at least with respect to propositions which are too well established to be conscientiously denied.[3]

Though in principle the courts clearly recognize the parties' power to establish binding propositions by their stipulations and admissions, it is equally clear that this power cannot be unlimited. When one tries to stake out the limits, however, neither judicial nor doctrinal authorities are particularly helpful. Under the "fact" doctrine, courts generally have been inclined to respect and enforce the parties' admissions and stipulations relating to foreign law; but even if one treats foreign law as matter of pure fact, one must remember that where a strong public interest is involved, e.g. in matrimonial cases, the parties have no power to settle the facts by admissions or stipulations.[4]

foreign law as fact

1. See, e.g., Usatorre v. The Victoria, 172 F.2d 434, 444 (2d Cir. 1949) (admission concerning proper interpretation of a provision of the Argentine Commercial Code); Autobuses Modernos, S.A. v. The Federal Mariner, 125 F.Supp. 780 (E.D.Pa. 1954) (stipulation as to validity of an assignment under Cuban law).

A fortiori, the parties can enter into valid stipulations concerning the existence and proper translation of foreign statutes. This is routine practice. See, e.g., the *First National City Bank* case, supra p. 72.

The parties may also, by stipulation or failure to object, permit the introduction of documentary and other evidence of foreign law which otherwise would have to be excluded. See, e.g., N. V. Stoomvaart Mattschaippij Nederland v. United States, 18 F.Supp. 567 (N.D.Cal. 1937), where long before the adoption of Rule 44.1 an exchange of correspondence between the U.S. Department of State and the Netherlands Minister in Washington was (by stipulation) admitted to prove a point of Netherlands law.

2. See Ezekiel v. Volusia S.S. Co., 297 F.2d 215 (2d Cir. 1961), cert. denied 369 U.S. 843, 82 S.Ct. 874 (1962).

Admissions with respect to the tenor of the applicable foreign law sometimes are constructive rather than explicit. Defendant's failure to deny a foreign-law allega-

tion contained in the complaint will, of course, have the effect of an admission. An example of an even more "constructive" admission is furnished by the case of Ganem v. Ganem De Issa, 269 So.2d 740 (Fla.App. 1972), cert. denied 414 U.S. 1113, 94 S.Ct. 844 (1973): Plaintiffs in support of their claim made certain allegations concerning the law of Colombia. In his answer, defendant denied these allegations; but when defendant subsequently refused to comply with certain discovery orders of the court, the court (under a Rule similar to FRCP Rule 37) struck out the answer. This, the majority of the appellate court held, had the effect that plaintiffs' allegations with respect to Colombian law stood admitted.

3. In Princess Pat, Ltd. v. National Carloading Corp., 223 F.2d 916 (7th Cir. 1955), plaintiff demanded an admission concerning certain Brazilian customs laws and regulations. Defendant's sworn statement that it did not possess sufficient information to form a belief regarding these Brazilian laws, was held to be an insufficient denial, and hence was treated as an admission of plaintiff's allegations of Brazilian law.

4. Suppose an annulment action is brought in State F, alleging that W was induced to marry H by the latter's fraudulent misrepresentations concerning his

On the other hand, the parties' power in a proper case to stipulate and admit propositions of foreign law is not automatically lost if the court concludes, under the impact of a provision such as Federal Rule 44.1, that foreign law is more akin to "law" than to "fact".

The modern approach is exemplified by Kountouris v. Varvaris, 476 So.2d 599 (Miss. 1985), a family dispute as to title to real property in Greece, governed by Greek law under Mississippi choice-of-law rules. Mississippi has a judicial-notice statute regarded as "an excellent method for determining the law of foreign jurisdictions." 476 So.2d at 607. Nevertheless, the court, id. at 608, acceded to the "insistence of all counsel . . . that we decide this case under Mississippi law," saying:

> It is . . . an unusual experience to have able counsel seemingly deliberately asking that we ignore rules of law that, to our minds, clearly apply. Our courts have authority, to be sure, to hear and adjudge personal controversies otherwise within their jurisdiction notwithstanding that the parties may stipulate to the application and enforcement of rules of law which are wrong and which, if contested, would have to be disregarded. In such actions our courts may enter personal judgments binding upon the parties. No doubt there are limits to this notion, but we do not perceive those to be reached here. If all parties wish to enter an unequivocal stipulation that Mississippi law regarding real property and powers of attorney shall govern this action on remand, they may do so. . . .

The parties could have reached the same result in that case if they had stipulated that on the relevant points Greek law is the same as Mississippi law. Generally, proper analysis of the cases [5] shows that, occasional loose dicta to the contrary notwithstanding, the parties' stipulations on matters of law as well as fact ordinarily will be honored, unless public policy forbids.[6] The effectiveness of a stipulation or admission relating to foreign law thus depends less on the categorization of the issue as "fact" or "law" than on considerations of public policy. The real problem is to delineate the types of situations in which public policy prevents the enforcement of such stipulations and admissions. The answer is relatively clear in some cases, and more doubtful in others:

(i) Contract cases clearly are governed by the principle of party autonomy. Since the parties as a rule (subject to limited exceptions) can effectively dictate the court's choice of the applicable law

---

wealth. Under F's conflict of laws rules, the question of the validity of the marriage is governed by the law of X (a foreign country), where the marriage was celebrated and where the parties lived at the time of such celebration. The parties stipulate that under the law of X a bridegroom's misrepresentation of his wealth makes the marriage voidable. It seems unlikely that the court in F would feel bound by this stipulation, even if it were regarded as one of "fact". See, e.g., Fraioli v. Fraioli, 1 A.D.2d 967, 150 N.Y.S.2d 665 (2d Dept. 1956).

5. Numerous cases are collected, though not convincingly analyzed, in 2 F. X. Busch, Law and Tactics in Jury Trials § 297 (1959); 83 C.J.S., Stipulations § 10e (1953 and Supps.); 73 Am.Jur.2d, Stipulations § 5 (1974); 92 A.L.R. 663 (1934).

6. In this connection, it is interesting to note that while FRCP Rule 36 in its original form provided for admissions "of the truth of any relevant matters of fact", the 1970 amendment eliminated the words "of fact".

in such cases,[7] it is plain that with equal effectiveness they can stipulate or admit the tenor of the governing foreign law.[8]

No to SIA

(ii) At the opposite extreme, it seems clear that in matrimonial cases,[9] in adoption and other status matters,[10] and presumably in criminal proceedings,[11] the parties have no power (or at most a severely restricted power) to bind the court by such stipulations or admissions.

(iii) In the context of other types of cases, it is more difficult to generalize regarding the parties' power to stipulate the foreign law. The burden of persuasion should always rest on the shoulders of the one who seeks to avoid the effect of an express [12] stipulation or admission knowingly made by the parties, especially by litigants who had the assistance of counsel. The burden, it is submitted, can be met only by showing that with respect to the issue at hand a strong public interest militates against party autonomy, and that such interest was not adequately represented by any of the parties to the stipulation.[13]

(3) *Evidence.* As shown above by the Fitzpatrick case and the materials following it, the older approach required that foreign law be proved as a fact. Failure to introduce competent evidence could have serious consequences for the party who bears the burden of proof. This latter aspect of the doctrine, and its modern modifications, will be discussed infra pp. 88–146.

(4) *Jury Question.* By carrying the "fact" doctrine to its logical extreme, one can arrive at the conclusion that the issue of foreign law is a jury question, at least when determination of the issue depends on the credibility of expert witnesses. Formerly this was asserted to be the prevailing rule. See the opinion in the Fitzpatrick case, supra. As the above survey of statutes has shown, however, this particular consequence of the "fact" doctrine has been eliminated by the legislators of almost all states.[14] Courts had rebelled against it even before the legislator intervened.

---

7. See Restatement, Second, Conflict of Laws § 187 (1971); Ehrenzweig, Treatise on the Conflict of Laws 467–70 (1962). In many cases, such recognition of the parties' autonomy is mandated by statute. UCC § 1–105.

8. See, e.g., Radosh v. Shipstad, 20 N.Y.2d 504, 509, 285 N.Y.S.2d 60, 64, 231 N.E.2d 759, 762, 763 (1967).

9. See supra n. 4.

10. See Tsilidis v. Pedakis, 132 So.2d 9, 13 (Fla. App. 1961).

11. Cf. Young v. United States, 315 U.S. 257, 259, 62 S.Ct. 510, 511, 512 (1942).

12. The problem of "tacit" stipulations, implied from the parties' failure to invoke foreign law, will be discussed later on. See infra pp. 88–120.

13. In tort cases, for instance, it would seem that normally there is no reason why a stipulation regarding the tenor of the applicable foreign law should not be honored. See Alfieri v. Cabot Corp., 17

A.D.2d 455, 235 N.Y.S.2d 753 (1st Dept. 1962), aff'd 13 N.Y.2d 1027, 245 N.Y.S.2d 600, 195 N.E.2d 310 (1963).

14. Where, as in most states, a statute provides that a question of foreign law (including foreign-country law) is for the court, it is error to submit such a question to the jury. De Sayve v. La Valdene, 279 App.Div. 784, 110 N.Y.S.2d 182 (1st Dept. 1952); see also same case after retrial 124 N.Y.S.2d 143, 147–8 (Sup.Ct.N.Y.Co. 1953), aff'd 283 App.Div. 918, 130 N.Y.S.2d 865 (1st Dept. 1954), appeal on constitutional grounds dismissed and leave to appeal granted, 307 N.Y. 861, 122 N.E.2d 747 (1954). Whether the error is reversible or harmless, can be a question of some intricacy. Compare the *Fitzpatrick* case, supra p. 43, with United States v. McClain, supra pp. 63–66. Even where the error is reversible, it would seem that a trial judge who erroneously has submitted the question to the jury, may still avoid a reversal if he treats the jury verdict as advisory, and

(5) *Appellate Review.* In jury cases, the power of an appellate court generally is limited to reviewing the lower court's rulings on the "law". Even in non-jury cases, the power of a higher court to review the trial judge's findings of "fact" often is subject to severe limitations. Under the traditional approach, therefore, most appellate courts used to refrain from reviewing foreign law questions in jury cases; in non-jury cases, such questions generally were reviewed only to the extent to which the appellate court had power to reexamine the trial judge's findings of fact.[15] This attitude may still prevail in the minority jurisdictions which do not permit judicial notice of foreign-country law. Modern judicial notice statutes, however, ordinarily authorize appellate as well as trial courts to examine such foreign law questions. The more modern ones of these statutes contain specific provisions to the effect that the trial court's determination of an issue of foreign-country law "shall be treated as a ruling on a question of law," or "shall be subject to review on appeal as a finding or charge on a matter of law" (see the statutes set forth supra). If the point has been properly raised and preserved by the appellant, such provisions make it mandatory for the appellate court to examine whether the trial court's foreign law determination appears correct in the light of the foreign law materials in the record and of such further materials as the parties may submit to the appellate court. Yet the extent to which the latter court will undertake supplementary foreign law research of its own probably remains a matter of discretion.[16] Furthermore, appeals on foreign-law questions, like appeals generally, are subject to stringent limitations of space for briefing and time for oral argument. These limitations are likely to inhibit a determination de novo by a court lacking background familiarity with the point of foreign-country law at issue.

Even in a case in which the trial judge did not rule on the foreign law (e.g., because the court, and perhaps the parties, proceeded on the assumption that the case was wholly governed by domestic law), a judicial notice statute may expressly authorize the appellate court to make its decision on the basis of foreign law. In this situation,

---

himself makes the requisite findings as to the foreign law. See Sulyok v. Penzinteze-ti Kozpont Budapest, 279 App.Div. 528, 111 N.Y.S.2d 75, 79 (1st Dept. 1952), modified on other grounds 304 N.Y. 704, 107 N.E.2d 604 (1952); Cf. Daniel Lumber Co. v. Empresas Hondurenas S.A., 215 F.2d 465, 468 (5th Cir. 1954).

15. See, e.g., Hanley v. Donoghue, 116 U.S. 1, 5–7, 6 S.Ct. 242, 244–5 (1885). For criticism of this traditional rule, see Nussbaum, The Problem of Proving Foreign Law, 50 Yale L.J. 1018, 1033–35 (1941).

Prior to the effective date of Rule 44.1, many federal courts held, in accordance with the traditional view, that a trial judge's findings concerning a point of foreign law could be reversed by a court of appeals only if "clearly erroneous" within the meaning of Rule 52(a); but the point was controversial. See the *First National City Bank* case, supra. For further references, see A. R. Miller, Federal Rule 44 and the "Fact" Approach to Determining Foreign Law, 65 Mich.L.Rev. 613, 689 (1967).

16. In exercising this discretion, an appellate court, and especially a court of last resort, may consider that its primary function is to state rules and principles in an authoritative manner, and thus to make the law certain and uniform within its territory. Appellate judges may feel that they do not really serve this function when they spend too much time and effort in order to ascertain a rule of foreign law, i.e., a rule which can be authoritatively settled only by the highest court of another country.

On the other hand, it has been argued that the existence of modern judicial notice statutes, which permit trial judges to make independent investigations of foreign law, increases the need for effective and thorough appellate review. See S. L. Cohn, The New Federal Rules of Civil Procedure, 54 Geo.L.J. 1204, at 1246 (1966).

however, difficult problems may arise from the parties' failure to comply with a requirement of timely notice such as that found in Rule 44.1, or otherwise properly to invoke the foreign law. These problems will be discussed in subsequent sub-chapters.

(6) *Summary Judgment.* Influenced by the "fact" approach, courts have held that if the affidavits submitted on a motion for summary judgment disclose the existence of an honest, genuinely debatable issue of foreign law, the motion would be denied.[17] But where the motion papers, which may include affidavits of foreign law experts, showed no substantial dispute as to the terms and the interpretation of applicable foreign laws, summary judgment has been granted.[18] The raising of a foreign law issue did not automatically prevent summary judgment; the party opposing the motion for summary judgment had to show that the issue was a substantial one.[19]

The operation of these rules, which were in part developed before the advent of liberal judicial notice statutes, is now being changed by the impact of such statutes. In a number of recent cases, federal courts have granted summary judgment even on questions of foreign-country law strongly disputed in the affidavits of the parties' experts. See Kunstsammlungen Zu Weimar v. Elicofon, 536 F.Supp. 829, 859 (E.D. N.Y. 1981), aff'd 678 F.2d 1150 (2d Cir. 1982), and e.g., Merican, Inc. v. Caterpillar Tractor Co., 596 F.Supp. 697, 700 (E.D.Pa. 1984): "Because this court's determination is treated as relating to a question of law . . . disagreement on the part of the experts would not foreclose the granting of a motion for summary judgment." Kashfi v. Phibro-Salomon, Inc., 628 F.Supp. 727, 737 (S.D.N.Y. 1986), illustrates this modern approach:[20]

> Disputes concerning the meaning of a foreign statute raise questions of law, rather than questions of fact. See Fed.R.Civ. P. 44.1. Summary judgment, therefore, is not precluded simply because foreign law is applicable. See Bassis v. Universal Line, S.A., 436 F.2d 64, 68 (2d Cir. 1970); Alosio v. Iranian Shipping Lines, S.A., 426 F.Supp. 687, 689 (S.D.N.Y. 1976), aff'd mem. 573 F.2d 1287 (2d Cir. 1977); Instituto Per Lo Sviluppo Economico v. Sperti Products, Inc., 323 F.Supp. 630, 635 (S.D.

---

17. See Byrne v. Cooper, 11 Wash.App. 549, 523 P.2d 1216 (1974); Werfel v. Zivnostenska Banka, 287 N.Y. 91, 38 N.E.2d 382 (1941); Read v. Lehigh Valley R. Co., 284 N.Y. 435, 444, 31 N.E.2d 891, 895 (1940); Croker v. Croker, 252 N.Y. 24, 26, 168 N.E. 450, 451 (1929); Mosbacher v. Basler Lebens Versicherungs Gessellschaft, 111 F.Supp. 551 (S.D.N.Y. 1951). Cf. Anderson v. A/S Berge Sigval Bergesen, 22 N.Y.2d 944, 295 N.Y.S.2d 161, 242 N.E.2d 393 (1968) (Motion denied where determination of choice of law issue depends on disputed questions of fact.)

18. See Pisacane v. Italia Societa Per Azioni Di Navigazione, 219 F.Supp. 424, 426 (S.D.N.Y. 1963). A fortiori, this is true under Rule 44.1. See Instituto Per Lo Sviluppo Economico Dell' Italia Meridionale v. Sperti Products, Inc., 323 F.Supp. 630 (S.D. N.Y. 1971).

19. Egyes v. Magyar Nemzeti Bank, 71 F.Supp. 560 (E.D.N.Y. 1947), aff'd 165 F.2d 539 (2d Cir. 1948); Komlos v. Compagnie Nationale Air France, 111 F.Supp. 393, 406 (S.D.N.Y. 1952), rev'd on other grounds 209 F.2d 436 (2d Cir. 1953).

If the motion for summary judgment is supported by the affidavit of a foreign law expert, and the opponent files no such affidavit, the movant's version of the foreign law may be accepted. See Regierungspraesident Land Nordrhein Westfalen v. Rosenthal, 17 A.D.2d 145, 146, 232 N.Y.S.2d 963, 965, 966 (1st Dept. 1962), motion for leave to appeal denied 12 N.Y.2d 648, 239 N.Y.S.2d 1025, 190 N.E.2d 27 (1963).

20. In addition to the cases cited in Kashfi, see In re Weiss-Wolf, Inc., 60 B.R. 969, 974 (Bkrtcy. S.D.N.Y. 1986).

N.Y. 1971). It is clearly within the authority of the court to interpret and apply a foreign statute. See Curtis v. Beatrice Foods Co., 481 F.Supp. 1275, 1285 (S.D.N.Y. 1980), aff'd mem. 633 F.2d 203 (2d Cir. 1980); 9 C. Wright & A. Miller, Federal Practice & Procedure § 2444 at 406–07 (1971).

If the experts have covered all the relevant points of foreign law in their affidavits, a court is not likely to be receptive to the suggestion that the experts' conflicting interpretations should be tested in the crucible of trial; the court will remember that "testifying" experts are subject to cross-examination by way of discovery under FRCP Rule 26(b) (4). The court may, of course, choose to postpone its ruling on a contested question of foreign law until such pre-trial interrogation of the experts has taken place.[20a]

One important point, however, has to be kept in mind: Under modern statutes and Rules, the court may go beyond the affidavits of experts and other papers submitted by the parties, and may conduct some foreign law research of its own. Such research may disclose that there are doubtful questions of foreign law which, although crucial, were not raised by the parties or their experts, or that the questions which the parties have raised are more complex than the expert's affidavits would lead one to believe. Such judicial discoveries may result in *denial* of the motion for summary judgment,[21] or perhaps in denial "without prejudice to renewal upon sufficient proof" of the applicable foreign law.[22]

Occasionally, the reverse situation occurs: The judge's own research, authorized by a judicial notice statute, may lead to the conclusion that a particular question of foreign law is not as doubtful as the experts' conflicting affidavits suggest, and that the motion should *be granted* because the dispute concerning such question is not a genuine one.[23] But where the foreign legal system involved is an alien one, a court in such a situation ordinarily will hesitate (although under a judicial notice statute it may have the power) to deprive the parties of the opportunity of testing the conflicting expert views in adversary proceedings. A fortiori, the courts remain reluctant to grant motions for summary judgment on the basis of their own explorations of a strange legal system when the parties have provided no information on the crucial issues of foreign law.[24]

20a. The motion for summary judgment will then be granted if it turns out that a party's factual allegations do not create a genuine issue of fact under the foreign law as thus ascertained. El Cid, Ltd. v. New Jersey Zinc Co., 575 F.Supp. 1513, 1520–24 (S.D.N.Y. 1983) and 588 F.Supp. 125, 126 (S.D.N.Y. 1984), aff'd 770 F.2d 157 (2d Cir. 1985) (table), cert. denied 474 U.S. 1021, 106 S.Ct. 573 (1985).

21. Cf. Majestic Co. v. Wender, 24 Misc. 2d 1018, 205 N.Y.S.2d 317 (Sp. T., Nassau Co., 1960).

22. See Boutin v. Cumbo, 259 F.Supp. 12, 14 (S.D.N.Y. 1966). Subsequently the motion was renewed in that case; this time

the parties submitted ample information, citing all of the relevant foreign authorities, and on the basis of these authorities the court granted the motion for summary judgment. See Boutin v. Cumbo, 278 F.Supp. 223 (S.D.N.Y. 1967).

23. See, e.g., Bassis v. Universal Line, S.A., 436 F.2d 64 (2d Cir. 1970).

24. See Prudential Lines Inc. v. General Tire Int'l Co., 440 F.Supp. 556 (S.D.N.Y. 1977); after the parties submitted sufficient foreign law materials, reargument was granted, 448 F.Supp. 202 (S.D.N.Y. 1978). See also Stone v. Stone, 29 A.D.2d 866, 288 N.Y.S.2d 393 (2d Dept. 1968).

(7) *Stare Decisis.* A judicial decision on a point of foreign law is generally held not to constitute a binding precedent.[25] Even if the previous decision deals with the law of the same foreign country, and with the same point, it is possible for the court in a subsequent case to arrive at a different conclusion, based upon a different record. In a jurisdiction, however, in which a statute authorizes the court to take judicial notice of the foreign law, a previous domestic decision dealing with the pertinent point of foreign law can be considered, and indeed may carry substantial weight.[26] Section 4 of the (English) Civil Evidence Act 1972 goes one step further, and expressly provides that English decisions "in citable form" are admissible as evidence as to the points of foreign law decided by them, and are controlling in this respect "unless the contrary is proved."

(8) *Unauthorized Practice of Law.* It has been argued that statutes prohibiting the unauthorized practice of "law" should not be construed as covering the activities of one who advises clients on foreign law only.[27] The argument, although dialectically it derives some support from the thesis that foreign law is a "fact," has been rejected.[28]

(9) *A Side-Effect in the Law of Contracts.* In those states which still adhere to the antiquated rule that a mistake of law is never a sufficient reason for avoiding a contract, the courts usually classify a mistake concerning foreign law as a mistake of "fact." [29] Thus, one old-fashioned, conceptualistic rule is used to mitigate the effect of another such rule.

2. THE OVER–ALL TACTICS OF FOREIGN–LAW LITIGATION: CONSEQUENCES OF FAILURE TO INVOKE OR PROVE THE APPLICABLE FOREIGN LAW

INTRODUCTORY NOTE

To ascertain the solution which a foreign legal system provides for a disputed problem of law normally requires considerable effort on the part of counsel; in many instances, he will need the assistance of a colleague who practices in the country in question, or for other reasons qualifies as an expert. For the client, these efforts mean substantial expense.

Once an action involving the foreign-law point is instituted, counsel may wish not only to educate himself on the foreign law, but in proper form to invoke and to prove such law in court. Thus, additional efforts by counsel and his expert informants may be required, and the resulting expenses to be borne by the client may grow to large amounts.

25. See, e.g., Estate of Leefers, 127 Cal. App.2d 550, 274 P.2d 239 (1954); Smith v. Russo Asiatic Bank, 160 Misc. 417, 290 N.Y.S. 471 (Sup.Ct.Albany Co., 1936); Lazard Brothers & Co. v. Midland Bank, [1933] A.C. 289 (House of Lords, 1932).

26. See Matter of Spitzmuller, 279 App. Div. 233, 109 N.Y.S.2d 1, 8 (1st Dept. 1951), aff'd 304 N.Y. 608, 107 N.E.2d 91 (1952), where the Appellate Division referred to an earlier New York case which (the court believed) established a rule of Italian law. Cf. Nicolas E. Vernicos Shipping Co. v. United States, 349 F.2d 465 (2d Cir. 1965).

27. E.g., a Mexican lawyer who, without being a member of the California Bar, maintains an office in Los Angeles where clients (not necessarily attorneys) are advised on Mexican law.

28. Bluestein v. State Bar, 13 Cal.3d 162, 118 Cal.Rptr. 175, 178, 529 P.2d 599 (1974); In re Roel, 3 N.Y.2d 224, 165 N.Y.S.2d 31, 144 N.E.2d 24 (1957). To the same effect, see Opinion of A.B.A. Committee on Unauthorized Practice of the Law, 22 Unauthorized Practice News 39 (1956).

29. See Williston On Contracts § 1592 (3d ed. by Jaeger, 1970).

Before he burdens his client with such expenses, a conscientious attorney will want to know the answers to the following questions:

What will happen if I do not invoke, and make no attempt to prove, the pertinent foreign law? Up to what point in the game will my opponent be able to inject the foreign-law point into the litigation? If he does, will I still have enough time effectively to meet the foreign-law point raised by him? If he does not raise any foreign-law point (i.e., if both sides fail to invoke and prove the foreign law), what will be the outcome of the lawsuit?

The materials which follow will show that although there are large numbers of reported decisions (and some statutes) bearing on these questions, the answers are far from simple.

CUBA RAILROAD CO. v. CROSBY
Supreme Court of the United States, 1912.
222 U.S. 473, 32 S.Ct. 132.

. . . Mr. Justice HOLMES delivered the opinion of the court.

This is an action for the loss of a hand through a defect in machinery, in connection with which the defendant in error, the plaintiff, was employed. The plaintiff had noticed the defect and reported it, and, according to his testimony, had been promised that it should be repaired or replaced as soon as they had time, and he had been told to go on in the meanwhile. The jury was instructed that if that was what took place the defendant company assumed the risk for a reasonable time, and, in effect, that if that time had not expired the plaintiff was entitled to recover. The jury found for the plaintiff. The accident took place in Cuba, and no evidence was given as to the Cuban law, but the judge held that if that law was different from the *lex fori* it was for the defendant to allege and prove it, and that as it had pleaded only the general issue the verdict must stand. 158 F. 144. The judgment was affirmed by a majority of the Circuit Court of Appeals. 170 F. 369, 95 C.C.A. 539.

The court below went on the ground that in the absence of evidence to the contrary it would "apply the law as it conceives it to be, according to its idea of right and justice; or, in other words, according to the law of the forum." We regard this statement as too broad, and as having been wrongly applied to this case.

It may be that in dealing with rudimentary contracts or torts made or committed abroad, such as promises to pay money for goods or services, or battery of the person or conversion of goods, courts would assume a liability to exist if nothing to the contrary appeared. Parrot v. Mexican Central Railway Co., 207 Mass. 184, 93 N.E. 590. Such matters are likely to impose an obligation in all civilized countries.*

---

* Where the complaint asserts "a rudimentary right generally recognized in civilized countries", as for instance "a conventional cause of action for negligence", the defendant must prove that such cause of action does not exist in the law of the particular country involved. See Rosenthal v. Compagnie Generale Transatlantique, 14 F.R.D. 33, 35 (S.D.N.Y., 1953). See also same case after reargument, 14 F.R.D. 336 (S.D.N.Y., 1953).

Rule

But when an action is brought upon a cause arising outside of the jurisdiction it always should be borne in mind that the duty of the court is not to administer its notion of justice but to enforce an obligation that has been created by a different law. Slater v. Mexican National R.R. Co., 194 U.S. 120, 126, 24 S.Ct. 581. The law of the forum is material only as setting a limit of policy beyond which such obligations will not be enforced there. With very rare exceptions the liabilities of parties to each other are fixed by the law of the territorial jurisdiction within which the wrong is done and the parties are at the time of doing it. American Banana Co. v. United Fruit Co., 213 U.S. 347, 356, 29 S.Ct. 511. See Bean v. Morris, 221 U.S. 485, 486, 487, 31 S.Ct. 703. That and that alone is the foundation of their rights.

Vested Right theory see p 98

. . .

We repeat that the only justification for allowing a party to recover when the cause of action arose in another civilized jurisdiction is a well founded belief that it was a cause of action in that place. The right to recover stands upon that as its necessary foundation. It is part of the plaintiff's case, and if there is reason for doubt he must allege and prove it. The extension of the hospitality of our courts to foreign suitors must not be made a cover for injustice to the defendants of whom they happen to be able to lay hold.

In the case at bar the court was dealing with the law of Cuba, a country inheriting the law of Spain and, we may presume, continuing it with such modifications as later years may have brought. There is no general presumption that that law is the same as the common law. We properly may say that we all know the fact to be otherwise. Goodyear Tire & Rubber Co. v. Rubber Tire Wheel Co., 164 F. 869. Whatever presumption there is is purely one of fact, that may be corrected by proof. Therefore the presumption should be limited to cases in which it reasonably may be believed to express the fact. Generally speaking, as between two common law countries, the common law of one reasonably may be presumed to be what it is decided to be in the other, in a case tried in the latter state. But a statute of one would not be presumed to correspond to a statute in the other, and when we leave common law territory for that where a different system prevails obviously the limits must be narrower still. [Citations.]

civil law countries' statutes should not be presumed be the same

Even if we should presume that an employé could recover in Cuba if injured by machinery left defective through the negligence of his employer's servants, which would be going far, that would not be enough. The plaintiff recovered, or, under the instructions stated at the beginning of this decision, at least may have recovered, notwithstanding his knowledge and appreciation of the danger, on the strength of a doctrine the peculiarity and difficulties of which are elaborately displayed in the treatise of Mr. Labatt. 1 Labatt, Master & Servant, ch. 22, esp. § 424. To say that a promise to repair or replace throws the risk on the master until the time for performance has gone by, or that it does away with or leaves to the jury what otherwise would be negligence as matter of law is evidence of the great consideration with which workmen are treated here, but cannot be deemed a necessary incident of all civilized codes. It could not be assumed without proof that the defendant was subject to such a rule.

[handwritten margin note: The law in the U.S. may not be the law in Cuba]

There was some suggestion below that there would be hardship in requiring the plaintiff to prove his case. But it should be remembered that parties do not enter into civil relations in foreign jurisdictions in reliance upon our courts. They could not complain if our courts refused to meddle with their affairs and remitted them to the place that established and would enforce their rights. A discretion is asserted in some cases even when the policy of our law is not opposed to the claim. The Maggie Hammond, 9 Wall. 435. The only just ground for complaint would be if their rights and liabilities, when enforced by our courts, should be measured by a different rule from that under which the parties dealt.

Judgment reversed.**

QUESTIONS

If a case similar to Crosby came before the U.S. Supreme Court today, how would the Court treat the problems arising from the parties' failure to invoke the foreign law?

(a) Would the parties' failure to meet the notice requirement of Rule 44.1 make it impossible for the Court to inform itself of the pertinent provisions of Cuban law? Cf. Ruff v. St. Paul Mercury Insurance Co., infra. Even if the notice requirement did not stand in the way, would the Supreme Court, unaided by the parties, be likely to study difficult questions arising under an alien legal system?

(b) When in spite of Rule 44.1 a federal court is unable or unwilling to examine the actual state of the pertinent foreign law, will it follow Crosby? Or will it have to look to state law for guidance in determining the consequences of the parties' failure to invoke the foreign law?

(c) Could the harsh result reached in Crosby have been avoided by treating "assumption of risk" as an affirmative defense, thereby throwing upon the defendant the burden of proving the Cuban law which would support such defense?

Some help in answering these questions will be found in the article that appears infra at pp. 96–115.

** When a judgment for the plaintiff is "reversed", without further explanation, this is sometimes understood to imply a final disposition, i.e., a dismissal of the complaint. See 14 Encyclopedia of Federal Practice 494 (1965, and Supps.). Inspection of the record in the Crosby case, however, has revealed that the Supreme Court's mandate provided for remand to the trial court, "with directions to grant a new trial", and that the trial court thereafter entered an order for a new trial. Such new trial does not appear to have taken place; the case was disposed of by an Order of Discontinuance. The record does not show the nature of the settlement or other events that led to this disposition.

LEARY v. GLEDHILL

Supreme Court of New Jersey, 1951.
8 N.J. 260, 84 A.2d 725.

VANDERBILT, C.J. From a judgment of the Law Division of the Superior Court entered on a jury verdict in favor of the plaintiff the defendant appealed to the Appellate Division of the Superior Court. We have certified the appeal on our own motion.

The plaintiff and the defendant were friends who had become acquainted while in the military service. They first met in 1943 and occasionally thereafter through 1945. They corresponded but did not meet again until Christmas, 1948, when the defendant visited the plaintiff in Germany where he was stationed. At that time the defendant was no longer in the military service but was in Europe attempting to sell tractors for the Franam Corporation. Prior to the defendant's trip to Europe he had corresponded with the plaintiff with reference to an investment in the Franam Corporation as one which would be very profitable. Their correspondence resulted in the plaintiff purchasing $1,000 worth of stock when the defendant went to see him in Germany, the defendant delivering to the plaintiff certificates of stock which he had brought with him to Europe in exchange for the plaintiff's check for $1,000.

In April, 1949, the plaintiff at the defendant's invitation visited him in Paris. The defendant had left the United States with $500 in his possession and after arriving in Europe had been in constant need of money to meet his expenses. In a conversation in a hotel in Paris the defendant told the plaintiff that he needed about $4,000 and that he could raise about $2,000 by selling his Cadillac car. In the plaintiff's presence the defendant made a telephone call to his wife in the United States and instructed her to sell the automobile. The defendant asked the plaintiff to help him, but did not mention anything about selling the plaintiff any shares of stock. The plaintiff said he would think it over for a few days and see what he could do. After returning to his base in Germany the plaintiff mailed the defendant a check payable to the defendant's order for $1,500 without indicating on the check or in the accompanying letter what the money was for. The defendant endorsed the check and converted it into traveller's checks. The parties did not see each other again until the day of the trial, although the plaintiff had made many attempts to see the defendant after they both had returned to the United States, seeking him at his home and calling him on the telephone at various times, but always without success.

The plaintiff instituted this suit against the defendant on two counts, the first for $1,000 and the second for $1,500, but at the outset of the trial the plaintiff moved for a voluntary dismissal of the first count and the pretrial order was amended accordingly. The issue as stated in the amended pretrial order was limited to whether the money given by the plaintiff to the defendant was a loan or an investment in a business venture. At the trial the plaintiff testified that the check for $1,500 was a personal loan to the defendant but this the defendant denied, contending that he had never borrowed any money from the plaintiff. At the end of the plaintiff's case and again at the end of the entire case the defendant moved for an involuntary dismissal on the ground that the plaintiff's proofs were insufficient, there being no promise to repay, no demand for repayment, and no pleading or proof of the law of France where the transaction occurred. These motions were denied, the trial court holding that while it would not take judicial notice of the law of France it would proceed, first, on the presumption that the law involving loans is the same there as in other civilized countries, and, secondly, on the ground that the issue with respect to the law of France had not been set forth in the pretrial order. When the case was submitted to the jury, the defendant objected to the charge on the ground that it did not instruct the jury to find as a fact what the law of France was. The jury returned a verdict in favor of the plaintiff in the sum of $1,500, and from the judgment entered thereon the defendant took this appeal. It is significant that the defendant never proved or even attempted to prove either the delivery of any stock to the plaintiff or a tender thereof. Neither did the defendant attempt to prove or even suggest that the law of France was such as to preclude recovery in the circumstances.

[In the next part of the opinion the Court points out that in the view which the jury took (and was justified in taking) of the evidence, the defendant received the $1,500 as a loan and impliedly promised to repay such loan upon demand. Under the law of New Jersey, the plaintiff—even though he made his demand for the first time in the complaint—has a good cause of action for $1,500. The Court then turns to defendant's argument that plaintiff should lose because he failed to plead and prove the applicable French law.]

A court will in general take judicial notice of and apply the law of its own jurisdiction without pleading or proof thereof, the judges being deemed to know the law or at least where it is to be found, 9 Wigmore on Evidence (3rd ed., 1940), 551. Under the common law of England as adopted in this country, however, the law of other countries, including sister states, would not be so noticed and applied by a court, but it was deemed an issue of fact to be pleaded and proved as other material facts had to be. [Citations]. This common law rule had two great disadvantages; it made every jury pass on questions of law quite beyond its competence and the decision of the jury as to the foreign law was unappealable at common law as were its findings on all questions of fact.

The courts, however, were reluctant to dismiss an action for a failure to plead and prove the applicable foreign law as they would have dismissed it for a failure to prove other material facts necessary to establish a cause of action or a defense. Accordingly the courts frequently indulged in one or another of several presumptions: that the common law prevails in the foreign jurisdiction; that the law of the foreign jurisdiction is the same as the law of the forum, be it common law or statute; or that certain fundamental principles of the law exist in all civilized countries. As a fourth alternative, instead of indulging in any presumption as to the law of the foreign jurisdiction, the courts would merely apply the law of the forum as the only law before the court, on the assumption that by failing to prove the foreign law the parties acquiesce in having their controversy determined by reference to the law of the forum, be it statutory or common law. By the application of these various presumptions the courts have in effect treated the common law rule that foreign law could not be noticed but must be pleaded and proved as if it were a matter of fact merely as a permissive rule whereby either party could, if it were to his advantage, plead and prove the foreign law. Thus the failure to plead and prove the foreign law has not generally been considered as fatal. . . .

[Turning to New Jersey authorities, the Court refers to the presumption that if the state or country in question is a common law jurisdiction, its common law is the same as the forum's.]

While the application of the presumption that the common law exists in the foreign jurisdiction works well in many cases, it does not produce sound results in a case where the common law on the subject involved has been substantially changed by statute here and in the foreign state. For example, if a case involved the capacity of a married woman to contract or to hold and convey property, resort to the common law to decide the case might well result in a decision contrary to long established statutory enactments here and in the foreign jurisdiction altering the common law rule. While the presumption as to the existence of the common law in the foreign jurisdiction has the advantages of having been long indulged in by the courts of this and other states, . . . in a proper case consideration might well be given to rejecting it in favor of the presumption that the foreign law is the same as the law of the forum, be it statutory or common law, or even more preferable, in favor of the presumption that the parties by their failure to plead and prove the foreign law acquiesce in the application of the law of the forum as the only law before the court.

In the instant case the transaction occurred in France. Our courts may properly take judicial knowledge that France is not a common law, but rather a civil jurisdiction. It would, therefore, be inappropriate and indeed contrary to elementary knowledge to presume that the principles of the common law prevail there. This does not mean, however, that the plaintiff must fail in his cause of action because of the absence of any proof at the trial as to the applicable law of France. In these circumstances any one of the other three presumptions may be indulged in, i.e., that the law of France is the same as the law of the forum; that the law of France, like all civilized countries, recognizes certain fundamental principles, as, e.g., that the taking of a loan

[handwritten margin note: presumption that one repays on loan]

creates an obligation upon the borrower to make repayment; that the parties by failing to prove the law of France have acquiesced in having their dispute determined by the law of the forum.

The court below based its decision upon the presumption that the law of France in common with that of other civilized countries recognizes a liability to make repayment under the facts here present, and its decision is not without substantial merit in reason and support in the authorities, see, for example, Cuba Railroad Co. v. Crosby, 222 U.S. 473, 32 S.Ct. 132, 56 L.Ed. 274 (1912), and Parrot v. Mexican Central Railway Co., 207 Mass. 184, 93 N.E. 590 (1911). The utilization of this presumption has decided limitations, however, for in many cases it would be difficult to determine whether or not the question presented was of such a fundamental nature as reasonably to warrant the assumption that it would be similarly treated by the laws of all civilized countries. The presumption that in the absence of proof the parties acquiesce in the application of the law of the forum, be it statutory law or common law, does not present any such difficulties for it may be universally applied regardless of the nature of the controversy. This view, moreover, is favored by the authorities, see the notes in 67 L.R.A. 33 and 34 L.R.A.,N.S., 261, . . . and appears to have been followed in at least one instance in this state, Sturm v. Sturm, 111 N.J.Eq. 579, 587, 163 A. 5 (Ch.1932), a case in which the law of Austria was involved.* We are of the opinion, therefore, that in the instant case the rights of the parties are to be determined by the law of New Jersey which unquestionably permits recovery on the facts proven.

[handwritten margin notes: ① ① ② "passed on positive event" rule]

We recognize, of course, that in certain cases there might be present factors which would make it unreasonable for the court to indulge in any presumption and where the court in the exercise of its sound discretion might require proof of applicable foreign law to be laid before the court, but such is certainly not the situation here. The defendant is in no way prejudiced by the application of the law of this State. If he had desired to raise an issue as to the foreign law, he might have done so in his answer or at the pretrial conference or, with permission of the court, at the trial itself, and himself have introduced proof as to the law of France. It is against the letter and the spirit of our practice to permit him to make the failure of the plaintiff to plead

---

* The Court's reliance on the *Sturm* case is misplaced. The parties in that case were husband and wife, who many years previously had gone through a marriage ceremony in Austria, and had lived together there and had a child. When W sued H for separate maintenance, the latter denied the existence of the marriage on the ground that in connection with the celebration of the marriage certain formalities allegedly required by Austrian law had not been observed. At the trial both parties introduced evidence concerning the validity of the marriage under Austrian law.

The court held in W's favor, *not* on the ground of the parties' acquiescence in the application of New Jersey law (nobody had acquiesced), but for the reason that H's evidence concerning Austrian law, which was strongly disputed, was insufficient to overcome the strong presumption in favor of the validity of a consummated ceremonial marriage.

It would be difficult to imagine a foreign-law case more different from Leary v. Gledhill.

and prove foreign law the basis of a surprise motion addressed to the court either in the course of or at the conclusion of the case.

The judgment below is affirmed.**

CALIFORNIA EVIDENCE CODE

§ 311. Procedure when foreign or sister-state law cannot be determined

If the law of an organization of nations, a foreign nation or a state other than this state, or a public entity in a foreign nation or a state other than this state, is applicable and such law cannot be determined, the court may, as the ends of justice require, either:

(a) Apply the law of this state if the court can do so consistently with the Constitution of the United States and the Constitution of this state; or

(b) Dismiss the action without prejudice or, in the case of a reviewing court, remand the case to the trial court with directions to dismiss the action without prejudice. (Stats.1965, c. 299, § 311.)

RUDOLF B. SCHLESINGER, A RECURRENT PROBLEM IN TRANSNATIONAL LITIGATION: THE EFFECT OF FAILURE TO INVOKE OR PROVE THE APPLICABLE FOREIGN LAW

59 Cornell L.Rev. 1 (1973).*

[Some footnotes omitted, others renumbered.]

I. INTRODUCTION: THE ELEMENTS OF COMPLEXITY

When, under the forum's choice of law rules, some or all of the substantive issues in a case are governed by the law of another country, but the parties fail to give timely notice of the foreign law or to show what it is, how is the court to arrive at a decision? This question presents itself with considerable frequency. The courts and legal writers have paid a great deal of attention to the matter;[1] but the voices of those who have treated the problem are not in harmony, and by virtue of the remarkable discordance of some of the suggested approaches the whole subject has acquired the reputation of being controversial and confused. It may be useful, therefore, as a first step to analyze the elements of the existing confusion. At least three such elements can be discerned.

** Noted 37 Cornell L.Q. 748 (1952).

* This is a revised and updated version of the article originally published in the Cornell Law Review.

As a member of the U.S. Government's Advisory Committee on International Rules of Judicial Procedure (see Act of September 2, 1958, Pub.L. No. 85–906, 72 Stat. 1743), the author was one of the draftsmen of Rule 44.1 of the Federal Rules of Civil Procedure. It goes without saying, however, that the views expressed herein are those of the author and do not necessarily reflect the thinking of any of the other individuals or groups that had a hand in formulating and promulgating Rule 44.1.

1. See supra pp. 53–55, 89–96.

A. Simplistic "Single Rule" Response to Diverse Problems

The basic problem is invariably defined in abstract language such as "failure to invoke or prove the applicable foreign law." This abstraction covers a great deal of ground. It applies to a variety of situations which in functional and practical terms, and in terms of simple justice, do not necessarily call for uniform treatment.

A litigant's failure to give notice and to provide information as to the applicable foreign law may be due to many diverse reasons. Perhaps his lawyer is incompetent, and hence does not realize that a case involving foreign elements cannot be handled like an ordinary domestic case. Or maybe the lawyer has recognized that there is a possible foreign law problem, but has wrongly assumed that the court either would apply the forum's own domestic law, or would place the burden of invoking and proving the foreign law on his opponent. In other cases, the lawyer failing to plead and prove the foreign law may have looked at the foreign law and found it less favorable to his client than the internal law of the forum. Regardless of the rules on choice of law and burden of proof, he may speculate that his less sophisticated opponent will handle the case as a domestic one until it becomes too late for either party to invoke the foreign law. Sometimes the lawyers on both sides—each analyzing the forum's internal law, the choice of law rule and the burden of proof in a different manner—try to outsmart each other in this way. In still other cases, an attorney may soundly conclude that to prove the foreign law, or to submit materials relating to it, is simply too expensive for his client. The assumption that a single and simple rule will do justice to all of these motley situations surely is one of the causes of the existing confusion.

B. Antithetical Theories

The second element of confusion results from the scholars' inability, thus far, to develop a viable theory for dealing with our problem. In every legal system it has long been the habit of courts and scholars to pose the problem in the form of the question whether foreign law should be treated as fact or law.[2] This is most unfortunate, because either of these theoretical characterizations, if consistently applied, leads to absurd results. The ultimate absurdity reached under the "fact" theory is that issues of foreign law have to be determined by the jury.[3] It is no less faulty, however, indiscriminately to equate foreign law with domestic "law." Since the ascertainment and interpretation of foreign law require skills which the court simply does not possess,

2. See Kegel, Zur Organisation der Ermittlung Ausländischen Privatrechts, 1 Festschrift für Nipperdey 453 (1965); Sass, Foreign Law in Civil Litigation: A Comparative Survey, 16 Am.J.Comp.L. 332 (1968); Zajtay, The Application of Foreign Law, in 3 International Encyclopedia of Comparative Law 14-1 (1972); Zajtay, Le traitement du droit étranger dans le procès civil—Étude de droit comparé, 4 Rivista di Diritto Internazionale Privato e processuale 233 (1968).

3. See supra pp. 43–48, 84. One twentieth-century example is Garza v. Klepper, 15 S.W.2d 194, 199 (Tex.Civ.App.—San Antonio 1929), writ refused.

the procedural treatment of a foreign law question cannot be quite the same as that of a question of domestic law. The soundest approach would be to give up all attempts to characterize foreign law as either "fact" or "law" and to start writing a new theory on a clean slate. But in the United States, at least, common-law doctrines, and some of the pertinent statutes, reflect the heritage of the fact theory to such an extent that in dealing with existing law we cannot afford completely to dismiss that unsound theory from our minds.

The difficulties flowing from the legacy of the fact-law dichotomy have been intertwined with, and compounded by, locally surviving relics of the vested rights theory. As preached by Holmes [4] and Beale,[5] this doctrine had, until a few decades ago, a strong impact on the case law in this area.[6] According to the apostles of that theory, it is axiomatic that a foreign cause of action is an *obligatio* created by the command of a particular foreign sovereign.[7] The cause of action does not exist apart from the foreign law which creates and defines it. For those accepting this premise, and combining it with the "fact" theory, it followed with logical necessity that a plaintiff who alleged a cause of action governed by foreign law, but failed to allege and prove the relevant command of the foreign sovereign, had failed to show one of the material "facts" of his case and thus had to lose. The same fate befell a defendant who failed to allege and prove the foreign law on which an affirmative defense was based.[8]

The vested rights theory is now rejected by most states, including those where cases involving foreign-country law are most frequently litigated.[9] Two of the mainstays of that doctrine, the lex loci delicti rule for torts and the lex loci contractus rule for contracts, have been characterized as "hoary" and "wooden," respectively, in Allstate Ins. Co. v. Hague, 449 U.S. 302, 315 note 21 and 316 note 22 (1981). Some observers are likely to question the Court's description of the governmental-interests approach as the "dominant" one in state courts today, id. 308, note 10. Nevertheless, and despite much continuing debate within the governmental-interests (or "functional approach") camp, those adhering to the "new method" are in basic agreement with the leading anti-Bealean, the late Professor Brainerd Currie, that the law of the forum is never effectively displaced unless the applicable foreign

---

4. See Cuba R.R. Co. v. Crosby, *supra.*

5. 3 J. Beale, A Treatise on the Conflict of Laws 1968–69 (1935).

6. See, e.g., Philp v. Macri, 261 F.2d 945 (9th Cir. 1958); Cosulich Societa Triestina Di Navigazione v. Elting, 66 F.2d 534 (2d Cir. 1933); Industrial Export & Import Corp. v. Hongkong & Shanghai Banking Corp., 302 N.Y. 342, 98 N.E.2d 466 (1951); Riley v. Pierce Oil Corp., 245 N.Y. 152, 156 N.E. 647 (1927).

7. See Slater v. Mexican Nat'l R.R., 194 U.S. 120, 126, 24 S.Ct. 581, 582 (1904).

8. See Tidewater Oil Co. v. Waller, 302 F.2d 638 (10th Cir. 1962); Eisler v. Soskin, 272 App.Div. 894, 71 N.Y.S.2d 682 (1st Dep't 1947), aff'd, 297 N.Y. 841, 78 N.E.2d 862 (1948). See also infra n. 21.

9. R. J. Weintraub, Commentary on the Conflict of Laws 318–323 (3d ed. 1986), cites (as of July 1, 1985) authorities from thirty states, Puerto Rico, and the District of Columbia rejecting the lex loci delicti rule, and decisions from eleven states retaining it. The count now appears to be 33 to 10, see O'Connor v. O'Connor, 201 Conn. 632, 519 A.2d 13 (1986).

opposite Justice Holmes opinion in Cuba

law has been invoked in proper and timely fashion. As Judge Mansfield put it, in Vishipco Line v. Chase Manhattan Bank N.A., 660 F.2d 854, 860 (2d Cir. 1981):

> . . . [W]ith the decline of the vested rights theory, see Currie, *On the Displacement of the Law of the Forum*, 58 Colum.L.Rev. 964, 1001 (1958), [the movement has been away from a mandatory application of the forum's choice of law rules and toward the adoption of a discretionary rule. While, as the Advisory Committee's notes to Rule 44.1 make clear, a court is still permitted to apply foreign law even if not requested by a party, we believe that the law of the forum may be applied here, where the parties did not at trial take the position that plaintiffs were required to prove their claims under Vietnamese law, even though the forum's choice of law rules would have called for the application of foreign law.

conflict of laws analytical approach Noted in class

Disagreement between scholarly camps concerned not only the solution of the problem, but even extended to its nature and curricular allocation. The "fact" theory, with its emphasis on establishing the foreign law by formal proof or by certain presumptions, had the effect of largely allocating the whole problem to the field of Evidence.[10] Those scholars, however, who prefer to formulate the problem in terms of "displacement of the law of the forum," claim that it constitutes an important and indeed a basic Conflict of Laws issue.[11]

Fact = ? Evidence. Law := conflict of law issue.

More recently, leading authorities on the law of Evidence have advocated yet another classification. Influenced by the impact of Rule 44.1 and of its progeny, they have adopted the view that feeding foreign-country law into the judicial process is "more appropriately an aspect of the law pertaining to procedure."[12] This debate about the proper allocation of the problem, which at first blush appears to be mere academic infighting, is not without practical significance; in the federal courts, the *Erie* doctrine and the terms of the Enabling Act[13] make it necessary to determine whether the problem is "procedural" or "substantive."

C. *The Complex Structure of the Pertinent Legal Rules*

In every American jurisdiction, there has been a considerable growth of common-law rules concerning the consequences of a failure to plead or prove the applicable foreign law. In the majority of jurisdictions—including all of those which have a considerable volume of

10. See, e.g., McCormick, Handbook of the Law of Evidence § 335, at 942 (3d ed. 1984).

11. See, e.g., Ehrenzweig, The Lex Fori—Basic Rule in the Conflict of Laws, 58 Mich.L.Rev. 637, 678–79 (1960).

12. McCormick, supra note 10, at 945, also citing Note on Judicial Notice of Law, Adv.Com.Note, Fed.R.Evid. 201. The Mc-Cormick treatise now somewhat futuristically suggests that "the electronic bleeps sounded by today's data processing equipment are actually tolling the intellectual death knell of this discrete subject-matter hitherto dealt with as a subdivision of the law of evidence." Id. at 945.

13. See 28 U.S.C. § 2072 (1970).

foreign law litigation—we also find judicial notice statutes that have been superimposed upon the common-law rules.[14]

The complexity arising from this interaction of judge-made and statutory law is further enhanced by the fact that all of the rules specifically dealing with the problem of invoking or proving the applicable foreign law have to be read against the backdrop of other, more general rules of procedure. Especially important are those procedural rules which determine when and how a foreign law issue has to be raised in order to be considered by the trial judge and to be preserved for appellate review.

In order to chart a path through this complex maze of legal rules— judge-made and statutory, specific and general—the discussion which follows will initially separate (1) the common-law background, (2) the judicial notice statutes, and (3) the relevant procedural rules of a more general nature. Only on the basis established by such separate analysis, can we examine the interaction of the three sets of rules.

II. SURVEY OF EXISTING LAW

A. *The Common Law*

1. **Conventional Analysis: Split Among Conflicting "Rules"**

The common-law rules are presented by most of the commentators as reflecting a basic split, and a superficial examination seems to lend some credence to the conclusion that the courts are divided. On the one hand, there are decisions influenced by the vested rights theory and thus leaning toward the rule that a cause of action or a defense based on foreign law is lost if the party asserting it fails to plead and prove the applicable foreign law. The classical example is Cuba Railroad Co. v. Crosby, *supra*.

The courts, however, have always recognized important exceptions to the orthodox rule applied [15] in the *Crosby* case. Under the exceptions, the internal law of the forum will be applied whenever it is reasonably probable that the foreign law in question is similar to domestic law. Such likelihood of similarity exists (1) when the foreign country belongs to the common-law orbit,[16] and (2) in any event, whenever the point at issue is so fundamental that even a country outside of the common-law orbit may reasonably be presumed to have adopted a solution similar to our own.[17]

14. See supra pp. 78–81.

15. Perhaps misapplied would be more accurate. See text at nn. 19–21 infra.

16. Judge Learned Hand has stated:

The extent of our right to make any assumptions about the law of another country depends upon the country and the question involved; in common-law countries we may go further than in civil law; in civilized, than in backward or barbarous.

E. Gerli & Co. v. Cunard S.S. Co., 48 F.2d 115, 117 (2d Cir. 1931).

17. See, e.g., Parrot v. Mexican Cent. Ry., 207 Mass. 184, 93 N.E. 590 (1911). Further references are collected in Arams v. Arams, 182 Misc. 328, 45 N.Y.S.2d 251 (Sup.Ct.1943).

[handwritten margin notes: "B/c of reasonable notice clause → raising for 1st time on appeal is not reasonable notice."]

In spite of these wide-ranging exceptions, the orthodox rule has been criticized as harsh. *Quaere*, however, whether the occasional harshness of judicial decisions using the orthodox approach stems from the rule itself or from its misapplication. If a case like *Crosby* came up today in the federal courts, the orthodox common-law approach would not lead to a harsh result. Today, the defendant would be prevented by Rule 44.1 and by several other provisions of the Federal Rules of Civil Procedure [18] from raising the Cuban law point on appeal. Thus, the plaintiff would win. Even in 1912, the plaintiff would have won if Justice Holmes had realized that "assumption of the risk" is an affirmative defense and that the burden of proving the Cuban law supporting this affirmative defense was on the defendant.[19] This was a case in which the plaintiff had a so-called fundamental cause of action—one presumed to be recognized in all civilized legal systems— while the affirmative defense was nonfundamental [20] and thus dependent on a proper showing of the applicable foreign law.[21] It follows that correct application of the orthodox rule and its recognized exceptions would have led to the correct result: affirmance of the judgment for the plaintiff.

[handwritten margin note: "Analysis of the Crosby case ... mentioned by Weeks"]

Another famous case often cited by the critics of the orthodox approach is *Walton v. Arabian American Oil Co.*[22] Walton was an American citizen who was temporarily in Saudi Arabia. While there, he suffered serious injuries in an automobile accident when his car collided with one of the defendant's trucks. Neither the plaintiff nor the defendant, an American corporation, attempted to prove the applicable law of Saudi Arabia. Under the New York conflict of laws rules as they stood at the time of the *Walton* case, the substantive law of the place where the tort occurred was controlling.[23] Thus, the burden was

---

18. The defendant in the *Crosby* case raised the foreign law point for the first time after trial, in a motion for judgment notwithstanding the verdict. If the case came up today, it would be arguable that, regardless of the merits of the foreign law point, the defendant had waived its objection concerning that point, and that the intermediate appellate court was authorized and indeed compelled by Federal Rules of Civil Procedure 12(h)(2) and 51 to affirm the judgment for the plaintiff. Cf. Black, Sivalls & Bryson, Inc. v. Shondell, 174 F.2d 587 (8th Cir. 1949).

19. See James, Assumption of Risk: Unhappy Reincarnation, 78 Yale L.J. 185, 195–96 (1968) and authorities cited therein.

20. Clearly, it cannot be taken for granted that assumption of risk as a complete defense is universally recognized by civilized legal systems. In our own country, the defense has been abolished, by statute or judicial decision, in a number of jurisdictions. See Prosser & Keeton on the Law of Torts 493–95 (5th ed. 1984). Even in states where the defense still exists, it would be unlikely to prevail in a case in which, as here, the defendant employer promised to repair the defective machinery and requested the employee to continue its use in the meantime. See id. at 492.

21. See cases cited supra n. 8.

On the other hand, when the plaintiff's cause of action and defendant's affirmative defense both were based on "fundamental" principles, and the plaintiff sought to counter the defense by a reply not borne out by such principles, the burden of proving the foreign law (i.e., the foreign law supporting the reply) was held to be on the plaintiff. See E. Gerli & Co. v. Cunard S.S. Co., 48 F.2d 115 (2d Cir. 1931); Mangrelli v. Italian Line, 208 Misc. 685, 144 N.Y.S.2d 570 (Sup.Ct.1955).

22. 233 F.2d 541 (2d Cir. 1956), cert. denied 352 U.S. 872, 77 S.Ct. 97 (1956).

23. Id. Prior to Babcock v. Jackson, 12 N.Y.2d 473, 240 N.Y.S.2d 743, 191 N.E.2d 279 (1963), New York generally applied the

thought to be on the plaintiff to prove the applicable Saudi Arabian law. Because he did not do so, the trial judge dismissed the action. This judgment was upheld reluctantly by the court of appeals. The result in *Walton* was not quite as revolting as that in *Crosby*, because in the *Walton* case the plaintiff's counsel had been warned repeatedly by the trial judge that the plaintiff would lose if he did not prove the law of Saudi Arabia. Whatever harshness remained was, perhaps, the result of the rigid choice of law rule prevailing at that time, and not of the orthodox approach to the consequences of failure to prove the foreign law. In 1971, the United States District Court for the Southern District of Texas had to deal with a case the facts of which were virtually identical with those of *Walton*, except that the accident occurred in Libya rather than in Saudi Arabia.[24] In that case, the problem of invoking and proving Libyan law was avoided because the court, focusing on the parties' common nationality and domicile, decided that Texas was the state of the most significant relationship,[25] and hence applied the substantive law of Texas. Thus, by adopting a more flexible choice of law rule, the court was able to hold in favor of the plaintiff and to obviate repetition of the *Walton* scenario.[26]

We must now turn to a different line of cases which, to the superficial observer, seems irreconcilable with *Crosby* and its offspring. In these cases, which are quite numerous,[27] failure to invoke or to prove the otherwise applicable foreign law led the courts to apply the domestic law of the forum.[28] Sometimes, as in Leary v. Gledhill, this result is explained in terms of the parties' acquiescence. On other occasions, it has been said that domestic law should be applied because it is the only law the court knows; or the case was decided in accordance with the forum's internal law without any explanation at all.[29] Those who follow the teachings of Professors Ehrenzweig or Currie will, of course,

rule of lex loci delicti to all substantive issues arising in a tort case.

24. Couch v. Mobil Oil Corp., 327 F.Supp. 897 (S.D.Tex.1971).

25. Cf. Restatement (Second) of Conflict of Laws §§ 6, 145, 146 (1971).

26. Even if, as a matter of choice of law, the court had held that some of the relevant substantive issues in the case were governed by the law of Libya, a satisfactory result—more satisfactory than the result in *Walton*—could have been reached under the modern approach explained below. In light of the fact that the defendant had much easier access to the sources of the applicable foreign law than the plaintiff, a modern court might well place the burden of proving such law on the defendant, with the understanding that the substantive law of the forum will be applied if that burden is not met. See note 44 and accompanying text infra. In other words, tinkering with choice of law rules is not the only method by which a court today

could avoid the harshness of the *Walton* result.

27. See cases collected in §§ 3–6 of Annot., 75 A.L.R.2d 529 (1961), and in Restatement, supra note 25, at § 136, Reporter's Note on comment *h* (1971) (with references concerning rule in England).

28. This approach might be called the forum-law approach, as distinguished from the orthodox approach exemplified by *Crosby*.

29. We agree . . . that the general, if not universal, rule is that the rights of succession of a husband to personal property of his wife is [*sic*] governed by the law of the domicile of the owner at death. . . . [I]n the instant case, there was no pleading or proof as to what, if any, marital rights Wackwitz would have, or what conduct, if any, on his part would forfeit such rights under the laws of his wife's domicile. We cannot judicially notice the law of Germany. . . . In the absence of proof of such law we must apply the law of Missouri.

explain all these decisions on the ground that, as a matter of choice of law doctrine, the forum's internal law remains the rule of decision unless it is displaced by a properly invoked foreign law.

This approach, too, contains some seeds of unfairness. Suppose the plaintiff has cleverly chosen a forum that has little connection with the transaction, but whose domestic law favors the plaintiff's side. If the court is willing to substitute its own law for the properly applicable but unproved foreign law, then the plaintiff by this maneuver has successfully relieved himself of the burden and expense of proving the foreign law, and has thrown that burden on the defendant.

Again, it is important to recognize that even those courts which pay unqualified lip service to the forum-law rule, do not apply it in all cases. There are situations in which it would be patently absurd to substitute domestic law for the applicable foreign law. Suppose, for instance, that the plaintiff sues for breach of contract, and the defendant seeks to excuse his nonperformance by asserting that performance on his part became impossible due to an embargo imposed by the government of Ruritania. If in this case the defendant fails to prove the Ruritanian statute or decree imposing the embargo, he will lose. It would be unjustifiable to let him substitute the law of the forum on this point. Even Currie and Ehrenzweig do not contend otherwise; in their opinion, the explanation is that in such a case the Ruritanian embargo provisions do not constitute the rule of decision, but a mere "datum." [30] However, since the borderline between a "datum" and a rule of decision has never been staked out with any precision, this is not an explanation, but merely a statement of the result. The significant fact is that in the view of all courts and all scholars there are *some* cases in which it is inappropriate to substitute domestic law for the otherwise applicable foreign law. [31]

Lane v. St. Louis Union Trust Co., 356 Mo. 76, 82, 201 S.W.2d 288, 291 (1947); see Savage v. O'Neil, 44 N.Y. 298, 300–01 (1871).

30. See A. A. Ehrenzweig, A Treatise on the Conflict of Laws 362 (1962); Currie, On the Displacement of the Law of the Forum, 58 Colum.L.Rev. 964, 1012–14 (1958), reprinted in B. Currie, Selected Essays on the Conflict of Laws 3, 58–61 (1963); Traynor, Conflict of Laws: Professor Currie's Restrained and Enlightened Forum, 49 Calif.L.Rev. 845, 873–75 (1961).

31. The following hypothetical situation, inspired by the facts of an actual case, may serve as a further illustration. Suppose Mr. and Mrs. Meyer, natives and nationals of Austria, were domiciled in that country until early 1972, when they immigrated into the United States and became domiciliaries of New York. Their marriage was celebrated in Austria in 1971, a short time before their emigration. In 1973, Mr. Meyer brings an annulment ac-

tion against Mrs. Meyer, in a New York court, on the alleged ground that she induced him to marry her by fraudulent misrepresentations concerning her willingness to bear children. The facts alleged by the plaintiff—facts which under New York law would make the marriage voidable—are proved at the trial to the satisfaction of the court. But neither party presents any evidence or materials concerning the pertinent provisions of Austrian law, and the court is unwilling (and perhaps unable) independently to investigate the relevant Austrian sources and authorities. Clearly, the annulment action must fail. It would be indefensible (and unconstitutional) to judge the initial validity of this Austrian marriage by the substantive standards of New York law. Phillips Petroleum Co. v. Shutts, 105 S.Ct. 2965, 2980, 472 U.S. 797, 821–22 (1985); Allstate Ins. Co. v. Hague, 449 U.S. 302, 312–313, 101 S.Ct. 633, 639–40 (1981), citing further authority. The constitutional defect is subject to waiver *by*

It follows that the orthodox rule and the forum-law rule are not as irreconcilable as appears at first blush. When the two allegedly conflicting "rules" *and their "exceptions"* are compared, it becomes clear that almost all of the relevant decisions, in spite of their differences in articulation, can be reconciled in terms of the results reached.

2. Suggested Analysis: A Multi-Factor Approach

In contract cases, it will sometimes be arguable that the parties' failure to invoke the foreign law amounts to conscious and genuine acquiescence in the application of domestic law. This may be regarded as a contractual choice of the applicable law, and today such a choice will normally be honored by American courts;[32] it certainly must be honored in a case governed by the Uniform Commercial Code, provided there is some reasonable relation between the transaction and the forum state.[33]

At the opposite extreme, there are situations in which it would violate basic dictates of fairness and common sense to apply domestic law to legal phenomena wholly and ineradicably rooted in a foreign legal system. In these latter situations, application of domestic law smacks of unconstitutionality.[34]

Between these extremes, however, there is a large middle field, where the consequences of the parties' failure to invoke or prove the foreign law cannot and should not be treated by way of a simple, definite rule. The older cases, whether they favored or opposed *Crosby*, often attempted to formulate rigid rules,[35] and most of the text writers still follow this obsolete method. In the more modern cases, however, an entirely different trend is discernible. Flexibility is the new watchword. In a 1968 case, the Supreme Court of Vermont announced that substitution of domestic law for the uninvoked foreign law "is justified

---

the defendant, but on the subconstitutional level, even an express stipulation of the parties calling for application of New York law would not be honored by a New York court in a matrimonial case. See, e.g., Fraioli v. Fraioli, 1 App.Div.2d 967, 150 N.Y.S.2d 665 (2d Dep't 1956). Thus, the plaintiff must lose because he has failed to prove one of the essential elements of his cause of action.

In this hypothetical, it seems rather doubtful whether the Austrian law can be called a mere "datum." Concerning the issue of the validity of the marriage, Austrian law appears to be the rule of decision. But that is only an unimportant semantic quibble. What is important is to recognize that substitution of forum law for the uninvoked or unproved foreign law does not solve all of the cases, just as we have seen that the orthodox approach of deciding against the party who has the burden of proof does not always lead to sound results.

32. See Restatement (Second) of Conflict of Laws § 187 (1971).

33. See Uniform Commercial Code § 1–105.

34. See supra note 31. The *Hague* formula, as reiterated in *Shutts*, 105 S.Ct. at 2980, precludes the application of forum law to claims in which the forum has no "interest," and which are "unrelated" to it. Note, however, that federal constitutional constraints on choice of law operate only to the extent that they are invoked. If Phillips had not seasonably raised a federal constitutional question in this respect, and preserved error, the lower courts' application of forum law would have become unassailable constitutionally.

35. Compare Western Union Tel. Co. v. Brown, 234 U.S. 542, 34 S.Ct. 955 (1914), with McLoughlin v. Shaw, 95 Conn. 102, 111 A. 62 (1920).

so long as it is reasonable and does not impose oppressive consequences." [36] Judge Wisdom, speaking for the United States Court of
Appeals for the Fifth Circuit, put it even more bluntly: "In the interest
of arriving at a just adjudication, the trial judge should have discretion
in determining whether the law of the forum, with or without the
disguise of a presumption, should prevail." [37] The New York Court of
Appeals, which previously had vacillated between the forum-law rule
and the *Crosby* rule,[38] finally adopted a similarly flexible approach in
Watts v. Swiss Bank Corporation.[39]

Flexibility, of course, does not leave the courts without guideposts.
In determining whether to apply domestic law or to decide the case
against the party bearing the burden of proof, the courts are aided by a
number of identifiable factors such as the following:

(a) *The Degree to Which a Strong Public Interest is Involved in
the Parties' Dispute.* If there is no such public interest, the forum-
law approach normally is preferable.[40] This is true not only in
contract cases (in which the parties' acquiescence in the application
of forum law may amount to a choice of law agreement),[41] but
equally in noncontract actions, provided the dispute touches nobody's interests except the private concerns of the parties.[42] When,
on the other hand, there is a strong public interest, as in matrimonial or criminal cases, it is clear that the parties should not have
the power by their action or inaction to determine the applicable
law. In cases of the latter kind, therefore, little or no weight
should be accorded to the fact that the parties have "acquiesced" in
the application of domestic law.[43]

(b) *The Parties' Access to Foreign Law Materials.* In some
cases, especially when exotic legal systems are involved, the court
should give some consideration to the parties' relative ability to
procure information concerning the foreign law (*e.g.*, Aramco's
access to the law of Saudi Arabia in 1955, as opposed to Leo
Walton's.) [44]

36. Pioneer Credit Corp. v. Carden, 127
Vt. 229, 234, 245 A.2d 891, 894 (1968).

37. Seguros Tepeyac S.A., Compania
Mexicana de Seguros Generales v. Bostrom, 347 F.2d 168, 175 (5th Cir. 1965).

38. The vacillating course of the earlier
New York decisions is traced in Justice
Walter's scholarly opinion in Arams v.
Arams, 182 Misc. 328, 45 N.Y.S.2d 251
(Sup.Ct.1943).

39. 27 N.Y.2d 270, 317 N.Y.S.2d 315,
265 N.E.2d 739 (1970).

40. See Kalyvakis v. T.S.S. Olympia,
181 F.Supp. 32, 36 (S.D.N.Y.1960).

41. See nn. 32 and 33 supra.

42. A caveat should be noted: The criterion stated in the text may prove difficult to apply in some types of cases, especially tort cases. At first blush, most tort
actions perhaps appear to be purely private disputes; but the public interest may
enter, e.g., when a breadwinner has been
killed or incapacitated, and a tort recovery
is the only way to keep his dependents off
the welfare rolls. It is hard to deny, also,
that the public interest becomes involved
in a tort case when the defendant invokes
the protection of a workers' compensation
statute. Cf. Tidewater Oil Co. v. Waller,
302 F.2d 638 (10th Cir. 1962).

43. See A. Ehrenzweig, Private International Law 182–83 (1967); Nussbaum, The
Problem of Proving Foreign Law, 50 Yale
L.J. 1018, 1040–42 (1941). See also supra
n. 31.

44. Walton v. Arabian Am. Oil Co., 233
F.2d 541, 545 (2d Cir. 1956), cert. denied

(c) *Forum Shopping.* The forum chosen by the plaintiff may be highly artificial as well as inconvenient to the defendant. If this does not lead to a discretionary dismissal under the doctrine of forum non conveniens, it should in any event be treated as a factor which strongly militates (a) against rewarding the forum-shopping plaintiff by the application of domestic law,[45] and (b) in favor of judicial prodding to produce proof of the appropriate foreign-country rule.[46]

(d) *The Strength and Clarity of the Forum's Choice-of-Law (or Other) Rule Pointing to the Foreign Law.* Where the transaction and the parties have no substantial connection with the forum, and the application of the forum's internal law thus would be artificial and far-fetched, the court may feel some reluctance to apply such law, even though no foreign law has been invoked. Such reluctance will be particularly strong when the plaintiff is guilty of forum shopping (see supra), or when the parties have entered into their transaction in reliance on the foreign law.[47] But where, as is frequently the case, the parties or the facts have substantial contacts with the forum, and it is at least arguable that under modern, flexible choice-of-law doctrines the internal law of the forum might be applicable, the court—without necessarily determining the choice-of-law issue—will apply its own substantive law rather than the uninvoked or belatedly invoked foreign law.[48]

352 U.S. 872, 77 S.Ct. 97 (1956). For background, see B. Currie, supra note 30, at 3–4, 19–20 and 44–45. The Saudi Arabian road traffic legislation of 1942, in effect at the time of the accident, cited id. at 45 note 102, had been enacted at the behest of Aramco. See Hart, Application of Hanbalite and Decree Laws to Foreigners in Saudi Arabia, 22 Geo.Wash.L.Rev. 165, 167–69 (1953). (This legislation did not, however, deal with civil liability or the key issue of *respondeat superior.*) Today, Saudi Arabian law is much further developed, and accessible in translation, see, e.g., A. P. Keesee, Commercial Laws of the Middle East, vol. 2: The Kingdom of Saudi Arabia (1980). With the aid of such materials and the assistance of affidavits by experts, questions of contemporary Saudi Arabian law have even been decided on motions for summary judgment. Merican, Inc. v. Caterpillar Tractor Co., 596 F.Supp. 697, 700–704 (E.D.Pa. 1984).

45. If the forum lacks a substantial connection with the transaction or the parties, application of its own substantive law may—at least in theory—be unconstitutional. See note 34 supra. It should be noted, however, that cases may arise in which the forum chosen by the plaintiff is not so completely contactless as to bring this rule of constitutional law into play, but in which the forum nevertheless is a highly artificial one, selected with a keen eye for advantages to be gained by forum shopping. In such a case, the artificiality of the forum should at least constitute a *factor* militating not only against the forum's exercise of jurisdiction, but also against application of its own internal substantive law.

46. Whenever Federal Rule 44.1 or its cognates apply, even exotic foreign law can be proved without undue difficulty or expense. See, e.g., Kaho v. Ilchert, 765 F.2d 877 (9th Cir. 1985) (customary adoption law of Tonga). A simple letter by foreign counsel (even house counsel), if plausible and uncontradicted, suffices to establish a proposition of foreign law. Swiss Credit Bank v. Balink, 614 F.2d 1269 (10th Cir. 1980); United States v. First Nat. Bank of Chicago, 699 F.2d 341, 343–45 (7th Cir. 1983).

47. See Restatement, Second, Conflict of Laws § 136, com. h (1971).

48. See, e.g., Cousins v. Instrument Flyers, Inc., 44 N.Y.2d 698, 700, 405 N.Y.S.2d 441, 443, 376 N.E.2d 914, 915 (1978); Commercial Insurance Co. of Newark v. Pacific-Peru Construction Corp., 558 F.2d 948, 952 (9th Cir. 1977); Stein v. Siegel, 50 A.D.2d 916, 917, 377 N.Y.S.2d 580, 582–83 (2d Dep't 1975); Seattle Totems Hockey Club,

A somewhat different situation is presented where the foreign law comes into play, not on the ground that it is the applicable law under the forum's choice-of-law rules, but simply because it constitutes a material part of the basis of plaintiff's claim under the forum's own internal law. For example, "if suit is brought against an attorney to recover damages sustained by reason of his alleged negligence in failing correctly to ascertain a foreign law, the plaintiff must establish as part of his case the content of that foreign law."[49] In such a situation it would be nonsensical to apply the forum's own internal law in lieu of the uninvoked foreign law. The plaintiff who in this kind of situation does not invoke and prove the foreign law, has failed to show that he has a claim, and consequently must lose.[50] A similar result will follow in a case where the alien plaintiff's claim depends on a reciprocity requirement,[51] and the plaintiff fails to show that his country would grant reciprocal treatment to an American citizen.[52]

(e) *The Nature of the Foreign Legal System and of the Issue Involved in the Case.* Finally, and perhaps most importantly, a judge's readiness to substitute forum law for the otherwise applicable foreign law will be enhanced if he can rationally assume that with respect to the point at issue the two laws do not radically differ from each other. Such an assumption may be based on the fact that the foreign legal system in question belongs to the common-law orbit.[53] Sometimes an assumption of similarity may be warranted even though the foreign system in question is part of an alien world, e.g., that of the civil law. To the extent that the issue at hand appears to be governed by a "fundamental principle," forum law may be applied on the theory that, unless the contrary is shown, the law of the foreign country in question, and perhaps the laws of all civilized nations, can be expected to be in harmony with the forum's law on that issue.[54]

[margin note: shifts burden of coming forward w/ foreign law]

In connection with the last point, a judicial notice statute can play an important role. Formerly, courts had to rely on an uninformed judicial hunch when they assumed (or refused to assume) that a particular cause of action or defense was based on fundamental principles of law presumably recognized by the foreign legal system in question or indeed by all civilized nations. Under a judicial notice statute, however, a court may undertake what Judge Breitel has referred to as "cursory independent research" concerning the foreign law.[55] Such cursory research perhaps will not enable the court exhaus-

Inc. v. National Hockey League, 783 F.2d 1347, 1355 note 9 (9th Cir. 1986).

49. Restatement, Second, Conflict of Laws § 136, com. h (1971).

50. Ibid.

51. See supra p. 28.

52. See Restatement, Second, supra n. 49.

53. See supra, text at n. 16.

54. See supra, text at n. 17.

55. See Watts v. Swiss Bank Corp., 27 N.Y.2d 270, 275, 317 N.Y.S.2d 315, 319, 265 N.E.2d 739, 742 (1970).

[handwritten margin note: see Martin-Dale - Hubbell [Summary of Foreign Law]]

tively to resolve the foreign law issue; but if it discloses that on the point in question there is no real clash between domestic law and the governing foreign law, this will constitute a potent factor against using the *Crosby* approach and in favor of relying on forum law as the rule of decision.[56]

It is submitted that if these variables are kept in mind, the actual results reached (although perhaps not the language used) in most of the reported cases can be reconciled. Thus, in the place of two allegedly conflicting "rules," there emerges a flexible but unified approach. In the hands of present-day courts, this approach most frequently leads to the application of forum law.[57] It should not be assumed, however, that forum law automatically can be substituted in every case in which there has been a failure to invoke or ascertain the applicable foreign law. Although perhaps not overly numerous, there are situations— especially those which involve marriage and family, or a transaction totally unconnected with the forum—in which, despite the parties' "acquiescence," the factors listed above may point away from the forum-law solution.

[handwritten margin note: flexible approach recommended]

B. Judicial Notice Statutes

Almost three-quarters of the states, including all but one of those in which transnational litigation occurs with some frequency, have enacted statutes or Rules either providing for "judicial notice" of foreign-country law or in other ways authorizing the court, in determining foreign law, to consider any relevant material or source, regardless of admissibility under technical rules of evidence, and regardless also of whether or not such material was submitted by a party.[58] These

56. Ibid.

57. In addition to the cases cited in nn. 10, 17, 48 and 55, supra, note 72 infra, and in Wachs v. Winter, infra, pp. 111–112, see Walter v. Netherlands Mead N.V., 514 F.2d 1130, 1137 (3 Cir. 1975), cert. denied 423 U.S. 869, 96 S.Ct. 133 (1975); Fairmont Shipping Corp. v. Chevron International Oil Co., 511 F.2d 1252, 1261 (2 Cir. 1975); Bartsch v. Metro-Goldwyn-Mayer, Inc., 391 F.2d 150, 155 (2 Cir. 1968), cert. denied 393 U.S. 826, 89 S.Ct. 86 (1968); Gangel v. Degroot, PVBA, 41 N.Y.2d 840, 393 N.Y.S.2d 698, 362 N.E.2d 249 (1977).

The tendency to resort to forum law whenever possible, is particularly strong in California. By way of an apparently well-considered dictum, the Supreme Court of California said: "In short, generally speaking the forum will apply its own rule of decision unless a party litigant timely invokes the law of a foreign state." Hurtado v. Superior Court, 11 Cal.3d 574, 581, 114 Cal.Rptr. 106, 110, 522 P.2d 666, 670 (1974). This is in line with Professor Currie's theories (see text at n. 9, supra), to which the

California Supreme Court has adhered since 1974. See also infra n. 65.

58. For a brief survey of these statutes, see supra pp. 78–81. The impact of the Federal Rules on state procedural law generally is analyzed by J. B. Oakley & A. F. Coon, The Federal Rules in State Courts: A Survey of State Court Systems of Civil Procedure, 61 Wash.L.Rev. 1367 (1986).

As applied to the ascertainment of foreign law, the term "judicial notice" may well be inappropriate. A few of the pertinent enactments, such as Federal Rule of Civil Procedure 44.1, have been deliberately drafted so as to avoid that term. For good or for ill, however, most of the relevant statutes in fact speak of "judicial notice."

Courts and legal writers generally refer to all of the relevant enactments, whether or not the term "judicial notice" is used therein, as judicial notice statutes. For the sake of brevity and convenience, the same usage will be followed here.

judicial notice statutes are, however, superimposed on common-law doctrines, which may retain some vitality in situations in which the statutory provisions do not lead to actual notice being taken of the foreign law.

1. Interaction of Judicial Notice Statutes and Decisional Law

Even in a jurisdiction which has a judicial notice statute, the statute is not a solvent for every foreign law case. Most of the statutes are permissive only, so that the court's determination whether or not to take judicial notice of the foreign law is a discretionary one. In exercising this discretion, courts naturally are disinclined to engage in independent research concerning a strange legal system if they receive no help from counsel. Even when the statute is drafted in mandatory terms, the result is not very different.[59]

Point 1

A few of the statutes, moreover, use pleading or notice requirements as a restriction on judicial notice. Under a bifurcated judicial notice rule of the New York type,[60] it may be arguable that the parties' failure to invoke the foreign law merely has the effect of making judicial notice of foreign law permissible rather than mandatory. But in those jurisdictions which have adopted Rules or statutes patterned after FRCP Rule 44.1, the notice requirement enunciated in the first sentence of that Rule may have stronger teeth. In Ruff v. St. Paul Mercury Insurance Co. (infra p. 124), the Second Circuit held that a court cannot even look at the foreign law unless it has been seasonably invoked, in the form of a written notice, by one of the parties.[61]

The *Ruff* case serves as a reminder that even in jurisdictions where a judicial notice statute is in existence, situations arise in which the court either lacks the power to take judicial notice, or as a matter of discretion will refuse to do so. In cases of this sort, the judicial notice statute in effect becomes inoperative; and just as in the old common-law days, the court is then faced with the question of how it should react to the parties' failure to invoke or prove the foreign law. Most of the statutes are silent on this point.[62] To find an answer, the court must turn to decisional rules—the same rules which would govern in the absence of a judicial notice statute. It follows that these decisional rules continue to play an important role even in those jurisdictions which have adopted a modern statute.

In California and New Jersey, the judicial notice statute itself contains an express direction, telling the court what to do in case the foreign law is neither proved nor judicially noticed.[63] The New Jersey

---

59. See supra p. 79.

60. See infra pp. 121–122.

61. Older New York and Massachusetts authorities in point are discussed by O. Sommerich & B. Busch, Foreign Law—A Guide to Pleading and Proof 64–74 (1959).

62. California and New Jersey, however, provide for this contingency in their judicial notice statutes. See text infra.

63. Cal.Evid.Code § 311 (West 1966), supra p. 96; N.J.Stat.Ann. § 2A:84A-16R.9(3) (1976).

statute favors application of domestic law in such a case,[64] while the much more sophisticated California provision (see supra p. 96), by vesting the court with a great deal of discretion, arrives at a result similar to that which has been reached by the most recent and most enlightened judicial decisions in other jurisdictions.[65] Although essentially declaratory of decisional law, the California statute has two original and valuable features. It warns the court of the constitutional doubts which may be created by imposing domestic law on a legal relationship which lacks any reasonable contact with the forum; [66] and it provides that when an action is dismissed because of the plaintiff's failure to prove the pertinent foreign law, the dismissal should be without prejudice.[67] ——➤ Noted

2. **Unproved and Unnoticed Foreign Law in the Federal Courts**

A special problem confronted the draftsmen of Federal Rule 44.1. It was realized that it would be conducive to clarity if the Rule spelled out the consequences that ensue when the foreign law is neither proved nor judicially noticed. But there was a hitch. Although the provision authorizing a court to take judicial notice can be viewed as a rule of adjective law, and thus covered by the Enabling Act, a rule spelling out the consequences of failure to take judicial notice is more difficult to characterize. A rule of the latter kind might be thought to be a choice-of-law rule and thus beyond the scope of the Supreme Court's rule-making power.[68] Because of this doubt, the draftsmen refrained from

64. "In the absence of an adequate basis for taking judicial notice of the law of any jurisdiction other than this State, and the United States, the judge shall apply the law of this State." N.J.Stat.Ann. § 2A:84A–16R.9(3) (1976).

65. See supra nn. 36–39 and accompanying text.

Although the statute (Cal.Evid.Code § 311) was carefully drafted, some difficulty—not foreseeable by the draftsmen—was subsequently created by the California Supreme Court's Hurtado dictum, quoted supra n. 57. In that dictum, the Court did not refer to § 311, and one wonders whether the dictum, which downplays judicial discretion and prescribes a more rigid forum-law approach, is wholly consistent with the statute. When faced with the question, the Court perhaps will say, in accordance with Professor Currie's theories, that forum law furnishes the rule of decision unless and until it is displaced; that it becomes displaced only when some foreign law is properly invoked; that until thus invoked, the foreign law is not "applicable"; and that § 311 speaks only of "applicable" foreign law. If California courts should take this position, they would have to distinguish between (a) a case where the

foreign law has not been invoked, and (b) a situation in which a party has invoked the foreign law but has failed to supply any helpful foreign-law materials, with the consequence that the court declines to take judicial notice of the foreign law. Situation (a) would be controlled by the Hurtado dictum, which means that "generally speaking" (and subject to constitutional limitations) the court would have to apply forum law. In situation (b), on the other hand, § 311 would govern, and the court would have the somewhat broader and more clearly defined discretionary powers spelled out in that provision.

66. See supra n. 34 and accompanying text.

67. Even in the absence of a statutory direction, a wise trial judge normally will dismiss "without prejudice" in such a case. See, e.g., Industrial Export & Import Corp. v. Hongkong & Shanghai Banking Corp., 302 N.Y. 342, 98 N.E.2d 466 (1951). Nevertheless, since some trial judges perhaps are not as wise and experienced as others, the statutory reminder is valuable.

68. Under 28 U.S.C.A. § 2072 (1970), the Supreme Court may promulgate *procedural* rules but may not use its rule-mak-

determining, in the Rule itself, the consequences which follow when the foreign law is neither proved nor judicially noticed. This left a gaping hole in the Rule. *44.1*

In line with older authority, it was at least arguable that this hole would have to be filled, at least in a diversity case, by reference to state law.[69] However, Professor Arthur Miller, in his well-known "Death-Knell" article, developed plausible arguments in support of the position that federal decisional law rather than state law should determine the matter in the federal courts.[70] It might still be too early to tell whether this latter view will ultimately prevail, for in many of the federal court opinions dealing with the issue, the Erie point is overlooked, and the reader is left to wonder whether the result (e.g., that the substantive law of the forum should be applied, since the parties failed to invoke any other law) was inspired by federal or state authorities.[71]

Nevertheless, there is a clearly discernible, unbroken line of authority for the proposition that in conflict-of-laws cases where the parties have failed to raise foreign-law issues as prescribed by the first sentence of Rule 44.1, federal courts will usually, pursuant to *federal* procedural law, apply the internal law of the state in which they sit. Thus, the current edition of a leading text on federal civil procedure baldly states: "If the parties fail to give notice to the court that foreign law is applicable, the court is not obliged to take judicial notice thereof, and may apply the law of the forum state." [72]

Wachs v. Winter, 569 F.Supp. 1438, 1442–43 (E.D.N.Y. 1983), well demonstrates and documents the current (and so far as can be ascertained, unanimous) practice of federal courts in this regard. After quoting the text of Rule 44.1 in support of the proposition that a federal

---

ing power to "abridge, enlarge or modify any substantive right."

69. See Krasnow v. National Airlines, 228 F.2d 326, 327 note 3 (2d Cir. 1955), where the court assumed "*arguendo*, and without expressing an opinion, that state rules concerning judicial notice of foreign law, like state conflict of laws rules, must be followed in an action in a federal court involving state-created rights." Note that the federal-system underpinnings of Erie R.R. v. Tompkins, 304 U.S. 64, 58 S.Ct. 817 (1938) do not support the extension of the rule of Klaxon Co. v. Stentor Elec. Mfg. Co., 313 U.S. 487, 61 S.Ct. 1020 (1941), to diversity cases where foreign-country law is arguably applicable. In Day & Zimmerman, Inc. v. Challoner, 423 U.S. 3, 96 S.Ct. 167 (1975), the Supreme Court nevertheless peremptorily mandated the application of forum choice-of-law rules in international conflicts cases as well.

70. See Miller, Federal Rule 44.1 and the "Fact" Approach in Determining Foreign Law: Death Knell for a Die-Hard Doc-

trine, 65 Mich.L.Rev. 613, at 702–15, 723–31, 746–48 (1967).

71. See M. Pollack, Proof of Foreign Law, 26 Am.J.Comp.L. 470, 472–473 with note 16 at 473 (1978).

72. 5 Moore's Federal Practice ¶ 44.1.03, p. 88 (1985–86 Suplement, J. D. Lucas ed. 1985), citing Vishipco Line v. Chase Manhattan Bank, N.A., 660 F.2d 854 (2d Cir. 1981), cert. denied, 459 U.S. 976 (1982); Clarkson Co. Ltd. v. Shaheen, 660 F.2d 506 (2d Cir. 1981), cert. denied, 455 U.S. 990 (1982).

Note, however, Moore's careful formulation to the effect that the court is *not obliged* to take judicial notice of the foreign law. In Wachs v. Winter (quoted in the text, infra) the court similarly emphasized that it was *not obligated* to do so. Whether in an unusual case a federal court *may* take judicial notice of foreign law in spite of the parties' failure to comply with the first sentence of Rule 44.1, is a different question, to be taken up infra immediately following the Ruff case.

court sitting in diversity "is not required to take judicial notice of the law of foreign countries," the court went on to say:

> If the parties fail to raise the issue of choice of law, the court is not obligated to do so on its own. Vishipco Line v. Chase Manhattan Bank, N.A., 660 F.2d at 860; Commercial Insurance Company of Newark, New Jersey v. Pacific-Peru Construction Corp., 558 F.2d 948, 952 (9th Cir. 1977); Bartsch v. Metro-Goldwyn-Mayer, Inc., 391 F.2d 150, 155 n. 3 (2d Cir.), cert. denied 393 U.S. 826, 89 S.Ct. 86, 21 L.Ed.2d 96 (1968). There is no evidence that either side has argued for application of foreign law. See Luckett v. Bethlehem Steel Corporation, 618 F.2d at 1378 n. 3. The failure of the parties to alert the court in pleadings or otherwise constitutes a waiver of this issue. See Morse Electro Products Corp. v. S. S. Great Peace, 437 F.Supp. 474, 487–88 (D.N.J. 1977). When both parties have been silent on the issue of which law to apply, it can be said that they have acquiesced in the application of the forum law. See Clarkson Company Limited v. Shaheen, 660 F.2d 506, 512 n. 4 (2d Cir. 1981), cert. denied 455 U.S. 990, 102 S.Ct. 1614, 71 L.Ed.2d 850 (1982). This view agrees with that of the Restatement (Second) of Conflict of Laws which calls for the application of forum law (i.e., New York law) where no or little information regarding the foreign law has been supplied. Id. at § 136, comment h at 378; accord, In re Air Crash Disaster Near Chicago, Illinois on May 25, 1979, 644 F.2d 594, 631 (7th Cir.), cert. denied 454 U.S. 878, 102 S.Ct. 358, 70 L.Ed.2d 187 (1981).

It seems likely that this approach will ultimately prevail in federal courts as a judicially-developed rule of federal civil procedure inspired by the internal logic of Rule 44.1, and reinforced by practical considerations. States with rules or statutes patterned upon Rule 44.1 are likely to follow this interpretation, except perhaps in some family law cases (which have traditionally escaped federal diversity jurisdiction).

3. Judicial Notice of Uninvoked Foreign Law

In those cases in which the court actually utilizes its statutory power to take judicial notice of foreign law, the problem of the consequences of the parties' failure to invoke and prove that law becomes moot. True, when the foreign law in question belongs to an alien system, and the parties have given the court no aid in ascertaining it, the court normally will decline to ascertain the foreign law by its own independent efforts; but unless the point is precluded on grounds of lateness, this is generally a matter of discretion. The terms of most judicial notice statutes—except those patterned after FRCP Rule 44.1— make it quite clear that the parties' failure to invoke the foreign law does not prevent the court from judicially noticing it, and that the court, even though totally unaided by the parties, has the *power* to undertake its own research.[73] Even Professor Currie, who strongly

---

73. The New York Rule (supra p. 57) is particularly clear on this point: "Every

court may take judicial notice *without request* of . . . the laws of foreign countries

opposed the utilization of uninvoked foreign law, and who for this reason criticized the sweeping language usually found in judicial notice statutes, conceded that his criticism was presented *de lege ferenda*.[74]

Although under most judicial notice statutes the court thus has the power independently to dig up foreign law points never invoked by a party, the question remains whether the court may and should decide the case without having given the parties an opportunity to respond to the results of the court's own foreign law research. The reader will recall the previous discussion of this point (supra pp. 60–61; 70–72).

C. *Other Pertinent Procedural Rules*

In many cases, of course, the initiative in finding and presenting the foreign law will be taken by the parties, and not by the court. When the parties make an intelligible presentation of the relevant sources and materials, the court in general will be inclined to make use of the powers conferred by the judicial notice statute. But frequently it happens that the parties and the court neglect a decisive foreign law point until after the trial. Perhaps the point is raised by the parties, or discovered by the court, for the first time in connection with a post-trial motion, such as a motion for judgment n.o.v. or for a new trial.[75] Or— and this is not infrequent—the foreign law points turn up for the first time on appeal.[76] Is the point now waived or precluded by lateness?

The answer to this question depends, in the first place, on whether the statute contains a notice requirement, and whether the courts have added teeth (or perhaps dentures) to that requirement. In this respect, the judicial notice statutes differ among each other. On the one hand, there is Federal Rule 44.1, with its express notice requirement, which, at least in the Second Circuit, has been taken so seriously that the foreign law point is dead unless introduced in good time.[77] On the other hand, state statutes not patterned after Federal Rule 44.1 either have no notice requirement at all, or provide that the parties' failure to give timely notice does not preclude the court from looking into the foreign law.[78]

This, however, is not a complete answer to the question of preclusion. Even when, as in New York and a number of other states, the judicial notice statute itself contains no preclusionary rule, belated resort to the foreign law may be precluded by general principles of

---

or their political subdivisions." (Emphasis added). The reader will recall that on the basis of this Rule the court in the Frummer case, supra, did not hesitate to take judicial notice of English law, even though neither party had referred to it.

In California, on the other hand, where the relevant statute (Evidence Code Sec. 452) is neutral on this point, it may be thought that the Hurtado dictum, quoted supra n. 57, forecloses judicial notice of uninvoked foreign law. See also supra n. 65.

74. See Currie, supra n. 30, at 981 (1958).

75. See, e.g., the Frummer case, supra.

76. See, e.g., the Ruff case, infra. See also Sonnesen v. Panama Transp. Co., 298 N.Y. 262, 82 N.E.2d 569 (1948), reargument denied 298 N.Y. 856, 84 N.E.2d 324 (1949), cert. denied 337 U.S. 919, 69 S.Ct. 1157 (1949).

77. See the *Ruff* case, infra.

78. See supra n. 73.

procedure. Suppose, for instance, that in a jury case the judge has instructed the jury in accordance with domestic law, and the parties have failed to raise the foreign law issue by timely requests or exceptions. In such a case, it might well be too late to argue on appeal that the judge committed error by charging the jury in accordance with the law of the forum.[79]

Even in a nonjury case, a foreign law issue may be similarly precluded if raised too late. Suppose, for instance, that in an action brought in a state court the complaint alleges invasion of privacy. Although the allegedly tortious acts occurred in Ruritania, where the plaintiff lived at the time, the case is tried on the assumption that it is governed by the law of the forum. After a trial without a jury, the court holds for the plaintiff. On appeal, the defendant for the first time claims that the law of Ruritania controls, and he submits ample materials demonstrating that under the law of that country an invasion of privacy such as shown in this case is not actionable. Even though the forum state's judicial notice statute contains no notice requirement, the point may be precluded. It is true, of course, that pursuant to the classical rule the defendant may at any time, and even for the first time on appeal, point to the legal insufficiency of the complaint.[80] But the classical rule has been changed in a number of states.[81] Under the influence of Federal Rule 12(h),[82] several states now provide that after the end of the trial a defendant may no longer attack the sufficiency of the complaint unless he has previously raised the objection.[83]

These preclusionary rules are technical and refined. Suppose that in the hypothetical invasion of privacy case the trial court, although applying domestic law, for some reason had dismissed the complaint, and the plaintiff had appealed. In that event, it might be possible for the defendant, *as appellee*, to urge affirmance on the basis of Ruritanian law. Some cases, at least, seem to suggest this distinction in favor of the appellee.[84]

In many jurisdictions, moreover, there is a more general rule that prohibits the parties, or at least the appellant, from raising new points of any kind for the first time on appeal.[84a] True, this rule is applied

79. See, e.g., FRCP Rule 51; N.Y. CPLR §§ 4017, 4110 b, 5501.

80. See Clark on Code Pleading 533, 736–37 (1947).

81. See, e.g., Ariz.R.Civ.P. 12(i); N.C.R. Civ.P. 12(h); Vt.R.Civ.P. 12(h).

82. See Black, Sivalls & Bryson, Inc. v. Shondell, 174 F.2d 587 (8th Cir. 1949).

83. See, e.g., Dale v. Lattimore, 12 N.C. App. 348, 183 S.E.2d 417 (1971).

In a jurisdiction in which foreign law does not have to be pleaded, or failure to plead it is not fatal, the objection may be thought to go to the sufficiency of the evidence rather than to the sufficiency of the complaint. Even so, however, the objection may be precluded by the defendant's failure, at the time when he moved for dismissal at the end of the plaintiff's case or at the end of the whole case, to specify the foreign law point as a ground for such motion. See, e.g., J. Weinstein, H. Korn & A. Miller, New York Civil Practice ¶ 4401.09 (1963).

84. See Southard v. Southard, 305 F.2d 730 (2d Cir. 1962); Archer v. United States, 217 F.2d 548 (9th Cir. 1954), cert. denied 348 U.S. 953, 75 S.Ct. 441 (1955).

84a. See, e.g., 14 Cyclopedia of Federal Procedure § 67.09 (3d ed. 1983 Reprint).

with considerable flexibility, and it is generally thought that an appellate court, in its discretion, can disregard the rule whenever its strict application would lead to injustice.[85] In spite of its flexibility, however, the rule lurks in the appellate practice of most jurisdictions. A lawyer devising litigation strategy in a foreign law case thus should keep in mind that even under the most liberal judicial notice statute, it may be dangerous to hold a foreign law point in reserve for an eventual appeal.

In any event, in order properly to appraise the consequences of a failure to invoke or prove the applicable foreign law, one must realize that the pertinent common-law rules [86] interact not only with judicial notice statutes but also with other, more general rules of trial and appellate procedure, and that under rules of the latter kind a foreign law point may be precluded unless seasonably raised.[87]

LOEBIG v. LARUCCI

United States Court of Appeals, Second Circuit, 1978.
572 F.2d 81.

[Some of Court's footnotes omitted, others renumbered.]

MOORE, Circuit Judge. This diversity action arose from a traffic accident in Nuremberg, Germany. The jury found in favor of defendant Larucci, and plaintiff Loebig's complaint was dismissed on April 7, 1977. From the judgment entered upon the verdict of no cause for action, plaintiff appeals. The only question presented concerns the specificity of the jury charge—whether the district court erred in refusing specifically to charge the substance of the New York Vehicle and Traffic Law regarding the standard of care to be used when entering intersections. Appellant contends that the court erred by failing to read either the applicable statute or the suggested charge based on the statute, which provided that a driver should drive at an appropriate reduced speed when approaching an intersection.

I.

On April 26, 1971, in the City of Nuremberg, Germany, Loebig was the passenger on a Honda motorcycle owned and operated by Larucci. Larucci was a resident of Schenevus, New York, and at the time was stationed in Germany as a member of the United States Army. Loebig was a resident of Pittsburgh, Pennsylvania, and was an American civilian having been discharged from the military service in April, 1970. Since the complaint alleged an amount in controversy in excess

85. See Jannenga v. Nationwide Life Ins. Co., 288 F.2d 169 (D.C.Cir. 1961), noted in 14 Stan.L.Rev. 162 (1961). See also H. Cohen & A. Karger, The Powers of the New York Court of Appeals §§ 161–69 (1952); 14 Cyclopedia of Federal Procedure, supra n. 84a.

86. See supra, text at nn. 15–57.

87. In the original version of this article, the foregoing analysis was followed by some suggestions to improve the judicial handling of the many cases in which the parties have failed to invoke or prove the applicable foreign law. These suggestions are not reproduced here; the interested reader will find them in 59 Cornell L.Rev., at 23–26 (1973).

of $10,000, this is a case of diversity jurisdiction under 28 U.S.C.A. § 1332.

At the time of the accident, about 5:55 P.M., Larucci was driving his motorcycle in an easterly direction on Bayern Street, a four-lane road with a median strip. As he approached the intersection, the traffic signal in the east-west direction was green, and his speed was "thirty or thirty-five miles an hour." [1] . . . The street in Larucci's direction of travel contained heavy traffic. As he approached the intersection without reducing his speed, Larucci noticed a car, operated by Robert Morrison, stopped at the intersection facing west. When Larucci's motorcycle was only about 15 feet from Morrison's car, Morrison pulled out abruptly, attempting to turn left toward the south. The two vehicles collided, and both riders of the motorcycle were hurled through the air. Loebig sustained serious injuries to his head and body, which served as the basis for this suit. Morrison admitted not seeing the motorcycle and was issued a citation for failure to yield the right of way.

II.

At the close of the evidence, both parties made requests to charge which included recital of specific sections of the New York traffic law, N.Y.Veh. & Traf.Law (McKinney) § 1 et seq. The appellee requested charges concerning § 1141 (vehicle turning left), § 1162 (starting parked vehicle), and § 1190 (reckless driving). . . . The appellant requested a charge concerning § 1180(a), (e) (appropriate speed entering intersection).[2]

In the discussions of the charge among the attorneys and the court, the court said,

> "I did read your requests, and I think that you are both agreed that we are going to instruct the jury upon the New York State Law regarding negligence, and contributory negligence, and I don't know about all of these other statutes. You have a lot of statutes here." . . .

Although appellee's attorney agreed to stipulate to withdraw his request concerning the statutes, appellant's attorney refused to stipu-

---

1. The speed limit was thirty-one or thirty-seven miles per hour, depending on interpretation of the military police report. . . .

[No mention was made by the parties of any other specific applicable German traffic statutes. The speed limit within German municipalities, unless posted differently, is 50 km, or about 31.5 miles. Ed.]

2. Sections 1180(a) and (e) read as follows:

(a) No person shall drive a vehicle at a speed greater than is reasonable and prudent under the conditions and having regard to the actual and potential hazards then existing. . . .

(e) The driver of every vehicle shall, consistent with the requirements of subdivision (a) of this section, drive at an appropriate reduced speed when approaching and crossing an intersection or railway grade crossing, when approaching and going around a curve, when approaching a hill crest, when traveling upon any narrow or winding roadway, and when any special hazard exists with respect to pedestrians, or other traffic by reason of weather or highway conditions.

late to "throw out" his charge request relating to § 1180(a), (e). The court noted:

> ". . . I will refuse number one of the Plaintiff, and take all of the statute out because to me it just doesn't make sense to give New York statutory law by reading the law, or by some interpretation concerning an accident that happened over in Germany." . . .[3]

The judge then made a general charge concerning the proper standard of care to be used in the operation of a motor vehicle. This charge included consideration of the speed of the appellee's vehicle. The court charged:

> "Consider all of the circumstances that were described by Mr. Larucci, and the time of day, and the visibility, and the speed he maintained, and the traffic conditions and the observations that he had of the intersection as he came into it.
>
> . . .
>
> "Each of them [Morrison and Larucci] was under a duty to maintain a reasonable safe rate of speed, and to have his automobile or motorcycle under reasonable control, and keep a proper lookout under the circumstances then existing, and to see if he was aware of what was in his view, and use reasonable care to avoid an accident." . . .

III.

In determining the propriety of the charge, the applicable substantive law must be determined. This court is bound by the choice of law rules of the forum state, New York. Klaxon Co. v. Stentor Electric Manufacturing Co., 313 U.S. 487, 61 S.Ct. 1020, 85 L.Ed. 1477 (1941); Rosenthal v. Warren, 475 F.2d 438, 440 (2d Cir. 1973).

[The opinion then discusses the New York choice-of-law rule, and concludes that the New York courts would treat the issue of defendant's exercise of due care in the operation of his motorcycle as governed by the law of the place of the accident.]

Thus, in this case, German law is the applicable law for determining the proper standard of care for the appellee.

Rule 44.1 of the Federal Rules of Civil Procedure permits parties to present information on foreign law, and the court may make its own

---

3. In response to the judge's comments, appellant's lawyer somewhat cryptically answered, "That is fine, Your Honor". (58a). This could be interpreted as the lawyer failing to take exception to the charge. The next day, after the charge was given to the jury, appellant's lawyer had "[n]o objections" and "[n]o further requests" to charge. . . . However, before beginning court on the day of the charge, counsel met in chambers with the judge. The judge, in refusing certain of appellee's requests for charge, stated to appellee's lawyer, "[A]nything that I refuse here now, you have an exception to automatically, if it becomes a question on appeal." . . . Since appellant's lawyer may well have believed that the statement was also addressed to him, for purposes of this appeal we assume that exceptions were properly taken by the appellant.

determination of foreign law based on its own research, but it is not mandatory that it do so. In the district court appellant did present a brief in which he conceded that German law is applicable as to the standard of care. Appellant further argued that German law is the same as New York law in this regard. The brief stated:

"Section 276 of the [German] Civil Code defines negligence as the failure to use the care requisite in one's dealings with others. The standard is 'that degree of care which is considered proper in the circumstances by ordinary prudent persons.' [Citation]." Brief on Behalf of Plaintiff at 4.

Appellant continued in describing that standard of care:

"Relevant to this case are the developed rules that 'the driver of a motor vehicle must maintain a speed low enough to avert accidents and traffic disturbances.' [Citation] . . ." Id. at 5.

In conclusion the appellant submitted "that the above stated standard of care and applicable doctrines should be applied in this case." Id. If this is deemed to be an offer of proof of applicable law, then the charge to the jury was a fair description of German law as proved by the appellant.

Assuming that this was not a complete offer of proof as to German law, the problem remains—determining the proper law to apply. In cases involving the law of common law countries, New York courts generally assume that the foreign law is the same as New York law. "If the contract were made or the tort committed in a state or country the foundation of whose jurisprudence is known to be the common law the presumption is indulged that the common law still prevails there and that it is the same as the common law of New York. . . ." Arams v. Arams, 182 Misc. 328, 45 N.Y.S.2d 251, 254 (Sup.Ct.N.Y.Co. 1943). Such a presumption generally is not indulged with respect to a civil law country; New York courts have not presumed the law of a civil law country to be the same as New York law. Riley v. Pierce Oil Corp., 245 N.Y. 152, 156 N.E. 647 (1927); Bril v. Suomen Pankki Finlands Bank, 199 Misc. 11, 97 N.Y.S.2d 22, 37 (Sup.Ct.Erie Co.1950); Savage v. O'Neil, 44 N.Y. 298, 300 (1871).[4]

When there is no presumption that New York law is the same as foreign law and no evidence has been presented as to foreign law, New York courts have decided the cases in accordance with New York law. *Savage*, supra; *Bril*, supra; *Arams*, supra; Smith v. Compania Litografica de La Habana, 127 Misc. 508, 512, 217 N.Y.S. 39 (Sup.Ct. Kings Co.1926).[5] In Watts v. Swiss Bank Corp., 27 N.Y.2d 270, 317

4. In at least one case, a New York court has presumed that the law was the same. Revillon v. Demme, 114 Misc. 1, 185 N.Y.S. 443 (Sup.Ct.Kings Co.1920).

5. This practice has not been universally followed in New York. In Riley v. Pierce Oil Corp., 245 N.Y. 152, 156 N.E. 647 (1927), the complaint was dismissed, in an action for conversion of oil extracted from the ground, because the plaintiff did not show the law of Mexico where the conversion allegedly occurred. That case was similar to Cuba Railroad Co. v. Crosby, 222 U.S. 473, 32 S.Ct. 132, 56 L.Ed. 274 (1912) where an employee suing his employer for injuries sustained in Cuba could

Choice of law rules are generally not mandatory — may contract for law of a particular forum although court would not on its own choose that foreign

FOREIGN LAW IN OUR COURTS 119

N.Y.S.2d 315, 265 N.E.2d 739 (1970), Judge (now Chief Judge) Breitel stated that "under modern principles, in the absence of manifest injustice, a total failure to raise or prove foreign law should not inevitably prevent the application of forum law". Id. at 276, 317 N.Y.S.2d at 320, 265 N.E.2d at 743. The court found that "court[s] will allow the parties by default in pleading or proof to agree or acquiesce that forum law is applied". (Citations omitted.) Id. In the case at bar the parties at least acquiesced in the application of New York law by their failure to prove German law and their requests to charge based on New York law.

In following New York law, certainly New York courts would assume that the general negligence standard of care would be applicable. It is unlikely, however, in a case arising out of an accident in Germany, that the courts would add the statutory refinements to the standard of care to include the apparent slight extra duty of care in approaching intersections. Although New York law may be applicable *rule* in the absence of proof of German law, strict statutory refinements in New York law should not be held binding as the standard of care for operation of a vehicle in Germany.

In addition, the appellant failed to prove any statutory necessity in Germany for drivers to reduce their speed as they approach intersections. Appellant also presented a brief indicating that the general negligence law of Germany was the same as that of New York. These two facts are sufficient to hold the appellant to have consented to the application of only so much of the New York law, regarding the standard of care, as the district court considered was consistent with German law. . . .

Affirmed.

NOTES AND QUESTIONS

(1) Did the Court in the principal case follow the older view—that in a diversity action the consequences of failure to invoke or prove the applicable foreign law are governed by state law—or the contrary view of Professor Miller? If the former, how is this approach to be reconciled with the same court's decision in Vishipco, quoted supra on p. 99?

(2) In the principal case the Court apparently held that in the absence of sufficient information on the applicable German law the district judge committed no error when he (a) instructed the jury in accordance with the forum's general doctrine concerning the standard of care to be observed by a motorist, but (b) declined to include in his

not recover without proving that the law of Cuba imposed liability upon the employer. Like *Cuba Railroad, Riley* dealt with a refinement in the law—the case depended upon Mexico's conception of the nature of oil rights. The case at bar is, on the other hand, in the class of "rudimentary contracts or torts made or committed abroad . . . [where] courts would assume a liabil- ity to exist if nothing to the contrary appeared" because "[s]uch matters are likely to impose an obligation in all civilized countries." 222 U.S. at 478, 32 S.Ct. at 132. The question here is not whether Germany would apply negligence law, but what standard of care is encompassed by negligence law.

jury instructions any reference to a forum statute specifically requiring reduction of speed at intersections.

How do you explain the seeming inconsistency between (a) and (b)? In this connection, consider the following:

(a) As to the general principle of due care prevailing in German law, the Court by "cursory independent research" (see supra p. 107) could have confirmed that in all likelihood such principle was similar to that recognized in New York. Therefore (there being no factors present in this case that would strongly militate against application of forum law), New York law was applied in dealing with this point.

(b) New York Vehicle and Traffic Law § 1180(e), on the other hand, imposes a "peculiar obligation".* This provision obviously found favor with the New York legislator; but there is no reason for assuming that other jurisdictions are likely to have enacted a similar rule. As the issue is clearly governed by German law, the question arises whether it is sensible to indulge in the presumption that § 1180(e) has a German counterpart. The Court answers this question in the negative, and thus throws upon the plaintiff the burden of proving the existence, in German law, of such a peculiar statute.

(3) Does the principal case call for a modification of the analysis set forth in the article immediately preceding the case? Or does the case confirm that analysis?

3. THE PRE–TRIAL PHASE: PLEADING AND NOTICE–GIVING IN FOREIGN LAW CASES

AN UNREPORTED CASE

P, a high official of the Government of Ruritania (a civil-law country), brought an action in a New York court against D, an American corporation with headquarters in New York City which conducts a world-wide publishing business. The complaint alleged that D had published a magazine article ridiculing P as an incompetent official, and that the publication of this article had occurred (among other places) in Ruritania, where P was domiciled at all times. The alleged defamatory statements, which assertedly caused grave damage to P's reputation, were set forth in the complaint; but the complaint was silent with respect to the law of Ruritania. D moved to dismiss the complaint on the ground that it failed to state one of the essential elements of P's cause of action, namely the controlling Ruritanian law.[1]

---

* Restatement, Second, Conflict of Laws § 136, com. (h), at 380 (1971).

1. The reader may assume that the question of the sufficiency of the complaint is governed by Ruritanian law. See Restatement, Second, Conflict of Laws §§ 149, 150 (1971). If the forum's domestic law controlled, the absence of any allegation of malice (or reckless disregard of the truth) probably would vitiate the complaint under the rule of New York Times v. Sullivan, 376 U.S. 254, 84 S.Ct. 710 (1964).

For purposes of the case stated in the text, supra, it is further assumed that an American court would not apply the constitutional principles of New York Times v.

While the court had the motion under consideration, the case was settled. What would have been the court's decision, if it had become necessary to determine the motion? The Notes and Questions which follow, contain some hints that may be helpful in resolving this problem.

Pleading and Notice Giving

NOTES AND QUESTIONS

(1) If this problem arose in one of the minority states which have not adopted an applicable judicial notice statute, the court either would treat the complaint as failing to state a material "fact," or it would apply the substantive law of the forum. In this particular case, it would make no difference whether the court uses one or the other of these two approaches; [1a] either way, the complaint would be dismissed (or the demurrer sustained), although perhaps with leave to amend.

(2) What would be the answer in a forum state where there is a simple judicial notice statute, i.e., a statute which, while authorizing judicial notice of foreign-country law, is silent on the pleading point? In such a jurisdiction, the determination of the motion probably would depend on whether or not the court is willing to take judicial notice of Ruritanian law. If the court, aided perhaps by materials which P in opposing the motion has informally submitted, takes such notice, and finds that under Ruritanian law the complaint states a good cause of action, the motion should be denied. A party who has failed to plead a material fact, may be prevented from introducing any formal evidence to prove such fact; but the taking of judicial notice is not similarly dependent on the pleadings.[1b] Nor does this result inflict any hardship on D. If D, in order to draft his answer or to prepare for trial, needs further information concerning the Ruritanian law on which P relies, it can make a motion to make more definite, or request a bill of particulars.[2]

On the other hand, the court may decline to take judicial notice; almost certainly this will be the court's reaction if P fails to submit helpful information on the relevant aspects of Ruritanian law. In that event, the judicial notice statute has no further impact on the decision, and the motion will have to be determined in the same way as in a state having no such statute.

pleading rule NY *

(3) In New York, the problem is more difficult, because it involves the interplay between the judicial notice provision (R 4511, supra) and an express pleading requirement (R 3016(e), supra).[3] When one at-

pleading law of foreign country, substance of the law must be stated

Sullivan to an alleged libel published in, and governed by the law of, a foreign country. The point, however, is not entirely free from doubt. See Deroburt v. Gannett Co., Inc., 83 F.R.D. 574 (D.Haw. 1979); F. K. Juenger, Trends in European Conflicts Law, 60 Cornell L.Rev. 969, 984 (1975).

1a. The reason is that this particular complaint fails to state a good cause of action under the domestic law of the forum. See supra n. 1. If the facts alleged in the complaint constituted a valid cause of action under forum law, the matter would be a bit more complicated; in that event it would become crucial for the court

to choose between the Crosby approach (which would lead to dismissal of the complaint) and the forum-law approach (under which the complaint, being good according to forum law, would be upheld).

1b. See Pfleuger v. Pfleuger, 304 N.Y. 148, 106 N.E.2d 495 (1952).

2. Ibid. See also Haines v. Cook Electric Co., 20 A.D.2d 517, 244 N.Y.S.2d 483 (1st Dept. 1963).

3. The pleading requirement was added by legislative second-guessers against the advice of the original draftsmen of the

tempts to reconcile these provisions, two antithetical lines of reasoning suggest themselves:

(a) Rule 3016(e) deals with pleading, while the whole of Rule 4511, including the notice provision in the last sentence of subdivision (b), addresses itself to proof and to judicial notice as a substitute for proof. This is shown not only by the wording of the two Rules but also by their systematic location in the CPLR. It follows that a motion raising purely a pleading problem should be determined pursuant to R 3016(e), without regard to R 4511.

(b) Rule 3016(e) is controlling in a case in which the court is not compelled, and does not choose, to take judicial notice.[4] But if in the above case the plaintiff—in his papers in opposition to the motion—furnishes sufficient information on Ruritanian law and gives notice of his intention to request judicial notice, the court may *have to* comply with such request pursuant to R 4511(b), and is in any event free to do so. As pointed out above, the pleading requirement becomes irrelevant once the court takes judicial notice of Ruritanian law.

Do you find (a) or (b) more convincing? Does Frummer v. Hilton Hotels International, supra, support either line of argument?[5]

Even on the assumption that argument (b) ultimately will prevail, it is certainly not safe for a pleader to omit allegations of foreign law if his cause of action, or his defense,[6] depends on the law of a civil-law country.[6a] As we have seen, the common-law approach asserts itself whenever the court refuses to take judicial notice of the foreign law; and there is always a possibility of such refusal. True, a portion of R 4511(b) is couched in mandatory language ("shall"); but the court may find that the information furnished by a party is not "sufficient", or that the notice given has been inadequate.

(4) The preceding Notes suggest that in most states a party may, under certain circumstances, still suffer adverse consequences if his complaint or other pleading fails to allege the foreign-country law on which he relies.[7] Thus, there presents itself a practical how-to-do-it question. What degree of particularity is required in alleging foreign law?

CPLR. See 3 Weinstein-Korn-Miller, New York Civil Practice ¶3016.15 (1968).

4. See, e.g., Taca International Airlines, S.A. v. Rolls Royce, 47 Misc.2d 771, 263 N.Y.S.2d 209 (Sp.T.N.Y.Co. 1965).

5. Argument (b) seems to be supported not only by the majority of commentators, but also by Dresdner Bank v. Edelmann, 129 Misc.2d 686, 493 N.Y.S.2d 703 (Sup. Ct., N.Y. County, 1985), and perhaps by dicta in Gevinson v. Kirkeby-Natus Corp., 26 A.D.2d 71, 270 N.Y.S.2d 989 (1st Dept. 1966); but the controversy is not yet authoritatively resolved.

6. Where the validity of a defense depends on foreign law, but such law is neither properly alleged nor judicially noticed, a motion to strike the defense as insufficient will be granted, with or with- out leave to amend. See Sinai v. Levi, 208 Misc. 650, 654–55, 144 N.Y.S.2d 316, 320–21 (City Ct., N.Y.Co. 1955).

6a. What is said in the text, supra, is particularly true in a case where the pleader's cause of action or defense is invalid under forum law, and where, consequently, even the forum-law approach leads to the granting of a motion to dismiss the complaint or to strike the defense as insufficient in law. See supra n. 1a.

7. The statement in the text probably applies to all states, with the possible exception of those which have adopted statutes or Rules modeled after Federal Rule 44.1. The (somewhat different) notice requirement of the latter Rule will be discussed infra.

Some courts have seemed inclined to dismiss a complaint, or strike a defense, unless the relevant foreign code sections, statutes, and perhaps even judicial decisions, are set forth *in haec verba*. The prevailing view, however, appears to be that, as against a motion to dismiss or to strike, a pleading is sufficient if it states the ultimate "fact", i.e., the *substance* of the foreign law; an opponent who needs more detailed information may seek it by corrective motion, by requesting a bill of particulars, or by discovery devices.[8] In New York, Rule 3016(e) expressly confirms the view that "the substance of the foreign law relied upon" should be pleaded; nevertheless, in exceptional circumstances New York courts may dismiss a complaint, or strike a defense, unless it contains "specific reference to the code or other provision of law relied upon to facilitate research by adverse party and the court." [9]

Suppose in the above Unreported Case the complaint is dismissed, with leave to file an amended complaint properly setting forth the applicable Ruritanian law. In drafting the amended complaint, how would you formulate the paragraph alleging the foreign law?

The simplest and most sensible form of pleading the substance of the pertinent foreign law (subject to possible amplification by bill of particulars) would be an allegation that "D's aforesaid acts constitute an actionable wrong under the law of Ruritania." At least one lower court, however, has frowned upon a complaint containing a foreign law allegation thus phrased.[10]

(5) If in the above Unreported Case the action had been brought in a federal District Court, would the complaint be dismissed because of its lack of allegations concerning Ruritanian law? See Rule 44.1 and the Advisory Committee Note, supra.

Note that under Rule 44.1 the form of defendant's 12(b)(6) motion may influence the subsequent proceedings. If in his motion papers the defendant expressly alludes to the complaint's failure to allege the applicable Ruritanian law, this allusion may be regarded as an invocation, by the defendant, of "an issue concerning the law of a foreign country" within the meaning of the first sentence of Rule 44.1. Thus the Rule's notice requirement is satisfied (see the Advisory Committee Note, supra), and the court now has the power to consult Ruritanian law; probably it will do so if the plaintiff, alerted by defendant's motion, submits adequate information concerning such law.

If, on the other hand, defendant's 12(b)(6) motion does not mention Ruritanian law (and plaintiff does not refer to it in opposing the motion), the first sentence of Rule 44.1 arguably precludes the court from looking at Ruritanian law.[11]

8. See O. C. Sommerich and B. Busch, Foreign Law—A Guide to Pleading and Proof 29–38 (1959), where helpful sample pleadings are set forth. For other samples, emphasizing greater and perhaps excessive particularity, see McKenzie and Sarabia, The Pleading and Proof of Alien Law, 30 Tul.L.Rev. 353, 361–64 (1956).

9. Taca International Airlines v. Rolls Royce, supra n. 4, at 772.

10. Andretto Bank A.G. v. Goodbody & Co., 15 Misc.2d 395, 181 N.Y.S.2d 343 (Sp. T.N.Y.Co. 1958). On the other hand, an allegation of special damages is not necessary unless Ruritanian law treats special damages as a pre-condition of recovery in a libel action of this kind. See Andretto Bank A.G. v. Goodbody & Co., 10 A.D.2d 696, 197 N.Y.S.2d 793 (1st Dept. 1960).

11. It does not follow, however, that defendant's 12(b)(6) motion would be granted. The first sentence of Rule 44.1 makes it clear that the required "notice" does not have to be given in the pleadings. The

This leads to a broader question: Does the notice requirement in the first sentence of Rule 44.1 have any teeth? The case which follows has a bearing on this question.

RUFF v. ST. PAUL MERCURY INSURANCE CO.

United States Court of Appeals, Second Circuit, 1968.
393 F.2d 500.

Before LUMBARD, Chief Judge and WATERMAN and KAUFMAN, Circuit Judges.

PER CURIAM. The sole issue on appeal is whether a work-connected disability which appellant sustained in Liberia due to contracting poliomyelitis, which concededly is an endemic disease in Liberia, entitles him to benefits under the terms of an insurance policy which his employer had taken out for the benefit of appellant and its other employees serving in foreign countries.

Charles Ruff, a Pennsylvania citizen, commenced this action in the Southern District against the St. Paul Mercury Insurance Company, a Minnesota corporation, for specific performance of an employer's liability insurance policy issued to Ruff's employer, the Institute of International Education, Inc. Admitting that Ruff, who was teaching law at the Arthur Grimes School of Law of the University of Liberia, was covered by the policy, the insurer pleaded as an affirmative defense that Ruff's injury, resulting from endemic disease, was excluded from coverage under the terms of the policy. Judge Wyatt sustained the defense and dismissed the complaint.

[After an analysis of the pertinent provisions of the policy, the court approves Judge Wyatt's conclusion that disabilities due to endemic disease were specifically excluded from coverage.] While the result is not one which we like to reach, we cannot rewrite the policy because of our sympathy for Ruff.

Ruff's other contention, that this court should take judicial notice of the Liberian Workmen's Compensation Act and apply its provisions to invalidate the limitation against recovery for endemic disease, is not properly before us. A party must give "reasonable written notice" in the district court proceedings in order to raise an issue concerning the law of a foreign country on appeal. Fed.R.Civ.P. 44.1. No written

plaintiff, therefore, may still have time to give such notice. See Grice v. A/S J. Ludwig Mowinckels, 477 F.Supp. 365, 367 (S.D. Ala. 1979), where the reason for the rule is colorfully explained. Moreover, even if the Ruritanian law is treated as uninvoked, it must be remembered that under general principles of notice-pleading the plaintiff has stated a claim sufficient to defeat a 12(b)(6) motion unless it is *inconceivable* that, consistent with the allegations of the complaint, plaintiff can prove facts giving rise to a claim. In the above Unreported Case, it is not inconceivable that at the trial plaintiff might prove malice, even though no malice is alleged in the complaint. Thus a 12(b)(6) motion is likely to fail even if the court cannot, or does not, look at Ruritanian law in disposing of the motion.

notice that appellant intended to rely upon Liberian law was given in the district court.*

In any event, were we to consider Liberian law in deciding this appeal, we do not see how it could change the result. While Ruff might have a cause of action against his employer under Liberian law and Coverage B of the endorsement obligates the insurer "To pay on behalf of the insured all sums which the insured shall become legally obligated to pay as damages because of bodily injury caused by accident or disease . . . sustained by an employee . . . arising out of and in the course of his employment. . . .", the scope of that coverage . . . is limited by the specific provision in Section 4 that "The provisions of this policy shall not apply to injury or death due to or arising out of endemic disease." **

The judgment is affirmed.

NOTES AND QUESTIONS

(1) The judges who decided the principal case admittedly realized that the result reached by them was a harsh one. They probably felt that to hold otherwise would render the Rule's notice requirement toothless. *Quaere*, however, whether the notice provision really loses all of its teeth if construed differently, e.g., as meaning that nonobservance of the notice requirement should make the court *reluctant* to take judicial notice, but would not completely destroy its *power* to do so. See, in this sense, Stuart v. United States, 813 F.2d 243, 251 (9th Cir. 1987), and Valdes v. Leisure Resource Group, Inc., 810 F.2d 1345, 1349 n. 2 (5th Cir. 1987).

(2) What exactly is the effect of a party's failure to comply with the notice requirement of Rule 44.1? Does such failure make itself felt only on appeal, or can it affect the outcome of the case in the district court? [1]

When an issue is governed by the law of country X, and the parties' failure to give timely notice makes it impossible for the court to

* This holding—that by his counsel's failure to give seasonable notice pursuant to Rule 44.1 the plaintiff is precluded from relying on the Liberian Workmen's Compensation Act—is the first of the two alternative holdings on which the decision rests.

** This paragraph of the opinion contains the second alternative holding, to the effect that even if the court were to take judicial notice of the Liberian law, plaintiff would still lose in this action against the insurance company, because Liberian law, although it might enlarge the liability of the employer, under fundamental choice-of-law principles could not change the effect of an insurance policy issued by an American insurer to an American insured (i.e., Ruff's employer).

The combined effect of the Court's two alternative holdings seems to be that the plaintiff might have won his case if (1) he had sued his employer rather than the insurance company, and if (2) he had given timely notice of his intention to raise an issue concerning Liberian law.

1. In order to answer this question, re-read the Note of the Advisory Committee, supra p. 60. In First Nat. Bank of Arizona v. British Petroleum Co., 324 F.Supp. 1348 (S.D.N.Y. 1971), the court permitted the defendant to raise an issue of Iranian law seven years after the commencement of the action, noting that defendant had not been aware of the issue for most of that time, and that plaintiff suffered no prejudice by the lateness of the notice. Significantly, the court remarked (at 1355) that its decision would be different if defendant had delayed "solely for strategic reasons".

consider the law of X, the case must nevertheless be decided. In order to arrive at a decision, the court will resort either to the Crosby approach or to the forum-law approach. See supra pp. 88–120, and especially pp. 100–108. In the principal case, it is arguable that the plaintiff must lose under either approach. In many situations, however,[2] the difference between the two approaches is just as crucial in a federal court as it would be in a state court.

(3) Often a party will give only minimal notice under Rule 44.1, e.g., by stating that "Plaintiff's cause of action is based on the law of Ruritania." Perhaps the court, which has broad discretion in this respect, will treat such notice as meeting the Rule's requirement, although the defendant has been given no information concerning the theories of Ruritanian law, or the authorities, on which plaintiff expects to rely. How can a defendant (or a plaintiff, in case the defendant has given notice of his intention to invoke foreign law in support of a defense) protect himself against surprise in such a situation?

Bills of particulars no longer exist in federal courts; but by a motion for a more definite statement, a pleader may be compelled to disclose at least the substance of the foreign law which he will invoke.[3] More frequently, parties seek to resort to interrogatories and other forms of discovery in order to obtain an advance look at the opponent's arsenal of foreign authorities. In Owens-Illinois, Inc. v. Commissioner, 76 T.C. 493, 496 (1981), the United States Tax Court said:

> In view of the flexibility intended by rule 44.1, FRCP, and our Rule 146, it is clear that issues of foreign law can be framed, molded, and even settled prior to trial in a number of ways, one of the most important of which is discovery. Interrogatories to parties and requests for admissions can be used to refine and sharpen disputed issues and assemble information relating to foreign matters. 9 C. Wright & A. Miller, Federal Practice and Procedure: Civil, sec. 2444 (1971). In our view, discovery is an appropriate tool to enable a party to make a reasoned judgment as to the applicability of foreign law.

> The unique character of foreign law, as well as the high cost of obtaining materials and experts, leads us to conclude that, at the least, a party should be able to use discovery to find the periphery of the foreign law in issue. We reach this conclusion even if it should result in a slightly wider scope of inquiry than is available on issues of domestic law. A. Miller, Federal Rule 44.1, 65 Mich.L.Rev. at 666. All parties should know the elements of the specific foreign laws upon which one of the parties relies.

The court went on to hold, however, that in view of the work product doctrine, its discovery order extended only to relevant materials not prepared in anticipation of litigation and not protected by privilege. Id. at 497. It concluded, nevertheless, by pointing out that under the Tax Court's discovery rule molded after Federal Rule 26, the party seeking

---

2. Especially where the claim or defense in question would be valid under the domestic law of the forum.

3. Keasbey & Mattison Co. v. Rothensies, 1 F.R.D. 626 (E.D.Pa. 1941); United States v. National City Bank, 7 F.R.D. 241 (S.D.N.Y. 1946). These decisions are based on Rule 12(e), which in terms applies only if the 44.1 notice is contained in a pleading; it is arguable, however, that by analogy the same principle should operate in a case where the notice happens to have been given outside of the formal pleadings.

discovery "apparently could get more information than we are permitting at this stage . . . with respect to petitioner's foreign law expert or experts." Id. at 499.

Rule 26 distinguishes between two types of expert witnesses: (1) those whom a party expects to call as expert witnesses at trial (testifying experts); and (2) those who have been retained in connection with litigation but are not expected to testify (non-testifying experts). Opposing parties can elicit, by interrogatory, the names of testifying experts, as well as statements as to the subject matter and "the substance of the facts and opinions" to which the expert is expected to testify, and a "summary of the grounds" for each opinion. Rule 26(b)(4)(A)(i). The court can also order the testimony of such experts on deposition, id. (ii), and such requests are, to our knowledge, never denied as to experts who are expected to testify as to key issues of foreign-country, international, or former-sovereign law. The identity of testifying experts is, as a rule, disclosed voluntarily or with minimal judicial pre-trial prodding.

The position of non-testifying experts is different. It seems established now that their identity can be discovered upon interrogatory,[4] but the opinions held by non-testifying foreign-law experts can be discovered by the opposing party only "upon a showing of exceptional circumstances under which it is impracticable for the party seeking discovery to obtain facts or opinions on the same subject by other means." Rule 26(b)(4)(B). This "heavy burden"[5] was judicially deemed to have been met in an unreported case involving a foreign-law expert who happens to be a co-author of the present edition.[6]

It should be remembered, moreover, that in many situations, and especially in foreign law cases, the most efficient "discovery" tool may be a motion for summary judgment. Perhaps the motion will be unsuccessful; but in defeating it, the movant's adversary necessarily will have disclosed much of his factual evidence and of his foreign law materials.[7]

4. THE TRIAL PHASE: TECHNIQUES OF PROVING FOREIGN LAW

A. DOCUMENTARY EVIDENCE INCLUDING OFFICIAL CERTIFICATES

INTRODUCTORY NOTE

As has been noted supra p. 80, even those states that do not authorize their courts to take judicial notice of foreign-country law,

4. C. A. Wright & A. R. Miller, 8 Federal Practice and Procedure § 2032 (1970), with further references in note 81 thereat (Supp. 1986, p. 116).

5. Barkwell v. Sturm Ruger Co., Inc., 79 F.R.D. 444, 446 (D. Alaska 1978).

6. State of New Mexico ex rel. Reynolds v. Aamodt, No. A 83 CA 482 (W.D. Tex.

Sept. 16, 1983). The case itself is reported in 618 F.Supp. 993 (D.N.M. 1985).

7. See the last two sentences of FRCP Rule 56(e), as amended in 1963. See also the discussion of motions for summary judgment, supra p. 86.

usually permit the parties to prove a *foreign statute* by way of documentary evidence, subject to some safeguards of authenticity but without the necessity of putting an expert witness on the stand.

The admissibility of other documents often relied upon to prove foreign law, such as *case reports* and *treatises*, cannot be resolved quite so easily. In the absence of a judicial notice statute, it is of course possible to render such documents admissible by stipulation;[1] but when a stipulation cannot be obtained, it may happen that technical objections to the introduction of such documents will prevail under strict rules of evidence. The party seeking to prove the foreign law thus will be compelled to use the more expensive method of presenting an expert witness. Through the examination of a witness who qualifies as an expert on the law of Ruritania, judicial decisions of Ruritanian courts normally can be introduced into the record (see the Fitzpatrick case supra). But the admissibility of a treatise remains a matter of controversy, even when the treatise is used in examining or cross-examining an expert witness.[2]

All of these difficulties in proving written sources and authorities concerning foreign law have been totally removed in the majority jurisdictions that have adopted an applicable judicial notice statute. Such a statute or Rule makes it possible for the parties to submit, and for the court to use, any relevant document. This includes not only copies of statutes, without regard to any formal authentication,[3] but also case reports, treatises[4] and, of course, affidavits or even letters of experts not present in the courtroom.[5]

From a tactical point of view, a party may still find it advantageous to present his version of the foreign law through an expert witness testifying in open court; and this remains the prevailing practice in big and important actions. But in cases where the expense of retaining expert witnesses is not warranted, or where a party cannot afford such expense, the majority jurisdictions now make it possible to prove the foreign law through the informal and relatively inexpensive presentation of written or printed materials. The parties (and, in case he conducts independent research, the judge) are completely free to utilize any document that tends to prove or disprove the disputed proposition of foreign law.

The subject of documentary evidence of foreign law thus has been enormously simplified in the majority of jurisdictions. There remains, however, one kind of document, frequently used for the purpose of proving foreign law, which raises some peculiar problems: a certificate

1. See, e.g., Witt v. Realist, Inc., 18 Wis. 2d 282, 118 N.W.2d 85, 89 (1962).

2. See McCormick on Evidence, § 321 (3d ed. by E. W. Cleary, 1984). In some jurisdictions, there are specific statutes dealing with the use of treatises in the examination and cross-examination of expert witnesses. See, e.g., Fed.R.Evid., Rules 703 and 803(18); Cal.Evid.Code, §§ 721, 802–804.

3. See, e.g., Ramirez v. Autobuses Blancos Flecha Roja, 486 F.2d 493 (5th Cir. 1973).

4. See Fitzgerald v. Texaco, Inc., 521 F.2d 448, 454 (2d Cir. 1975), cert. denied 423 U.S. 1052, 96 S.Ct. 781 (1976); Ramsay v. Boeing Co., 432 F.2d 592, 602 (5th Cir. 1970).

5. See, e.g., Alosio v. Iranian Shipping Lines, S.A., 426 F.Supp. 687, 689 (S.D.N.Y. 1976); Swiss Credit Bank v. Balink, 614 F.2d 1269 (10th Cir. 1980); United States v. First Nat. Bank of Chicago, 699 F.2d 341, 343–45 (7th Cir. 1983).

issued by a governmental authority in country *A* concerning some point of the law of *A*, intended to be used in litigation which, although it involves an issue governed by the law of *A*, is pending in country *B*. Many foreign governments, sometimes pursuant to international treaties,[6] routinely issue such official certificates or opinions concerning their own law for use in litigation in other countries.[7] Our courts, therefore, are frequently faced with such certificates, especially when the foreign government is interested in the litigation.[8] The case which follows presents an example.

U.S. S.C. allows Soviet certificate although it is contrary to U.S. policy ⋆ Important Case

---

UNITED STATES v. PINK, SUPERINTENDENT OF INSURANCE OF THE STATE OF NEW YORK

Supreme Court of the United States, 1942.
315 U.S. 203, 62 S.Ct. 552.

Certiorari, 313 U.S. 553, 61 S.Ct. 960, to review a judgment affirming the dismissal of the complaint in a suit by the United States. . . .

Mr. Justice DOUGLAS delivered the opinion of the Court.

This action was brought by the United States to recover the assets of the New York branch of the First Russian Insurance Co. which remained in the hands of respondent after the payment of all domestic creditors. The material allegations of the complaint were, in brief, as follows:

The First Russian Insurance Co., organized under the laws of the former Empire of Russia, established a New York branch in 1907. It deposited with the Superintendent of Insurance, pursuant to the laws of New York, certain assets to secure payment of claims resulting from transactions of its New York branch. By certain laws, decrees, enactments and orders, in 1918 and 1919, the Russian Government nationalized the business of insurance and all the property, wherever situated, of all Russian insurance companies (including the First Russian Insurance Co.), and discharged and cancelled all the debts of such companies and the rights of all shareholders in all such property. The New York branch of the First Russian Insurance Co. continued to do business in New York until 1925. At that time, respondent, pursuant to an order

---

6. See Cappelletti and Perillo, Civil Procedure in Italy, 410–11 (1965); H. L. Jones, International Judicial Assistance, 62 Yale L.J. 515, 547 (1953). This country is not now a party to any such treaty; but the future may possibly witness a change in this respect. See infra, Notes following the *Pink* case.

7. See Sommerich and Busch, The Expert Witness and the Proof of Foreign Law, 38 Cornell L.Q. 125, 145–7 (1953); Stern, Foreign Law in the Courts, 45 Calif.L.Rev.

23, 37–8 (1957); Nussbaum, The Problem of Proving Foreign Law, 50 Yale L.J. 1018, 1028–30 (1941).

8. See Domke, Some Aspects of the Protection of American Property Interests Abroad, 4 N.Y. City Bar Ass'n Record 268, 271 (1949). Sometimes, the foreign government in its certificate attempts to cover not only rules of law, but also "internal conditions". Cf. In re Siegler's Will, 284 App.Div. 436, 132 N.Y.S.2d 392 (3d Dept. 1954).

of the Supreme Court of New York, took possession of its assets for a determination and report upon the claims of the policyholders and creditors in the United States. Thereafter, all claims of domestic creditors, i.e., all claims arising out of the business of the New York branch, were paid by respondent, leaving a balance in his hands of more than $1,000,000. In 1931, the New York Court of Appeals (255 N.Y. 415, 175 N.E. 114) directed respondent to dispose of that balance as follows: first, to pay claims of foreign creditors . . .; and second, to pay any surplus to a quorum of the board of directors of the company. Pursuant to that mandate, respondent proceeded with the liquidation of the claims of the foreign creditors. Some payments were made thereon. The major portion of the allowed claims, however, were not paid, a stay having been granted pending disposition of the claim of the United States. On November 16, 1933, the United States recognized the Union of Soviet Socialist Republics as the *de jure* Government of Russia and as an incident to that recognition accepted an assignment (known as the Litvinov Assignment) of certain claims.[1]

[Under the terms of the Litvinov Assignment, the Government of the U.S.S.R. assigned to the U.S. Government "the amounts admitted to be due or that may be found to be due" the assignor, "as the successor of prior Governments of Russia, or otherwise, from American nationals, including corporations, companies, partnerships, or associations. . . ."]

Thereafter, the present suit was instituted in the Supreme Court of New York. . . . The complaint prayed, *inter alia*, that the United States be adjudged to be the sole and exclusive owner entitled to immediate possession of the entire surplus fund in the hands of the respondent.

Respondent's answer denied the allegations of the complaint that title to the funds in question passed to the United States and that the Russian decrees had the effect claimed. . . .

The answer was filed in March, 1938. In April, 1939, the New York Court of Appeals decided Moscow Fire Ins. Co. v. Bank of New York & Trust Co., 280 N.Y. 286, 20 N.E.2d 758. . . .

The judgment in that case was affirmed here by an equally divided Court. 309 U.S. 624, 60 S.Ct. 725. . . .

The New York Court of Appeals held in the Moscow case that the Russian decrees in question had no extraterritorial effect. If that is true, it is decisive of the present controversy. For the United States acquired, under the Litvinov Assignment, only such rights as Russia had. Guaranty Trust Co. v. United States, 304 U.S. 126, 143, 58 S.Ct. 785. If the Russian decrees left the New York assets of the Russian insurance companies unaffected, then Russia had nothing here to

1. See Establishment of Diplomatic Relations with the Union of Soviet Socialist Republics, Dept. of State, Eastern Europe- an Series, No. 1 (1933) for the various documents pertaining to recognition.

assign. But that question of foreign law is not to be determined exclusively by the state court. The claim of the United States based on the Litvinov Assignment raises a federal question. United States v. Belmont, 301 U.S. 324, 57 S.Ct. 758. This Court will review or independently determine all questions on which a federal right is necessarily dependent. [Citations.] Here, title obtained under the Litvinov Assignment depends on a correct interpretation of Russian Law. As in cases arising under the full faith and credit clause (Huntington v. Attrill, 146 U.S. 657, 684, 13 S.Ct. 224; Adam v. Saenger, 303 U.S. 59, 64, 58 S.Ct. 454), these questions of foreign law on which the asserted federal right is based are not peculiarly within the cognizance of the local courts. While deference will be given to the determination of the state court, its conclusion is not accepted as final.

We do not stop to review all the evidence in the voluminous record of the Moscow case bearing on the question of the extraterritorial effect of the Russian decrees of nationalization, except to note that the expert testimony tendered by the United States gave great credence to its position. Subsequently to the hearings in that case, however, the United States, through diplomatic channels, requested the Commissariat for Foreign Affairs of the Russian Government to obtain an official declaration by the Commissariat for Justice of the R.S.F.S.R. which would make clear, as a matter of Russian law, the intended effect of the Russian decree nationalizing insurance companies upon the funds of such companies outside of Russia. The official declaration, dated November 28, 1937, reads as follows:

> "The People's Commissariat for Justice of the R.S.F.S.R. certifies that by virtue of the laws of the organs of the Soviet Government all nationalized funds and property of former private enterprises and companies, in particular by virtue of the decree of November 28, 1918 (Collection of Laws of the R.S. F.S.R., 1918, No. 86, Article 904), the funds and property of former insurance companies, constitute the property of the State, irrespective of the nature of the property and irrespective of whether it was situated within the territorial limits of the R.S.F.S.R. or abroad."

The referee in the Moscow case found, and the evidence supported his finding, that the Commissariat for Justice has power to interpret existing Russian law. That being true, this official declaration is conclusive so far as the intended extraterritorial effect of the Russian decree is concerned.* This official declaration was before the court below, though it was not a part of the record. It was tendered pursuant   *⇒ BUT*

---

* Note the transposition of categories here involved: The (obvious) power of the Commissariat (Ministry) of Justice to interpret domestic laws, e.g., by the equivalent of Attorney Generals' Opinions, is regarded as encompassing the power to issue *generally binding* (in civil-law parlance: authentic) interpretations. No known system of government, from the Roman Empire to the present, has vested such power in a cabinet ministry or its equivalent. For details, see infra pp. 133–134.

to § 391 of the New York Civil Practice Act, as amended by L.1933, c. 690.** In New York, it would seem that foreign law must be found by the court (or in the case of a jury trial, binding instructions must be given), though procedural considerations require it to be presented as a question of fact. Fitzpatrick v. International Railway Co., 252 N.Y. 127, 169 N.E. 112; Petrogradsky M. K. Bank v. National City Bank, 253 N.Y. 23, 170 N.E. 479. And under § 391, as amended, it is clear that the New York appellate court has authority to consider appropriate decisions interpreting foreign law, even though they are rendered subsequently to the trial. Los Angeles Investment Securities Corp. v. Joslyn, 282 N.Y. 438, 26 N.E.2d 968.*** We can take such notice of the foreign law as the New York court could have taken.[2] Adam v. Saenger, supra. We conclude that this official declaration of Russian law was not only properly before the court on appeal, but also that it was embraced within those "written authorities" which § 391 authorizes the court to consider, even though not introduced in evidence on the trial. For, while it was not "printed," it would seem to be "other written law" of unquestioned authenticity and authority, within the meaning of § 391.

We hold that, so far as its intended effect is concerned, the Russian decree embraced the New York assets of the First Russian Insurance Co.

The question of whether the decree should be given extraterritorial effect is, of course, a distinct matter. . . .

** At the time of the Pink decision, § 391 read as follows: "A printed copy of a statute, or other written law, of another state, or of a territory, or of a foreign country, or a printed copy of a proclamation, edict, decree or ordinance, by the executive power thereof, contained in a book or publication purporting or proved to have been published by the authority thereof, or proved to be commonly admitted as evidence of the existing law in the judicial tribunals thereof, is presumptive evidence of the statute, law, proclamation, edict, decree or ordinance. The unwritten or common law of another state, or of a territory, or of a foreign country, may be proved as a fact by oral evidence. The books of reports of cases adjudged in the courts thereof must also be admitted as presumptive evidence of the unwritten or common law thereof. The law of such state or territory or foreign country is to be determined by the court or referee and included in the findings of the court or referee or charged to the jury, as the case may be. Such finding or charge is subject to review on appeal. In determining such law, neither the trial court nor any appellate court shall be limited to the evidence produced on the trial by the parties, but may consult any of the written authorities above named in this section, with the same force and effect as if the same had been admitted in evidence."

In 1943, after the Pink decision, this provision was further amended and in part transferred to C.P.A. § 344–a, which was the predecessor of present Rule 4511 of the CPLR.

*** Accord: Graybar Electric Co. v. New Amsterdam Casualty Co., 292 N.Y. 246, 54 N.E.2d 811 (1944). In a case coming up from the federal courts, the Supreme Court likewise (but without statutory authority) took notice of a Mexican decision rendered only one month before the argument in the Supreme Court. Steele v. Bulova Watch Co., 344 U.S. 280, 285–9, 73 S.Ct. 252, 255–7 (1952).

2. Hence, the denial of the motion of the United States to certify the official declaration as part of the record of the Moscow case in this Court (281 N.Y. 818, 24 N.E.2d 487) would seem immaterial to our right to consult it. [Court's footnotes renumbered.]

NOTES AND QUESTIONS

(1) For a recent case carrying the *Pink* line of reasoning one step further, and holding that an opinion of the Attorney General of Mexico is conclusive on a point of Mexican law, see D'Angelo v. Petroleos Mexicanos, 422 F.Supp. 1280 (D. Del. 1976), aff'd without opinion 564 F.2d 89 (3d Cir. 1977), cert. denied 434 U.S. 1035, 98 S.Ct. 770 (1978).

The court concluded, on the basis of expert evidence, that the Attorney General of Mexico was authorized to "issue official expert opinions in response to a proper request." It also noted agreement of the experts to the effect that under Mexican law, the judiciary is the exclusive arbiter of property rights. 422 F.Supp. at 1284–85. Since the substance of the Attorney General's opinion was uncontroverted, it could, of course, have been regarded as highly persuasive, and accepted on that basis. The court went out of its way, however, to hold that the Mexican Attorney General's opinion was an "official declaration" of the Mexican government, and that it was therefore *binding* on the court by virtue of *Pink.*

(2) Note that there is a strong element of self-interest in d'Angelo (recognition abroad of the effects of the Mexican oil expropriations of 1938; protection of the leading Mexican state enterprise and taxpayer). Soviet self-interest in *Pink* was even stronger: The "amounts . . . that may be found to be due" the Soviet Union, and assigned to the United States by the Litvinoff Assignment, were to be credited toward the satisfaction of United States claims against the Soviet Union. Even more to the point, a 1922 circular of the R.S.F.S.R. People's Commissariat of Foreign Affairs had declared that the nationalization decrees of that Republic, adopted less than three years earlier, regulated "only property relations in the territory of the R.S.F.S.R." Translation in V. Gsovski, 1 Soviet Civil Law 300 (1948). The 1937 certificate relied on in the principal case was thus directly contradicted by an earlier official statement of the same government, which (to put it mildly) had at least the same probative value.

(3) In d'Angelo, 422 F.Supp. at 1285, the court found that "under Mexican law the judiciary has no power to issue advisory or consultative opinions." If Mexican law had been different in this respect, what effect should have been given to an advisory opinion by the Supreme Court of Mexico? In Kunstsammlungen Zu Weimar v. Elicofon, 536 F.Supp. 829, 855 (E.D.N.Y. 1981), aff'd 678 F.2d 1150 (2d Cir. 1982), the court followed an advisory opinion of the Supreme Court of the German Democratic Republic which stated that the latter tribunal had abandoned its prior jurisprudence on a point at issue. See 1984 Recht in Ost und West 300. This advisory opinion was surely persuasive authority on G.D.R. law as it then stood. Note, however, that at least one highly respected court (the Supreme Judicial Court of Massachusetts) has repeatedly departed from its own advisory opinions in subsequent cases. F. Frankfurter, A Note on Advisory Opinions, 37 Harv.L.Rev. 1002, 1006–1007 (1924).

(4) Finally, consider so-called authentic interpretations of law. Civil-law learning in point is encompassed in the 1983 Code of Canon Law:

"Can. 16—§ 1. Laws are authentically interpreted by the legislator and by the one to whom the legislator has granted the power to interpret them authentically.

"§ 2. An authentic interpretation communicated in the form of a law has the same force as the law itself and must be promulgated. Furthermore, if such an interpretation merely declares what was certain in the words of the law in themselves, it has retroactive force; if it restricts or extends the law or if it explains a doubtful law, it is not retroactive.

"§ 3. However, an interpretation contained in a judicial decision or an administrative act in a particular matter does not have the force of law and binds only the persons and affects only those matters for which it was given."

For Roman-law background, see P. Gaudemet, L'Empereur, Interprète du Droit, 2 Festschrift für Rabel 169 (1954). In early-nineteenth century constitutional practice, the power to interpret the law authentically was conferred upon the Legislative branch. See, e.g., Spanish (Cortes) Constitution of 1812, articles 131 and 161 *decimo*, alluded to in defendant's third argument in Breedlove v. Turner, infra pp. 599–606, 601–604, and the survey of Swiss cantonal (state) constitutions in D. Jenny, Zur Lehre und Praxis der authentischen Interpretation, 106 Zeitschrift für Schweizerisches Recht (n.s.) 213 (1987). Some absolutist regimes experimented unsuccessfully with authentic interpretation by royal commission, see Roscoe Pound, The Spirit of the Common Law, infra pp. 623–626. At the time material in *Pink*, the Constitution of the R.S.F.S.R of January 21, 1937, article 33c, conferred the power to issue (binding) interpretations of law upon the Presidium (or standing committee) of the Supreme Soviet, i.e., the *Legislature* of that Republic. This followed the model of the Stalin Constitution of 1936 (article 49c). See generally, A. Vyshinsky, The Law of the Soviet State (transl. by Babb and Hazard) 416 (1948). It follows that the official certificate before the Court in *Pink* was *not* conclusive under Soviet law.

(5) Note that the *Pink* case came up from the New York courts, and that, consequently, the Supreme Court felt authorized, under the New York statute, to take *judicial notice* of the Commissar's certificate.

(a) Would the New York statute invoked by the Court have authorized judicial notice of the certificate even if the court had not treated it as conclusive?

(b) Do the more modern statutes permit judicial notice of such a certificate even though it is not conclusive? The question is important, because as a rule the foreign government officials issuing such certificates have neither the power nor the intention to give their certificates conclusive effect.

(c) In the absence of an applicable judicial notice statute, when the foreign law has to be proved in accordance with ordinary rules of evidence, would a certificate issued by a foreign government concerning a point of its law be admissible?[1]

(d) Assuming that such a certificate is admissible or that it can be considered under a judicial notice statute, what weight should

---

1. The authorities seem to be in conflict. See Stern, Foreign Law in the Courts, 45 Calif.L.Rev. 23, 37–8 (1957).

be accorded to the statements contained therein? Should such weight depend on the issuing government's reputation for veracity and objectivity? [2]

(6) Lawyers in civilian countries, when conducting litigation in their own courts that involves points of American law, often request American counsel to obtain an "official" declaration of such law. These requests reflect their belief that there exists in this country a governmental practice similar to that which would be followed by their own government in the converse case.[3] Is it possible for American counsel to comply with such a request? [4] *Generally, no.*

Suppose the foreign court, through diplomatic or other proper channels, requests the U.S. State Department to obtain an opinion on the pertinent point of American law from the U.S. Attorney General or, if the point is one of state law, from the attorney general of the particular state. If the U.S. State Department attempted to comply with the request, could it obtain such an opinion? State laws are not uniform concerning the power of the state attorney general to answer an inquiry which the U.S. State Department makes on behalf of a foreign court; but the Attorney General of the United States probably lacks power to answer such an inquiry.[5]

(4) As mentioned in the Introductory Note preceding the Pink case, there are *international treaties* encouraging and regulating the use of official certificates for the purpose of proving foreign law. An important multilateral treaty of this kind, the *European Convention on Information on Foreign Law*,[6] which was concluded under the auspices of the Council of Europe, has been ratified by many European nations.

---

2. See Zwack v. Kraus Bros. & Co., 133 F.Supp. 929, 936 (S.D.N.Y. 1955), aff'd on this point 237 F.2d 255, 260 (2d Cir. 1956); In re Siegler's Will, 284 App.Div. 436, 132 N.Y.S.2d 392 (3d Dept. 1954).

Even where no political issues are involved, and the government that has issued the certificate is a decent one, the evidentiary value of such a document may be questionable. "The experience of other countries shows that the evidence obtained by means of official certificates is of a mediocre kind." J. K. Grodecki, Recent Developments in Nullity Jurisdiction, 20 Mod.L.Rev. 566, 584 (1957). The problem of expense, however, should not be forgotten. Where the amount involved in the litigation is modest, and the parties cannot afford the expensive services of an expert, "mediocre" evidence may be better than none, especially if the court, under a judicial notice statute, can independently examine the accuracy of the statements made in the certificate.

3. In 1 Rabel, The Conflict of Laws—A Comparative Study 443 (2nd ed. by U. Drobnig, 1958), it is reported that a Swiss court once tried to consult the Supreme Court of the United States on a point of "American" divorce law, but was informed that neither courts nor administrative agencies in the United States are prepared to give such advice for purposes of litigation pending abroad.

Could a state by statute authorize its courts to answer questions involving the law of that state which have been certified to it by a foreign court? An affirmative answer is suggested by the analogy of state statutes providing for state court answers to questions certified by federal courts. See the authorities collected in C. A. Wright, A. R. Miller and E. H. Cooper, 17 Federal Practice and Procedure § 4248 note 29 (1978) as supplemented by 1986 Pocket Part, p. 199. As yet, however, no statute authorizing this form of international judicial co-operation appears to have been enacted.

4. See generally H. Smit, International Cooperation in Litigation: Europe 9–10 (1965).

5. The pertinent statute, 28 U.S.C.A. § 512 (1968), apparently has been construed to mean that the Attorney General is neither required nor authorized to render an opinion in answer to an inquiry made by the head of another executive department, unless the inquiry relates to a question "arising in the administration" of that department.

6. ETS 62, 1968, published also in 9 Int'l Legal Materials 477 (1970). The Con-

It provides that through "national liaison bodies" (usually a department of the Ministry of Justice) a court in participating country X, when it has to decide a question involving the law of participating country Y, can address an inquiry to an official body of Y. As expressly stated in article 8 of this Convention, "information given in the reply shall not bind the judicial authority from which the request emanated."

Normally, the appropriate national liaison body (i.e., a government agency) will itself answer the inquiry, or procure an answer from another official agency; but it "may, in appropriate cases or for reasons of administrative organization, transmit the request to a private body or to a qualified lawyer to draw up the reply." (Art. 6, par. 2). The last-quoted provision would render it feasible for the U.S. to accede to the Convention.[7] Such accession is possible even for a non-member of the Council of Europe if invited by the Committee of Ministers of the Council; but the U.S. Department of State and its Advisory Committee on Private International Law at present appear to be disinclined to seek such accession.

NOTE ON PROOF OF FOREIGN OFFICIAL RECORDS

The certificate method of proof of foreign law is widely used, and indeed indispensable, when foreign official records are sought to be used as evidence.

Very frequently it becomes necessary in judicial and administrative proceedings, even in proceedings involving purely domestic issues, to prove births, marriages, deaths, and other publicly recorded events which occurred abroad. Normally, the only practicable method of proof is to offer a copy of the foreign record, attested by the custodian of the original record (e.g., a city clerk, vital statistics officer, or registrar of civil status) or by some other official authorized to make such attestation.[1]

Statutes in many jurisdictions make such a copy (e.g., a birth certificate) admissible, provided (a) that the attesting officer's signature is genuine, (b) that the attesting officer is shown to hold the office he purports to hold, and (c) that the holder of such office is the custodian of the original record or otherwise authorized to attest the copy. If the original record is one that is kept in a foreign country, it is clear that points (b) and (c) involve questions of foreign law. Formerly, most of the pertinent statutes provided that points (a), (b), and (c), including their foreign law aspects, had to be proved by an official certificate, and

vention entered into force in December 1969.

An Additional Protocol, 17 Int'l Legal Materials 797 (1978), makes the Convention applicable in criminal cases, and also authorizes public legal aid offices (as well as judicial authorities) to use the Convention machinery for the purpose of obtaining information on foreign law.

7. In most instances the information on "American" law desired by a foreign court would involve questions of state law. The U.S. "liaison body" (presumably an office within the U.S. Department of Justice) probably would be unwilling to provide in-

formation on the law of one of the states; but the provision of the Convention quoted in the text, supra, would make it possible for the U.S. "liaison body" to obtain such information from an appropriate public or private source (e.g., the State Attorney General's office, or an attorney-supervised clinical program of a law school) located in the respective state, for transmission to the "liaison body", and ultimately to the court, in the requesting country.

1. In civil-law countries, a notary usually is authorized to attest the correctness of such copies, regardless of whether he is the custodian of the original.

that the only persons authorized to issue such a certificate were United States foreign service officers. This led to many difficulties, not the least of which stemmed from the fact that a U.S. consul, though stationed in Ruritania, is apt to be unfamiliar with the law of Ruritania and thus unable to make a certification which involves issues arising under that law. These difficulties are overcome by the more sophisticated and more flexible provisions of FRCP Rule 44(a)(2), as amended in 1966.

Since the problem is of great importance in practice, it is suggested that the reader acquaint himself with amended Rule 44, and with the explanatory Note of the Advisory Committee, which appears in 39 F.R.D. 69, at 115–17 (1966).[2] Many states have adopted provisions substantially similar to Rule 44.[3]

The United States is now a party to the Hague Convention Abolishing the Requirement of Legalisation for Foreign Public Documents, of October 5, 1961, T.I.A.S. 10072 of October 15, 1982. "Legalisation" as used in that convention is defined as "only the formality by which the diplomatic or consular agents of the country in which the document has to be produced certify the authenticity of the signature, the capacity in which the person signing the document has acted and, where appropriate, the identity of the seal or stamp which it bears." (Article 2). The contracting states (by now some thirty-six in number) undertake not to require such diplomatic or consular super-validation, but they *may* require, in lieu thereof, a certificate known as an "apostille," articles 3 and 4. The prescribed form of that document is contained in the annex to the convention, and is conveniently reproduced together with it in 28 U.S.C.A. Rule 44 Note pp. 87–93, as well as vol. 7 of annual editions of Martindale-Hubbell, Legal Directory under Part VII: Selected International Conventions to which the United States is a Party. These sources also list the offices from which an apostille may be obtained in the United States. Such documents are frequently required by other states adhering to the Convention.

Sometimes, neither official certification nor diplomatic or consular legalisation of a public document can be obtained because of lack of diplomatic relations or even more severe obstacles (e.g., non-recognition, occupation, or annexation of the country concerned). In Jacombe v. Jacombe, 105 C.L.R. 355, 357–59 (Australia 1961), a Latvian divorce decree was proved through a certified copy issued in 1939. The seal of the court and the identity, signature, and official capacity of the certifying officials were established through the testimony of a former judge of the same Riga court, now living in Australia.

2. For a collection of the cases in which Rule 44(a)(2) was applied, see Anno., 41 A.L.R.Fed. 784 (1979).

See also Rule 902(3) of the Federal Rules of Evidence. According to the Advisory Committee's Note, the latter provision "is derived from Rule 44(a)(2) of the Rules of Civil Procedure, but is broader in applying to public documents rather than being limited to public records."

For more extensive treatment of the whole problem, see H. Smit, International Aspects of Federal Civil Procedure, 61 Colum.L.Rev. 1031, 1059–71 (1961); id., International Litigation Under the United States Code, 65 Colum.L.Rev. 1015, 1042–43 (1965).

3. See, e.g., N.Y. CPLR Rule 4542, as amended in 1969 and 1972, and § 5.02 of the Uniform Interstate and International Procedure Act, 13 U.L.A. 461, 501–03 (1980). Provisions similar to Rule 44(a)(2) have been adopted also in most of the states whose civil procedure generally follows the model of the Federal Rules.

The copy of a foreign official record, even if admissible, is never conclusive; it is for the trier of the facts to determine its reliability.[4] In this connection, the court can take into consideration that the foreign record itself, under the foreign law, may be based on evidence which would be inadmissible under common law rules of evidence.[5] In addition, an attitude of healthy scepticism may be indicated if the original record is in the hands of an untrustworthy government, or if the authentication of the copy depends on the veracity of statements made by such government. A golden seal may cover a black untruth or forgery.

B. PROOF BY EXPERTS

(AA) NECESSARY QUALIFICATIONS OF A FOREIGN LAW EXPERT

MATTER OF MASOCCO v. SCHAAF
Supreme Court of New York, Appellate Division, Third Department, 1931.
234 App.Div. 181, 254 N.Y.S. 439.

[In this workmen's compensation case, the employer and his insurance carrier appeal from an award made to the claimant by the State Industrial Board.]

RHODES, J. The appeal presents the question whether the claimant is the widow of the deceased employee. It is undisputed that the parties went through the form of a religious marriage ceremony performed by a priest in a church at Guilano Di Roma, Italy, on October 29, 1921; that they thereafter cohabited together and a daughter was born of the marriage, such child being now deceased. It is the claim of the appellants that a religious ceremony of marriage is not recognized by the civil authorities as having any validity. Witnesses for each party testify that common-law marriages are not recognized in Italy.

At a hearing herein a copy of the marriage certificate showing such religious marriage, certified or "legalized" by the mayor of the town and other civil authorities, was offered and received in evidence. The secretary of the Italian Consulate of the city of Buffalo was called as a

---

4. In re Kohn's Estate, 124 N.Y.S.2d 861 (Surr.Ct.N.Y.Co. 1953); In re Kuehnert's Estate, 147 N.Y.S.2d 713 (Surr.Ct. Westch.Co., 1955). The rule may be otherwise with respect to a certificate of citizenship issued by a foreign government. Such certificate proves a governmental determination and not a physical fact like birth or death. See Murarka v. Bachrack Bros., 215 F.2d 547, 553 (2d Cir. 1954); Blair Holdings Corp. v. Rubinstein, 133 F.Supp. 496, 499 (S.D.N.Y. 1955).

5. See infra pp. 424–425. Problems of this kind are presented by foreign death

certificates, which may be based on hearsay evidence or on the operation of presumptions. See the New York cases cited n. 4, supra. To prove the unwitnessed deaths of concentration camp victims, it was found necessary to admit and to credit such documents; but the rights of the alleged decedent and the interests of local stakeholders must be properly safeguarded. See Matter of Goldstein's Estate, 299 N.Y. 43, 85 N.E.2d 425 (1949).

witness and testified that he knew the Italian law very well but was not a lawyer; that he was familiar with the requirements of a legal marriage in Italy and that the certificate, in his opinion, established a legal marriage in Italy; that after a religious ceremony, in order to legalize it, the parties go to the City Hall and register; that unless the marriage had been recognized as legal by the civil authorities, they would not have certified to the said certificate of marriage; that when parties have been married in church, although the marriage has not been legalized, they do not live in adultery; "they are still married in the church but the law don't recognize them. They live that way because they are used to go to the priest and get married."

There was other testimony introduced in behalf of the claimant in relation to their having lived together as husband and wife and having openly sustained that relation.

In opposition the appellants produced the deposition of a solicitor and barrister in Italy which states that the religious ceremony in Italy had no validity whatsoever, and that the marriage certificate referred to had no legal significance whatsoever. The deposition of another witness was produced who had served as Vice-Consul and holds the degree of Doctor of Law and Economic Sciences from the University of Milano. His deposition is to the same effect. The deposition of another witness was produced, who is described as an avvocato, and is of similar import. In addition the appellants called as a witness an attorney of the State of New York who stated that he has familiarized himself with the Italian law, but who apparently has not been admitted to practice in Italy. He produced a copy of what purported to be a pocket edition of the Five Italian Codes,[a] including the Civil Code, which he bought at a book store in the Via Nationale at Rome. It purports to be a printed copy of the Italian statutes published under the authority of a proclamation issued in 1865, signed by the first King, Victor Emanuel.[b] He testified that this was the law in force in the year 1923 and that the particular sections had not been amended except in so far as they were later modified by the Lateran Treaty of February, 1929, between the Vatican State and the Kingdom of Italy, and that under the Italian law no common-law relationship is recognized.

The foregoing is a resume of substantially all the pertinent evidence produced by the parties.[c]

a. In most civil law countries, the following are regarded as the five basic codes: Civil Code, Commercial Code, Code of Civil Procedure, Penal Code, and Code of Criminal Procedure.

b. The Italian Civil Code of 1865 remained in force until a new Civil Code (covering both "civil" and commercial law) was enacted in 1940.

c. Most of the evidence presented by the parties dealt with the law of Italy. The lawyers in the case obviously believed that the outcome of the proceeding depended wholly on the validity, under Italian law, of the 1921 ceremonial marriage. It should be noted, however, that the case could have been decided without reference to Italian law, because at the relevant time New York still recognized common law marriages; thus the claimant could have argued that—regardless of the validity of the ceremonial marriage of 1921—she entered into a valid common law marriage with the decedent while they lived together as husband and wife in New York. See H. W. Baade, Marriage and Divorce in Ameri-

I   The question now is whether there was sufficient evidence to support the finding of the Board that the claimant is the widow of the deceased.[d]

The law presumes morality and not immorality; marriage and not concubinage; legitimacy and not bastardy. Where there is enough to create a foundation for the presumption of marriage, it can be repelled only by the most cogent and satisfactory evidence. [Citations.] The cohabitation, apparently decent and orderly, of two persons opposite in sex, raises a presumption of more or less strength that they have been duly married. Gall v. Gall, 114 N.Y. 109, 21 N.E. 106.

If there was competent evidence supplementing the presumption and supporting the validity of the marriage, then it is unnecessary to examine the evidence to the contrary attacking the marriage, even assuming that the opposing evidence was competent. The answer to this question depends principally upon whether the witness Fareri, the secretary of the Italian Consulate, was qualified to testify as an expert. Whether in any case a witness is qualified to speak as an expert is a fact to be determined by the court upon the trial preliminary to his testifying, and ordinarily the decision of the trial court on this point, when there are any facts to support it, is not open to review in this court. [Citations.]

In 22 Corpus Juris, 541, section 636, relative to the competency of a witness to testify as to the law of a foreign country, it is stated that it is not necessary that the witness should be a lawyer. [Citations.][e]

In Lacon v. Higgins, alias Isaacs, 16 Eng.C.L. 425; 3 Starkie, 178, there was involved the validity of a marriage celebrated in France. The French Vice Consul, resident in London, was called as a witness. It did not appear that he was a member of the bar, but he was permitted to state that he was well acquainted with the laws and customs of France and testified concerning the validity of the marriage then in question.

Expert Foreign law witness need not be an attorney In Hecla Powder Co. v. Sigua Iron Co., 157 N.Y. 437, 52 N.E. 650, the United States Consul at Santiago de Cuba testified as to the Spanish law applicable to the island of Cuba. It does not appear that the witness was an attorney; however, the opinion states that the testimony was received without objection.

can Conflicts Law: Governmental Interests Analysis and the Restatement (Second), 72 Colum.L.Rev. 329, 364–68 (1972). New York would not have required a *new* (informal) agreement to marry, entered into *in New York*, see Matter of Haffner, 254 N.Y. 238, 172 N.E. 483 (1930). If counsel had made this argument, all the interesting points relating to proof of foreign law that are discussed in the opinion might have become irrelevant.

d. With respect to issues of fact arising in workmen's compensation cases, it has been held that "When conflicting infer-ences are possible, the finding of the Board prevails." Matter of Gordon v. New York Life Ins. Co., 300 N.Y. 652, 654, 90 N.E.2d 898, 899 (1950). See also McKinney's N.Y. Workm.Comp.Law, § 20.

e. Another court, citing the principal case, subsequently held that an expert on Honduran law need not be a member of the Honduras Bar. See Murphy v. Bankers Commercial Corp., 111 F.Supp. 608, 611 (S.D.N.Y. 1953). To similar effect see also United States v. Baumgarten, 300 F.2d 807, 808 (2 Cir. 1962).

In the case at bar the secretary of the Italian Consulate at Buffalo testified that he was familiar with the requirements for a legal marriage in Italy and that the marriage in question was valid, and further, in substance, that when the parties to a religious ceremony appeared before the proper civil authorities and caused proof of said marriage to be registered or legalized[f] said marriage then became legal and was recognized as legal and valid by the civil authorities; that when a religious marriage is not certified by the civil authorities, the contracting parties do not live in adultery. The witness testified that he had been two and one-half years with the Italian Consulate and that as such secretary he transacts the more important business of the Consul; that in his opinion the certificate produced constitutes a legal marriage in Italy and that he was able to say this as an official of the Italian Consulate of the city of Buffalo; that the certificate in question was a document taken from the records of the church where this marriage took place and was legalized by the proper civil authorities.

From the foregoing it seems that the witness, in his official capacity, was competent to testify and express an opinion as to the validity of the marriage in question. His official duties would naturally require considerable familiarity with Italian law affecting persons of Italian nationality and residence, rendering him peculiarly qualified to speak.

. . . Our courts will not assume judicial knowledge of foreign laws (Hanna v. Lichtenhein, 225 N.Y. 579, 122 N.E. 625),[g] but our courts will assume judicial knowledge of historical facts in relation to the laws of other countries as to whether they were derived from the Roman civil law or otherwise. Matter of Roberts, 8 Paige Ch. 446.

Section 391 of the Civil Practice Act permits proof of statutes of another country contained in a book or publication purported or proved to have been published by the authority thereof.[h] Whether or not the proof of the authenticity of the Italian Code was strictly sufficient, it was received without objection, the only question raised being to the competency of the opinion of the witness Di Bartolo concerning the law of Italy. We may, therefore, treat the Italian statute as sufficiently proven. [Citation.]

The attempted interpretation of the statute by the appellants' witnesses is not controlling.[i] The statute being in evidence, its con-

---

f. Note the pun: "Legalized," of course, does not mean "validated" in this context, but merely "authenticated." For general usage, see supra p. 137.

g. This case, like the principal case, was decided prior to the enactment of a modern judicial notice statute applicable to foreign-country law.

h. The same Section 391 also played a role in the *Pink* case, supra; it is set forth in a footnote appended to that case. The application of that section, which is now superseded by more modern statutes, was limited to the *written* law of a foreign country.

i. The witness' interpretation of the foreign statute is admissible opinion evidence if the witness is properly qualified as an expert. Fusco v. Fusco, 200 Misc. 1039, 107 N.Y.S.2d 286 (Sup.Ct.Onandaga Co., 1951). But the court determines the weight of the testimony. The court may reject the opinion of the witness if it is not "a reasonable inference from statute or from precedent or from the implications of a legal concept, such as contract or testa-

struction was for the court. Bank of China, etc. v. Morse, 168 N.Y. 458, 61 N.E. 774. See, also, cases cited and discussed in the opinion in O'Rourke v. Cunard Steamship Co., Ltd., 169 App.Div. 943, 154 N.Y.S. 29.

It will be observed that no decisions of the courts of Italy are cited. Neither are the provisions of the statute set forth in full in the record.[j] So far as presented, they appear to govern the manner of celebrating a civil marriage, but they do not in any wise refer to a religious ceremony nor specify the steps necessary to the recognition by the civil authorities of such religious marriage. Hence the statute, so far as set forth, does not necessarily cover the situation here presented. Its construction being the province of the court, the opinion of the witness as to its meaning was at best a conclusion of law. It may be remarked that an examination of the statutes of our State concerning marriage might give the impression that marriage in no other form is permitted here, but it has many times been held that a valid marriage may be contracted although none of the prescribed statutory requisites are followed. Similarly the Italian Code sheds no light on the method of validating a religious marriage, but it does not follow that there is no provision for its legalization.[k] From the Lateran Treaty, known as the Concordat, effective in 1929, it appears that immediately after a religious ceremony the priest will draw the marriage certificate, a complete copy of which must be forwarded within five days to the commune in order that it may be entered in the register of the civil status. While it is claimed the treaty is not retroactive, it may be that it is simply declaratory of the theretofore existing practice and law of Italy.[l]

ment or juristic personality." Petrogradsky Mejdunarodny Kommerchesky Bank v. National City Bank, 253 N.Y. 23, 34–5, 170 N.E. 479, 483–4 (1930; Cardozo, Ch. J.). The court may accept the expert's translations of statutes and code sections, without adopting his interpretation. In Re Hirschmann's Estate, 124 N.Y.S.2d 801 (Surr.Ct. N.Y.Co., 1953).

The principle underlying these cases is that the court may derive information and increased understanding of the foreign rule from the expert's testimony, but that the ultimate responsibility for construing and applying the foreign rule is the court's, not the expert's. This is especially important in cases turning on the effect which a particular document has under foreign law. Is it necessary to show the document to the expert? It has been held that this is not necessary, and that it is sufficient to have the expert explain (perhaps on the basis of abstract or hypothetical questions) the applicable rules of foreign law. Estate of Danz, 444 Pa. 411, 283 A.2d 282, 284 (1971). Whether this is the best possible practice, is of course another question.

j. Did the State Industrial Board *have to* reject the expert's opinion on the ground that it was insufficiently supported by citations of cases and code sections? See De Sayve v. De La Valdene, 124 N.Y.S.2d 143, 146–7 (Sup.Ct.N.Y.Co.1953), aff'd 283 App. Div. 918, 130 N.Y.S.2d 865 (1st Dept. 1954), appeal on const. grounds dism. and motion for leave to appeal granted 307 N.Y. 861, 122 N.E.2d 747 (1954). Could it be that appellants' experts were unable to cite cases for the simple reason that their interpretation of the 1865 Code was self-evidently correct and had never been challenged in an Italian court?

k. Should it be assumed that the Italian Code contains as incomplete a set of rules as the New York statute, and that the Code, like an American statute, must be read against the background of an all-permeating common law?

l. The assumption that in this respect the Concordat of 1929 was declaratory of pre-existing law (what "law"?), is incorrect. See Vergnani v. Guidetti, 308 Mass. 450, 32 N.E.2d 272 (1941); Rheinstein, Trends in Marriage and Divorce Law of Western

So far as the opinion of appellants' witnesses as to the law is concerned, without reference to an attempted interpretation of the Code, such opinion has no more weight than the opinion of claimant's witness and the Board has seen fit to accept as a fact the testimony in behalf of the claimant.

[handwritten margin note: interpretation of the code. No greater value than common law in experience...]

Appellants further claim that the marriage was void because the parties were second cousins and that such marriage is prohibited by the Italian Code. The only evidence of relationship presented is the statement contained in the marriage certificate, and by the same document it appears that the necessary dispensation was obtained from the Apostolic See.

From the provisions of the Italian Code, printed in the record, it appears that the King, when grave reason exists, may dispense with these impediments. If, therefore, a proper dispensation was obtained from the religious authorities and a religious marriage was thereupon celebrated which has been recognized as valid by the civil authorities, that is sufficient here.

The finding of the Board as to the marriage of the parties is amply supported by competent evidence.

The award to the claimant should be affirmed, with costs to the Industrial Board.

Countries, 18 Law & Contemp.Prob. 3, 15 (1953); Campbell, Fascism and Legality, 62 Law Q.Rev. 141, 144 (1946). In 1929, Italy and the Holy See concluded two agreements: a 27-article treaty regulating the political relations between these two powers as well as the status of Vatican City (Lateran Treaty), and a twenty-six article treaty which regulated the status of the Church in Italy and the relation of canon law (including matrimonial law, article 34) to Italian secular law (Concordat). See L. Schöppe, Konbordate seit 1800 at 161–87 (1964). More recently, Italy and the Holy See have revised the Concordat of 1929, including its provisions as to matrimonial law. J. Gaudemet, L'Accord du 18 Fevrier 1984 entre l'Italie et le Saint-Siège, 1984 Annuaire Français de Droit International 209, 215–16.

There remains the question whether the Concordat, as implemented by Italian Law No. 847 of May 27, 1929, by its terms retroactively validated a marriage such as the Masoccos'. In this connection, Professor Baade (in the article cited supra n. c) calls attention to Art. 21 of the latter enactment, which deals with previously celebrated religious marriages. It provides that such a marriage may be validated *if upon petition of both parties* the Court of Appeals by *decree* orders it civilly registered ("transcribed"). (Emphasis supplied)

It should be noted that neither the Concordat nor this legislative implementation provides for automatic retroactive validation of all pre-1929 religious marriages. Under the terms of Art. 21, such validation occurs only if (a) both spouses file an appropriate petition with the Court of Appeals, and (b) that Court enters a formal decree granting the petition. In the Masocco case, neither condition (a) nor condition (b) appears to have been met. The date of the case indicates that Mr. Masocco's fatal accident must have occurred before or very shortly after the effective date of the Concordat (June 7, 1929). Even if he was still alive at that time, it is highly unlikely that the Masoccos, relatively uneducated people who then lived in the United States, ever petitioned an Italian Court of Appeals for civil registration of their marriage. Thus it is virtually certain that they failed to comply with the requirements of the purely optional validation procedure provided by Art. 21. On these factual grounds, Professor Schlesinger is unable to agree with the argument of Professor Baade that the Concordat and its implementing legislation retroactively validated the Masoccos' marriage. Professor Baade replies that in the light of this legislation, Italy had no governmental interest in invalidating this marriage at the time here material.

NOTES AND QUESTIONS

(1) If the principal case arose today, would the provisions of CPLR Rule 4511 (supra p. 57) lead to a different result? [1]

(2) Massucco v. Tomassi, 78 Vt. 188, 62 A. 57 (1905): "An Italian priest was permitted to testify that a marriage by religious ceremony alone did not constitute a legal marriage in Italy. In this there was no error, as the record shows that the court first found that the witness was duly qualified to testify upon the subject."

(3) Banco De Sonora v. Bankers' Mutual Casualty Co., 124 Iowa 576, 100 N.W. 532 (1904): The principal issue in this case was whether one Dato, at the age of 17, was a minor or an "adult" under the law of the State of Sonora, in the Republic of Mexico. "The plaintiff pleaded that the 'civil law, in distinction from the common law, is the foundation of the laws of Mexico.' It called as witness an attorney, who testified, in substance, that he was not acquainted with the laws of the Republic of Mexico nor of the State of Sonora, but that he had been a student of the history of law and government and from his studies knew in a general way the countries having a civil law or a Justinian Code as the basis of their jurisprudence, and that Mexico was one of these; that the country had a constitution and statutory laws in system like those of the United States; and that Bouvier's Law Dictionary is accepted authority on legal definitions. The parts of this dictionary stating that the civil law is the foundation of the law of Mexico and certain other countries, and that 'an adult, under the civil law, is a male infant who has attained the age of fourteen years,' were introduced in evidence. All this evidence was received over the defendant's objection. That concerning the dictionary and its definition of an adult under the civil law was rightly admitted. Otherwise the witness did not show himself competent to testify. No evidence of the written law was introduced. The statute authorizes proof of the unwritten law of a foreign country by parol. Section 4657; Crafts v. Clark, 38 Iowa 237. But this must be given by persons familiar with the laws of such country, or who are at least in a situation rendering such knowledge probable. [Citations.]

As to whether the civil law is the foundation for Mexican jurisprudence, the histories are quite as accessible to the court as to the witness. Probably judicial notice should be taken of the fact as a matter of history. But this extends no farther than that the general system of jurisprudence prevails, without taking notice of details. The extent of its adoption we are not bound to know, for, in its adjustment to the situation and conditions of a people on this continent, doubtless many changes were made. Was the entire body of the Justinian Code adopted? Or this with modifications essential to meet the necessities and demands of modern civilization? This was a matter for specific proof with respect to the particular issue. We know that Mexico was a Spanish province for about 300 years, and then became, and still is, a republic. At no period of its history has it been under British sovereignty. Its institutions are Latin, and not Anglo-Saxon, and the common law is not presumed to be in force in any State or country where

---

1. Concerning the applicability of the CPLR in workmen's compensation cases, see McKinney's N.Y.Workm.Comp.Law, § 23, and Rules, Regulations and Procedures Promulgated Under Workers' Compensation Laws (as amended to April 30, 1986) § 300.18(i).

English institutions have not been established. [Citations.] . . . Reversed."

(4) Even without the aid of a modern judicial-notice statute or rule, it has been held that a person of learning, such as an exceptionally well-trained foreign-law librarian, may be qualified to testify concerning the law of a number of countries, although he has never practiced there.[2] Section 4(1) of the (English) Civil Evidence Act 1972 provides, in this respect:

> It is hereby declared that in civil proceedings a person who is suitably qualified to do so on account of his knowledge or experience is competent to give expert evidence as to the law of any country or territory outside the United Kingdom, or any part of the United Kingdom other than England and Wales, irrespective of whether he has acted or is entitled to act as a legal practitioner there.

See Practice Direction, [1973] 3 All E.R. 912.

(5) Note that in jurisdictions which have adopted Rule 44.1 or its equivalent, the issue of expert qualification goes to weight and possibly to relevance: the court may consider "*any* relevant material or source, including testimony, whether or not . . . . admissible under the Federal Rules of Evidence" (emphasis added). Relevance is thus the ultimate test for admissibility. Under the sway of the older system, however, the following questions arose:

Is a lawyer who has practiced in one civil law country, qualified to testify concerning the law of any other civil law country? Assuming he is qualified, would his testimony be entitled to the same weight as that of a practitioner duly admitted in the particular foreign country? See Usatorre v. The Victoria, infra p. 653.

(6) If the litigation involves the law of Ruritania, and no experts sufficiently familiar with that law can be found at the forum, it may be necessary to procure statements from, or to take the depositions of, expert witnesses in Ruritania. On the other hand, if Ruritanian experts are available at the place of trial, the court ordinarily will refuse to order that such testimony be taken by deposition. This for the reason that viva voce testimony at the trial, which can be tested by cross-examination, is much to be preferred to testimony by deposition. See, e.g., Estate of Kovacs, 130 N.Y.L.J. 1531, Col. 7, Dec. 22, 1953 (Surr. Ct.N.Y.Co.). Cf. American Infra-Red Radiant Co. v. Lambert Industries, Inc., 32 F.R.D. 372 (D.Minn. 1963).

It has been suggested earlier that modern enactments such as Rule 44.1, which authorize the use of any relevant material or source concerning foreign law, may in the future lead the courts to authorize the taking of depositions even though competent experts are locally available.[3] It is equally conceivable, however, that these modern enactments will have the opposite effect. They make it possible to procure the evidence of an expert (even though he may be living in Ruritania) by informal and relatively inexpensive means, ordinarily in the form of an affidavit or even a more informal communication. Therefore, in a

---

2. See In re Estate of Spoya, 129 Mont. 83, 282 P.2d 452, 455–6 (1955), and authorities there cited. In Bostrom v. Seguros Tepeyac, S.A., 225 F.Supp. 222, 230 (N.D. Tex. 1963), aff'd in part and rev'd in part, on other grounds 347 F.2d 168 (5 Cir. 1965), reh. denied 360 F.2d 154 (5th Cir. 1966), the same witness was unjustly criticized.

3. See A. R. Miller, Federal Rule 44.1 and the "Fact" Approach to Determining Foreign Law, 65 Mich.L.Rev. 613, 644 (1967).

jurisdiction where Rule 44.1 or a similar enactment is in force it is *less* necessary than at common law to resort to formal deposition procedure in order to *obtain* foreign law materials. Establishing their legal significance is another matter.

(7) As already stated above in note (5), the question of the qualification of expert witnesses on foreign-country law arises under Rule 44.1 (or rules or statutes patterned after it) mainly when determining the weight (or in extreme cases, even the relevancy) of the testimony proffered.

An adverse ruling on admissibility of proffered "expert" testimony is nevertheless essentially a ruling on relevance, reviewable on appeal together with the trial court's ruling on the question of foreign-country law itself. The latter, of course, is the main issue. Quite unsurprisingly, in this situation, there is a dearth of post-Rule 44.1 federal appellate authority on the admissibility of the testimony of expert witnesses on foreign-country law whose qualifications have been challenged.

(8) On the other hand, in the (minority) states which have no judicial notice statute, the testimony of a witness who is not "qualified" as an expert must be rejected as incompetent and hence inadmissible evidence. The trial court, however, has broad discretionary powers in determining whether a witness is properly qualified as an expert.[4]

This is overlooked by most text-writers, who, in discussing the cases, state that a certain type of expert was held "qualified," while another type was held "not qualified." Careful analysis of the cases shows that we must distinguish, not between two kinds of witnesses ("qualified" and "not qualified"), but between three categories: (a) There are some experts whose qualifications are so clear and so strong that it would be reversible error for the trial court to reject their testimony on the ground of insufficient qualifications. E.g., a member of the Bar of the foreign country in question, who has practiced there for a substantial period during the recent past.[5] (b) At the other extreme, there is the witness whose qualifications are so clearly nonexistent that it would be error to admit his testimony, and reversible error to rely on it. This category is exemplified by the "expert" in the Banco De Sonora case, supra. (c) Between these two categories, there is the large intermediate group of experts whose qualifications are fairly debatable. The testimony of witnesses in this intermediate group may be admitted or rejected in the discretion of the trial court. The same expert may be found "qualified" by one trial judge, and "not qualified" by another. On appeal, the decisions of both trial judges may be upheld.[6]

(BB) LEGAL EDUCATION IN CIVIL LAW COUNTRIES AND ITS BEARING UPON THE QUALIFICATIONS OF CIVIL LAW EXPERTS

INTRODUCTORY NOTE

(1) The materials in this sub-chapter deal with legal training and—in a preliminary way—with structure and organization of the legal

---

4. See, e.g., In re Spoya's Estate, supra n. 2. The principal case, also, serves as a vivid illustration.

5. See Panama Electric Ry. Co. v. Moyers, 249 Fed. 19, 22 (5th Cir. 1918).

Another example is furnished by the eminent experts who testified on Panamanian law in the First National City Bank case, supra.

6. For an example, see supra n. 2.

profession.[1] For reasons of space, these materials refer to civil law countries only, although it would not be without interest to compare systems of legal education within the common law world. There are marked differences in general education as well as legal education between the United States, on the one hand, and most parts of the British Commonwealth, on the other.[2] In part, but only in part, these differences are due to the fact that in the United Kingdom and in some of the present and former Commonwealth countries the legal profession is divided into solicitors and barristers.[3]

(2) The literature on legal education in civil-law countries—even if one limits one's attention to writings in English—has become extremely voluminous in recent years.[4] The most cursory examination of this literature shows that the systems of legal training prevailing in the various civil-law countries are not uniform. Nevertheless, common historical roots and the strong influence exerted by some leading systems have produced certain features which can be called typical in the sense that they (a) are shared by most, or at least a significant number, of the civil-law countries, and (b) set the training of our civil-law brethren apart from our own. The materials which follow, although limiting detailed coverage to two countries, are intended to highlight these typical features.[5]

(3) One of the typical, and indeed uniform, features of civilian legal education is the monopoly of the university; in order to become a full-fledged member of the legal profession in a civil-law country, a candidate must receive all or a substantial part of his training at a university.[6] Since some of the materials which follow thus necessarily deal with various aspects of university life, a *caveat* must be voiced at the outset: Since the late 1960s, universities everywhere have been buf-

1. For further materials on the legal profession in civil-law countries, see infra pp. 341–352.

2. For a broad-based comparative study, see Q. Johnstone and D. Hopson, Lawyers and Their Work—An Analysis of the Legal Profession in the United States and England (1967).

For more recent descriptions of legal education in England, with emphasis on changes that have occurred during the last two decades, see M. J. Berger, A Comparative Study of British Barristers and American Legal Practice and Education, 5 Nw.J. Int'l L. & Bus. 540 (1983); Ph. S. James, English Legal Education and Practice, 27 N.Y.L.Sch.L.Rev. 881 (1982); K. M. Teeven, An American Lawyer's View of English Legal Education, 11 No. Kent.L.Rev. 355 (1984).

3. Informative discussions of this divided system can be found in Johnstone and Hopson, supra n. 2, at 357–98, and in the article by Berger, supra n. 2.

4. See the selective bibliography in 1973 International Legal Education Newsletter, No. 2. Every year, the Journal of Legal Education and other periodicals add numerous new items to the bulk of this literature, as a brief look at the standard bibliographical sources will reveal.

5. The reader who would like to study interesting variants of civilian legal education in countries other than those covered here, is referred, e.g., to J. M. Perillo, The Legal Profession of Italy, 18 J.Legal Ed. 274 (1966); T. G. Rickert, Some Notes on the Practice of Law in Spain, 6 Int.Law. 333 (1972); R. C. Maxwell and M. G. Goldman, Mexican Legal Education, 16 J.Legal Ed. 155 (1963); F. V. Perry, Understanding the Mexican Attorney: Legal Education and the Practice of Law in Mexico, 10 Int. Law. 167 (1976); K. S. Rosenn, The Reform of Legal Education in Brazil, 21 J.Legal Ed. 251 (1969); J. Laufer, Legal Education in Israel, 14 Buf.L.Rev. 232 (1965). See also supra n. 4.

6. By way of contrast to the civilian system, which involves a monopoly of the University, it should be noted that in the United States some law schools are not University-connected, and that in a number of states a person still can prepare himself for the Bar Examination by "reading law" in a law office. For some facts and figures on the latter alternative, see D. Loevy, Become a Legal Apprentice, 4 Student Lawyer No. 5, p. 40 (Jan.1976).

feted by the winds of change,[7] and many countries have undertaken ambitious efforts to restructure their universities. Some of these structural changes, and their effects upon legal education, are discussed in the materials that follow; but the process, of course, is an ongoing one, and further changes must be anticipated.

A reader who is aware of this *caveat*, however, will find that his time spent studying the present, still largely traditional systems of civilian legal education is not wasted. To the extent that future changes in university structure will affect the essentials of legal education in a given country, such changes will be understandable only to one who is basically familiar with the traditional system. Moreover, all those who today practice law in a particular country, are products of the past rather than the future version of that country's educational system; when we deal with such practitioners, and perhaps seek to appraise their qualifications as experts or consultants, we must be conversant with the fundamental features of the training they received, even though their sons (and daughters) may look forward to studying under a somewhat modified system.

P. HERZOG, EDUCATION AND TRAINING OF LAWYERS IN FRANCE *

There is no unified legal profession in France wholly analogous to the legal profession in the United States. The giving of legal advice, for instance, was not regulated at all until 1971. At that time, a new profession of *conseils juridiques* was created, whose members may give legal advice, but are not authorized to appear in court on behalf of their clients.[1] The preparation of legal documents relating to real property transactions and certain other matters is the monopoly of the *notaires*, whose role is vastly more significant than that of their common-law namesakes.** The *avocats* bear the closest resemblance to American lawyers. They may present oral arguments in all courts, except in the Supreme Court for civil and criminal matters (*Cour de cassation*) and in the Supreme Court for administrative litigation (*Conseil d'Etat*).[1a] *Avocats* also act as their clients' agents (in essence as solicitors) before the courts of first instance; but a special body of professionals, few in number, performs that function before the intermediate appellate courts (*cours d'appel*).[2] In addition, *avocats* may give legal advice to

---

7. See the comparative symposium on Student Power in Universities, 17 Am.J. Comp.L. 331 (1969), with contributions covering Germany, France, Italy, Turkey, Mexico, Costa Rica, England and the United States.

* This is an updated version, prepared by Professor Herzog, of the excerpt from Herzog, Civil Procedure in France (1967), that appeared in the fourth edition of this work at pp. 147–54.

(c) 1979 Peter Herzog.

1. French and EEC nationals may still give legal advice without abiding by the rules governing *conseils juridiques*, provided they do not use that title.

** See supra pp. 18–20 . . .

1a. A group of only about 60 attorneys called *avocats au Conseil d'Etat et à la Cour de cassation* has a monopoly for those courts.

2. These are called *avoués* at the *cours d'appel*. Until 1971, similar *avoués* also

their clients, prepare documents (except as to documents reserved for the *notaires*), etc. In fact, though in former times they were principally litigators, their role as counsellors is increasing in significance.[2a]

Traditionally, the educational and training requirements for the various branches of the French legal profession have differed substantially from one branch to the other. While in recent years there has been a tendency towards standardization, some differences remain. Here, only the education and training of the *avocats* will be described.[3]

To be admitted as an *avocat*, one must have a *maîtrise* (master's) degree or a *doctorat* in law from a French University.[4] Admission to the law program of a University ordinarily requires completion of one's secondary education in a *lycée* or *collège*, and the passing of the country-wide *baccalauréat* examination. French secondary schools put considerable emphasis on linguistic skill, logic and memory. Different types of secondary schools emphasize different fields of knowledge, but once a student has chosen a school, there is little room for making choices among course offerings. Formerly the French high schools in their final years were attended primarily by students having a middle-class background, who wanted eventually to obtain some form of university or other advanced education.[5] Recently, that situation has tended to change. An attempt has been made to encourage more members of lower-class families to complete the lycée or collège and to go on to university studies. In the very recent past, this has been followed by an endeavor to broaden the whole base of French secondary education.

Currently, the possession of the *baccalauréat* diploma is sufficient for admission to the law curriculum of most French universities.[6] Since the great university reform of 1969,[7] the teaching duties at the

acted as the parties' agents before the courts of first instance. [See infra pp. 344–345 . . .]

2a. For a discussion of that trend and of some resulting changes and problems, see Legris, *Avocats*, L'Express, August 9, 1985, pp. 41–46. The Article notes that of the 5600 *avocats* in Paris some 2500 regularly appear in court.

3. As to the various legal professions in France, see, e.g., Herzog & Herzog, The Reform of the Legal Professions and of Legal Aid in France, 22 Int. & Comp.L.Q. 462 (1973). [See also infra pp. 341–352]

4. Law No. 77–685 of 30 June 1977, J.O. July 1, 1977, p. 3433, 1977 Dalloz Législation 262, art. 1 (hereinafter cited as Law No. 77–685).

5. Even more prestigious than the universities are certain so-called *grandes*

écoles in France which dispense university level education to rather small numbers of students chosen by competitive examination, such as the *Polytéchnique* or the *Normale Supérieure*.

6. While legally the *baccalauréat* is still the only condition for admission, a few universities which are encountering particularly large numbers of applicants, have begun to practice some selection, based on grades. In some special situations, the diploma can be dispensed with.

7. This reform was accomplished by the so-called *loi d'orientation de l'enseignement supérieur*, Law No. 68–978 of November 12, 1968, 1969 Dalloz Législation (hereinafter D.L.) 317. The title of the law is almost untranslatable; it could be rendered as law for the restructuring of higher education.

universities are generally assigned to a number of so-called *Unités d'Enseignement et de Recherches* (UER's-teaching and research units), organized somewhat along the lines of American university departments, rather than to *facultés* (faculties) of much larger size. The university reform of 1969 was designed to decentralize French higher education by transferring much of the power over academic matters from the Ministry of National Education to elected bodies with faculty and student representation. The impact of this reform on basic legal studies has been modest. Because of professional licensing requirements, these basic studies are still fairly uniform throughout France.[7a] But there has been a proliferation of quite varied graduate programs. Instruction in the universities tends to be predominantly through formal lectures for which no day-to-day preparation is required. Class size, especially in Paris in the basic courses, is extremely large.[8] Students frequently do not attend, preferring instead to study from mimeographed transcripts of the lectures (*polycopiés*) conveniently put out by most faculty members in charge of large courses. For some years now, however, students also have had to attend small group sections, usually conducted by teaching assistants, in which matters covered in a given course are discussed in some depth and where not only attendance but also preparation (by reading assignments) and homework are required. Examinations, which may be written or oral, normally are given at the end of each academic year.

Since French law students come to the University directly from a secondary school, they basically resemble American undergraduates, though they are likely to be about a year older than the average

For a comment, see D. G. Carreau, Toward "Student Power" in France? 17 Am.J. Comp.L. 359 (1969). The law had a checkered career. A Law No. 80–564 of July 21, 1980, J.O. July 22, 1980, p. 1850, 1980 D.L. 314 attempted to reduce the influence of left-wing dominated student groups and made some other "conservative" changes. It was abrogated after the electoral success of the socialists in 1981. Law No. 81–995 of November 9, 1981, J.O. November 10, 1981, p. 3071, 1981 D.L. 368. Further changes were made by Law No. 84–52 of January 26, 1984, J.O. January 27, 1984, p. 431, 1984 D.L. 161. That law, as originally adopted by the French Parliament, contained a provision which would have diluted the voting strength of French professors in the elected university councils by combining their representatives with those of other university employees having scholarly or scientific functions; but that provision, and several others, were declared unconstitutional as violating academic freedom. Arthuis et autres, Constitutional Council, January 20, 1984, 1984 Dalloz Jurisprudence (hereinafter D.J.) 593 (with a note by Prof. Luchaire). The law thus had

to be promulgated without these provisions. The conservative government elected in March, 1986 wanted to change the law again—in a more conservative direction, but was stymied by student protests.

7a. The various law departments are free, however, to offer a modicum of elective and even innovative courses to their upper-class students. An interesting experimental program of this kind is described in the instructive article by A. Sultan, Teaching American Law to French Law Students—in English, 29 J.Legal Ed. 577 (1978).

8. In basic courses, in Paris, class size may exceed 1000. This minimizes real contact between students and teachers, which is further reduced by the fact that few universities provide office space for their faculty members, unless they also happen to have an administrative position; faculty members thus do much of their work at home. The situation is somewhat different in the later years of law study, when students tend to take more specialized elective courses with often a much smaller enrollment.

American college freshman, and to have a somewhat broader cultural background. There is thus an obvious need to include broadening (and not only technical legal) materials in the curriculum. The first two years of the curriculum (known as the first cycle) therefore contain a number of courses of an introductory nature in political science, legal history and the like, as well as some more technical legal courses.[9] Completion of the first cycle leads to a "general studies" diploma, which serves, for instance, to qualify the candidate for some civil-service positions.

Until recently, the "first cycle" was followed by another two-year period of legal studies, called the "second cycle," at the end of which the student would obtain the *licence* degree. The latter was the basic law degree, making the candidate eligible to take the bar examination, the entrance examination for the institute of judicial studies,[10] or similar professional examinations. Because of the undergraduate nature of French legal education,[11] it has always attracted large numbers of students not necessarily destined for a legal career. In spite of a very substantial dropout rate (probably in excess of 50%) the number of students obtaining, in the form of the *licence* degree, the basic legal qualification for access to the profession of *avocat* was thus quite large. A change occurred in 1976–77. A decree of the Under Secretary for University Affairs reduced the time needed for obtaining the *licence* degree from four to three years, and provided that students continuing their legal studies for one year beyond the *licence* would obtain a master's degree (*maîtrise*).[12] Concurrently, the statute governing the profession of *avocat* was changed to provide that the *maîtrise* was required for access to the Bar.[13] The reason for the change apparently was the desire to effectuate a kind of selection among students: those interested in law merely for its general educational value or for its usefulness in business or related careers could seek employment earlier (after having obtained the *licence*), and thus would not compete with

---

9. The most basic of these is *droit civil*, which covers all the non-commercial private-law subjects (introduction to law, family law, property, contracts, torts, etc.) and actually is spread over several years. The rules concerning the "first cycle" are contained in a decree (*arrêté*) of the Minister of Education of March 1, 1973, J.O. March 3, p. 2367. For a detailed description of the French law curriculum, including its historical development, see T. Carbonneau, The French Legal Studies Curriculum: Its History and Relevance as a Model for Reform, 25 McGill L.J. 445 (1980); J. Y. Nagourney, Approaches to Legal Education: France, 5 Comparative Law Yearbook 45 (1981).

10. This institute trains law graduates who wish to follow a career as judges or prosecutors. In France, as in most civil-law countries, judges as well as prosecutors are career officials and members of a special kind of civil service. See J. P. Richert, Recruiting and Training Judges in France, 57 Judicature 145 (1973). See also infra pp. 180–182.

11. The statement in the text, supra, refers only to basic legal education. It should be noted that in France as elsewhere there are also opportunities for graduate legal studies (beyond the *licence* and *maîtrise*), designed either for those seeking an academic career or for practitioners who desire to specialize in a particular field of law. Various kinds of doctoral degrees (including special ones for foreigners) are available.

12. Decree (*arrêté*) of January 16, 1976, J.O. January 20, 1976, p. 528, cf. *arrêté* of April 7, 1977, J.O. April 22, p. 2342.

13. See supra note 4.

those seriously interested in a legal career during the final year of legal studies.

For well over a century, the formal legal education of a French *avocat* ended with the award of the university diploma. After it had been obtained, the prospective *avocat* had to take a qualifying examination. The candidates who passed received the *certificat d'aptitude à la profession d'avocat* (qualifying certificate for the profession of lawyer, in France usually referred to as CAPA) and then took an oath of office as lawyers whereupon they were awarded the title of *avocat stagiaire*, that is, probationary lawyer.

The *avocat stagiaire* was permitted to handle any cases and could have his or her [14] own clients but, during a probationary period called *stage*, which lasted at least three years but could be extended to five years, had to use the title *avocat stagiaire*, not the title of *avocat* simply, and had to work out of the office of an established *avocat*. The idea was that the established *avocat* would provide some guidance and supervision to the neophyte in the office, and the latter would do some legal work for his (or her) mentor for some modest compensation. The young person's status in relation to the older *avocat* was viewed more as that of an independent contractor than as that of an employee. For obvious reasons, the *avocat stagiaire*'s own cases tended, in the beginning, to consist mainly of assigned counsel matters under the French scheme of legal aid, for which, at that time, no compensation was payable.

If the *avocat stagiaire* performed his duties (which included attending occasional lectures for young lawyers organized by the Bar) adequately, a certificate of successful completion was issued to him by a decision of the local Bar and the young lawyer became a full-fledged *avocat*.[15]

This traditional system began to work less well when the compensation paid the *avocats stagiaires* started to rise and their mentors accordingly expected a better performance, and when, in addition, the increasing complexity of the law made it more and more difficult for the *avocats stagiaires* to handle their own cases well. Accordingly, regional institutes for professional education (*centres de formation professionnelle*) were created by the 1971 statute which reorganized the

14. The increase in the number of women law students in France began long before it did in the United States. Currently, nearly half of all French law students are women. Women constitute a considerable percentage of the younger French *avocats* and *conseillers juridiques* as well as of the younger judges, though the number of women *notaires* has remained quite small.

15. In France the Bar is "integrated". The local bar associations (*ordres*) exercise disciplinary and various other "public" functions, though subject to review by the courts. Unlike the situation in some other European countries, there is no overall *ordre* at the national level, though there is a "Conference of Bar Presidents", which does not, however, currently include the Paris Bar. In addition, several "unofficial" associations of lawyers exist. There is also a European Community-wide lawyers' organization, the Consultative Committee of the Bars and Law Societies of the European Community (CCBE). See J. A. Crossick, The B.C.B.E.: An E.E.C. Bar Association?, 67 A.B.A.J. 170 (1981).

legal professions in France.[16] It is that statute which contains the basic rules concerning the profession of *avocat*. The institutes were operated jointly by the universities and the organized Bar and provided additional, more practical training to the French law students intending to take the qualifying examination as well as, subsequently, to the *avocats stagiaires*. Within a brief time, however, it was felt that even this did not provide sufficient practical training in a supervised setting. Accordingly, a law enacted in 1977 [17] provided that the prospective *avocat*, after having obtained the *maîtrise*, would receive some additional practical and theoretical training in accordance with measures to be enacted by an implementing decree. After some delay due to financial problems, that decree was finally enacted in 1980 and amended in 1981 and 1983.[18]

Pursuant to the decree, a person seeking to become an *avocat* must, after having received the required university diploma, apply to take the entrance examination to a one-year professional education program given by one of the regional institutes mentioned above. The entrance examination is partly oral and partly written. It tests not only the candidates' knowledge of the law but also their general culture—a matter usually considered quite important in France—and even their knowledge of a foreign language. The examination may not usually be taken more than three times. Instruction at the institutes is gratuitous, though a payment for the cost of instruction may be demanded as a sanction for misconduct. Assistance with living expenses is available. The instruction at the institute consists of class-room sessions largely in the nature of work on simulated clinical problems (including the drafting of contracts, the preparation of procedural documents, and the like) and of lectures on professional ethics; in addition, each student must spend part of his or her time as an intern in the office of an *avocat* designated by the center; for not more than half of that period a student may, instead, act as an intern in the legal department of a business firm, in an administrative agency, a court or the like, even in a foreign country. As intern in the office of an *avocat*, the prospective lawyer should participate in client interviews, accompany his mentor to court, etc. With the permission of the presiding judge, the intern may also address the court, of course under the control of his mentor. Thus the student is provided with a form of actual clinical experience.[19]

16. Law No. 71–1130 of December 31, 1971, J.O. Jan. 5, 1972, p. 167, 1972 D.L. 38.

17. *Supra* note 4.

18. Decree No. 80–234 of April 2, 1980, J.O. April 3, 1980, p. 838, 1980 D.L. 172, amended by Decree No. 81–887 of September 28, 1981, J.O. October 1, 1981, p. 2678, 1981 D.L. 343 and Decree No. 83–1036 of December 3, 1983, J.O. December 6, 1983, p. 3524, 1984 D.L. 2. Earlier implementing rules were enacted by Decree No. 72–468 of June 9, 1972, J.O. June 11, 1972, p.

5884, 1972 D.L. 268, modified in particular by Decree No. 83–210 of March 17, 1983, J.O. March 22, 1983, p. 838, 1983 D.L. 186 and by Decree No. 85–1123 of October 22, 1985, J.O. October 23, 1985, p. 12255, 1985 D.L. 557.

19. Since the system works through the use of practicing lawyers who take a neophyte under their wing (something that is relatively easy in France as the numbers involved are small; currently, only about 250 new *avocats* are admitted in Paris each year, see Legris, *supra* note 2a), rather

At the end of the one-year training period, the student must submit a written report summarizing his or her work experiences. This is followed by an examination which includes a written element involving the preparation of an opinion letter or legal document of some kind, and an oral element consisting of an oral argument before the examining board on some legal issue. The candidate is given three hours to prepare this argument. The examination continues with questions by the board on legal ethics and a discussion of the summary prepared by the candidate on his or her work experience during the internships. Furthermore, the examining board has before it the assessments that were given each candidate by the individuals or firms for which he acted as intern. An examination that was totally failed may normally be repeated only once, after an additional one-year training period, though in the case of a partially failed examination, the failed part alone may be retaken. If the examination has been passed, the successful candidate receives the CAPA, i.e. the document which formerly was issued shortly after the end of the formal university education.

After the award of the *certificat*, the young lawyer must take the oath of office. In it, he or she swears to act with dignity and independence, as well as conscientiously and humanely when representing or advising clients.[20] Once the oath has been taken, the new lawyer may use the title *avocat*, but this does not mean that the previous rules as to the probationary period (*stage*) have been entirely eliminated. The new *avocat*, though authorized to engage in any professional activities and no longer required to use the word *stagiaire* after the title *avocat*, must still undergo a probationary period of at least two, but not more

than through "in-house" clinics, and also makes considerable use of what one might call simulated clinics, the practical training received through the institute is less heavily oriented towards problems of the indigent than is often true in clinical education in the United States. Students might, for instance, be asked to prepare and discuss a contract involving an export sale. It should be noted, also, that for certain individuals who have worked in the field of law for a specified period of time (law teachers with a doctoral degree who have been teaching for five years, house counsel with eight years practice, certain judges, etc.) the training period at the training institute and subsequent examination can be waived and the trial period (*stage*) can be reduced to one year. Decree No. 85–1123, *supra* note 18, arts. 1, 4, 5.

20. Law No. 82–506 of June 15, 1982, J.O. June 16, 1982, p. 1899, 1982 D.L. 277. If this oath or the general rules of ethics are violated in court, the offending lawyer is nevertheless not to be summarily punished by a contempt-like procedure, but to be referred to the disciplinary authorities (the organized Bar, with *de novo* review before the intermediate appellate court), which must act expeditiously.

The obligation to act with "dignity" probably requires French lawyers to act with more restraint than might be usual for some of their more aggressive American brethren. Thus it was held that a lawyer who wrote a letter to his client criticizing a decision of the disciplinary authority as interfering with his representation of the client could be disciplined, because the client was a newspaper publisher and the lawyer thus knew that his letter, critical of the legal processes of the organized Bar, was likely to be published. X. c. Procureur général, Cass. civ. (1st ch.), December 4, 1979, 1981 D.J. 328 (with a note by Mr. Brunois). Furthermore, contingent fee contracts are a violation of professional ethical standards and subject to being declared void by the court. *See* X., Cour Versailles, January 14, 1980, 1980 D.J. 422. See also infra pp. 353–354.

than five years.[21] For a least one year during that period (but more is usual) the new *avocat* must work as either a "collaborator" or even a partner in the office of an *avocat* or of an *avoué* or a *conseil juridique*. The balance of the period may be spent in certain other legal activities, such as by working in a corporate law office, in certain public agencies or even in the office of a lawyer in a foreign country. In addition, the young lawyers must, during the probationary period, participate in continuing legal education programs organized for them by the regional institutes mentioned above.

As a practical matter, most young lawyers will spend most of the probationary period as "collaborators" of established *avocats*. As noted, the relation between "collaborator" and established *avocat* was traditionally viewed as a kind of independent contractor relationship, in line with the notion, expressed also in the oath taken by French lawyers, that they must be "independent". The increasing complexity of the law and the growth of law partnerships in France, though not nearly reaching the size of American firms and still being much less numerous [22], meant that the relationship between "collaborator" and established *avocat* came to resemble more and more that between a young associate in an American law firm and a partner. In one instance in which the young "collaborator" was limited to rather routine work and cut off from any direct contact with clients, a French court held some years ago that the "collaborator" had to be deemed an employee.[23] This upset the French Bar, since it implied that all the provisions of French labor law governing employees would become applicable, including those (subsequently modified in 1986) that greatly restrict an employer's power to terminate the employment. Accordingly, the French Parliament adopted a statute stating that the relationship between *avocat* and "collaborator" was not an employment relationship.[24] Nevertheless, the relationship remains ambiguous. It would undoubtedly be best to recognize that generally an employment relationship exists, but that it cannot be governed by all of the statutory rules on employment, designed to operate in a different context.[25]

---

21. The new rules are contained in Decree No. 83–210, modifying Decree No. 72–468, both *supra* note 18. There are some tax advantages in not terminating the probationary period until legally required; thus many young lawyers continue it for five years, though the mandatory minimum period was reduced from three to two years by Decree No. 83–210.

22. Thus there are some 5600 *avocats* in Paris and 1540 law offices involving more than one *avocat*, but of these the vast majority, 1020, include only two, and only 130 include five or more *avocats*; a very few offices have slightly over thirty *avocats*. Legris, *supra* note 2a, at 42. Group practice in France may take the form of an office sharing arrangement (*association*), which must, however, be evidenced by a

written contract, or of a formal partnership (*société civile professionnelle*).

23. X.c. Assoc. d'avocats Y., Cour Paris, February 23, 1977, 1977 D.J. 193 (with a note by Jestaz discussing the legal nature of the relation).

24. Law No. 77–685, *supra* note 4, art. 3. Though the law stated that it was retroactive, it was held to be not applicable to the case mentioned *supra* note 23. Conseil de l'ordre c. Dame B., Cour Paris, November 7, 1977, 1977 D.J. 652 (with a note by Jestaz).

25. For a detailed discussion of the relationship (but not reflecting some recent changes) see T.T.T. Trai Le, *Professional Independence and the Associate in a Law*

At the end of the probationary period, the training institute, after hearing the comments of the competent Bar council, issues a certificate of successful completion of the probationary period to the young *avocat* if his or her performance has been satisfactory.[26] He or she may now set up an independent office [27] or practice law (as during the probationary period) as a "collaborator" or partner of another *avocat* or partnership of *avocats*; but with minor exceptions (university teaching, temporary replacement of certain judges, part-time functions in certain lower courts) a French *avocat* may not accept paid employment and thus could not, for instance, accept a position in the legal department of a corporation.[28] Furthermore, under traditional French rules, an *avocat* may have only *one* office. The latter rule, however, has suffered some modification as a result of the provisions on the "right of establishment" contained in the Treaty establishing the European Economic Community, which prohibit any discrimination on account of nationality or residence.[29] On the basis of these provisions, the Court of Justice of the European Communities ruled that a lawyer from a Member State of the Community who had an office in his home State could not be prevented from establishing an additional office in another Member State if he fulfilled all normal conditions for admission to the Bar there.[30] Accordingly, the French *Cour de cassation* held that a German lawyer who had an office in Germany, and who fulfilled all the French requirements for admission as *avocat*, had to be admitted in France, in spite of the rule which, in other circumstances, prohibits an *avocat* from having more than one office.[31]

The last-mentioned case is just one example of the direct impact of European Community law on the French Bar. Of course, European Community law also has indirectly affected French lawyers because it has added a transnational dimension to French law and thus forced

Firm: A French Case Study, 29 Am.J. Comp.L. 647 (1981).

26. The certificate is rarely refused. If it is refused, the probationary period may be extended twice for one year. Decree No. 72–468 as amended, *supra* note 18, arts. 39, 40. Only an individual admitted to the French Bar and a regular member of the local *ordre* or serving out the *stage* period locally may use the title *avocat*, which is to be followed by the name of the local *ordre* with which the *avocat* is affiliated. An individual also admitted abroad may indicate this as well. Decree No. 85–1123, *supra* note 18, art. 7.

27. On the extent to which group practice (by way of an office sharing arrangement (*association*) or a formal partnership (*société civile professionnelle*) is significant, see *supra* note 22.

28. Law No. 71–1130, *supra* note 16, art. 7, as amended by Law No. 85–99 of January 25, 1985, J.O. January 26, 1985, p. 1117, 1985 D.L. 166; Decree No. 72–468, *supra* note 18, as amended by Decree No. 79–1014 of November 26, 1979, J.O. November 30, 1979, 1980 D.L. 8, art. 62.

29. Treaty Establishing the European Economic Community, done at Rome, March 25th, 1957, arts. 52, 59. (Official English text in Office for Official Publications of the European Communities, Treaties establishing the European Communities (2d ed. 1978)).

30. Ordre des avocats v. Klopp, Court of Justice of the European Communities, Case No. 107/83, July 12, 1984, 1984 E.C.R. 2971.

31. Ordre des avocats c. Klopp., Cass. Civ. (1st ch.), January 15, 1985, 1985 D.J. 316. It should be noted that normally French nationality is required for admission to the French Bar, but this rule does not apply to nationals of Member States of the European Communities.

French lawyers to deal with more complex legal issues and to familiarize themselves with events beyond French borders. The growing involvement of France in world trade has had a similar effect. Partially in reaction to this trend, a recent French decree permits French *avocats*, with the permission of the local Bar, to have foreign lawyers in their office for a *stage* period of one to three years, though this does not give the foreign lawyer any right to be admitted to the French Bar. Furthermore, foreign law students may be admitted as auditors at the training institutes mentioned above. While this was primarily intended to assist the foreign students to gain some knowledge of French law, it would also tend to improve the knowledge of foreign law and foreign cultures of those French students and lawyers who come into contact with them. Finally, French nationals and nationals of Common Market countries who have been active in a career in their home country analogous to that of an *avocat* in France (such as a barrister, solicitor or advocate in the United Kingdom, *Rechtsanwalt* in Germany, etc.) for a specified period, may now be admitted to practice in France without fulfilling the above-described requirements, provided they show that their practical experience has given them an adequate knowledge of French law and pass an examination to demonstrate such knowledge.[32]

NOTES AND QUESTIONS

(1) As the foregoing materials indicate, the academic part of legal education in France, as in most civil-law countries, is (to use our expression) "undergraduate." This, of course, marks a significant contrast between our system of legal education and that of our civilian brethren. It seems difficult to explain this contrast in terms of differing present-day social conditions or of divergent policy objectives. Thus one suspects that the reasons for the contrast can be discerned only by the student of history. Does the history of universities and of other (academic or professional) educational institutions perhaps shed some light on the matter?

(2) In France, as in most civil-law countries, a candidate's legal training is divided into an academic and a practical phase.

With respect to the practical (or apprenticeship) phase, two significant features should be noted:

(a) The kind of practical training which a candidate receives during that phase, depends on which branch of the legal profession he intends to enter. If he has his eye on a judicial career, he must try to get into the Institute of Judicial Studies (see supra). If his aim is to become an *avocat*, he has to attend a professional training

---

32. Decree No. 85–1123, *supra* note 18, arts. 2 (*stage* permitted for foreign lawyers), 6 (admission of law professionals having practiced abroad if French or EEC nationals), 10 (foreign law students as auditors at training institutes). Detailed rules on the (rather short) examination to be taken by lawyers from other common market countries who wish to be admitted in France are contained in a regulation (*ar-* *rêté*) of the Minister of Justice of December 24, 1986, J.O. January 7, 1986, p. 338, 1986 D.L. 170. The rules on the admission of lawyers from other Common Market countries were apparently designed as a way of facilitating the right of establishment of lawyers under Common Market rules, though implementing provisions on that point at the European Community level are still lacking.

institute, and is then subject to a probationary period. If he aspires to some other type of legal career, e.g., that of a *Notaire*, again his practical training will be of a different specialized nature. This means that under the French system a young law candidate must choose his *particular branch* of the legal profession *before* he enters the practical phase of his training.

(b) Under the French system the *avocat*, even during the probationary period, is a member, although a junior member, of the Bar. Thus he initially obtains such membership, with many of its privileges and responsibilities, at the average age of 24 or 25, and before he has acquired much practical experience.

On both of these points, as the reader will soon discover, the German system differs from the French.

RHEINSTEIN, LAW FACULTIES AND LAW SCHOOLS: A COMPARISON OF LEGAL EDUCATION IN THE UNITED STATES AND GERMANY

[1938] Wis.L.Rev. 5.

[Footnotes omitted.]

. . . While the common law of England and America was essentially shaped by judges, the civil law of the Continent of Europe was built by university professors. The Curia Regis of the English king was the centralizing agency, which, out of innumerable customs of cities, manors, counties, guilds, forests, stannaries, of the Church and of the navy, of the constables' courts and of the law merchant, molded the common law of England. No royal, papal, or imperial court attained such a role on the Continent. The elaboration of a common law on the basis of the law of ancient Rome was the work of the universities, of the scholars of Pavia, Bologna and Padua, of Paris and Bordeaux, of Leyden, of Prague, Vienna, Budapest, Cracow, of Copenhagen, of Leipzig, Heidelberg, Ingolstadt and Halle, of Berne, Zurich and Geneva. In the fourteenth century, a young man who aspired to a career in the service of his prince, or who intended to practice before the prince's boards and tribunals as an advocate, or as a notary, went to the Italian seats of learning. In later times, the princes provided their young men with universities in their own territories, but in all universities the same Corpus Juris was taught by the professors. The Corpus Juris, the work of the sixth century, was to be adapted to the needs of new times. This task was fulfilled by the professors who were creative men of great learning and authority. No court had a territory sufficiently large to obtain the same authority as a unifying agency as the universities. The professors' influence and authority is illustrated by the fact that the judges, who had been their pupils, became accustomed to ask the professors' opinions in difficult cases. Finally, the faculties of law attained, even formally, the position of appellate courts to which parties could appeal from the supreme courts of the territories. The "transmission of the docket" of a case from a court of "ultimate" appeal to a law faculty became a fixed institution; professors became the highest judges. Even where their jurisdiction was limited to the territory of a single prince, the law professors would migrate from one faculty to another and uphold a common tradition and a common law.

The importance of the institution of *Aktenversendung* can hardly be overestimated. It brought the law professors into continuous contact with the facts of life and the actual problems of legal practice; it was a consequence as well as a cause of their enormous influence on the development of the law. Its memory still lingers on in the habit of attorneys of laying before the courts professors' learned opinions on difficult questions of law, a practice which not only provides leading professors with considerable fees, but which also makes them influential amici curiae.

For centuries, even officially, teaching was only part of the law professors' manifold activities. They were also judges, legal advisers, scholars, and as scholars they primarily felt themselves. Their principal ambition was, and still is, to be known as authors of influential books, to be quoted as authorities, to elaborate theories, to adapt the law to the changing needs of time and place. The students might listen to the words of truth the professor would reveal to them in his lecture. Occasionally, a young man would be used by a professor as a "famulus", or a professor would condescend to a formal disputation.*

In America, legal education originated in the office of the attorney who would explain to his apprentice legal questions as they happened to arise in his practice, or who would occasionally discuss with him a chapter from Blackstone. If one of these practitioners had more pedagogic talents than others, apprentices would prefer to "read law" with him. In the course of time some lawyers discovered that pupils provided a welcome supplementary source of income. They specialized in this line. There finally emerged small schools, such as the Litchfield School, conducted by practitioners for practitioners, trade schools where young men could learn the techniques of practice and pleading, the arts of drafting instruments and of winning law suits. Such is still the spirit of the modern night schools, and such also was the spirit of the first successful American university law school, Harvard, before Story, Langdell and his colleagues recognized the law professor's responsibility as a scholar. Under the leadership of these men and such others as

---

* The reader who is looking for a more extensive historical explanation of some of the principal features of continental (especially German) legal education, is referred to the excellent article by H. Peter, Die juristische Fakultät und ihre Lehrfächer in historischer Sicht, 16 Studium Generale 65 (1963), published also, in slightly abbreviated form, in 1966 JuS 11.

The more general discussion of the history of the civil law, infra pp. 245–310, will throw further light on the historical roots of many present-day aspects of legal education in civil law countries.

Chancellor Kent at Columbia, American law professors began to criticize, to refine, and to overhaul the law of the United States.**

NOTE

In modern days, European professors have come to devote a large part of their energies to teaching. Among American law professors, on the other hand, many have attained prominence as scholars; some of them exercise considerable influence upon the development of the law as authors of textbooks and Restatements, as draftsmen of Uniform Laws, as consultants to legislative bodies, as attorneys in landmark cases, and generally as leading advocates of social and political reforms. Thus, the dissimilarities between European law faculties and many American law schools have become less marked. In some ways, however, the scholarly tradition of European universities, as compared to the professional (trade school) origin of American law schools, still makes for differences in atmosphere, which are vividly described by Parker, The Good Law School: Pipe-dreams of a Lawyer from Two Continents, 42 A.B.A.J. 1123 (1956). For refreshingly irreverent notes on the self-images of American legal academe, see A. L. Konefsky & J. H. Schlegel, Mirror, Mirror on the Wall—Histories of American Law Schools, 95 Harv.L.Rev. 833 (1982). A. W. B. Simpson, The Rise and Fall of the Legal Treatise: Legal Principles and the Forms of Legal Literature, 48 U.Chi.L.Rev. 632, 664 and 668–74 (1982) documents the backgrounds of English and American treatise writers.

THE TRADITIONAL SYSTEM OF LEGAL EDUCATION AND LEGAL CAREERS IN GERMANY (WITH SIDE–GLANCES AT OTHER CONTINENTAL COUNTRIES) [1]

I. Pre-legal Education

There is one feature of legal education which—as a result of the historical developments just alluded to—is common to all civil-law systems: the monopoly position which the University occupies (at least with respect to the first part of a future lawyer's training). In Germany, as in other civil-law countries, it is wholly impossible to become a full-fledged member of any branch of the legal profession without

---

** See also the lecture by Judge (later Chief Judge) Irving Lehman, The Influence of the Universities on Judicial Decision, 10 Cornell L.Q. 1 (1924). The early history of a nineteenth-century "small school" is described by H. W. Baade, Law at Texas: The Roberts-Gould Era (1883–1893), 86 Sw.Hist. Q. 162 (1982).

1. Much of the information presented on the following pages has been drawn from W. K. Geck, The Reform of Legal Education in the Federal Republic of Germany, 25 Am.J.Comp.L. 86 (1977); W. Schluter & W. O. Morris, A Comparison of Legal Education in the United States and West Germany, 72 W.Va.L.Rev. 317 (1970);

B. Shartel, Report on German Legal Education, 14 J. Legal Ed. 425 (1962) (based on a thorough report prepared by German experts which contains some interesting comparative data); W. Wengler, Law Studies in Western Germany, 18 J.Legal Ed. 176 (1965).

For interesting comparisons between the German system of legal education and our own, see G. Casper, Two Models of Legal Education, 41 Tenn.L.Rev. 13 (1973), and the article by Schluter and Morris, supra. See also D. Rueschemeyer, Lawyers and Their Society—A Comparative Study of the Legal Profession in Germany and in the United States (1973).

having studied law at a University. The nature and extent of a candidate's pre-legal education thus is dictated by the requirements for his admission to the University.

In order to enroll as a student in the Law Faculty (as in any other Faculty) of a German University, the candidate must present a "certificate of maturity" showing that he has completed his secondary education and has passed the rather demanding comprehensive examination (*Abiturientenexamen* or *Abitur*) that concludes his attendance at a secondary school. A German student thus enters the study of law immediately upon his graduation from a secondary school. In this respect, again, the German scheme is typical of the system prevailing in the overwhelming majority of civil-law countries. With the notable exception of Belgium, these countries generally do not interpose a period of "college" work, i.e. of more or less general education on the "higher" level, between secondary school and law study. There is no uniformity among civil-law countries, however, as to the quality and duration of primary and secondary education. In Germany, pre-University study is relatively long; generally it lasts thirteen years. Thus an average German student entering the University will be a year older than his American colleague who begins his freshman year in college.[2] It remains true, nevertheless, that in Germany, as in most other civil-law countries, law study at the University is essentially "undergraduate",[3] and that for the professionally-oriented German student the end of his general education and the time for choosing his profession comes somewhat earlier in life than for his opposite number on an American campus.

In the past, once a German student had acquired his "certificate of maturity," there were no further prerequisites to his enrollment in the University. Regardless of the high or low grades he had received in the *Abitur*—provided only that they were passing grades—a German student was able to register at the University of his choice. This traditional system of open admissions, coupled with very low tuition fees (which, moreover, can be waived in the case of a student of limited means), brought about such an enormous influx of students that the Universities could no longer absorb them. This led to agitation in favor of a numerical ceiling on admissions—a system known in Germany as *numerus clausus*. The introduction of such a system, however, raised serious constitutional problems. Almost all German Universities are what we would call State Universities, funded by taxpayers' money;[4]

---

2. A student who, upon having obtained a German "certificate of maturity", seeks to enter an American college, normally is granted sophomore or junior standing.

3. This, of course, tends to augment the number of law students, and also to affect the composition of the student body. Numerous young men and women, feeling that their education and their student life should not end at the age of 18 or 19, enter the University without a fixed professional goal. Being forced at the outset to choose among the several Faculties, many of them enroll in the Faculty of Law, although they do not (or at least not definitely) aspire to a legal career. In recent years, the number of law students has been further inflated due to the fact (discussed infra) that access to other fields of study, such as medicine, has been severely restricted.

4. For an instructive discussion of the legal and political framework of University

and the Constitution of the German Federal Republic protects the individual's "right to learn," which, it has been forcefully argued, includes his right of access to an institution of higher learning.[5] According to several decisions of the Federal Constitutional Court,[6] this right is not an absolute one; it may be limited by law to the extent— but only to the extent—that practical necessities reasonably justify such limitation.[7] In practice, this means that in most scientific and technological fields (including medicine) a limited supply of laboratories and other physical facilities justifies and indeed dictates a rigorous limitation of the number of students who can be admitted each year.

So far as law study is concerned, however, there is no similar dearth of physical facilities, and the lecture system of instruction (to be discussed infra) makes it possible for one professor to teach a very large number of students.[8] Thus, under the above-mentioned court decisions, it might be unconstitutional to impose too strict a form of *numerus clausus* upon law students, and as a consequence the recent modifications of the old system of open admissions have been relatively mild insofar as law study is concerned. A candidate for such study, especially one whose *Abitur* grades are less than excellent, today can no longer be sure that he will be admitted to the law school of his choice; but normally he will be able—at least after a waiting period—to gain access to *some* German law school.[9] Thus the flood-tide of entrants into law

governance in West Germany, see R. T. Cole, Federalism and Universities in West Germany, 21 Am.J.Comp.L. 45 (1973). As predicted in Professor Cole's article, a federal skeleton law incorporating general principles for the structure, organization and governance of German Universities has meanwhile been enacted. See Hochschulrahmengesetz of January 26, 1976 (BGBl III 223).

5. Every student who is refused admission to a German University can seek review of such refusal in an administrative court (see infra pp. 498 ff.). To the extent that questions of federal constitutional law are involved in such a case (see infra nn. 6 and 7), an ultimate appeal may lie to the Federal Constitutional Court. There is much litigation of this kind. See Cole, supra n. 4, at 49–50.

6. The leading cases are BVerfGE 33, 303 (1972), BVerfGE 43, 291 (1977), and BVerfGE 59, 1 (1981).

7. The Court's holdings, cited n. 6 supra, are more complex and more equivocal than the oversimplified statement in the text reveals. For detailed discussion, see U. Karpen (Ed.), Constitutional Aspects of Access to Higher Education (1978); U. Karpen & F. L. Knemeyer, Verfassungsprobleme des Hochschulwesens (1976).

8. During the last three decades, "about half a dozen new law faculties were found-

ed, a considerable number of new professorships created and the junior staff increased," but "these measures did not keep pace with the growing number of students." Geck, supra n. 1, at 93.

9. The mechanism used for this purpose in recent years has been a central admissions office (in Dortmund) for all German Universities. That office could assign a candidate either to the University of his choice, or to another (perhaps less popular) University. The hardship inherent in this assignment method is not as great as an American observer might assume, because qualitative differences among German law schools are far less pronounced than among their American counterparts (see infra). Moreover, the financial hardship imposed on a student assigned to a University far from his family's home is mitigated by fairly generous, publicly financed scholarships.

Whether the German Universities will continue to use the mechanism of a central admissions office, and what rules should govern the assignment of candidates to the various Universities (e.g., what role *Abitur* grades should play in this process), is a matter of constant political debate. The admissions system, although regulated in some detail in §§ 27–35, 72–76 of the federal statute cited supra n. 4, thus remains in a state of flux.

study has not been stemmed, with the result that the student-professor ratio in a German law school averages 120 to 1, and occasionally climbs to the unbelievable figure of 200 to 1.[10]

II. The Traditional System of Legal Education [10a]

(1) *Basic Features*

The outstanding characteristic of traditional legal training in Germany—as in the majority of civil-law countries—is that the training period is sharply divided into two distinct phases: first several years of theoretical study at a University, followed by a somewhat shorter period of "preparatory service", i.e. practical training as an apprentice.[11] At the end of each of these phases the candidate is subjected to a difficult comprehensive examination.

Federal law makes entry into any branch of the legal profession dependent upon successful completion of both phases.[12] The general framework of legal education thus has been fixed by federal legislation. The details, however, were traditionally left to be determined by the laws and regulations of the *Länder*. As to relatively minor matters, the regulations in the various *Länder* differed from each other; but by continuous consultation and cooperation among the governments of the *Länder* and other interested organizations, a high degree of nation-wide uniformity throughout the German Federal Republic was achieved and maintained.

An American reader may interject, at this point, that in spite of near-uniformity of state legislation and state regulations the actual curricula and methods of instruction (during the first phase of legal training) might well vary from University to University. With respect to German education, this raises a somewhat complex issue. In contrast to France, where until recently the curriculum of law schools was almost wholly fixed by governmental decree, the German system is based on an old and well-established tradition of academic autonomy. This means that in theory each academic institution is autonomous as regards the matter and the methods of instruction.[13] In practice, however, the scope of this autonomy has been quite limited. As there

---

10. See Geck, supra n. 1, at 91, 93.

10a. Attempts to reform the traditional system, and recently enacted modifications of that system, will be discussed infra, in Parts III and IV of this essay. Familiarity with the traditional system, however, is necessary before one can understand the attempted and actual reforms. Moreover, as the reader will observe when she or he comes to Parts III and IV, the more radical reform experiments have been abandoned, and the recently adopted actual modifications are relatively modest. It is safe to say, therefore, that in its essence (though not in every detail) the traditional system is still—or again—in effect today.

11. The historical reasons for the two-phase system of legal education prevailing in continental Europe are interestingly discussed by Casper, supra n. 1, at 14–16.

12. This is the traditional system, which now prevails again throughout the Federal Republic. For a discussion of the recent legislation by which some experimentation with one-phase legal education was temporarily permitted, see infra, III.

13. Since the founding of the German Federal Republic, this principle has been backed by a constitutional provision guaranteeing freedom of teaching and research.

are no examinations in lecture courses, nor as a rule any other semi-annual or annual University examinations,[14] a German law student is compelled, during all of the years of his studies at the University, to keep his eye primarily on the dreaded comprehensive examination which he will have to take at the end of the whole period. The subjects that will be covered in that examination, however, were fixed by (more or less uniform) state regulations. As a result, the Law Faculties of all German Universities were forced to build their curricula around those same subjects. In fact, if an observer of German legal education went to visit one University after another, he would have found relatively little variance in subjects and methods of instruction.[15] Thus it is easier to generalize concerning "German legal education" than it would be in speaking of "American legal education". [16]

(2) University Study

4 years of law school work b/f apprentice position

Federal law prescribes a minimum duration of 3½ years, i.e. of 7 semesters, for the academic phase of legal education; but Law Faculties generally recommend that 8 semesters be devoted to the task. Students often delay even longer; on average, they spend between nine and ten semesters studying law before they take the comprehensive examination concluding this phase of their training.

Those students who are financially able to do so, tend to remain at one University for only one or two semesters, and then to move on to other Universities.[17] Only the last two or three semesters must—by

14. There are periodical examinations for students who seek a waiver of tuition fees or other financial assistance; but these serve only to determine whether the candidate deserves such assistance. Students not seeking financial assistance sometimes are permitted to take the same examinations on a voluntary, non-credit basis; but few of them seem to avail themselves of the opportunity. As to comprehensive mid-study qualifying examinations, see infra, IV.

15. In part, this may be due, also, to the fact that although Germany has a federal form of government, its private law, criminal law and procedural law (in other words, the bulk of its "lawyers' law") is embodied in national codes. Thus, as compared to the United States, there may be less room for choice and for differences of opinion as to the principles and rules of positive law to be taught.

16. The statement in the text applies to the quality as well as the scheme of academic legal education. It is true that some German law schools manage to attract more famous professors and thus have acquired greater prestige than others. It is true, also, that some of the new, experimental one-phase law schools (see infra)

were widely considered to be inferior. But, subject to this qualification, a German law student can expect approximately the same quality of instruction no matter which law school he attends. Since all German Universities with law faculties still are what we would call State Universities, and the Ministries of Education of the various *Länder* by informal arrangements seek to minimize the Universities' competitive use of financial incentives, there is little difference among German law schools with respect to the level of faculty salaries. For similar reasons, the quality of the libraries and of other supporting services does not vary from University to University as dramatically as it does in the United States. Indeed, some newer universities have superior law libraries. It is not surprising, therefore, that differences in the quality of teaching and research are far less pronounced among the Law Faculties of the various German Universities than among American law schools.

17. Recent restrictions on admissions (see supra n. 9) have made such transfers somewhat more difficult. But by various methods, including a system of swapping assigned places, German law students still

virtue of regulations, or in any event for obvious practical reasons—be spent at the place where the student intends to report for the examination. Up to three semesters' credit may be given for study at foreign universities. (Some Swiss universities not only have German professors, but also offer courses in German law.)

As has been mentioned before, course offerings and course elections are heavily oriented toward the subjects which will be covered in the examination. The sequence in which these courses are taken is of considerable importance, and in order to provide some guidance in this respect most Law Faculties issue "recommended curricula". What follows is the curriculum recommended by the Faculty of Law of the University of the Saarland, which may be taken as fairly typical for its time: [18]

Study Program
For the Study of Law
(as of April 1975)

I. General and Compulsory Courses *

Weekly hours

First Semester

Introduction to law	3
General section of the private law code **	4
+ Workshop (supplementing the lecture)	2
General section of the criminal law code	4
+ Workshop (supplementing the lecture)	2
Constitutional law I (organization of the Federal Republic)	3
Introduction to economics (with graded tests) ***	3
	21

manage to move from one University to another.

18. See Geck, supra n. 1, at 111–15.

* These courses cover the subjects in which, according to official Examination Regulations, every student will be examined at the end of the period of his University study. The Examination Regulations differ somewhat, but not too drastically, from Land to Land.

Note that some subjects are taught in detail, while as to others only "Fundamentals" are taught. This, also, reflects the requirements of the Examination Regulations. The provision that as to certain subjects the candidate has to be familiar only with "Fundamentals", and not with details, is a relatively recent innovation (see infra).

** The General Section or General Part of the German Civil Code proclaims principles and rules of such generality that they

cut across the fields of Contracts, Torts, Property, Family Law, Decedents' Estates, and all other areas of substantive private law. See infra pp. 533–534. Needless to say, this course has no exact counterpart in the curriculum of an American law school with a common-law curriculum.

*** These subjects, like some of the elective subjects listed below, are not, strictly speaking, within the field of law. One must remember, in this connection, that a German law student has never gone to "college" and thus would have no opportunity, after the end of his secondary education, to receive formal instruction in economics and political science if he did not study those subjects as part of his legal education. Whether German law students (who tend not to study very hard during the early semesters, and to concentrate on technical legal subjects during the last 1½ or 2 years before the examination) derive

Second Semester

General section of law of obligations	4
Real property and chattels I	3
+ Workshop on law of obligations and property	2
Special sections of the criminal law code	4
Criminal law: practical course for beginners	2
Constitutional law II (basic rights)	3
+ Workshop (supplementing the lecture)	2
	20

Third Semester

Special sections of law of obligations I	3
Real property and chattels II	3
Private law: practical course for beginners	2
Constitutional law III (in its relationship to international law)	2
General theory of the state	3
Fundamentals of constitutional court procedures	2
Constitutional law: practical course for beginners	2
Fundamentals of court organization	1
	18

Fourth Semester

Special sections of law of obligations II	2
Fundamentals of family law	3
Fundamentals of inheritance law	3
Fundamentals of criminal procedure	3
Criminal law: practical course for advanced students	2
Special sections of administrative law	4
	17

Fifth Semester

Commercial law I	1
Labor law	4
Fundamentals of civil procedure	4
Private law: practical course for advanced students	2
General section of administrative law	4
Fundamentals of administrative law court procedures	2
	19

Sixth Semester

Commercial law II	3
Commercial law III (fundamentals of securities)	2
Constitutional and administrative law: practical course for advanced students	2
Fundamentals of bankruptcy and execution	3
Fundamentals of non-contentious procedure	1
Elective courses (cf. II below)	8
	19

much actual benefit from these course offerings, is another question.

Seventh Semester

Private law: elective practical course	2
Practical course preparing specifically for the written part of the first state examination	4
Review course in private law	2
Review course in criminal law	2
Review course in constitutional and administrative law	2
Elective courses (cf. II below)	4
	16

After the Seventh Semester (between semesters)
Review course in private law, criminal law, constitutional law and administrative law = 60 hours

During any semester: in addition to the foregoing program
One elective course from group 1 or 2 (cf. II below)

II.   Elective Courses *

Elective Group 1
Sixth Semester

Roman law	4
Medieval legal history	4

Seventh Semester

Recent private law history +	2
Recent constitutional law history +	2

Elective Group 2
Sixth Semester

Legal philosophy I +	3
Legal sociology I +	3
General theory of law I +	2

Seventh Semester

Legal philosophy II	1
Legal sociology II	1
General theory of law II +	2

Elective Group 3
Sixth Semester

Criminology I	4
Juvenile law	2
Law and practice of prisons	2

Seventh Semester

Criminology II	4

* According to the Examination Regulations, each student had to choose one of the seven groups of electives, and (as part of the comprehensive examination) was examined in the subjects which belong to the group chosen by him. He was free, of course, to attend lectures on subjects in other groups, and some of the elective courses (marked with a cross) are recommended to all students; but students tend to devote little time and energy to subjects in which they do not face an examination, i.e., to electives outside the chosen group.

Elective Group 4
Sixth Semester

Fundamentals of administrative practice	2
Administrative law (special section)—subject matter not included in the obligatory administrative law courses	4
Fundamentals of social security	2

Seventh Semester

Intensive study courses taken from the preceding electives	4

Elective Group 5
Sixth Semester

Economic law I (including economic administrative law)	2
Fundamentals of tax and budgetary law I	2
Patent and copyright law	4

Seventh Semester

Economic law II (including economic administrative law)	2
Fundamentals of tax and budgetary law II	2

Elective Group 6
Sixth Semester

Public international law	3
Law of international organizations	3
Law of the European communities	3

Seventh Semester

Intensive study courses taken from the preceding electives (including one 2-hour seminar)	3

Elective Group 7
Sixth Semester

Comparative law	3
Fundamentals of French law I	2
Private international law	3

Seventh Semester

Fundamentals of French law II	3
Intensive study courses taken from the preceding electives	1

If the total number of weekly hours suggested in this curriculum appears somewhat large to an American reader, he should keep in mind that most of the courses listed (in fact, all of them except those designated as first-year Workshops or as upper-class Practical Courses) consisted purely of lectures. For the student, these lecture courses traditionally require no preparation; in class (if he attends, and there is no check on his attendance), he is a passive listener while the professor delivers a monologue that is but rarely interrupted.[19]

In the Practical Courses there is traditionally, again, little oral give-and-take; but the students have to write papers, either in class (using only a text edition, without annotations, of the relevant codes) or at home on the basis of library research. These papers, normally based on hypothetical cases, are intended to give the students an opportunity to apply the knowledge gained in the lecture courses; but the large number of participants in the Practical Courses—often over 100—forces the professors to entrust the grading to relatively inexperienced assistants. Satisfactory completion of a certain number (usually 6 or 7) of Practical Courses is a pre-condition of admission to the comprehensive examination.[20]

In addition, most law faculties have been experimenting with various forms of discussion classes;[21] but as a rule such exercises require no preparation on the part of the students and are conducted by assistants. There are also seminars in which the discussion is led by a professor. Participation in a seminar, however, usually is reserved to those students who have excelled in a Practical Course.

The examination which a German law student has to take at the end of the first phase of his training, is truly comprehensive in the sense that it covers—in more or less detail—all of the compulsory subjects (see supra), plus the group of electives chosen by the candidate. The conduct of the examination is controlled, not by the law faculty, but by the Ministry of Justice of the particular State; accordingly, it is called the First State Examination. Although there are minor varia-

---

19. Some of the younger law teachers, especially those acquainted with American teaching methods, recently have begun to experiment with various ways of inducing a measure of student participation. Casebooks have been published in several fields. See W. Fikentscher, Rechtsunterricht und Entscheidungssammlungen, in Tübinger Festschrift für Eduard Kern 139, especially at 141 (1968). Using these casebooks or other materials, some of the professors give reading assignments to the students and often base their lectures on leading cases with which the students would be familiar if they had done their reading. It must be remembered, however, that there are no course examinations, and that traditional notions of "academic freedom"—deeply rooted in the history of German Universities and vigorously defended by student representatives—make it impossible for the professor to check on attendance or preparedness. Thus the new experiments benefit only those students—apparently a small percentage—who voluntarily avail themselves of the opportunities offered. According to E. A. Laing, Revolution in Latin American Legal Education:

The Colombian Experience, 6 Lawyer of the Americas 370 (1974), attempts to modernize law teaching through the case method and other methods requiring student participation and class preparation are open to the charge of being "Yankee-inspired." More recently an Austrian professor of Roman law has successfully published collections of cases and materials on the Roman law of torts for law students. H. Hausmaninger, Das Schadenersatzrecht der lex Aquilia (2d ed. 1980).

20. "This requirement of participation in practical exercises is the only device in the entire German system of legal education that is comparable to compulsory class attendance, examinations in specific courses, and various other methods of control that are common in the United States." Shartel, supra n. 1, at 439.

21. E.g., the first-year Workshops listed in the above curriculum of the University of the Saarland. These are study groups of moderate size (typically 20 to 30 students) who meet once or twice a week with an assistant to discuss the professorial lectures they have attended.

tions from state to state, the following description of the practice in
West Berlin may be regarded as typical:

> The first State law examination in Berlin includes four
> supervised papers, an important paper prepared at home, and
> an oral examination. The supervised papers are on civil law,
> criminal law, commercial or labor law, and constitutional or
> administrative law. In writing each one of these papers dur-
> ing five hours, the candidate has at his disposal the relevant
> legislative text but no textbooks or commentaries. A few days
> after writing the last paper, the candidate is handed the
> subject-matter for the work which is to be prepared at home
> during six weeks. Dealing with a more difficult legal problem,
> the candidate has to show here that he is capable, with the use
> of all the relevant literature, of preparing a fully constructed
> and carefully thought out legal opinion. Finally, there is an
> oral examination before a four-man board. A judge or senior
> civil servant usually takes the chair; the other members are as
> a rule two university professors, and another judge or a state
> prosecutor or a barrister. The oral examination, to which five
> candidates are summoned at a time, lasts about five hours.
> Each member of the board of examiners examines all the
> candidates in his specialized field. The orals [cover all exami-
> nation subjects.] The chairman of the board, as the last
> examiner, usually puts questions on procedural law and other
> branches. Immediately afterwards, the board, whose members
> have previously assessed the written work, decides on the
> results of the examination and informs the candidate.[22]

If successful, the candidate now has the right to use the title
Referendar and to enter the "preparatory service", which constitutes
the second part of his training.

(3) Apprenticeship Training

The normal period of the Referendar's "preparatory service", formerly of longer duration, recently has been set at two and a half years
after having been initially reduced to two.[23] During this period, the
Referendar has the status of a temporary civil servant [24] and he
receives an allowance for his and his dependents' support. Pursuant to
a training plan, the details of which have varied somewhat from state
to state but are now standardized by federal law, the Referendar
successively works, as a closely supervised assistant, in a number of

---

22. Wengler, supra n. 1, at 177.

23. Deutsches Richtergesetz § 5b, as repeatedly amended (up to 1984). The implementing Regulations of the *Länder* are cited in Schönfelder, Deutsche Gesetze,
footn.*** under § 5b of the Richtergesetz.

24. In the days of the Empire and the
Weimar Republic, there was a split among

the *Länder* concerning the status of a
Referendar. Under the old Prussian system, he was a *Beamter*, while in Bavaria
and some other states he was regarded as a
trainee not having the status (though
sometimes doing the work) of an official.

obligatory and elective training stations. The four obligatory training stations, each having a minimum duration of three months, are with a civil court, a criminal court or a prosecutor's office, an administrative agency, and a lawyer. Additionally, there are to be, as a rule, no more than three elective training stations of six months each. These include any one of the obligatory stations as well as legislative services, notaries, specialized tribunals, unions or employers' or other associations (e.g., chambers of commerce), "a supranational, international, or foreign station, or a foreign lawyer," and other stations suitable for appropriate training.[25] These provisions enable young German lawyers to spend part of their post-academic training with law firms or other suitable organizations in foreign countries, including the United States.

In addition, a law trainee attends group sessions devoted mostly to the analysis of difficult practical cases. These sessions perhaps are somewhat similar to the Practical Courses or Practical Exercises in which he previously participated as a University student; but now they are conducted by judges, administrative officials and other non-academic lawyers.

One important feature of the German "preparatory service" system has been that every Referendar receives virtually the same training, regardless of whether the career to which he aspires is that of a professor, a judge, a prosecutor, a public official, or an attorney.[26] This distinguishes the German system of apprenticeship from that prevailing, e.g., in France, where the apprenticeship program (and in part even the training received during the second half of University law study) varies depending on the special branch of the legal profession which the candidate seeks to enter. A young German lawyer thus may wait longer than his French colleague before he chooses the type of legal work in which he will engage.

At the end of his "preparatory service", the Referendar takes the Second State Examination, which again is administered by the State's Ministry of Justice. This time, all of the examiners are judges and officials rather than professors. Though similar in nature to the First State Examination, the final examination is more practice-oriented and even more comprehensive and difficult. In the case of a candidate who intends to enter a judicial or other official career (see infra), the grade received in this examination will strongly affect his chances of being appointed to such office, and also his future promotions. Upon having passed, the successful candidate now possesses the basic qualification necessary for entry into any branch of the legal profession.[27]

25. Richtergesetz, § 5b (1984 version).

26. Note, however, that during part of the training period a modicum of specialization is permitted, e.g. by working for an academic institution, or for a law firm or other organization outside of Germany.

27. Upon having passed the Second State Examination, the successful candidate used to receive the title of "Assessor".

This title is no longer official, but it is still widely used.

It should be noted that both "Referendar" and "Assessor" are non-academic professional titles. The degree of Doctor Juris (Dr. Jur.), on the other hand, is a purely academic one. Although it is not necessary for a judicial or official career, or for the practice of law, the doctoral degree

III. Attempts to Reform the Traditional System of Legal Education

Although large numbers of highly competent professionals were produced by the traditional system of German legal education, many critics have long spoken of a crisis of that system.

Some aspects of that crisis may be connected with the malaise and mood of rebellion which in the late 1960's began to make itself felt among students (not only law students) throughout the world.[28] There is no doubt, however, that the special problems of German legal education had reached the crisis stage long before the emergence of the radical student movement of the 1960's. For many decades, there had been intense and almost universal dissatisfaction, especially with the first (academic) phase of legal training.[29] How completely the traditional system has failed to keep up with the educational needs of German law students, is shown by the fact that the majority of those students have adopted the custom of more or less neglecting their University courses and of turning to private cram courses in order to acquire the bulk of the knowledge and skills that are necessary to pass the fearful First State Examination.[30] The "repetitors", who conduct these cram courses, usually are good lawyers and talented teachers; but they have no academic standing and are engaged in a business for profit.[31] Thus

is sought by many young German lawyers, including a large percentage of those who do not aspire to any kind of academic position. The reason may be, in part, that in German-speaking countries every person having a doctoral degree (not only a medical doctor) customarily is addressed as "Herr Doktor", so that possession of such a degree carries a measure of constantly perceptible prestige—fondly remembered by two of the editors.

In the last several decades, German law faculties have had to curtail the number of doctoral candidates, by admitting to such candidacy only those Referendars who have done relatively well in their First State Examination.

28. On the political atmosphere in German Universities (which is part of the background of ongoing attempts to reform legal education), see the two articles by H. L. Mason, Reflections on the Politicized University: The Academic Crisis in the Federal Republic of Germany, 60 AAUP Bulletin 299 (Sept.1974), and The Continuing Academic Crisis in West Germany, 64 AAUP Bulletin 12 (March 1978).

29. See W. O. Weyrauch, The Personality of Lawyers 96 ff. (1964). One can hear and read, also, some remarks that are critical of the "preparatory service" phase of German legal education; but usually these criticisms are mild compared to those di-

rected at the academic phase. For a bibliography of the enormous literature generated by the crisis of German legal education, see Geck, supra n. 1, at 116–19.

Outside of German, the German apprenticeship method has many admirers, even in the United States, and compulsory postgraduate training schemes of a similar nature have been advocated here. See, e.g., E. B. Stason, Legal Education: Postgraduate Internship, 39 A.B.A.J. 463 (1953). Cf. Report of the Committee on Continuing Legal Education, Association of American Law Schools, 1960 Program and Reports of Committees 42.

30. See Weyrauch, supra n. 29, at 101–08.

31. The courses conducted by the German "repetitor" are not comparable to the cram courses taken by many American law students during the last few weeks before the bar examination. The American law student (a) has completed the bulk of his training, and (b) has obtained a law degree on the strength (c) of many course examinations, *before* he takes his cram course, which is (d) very short, (e) mainly designed to acquaint the candidate with peculiarities of local law and procedure, and thus meant (f) to supplement the student's law school training rather than to serve as a substitute for it. In all of these respects the student gets his real training largely outside of the official educational system.[32] It is in the "repetitor's" cram course that the student, often for the first time, finds a small class conducted by a mature teacher; here he becomes acquainted with the give-and-take of genuine discussion and perhaps begins to realize that law is not merely an abstract system of precepts and concepts neatly expounded in a lecture, but also an attempt to find viable answers to the very real and ever-changing (and perhaps disordered) problems bred by the interaction of human beings and social groups. At the same time, the student is drilled in the subjects which he must master for the examination, and is given expert instruction regarding the idiosyncrasies of the individuals who are likely to be his examiners.

The last decades have witnessed a veritable avalanche of proposals for the reform of German legal education.[33] As a result, some changes have occurred; they can be divided into two categories, namely (a) modest, piecemeal reforms which have brought about some minor improvements in most German law schools but have not altered the fundamental features of the traditional system; and (b) radically innovative experiments conducted at only a few law schools.

(a) Several recent changes of the first kind already are reflected in the above description of University law study. The division of examination subjects into compulsory subjects and groups of electives is of relatively recent vintage. So is the provision that as to some of the compulsory subjects only the "Fundamentals" (and not the details) have to be mastered by the candidates in the First State examination. Thus the coverage of that examination, although it is still fairly comprehensive, has been somewhat limited. As will be seen infra, some of this is now codified.

The introduction of discussion classes, such as first-year workshops, also is a relatively new development. At the University of Frankfurt, it was announced in 1978 that first-year workshops, supplementing the lectures and devoted to the discussion of actual cases, in the future will no longer be conducted by junior academic personnel, but by judges, prosecutors, attorneys, and state officials.[34]

The careful reader of the suggested curriculum reproduced above will have noticed, moreover, that in an undisguised

the German "repetitor" courses are different.

32. To a considerable extent, the students have abandoned not only the courses offered by the official system, but also the textbooks and treatises written by their professors. Law students turn more and more to teaching tools specially prepared for their use (with heavy emphasis on cases) by non-academic authors, including "repetitors". Some of these books, espe-cially those written for advanced students, contain much useful analysis; but they are rarely (if ever) cited in "respectable" legal writings, and not to be found in University libraries. American law students, too, are familiar with this *genre* of legal literature.

33. For references see Geck, supra n. 29.

34. See Editorial, 1978 Bildung and Wissenschaft 203, 204.

effort to compete with the "Repetitor", the Law Faculties have sought to offer a seventh-semester "Practical Course preparing specifically for the written part of the first state examination" as well as an intersession review course covering the most important compulsory examination subjects.[35]

(b) Between 1971 and 1984, some German law schools have been experimenting with radically innovative models of *one-phase legal education*, i.e., models which seek to combine the academic and the practical features of legal training in a single, integrated system. The legal basis for this experiment was a 1971 amendment of § 5 of the Richtergesetz, which "authorized the states to combine university studies and practical training into one single unit or phase (*Einphasen-Ausbildung*), and to replace the first state examination either by an intermediary examination or by grades obtained during the course of studies." [36] While a number of *Laender* implemented relatively modest "one-phase" programs at new universities within a relatively traditional mold (e.g., Augsburg; Bielefeld), the City-State of Bremen attempted a more fundamental realignment of law training itself, in a manner somewhat reminiscent of the legal realism-*cum*-social engineering model advocated by Professors Harold Lasswell and Myres McDougal in this country towards the end of the second world war.[37] Professor Geck described this model as follows:

> This one phase experiment has been terminated

W. K. GECK, THE REFORM OF LEGAL EDUCATION IN THE FEDERAL REPUBLIC OF GERMANY *
25 Am.J.Comp.L. 86, 99–101 (1977).

The Bremen Model

. . . The Bremen model is based largely on the work of the "*Loccumer Arbeitskreis*," a private group of university professors, assistants, legal trainees, students and one judge who had made himself a name fighting for reforms of the judiciary. Let me briefly describe the *Loccum* tenets.

The *Loccum* program aims at emancipation. First the jurist himself is to be emancipated. The law of an industrial state in the 20th century is not so much a decision by the legislature which a judge or administrator merely applies on

---

35. See supra pp. 165–168.

36. W. K. Geck, The Reform of Legal Education in the Federal Republic of Germany, 25 Am.J.Comp.L. 86, 95 (1977).

37. H. D. Lasswell & M. J. McDougal, Legal Education and Public Policy: Professional Training in the Public Interest, 52 Yale L.J. 203 (1943).

* Reprinted by permission of the American Journal of Comparative Law and the American Association for the Comparative Study of Law.

The author of this article, who was familiar with American as well as German legal education, was Professor of Law at the University of the Saarland. We mourn his passing.

the basis of scholarship, legal experience and common sense. Since modern statutory law with its many general clauses leaves more and more possibilities of application open, the modern judge or administrator develops from an interpreter of the law into the real law-giver. Present-day problems do not require a servant of the statute, but a social engineer who forms the law and who does it with a special goal, the emancipation of the people. Traditional legal education does not prepare one for this task. The customary methods of interpretation—considering the wording of a norm, its context within the system, the intent of the norm and its legal history—seem inadequate. They help to stabilize the existing social and economic system. In order to bring about the necessary emancipating changes as a social engineer, the jurist should put the greatest possible emphasis on the social and economic background of each case he has to decide. A broad basis in economics and sociology is the first condition for the new jurist. Also the teaching methods must be thoroughly changed. University education as well as practical training have mainly been a one-way street of communication, with information fed by the professor, judge, administrator, etc. to the student or legal trainee. This has also contributed to the production of jurists who are faithful members of the establishment. Examinations are still virtually initiation rites to the establishment, as they force the candidate to adapt himself to the ruling system. Legal education and examination disregard modern psychology, as they prevent the future jurist from developing himself free of repression and from working in cooperation with others. Moreover, the whole traditional system of legal education is oriented towards the judiciary career and not towards the other legal professions.

The authors of the *Loccum* program, starting from these premises, suggested the following main changes. As a system like Augsburg does not really abolish the traditional faults, the whole legal training should take place at the university but at a university quite different from the traditional one. The study of law should be arranged, not according to the system of the subject matter, like the different books of the civil code, but according to practical problems; for instance, from the conclusion of a sales contract to a law suit resulting from it, and on to a judgment and its execution. The studying should take place in small groups, using the experience of modern psychology. Instead of the repressive comprehensive examinations, the student should prove his qualification by work done in individual courses, and by writing a final research paper on a subject of his own choice. After five years, the university should award a diploma giving the same qualification as the second state examination. . . .

Since April 1975, a new statute for the Bremen version of the single-phase education of the jurist has been in force. The aim of the training is to produce a jurist capable of practicing in a changing society under the rule of law and a democratic and social constitution. Through exemplary models and a critical understanding of scholarly methods, the prospective jurist is to gain the knowledge and the capability to learn which he will need in practice. Theory and practice must not be separated. Working in small groups is the preferred form of study and tutors are to play an important role.

This legal education is to last six years.* The first year is devoted to an integrated study of the social sciences. Law students have the same two courses as the students of economics and sociology. The first course deals with the position and activities of jurists and social science graduates in their professions and in society. The second one examines the structure of bourgeois society to the present day. Courses like this are chiefly supposed to teach the economic and social basis on which the legal order is founded, and which a lawyer has to take into consideration.

The specific legal training is divided into two phases, one of three and one of two years. During the first main period, three semesters are used for the main subject matter in private, labor, public, criminal and procedural law. This subject matter is of course so vast that the exemplary learning called for in the statute can only deal with very small segments of these fields. They are to be chosen according to their practical, social and systematic relevance. The law is always to be viewed in its social context and its methods are to be viewed critically. During the second part of the first main period, the

---

* The following is a schematic outline of the Bremen Model, as set forth by Professor Geck (25 Am.J.Comp.L. at 116):

Phase:	Duration:	Subject matter:
Integrated study of the social sciences	1 year	Courses: Jurists and social science graduates in their professions and in society. The structure of bourgeois society from the beginning of capitalism to the present day
Law studies: main period I	3 years 20 months	University studies: The main subject matter in private, labor, public, criminal and procedural law by exemplary method
	1 month 15 months	Introductory course to the Practical training in private, criminal, and administrative law at courts, an administrative agency and under an attorney at law
Law studies: main period II	2 years	Specialization (in labor and economic law, or in public administration or in social and criminal law)
	3 semesters 6 months	Studies at the university Practical training

total 6 years

student, after a one month introductory course, undergoes fifteen months of the same practical training as his fellows in Augsburg and those under the traditional model. Parallel to the practical training, there are to be complementary courses held jointly by professors and judges or other jurists in practice. Then the student goes back to the university for the second main period, devoted to specialization either in the fields of labor and economic law, or of public administration or social and criminal law. In his special field of interest, the student is to review critically the theories and methods he had become acquainted with earlier, to recognize the historical, social and political reasons for legal rules and decisions, and to work on suggestions and drafts for legal regulations and changes of existing regulations. The preferred working method in this stage is study by research, preferably on special projects of an interdisciplinary nature. Finally the student will take practical training for six months in his special field of interest.

. . .

IV. Federal Uniformity and Reform, 1981-84

Professor Geck goes on to discuss what, to him, seemed the most negative aspects of the Bremen Model: an essentially Marxist approach to the social sciences; an idiosyncratic grading method, neglect of essential "core" courses, and—through a combination of these factors with some others—the likely emergence of a "Bremen jurist" who has little in common with traditional jurists. On a purely budgetary level, there was also the question of cost effectiveness: "One-step" systems like that of Bremen required a much higher faculty-student ratio, and were thus attractive only if manifestly successful.[38]

We should add in fairness that despite or perhaps because of its unorthodox recruitment methods, the Bremen faculty attracted a number of innovative scholars, whose views received a measure of attention in the United States.[39] This does not, however, detract from the central objection to the "Bremen Model" which is implicit in Professor Geck's above-quoted remarks: Homogeneity of legal education in the Federal Republic of Germany is conceived to be an absolute requirement because the legal culture is based on the notion of *"Freizuegigkeit der Juristen,"* i.e., the uniformity of legal qualifications which makes it possible for lawyers in the Federal Republic of Germany freely to move from one part of the country to another. It is simply intolerable for Germans to envisage lawyers professionally qualified to be attorneys,

---

38. Geck, supra n. 1, at 101–105.

39. See C. Joerges, Relational Contract Theory in a Comparative Perspective: Tensions Between Contract and Antitrust Law Principles in the Assessment of Contract Relations Between Automobile Manufacturers and Their Dealers in Germany, 1985 Wis.L.Rev. 581, G. Teubner, Substantive and Reflexive Elements in Modern Law, 17 L. & Soc.Rev. 239 (1983), and the debate between Professors Blankenburg and Teubner, 18 L. & Soc.Rev. 273 and 291 (1984). Professors Joerges and Teubner are members of the Bremen law faculty, and well-known for their innovative research.

prosecutors, and judges in Bremen but not, automatically and simultaneously, in Bavaria or Berlin. Thus, the "Bremen Model" had to succeed on a national scale or not at all.

Whatever the ultimate verdict of legal and social historians, the legislative response has been unambiguously negative. The "one-phase" model survived the initial statutory deadline of 1981, but the Federal Minister of Justice was given authority to promulgate a regulation "establishing the grade and point scales for individual and comprehensive grades" in legal examinations.[40] This federalization of bar examination grade scales was followed, quite logically, by the federalization of law faculty curriculum structures and law training regulations, brought about by the Act of July 25, 1984.[41]

The key provision of that enactment is § 5, which restores the traditional requirements of university education followed by a first state examination, a preparatory training service, and a second state examination. As there are no exceptions from this scheme, the "one-phase" experiment has been terminated. The training period, as already mentioned, is set at two and a half years, and its stations as well as the duration thereof are now regulated by federal law. Very little is left in this regard to regulation by *Land* (state) law.[42]

University law study, too, is now federally regulated. The key provision is § 5a(2), providing:

> The objects of study are especially the core subjects Civil Law, Penal Law, Public Law, and Procedural Law, including the methods of legal science with their philosophical, historical, and social foundations. Additionally, the student devotes himself to elective subjects, which serve to broaden his studies and to deepen his understanding of the obligatory subjects connected with the electives.

Additionally, legal education is to "take account of adjudicative, administrative, and counselling practice." This is to be achieved by practical studies between semesters, totalling at least three months.[43]

Perhaps the most significant break with past tradition is the new federal legislative requirement of "performance controls" through examinations at an intermediate stage of university studies—as a rule, not later than at the end of the second year of study. These controls are to extend, at a minimum, to Civil Law, Penal Law, and Public Law. In the event of failure, these intermediate examinations can be repeated within a year. Their successful completion is a precondition for

40. Richtergesetz, § 5d (in effect from 1981 to 1984); Regulations of December 3, 1981 [1981] 1 BGBl 1243. Two questions: (1) Could you conceive of such a regulation (setting *federal* standards for *state* or *provincial* bar examinations) in the United States or in Australia or Canada? (2) Would you like to be the draftsperson?

41. Amending Richtergesetz §§ 5–5d and "grandfathering" those qualified under prior law as of September 16, 1984, id. § 109.

42. State law can authorize service at labor, administrative, social, or tax courts as the equivalent of some federally required training stations.

43. Richtergesetz § 5a(3).

participation in training programs designated by state law and, crucially, for admission to the first state examination.[44]

The next few years will show whether these intermediate examinations will, at least to some degree, stem the tide of those entering law study [45]. It should be kept in mind, however, that modest reforms of this kind do not really come to grips with the basic problem, i.e., the unfavorable teacher-student ratio. Unless and until that ratio is dramatically improved, legal education in Germany will continue to suffer from the twin evils bred by the relative scarcity of professorial manpower: the prevalence of lecturing as a teaching method [46] and the absence of course or term examinations.

NOTES AND QUESTIONS

(1) When we seek to compare the problems faced by the German experimenters with those which in the opinion of many critics exist in American legal education, one thing appears certain: Clinical training has always played a large role in the traditional German scheme; but that scheme has been criticized for its failure to *integrate* academic study and practical training. In this country, on the other hand, for a long time the main thrust of the critics' stance has been that *the quantity* of a future lawyer's clinical training (prior to his entry into the profession) is inadequate. But when in recent years the quantity of clinical offerings was increased in most American law schools, the problem of "feedback" was quickly recognized as a crucial one, and it became evident that American law schools, like their German counterparts, had some difficulty in attempting to integrate academic and clinical legal education. On both sides of the Atlantic it has been found that such integration necessarily involves a great deal of faculty supervision of the clinical work of individual students, and of small groups. Consequently, this is expensive education.

Is the need for pre-practice clinical training as great in this country as it is in Germany? Consider, in this connection, (a) that if the requirement of an apprenticeship period were eliminated, a German law candidate normally would be ready to become a full-fledged member of the profession at age 22, and (b) that the gap between book-learning and actual practice may be particularly wide in an environment where the academic part of law study consists primarily of the systematic presentation of concepts and precepts, and de-emphasizes the utilization of such concepts and precepts for the solution of actual cases.

(2) The organization of the legal profession in civil-law countries will be discussed in more detail at a later point. See infra pp. 341-352. However, without some knowledge of the range of legal careers toward which a candidate's legal training is directed, it would be difficult fully

44. Richtergesetz § 5a(4).

45. As to this, see Ostler, Neueste Entwicklungen in der Rechtswissenschaft, 1987 N.J.W. 281, and infra p. 183.

46. In recent years, German student organizations have attacked the lecture system not only as pedagogically ineffective, but also as silencing dissent from the professor's views and stunting the development of independent, critical thinking on the part of the student.

to understand and to appraise such training. For this reason, an outline of legal careers (that are open to a German candidate after he has passed the required examinations) is set forth in the materials which immediately follow.

LEGAL CAREERS IN GERMANY

Having passed the Second State Examination, a young German lawyer must choose the branch of the legal profession in which he will seek a career. The choice he makes is a much more definite one than that implicitly made by a recent graduate of an American law school who embarks on his first job. Although German law does not make it completely impossible for a lawyer in mid-career to switch from private practice to civil service or to teaching (or vice versa), such a switch may encounter certain—legal or practical—obstacles and delays. In any event, whatever the reasons may be, such switching is not in the continental and especially the German tradition. Since World War II, and in part perhaps as a result of the upheavals brought about by the war and its aftermath, there has been a little more flexibility in this regard; but a change-over from one branch of the profession to another is still exceptional, in contrast to the frequency and ease with which American lawyers move from private practice to official, business or academic positions and back again.

(1) Judges and Prosecutors

A candidate who has obtained a sufficiently good mark in his Second State Examination, may apply for appointment as a judge. In Germany, as in the overwhelming majority of civil law countries,[1] the judiciary is a career service, in which a successful applicant for appointment normally begins his career in the lowest court, hoping that in time, through successive promotions, he will become a member of a higher or highest court, or perhaps be called upon to preside over such a court or one of its panels.

An English or American lawyer, to whom the institution of a career judiciary may seem strange, should keep in mind that on the continent the institution is backed by a long tradition.[2] During the age of Absolutism the judicial system of many continental states—especially in Germany—was dominated by the notion that the judges were mere instruments of the monarch, and that the latter always had the residual power to change the decisions of his tribunals, or even to remove a judge with the same ease with which he could dismiss other civil "servants".[3] This power, though rarely exercised, remained absolute until the last decades of the 18th century. From then on, the

---

1. In Switzerland, however, there is no career judiciary. Swiss judges are elected, either by the (federal or cantonal) legislature or by the People.

2. See Schmidt-Räntsch, Deutsches Richtergesetz 35–50 (1973).

3. The situation was partly different in France, where even during the 18th century, and until the Revolution, the members of some courts were feudal office-holders, who for their own benefit exercised a measure of power independent of (and often in opposition to) the King. See infra p. 266.

German monarchs one by one first renounced the power to change judicial decisions, and subsequently (in Prussia as late as 1848) acquiesced in the adoption of constitutional provisions which guaranteed the personal independence of judges by protecting them from involuntary removal or transfer.[4] Such constitutional guarantees of judicial independence, later written into federal as well as state constitutions, to this day have remained a basic feature of the administration of justice in Germany.[5]

The judiciary, nevertheless, continued to be a career service. Thus the government, while powerless to remove or transfer a judge without his consent, retained plenary power over judicial appointments and promotions. Since the 19th century, this power traditionally has been wielded by highly-placed civil servants, usually in the Ministry of Justice. During the Empire and the Weimar Republic, appointments and promotions were governed by a merit system (based in part on the candidate's grade in the Second State Examination), and it happened only rarely that the Ministry abused its tremendous power for political or other improper purposes. During the Nazi period, however, such abuse became the rule, and this was one—though not the only one—of the methods by which the judiciary was made to fall into line. When after the demise of the Nazi regime the West German judicial system had to be rebuilt, strong arguments were made against leaving unchecked power over judicial careers in the hands of the government's executive branch. There emerged a compromise system of judicial selection. The members of the Federal Constitutional Court and of other federal courts of last resort are (as a matter of federal law) chosen by highly complex methods, under which the power of selection is shared by state and federal governments, and within the federal government by the executive branch and the two houses of Parliament.[6] As to most of the other judges (i.e., the bulk of the judiciary), the methods of appointing and promoting them are partly governed by state law, and there are differences from state to state; federal law, however, requires that a committee of judges participate in appoint-

4. A judge, however, remained subject to properly (i.e., judicially) conducted disciplinary proceedings for cause. Moreover, the constitutional guarantee of irremovability is not operative during a probationary period of limited duration (three to five years) at the beginning of a judge's career.

5. The statement in the text is subject to two exceptions, which relate (a) to the Nazi period, and (b) to post-World-War II conditions in what is now the German Democratic Republic.

6. G. N. Schram, The Recruitment of Judges for the West German Federal Courts, 21 Am.J.Comp.L. 691 (1973), discusses the relevant legal provisions and the politics involved in the selection of judges of the Federal Constitutional Court and

the highest courts of the five court systems. (As to what these five court systems are, see infra p. 499, n. 3.). Of the 15 members of the Italian Constitutional Court, five are elected by the highest judges of the country from among their number, five are appointed by the President of the Republic, and five are elected by joint session of both houses of Parliament. See T. Ritterspach, Constitutional Review in Italy, 4 Hum.R.L.Rev. 179, 181 (1983).

For a comparative study of judicial selection in England, the United States and West Germany, see U. Kayser, Die Auswahl der Richter in der englischen und amerikanischen Rechtspraxis (1969), interestingly reviewed by H. G. Rupp in 34 Rabels Z. 745 (1970).

ments to the higher judicial offices, and in some of the *Länder* such committees are given even greater powers. Thus it is fair to say that the Ministry, though it still keeps the judges' personnel records and surely influences their careers, no longer wields untrammeled power over judicial appointments and promotions.

In the last decades, especially since World War II, a similar trend has become noticeable in other civil-law countries as well.[7] In a number of such countries, including France[8] and more recently Turkey,[9] high-level committees wholly or partly consisting of judges have been granted many of the powers over judicial appointments and promotions which formerly rested exclusively in the hands of the Minister and his bureaucracy.[10]

Prosecutors, like judges, are career civil servants; this is true in the great majority of civil-law countries, including Germany. In some of those countries, again including Germany, the judicial and prosecutorial careers are not strictly separated. The entrance requirements are the same, and an individual may, perhaps by way of promotion, move from a prosecutorial position to a judicial one, or vice versa.[11] Even while he serves as prosecutor, he has permanent tenure; but—as distinguished from a judge—he has to take orders from his superior concerning his work, including the treatment of particular cases.[12]

7. For a broad-ranging comparative study see S. Shetreet & J. Deschênes (Eds.), Judicial Independence: The Contemporary Debate (1985).

The classical discussion of the problem of a career judiciary, stressing the inconsistency between constitutional "independence" and administrative dependence on a ministerial bureaucracy, is to be found in the slim but significant book by P. Calamandrei, Procedure and Democracy 35–44 (1956).

8. See G. L. Kock, The Machinery of Law Administration in France, 108 U.Pa.L. Rev. 366, 384 (1960); R. David, French law 54–58 (1972). For a more detailed discussion see J. Vincent, Procédure Civile 132–34, 188–89, 194–96 (18th ed., 1976).

9. See Comment, New Status for Turkey's Public Prosecutors, Bulletin of the International Commission of Jurists, No. 25 (March 1966) 36.

10. In the emerging European judiciary (as distinguished from the national judicial systems of individual European countries) there are no career judges. As was well said by M. Cappelletti (Ed.), New Perspectives for a Common Law of Europe, Introduction at 17 (1978):

"Judges of the European Court of Justice at Luxembourg, as well as their counter-parts both in the Commission and the Court of Human Rights at Strasbourg, are not career magistrates: their background is not one of an entire life spent in the judiciary; their appointment to those high adjudicatory bodies is not based on seniority in the judicial service; their personalities are far from bureaucratic and anonymous."

11. A transfer from a judicial position to a prosecutorial one requires the judge's consent, pursuant to the above-mentioned constitutional provision protecting judges against involuntary removal or transfer; but, especially where a promotion is involved, such consent normally is not refused. Concerning the frequency of such interchanges between judicial and prosecutorial personnel, the practice seems to vary from state to state and also from time to time. When a prosecutor is transferred to a judicial position, he may not, consistently with the impartiality guarantee of article 6(1) of the European Convention on Human Rights and Fundamental Freedoms, sit as a judge in a case in which he actively participated as a prosecutor. Piersack v. Belgium, 4 Hum.R.L.Rev. 207 (1983) (Eur. Court, October 1, 1982).

12. See Gerichtsverfassungsgesetz (Law Concerning Judicial Organization) § 146.

(2) Other Branches of the Legal Profession

Although the legal training and the two state examinations described above are formally designated as entrance requirements for the judicial service,[13] their successful completion will open the door to other legal careers as well. A successful candidate, who does not become a judge or prosecutor, may turn to any one of the other branches of the German legal profession:

(a) He may become **a member of the Bar**. This is now, by choice or necessity, the primary goal for most young German lawyers who have successfully completed both state examinations. The figures speak for themselves: 17,000 practicing lawyers around 1955, 27,000 at the end of 1975, and almost 49,000 by the end of 1985 (8.5 per cent of them women). The BRAK (Federal Bar Association) estimates that by 1996, there might be as many as 90,000 to 100,000 members of the Bar (out of a total of 110,000 to 120,000 fully qualified lawyers) in the Federal Republic of Germany.[14] The functions of German attorneys and notaries, and the organization of these branches of the profession, are discussed elsewhere in this book.[15]

(b) The young lawyer may become **an administrative official**. The great majority of higher administrative offices, both state and federal, and even municipal, are open only to candidates who are "Volljuristen", i.e., who have passed the Second State Examination. A candidate may seek a career in one of the specialized administrative services, such as the tax administration, or he may aspire to become a member of the "general administration". The latter organization, which has no precise counterpart in the United States, has jurisdiction in all administrative matters not specifically entrusted to a specialized agency; through this ever-present, stable, hierarchically structured organization of experienced administrators—headed by a Minister (usually the Minister of the Interior) and spread over the whole state—the state government is always able to implement a wide variety of laws and policies, old and new,[16] and effectively to supervise the activities of all units of local government. Retired civil servants receive generous pension benefits; but recently a tendency has developed among lawyer-retirees from the civil service to enter legal practice, for which they are of course formally qualified. Given the present and projected economic future of the legal profession, this is fiercely resisted by the practicing Bar.[17]

13. The number of judges, in relation to the population and also in relation to the number of attorneys, has been historically much higher in civil-law than in common-law countries. The reasons for this will become clear when we study civil-law procedure (infra pp. 337.).

14. These figures are supplied by F. Ostler, Neueste Entwicklungen in der Rechtsanwaltschaft, 1987 N.J.W. 281. The author, a well-known practitioner, predicts economic misery, except for "good and versatile lawyers, especially with knowledge of foreign languages and of tax and business law."

15. See supra pp. 18–20 and infra pp. 341 ff.

16. One of the advantages of this system is that it makes it unnecessary to build up a brand-new administrative organization every time a novel program calling for some kind of administrative activity is initiated.

17. See Ostler, supra note 14, at 282.

(c) Whether or not admitted to the Bar,[18] a person having the necessary legal training may obtain employment as *Syndikus* (house counsel) of a bank, insurance company or other business enterprise. In litigated matters, however, such house counsel will need the assistance of an independent attorney; this is true even if the house counsel is a member of the Bar, because German law prohibits an employed lawyer from representing his employer in court.[19]

It goes without saying, moreover, that in Germany, as elsewhere, it is by no means uncommon to use one's legal training as preparation for a career on the management side (rather than the law department) of a business concern.

(d) Relatively few young lawyers—as a rule only some of those who have attracted the attention of a professor by extraordinary achievement in a seminar or in the First State Examination—aspire to become law teachers. For these few, the doctoral degree is not merely a prestigious title, but a necessary requirement for entering their particular career.[20] After having written his doctoral thesis, and having obtained his doctorate, the future law teacher has to submit to a Law Faculty a second, even more ambitious scholarly work, his so-called *Habilitationsschrift*.[21] If this work is approved by the Faculty, the candidate is declared "habilitated", i.e., qualified to teach.[22] He is now eligible to be "called" to fill a professorial position in his field of specialization, if and when a vacancy occurs in one of the German law faculties. Once he has obtained such a position, he belongs to a group which traditionally has enjoyed a most elevated status.

"The group of legal scholars is small, probably not over three hundred for the whole of Germany. But its influence has been enormous in all the Continental countries and particularly in Germany. . . . Not only were all members of the bench and bar trained by such scholars during the last several centuries, but scholars carried on almost alone the work of adapting Roman law to modern conditions. . . . There is no country in the world where the scholar, and particularly the legal scholar, enjoys the prestige which he enjoys in Germany."[23]

---

18. See Rechtsberatungsgesetz § 6.

19. Bundesrechtsanwaltsordnung § 46.

20. Most German law teachers also have passed the Second State Examination, although this is not required.

Another customary (though not legally required) step along the academic path is service as an assistant to a professor, or at a university institute.

21. In exceptional cases, other legal writings of a scholarly nature sometimes are accepted in lieu of a *Habilitationsschrift*.

22. The reader will note that the candidate's ability to excel in scholarly research and writing is severely scrutinized in this selection process. Traditionally, there has been less emphasis on testing the candidate's effectiveness in the classroom, except for a test lecture (before the faculty) which may be required as part of the habilitation procedure.

As to the legal status and the (assertedly deteriorating) economic position of "habilitated" law teachers, see T. Köstlin, Der kostenlose Privatdozent?—Lehrverpflichtung und Art. 12 GG, 1987 DVBl. 123.

23. B. Shartel & H. J. Wolff, German Lawyers—Training and Functions, 42 Mich.L.Rev. 521, at 522–23 (1943).

This was written over four decades ago. At that time, the prestige of German law faculties as an elite group, small in number and traditionally holding a position of leadership in the development of the law,[24] was comparable to that of the English judiciary.[25] In the meantime, and especially since the 1960s, the number of professorial positions has been substantially increased,[26] and there has been a "gradual decline of the professor's status;"[27] but the force of tradition is strong in German society, and the members of German law faculties remain a respected and influential group.

NOTES ON LEGAL EDUCATION IN EAST GERMANY [1]

The following table[2] illustrates the fundamental difference between the legal professions in the two Germanies.

Lawyers in the Soviet Zone and GDR (including East Berlin)

Year	Number	Not Members of Lawyers' *Collegia*
1948	1158	
1951	901	
1959	863	448
1964	629	174
1981	562	35
1983	568	33

24. Until the end of the 19th century, academic writers had a near-monopoly as authors of influential treatises and commentaries. More recently, it can be observed that practitioners, judges and government officials (especially those who participated in the drafting of the laws forming the subject of their books), have made inroads on this monopoly. See E. J. Cohn, German Legal Science Today, 2 Int. & Comp.L.Q. 169, 186–87 (1953). Even with respect to textbooks for students, the monopoly is becoming eroded; see supra p. 173. Nevertheless, professorial authors still retain a pre-eminent position in German legal literature.

25. The historical developments which explain the status and influence of the academic branch of the legal profession in continental countries, and especially in Germany, are discussed supra pp. 158–159 and infra pp. 255–275.

26. This is due, in part, to the recent creation of a number of new Universities, e.g. at Bochum, Regensburg, Augsburg and Konstanz. Other reasons for the increase are discussed by W. K. Geck, The Reform of Legal Education in the Federal Republic of Germany, 25 Am.J.Comp.L. 86, 107 (1977).

27. Id. at 108.

1. See especially D. J. Meador, Impressions of Law in East Germany, Legal Education and the Legal Systems in the German Democratic Republic (1986) and, for background, I. Markovits, Pursuing One's Rights Under Socialism, 38 Stan.L.Rev. 681 (1986). The organization and functioning of the Bar is described by P. A. Brand, Der Rechtsanwalt und der Anwaltsnotar in der DDR, Ihre Stellung und Funktion im sozialistischen Rechtssystem (1985). For an authoritative brief survey of the current government-approved plan for legal education in the GDR, which was formulated in 1974 and implemented as of the academic year 1977/78, see W. Büchner-Uhder, Erfahrungen und Aufgaben bei der Ausbildung von Studenten an den rechtswissenschaftlichen Sektionen der Universitäten, 27 Neue Justize 195 (1978). K.-H. Lehmann, Reform der Juristenausbildung in der DDR, 1969 JuS 195; id., Die juristische Ausbildung in der DDR, 1968 JuS 341, with many further references; O. Kirchheimer, The Administration of Justice and the Concept of Legality in East Germany, 68 Yale L.J. 705, 711–13 (1959); and E. J. Cohn, German Legal Science Today, 2 Int. & Comp.L.Q. 169, 174–75 (1953), are of historical interest.

2. Brand, supra, n. 1, at 166.

Thus, while the number of practicing lawyers virtually trebled in the Federal Republic of Germany and is expected to double once more within the next decade (supra p. 183), it sank to barely half the 1948 figure in the GDR, and remains constant at about 565—for a country of 16.7 million. As a recent commentator notes: "Lawyers, so influential and omnipresent in capitalist societies, are in little demand under socialism." [3] It is true that in addition to the above-mentioned small number of members of the Bar there are an estimated 3,000 lawyers serving as house counsel of various state-owned enterprises in the GDR. Even so, the ratio of lawyers to the total population is dramatically lower in East Germany than in West Germany or in, e.g., the United Kingdom.[4]

The number of law graduates required for the economy and the administration of justice is determined by the central economic plan, and the Ministry of Higher Education sets the admission quotas for the four law faculties, currently at a total of 430 per year. Bifurcation of legal education and of career patterns occurs at this early stage, for two law faculties (Halle and Leipzig) teach the economic law curriculum, while the two others (Berlin and Jena) train *"Justizjuristen,"* i.e., prospective judges, prosecutors, and practicing lawyers. Jena, which by tradition is a small university, has a quota of only sixty entrants per year, most of whom, apparently, are headed for a prosecutor's career.[5] The selection process begins early and includes some active recruiting. Loyalty to the state and commitment to the system are important factors, social background less than in former years. As a rule, students will be expected to have had two years' work experience between high school and university study, but (obligatory) military service by men is credited for this purpose.[6]

The overall curriculum is four years, with practical training periods of four and twelve weeks, respectively, after the second and third years of study, plus a five-week period at the end of the fourth year for the completion of a written study project. Examinations are more frequent than in West Germany. The traditional training period after the first state examination was abolished as early as 1953, but lawyers entering into private practice have to serve an apprenticeship period of one year with their *collegia*, or government-organized lawyers' cooperatives.[7]

The obligatory study plan as approved by the Ministry of Higher Education contains separate curricula for prospective administration-of-justice lawyers (i.e., students at Berlin and Jena) and for budding economic lawyers (i.e., students at Halle and Leipzig). The first-year curricula show little difference, and contain a large proportion of courses on Marxism-Leninism. After that, there is increasing divergence, with courses on economic law, domestic and international, heavily represented in the Halle-Leipzig curriculum.[8]

Career patterns of law graduates are virtually predetermined by their initial university assignments (Berlin graduates have a somewhat wider choice between judicial, prosecutorial, and practicing law careers). There has been some suggestion that the career of an average

3. Markovits, supra note 1, at 754.

4. Markovits, id.; Meador, supra n. 1, at 146 and 174.

5. Meador, supra n. 1, at 113 and 71.

6. Id. at 105–108.

7. Brand, supra n. 1, at 79.

8. Meador, supra note 1, at 233–43.

economic law graduate as junior house counsel to a state enterprise is likely to be unexciting. There is, however, the countervailing consideration that in East Germany (unlike in West Germany, see supra p. 184) house counsel are qualified to act as counsel of record for their enterprises not only before state arbitration tribunals, but before the civil courts as well.[9] This is of course unfavorable to the practicing Bar, and may in part explain the surprisingly low number of practicing lawyers.

Academic careers and graduate legal education can be pursued not only at the four universities but also at the Academy for State and Law in Potsdam-Babelsberg. This is a training center for the diplomatic service and local government officials, and in addition has a law faculty for advanced study and research. Graduate legal studies for those aspiring to university careers are now standardized, and both the doctorate and a further qualification resembling the *Habilitation* are the usual steps.[10]

NOTES AND QUESTIONS

(1) In spite of evident contrasts, American legal education and the various continental systems are not so radically different as to preclude the mutual importation of ideas and techniques. Each side attempts to learn from the other; in recent years, this learning process has been further stimulated by the exchanges of academic personnel which are fostered by governmental[1] and foundation grants.

(2) It is quite possible to create a mixed system of legal training by utilizing both continental and American ideas. In Japan, for instance, we observe an interesting combination of the continental apprenticeship system[2] and of a number of American features adopted after World War II, e.g., some use of the case method and occasional recruitment of judges from the Bar.[3]

(3) A comparison of the French and German systems with each other, and with legal education in the United States, naturally suggests questions: Disregarding unimportant details, what are the essential similarities and differences? To what extent can the dissimilarities be

---

9. Markovits, supra note 1, at 754–55; Brand, supra n. 1, at 68–74.

10. Meador, supra note 1, at 89–104.

1. 22 U.S.C.A. §§ 2451–58 (1979 and 1987 Supp.).

2. During the apprenticeship phase of his training, the future Japanese lawyer is enrolled in the Legal Training and Research Institute; the essence of the Institute's curriculum is on-the-job training in the offices of judges, prosecutors and private practitioners. See Chin Kim, Clinical Legal Education: Japanese and U.S. Experience with Prosecutor Training Programs, in Chin Kim, Selected Writings on Asian Law 95, 97–101 (1982).

A striking feature of the Japanese system, which stands in sharp contrast to the German model, is the tiny percentage of candidates passing the examination that corresponds to the German First State Examination, i.e., the examination to be tak-

en at the end of the period of academic law study, and before admission to the second phase of legal education. See M. M. McMahon, Legal Education in Japan, 60 ABAJ 1376 (1974). In the decade from 1974 to 1983 the pass rate was consistently below 2%. See T. Hattori & D. F. Henderson, Civil Procedure in Japan, § 2.02[2] (1985). See also H. Tanaka, The Japanese Legal System 577 (1976). The number of judges, prosecutors and licensed attorneys thus is kept exceedingly small under the Japanese system. The reasons for this will be explained later. See infra pp. 332–333.

3. See Tanaka, op. cit. supra n. 2, at 566–88; Rabinowitz, The Historical Development of the Japanese Bar, 70 Harv.L. Rev. 61, 73–8 (1956); Nathanson, On Teaching Law in Japan, 9 J. Legal Ed. 300 (1957); Matsuda, The Japanese Legal Training and Research Institute, 7 Am.J. Comp.L. 366 (1958).

traced to (a) differences in the general educational system, (b) differences in the political system, (c) differences in the legal system, and (d) other institutional differences between the various countries involved in the comparison? Under which system are law students most likely to lead a happy life? Which system makes the best and most economical use of the time of teachers and trainees? Under which system is the competence of future lawyers most effectively tested?[4] Which system will produce legal craftsmen of superior technical skill? Is the time ripe for a more comprehensively international approach?[5]

It should be remembered, also, that during his training period the future lawyer may form attitudes toward the law, and toward its reform and development on the local, national and international level. He may learn to *accept* existing institutions and rules of law as the indisputable command of the sovereign; as the definitive embodiment of professional wisdom; or as an arsenal of weapons in the class struggle. Or, on the other hand, he may be induced to *question* these rules and institutions, and to regard them as mere techniques for the implementation of policies which may or may not be anchored in ultimate values and which (at least to the extent that they are not so anchored) are ever-changing and always open to re-appraisal. Which of these attitudes are apt to be instilled in the future lawyers of (a) France, (b) Germany (West and East), and (c) the United States?

(CC) THE ART OF EXAMINING AND CROSS-EXAMINING FOREIGN LAW EXPERTS

WOOD & SELICK, INC., v. COMPAGNIE GENERALE TRANSATLANTIQUE

United States Circuit Court of Appeals, Second Circuit, 1930.
43 F.2d 941.

Appeals from the District Court of the United States for the Southern District of New York.

Libel by Wood & Selick, Inc., and by A. Salomon, Inc., against the Compagnie Generale Transatlantique, for cargo damage. From decrees in admiralty by the District Court, in libelant's favor (32 F.2d 283), the respondent appeals.[a]

Affirmed.

4. In this context it is interesting to reflect, also, on the tremendous impact which the system of law examinations has on legal education everywhere. Are the examinations the tail that wags the dog of legal training? See W. Twining, Pericles and the Plumber, 83 L.Q.Rev. 396, 424 (1967).

5. Wetter, The Case for International Law Schools and an International Legal Profession, 29 Int'l & Comp.L.Q. 206, 212 (1980).

a. In traditional admiralty practice, a suit in admiralty was called a libel. The plaintiff was the libellant, and the defendant, the respondent. These terms have been abolished by the unification of the Admiralty Rules and the Federal Rules of Civil Procedure in 1966. See L. Colby, Admiralty Unification, 54 Geo.L.J. 1258, 1264–67 (1966); Haskins v. Point Towing Company, 395 F.2d 737, 738 note 1 (3rd Cir. 1968).

right being extinguished seems substantial

Before L. HAND, SWAN, and AUGUSTUS N. HAND, Circuit Judges.

L. HAND, Circuit Judge. These two appeals involve only the question of the statute of limitations. The libels were filed for damage to certain consignments of goods, shipped on the respondent's vessels under bills of lading, issued in France, and containing the following clause (Rule 18): "All litigations arising out of interpretation or execution of this contract or bill of lading shall be judged according to the French law at the Tribunal of the place indicated in the bill of lading, and the owners of the ship and claimants formally declare to accept its competency." The bills further provided: "Disputes resulting from the interpretation or execution of this bill of lading shall be submitted to the court provided for in Rule 18 of the Commerce Court of the Seine."

it provides seperate clauses for choice of forum and choice of law

The respondent proved the French law by its relevant sections, and by a competent French lawyer, and maintained that under it the limitation of one year was made a condition of the obligation, in the sense that the lapse of that period extinguished the right. Hence it argued that the local statute did not apply as part of the lex fori, and that as the libels had not been filed within a year, though within the time allowed by the local law, the suits must fail. The following sections of the French Codes are pertinent. Section 433 of the Commercial Code, which is under the title, "Prescription," provides: "The following are barred by prescription. All claims for delivery of goods, or for damages for average losses, or delay in the carriage of them, one year after the ship's arrival." This is all that there is in the Commercial Code, but the Civil Code under chapter five, which concerns the "discharge" (extinguishment), "of obligations," provides, section 1234: "Obligations are discharged" (s'éteignent), "by payment (or performance)—by novation—by voluntary release—by set-off—by merger—by loss of the subject matter—by being void or by rescission—by the effect of a condition in avoidance, which has been explained in the preceding chapter; by prescription which will form the subject of a special title." The only evidence in the record of that special title is the following two sections: Section 2220, "The right of prescription may not be waived" (renoncé), "beforehand; prescription which has been already acquired may be waived"; section 2223, "Judges may not of their own motion base their decisions upon grounds which depend upon prescription."

The testimony of the expert was exceedingly confusing, not due to any fault of his, but inevitable because of the attempt to import into the French law the refined notion which pervades our own, of a right barred of remedy, but still existing in nubibus. He based his opinion upon the reasoning that since section 1234 of the Civil Code provides that "prescription" shall extinguish or discharge obligations, and since section 433 of the Commercial Code establishes a prescriptive period of one year for suits like those at bar, it follows that the French law extinguished these obligations. When faced with the sections from the Civil Code dealing with prescription, he became however less clear. It was apparent that time alone did not for all purposes extinguish the obligation, for the defendant must claim the defense, and might renounce it by his conduct after the prescription was complete. Without in any sense meaning to question his competence, in the upshot his testimony does not materially help us. Each party relies upon a part here and a part there; we shall not cite it, nor indeed need we consider it, for it seems in the end to leave the interpretation of the Codes much as it would be on the words themselves.

We may at the start lay aside the clauses in the bills of lading, which apparently were intended to confine any litigation over the contracts to a French court. The respondent does not pretend that, so construed, these would be valid, and it is of course well settled that they would not. [Citations.] [b] If they were not so intended, but only meant to stipulate that the obligations of the contract were to be interpreted and executed according to French law, they did not incorporate the French law of prescription. "Interpretation" certainly cannot be stretched so far, and "execution" will serve no better. Its natural meaning is "performance", including excuses for performance; it would wrench that meaning quite out of measure to include within it the period within which suits must be brought. Without deciding how plainly a carrier must declare itself on such a question,[c] it suffices to say that the contracts were not definite enough, and we cannot reverse the decrees except by force of the French law itself.

It is well settled that ordinarily the statute of limitations of the forum controls. Walsh v. Mayer, 111 U.S. 31, 4 S.Ct. 260, 28 L.Ed. 338; Flowers v. Foreman, 23 How. 132, 149, 16 L.Ed. 405; Canadian Pacific Ry. v. Johnston (C.C.A.2) 61 F. 738, 745, 25 L.R.A. 470.[d] But a statute of the place where the right arose may impose upon it a condition which goes to its substance, and, when this is so, the condition will be

---

b. Contract clauses which not only *confer* jurisdiction upon a named court but at the same time purport to *deprive* all other courts of jurisdiction, are routinely used and enforced in many civil law countries. For a discussion of such clauses, and of the treatment they receive in American courts, see infra pp. 385–388.

c. Compare the principal case and Dorff v. Taya, 194 App.Div. 278, 185 N.Y.S. 174 (1st Dept., 1920) (general reference to "the law" of a named country) with Jones v. The Cunard S.S. Co. Ltd., 238 App.Div. 172, 263 N.Y.S. 769 (2d Dept., 1933) (reference to "the terms and provisions of the Hague Rules 1921" held sufficiently specific).

d. Today, a similar action would be subject to the one-year statute of limitations contained in the Carriage of Goods by Sea Act, 46 U.S.C.A. § 1303(6); but that Act was passed several years *after* the decision in the principal case. Cf. Y. F. Chiang,

The Applicability of COGSA and the Harter Act to Water Bills of Lading, 14 B.C. Ind. & Comm.L.Rev. 267 (1972).

In the absence (at that time) of a federal statute, the Court had to follow the general admiralty practice which, while using the term "laches", in effect tends to apply the state statute of limitations. See Gilmore and Black, The Law of Admiralty 768–76 (2d ed., 1975). If, as we may assume, the plaintiffs were residents of New York, the New York statute of limitations then in force provided for no "borrowing" of the French time limitation, and permitted the bringing of suit within six years from the accrual of the cause of action. See former N.Y.C.P.A. §§ 13, 48 and 55. (The present New York provision, CPLR § 202, is to the same effect.) Court and counsel in the principal case, therefore, were correct in assuming that the statute of limitations of the forum did *not* bar the action.

choice of law = choice of substantive law (Eric v. Thompkins)

observed elsewhere.[e] This has ordinarily come up in the case of statutory rights in which the limitation was imposed by the same statute which created the right itself [Citations.] But it is not necessary that the limitation should be in the same statute, so the purpose be plain to make it a condition. [Citation.] Since in France all obligations are presumably created by force of statute, we have therefore to decide how far the French law imposes such a condition upon the obligations created by bills of lading.

The embarrassment is, as we have said, that we have to interpret another system of law according to notions wholly foreign to it. It is indeed easy to say that as the French law recognizes nothing but the extinguishment of an obligation by lapse of time, we have nothing more to do than take all obligations there created as subject to such a condition. But the question does not seem to us quite so simple as that, for it is apparent that the right is not always extinguished, as, for example, if the obligor renounces the prescription, or fails to claim it. Our own statutes of limitation do in fact extinguish the right so far as they extinguish all remedies, for a right without any remedy is a meaningless scholasticism, and the distinction we make is more than formal only in that the applicable period varies with the law of the forum where the suit chances to be laid. At any rate it is permissible for us to say that if the assumed extinguishment which the French law imposes, is itself subject to conditions which assimilate it to our ordinary statutes of limitation, it makes no difference that it speaks of "extinguishment." We are to decide whether the defense falls within one class or the other recognized by us, and in that inquiry we are not necessarily concluded by the terms used; we may assimilate it rather to matter of remedy, just because it has those conditions which would so determine it in our law.[f]

It appears to us that this is the case here. For example, as mere matter of procedure the defendant under our law need not plead the limitation, when it is a condition upon the right.[g] [Citations.] The rule is otherwise when it merely bars the remedy, and section 2223 of the French Civil Code pro tanto makes the defense like that of our ordinary

= procedural under US law

e. ". . . The usual conflicts rule [that the statute of limitations is procedural and hence controlled by the law of the forum], is subject to an exception in the case of limitations affecting statutory rights of action which did not exist at common law. In such cases, the period of limitation is ordinarily said to be a condition to the right itself and not merely a bar to the remedy; hence, it is treated as a matter of substantive law. Accordingly, when such period of limitation has expired the law of the forum is inapplicable because, the right of action itself having ceased to exist, there is nothing left to sue upon. Thus, even under a statutory conflicts rule, as in New York, where a resident plaintiff's foreign cause of action is subject only to the New York statute of limitations, such action will nevertheless be barred if the period of limitation which is a condition to the foreign right has expired, even if the local statute of limitations has not yet run." Note, 40 Cornell L.Q. 589, 590 (1955). This approach, however, has been questioned by some of the more recent authorities. See infra p. 212.

f. More recently, the Second Circuit has given up this criterion. See Bournias v. Atlantic Maritime Co., Ltd., 220 F.2d 152 (2 Cir., 1955), discussed infra p. 211.

g. See Atkinson, Pleading the Statute of Limitations, 36 Yale L.J. 914, 926 ff. (1927).

statutes. While this perhaps does not go very far, it tends to put the French law in accord with the libelants' position, and we must not look for demonstration.

There is, however, a more solid basis for our conclusion. Even in form it is, strictly speaking, never possible to revive the old right, at least in cases of a liability in contract or tort. Revival rests in any event upon historical peculiarities of our procedure, and does not exist in cases of tort. [Citations.] While there are exceptions when the defendant has misled the plaintiff who has acted upon the strength of the promise, in such cases the question is really whether these facts create a contract not to use the defence, though this is usually disguised under the term, "estoppel." Moreover, even in cases of contract the new promise, which is said to revive the debt, does not really do so. Rather it creates a new obligation for which the old liability is regarded as a sufficient consideration. [Citations.] Thus a mere acknowledgment is ordinarily not enough unless a promise can be inferred from it (Williston, §§ 166, 167), and partial payment is good only in so far as a promise can in the same way be implied (Williston, § 174). Again, under most authorities the promise must be made before action brought [citations], which would not be true if the statute gave only a defence that could be "renounced," or "waived." While, indeed, it must be acknowledged that action is usually brought on the old debt, this is certainly anomalous, and should not disguise the substance.

Thus it appears that even in cases of contract, where alone the right can be revived, our statute more truly treats it as extinguished than if the defence were merely "waived." We do not know what is meant by the language of section 2220 of the French Civil Code, relating to prescription, for we are not advised how the obligor may "renoncer" the defence; but certainly it is difficult to suppose that the right is more completely gone than under our law. We are surely not to assume that it is necessary to make a new contract under the French law, and yet that is the substance of what we ourselves require. If we were to guess, we should assume that any one of those situations which we vaguely class as "waiver" would serve, which they do not with us. Thus we are justified in treating "prescription" under section 1234 as more nearly analogous to a statute "barring the remedy" than to one "extinguishing," or "a condition upon," the right. The respondent had the burden of establishing the defense, and at least on this record we cannot say that it has proved that the French law goes far enough. . . .

. . . On this record, whatever might be the conclusion on other evidence, the District Judge was right. . . .

The Expert's Testimony in the Wood & Selick Case

The following is taken from the Record which was before the Circuit Court of Appeals in the above case (the bracketed numbers are folio numbers of the Record):

UNITED STATES DISTRICT COURT,

Southern District of New York

A. SALOMON, INC.,
          Libellant,
         AGAINST
COMPAGNIE   GENERALE
   TRANSATLANTIQUE,   [185]
Respondent.

WOOD & SELICK, INC.,
          Libellant,   [186]
         AGAINST
COMPAGNIE   GENERALE
   TRANSATLANTIQUE,
Respondent.

JEAN C. MANCINI, called as a witness on behalf of the respondent, having been duly sworn, testified as follows: [187]

Mr. Longley [attorney for the plaintiff or "libellant"]: Let the record appear that we except to the witness testifying, on the ground that it is immaterial. I will admit the witness is well qualified as an expert in French law.

Mr. Garity [attorney for the defendant or "respondent"]: Just for the purpose of the record I will ask a few questions.

Direct Examination by Mr. Garity:

Q. Are you a lawyer admitted to practice under the laws of the Republic of France? A. Yes, sir. [188]

Q. Are you a French citizen? A. Yes, sir.

Q. Have you a law degree delivered to you by the Republic of France? A. Yes, sir.

Q. Where and when did you obtain this degree? A. In Paris, in 1918.

Q. Are you qualified to practice law in France and to appear before the Courts of France? A. I am.

Q. Have you a law office in Paris? A. I have.

Q. Are you connected with any French official institution in this city? A. I am one of the directors of the French Chamber of Commerce.   [189]

Q. You have a law office in this city? A. I have a law office in this city.

Q. And have practiced before the Courts in France? A. I have.

Q. Are you familiar with the laws of France covering bills of lading issued by steamship companies in France? A. Yes, I am.

Q. There are certain requirements under the French law that must be complied with in order to make these bills of lading valid? A. Yes.

Q. What are those requirements? A. The law requires that the bill of lading shall bear the name of the consignee, the name of the shipper, and the name of the ship master.   [190]

Q. Will you look at these bills of lading and tell me if they are valid bills of lading under the laws of the Republic of France? A. I have looked at them and they are.

Q. Will you look at rule 18 and article 14 and say in contemplation of what law the parties contracted? A. The French law.

Q. These bills of lading - - -

The Court: How does he know that, is that indicated by the wording? The contract speaks for itself. Go ahead.   [191]

Q. Are these bills of lading binding on the parties under the French law? A. Yes, sir.

Q. Is there any provision of the French law within which time suit must be instituted?

By the Court:

Q. Has the French law got a statute of limitations? A. Yes, sir.   [192]

Q. A general statute? A. Yes, sir.

Q. What is the general statute of limitations? A. It is one year.[h]

Q. Do you know the wording of the French statute? A. I do not understand the question.

Mr. Garity: Do you know the wording?

The Witness: Yes, I know.

Q. Have you got it? A. Yes.

Q. Let us have the French statute. What section is it, do you know? A. Yes, your Honor, here it is.

Q. 433? A. 433.   [193]

h. The general prescription period is *thirty* years. French Civil Code, article 2262; see infra, pp. 206–207.

Q. Read section 433. A. It is in French, but there is a translation.

Q. I notice that it says "Prescription"? A. Yes.

Q. What does the word "prescription" mean? A. Limitation.

Q. Limitation? A. Yes, sir.

Q. What does the word mean, prescription? A. It means limitation.

Q. All right then, this is article 433? A. Article 433.[i] [194]

Q. Continue. A. Are extinguished—

Q. Where do you get the word extinguished? A. That is it here.

Q. I asked you what the word prescription meant, and you did not say extinguished, you said limitation, what does the word prescribe mean? A. Extinguish.

Q. What is the French word for extinguish? A. Eteindre.

Q. Prescription does not mean that? A. Yes, your Honor, prescription is a way of distinguishment, extinguishment of the obligation. [195]

Q. Do you know Latin? A. Yes.

Q. Does the word prescribe mean the thing that the word prescribe would etymologically? A. Yes, sir.

Q. Prescribe does not mean extinguish, does it? A. But it is in the Code.

Q. What? A. In our Code prescription means—

Q. I am not asking for the effect, I am asking you to read that. Show me the French for "the obligations, are extinguished on payment," show us that, that is the important part of this case? A. Section of the Code, article 1234.

Q. We will get at 1234, do you speak French? [196]

Mr. Garity: Not fluently enough to discuss that, your Honor. If your Honor please, I think that this certificate of the translation we have been given of it will show that that does mean a distinction is made between that and limitation. [197]

The Court: Chapter 5, for the extinguishment of obligations.[j] That is a different section and is entirely different from this other section that you referred to. Here, this is what prescription means, is it not?

Mr. Garity: I cannot testify to it.

The Court: What do you want to show me?

The Witness: That prescription here is shown.

---

i. For (mis)translation of the pertinent parts of that article, see infra p. 197.

j. Book III, Title III, Chapter V of the French Civil Code (articles 1234–1314), entitled "Extinction of Obligations." For an outline of this code, see infra pp. 531–532.

Mr. Garity: That is the French Civil Code, is it not?

The Witness: It is the Civil Code.   **[198]**

By the Court:

Q. What is the word éteignent? A. Extinguishment.

Q. What is the difference between éteignent and prescription? A. This is the verb, this is the substantive, and this is the verb.

Q. The same meaning? A. The obligations are extinguished, and this is the extinguishment, this is the substantive, and this is a verb.

Q. Are you sure they are different words? A. This is a noun and this is a verb.[k]

Q. Read chapter 5 of the Civil Code? A. Chapter 5?   **[199]**

Q. I mean the translation of 5. A. Do you want me to translate all of this part?

Q. Go ahead. A. The obligations are extinguished by payment, by novation, by voluntary release, by amalgamation, by laws of the chattel, by an annulment of rescission, by the reversal of the desultory conditions, and by prescription which shall be treated in a special division.[l]

Q. That is article 1234, chapter 5. Is there any special provision of the law then? A. Yes, your Honor.   **[200]**

Q. What is it? A. Prescription.

Q. Where is it? A. In the Civil Code, your Honor.

Q. Commercial Code, is it not? A. No, Civil Code.

Q. What section? A. Third book, 12th Division.

The Court: You see they are now drawing the distinction whether it is a statute of limitations, or whether it goes to the obligation.   **[201]**

Mr. Garity: For the purpose of the record, your Honor, will you have him dictate that?

The Court: Yes.

Q. Article 2220 of the Civil Code reads how? A. Article 2220, one cannot renounce beforehand to the prescription, one can renounce to the prescription when secured.

k. Eteignent (tr. v. éteindre) = extinction (n). Article 433 of the Commercial Code then in effect started with "Sont prescrites" (tr. v. prescrire) = prescription (n). Testimony of this "quality" would hardly be tendered today, especially if the opposing party's expert were in court to assist with cross-examination, see infra pp. 198–199.

l. A more accurate translation of Art. 1234 of the French Civil Code appears in Judge L. Hand's opinion, supra. Today, the court and the experts would normally follow the translation in J. H. Crabb, The French Civil Code 233 (1977).

Q. Now, are there any further provisions that bear on this thing? The Commercial Code, did you read that into the record?   [202]

Mr. Garity: I think the record should be made clear by having article 433 of the Code in there.

The Court: What Code is that?

The Witness: The last one was the Civil Code.

The Court: And now what are you reading?   [203]

The Witness: Now I am going to read from the Code of Commerce.

The Court: Read from the Commercial Code, section 433. Do you see the point now?

Mr. Longley: I see the point, but I say it does not apply.

The Witness: Article 433: *Are extinguished* [m] all actions in payment of the freight, and every claim in delivery of the goods and for damaged goods or delay in the transportation one year after the arrival of the ship.   [204]

By Mr. Garity:

Q. Is it necessary to refer to this article 433 in the bill of lading? A. No.

Q. Did I understand you to say that in your opinion under the laws of France by article 433 an action for damage to cargo is extinguished unless the action is started within one year, is that correct? A. Yes.

Q. Now, you were talking to his Honor about prescription, what do you mean by that? Do you mean that the right under the contract or the remedy under the contract is extinguished if suit is not instituted within a year? A. It is the right which is extinguished.   [205]

Q. The right is extinguished? A. Yes.

Q. Rights under the contract are extinguished unless action is started within a year, is that your interpretation of the French law? A. Yes, sir.

Q. Is that based on the statutes you have just read to us? A. Yes, sir.   [206]

[Folio numbers 206–12 of the record have been omitted. They are reproduced at pp. 200–202 of the Fourth Edition (1980) of the present work.]

.   .   .

m. French: Sont prescrites (emphasis in text supplied). For derivation, see supra note k. The corresponding provision of article 433 of the Commercial Code has now been replaced by article 26 of Law No. 66–420 of June 18, 1966, which provides that claims for damage to cargo "sont prescrites par un an."

By Mr. Longley:

Q. What is your understanding of the difference between substantive law and a question of remedy? A. In civil law the substantive law is a public order you cannot renounce.[n] It is a right given you by the substantive law which you cannot renounce. But you could renounce a right given you by a remedy. I mean the substantive law is compulsory, you cannot renounce, by prior agreement. That is my understanding of the difference between remedy and the substantive law as far as this question is concerned.   **[214]**

By Mr. Garity:

Q. If there was a clause in the bill of lading attempting to renounce the effect of this section 433, would it be a valid clause under the French law? A. It will not be a valid clause because the civil law says you cannot renounce the prescription beforehand.   **[215]**

Q. All these sections you have referred to were in force during 1920 at the time these shipments arrived in this country? A. Yes.

Q. All of those sections? A. Yes, sir.

(Further argument off the record.)

Mr. Garity: That is all.

Mr. Longley: That is all.

The Court: I will give you until the 15th of January [1928] for briefs.   **[216]**

NOTE ON EXPERT ASSISTANCE IN CROSS-EXAMINATION

We have just seen that the respondent's (defendant's) expert mistranslated key statutory sources and misstated basic propositions of French law. Mistranslations can be corrected by opposing counsel with the requisite linguistic skills; misstatements of law can only be checked by counsel having detailed knowledge of the foreign legal system involved. Even experienced trial lawyers in major metropolitan centers usually lack such skills and familiarity, especially in combination. It is vital, therefore, that opposing counsel be assisted by his foreign law expert in the course of cross-examination.

This raises the question of the applicability of "the Rule." Rule 615 of the Federal Rules of Evidence provides that at the request of a party the court shall, and that on its own motion it may, "order witnesses excluded so that they cannot hear the testimony of other witnesses." This rule does not, however, "authorize exclusion of . . . a person whose presence is shown by a party to be essential to the presentation of his cause." As stated in a leading commentary, this exception "may perhaps most frequently be invoked in the case of expert witnesses." J. B. Weinstein & M. A. Berger, 3 Weinstein's

n. Article 6 of the French Civil Code provides, in terms: "One may not by particular agreements derogate from laws affecting public order and morality." This rule reflects the familiar maxim, ius publicum privatorum pactis mutari non potest. Dig. 2, 14, 38 (Papinian). It has nothing to do with "substance" and "procedure," since it also encompasses "procedural" rules not subject to the disposition of the parties (e.g., the language of proceedings).

Evidence ¶615[02], p. 615–11 (1985) (footnote omitted). One of the co-authors of the present edition has testified as an expert witness on foreign law in federal courts for two decades, and has always sat at counsel table during the cross-examination of opposing experts. Counsel will usually agree in advance (in obvious mutual self-interest) to "waive the Rule" as to expert witnesses on foreign law, but this might not always be the case. It is hoped that the above annotated account of Me. Mancini's testimony in Wood & Selick, supra, will aid trial courts, if called upon, to exercise their discretion in this matter so as to afford the parties (represented by counsel aided by experts) their full day in court.

What follows is the continuation of the trial record in the Wood & Selick case.

Wood & Selick, Inc. v. Compagnie Generale Transatlantique

Woolworth Building, May 2nd, 1928.

At 4:00 o'clock, P.M.

Present:—Hon. William Bondy, U.S.D.J.
Appearances:

Messrs. Bigham, Englar & Jones, by Mr. H. N. Longley
and Mr. E. G. B. Fox, Proctors for the Libellant.

Joseph P. Nolan, Esq., by Mr. Edward J. Garity,
Proctor for the Respondent.

Jean C. Mancini, a witness called on behalf of the respondent, being first duly sworn, testified as follows: [217]

Mr. Longley: If your Honor please, in this case you will recall the question of the French law is involved. At the trial, as certain portions of the French Statutes were put in the record, by agreement of my brother, we will read in another section of the code, which we wish to offer as part of the record in the case and that section to which I refer is Section 2223 of the French Civil Code reading as follows: "A judge cannot put forward a plea of prescription of his own 'motion'." That is all we have to offer. My brother wishes to examine his witness, Mr. Mancini, to explain what that section of the code means.   [218]

Mr. Garity: Did you finish your statement?

Mr. Longley: Yes.

Mr. Garity: Well, I have no objection to admitting that a correct translation of this section is that a judge cannot put forward the plea of prescription on his own motion. But I object to the admission of this in evidence on the ground it is irrelevant and immaterial.   [219]

The Court: I thought you said it was conceded?

Mr. Longley: It is conceded as far as formal proof is concerned. I did not know that my brother had any objection.   [220]

Mr. Garity: I object to it on the ground it is immaterial and irrelevant in this issue.

Direct Examination by Mr. Garity:

Q. Mr. Mancini, you have previously testified that Section 433 of the French Code affects the prescription of a person's rights. Is that so? A. That is right.

Q. Are you familiar with Section 2223 of the French Civil Code? A. Yes, I am.   [221]

Q. Does that in any way affect the extinguishment of a right as has been previously testified to under Section 433? A. No. It does not.

Q. Will you explain the effect of Section 2223? Is this an Article or Section? A. Article.

The Court: That is as to the effect of it?

Mr. Garity: Yes.

The Court: You know what it means?

Mr. Garity: Yes, under the French law.

A. It means that if the prescription is not raised by the parties, the judge has no right to raise it. But it does not mean that the prescription is not the extinguishment of a right. [222]

Q. Mr. Mancini, when you say that it is not the extinguishment of a right, how do you explain that?

The Court: Just let me ask you a question. A prescription is nothing like anything in the American law?

The Witness: I do not think so. [223]

The Court: Do you know what limitation means?

The Witness: Yes, sir.

The Court: Do you know what is called expiration of limitation?

The Witness: Yes.

The Court: Is the French prescription the same as limitation?

The Witness: Yes.

The Court: This means in American law that a party who does not plead limitation waives it? [224]

The Witness: Yes.

The Court: Is that what this clause means, that it is waived?

The Witness: Yes.

The Court: The Court cannot raise the question of prescription if the party himself does not?

The Witness: Yes.

The Court: Is that what that means?

The Witness: Yes.

The Court: Is that right?

Mr. Garity: No. [225]

The Court: If it is not, set me right. Is that what you understand it to mean?

Mr. Longley: I think there was an inconsistency between his answers made to you and his answers made to my brother.

The Court: Did you read all those provisions, 2219?

Mr. Garity: Those other provisions there?

The Court: Right before that?

Mr. Garity: Yes. But I do not think that any of them have any application to this.   [226]

The Court: But if it has, I think you would know it.

Mr. Longley: I think the only one is 2223. That is the only one we have raised any point on.

The Court: Without reading the other one I don't know what it means.   [227]

Mr. Garity: Mr. Mancini said in this testimony that the judge has no right to raise this question of prescription himself.

The Court: That is right. If a party does not waive [sic] the statute of limitations, it is not waived [sic], the Court cannot, so he cannot raise the statute to bar the claim. Is that right?

Mr. Garity: I understand he has so testified. Yes.

The Court: That is about the effect of it.   [228]

Mr. Garity: Yes. That is so.

The Court: Do you want to bring anything else up?

Mr. Garity: If your Honor please, we have already had testimony in the case that this Section 433 of the Code extinguished a right, but was not the extinguishment of remedy.

The Court: What is 433?

Mr. Garity: That is not in there.

The Court: Is it in this Code?

The Witness: No. It is not there. It is a different Code.°[229]

Mr. Garity: Is 433 in there (handing paper to the witness)?

The Witness: It is there.

The Court: (Having perused paper) Go ahead.

Q. You have previously testified concerning the effect of Section 433 in this case. Do you recall such testimony? A. Yes.   [230]

The Court: In that action upon a plea what are the judges under, where 433 comes? Show me? Give them?

The Witness: Code of Commerce.

Q. Mr. Mancini, do you recall such testimony? A. I do.

Q. Do you testify that this section affects right or a remedy under a contract?

Mr. Longley: I object to that question as leading.

The Court: They asked him what he testified to. It didn't make any difference.   [231]

o. Should confusion as to the interrelationship of the Civil Code and the Commercial Code continue until this point? See infra, pp. 208–209.

Mr. Garity: I was just going to try to lead up to the main point.

The Court: Did you testify?

The Witness: I testified that that affects the right.

Q. Does this Section 2223 of the French Civil Code in any way make you change your statement that you have previously made as regards the effect of Section 433? A. No. Not at all.   [232]

Q. How can you explain the fact that if the judge cannot of his own motion raise the question of prescription that Section 433 of the Commerce Code affects a right rather than a remedy? A. The Code says that a prescription is a way of extinguishment of an obligation. From the authorities in France we find that the meaning of the prescription is an extinguishment of right. I remember. I can quote from his work, which is stated in the very precise manner, that the prescription is an extinguishment of a right. Therefore Article 2223 cannot go against what we have seen in the Code and what the authority has been. Furthermore, I understand that such article means that the judge cannot raise the prescription by himself if it is a right, because if a party does not want to take advantage of a right the Court cannot force such party to take it.   [233]

The Court: Well, under 2223, if a party does not take advantage of it, then the right exists to be enforced.

The Witness: Yes. The right exists.   [234]

The Court: That is under 2223. What is the other section?

Mr. Garity: 433.

The Court: Now, if a prescription under 433 takes effect, and nobody alludes to it, could the party recover?

The Witness: The rights still exist.

The Court: The rights still exist under 433 too?

The Witness: Yes.

The Court: The rights still exist?

The Witness: Yes.   [235]

The Court: So in both instances it is only the remedy that is affected.

The Witness: It is only the remedy that is affected under 2223.

The Court: The right—

The Witness: No. Under 433 there is no remedy. Under Section 433 it is a right.

The Court: Suppose you get a right which you otherwise would have if it were not for 433, if you understand me, if it were not for 433 you would have a right. You can enforce that right, can't you?   [236]

The Witness: The right is extinguished.

The Court: You cannot sue?

The Witness: No. You can sue. But the right is extinguished.

The Court: If you do, what would the Judge say?

The Witness: If you sue after a year, the Judge cannot raise the prescription by himself. He will judge the case.   [237]

The Court: What?

The Witness: He will take the case.

The Court: Yes. But even if it is a right under 433 what should he do? Take the case and give relief?

The Witness: Right.

The Court: If he has no right how can you give relief?

The Witness: Because the party did not take his right.

The Court: If a right was extinguished, the judge cannot give any relief, can he, if there is no right?

The Witness: Why—   [238]

The Court: You say he can?

The Witness: Yes.

The Court: You understand what I mean?

The Witness: Yes.

The Court: If the right is extinguished, the party does not plead prescription, what would the judge do?   [239]

The Witness: The judge cannot raise the prescription.

The Court: Can he give relief to the plaintiff?

The Witness: Well, the judge will decide that. The case must be judged.

The Court: Must be what?

Mr. Longley: Must be judged.

The Court: Must be judged?

The Witness: Yes.

The Court: How would he judge it?

The Witness: They will judge without taking any account of the prescription.

The Court: Do you understand what I mean?

The Witness: Yes.

The Court: Is that your understanding of it?

Mr. Longley: Exactly.   [241]

The Court: I do not know how relevant it is on the question of a contract. But if a man has a claim and is prescribed under 433 and depends on it, then he can recover as I understand it. Unless the other side plead prescription he can recover. Is that your understanding?

Mr. Garity: He has so testified, Judge.

The Court: Have you any understanding of it?

Mr. Garity: No. I understand this, Judge, he has so testified. I had better ask questions rather than make statements though, hadn't I?

The Court: You may ask the witness questions if you want to. **[242]**

Q. Does Section 2223 have any application when the defendant sets up the provisions of 433? A. No.

Q. When the defendant does set up the provisions of Section 433, what will the Court do? A. If the defendant claims that there is prescription, the Court will give,—the Court will dismiss the case.**[243]**

The Court: That is a different case. The case you are putting forward, the plaintiff himself is urging prescription.

Mr. Garity: Yes, as in this instance, we have set up prescription. We plead for the defense.

The Court: I understand that.

Mr. Garity: That is to say we plead that. The other case has no relevancy in this particular case.

The Court: You raise the plea?

Mr. Garity: We are pleading it. **[244]**

The Court: Section 2223 applies to a case where it is not pleaded.

Mr. Garity: Where it is not pleaded.

The Court: And there the Judge cannot raise it. What that means is immaterial, because in this case before me, I understand it is pleaded. Do I get the fact right?

Mr. Garity: I did not ask the witness. It was just for that reason that I objected to any admission of the evidence. **[245]**

The Court: I understand.

Mr. Longley: I desire to ask Mr. Mancini one question.

By Mr. Longley:

Q. Section 433, I take it in your testimony, is a statute providing a defendant a statutory defense to a claim which may be filed or a suit which may be filed after the statutory period has elapsed, under the French Law. That is the situation, is it not? A. Yes, sir. **[246]**

Mr. Longley: That is our case, if your Honor please.

By Mr. Garity:

Q. Mr. Mancini, is that statutory defense directed to a remedy which is open to a defendant or to a right under a contract? A. It is directed to a right.

Q. Why do you say it is directed to a right rather than to a remedy? A. For two reasons: The first is because in the Code itself there are two provisions of the law: One for the right and the other for the remedy.   [247]

The provision for the right is 433, and the provision for the remedy is 435.

[The witness had previously testified that since article 433 of the Commercial Code was contained in (Book II), Section 13 thereof, entitled "Of Prescriptions," and since article 435 was contained in Section 14 thereat, stated by him to be entitled "Remedies," it followed that article 433 was substantive, not procedural. He now reiterated this testimony, and again was unable to cite authority in support. Section 14 is in reality entitled "Fins de non-recevoir," more accurately translated as "pleas in bar." Article 435 as then in effect stated, in substance, that claims against the master and the underwriters and similar claims were "non-receivable" if the merchandise had been received or paid for without protest made within twenty-four hours of receipt, followed by suit within a month thereafter. This is so-called délai préfixe, see text—note (3) following this case.]

. . .

The Court: Do you base your opinion on anything else?

The Witness: Now I have another reason in addition to that.

The Court: What is it?

The Witness: In the French Code it is this statement here that prescription is extinguishment of obligation. Then I went to the authorities and I took the best authority of it in France.   [253]

The Court: What is the name of it?

The Witness: Colin Capitant.

The Court: What is the name of the book?

The Witness: Course of French Civil Law.

The Court: In French.

The Court: Did you examine that?

The Witness: Yes and I found under page—   [254]

The Court: Is that book an authority?

The Witness: That is the best authority abroad.

The Court: Yes. The best authority?

The Witness: Yes. The best authority, and I found in volume 2, page 130, under the title "Prescription,"—may I read it?

The Court: Yes. What did you find?

The Witness: I found that the prescription is a way of extinguishment of a right of patrimony resulting in [sic] the nonexercise of these rights by their owners during a certain lapse of time which is in principle of thirty years.   [255]

The Court: Thirty years?

The Witness: In principle.

The Court: What?

The Witness: In principle thirty years. When there is no provision of the law within thirty years but in this case there is a provision of the law.

The Court: That is a provision of thirty years. Is that a translation by you? [256]

The Witness: That is a translation.

The Court: You are speaking of the rights of patrimony?

The Witness: Yes.

The Court: That is you said prescription is a way of extinguishment of a patrimony? [257]

The Witness: I have given an explanation.

The Court: Patrimony under the French law?

The Witness: Is where the man's property and rights are involved. That is what this is. I could not find any translation of the French words. The translation is patrimony.[p]

Q. Did you say that patrimony under the French Law means extinguishment of all the rights? A. Means the whole of the rights of a man. [258]

Q. Of the man's what? A. With respect to his property.

Q. And the prescription of patrimony means the prescription of the entire rights?

The Court: The next paragraph helps you out. What is that?

The Witness: The rights of actions susceptible of prescription. That is the way of extinguishment applies [sic] to all the rights of patrimony, the rights of claims, and the rights on property of third parties. Not only the rights of patrimony are extinguished by the non-use, but also all the real or personal actions attached to these rights. [259]

The Court: Have you any other reasons upon which you base it?

The Witness: Well, I base it on the books and on the authority and the Code.

. . .

The Court: . . . you are willing to state what he says is the law?

Mr. Longley: I am willing to rest our case on Mr. Mancini's testimony.

p. The difficulty of the witness in this respect is understandable. Patrimoine (Fr.) = patrimonio (Sp.) = Vermögen (Ger.) describes "property" rights as contradistinguished from "moral" or "personal" rights, but includes liabilities as well as assets. "Net worth" or "estate" are kindred but not exactly parallel concepts. See generally A. N. Yiannopoulos, Property 315 et seq. (vol. 2 of Louisiana Civil Law Treatise, 1980).

NOTES AND QUESTIONS

(1) As the above record amply demonstrates, courts and counsel in the United States frequently have considerable difficulty in understanding the relationship between the Civil Code, the Commercial Code, and (where pertinent) special legislation, e.g., as to company law, bills, notes, and checks, or general contract terms. The following statement of German civil, commercial, and company law illustrates the pattern used by one of the co-authors of the present edition in order to overcome these difficulties:

GERMAN COMPANY LAW

German private law is codified in the Civil Code (BGB). That code is divided into a General Part and four additional books dealing, in the order indicated, with Obligations, Things (Property), Family Law, and Successions. Provisions covering legal transactions as such, e.g., self-dealing (§ 181 BGB) are found in the General Part. Basic rules on liability in contract and in tort (§§ 242, 276–77; 823 et seq.), and on the law of partnership (§§ 705–740) are found in the book on Obligations. The Civil Code provides the general rules for private law transactions, comparable in this respect with the common law in Texas.

The law of private limited-liability companies (Gesellschaft mit beschraenkter Haftung = GmbH) is codified in the GmbH Law (GmbHG), which is a separate enactment. The law of commercial partnerships (offene Handelsgesellschaft = oHG), of limited partnerships (Kommanditgesellschaft = KG), and of silent partnerships (stille Gesellschaft) is found in §§ 105–160, 161–177a, and 335–342, respectively, of the Commercial Code (HGB). The provisions of the Civil Code regarding associations (§§ 705–740) are applicable to commercial partnerships to the extent not otherwise provided, § 105(2) HGB. The provisions relating to commercial partnerships (§§ 105–160 HGB) are applicable, in turn, to limited partnerships unless otherwise provided, § 161(2) HGB. There is no corresponding general reference for silent partnerships.

All three of these enactments are federal laws, applicable throughout the Federal Republic at all times here material. Their interpretation is ultimately the responsibility of the Federal (Supreme) Court (BGH), the highest West German tribunal in civil and commercial matters, and was until 1945 the responsibility of the Supreme Court of Germany (RG). Reference will be made to the decisions of these courts as occasion arises. While there is considerable dispute as to the nature and place of judicially-developed law in West Germany, seasoned observers note more similarities than differences between *stare decisis* as now used in the United States and German adherence to leading decisions of the BGH. See, e.g., J. P. Dawson, *The Oracles of the Law* 500–501 (1968).

After reading the following notes, try to draft a similar statement on French law which might have been used by Me. Mancini in order to show the Court in Wood & Selick, supra, how articles 1234 and 2223 of

Courts do not want to see forum shopping
So law may say if claim barred in foreign state
it is also barred
here

FOREIGN LAW IN OUR COURTS 209

the French Civil Code and articles 433 and 435 of the French Commercial Code related to each other.
→ Noted

(2) If an American lawyer who has had some training in comparative law were to look into the questions of French law raised by the principal case, he could—by cursory research—find the following data: *Similarities in French American law*

(a) The defense of prescription must ordinarily be pleaded (Code Civil, art. 2223) and is waivable, though not in advance (arts. 2220, 2221, 2224).

(b) After the period of prescription has run out, there remains what is known in the civil law as an *obligatio naturalis*, i.e., an obligation which cannot be enforced. A voluntary performance of such "obligation" does not constitute a gift. An obligor who made payment in ignorance of the prescription, is not entitled to restitution (*condictio indebiti*); the payee is not unjustly enriched, because the payor, though he could not be sued, was still "obligated" to pay.[1]

(c) There is controversy among French scholars as to whether prescription bars the right or the remedy. The theory which claims that the right is barred, is based mainly on the literal meaning of "extinguish" in Art. 1234 of the Code Civil. It is, however, the other theory, according to which only the remedy is barred, which has the weight of authority behind it. Among modern, sophisticated authors the view seems to be gaining ground that it is impossible to devise a unitary label accurately stating the nature and effect of prescription, and that prescription may have to be treated as procedural or remedial for some purposes, but as substantive for others.[2]

(3) In his opinion, Judge L. Hand referred to the "refined notion" of our law, according to which some statutory time limitations (especially those in wrongful death statutes) extinguish the right, while others merely affect the remedy. On the basis of the expert testimony in the record, he thought that this refined notion was "wholly foreign" to the French system. In reality—but this was not brought out in the examination of the expert—the pertinent French notions are no less refined than ours; in fact, they are more refined.[3] While we distinguish between two kinds of statutory time limitations, the French recognize at least three different types:

(i) Regular prescription (see supra).

(ii) In some instances of short statutory limitation periods the rule prevails that the expiration of the time limit creates merely a presumption of payment, and that the presumption can be rebutted in certain ways.[4]

1. See French Civil Code Art. 1235, and the interesting discussion by Constantinoff, Two Creations of Praetorian Jurisprudence Under French Law, 24 Tulane L.Rev. 302, 307–10 (1950). See also 1 M. Ferid, Das französische Zivilrecht, Secs. 1F2 and 1F97–102 (1971). Art. 63 of the Swiss Code of Obligations, infra p. 711, announces a similar rule. In our law, the rule (although not the terminology) is essentially the same. See Restatement of the Law of Restitution, Sec. 61 and Illustr. 4 (1937).

2. See, e.g., G. Marty and P. Raynaud, Droit Civil, Vol. II 1, § 876 (1962).

3. Because of these (perhaps excessive) subtleties, the subject of statutory time limitations is known to be complex in French law; a number of pertinent points, including some of those briefly mentioned here, are embroiled in controversy.

4. Marty and Raynaud, supra n. 2, at § 877; Ferid, supra n. 1, at Secs. 1F103–105.

(iii) On the other hand, there is a type of statutory time limit, called *délai préfixe*, which is more drastic in its effect than ordinary prescription. While details are controversial, it is clear that at least in some instances the debtor cannot waive the benefit that has accrued to him from the expiration of a *délai préfixe*, and that in those instances it is unnecessary for him to invoke the statutory time limit by way of an affirmative defense.[5]

Art. 433 of the Commercial Code, the provision involved in the principal case, apparently is not regarded as belonging to either of the two special categories (ii) and (iii). Article 435, see supra p. 206, is a *délai préfixe*.

(4) Which of the points mentioned in notes (2) and (3) would you have sought to bring out if you had been the attorney for the defendant? If you had been the attorney for the plaintiff?

(5) Consider whether the defendant would have had a tenable position if it had argued as follows: The French Codes are not isolated statutes superimposed upon a body of unwritten law; they form a unit, a complete and self-sufficient system of law of which the Code Civil and the Code de Commerce form integral parts. It follows from this very nature of the Code system that every right created by such system bears in itself the conditions and qualifications expressed in any part of that same system. An American court, asked to enforce a right created by the French legal order, should not enforce it without regard to such inherent conditions and qualifications.

Does Judge Hand's opinion meet the argument stated in the preceding paragraph? If there were no authority on the point, would you find the argument persuasive? [5a]

(6) The foregoing question raises a point of comparative law and of conflict of laws. The close interrelation of the two subjects (see supra, p. 25 ff.) is again demonstrated by the principal case. Part of the difficulty faced by counsel and expert was due to the elusive nature of the conflict of laws rule regarding foreign limitation statutes then prevailing. It was correctly assumed by all that the one-year "prescription" provided in art. 433 of the French Commercial Code would be treated as substantive, and hence as controlling, if it could properly be called a condition of the libellant's rights, but that art. 433 would be regarded as procedural and would not be applied by an American court if it were an ordinary statute of limitations destroying the remedy rather than the right. The *criterion* which determines ("characterizes," "classifies," or "qualifies") the substantive or procedural nature of art. 433 is a matter of the forum's own conflict of laws. But the legal *institution* to which the criterion is to be applied (in this case the institution of prescription pursuant to art. 433), is an institution of French law, so that French law determines its features and incidents.

---

5. See 28 Baudry-Lacantinerie and Tissier, Traité Théorique et Pratique de Droit Civil, as translated in Vol. 5 of the Civil Law Translations published by the Louisiana State Law Institute (J. Mayda, Translator), at pp. 26, 30 (1972); 12 Aubry and Rau, Droit Civil Français, as translated ibid, at 421, 423; Marty and Raynaud, supra n. 2, at § 859; 7 Planiol-Ripert,

Traité Pratique de Droit Civil Français § 1403 (1954, and 1962 Supp.).

5a. See W. L. M. Reese, Dépeçage: A Common Phenomenon in Choice of Law, 73 Colum.L.Rev. 58 (1973); R. A. Leflar, American Conflicts Law 221–22 (3d ed., 1977).

The latter must be developed through the testimony of an expert; but counsel cannot ask the right questions unless he knows precisely what the criterion is.[6]

Defendant's counsel apparently thought that the criterion is predicated on whether the French, in unspecified contexts, *label* their prescription as substantive or procedural.[7] Libellant's counsel, on the other hand, correctly anticipated the criterion which the appellate court ultimately used. Thus, the few questions he asked turned out to be the decisive ones.

(7) The sophisticated and perhaps overly refined criterion announced by the Second Circuit in the principal case was followed by some other courts,[8] but the Second Circuit itself abandoned it some time ago for maritime cases.[9] In Bournias v. Atlantic Maritime Co., 220 F.2d 152 (2d Cir., 1955), the Court of Appeals for the Second Circuit modified the views expressed in the principal case and announced a new criterion, predicated on whether the foreign time limitation is *specifically* directed to the right in question.[10] Under this rule, it would be necessary to present expert testimony concerning the "specificity" of the foreign prescription statute. Along what lines would you question the expert in order to prove or disprove that art. 433 of the French Commercial Code is "specifically" directed to causes of action for damage to cargo shipped under an ocean bill of lading? [11]

6. In cases where the forum's choice-of-law rule is clear, counsel and experts are more likely to understand, and to focus on, the precise question of foreign law to be explored. In such cases, the experts' testimony is apt to be more helpful. For an example, see Diaz v. Southeastern Drilling Co. of Argentina, S.A., 324 F.Supp. 1 (N.D. Tex. 1969), aff'd 449 F.2d 258 (5th Cir. 1971).

7. There is some support for this position. See Goodwin v. Townsend, 197 F.2d 970, 972–3 (3d Cir., 1952); Matter of Tonkonogoff's Estate, 177 Misc. 1015, 32 N.Y.S.2d 661 (Surr.N.Y.Co. 1941; Foley, S.).

8. See, e.g., Ramsay v. The Boeing Co., 432 F.2d 592 (5th Cir. 1970). In this wrongful death case, the defendant invoked a Belgian statute imposing a five-year time limitation upon any claim arising from a tort which at the same time constitutes a crime. Faced with the question whether this Belgian time limitation is substantive or procedural, the court surveyed the controversial views expressed in the cases concerning the proper criterion to be applied, and then (purporting to determine the question under the choice-of-law rules of Mississippi) chose the Wood & Selick criterion as the soundest one. As the expert testimony showed that under Belgian law this particular statutory time limitation cannot be waived, and that it must be applied by the court *ex officio*, it was treated as substantive under the Wood & Selick test, with the result that it had to be applied in the case at bar.

Cf. Gillies v. Aeronaves de Mexico, 468 F.2d 281 (5th Cir. 1972) (Action for severance pay under Mexican law, including wages for the period from the day of discharge to the date of the judgment. *Held*, under Florida law, that where defendant is subject to continuously accumulating claims but plaintiff is required to bring his action within two months, the time limit is substantive because of its obvious connection with plaintiff's substantive claims, the further accumulation of which the time limit is designed to stop).

9. In diversity cases the question is governed by state law. See Klaxon Co. v. Stentor Electric Mfg. Co., 313 U.S. 487, 61 S.Ct. 1020 (1941). See also the cases cited in n. 8, supra.

10. "Was the limitation directed to the newly created liability so *specifically* as to warrant saying that it qualified the right?" Bournias v. Atlantic Maritime Co., Ltd., supra, at 156, quoting from Davis v. Mills, 194 U.S. 451, 454, 24 S.Ct. 692, 694 (1904).

To the same effect see Kalmich v. Bruno, 553 F.2d 549 (7th Cir. 1977), a case in which the court had to determine whether certain time limitations imposed by the law of Yugoslavia were substantive or procedural.

11. The Bournias opinion (at 157), intimates that Wood & Selick would have been decided the same way under the new test,

(8) It is plain that the difficulties encountered in the principal case largely stem from the traditional choice-of-law rule which characterizes statutes of limitations in general as "procedural", but exceptionally treats *some* (precariously differentiated) time limitations as "substantive". One way to avoid this conundrum would be to get away from the basic rule which labels the statute of limitations as procedural and hence governed by the law of the forum. More recently, as part of the ongoing "revolution" in conflict-of-laws thinking, attempts have been made to do away with the basically "procedural" characterization of the limitation issue. In Keeton v. Hustler Magazine, Inc., 465 U.S. 770, 778, n. 10, 104 S.Ct. 1473, n. 10 (1984), the Supreme Court noted considerable academic criticism of the rule that permits a forum State to apply its own statute of limitations regardless of the significance of contacts between the forum state and the limitation. The same year saw the enactment, for England, of the Foreign Limitations Act 1984, which as stated in its caption provided "for any law relating to the limitation of actions to be treated, for the purposes of cases in which effect is given to foreign law or to determinations by foreign courts, as a matter of substance rather than as a matter of procedure." That enactment largely reflects the recommendations contained in Working Paper No. 75 of the Law Commission, entitled "Classification of Limitation in Private International Law" (1980). See generally Stone, Time Limitation in English Conflict of Laws, 1985 Lloyd's Maritime & Comm. L.Q. 497.

In 1986, and again in 1987, the reporter of the Restatement (Second) of Conflict of Laws proposed a far-reaching amendment of § 142 of that Restatement;[12] but both times the proposal encountered opposition on the floor of the American Law Institute meetings. The members of the Institute seem to be generally inclined towards the view that issues relating to the statute of limitations should be governed by the law which, with respect to such issues, has the most significant relationship to the parties and the occurrence; but as of June, 1987, there is as yet no agreement as to the extent (if any) of the (presumptive) interest of the forum to apply its own period of limitation.

How would the principal case be decided now, assuming that the Second Circuit would follow what appears to be the new trend in choice-of-law thinking on statutes of limitations?

(DD) PROOF OF FOREIGN-COUNTRY LAW IN THE EIGHTIES

Introductory Note

The case which follows illustrates the way proof of foreign-country law is handled today by sophisticated lawyers and by a diligent, well-

---

i.e., that art. 433 of the French Commercial Code is not sufficiently specific to be labelled a condition rather than a statute of limitations. Does a mere reading of art. 433 bear this out? Would it be necessary to consider other provisions of the same Code, or to compare the coverage of art. 433 with that of the less specific Civil Code provisions dealing with prescription?

Cf. Pisacane v. Italia Societa di Navigazione, 219 F.Supp. 424 (S.D.N.Y. 1963) (Ital-

ian one-year limitation of "rights arising under contracts of transportation of persons" probably non-specific under Bournias test.)

12. See Restatement of the Law (Second), Conflict of Laws, 1986 Revisions, pp. 173–183; id., Supplement dated March 31, 1987.

informed U.S. district judge in a major metropolitan center. Note that the case involves German law, which, along with Mexican law, is the foreign-language legal system most frequently coming into play in American courts. Note also that there is a ready supply of "German lawyers who speak and read English and have a background in American law." Usually, these are *German* lawyers with American M.C.J. or LL.M. degrees; but in recent years, a number of German practitioners with such American post-graduate degrees have been admitted to practice in the United States (especially in New York) in the usual manner, i.e., upon examination.

Finally, note Judge Metzner's pointed complaint about some of the translations of German legal materials by "American translation services without any indicated knowledge of either German or American law", which in "many instances . . . were stilted and awkward and failed to make any sense". Why didn't the parties use German lawyers with knowledge of American law as translators? In more practical terms, how do the fees of (lay) translators compare to those of (multilingual) lawyers? Is there a middle way for economy-minded litigants?

PANTONE, INC. v. HERTZ AUTOVERMIETUNG GmbH

United States District Court, Southern District of New York, 1983.
572 F.Supp. 748 and 575 F.Supp. 789.

[October 5, 1983]

METZNER, District Judge:

The court has completed a two-day hearing in which it heard testimony from experts presented by the respective parties as to the German law to be applied to the issues in this litigation. This hearing followed a three-day hearing on the applicable German law held in March 1981 before Judge Lowe. The court has read thirteen briefs and folders of translations of German law, and the transcript of the testimony previously heard by Judge Lowe.

Fed.R.Civ.P. 44.1 requires that the court determine foreign law as a matter of law. In reaching such a determination, the court must perforce make factual determinations as to the German law. What is the German law where there is disagreement between the experts as to the English translation of the German law? Which expert does one follow where there is disagreement as to the German law either substantively or procedurally?

The two experts who testified were German lawyers who speak and read English and have a background in American law. Some of the translations were made by American translation services without any indicated knowledge of either German or American law. In many instances the translations were stilted and awkward and failed to make any legal sense.

The individual plaintiff, Lawrence Herbert, is the president and sole stockholder of the corporate plaintiff, Pantone, Inc. Hertz Germany and Hertz France are named as defendants, but counsel have stipulated for the purposes of this trial that they will be considered as one. The defendant will be Hertz Germany (Hertz).

On May 17, 1974, Herbert rented a car from Hertz in Frankfurt, Germany, and agreed to return the car in two days to a Hertz office in Paris. He used his American Express card which had been issued to "Lawrence Herbert, Pantone, Inc." On the following day, May 18, Herbert returned the car to a Hertz office in Paris, entered the mileage in the appropriate blocks on the printed rental agreement, left the keys in the car, and went into the Hertz office. Herbert alleges that no one was in the office, but a person in a Hertz uniform came from the parking area and Herbert gave him the rental documents and left.

The Hertz records did not reflect that the car was ever returned, and on June 17, 1974, Hertz considered the car to have been stolen. Hertz submitted a bill to American Express Company showing a rental period from May 17, 1974 to June 30, 1974. On July 2, Hertz sent a cablegram to Herbert in New City, New York, requesting information concerning the whereabouts of the car. Two days later on July 4, 1974, without having received any reply to the cablegram, Hertz filed a penal report with the West German police requesting that Herbert be prosecuted for misappropriation of the car. This form also provided space for informing the police if the car were located: "The car reported as misappropriated with this information with the characteristic _____ could be found again and is again in our possession since _____."

Herbert claims that he answered the July 2 request from Hertz on July 11, and told them that the car had been left at the Hertz office near the Hotel Hilton on May 18. Hertz denies having received this communication. On August 4, Hertz was notified that the car had been found by the police in Paris. Hertz did not inform the German police of this fact.

On August 28, the German police issued a warrant to arrest Herbert which stated that Herbert had rented the car from Hertz, that he did not intend to pay for the use of the car or return it, and that "the car has not yet been returned to date."

The police record reflects that on September 4, a form notice was sent to Hertz reporting that the investigative procedure had been suspended because of lack of knowledge of Herbert's whereabouts. The form requested that Hertz notify the police if it learned of Herbert's whereabouts. Hertz denies having received this communication as well.

On October 19, American Express notified Hertz that Pantone disputed the amount of the bill. On October 21 Hertz wrote to Herbert at Pantone that it had no record of the return of the automobile and that it had not received any reply to its cablegram of July 2. The letter added that the French police had found the car on August 7, and requested Herbert to furnish detailed information as to what happened when the car was checked in.

On November 1, Herbert replied to Hertz giving the requested information, but ignored the statement that Herbert had not replied to the cablegram of July 2. Herbert ended by stating that he would not pay more than a one-day rental charge plus mileage. On November 5, Hertz replied to Herbert at Pantone, stating that "there was a big mistake with Hertz Paris," "We are very sorry that all this happened and want to express our sincere apologies," and finally, "Now we hope that the matter was cleared to your satisfaction and that this incident does not reflect upon our good business relations." Hertz did not inform the German police of this agreement with Herbert.

Two and a half years later, on January 21, 1977, Herbert arrived at the Cologne Airport in Germany, where he was promptly arrested on the previously issued warrant. He was searched at the airport and again after being transported to the jail in Cologne. Herbert claims that the police menaced him with guns and that he was treated in the jail as a common criminal. Upon the intervention of an attorney retained to represent Herbert, he was released from jail the following morning at 11:30 A.M.

Herbert seeks damages for pain and suffering incident to the arrest which he claims flow directly from the way Hertz handled this matter. This pain and suffering, he claims, includes a traumatic neurosis which has destroyed his self-image. Further, Herbert claims that he has lost his ability to manage Pantone effectively, and that, specifically, his fear of being in West Germany has resulted in his inability to market Pantone's Color Data System in Europe.

The second claim is presented by the corporate plaintiff Pantone for damages in contract. Under German law there are three statutory bases for recovery for breach of contract. See Palandt, Commentary on Civil Law, § 276 n. 7(a)(aa), at 301. The courts have developed additional bases for recovery encompassed in the concept of "positive Vertragsverletzung," or "pVV," relying on the German Civil Code, the Burgerliches Gesetzbuch ["BGB"] §§ 242, 276. PVV creates ancillary duties for the contracting parties, among which is the "duty to act during the course of the contractual relationship in such a fashion that the person, property and other legal interests of the other party are not injured." Palandt, § 242 n. 4B(b), at 202. Defendant's expert has conceded that Pantone may recover under pVV provided that Pantone was the contracting party for the rental of the car and that Hertz was under a duty to notify the police of the resolution of the matter with Pantone and Herbert.

Pantone claims that the trauma suffered by plaintiff Herbert, its chief executive and chief operating officer, caused the failure of its European marketing efforts for its Color Data System. Herbert was unable to attend a scheduled meeting with representatives of Pantone's West German public relations and advertising firms on January 22, 1977, and because of his fears was unable to remain at Pantone's March, 1977, Frankfurt show for more than one day, or to remain in

Germany for more than one day of a two-week show in Dusseldorf the following June. Pantone claims that Herbert's singular technical expertise and his status as chief executive officer of Pantone made him the only Pantone employee who could sell the system effectively.

There is no doubt that under German law plaintiffs' complaint on its face can successfully withstand a motion to dismiss.

We turn now to the defenses raised by Hertz. The first of these is known under German law as the right of error.

One who instigates legal proceedings later determined to be unfounded may not be held liable for instituting the action unless a deliberate unethical injury is inflicted by unfair means. Judgment of March 13, 1979, Bundesgerichtshof, Grosse Senate fur Zivilsachen ["BGHz"], 1979, 1979 BGH NJW 1351 [the "1351 case"]; Judgment of October 3, 1961, BGHz, 1961, 36 BGH 18, 1961 NJW 2254. Even negligence in instituting the proceedings will not vitiate the defense. The right of error rests on a policy that the public should be afforded easy access to the judicial system and not be deterred by the possibility of suit for instituting the proceedings. 1351 case.

Holding

I hold that German law sustains a defense of right of error to a claim for injury based on the filing by Hertz of the complaint with the police department. This is true notwithstanding the fact that the defendant filed the complaint without waiting a reasonable time for an answer to its cablegram of July 2, 1974, inquiring as to where Herbert left the car.

Herbert also predicates his tort claim on the failure of Hertz to notify the police that the car had been found and the matter concluded according to Herbert's claim that the car had only been used by him for one day.

The policy considerations underlying the right of error defense are not applicable to this claim. The denial of the defense here will not discourage German litigants from seeking judicial relief. Hertz is charged with failure to notify the police of the information in its possession which could have aborted the criminal proceedings which it instigated.

The 1351 case furnishes the basis for this ruling. That case arose under BGB § 823, which provides liability when a person negligently or willfully, and unlawfully, injures another.[a] In 1351 an attorney was held liable for continuing civil litigation to collect a debt after he had received payment from the debtor. The court stated that the right of error defense requires critical limitation:

> "It must cease at the point where . . . his freedom of decision and action is not restricted to an unreasonable extent by the risk of liability. In the instant case this boundary was overstepped. For the requirement that he should note an easily checked notification

a. A translation of this provision appears infra p. 553.

that his legal proceedings have in the interim become unjustified and act accordingly does not constitute a serious encroachment on his right of access to legal process."

Under the spirit of that decision the German courts would hold on the facts of this case that to require Hertz to notify the authorities would "not constitute a serious encroachment on [its] right of access to legal process." I find that the instant case is not distinguishable from 1351 even though the latter involved a civil proceeding, while Hertz filed a criminal complaint.

While it is true that the German authorities had complete discretion as to whether the complaint should be followed up, Hertz was under an obligation to furnish the police with facts later acquired that Herbert may not in fact have misappropriated the car. Defendant's expert has testified that had Hertz notified the authorities of these facts, the prosecution would not have proceeded. Furthermore, the correspondence between Pantone and Hertz indicates that Hertz no longer considered Herbert an automobile thief.

Hertz's statement of misappropriation, and its request for prosecution of Herbert, put in motion the procedures for apprehension. Prosecution can only follow apprehension. Hertz must have been aware of its obligation since the very notification requesting prosecution contained places for Hertz to indicate that the car had been returned.

Defendant further attempts to distinguish the 1351 case on the basis that Hertz did not know that a warrant of arrest had been issued. It argues that in 1351 the lawyer was chargeable with knowledge of payment by the debtor and therefore should have discontinued the litigation.

It makes no difference whether Hertz knew or did not know of the issuance of the warrant since the duty imposed was to advise the police of the facts so that the latter could properly exercise their discretion as to the continuation of the proceedings.

Consequently, the defense of right of error is inapplicable to Herbert's tort claim for the failure to notify the police.

The parties do not dispute the facts concerning Hertz's charge that Pantone was not the contracting party and therefore cannot recover on its pVV claim. They do dispute the proper application of German law to the rental contract.

Pantone's credit card was imprinted on the rental contract to indicate the party to be charged. Herbert's name was placed on the contract as the renter of the vehicle. Obviously, a corporation cannot drive a car, only an individual can do that. Hertz checked Pantone's credit, and, contrary to its assertion that Pantone was only a guarantor of payment, it is clear that Pantone was the primary obligor.

Under German law one looks to the true intent of the parties, as evidenced by their acts in executing the contract, to determine the parties to the contract. BGB §§ 133, 164(1). The car was rented for use in Pantone's business. Hertz rented that car to Pantone, relying solely on Pantone to pay the cost.

Defendant relies on a case, Judgment of October 13, 1975, BGHz, 1975, 65 BGHz 213, which we will call the check case. That case is not helpful to Hertz because the face of the check did not indicate to the payee that the husband was to be liable for payment of the check. In the instant case, Pantone's name, with its account number, appears on the face of the document, and Hertz, in fact, checked Pantone's credit. Similarly, the second case relied on by Hertz, Judgment of January 27, 1975, BGHz, 1975, 1975 NJW 775, is not on point. That case stands for the proposition that the burden of proof in the instant case would be on Herbert to establish that he acted in the name of Pantone.

> "Thus . . . [Herbert] has to prove either that he expressly acted in the name of [Pantone] or that his intent to act as an agent was obvious under the circumstances."

Here the intent to act as agent "was obvious under the circumstances."

As defendant's expert has stated on the record, if Pantone is a proper party, then on the facts of this case it would be entitled to damages on the theory of pVV if Hertz had a duty to notify the police of the events which followed the initial complaint. I have held that on the facts of this case such a duty existed. Thus, on this claim, the only issue for the jury is the amount of damages to be awarded.

The parties agree that the question of contributory negligence exists in this litigation and that, under the German law, comparative negligence is a partial defense to both the tort and contract claims.

Defendant relies on a defense to the tort claim provided by the German law to the effect that an employer is not liable for the torts of its employees where the employer has properly selected and supervised them. This, of course, raises an issue of fact to be submitted to the jury.

Finally, there has been discussion regarding the defense of disclaimer. The contract had a disclaimer clause which stated:

> "Hertz cannot be held responsible for any damage, not covered by insurance, to a third person in connection with the operation of the rented vehicle, as well as the loss or damage to articles stored or left in the vehicle during the rental period, nor for any possible damage or inconvenience caused by the belated delivery of the vehicle, possible motor trouble or any other causes."

The experts were far apart in their statements as to the interpretation of this clause. They referred to cases which seem at odds to one another. Time has been given to the parties to submit additional material, which has just been received, and the court reserves decision on that question.

So ordered.

[October 31, 1983]

METZNER, District Judge:

Section 7 of the rental agreement between Pantone, Inc. (Pantone) and Hertz Autovermietung GmbH (Hertz) contains a disclaimer clause which defendant asserts bars recovery in this case by Pantone.[b] The Pantone claim arises under the contractual concept of pVV in German law. This concept is fully discussed in this court's opinion of October 5, 1983, 572 F.Supp. 748. The clause reads as follows:

> "HERTZ cannot be held responsible for any damage, not covered by insurance, to a third person in connection with the operation of the rented vehicle, as well as the loss or damage to articles stored or left in the vehicle during the rental period, nor for any possible damage or inconvenience caused by the belated delivery of the vehicle, possible motor trouble or *any other causes.* The Renter agrees to exonerate HERTZ from all responsibility in this connection and to indemnify, hold harmless and defend HERTZ against any loss, liability and expense, including reasonable attorney's fees, which may arise out of or in connection with any such damage and/or loss."

(Emphasis added.)

While the defendant contends that this disclaimer clause applies to Herbert's tort claim as well, the contention is without merit since it has been held that Pantone was the party contracting with Hertz.

Pantone challenges the claim that the disclaimer clause bars this action, making two arguments. First, it asserts that under West German law the clause as written is unenforceable because it seeks to disclaim too wide an ambit of liability. Second, the plaintiff claims that even if the disclaimer clause is indeed enforceable under German law, it would not be interpreted to include negligent injury of the type here encountered. The court has relied only on cases for which the parties have furnished English translations.

Dispute centers around the section's disclaimer of liability "for any possible damage or inconvenience caused by the belated delivery of the vehicle, possible motor trouble, or any other causes." In May of 1974, when the parties entered into the contract which contained the clause, German law prohibited only those disclaimers which by their wording were intended to exempt a party from liability for his intentional torts and intentional violations of the contract. BGB § 276(2). Disclaimers of purely negligent actions were valid. 1979 NJW 2148.

The parties agree that on their face the words "or any other causes" comprehend causes arising both from intentional and from negligent action. Defendant argues, however, that despite the broad coverage of the clause, a German court would enforce the clause for

---

b. For a more general discussion of the treatment of disclaimer clauses in civil-law systems, and especially in German law, see infra pp. 714–725.

negligent torts and breaches of contract, deeming the parties to have intended to enter into a valid agreement, citing BGB §§ 133, 157.

Defendant has cited a decision of a German intermediate appellate court to support its position that the clause should be upheld to the extent that it disclaimed liability for negligence. In the Judgment of May 22, 1981, OLG München, 1981, 1981 NJW 1963, the appellate court construed a disclaimer clause under the new German sales law, the AGB-Gesetz (AGBG). While that law was not in effect in 1974, when the car rental contract was signed, the parties agree that court decisions handed down interpreting the AGBG are illuminative for purposes of construing the 1974 clause. The Munich court's reasoning supports the contention that the disclaimer clause at issue should be read to disclaim liability only for negligence, and therefore be enforced to bar Pantone's claim.

A later decision of the West German Supreme Court (BGHz), however, rejects the Munich court's reasoning. The Judgment of January 20, 1983, BGHz, 1983, 1983 NJW 1322, also considered a disclaimer clause under the AGBG. In the 1983 case, a disclaimer clause was held unenforceable in toto when it excluded liability for intentional as well as for negligent actions. The court wrote that since the clause was partially invalid as written, it could not be enforced at all.

We must follow the recent decision of the highest court in Germany. Even before the AGBG was enacted, the German courts would not stretch to provide meanings to ambiguous clauses which would permit the drafter the widest possible benefit consistent with legal limitations; instead, whole clauses were struck. *See* cases cited in the Judgment of May 17, 1982, BGHz, 1982, 1982 BGH NJW 2309.

The disclaimer clause is invalid as overbroad, and should not bar plaintiff's claims in this action.

In view of this disposition of the matter, it is unnecessary to discuss plaintiff's second contention as to interpretation. However, this court would point out that the parties have failed to furnish the court with adequate citation to West German law upon which to decide the issue.

So ordered.

NOTES AND QUESTIONS

What do you think of this nimble use of German case law? Should there have been a discussion of *stare decisis* in German law (infra, pp. 608–651)? Or isn't the court in the principal case right in following the most recent decision of the highest German court for the simple reason that it cannot be expected to do better by independent research?

(EE) COURT-APPOINTED EXPERTS

INTRODUCTORY NOTE

Whenever the resolution of an issue arising in a lawsuit calls for expert knowledge, the legal systems of the common-law orbit tend to rely on partisan experts, retained and paid by the parties. This practice, which stands in marked contrast to that prevailing in the civil-law world,[1] has been criticized by scholars and law reformers,[2] and occasionally—at least by implication—even in judicial opinions.[3] The principal grounds for such criticism are (a) that the testimony of a biased expert cannot be reliable, and (b) that partisan experts are expensive and hence beyond the reach of impecunious parties. In connection with the latter point, it must be noted that the difficulty cannot be avoided by the expedient of making the expert's fee contingent upon success. The Code of Professional Responsibility makes it a disciplinary offense for a lawyer to arrange for a contingent fee payable to a witness, including an expert witness.[4]

The criticisms leveled against the system of partisan experts have led to enactments such as the one which immediately follows.

FEDERAL RULES OF EVIDENCE

Rule 706. Court appointed experts

(a) *Appointment.* The court may on its own motion or on the motion of any party enter an order to show cause why expert witnesses should not be appointed, and may request the parties to submit nominations. The court may appoint any expert witnesses agreed upon by the parties, and may appoint expert witnesses of its own selection. An expert witness shall not be appointed by the court unless he consents to act. A witness so appointed shall be informed of his duties by the court in writing, a copy of which shall be filed with the clerk, or at a conference in which the parties shall have opportunity to participate. A witness so appointed shall advise the parties of his findings, if any; his deposition may be taken by any party; and he may be called to testify by the court or any party. He shall be subject to cross-examination by each party, including a party calling him as a witness.

---

1. See 1936 Report of the New York Law Revision Commission, Study Relating to Expert Witnesses, pp. 805, 834–37.

The civil-law practice will be discussed infra, at pp. 442–443. Until we reach that point in the course, the reader should suspend judgment on the question whether a system relying mainly on court-appointed experts is necessarily superior to the adversary examination and cross-examination of partisan experts.

2. For references see Note, 30 Hast.L.J. 209, 216 (1978).

3. See, e.g., United States v. McClain, 545 F.2d 988, 1005 (5th Cir. 1977); Usatorre v. The Victoria, infra p. 653.

4. See Person v. Association of the Bar of the City of New York, 554 F.2d 534 (2d Cir. 1977), cert. denied 434 U.S. 924, 98 S.Ct. 403 (1977), where a constitutional attack against this provision of the Code of Professional Responsibility was rejected.

(b) *Compensation.* Expert witnesses so appointed are entitled to reasonable compensation in whatever sum the court may allow. The compensation thus fixed is payable from funds which may be provided by law in criminal cases and civil actions and proceedings involving just compensation under the fifth amendment. In other civil actions and proceedings the compensation shall be paid by the parties in such proportion and at such time as the court directs, and thereafter charged in like manner as other costs.

(c) *Disclosure of Appointment.* In the exercise of its discretion, the court may authorize disclosure to the jury of the fact that the court appointed the expert witness.

(d) *Parties' Experts of Own Selection.* Nothing in this rule limits the parties in calling expert witnesses of their own selection.

NOTES AND QUESTIONS

(1) Additionally, Rule 53 of the Federal Rules of Civil Procedure authorizes reference of a particular issue to special masters upon a showing that "some exceptional condition" *requires* such a reference. The reference of particular issues to special masters is expressly stated to be "the exception but not the rule," id. (b), and has apparently been used for foreign-law issues in only two reported cases four decades apart from each other. Heiberg v. Hasler, 1 F.R.D. 737 (E.D.N.Y. 1941), 45 F.Supp. 638 (E.D.N.Y. 1942); Corporacion Salvadorena de Calzado, S.A. v. Injection Footware Corp., 533 F.Supp. 290 (S.D. Fla. 1982).

(2) Another, unusual expedient is described by H. J. Stern, Judgment in Berlin 205 (1984): In United States, as the United States Element, Allied Kommandantura, Berlin v. Tiede & Ruske (1979), 19 Int'l Legal Materials 178 (1980), the United States Court for Berlin (an ad hoc tribunal) appointed a German law professor as its "legal adviser expert in German law." (The author of the book just cited was the judge ad hoc). For further background, see Lowenfeld, Book Review, 83 Mich.L.Rev. 1000 (1985).

(3) It has been argued that foreign-country law should be proved in the United States primarily through court-appointed experts or special masters, mainly because experts retained by the parties are likely to present "corrupt (i.e., partisan, slanted, or sometimes misrepresented) 'expert' versions of foreign law." J. H. Merryman, Foreign Law as a Problem, 19 Stan.J. Int'l L. 151, 158; 164–68; 172–73 (1983). Do you get that impression from the Pantone case, supra? For an entirely different view as to reliability of legal experts retained by the parties, see H. W. Baade, Proving Foreign and International Law in Domestic Tribunals, 18 Va.J. Int'l L. 619, 642 (1978), and infra Note (8).

(4) Even in the absence of enactments such as federal Rule 706, it is recognized that a trial judge who distrusts the testimony of partisan experts has the power to call an expert of his own.[1] But this common-law power is almost never exercised, because in the absence of an

1. Some of the authorities are collected in the Advisory Committee Note appended to Federal Rules of Evidence, Rule 706.

appropriate statute the court lacks the authority to provide for the expert's compensation.[2] This difficulty can be overcome only by statutory provisions such as subd. (b) of the federal Rule reproduced above.

(5) Statutes or Rules similar to federal Rule 706 have been adopted in California and a few other states;[3] but no such enactment can be found in the majority of states.

In the majority jurisdictions the courts still face the difficulty that they cannot adequately compensate a court-appointed expert. Could this difficulty be met by appointing the expert as a master or referee?[4] It has been suggested that whether a particular appointee is an expert witness or a master, must be determined by looking at his actual functions, and not by the use of a label.[5]

(6) Even in jurisdictions which have enacted Rules or statutes similar to federal Rule 706, the court's power to appoint an expert witness is purely discretionary and is infrequently exercised. The common-law tradition of an adversary procedure continues to assert itself. But in cases where a party's financial inability to hire an expert threatens to defeat a meritorious cause of action, a provision such as Rule 706 makes it possible for the court to prevent injustice. Note, especially, the last sentence of subd. (b).

(7) The problem of the impecunious litigant who cannot afford to hire an expert could be solved, also, by an alternative method. Instead of authorizing the appointment of an official expert, one might provide public funds for the compensation of the poor litigant's own expert. This method is widely used in criminal cases,[6] but not in civil matters.

(8) Foreign law is only one of many scholarly or scientific subjects on which expert witnesses are asked to testify. It is submitted that the need for court-appointed experts is less pressing in foreign-law cases than in other types of cases calling for expert testimony.[7]

When partisan medical experts testify before a jury, their conflicting views may confuse the triers of the facts, and in any event are not likely to be subjected to knowledgeable scrutiny. Recognizing this, some jurisdictions have made provision, especially in personal injury cases, for the victim's examination by an impartial medical expert.[8] By way of contrast, issues of foreign law are determined by the judge rather than the jury in almost all jurisdictions; and under judicial notice statutes, where they exist, the judge has the power to evaluate the conflicting testimony of partisan experts in the light of his own

alternative

2. See Walton v. Arabian American Oil Co., 233 F.2d 541, 546 (2d Cir. 1956).

3. See Cal.Evid.Code §§ 730–733. For further references see Advisory Committee Note, supra n. 1, and Note, 30 Hast.L.J. 209, 216 (1978).

4. See Beuscher, The Use of Experts by the Courts, 54 Harv.L.Rev. 1105, 1111–20 (1941); J. Basten, The Court Expert in Civil Trials—A Comparative Appraisal, 40 Mod.L.Rev. 174, 189–90 (1977) (comparing English and American practice). Cf. Heiberg v. Hasler, 1 F.R.D. 735 (E.D.N.Y. 1941), with a postscript in 45 F.Supp. 638 (E.D.N.Y. 1942).

5. United States v. Cline, 388 F.2d 294, 296 (4th Cir. 1968).

6. See, e.g., Criminal Justice Act of 1964, as am. 1986, 18 U.S.C.A. § 3006A(e).

7. For a different view, see Nussbaum, Proof of Foreign Law in New York, 57 Colum.L.Rev. 348 (1957). The proposal made in that article—to create an official panel or roster of impartial foreign-law experts—has not been adopted in any American jurisdiction.

8. See supra n. 1.

supplementary research and of his careful (and not entirely inexpert) examination of the sources and authorities presented by the experts.

When a party cannot afford a foreign-law expert, modern judicial notice statutes may make it possible for such a party to prove the foreign law by less expensive means. Thus it is clear that in foreign-law cases (in contrast to cases where medical or engineering evidence is required) the appointment of an official expert often is not the only way in which a poor litigant can be saved from a miscarriage of justice.

(9) Finally, there is the question whether a foreign-law expert, his as yet unpublished manuscripts, and his unpublished notes in support of published work, are subject to compulsory process, testimony, and discovery in cases where the expert has not been retained by, and has no other connection with, either of the litigating parties. Summoning an expert witness (if permissible) will not aid an impecunious party, as the expert is entitled to "a reasonable fee for testifying," including, where appropriate, "a charge for a portion of the expenses of the original research." Wright v. Jeep Corp., 547 F.Supp. 871, 877 (E.D. Mich. 1982). Moreover, the expert cannot, in the face of the Thirteenth Amendment, be compelled to do additional research for the case at hand. There is, however, the possibility that his research notes and materials (if relevant) might be subject to compulsory production. Courts have been reluctant, so far, to develop a "scholar's privilege" extending to such records. See In re Grand Jury Subpoena Dated January 4, 1984, 750 F.2d 223 (2d Cir. 1984); Dietchman v. E. R. Squibb & Sons, Inc., 740 F.2d 556 (7th Cir. 1984); Dow Chemical Company v. Allen, 672 F.2d 1262 (7th Cir. 1982).

5. A COMPARATIVE SIDE–GLANCE: THE PROCEDURAL TREATMENT OF FOREIGN LAW IN OTHER LEGAL SYSTEMS

GERMAN CODE OF CIVIL PROCEDURE

Sec. 293. The law prevailing in another country . . . needs to be proved only in so far as it is unknown to the court. In ascertaining [such law] the court is not confined to the evidence adduced by the parties; it may use, also, other sources of information and may make any orders necessary for their utilization.

NOTES AND QUESTIONS

(1) On its face, Section 293 is not free from ambiguity. In order to ascertain its precise meaning, a German lawyer would use one or several of the "Commentaries" on the Code of Civil Procedure. These Commentaries are not mere annotated editions of the Code; they are systematic treatises, organized in the same way as the Code itself, so that each code section is immediately followed by a systematic commentary which, inter alia, contains references to judicial decisions and legal writings.

The two most authoritative Commentaries on the German Code of Civil Procedure, in their annotations appended to Section 293, provide the following information:

(a) Although the Code uses the word "may", the Baumbach Commentary,[1] citing judicial decisions, points out that a judge, when dealing with foreign law, "is under a duty to ascertain it *ex officio.*" There appears to be no dispute on this point.

(b) Again referring to judicial decisions, the same Commentary says that when Section 293 speaks of evidence, "that means only that in exploring foreign law the court may call upon the parties to assist; . . . it does not mean that the alleged rule of foreign law [if it remains unproved] will be regarded as non-existent . . . or that foreign law is treated like a fact that needs to be proved."[2]

(c) The duty to ascertain the foreign law *ex officio* places a heavy burden on a German court.[3] How do the courts meet this burden? The current edition of the comprehensive Stein-Jonas Commentary[4] discusses this question in considerable detail. The commentator (Professor Dieter Leipold of Freiburg) starts with the premise that the method for ascertaining foreign law is largely left to the discretion of the court. There is no need to adhere to the limits and forms for proof of fact. Professor Leipold distinguishes between three methods: personal research by the judge, informal requests for information, and strict proof by expert opinion, tested by examination in open court if requested by a party.[5] Personal research[6] is limited essentially to German-language countries. Informal requests for information from German or foreign embassies, consulates, or government departments are described as unpromising. The major sources of reliable information are still the university and Max Planck institutes of comparative law.[7] The author

1. Baumbach, Lauterbach, Albers and Hartmann, Zivilprozessordnung, Sec. 293, Anno. 1B (44th ed., 1986).

2. Id., Anno. 2 [citations omitted].

3. Some German courts, especially in large metropolitan centers where much transnational litigation occurs, have attempted to deal with this problem by assigning all foreign-law cases to special panels of judges, the idea being that the members of such panels will become foreign-law and conflict-of-laws specialists. See K. Siehr, Special Courts for Conflicts Cases: A German Experiment, 25 Am.J. Comp.L. 663 (1977).

4. Stein & Jonas, Kommentar zur Zivilprozessordnung, Vol. II-1, Sec. 293, Annos. 1–109 (pp. 227–52) (20th Ed., 1987) (Author: D. Leipold.)

5. Id. ¶¶37–38, p. 237.

6. A court of the Swiss Canton of Zurich (applying a code provision similar to Sec. 293 of the German Code) sent one of its members to Paris in order to study a question of French law which had arisen in a case before the court. The parties had agreed to bear and to advance the expense of this judicial exploration trip. On appeal, it was held that this was a proper method of ascertaining the foreign law. Kassationsgericht of the Canton of Zurich,

Oct. 12, 1951, 11 Schweizerisches Jahrbuch fuer Internationales Recht 302 (1954). The procedure employed in the Zurich case was no doubt unusual; but it illustrates the wide range of the methods which the court, in its discretion, may use in order to educate itself on a question of foreign law.

7. Leipold, supra Note 4, ¶41, pp. 237–38. Concerning the organization of the leading German Institutes of this kind, and their methods of operation, see E. Rabel, On Institutes for Comparative Law, 47 Colum.L.Rev. 227 (1947); H. W. Baade, Aus der Gutachtenpraxis des Instituts für Internationales Recht seit 1955, 8 Jahrb.f.Int. Recht 295 (1959); R. A. Riegert, The Max Planck Association's Institutes for Research and Advanced Training in Foreign Law, 25 J.Legal Ed. 312 (1973). The last-cited article contains references to the same author's previous papers describing the individual Max Planck Institutes, and interestingly compares those Institutes with research organizations in the U.S. and elsewhere.

For a somewhat skeptical appraisal of the value of Institute opinions, see A. A. Ehrenzweig, Private International Law 191 (1967); id., Treatise on Conflict of Laws 365 (1962). If he wishes, however, the reader can form his own judgment concerning the value of the opinions which German Com-

also mentions, but does not strongly recommend, obtaining information through the European Convention on Information on Foreign Law, which according to him is used only hesitatingly by German courts.[8]

In a drastic departure from prior editions, Professor Leipold now regards the informal use of university or Max Planck institute opinions as permissible only in answer to "abstract" legal issues but not if the opinion comments on the facts of the case at hand. In cases of the latter kind, following a decision of the Federal (Supreme) Court of July 10, 1975, the parties are entitled to summon the expert and to question him in open court.[9]

As regards the participation of the parties, Professor Leipold states that they may be directed by supervisory order [10] to assist the court in its efforts to ascertain the foreign law. He adds that while this mode of procedure is not mandatory, it is manifestly in the interest of a party relying on a proposition of foreign law to assist in the ascertaining of that rule because if it cannot be ascertained, the proposition of foreign law relied on may not be applied.[11]

(2) It has been asserted by American writers that FRCP Rule 44.1 has converted a foreign-law question from one of fact to one of law. Is this assertion borne out by a comparison between Rule 44.1 and the German doctrine? Does Rule 44.1 have the purpose and effect of making the practice in our federal courts basically similar to that of the German courts? [12]

Is the solution of practical problems relating to the ascertainment of foreign law really promoted by attempts to classify the law of other nations as "fact" or "law"?

(3) Note that § 293 applies only if one or more issues in the case are *governed by foreign law*. Recent decisions of German courts seem to indicate, however, that—at least in a contract case—all issues are automatically governed by German law unless one of the parties clearly invokes the law of another country. See BGH decision of January 15, 1986, reported in 6 IPRax 292 (1986), sharply criticized in a comment by Professor H. Schack, id. at 272.

parative Law Institutes render at the request of German courts. In recent years, these opinions have been (selectively) reported in the series entitled "Gutachten zum internationalen und ausländischen Privatrecht" (abbr. IPG).

8. Leipold, supra Note 4, at ¶¶42 and 81, pp. 238 and 246. The European Convention on Information on Foreign Law (see supra p. 135) has entered into force for the Federal Republic of Germany and for a large number of other European nations, plus Costa Rica. Under the terms of that Convention a German court, when faced with a question involving the law of country X, could now channel an inquiry concerning such law to the appropriate authorities of X (provided that X, also, adheres to the Convention). For comments on the various provisions of the Conven-

tion, see Leipold, supra Note 4, ¶¶72–81, pp. 245–47. The text is reproduced id. at 247–51.

9. Id. ¶¶43–44, p. 238, citing BGH, 1975 NJW 2142, 2143. Note, however, that even where the institute's opinion contains comments on the facts of the case, the expert (i.e., the author of the opinion) has to testify in open court only if a party requests it. Experience has shown that German lawyers, either for tactical reasons or because of unfamiliarity with the 1975 decision just cited, rarely make such a request.

10. For a discussion of such supervisory orders see infra pp. 418–431.

11. Leipold, supra note 4, ¶¶47–48, p. 239.

12. See supra pp. 62–63.

By thus adopting the "homeward trend" that has long been displayed in American cases such as *Hurtado* (supra p. 108), the German court reduces the number of situations in which § 293 compels judicial exploration of foreign law. See also the decision of the Supreme Court of Italy of May 4, 1985, reported in 22 Riv.Dir.Int. Privato e Processuale 648, 651 (1986), applying Italian law to a contract held to be governed by Libyan law which, however, had not been determined below. Reversing the trial court's dismissal for plaintiff's failure to establish Libyan law, the Court said:

> Taking into account the general principle that the legal order does not know of *lacunae* and that it is not permitted to the judge to respond to party demands by *non liquet*, it appears unavoidable that the judge arrives at the substitution (and application) of the known for the unknown, on the basis of the presumption that the different legislative systems are all inspired by common principles of a most general kind.

(4) The reader who is interested in comparing our treatment of the subject with the relevant doctrines, not only of Germany, but of a large number of civil-law and socialist systems, is referred to: S. L. Sass, Foreign Law in Civil Litigation: A Comparative Survey, 16 Am.J.Comp. L. 332 (1968); I. Zajtay, The Application of Foreign Law (Vol. III, Ch. 14 of the International Encyclopedia of Comparative Law, 1972); G. Kegel, Zur Organisation der Ermittlung ausländischen Privatrechts, in 1 Festschrift für Nipperdey 453 (1965); Kerameus, Revisibilitaet Auslaendischen Rechts, Ein Rechtsvergleichender Ueberblick, 99 Zeitschrift fuer Zivilprozess 116 (1986). Each of these excellent studies contains a wealth of further references.[13]

(5) Finally, consider the following comment by Mustill, L.J., in Muduroglu Ltd. v. T. C. Ziraat Bankasi (C.A.), [1986] 3 W.L.R. 606, 625:

> [A] few comments may be made on the trial of foreign law in an English court. First, many actions are brought each year in which some aspect of the relationship between the parties is governed by foreign law. This is so particularly in the Commercial Court, because of the large proportion of foreign litigants who choose, or are brought, to appear before the court. Secondly, so far as my own experience has shown, most of these cases are decided solely in accordance with English law, not so much because the court has applied the presumption that foreign law is the same as English law, but because in so many practical respects there is insufficient difference between the commercial laws of one trading nation and another to make it worthwhile asserting and proving a difference. There does, however, remain a residue of cases where

---

13. The rules concerning the ascertainment of foreign law which are in force in a given country, are bound to reflect many of the more general characteristics of that country's system of procedure, evidence and conflict of laws. Thus the reader may find the comparative readings suggested in the text even more instructive after he has acquainted himself with the basic judicial institutions of civil-law countries (infra pp. 337–530).

Most legal systems recognize that at least in the more difficult cases a court cannot satisfactorily resolve a problem of foreign law without expert advice. It stands to reason, therefore, that everywhere the rules relating to the ascertainment of foreign law must be viewed in the context of a given legal system's basic treatment of the problem of expert testimony. The differences between the civil-law and the common-law approach to this problem will be discussed infra pp. 441–443.

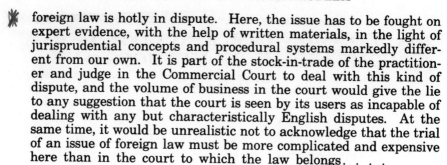 foreign law is hotly in dispute. Here, the issue has to be fought on expert evidence, with the help of written materials, in the light of jurisprudential concepts and procedural systems markedly different from our own. It is part of the stock-in-trade of the practitioner and judge in the Commercial Court to deal with this kind of dispute, and the volume of business in the court would give the lie to any suggestion that the court is seen by its users as incapable of dealing with any but characteristically English disputes. At the same time, it would be unrealistic not to acknowledge that the trial of an issue of foreign law must be more complicated and expensive here than in the court to which the law belongs. . . .

B. COMMON LAW AND CIVIL LAW— COMPARISON OF METHODS AND SOURCES

I. COMMON LAW AND CIVIL LAW JURISDICTIONS DISTINGUISHED

1. NATURE AND SIGNIFICANCE OF THE DISTINCTION

— Spent one class period on this case

— see page 597

IN RE SHOOP
Supreme Court of the Philippine Islands, 1920.
41 Phil. 213.

. . . MALCOLM, J.[a] Application has been made to this court by Max Shoop for admission to practice law in the Philippine Islands under paragraph four of the Rules for the Examination of Candidates for Admission to the Practice of Law, effective July 1, 1920. The supporting papers show that the applicant has been admitted to practice, and has practiced for more than five years, in the highest court of the State of New York.

The Rules

That portion of the rules of this court, in point, is as follows:

"Applicants for admission who have been admitted to practice in the Supreme Court of the United States or in any circuit court of appeals or district court, therein, or in the highest court of any State or territory of the United States, which State or territory by comity confers the same privilege on attorneys admitted to practice in the Philippine Islands,

Philippine Law calls for comity to allow an attorney to practice

---

a. Many of the questions presented by this case had been discussed, four years earlier, in an extensive article by Malcolm, Philippine Law, 11 Ill.L.Rev. 331, 387 (1916–17).

To look at the names of the judges who participated in deciding this case, is not without interest. It appears that "there was a well-established policy throughout the period of American administration to maintain marginal but majority control [of the Supreme Court] by allocating five seats to Americans and four (including the Chief Justiceship) to Filipinos." A. B. Salmonte,

The Philippine Supreme Court: A Study of Judicial Background Characteristics, Attitudes, and Decision-Making, in G. Schubert & D. J. Danelski, Comparative Judicial Behavior 157, 162 (1969). For an interesting discussion of the history of that policy, see ibid. The author quotes a 1909 telegram from the Governor General to the U.S. Secretary of War, reading: "Believe that the appointment of Filipinos to the Supreme Court, making the majority of that body native, would have very disastrous effect upon capital and those proposing to invest here. . . ."

and who can show by satisfactory affidavits that they have
practiced at least five years in any of said courts, may, in the
discretion of the court, be admitted without examination."

The above rule requires that New York State by comity confer the
privilege of admission without examination under similar circumstances to attorneys admitted to practice in the Philippine Islands.
The rule of the New York court permits admission without examination, in the discretion of the Appellate Division, in several cases, among
which are the following:

> "2. Any person admitted to practice and who has prac-
> ticed five years in another country whose jurisprudence is
> based on the principles of the English Common Law." [b]

This court is advised informally that under this rule one member of
the bar of the Philippine Islands has been admitted to practice, without
examination, in the State of New York, and one member of the same
bar has been refused such admission, the latter being the more recent
case. The rulings of the New York court have not been brought to the
attention of this court authoritatively, but assuming that reports of
such rulings by the New York court are true, in view of the apparent
conflict, it seems proper to enter upon the consideration of whether or
not under the New York rule as it exists the principle of comity is
established. It must be observed that under the rules of both jurisdictions, admission in any particular case is in the discretion of the court.
Refusal to admit in any particular case is not necessarily conclusive as
to the general principles established by the rules.

. . . What is "jurisprudence based on the principles of the English
Common Law?" . . .

Common Law in the United States

We must assume that the New York court, in using this phrase,
considered that the jurisprudence of New York State was based upon
the principles of the English Common Law. We should, therefore,
consider to what extent the English Common Law principles apply to
New York. In a case in 1881 we find the following:

> "And the Common Law of England was the law of the
> colony at that date (April 19, 1775), so far as it was applicable
> to the circumstances of the Colonists. And it has since contin-
> ued so to be, when conformable to our institutions, unless it

b. For a summary of the comparable
(and largely similar) rules presently in effect, see Pascual v. State Bd. of Law Examiners, 79 A.D.2d 1054, 435 N.Y.S.2d 387,
388 (3d Dep't 1981), motion for leave to
appeal denied 54 N.Y.2d 601, 442 N.Y.S.2d
1027, 425 N.E.2d 901 (1981). New York
now requires, additionally, graduation
from a law school substantially the equivalent of an "approved" law school in the
United States. This requirement is established or denied by the Board with the aid
of consultants who are experts in the law
of the foreign country in question. As
reported 435 N.Y.S.2d at 388, only two
Philippine law schools were at that time
considered by the consultants to be the
substantial equivalents of "approved" law
schools.

was established by an English statute which has since been abrogated or was rejected in colonial jurisprudence, or has been abolished by our legislation." Cutting v. Cutting, 86 N.Y., 522, p. 529. . . .

In Morgan v. King (30 Barber [sic], N.Y., 9), the New York court said that in adopting the English Common Law, New York adopted:

"The written law of England as a constantly improving science rather than as an art; as a system of legal logic, rather than as a code of rules,—that is, that the fundamental principles and modes of reasoning and the substance of the rules of the Common Law are adopted as illustrated by the reasons on which they are based, rather than the mere words in which they are expressed." c   . . .

The above statements of the New York court clearly indicate the scope of the English Common Law in that state. In most of the States, including New York, codification and statute law have come to be a very large proportion of the law of the jurisdiction, the remaining proportion being a system of case law which has its roots, to a large but not an exclusive degree, in the old English cases. In fact, present day commentators refer to American jurisprudence or Anglo-American jurisprudence as distinguished from the English Common Law.

Accordingly, in speaking of a jurisprudence which is "based on the English Common Law," for present purposes at least, it would seem proper to say that the jurisprudence of a particular jurisdiction *is based* upon the principles of that Common Law, if, as a matter of fact, its statute law and its case law to a very large extent includes the science and application of law as laid down by the old English cases, as perpetuated and modified by the American cases.

Common Law Adopted by Decision   → *Not even England*

The concept of a common law is the concept of a growing and ever-changing system of legal principles and theories, and it must be recognized that due to the modern tendency toward codification (which was the principle of the Roman and Civil Law d), there are no jurisdictions today with a pure English Common Law, with the exception of England itself.e   In the United States the English Common Law is *Novel* blended with American codification and remnants of the Spanish and French Civil Codes. There a legal metamorphosis has occurred similar to that which is transpiring in this jurisdiction today. Some of the western states, which were carved out of the original Louisiana territory, have adopted the Common Law by decision. [Citations.]

c. This is a paraphrase rather than an exact quotation of the language used by James, J., in Morgan v. King, 30 Barb. 9, 14–15 (N.Y.Sup. 1858), reversed on other grounds 35 N.Y. 454 (1866).

d. Is this statement correct in respect of classical Roman law? See infra, p. 286.

e. Is it correct to assume that in England "pure English common law" is in force today, or was in force at the time this opinion was written?

Louisiana has long been recognized as the one State of the Union which retained a portion of the Civil Law. In a case in 1842 in Louisiana, the court considered the question of whether a protest on a promissory note had been made within the required time. The court rejected the straight Civil Code rule, and adopted the custom of New Orleans, which was the law of the sister States, saying:

> "The superior court of the late territory of Orleans very early held that although the laws of Spain were not abrogated by the taking possession of the country by the United States, yet from that event the commercial law of the Union became the commercial law of New Orleans; and this court has frequently recognized the correctness of these early decisions, principally in bills of exchange, promissory notes and insurance." Wagner v. Kenner, 2 Rob. [La.], 120.[f] . . .

Louisiana, by statute, adopted certain common law rules, and with reference to these the court said, in State v. McCoy (8 Rob. [La.], 545):

> "We concur with the counsel in believing that the legislature in adopting the Common Law rules of proceeding, method of trial, etc., adopted the system as it existed in 1805, modified, explained and perfected by statutory enactment, so far as those enactments are not found to be inconsistent with the peculiar character and genius of our government and institutions."

From this brief survey of the extent of the English Common Law basis in the States, we may conclude—(1) that the New York Court in referring to a jurisdiction whose jurisprudence is based on the English Common Law, uses the phrase in a general sense; and (2) that such Common Law may become the basis of the jurisprudence by decision of the courts where practical considerations and the effect of sovereignty gives ground for such a decision. If, in the Philippine Islands, a comparatively young jurisdiction, English Common Law principles as embodied in Anglo-American jurisprudence are used and applied by the courts to the extent that such Common Law principles are not in conflict with the local written laws, customs, and institutions as modified by the change of sovereignty and subsequent legislation, and there is no other foreign case law system used to any substantial extent, then it is proper to say in the sense of the New York rule that the "jurisprudence" of the Philippine Islands is based on the English Common Law.

In the Philippine Islands

The extent of the English or the Anglo-American Common Law here has not been definitely decided by this court. But when the

---

f. For background on the Civil Law in Louisiana see supra, pp. 13–15. The Custom (coutume) of Paris was in effect in French Louisiana until it was replaced by the law of Castile and of the Indies in 1769. There was no such thing as the "custom" (coutume) of New Orleans properly speaking. Presumably, the reference is to commercial custom prevailing in New Orleans under United States rule. See R. H. Kilbourne, Jr., Louisiana Commercial Law: The Antebellum Period (1980). As to coutumes in pre-revolutionary French law (ancien droit), see infra p. 265.

subject has been referred to by this court there has been a striking similarity to the quotations from the American decisions above cited with reference to the English Common Law.

In Alzua and Arnalot v. Johnson, 21 Phil., 308, this court, in passing upon an objection of counsel, that while a certain rule was universally recognized and applied in the courts of England and the United States, it was not the law in the Philippine Islands, said:

"To this we answer that while it is true that the body of the Common Law as known to Anglo-American jurisprudence is not in force in these Islands, 'nor are the doctrines derived therefrom binding upon our courts, save only in so far as they are founded on sound principles applicable to local conditions, and are not in conflict with existing law' (U.S. v. Cuna, 12 Phil., 241); nevertheless many of the rules, principles, and doctrines of the Common Law have, to all intents and purposes, been imported into this jurisdiction, as a result of the enactment of new laws and the organization and establishment of new institutions by the Congress of the United States or under its authority; for it will be found that many of these laws can only be construed and applied with the aid of the Common Law from which they are derived, and that to breathe the breath of life into many of the institutions introduced in these Islands under American sovereignty recourse must be had to the rules, principles, and doctrines of the Common Law under whose protecting aegis the prototypes of these institutions had their birth." . . .

"And it is safe to say that in every volume of the Philippine Reports numbers of cases might be cited wherein recourse has been had to the rules, principles and doctrines of the Common Law in ascertaining the true meaning and scope of the legislation enacted in and for the Philippine Islands since they passed under American sovereignty." Pp. 331, 333.

And later in speaking of the judicial system of the Philippine Islands (page 333):

"The spirit with which it is informed, and indeed its very language and terminology would be unintelligible without some knowledge of the judicial system of England and the United States. Its manifest purpose and object was to replace the old judicial system, with its incidents and traditions drawn from Spanish sources, with a new system modelled in all its essential characteristics upon the judicial systems of the United States. It cannot be doubted, therefore, that any incident of the former system which conflicts with the essential principles and settled doctrines on which the new system rests must be held to be abrogated by the law organizing the new system."

In U.S. v. De Guzman, 30 Phil., 416, the court spoke as follows:

"We have frequently held that, for the proper construction and application of the terms and provisions of legislative enactments which have been borrowed from or modelled upon Anglo-American precedents, it is proper and ofttimes essential to review the legislative history of such enactments and to find an authoritative guide for their interpretation and application in the decisions of American and English courts of last resort construing and applying similar legislation in those countries. . . ."

In U.S. v. Abiog and Abiog, 37 Phil. 137, this court made this further statement on the subject:

". . . What we really have, if we were not too modest to claim it, is a Philippine Common Law influenced by the English and American Common Law, the *derecho comun* of Spain and the customary law of the Islands and builded on a case law of precedents. Into this Philippine Common Law, we can properly refuse to take a rule which would estop other courses of reasoning and which, because of a lack of legal ingenuity would permit men guilty of homicide to escape on a technicality."

At this juncture, three years after the last quoted comment, the influence of English and American jurisprudence can be emphasized even more strongly. A survey of recent cases in the Philippine Reports, and particularly those of the last few years, shows an increasing reliance upon English and American authorities in the formation of what may be termed a Philippine Common Law, as supplemental to the statute law of this jurisdiction.[g] An analysis will show that a great preponderance of the jurisprudence of this jurisdiction is based upon Anglo-American case law precedents,—exclusively in applying those statutory laws which have been enacted since the change of sovereignty and which conform more or less to American statutes, and—to a large extent in applying and expanding the remnants of the Spanish codes and written laws.

Philippine Statute Law

Introductory to analyzing what Spanish written laws remain in force to-day, we will consider in a general way those Spanish laws which were in force at the time of the change of sovereignty.

Spanish law became highly codified during the nineteenth century. All of the laws of Spain were, however, not made applicable to the

---

g. Concerning similar problems in Puerto Rico, see Ramos, Interaction of Civil Law and Anglo-American Law in the Legal Method in Puerto Rico, 23 Tulane L.Rev. 1, 345 (1948–49). R. Graffam, The Federal Courts' Interpretation of Puerto Rican Law: Whose Law Is It, Anyway?, 47 Rev.Col.Abog.P.R. 111, 125–27 (1986), notes that in recent years, Puerto Rico has moved in the opposite direction. See also infra notes s and t.

Philippine Islands: only those were effective here which were extended by royal decree. The chief codes of Spain made effective in the Philippines were as follows:

Penal Code --- 1887

Code of Commerce -- 1888

Ley Provisional, Code of Criminal Procedure, and Code of
  Civil Procedure --- 1888

Civil Code -- 1889 [h]

  (Except portion relating to marriage, thus reviving a portion of Marriage Law of 1870)

Marriage Law --- 1870

Mortgage Law --- 1889

Railway Laws -- 1875 and 1877

Law of Waters -- 1866

In addition to these there were certain special laws having limited application: Las Siete Partidas; Las Leyes de Toro; Leyes de las Indias; La Novisima Recopilacion; Mining Law; Notarial Law; Spanish Military Code, and the Copyright Law.[i]

The foregoing were written laws which, by change of sovereignty, acquired the force of statute law in the Philippine Islands. There was no properly called Common Law or Case Law of Spain to accompany and amplify these statutes, although there were, of course, the customs of the people of the Islands, which constituted, in a sense, unwritten law. Spanish jurisprudence does not recognize the principle of *stare decisis*; consequently, there could be no Common Law in any sense analogous to the English or American Common Law.[j] Article 6 of the Civil Code provides:

"When there is no law exactly applicable to the point in controversy, the customs of the place shall be observed, and in the absence thereof, the general principles of law." [k]

In order to determine the general principles of law "judicial decisions cannot be resorted to". (2 Derecho Civil of Sanchez Roman, pp.

h. On the history of the Spanish Civil Code, and its roots in the Code Napoleon, see H. W. Baade, Marriage Contracts in French and Spanish Louisiana: A Study in "Notarial" Jurisprudence, 53 Tulane L.Rev. 3, at 90–91 (1978).

i. The Recopilación de Leyes de los Reinos de las Indias (R.I.) establishes the order of precedence (*prelación*) between pre-nineteenth century sources, see id. at 41. The R.I. would come first, the Siete Partidas, last, and the other Castilian compilations, in between. The Novisima Recopilación was applicable to the Philippines, but in view of the date of its adoption (1805) its effect in, e.g., Argentina and Mexico, remains controversial.

j. Pre-codification Castilian law, which supplies most of the substance of the Spanish Civil Code of 1889, is (and was) commonly referred to as *derecho comun*. See the terminology in Abiog v. Abiog, quoted in the principal case, supra p. 234.

k. The new Preliminary Title of the Spanish Civil Code, enacted in 1974, replaced article 6 with a new (but essentially similar) authoritative listing of the sources of Spanish civil law. See translation and discussion infra, pp. 652–653. For a discussion of the Spanish provision quoted in the text, see Diokno, What Are "Los Principios Generales del Derecho" in Article Six of the Spanish Civil Code, 10 Phil.L.Jour. 1 (1930).

79–81; 1 Manresa, p. 80.)[1]   A lower court of Spain is at liberty to disregard the decisions of a higher court. This is the general continental rule. (Holland's Jurisprudence, 11th Ed., pp. 68–70.)[m]

"The Partidas is still the basis of Spanish Common Law, for the more recent compilations are chiefly founded on it and cases which cannot be decided either by these compilations or by the local *fueros* [customary laws] must be decided by the provisions of the Partidas." (IV Dunham, History of Spain, p. 109).[n]

The Partidas is a code law and cannot in any proper sense be considered as Common Law. It specifically provided, however, for recourse to customs when the written law was silent. The customs to which resort is to be had are the customs of the particular place where the case arises; [o] the customs of one locality in Spain having no effect

l. This is a correct quotation from a respected and influential treatise; but the question is highly controversial among legal writers in Spain. See Brown, The Sources of Spanish Civil Law, 5 Int. & Comp.L.Q. 364, 367–72 (1956).

m. The last two sentences in the text illustrate the danger of over-generalization which is ever-present in comparative law. In many continental countries, such as Germany and France, a lower court is *in theory* free to disregard prior decisions of higher courts, even though in practice the lower courts ordinarily hesitate to invite a reversal by exercising this freedom. So far as Spain is concerned, however, the statement in the text is not even theoretically correct. Article 1692 of the Spanish Code of Civil Procedure provides that an appeal to the Supreme Court may be based on the lower court's violation of "a law" (written law) or of a *doctrina legal*. The latter term has been defined by the Supreme Court as meaning a doctrine which has been followed and applied by that Court in more than one decision. The question of the extent to which the notions of "general principles of law" and of "*doctrina legal*" overlap and perhaps conflict, has given rise to fascinating academic controversies. Article 1(6) of the Spanish Civil Code, infra p. 652, now provides that *doctrina legal* "complements" the legal system.

n. Does this statement indicate that (in the absence of an applicable *doctrina legal*) the Siete Partidas, promulgated by Alfonso X of Castile and Leon in 1265, must be looked to today as one of the important repositories of the "general principles of law"? Cf. Geigel v. Mariani, 85 P.R.R. 43, 50 (1962), where a provision of the Siete Partidas was relied upon to answer a question left open in the Code.

In the hierarchy (*prelación*) of sources of pre-codification Spanish ultramarine law,

the Siete Partidas ranged last, see note i supra. Nevertheless, this text (a legal manual in the form of a code) had a tremendous influence on the development of the law not only in Spain, but also throughout Spanish-America, including the Southwestern part of the United States (supra pp. 12–14). For an English translation see Scott, Lobingier and Vance, Las Siete Partidas (Commerce Clearing House, 1931). A summary of the contents of the Partidas, with a brief but masterful historical introduction by the late Max Radin, is to be found in Nichols, Las Siete Partidas, 20 Calif.L.Rev. 260 (1932).

o. In Spain, the victory of central Government and unified law over regional customs and privileges was less complete than in Germany and especially in France. Arts. 12 and 13 of the Spanish Civil Code preserve the local laws and customs (the so-called "foral laws") of Aragon, the Balearic Islands, Catalonia and several other provinces. The foral laws thus preserved are not as comprehensive as a modern civil code; they deal mainly with matters of testate as well as intestate succession, and with matrimonial property regimes. But as to points covered by it, an applicable foral law prevails over the provisions of the national Civil Code. The latter thus becomes a mere subsidiary source of law in those provinces whose foral laws have been preserved. See Brown, loc. cit. supra, at 372–377. For comprehensive discussion, referring also to the recent official compilations of most of the foral laws, see Hierneis, Das besondere Erbrecht der sogenannten Foralrechtsgebiete Spaniens, especially the introductory chapter, pp. 1–81 (1966); J. Cadarso Palau & J. W. Fernandez, The Spanish Constitution of 1978: Legislative Competence of the Autonomous Communities in Civil Law Matters, 15 Vand.J.Transnat.L. 47, 48–57 (1982).

on the application of law in another place. 1 Manresa, pp. 77, 79; Civil Code, art. 6; Code of Commerce, art. 2. Accordingly, the Spanish customary law could not have any force here. The law or custom cannot be migratory. Manresa does not define what is meant by "general principles of law," but from his discussion under article 6 of the Civil Code it appears how far from a case law system is Spanish jurisprudence. He formulates the rule that courts are governed: first, by written law; second, by the customs of the place; third, by judicial decision; and fourth, by general principles of law. In fact, in urging that resort to judicial decisions should come before resort to general principles of law, Manresa rather implies that the practice of the courts is the contrary.[p]

English Common Law is quite a different conception. While it grew out of the early Anglo-Saxon customs, it came in time to be a case law of binding force which controlled custom. In fact, it became so binding that it was found necessary, in order to effect justice in particular cases, to establish the Court of Chancery, which became the court of equity. The English Common Law recognizes custom only so far as it does not conflict with the well settled principles of that law. Under the Spanish system, on the other hand, when the written law is silent, before considering precedents in the cases the court is governed by the customs of the locality at the time.

Consequently, by the change of sovereignty there was no body of case law or common law of Spain which could be considered as existing in connection with the written law retained in force in these Islands. The only amplification of that written law was the local customs of the people of the Islands. This is particularly true of Spanish decisions rendered since the change of sovereignty, which do not preclude the local courts from exercising an independent judgment. Cordova v. Rijos, 227 U.S. 375, 33 S.Ct. 350.

Spanish Statute Law

The Spanish statute law, as amplified by Spanish commentaries but without a background of Spanish precedent or case law, was by the change of sovereignty, severed from Spanish jurisprudence and made effective in this jurisdiction to the same extent as if Congress had

It should be noted that the regional *fueros* are written sources of law. They originated as customs, but were reduced to writing long before the age of codification. Spanish lawyers clearly distinguish between (a) the *fueros*, which are a form of written regional law, and (b) *costumbres*, i.e., unwritten customs. The latter, although under certain conditions theoretically recognized as sources of law, play no significant role in Spanish legal practice; but the *fueros*, as pointed out above, are of enormous practical importance in certain parts of Spain.

The opinion in the principal case, by failing to mention the distinction between *fueros* and *costumbres*, is somewhat confusing at this point.

p. The statement by Manresa to which reference is made in the text, undoubtedly is one of that famous author's contributions to solving the controversial problem of the relationship between "general principles of law" and "doctrina legal". For a fuller discussion of Manresa's theory see Brown, loc. cit. supra, at 371.

enacted new laws for the Philippines modelled upon those same Spanish statutes. This retention of the local private law was merely in
accordance with the principles of International Law in that regard.q
However, by the mere fact of the change of sovereignty, all portions of
that statute law which might be termed political law were abrogated
immediately by the change of sovereignty. Also, all Spanish laws,
customs, and rights of property inconsistent with the Constitution and
American principles and institutions were thereupon superseded.
Sanchez v. United States, 216 U.S. 167, 30 S.Ct. 361.

. . . [The court refers to a great number of Spanish statutes which
were repealed and replaced by new enactments.] Even the Spanish
Civil Code r has been largely modified as will appear from the table in
the note below.[2]

q. International law would not have
prevented the new Sovereign from subsequently repealing all of the Spanish codes.
In fact, however, there was no such wholesale repeal. Compare the methods employed in the Philippines with the laws
adopted for the Trust Territory of Saipan,
where by one stroke of the legislative pen

the common law was substituted for the
pre-existing civilian code system. Cf. Cald-
well v. Carmar Trading Co., 116 F.Supp.
546 (D.C.Haw.1953).

r. Compare the outline of the Spanish
Civil Code, reproduced here, with that of
the French Civil Code, infra pp. 531–532.

2. [Footnote by the court.]

CIVIL CODE

Book and title		Subjects	Status	By what law affected
BOOK I				
Preliminary	1.	General rules for the application of laws	Modified	Act No. 2711
Title I	2.	Citizenship	Repealed	By change of sovereignty; Acts of Congress, July 1, 1902, Aug. 29, 1916; Act No. 2927
Title II	3.	Status of persons, natural or juridical	Slightly modified	Code of Civil Procedure
Title III	4.	Domicile	In force	
Title IV	5.	Marriage	Never in force in Philippine Islands	See Marriage Law, 1870; G.O. No. 68; Act No. 2710
Title V	6.	Paternity and filiation	Slightly modified	Code of Civil Procedure
Title VI	7.	Support	In force	
Title VII	8.	Parental authority (with regard to persons and property of children).	Modified	Do.
	9.	Adoption	Repealed	Do.
Title VIII	10.	Absence	Modified	Do.
Title IX	11.	Guardianship	Repealed	Do.
Title X	12.	Family council	do.	Do.
Title XI	13.	Emancipation and majority	Modified	Code of Civil Procedure; Act No. 1891
Title XII	14.	Registry of civil status	Never in force in Philippine Islands	See G.O. No. 68 and Act No. 2711

2. [Footnote 2 continued]

Book and title	Subjects	Status	By what law affected
BOOK II			
Title I–III . . . . 15.	Property, ownership, and its modifications	Slightly modified	Code of Civil Procedure
Title IV . . . . 16.	Special properties	Modified	Act No. 2152; Act of Congress, July 1, 1902
Title V . . . . 17.	Possession	Slightly modified	Code of Civil Procedure
Title VI . . . . 18.	Usufruct	do. . . . . Do.	
19.	Use and habitation	In force	
Title VII . . . . 20.	Easements	do.	
Title VIII . . . . 21.	Register of deeds	Largely modified	Mortgage Law; Act Nos. 496 and 2711
BOOK III			
Title I . . . . 22.	Occupancy	In force	
Title II . . . . 23.	Donations	Slightly modified	Act No. 496
Title III . . . . 24.	Wills	Mostly repealed	Code of Civil Procedure
25.	Inheritance	Slightly modified	Code of Civil Procedure
26.	Executors	Repealed . . . . . . Do.	
27.	Intestate succession	Slightly modified	Do.
28.	Property subject to reversion	In force . . . . Do.	
29.	Accretion (in-succession)	do. . . . . Do.	
30.	Acceptance and repudiation of inheritance	Mostly repealed	Do.
31.	Collation	Slightly modified	Do.
BOOK IV			
Title I . . . . 32.	Partition	Modified . . . . Do.	
33.	Obligations	Slightly modified	Do.
Title II and III . . . . . 34.	Contracts (including also dowry, paraphernal property, conjugal property, separation of property of spouses).	Slightly modified	Do.
Title IV and V . . . . . 35.	Purchase and sale, and barter	do. . . . . Do.	
Title VI . . . . 36.	Lease	do. . . . . Do.	
37.	Labor contracts	do. . . . . Do.	
38.	Carriers	do.	
Title VII . . . . 39.	Census	do.	
Title VIII . . . . 40.	Partnership	do.	
Title IX . . . . 41.	Agency	do.	
Title X . . . . 42.	Loans	do.	
Title XI . . . . 43.	Bailments	do.	
44.	Sequestration	Repealed . . . . . . Do.	

Cases under American Derived Statutes

It thus appears that the bulk of present day Statute Law is derivative from Anglo-American sources; derivative within the sense of having been copied, and in the sense of having been enacted by Congress or by virtue of its authority. This court has repeatedly held that in dealing with the cases which arise under such statute law the court will be governed by the Anglo-American cases in construction and application. [Citations.]

To illustrate more clearly the scope of the use of Anglo-American cases in this connection, a brief analysis of some of the more recent decisions of this court is advisable. For convenience the cases will be taken up in the note by subjects. [The voluminous Note is omitted.] In all of them, Anglo-American decisions and authorities are used and relied upon to a greater or less degree. Although in many cases the use is by way of dictum, nevertheless, the net result is the building up of a very substantial elaboration of Anglo-American case law.

From the foregoing selection of the more recent and typical cases, it appears how broad is the scope of the use of Anglo-American authorities and precedents in the field of law subjects affected by American derived legislation. In the application of those statutes in the many cases which come before the court, there is bound to be developed a substantial common law. There is no question that this exists. We are merely concerned with its extent and source.

Cases under Spanish Statutes

In addition to the subjects covered above, there is a wide field of use of Anglo-American cases in the interpretation and application of the remnants of the Spanish statutes. Such is of even greater importance in showing the real permanency of the hold which Anglo-American Common Law has fastened upon the jurisprudence of this jurisdiction. . . .

2. [Footnote 2 continued]

Book and title		Subjects	Status	By what law affected
Title XII	45.	Insurance	Modified	Act No. 2427
	46.	Gambling	Repealed	Act No. 1757
	47.	Life annuities	In force	
Title XIII	48.	Compromise	do.	
	49.	Arbitration	Repealed	Code of Civil Procedure
Title XIV	50.	Suretyship	In force	
Title XV	51.	Pledge	Modified	Act No. 1508
	52.	Mortgage	do.	Mortgage Law; Act No. 496; Code of Civil Procedure
	53.	Antichresis	In force	
Title XVI	54.	Quasi-contracts	do.	
	55.	Torts	do.	
Title XVII	56.	Preference of credit	Mostly repealed	Act No. 1956
Title XVIII	57.	Prescription	do.	Code of Civil Procedure

To illustrate the scope of the use of Anglo-American cases in connection with the remaining Spanish statutes, a brief analysis of the more recent cases under a few of the principal subjects, will be appropriate. [Note omitted.] Frequently in these cases reference to Anglo-American precedents is for the purpose of showing that Spanish law and the Anglo-American law is the same, and frequently it is for the purpose of amplifying or extending the Spanish statutes.[s] In most cases it is for the purpose of applying those statutes to the particular case before the court; but whatever the use, the fact remains that through the influence of these cases a broad exposition of American case law is made. . . .

The foregoing two groups of cases in combination, those under the subjects covered by Spanish statutes and those under the subjects covered by American-Philippine legislation and effected by the change of sovereignty, show conclusively that Anglo-American case law has entered practically every one of the leading subjects in the field of law, and in the large majority of such subjects has formed the sole basis for the guidance of this court in developing the local jurisprudence. The practical result is that the past twenty years have developed a Philippine Common Law or case law based almost exclusively, except where conflicting with local customs and institutions, upon Anglo-American Common Law. The Philippine Common Law supplements and amplifies our statute law.

Collateral Influences

This conclusion is further justified by the practical situation which has surrounded the Bench and Bar of the Philippine Islands for many years and which there is every reason to believe will continue unabated in the future.

This court has, in an increasing degree during the past twenty years, cited and quoted from Anglo-American cases and authorities in its decisions. The following analysis of the citations of the last twenty volumes of the Philippine Reports show this graphically. [Table omitted.]

The American citations are over ten times as numerous as the Spanish citations. (In Vol. 1 there were 63 Spanish to 53 United States.) Add to this the cumulative effect of perpetuating this ratio through the citations of Philippine cases in which American cases have been cited, and it is obvious that Spanish decisions have had comparatively slight effect in the development of our case law.

It is a fact of considerable practical importance that there are no digests of Spanish decisions to aid the study of Bench and Bar. On the

---

s. The Supreme Court of Puerto Rico now publishes its decisions in Spanish, and freely refers to post-1898 Spanish authorities and decisions. See, e.g., De Jesus Diaz v. Carreno, 112 D.P.R. 631, 636–38 (1982). The Court has, by extrajudicial comment, expressed its displeasure at unnecessary references to "continental" (United States) law. See also, below, note t.

other hand, the local libraries contain both digests and reports of the Federal Courts and Supreme Court of the United States, and of most of the State courts, and also many reports of the English courts. Added to this is a liberal supply of English and American text books. The foregoing not only has a natural influence on the results of the work on the Bench, but it has a very decided influence on the development of the present Bar of the Philippine Islands; each year adds to the preponderance of lawyers trained chiefly from a study of Anglo-American case law.[t]

The fact that prolific use of Anglo-American authorities is made in the decisions of this court, combined with the fact that the available sources for study and reference on legal theories are mostly Anglo-American, present a practical situation at this moment from which this court can draw but one conclusion, namely, that there has been developed, and will continue, a common law in the jurisprudence of this jurisdiction (which for purposes of distinction may properly be termed a Philippine Common Law), based upon the English Common Law in its present day form of an Anglo-American Common Law, which common law is effective in all of the subjects of law in this jurisdiction in so far as it does not conflict with the express language of the written law or with the local customs and institutions.

Conclusions

We may summarize our conclusions as follows:

. . . (2) In interpreting and applying the bulk of the written laws of this jurisdiction, and in rendering its decisions in cases not covered by the letter of the written law, this court relies upon the theories and precedents of Anglo-American cases, subject to the limited exception of those instances where the remnants of the Spanish written law present well-defined civil law theories and of the few cases where such precedents are inconsistent with local customs and institutions.

(3) The jurisprudence of this jurisdiction is based upon the English Common Law in its present day form of Anglo-American Common Law to an almost exclusive extent.

(4) By virtue of the foregoing, the New York rule, given a reasonable interpretation, permits conferring privileges on attorneys admitted to practice in the Philippine Islands similar to those privileges accorded by the rule of this court.

t. For an account of the initial phase of that process, see A. L. Garcia Martinez, La Americanizacion de Filipinas—la Justicia—la Imposición del Idioma Inglés en los Tribunales en el Periodo 1898–1906, 45 Rev.Abo.P.R. 143 (1984). As shown by Schneider v. Colegio de Abogados de Puerto Rico, 565 F.Supp. 963, 965–71 (D. Puerto Rico 1983), rev'd sub nom. Romany v. Colegio de Abogados de Puerto Rico, 742 F.2d 32 (1st Cir. 1984), the situation in Puerto Rico is somewhat different. See, as to the history of the Puerto Rican bar, Colegio de Abogados v. Schneider, 122 D.P.R. 540, 544–45 (1982), and as to precedent for its "tradición civilista" id. 550–51. As the Court said in People v. Superior Court, 92 P.R.R. 580, 588–89 (1965), Puerto Rico continues to be part of Hispanic culture, and "the means of expression of our people is Spanish."

Accordingly, the supporting papers filed by the applicant in this case showing to the satisfaction of the court his qualifications as an attorney-at-law, his petition is hereby granted and he is admitted to the practice of law in the Philippine Islands. Our decision is based upon our interpretation of the New York rule, and it does not establish a precedent which may be controlling on this court with respect to future applications if our interpretation is not borne out by the future enforcement of that rule by the New York court. So ordered.

MAPA, C.J., JOHNSON, ARAULLO, STREET, AVANCENA, and VILLAMOR, JJ., concur.

Petition granted.

[handwritten: Philippines will follow NY rule so long as there is comity.]

NOTES AND QUESTIONS

(1) What are the criteria by which the Court in the foregoing case determines whether its jurisprudence is based on the common law or the civil law? Compare the Court's criteria with those developed in R. Parker, The Criteria of the Civil Law, 7 Jurist 140 (1947). *[handwritten: Question]* *[handwritten: ① It follows Anglo-American case law system p 282]*

As to what are the correct criteria to be used in distinguishing between common law and civil law, the reader should suspend judgment until after (s)he will have studied the bulk of the materials in this book. *[handwritten: ② cases in Phillipine Reports ·233]*

(2) The question whether a given territory is a common-law or a civil-law jurisdiction, is often of more than academic interest. It becomes a question of practical importance, for instance, in cases in which there has been a failure to plead or prove the law of the particular jurisdiction. As the reader will remember (see supra pp. 88-120), the court in such a situation must choose between the Crosby approach and the forum-law approach, and in making that choice the court may be influenced by the common-law or civil-law character of the legal system in question. See, e.g., Kennard v. Illinois Central R.R. Co., 177 Tenn. 311, 148 S.W.2d 1017 (1941). *[handwritten: Reports make recourse to rules, principles + doctrines of common law.]* *[handwritten: ③ Look to legislation in U.S. history + to interpret their laws.]*

Under a permissive judicial notice statute (see supra pp. 55-81), the court in the exercise of its discretion will be more easily inclined to notice the foreign law if it is the law of a common-law jurisdiction.[1] In this context, again, it becomes a matter of practical significance whether the foreign state or country in question belongs to the civil-law or the common-law world. *[handwritten: ④ statute law taken from U.S. and construed by U.S. cases]*

(3) Being caught in the dynamic process of amalgamation of common-law and civil-law elements in the legal system of the Philippines, the Supreme Court of the Islands became highly skilled in the use of the comparative method, and its opinions, even though they show a certain amount of wavering between civil-law and common-law methods,[2] contain many valuable contributions to our subject. Frequently, the decisions of the Court demonstrate that the common law and the civil law, in spite of differences in terminology and technique, ultimately reach identical results. See, e.g., Cuyugan v. Santos, 34 Phil. 100 *[handwritten: ⑤ Only of digests of common law cases (no Spanish)]*

---

1. Under the Maryland statute (see supra, p. 79), even the *power* of the court to take judicial notice of the law of a foreign country depends on whether such country is a common-law jurisdiction.

2. See Gamboa, An Introduction to Philippine Law 75-78 (7th ed., 1969).

(1916).   The opinions of a Court in the Far East thus furnish evidence of the essential unity of "Western" civilization.[2a]

(4) On July 4, 1946, the Philippine Islands became an independent nation.   This historic event, however, did not bring about a radical change in legal methods.   American legal materials continue to be generally available to Philippine judges, lawyers and law students, while Spanish authorities, especially judicial decisions, are somewhat difficult to obtain.[3]

There are, moreover, several other factors which strengthen the common-law component of the Philippine legal system:

(a) *Legal education* follows the American pattern.   Some use is made of American casebooks, and new teaching tools published by Philippine law teachers not only tend to adopt the American style of "Cases, Text and Materials", but often contain American as well as Philippine cases.   Young lawyers in the Philippines, in their formative years, thus become accustomed to American legal folkways.

(b) At the time of the change of sovereignty in 1898, Spanish *public law* was in large measure automatically superseded by a new Anglo-American body of public law.[4]   Upon independence, the Philippines stabilized their public law on a common-law basis by incorporating Anglo-American principles into their own Constitution.[5]

(c) Civil and criminal *procedure*, and the organization of the judiciary, follow the American model.[6]   Although the jury system has not been adopted, the admissibility of evidence is governed by

2a.   It is interesting to note, also, that even today United States Supreme Court decisions which (before Independence) were rendered in cases originating in the Philippines, occasionally provide guidance as to rules of Spanish public land law affecting land titles in California and other parts of the United States.   See, e.g., the reference to Jover y Costas v. Insular Government, 221 U.S. 623, 31 S.Ct. 664 (1911), in the recent case of Summa Corp. v. California ex rel. State Lands Comm'n, 466 U.S. 198, at 201, n. 1, 104 S.Ct. 1751, 1753–54 (1984).

3.   See N. J. Quisumbing, L. A. L. Javellana and Y. Quisumbing-Javellana, Philippine Legal Bibliography 69–70 (1953).

It is interesting to note, also, that F. B. Moreno, Philippine Legal Bibliography (1973), devotes a large section (pp. 109–51) to U.S. legal materials, while the Spanish Law Reports are mentioned only briefly, in an almost off-hand fashion (pp. 91–92).

4.   Gamboa, The Meeting of the Roman Law and the Common Law in the Philippines, 4 Seminar 84, 96–97 (1946); Gilmore, Philippine Jurisprudence—Common Law or Civil Law, 16 A.B.A.J. 89 (1930).

5.   Even the 1973 Philippine Constitution, while quite different from ours in the distribution of political power, still retained many provisions patterned on the American model, and the commentators stated that construction of the Constitution should be governed by American-derived principles.   See 1 J. G. Bernas, Constitutional Rights and Duties 19 (1974); E. M. Fernando, The Constitution of the Philippines 27–30 (1974).

To what extent actual practice was in harmony with that Constitution is another question; this, however, is a problem not limited to the Philippines.   See infra pp. 880–890.

6.   See G. W. Pugh, Aspects of the Administration of Justice in the Philippines, 26 La.L.Rev. 1 (1965); Gamboa, supra n. 2, at 421–63.

It is interesting to note, however, that one important feature of civilian procedure, i.e., the victim's right to intervene and to seek damages in a criminal proceeding (see infra pp. 492–497), has been preserved in the Philippines.   See A. F. Tadiar, The Administration of Criminal Justice in the Philippines, 47 Phil.L.J. 547, 557–8, 570–76 (1972).

American-derived rules.[7] This basic character of Philippine adjective law has not changed in recent years.

(d) The Spanish-derived *substantive private law* never suffered wholesale abrogation. The new Civil Code of 1949–50, an enactment reflecting thorough revision,[8] retains much of the basic structure of its Spanish predecessor. The old Code of Commerce is still in force,[9] although many of its provisions, especially those dealing with negotiable instruments and with corporations, have long been replaced by more modern, American-influenced statutes.[10] Thus, on the face of the principal codes, the substantive private law of the Philippines in part has retained the appearance of a civilian system. But the tendency mentioned in the Shoop case, supra, to infuse common-law methods into the application and construction of the codes themselves, now receives additional impetus from Art. 8 of the new Civil Code, which expressly provides that "judicial decisions applying or interpreting the laws or the Constitution shall form a part of the legal system of the Philippines."[11]

2. THE DISTINGUISHING FEATURES OF THE "CIVIL LAW"—THEIR HISTORICAL ROOTS

A. THE PRE–CODIFICATION PERIOD

now (Guyana)
* discussed

Important to note sources of law examined

DEMERARA TURF CLUB, LTD. v. WIGHT
Judicial Committee of the Privy Council, 1918.
[1918] A.C. 605.

The judgment of their Lordships was delivered by

cause of action

SIR WALTER PHILLIMORE. The plaintiff in this case, the present respondent [Wight], brought an action to enforce specific performance of an alleged contract of sale whereby he contended that he became the purchaser of certain real estate in the Colony of British Guiana which was the property of the defendant company.

The Chief Justice of British Guiana, Sir Charles Major, gave judgment for the defendant company, dismissing the action with costs.

7. See the annual surveys of decisions on Evidence in the Philippine Law Journal. As they operate without a jury, Philippine courts apply the rules of evidence in a spirit of liberality, not unlike that exhibited by American courts in non-jury cases. See Pugh, supra n. 6, at 15–16.

8. See 1 Paras, Civil Code of the Philippines Annotated (9th ed., 1978), where at p. 9 the author remarks that "The new Civil Code contains 2270 articles, 43% of which are completely new provisions." Some of the new provisions, such as the Title dealing with express and implied trusts (Arts. 1440–57), clearly reveal their Anglo-American ancestry. See Gamboa, supra n. 2, at 248–52.

9. Title Two of the Code of Commerce preserves the commercial register, a typically civilian institution (see infra pp. 696–702).

10. See 1 Agbayani, Commentaries and Jurisprudence on the Commercial Laws of the Philippines 3–4, 79 (1964); 3 id. 1137 (1964).

11. For discussions of this provision, and of the stare decisis rules derived from it, see Gamboa, supra n. 2, at 12–13, and especially Paras, supra n. 8, at 39–44.

On appeal the Supreme Court, Berkeley and Hill JJ., reversed the decision of the Chief Justice, and ordered the defendant company to transport and deliver to the plaintiff the property in dispute on payment of the sum of 16,005 dollars and one-half the costs of transport,[a] and ordered the defendant company to pay the plaintiff's costs in both Courts. The company appeals from this decision.

The story is a short one. Some matters were controverted in the evidence; but the facts as found by the Chief Justice, and not disputed in the Court of Appeal or before their Lordships, are as follows: The company was in liquidation, and one Cannon, the liquidator, who was also a licensed auctioneer, obtained leave from the Court to sell the real property of the company, 55 acres of land known as Bel Air Park with the buildings thereon. Cannon was to be the auctioneer, making no charge for his services.

The sale was advertised as a sale at public auction by the liquidator in the grand stand of the club. On the appointed day, December 4, 1914, the auctioneer began the proceedings by reading out the conditions of sale, which were as follows:—

"Conditions on which the undersigned will offer for sale at public auction on Friday, the 4th December, 1914, at 1 o'clock P.M., on the premises (in the grand stand), by order of Mr. N. Cannon (as liquidator of the Demerara Turf Club, Limited), 55 acres of land known as Bel Air Park, with all the buildings, erections, fixtures, and fittings thereon:—Article 1: The purchaser or purchasers shall provide good and sufficient securities to the satisfaction of the auctioneer, who shall sign these conditions of sale along with the said purchaser or purchasers, and shall be bound as they do hereby bind and oblige themselves jointly and severally with such purchaser or purchasers to pay the purchase-money. Article 2: Payment of the purchase-money shall be paid to the auctioneer as follows: 10 per cent. in cash on the knock of the hammer, and the balance on the passing of the transport. Article 3: The purchaser or purchasers shall pay to the auctioneer in cash on the knock of the hammer the church and poor money payable on the sale. Article 4: Possession will be given on the passing of the transport, the cost, including the revenue stamp, to be divided between the seller and the purchaser. Article 5: Two or more persons bidding at the same time, or any dispute arising, the auctioneer reserves to himself the right of deciding and settling the same in such manner as he may think fit."

A bid of 15,000 dollars was made, and a second bid of 15,005 dollars. Then came a third bid of 16,000 dollars, and then the plaintiff bid 16,005 dollars. No further bid was made. Cannon then said, "I am

---

a. To "transport" means to convey the property. It is a literal translation of over-dracht (Dutch) = Uebertragung (German), usually translated as "transfer." See also R. W. Lee, An Introduction to Roman-Dutch Law 139 (1953). In New York, the term "transport" was used in a similar sense during the Dutch period.

sorry, gentlemen, but I cannot sell at that price." The plaintiff says that he said, "The Turf Club is mine," using consciously or unconsciously a phrase common at Dutch auctions by way of a descending scale. If he did say so Cannon did not hear him; and without more being said the company dispersed. There was some correspondence afterwards, and then the plaintiff brought his action on March 23, 1915.

It is to be noted that there was, on the one hand, no intimation either beforehand or at the auction that there was a reserved price, or that the vendor reserved the right to bid; nor, on the other hand, was there any intimation that the sale was to be without reserve, or that the property would be knocked down to the highest bidder.

In these circumstances their Lordships have to determine what was the nature of the business which was entered upon when this property was put up for sale.

It is contended on behalf of the plaintiff that this matter is concluded by law; that by the Roman-Dutch law [b] which rules, or at the time ruled, in British Guiana,[c] the auctioneer who puts up property for sale thereby makes an offer, that each bidder is an acceptor, that by each bid a provisional contract is made, one liable to be displaced or superseded by a higher bid, but forming unless so displaced or superseded a contract binding on both parties. Alternatively the contention is expressed in this way: that the auctioneer when he puts up property for auction tacitly promises to accept the highest bid, and is bound to accept it, and that his verbal or physical acceptance is a mere formality which he is bound to give. Hill J. apparently decided for the plaintiff on both grounds; Berkeley J. probably on the second only.

It is to be observed that this is not an action for damages for not accepting a bid or for withdrawing the property from sale. It is an action which proceeds upon the assumption that there was a sale. For the plaintiff, therefore, to succeed, either the bidder must be an acceptor, or the auctioneer's acceptance of the last bid must be a mere formality.

b. Roman-Dutch law is usually defined as the system of law which prevailed in The Netherlands (or, more precisely, in the province of Holland) from the middle of the 15th century until the age of codification. See R. W. Lee, An Introduction to Roman-Dutch Law 2 (1953); Hahlo and Kahn, The Union of South Africa 13 (1960).

The substantive private law of The Netherlands was codified in 1838. In those overseas territories, however, which the Dutch had lost prior to 1838 (including the former Dutch possessions in South Africa, Ceylon and British Guiana), these 19th century Dutch codes were never introduced; to the extent that the new Sovereign retained the prior law in those territories, it was preserved in the form of uncodified Roman-Dutch law.

c. The three Dutch settlements later united as British Guiana were captured in 1803 and ceded to Britain in 1814. The then existing system of law (i.e. Roman-Dutch law, see preceding fn.) was retained for over a century; but in 1916, after the commencement of the present action, the Civil Law of British Guiana Ordinance abrogated most of the Roman-Dutch law, except that relating to real property and intestate succession. See M. Shahabuddeen, The Legal System of Guyana 202–203 (1973). As to post-independence developments in the legal system of this former British colony, see id., passim, and J. N. Hazard, Guyana's Alternative to Socialist and Capitalist Legal Models, 16 Am.J. Comp.L. 507 (1968).

It is contended on behalf of the defendant company that there is no settled rule of Roman-Dutch law to the effect asserted by the plaintiff, and no rules of Roman-Dutch law which apply to such auctions as this was, and that in any case, this being a voluntary sale, the auctioneer could make his own arrangements, and that the nature of the business for which he was arranging was sufficiently indicated by the use of the phrase "knock of the hammer" in the second and third of the conditions of sale, which showed that the bidder was to be deemed the offerer and the auctioneer, if he so willed, the acceptor. It is no doubt true that the auctioneer could make his own terms on which he proposed to conduct the sale; but it is also true that if there was a silence as to any term or a doubt what the term was, it is material to know what is the underlying law, or the law which would prevail in the absence of any special term.[d]

Their Lordships therefore proceed to examine whether there is any rule of Roman-Dutch law applying to auctions of this nature, and if so what its effect is. All the judges in the Courts below seem to have thought that there is a rule of Roman-Dutch law upon this point, but they have differed in their view of its effect. There are no decided cases which can be quoted as authorities and there is no Code, Statute, or Ordinance. The law has to be extracted from the works of writers of authority. These start by referring to the Roman law.

In the Roman law itself, though sales by auction and the letting of tolls by auction were well known, there is no direct guidance to be found. There are references to auctions, but no rules of law, to be found in the Digest.[e] In the Code there are two passages (lib. 10, tit. 3,

---

d. Needless to say, the same problem poses itself in modern legal systems. For a comparative discussion of present-day solutions in common-law as well as civil-law countries see 1 Schlesinger (Gen.Ed.), Formation of Contracts—A Study of the Common Core of Legal Systems 82–83, 391–429 (1968).

e. Justinian's Corpus Juris Civilis, the most influential legislative pronouncement of all times, is divided into four parts:

(a) The Institutiones, four books written in textbook style, but given the force of law.

(b) The Digesta or Pandecta, the longest and most important part of the whole work, arranged in 50 books and constituting a compilation of excerpts (edited and sometimes revised by Justinian's commission) from the opinions and writings of the 38 most famous Roman jurists of prior centuries, especially Ulpianus, Paulus, Papinianus, Gaius and Modestinus.

(c) The Codex, a compilation of prior imperial decrees, again edited and in part revised by Justinian's commission under the chairmanship of Tribonianus.

(d) The Novellae, a collection of decrees and rescripts issued by Justinian after 534 A.D., i.e. after the three original parts of the work were completed.

See Wenger, Die Quellen des römischen Rechts 576–679 (1953), where the reader will find massive further references.

Concerning the nature and significance of the older jurists' opinions (*responsa*) which formed part of the raw material of the Digest, see A. A. Schiller, Jurists' Law, 58 Colum.L.Rev. 1226 (1958); id., The Nature and Significance of Jurists Law, 47 B.U.L.Rev. 20 (1967). See also F. H. Lawson, Many Laws (Vol. 1 of Selected Essays) 124–46 (1977).

Although the Corpus Juris is not free from obscurities and contradictions, there is universal agreement that the commission chaired by Tribonianus, which completed the compilation within the unbelievably short period of approximately three years, must be credited with a triumphal intellectual accomplishment. For an in-

s. 4; lib. 11, tit. 31, s. 1); [f] but these relate to necessary or judicial sales, and, moreover, have no bearing on the point in question.

The writers on Roman-Dutch law endeavour to help themselves out by the analogy of the Roman law as to sales by addictio in diem.[g] This analogy is noticed in the judgments of the judges in the Court below; but as it was agreed at the Bar before their Lordships, is a misleading analogy. It is unnecessary, as there was this agreement, to explain at length why no assistance can be got from the analogy, and why, indeed, confusion will arise if it is attempted to bring sales by auction under the law as to sales by addictio in diem. The writers on Roman-Dutch law also avail themselves of the writings of commentators of other European nations, such as Bartolus, who was an Italian, and Choppinus, who was a Frenchman from Anjou. How far they can be used as authorities on Roman-Dutch law may be doubted.[h] They, too, found themselves on the law as to sales by addictio in diem.

The authority principally relied upon in the Courts below and before their Lordships is Matthaeus, an author of much learning and repute, and quoted as an authority by later writers who are accepted authorities on Roman-Dutch law. He wrote a treatise on auctions. His book De Auctionibus was published at Utrecht in 1653. His work is founded on the Roman law [i] and the European commentators upon it

structive and entertaining account of the politics behind the Corpus Juris, and of the imprint which the personalities of Justinian and of Tribonianus left upon the great work, see A. M. Honoré, The Background of Justinian's Codification, 48 Tul.L.Rev. 859 (1974). The same author also has presented us with a book-length treatment of the subject. See A. M. Honoré, Tribonian (1978).

f. For English translations of these sections of the Codex see 15 Scott, The Civil Law 93, 187 (1932). More recent translations of the Institutes and the Digests are J. A. C. Thomas, The Institutes of Justinian (1975), and A. Watson, ed., The Digest of Justinian (4 vols., 1985).

g. "An agreement between buyer and seller giving the latter the right to declare the sale annulled, if, within a certain time, he received an offer of a higher price (*adiectio*) for the object sold. In such a case the first buyer had the possibility to increase his bid and to keep the thing.—D. 18.2." A. Berger, Encyclopedic Dictionary of Roman Law, in Transactions of the American Philosophical Society, N.S., Vol. 43, Part 2, at p. 348 (1953).

h. Is this doubt well-founded? See Hahlo and Kahn, The Union of South Africa 36 (1960), where it is pointed out that even today, when dealing with a doubtful point of Roman-Dutch law, South African courts not infrequently refer to outstand-

ing treatises whose authors in their day may have been Italians, Frenchmen, Spaniards or Germans.

The Court is here speaking of the 17th century. Long before that time, Roman law scholars had created a *jus commune*, a body of learning common to the whole of continental Europe. See infra pp. 255–275. The Court itself, in a later part of the opinion, regards the authority of the Dutch author Matthaeus as weakened by the fact that his view was contradicted by that of other, *non-Dutch* scholars.

i. "Roman Law" in this context means Justinian's Corpus Juris. To the modern mind, this may seem a startlingly narrow definition, in view of the fact that the Corpus Juris was itself the culmination of an unbroken historical development spanning the preceding ten centuries—a development that can be traced back at least to the Twelve Tables (451 B.C.). By incorporating the writings of older jurists in the Digest, the Corpus Juris on its face reveals its indebtedness to the work of men who lived several centuries before Justinian's day. Nevertheless, it was only during a relatively brief spell of 16th century humanism, and then again in the last 150 years, that substantial and sustained scholarly efforts were devoted to the pre-Justinian history of Roman law. During most of the period from the 11th to the 19th century, the Corpus Juris was regarded as a

from Bartolus onwards.[j] He also makes frequent reference to local Ordinances as precedents.

Unfortunately, however, for its value as a guide in the present case, the principal scope of the work is to treat of public (so called) or necessary sales; that is, sales made under the authority of a Court of justice, either of confiscated property or of property taken in execution of a civil judgment. Private or voluntary sales are matters of subsidiary treatment only. This is stated on the title page, and in bk. i, ch. 4, ad finem. And there is another reason. Voluntary sales by auction, using the word "auction" for a sale by increasing bids and "reduction" (as it will be convenient to do) for sales by decreasing bids, were, and apparently still are, unknown in Holland, except as tentative or provisional transactions. Two classes of competitive sales are known in Holland. Necessary sales are in the ordinary form of auction sales, but at the close of the day no contract binding the vendor is created between him and the highest bidder; for all the authorities, including Matthaeus, are agreed that further offers may be, and, indeed, must be, taken till the last moment when the decree of the Court is made, till the seal of the Court has been lifted from the wax, as it is picturesquely expressed.

As to voluntary sales, those at any rate of land, they take two days. The first day there is an auction, and the highest bidder receives a "treckgelt" or "strijckgelt," "premium quod datur augenti pretium," as Matthaeus calls it (lib. 1, ch. 1, s. 6, and ch. 9, s. 11). In consideration of this "premium" [presumably a modest sum of money] the bidder is provisionally bound, but the vendor is not bound. On the second day the vendor makes a starting price, usually one-third higher than the highest bid of the previous day, and then descends (the process being called "afstach") till some bidder calls out "Mine" (see "Matthaeus," lib. 1, ch. 12, s. 1). This process is so prevalent that a verb has been coined, "mijnen" "to mine," meaning to bid, and bidders of all sorts are called "mijnders" (lib. 2, ch. 2, s. 5). Hence, too, comes the English phrase a "Dutch auction." The vendor is apparently not bound to keep reducing, but can withdraw at any stage. If, however, he chooses, he can descend to the level reached by the highest bid at the first day's sale,

book of authority, a tool for lawyers rather than an object of the historian's study and research.

After modern codifications deprived the Corpus Juris of its authoritative stature in most civil-law systems, Roman law scholarship assumed its present, predominantly historical bent. Today, the efforts of students of "Roman law" are largely concentrated on aspects previously neglected: pre-Justinian developments, including Greek and other "foreign" influences, and detailed study of (a) changes made in the older texts by Tribonianus and his col-

leagues (interpolations) as well as (b) changes in original older texts which—already prior to Justinian's day—had been made by commentators of the intermediate period (glossemes). It is clear, however, that the Privy Council does not use the term "Roman law" in this modern, academic sense, but rather as more or less synonymous with the Corpus Juris.

j. Concerning the three schools of older writers with whose works Matthaeus presumably was familiar, see infra pp. 270–271.

and if no one else bids, compel the bidder of the first day to complete his bargain.   *→ Descending Dutch Auction theory*

Though Matthaeus refers but slightly and allusively to this practice, he certainly knew of it. But the difficulty is to fit those observations of his, on which the plaintiff and the judges in the Supreme Court rely, to either form of competitive sale. Necessary sales are by way of auction, but it is clear that the highest bidder at the auction cannot claim to have bought the property, though he may be bound to complete his purchase. In voluntary sales the first step is by way of auction, but the highest bidder cannot claim to have bought the property, though he may in a certain event be bound to complete his purchase. During the second stage of reduction it may be that the vendor offers the property at every price which he names. If the observations of Matthaeus on which reliance is placed are intended for a sale by reduction, they have no application to the case before their Lordships. If they contemplate a sale by auction, they are theoretical merely.   *case here was not a reduction auction*

These observations of Matthaeus are to be found in bk. 1, ch. 10, De Licitationibus,[k] ss. 44–48. In s. 40 he is drawing the distinction between necessary and voluntary sales, and insisting as against other authorities that in necessary sales there is no concluded bargain till the seal of the Court has been attached.

Contrariwise in voluntary sales, the matter is completed, "simul augendi seu adjiciendi facultas praecisa sit."[1] But this passage leaves it an open question when the "facultas" is "praecisa." It may be by the last bid, or it may be by acceptance of the last bid. In s. 41 he appears to admit of the prolongation of the auction from day to day till the vendor is satisfied. In s. 43 he discusses the question whether a bidder can withdraw his bid, and concludes, in contradiction to other authorities, which he quotes, that he cannot. But whether this means that he cannot withdraw when once the words are out of his mouth, or that he cannot withdraw when his bid has been accepted, or has been taken as a bid so that a further bid is made upon it, does not appear.

Lastly, in s. 48 he puts the question whether, after bids have been made, but there has been no acceptance by the vendor, "post licitationes facta ante tamen addictionem,"[m] the vendor can withdraw. He states, and states correctly, that the authority of Bartolus and of Damhouder is against him; but he concludes, and this is the passage mainly relied upon, that the vendor cannot withdraw. His reasons are that it would be absurd that the bidder should be bound and not the vendor, and that he who proclaims that he is going to hold a sale by auction tacitly promises that the property shall be sold to the winning

k. Licitatio means bid.

l. As soon as the power to make a higher bid or to knock down [the property] has been cut off.

m. The word "facta" probably should read "factas". The phrase means "after the bids have been made but before the knocking down".

bidder "ei qui vicerit licitatione." [n]   As to the first reason, it may be observed that there are cases where it will happen that the bidder is bound while the vendor is not: as to the second reason, that, pushed to its logical conclusion, it would extend to prevent the vendor from withdrawing the property before any bid was made, as it would disappoint the company, or from announcing that there is a reserve, or from stating any conditions of sale which he has not previously advertised, unless indeed they be in common form.

full

It is further to be noticed, as the Chief Justice points out in his judgment, that Matthaeus does not take the view that the auctioneer offers and the bidder accepts.   There are Continental writers on jurisprudence who take this view; for instance, Puchta, Pandekten (6th ed., by Rudolph, Leipzig, 1852, s. 252).   Voet also is claimed for it; [o] and it is certainly the view of his translator and editor, Berwick; and it is the view to which Hill J. expressly gives his assent.   But it is not that of Matthaeus.   He takes the more common view that the bidder offers and the auctioneer accepts; but he thinks, for the reason which he gives, that the auctioneer has tacitly promised to accept.

Remembering that there were in the Dutch usage of his time no conclusive auctions with rising bids, their Lordships think that Matthaeus, if he was writing of such auctions, was writing as a professor of jurisprudence and not as a witness bearing testimony to the existing Roman-Dutch law.[p]

n. Literally, "to the one who shall have won out in bidding".

o. Johannes Voet (1647–1713) was one of the most famous Dutch jurists.   His Commentarius ad Pandectas, to this day one of the principal authorities on Roman-Dutch law, has been translated into several modern languages.   The most recent English translation by Judge Percival Gane (8 Vols., 1955–58) contains explanatory annotations and references to South African cases which are kept up to date by supplements.

For a list of the other famous 17th and 18th century Dutch authors who have become the leading oracles of Roman-Dutch law (a list which does not include Matthaeus), see R. W. Lee, An Introduction to Roman-Dutch Law 15–18 (1953). See also R. Feenstra & C. J. D. Waal, 17th Century Leyden Law Professors and Their Influence on the Development of the Civil Law: A Study of Bronchorst, Vinnius and Voet (1975), and most recently G. F. Margadant, La Secunda Vida del Derecho Romano 253–63 (1986).

The three authors Matthaeus (grandfather, father and son), of whom the middle one wrote the book "De Auctionibus", are not quite in the same class as Voet; but the fact that Voet expressed some admira-

tion for their writings, and often cited "De Auctionibus" with approval, by reflection bestowed some of Voet's tremendous authority upon Matthaeus.   See Vol. 1 of Gane's Voet translation, Introduction p. XVIII (1955).   It should be noted, however, that on the point presently under consideration Matthaeus and Voet, while reaching similar results, propounded different theories.

p. With deference, it is suggested that the opinion, which up to this point has shown considerable understanding of the sources and methods of the civil law, here betrays its author's common-law upbringing.   In the view of a civilian, Matthaeus is an authority for the very reason that he was a renowned "professor of jurisprudence".   Concerning what kind of "existing" Roman-Dutch law should he have borne witness?   We must remember that we are not dealing with a case-law system.   Had he referred to an "existing" local statute or custom, the question would arise whether the local law of that particular locality was exported to the overseas settlements now constituting British Guiana.   As to this question, see Margadant, cited in the preceding note, at 344–48.   In all probability there was no relevant local statute or custom in Matthaeus' day.

As to other writers, Bartolus, so far as he is an authority to be quoted on Roman-Dutch law, takes, as Matthaeus admits, the contrary view. So does Damhouder, a practising lawyer and writer in Holland. Grotius is quoted on other points by Matthaeus, but has made, apparently, no statement on this point. Voet, it is suggested, favours Matthaeus's view; but it is not clear that he does, and he has very much involved himself with addictio in diem. Van Leeuwen and Van der Linden q are apparently silent on the point. Sir Andries Maasdorp in his Institutes of Cape Law (vol. 3, p. 130) certainly expresses himself to the effect that the sale is not completed till the fall of the hammer. On the other hand, Burge in his Foreign and Colonial Law (vol. 2, p. 576) and Nathan in his Common Law of South Africa (vol. 2, p. 718) translate and accept Matthaeus.

The industry of counsel has furnished their Lordships with quotations from several other writers not mentioned in the judgments of the Courts below; but they are chiefly interesting for their full statements as to Dutch usage and for their silence on the point in question.

One modern author, S. J. Fockema Andreae, in a work published at Haarlem in 1896, speaking of the usage of lighting a candle for the period of the auction, says that the last bidder before the candle burnt out is the purchaser, if his offer be accepted. *Ruling*

On the whole, their Lordships are of opinion that there is no rule of Roman-Dutch law which prescribes that at sales by auction the bidder is the acceptor. In sales by reduction it may be otherwise. Neither is there any rule that the highest bidder can insist that the property shall not be withdrawn from sale and claim to have bought it. This being so, the matter is governed by the provisions in the conditions of sale, and they indicate with sufficient clearness that the offer will come from the bidder, and that there is no bargain till it has been accepted by the auctioneer, and they do not indicate that the auctioneer is bound to accept the highest bid.

Their Lordships will therefore humbly advise His Majesty that this appeal should be allowed, that the judgment of the Supreme Court should be reversed and that of the Chief Justice restored, and that the appellant company should have its costs in the Court below and of this appeal. *highest bidder not entitled to property until bid is accepted by auctioneer*

NOTE

The reader will have noted that in the principal case a court sitting in London in 1918, passing on a matter which had occurred a few years

Thus we are brought to the decisive question: What are the sources and authorities which we must use to inform ourselves of "existing" non-local law in an uncodified civil-law system? The Corpus Juris itself being silent on the point at issue, it would seem that "existing" law, or at least strong evidence thereof, flowed from the pens of professorial writers such as Matthaeus.

q. J. Van der Linden (1756–1835) was regarded as a pre-eminent authority on Roman-Dutch law in South Africa. See G. M. Moris, trans., Van der Linden's Institutes of the Laws of Holland (2d ed. 1922). The Transvaal Constitution of 1859 declared his treatise to be "the Legal Code (wetboek) of this State" (article 52, sec. 1).

earlier in the Caribbean region, used as its principal authorities (a) a compilation of laws promulgated in the year 534 A.D. by a Byzantine emperor holding court in Constantinople, and (b) the writings of a Dutch author who lived in the 17th century. The case thus furnishes a dramatic—though by no means unique—illustration of the hardy persistence and world-wide extension of Roman-inspired civil law.

Lest the reader jump to exaggerated conclusions, it should be pointed out right away that today there are very few countries in which Justinian's Corpus Juris, or the writings of civilian authors who lived in centuries long past, would still be recognized as primary sources of present-day law.[1] In the overwhelming majority of civil-law countries, relatively modern codes enacted during the last two centuries have replaced the older sources of law. These codes, as will be explained below (pp. 275–289), to some extent marked a conscious break with the past. Nevertheless, they did not—Athena-like—spring from the head of Zeus. Each of the codes was drafted by lawyers—practitioners or professors—, and these members of the legal profession, though acting as draftsmen for reform-minded rulers or legislatures, invariably had acquired their training and experience under the older system and thus were steeped in traditional learning.

Speaking metaphorically, one might say that each of the modern code systems was a new edifice, but that the building-blocks used for its construction largely consisted of pre-existing concepts and precepts. A student seeking to gain a true understanding of modern civilian code systems will do well, therefore, to familiarize himself with the principal sources, methods and trends of pre-code civil law.[2]

On a more practical level, the principal case demonstrates the high level of classical education and even civil-law learning of British jurists called from time to time to serve on ad hoc boards of the Judicial Committee of the Privy Council. In the 1820s, when faced with an appeal involving Roman-Dutch law, the Privy Council sent the printed record to a Dutch lawyer in Amsterdam for an opinion on "the law of Holland as administered in Demerara." Freyhous v. Forbes, 1 Knapp 117, 12 Eng.Rep. 265 (1827). Soon thereafter, however, it acquired the ability to deal with such appeals with the aid of the civil-law bar of the Doctors' Commons.[3]

---

1. Scotland, South Africa, Sri Lanka and Andorra are countries which have preserved essentially civilian and yet uncodified systems of law. See infra pp. 290–291. As to Guyana see supra p. 247.

2. See A. Watson, The Making of the Civil Law, passim and especially ch. 2, entitled "The Block Effect of Roman Law" (1981).

3. See L. Moccia, English Law Attitudes to the "Civil Law", 2 J. Legal Hist. 157 (1981); B. P. Levack, The Civil Lawyers of England, 1603–1641: A Political Study (1973); G. D. Squibb, Doctors' Commons: A History of the College of Advocates and Doctors of Law (1977).

H. COING, THE ROMAN LAW AS IUS COMMUNE ON THE CONTINENT

89 L.Q.Rev. 505 (1973).[a]

[Some footnotes omitted, others renumbered.]

. . . The question . . . is "What developments gave Roman Law such outstanding significance in the Europe of modern times?"

I.

One might imagine that the role Roman Law played in European history was a direct consequence of the fact that the Romans once dominated many parts of Europe. This was certainly not the case. When the Roman armies had left Britain, Western and Southern Germany and finally France at the end of Antiquity, new barbarian states were organized on the former Roman territory. The influence of Roman legislation did not cease completely but during the centuries which followed slowly withered away. We cannot follow here the different stages of this process nor state in which regions and to what extent there remained certain survivals of Roman Law. But there is one fact of great historical importance. In the sixth century, the East Roman Emperor Justinian brought about the great summary of antique Roman Law which is called the *Corpus Iuris Civilis*—the law-book which is the main source of our knowledge of ancient Roman Law. But this great piece of legislation could not at the time be introduced into the Latin West, since Justinian's Empire was restricted mainly to the eastern half of the ancient Roman Empire [b] and included, as far as the West was concerned, only [a part of] Italy. Although Justinian greatly widened the frontiers of his Empire, he never ruled in Northern France, Germany or Great Britain.[c]

a. Reprinted by permission of Sweet & Maxwell, Ltd., and the Law Quarterly Review.

b. In the Eastern Empire, Justinian's codification had the force of law. During subsequent centuries, Greek translations and adaptations of the (originally Latin) Corpus Juris, together with commentaries based upon it, remained the basis of the Byzantine legal system. Even after the Byzantine Empire had been overrun by the Turks in the 15th century, somewhat atrophied versions of the Corpus Juris survived as the law governing the affairs of the non-Islamic subjects of the Turkish Empire; and when Greece and other Eastern European countries regained their independence from the Turks in the 19th century, the Corpus Juris naturally formed the basis of the legal systems of the reborn nations. In Greece, as in some other countries of the area, Justinian's legisla-tion thus remained in force until it was replaced by modern codes during the present century. See W. Kunkel, An Introduction to Roman Legal and Constitutional History 178–81 (2d ed., transl. by J. M. Kelly, 1973); S. L. Sass, Medieval Roman Law: A Guide to the Sources and Literature, 58 L.Lib.J. 130, 131–34 (1965).

c. In spite of temporary military victories, Justinian and his successors ultimately failed in their attempt to "reconquer" the Western Empire from the Germanic tribes which had swarmed over Western Europe and had captured Rome itself in 476 A.D. The Germanic rulers of Western Europe (not unlike the Arab conquerors a few centuries later) believed in the principle of "personal law," which meant that within each territory the Germanic subjects lived under their own inherited laws and customs, while the indigenous population continued to live under Roman law.

It is necessary therefore to turn to other factors and times to explain the historical influence Roman Law had on modern European legal development.   And here we have to take into consideration a period of the later Middle Ages and, in this period, three developments in particular.   The first is the development in education: the history of the law schools in the universities of medieval Europe.   The second is concerned with the development of State and administration in the same period.   Thirdly we have to look at the development of ideas about law in this period.

256 – 264 : What brought Roman law back to prominence in Europe

II.

The first subject to be considered is the origin of the medieval universities.

(1) It is well known that universities as a social institution in education owe their existence to medieval civilisation.   There is quite a difference between the character of a modern university and a university of the thirteenth or fourteenth century.   The modern university unites research with teaching.   The main task of the medieval university was to introduce the student to traditional knowledge as laid down in a certain number of books of authority.   It is characteristic of the medieval university that the knowledge it had to impart to its students and the books of authority it used for this purpose, were taken from a civilisation which had long since passed away and which, nevertheless, was considered as the origin and model of all spiritual culture: Greco-Roman antiquity.   In the medieval university, philosophy was at first taught on the basis of platonic tradition and, from the thirteenth century, on that of the writings of Aristotle, mainly known by translations from the Arabic countries.   The same author, Aristotle, together with texts of Galenus, was used in the courses on medicine.   In the Divinity Schools one used a compilation of the Fathers of the Church, the *Sententiae* of Lombardus.   It is true that with the progress of time, medieval science itself produced a vast literature, *e.g.* the great *Summa Theologica* of Thomas Aquinas, but even these writings were the fruit

A remnant of Roman law thus survived in the West. Some of the Germanic rulers enacted Roman law codes for their non-Germanic subjects, e.g., the *Lex Romana Visigothorum* and the *Lex Romana Burgundionum*; and in time some elements of Roman law even entered into legislation governing the Germanic subjects. It must be remembered, however, that the period from the 5th century to the 10th was one of intellectual decline. As a result, the "vulgarized" Roman law of that period had none of the intellectual finesse of the Corpus Juris. See W. Kunkel, An Introduction to Roman Legal and Constitutional History 177 (2d ed., transl. by J. M. Kelly, 1973).

Although the matter is somewhat controversial among Roman law scholars, Professor Coing thus seems to be correct in implying that Roman law as a vibrant intellectual force was not reawakened in Western Europe until the rediscovery (see infra) of the Corpus Juris itself and the beginnings of law teaching at the University of Bologna near the end of the 11th century. See S. L. Sass, Medieval Roman Law: A Guide to the Sources and Literature, 58 L.Lib.J. 130, 138–40 (1965). For another brief but instructive account of the survival and reawakening of Roman law in Europe, see W. Hug, The History of Comparative Law, 45 Harv.L.Rev. 1027, 1034–38 (1932).

of the discussion the medieval mind conducted with the authors of Antiquity.

It is in harmony with this general feature of the medieval universities that legal education, which began in the twelfth century, was based on the greatest collection of legal materials Antiquity had left to posterity, the *Corpus Iuris* of Justinian. Modern research has shown that there may also have been political considerations which led the legists of Bologna to turn to the *Corpus Iuris Civilis*, since the medieval emperors considered themselves the successors of the Roman *imperatores*, and their partisans welcomed arguments drawn from the *Corpus Iuris* in the great struggle against the Papacy. But it is the great authority of ancient civilisation in general that is the most convincing explanation for the attitude the medieval law schools took.

The first medieval universities were not founded by act of State or church but slowly grew out of groups of students gathering around and entering into contract with individual professors. These first universities were generally restricted to one or two main subjects. They did not aim at comprehensive scientific education as most modern universities do. Theology and philosophy were taught at Paris, medicine at Salerno and Montpellier. For law, it was an Italian university which took the lead: Bologna. Here, law courses began at the end of the eleventh century, and an organized curriculum including examinations for different degrees developed during the following century. The subject taught was at first only the *Corpus Iuris* of Justinian.[d] . . . Canon Law, that is the law of the medieval Roman Catholic Church, was added in the twelfth century; about 1140 the Bolognese monk Gratianus completed the great collection of Canon Law materials called the *Decretum*. To this, several official collections of Papal Decretals were added in later times. Thus Bologna had two law faculties, one devoted to Roman Law (the Legists), the other to Canon Law (the Canonists). The totality of the legal material taught at Bologna was described by the term *ius utrumque*, i.e. both laws, Roman Law and Canon Law.

The educational system worked out in Bologna became the model for all legal instruction given at universities in Europe during the Middle Ages. It is most important to understand this fact if we wish to comprehend the significance Roman Law acquired on the European continent.

Already in the twelfth century Bologna had developed into an international centre of legal studies. This can be seen in the fact that the emperor Frederick Barbarossa in 1158 gave by the so-called Authentica "Habita" very important privileges to the students of

d. During the centuries of intellectual decline and "vulgarized" Roman law (see supra), much of the Corpus Juris was virtually unknown in Western Europe. Lawyers of that period would not have been equipped to understand its finer points. But toward the end of the 11th century— the beginning of an intellectual renaissance—the Digests were discovered when an ancient manuscript containing its text came to light in a library at Pisa. See H. J. Berman, The Religious Foundations of Western Law, 24 Cath.U.L.Rev. 490, 492 (1975).

Bologna. The Emperor promises the students protection during their journey from their home country to Bologna. He grants them exemption from the city jurisdiction of Bologna, giving them a choice between the jurisdiction of the Bishop and of their own professors. Furthermore, he lays down that no reprisals can be taken against a member of a student community. This last privilege calls for a few words of explanation. The Middle Ages considered it lawful that a citizen of one community, let us say the city of Cologne, should be held responsible in a foreign city for the debts any citizen of Cologne had incurred to a citizen of that foreign city. So a student from Cologne or Montpellier coming to Bologna had to run the risk that the city judges of Bologna would compel him to pay for the debts any of his countrymen had incurred in the city of Bologna. The imperial privilege abolished this institution of reprisals as far as students were concerned. Now, if the emperor found it necessary to provide for the students of Bologna by such specific legislation, there must have been at the time a considerable number of foreign students in Bologna.

In fact, modern research, undertaken especially by the Swiss historian Stelling-Michaud, had shown that in 1269 more than a thousand foreign students were present at Bologna.[1] That would be a considerable number even for a modern law school. But Bologna was not only a great international centre of legal studies. It also became the model for all the law schools which were organised at medieval universities.

As has already been mentioned, a number of medieval universities grew up during the twelfth and thirteenth centuries, some of them out of former educational institutions like cathedral schools. The latter is for example true for the great French Universités de loi, Orléans and Angers. In part they came into existence by migrations of doctors and students from one place to another. That for example is true for Cambridge (1209) and Padua (1224). But most later medieval universities were founded by a planned act of the political powers of the time, by princes or cities. The first of this type of university is Naples, founded in 1224 by the famous emperor Frederick II. Other examples are provided by Salamanca (ca. 1220), Cologne (foundation of the city 1388), Prague (1356), Cracow (1383). These planned and organised universities mostly had the four classical faculties: arts or philosophy, divinity, medicine and law. In total, up to 1500 about seventy new universities were organised.

Now the important fact for legal history is that as far as their law schools were concerned, all these universities more or less followed the model worked out by Bologna. In some cases, this was decided by the universities themselves. This is for example true for the Aragonese university of Lerida (founded 1300). On others it was imposed by papal legislation. Thus, for example, it was laid down for the university of Perugia in 1318 that the law curriculum and examinations in law

1. Stelling-Michaud, L'Université de Bologna, Geneva 1955.

should follow the example of Bologna. Moreover, in statutes of new universities reference is made to the university of Bologna. This is for example the case for the university of Toulouse, founded in 1229, although it is not yet completely clear what such references really meant for the university in question. Whatever may have been the legal basis, what interests the legal historian is the fact that all these law schools—this applies also to medieval Oxford and Cambridge—did follow the model of Bologna and taught Roman and Canon Law to the exclusion of local or territorial law. The result was that all over Europe a new professional group came into existence: the lawyers, the *juristae*. They all had had the same training, the *ius utrumque*;[e] they all used the same method, the method of scholastic legal interpretation, and they all had at their disposal the same international literature on Roman and Canon Law.

It is the social function of this new group to which we have now to turn to understand the influence it exerted on late medieval culture.

III.

It is at this point that the development of state administration comes in. We can start with the simple question: where did the members of the new profession look for a place in society? The answer to this question will lead us to answer the sociological question—what social function did the new profession exercise in medieval society?

There is no doubt that in the later centuries of the Middle Ages, quite a few of the universities founded in this period were created because princes or cities wished to have a place where lawyers could be trained to help in their administration. This is true for example for the university of Cologne (1388) as well as for Rostock and Greifswald. It also applies to many universities founded in this time by princes in order to develop their territory. This demand for lawyers is to be explained by the fact that in these centuries the church as well as the different medieval states were changing and widening their administrative and judicial systems. It is in this period that origins of the modern administrative state are to be found. Slowly and step by step, medieval feudalism is replaced by a centralised administrative system handled by civil servants at the centre as well as on the level of the local administration, and it was in these new or transformed judicial and administrative bodies that the new profession of lawyers found its place in society.

The first great organisation which called in the lawyers was the Roman Catholic Church. Modern research seems to have established that the number of lawyers holding church offices grows steadily during the fourteenth and fifteenth century. This has been shown especially for England in the two ecclesiastical provinces of Canterbury

e.   J.U.D. stands for juris utriusque doctor = doctor of both laws. The two laws were, of course, civil law and canon law.

and York. More important was the fact that from the second half of the twelfth century the church began to reorganise its judicial system. This reorganisation was a long process. It ended only in the middle of the fourteenth century. The aim of this reform was to introduce the "learned law" into the procedure as well as the substantive rules of the ecclesiastical courts, and this, of course, meant that university-trained lawyers had to fill the role of judges as well as advocates. It is well known how extensive was the jurisdiction of ecclesiastical courts in the later Middle Ages. Their jurisdiction was by no means restricted to purely ecclesiastical questions in the modern sense of the word. It not only extended to all matters of marriage and divorce and consequently of "status," but covered also all questions concerning wills and many cases of general contracts. This powerful organisation, then, was the first stronghold of the new legal profession in Europe.[f]

But states and cities followed. We first find the lawyers as general counsellors. This applies as well to kings and princes as to free cities. A famous example is the fact that King Edward I of England hired the services of the son of the famous glossator, Accursius;[g] for a decade he served as a general counsel. But the same phenomenon more or less is to be observed at all the great courts of Europe. Even the emperors of the Holy Roman Empire, backward as their administrative system was, had some lawyers in their council from the thirteenth century onwards.

As the administrative organisation of the medieval state developed, lawyers began to fill places in the new administrative organisation and especially in the Central Courts which were set up. In many instances, they replaced the noblemen who in feudal times had been members of these courts. This too was a slow development and there were quite big differences in space and time if we compare the individual European states. We find that by about 1180 some Italian city-states had university-trained lawyers as judges in their courts. . . . In Germany, it was not until the fifteenth century that the same development took place at the central courts as well as the territorial ones. This development was confirmed when in 1495 it was laid down for the newly organised central court, the *Reichskammergericht*, that half of the judges had to be university-trained lawyers, the other half being taken from the nobility. . . .

IV.

The lawyers, thus firmly established in the new civil service, began in the exercise of their new [administrative and judicial] functions to apply the law they had learned at the university, that is the Roman Canon Law. This is easily to be explained as far as church administration and ecclesiastical courts are concerned. It was quite natural that

f. For a comprehensive recent account, see H. J. Berman, Law and Revolution, The Formation of the Western Legal Tradition, pt. I: The Papal Revolution and the Canon Law (1983).

g. For a discussion of the role which Accursius and the other "glossators" played in the development of the civil law, see infra p. 270.

ecclesiastical courts applied Canon Law, and Canon Law itself was based on Roman Law. But things were different for the lawyers in the service of states and free cities. All the states, territories and cities had, of course, their own law laid down in statutes or customs. Here then the question arises how a judge or administrator could apply the Roman Canon Law instead of restricting himself to the local norms.

To explain this phenomenon, we have to turn to the ideas of law prevailing in this period. The theories developed by Austinians [h] are of no assistance in understanding the attitude of the lawyer of the fourteenth or fifteenth century towards the sources of law. According to those theories legal rules are norms laid down by the sovereign for the subjects, for the citizens of the state. There is according to this view no law except what is contained in the orders of the sovereign. Consequently, no judge and no administrator is entitled to apply a rule which is not recognised by the sovereign, and the legal system is strictly territorial, strictly tied to the boundaries of the individual state. Although Austin and his school have presented this theory as a general theory of law, the historian must admit that it expresses only the attitude lawyers adopted in the nineteenth century and especially since the French Revolution when the idea of national sovereignty began to gain strength. The ideas of the Middle Ages and even of the Ancien Régime, of the time before the French Revolution, were quite different. Views prevailing then can be described by the term "Pluralism" as applied to legal sources. Pluralism means first that unity of law in the modern sense is absent. There are different rules for different cities and territories and different rules for the individual professional groups like merchants, nobility, peasants, etc. But Pluralism of legal sources also means that a judge who has to decide a specific case, has to look for rules not only in the orders of the sovereign, but can apply rules which he finds in any book of authority, whether this has been expressly recognised by the sovereign or not. It is more important for him to find an appropriate rule than to be sure to confine himself to following the orders the sovereign has given.

It was this basic attitude of the medieval period which made it possible for the *juristae* to apply the law they had learned at the university, the Roman Canon Law, in daily practice. The Italian law professors elaborated a convenient theory of sources of law. Broadly speaking, this theory was that a judge must first apply local customs and statutes, but whenever he could not find an appropriate rule to decide the case before him in this legal material, he could turn to Roman Canon Law and fill the gaps found in territorial or local law by the rules of Roman Law. He also was entitled according to this theory to construe local customs and statutes within the framework of Roman

h. The reference is to legal positivism, as set forth in J. Austin, The Province of Jurisprudence Determined (1st ed. 1832). For representative recent works in this tradition, see H. L. A. Hart, The Concept of Law (1963); J. Raz, The Concept of a Legal System (1980); N. MacCormick & O. Weinberger, An Institutional Theory of Law: New Approaches to Legal Positivism (1986).

Law. This, of course, was a quite natural intellectual attitude for a time which did not look on Antiquity as a historical period long gone but rather as a model to be applied immediately to the present day. There were different opinions as to what the basis of the authority of Roman Law was. Most widely accepted was the idea that Roman Law was to be considered as *ratio scripta* (written reason) and as such applied in every country. In the medieval empire, there was a legend that one of the medieval emperors, Lotharius, had expressly introduced Roman Law.

Later on, with the beginning of historical criticisms at the Renaissance, this theory was replaced by the idea that Roman Law was received by the custom of the courts. But whatever argument was used, the practical outcome was that Roman Law was generally considered as a subsidiary to which one could turn if local law failed to answer a problem. As the famous medievalist, Kantorowicz, has said, Roman Law was a kind of treasure-house where everybody could enter and find what he needed to solve a legal problem.[2] An event which took place in the second half of the thirteenth century in Northern Germany will illustrate this. The city of Lübeck asked the city of Hamburg what rules were applied in Hamburg to a certain question of maritime law. The head of the Chancery of the City of Hamburg could not find any specific rules in the Hamburg statute book or custom. But as he was a learned lawyer, he translated certain passages of the Digest of Justinian into German and in his answer to the citizens of Lübeck stated it as the law of Hamburg. The latter from that time on followed the rule of the Digest.[3] The general result of this process was that the lawyers on the Continent applied a mixed legal system whose components were on one hand local statutes and customs and on the other hand the law books of Justinian and the Canon Law.

V.

On the whole, this result was reached by the end of the Middle Ages. It led on the Continent of Europe first to the *juristae*, the university-trained lawyers, a uniform professional group having the same scientific background. Furthermore, it led to a unified legal literature based on Roman Canon Law and allowing scientific discussion of common problems all over the Continent. In the library of the Canon Law College of the university of Coimbra in Portugal are the writings of a German legal author, Carpzow, with handwritten notes of a Portuguese judge who evidently used the book in his own practice. It is again well known that German bankruptcy law has its historical origin in the writings of a Castilian judge of the seventeenth century, Salgado de Samoza. Also, decisions of the Court of Appeal of Hanover dating from the eighteenth century show that the judges used the works of Argentré, a famous French commentator on local custom of

---

2. Kantorowicz, Bractonian Problems, p. 126.

3. See Reincke, "Frühe Spuren Römischen Rechts in Nieder-Sachsen." Festschrift Haff, pp. 174–184.

the sixteenth century, to decide cases about the inheritance of Hanoverian peasants.[i]

There were, of course, within the framework of this Common Law on the Continent developments and changes, notably the influence of the enlightenment and of the so-called Natural Law Movement in the eighteenth century.[j] Yet on the whole the system of *Ius Commune* on the Continent lasted up to the eighteenth century and was finally changed only by the modern national codifications, especially by the influence of the legal ideas of the French Revolution whose outcome on the Continent was the modern national state. Since then, the law on the Continent has been split up into a series of national systems. Still, one cannot deny the common background all these systems have, and modern writers on Comparative Law rightly speak of the Continental legal systems as a family of laws which can be opposed as a unit to the great systems of the English-speaking nations, the English Common Law. In this sense we can still say today that Roman Law on the Continent is a kind of *ratio scripta*. It has given to Continental lawyers their underlying basic notions and Roman legal expressions still are the *lingua franca* of Continental lawyers.

Finally, what of the position of England in this whole development of Roman Law since the Middle Ages? It would certainly be wrong to say that England was never touched by these developments in legal ideas and practice. It has been clear since Maitland's writings [4] that ecclesiastical courts in medieval England followed the Roman Canon Law. It is also clear that the medieval law-schools in Oxford and Cambridge taught Canon and Roman Law. What is more, in the twelfth and thirteenth century there were English judges having a broad background of knowledge of the Roman Canon Law.[k]

Bracton's famous book *De Legibus Angliae* is proof enough. We also know that up to the end of the eighteenth century there were courts in England which not only followed Roman Canon procedure but also based their judgment, as far as substantive law is concerned, on *Ius Commune*. This is true for the High Court of Admiralty and the Curia Militaris, the Court of the Constable and Marshal.[l]

---

i. The Court of Appeals at Celle started its eighteenth-century library collection with an appropriation of 140 *Thalers*. A glossed edition of the Corpus Juris Civilis cost 40 *Thalers* at that time. Baade, Book Review, 14 Int'l J. Legal Inf. 264, 265 (1986).

j. For elaboration of this point see infra pp. 273-275.

4. Maitland, Canon Law in the Church of England.

k. For a case study in point, see R. Helmholtz, Support Orders, Church Courts, and the Rule of *Filius Nullius*: A Reassessment of the Common Law, 63 Va.L.Rev. 431 (1977).

l. Professor Coing's enumeration of the successive waves of civil-law influences upon the law of England is not meant to be exhaustive. For additional references, see supra p. 254. In addition, one must remember that in the formative years of the equity courts the Chancellors, who at that time tended to be clerics, adopted a Romano-canonistic form of procedure as well as a number of substantive principles derived from canon law. See E. Re, The Roman Contribution to the Common Law, 29 Fordham L.Rev. 447, especially at 479–83 (1961); J. Barton, Roman Law in England 50–53 (1971). The absorption of the law merchant into the common law (see infra p. 303) also has to be mentioned in this

English law easier to develop and maintain on an island

Despite all this, the fact remains that the English Common Law developed independently and is a legal system of its own, not based on Roman Canon Law. Where are we to look for the explanation of this specifically English development? Modern research is inclined to see the answer in the fact that the English Monarchy after the Norman conquest was the most centralised and powerful state in Europe and, in a certain sense, had the most progressive administrative and judicial organisation.[5] At the time when the Roman Canon Law began to expand over the Continent—the critical period being the beginning of the thirteenth century—when the Church had begun to reorganise its court system, the English Monarchy, and the English Monarchy alone, had organised a permanent system of central courts at Westminster whose judges used to apply English statutes and feudal customs and to follow their own precedents. As a result, Roman Law, as Van Caeneghem has put it, in a sense came to England too late. When the other European countries adopted Roman Law as *ratio scripta* or as imperial law, the English Monarchy already had a system of central courts with traditions of its own. So, even in terms of the theory of legal sources of the Continental lawyers there was not much room for Roman Canon Law, the main ground being covered by legal rules developed in England itself. *different legal beginning from continental Europe*

There is a second factor to be considered. We have seen that the Continental rulers in the course of the thirteenth, fourteenth and fifteenth centuries began to appoint university-trained lawyers to their courts. The same, perhaps, could have happened in England too. But here we encounter one of the accidents which again and again we find in history and in the last resort cannot explain. Edward I organised a training for the judges of his courts which was independent of the law schools of Oxford and Cambridge. The English lawyer, consequently, was not a lawyer trained at universities; he was educated at the inns of court and the court itself. English lawyers as a professional group were separated from the *juristae* of the universities and developed their professional knowledge on different lines. Nevertheless, the English Common Law has never been completely separated from legal development on the Continent. There has always in the course of centuries

context. Nor should one forget Blackstone's heavy reliance on civil-law authorities. See B. Nicholas, Rules and Terms—Civil Law and Common Law, 48 Tul.L.Rev. 946 (1974). See also infra p. 281. During the 19th century, finally, the Code Napoleon and other civilian codes not merely inspired Bentham and his followers, but on numerous occasions directly influenced decisions handed down by English courts. For instance, the key sentence in Hadley v. Baxendale, 9 Ex. 341, 156 Eng.Rep. 145 (1854) (known to every law student as the leading case on contract damages) is a paraphrase of Art. 1150 of the French Civil Code.

The student of American legal history has to remember that, in addition, both Roman and modern civilian ideas were imported into this country during the first half-century of the Republic (see supra p. 8) and in more limited measure again in recent times (e.g., in connection with the Uniform Commercial Code, see supra pp. 16–17).

5. See especially Van Caeneghem, Royal Writs in England from the Conquest to Glanville (publ. Seld.Soc. LXXVII).

been give and take from [England] to the Continent and vice versa. . . .[m]

DEÁK AND RHEINSTEIN, THE DEVELOPMENT OF FRENCH AND GERMAN LAW

24 Geo.L.J. 551 (1936).

[Some footnotes omitted, others renumbered.]

I. The Development of the Law of France

Although France achieved political unity, under a comparatively strong central authority, several centuries before the various German states were consolidated into the Reich, uniformity of law was not accomplished until the beginning of the nineteenth century. German legal uniformity followed closely on the heels of political consolidation. On the other hand, mediaeval France, although a "nation," in the modern sense of the word, for several centuries before codification, presents to the legal historian a kaleidoscope of various legal systems existing contemporaneously, yet independently in the various provinces and districts.

Pre-revolutionary France, living under what French legal historians designate as the period of "ancient law" (*l'ancien droit*),[a] may be divided into two geographical zones. In the south (the *Midi*), Roman law was paramount and that section is therefore designated by French legal historians as the country of written law (*pays de droit écrit*). In the various provinces of the north, local customs were in force and this area has been termed the country of customary law (*pays de coutume*). This geographical division should not be regarded as a complete cleavage; like every generalization, it is subject to qualifications. The *pays de droit écrit* had some customary law (e.g., the *coutume de Bordeaux*), though it was strictly local and considerably less elaborate than in the northern provinces. On the other hand, the *pays de coutume* recognized at least the persuasive authority of Roman law, especially when customary law was silent. Roman law, furthermore, was to a large extent the common background of legal learning and of law teaching in the Universities, even in the North of France.

The customs were numerous and varied.[b] Some called *coutume générale*, of which there were about sixty, were in force in an entire

---

m. This last point was further developed by the same author in a more recent paper. See H. Coing, European Common Law: Historical Foundations, in M. Cappelletti (Ed.), New Perspectives for a Common Law of Europe 31 (1978).

a. *Ancien régime* and *ancien droit* are commonly used as references to French government and law before the Revolution of 1789. "Ancient law" is, even today, not an entirely accurate translation of *ancien droit*, i.e., pre-revolutionary French law.

b. It is true that the customs were "numerous and varied." For an exhaustive listing, see A. Gouron & O. Terrin, Bibliographie des Coutumes de France (1975). But since historically they derived from similar sources and developments, the differences between them involved largely matters of detail. In many important re-

province, or in a large district (e.g., *coutume de Paris, coutume de Normandie, coutume d'Orléans*). It may be noted that the influence of the *coutume de Paris* was extended beyond the geographical limits of its actual authority. Others were in force only in a city or a village; these are called *coutumes locales,* of which there were some 300. In view of their number, and in view of the fact that the customs were originally not reduced to writing, there must have been considerable confusion and uncertainty. To remedy the situation, Charles VII, in his ordinance of Montils-les-Tours, 1453, ordered the official compilation of all customs. More than a century was necessary to accomplish this task; but by the end of the sixteenth century the bulk of French "customary" law was, in fact, reduced to written law.

An additional factor, still further emphasizing the particularism of ancient French law, was the power of the *Parlement* of Paris and the thirteen provincial *Parlements*—in the exercise of their judicial functions—to resolve moot questions. In exercising this power, they often adopted conflicting views. These decisions, called *arrêts de règlement,* were not rendered in actual litigation, but declared the position the *Parlement* would take in the future in similar cases. This was, of course, a form of judicial legislation, although it was limited both in substance (i.e., the *Parlements* had no power to modify the existing law) and in extent (i.e., within the jurisdiction of the respective *Parlements*).[1]

Despite the existence of numerous customs, the royal ordinances issued in exercise of the King's legislative power had a certain unifying force. These ordinances were, as a rule, in force throughout the kingdom. Their unifying effect was somewhat impaired by the occasional refusal of some of the provincial *Parlements* to execute them by "registration" within their respective jurisdictions; their reluctance

spects (except, most prominently, in matrimonial property law) they reflected common principles. See R. Rodière, Introduction au Droit Comparé 84–85 (1979).

1. The *Parlement* of Paris, which emerged as the judicial branch from the King's court (*curia regis*) and which became independent toward the end of the thirteenth centry, and the various provincial *Parlements* established between 1443 and 1775 (Toulouse, Grenoble, Bordeaux, Burgundy, Brittany, Normandy, Aix, Trevaux, Bearn, Metz, Besançon, Douai, and Nancy) were chiefly courts of justice. At the same time they exercised legislative as well as administrative powers. Concerning the history and functions of these *Parlements,* see Brissaud, History of French Public Law [Continental Legal History Series, vol. 9] (1915) §§ 403–419.

It may be noted that this power of the provincial *Parlements,* or rather its abuse,

became a fertile source of discontent. Thus may be explained, in part, the hostility to judicial legislation, in the revolutionary and Napoleonic era, and the disregard of precedent as a source of law until very recent times. See in this connection Art. 5 of the French Civil Code, which requires courts to decide only the actual case before them and enjoins them from rendering decisions laying down general principles. [See infra p. 625.]

[It is interesting to note that to the legislative power of the pre-revolutionary French *Parlements* there is a close present-day parallel, not in France but—in Soviet Russia. See B. Rudden, Courts and Codes in England, France and Soviet Russia, 48 Tul.L.Rev. 1010, 1013 (1974). Cf. S. Frankowski, Polish Supreme Court Directives as Sources of Criminal Law, in W. E. Butler, Ed., Anglo-Polish Legal Essays 55–74 (1982). Ed.]

was, however, usually overcome by the pressure of royal authority. . . .

To complete this picture, mention should be made of the canon law
which also exerted profound influence on some branches of French law,
especially in the field of family law.

The advent of the Revolution marks the end of the period of
"ancient" law and, at the same time, the beginning of the transitional
period commonly called the period of "intermediary" law (*droit in-
termédiaire*). Revolutionary legislation aimed chiefly at reform in the
field of public law and of political institutions. Its main accomplishments were the abolition of ancient privileges, the establishment of
equality before the law, the guarantee of individual liberty, and the
protection of private property. . . . c

II. The Development of the Law of Germany

The law of mediaeval Germany consisted mostly, as did mediaeval
law generally, of customs and tradition. Although originating in common Germanic ideas, they were locally developed in each part of the
vast territories of Central Europe which made up the "Holy Roman
Empire of the Germanic Nation." Many of these customs prevailed
over large stretches of territory, others were confined to a single city,
village, or manor, or to a special group of persons. Many were
privately collected and expanded in law books, some of which, in the
course of time, attained quasi-statutory force similar to the English
books of authority.[2]

While in mediaeval England the customs and rules which were
applied by the royal courts at Westminster gradually supplanted all
local customs and became the Common Law of the Realm, the central
power in the Empire did not attempt such an undertaking until the law
of Rome (i.e., Justinian's *Corpus Juris*), had so effectively encroached
upon the native Germanic laws that it had come to be regarded as the
Common Law of the Empire.[3] With this infiltration virtually an
accomplished fact, the period of Roman law dominance, from the
fifteenth to the end of the nineteenth century, began. When, in 1495, a
central imperial court, the *Reichskammergericht*, was established, its
judges were ordered to decide the cases coming before them "according
to the Common Law of the Empire," i.e., according to Roman law.

c. The philosophical roots of this revolutionary legislation are traced in the essay by C. J. Friedrich, The Ideological and
Philosophical Background, which forms
part of the symposium (Schwartz, Ed.), The
Code Napoleon and the Common-Law
World, pp. 1–18 (1956). The same essay
interestingly discusses the subsequent process of consolidation, moderation and compromise by which Napoleon, working with
a small team of lawyers—men of great
professional competence but reared in
traditional, pre-revolutionary legal learning—transformed the laws of the Revolution into a workable system of codes.

2. The most influential of these books
was Eike von Repgow's Mirror of Saxon
Law (Sachsenspiegel) about 1225.

3. As to this process of the "Reception"
of the Roman Law, its causes and consequences, see the article by Seagle in 13
Encyclopedia of the Social Sciences 153,
and the literature there quoted. [See also
supra, pp. 255 ff., and infra pp. 269–275.]

However, the Roman law did not completely supplant the local laws. The *Usus Modernus Pandectarum* was rather an amalgamation of Roman law with the old local customs, in which Roman law, being more comprehensive and elaborate, was the dominating element. The result of this amalgamation was different in the various parts of the country. The differences among the local customs and precedents were increased through territorial legislation, which assumed considerable importance with the growing independence of the territorial rulers. Natural law philosophy, the merging of various smaller states into larger political units, and the rise of absolute monarchy led to more or less comprehensive territorial codifications which, however, partly preserved the pre-existing law as a "subsidiary" source to be applied in the absence of statute. When the Empire was formally dissolved in 1806, state legislation had been supreme for a considerable time, and when, in 1871, the new *Reich* was created, the country was governed by a multitude of laws, much as pre-revolutionary France had its multitude of customs.

. . . All these different laws were linked together by a common jurisprudence, developed by the universities, which taught the common features and foundations rather than the details of the various local laws. This policy of the universities resulted in some measure of uniformity of German law, despite all the actual differences, so that there was a *German* legal profession, with a universal legal terminology and system, based mostly on "Romanist" learning.[4]

This academic molding process was assisted by legislation after the middle of the nineteenth century, first by the adoption of uniform statutes in the various German states, then, after 1866, by federal legislation. . . .

The most important step in the process of unification was the enactment, on August 1, 1896, of the Civil Code (*Bürgerliches Gesetzbuch, BGB*). The Code, covering almost the entire field of private law, abolished all the various local laws and replaced them with a uniform legal system. It came into force on January 1, 1900, accompanied by an Introductory Law. . . .

As in France the Civil Code of 1804 marks the beginning of the period of modern French law, so in Germany, the adoption of the *Bürgerliches Gesetzbuch (BGB)* almost a century later meant a fresh start for German law. It should be noted, however, that the break in evolution in Germany was less violent than in France. Codification in Germany was a molding process following political unification; it was not blended with antagonism toward an old order, the institutions of which were swept abruptly away by revolution. . . .

4. The "Romanists" were the leading group among the scholars. Their methods and, above all, their "system," i.e., their classification of the legal institutions, acquired universal significance. The great leaders of the German jurisprudence of the nineteenth century, Savigny, Puchta, Regelsberger, Windscheid, Ihering, and Dernburg, were Romanists. Among the Germanists, Eichhorn, and later, Otto von Gierke were most conspicuous.

SOME FEATURES OF PRE–CODE CIVIL LAW *✱ Noted summary*

At this point, the reader may feel that an image of pre-code civil law is emerging in his mind. He should, however, be aware of the dangers inherent in all generalizations. In speaking of "pre-code civil law", we refer to a galaxy of legal systems which, although sharing a common European tradition, were widely separated from each other in time and space.[1]   *developed over 10 – 12 centuries*

An attempt will be made later on (infra pp. 295–308) to brave the dangers of generalization and to discuss certain traditions and features believed to be common to all or most of the civil-law systems. At this point, however, attention must be called to some necessary qualifications and distinctions:

(1) That there are important *differences from country to country*, has been shown by the preceding materials, especially the excerpts from the article by Deák and Rheinstein. These differences relate, inter alia, to the depth of Roman law influence; the time when the "reception" of Roman law occurred; the relative strength of central and territorial political power; the predominance of one or the other of the doctrinal schools (see infra); the revolutionary or evolutionary nature of change; and the earlier or later date of modern codification on a national scale.

(2) When we speak of the history of civil law prior to the age of modern codifications, we have in mind a period which lasted from 534 A.D. until the 19th century. It may be a truism (but it is important to remember) that although the pace of change was slower than in our day, *the law did not stand still during that period.*

A comprehensive description of the development of legal institutions in continental Europe during those 13 centuries would fill many volumes.[2] No attempt is made here to present such an encyclopedic history. What follows is merely an endeavor (a) to emphasize those successive developments in the teaching of Roman or Roman-influenced law which have left a permanent imprint on civil-law methods, and (b) to remind the reader that modern civil law was shaped not only by the Roman law tradition but also by

1. Concerning the geographic expansion of the civil law see infra pp. 310–337.

2. For ample documentation see Cappelletti-Merryman-Perillo, The Italian Legal System 4–41 (1967); S. L. Sass, Medieval Roman Law: Sources and Literature, 58 L.Lib.J. 130 (1965); G. Margadant, La Secunda Vida del Derecho Romano (1986).

The student who seeks extensive information on European legal history from Justinian to the present, will find that in the past many of the best-known works were written in terms of national (e.g. French or German or Spanish) legal history, thus making it relatively difficult for the reader to gain an overview of European trends and developments. Valuable recent works dealing with European rather than national legal history are Koschaker, Europa und das römische Recht (1953), Wieacker, Privatrechtsgeschichte der Neuzeit (2d ed. 1967) and H. Coing, Ed., Handbuch der Quellen und Literatur der neueren europaeischen Rechtsgeschichte (6 vols. to date, 1973–86). The Max Planck Institut at Frankfurt, founded by Professor Helmut Coing, is devoted to research on *European* (not merely German) legal History. See R. A. Riegert, The Max Planck Institute for European Legal History, 22 Southwestern L.J. 397 (1968). The Institute publishes a series of monographs entitled Ius Commune. Twenty-nine volumes have appeared in this series between 1967 and 1986. A brief but stimulating overview is presented in the article by P. J. Zepos, The Legacy of Civil Law, 34 La.L.Rev. 895 (1974).

forces that were more or less independent of that tradition, and sometimes openly opposed to it.

(a) As we have gathered from Professor Coing's article, supra, the end of the 11th century was a crucial point in the development of the civil law. Beginning at that time, and for centuries thereafter, successive generations of influential scholars fashioned a modernized Roman law, a *jus commune*, which became one of the strongest elements of a common European culture. In referring to the accomplishments of these scholars, one usually distinguishes between three schools:

(aa) The *glossators* were law teachers of the 11th, 12th and 13th centuries. Irnerius, the founder, and the other most important representatives of this school taught at Bologna, where thousands of students from every part of Europe sat at their feet.[3] Many of the Italian law teachers referred to as glossators, and not a few of their former students, also taught at other Universities throughout Europe.[4] The principal scholarly accomplishment of the glossators consisted of *glossae*, or annotations appended to the text of the Corpus Juris. Accursius (1182–1259) combined several previous glossae into the famous *Glossa Ordinaria*. It was in this annotated form that the Corpus Juris was used in practice for several centuries thereafter.[4a]

(bb) The 14th and 15th century *commentators* (formerly also referred to as post-glossators) like their predecessors were largely centered in Italy; but their influence, again as in the case of the glossators, reached to the far corners of the Christian world. Bartolus de Sassoferrato (1314–1357) was the greatest representative of this school. While the glossators had not ventured beyond mere exegesis and systematization of the Roman texts, the commentators' approach was primarily a practical one. They sought to adjust the law to the needs of their own time, often by taking great liberties in interpreting the Corpus Juris and in reconciling conflicting (or seemingly conflicting) passages of the original Justinian compilation as well as the glossa. In their effort to modernize the law, the commentators also took note of legal materials outside the Corpus Juris, such as statutes and local and commercial customs.

[Margin handwritten note: Wanted to modernize the Roman Law]

3. See H. Rashdall, The Universities of Europe in the Middle Ages 87–267 (2d ed. F. M. Powicke and A. B. Emden, 1936).

While the majority of the law students at Bologna came from continental countries, some of them were English clerics and laymen. It is known, for instance, that Bracton "learned a great deal" from Azo, a famous glossator who taught at Bologna in the early part of the 13th century. Plucknett, A Concise History of the Common Law 296 (1956). See also Kantorowicz, Bractonian Problems (1941). For further references concerning the question of the glossators' influence on the development of English law see Wieacker, supra n. 2, at 111.

4. Italian law teachers traveled not only to other continental countries, but also to England. In the middle of the 12th century the Italian Glossator Vacarius founded the law school at Oxford. See Cappelletti-Merryman-Perillo, supra n. 2, at 33; Koschaker, supra n. 2, at 74–75.

4a. The scholastic method employed by the glossators also left a lasting imprint on the civil law. See H. J. Berman, The Origins of Western Legal Science, 90 Harv.L. Rev. 894, 908–30 (1977).

The commentators' influence on legal practice throughout Europe was strong and sustained. A Spanish statute of 1449, for example, directed the courts to follow the views of Bartolus and his pupil Baldus in any case not governed by the terms of a written law. Even in the absence of such a statutory direction, the writings of Bartolus and Baldus were similarly authoritative in other countries, especially in 16th century Germany.[5]

(cc) The *humanists,* whose principal seat of learning was the French University of Bourges, during the 16th and 17th centuries sought to cleanse the Roman texts of the glossators' and commentators' incrustations, and by going back to the sources of the classical period of Roman law (100 B.C. to 250 A.D.) even to uncover the interpolations of Tribonianus and his commission. The humanists, who were excellent classical scholars, poked fun at the commentators' ignorance of Greek and the inelegance of their Latin. Some of the harsh criticisms which the humanists directed against the commentators, have been enshrined in world literature by Rabelais. But since the endeavors of many of the humanists, in spite of their unquestionable scholarly merit, were antiquarian rather than practice-oriented, their *mos gallicus* gained less influence in most parts of Europe than the *mos italicus* of the commentators.

When we speak of the more modern era, especially of the 17th century, it becomes increasingly difficult to label each of the important scholars as a member of a particular school. Some of the great Dutch law teachers, for instance, who were to become the outstanding oracles of Roman-Dutch law,[6] combined the classical learning postulated by the *mos gallicus* with the practical methods and objectives of the *mos italicus*.[7] To varying degrees, moreover, they began to exhibit a critical attitude toward traditional Roman Law learning, under the influence of the new "school" of natural law, to which reference will be made below.

(b) Not all of the crucial stimuli of legal development (during the pre-codification era of civil law) came from the Roman heritage. Only a brief listing of the non-Roman impulses is possible here. The following appear to be particularly important:

(aa) In northern Europe, *local and regional customs of Germanic origin* played a significant role until the age of codification, as explained in the above excerpts from the article by Deák and Rheinstein. The Langobards and Visigoths, moreover, carried some of their customs into parts of Italy and Spain.

(bb) Both in public law and in the law of real property, the *feudal epoch* gave rise to social and legal institutions unknown to antiquity. It was only by a dazzling display of ingenuity, and indeed a bit of legerdemain, that the commentators were

5. See Koschaker, supra n. 2, at 104–5.

6. See Demerara Turf Club Ltd. v. Wight, supra; Margadant, supra note 2, at 251–66.

7. See Koschaker, supra n. 2, at 117–8; H. Coing, Das Schrifttum der englischen Civilians und die kontinentale Rechtsliteratur in der Zeit zwischen 1550 und 1800, in V Ius Commune 1, at 4–8 (1975).

able to fit some of these institutions into their Romanist system and into the terminology of the Corpus Juris.[8]

(cc) *The law of the Church,* the "jus canonicum", was an independent system, co-existing with the "jus civile" taught by the glossators and commentators.[9] The two systems influenced and supplemented each other in many ways.[10]

The views of the Church were, of course, paramount with respect to those subjects of which the ecclesiastical courts had jurisdiction, such as matrimonial and testamentary matters. Beyond that, ecclesiastical jurisdiction often could be founded on the allegation that defendant's conduct, e.g. his non-performance of a promise, constituted a sin. On this jurisdictional basis, Bartolus reports, the ecclesiastical tribunals of his time "daily" enforced promises for the breach of which there would have been no remedy, or no adequate remedy, in the secular courts.[11] As a rule, such decrees of ecclesiastical courts surely were obeyed; a recalcitrant party would have faced excommunication, with its secular as well as spiritual consequences. Canon law, as enforced by ecclesiastical tribunals, thus significantly supplemented, and in effect changed, the Roman-derived law of contracts.[12]

In many areas of law, the views of the Church, as reflected in the jus canonicum, also had a strong impact on the jus civile itself. Again, the law of contracts furnishes an apt illustration. Under the Roman system of contract law, the details of which need not be restated here,[13] only certain categories of contracts were enforceable. An executory contract which did not fit into any of these categories, was called nudum pactum and was not actionable (although it could be pleaded by way of defense). Under the influence of canon law, the glossators and commentators attempted to liberalize this somewhat rigid Roman system, and to bring it closer to the expansive canon law interpretation of "pacta sunt servanda". As one might expect, however, these attempts to reconcile two irreconcilable approaches led to much refinement, controversy and confusion,[14] with the result that concerning this particular subject the jus civile was, and for several centuries remained, in a very unsatisfactory state. The modern civil-law solution of the

8. See Wieacker, supra n. 2, at 83–85.

9. The degree of Doctor Utriusque Juris—to this day conferred by many European law faculties—still bears witness to this former duality of legal systems.

10. See Wieacker, supra n. 2, at 71–80; H. J. Berman, The Religious Foundations of Western Law, 24 Cath.U.L.Rev. 490 (1975).

11. See H. Coing, English Equity and the Denunciatio Evangelica of the Canon Law, 71 L.Q.Rev. 223, 231 (1955).

12. As the reader may have surmised, the parallel between this continental development and the subsequent growth of English equity is not accidental. See Coing, ibid. See also H. J. Berman, Law and

Revolution, The Formation of the Western Legal Tradition 245–50 (1983).

13. See R. W. Lee, Elements of Roman Law 290–344 (1956).

14. Even eminent 19th century Romanist scholars encountered great difficulty when they attempted to disentangle the medieval law teachers' views on the question whether and under what circumstances executory contracts (outside of the categories recognized as enforceable in Roman Law) should be enforced. Compare, e.g., Seuffert, Geschichte der obligatorischen Verträge (1881) with C. Karsten, Die Lehre vom Vertrage bei den italienischen Juristen des Mittelalters (1882, reprinted 1967).

problem emerged from two other sources, i.e. the law merchant and the teachings of the "natural law" school.[15] Both of these sources, to which further reference will be made instantly, were of non-Roman origin.

(dd) *The law merchant*, the history and present-day significance of which are discussed infra pp. 301–304, was another independent system co-existing with the Roman-derived jus civile. In many instances the rules of the law merchant were superior to those taught by the Romanists. Thus, in transactions among merchants, there was never much doubt concerning the enforceability of executory contracts, even non-typical ones. In time, it became clear that—in this instance as in others—the solution adopted by the law merchant was the most desirable one, and that solution was then gradually taken over into the general law.

(ee) Beginning in the 1500s, and coming to a climax in the 17th and 18th centuries, increasingly rationalistic and secularized versions of *natural law thinking* exerted a powerful influence on law-teaching and legal institutions.[16] Insofar as private law was concerned, this influence made itself felt in two ways:

First, with respect to the substance of legal rules, the authority of the Corpus Juris was challenged. Medieval scholars, when seeking to adjust Roman law to the conditions of their own time, had done so by interpretation, even bold interpretation, of the ancient texts; but they had not questioned the authoritative nature of those texts. Now a different attitude emerged. The legal scholars of the "natural law" era, which in part coincided with the "humanist" period, were conversant with Roman law, and they made ample use of the rich casuistry of the Roman texts as indicative of the practical legal problems to be resolved. In many instances, they even adopted the Roman solution; but they felt no longer bound to do so. In their view, the Corpus Juris had ceased to govern *ratione imperii*. Whatever persuasive force it retained—and that force was still considerable—, it had to exercise *imperio rationis*, by virtue of the rational superiority of a particular rule or principle announced by the Roman jurists.[17] On many points, such as the question of the enforceability of a nudum pactum, the Roman solution was regarded as unreasonable and was, therefore, rejected by the followers of the new school.[18]

15. Concerning the treatment of the problem in the modern civil-law codifications, and the sources used by the codifiers, see infra pp. 279–281.

16. See Bodenheimer, Jurisprudence 31–59 (Rev.Ed.1974); Wieacker, supra n. 2, at 249 ff.

17. Already before the advent of the great national codifications, this attitude of the natural law thinkers not only influenced the jus commune, but also had a strong impact on legislation. For instance, in Portugal (and Brazil), where an older statute had given the force of law to the opinions of Accursius and Bartolus, the Law of Sound Reason, enacted in 1769, provided that gaps in the written law should in the future be filled by resort to reason rather than by invoking the Roman law learning of the medieval Doctores. See Orlando Gomes, Historical and Sociological Roots of the Brazilian Civil Code, 1 Inter-American L.Rev. 331, 332–3 (1959).

18. In this particular instance, as we have seen above, the solution favored by the school of natural law had the support, also, of canon law and of the law merchant. The natural law scholars did

Secondly, and perhaps even more importantly, the legal thinkers of the natural law period revolutionized the methods of systematization. Prior to the 17th century, the civil law had been far less systematic than is commonly believed. The spirit of classical Roman law was pragmatic and casuistic, and even the sophisticated compilers of the Corpus Juris excelled more in practical wisdom than in system-building.[19] The medieval scholars, especially the commentators, improved the systematic treatment of certain subjects; but like the Roman jurists, they thought primarily in terms of specific problems or topics rather than in terms of an overall system. It was not until the natural law era that scholars began to build coherent and comprehensive systems of private law.[19a] The method of system-building used during the 17th and 18th centuries was deductive.[20] Employing a small number of very general concepts and precepts as his starting point, the system-builder of that period deductively developed successive ranges of less and less general abstractions, categories and principles until finally, on the lowest level of abstraction, he laid out the specific rules governing concrete fact situations. The influence of this method upon the legal thinking of the immediate pre-codification period, and on the structure and spirit of some of the modern codes, has been profound. Later in this course, especially when we study the structure of the German Civil Code, we shall have occasion to trace its continuing present-day effect.

At the beginning of the 19th century, to be sure, the historical school revolted against the allegedly lifeless rationalism of the preceding period. Even in Germany, however, where under Savigny's leadership this revolt was particularly

---

not hesitate, however, to discard Roman rules even in instances where their own solutions were unsupported by prior doctrine or practice, and had to be based exclusively on "reason".

For further examples of practical legal problems which the natural law scholars proposed to resolve in a manner different from, and often diametrically opposed to, the classical Roman solutions, see infra pp. 279–286.

19. The Institutiones, serving primarily an educational function, were organized in a simple but understandable manner. In dealing with private law, they followed the Institutiones of the great classical jurist Gaius (about 160 A.D.) by focusing, successively, on *persons, property, wills, intestate succession,* and *obligations.* The "system" or organizing principle of the more important Digest, on the other hand, was so obscure that it remained hidden to post-Roman scholars until it "was discovered by Bluhme in a brilliant study published in 1820". Yntema, Roman Law and Its Influence on Western Civilization, 35 Cornell L.Q. 77, at 81 (1949).

19a. Without the foundations laid by these system-building scholars, the subsequent codification of the civil law would have been impossible.

The very idea of a comprehensive, systematic code is itself a creature of the Age of Reason. The emergence of this idea, and the early, pre-Napoleonic attempts to implement it, are traced by J. Maillet, The Historical Significance of French Codifications, 44 Tul.L.Rev. 681 (1970) and by R. Batiza, Origins of Modern Codification of the Civil Law: The French Experience and Its Implications for Louisiana Law, 56 Tulane L.Rev. 477, 478–578 (1982).

20. The reader may wonder why a deductive and speculative method remained dominant in philosophy and law during the very period that witnessed the first triumphs of modern science. The question cannot be answered with certainty. The fact appears to be that the mathematical aspects of the scientific advances of the era received more attention than the experimental ones. See Wieacker, Privatrechtsgeschichte der Neuzeit 254–57 (1967).

strong, it did not lead to antiquarian reconstruction of ancient Roman or Germanic law. The commanding academic voices who developed and in some measure unified German law during the 19th century (see supra p. 268), postulated greater respect for grown legal institutions than had been shown by the rationalists; but the latters' method of systematization was used and indeed perfected by Savigny and the other representatives of the German Pandektenwissenschaft. It is to this systematicity—never surpassed or equalled anywhere—that the 19th century German legal scholars owed the world-wide influence of their writings, and of the B.G.B. which was the ultimate embodiment of their teaching.[21]

(3) The relative strength of Roman and non-Roman influences upon the development of the civil law during the pre-code era varied not only from country to country and from period to period, but also *from subject to subject.*[22] We have seen, for instance, that in the 17th and certainly in the 18th century the Roman rule against affirmative enforceability of the nudum pactum had been abandoned by most of the leading authorities. At the same time, the essence of the Roman doctrine of negotiorum gestio (see supra p. 5) was preserved intact by Pothier and other influential writers, with the ultimate result that it was written into the modern codes.[23]

Further examples of Roman and non-Roman elements utilized by the codifiers will appear in the materials which follow.

B. THE NATIONAL CODIFICATIONS—TRADITIONAL AND MODERN ELEMENTS IN THE CIVIL LAW

FRENCH LAW OF MARCH 21, 1804

[During 1803 and the early part of 1804, the various parts of the French Civil Code had been enacted by way of thirty-six separate statutes. The law of March 21, 1804 re-promulgated the Code as a whole [24]].

Article 7. From the day when these laws [constituting the Code] become effective, the Roman laws, the ordinances, the general and local customs, the charters and the regulations all cease to have the force

---

21. Everybody agrees that as an intellectual accomplishment the system-building of 18th and 19th century legal scholars commands our admiration. The question remains, however, whether rigid systematicity and the concomitant employment of highly abstract, pervasive concepts and precepts will always make it easier to reach sound results. See 1 Schlesinger (Gen.Ed.), Formation of Contracts—A Study of the Common Core of Legal Systems 52–53 (1968). The reader should keep this question in mind when, in later parts

of this course, he encounters cases arising under the present codes, especially under the German B.G.B.

22. See Zepos, supra n. 2, at 903–04.

23. See Dawson, Negotiorum Gestio: The Altruistic Intermeddler, 74 Harv.L. Rev. 817, 820–23 (1961), where it is pointed out, also, that in matters of detail the various code versions of negotiorum gestio differ from each other.

24. See R. Batiza, supra n. 19a, at 572.

either of general or of special law concerning the subjects covered by the present code.

H. C. GUTTERIDGE: COMPARATIVE LAW *
2nd ed. 1949. P. 77.

[Some of author's footnotes omitted.]

When called on to deal with foreign law an English lawyer passes from an environment of case law into a "world governed by codes". His first step must, therefore, be to examine the relevant provisions of the codified law, and it will be necessary for him to remember that there are certain differences between the continental codes and English codifying statutes such as the Sale of Goods Act, 1893. A continental code is intended to lay down new rules and is not conceived as resting on a pre-existing body of law.** The history of a rule of continental law is, consequently, not a matter of very great importance save in exceptional cases. "Whereas an English lawyer seeking to interpret a legal principle will look first to its pedigree, a continental lawyer will search for its policy." [3]

THE CODES' BREAK WITH THE PAST

For many years legal scholars have engaged in lively and sometimes controversial discussions of the extent to which the codes have turned the modern civil-law systems away from their past. It would seem, however, that unhelpful generalities can be avoided only if the issue is broken down into two related but distinct questions:

(1) What models and sources *inspired the draftsmen* when they prepared the codes?

(2) How much influence did the pre-code sources—as such—retain *after the adoption of the codes*?

(1) The draftsmen invariably were men who had attained prominence by teaching or practicing under the pre-code system or systems, with which they were intimately familiar. On the other hand, their mandate in each instance was to bring about revision as well as national unification of diverse local laws. Thus, subject to whatever

---

* By permission of Cambridge University Press.

** "So strong was this feeling that the Code must be treated as *res nova* that one of the early commentators, Bugnet, said, 'I know nothing of civil law; I only teach the Code Napoleon'. This fear lest the past should slink back again by a side-door explains Napoleon's remark *mon code est perdu* when he heard of the publication of the first commentary. And it is remarkable to-day how rarely in the application and interpretation of the French Code, the attention of the judge is invited to any legislative text or judicial decision prior in date to 1804." Amos, The Code Napoleon and the Modern World, 10 J.Comp.Leg. & Int. Law (3rd Ser.) 222, 224 (1928).

3. Walton and Amos, Introduction to French Law, p. 4. [The reference here is to the first edition. The current third edition, by F. H. Lawson, A. E. Anton and L. N. Brown (1967), at p. 7, contains a very similar though slightly more guarded statement.]

political controls were operative at the time, they were authorized and indeed directed to use independent judgment.[1]

The statement just made requires one important qualification. Into many of the civil law countries, the civil code or the whole code system of another nation was imported as a result either of military conquest or of cultural influence.[2] In this way, as we shall see, so-called code families have come into existence (see infra, p. 546). Thus, when we speak of the codifiers' exercise of independent judgment, we must limit our statement to the seminal codes.

The draftsmen of the various seminal codes, in exercising their independent judgment, very often reached different conclusions regarding the same point.[3]

(a) The various codes are significantly different in their systematic structure. In this connection, it is instructive to compare the tables of organization of the civil codes of France and Germany, which appear infra at pp. 531–540.[4] While the Napoleonic Code, in spite of some refinements,[5] still clings rather strongly to the simple Roman system embodied in Justinian's Institutiones,[6] the organization of the German Civil Code shows much less dependence on the somewhat primitive structural thinking of the Romans. Not only its General Part, with its highly abstract, pervasive concepts and precepts, but the whole struc-

---

1. The statement in the text is true not only with respect to draftsmen commissioned by an absolute ruler (as in the case of the Code Napoleon and the Austrian General Civil Code of 1811), but also regarding draftsmen operating within the framework of a representative constitutional system (as in the case of the German as well as the Swiss Civil Code).

Napoleon commissioned a group of four eminent lawyers, the most influential of whom was Portalis, to prepare a draft of the French Civil Code. Although subsequently the draft was debated and somewhat modified in the course of sessions of the Council of State presided over by Napoleon himself, it is clear that the draftsmen's approach, and the sources used by them, remain a subject of great interest. It is, therefore, fortunate that two brilliant and highly informative statements made by Portalis concerning the nature and sources of the Code are now available in English translation. See M. S. Herman, Excerpts from a Discourse on the Code Napoleon by Portalis, 18 Loyola L.Rev. 23 (1972); and A. Levasseur, Code Napoleon or Code Portalis?, 43 Tul.L.Rev. 762, 767–74 (1969).

For interesting details concerning the manner in which the Austrian, German and Swiss codes were prepared, see W. Lorenz, Some Comments on the Austrian, German and Swiss Legal Systems, with Particular Reference to the Law of Contracts, in 1 Schlesinger (Gen.Ed.), Forma-

tion of Contracts—A Study of the Common Core of Legal Systems 251–59 (1968). See also Schlesinger, The Uniform Commercial Code in the Light of Comparative Law, 1 Inter-American L.Rev. 11, 28–31 (1959).

2. See supra pp. 8–12.

3. In part, this can be explained by differences in national circumstances and by the fact that some codes were passed much later than others. This, however, is only a partial explanation. To a considerable degree, the differences between the various codes must be ascribed to deliberate choices made by the codifiers—choices that often were personal and accidental in the sense that they were not necessitated by national circumstances or the spirit of the time. In any event, whatever the reasons, the fact is that as a result of codification the differences inter sese among civil law systems have become much more pronounced than they were in pre-code days. We shall come back to this point at pp. 306–307.

4. The reader may find it interesting, also, to extend the comparison to the Spanish Civil Code. For the latter Code's table of organization, see supra pp. 238–240.

5. The refinements, especially in subdividing the area of Obligations, largely reflect the systematic thinking of Pothier (1699–1772). See S. Jorgensen, Vertrag und Recht 67–68 (1968), where further references can be found.

6. See supra p. 274.

ture is imbued with the systematic, speculative thinking of the 18th and 19th century scholars of whom we have spoken above.

(b) Similarly, the style and diction of each of the leading codes reflect intellectual and political forces having at least some of their roots in the past, i.e. in the era preceding the particular codification. The Napoleonic Code, still strongly influenced by 18th century rationalism, displayed an optimistic faith in human Reason by being written in elegant and simple language, which was expected to be fully understood by the citizens. The draftsmen of the German B.G.B., on the other hand, doubtless were influenced by 19th century admiration of scientific method. Clearly, they addressed the legal profession rather than the ordinary citizen when they employed the many highly abstract, technical terms and the countless system-breathing cross-references for which their Code is famous. The Swiss Civil Code, although prepared only a short time after the German and influenced by the latter, again reverted to simple and predominantly non-technical language, in an attempt—inspired by democratic ideals—to bring justice closer to the people. Unlike the Napoleonic Code or the B.G.B., it is substantially the work of a single draftsman, Professor Eugen Huber, then of the University of Basel.[6a]

(c) In fashioning specific principles and rules, the codifiers were free to choose among many models and other sources of inspiration. Even a superficial and schematic list of such sources would have to include the following:

(aa) Roman law, both in its classical form and as developed through the centuries.

(bb) The non-Roman elements of pre-code civil law, which have been discussed above: customs of Germanic or feudal origin; canon law; the law merchant; and the scholarly writings originating from the school of natural law and the Pandektenwissenschaft.

(cc) Codes or compilations previously adopted in parts of the national territory.[7]

(dd) Comparative studies of foreign systems, especially of the leading codes previously adopted in other countries.

(ee) Original solutions devised by the draftsmen, either by way of free, non-imitative invention, or by fashioning a novel combination of elements borrowed from several older sources.

Even if one focuses on a single code, any attempt to generalize concerning the relative strength of these various sources of inspiration

---

6a. Professor Huber had previously abandoned a distinguished career as a journalist because he disagreed with the anti-labor editorial policy of his employer, a leading Swiss daily.

7. See the article by Deák and Rheinstein, supra. Local codes previously enacted in some of the German kingdoms and principalities constituted a particularly important source for the draftsmen of the German Civil Code. See Lorenz, supra n. 1. In this connection, it must be remembered that throughout most of the 19th century some major regions of Germany lived under a code system modelled on the French. Originally that system may have owed its adoption, at least in part, to Napoleon's armed might; but in Baden, and some other parts of Germany not far from the French border, it was voluntarily retained after Napoleon's downfall. The draftsmen of the German Civil Code thus had to consider a version of the Code Napoleon as the "local" law then existing in some German provinces, and not merely as a foreign system to be examined by way of comparative studies.

is difficult and often hazardous.[7a] In order to get the "feel" of the sources drawn upon by the codifiers, one must select specific problems and examine the historical background of the treatment which these problems have received in particular codes.[8] This is the purpose of the illustrations which follow.

Illustration 1 (Formation of Contracts)

On the eve of the age of codification, the recognized oracles of the civil law had reached a measure of agreement concerning the question of the enforceability of non-typical as well as typical contracts. As we have seen above, the classical Roman view (that only certain types of contracts should be enforced) had been rejected. Under the influence of canon law, the law merchant and natural law, it had become recognized that in principle any agreement of two parties, voluntarily entered into and meant to create legal obligations, should be enforced as a contract,[9] regardless of the presence or absence of what a lawyer brought up in the common law would call "consideration".[10]

In view of this state of the authorities of the immediate precodification period, it is not surprising to find that the same general principle—often referred to as the principle of freedom of contract, although it deals with only one aspect of such freedom—was taken over into all of the codes.[11]

7a. An example is provided by the Civil Code of Louisiana. The reader will recall that there is a heated scholarly controversy concerning the question whether the draftsmen of the predecessor of the present Code were predominantly inspired by Spanish or by French sources. See supra p. 14, text at n. 48.

8. Research of this kind is sometimes facilitated by the fact that the draftsmen usually left an ample documentary record of their preparatory work. See infra p. 585. Nevertheless, until recently most legal scholars in code countries have been only mildly interested in investigations of this kind, because (for reasons to be discussed below) the results of such historical research would be of little use in present-day practice. During the last three decades, however, there has been a massive awakening of scholarly interest in the law of pre-code Europe. See Kaser, Der römische Anteil am deutschen Bürgerlichen Recht, 7 Juristische Schulung 337, especially at 344 (1967) and the materials cited supra p. 269, note 2. Although everyday legal practice is still virtually unaffected by these scholarly endeavors, they are likely to be intensified because they may serve to underpin the partial re-unification of the legal systems of a politically more integrated future Europe. See Neumayer, The Role of a Uniform Legal Science in the Harmonization of the Continental Legal Systems, in R. A. Newman (Ed.), Essays in

Jurisprudence in Honor of Roscoe Pound 649 (1962).

For references to a considerable number of recent studies exploring the dogmatic history of specific legal institutions, see K. Luig, Überwiegendes Mitverschulden, in II Ius Commune (H. Coing, Ed.) 187, 188–89 (1969).

9. Needless to say, in many instances the application of this principle was subject to form requirements. Moreover, as in any highly developed legal system, there were rules dealing with the pathological situations in which illegality, duress, fraud or mistake might be involved. For present purposes, we are assuming the absence of such problems.

10. Thus, long before the great codifications, the civil law had come to recognize the validity and enforceability of a contractual promise to make a gift (a type of promise in which the Church had always shown a considerable interest), subject to the requirement of notarial or other form, e.g., registration. J. P. Dawson, Gifts and Promises (1980); Baade, Donations Reconsidered, 59 Tex.L.Rev. 179, 181 (1980).

11. The doctrine of consideration is peculiar to the common law and is not recognized in the civil-law systems. See A. G. Chloros, The Doctrine of Consideration and the Reform of the Law of Contract, 17 Int. & Comp.L.Q. 137 (1968); Lorenzen, Causa and Consideration in the Law of Contracts,

The adoption of this principle, which made the parties' *consensus* the central and decisive element of the law of contracts, rendered it necessary to deal with the often difficult question of the manner in which such consensus comes about. The Roman jurists, who had never developed a unitary contract theory,[12] left this question unanswered. Even in post-Roman days, so long as most consensual transactions were concluded inter praesentes, legal scholars did not feel called upon to devote much deep and systematic thought to the subject of formation of contracts. But when, with expanding trade and travel, contracts inter absentes became a matter of routine, the need for legal rules concerning the mechanics of formation made itself felt. In response to this need, Grotius (1583–1645) developed the modern doctrine of offer and acceptance. From his works, and those of other natural law authors, the doctrine found its way into most of the great codes.[13]

This, however, was not yet the end of the story. Grotius had favored the rule that normally an offer should be revocable until accepted.[14] Some of the earlier codes adopted this rule, along with other aspects of the doctrine of offer and acceptance which Grotius had developed as a matter of natural law. In France, also, the natural law view favoring revocability of offers exerted some influence, even though the Code Napoleon was silent on the point.[15] As a result, some civil-law systems still adhere to the view that, in principle at least, an offer is revocable until accepted.

In Germany, however, somewhat different influences made themselves felt. The civil codes of Prussia (1794) and of Saxony (1863) made the offer irrevocable in cases where the offeror had set a time limit for acceptance.[16] The Commercial Code of 1861, going a step further, extended the rule of irrevocability to all offers regardless of whether or not they specified such a time limit;[17] where no time limit was specified, the offer was to remain irrevocable for a reasonable time. This, in essence, was the rule later embodied in the German Civil Code.[18]

The foregoing sketch, though over-simplified, shows that in fashioning the modern rules of offer and acceptance,[19] the codifiers drew on

28 Yale L.J. 621 (1919); Mason, The Utility of Consideration, 41 Colum.L.Rev. 825 (1941).

For a recent American decision enforcing a promise to make a gift, where the promise was made in notarial form (see supra p. 18) and was governed by German law, see In re Estate of Danz, 444 Pa. 411, 283 A.2d 282 (1971).

12. See Schulz, Classical Roman Law 465–68 (1951); R. W. Lee, Elements of Roman Law 345 (1956); 1 Kaser, Das römische Privatrecht 229 (2d ed. 1971). Regarding the complexities and confusion that arose during the post-classical period, see 2 Kaser, id. 362 ff. (2d ed. 1975).

13. The one big exception is the French Civil Code, which—strange to relate—contains virtually no provisions on the subject of offer and acceptance. The reason for this omission seems to be that Domat and Pothier, the two authors on whose works

the French codifiers relied most strongly, had been somewhat neglectful in treating this particular subject. See Bonassies, Some Comments on the French Legal System, with Particular Reference to the Law of Contracts, in 1 Schlesinger (Gen. Ed.), Formation of Contracts—A Study of the Common Core of Legal Systems 243 (1968).

14. See Wieacker, Privatrechtsgeschichte der Neuzeit 295 (1967).

15. See the report by Professor Bonassies in 1 Schlesinger, op. cit. supra n. 13, at 769 ff., especially 770.

16. See Lorenz, supra n. 1, at 254.

17. Id. at 255.

18. See §§ 145–149; see also infra pp. 659–660.

19. For a comparative and more detailed discussion of the pertinent modern rules, see 1 Schlesinger, supra n. 13, at 109–11, 745–91.

almost all of the types of sources enumerated above. Roman law did not play a significant role in this instance; yet it furnished some of the basic terms and concepts, especially the all-important notion of consensus.[20]

France rejects strict liability

Illustration 2 (A Problem of Strict Liability in Tort)[21]

The Louisiana Civil Code of 1870, as amended, in Art. 177 makes the "master" liable "for the damage caused to individuals or to the community in general by whatever is thrown out of his house into the street or public road." This liability does not depend on proof of negligence. In a case not covered by the language of Art. 177, but arguably coming within its spirit,[22] the Court of Appeals for the Fifth Circuit delved deeply into the historical antecedents.[23] On the basis of this research, the Court concluded that the rule of Art. 177 is of Roman origin.[23a] It can be found, in terms substantially similar to those of the Louisiana Code, in Justinian's Digest as well as in the Institutiones. From there, through the Siete Partidas (see supra, p. 236) and the writings, among others, of the 17th century French author Domat, it found its way not only into the Louisiana codes of 1808, 1825 and 1870,

---

20. See Kreller, Römisches Recht—Grundlehren des Gemeinen Rechts 269 (1950).

21. This illustration is based on Williams v. Employers Liability Assurance Corp., 296 F.2d 569 (5th Cir. 1961), cert. den. 371 U.S. 844, 83 S.Ct. 76 (1962). Judge Wisdom's scholarly opinion in that case contains a wealth of references, and no further citations will be given here.

22. The facts of the case, supra n. 21, were simple and tragic. The plaintiff, a widow 43 years of age, who worked in a large office building owned and operated by defendant, was brutally assaulted and sexually abused by a young hoodlum who had followed her into the ladies' room. As a result, she suffered physical injuries and severe nervous disorders. Alleging that defendant, in operating the building, had taken insufficient precautions against intrusions by hoodlums, plaintiff sought damages from defendant. The trial court submitted the issue of negligence to the jury (which found no negligence on defendant's part), but refused to charge that Art. 177, directly or analogously applied, would impose liability on the defendant even if its conduct were not proved negligent. Whether this refusal to charge constituted error, was the main issue on appeal.

23. At the end of its historical excursion, the Court affirmed the District Court's judgment for defendant, on the ground that the rule embodied in Art. 177 was never intended to protect a person inside the building.

One might question whether a civil-law court sitting in a country free from common-law influences would have devoted the same amount of effort to historical research. See text infra under (2). On the other hand, judges trained in the civil law probably would have examined the question—not even mentioned in the Court's lengthy opinion—whether a principle of strict liability sufficiently broad to cover this fact situation might be analogously derived, not from Art. 177 alone, but from the whole galaxy of strict liability provisions to be found in various parts of the Civil Code.

23a. Seemingly disagreeing with Judge Wisdom's conclusion, Professor Batiza has stated that Art. 177 was almost verbatim lifted from Blackstone. See R. Batiza, The Louisiana Civil Code of 1808: Its Actual Sources and Present Relevance, 46 Tul.L. Rev. 4, at 28, 51 and 137 (1971). But although Blackstone classified (or perhaps misclassified) the subject as forming part of the law of Master and Servant, he expressly admitted that he formulated the rule on the basis of civil-law authorities. 1 Bl. Com. *419 note m, citing Dig. 9, 3, 1, and Inst. 4, 5, 1. The odd location of article 177 of the Louisiana Civil Code and of Blackstone's reference in the master-and-servant section is readily explained by the close connection of this topic to the law of slavery in Rome and in ante-bellum Louisiana. See also next footnote. Thus Judge Wisdom's conclusion—that the rule was of Roman origin—may be right regardless of whether the Louisiana draftsmen derived it directly from the civil-law authorities to be mentioned in the text, infra, or indirectly via Blackstone.

but also into the Civil Codes of Spain and some other civil-law countries, especially in Latin America.[23b]

As generally understood, this Roman-derived rule makes the person in possession of the house (not necessarily the owner) absolutely or at least presumptively liable for any injury or damage caused by an object thrown or poured from the house, even though the victim may be unable to show whether the physical act was committed by the defendant himself, a member of his family, a servant, a tenant or sub-tenant, or a stranger. Typically Roman in its casuistic and practical approach to a rather specific problem, at first blush the rule seems basically sound. We find, however, that the French Civil Code, and following it a majority of the modern codes, rejected the rule, thus allowing recovery only if the victim can prove negligence on the part of the defendant or of a person for whose conduct the defendant is vicariously liable. As stated in the Court's opinion,

> A preliminary draft of the Code Napoleon, used by the Louisiana codifiers as a source for the Code of 1808, did attempt to codify the law [i.e. the Roman law] relating to things thrown from houses. The Conseil d'État rejected the proposed provisions. The Code Napoleon, a code to reform the law, perhaps influenced by contemporary philosophical interest in individualism, free will, and moral responsibility, takes the approach that the liability of a master for things thrown out of a house must be based on culpability within the general principle of no liability without fault.[24]

The Court does not intimate that concerning the specific point in question the French codifiers were influenced by 17th or 18th century legal authors. On the contrary, the opinion demonstrates by apt quotations that Domat, perhaps the most original and influential of the pre-code French authors, had emphatically and approvingly restated the Roman rule. Thus, if we accept the results of the Court's painstaking historical research, we must conclude that the French codifiers broke with tradition in passing on this issue. Whatever their philosophical or other reasons may have been, they fashioned a novel solution, reversing whatever precedent could be found in the pre-code sources.

The upshot, again, is that the modern civil-law codes, in spite of basic similarities in methods and concepts, reached divergent results concerning the specific point at issue. Some of them, probably a minority, have adhered to the essence and almost to the very words of the rule stated by Justinian.[25] In the other codes, the opposite rule has

---

23b. The history of the rule in pre-code civil law is interestingly traced by Stein, The Actio de Effusis vel Dejectis and the Concept of Quasi-Delict in Scots Law, 4 Int. & Comp.L.Q. 356 (1955) (commenting on a 1954 case which turned on the question whether the rule mentioned in the text had been received into Scots law).

24. 296 F.2d, at 575–6. In addition to the philosophical reasons suggested by the Court, the codifiers may have had more specific practical grounds for abolishing the Roman rule. In the age of firearms, a

rule imposing absolute or quasi-absolute liability on the owner of the building can lead to rather harsh results, e.g., in the case of a sniper hiding out in the building and killing or injuring people in the street. For further discussion, see A. Watson, Failures of the Legal Imagination, ch. 1 (to appear in 1988).

25. The Louisiana Civil Code belongs to this group. The reasons why on this particular issue the Louisiana codifiers did not follow the French model, are thoroughly explored in Judge Wisdom's opinion.

been adopted, following a re-examination in which policy considerations prevailed over tradition.

Illustration 3 (The Fate of the Bona Fide Purchaser of Chattels)

Every developed legal system must resolve the conflict between two innocent parties which occurs in the typical "bona fide purchaser" situation. In the discussion which follows, the original owner will be referred to as *A*. The bailee or thief who, acting as if he had title, purports to transfer such title and delivers possession of the chattel to a third person, will be called *B*. The third person, i.e. the purchaser, will be named *C*.

The civil-law systems began very early to face up to the problem. Again, the trail begins in ancient Rome. Roman law clearly resolved the issue in favor of *A*; he had the right to recover his chattel from *C*, even though the latter had paid value and had acted in good faith.[26] In case *C* had possession of the chattel for at least a year prior to the commencement of *A*'s action, he might try to defend on the ground of usucapio (comparable to adverse possession); but a person in the position of *C* could successfully invoke this defense only in exceptional fact situations, because usucapio did not apply to a chattel which the owner had lost through larceny, and a bailee's embezzlement was regarded as an instance of larceny. Thus *C* could defend on grounds of usucapio only in the rare case in which *B* was neither a thief nor an embezzler (e.g., when *B* had made an honest mistake in disposing of the chattel). Even in such a rare case, *C* could prevail only if he had had possession of the chattel for at least a year, and if he had acted bona fide. In the light of later developments, it is important to note that in this way, through the usucapio doctrine, Roman law injected the notion of bona fides into the handling of our problem.

The rule prevailing in Germanic customary laws—first reliably reported in the 12th century, but probably of much older origin—was more favorable to *C*. Under this rule, a basic distinction was drawn depending on whether *A* had lost possession of his chattel against his will (e.g. by theft), or whether he had entrusted it to a bailee of his choice. In the former situation, *A* ordinarily prevailed over *C*, even under Germanic law. But where *A* had entrusted his chattel to bailee *B*, he had a cause of action only against *B*, and never against *C*. The theory was that *A*, who had voluntarily parted with his chattel, should not be able to recover it from anyone other than the person in whom he

On another, somewhat comparable issue of tort liability, involving the responsibility of the owners of dogs and other domestic animals, the French Code and the Louisiana Code are in agreement. In similar language, both codes have adopted a principle of strict liability for damage caused by the animal. In a recent, exceedingly interesting opinion, the Supreme Court of Louisiana held that the relevant Louisiana provision should be given the same (rather strict) interpretation which the French courts and commentators have placed on the comparable article of the French Code. As a result, the Court rejected the common-law approach under which, it is often claimed, "the dog gets the first bite free". See Holland v. Buckley, 305 So.2d 113 (La. 1974).

26. The rule was expressed in axiomatic and striking language: "Ubi rem meam invenio, ibi vindico", or "Nemo plus juris ad alium transferre potest quam ipse habet". Common law courts have used similar expressions; cf. the opinion of Willes, J., in Whistler v. Forster, 14 C.B.(N.S.) 248, 257, 143 Eng.Rep. 441, 445 (1863); Handley Motor Co. v. Wood, 237 N.C. 318, 75 S.E.2d 312, 316 (1953).

had put his trust. Thus C could keep the chattel, and A was relegated to an action against bailee B. Under Germanic law, this was so regardless of whether C had acted in good or bad faith. Nor did the length of the period of C's possession make any difference. The operation of the rule protecting C did not depend on the passage of time; C prevailed even if he was sued by A the day after he (C) had obtained the chattel from B.

From the 15th to the 19th century, the Roman view and the Germanic rule competed for predominance in Germany, The Netherlands and Northern France.[27] Occasionally, there were attempts to work out a compromise solution with special attention to the protection, developed in the law merchant, of purchases in an open market—in English legal parlance, the market overt.[28]

Most of the draftsmen of modern codes were familiar with the conflict between the two rules, and their tendency was to combine the best features of both. A few countries, including Spain and some of the Latin American republics, essentially adopted the Roman approach, subject to relatively minor exceptions.[29] In the majority of civil-law countries, however, a careful weighing of policy considerations [30] led to a different solution. Although far from identical in their details,[31] all of the codes of the majority group—which includes France,[31a] Germany [31b] and Switzerland [31c]—contain the following essential features:

27. See Eckhardt and Jessen, Fahrniserwerb vom Nichtberechtigten, in 3 Rechtsvergleichendes Handwörterbuch 307, 308 (1931); J. G. Sauveplanne, The Protection of the Bona Fide Purchaser of Corporeal Movables in Comparative Law, 29 Rabels Z. 651, 655 (1965).

28. See B. Kozolchyk, Transfer of Personal Property by a Nonowner: Its Future in Light of its Past, 61 Tul.L.Rev. 1453, 1484–86 (1987). On the market overt in the City of London, see the authorities collected in Reid v. Commissioner of Police of the Metropolis, [1973] 1 Q.B. 551 (C.A.).

29. In the Spanish Civil Code, the relevant provisions are derived in part from the Code Napoleon, and in part from the Siete Partidas, with the result that these provisions are not free from ambiguity. See Comment, Sales of Another's Movables—History, Comparative Law and Bona Fide Purchasers, 29 La.L.Rev. 329, 335–37 (1969). As interpreted by the Spanish Supreme Court, the Code provisions essentially embody the Roman rule, but with some exceptions. A particularly important exception is stated in Art. 85 of the Spanish Commercial Code, which grants immediate protection to C if in good faith he has bought goods in a shop or department store. See Sauveplanne, supra n. 27, at 657–8. Needless to say, this provision invites comparison with UCC § 2–403.

For broad-based comparative studies, in addition to those cited in n. 27 supra, see J.

G. Sauveplanne, Security Over Corporeal Movables 15–19 (1974), and Zweigert, Rechtsvergleichend-Kritisches zum gutgläubigen Mobiliarerwerb, 23 Rabels Z. 1 (1958).

30. For interesting discussions of these policy considerations, see Zweigert, ibid.; Wolff-Raiser, Sachenrecht 247–50 (1957); Baur, Lehrbuch des Sachenrechts 460–61 (1975).

31. For instance, the various codes of the majority group differ among each other concerning the time limitation to which A's action against C (provided such action is otherwise well-founded under the facts of the case) will be subjected. See Sauveplanne, supra n. 27, at 680. For a discussion of other differences see infra n. 32.

31a. For a recent exposition of the relevant French rules see C. S. P. Harding & M. S. Rowell, Protection of Property Versus Protection of Commercial Transactions in French and English Law, 26 Int. & Comp.L.Q. 354, 356–63 (1977).

31b. See German Civil Code, §§ 932–35 and German Commercial Code, §§ 366–67, discussed by E. J. Cohn, Manual of German Law, § 362 (2d ed. 1968), and in Kunstsammlungen zu Weimar v. Elicofon, 536 F.Supp. 829, 839–43 (E.D.N.Y. 1981), aff'd 678 F.2d 1150 (2d Cir. 1982).

31c. An English translation of the relevant Swiss provisions appears infra p. 818.

(i) In accordance with the Germanic approach, a basic distinction is drawn depending on whether *A* voluntarily parted with possession. If he did not, i.e. if the chattel was stolen from him or lost by him, then *A* prevails over *C*; this, at least, is the ordinary rule, subject to varying exceptions.[32] On the other hand, if *A* entrusted his chattel to *B*, and the latter without authority transferred and delivered it to *C*, in that event *A* normally cannot recover the chattel from *C*. Thus, in essence, the old Germanic rule is followed.

(ii) Invariably, however, the qualification is added that even in the case where *A* had entrusted his chattel to *B*, no protection is accorded to *C* if he acted in bad faith.[33] This qualification, which was not recognized under the Germanic rule, was derived from the above-mentioned Roman doctrine of usucapio.[34]

One may fairly say, therefore, that in this instance the majority of the codifiers relied on traditional principles, largely of Germanic and to a lesser extent of Roman origin. If, however, one takes a closer look at the pertinent rules as they appear today in the various codes belonging to this group, one finds that in important details they differ from each other.[34a] Why is this so, in spite of the fact that in dealing with the present topic the draftsmen of all these codes were utilizing the same sources? The answer, clearly, must be that in fashioning a new principle by a combination of Germanic and Roman elements, and in devising the specifics necessary to make the new principle work, the draftsmen of each of the new codes had to resolve numerous questions of policy and of drafting technique. By the time each group of draftsmen had independently and creatively developed its own answers to

32. The most important exceptions are the following:

(a) Even though the chattel was stolen from *A* or lost by him, most of the codes protect *C* if he has acquired the chattel in a public auction. But the manner in which *C* is protected in such a case, differs from country to country. Under German and Austrian law, *C* acquires good title if he is a bona fide purchaser; the French and Swiss codes, on the other hand, while compelling *C* to surrender the chattel to *A* if the latter brings a timely action, provide that in such a situation the surrender be conditioned upon *C* receiving from *A* the amount which *C* in good faith paid for the chattel. See Sauveplanne, supra n. 27, at 683–4; H. P. Dunkel, Öffentliche Versteigerung und gutgläubiger Erwerb 1–2 (1970).

(b) The German Civil Code, and similarly the Swiss Civil Code (see infra p. 818), contain special provisions covering the case in which bearer securities have been lost by *A*, or stolen from him. By way of an exception to the rule that in the case of lost or stolen chattels *A* prevails over *C*, both codes protect *C*, the bona fide purchaser, where the chattel is a bearer security. It should be noted,

however, that if *A* discovers the loss or theft in time, he can (in most civil-law countries) have the numbers of the lost or stolen securities published in an official gazette. A purchaser who acquires a bearer security after such publication, may be precluded from asserting good faith. See, e.g., § 367 of the German Commercial Code.

33. Most of the codes spell out the requirement of good faith. In France, where the elegant but cryptic phrasing of Art. 2279 c.c. ("En fait de meubles, la possession vaut titre") leaves the point in doubt, the courts have read the requirement into the Code.

34. See Kaser, supra n. 8, at 342.

34a. See nn. 31 and 32 supra.

To overcome some of the difficulties created by these differences, and also by the divergencies between the civil-law and the common-law approaches to the problem, the International Institute for the Unification of Private Law has proposed an international convention. See Unidroit, Draft Convention Providing a Uniform Law on the Acquisition in Good Faith of Corporeal Movables (1975). A helpful explanatory report by Professor Sauveplanne forms part of that publication.

these questions, it had—while making considerable use of ancient building-blocks—constructed an essentially new building, a building somewhat similar to, and yet distinct from, the edifices created by the code architects of other nations.[35]

Having studied these illustrations, which may be taken as typical,[36] the reader can form his own judgment concerning the relative strength of the traditional and the innovating thoughts which interacted in the minds of the codifiers. On one point, however, there can be no reasonable difference of opinion: The old adage, all-too-frequently repeated, that the civilian codes presently in force are merely a modernized version of Roman law, is simply nonsense. In many respects, the solutions adopted by the codifiers were not traditional; and of the traditional ones, many were not Roman.[37] Professor Reginald Parker was probably right when he said: "I seriously believe it would not be difficult to establish, if such a thing could be statistically approached, that the majority of legal institutes, even within the confines of private law, of a given civil law country are not necessarily of Roman origin." [38]

It should be remembered, moreover, that classical Roman law "was never codified in a modern sense, and is, therefore, in many respects more similar to common-law sources than to a civil code".[39] Indeed, it has been shown by an imposing array of evidence that in its basic law-making methods, and also in many particulars, classical Roman law is closer to the common law than to the modern civilian codes.[40]

Some of the institutions of Roman law which were eliminated from the civil law by the codifiers, have survived in the Anglo-American system, especially on the equity side. Our pretrial discovery, for instance, is directly traceable to Roman and Canon law.[41] Corresponding devices in modern continental systems of procedure are much weaker.[42] Every international practitioner knows that the existence, under our law, of potent devices for the extraction of factual information from an unwilling opponent, and the non-existence or weakness of

35. The draftsmen of the Italian Civil Code of 1942, one of the most recent civilian codes, went further and discarded all of the traditional approaches. They fashioned an original solution (Arts. 1153–57), according to which the bona fide purchaser (C) acquires good title regardless of whether A's loss of possession was voluntary or involuntary. For application, see Winkworth v. Christie Manson and Woods, Ltd., [1980] Ch. 496.

36. For further illustrations see supra pp. 272–273. See also the next-following footnote.

Yet another instructive illustration, relating to transfer of ownership and risk in sales, can be found in A. Watson, Legal Transplants—An Approach to Comparative Law 82–87 (1974).

37. In addition to the examples already given, the following have been mentioned as institutions found in the modern codes but non-existent or only primitively developed in Roman law: assignability of claims; negotiability of instruments; and

the law of agency. See Parker, Book Review, 42 Cornell L.Q. 448–9 (1957).

With respect to the law of agency, the reader will be able to verify the correctness of Professor Parker's statement when he studies the materials which appear infra at pp. 768–775.

38. Parker, ibid.

39. Ehrenzweig, A Common Language of World Jurisprudence, 12 U. of Chi.L. Rev. 285, 289 (1945).

40. See Pringsheim, The Inner Relationship Between English and Roman Law, 5 Camb.L.J. 347 (1935); Moses, International Legal Practice, 4 Fordh.L.Rev. 244, 253–5 (1935).

For a brief discussion of the successive waves of Romanist influence on English law see supra p. 263 ff.

41. See Millar, The Mechanism of Fact Discovery: A Study in Comparative Civil Procedure, 32 Ill.L.Rev. 261, 424 (1937).

42. See infra pp. 426–428.

such devices in civil-law countries, constitutes one of the significant facts of life in international litigation. Where choice is possible between a civil-law and a common-law forum, this procedural difference will loom large in the parties' strategic planning. The difference exists because the influence of the Roman *interrogatio* and the canonical *positio* remained unbroken through centuries of discovery practice in chancery and admiralty,[43] while the draftsmen of the classical continental codes, seeking to protect individual privacy, consciously abolished or weakened the older devices for discovery.[43a]

On the other hand, the civil law has remained more Roman than the common law in its terminology and in its techniques of conceptualization and classification. Without Roman terms and concepts, and without the wealth of illustrative material found in the practical solutions devised by the Roman jurists, the progressive systematization of the civil law at the hands of glossators, commentators, humanists, natural law scholars and pandectists would not have been possible. It is the continental jus commune thus developed over the centuries, and its influence upon the codes, together with the method of codification itself, which has preserved the "civil-law systems" as an identifiable group, a group which (except in the case of some mixed systems) is clearly set apart from the common-law family.

(2) Up to this point, we have attempted to assess the role which traditional and non-traditional elements played in the thinking of the codifiers. Now we turn to the related but distinct question of the extent to which the single, dramatic event of codification marked a break with the pre-code past for the generations of lawyers who in the various civil-law countries have practiced, and are still practicing, under the codes.

The answer to this latter question is relatively simple. In each of the countries of the seminal codes, codification meant not only national unification, comprehensive revision, and intensive restructuring of the whole body of private, criminal and procedural law,[44] but also the enactment of a new and authoritative text.[45] In order to accomplish all

---

43. The civil-law origin of discovery was stressed by Story, J., in Sherwood v. Hall, 3 Sumn. 127, Fed.Cas. No. 12,777 (1837), and again by Jackson, J., concurring in Hickman v. Taylor, 329 U.S. 495, 515, 67 S.Ct. 385, 396 (1947). See also Millar, Civil Procedure of the Trial Court in Historical Perspective 201–2 (1952).

43a. Only most recently, and with considerable caution, have civil-law legislators taken steps to strengthen their discovery devices. See infra pp. 426–428.

44. The public law of the civil-law countries, and especially their administrative law, developed in a different manner. It has never been comprehensively codified. The French system of administrative law has been created essentially by case law (see infra pp. 502 ff.), while in Germany the subject was first systematized by legal scholars. Over the years, there has been a tremendous increase in the number of statutes dealing with administrative law; in

some countries, especially in Germany, these statutes tend to become more and more systematic. Nevertheless, it remains true that private law, criminal law, and civil as well as criminal procedure are truly codified in civil-law countries but that public law (except for constitutional law) is not.

45. The last-mentioned aspect of codification is not a mere technical matter of legal method. Civilians are apt to regard complete codification of the law as an important bulwark against official (especially judicial) arbitrariness. See Schlesinger, The Uniform Commercial Code in the Light of Comparative Law, 1 Inter-American L.Rev. 11, 19–21 (1959). This attitude is particularly strong in France, where in pre-revolutionary times the judiciary had been guilty not only of corruption but also of usurpation and abuse of law-making powers. See supra p. 266.

of these objectives of codification, it was imperative, in applying the codes, to treat their provisions as the exclusive source of binding authority, subject only to legislative amendment, and not to let the old law slink back under any pretense.

In some of the early attempts at codification, especially the Prussian Code (Preussisches allgemeines Landrecht) of 1794, the draftsmen tried to provide specific rules for every conceivable fact situation, and expressly prohibited the courts from amplifying those rules by "interpretation". Although the Prussian Code was a document of excessive length, containing many thousands of sections, it turned out soon after its enactment that there were fact situations which had not been foreseen by the draftsmen and which, consequently, were not covered by the provisions of the Code.[46] The primitive method by which the Prussian draftsmen had sought to secure their Code's status as the exclusive source of law, thus clearly failed.

The methods by which 19th century codifiers sought to accomplish the same purpose, were less direct but more sophisticated. Many of the 19th century civil codes contain explicit directions enumerating the subsidiary sources of law (e.g., analogy, customs, natural law) to be used in cases not covered by the substantive provisions of the Code.[47] Thus, in theory at least, it can be maintained that the courts resort to these other sources only by virtue of the Code's own mandate, and that within the scope of its subject-matter the Code governs the disposition of a case even when its substantive provisions are silent. Moreover— and this is of still greater significance—modern codes seek to cover a wide range of unforeseen fact situations by way of substantive provisions of utmost generality and flexibility. These so-called "general clauses" of the codes may provide, for instance, that all immoral transactions are void, or that every obligation must be performed in good faith.[48] Thus, even when faced with a novel and unforeseen case, and fashioning what in effect may be a new solution, a civil-law court as a rule purports merely to "interpret" and "apply" a provision— though perhaps a broadly worded one—of the Code.

This theoretical adherence to the ideal of a comprehensive Code, supposedly constituting the exclusive source of law in a broadly defined area of the legal order, did not prevent the courts in civil-law countries from developing decisional law.[49] But the fact that now, in contrast to pre-code days, judicial law-making as well as scholarly exposition almost invariably had to be masked as mere "interpretation" of a text of unquestionable authority, and had to be fitted into the structural framework of the Code, nevertheless produced important practical consequences.

In every civil-law country, codification had a profound effect on legal education and legal literature. The curricula of the law faculties had to be reshaped, and new textbooks and treatises had to be prepared, in order to adjust them to the systematic arrangement and the substantive innovations of the codes.[50] Gradually, as it was replaced by more

46. For further discussion of this point see infra pp. 624–625.

47. See infra pp. 651–653.

48. For extensive materials concerning the function of these general clauses in

modern civil-law systems, see infra pp. 567 ff., 702 ff.

49. See infra pp. 597–657.

50. Practitioners in code countries are thoroughly familiar with the arrangement

current tools, the pre-code legal literature thus lost its practical value for lawyers and law students.

There was a steep decline, also, in the courts' reliance on pre-code authorities. It is true that in some code countries this decline was less abrupt than might have been expected. So long as members of the generation learned and experienced in pre-code law wielded controlling influence on Bench and Bar, judicial decisions continued to refer to pre-code authorities, sometimes in open defiance of code provisions specifying the sources of law which should, or should not, be resorted to.[50a] But as the post-code generations of law students, brought up on code-oriented lectures and teaching tools, moved into the judicial and other branches of the profession, pre-code authorities were virtually forgotten.[51] Even in scholarly writings, insofar as they dealt with existing law,[52] references to pre-code developments became less and less frequent.

It is in this sense that we can speak of the code systems' break with the past. This break occurred in virtually every civil-law country. Depending on political circumstances, however, there were considerable differences from nation to nation regarding the timing, and the degree of abruptness, of the change. In France, the five basic codes were enacted in rapid succession at the beginning of the 19th century. In Germany, codification on a national scale took place during the latter part of the 19th century, and in a much more gradual manner. The first of the basic codes, adopted by the great majority of the German states during the 1860s before the advent of political unification of the Reich, was the Commercial Code.[53] It was followed in the 1870s by the Penal Code and the two procedural codes; but the Civil Code, although preparatory work on it started in 1874, was not enacted until 1896, and went into effect January 1, 1900.[54]

[handwritten margin notes: Germany · B&B · 1871 unified under Bismark]

of their codes, and thus find it convenient to use tools which closely follow that arrangement. In some parts of the civil-law world, especially in Germany and German-influenced countries, the most popular research tool of lawyers and judges is the code "commentary". As has been mentioned before, the leading commentaries are not merely annotated text editions, but constitute elaborate treatises, which offer thorough discussion as well as massive references, following in each instance the relevant code sections. This type of legal exposition is readily traced to the Commentators of fourteenth-century Italy (supra p. 270) who in turn followed the style of classical Roman jurists' commentaries on the Praetorian edict.

50a. In France, this was facilitated by the publication, immediately after codification, of code editions which in effect were concordances of code provisions and pre-existing law (Roman law, customs, statutes etc.). See, e.g., H. J. B. Dard, Code Napoléon, avec des notes indicatives des Lois Romaines, Coutumes, Ordonnances, Édits et Déclarations qui ont rapport à chaque arti-cle (1808). But legal tools of this kind soon became obsolete, and were replaced by treatises and other literary aids wholly based on the Code itself, and reflecting *its* interpretation by scholars and courts.

51. Legal authors occasionally report an instance in which a modern court referred to a pre-code authority. See, e.g., David and DeVries, The French Legal System 93 (1958). The rare and exceptional nature of such instances, however, confirms the fact that resort to pre-code authorities is not a routine technique in civil-law countries.

52. Legal history, of course, remained a subject of academic teaching and research in civil-law countries even after codification. But in the late 19th and early 20th century the work of the legal historians, though on a high level of scholarship, became an academic specialty totally removed from legal practice. See supra n. 8 and infra pp. 294–295.

53. See Lorenz, supra n. 1.

54. For details and further references see Lorenz, ibid.

The Remaining Enclaves of Uncodified Civil Law

It was stated above that codification, and the consequent break with the past, occurred "in virtually every civil law country". There are a few—very few—exceptions.* Scotland [1] preserved its civil-law system in uncodified form.[2] The Roman-Dutch law of South Africa,[3] Sri Lanka (formerly Ceylon),[4] and British Guiana [5] equally resisted the trend toward codification.[6] As a result we find that a case coming up in a Scottish or South-African court today may turn on the interpretation of a passage from Justinian's Corpus Juris,[7] or from the works of an authoritative 17th century writer.[8]

The principality of Andorra is another jurisdiction—this one in continental Europe—where uncodified civil law has remained in force

* The substantive law of pre-communist *Hungary* was only partly codified, and the gaps in the written law were filled by customary law and by judicial decisions; the opinions of the highest court sitting en banc were binding on all courts. See Zajtay, Introduction à l'étude du droit Hongrois (1953); A. Csizmadia, Hungarian Customary Law Before the Bourgeois Rebellion of 1848, 4 J. Legal Hist. 3 (1983); von Szladits, "Ungarn", in 1 Rechtsvergleichendes Handwoerterbuch fuer das Zivil- und Handelsrecht des In- und Auslandes 276–86 (1929). Therefore, Hungary had to be counted among the exceptions (civil law without a civil code) so long as it belonged to the civil-law orbit. Today, its legal system reflects its position as a member of the socialist bloc. See infra pp. 328–29. In 1959, Hungarian private law was codified. See Wagner, Some Comments on the Legal Systems of Communist Countries, With Particular Reference to the Law of Contracts, in 1 Schlesinger (Gen. Ed.), Formation of Contracts—A Study of the Common Core of Legal Systems 213, at 218–19 (1968).

1. For information on the Scottish legal system see, e.g., T. B. Smith, Scotland: The Development of Its Laws and Constitution (1962); A. Watson, Legal Transplants—An Approach to Comparative Law 44–56 (1974).

2. In varying degrees, both Roman-Dutch law and Scots law have been subjected to an infiltration of common law rules and common law techniques. See the writings cited supra n. 1 and infra n. 3. See also infra p. 320.

3. The law of South Africa "still breathes the spirit" of the reception of Roman law. Beinart, Roman Law in South African Practice, 69 So.Afr.L.J. 145, 151 (1952).

For further references, see Dannenbring, Heutiges römisch-holländisches Recht—

Vom Privatrecht der Republik Südafrika, 6 ZfRV 56 (1965); Leyser, Some Comments on the South African Legal System, with Particular Reference to the Law of Contracts, in 1 Schlesinger (Gen.Ed.), Formation of Contracts—A Study of the Common Core of Legal Systems 321 (1968); H. R. Hahlo & E. Kahn, The South African Legal System and Its Background (1968); R. W. Lee, The Roman-Dutch Law in South Africa: The Influence of English Law, 1 Colombo L.Rev. 1 (1969).

4. See Jennings and Tambiah, The Dominion of Ceylon—The Development of Its Laws and Constitution 179 ff. (1952); T. B. Smith, Studies Critical and Comparative XXIX–XXXII (1962); 1 Weeramantry, The Law of Contracts 23–68 (1967); T. Nadaraja, The Legal System of Ceylon in Its Historical Setting (1972); L. M. J. Cooray, The Reception of Roman-Dutch Law in Ceylon, 7 Comp. & Int'l J.So.Afr. 295 (1974).

5. See supra pp. 245–253. On various civil-law (not only Roman-Dutch) influences persisting in the area, see also Patchett, Some Aspects of Marriage and Divorce in the West Indies, 8 Int.Comp.L.Q. 632, 633 (1959).

6. All three of these territories formerly were Dutch colonies; but they were politically separated from the Netherlands prior to the codification of Dutch law. See supra p. 247.

Concerning the interaction of common law and civil law in these countries, see the authorities cited in ns. 3–5 supra. See also infra p. 320.

7. See, e.g., Cantiere San Rocco S.A. v. The Clyde Shipbuilding & Engineering Co., Ltd., [1923] S.C. (H.L.) 105, as well as the delightful case of Mustard v. Patterson, (1923) Sess.Cas. 142.

8. See supra pp. 245–253; Glazer v. Glazer, [1963(4)] S.A.L.R. 694.

Have percise definition of common law and civil law.

to this day.[8a] In the decisions (including recent decisions) of the courts of Andorra, many references to Roman law and Canon law can be found.[8b] In some respects, the law of Andorra is similar to that of neighboring Catalonia. In this connection, the reader will recall (see supra p. 236) that Catalonia is one of those Spanish provinces where pre-code customs (*fueros*) have been preserved as the primary source of law, and where the national Civil Code governs only those issues of private law that are not covered by such customs.

The Meaning of "Codification" *

In the vast majority of civil-law countries, the bulk of private, penal and procedural law is enshrined in codes. For the historical reasons explained on previous pages, the codes were intended to be authoritative, systematic *and comprehensive* statements of the law on each of these subjects.

The feature of comprehensiveness is particularly striking in the procedural codes. In the area of substantive private law, the codifiers provided for flexibility and future growth by incorporating a certain number of broad, elastic formulations into the codes themselves (see supra p. 288 and infra pp. 702 ff.). The adjective codes, however, are meant to be essentially all-inclusive statements of judicial powers, remedies and procedural devices.

In common law jurisdictions, too, procedure is generally "codified";[9] but the continued influence of the unwritten law is preserved by statutory safety valves such as § 140–b of the New York Judiciary Law which provides that "The general jurisdiction in law and equity which the supreme court [of the state] possesses under the provisions of the constitution includes all the jurisdiction which was possessed and exercised by the supreme court of the colony of New York at any time, and by the court of chancery in England on the 4th day of July, 1776;. . . . ." Such reference to the powers which in bygone days the courts possessed by virtue of their own pronouncements at law and in

---

8a. See B. Bélinguier, La condition juridique des Vallées d'Andorre 9 (1970); J. Anglada Vilardebo, Andorra, in Int.Enc. Comp.L., Vol. I, pp. A29–32 (1970); A. H. Angelo, Andorra: Introduction to a Customary Legal System, 14 Am.J.Leg.Hist. 95 (1970).

8b. See P. Ourliac (Ed.), La Jurisprudence Civile d'Andorre (1972), a collection of decisions handed down by the highest court of Andorra between 1947 and 1970, with annotations by the editor.

* In later chapters of this book, when dealing with present-day legal phenomena, many characteristics of code law in civilian systems will be explored. At this point, no more is intended than to take a first look, from a comparative and historical perspective, at one of the features of a codified system.

For comparative studies of more comprehensive scope, see S. A. Bayitch, Codifica-tion in Modern Times, in A. N. Yianno-poulos (Ed.), Civil Law in the Modern World 161 (1965); W. J. Wagner, Codifica-tion of Law in Europe and the Codification Movement in the Middle of the Nineteenth Century in the United States, 2 St. Louis Un.L.J. 335 (1953).

9. In the United States, the codification movement is a nineteenth-century phe-nomenon, heavily influenced by Bentham. David Dudley Field was the most impor-tant protagonist of that movement, but not its originator. See D. Van Ee, David Dud-ley Field and the Reconstruction of the Law (1986); C. M. Cook, The American Codification Movement, A Study in Ante-bellum Legal Reform (1981). Field was familiar with the leading civilian codes. See the article by W. J. Wagner cited in the preceding footn., at 349.

equity, makes us feel that at least some of such powers are "inherent" and quite independent of any statute.[10]

For the continental lawyer it is hard to understand that judicial powers and remedies can exist without an express basis in the written law.[10a] This becomes apparent, for example, in cases in which civilian courts are asked to enforce American judgments.[11] Many countries, including a number of civil-law jurisdictions, enforce foreign judgments only on condition of reciprocity. Therefore, if a New York judgment is sought to be enforced in Ruritania, the Ruritanian court probably will examine the question whether a New York court in the converse case would enforce a Ruritanian judgment. Actually, as we know, the anwer to this latter question has long been in the affirmative, because for more than half a century New York has recognized foreign-country judgments as ordinarily conclusive.[12] This liberal New York rule, however, originally was a creature of decisional law, and until 1970 was not embodied in the CPLR (Civil Practice Law and Rules) or any other statute.[12a] Thus prior to 1970 it could happen, and in practice it did happen,[13] that the court in Ruritania (a civil-law jurisdiction), having carefully examined the pertinent New York "code", inferred from its silence that New York had made *no* provision for the enforcement of foreign judgments.[14] The result of such a mistaken inference was that prior to 1970 New York judgments were refused enforcement in Ruritania under the Ruritanian reciprocity rule,[15] although as a matter of fact Ruritanian judgments were routinely enforced in New York.

To remedy this situation, the Commissioners on Uniform State Laws proposed, and New York as well as a number of other states

---

10. See R. Dale Vliet, The Inherent Power of Oklahoma Courts and Judges, 6 Okla.L.Rev. 257 (1953). The list of inherent powers presented in that article would make a civilian rub his eyes in disbelief. For other examples see, e.g., Ochs v. Washington Heights Federal Savings & Loan Ass'n, 17 N.Y.2d 82, 268 N.Y.S.2d 294, 215 N.E.2d 485 (1966); Matter of Steinway, 159 N.Y. 250, 53 N.E. 1103 (1899); Cf. Petition of Petrol Shipping Corp., 360 F.2d 103 (2d Cir. 1966), cert. denied 385 U.S. 931, 87 S.Ct. 291 (1966).

10a. The one, highly exceptional and much-commented-on example of a judge-made remedy in the civil law is the French *astreinte.* See infra p. 669. Recently, however, even this lonely example has disappeared; in 1972, the *astreinte* was given a statutory basis.

11. See Kulzer, The Uniform Foreign Money-Judgments Recognition Act, in the Thirteenth Annual Report of the Judicial Conference of the State of New York, Leg. Doc. (1968) No. 90, at 194 ff.; Nadelmann, Non-Recognition of American Money Judgments Abroad and What to Do About It, 42 Iowa L.Rev. 236 (1957); id., Reprisals Against American Judgments?, 65 Harv.L. Rev. 1184 (1952); id., The United States of America and Agreements on Reciprocal Enforcement of Foreign Judgments, 1 Nederlands Tijdschrift Voor International Recht 156, 158-9 (1954).

12. Johnston v. Compagnie Generale Transatlantique, 242 N.Y. 381, 152 N.E. 121 (1926); Cowans v. Ticonderoga Pulp & Paper Co., 219 App.Div. 120, 219 N.Y.S. 284 (3d Dep't 1927), aff'd on opinion below 246 N.Y. 603, 159 N.E. 669 (1927).

12a. In 1970, New York adopted the Uniform Foreign Money-Judgments Recognition Act (see infra n. 16) as Art. 53 of its CPLR.

13. See Nadelmann, supra n. 11; J. T. Clare, Enforcement of Foreign Judgments in Spain, 9 Int.Lawyer 509, 514 (1975).

14. The more sophisticated courts in civil-law countries seem to understand that in a common-law jurisdiction a foreign judgment may be enforceable although the "code" is silent on the point. See the September 30, 1964, decision of the German BGH reported in NJW 1964, 2350. Proof of reciprocity in the absence of statute may, however, be prohibitively expensive if, e.g., the pertinent decisional materials have to be formally certified in translation.

15. See Nadelmann, supra n. 11.

enacted, the Uniform Foreign Money-Judgments Recognition Act.[16] As the Commissioners pointed out in their Prefatory Note, the Act merely "states rules that have long been applied by the majority of courts in this country."[17] The purpose of the Act is simply to ease the burden of a litigant who, in seeking enforcement abroad of an American judgment, may have to inform the foreign court of the rules which would be applied here in a converse case.[18] The Act, in other words, owes its very existence to the sponsors' recognition of the fact that courts in civil-law countries find it difficult to comprehend the notion of procedural common-law rules surviving the enactment of a "code" of procedure.

As the example shows, the very meaning of the word "code" depends on whether it is used by civilians or by lawyers brought up in the common-law tradition. In the eyes of the latter a code is supplemental to the unwritten law, and in construing its provisions and filling its gaps, resort must be had to the common law.[19] Though perhaps gradually changing,[20] this attitude is still dominant in the common-law world. To the civilian, on the other hand, a code is a comprehensive, and in the area of procedure often an all-inclusive, statement of the law.[21] In its interpretation, the court is always conscious of the interrelation of all the provisions contained in the whole code, and indeed in the entire code system. The intention of the legislator, where

---

16. 13 ULA 261 (1986). In addition to New York, fifteen other states (including California, Illinois, Michigan, and Texas) have adopted the Act. See Fairchild, Arabatzis & Smith v. Prometco (Prod. & Metals), 470 F.Supp. 610 (S.D.N.Y. 1979).

17. Ibid.

18. See Prefatory Note, ibid. The Massachusetts and Texas variants of the Act contain the requirement of reciprocity, but in Texas, the judgment debtor has the burden of showing the *lack* of reciprocity. Hunt v. BP Exploration Co. (Libya) Ltd. (II), 580 F.Supp. 304 (N.D.Tex. 1984). The formulation of the reciprocity requirement in the Texas variant was chosen in order to allay doubt abroad as to the readiness of Texas to recognize foreign-country decisions. The draftsman failed in his attempt to exclude the reciprocity requirement entirely.

19. For an instructive discussion of codification in common-law jurisdictions, see Patterson, The Codification of Commercial Law in the Light of Jurisprudence, 1955 Report of the New York Law Revision Commission at pp. 41, 67–74, N.Y.Leg.Doc. (1955) No. 65–A, pp. 11, 37–44. Professor Patterson calls attention to § 5 of the California Civil Code, which expressly provides: "The provisions of this code, so far as they are substantially the same as existing statutes or the common law, must be construed as continuations thereof, and not as new enactments." Concerning the supplementary nature of the California Civil Code, see also Harrison, The First Half-Century of the California Civil Code, 10

Calif.L.Rev. 185 (1922); Van Alstyne, The California Civil Code, in West's Anno.California Codes, Civil Code, Sections 1 to 192, pp. 1 ff. (1954). See generally E. Bodenheimer, Is Codification an Outmoded Form of Legislation? 30 Am.J.Comp.L. (Supplement) 15, 16–18 (1982).

20. See W. J. Wagner, Codification of Law in Europe and the Codification Movement in the Middle of the Nineteenth Century in the United States, 2 St. Louis L.J. 335, 358–59 (1953).

In the United Kingdom, there was a period in the late 1960s when the English and Scottish Law Commissions appeared to pull in the direction of civilian-style codification of the law of contracts. See Chloros, Principle, Reason and Policy in the Development of European Law, 17 Int. & Comp. L.Q. 849, especially at 863–4 (1968). More recently, however, much of the momentum towards such codification has been lost, even though the meaning of the term "code" continues to be debated. See J. H. Farrar, Law Reform and the Law Commission 37–39, 57–62 (1974).

21. Even in the field of adjective law, civilian judges will occasionally twist the language of the Code in order to avoid a shocking result; the pre-1972 French practice with respect to *astreintes* (see supra n. 10a) provides an example. But civilians always realize the anomalous and exceptional nature of such a development, and as a rule never dream of looking for a rule of procedure not derived from a written text.

it can be ascertained, will not be disregarded.[22] Primarily, however, code construction is grammatical, logical and teleological;[23] in any event, it is relatively free from historical reminiscences reaching back into the period prior to the preparation of the code.[24]

It stands to reason, therefore, that for the bread-and-butter purposes of the legal practitioner in a modern civil-law country, familiarity with the older history of his legal system is hardly necessary—certainly less necessary than for his common law colleague who even today may win a case by citations from the Year Books.[25]

Thus, at least at first blush, it may strike us as paradoxical that in most civil-law countries a law student has to take several compulsory courses on Roman Law and other historical subjects, while the great majority of his American confreres, whose legal system has never undergone a sharp break with the past, may graduate from law school without having taken any course in Legal History. Several explanations may be offered for this apparent paradox. First of all, law students in civil-law countries are what we would call "undergraduates" (see supra pp. 147 ff.); thus the lectures on Legal History attended by them may be comparable to certain college courses in the areas of history and government rather than to any part of the law school curriculum in the United States.[26] It should be noted, in

22. Resort to legislative materials is frequent in many civil-law countries, especially during the years when a code is relatively young, and other authoritative materials for the interpretation of ambiguous provisions are not yet available. The thorough preparation by high government officials, scholars and legislative committees which usually preceded the enactment of the modern codes, provides a civil-law court with valuable materials throwing light on the intention of the legislator. The German case, infra, p. 584, furnishes an illustration.

For a comparison of the techniques of drafting and initiating legislation in this country and in continental countries, see Cardozo, A Ministry of Justice, 35 Harv.L. Rev. 113 (1921), and, with particular reference to the preparation of codes, Schlesinger, The Uniform Commercial Code in the Light of Comparative Law, 1 Inter-Am. L.Rev. 11, at 27–31 (1959).

On methods of legislative drafting and law-making in France and Germany today, see W. Dale, Legislative Drafting: A New Approach 83–96, 106–16 (1977). As to the role of the French Conseil d'Etat in the law-making process, see also infra pp. 499–500.

23. The volume of scholarly writings on methods of code interpretation in civil-law systems is colossal. A classic account—indeed "the" classic account according to some scholars—is François Gény's Méthode d' interprétation et sources en droit privé positif (2d ed. 1919). An Eng-

lish translation of this work, prepared by Professor Jaro Mayda, was published under the auspices of the Louisiana State Law Institute in 1963. In Gény's own footnotes, and in Professor Mayda's elaborate Introduction, the reader will find massive further references.

For a brief discussion of French and German methods of statutory interpretation, see Dale, supra n. 22, at 298–303, 306–08.

24. See M. Franklin, The Historic Function of the American Law Institute: Restatement as Transitional to Codification, 47 Harv.L.Rev. 1367, 1377 (1934), quoted by the court in Shelp v. National Surety Corp., 333 F.2d 431, 435 (5th Cir. 1964); Patterson, op. cit. supra n. 19, N.Y.Leg. Doc. (1955) No. 65–A, at 31. See also supra p. 289.

25. See, e.g., Murphy v. Extraordinary Special and Trial Term of the Supreme Court, 294 N.Y. 440, 63 N.E.2d 49 (1945).

26. Moreover, continental legal education is more leisurely, and the theoretical and practical aspects of law study are more distinctly separated. A continental law student, who is certified to have completed his pre-law education at age 18 or 19, and whose legal education may take as long as seven years (typically four or five years of theoretical study and two or three years of apprenticeship), is not terribly rushed. Thus he will have more time than his American colleague to devote to "broadening" or "perspective" courses. (Whether the average continental law student actu-

[handwritten annotations in top margin: 30 years war — Protestants defeated Catholics / 1648 — ended peace of Westphalia / Demise of Holy Roman Empire / end of Feudal system / Rise of the Nation-state]

addition, that a student of the common law, reading through cases and other materials often stemming from former periods, absorbs a certain amount of historical knowledge even though he does not take a course labeled "Legal History." [27] The civilian, whose courses and textbooks on present-day law are code-centered and do not contain many references to pre-code developments, would find himself in a complete historical vacuum if he did not have the benefit of courses specially devoted to legal history. [28]

From the foregoing discussion, the reader may have concluded that historical studies are of limited "practical" value to a lawyer faced with problems arising under a modern civil-law system. History, however, provides important clues to an understanding of the differences between common law and civil law. To present and to analyze some of these clues, is the purpose of the materials on the next-following pages.

COMMON LAW AND CIVIL LAW—A HISTORICAL COMPARISON *

I. *Case Law and Code Law*

In his "History of the English Speaking Peoples", Winston Churchill again and again drives home an important point: the focal rôle which the common law played in the process by which England was welded into a nation. It was the common law which brought about national unification of England's legal system. Neither reception of a professorial "Roman" law nor subsequent codification was needed in England to unify the law on a national scale.

The historical processes by which the leading continental countries attained nationally unified law, differ in at least two respects from those to be observed in English history:

(1) In England, unification was accomplished by the *Bench and Bar* of a *powerful central court* which succeeded in gaining the respect of the nation. Although they represented the central Government, and wielded the tremendous power of judicial lawmaking which became the mainspring of the common law, the royal judges by preserving the jury system [1] were able to dispense the people's own justice. Judicial

---

ally attends these courses, and whether as a rule they are effectively taught, is another question. See supra pp. 164–179).

27. Whatever its title, a course dealing, e.g., with estates in land or with the law-equity dichotomy necessarily must reach back into centuries long past.

28. See Gorla, Book Review, 6 Rivista di Diritto Civile I 558, 561 (1960).

* One of the purposes of this essay is to review and summarize some of the most important points emerging from the preceding materials. The reader is warned, however, that in order to derive substantial benefit from this somewhat summary

discussion, he has to be familiar with the more detailed historical data presented above.

1. Of course, the ancient jury system underwent important changes; but these came about gradually and organically. See Millar, Civil Procedure of the Trial Court in Historical Perspective 20–23 (1952), and 1 Holdsworth, History of English Law 315 ff. (1956), where it is pointed out, also, that it was Roman-canonistic influence during the 12th and 13th centuries which eliminated the jury from civil procedure, and to a large extent from criminal procedure, in the continental countries.

arbitrariness was checked by the jury, and later by the rule of stare decisis.[2]

During the critical revolutionary period in English history, Bench and Bar of the common law courts successfully defended the law—their law, which they had created, and of which they were the institutional representatives—against the encroachments of the Stuart Kings. "The law", which was the matrix of the writs of habeas corpus, certiorari and mandamus, was perceived to favor the liberties of the subject during the constitutional crisis of the early seventeenth century.[3] In the eighteenth and nineteenth centuries, the common law courts were able to align themselves with the forces which transformed England from a feudal agricultural society into a commercial and industrial nation. England's legal institutions, still centered on a powerful and respected judiciary,[4] thus entered the modern age almost entirely without a violent break in continuity.[5]

Continental courts, by way of contrast, were unable to create nationally unified law. The reasons why no court on the continent attained the stature of the English Curia Regis, can be found in the divisive struggles between ecclesiastic and secular power, and between overlord sovereignty and local or regional independence which characterize the medieval period in continental history.[6] In the absence of authoritative precedents set by a powerful central court, lawyers and judges had to turn to other sources of authority. Roman law was favored as such a source not only by the Church, which had absorbed much of the Roman system into its Canon Law, but also by the Emperor who under the theory of "Continuous Empire" claimed to be the legitimate heir of Justinian's imperial power and who could but benefit from the Byzantine doctrine: that only a written text approved by the Ruler was "the law". Nor were the other kings and princes of

2. See Tunc, The Grand Outlines of the Code Napoleon, 29 Tulane L.Rev. 431 (1955).

3. Those courts, on the other hand, which did not follow the common law but operated without a jury and under the inquisitorial procedure imported from the continent (e.g., the Star Chamber) became the very symbols of oppression. English civil lawyers were tarred with the same brush. D. R. Coquillette, Legal Ideology and Incorporation I: The English Civilian Writers, 1523–1607, 61 B.U.L.Rev. 1, 77–86 (1981).

4. To this day, continental writers marvel at what many of them call the *Richterkoenigtum* (king-like stature of judges) prevailing in Anglo-American countries. See 2 W. Fikentscher, Methoden des Rechts 4–5 (1975). For an excellent comparative study, seeking to make the English system of administration of justice understandable to a continental audience, see

E. J. Cohn, Richter, Staat und Gesellschaft in England (Schriftenreihe der Juristichen Studiengesellschaft Karlsruhe No. 37/38, 1958).

5. Even the Commonwealth was less disruptive in this respect than might be thought. S. F. Black, The Courts and Judges of Westminster Hall During the Great Rebellion, 1640–1660, 7 J. Legal Hist. 23 (1986).

6. True, there were similar struggles in medieval England; but relatively soon after the Norman Conquest, and several centuries before the emergence of a strong and stable national government in any continental country, the English kings gained the upper hand in their political and military battles against the centrifugal forces. See A. R. Hogue, Origins of the Common Law 19, 57–64 (1966). Thus, almost from its beginning, the English Curia Regis had a political power base far stronger than that of any court on the continent.

Europe, much as their claims to power competed with those of the Emperor, averse to the absolutist implications of this doctrine, believed to be enshrined in the Corpus Juris.

The seat of Roman law learning was in the Universities. While in England the Bench and Bar of the common law courts provided for the professional training of young lawyers practicing before the secular tribunals,[7] the continental rulers had to turn to the law faculties to supply them with men trained to become judges, lawyers and administrators. The Universities, in exchange for generous charters and privileges, willingly complied, and turned out large numbers of *doctores* well versed in Latin and in Roman law. Thus it came about, as we have seen before,[8] that a Roman-influenced, university-taught and university-developed *jus commune* became dominant (although perhaps in varying degrees) in almost every part of the continent. This domination (the exact period of which, again, varies from country to country) lasted for several centuries, from the middle ages to the late 18th and early 19th century.

During this whole period, continental courts failed to play a leading role in the development and the national unification of the law. True enough, when sufficiently supported by the political power of the local potentate, certain courts were able, for limited periods of time, to attract eminent men to the judiciary and under their leadership to assert real influence.[9] But this influence, while perhaps not strictly confined to the court's own territory, always remained relatively short-lived. The university still retained the monopoly of instructing the fledgling lawyers, and in their lectures and writings the professors paid scant attention to the decisions of contemporary courts. When they needed practical examples to illustrate their points, they generally preferred the rich casuistry of classical Roman law—i.e., disputes the facts of which had occurred about a thousand years earlier—over the cases decided in their own time.

Continental courts, moreover, never gained the prestige necessary for sustained leadership in the development of the law. By their Roman-canonistic, inquisitorial procedure,[10] by their failure to fashion legal remedies against official oppression,[11] and by their frequent ob-

---

7. See Radcliffe and Cross, The English Legal System 387–90 (6th ed. by Hand and Bentley, 1977); Chroust, The Legal Profession During the Middle Ages: The Emergence of the English Lawyer Prior to 1400, 31 Notre Dame Law. 537, especially at 579–81 (1956).

8. See supra pp. 255–275.

9. As an example one might mention the Supreme Court, also called Senate, of Piedmont and Savoy during part of the 17th and 18th centuries. See the fascinating studies by Gorla, I "Grandi Tribunali" italiani fra i secoli XVI–XIX: un capitolo incompiuto della storia politico-giuridica d'Italia, published in Quaderni del Foro Italiano (1969), and Die Bedeutung der Präzedenzentscheidungen der Senate von Piemont und Savoyen im 18. Jahrhundert, in Ius Privatum Gentium—Festschrift für Max Rheinstein 103 ff. (1969). See also G. Gorla & L. Moccia, A "Revisiting" of the Comparison Between "Continental Law" and "English Law" (16th–19th Century), 2 J. Legal Hist. 143 (1981).

10. See supra n. 1.

11. Frequently, the courts themselves were instruments of oppression. See, e.g., supra p. 266.

future civil law countries lost respect.

struction to reforms desired by their own governments,[12] they lost popular support and respect.[13] In France, in particular, they became identified with the hated *ancien régime*, and with it were swept away in the French Revolution. The Revolution, at the same time, released strong feelings of nationalism. New national law and new democratic (or at least non-feudal) courts had to be created.[14] They were created *by legislation*. Not a court, but a code became the instrument and symbol of the national unification of law in continental countries. Historically, therefore, it is true, though perhaps an over-simplified truth, that the common law postulates a law created by the courts, while to the civilian the court is merely a creature of legislated law.[15]

Compare

(2) Another significant difference between the English and the continental way of attaining nationally unified legal systems becomes apparent if we consider the time element.

The growth of the common law has been a slow, gradual process which has continued from the time of William the Conqueror to this day. The institutions of the common law, therefore, bear the imprint of many different ages. Each of the modern continental legal systems, on the other hand, was shaped into a nationally unified structure at one stroke, by a more or less revolutionary act of codification.[16] Each code, consequently, breathes the spirit of the particular age in which it was born.

The influential codes of France (1804) and of Austria (1811) were products of the age of enlightenment and of rationalism. That was an era which extolled reason over tradition. Reasonable rather than traditional solutions were sought by the draftsmen of the codes. True, the draftsmen were learned in, and greatly influenced by, the laws and

---

12. See Riesenfeld, The French System of Administrative Justice, 18 B.U.L.Rev. 48, at 56 (1938), where further references can be found.

13. In Germany, the "Doctores" and their Latin jurisprudence always were felt to be a foreign-imported, non-German element. The importance of this factor is a matter of scholarly controversy. Probably it was the academic flavor of Pandectist law, and its inadequate procedure, rather than its foreign origin, which made it objectionable.

14. In other European countries, outside of France, the development was less violent and less abrupt (see the article by Deák and Rheinstein, reprinted supra); but the direction was the same. It must be remembered, moreover, that Napoleon's armies carried much of the spirit of the French Revolution across vast stretches of the continent.

15. Viewed from a purely logical standpoint, this may sound like the story of the chicken and the egg. But logical or not, these historically conditioned attitudes are

very real forces in a society. They produce important practical effects, of which the relatively modest social standing and the low rate of compensation of judges in many civil law countries may be mentioned as examples.

16. Even in countries such as Prussia and Austria, where codification was not preceded by political revolution in the ordinary sense of the word, the codes of the late 18th and early 19th century were the result of a "revolution at the top", i.e., a revolution in the thinking of the rulers. See Thieme, Das Naturrecht und die europaeische Privatrechtsgeschichte, especially 17–18, 38–43 (2nd ed. 1954), where the influence of natural-law philosophy upon the great continental codifications is traced and discussed. For a more general discussion of the intellectual and political forces responsible for the emergence and continuing importance of codes in many legal systems, see M. Damaska, On Circumstances Favoring Codification, 52 Rev. Jur.U.P.R. 355 (1983).

legal writings of the pre-code period (see supra pp. 276–287); but traditional solutions which did not stand the test of reason, as seen in the light of the political and social views prevailing at the time, were eliminated without regret. The codes which thus emerged, were no mere restatements but important vehicles of innovation.

The very idea of codification rests on the sanguine 18th century belief in the ability of the human mind by its reason to project the solution of future controversies, and to do so in a systematic and comprehensive manner. The great legal compilations of older periods, including Justinian's *Corpus Juris*, the *Siete Partidas* and the German *Sachsenspiegel*, had been restatements rather than codes. It remained for rulers and lawyers who understood the philosophy of rationalism, the teachings of the French Revolution and the practical needs of the 19th century to develop the technique of a true code, i.e., of a systematic, authoritative and direction-giving statute of broad coverage, breathing the spirit of reform and marking a new start in the legal life of an entire nation. This *technique* is still part of the civilian mentality, even in those civil-law countries in which the codes' *positive provisions*, adopted or revised at a later date, reflect philosophies of more recent vintage.

II. Differences in Classification—The Great Dichotomies

The common law had grown into a system at a time when men's ideas about law were still encased within rigid formulas. The eternal need for flexibility had to be met, at least in part, outside of "the law"; and this function was taken over by the Court of Chancery. The latter Court also served a political purpose by becoming a seat of countervailing power, used by the King as an antidote to the power of the common law courts. Thus originated the division between law and equity which is still one of the outstanding features of Anglo-American law.

On the continent, there was no central court possessing such independent power and prestige as to provoke the creation of another central court intended to constitute an antidotal or countervailing instrument of judicial power. Furthermore, we must again remember that modern civil law, i.e., code law, is essentially a product of the last two centuries, a period sufficiently free from ancient formalism so that the draftsmen of the codes have been able to combine both strict rules of law and broad equitable principles in a single unified structure.[17] Thus, no need was felt for a separate system of equity courts and of equity jurisprudence. The result is that the law—equity division is unknown in modern civil law.[18]

17. The broad, general provisions, inserted into the codes in order to assure flexibility and to provide for unforeseen and unforeseeable situations (see supra pp. 287–288 and infra pp. 702–766), constitute the modern civil law counterpart of many of our "equitable" doctrines.

18. This in spite of the fact that in classical Roman law there co-existed two bodies of law and of institutions which bore

On the other hand, and again for reasons which only history can explain, civilian thinking is completely dominated by two great dichotomies—dichotomies which, though not unknown to us, traditionally play a much more limited role in common-law systems.

In a civilian mind, all law is automatically divided into private law and public law. This dichotomy, recognized by Ulpian (d. 223 A.D.) and reflected in Justinian's digest (Dig. 1, 1, 1, 2) was never questioned by Roman law scholars from Irnerius to Savigny and was left intact by the codifiers. Its direct effect was drastic: Civil lawyers concentrated on *private* law, and neglected public law (except for criminal law and procedure). Public law came into its own in the sixteenth century; public-law text collections and treatises started appearing in the seventeenth century, and public-law chairs were established at Continental universities even more recently.[18a] Constitutional and administrative law, as discrete subjects of academic study, date from the nineteenth century.

The codes, if anything, deepened the chasm between the two spheres of the law, by reshaping private law in codified form, while leaving public law (except constitutional law, criminal law and procedure)[19] in its generally uncodified condition. It must be noted, moreover, that some important civilian countries live under a federal system of government. When such a country in accordance with constitutional provisions enacts a *national* civil code (such as the codes of Germany, Switzerland and Brazil), it thereby federalizes its private law, while a large part of its public law necessarily remains state law. This, again, adds emphasis to the dichotomy between public and private law.[20]

From a practical standpoint, the great importance of the dichotomy lies in its jurisdictional aspect. Under the influence of Montesquieu's doctrine of separation of powers, and, more specifically, in reaction to the interference of the French *parlements* with Royal reforms, it has become an established principle in most continental countries that—

a striking resemblance to English "law" and "equity". See Pringsheim, The Inner Relationship Between English and Roman Law, 5 Camb.L.J. 347, 357 (1935).

18a. See H. Gross, Empire and Sovereignty, A History of the Public Law Literature in the Holy Roman Empire, 1599–1804 (1975); D. Wydunckel, Ius Publicum (1984), and the contributions and discussions in R. Schnur, Ed., Die Rolle der Juristen bei der Enstehung des Modernen Staates (1986).

19. Some continental scholars, especially in Germany, contend that even Civil Procedure belongs to the sphere of public law, because procedural law essentially regulates the relationship between the parties, on the one hand, and the court (i.e., an organ of the state), on the other. The question is controversial among academicians. It may become of practical significance under a federal constitution listing "private law" as one of the subjects of national legislative jurisdiction. See, for instance, the Swiss case infra pp. 710 ff.

20. The historical roots as well as the present-day significance of the dichotomy are interestingly discussed by Merryman, The Public Law-Private Law Distinction in European and American Law, 17 J.Pub.L. 3 (1968). See also the provocative comment in the article by E. M. Wise, Prolegomena to the Principles of International Criminal Law, 16 N.Y.Law Forum 560, 563–4 (1970). For a discussion of the dichotomy with particular reference to the formerly Spanish territories in the Western Hemisphere, see Batiza, The Unity of Private Law in Louisiana Under the Spanish Rule, 4 Inter-Am.L.Rev. 139, especially at 155 (1962).

apart from criminal matters—the jurisdiction of the ordinary courts is limited to disputes governed by private law. This jurisdictional restriction, like the dichotomy which it reflects, is regarded as so fundamental that it is highly resistant to change. It has remained, to this day, a basic feature of most civil-law systems, even though in the course of the 19th and 20th centuries an ever-widening range of public law disputes, that is disputes regarding the validity and propriety of administrative and other official acts, gradually became justiciable. Since the ordinary courts, for the reasons just indicated, could not deal with these disputes, separate administrative courts had to be created to perform the adjudicatory function in public law matters.[21] The co-existence of at least two separate judicial systems—of ordinary courts and of administrative courts—thus became an important feature of the legal order in most civil-law countries.

The comparable development of the common law occurred much earlier in point of time and was little affected by the theoretical distinction between public and private law. By habeas corpus, certiorari, mandamus and prohibition, and by tort actions against public officials (sued in their individual capacity, to be sure), the common law courts asserted, and through centuries of political and indeed military struggles successfully preserved, their power to curb abusive official action. As a result of these struggles, which reached their points of climax in the days of Magna Carta and later of Lord Coke, the common law established the basic principle that the same court which decides a private dispute between two individuals also reviews the lawfulness of administrative acts.[21a] The different development in the civil law countries is not surprising if we remember that in those countries the law was not shaped by a powerful central court.

Another dichotomy which is of the greatest practical importance for civilian lawyers, is that between "civil"[22] and commercial law.

21. See infra pp. 498 ff. For a concise history of the French system, which has served as a model in a number of other civil-law countries, see Riesenfeld, supra n. 12, at 55–67.

Separate administrative courts must not, of course, be confused with separate constitutional courts (see infra pp. 375–380; the latter are the product of much more recent (post-World-War I) developments in certain civil-law countries. See Deener, Judicial Review in Modern Constitutional Systems, 46 Am.Pol.Sc.Rev. 1079, especially 1086–87 (1952).

21a. Along with parliamentary sovereignty, this was one of the basic constitutional principles championed by A. V. Dicey. See the contributions to the All Souls Public Law Seminar: Dicey and the Constitution, 1985 Pub.L. 583–723, especially R. Errera, Dicey and French Administrative Law; A Missed Encounter?, id. at 695. Cf.

H. Woolf, Public Law—Private Law: Why the Divide?, 1986 Pub.L. 220. Despite continued adherence to the basic notion that public-law disputes ultimately must be decided by ordinary courts (whether trial or appellate courts), common-law countries today (1) increasingly recognize public law as a discrete category, and (2) frequently provide for the *initial* adjudication of public-law disputes by administrative agencies or tribunals. For additional discussion of this point, and further references, see infra pp. 498–499.

22. The word "civil" has different meanings in different contexts. We speak of civil-law countries, as distinguished from common-law jurisdictions and other legal systems. "Civil" also may connote the opposite of "criminal", as in the context of the term civil procedure, in contrast to criminal procedure. In yet other contexts, the system of "civil" law may be be con-

Historically, this division reaches back into the middle ages. Roman law, as developed and perhaps corrupted in medieval times, became unsuitable as a basis for business transactions. This was due to several features of that system of law, such as irksome interference with freedom of contract (see supra pp. 272–273); restrictions on assignments and powers of attorney; usury laws which sharply limited and often prohibited the taking of interest; over-indulgent protection of debtors; failure to recognize the mercantile concept of negotiability; and, above all, a cumbersome, expensive and irritatingly slow procedure.[23] In order to avoid these fetters of an inadequate general law, the guilds and corporations of merchants developed a customary law of their own; in time they gained from secular as well as ecclesiastic authorities grudging recognition of the principle that this customary commercial law within its proper sphere should prevail over the general law.[24] According to medieval views, the guild or corporation had the power to codify its corporate customs, and these codifications became known as *statuta mercatorum*. Confirmation of the *statuta* by the sovereign was frequently sought and granted; but it was the prevailing view that the *statuta* had the force of law even in the absence of such confirmation.[25]

The *statutum* conferred on the individual member of the guild a status which he took with him wherever he traveled and which, at least in principle, had to be respected by any court before which he might appear. This liberal rule of conflict of laws made it incumbent upon the courts dealing with commercial matters to familiarize themselves with the *statuta* of many trades and countries, with the result that by this practical use of "comparative law" the commercial customs and laws of the Western world became more and more unified.[26]

The guilds also had the power to elect their own judges.[27] The jurisdiction of these special courts, originally limited to internal affairs

---

trasted to that of canon law or of military law. Occasionally, and perhaps not too accurately, the term "civil" is used as synonymous with "private", i.e., as opposed to "public". The civilians, finally, often speak of "civil law" as opposed to commercial law. In this latter sense, "civil law" may be defined as comprising the whole area of substantive private law which remains if one excludes commercial law; this is the meaning of the term "civil law" as here used in the text.

23. See Goldschmidt, Universalgeschichte des Handelsrechts 137–42 (1891); Goldschmidt, Handbuch des Handelsrechts 367–68 (1874).

24. See Endemann, Beitraege zur Kenntnis des Handelsrechts im Mittelalter, 5 Zeitschrift fuer das Gesamte Handelsrecht 333, 350–53 (1862). Some of the English-language literature on the history of the law merchant is listed by Plucknett, A Concise History of the Common Law (5th ed. 1956) 657 ff.

25. See Endemann, supra n. 24.

26. The most influential *statuta* were those adopted by the merchants' guilds in the great Italian centers of commerce during the 14th and 15th centuries. Concerning the migration of these *statuta*, and the gradual process of unification of commercial law throughout medieval Europe, see Rehme, Geschichte des Handelsrechts, in Vol. 1 of Ehrenberg's Handbuch des gesamten Handelsrechts, pp. 94–97 (1913); Schmitthoff, International Business Law: A New Law Merchant, in 1961 Current Law and Social Problems (Un. of Toronto Press) 129, 132–35.

27. See Endemann, loc. cit. supra n. 24, at 355 ff. In addition to these guild courts, whose jurisdiction (over their members) originally had a *personal* basis, there existed many a merchants' court having *territorial* jurisdiction over a market place, a fair or a port. Those among the latter courts which sat in port towns, are part of the ancestry of modern admiralty courts. See

of the guild, was later broadened to include all cases involving commercial disputes between merchants. The procedure of the merchants' courts was fair, rational and expeditious, in sharp contrast both to the primitive forms of trial (battle, ordeal, or wager of law) which until the reception of Roman law prevailed in Germanic countries, and to the delays and subtleties of canonistic procedure which in non-commercial matters dominated procedural thinking on the continent from the middle ages until the 19th century.[28]

The main characteristics of the substantive law which was created by the commercial courts, were emphasis on freedom of contract and on freedom of alienability of movable property, both tangible and intangible; abrogation of legal technicalities; and, most importantly, a tendency to decide cases *ex aequo et bono* rather than by abstract scholastic deductions from Roman texts. No wonder, then, that commercial law was a highly successful institution. Cosmopolitan in nature and inherently superior to the general law, the law merchant by the end of the medieval period had become the very foundation of an expanding commerce throughout the Western world.

Commercial law as a separate branch of private substantive law, coupled with the special jurisdiction and procedure of commercial courts, thus was well established before the time of the great codifications. In Napoleon's code system, and in most of the later codifications, the dichotomy between "civil" and commercial law was preserved by the enactment of separate commercial codes, and by provisions (either in the code of commerce or in the procedural codes) perpetuating the separate commercial courts.[29] The continuing present-day significance of the dichotomy for the legal systems of civilian countries will be illustrated in later parts of this book.

In England, the law merchant was absorbed into the common law during the 17th and 18th centuries.[30] The common law courts, always jealous of competing judicial bodies, proved powerful enough to displace the special commercial courts. In the process, many of the merchants' substantive rules and customs, especially those dealing with negotiable

Gilmore and Black, The Law of Admiralty 5–6 (2d ed., 1975). But the guild courts (exercising personal jurisdiction over members, and later over all merchants) rather than the market and port tribunals must be regarded as the most important forerunners of modern commercial courts in civil-law countries.

28. See Goldschmidt, Handbuch des Handelsrechts 368 (1874); W. Mitchell, An Essay on the Early History of the Law Merchant 12–16 (1904).

29. See Schlesinger, The Uniform Commercial Code in the Light of Comparative Law, 1 Inter-Am.L.Rev. 11, 36 ff. (1959).

Some civil-law countries, such as Switzerland and Italy, no longer have a sepa-

rate commercial code. But such attempts to create a "unitary" private law constitute a minority position in the civil-law world.

The question whether the traditional systematic separation of "civil" and commercial law should be preserved, has long been the subject of lively debate among civilian scholars and law reformers. For an excellent multinational collection of essays on the present status and the future of the dichotomy between "civil" and commercial law, see M. Rotondi, L'Unité du Droit des Obligations (Vol. 3 of Inchieste di Diritto Comparato, 1974). See also infra pp. 542–543.

30. See Schlesinger, supra n. 29, at 40–41.

instruments, were transformed into common law rules.[31] This incorporation of commercial law into the fabric of the common law was
facilitated by the fact that an inductive, pragmatic method was common to both systems.[31a] For the same reason, the merchants' resistance to the process of absorption was not too strenuous. On the
continent, on the other hand, where at that time the general law was
still largely dominated by scholastic thinking and by canonistic procedure, and where the courts of general jurisdiction were much weaker
and less respected, the merchant class successfully resisted the merger
of "civil" and commercial law.

III. Surviving Traces of Pre-Codification Law in the Civil-Law World

Before the age of the great codifications, continental law had three
principal characteristics:

(a) In most countries of the continent, it was still strongly
Roman-influenced.

(b) It was University-taught law.

(c) Based on a largely Romanistic University tradition which
transcended regional and national frontiers,[32] it was, to a considerable extent, a *jus commune* prevailing throughout most of the
European countries and their overseas possessions.[33]

The first of these characteristics has become greatly attenuated in
modern, codified civil law. We have seen (supra pp. 275–280) that
codification deprived the Corpus Juris of whatever authoritative status
it previously possessed. Looking at the historical antecedents of pres-

---

31. See Plucknett, A Concise History of
the Common Law (5th ed. 1956) 664, 668–
69; S. Lowry, Lord Mansfield and the Law
Merchant: Law and Economics in the 18th
Century, 7 Journal of Economic Issues 605,
615–19 (1973); D. R. Coquillette, Legal Ideology and Incorporation II: Sir Thomas
Ridley, Charles Molloy, and the Literary
Battle for the Law Merchant, 1607–1676,
61 B.U.L.Rev. 315 (1981); and Ideology and
Incorporation III: Reason Regulated—The
Post-Restoration English Civilians, 1653–
1735, 67 B.U.L.Rev. 289 (1987).

31a. More recently, a specialized Bar
and Bench (now formally organized in the
Commercial Court) has kept England's judicially-developed commercial law responsive to commercial needs.

32. It was only in the late 17th and
18th centuries that a few University chairs
for the teaching of local law slowly began
to be created in France, Germany and
Spain. Until then, the law faculties
taught exclusively Roman law and Canon
law, with the result that both students and

teachers could move freely from one European University to another without changing their intellectual habitat. See David,
Considérations sur l'unification des droits
Européens, in Annuaire 1957 of the Institut Universitaire d'Etudes Européennes
de Turin, pp. 5, 9–10.

33. Of course, there were countless local statutes and ordinances of considerable
diversity, as well as local customs reduced
to writing. In cases not clearly covered by
these local enactments, however, the *jus
commune* controlled.

There were occasional attempts, especially during the 17th and 18th centuries, by
local statutory provisions to establish a hierarchy of authoritative oracles of the *jus
commune*, and thus to bring local influences to bear on the application of the *jus
commune* itself; but these provisions
(called Laws of Citation), although they led
to some local variations of legal method,
did not destroy the cosmopolitan quality of
the *jus commune*.

ent-day civil law systems, we have found that Roman law is just one of a number of strands which are intricately interwoven in those systems.

It remains to explore the question to what extent the two other characteristics of pre-code civil law, its professorial and its transnational nature, have survived the surgical process of codification.

(1) Prior to the Age of Reason, the law faculties had long held a position of leadership in the development of the law. This was natural during a period when the most important sources of the law were enshrined in Latin texts and writings accessible only to the well-trained scholar. During the 17th and 18th centuries, however, the traditional methods and sources were questioned with increasing vigor. The movement toward codification itself arose from this critical attitude; it was aimed at changing the traditional legal method which, in the eyes of the critics, relied too heavily on the accumulated cobwebs of centuries of professorial learning.

This new spirit, not surprisingly, tended to diminish the law faculties' position of leadership in the development of the law. In some countries, such as France, academic lawyers were not even asked to participate in the drafting of the codes. Elsewhere, e.g., in Germany and Switzerland, law professors did help to prepare the codes, either as single draftsmen [34] or as members of a drafting team; but their proposals, of course, required the approval of legislative committees and of the legislature itself. The days when the professors literally were making law *ex cathedra*, were gone.

Academic influence on the law, to be sure, was by no means broken. The codes needed interpretation, and the authors of the majority of influential commentaries, treatises and monographs were members of law faculties.[35] So long as a code is relatively new, the opinions of academic commentators (*la doctrine*, as the French expression goes) may constitute the only available guide in the application of the code and in filling its gaps. Even later, when most of the important controversial questions arising under the code have been settled by court decisions (i.e., by *la jurisprudence*, as the French would call it), the commentator's role in collecting, explaining, systematizing and often criticizing the judicial decisions remains a significant one.[36] There is no doubt that to this day the authority of leading textbooks and commentaries in civil-law countries is considerably stronger than in the common-law world.[37] We shall come back to this point in connection with the question of the persuasive force of judicial and non-judicial authorities (infra pp. 597–657, especially 644–645).

---

34. The original draft of the Swiss Civil Code of 1907 was written by Professor Eugen Huber.

35. Even in civil-law countries, of course, professors have no monopoly of legal writing. See supra p. 185.

36. In criticizing judicial opinions, civilian legal writers are both bolder and more influential than their counterparts in the common law world. See Moses, International Legal Practice, 4 Fordh.L.Rev. 244, 265–66 (1935).

37. The unflattering term "secondary authority" is unknown in the civil-law orbit.

Another surviving trace of the formerly dominant position of the law faculties may be found in the fact that the young civilian, unlike his counterpart in some common-law countries, simply cannot become a lawyer without having passed a course of University study.[38] He cannot enter the profession by "reading law".[39]

(2) Of all of the characteristics of pre-code civil law, its transnational nature was the one most radically changed by codification. The important codes enacted in the civil-law world during the 19th and 20th centuries were national codes. *Within* the enacting nation state, codification usually meant unification of diverse laws. But *as between* one nation state and another, the national codifications had the effect of impeding the interchange of legal thought and experience. Judges, practitioners and academicians in each country began to concentrate their efforts on the interpretation and development of their own code system, without paying much attention to the similarly isolated developments in other countries living under different codes.[39a] Linguistic and conceptual barriers between the lawyers of various civil-law countries thus were bound to grow, with the result that the civil-law orbit has lost its former coherence to a much greater degree than has been the case in the common-law world. Only rarely can we speak today of "the civil-law rule" on a given point,[40] and the experience of international practitioners shows that the differences *inter sese* among civil-law systems are even more pronounced than those among common-law jurisdictions.[41]

The intellectual isolation of each national legal system which resulted from the codifications, was somewhat mitigated by the fact that some outstanding codes were used as models by legislators in other countries.[42] Thus, so-called "code families" (see infra pp. 546–547) came into existence.

38. Even in communist countries, where this University monopoly was temporarily broken, the tendency seems to be toward restoring it once the "revolutionary phase" of the regime is past. See, e.g., Hager, Soviet Legal Education, 5 Duquesne L.Rev. 143, 144–5 (1967). D. J. Meador, Impressions of Law in East Germany: Legal Education and Legal Sytems in the German Democratic Republic 54–88; 146–159 (1986).

39. See supra, text at n. 7, for the historical reasons.

39a. Leading 19th century scholars were quick to recognize that the differences among the various codes call for comparative studies, and that the intellectual isolation of national legal systems brought about by national codification would become complete without "comparative jurisprudence". See the striking comment by Jhering, quoted (in English translation) by K. Zweigert and K. Siehr, Jhering's Influ-

ence on the Development of Legal Method, 19 Am.J.Comp.L. 215, at 218 (1971).

40. Comparative studies concerning a controversial point, on which there is a division of authority, often show that there are both civil-law and common-law jurisdictions in each camp.

41. See Moses, loc. cit. supra n. 36, at 256.

42. This point is, of course, connected with the general subject of migration and reception of laws, discussed supra pp. 8–12.

During the 19th century, when all developed legal systems had to struggle with new problems created by the industrial revolution, it became customary for European legislators and their advisers, as part of their work in preparing national legislation, to conduct comparative studies of other countries' legislative experience. See H. Coing, European Common Law: Historical Foundations, in M. Cappelletti (Ed.), New

As between two civilian codes which do not belong to the same code family, differences in positive rules and principles, and even in the system of the codes, are apt to be marked. If, nevertheless, judges and legal writers continue to use the generic term "civil law", they must feel that in spite of the differences between the various codes there is a common approach or way of thinking, perhaps a common method and terminology, which binds all civilians together and sets them apart from those who practice under different systems. In studying the materials presented in the following parts of this book, the reader should attempt to identify the mental processes which in this sense may be attributed to the "civil law" rather than to the legal system of an individual civilian nation. He may find that the features common to all civil-law systems can be divided into two categories. Some arise from the very nature of a codified system of law. Others, it is submitted, are surviving traces of the transnational, professional, Romanistic law of pre-code days.

Revival of the transnational features of the civil law is becoming a highly practical issue for European lawyers, in the face of the increasing economic integration of the continent and of the growing importance of supranational European organizations. These organizations, especially the European Economic Community and the Council of Europe, are engaged in large-scale efforts to unify or to harmonize the law in certain specific areas; [42a] but although a modicum of new transnational law is in the process of being created in this manner,[42b] it is clear that the bulk of the written law governing private and business affairs on the European continent remains firmly based on the various national codes. The task of supplementing the specific texts of treaties and supranational regulations by the creation of a new *jus commune* for Western Europe thus has to be performed outside of the codes, by Bench and Bar, scholars and teachers.[43]

Perspectives for a Common Law of Europe 31, 38–42 (1978).

42a. See supra p. 32. In these efforts, it may well prove useful to learn from the experiences gained during 200 years of American federalism. A massive research project devoted to such utilization of American experience is presently in progress. See M. Cappelletti, M. Seccombe & J. Weiler (Gen. Eds.), Integration Through Law, a six-volume work some parts of which were published in 1985 and 1986.

42b. In this process, the Court of Justice of the European Communities plays a crucial role. In the areas subject to its jurisdiction, the Court—using the comparative method—has consciously set about to create a new *jus commune*. See W. Lorenz, General Principles of Law: Their Elaboration in the Court of Justice of the European Communities, 13 Am.J.Comp.L. 1 (1964); H. G. Schermers, The European Court of Justice: Promoter of European

Integration, 22 Am.J.Comp.L. 444, especially at 454–55 (1974); M. Akehurst, The Application of General Principles of Law by the Court of Justice of the European Communities, 1981 Brit.Y.B. Int'l L. 29.

43. See Coing, supra n. 42, especially at 44; David, supra n. 32; Lorenz, supra n. 42b; Neumayer, The Role of a Uniform Legal Science in the Harmonization of the Continental Legal Systems, in Essays in Jurisprudence in Honor of Roscoe Pound (Ralph A. Newman, Ed., 1962), at 649 ff.

Legal scholars increasingly recognize that, as a necessary underpinning for the efforts to reconstitute a truly European law, *European* legal history (as distinguished from the national legal history of individual nations) should become a subject of intensive study. See Neumayer, ibid.; Coing, Die Bedeutung der europäischen Rechtsgeschichte für die Rechtsvergleichung, 32 Rabels Z. 1 (1968); Riegert,

Attempts to re-create such a *jus commune* of the European continent had hardly begun during the third quarter of the 20th century when the task was rendered even larger—and more complex—by the rush of events. Now that the United Kingdom and the Irish Republic have joined the Common Market, and that the necessity of closer economic and political co-operation among major industrial nations—in North America and the Far East as well as in Europe—has been widely recognized, it is becoming apparent in the European Community and elsewhere that a purely civilian *jus commune* no longer meets the needs of our time, and that the search for a common core of legal systems will have to encompass the common-law as well as the civil-law orbit.[44]   In examining the materials which follow, the reader will be able to form his own opinion as to the feasibility of finding and formulating such a common core in various areas of law.

At this point, and on the basis solely of the historical survey just completed, a preliminary observation may be ventured: We have found that the basic differences between common-law and civil-law systems have their roots in the political and social conditions of bygone ages, and not in the realities of our day. No present-day schism separates the social, religious, moral and political presuppositions of the common law from those of the civil law. The terminological and institutional divergencies between the two systems, though they have become realities for the international practitioner and for the student of comparative law, are realities forced on us by by the dead hand of the past. Behind the façade of these divergencies, it seems reasonable to expect, comparative studies will uncover more and more similarities in the actual handling of 20th century problems.[45]

COMMON LAW AND CIVIL LAW—ANOTHER OPINION

The above survey, while emphasizing the differences between the civil-law and common-law "cultures," has ended with the prediction that the future will see a measure of convergence between these two systems, and the emergence of a "common core" of legal rules shared

The Max Planck Institute for European Legal History, 22 Southwestern L.J. 397 (1968).

44. The point briefly indicated in the text has been stated more elaborately by Rudolf B. Schlesinger in his Introduction to the two volumes entitled Formation of Contracts—A Study of the Common Core of Legal Systems (Schlesinger, Gen.Ed., 1968), especially at pp. 5–17. See also the important recent writings by G. Gorla cited in M. Cappelletti's Foreword (p. XIII) to Vol. 1, Book 1, of the work cited supra n. 42a. Similar thoughts, with strong emphasis on the role of legal education and legal scholarship in elucidating the common core of legal systems, have been expressed by R. Sacco, Droit Commun de l'Europe, et Composantes du Droit, in M. Cappelletti (Ed.), New Perspectives for a Common Law of Europe 95, especially at 107–09 (1978). Cf. J. G. Wetter, The Case for International Law Schools and an International Legal Profession, 29 Int'l & Comp.L.Q. 206 (1980).

45. The method of research by which a "common core" was found and formulated in the area of formation of contracts (see supra n. 44), may well prove fruitful in other areas as well. See, e.g., B. H. Greene, Book Review, 53 Minn.L.Rev. 187, 198–99 (1968); J. M. Perillo, Book Review, 37 Fordh.L.Rev. 144, 149 (1968); J. Wolff, Book Review, 57 Georgetown L.Rev. 208, 213 (1968).

by advanced industrial society on a global scale. Quite a different perspective is offered, against the same background, by Professor Alan Watson. A well-known scholar of Roman law, with particular emphasis on the Republican period, he has more recently turned his attention to comparative law.[1]

Professor Watson has been kind enough to prepare the following summary of his views for inclusion herein:

"For Watson, Comparative Law is a study of the connections between systems which have some relationship. As a practical subject Comparative Law is a study of the legal borrowings or transplants that can and should be made; Comparative Law as an academic discipline in its own right is the other side of the coin, an investigation into the legal transplants that have occurred: how, when, why and from which systems have they been made; the circumstances in which they have succeeded or failed; and the impact on them of their new environment. Comparative Law as an academic discipline therefore necessarily entails a large historical component.

"As a matter of observable fact, he argues, borrowing has been the most fruitful source of legal change in the Western world. Consequently, by examining a number of related systems over centuries one can observe and explain patterns of development. For example, most Western legal systems nowadays are classified either as civil law systems (defined by Watson as those that accepted Justinian's *Corpus Juris Civilis* in whole or in part as law of the land or as directly highly persuasive) or as common law systems, and the types have markedly different characteristics: most civil law systems are codified, they distinguish, to a much sharper degree than do common law systems, public law and private law, commercial law and private law; they have a career judiciary; they traditionally ascribe higher prestige to legal academics; and they are much more rule conscious. The characteristic differences between the types of system (which also have important practical effects) cannot easily be related to political, social and economic conditions since in these regards Quebec for instance is akin to New Brunswick rather than the Dominican Republic which in legal structure it more resembles. They result in Watson's opinion from the different attitudes to the *Corpus Juris Civilis* in the civil law and the common law systems. The legal tradition, maintains Watson, has a vast importance in legal growth, an importance that is usually grossly underestimated.

"When, as Watson does, one adds to the picture the claim that legal rules are frequently and for long stretches of time dysfunctional; ill-adapted to meet the needs and desires of the society at large, its ruling elite or any recognisable group, then one can see, he insists, that law exists as culture as well as on the level of practical reality. Comparative Law, involving the study of many systems sharing the same legal traditions over centuries, is a powerful tool and, in Watson's view, the only satisfactory tool for unravelling the causes of legal change and,

1. See especially the following: *Legal Transplants, An Approach to Comparative Law* (1974); Legal Transplants and Law Reform, 79 L.Q.Rev. 79 (1976); *Society and Legal Change* (1977); Comparative Law and Legal Change, 1978 Camb.L.J. 313; *The Making of the Civil Law* (1981); Legal Change: Sources of Law and Legal Culture, 131 U.Pa.L.Rev. 1121 (1983); *Sources of Law, Legal Ambiguity and Legal Change* (1985); and Failures of the Legal Imagination (to appear 1988).

just as important, the nature of the relationship between law and the society in which it operates."

Notes and Questions

(1) Regarding the purposes of the study and practice of comparative law, Professor Watson's views clearly differ from those presented in the Introduction to this book (supra pp. 1–43). Can you spell out the differences?

(2) In attempting to supply a historical explanation for the contrasting features of civil law and common law, Professor Watson emphasizes the autonomous intellectual history of the law, and minimizes the degree to which that intellectual history may have been impacted by social and political events. Is it (a) possible and (b) fruitful to view a legal system as the mere embodiment of an intellectual tradition, and for purposes of scholarly study to isolate that tradition from the social and political problems to which at all times the law had to respond, and to the solution of which we are trying to direct the law today? Will comparativists who subscribe to Professor Watson's views be the kind of law reformers we want for the improvement of our own legal system?

3. GEOGRAPHIC EXPANSION OF COMMON LAW AND CIVIL LAW

NOTE

(1) The Problem of Classifying Legal Systems

It is difficult to engage in an intellectual interchange involving a multilateral comparison of legal systems without being able to group the systems and to apply identifying labels to each group. Nor can one meaningfully discuss the geographic expansion of common law and civil law without a sense of what other groups of legal systems can be discerned in the modern world. Thus it is understandable that scholars interested in comparative law have expended much time and effort in trying to arrive at a systematic classification of legal systems on a global scale. To date, unfortunately, these endeavours have produced little standardization and much controversy. One reason for this situation is related to the fact that classification is never an end in itself: when we classify legal systems, we do so for a specific purpose, and it cannot be taken for granted that a classificatory scheme that is suitable for one purpose will prove equally useful in other contexts. Another reason is that we can attempt to compare particular segments of legal systems (e.g., private or public law) or legal systems as a whole. Still another reason is that—even granted the same purpose and scope of comparison—there is disagreement concerning the threshold problem of the criteria to be used. Thus, in classifying legal systems as a whole, some rely on criteria related to the form of law and on considerations peculiar to legal science, while others use extra-juridical criteria, such as the type of civilization, political ideology and the like. Older attempts to use a single criterion [1] have been followed more recently by

1. Some of the better-known classifications are those by cultures (Schnitzer), by races and languages (Esmein and Sauser-Hall), by historical origins (Glasson and Sarfatti), and by legislative families (Lévy-Ullman). See 1 Arminjon-Nolde-Wolff, Traité de Droit Comparé 42–47 (1950); 1 Schnitzer, Vergleichende Rechtslehre 133–

*Aspects of Civil law + Common law in almost all legal systems
(e.g. influential in countries w/ Islamic law)*

suggestions that either a composite criterion, such as the "style" of legal systems,[2] or a combination of several criteria [3] be used. But while this approach may have yielded more satisfactory results in some respects, it has generated new controversies. For example, the choice of the elements of composite criteria, and the mutual relationship among these elements, have become new bones of contention.[3a] All in all, in spite of valiant efforts to identify "determinative elements" of world legal systems, the taxonomic fundamentals of comparative law are still in their infancy.

Most Western comparativists distinguish three large groups of legal systems—civil law, common law and socialist law. Almost every legal system presently in existence has at least some characteristics affiliating it, more or less strongly, with one or several of these three groups, each of which is characterized by features of European origin. But it should be pointed out immediately (and the observation will recur throughout our discussion) that this trichotomous scheme of classification, though useful as a rough orientation, does not exhaust the rich variety of laws one finds in the modern world. Especially in Asia and Africa there are several legal systems which, although in some ways connected with one or more of the principal groups, retain important elements of non-European origin. Until recently in general decline, these native elements are on the ascendancy in some parts of the world. This is particularly true of Islamic countries.

By way of broad initial generalization it can be said that the whole of continental Europe this side of the "Iron Curtain" (with the possible exception of Scandinavia) and the countries of continental South and Central America (with the possible exception of Nicaragua and Guyana) are looked upon as the core of the civil-law jurisdictions. The common-law orbit may be considered roughly—very roughly, as we shall see—co-extensive with the English-speaking world. The group of socialist legal systems also has its core and its periphery. The former includes the Soviet Union, the other Warsaw Pact nations and two additional European countries (Albania and Yugoslavia) which are not members of that Pact. Among Asian nations, the People's Republic of China,

---

42 (1961). For a critique of these classificatory attempts, see L. J. Constantinesco, Traité de Droit Comparé, vol. 3, 80–105 (1983).

2. See K. Zweigert & H. Kötz, An Introduction to Comparative Law 62–66 (Transl. by T. Weir, 1977). According to these authors, the elements determining the style of a legal system are (1) historical origin; (2) method of legal reasoning; (3) particularly characteristic legal institutions; (4) nature and treatment of sources of law; and (5) ideological factors. Another composite criterion is that of "legal tradition". See, e.g., M. A. Glendon, M. W. Gordon, C. Osakwe, Comparative Legal Traditions 4 ff. (1982).

3. See R. David & J. E. C. Brierley, Major Legal Systems in the World Today 20 (3d ed., 1985), where it is suggested that two independent criteria be used: (a) legal method and (b) the philosophical, political and economic fundamentals of the legal

order. It will be noted that there is relatively little difference between this view and that of Professors Zweigert and Kötz (supra n. 2), except that the latter, in the first four determinants of "style" listed by them, subdivide the concept of legal method into several component elements.

3a. It has thus been argued that historical origin only explains characteristics of a legal "style", but cannot be regarded as a stylistic element. See, e.g., Constantinesco, supra n. 1, especially at 128; A. Malmstrom, The Significance of Legal Systems, Scandinavian Studies in Law 127 (1969).

Sociologists of law have faulted most of these classifications for focusing too much on legal doctrine. See, e.g., G. Gurwitch, Sociology of Law, Chapt. 4 (1962); A. Podgorecki, C. J. Whelan and D. Khosla, Legal Systems and Social Systems; I. Markovits, Hedgehogs or Foxes, 34 Am.J.Comp. Law 113, 132 (1986).

Kampuchea, Mongolia, North Korea and Vietnam are usually included in the core group; so is one country in the Western Hemisphere—Cuba. But the reach of socialist law is not limited to this territory: there are several developing nations, most of them in Africa, which have introduced so many features of socialist law into their legal systems that they can be classified as evolving or peripheral socialist law jurisdictions. Needless to say, these groupings are by no means immutable: they have changed in the past, and they will continue to change in the future. Even at a fixed point in time, such as the present, the commonly accepted groupings are subject to certain qualifications, some of which will be discussed below.

Especially when we deal with countries outside of the core areas of the three principal groups, even the most elemental generalizations become treacherous. The interpenetration of common, civil, socialist and non-European law in many parts of the world produces mixed systems which elude easy classification. In spite of these difficulties, an attempt will be made on the following pages to present a rough outline of the legal map of the world; this will be done by way of briefly indicating, with reference to a number of mixed systems, the features which indicate or counter-indicate their affiliation with a given group.

Before the legal systems of particular countries or areas are discussed in this fashion, however, a few points of caution should be noted:

(i) Earlier in this chapter we observed that the contrast between common and civil law mainly draws on divergent ways of handling legal materials, organizing the law, making arguments, structuring the legal process, and similar factors of a legal-technical nature. When we extend the comparison to socialist law, the focus changes: now the emphasis is on features related to extra-juridical factors, such as the socio-economic organization, political structure and ideology. The label "socialist law" refers to legal systems of those states that have socialized the means of production, expanded the role of the state or state-affiliated organizations in all spheres of social life, established a "vanguard party", and adopted Marxism as their official ideology.

Clearly, then, the conventional trichotomy—common law, civil law, socialist law—rests on classificatory criteria that are not consistently applied. If one were consistently to use the criterion of economic, social and political fundamentals of the legal order, socialist law would have to be contrasted with a type of law originating from private ownership of productive capital, a limited role of government in society, and similar considerations.[3b] Conversely, if one were consistently to apply

---

3b. Comparativists from socialist countries juxtapose socialist to capitalist law, and are thus not vulnerable to the criticism of inconsistency in applying their basic classificatory criterion of "socio-economic formation". But their portrayal of these two families of law is often marred by political propaganda. For interesting discussions from the socialist side, see G. Eörsi, Comparative Law (1979); Z. Peteri, Le Droit Comparé et la Théorie Socialiste de Droit, in Z. Peteri (Ed.), Legal Theory, Comparative Law, 318–345 (1984). A well-known Soviet scholar suggests that while the distinction between socialist and capitalist systems should furnish the principal

classification, it makes sense to subdivide the capitalist systems into common law and civil law. See V. A. Tumanov, On Comparing Various Types of Legal Systems, in W. E. Butler & V. N. Kudriavtsev, Comparative Law and Legal System: Historical and Socio-Legal Perspectives 69, 76 (1985). For many practical purposes, this view accords with the usual trichotomy.

In the West, also, suggestions have been made that a classificatory scheme be set up contrasting socialist law with a type of law encompassing both common and civil law jurisdictions of Western pluralist countries. See C. M. Lawson, The Family Affinity of

classificatory criteria pertaining to technical-legal factors, jurisdictions generally classed as "socialist" could hardly qualify as a distinctive third group on the same plane with common and civil law. In fact, because countries that call themselves socialist appeared mostly in areas of the world that used to belong to the civil-law orbit, a lawyer trained in civil law finds, at the level of legal form, much that is familiar to him in communist systems: many legal concepts are recognizable, techniques of using legal materials are similar, and so are ways of drafting codes, structuring procedural institutions, and the like.[3c] On the other hand, many distinctive features of the common law appear equally alien to lawyers brought up in socialist countries and to lawyers trained in those Western pluralist countries that belong to the civil-law group.[3d]

Although the weakness of the conventional trichotomy is quite transparent, we shall not try to remedy it here: the scheme can still be used as a rough orientative tool.

(ii) In comparing and grouping legal systems, we are accustomed to speak of *national* systems. It is true that today all legal systems, to varying degrees, contain elements of international or supranational law.[3e] In many instances, such elements have been imported into a national legal system by treaties and other cooperative arrangements seeking unification or harmonization of law on a regional or international plane. As has been shown, however,[4] the supranational elements of existing legal systems, important as they may be in certain areas of legal practice,[4a] usually constitute no more than a small

Common Law and Civil Law Systems, 6 Hastings Int. & Comp.L.Rev. 85 (1982); M. Ancel, La Confrontation des Droits Socialistes et des Droits Occidentaux, in Z. Peteri, supra 13–24. For a thoughtful treatment of this theme, see I. Markovits, Socialist v. Bourgeois Rights, 46 Univ. Chicago L.Rev. 612 (1978).

3c. See, e.g., O. Joffe and P. B. Maggs, Soviet Law in Theory and Practice 1 (1983). Generally speaking, the association of socialist law with civil-law forms is more a matter of historical contingency than intrinsic affinity. There is no doubt, for example, that property arrangements as to socialized means of production could as easily be expressed with common-law as they are with (adapted) civil-law property concepts. Much as capitalism flourished both under common and civil law, so socialism, at least under most of its definitions, appears to be able to function with widely divergent legal techniques.

3d. For their part, some lawyers trained in common-law jurisdictions tend to lump Eastern and Western European continental countries into the same classificatory niche of "continental law". See, e.g., R. J. Aldisert, Rumbling through Continental Legal Systems, 43 U. of Pittsburg L.Rev. 935, 961–981 (1982).

3e. For an account of the growing influx of international law elements into na-

tional legal systems, see V. P. Nanda, Application of Customary International Law by Domestic Courts, 12 N.Y.Law Forum 185 (1966), where a wealth of further references can be found.

As to supranational elements in modern legal systems, especially those of continental Europe, see P. Hay, Federalism and Supranational Organizations—Patterns for New Legal Structures (1966); J. P. Warner, The Relationship Between European Community Law and the National Laws of Member States, 93 L.Q.Rev. 349 (1977). See also J. A. Usher, European Community Law and National Law—the Irreversible Transfer? (1981).

4. See the discussion of "unification", supra pp. 31–34. For a general treatment of the work of the EEC Commission on the Harmonization of Laws, see G. Close, Harmonization of Laws: Use and Abuse of the Powers under the EEC Treaty? 3 European L.Rev. 461 (1978).

4a. E.g., in those areas of criminal procedure and administrative law in which the protection of human rights is a paramount issue. See A. L. del Russo, The European Bill of Rights: The First Decade of International Protection of Human Rights, 4 Santa Clara Law. 8 (1963); M. Cappelletti & W. Cohen, Comparative Constitutional Law 145–49, 237–49, 429–41 (1979).

portion of the total body of precepts and concepts of which a legal system is composed.[5]   Except in Scandinavia, where regional unification of broad areas of the law has been achieved,[6] one observes everywhere that the bulk of the norms and notions studied in law schools and applied in legal practice represents the law of a nation-state or of its subdivisions, and is not (or not yet) the product of international cooperation in the lawmaking process.[7]   It is true that in the European Community there are "directly applicable" provisions of community law.   But even where these provisions create a new claim enforceable in national courts, the remedies used in these courts to implement such claims may reflect national law.[7a]   Thus, in spite of manifold outside influences to which all modern legal systems have been and continue to be exposed, each of them retains its identity as a national system.

(iii) Almost every legal system consists of several layers, each layer being attributable to a different period of history.   In the case of countries whose history (especially in relatively recent times) has been marked by violent upheavals, such as revolution, conquest or massive immigration,[8] each of these layers may be derived from a wholly different culture; thus the various layers may be so distinct from each other that they are apparent even to the superficial observer.   In other instances, where the internal development of a country has been characterized by evolution rather than by revolution or other upheaval, the successive layers of legal accretion may be more difficult to discern; but they exist nevertheless.

If the legal system of a nation is sought to be classified by the use of a single label, that label often will describe only one of the layers which are superimposed on each other in the national legal order.   By leading us to disregard the other layers, such a single-label method of classification may produce somewhat inaccurate impressions.[9]

5.   It should not be forgotten, moreover, that supranational institutions do not develop in a vacuum.   Frequently they contain features borrowed from national models, and for one unacquainted with the models these features are difficult to understand.   For example, the interplay of administrative powers and judicial review in the European Community can be profitably studied only by a person who is reasonably familiar with the administrative law of the member-nations, especially of France.

6.   See infra at n. 85.

7.   With specific reference to the European Community it has been pointed out that in practice the emerging Community law is of interest primarily to certain specialists, and that the bulk of every-day lawyers' law is still governed by the national laws of the several member nations. See E. J. Cohn, The Rules of Arbitration of the United Nations Economic Commission for Europe, 16 Int. & Comp.L.Q. 946, at 981 (1967).

On the whole, this observation made by Professor Cohn in 1967 still holds true today.   But it must be noted that Commu-

nity law and international conventions sponsored by the Council of Europe have begun to intrude into ordinary, bread-and-butter areas of legal practice, such as products liability, corporation law, patents and trademarks, and enforcement of foreign judgments.

7a.   See N. Green, The Treaty of Rome, National Courts and English Common Law, 48 Rabels Z. 509 (1984) citing a recent decision of the House of Lords and a comparable 1979 decision of the BGH.

8.   The recent history of Israel exemplifies an upheaval connected with large-scale immigration.   Upheavals connected with revolutionary change are illustrated by the difficulties the Soviet regime experienced in the twenties in imposing its new law in Asia.   See G. J. Massell, Law as Instrument of Social Change in a Traditional Milieu, 2 Law and Soc.Rev. 179–228 (1967).

9.   That at least for some purposes the single-label method is inadequate, becomes apparent in any discussion, however brief and general, of the present legal systems of Latin American, Asian and African nations.   See the discussion in part (2) of this Note.   See also, as a particularly striking

[handwritten margin notes: Colonial rule of law as opposed to geographically contained law / most classification focus on private law not public law / [come up w/ a classification scheme for comparing various laws to legal systems] / non-trivial]

(iv) One who applies group labels to particular legal systems should be aware of yet another element of inaccuracy. Every legal system, as we have seen,[10] to a greater or lesser extent contains features that are not home-grown but borrowed from other systems. Such borrowings may be limited to a specific subject, as exemplified by Germany's adoption of basic notions of American antitrust laws. Where this occurs, the resulting imprecision of applying single-group labels is negligible. But in many countries a large portion or almost the whole of the legal system may be borrowed or imported. This is true of most legal systems outside of Europe. A country having such a substantially imported legal system does not always derive all parts of its system from the same group of laws. The area-by-area survey which follows will show that there are many countries which by such borrowing have introduced both common-law and civil-law elements into their legal systems. And as comparativists lack a clear understanding of the features that are indispensable to the affiliation of a legal system to a larger group, countries that engage in such large-scale eclectic borrowings present serious classificatory difficulties.

(v) It should also be noted that those who seek to classify legal systems, frequently pay exclusive attention to the area of private law. The classificatory schemes thus produced are apt to be uninformative or misleading regarding the character of a nation's public law.

(2) Tentative Area-By-Area Survey [11]

The point made in the preceding paragraph is well illustrated by the legal systems of continental Latin America. The Spanish and Portuguese conquerors introduced legal systems rooted in the civil law; most of the nineteenth and twentieth century codes, though adopted after emancipation, continued this tradition by following European models. The legal systems of Latin America thus are generally classified as belonging to the civil-law orbit. Their fundamental civil-law character has been judicially noticed by courts in the United States.[12]

example, the discussion of the Philippine legal system in the *Shoop* case and the Notes following it, supra pp. 229–245.

10. See supra pp. 8–15.

11. The attention of readers who are not satisfied with this cursory overview is directed to more elaborate surveys of the world's legal systems, past and present. The best-known work of this kind is Wigmore's Panorama of the World's Legal Systems (3 vols. 1928); although in part obsolete, that magisterial and richly illustrated treatise contains much that is of lasting and absorbing interest. More recent surveys of universal or near-universal scope, all of them valuable though differing among each other in arrangement and depth, can be found in the works cited supra, nn. 2 and 3, as well as in K.R. Redden (Gen.Ed.), Modern Legal Systems Cyclopedia (10 Vols., 1984/85) and in Derrett (Ed.), An Introduction to Legal Systems (1968). A great deal of information on the mixed legal systems of Asia and Africa can be found also in M. B. Hooker, Legal Pluralism: An Introduction to Colonial and Neo-Colonial Laws (1975). Moreover, the International Encyclopedia of Comparative Law, in its Vol. I (V. Knapp, Chief Editor), offers National Reports, in alphabetical order, briefly describing the principal features of each legal system. Most (although not all) of these National Reports, each of which contains a useful bibliography, already have been published. More summary descriptions, with emphasis on the organization of Bench and Bar, can be found in C. E. Rhyne (Ed.), Law and Judicial Systems of Nations (3rd ed., 1978).

The Area-by-Area Survey presented on the following pages is intended as a mere thumb-nail sketch. In view of the availability of the comprehensive surveys and reference works mentioned above, no attempt will be made here to offer exhaustive references to the (enormously large) relevant literature.

12. See, e.g., supra p. 144.

Yet, the common law (especially as reflected in the U.S. Constitution) has had a considerable impact on Latin American legal systems, primarily in the area of public law.[13] The notions of due process and habeas corpus, for example, have been incorporated into the constitutions and statutes of a number of Latin American nations.[14] Even in the field of private law, it seems that common-law influences are not lacking, and in fact are growing of late, spearheaded by the relatively recent adoption of the express trust in a number of Central and South American countries.[15]

The same mixed character of law in a large portion of the Western Hemisphere is evident to an even greater extent in Puerto Rico (see supra p. 15) as well as in Louisiana and Quebec, often referred to as civil-law enclaves in the common-law world. Of the two last-mentioned jurisdictions, perhaps Quebec has better resisted the encroachment of the common law,[16] although much of the commercial law of the province, codified as well as uncodified, reflects English influence.[17] Even Louisiana, laboring under the decadence of the French language and the impact of a federal system, still maintains a civil-law flavor in juridical method as well as in legal substance.[18]

Common-law influences have been felt, also, in areas geographically remote from the United States and Great Britain. These areas are by no means contiguous; to a large extent, their shape and location

13. It is because of the traditional classification's focus on private law that the "civil law" label is pinned with ease on Latin American systems. A comparative study of public law might require a different scheme. See J. A. Jolowicz, Development of Common and Civil Law, Lloyd's Maritime and Commercial Law Quarterly 87, 95 (Feb. 1982).

14. In practice, these borrowed institutions may assume a somewhat different character on Latin American soil. Nevertheless, they remain a genuine link between the legal systems of North and South America. See Jaffin, New World Constitutional Harmony, 42 Colum.L.Rev. 523 (1942); B. M. Carl, Erosion of Constitutional Rights of Political Offenders in Brazil, 12 Va.J.Int.L. 157 (1972); D. S. Clark, Judicial Protection of the Constitution in Latin America, 2 Hastings Const.L.Q. 405 (1975); D. B. Furnish, The Hierarchy of Peruvian Laws: Context for Law and Development, 19 Am.J.Comp.L. 91 (1971); P. P. Camargo, The Claim of "Amparo" in Mexico: Constitutional Protection of Human Rights, 6 Cal.West.L.Rev. 201 (1970); Note, The Writ of Amparo: A Remedy to Protect Constitutional Rights in Argentina, 31 Ohio St.L.J. 831 (1970). The impact of political realities upon constitutional safeguards is discussed in A. S. Grebert and S. Y. Nun, Latin American Law and Institutions 69–82 (1982).

15. See Eder, The Impact of the Common Law on Latin America, 4 Miami L.Q. 435, 438–40 (1950). What has been said in n. 14, supra, applies equally to the transplantation of the trust. See B. Kozolchyk, Fairness in Anglo and Latin American Adjudication, 2 B.C.Int. & Comp.L.Rev. 219, 225–27 (1979).

For references to other common-law institutions which influenced the private law of Latin American countries, see Eder, A Comparative Survey of Anglo-American and Latin-American Law (1950). See also Clagett, The Administration of Justice in Latin America (1952); Recasens Siches and others, Latin American Legal Philosophy (1948).

16. The persistence of French language, culture and traditions, as well as the greater continuity of Quebec's legal history (as compared to the repeated upheavals in Louisiana) aid in explaining this phenomenon. On the legal system of Quebec, see generally Castel, The Civil Law System of the Province of Quebec, especially Ch. 1 (1962).

The ongoing reform of the Civil Code of Quebec is discussed in L. Baudouin, The Reform of the Civil Code of Quebec, 52 Revista Juridica de la Universidad de Puerto Rico 149 (1983).

17. See Castel, id. at 171–72.

18. See supra 13–15. . . . However, if the conventional focus were not on the area of private law, one could hardly consider Louisiana an oasis of civil law.

reflects the crazy-quilt pattern of former British conquests in Asia and Africa.

During the colonial period the British rulers usually adhered to the policy that with respect to matters of family law, marital property, succession upon death, and related questions of land tenure, the personal law of the individuals involved should be applied. Islamic law,[19] Hindu law and other non-European systems thus continued to be of great importance throughout the British empire insofar as the personal relations and property interests of the indigenous populations were concerned. Even with respect to these matters, however, common-law influences made themselves felt, because disputes often were decided by British judges [20] (the Privy Council acting as court of last resort); as a rule these judges were empowered by statute or ordinance to interpret—and sometimes even to correct or reject—the parties' personal law in the light of the court's notions of "justice, equity and good conscience." [21] In other fields of law, relating especially to contracts,[22] commercial law, procedure and evidence, the common law tended to displace the non-European systems either entirely or to a very large extent.[23]

mentioned

19. The influence of Islamic law has been considerable, not only in the so-called Near East countries and in South and South East Asia, but also in large parts of Africa. See J. N. D. Anderson, Islamic Law in Africa, especially pp. 3–7 (1954).

20. It is true, of course, that the tribal, "native" or local courts as well as the religious tribunals (especially the Sharia courts administering Islamic law) which function throughout the Asian and African parts of the British Commonwealth, normally are presided over by judges who are not Europeans and who as a rule are not trained in the common law. In some countries, especially in Africa, where much of the law applied by such courts consists of tribal customary law, local African judges are further insulated from the common law by statutes prohibiting professional counsel from appearing in these courts. It must be remembered, however, that frequently an appeal will lie from the decisions of the local courts to a higher tribunal staffed with "learned" judges. The local court's ruling on a point of customary law is often treated as a finding of fact, not freely reviewable on appeal. See Allott, Essays in African Law 87 (1960). But where, by frequent proof in the courts, a particular custom becomes "notorious", it can be judicially noticed and thus becomes "law" for purposes of appellate review. Id. at 88–94. Thus the customary law, even where it is administered in the first instance by chiefs or other indigenous judges, may come under common-law influence through the appellate process. See Hooker, supra n. 11, at 137–39.

21. See Hooker, id. at 58–61, 86–87, 109; Derrett, Justice, Equity and Good Conscience, in J. N. D. Anderson (Ed.), Changing Law in Developing Countries 114 ff. (1963). It is also true that in matters of family law and successions it was often left to the individuals concerned to decide whether to opt out of the indigenous system and become subject to common law. Moreover, in dealing with cases involving more than one "personal law", the appellate courts—again using common-law techniques—developed highly sophisticated conflicts rules.

22. See, e.g., Saxena, Some Comments on the Indian Legal System, with Particular Reference to the Law of Contracts, in 1 Schlesinger (Gen. Ed.), Formation of Contracts—A Study of the Common Core of Legal Systems 281–93 (1968).

23. Sometimes, when they acquired a territory originally colonized by another European power, the British retained the legal system previously established, i.e., a system the European component of which was derived from the civil law rather than the common law. Examples are Roman-Dutch law in South Africa and Ceylon (now Sri Lanka) and French law in Quebec. See also the reference, supra p. 247, to Roman-Dutch law in British Guiana. For a peculiar mixture of imported European law in present-day Botswana, see H. Barton, J. Gibbs, V. Li and J. H. Merryman, Law in Radically Different Cultures 81–82 (1983). These instances, however, are exceptional; as a rule, it was the common law which furnished the European component of the legal systems prevailing in

The strong influence of the common law in the Asian and African parts of the British Commonwealth, though originally imported during a period of occupation or colonization, generally has persisted after the end of that period. It appears, indeed, that upon gaining independence most of the former colonial countries, tending to modernize their law in the interest of economic development, sweep out some of the customary and religious elements and strengthen the Western or Western-influenced components of their legal systems.[24]   Among other examples,[25] one might cite India's abolition of the caste system, and the ambitious attempt made by the same country to modernize and "codify" the customary law pertaining to family relations and family property.[26] The newly independent Commonwealth nations, moreover, invariably face fundamental problems of constitutional law. Almost all of them have adopted written constitutions. The draftsmen of these documents and the judges interpreting them usually are familiar, not only with British traditions, but also with at least some aspects of American constitutional law. Sometimes, they have to choose between (somewhat conflicting) British and American solutions, thus strengthening the basic common-law orientation of their public law, whether their preference in the particular case be for Dicey or for Holmes and Brandeis.[27]

Asian and African countries under British control.

24. It is true that almost all newly independent countries established their own supreme court and renounced the jurisdiction of the Privy Council. But law teachers and legal writers tend to be Western-trained. So are most of the judges of the higher and highest courts, even though they may be of non-European descent. As a result, the courts in many of the newly independent nations of the British Commonwealth strongly adhere to common-law techniques, especially to the doctrine of stare decisis. Indeed, in some of those countries one can observe that stare decisis is more rigidly applied than it is (since 1966) in the English courts.

The discussion of this topic will be taken up again infra at nn. 112–132.

25. Such examples can be found in Asia as well as in Africa. See, e.g., A. Allott, New Essays in African Law 45 (1970); Z. Mustafa, The Common Law in the Sudan 182–228 (1971); Guttmann, The Reception of the Common Law in the Sudan, 6 Int. & Comp.L.Q. 401 (1957); Buss-Tjen, Malay Law, 7 Am.J.Comp.L. 248 (1958); Maung Maung, Lawyers and Legal Education in Burma, 11 Int. & Comp.L.Q. 285 (1962). But see infra, text at nn. 27a and 27b.

26. The statutes comprising this "codification" were enacted between 1955 and 1961. See Derrett, Introduction to Modern Hindu Law 559–610 (1963); K. S. Sidhu, An Institutional and Historical Study of Property in Land in Relation to Punjab Customary Law (unpubl. thesis, Cornell Law Library, 1957), pp. 172–82, 224–29,

240. One of the important objectives of this legislation was to get rid of archaic restrictions upon the alienability of real property. See the instructive discussion by Derrett, Statutory Amendments of the Personal Law of Hindus Since Indian Independence, 7 Am.J.Comp.L. 380 (1958).

There are remnants of civil-law influence in those small parts of India that were formerly Portuguese or French. See K. M. Sharma, Civil Law in India, 1969 Wash.U.L.Q. 1. It does not seem, however, that these civil-law pockets have substantially affected the overall legal development of independent India.

27. See, e.g., Mustafa, supra n. 25, at 212–13. Concerning India, see Alexandrowicz, Constitutional Developments in India (1957); Tripathi, Foreign Precedents and Constitutional Law, 57 Colum.L.Rev. 319, 334–42 (1957). The amalgamation of Islamic and secular (common law) elements in the public law of Pakistan is interestingly discussed by McWhinney, Judicial Review 140–52 (4th ed., 1969). Relevant comparative materials can be found in the casebook by T. M. Franck, Comparative Constitutional Process—Fundamental Rights in the Common Law Nations (1968), and also in the proceedings of the Roundtable on the Rule of Law in Oriental Countries, held in 1957 in Chicago under the auspices of the American Foreign Law Association in cooperation with the International Association of Legal Science, and published in the Annales de la Faculté de Droit d' Istanbul (8e annèe, t. IX), no. 14, 1960; for a brief summary by the General Reporter see Schlesinger, The Rule of Law

Countervailing tendencies should be recognized, however, in several former British possessions. Some of these countries have adopted elements of a socialist character in their law, while others try to preserve and adapt indigenous legal institutions.[27a] In the Sudan, President Nimeiri declared in 1983 that henceforth the country was to be governed by Islamic law. Since then a number of new codes, essentially based on Islamic notions, have been enacted.[27b] The situation is in a state of flux, and it remains to be seen to what extent Western legal institutions will be displaced by adapted religious and socialist legal ideas.

The American impact upon the law of the Philippines has been strong and apparently lasting.[28] Japan, essentially a civil-law country, in many ways shows the strong American influence of the postwar period, especially in its judicial organization and its constitutional and administrative law.[29] Common-law institutions, such as habeas corpus, have been superimposed also on the legal order of South Korea, another civil-law country.[30]

On the other side of the globe, we find in Liberia a legal system essentially patterned after its United States model.[31] In the interior of the country, tribal affairs are still administered according to tribal laws and customs to the extent that the latter do not conflict with statutes or administrative regulations.[32] Apart from the tribal communities, however, the country lives under a legal system originally derived from American sources and recently modernized with the assistance of American consultants.[33] Relatively ancient features of Anglo-American law, such as strict common law pleading, were preserved much

in Oriental Countries, 6 Am.J.Comp.L. 520 (1957).

27a. See D. N. Smith, Man and Law in Urban Africa, 20 Am.J.Comp. Law 223 (1972); H. Barton, J. Gibbs, V. Li and J. H. Merryman, supra n. 23, at 96–101; D. Weisbrot, Customizing the Common Law: the True Papua New Guinea Experience, 67 ABAJ 727 (1981).

27b. During Nimeiri's rule an amendment to the Constitution has been proposed that included the following provision: "Any legislation or law which conflicts with a definitive rule of Islamic Sharia is void, and any citizen may challenge the laws on this ground before the Supreme Court". See C. N. Goodwin, Sudan's Legislative Revolution, ILN (Int. Lawyers' Newsletter) No. 6, pp. 3–4 (1984). What will be the future of the law in the Sudan, torn by the differences between the non-Islamic south and the Islamic north, is extremely uncertain. See C. N. Gordon, The Islamic Legal Revolution: The Case of Sudan, 19 Int. Lawyer 793 (1985).

28. See supra pp. 229–245. After World War II, the common law has replaced the civil law also in some of the formerly Japanese islands in the Pacific.

29. A significant shift from civil-law to common-law institutions is indicated by

Article 76, par. 2 of the Japanese Constitution, which provides that "no extraordinary tribunal shall be established, nor shall any organ or agency of the Executive be given final judicial power." This has the effect of abolishing continental-style administrative courts (to be discussed infra pp. 498–519 ff.); the function of judicial review of administrative acts was transferred to the regular law courts. The problems of transition caused by this shift have been severe. See Ichiro Ogawa, Judicial Review of Administrative Actions in Japan, 43 Wash.L.Rev. 1075 (1968). It should be borne in mind, however, that the practical operation of the Japanese system of judicial review of administrative acts is quite different from the American. See M. Schaar, Verwaltungsrecht, in P. Eubel (Ed.), Das japanische Rechtssystem 85, 95–98 (1980).

30. See Sang Hyun Song, Introduction to the Law and Legal System of Korea (1983).

31. See Konvitz & Rosenzweig, Liberia, in Allott (Ed.), Judicial and Legal Systems in Africa 122–25 (2d ed., 1970).

32. Ibid.

33. See supra p. 11.

longer in Liberia than in the United States, where the pace of statutory change has been quicker. More recently, however, Liberian civil procedure was revised in the light of modern developments in the United States,[34] and this was followed by a thorough revision of the entire body of the country's statute law, benefiting from American experience.[35]

The common law has worked, also, upon the uncodified civil law systems of Scotland, South Africa, Sri Lanka and Guyana.[36] Scots law retains much of its original character,[37] particularly in the traditional fields of contracts, torts, property and inheritance; but centralized legislative and judicial control, combined with the economic integration of the United Kingdom, have had the effect of anglicizing many facets both of substance and procedure.[38] The law of South Africa, likewise, has been influenced by the common law; but it has preserved its basic Roman-Dutch character.[39] Unlike Scots law, South African law is no longer subject to legislative and judicial controls exercised in Britain,[40] and this fact, coupled with political sentiments, may assure the survival of the interesting Roman-Dutch system for the visible future.[41] In Sri Lanka,[42] and even more in Guyana,[43] on the other hand, the common law has widely replaced the former Roman-Dutch system.

34. See Konvitz and Rosenzweig, Background and Summary of the New Civil Procedure Law, 1 Liberian Law Journal 3 (1965).

35. The Liberian Code of Laws of 1956, prepared by the Liberian Codification Project at Cornell University, was a systematic rearrangement of existing laws. The new Code, on which the Project (under the direction of Professor Konvitz) worked for many years in co-operation with leading Liberian lawyers and officials, must be regarded as a revision rather than a mere rearrangement.

For additional references concerning common-law influences in Africa and Asia, see L. E. Trakman, The Need for Legal Training in International, Comparative and Foreign Law: Foreign Lawyers at American Law Schools, 27 J. Legal Ed. 509, 511–12 (1976).

36. The reasons why a small number of civil-law systems escaped codification, have been indicated supra p. 290. For a more complete listing and an informative discussion of the somewhat exceptional civil-law jurisdictions in which a code system of the civilian type has never been adopted, see T. B. Smith, Studies Critical and Comparative IX–XXXVII (1962).

Attempts to introduce particular common-law institutions into such a predominantly civilian system sometimes are made by statute. The difficulties engendered by legislation of this kind are illustrated in the article by T. B. Smith, Exchange or Sale?, 48 Tul.L.Rev. 1029, especially at 1036–41 (1974).

37. See supra p. 290.

38. English influence has been particularly marked in those areas in which Roman law was defective and failed to provide adequate solutions, e.g., in agency and trust situations. Along with English rules of substantive law, some common-law notions of stare decisis seem to have infiltrated into Scots law, a development regretted by some Scots lawyers. See T. B. Smith, English Influences on the Law of Scotland, 3 Am.J.Comp.L. 522 (1954); Cooper, The Common Law and the Civil Law—A Scot's View, 63 Harv.L.Rev. 468 (1950).

39. See Leyser, Some Comments on the South African Legal System, in 1 Schlesinger, Formation of Contracts—A Study of the Common Core of Legal Systems 321–3 (1968). For further references see supra p. 290.

40. Appeals from South African courts to the Privy Council have been abolished. See Leyser, ibid.

41. South Africa's notorious system of racial legislation is not inherited from traditional Roman-Dutch or common law sources. It is a relatively recent statutory accretion. See E. S. Landis, South African Apartheid Legislation, 71 Yale L.J. 1, 437 (1961–62).

42. See supra p. 290. For a case study of common-law influences upon the originally Roman-Dutch system of Ceylon, see L. W. Athulathmudali, The Law of Defamation in Ceylon—A Study of the Inter-Action of English and Roman-Dutch Law, 13 Int. & Comp.L.Q. 1368 (1964). See also

43. See note 43 on page 321.

A "mixed" legal system of singular complexity prevails in Israel.[44] Matters of personal status, especially of marriage and divorce, are still left to the (frequently exclusive) jurisdiction of Jewish, Moslem and Christian religious courts; subject to some legislative inroads, these courts apply the traditional law of their respective communities. Otherwise, the legal system is a secular one; but its various parts stem from different cultures and periods. Before it became a British Mandate in the wake of World War I, Palestine was a province of the Ottoman Empire. Some remnants of the law of that period, which itself reflected a mixture of Islamic and French sources, are still in force today.[45] During the Mandate era, some areas of the law— especially procedure, evidence and torts—were thoroughly anglicized, partly by legislation and partly by judicial importation of common law and equity.[45a] Since the founding of the State of Israel in 1948, new legislation enacted by the Knesset has come to play an ever-increasing role. Aiming at the creation of a national and independent legal system, the Government embarked on an ambitious program of codification.[46] After some initial study and debate, however, it was decided not to prepare a comprehensive Civil Code, to be enacted at a single stroke. Instead, the codifiers have successively tackled various branches of substantive private law. The Law of Succession, enacted in 1965, marked the first major step along this road.[47] This was followed by the codification, in stages, of some parts of the law of property and of the major areas of contract law. As their sources and models, the codifiers used traditional Jewish law, common law and the codes of the civil-law world.[48] In interpreting the new enactments, some of which contain an "autarchy clause",[48a] the courts seem to be somewhat torn between the common-law method of falling back on pre-code case law and the civilian approach of treating the code as a new start.[48b] There is little doubt, however, that at least in the area of substantive private law the

Source of law

L. J. M. Cooray, The Reception of Roman-Dutch Law in Ceylon, 7 Comp. & Int'l J.So. Afr. 295 (1974).

43. See supra p. 247.

44. See, e.g., D. Friedmann, The Effect of Foreign Law on the Law of Israel (1975); G. Tedeschi & Y. S. Zemach, Codification and Case Law in Israel, in J. Dainow (Ed.), The Role of Judicial Decisions and Doctrine in Civil Law and in Mixed Jurisdictions 272 (1974); U. Yadin, Judicial Law-making in Israel, id. at 296.

45. See Friedmann, supra n. 44. The most important enactment of that period was the Ottoman code of civil law, the *Mejelle*. This code, although somewhat French-influenced in its structure and later in its application, was essentially a compilation of rules of Moslem law. In 1984 the *Mejelle* was repealed, but some other remnants of Ottoman law are still in force.

45a. See, e.g., H. W. Baade, The Eichmann Trial: Some Legal Aspects, 1961 Duke L.J. 400, 403, where further references can be found. See also supra n. 44.

46. See Yadin, The Law of Succession and Other Steps Towards a Civil Code, in

Tedeschi and Yadin (Eds.), Studies in Israeli Legislative Problems 104 ff. (1966).

47. Ibid.

48. See G. Shalev & S. Herman, A Source Study of Israel's Contract Codification, 35 La.L.Rev. 1091 (1975); U. Yadin, The New Statute Law of Contracts, 9 Is.L. Rev. 512 (1974).

It may be worth noting, in this connection, that a number of the Israeli lawyers playing a part in the preparation of the various codes received their original legal training in civil-law countries.

48a. Such a clause precluded resort to Art. 46 of the Palestine Order-in-Council, 1922, which (until its repeal in 1980) called upon courts to "exercise their jurisdiction in conforming with the substance of the common law and the doctrines of equity in force in England."

48b. Among Israeli legal scholars there is much debate on how the codes should be interpreted, and how their gaps should be filled. So far as the courts are concerned, it is noticeable that the majority of the present judges have been brought up on the case-law method; but with the advent

ongoing process of codification tends to weaken the common-law ties of Israel's mixed legal system, and in time to move it somewhat closer to the civil-law camp.[48c]

The civil law, even though it has its core areas in continental Europe and Latin America, has spread into many parts of Asia and Africa. Japan,[49] having adopted the main structure of the German code system more than eighty years ago,[50] subsequently felt a measure of common-law influence following World War II.[51] It remains true, nevertheless, that a German-trained member of the legal profession encounters much less difficulty in comprehending Japanese legal materials than a lawyer brought up in the common law; in this sense, Japan is still a civil-law country. The same is true of South Korea.[52] German law also influenced the legal system of pre-communist China,[53] and this German influence remains clearly noticeable in the basic codes of the Republic of China (Taiwan).[54]

of a new generation of judges, who in their formative years have become familiar with the codes, some subtle changes in legal method may occur. Moreover, as the codes' total coverage grows more comprehensive, one may expect a greater willingness on the part of the courts to resort to analogy and generally to become more civilian in treating the codes as an integrated system.

48c. In the areas of procedure and evidence, Israeli law thus far has retained its strong common-law orientation. The same is true of the field of torts; in dealing with automobile accidents, however, Israel went its own way by enacting a statute which imposes strict liability on the driver and owner but limits the amount of damages recoverable by the victim. "The ambit of the tort of negligence has, thus, been considerably curtailed." Friedmann, supra n. 44, at 125.

49. For English-language introductions to the Japanese legal system see, e.g., H. Tanaka (assisted by M. D. H. Smith), The Japanese Legal System (1976); Y. Noda (transl. by A. H. Angelo), Introduction to Japanese Law (1976); D. F. Henderson, Foreign Enterprise in Japan: Laws and Policies (1973). See also C. R. Stevens, Modern Japanese Law as an Instrument of Comparison, 19 Am.J.Comp.L. 665 (1971); L. W. Beer & H. Tomatsu, A Guide to the Study of Japanese Law, 23 Am.J.Comp.L. 284 (1975); M. K. Young, The Japanese Legal System: History and Structure, in Kitagawa (Ed.), Doing Business in Japan, vol. 2 (1984). The most comprehensive and richly documented description of the Japanese legal system in a Western language is P. Eubel, supra n. 29.

Helpful discussions of a comparative nature will be found in two articles by T.

Taniguchi, Fremder Einfluss auf das japanische Recht, 3 Japan Annual of Law and Politics, 25 ff. (1955), and La loi et la coutume au Japon, in Études Juridiques offertes à Léon Julliot de la Morandière 571 ff. (1964).

50. The process by which a predominantly German-inspired Civil Code was adopted in Japan, was somewhat akin to the choice of a compromise candidate. For details of the irreconcilable controversy between the English and the French schools, and the eventual adoption of the German Code, see Takayanagi, Contact of the Common Law with the Civil Law in Japan, 4 Am.J.Comp.L. 60 (1955).

51. See supra, text at n. 29.

52. For a discussion of the 1960 Civil Code, see Sang Hyun Song, Introduction to the Law and Legal System of Korea 382–84 (1983); Kim Chung Han, The New Civil Code of Korea, 4 The Justice 3 (1960); Kyu-Chang Cho, Koreanisches Buergerliches Gesetzbuch XVIII–XX (1980). See also supra n. 30.

53. See Pound, The Chinese Civil Code in Action, 29 Tulane L.Rev. 277 (1955); Escarra, Le Droit Chinois (1936).

54. The Civil Code, in particular, is substantially patterned after that of Germany. See H. H. P. Ma, General Features of the Law and Legal System of the Republic of China, in Cosway, Ma & Shattuck, Trade and Investment in Taiwan: The Legal and Economic Environment in the Republic of China 8 (1973). See also the second (1985) ed. of the same work, by H. H. P. Ma.

For a concise overview of the legal system of the Republic of China, see P. M. Torbert, The Legal Status of U.S. Corporations and Individuals in Taiwan, 1 Hast. Int. & Comp.L.Rev. 263, 268–72 (1978).

Eclectic importation and adaptation of codes stemming from various civil law countries may be said to characterize the Turkish legal system.[55] Turkey virtually copied the Swiss Civil Code and the Swiss Code of Obligations, and subsequently adopted a revised Commercial Code which, although largely German-inspired, was carefully integrated into the (Swiss) scheme of the two older codes.[56] The Turkish Penal Code follows the Italian model, while the Code of Criminal Procedure shows German influence and the Code of Civil Procedure is patterned after the procedural code of the Swiss Canton of Neuchatel.[57] The system of administrative courts and of (uncodified) administrative law is distinctly French-influenced.[58]

Similar eclecticism marks the legal systems of some other developing countries which, like Turkey, remained free from colonial rule but independently decided to follow Western models in modernizing their law.[59] Thailand, for example, has enacted a Penal Code derived from French, Japanese, English and indigenous sources,[60] while the draftsmen of its Civil Code drew inspiration mainly from the codes of France, Germany and Switzerland.[61]

As another example, one can mention Ethiopia, where a similarly variegated bouquet of Codes, prepared by French, Swiss and other European scholars, was adopted during the reign of the late Emperor.[62] Prior to the revolution of 1974, Ethiopian law students seeking to master this essentially civilian code system—which had never become the actual living law in the more remote areas of the country—were instructed in a local law school. The faculty was at the time largely

---

55. See generally T. Ansay and D. Wallace, Introduction to Turkish Law (2d ed., 1978).

56. See Hirsch, Der Einfluss des schweizerischen Rechts auf das neue Tuerkische Handelsgesetzbuch, 52 Schweizerische Juristenzeitung 325 (1956); Ansay, Turkey: New Commercial Code, 6 Am.J.Comp.L. 106 (1957).

57. See Karlen and Arsel, Civil Litigation in Turkey 7–8 (1957).

58. See R. Aybay, Administrative Law, in the work cited supra n. 55, at 53 ff.

Some of the problems of adjustment which arose as a result of Turkey's importation of foreign codes, are interestingly discussed by Hamson, The Istanbul Conference of 1955, 5 Int. & Comp.L.Q. 26 (1956), and by Hooker, supra n. 11, at 364–71. See also the discussion infra, in part (3) of this Note. On the whole, however, Turkey is one of a few countries where Western institutions were successfully introduced into a traditional Moslem milieu. This is often attributed to the charismatic influence of Atatürk. See G. J. Mussell, The Surrogate Proletariat at 392 (1974).

59. When a developing country which is not under colonial rule, independently embarks on a program of modernizing and Westernizing its legal system, it has a choice between civil-law and common-law models. Experience has shown that such countries tend to look to the civil law, probably for the reason that the civil-law models present themselves in the conveniently packaged form of codes.

60. See T. Masao, The New Penal Code of Siam, 18 Yale L.J. 85 (1908).

61. See F. C. Darling, The Evolution of Law in Thailand, 32 Rev.Pol. 197 (1970). The influence of French law was particularly strong, due to the predominance of French advisors during the codification process, and to the large number of Thai lawyers who had received their legal training in France. Even today, the French language is a required part of the law school curriculum in Thailand. See Darling, id. at 216. For further references see Chin Kim, The Thai Choice-of-Law Rules, 5 Int. Lawyer 709 (1971).

62. See N.J. Singer, The Ethiopian Civil Code and the Recognition of Customary Law, 9 Houston L.Rev. 460 (1972); J. Vanderlinden, An Introduction to the Sources of Ethiopian Law, 3 J. of Eth.L. 227 (1966); R. David, A Civil Code for Ethiopia, 37 Tul.L.Rev. 187 (1963); id., Les sources du code civil Éthiopien, 14 Rev.Int. Dr.Comp. 497 (1963); F. F. Russell, The New Ethiopian Civil Code, 29 Brooklyn L.Rev. 236 (1963); id., The New Ethiopian Penal Code, 10 Am.J.Comp.L. 265 (1961).

American and had developed an American approach to teaching and research.[63] After the downfall of the Emperor, the new regime passed a series of "basic laws" which expressed the regime's socialist orientation (e.g., nationalization of land and industry), and appointed a legislative commission to suggest reforms of the codes in the spirit of socialist values and policies.[64] American law teachers were replaced by Ethiopians and a sprinkle of East Europeans.[65] What direction legal development will take remains to be seen.[66]

The Code Napoleon has enjoyed a wide sphere of influence, not limited to the traditional civil-law areas of Europe and Latin America.[67] Throughout the vast area of North and West Africa as well as the Near East (except in Turkey and Israel) French influence has been stronger than that of any other western legal system; but the depth of its penetration has varied from period to period and from country to country.[68] Generalizations, even if limited to the predominantly Arab countries of the area, have to be formulated with caution.[69] There are a few nations, such as Saudi Arabia, Oman and the Arab Republic of Yemen, where the law is still largely based on the Koran and other religious sources.[70] In most of the legal systems of the region, however,

---

63. See J. C. N. Paul, Fourth Annual Report from the Dean, 4 J. of Eth.L. 21 (1967); J. Vanderlinden, Civil Law and Common Law Influences on the Developing Law in Ethiopia, 16 Buff.L.Rev. 250 (1966). See also R. A. Sedler, Legal Education: Ethiopia, 7 For.Exch.Bull. No. 1, p. 7 (1965), where the following observation is made: ". . . teaching in the areas covered by the codes—all private and penal law—calls for a knowledge of continental law. It is very difficult to obtain continental-trained lawyers who can teach in English [the country's second language]; consequently there is a great need for American or British lawyers who have training in comparative law and are bilingual [in the sense that they can work with French or French-derived legal materials]".

64. See F. Nahum, Socialist Ethiopia's Achievements as Reflected in Its Basic Laws, 11 J. of Eth.L. 83–88 (1980).

65. See D. Haile, Annual Report from the Dean, 12 J. of Eth.L. 112–113 (1982)

66. Some comparativists already include Ethiopia among socialist systems. See M. A. Glendon, M. W. Gordon and C. Osakwe, supra n. 2 at 284.

With respect to Eritrea, it is perhaps even more difficult to predict the future course of political and legal developments. Although incorporated into Ethiopia in 1952, Eritrea later struggled for independence. In its legal system, one encounters not only a separate body of local customs but also some remnants, not found in Ethiopia proper, of Italian and British law. See F. F. Russell, Eritrean Customary Law, 3 J.Afr.L. 99 (1959). Regarding the comparable situation in the Somali Republic, see

M. R. Ganzglass, A Common Lawyer Looks at an Uncommon Legal Experience, 53 A.B.A.J. 815 (1967).

67. See Limpens, Territorial Expansion of the Code, in B. Schwartz (Ed.), The Code Napoleon and the Common Law World 92 ff., especially 101–2 (1956); I. Zajtay, Les destinées du Code Civil, 6 Rev.Int.Dr.Comp. 792 (1954). The latter article appears also in I. Zajtay, Beiträge zur Rechtsvergleichung 109 ff. (1976).

68. French influence has remained particularly strong in Lebanon and (at least until recently) in Iran, although the codes of the latter country reflect a measure of eclecticism. See H. J. Liebesny, Stability and Change in Islamic Law, 21 Middle East Journal 16, at 28, 30 (1967); W. G. Wickersham & M. M. Nsouli, Legal System of Lebanon: Summary and Bibliography, 5 Int.Lawyer 300 (1971); G. B. Baldwin, The Legal System of Iran, 7 Int.Lawyer 492 (1973). For a comprehensive survey of codifications of private law in Arab states, see F. Castro, La Codificazione del Diritto Privato negli Stati Arabi Contemporanei, 31 Rivista di Diritto Civile 387–447 (1985).

69. The article by Liebesny, supra n. 68, offers an excellent brief survey covering most of the countries of the area. For thorough treatment and documentation, see S. H. Amin, Middle East Legal Systems (1985); N. H. Kittrie (Ed.), Comparative Law of Israel and the Middle East (1971), and H. J. Liebesny, The Law of the Near and Middle East: Readings, Cases and Materials (1974).

70. See G. Baroody, Shari'ah—The Law of Islam, 72 Case and Comment, March–April 1967, at 3 ff.; Hart, Application of

one observes a mixed pattern. Some version, often a considerably reformed version, of Islamic law is apt to govern matters of family law, including perhaps certain related problems of property and succession; the jurisdiction of religious courts over such matters has been preserved in some but not all of the countries in question. In other fields, especially in the law of obligations and in the area of commercial law, civil-law influence—traditionally of the French variety—has become predominant. One must note, however, the current pressures to depart from Western law whenever it appears to conflict with basic principles of Islamic law.[71]

It is along these lines that the Civil Codes of Egypt (1949),[72] Syria (1949), Iraq (1951, eff. 1953) and Libya (1954), all of which are modern in style and organization, seek to achieve a synthesis between Islamic teachings and the legal institutions of the West.[73] To the extent that they follow western models, modern Near-East legislators—differing in this respect from earlier codifiers who derived their civil-law learning exclusively from French sources—tend to be selective; [73a] but while the Code Napoleon is no longer blindly followed, it is still the most potent source of western influence upon draftsmen of private law codes in the Arab world.[73b]

The growing amalgamation of civil law and Islamic law in the Near East is well illustrated by Art. I of the Iraqi Civil Code, which reads as follows:

> Section 1. The code governs all questions of law which come within the letter or spirit of any of its provisions.

Hanbalite and Decree Law to Foreigners in Saudi Arabia, 22 Geo.Wash.L.Rev. 165 (1953). Although the basically Islamic character of the Saudi Arabian legal system remains unchanged, the country's oil wealth in recent years has led to the enactment of much modern legislation, some of which is based on Western models. See N. H. Karam, Business Laws of Saudi-Arabia (1979); J. Asherman, Doing Business in Saudi-Arabia, 16 Int. Lawyer 321 (1982); T. M. Hill, The Commercial Legal System of the Sultanate of Oman, 17 Int. Lawyer 507 (1983).

The Islamic tradition, modified in part by codes and other statutes, also plays a dominant role in the legal system of Afghanistan. See A. S. Sirat, The Modern Legal System of Afghanistan, 16 Am.J. Comp.L. 563 (1968). Whether and to what extent this will change under the present Marxist regime, remains to be seen.

71. See G. F. Borden, Legal Counselling in the Middle East, 14 Int. Lawyer 545, 560 (1980); H. Barton, J. Gibbs, V. Li and J. H. Merryman, supra n. 23 at 36.

72. This Code went into effect upon abolition of the Mixed Courts, as to which see Brinton, The Mixed Courts of Egypt (rev. ed. 1968). Until 1949, Egypt had a Civil Code for the Mixed Courts (1875) and a Civil Code for the National Courts (1883),

both of which largely followed the Code Napoleon. The 1949 Code thus marks a partial recession of foreign and especially of French influence.

In 1980 the Constitution was amended to make Islamic law the principal source of legislation, and several courts have invalidated contracts with interest provisions on the ground that such provisions violate Islamic law. See H. Barton, J. Gibbs, V. Li and J. H. Merryman, supra n. 23 at 36.

73. In addition to the writings cited in n. 69, supra, and to the Practising Law Institute publication mentioned in n. 70, supra, see Gamal Moursi Badr, The New Egyptian Civil Code and the Unification of the Laws of the Arab Countries, 30 Tulane L.Rev. 299, 303–4 (1956); R. Khany, The Legal System of Syria, 1 Comp.L.Yearbook 137 (1977, publ. 1978).

73a. See F. J. Ziadeh, Law of Property in Egypt: Real Rights, 26 Am.J.Comp.L. 239, 246 (1978).

73b. This is illustrated by the Egyptian Civil Code's provisions on land law, which apparently were inspired by somewhat archaic rules embodied in the Code Napoleon. See ibid., and D. F. Forte, Egyptian Land Law: An Evaluation, 26 Am.J.Comp. L. 273 (1978).

Section 2. If the Code does not furnish an applicable provision, the court shall decide in accordance with customary law, and failing that, in accordance with those principles of Muslim law (Shari'a) which are most in keeping with the provisions of this Code, without being bound by any particular school of jurisprudence, and, failing that, in accordance with the principles of equity.

Section 3. In all of this, the Court shall be guided by judicial decisions and by the principles of jurisprudence in Iraq and in foreign countries whose laws are similar to those of Iraq.[74]

The "similar laws" of foreign countries to which Sect. 3 refers, are said to be the codes and judicial decisions of Syria, Egypt and France.[75]

The Islamic tradition is a factor, though a less potent one, also in Indonesia, another oriental country touched by civil law influence. There, the Dutch introduced the so-called "dualist" system; the majority of the indigenous population lived under their own customary law ("Adat" law, varying from region to region), while Europeans, non-native orientals and others who voluntarily accepted European law were governed by Dutch codes.[76] There was, also, a dual court system. Upon gaining independence, the Indonesian Republic created a substantially unitary court system;[77] but the dualism of the substantive law, while greatly reduced by the enactment of unitary statutes covering certain important areas (especially of business law),[78] has not been completely eliminated.[79] As a result, Indonesian lawyers and law

---

74. See Jwaideh, The New Civil Code of Iraq, 22 Geo.Wash.L.Rev. 176, 181 (1953). For a discussion of this provision, and of similar provisions in the Civil Codes of Egypt, Syria and Libya, see also Liebesny, supra n. 68, at 31.

The Code's reference to "principles of equity" was inspired by Art. 11 of Egypt's former Civil Code for the Mixed Courts (see supra n. 72), which provided that "in case of silence, insufficiency and obscurity of the law, the judge shall follow the principles of natural law and equity." See G. M. Wilner, The Mixed Courts of Egypt: A Study on the Use of Natural Law and Equity, 5 Georgia J.Int. & Comp.L. 407 (1975).

75. See Jwaideh, supra n. 74.

76. See Ter Haar, Adat Law in Indonesia, with an instructive Introduction by Hoebel and Schiller (1948); Leyser, Legal Developments in Indonesia, 3 Am.J.Comp. L. 399 (1954).

The codes for the East Indies were not entirely but very largely identical with the French-influenced codes adopted in Holland in 1838. The Netherlands East Indies Civil Code of 1847, for example, was essentially based on Holland's own Civil Code of 1838, which in turn was a derivative of the

Code Napoleon. Subsequent amendments of the Holland codes were not always incorporated into the East Indies codes.

77. Religious courts, however, exercising jurisdiction over Moslems in matters of family law (with the Islamic High Court as appellate court) were preserved. Recently, and very largely as a result of the Marriage Law of 1974, there has been a notable increase in the power and stature of these courts. See J. S. Katz & R. S. Katz, Legislating Social Change in a Developing Country: The New Indonesian Marriage Law Revisited, 26 Am.J.Comp.L. 309, 317 (1978).

78. See the series of English-language monographs directed by Professors Mochtar Kusumaatmadja and Sudargo Gautama (J. Katz & R. Katz, Advisors) and published by Padjadjaran University Law School under the title Survey of Indonesian Economic Law (1973-74).

79. See S. Gautama & R. N. Hornick, An Introduction to Indonesian Law: Unity in Diversity (1974); E. Damian & R. N. Hornick, Indonesia's Formal Legal System, 20 Am.J.Comp.L. 492 (1972) (with bibliography); D. S. Lev, The Lady and the Banyan Tree: Civil Law Change in Indonesia, 14 Am.J.Comp.L. 282 (1965).

students still have to familiarize themselves with the intricacies of interpersonal "conflict of laws" problems.[80]

A survey of civil-law and common-law jurisdictions, even a most hurried one, would not be complete without some reference to the special position of the Scandinavian legal systems.[81] Eluding classification as belonging to either group,[82] Scandinavian law has some of the characteristics of both.[83] It is progressive and largely embodied in fairly systematic statutes, some of them of broad coverage; these statutes, however, are not organized as a comprehensive whole such as the code systems of typical civil-law jurisdictions. There are differences *inter sese* between the laws of the various Scandinavian nations; but many uniform statutes have been enacted by all or most of them, governing such matters as marriage, sales, checks, insurance, trademarks and air traffic. Social security has been a subject of inter-Scandinavian coordination, and uniform rules of conflict of laws for all five Scandinavian nations were adopted by treaty.[84] Scandinavian lawyers and legislators thus created a model of cooperation among sovereign states which deserves close study by those facing similar problems in other parts of the world.[85]

In appraising the world-wide influence of the civil law, it must be remembered, finally, that certain civil-law elements remain alive in the legal systems of those nations which today belong to the communist orbit.

80. This phenomenon is by no means limited to Indonesia. A measure of "dualism" or "pluralism"—i.e., an approach postulating different law for different groups within a nation state—continues to characterize most of the legal systems of the southern hemisphere. We shall come back to this point in our discussion of the legal systems of developing countries. See infra, text at nn. 112–132.

81. See, generally, Orfield, The Growth of Scandinavian Law (1953); R. B. Ginsburg, A Selective Survey of English Language Studies on Scandinavian Law (1970).

For an interesting birds-eye view of the essential features of the Swedish legal system, see J. B. Board, Jr., Legal Culture and the Environmental Protection Issue: The Swedish Experience, 37 Albany L.Rev. 603 (1973).

82. Some scholars classify Scandinavian law into a distinct group independent of both common and civil law. See B. Gomard, Civil Law and Scandinavian Law, 5 Scandinavian Studies in Law 29 (1961); S. Jorgensen, Les traits principaux de l' évolution des sources du droit Danois, 1971 Rev.Int. de Droit Comparé 65. See also S. Jorgensen, Grundzüge der Entwicklung der skandinavischen Rechtswissenschaft, 25 Juristenzeitung 529 (1970) (emphasizing the independence of Scandinavian legal scholarship).

To others, Scandinavian law is but a branch of "continental" legal systems which are contrasted with common law. See, e.g., F. Wieacker, Privatrechtsgeschichte der Neuzeit, 496, 505 (2nd ed., 1967).

83. Common-law as well as civil-law characteristics can be found, for instance, in the Swedish Code of Civil Procedure of 1948. See Ginsburg and Bruzelius, Civil Procedure in Sweden (1965). See also infra p. 526.

The Scandinavian courts' attitude toward precedents has been described as an intermediate one, midway between stare decisis and the corresponding doctrines of the civilians, which will be discussed below (pp. 597 ff.). See von Eyben, Judicial Law Making in Scandinavia, 5 Am.J.Comp.Law 112 (1956).

84. See Orfield, supra n. 81, at 302–6; H. A. Schwarz-Liebermann, Droit Comparé 241–45 (1978).

The working methods of legislative cooperation among the Nordic countries are interestingly described and illustrated by S. Jorgensen, Abbestellungsrecht und nordische Gesetzeszusammenarbeit, 1971 Zeitschrift für Rechtsvergleichung 12.

85. See S. Petrén, Nordic and International Lawmaking, 12 Scandinavian Studies in Law 69 (1968); N. E. Holly, Legal and Legislative Co-operation in the Scandinavian States, 49 A.B.A.J. 1089 (1963).

As to the continuing strength of these civil-law elements, the communist legal systems differ widely from one another. At one extreme, there is the People's Republic of China, where even before the advent of communism the dominance of legal institutions imported from the West [86] (mainly from civil-law countries) was less than solidly established and perhaps only skin-deep.[87] All outside influences (including the influence of Soviet law which served as a model during the early post-revolutionary era) were further weakened in the period of Mao's "legal nihilism". After Mao's death there began a revival of interest in the legal ordering of society, including a program of national codification.[87a] Many important pieces of legislation have been enacted, most of them showing definite traces of civil-law drafting techniques.[88] But these tokens of civil-law influence may turn out to be superficial: they compete with socialist legal institutions and with traditional attitudes that do not encourage the growth of Western legal infra-structures, including a truly influential legal profession.[89]

At the opposite extreme there are the countries of Eastern and Southeastern Europe which (with the exception of Albania)[90] truly belonged to the civil-law world until the 1940's.[91] Under communism, the ideological thrust of those countries' legal systems has been radical-

---

86. See supra n. 53.

87. See H. C. Darby, The Chinese Legal System: Historical Background, 10 Civil & Military L.J. (New Delhi, 1974); L. T. Lee & W. W. Lai, The Chinese Conceptions of Law: Confucian, Legalist, and Buddhist, 29 Hast.L.J. 1307 (1978).

87a. Recently (to take effect Jan. 1, 1987) the important "General Principles of Civil Law of the P.R.C." have been enacted. For an English translation (by W. Gray & H. R. Zheng) see 34 Am.J.Comp.L. 715 (1986). See also H. R. Zheng, China's New Civil Law, 34 Am.J.Comp.L. 669 (1986); E. J. Epstein, The Evolution of China's General Principles of Civil Law, id. at 705.

88. A list of these statutes can be found in D. F. Forte, Western Law and Communist Dictatorship, 32 Emory L.J. 136, 215 (1983). See also F. H. Foster, Codification in Post-Mao China, 30 Am.J.Comp.L. 395–428 (1982); M. Kato, Civil and Economic Law in the P.R. of China, id. at 429–457; Shao-Chuan Leng and Hungdah Chiu, Criminal Justice in Post-Mao China (1985); Chin Kim, The Modern Chinese Legal System, 61 Tul.L.Rev. 1413 (1987). For a very instructive discussion of the efforts to rebuild China's legal system, see T. A. Gelatt and F. E. Snyder, Legal Education in China: Training for a New Era, 1 China Law Reporter 41 (1980). It is interesting to note that the study of laws of capitalist countries has been officially encouraged as part of a search for useful legal ideas. See Beijing Review, April 6, 1981 at 14–16.

On the basic direction of the legal systems of P. R. China, Vietnam and North Korea, see Chin Kim, Recent Developments in the Constitutions of Asian Marxist Socialist States, 13 Case Western Res.J. of Int.L. 483 (1981).

89. For a sceptical view about the prospect that China would successfully adopt Western Law, see V. Li, The Drive to Legalization, in J. H. Barton, J. L. Gibbs, V. Li and J. H. Merryman supra n. 23. *But see* W. Gray, China's Changing Legal Climate, 31 Law Quadrangle Notes, No. 2, p. 1, at p. 2 (1987), where it is pointed out that today "the number of students studying law in full- or part-time programs is probably close to 100,000. In-service education for China's judges, very few of whom have had formal legal education, has been instituted, and an extensive legal literature is now appearing."

90. In spite of the adoption of some codes influenced by French and Italian models, it seems that Islamic and Ottoman influences were predominant in the precommunist legal system of Albania. See Kolaj and Pritsch in 1 Rechtsvergleichendes Handwoerterbuch fuer das Zivil- und Handelsrecht des In- und Auslandes 1–5 (1929); Hooker, supra n. 11, at 410.

91. Except for Hungary, all of the countries in question had adopted typical civilian code systems, modeled on the Austrian or some other classical continental patterns. Some countries, notably the Kingdom of Yugoslavia, had preserved enclaves of Islamic law (relating to personal status) for the benefit of their sizable Moslem minorities.

ly changed, and the same is true of those sectors of the law that reflect the socio-economic character of the state. But on the working level, those countries have preserved most of the concepts and techniques, and a considerable number of the actual institutions, which had been part of their civil-law heritage.[92] Thus, in spite of the chasm that separates the pluralist West from the communist East in terms of economic structure, political organization and ideology, a lawyer trained in the civil law will experience little difficulty orienting himself in the legal systems of the communist countries located to the West and Southwest of the Soviet Union.[93]

Without much exaggeration, a similar statement could be made regarding the legal system of the Soviet Union itself. Although its older historical roots are quite different from those of the law of Western and Central Europe, the Russian legal system came under the strong influence of western civilian codes during the last half-century preceding the October Revolution of 1917.[94] Present-day Soviet codes of civil and criminal procedure, and indeed the civil codes of the various Soviet Republics,[95] do not mark a sharp break with traditional civilian techniques.[96] A lawyer brought up in the civil law may dislike the

---

92. See David & Brierley, supra n. 3, at 181–84.

One of the principal legacies of the civil law to the socialist legal systems of Eastern Europe is the technique of codification. See F. J. M. Feldbrugge (Ed.), Codification in the Communist World (1975).

93. Much relevant material, and many references, can be found in Professor W. J. Wagner's introductory comments on the Polish legal system, and on the legal systems of other communist countries, in 1 Schlesinger, op. cit. supra n. 22, at 213–23 and 311–17. See also W. J. Wagner, Polish Law Throughout the Ages (1970).

The Yugoslav legal system has developed along lines which in many respects differentiate it strongly from the legal systems of other socialist countries. An important source of differences is the fact that the Yugoslavs have rejected rigid central planning (by state agencies) of the economy and the management of economic organizations. Yugoslav law expresses the new economic organization by stating that the productive capital belongs to society ("social ownership") rather than to the state or to private individuals and groups: people working in enterprises have the right to manage and use the "socially owned" capital. An American court has tried to explain the resulting arrangements by a partial recourse to the common-law trust device. See Edlow Int. Co. v. Nuklearna Elektrarna Krsko, 441 F.Supp. 827 (D.D.C. 1977). Notwithstanding all the peculiarity of the Yugoslav brand of socialism, the statement in the text, supra, applies to that country as well as to Warsaw Pact countries. Concerning pronounced civil-

law features of the 1978 Yugoslav Statute on Obligations, see K. Muscheler, Deutsch-Jugoslawisches Juristentreffen, Mitteilungen der Gesellschaft für Rechtsvergleichung, No. 18 (May 1981), p. 320.

94. See S. Kutcherov, Courts, Lawyers and Trials Under the Last Three Tsars (1953); K. Grzybowski, Legal Science During the Last Century: Russia, in M. Rotondi (Ed.), Inchieste di Diritto Comparato—La Scienza del Diritto nell' Ultimo Secolo, at 623–43 (1976); H. J. Berman, The Comparison of Soviet and American Law, 34 Ind.L.J. 559, 562–63 (1959).

95. For an excellent English translation, see W. Gray and R. Stults, The Civil Code of the Russian Soviet Federated Socialist Republic (1965). See also W. E. Butler, Collected Legislation of the USSR & the Constituent Union Republics (1979).

96. See, e.g., the numerous references to "Romanist tradition" in J. N. Hazard, Communists and Their Law (1969).

In matters of technical detail, the civilian tradition is apparent at every step. As one of many examples, one might mention the list of transactions requiring the formality of a notarial act. See Hazard, Butler & Maggs, The Soviet Legal System 69–71 (3rd ed., 1977). Socialist legal scholars seem to agree that "legal forms" in bourgeois and socialist law may be similar. See I. Szabo, The Socialist Conception of the Law, in International Encyclopedia of Comparative Law, Vol. II, Ch. 1, p. 59 (1970).

It should be kept in mind, however, that many traditional civilian techniques and institutions undergo a more or less subtle

ideology that permeates the text or the implementation of these codes;[97] but their structure, terminology and technique will appear reasonably familiar to him.[98]

At the end of this brief survey, the reader may be tempted to proceed to quantitative generalizations, in terms of the number of people affected by the civil law. It is safe to say that well over half a billion people today live under legal systems which are essentially of the civil-law type.[99] The lives of additional hundreds of millions are governed by systems of legal order in which civil-law elements, though conjoined with norms of communist, non-European or common-law provenience, nevertheless play an important role. The total impact of the concepts and precepts usually grouped together under the "civil-law" label thus is truly enormous. As we have seen, this impact is felt in every part of the globe.

(3) The Limited Usefulness of the Common Law— Civil Law—Socialist Law Trichotomy: A Brief Look at Alternative Groupings

The above survey is based on a trichotomous grouping—common law, civil law and socialist law—, and there can be no doubt that this grouping is useful in that it facilitates our discourse on many subjects. That this is so, is due to a reason which has been stated above but is worth repeating: that almost every legal system presently in existence has at least some features affiliating it, more or less strongly, with one or several of these three groups.

Clearly, however, it is possible to develop other groupings, based on a variety of criteria. Experience shows that such other groupings are frequently useful and that for certain purposes they are indeed indispensable as supplemental tools of categorization. For instance:

(a) For some purposes, it is undoubtedly useful to lump together all those legal systems which are strongly influenced by a

change of purpose when used in the Soviet system: policies pursued in the new context are different. There is little doubt, for example, that in the Soviet system the requirement of a notarial act reflects a stronger degree of state supervision than would be the case in a Western civil-law country.

97. Concerning the impact of ideology on the Soviet administration of justice, see W. J. Wagner, The Russian Judiciary Act of 1922 and Some Comments on the Administration of Justice in the Soviet Union, 41 Ind.L.J. 42o (1966).

For a broad-based discussion of the jurisprudential underpinnings of socialist law, see D. A. Funk, Lessons of Soviet Jurisprudence: Law for Social Change Versus Individual Rights, 7 Ind.L.Rev. 449 (1974). See also I. Markovits, Socialist vs. "Bourgeois" Rights, 46 Univ. Chicago L.Rev. 612 (1978).

98. The problem of the comparability of socialist and nonsocialist legal institutions has spawned a voluminous literature.

Comparativists from socialist countries usually stress the uniqueness of their system and the limits of comparability. See, e.g., I. Szabo, supra note 96 at 59–61; A. A. Tille, Socialisticheskoe Sravnitelnoe Pravovedenie (1975). For Western views, see Hazard, Socialist Laws and the International Encyclopedia, 79 Harv.L.Rev. 278 (1965); 1 Schlesinger (Gen. Ed.), Formation of Contracts—A Study of the Common Core of Legal Systems 22–29 (1968); D. Loeber, Rechtsvergleichung zwischen Ländern mit verschiedener Wirtschaftsordnung, in 26 Rabels Z. 201 (1961). See also F. Mádl, A Comparative Law Synthesis Theory v. Private Transnational Law as a New Concept in Private Law, 2 Comp.L. Yearbook 1 (1979); M. Bogdan, Different Economic Systems and Comparative Law, 2 Comp.L. Yearbook 89 (1979).

99. The comparable figure for the common law may be close to a billion, if one includes India and Pakistan among the common-law jurisdictions.

particular religion, and to distinguish them from secular legal systems. The prime example (although not the only one) is "Islamic law." As we have seen above, there are very few countries today where traditional Islamic notions dominate all fields of law; but in many Asian and African legal systems the Islamic component is of great importance for some areas of law, especially for matters involving the family. International practitioners and scholars engaged in comparative legal studies thus would find their discourse severely hampered if they could not utilize the category of "Islamic law."

This category, based on a religious criterion, thus supplements the basic trichotomy; and to a considerable extent it cuts across the trichotomy, because there are socialist as well as civil-law and common-law countries whose legal systems contain an Islamic component.

(b) For some purposes, the legal systems of nations having a federal structure can and should be viewed synoptically, and distinguished from unitary systems. Important scholarly studies have been made possible by the use of this grouping; [100] and every experienced international practitioner realizes that he cannot even begin to conduct research on a question arising under the law of Ruritania unless he knows whether Ruritania has a federal or a unitary structure.[101]

The categories of "federal" and "unitary" legal systems again cut across the basic trichotomy. There are both federal and unitary systems in the orbits of the common law, of the civil law, and of socialist law.

(c) For certain purposes, it has been found useful to group together those legal systems which provide for judicial review of legislative acts, and to contrast them to the systems lacking such review.[102] Needless to say, such a classification again cuts across the basic trichotomous division.[103]

More broadly, one can classify legal systems by using as a criterion the relative influence which the various branches of

100. See, e.g., the 1970 Colloque of the International Association of Legal Science entitled "Federalism and Development of Legal Systems" (publ. 1971, with a Foreword and Summary by J. N. Hazard; national reports from West Germany, Canada, U.S.A., India, Czechoslovakia, U.S.S.R. and Yugoslavia); E. McWhinney, Federalism and Supreme Courts, and the Integration of Legal Systems (1973).

101. An illustration from the civil-law world is presented by the Swiss case of Haass v. Wyler, infra pp. 710 ff. The federal system of West Germany is ably discussed by P. M. Blair, Federalism and Judicial Behaviour in West Germany (1981).

102. See, e.g., R. David, Sources of Law (Vol. II, ch. 3 of the International Encyclopedia of Comparative Law) Secs. 64–84 (1984); M. Cappelletti and W. Cohen, Comparative Constitutional Law: Cases and Materials (1979); Constitutional Judicial Review of Legislation: A Comparative Law Symposium, 56 Temple L.Q. 287–438 (1983).

103. In the European heartland of the civil-law orbit elaborate systems of judicial review spread following the Second World War (e.g., Italy, West Germany). In recent years there occurred another expansion of judicial review on the Iberian peninsula. Concerning the spread of judicial review in Latin America, see D. C. Clark, supra n. 14. In the socialist orbit we encounter special constitutional courts only in Yugoslavia, and a limited possibility of constitutional review in Roumania and (since the beginning of 1986) in Poland. See H. Roggemann, Zur Entwicklung sozialistischer Verfassungskontrolle—das neue Verfassungsgericht in Polen, Zeitschrift fuer Rechtspolitik 1986, pp. 137 ff.

government have upon the development of the law. That the relative influence of the legislature and the courts is often used as a criterion, or part of a criterion, is well known to everyone who has even begun to familiarize himself with judicial and scholarly attempts to differentiate between the common law and the civil law.[104] What is frequently overlooked, is that in many legal systems the executive branch has important law-making functions. This can be so even in a democratic country such as France.[105] Thus, one might—for certain practical as well as scholarly purposes—classify legal systems according to the relative strength of the *executive* (as well as legislative and judicial) influence upon the development of the law.[105a]

(d) Significant insights into the nature and the function of legal systems may be lost for one who, through exclusive reliance on traditional schemes of classification, fails to pay sufficient attention to the fact that the importance of law as an ordering device is not everywhere the same. We think of law as essentially independent of (although fed by) custom, morality and other social norms; we also assume that law carries everywhere roughly the same weight as a social force. But the concept of law and law's impact on social life are not invariables; many sociologists and anthropologists claim that law as an autonomous, systematic body of norms is peculiarly Western. It is only in the West that law—so understood—plays a significant role in the actual life of individuals and groups.[105b]

Evidence for the proposition that in non-Western cultures the law plays a much more limited role than in Anglo-American or Western European countries, can be found not only in the great majority of developing countries—the legal systems of which will be discussed under (e) infra—, but even in a country as highly developed and industrialized as present-day Japan. To a much greater degree than its Western counterparts, Japanese society still functions on the basis of non-legal restraints and conventions, and

104. In this connection, the reader will recall the reasoning of Malcolm, J., in the *Shoop* case, supra.

105. See Kahn-Freund, Levy & Rudden, A Source-book on French Law 16–67 (2d ed., 1979); B. Nicholas, Loi, Reglement and Judicial Review in the Fifth Republic, 1970 Public Law 251; G. Bermann, French Treaties and French Courts: Two Problems in Supremacy, 28 Int. & Comp.L.Q. 458, 481 (1979).

A special problem arises in socialist legal systems because of the ubiquitous presence of the communist party. Thus, for example, the *actual* legislative initiative is regularly exercised by the Party's Politbiro. See O. Ioffe and P. B. Maggs, supra n. 3c at 99. The Party's control over the executive is also indubitable.

105a. Following the German sociologist Max Weber, many legal scholars have attempted, also, to classify legal systems according to the role played in their develop-

ment by "key groups" such as judges or scholars. See, e.g., H. Bernstein, Rechtsstile und Rechtshonoratioren; ein Beitrag zur Methode der Rechtsvergleichung, 34 Rabels Z. 343 (1970); J. P. Dawson, The Oracles of the Law (1968).

105b. See H. Berman, Law and Revolution 7–8 (1983); G. Sawer, The Western Conception of Law, in 2 International Encyclopedia of Comparative Law, chapt. 1, 46–47 (1975); L. J. Constantinesco, supra n. 1 at 267 ff. Professor A. Bozeman, in her provocative book "The Future of Law in a Multicultural World" (1971), argues that the adoption of autonomous Western Law by Asian and African countries, be it in its civil-law or common-law variant, is merely "rhetorical". But even in Europe, it may be that law is more of a vital social force in the pluralist West than in the communist East. See I. Markovits, supra n. 3a at 133–134.

recourse to the legal process, which may involve some loss of face for all concerned, is thought of merely as a last resort.[106] Among the members of the present generation this attitude is said to undergo a modicum of change; [107] but this is a slow process. One of the effects of the traditional attitude is that in Japan there is much less litigation and hence less need for lawyers' services than in the West.[108] "According to statistics published in 1965, people in California . . . filed fourteen lawsuits for every one filed in Japan." [109] And in 1976 it was reported that there were only 11,000 members of the Bar in Japan, serving a population of nearly 112 million. In contrast, with a population of less than double that of Japan, the United States at that time had over 350,000 attorneys actively engaged in the practice of law. It should be recognized, however, that numerous licensed specialists other than attorneys are available to the Japanese public for legal advice and drafting of documents in *non-litigated* matters.[110]

106. The same attitude, which at least in part is traceable to the teachings of Confucius, can be found in traditional China. Remnants of this attitude, which leads to a preference for conciliation over litigation, are said to be noticeable in the present (communist) system of mainland China. See, e.g., Lau v. Kiley, 563 F.2d 543, 551 (2d Cir. 1977), where the following language is quoted from an article by Professor Victor H. Li:

> The non-legal background of the Communists was reinforced by the traditional attitude of paying little attention to law. Although a formal legal system had existed in China for many centuries, whenever possible people avoided resorting to it.

107. In part, the change may be due to the fact that in most tort cases the victim nowadays confronts a faceless insurance company rather than an individual as his opponent.

108. See The Wall Street Journal of April 14, 1983 at p. 28. Not only private law litigation, but also public law litigation (including attempts to have administrative action reviewed by the courts) is less frequent in Japan than in other highly industrialized nations. See M. K. Young, Judicial Review of Administrative Guidance: Governmentally Encouraged Consensual Dispute Resolution in Japan, 84 Colum.L. Rev. 923, 951–953 (1984).

Fairly recently, a noted Japanese scholar has written that in the minds of his countrymen:

> ". . . the word law is always associated with prison, the symbol of severity. They do not understand how, in other countries, the law is personified by a

goddess like Dike or Justitia. To bring someone before a court is in itself a shameful act, because resort to the law shows that the plaintiff thinks that his opponent is an abnormal person with whom it is impossible to reach friendly agreement through mutual talk. . . .

> "Even among the cases brought before the courts a great number is finally resolved by conciliation. CCProc. art. 136 provides that 'at any time the court may conciliate the parties . . . .'. Moreover, a plaintiff can, at the start, require the court to deal with the conflict according to the mediation procedure. The rules concerning mediation procedure are laid down by Law no. 222 of 9 June 1951. The percentage of requests for mediation is very high, compared to that of requests for judgment."

Y. Noda, The Far Eastern Conception of Law, in International Encyclopedia of Comparative Law, Vol. II, Ch. 1, at 120, 133 (1971). See also Chin Kim and E. M. Lawson, The Law of the Subtle Mind: The Traditional Japanese Conception of Law, 28 Int. & Comp.L.Q. 491 (1979).

109. M. M. McMahon, Legal Education in Japan, 60 A.B.A.J. 1376, 1380 (1974).

110. See 13 The World Jurist No. 6, p. 4 (Nov.–Dec. 1976). See also C. R. Stevens, Modern Japanese Law as an Instrument of Comparison, 19 Am.J.Comp.L. 665, 679 (1971).

In this connection, the reader will recall our previous discussion of the exceedingly low pass-rate in Japanese bar examinations. See supra p. 187. Concerning specialists other than attorneys, see T. Hattori and D. F. Henderson, Civil Procedure in Japan, § 2.09 (1983).

Because its formal (last-resort) precepts are largely patterned after Western models,[111] Japan's legal system ordinarily is classified in terms of its "civil-law" or "common-law" elements. For some purposes, especially in the context of a discussion of technical legal problems, this may be quite proper. But in other contexts, whenever the actual role of law as a solvent of disputes and other societal problems is at issue, such a classification—unless supplemented and qualified by other classificatory endeavors—can be seriously misleading.

(e) The interaction between law and economic development has become a much-discussed topic in recent years. Thus far, most of the steadily growing literature on the subject consists of studies focusing on a single "less developed country" (LDC) or on a regionally defined group of such countries; but comparative discussions are beginning to appear,[112] using classificatory labels that are predicated on a country's economic or socio-economic development and thus cut across most of the other schemes of classifying legal systems.

Some of those who use the new labels probably hope to arrive at generalizations that are valid for all LDCs, and will help to clarify the role of law in the development process. Perhaps such generalizations will emerge in time. They would be useful because they might make it possible to transfer experience from one LDC to another. But the task is rendered extremely difficult by the fact that any study relating to all of the LDCs—in Asia, Africa, and Latin-America—necessarily has to deal with a forbidding array of political, social and cultural variables.

It is commonplace for western observers somewhat regretfully and patronizingly to comment on the obstacles which in most of the LDCs seem to impede the effective use of law as an instrument of economic development. But the nature of these obstacles is not everywhere the same. There may be flaws in what is formally proclaimed as "law"; [113] or a law which on its face seems perfectly sound to the outside observer, fails to accomplish its purpose because of lack of implementation.[114]

Lack of implementation, again, may be due to a variety of causes. Perhaps the formally enacted "laws" have not been effec-

---

111. See the Area-by-Area Survey, supra.

112. See, e.g., the International Legal Center's reports on "Law and Development" (1974) and on "Legal Education in a Changing World" (1975).

113. The formally established law of land tenure may stand in the way of obtaining agricultural credit, or in other ways inhibit the efficient use of land; or the rules of commercial law may be unsuited as a basis for a modern credit system. See B. Kozolchyk, Toward a Theory on Law in Economic Development: The Costa Rican USAID-ROCAP Law Reform Project, 1971 Law and Social Order (Ariz. State Un.L.J.) 681; id., Commercial Law Recodification and Economic Development

in Latin America, 4 Lawyer of the Americas No. 2, pp. 1 ff. (1972); L. M. Hager, The Role of Lawyers in Developing Countries, 58 A.B.A.J. 33 (1972).

114. For examples, reference may be made again to the articles cited in the preceding footnote. See also B. Kozolchyk, Law and the Credit Structure in Latin America, 7 Va.J.Int.L. 1 (1967).

The problems that arise when actual practice diverges from the law in the books are of course not limited to LDCs. See infra pp. 880 ff. But experience seems to show that they tend to be particularly acute in developing countries. See Hager, supra n. 113, at 35, where further references can be found.

·tively communicated to the citizenry, or even to the judges and other officials expected to enforce them.[115] Or they are so unresponsive to the particular social needs of the country that it becomes customary to circumvent them.[116] Or again, the role of law in the particular society may be so completely eclipsed by other cultural forces that the voice of the law is never loud and clear.[117]

Yet, an unqualified statement to the effect that law is impotent as an instrument of modernization, also would be an unwarranted generalization. Experience has shown that even in a society not attuned to western-style law, desirable social change can be brought about by legislation, provided the legislator is sophisticated enough to keep modernization within culturally tolerable limits,[118] and whenever possible to utilize respected existing institutions as agents of reform.[119] Unfortunately, however, many efforts to change indigenous institutions suffer from shortsighted Western ethnocentricity and from insensitivity to native values.[119a]

The subject is one of vital importance for the Third World. It deserves to attract the increased attention of those trained in comparative law.[120] An introductory coursebook, however, is not the place to pursue these problems in greater depth. Certain it is that much further research of an interdisciplinary as well as comparative nature will be required before we shall be able to pass final judgment on the value of endeavors to group legal systems in terms of economic development.

(f) A less ambitious (and less controversial) scheme of grouping legal systems is predicated on the fact, previously mentioned in our discussion, that the systems of most of the developing countries in Asia and Africa are "pluralistic." In this context, as the reader will recall, the term "pluralism" means that different groups of a nation's population are to some extent subject to different laws, with the result that interpersonal (as distinguished from interterritorial) conflict-of-laws problems arise in many situations. In this sense it is possible to classify national legal systems as pluralistic or unitary.[121]

---

115. See J. H. Beckstrom, Transplantation of Legal Systems: An Early Report on the Reception of Western Laws in Ethiopia, 21 Am.J.Comp.L. 557 (1973); id., Handicaps of Legal-Social Engineering in a Developing Nation, 22 Am.J.Comp.L. 697 (1974).

116. In addition to the articles cited supra nn. 113 and 114, see K. S. Rosenn, The Jeito—Brazil's Institutional Bypass of the Formal Legal System and Its Development Implications, 19 Am.J.Comp.L. 514 (1971).

117. See the discussion at the beginning of (d) supra.

118. See J. S. Katz & R. S. Katz, The New Indonesian Marriage Law: A Mirror of Indonesia's Political, Cultural and Legal System, 23 Am.J.Comp.L. 653 (1975), supplemented by the same authors' follow-up report, Legislating Social Change in a Developing Country: The New Indonesian Marriage Law Revisited, 26 Am.J.Comp.L. 309 (1978).

119. In modernizing the law of marriage and divorce, the Indonesian legislator successfully used the religious courts as agents of reform. See Katz & Katz, supra n. 118, especially the second article. Voices are heard in the Philippines urging that still surviving indigenous legal institutions be introduced into the "formal" legal system which was discussed supra pp. 229–245. See O. J. Lynch, The Philippine Indigenous Law Collection, 58 Philippine L.J. 458 (1983).

119a. For a scathing criticism of this attitude, see J. A. Gardner, Legal Imperialism: American Lawyers and Foreign Aid in Latin America (1980), reviewed by R. J. Radway in 16 Int. Lawyer 420 (1982).

120. See Hager, supra n. 113.

121. The term "unitary" has more than one meaning. It may be used, also, as

[handwritten margin note: Interpersonal Not Interterritorial]

In many countries, especially Islamic ones, the roots of plural-ism reach far back into history. Like their Germanic predecessors, the Arab conquerors of the middle ages recognized that everyone, conqueror and conquered alike, should live under his own personal law. Applying this principle, they ordained that the law applicable to a person (and the jurisdiction of religious courts over him) should be determined by that person's religion.[122] In Islamic countries, and especially in the Ottoman Empire, the tradition of pluralism thus established was continued until the twentieth century.[123]

In the nineteenth century, and the first half of the twentieth, colonialism became the principal force behind the spread and preservation of pluralistic legal systems throughout the southern hemisphere. "Natives" and "Europeans" became subject to differ-ent laws.[124]

Because it is in part (though not entirely)[125] a legacy of the colonial era, the pluralistic approach has come under severe criti-cism in the newly independent countries. In spite of such criti-cism, it seems that complete internal unification of the legal system is a long way off in many Asian and most African nations. But the significance and the divisive impact of pluralism are nevertheless diminishing in most of the developing countries. Braving the ever-present hazards of generalization, one may ascribe this to the following factors:

(aa) In the fashioning and operation of internal conflicts rules, the emphasis gradually is shifting from affiliation with racial or tribal groups to more objective criteria such as geo-graphic situs and the actual or presumed intention of the parties.[126]

(bb) As we have seen, many of the developing countries have restricted the pluralist approach to matters of family law and closely related subjects. In other areas, especially in the law of obligations and of commercial transactions, we usually find that modern law patterned after European models, wheth-

characterizing the legal system of a coun-try not having a federal structure. See supra under (b). In the present context, however, "unitary" means the opposite of "pluralistic".

122. See H. J. Liebesny, Comparative Legal History: Its Role in the Analysis of Islamic and Modern Near Eastern Legal Institutions, 20 Am.J.Comp.L. 38, 39–41 (1972).

123. See W. Yale, The Near East—A Modern History 19 (1958).

124. In substance, this was true in all of the colonial empires, although colonial policy was not everywhere the same. For a detailed treatment of the impact of Brit-ish, French and Dutch colonial policy on the legal systems of the former colonies, see Hooker, supra n. 11.

125. The discussion in the text at nn. 122 and 123, supra, has shown that plural-istic legal systems have existed in pre-colo-nial and non-colonial environments. See also Rheinstein, Problems of Law in the New Nations of Africa, in Geertz (Ed.), Old Societies and New States 220, at 222–5 (1963).

126. To some extent, this is true even with respect to matters traditionally gov-erned by personal status. See Rheinstein, id. at 235: "Clear-cut rules will be neces-sary in all parts [of Africa] to render it possible for an individual to change his subjection to the law of one group to that of another. The African who moves from the bush into the city and adopts the ur-ban, modern way of life cannot for all times remain subject to the tribal customs of marriage, succession, or land tenure. In the regions of French and Belgian legal traditions such rules seem to exist. By being registered as an évolué, an African ceases generally to be dominated by tribal custom and comes to be regulated in his civil matters by the 'modern' law."

er of the civil-law or the common-law variety, is applied as the law of the land, regardless of the parties' group affiliations.[127]

(cc) Through codification, restatement of rules of customary law and similar techniques, even indigenous law may become Western in form. In the process, its nature or substance is frequently changed.[128]

(dd) Upon the indigenous and imported sectors of their legal systems, most developing countries are superimposing a third sector of legal ordering: statutes and regulations, often of a so-called socialist character,[129] which are concerned with political processes and economic planning.[130] These statutes and regulations, which belong to the sphere of public law, ordinarily are of nation-wide application [131] and thus have the effect of further reducing the relative significance of those vestiges of pluralism that may persist in the private law of a developing nation.[132]

II. PROCEDURE IN CIVIL LAW COUNTRIES

REFERENCE

The materials in this chapter are focused on the procedural institutions of "Ruritania", a typical civil-law country. The emphasis will be on institutions and principles that are common to most or at least several of the civilian systems, and little attention will be paid to local peculiarities. Although there will be many illustrative references to the law of particular countries—i.e., of countries which, unlike Ruritania, belong to the real world—, the principal aim of the discussion will be to construct a *model* exhibiting the *typical* features of procedure in civil-law systems.

127. See, e.g., Farnsworth, Law Reform in a Developing Country: A New Code of Obligations for Senegal, 8 J.Afr.L. 6 (1964).

128. See Macneil, Research in East African Law, 3 East Afr.L.J. 47, 67 (1967); Tanner, The Codification of Customary Law in Tanzania, 2 East Afr.L.J. 105 (1966); M. Galanter, The Aborted Restoration of "Indigenous" Law in India, 14 Comp. Studies in Society and History 53 (1972). See also supra at nn. 20–26, 45.

129. In some African countries, it should be noted, certain aspects of the legal and political system are directly and avowedly influenced by the communist model. See Hazard, Mali's Socialism and the Soviet Legal Model, 77 Yale L.J. 28 (1967). The statement in the text, however, is not limited to those countries. An element of national economic planning can be discerned in the legal system of every developing nation, regardless of its leaders' attitude toward marxism as a political creed.

130. See Seidman, Law and Economic Development in Independent, English-Speaking, Sub-Saharan Africa, 1966 Wis.L. Rev. 999.

131. The fact that these laws are of nationwide application, does not always assure their effectiveness. The difference between book law and living law (see supra at nn. 114 to 116 and infra pp. 880 ff.) must be kept in mind. For an interesting discussion of the role of corruption and of its impact on the implementation of economic planning in a developing country, see S. Ottenberg, Local Government and the Law in Southern Nigeria, in D. C. Buxbaum (Ed.), Traditional and Modern Legal Institutions in Asia and Africa 26 ff. (1967).

132. Scholars whose attention is focused exclusively on the private law of a given country, thus are apt to overemphasize the pluralist and to underestimate the nationally unified elements in that country's legal system. Cf. supra n. 13, and text at nn. 8–9.

The reader may find it desirable, along with his study of Ruritanian procedure, to acquaint himself with the actual procedural system (including the non-typical and purely local features) of a selected civil-law country. Many valuable English-language materials, in the form of succinct surveys, are available for this purpose.[1] Only some of these can be mentioned here:

An instructive treatment of *German* civil procedure, illustrated by very helpful forms (of a complaint, an answer, the minutes of several successive hearings, and a judgment), can be found in 2 E. J. Cohn, Manual of German Law 161–254 (2d ed., 1971).[2] That treatment is no longer entirely up-to-date, but is helpfully supplemented by two recent articles: W. B. Fisch, Recent Developments in West German Civil Procedure, 6 Hastings Int. & Comp.L.Rev. 221 (1983); and P. Gottwald, Simplified Civil Procedure in West Germany, 31 Am.J.Comp.L. 687 (1983).[2a]

A great deal of information concerning the *Austrian* Code of Civil Procedure of 1895, which has influenced procedural law in many other countries and is generally acclaimed as an enlightened piece of legislation, is contained in two articles which happily supplement each other: A. Lenhoff, The Law of Evidence—A Comparative Study Based Essentially on Austrian and New York Law, 3 Am.J.Comp.L. 313 (1954), and A.

1. The reader who is not satisfied with a brief survey and prefers a book-length treatment, has excellent single-country treatises available to him. See, e.g., Takaaki Hattori & D. F. Henderson, Civil Procedure in Japan (1983, with 1985 Supp.). Older treatises, though partly obsolete, can still be useful as starting points for research. See, for instance, Cappelletti and Perillo, Civil Procedure in Italy (1965); Ginsburg and Bruzelius, Civil Procedure in Sweden (1965); P. Herzog (with the collaboration of M. Weser), Civil Procedure in France (1967). A loose-leaf service on Italian procedure is available as part of the new series by R. E. Myrick (Ed.), World Litigation Law & Practice (1986). For another extensive English-language description of a civilian system of procedure largely following the French pattern (adopted from the Code of the Swiss Canton of Neuchatel) see Karlen and Arsel, Civil Litigation in Turkey (1957).

The comparative literature on civil procedure is vast. For comparative discussions of reforms and recent tendencies, see, e.g., M. Storme & H. Casman, Towards a Justice with a Human Face (1978); M. Cappelletti & D. Tallon, Fundamental Guarantees of the Parties in Civil Litigation (1973); M. Cappelletti, Social and Political Aspects of Civil Procedure—Reforms and Trends in Western and Eastern Europe, 69 Mich.L.Rev. 847 (1971).

Concerning the historical background, see C. H. Peterson, An Introduction to the History of Continental Civil Procedure, 41 U. of Colo.L.Rev. 61 (1969); Cappelletti & Perillo, op. cit. supra, at 25–46; R. C. Van Caenegem, History of European Civil Procedure, in International Encyclopedia of Comparative Law, Vol. XVI, Ch. 2 (1971). For a brilliantly condensed attempt to explain the main differences between English and continental civil procedure in historical terms, see R. David, English Law and French Law 57–58 (1980).

2. The forms are at pp. 191–97. Equally helpful translations of German procedural forms appear in the interesting article by S. B. Jacoby, The Use of Comparative Law in Teaching American Civil Procedure, 25 Clev.St.L.Rev. 423 (1976).

For older (but still useful) surveys of German civil procedure, see Schopflocher, Civil Procedure: A Comparative Study of Some Principal Features Under German and American Law, [1940] Wis.L.Rev. 234; Harris and Schwarz, Comparative Law: Important Contrasts in the Administration of Justice in the United States and Western Germany, 30 Texas L.Rev. 462 (1952); Kaplan, Von Mehren and Schaefer, Phases of German Civil Procedure, 71 Harv.L.Rev. 1193, 1443 (1958).

2a. For an argument that reformers of our own system (or systems) of civil procedure should take a close look at the German model, see J. H. Langbein, The German Advantage in Civil Procedure, 52 U.Chi.L.Rev. 823 (1985).

Homburger, Functions of Orality in Austrian and American Civil Procedure, 20 Buff.L.Rev. 9 (1970).[3]

A reader who limits himself to materials in English, may encounter a little more difficulty in studying *French* civil procedure. There are some excellent English-language surveys of French practice under the old Code of Civil Procedure;[4] but these are seriously out of date. In the early 1970s, that Code was drastically revised. Obviously preceded by comparative studies, the revision brought French law more clearly into line with the basic principles of civil procedure prevailing in other continental countries, especially in Germany. Occurring in installments, the revision took the form of several successive decrees, which were issued between 1971 and 1973. Subsequently, Decree No. 75–1123 of December 5, 1975, brought all of the new provisions together in the integrated form of a new Code of Civil Procedure. As yet, there is no comprehensive English-language description of French practice under the new Code; but some of its features are interestingly discussed in a recent article: J. Beardsley, Proof of Fact in French Civil Procedure, 34 Am.J.Comp.L. 459 (1986).[5]

A reader who would like to acquaint himself with a *Latin-American* variant of civil-law procedure, will find up-to-date information in the article by K. S. Rosenn, Civil Procedure in Brazil, 34 Am.J.Comp.L. 487 (1986).

The dialogue which follows, it should be stressed again, does not aim at the systematic presentation of the civil procedure of any single country; but in connection with the discussion of specific issues some significant aspects of the procedural codes of Germany, France and other (European and non-European) civil-law countries will be mentioned.

1. THE COURSE OF A CIVIL LAWSUIT—ESSENTIAL ELEMENTS OF PROCEDURAL INSTITUTIONS IN MODERN CIVIL LAW COUNTRIES

A Fictional Dialogue Concerning a Not-Too-Fictional Case[6]

The following is the transcript of a conference taking place in a big midwestern city, in the office of Malcolm Smooth, Esq., General Coun-

3. Additional information on civil procedure in Austria (and in Israel), with instructive *forms*, is presented by F. R. Lacy, "Civilizing" Nonjury Trials, 19 Vand.L. Rev. 73 (1965). The Yugoslav law of procedure, which even today shows considerable traces of Austrian influence, is discussed in the article by F. R. Lacy, Yugoslavia: Practice and Procedure in a Communist Country, 43 Ore.L.Rev. 1 (1963).

4. See G. L. Kock, The Machinery of Law Administration in France, 108 U.Pa.L. Rev. 366 (1960); G. W. Pugh, Cross-Observations on the Administration of Civil Justice in the United States and France, 19

U.Miami L.Rev. 345 (1965). Older articles on the same subject are cited by Pugh, id. at 351.

5. There is, moreover, an English translation of the new French Code of Civil Procedure, with a brief introduction. See F. Grivart de Kerstrat & W. E. Crawford, New Code of Civil Procedure in France (1978).

6. The case of Haifisch v. International Dulci-Cola Corporation reflects the composite facts of several actual lawsuits, which in the end were determined by settlements or unreported decisions; but all names,

sel of the giant International Dulci-Cola Corporation. In addition to Mr. Smooth, the conference participants are Donald Edge, Esq., Assistant General Counsel, and Dr. André Comparovich, Professor of Law at a famous law school.

Smooth: Let me say, first of all, how happy we are that you, Professor Comparovich, have accepted our retainer, and that you are willing to act as our consultant on difficult problems of foreign law. As you know, our company has branch offices or subsidiaries in almost every country of Europe, East Asia and Latin-America. This produces quite a few legal problems. The specific reason why we have asked you to come here for this conference today, is that recently both our company and some of our American personnel have become involved in a lot of litigation abroad. Of course, this office receives regular reports concerning such litigation, and we are supposed to provide some overall direction and coordination.

Edge: In addition, if things go wrong in the foreign courts, we are the ones who have to answer the questions of top management here.

Smooth: Quite so. Moreover, it seemed to me that if we had a better understanding of litigation in civil-law countries, maybe sometimes we could avoid such litigation, or at least prepare for it more efficiently than we now do.

Comparovich: Of course. Every time you enter into a deal or operation which might possibly become the subject of litigation in country X, you have to have the law of X in the back of your mind, and you have to procure and preserve the kind of evidence which will stand up in the courts of X. This is fundamental.

Smooth: In addition, I should mention that our company, and Mr. Edge and I as individual lawyers and members of Bar Association committees, are very much interested in procedural reform in our own State; and perhaps we could get a few ideas from the civil-law world. Unfortunately, however, we are quite puzzled by what we see of the jurisdictional and procedural principles which courts in civil-law countries seem to apply. You are known as a great expert on comparative civil procedure, and perhaps you can dispel our ignorance.

Comparovich: I shall try my best. But how do we proceed?

Smooth: From among the many foreign lawsuits in which our company has been involved in recent years, I have picked one case, *Haifisch v. International Dulci-Cola Corporation*, in which a number of puzzling developments took place—at least puzzling to us. I would suggest that we tell you the whole history of that case from start to finish, and that you give us a running comment on each phase of the case. By this kind of *post mortem* we shall cover a lot of ground; and if you care to, you might at any time interject, or add at the end, some remarks of a more general nature.

Comparovich: This plan is agreeable to me. What were the facts of the case?

Edge: About five years ago, we contemplated a reorganization of our subsidiary in Ruritania. We contacted Mr. Haifisch (H), a Ruritanian lawyer who then resided in New York, and inquired whether and on what terms he would be willing to do the legal work in connection with the planned reorganization. After some initial correspondence, H flew here from New York, at our expense, and we conferred with him for several hours, going over the problems involved in the reorganization, and negotiating about his fee. No definite agreement was reached, at least not according to our recollection. The reorganization project was subsequently abandoned, and we so informed H. Thereupon, H sent us a bill in the amount of 800,000 Ruritanian Guilders (equivalent to $95,000), allegedly in accordance with the statutory fee schedule of Ruritania, which is said to be based on the amount involved in the lawyer's activity.

Comparovich: May I interrupt you right here?

Smooth: Please feel free to interrupt us at any time. Your running comment on our tale is exactly what we want.

Comparovich: Whenever you have a legal problem abroad, the most important step is the intelligent selection of foreign counsel and the making of appropriate arrangements concerning his compensation. This is not only the most important step, but also, as a rule, the first one in point of time.[7] Therefore, it might not be illogical for me to address my first remarks to this subject.

A. SELECTION OF COUNSEL—ORGANIZATION OF THE LEGAL PROFESSION [7a]

Comparovich (continuing): Sometimes, when you have a problem arising under the law of country X, you may find a member of the Bar of X, having an office in New York or elsewhere in this country.[8] More

---

7. Though frequently involving problems of foreign law (especially with respect to the foreign lawyer's fees), this first step usually has to be taken by American counsel without the help of a foreign lawyer.

7a. The materials in this section focus principally on countries located in Western Europe. But it should be kept in mind that the legal professions of non-European countries, including Third World countries, generally are "patterned on Western models. . . . They evolved as a consequence of the introduction of European legal systems through colonial governments, or (as in Latin America and countries like Ethiopia, Thailand or Liberia) through the efforts of 'modernizing' rulers and elites to import Western legal structures." C. J. Dias & J. C. N. Paul, Lawyers, Legal Professions, Modernization and Development,

in C. J. Dias, D.O. Lynch & J. C. N. Paul (Eds.), Lawyers in the Third World: Comparative and Development Perspectives 11 (1981).

8. There are many foreign attorneys who, like Mr. Haifisch, have offices in the United States, just as American lawyers and law firms in increasing numbers are practicing in foreign countries. For data illustrating the explosive recent growth of this kind of transnational legal practice, see John Bassett Moore Society of International Law, Directory of Opportunities in International Law (7th ed., 1984).

When a lawyer seeks to practice in a country other than the one where he was originally admitted, serious problems concerning his status are apt to arise. A concise overview of these problems is pre-

frequently, however, you will have to retain local counsel in X. In any event, you cannot even begin to look for the right individual unless you have some knowledge concerning the organization of the legal profession of X.[8a]

In this country, not having adopted the English-type division of functions between solicitors and barristers, we are not accustomed to legally enforced specialization among members of our profession. In some of the civil-law countries, the situation is quite different.

The French system, for example, traditionally has been one of extreme specialization.

Smooth: We learned that the hard way. When we litigated a relatively simple matter before a French court in 1968, we were told that we needed two lawyers, an *avoué* to draft the pleadings and do all the other paperwork, and an *avocat* to argue [9] in court.[10] But somebody told me that all this was changed in the early 1970s.

Comparovich: By a Law of December 1, 1971, which went into effect in 1972, the organization of the French legal profession was quite drastically modified. The new, modified system, however, is difficult to understand for one who is not familiar with the traditional, pre-1972 structure of the profession.

Smooth: The best way to proceed, then, might be: first to explain the pre-1972 system, and to follow this up with a summary of the 1972 changes.

Comparovich: Excellent idea. For the pre-1972 period, I can answer your question by quoting from an article by a prominent French lawyer. In that article, he listed the various types of (unlicenced as

sented by D. Campbell, A Lawyer Abroad: Regulatory Ambiguities of Foreign Practice, in J. W. Williams (Ed.), Career Preparation and Opportunities in International Law 105 (2nd ed., 1985). For more comprehensive comparative discussions and further references see L. S. Spedding, Transnational Legal Practice in the EEC and the United States (1987); T. Kosugi, Regulation of Practice by Foreign Lawyers, 27 Am.J.Comp.L. 678 (1979); Comment, 83 Colum.L.Rev. 1767 (1983). We shall come back to this point infra at ns. 17d–20.

8a. An American lawyer upon whose recommendation his client has retained X as foreign counsel, is not automatically responsible for any mistake X may make; but he is liable if he has failed to exercise due care in selecting X. See M. W. Janis, The Lawyer's Responsibility for Foreign Law and Foreign Lawyers, 16 Int. Lawyer 693, 698 ff. (1982).

9. The French word for oral argument is *plaidoirie*. The latter term, when trans-

lated into English, often is rendered as "pleading". This is utterly incorrect. When the French speak of an *avocat qui fait la plaidoirie*, they refer to a lawyer who orally addresses the court; the expression has nothing whatever to do with written pleadings (which under the traditional, pre-1972 system were drafted and filed by an *avoué*).

10. Neither the traditional nor the present system limits the *avocat* to the handling of litigated matters; he may also give advice, or draft contracts or other documents. But insofar as he acts as counselor, the *avocat* must compete with other (unlicenced as well as licenced) types of lawyers. As an advocate, he has always had a monopoly in the sense that in the civil courts of general jurisdiction and the intermediate appellate courts nobody but an *avocat* could present an oral argument for a client. In essence, this is still the position today.

well as licenced) lawyers who, in addition to the *avocats*, were then found practicing in France. Here is the quotation: [11]

> Lepaulle, Law Practice in France, 50 Colum.L.Rev. 945, 947–8 (1950): At the outset, it must be borne in mind that there is no law predicating the exercise of the legal profession on certain qualifications. Any person, whether trained in law or not, with or without a criminal record, is authorized to practice law: that is, to advise clients on legal matters, draft documents, and represent parties in those jurisdictions where advocates and "*avoués*" have no monopoly.[12] The public usually calls them "*agents d'affaires*," although they sometimes prefer the title of "*conseils juridiques*," "*jurisconsultes*," "*conseillers fiscaux*," or "*contentieux*." Some of them have organized reliable firms.[12a]
>
> The "*agréés*" are a type of *agent d'affaires* specializing in commercial cases before a definite commercial court and are limited in number. They must receive the consent of the court in order to practice, and such consent is never given except to the successor of a retiring *agréé*. They number fifteen in the Commercial Court of the Seine, and their standing is excellent.
>
> The "*officiers ministériels*" are lawyers appointed by the State, who are limited in number and have a monopoly in certain matters. They have an official rate of fees and buy the good will of their office from their predecessor. They are divided into the following classes:
>
> 1. *Notaires.* The French "*notaire*," who probably came into existence before St. Louis, is a trained lawyer who has nothing to do with litigation, but who has a monopoly for drawing marriage settlements and mortgages; he is usually retained for drawing deeds of sale of real estate and for administering estates. In Paris there are 149 *notaires*, a number officially fixed. A will is filed in a notary's office and

---

11. All of the footnotes accompanying the quotation (nn. 12–17 infra) are by the authors of this casebook.

12. The courts where there is no monopoly of *avocats* and *avoués* are essentially those of limited or inferior jurisdiction. Concerning the *avoués*' and *avocats*' traditional monopoly of representing clients before courts of general jurisdiction and appellate courts, see G. W. Pugh, supra n. 4, at 354–55.

12a. On the important question whether and to what extent unlicenced persons may engage in the practice of law, the legal systems of the world have developed a great variety of approaches. At one extreme we find the usual American approach of outlawing and indeed criminalizing any act that constitutes the unauthorized practice of law. The traditional French rule, stated in the text, and (with minor modifications, see infra) still followed today, stands at the opposite extreme. Most other legal systems have taken a position somewhere between these extremes. The dividing line between common law and civil law does not seem too significant in this respect. The German approach, for instance, is closer to ours than to the French. See infra n. 20.

remains there, so that the office serves the function of a probate registry.[13]

2. *Avoués.* "*Avoués*" are divided into two classes: Civil Court and Court of Appeal. They can practice only before the court to which they have been appointed. The lower courts of general jurisdiction are the commercial courts, which deal with commercial cases, and the civil courts for all other matters. The *avoués must* represent the litigants in civil courts. This means that they file all pleadings in their clients' names, but as a general rule, they have no right to address the court except for temporary motions or before some exceptional jurisdictions. There are 151 *avoués* of first instance at Paris, and again the number is fixed. The *avoués* of the Court of Appeal have similar functions before that court, which hears both civil and commercial cases, but they never address the court. There are fifty-one *avoués* before the Court of Appeal of Paris.

The *avoués* do what the advocates do not; they represent their clients, and act as their agents, signing the pleadings in their behalf, making offers in their name, handling money and receiving funds for them, taking care of such matters as service of process, notification, and execution.[14]

3. *Advocates before the Court of Cassation and the State Council.*[15] These special advocates, who are also *officiers ministériels*, buy their office and fulfill the functions of both the *avoué* and *avocat* before the Court of Cassation and the State Council. They do not appear before any other courts and other advocates cannot appear before these two courts.[16] Their number is limited to sixty.[17]

Edge: Has the 1972 reform merged all these branches of the legal profession into a single one?

Comparovich: No. The reform was a limited one, and after the restructuring of 1972 the organization of the French legal profession has remained at least as complex as it had been prior to the reform.

13. For further materials and references concerning the role of notaries in civil-law countries see supra pp. 18–20.

14. For more detailed information on the traditional status and functions of the *avoué*, see Buerstedde, Der Avoué in Frankreich, 17 JZ 660 (1962).

15. The State Council (Conseil d'Etat) acts as the highest administrative court. See infra pp. 449–500.

16. Even in countries in which there is less specialization than in France (e.g., in Germany), one finds that practice before the court of last resort in civil cases is restricted to a few members of a special Bar. As a rule, only questions of law can be argued before courts of last resort. In civil-law countries, where the lower courts do not separate issues of fact from issues of law as neatly as we do (see infra pp. 416–417), it may be felt that the ordinary practitioner lacks the training necessary for arguing a purely legal question which must be drained of all factual issues.

17. The reader who seeks additional information on the traditional fragmentation of the French legal professions is referred to Simmons, French Lawyers' Special Fields, 30 Tulane L.Rev. 101 (1955). For further interesting information on the history of the French Bar see Trai Le, infra n. 17a, at 64–68.

Smooth: What, then, were the changes brought about by the 1972 reform?

Comparovich: The details are spelled out in several law review articles, written in English.[17a] For this reason, I shall limit myself to a very brief outline of the major changes.

First, in the trial courts the professions of *avocat* and *avoué* were merged, so that a litigant now needs only one lawyer. This one lawyer, who calls himself an *avocat*, does both the paper work and the arguing in court, i.e., he performs the functions formerly exercised by an *avoué* and an *avocat*. But this merger, though significant and beneficial from the client's point of view, is far from complete.

Edge: I noticed that when you spoke of the merger, you limited your statement to the trial courts. Is the old system still intact on the appellate level?

Comparovich: I can see that you are a careful listener. In the appellate courts, the old system indeed has remained intact. Before the intermediate appellate court (*cour d'appel*), the client still needs both an *avoué* and an *avocat*; and if the case goes to the court of last resort, i.e., the Court of Cassation or the State Council, he needs yet another lawyer, one admitted to the special Bar of those courts.[17b] In other words, the *avoués* admitted to the intermediate appellate courts, and the advocates admitted to practice before the courts of last resort, continue as separate branches of the profession.

Edge: I can see now why it is impossible to understand the "new" system without knowing the old one. Has the merger remained incomplete even if one focuses exclusively on the trial court level?

Comparovich: Even with respect to trial courts—or courts of first instance, as the civilians would call them—, French law still distinguishes between the functions of an *avoué* and the functions of an *avocat*, although the same person now performs all of these functions.

Edge: Is that a purely theoretical distinction, designed to make French law students think like good civilian lawyers, or does it have practical consequences?

Comparovich: It has very practical consequences. For instance, a member of the newly "merged" profession may perform *avocat*-functions anywhere in France (as has always been true of the *avocats*); at the same time, however, he can perform *avoué*-functions only before the courts of his particular locality.

Smooth: My eye! Suppose a Paris lawyer has a case in Toulouse. What is he supposed to do?

17a. See P. Herzog & B. E. Herzog, The Reform of the Legal Professions and of Legal Aid in France, 22 Int. & Comp.L.Q. 462 (1973); Trai Le, The French Legal Profession: A Prisoner of Its Glorious Past?, 15 Cornell Int.L.J. 63 (1982).

17b. See supra, text at nn. 15–17.

Comparovich: For the *avoué*-functions he must retain a colleague in Toulouse. But he (the Paris lawyer) may, if he desires, present the oral argument before the Toulouse court.

A statute passed in 1984 now permits a lawyer admitted to practice before any court of first instance in the greater Paris region to exercise *avoué*-functions throughout that region. Subject to this minor exception, however, the exercise of *avoué*-functions remains strictly localized.

In parenthesis, I might mention that the civil-law systems are divided on the question whether a lawyer, once admitted to the Bar, should be able to appear only before the courts of his local bailiwick (as in Germany), or whether his admission entitles him to make an appearance anywhere within his state or nation. One can easily understand a system of purely local admission, or a system of nation-wide admission. What makes the position of a French lawyer a bit complicated, is that he is simultaneously subject to both systems—the local system for his *avoué*-functions, and the nationwide system for his *avocat*-functions.

Smooth: I am happy to learn that our legal system is not the only one that has developed a genius for complexity. Carrying the French theory—of separating the *avoué*-functions from the *avocat*-functions—a step further, does one not reach the conclusion that a lawyer performing both functions is entitled to two separate fees?

Comparovich: That is a correct conclusion under present French law. We shall come back to this point in a few minutes when we turn to the topic of attorneys' fees.

Edge: I read somewhere that before the 1972 reform the offices of *avoués* were inheritable and saleable. Is that true?

Comparovich: In order to become an *avoué*, a candidate had to meet stringest requirements of professional training, and in addition had to be presented for the office by the former holder or his heirs. Needless to say, the would-be new office-holder normally had to pay a price for such "presentation". Thus the answer to your question is in the affirmative. In fact, the offices of the *avoués* admitted to practice before intermediate appellate courts are still inheritable and saleable. Their economic value is due to the fact that the number of such offices is severely limited.

Edge: But insofar as the trial-court-*avoués* are concerned, the 1972 merger has done away with the system of limited numbers of such offices, and thus has destroyed their inheritability and saleability. Was this fair treatment of the individuals who at that time owned such offices?

Comparovich: It was recognized that the 1972 merger deprived such individuals of property, and they received compensation. The amount of the compensation is a multiple of prior years' earnings, *as reported to the tax authorities*. Some of the former *avoués* are said to have been unenthusiastic about this method of computing their compensation.

Edge: Are all the other special branches of the legal profession, as listed in the Lepaulle article, still in existence?

Comparovich: Yes, with the exception of the *agréés*, the small group of practitioners who formerly specialized in commercial-court litigation.

While the abolition of the separate group of *agréés* somewhat reduces the number of such groups, it is important to note that the 1972 reform also *added* a new category of licensed legal professionals. This brings me to the second important aspect of that reform: the creation of a new licensed profession of legal adviser (*conseil juridique*). A member of this new branch of the legal profession can give legal advice and draft documents; but he cannot represent a client in litigation. He is purely an office lawyer.

Edge: How does one become a *conseil juridique*?

Comparovich: Except for individuals covered by a grandfather clause of the 1971/72 statute, the educational and other requirements are very similar to those that have to be met by one aspiring to be an *avocat*. A *conseil juridique* thus is now a member of a learned profession. He is, moreover, subject to a form of professional discipline.

Smooth: Should our French subsidiary retain a firm of *conseils juridiques* for its day-to-day flow of non-litigated legal matters?

Comparovich: As you know, the *avocats* may handle non-litigated as well as litigated affairs. In the past, they used to concentrate mainly on litigation; but this has changed in recent years. Now there are many firms of *avocats*, some of respectable size,[17c] that are perfectly able to handle the legal affairs of large corporate clients, and are indeed anxious to do so. Thus there is real competition between *conseils juridiques* and *avocats* for the legal business (other than litigation) of clients such as your French subsidiary.

Some members of the French legal profession, dissatisfied with this state of affairs, have proposed to merge *avocats* and *conseils juridiques* into a single branch of the profession, or at least to permit the establishment of mixed law firms, which would include both *avocats* and *conseils juridiques* in the membership of a single firm. These proposals, however, like many other suggestions for reforms more radical than those of the early 1970s, are still in the talking stage.

Smooth: To come back to the problem our French subsidiary faces in choosing counsel: The essence of what you are telling us seems to be

---

17c. Until the 1950s, a French *avocat* was not permitted to form a partnership. Thus he was forced to practice as a solo practitioner, assisted perhaps by an *avocat stagiaire* (see supra pp. 152–157 ff.). Since then, however, the restrictions against forming partnerships have been gradually lifted. By now, there are many partnerships (firms) of *avocats*. Some of them, expecially in Paris, are quite sizeable, though perhaps not by New York standards.

that at our option we can retain either a firm of *avocats* or a firm of *conseils juridiques*. Which way would you advise us to jump?

Comparovich: Some people will tell you to hire a firm of *avocats*, because they can handle litigation as well as non-litigated matters. With equal plausibility, however, one can argue that the *conseils juridiques'* inability to handle litigation is an element of strength, because it enables them, whenever litigation becomes unavoidable, to choose the trial counsel best suited for the particular case at hand, and to make that choice from a wide field.

My own feeling is that all these arguments are a bit theoretical, and that your subsidiary should retain the law firm consisting of the best individual lawyers, regardless of whether they have qualified as *avocats* or as *conseils juridiques*.

Smooth: Could our subsidiary retain one of the American law firms in Paris?

Comparovich: Yes. Before 1972, American lawyers and law firms in France were able to handle non-litigated matters because the traditional French rule permitted *anybody* to give legal advice and to prepare legal instruments. Since 1972, the provisions governing the practice in France of non-French attorneys have become quite complex.[17d] By way of mild oversimplification, however, one can say that American lawyers now can practice in France as *conseils juridiques*. An American law degree, coupled with some apprenticeship in a French law firm, normally will meet the educational requirements, and quite a number of American lawyers and law firms are practicing today as *conseils juridiques*.[17e]

Smooth: Don't the French insist on reciprocal treatment of French lawyers who wish to practice in this country?

Comparovich: They do—and hereby hangs a tale. The French statute and regulations threatened to subject any foreign lawyer from a non-Common-Market country to severe disadvantages unless his own country would, under comparable conditions, grant French lawyers a status similar to that of a *conseil juridique*. Most of the American

---

17d. For references concerning details, see supra ns. 8 and 17a. See also S. M. Cone, The Regulation of Foreign Lawyers 68–70 (3rd ed. 1984).

Non-French lawyers from other Common Market countries enjoy special privileges not shared by American lawyers. Properly qualified nationals of such countries may not be denied admission to any of the legal professions on the ground of lack of French citizenship. See Reyners v. Belgium, [1974] E.C.R. 631, CCH Comm. Mkt. Rep. ¶8256. The case is reproduced also in E. Stein, P. Hay & M. Waelbroeck, European Community Law and Institutions in Perspective: Text, Cases and Materials 533 ff. (2d ed., 1976). Moreover, lawyers from other Common Market countries may temporarily provide services in France pursuant to the March 22, 1977 Directive of the Council of the European Communities, implemented in France by Decree 79–233, 1979 D.L. 146.

For a comprehensive study of the mobility of lawyers within the EEC, see L.S. Spedding, Transnational Legal Practice in the EEC and the United States (1987).

17e. American lawyers and law firms established in France before 1972 derive a somewhat privileged position from grandfather provisions in the applicable statute and regulations. See n. 17d, supra.

lawyers and law firms exposed to this threat were from New York, and understandably they launched a massive lobbying offensive in order to have reciprocal legislation enacted in New York.[17f] Their efforts were crowned by success. A 1974 New York statute,[17g] implemented by Court of Appeals Rules,[17h] permits a foreign lawyer to become a Legal Consultant in New York. As such, he may give legal advice to clients; he may also prepare legal instruments except those relating to real estate, decedents' estates and matrimonial relations (i.e., those which in a civil-law country normally would be prepared by a notary rather than a *conseil juridique*).[17i] Thus New York has granted foreign lawyers the kind of reciprocity the French are insisting on. During the first decade of the New York statute's operation, more than seventy foreign lawyers, possessing specialized knowledge of the laws of about thirty different countries, were licensed as foreign legal consultants.[17j]

Smooth: Have other jurisdictions in the United States followed the example of New York? [17k]

Comparovich: Thereby hangs another tale—a tale again illustrating the world-wide interaction of legal institutions.

The French Government apparently took the view that so long as French lawyers could practice as legal consultants in New York, a condition of reciprocity existed between France and the United States. As a result, the favorable treatment accorded to New York lawyers was extended by the French to lawyers from other states. Thus the other states got a free ride on New York's coat-tails and initially felt under no pressure to enact "foreign legal consultant" legislation of their own.

The situation, however, changed quickly when in the early 1980s increasing numbers of American law firms—not only in New York but in other jurisdictions as well—developed plans to open branch offices in the Pacific rim, and especially in Japan. As part of U.S.-Japanese trade negotiations, protracted discussions took place concerning the "import" and "export" of legal services. In these discussions the Japanese emphasized reciprocity, and—understandably less willing

---

17f. The reader will recall (from our study of the Shoop case, supra) that a foreign lawyer from a common-law country may under certain conditions be admitted in New York as a full-fledged member of the Bar, without having to take the bar examination. Lack of U.S. citizenship, of course, does not disqualify him. In re Griffiths, 413 U.S. 717, 93 S.Ct. 2851 (1973). Lawyers from civil-law countries, on the other hand, have to pass the bar examination in order to become regular members of the New York Bar. For them, the alternative of becoming admitted as legal consultants (which does not hinge on passing an examination) may be particularly attractive.

17g. McKinney's N.Y. Judiciary Law § 53(6), as added by L.1974, Ch. 231.

17h. Part 521 of the N.Y. Court of Appeals Rules for the Admission of Attorneys, 22 N.Y.C.R.R. Part 521, as last amended in 1983.

17i. For details see Cone, supra n. 17d, at 30–31; W. R. Slomanson, Foreign Legal Consultant: Multistate Model for Business and the Bar, 39 Albany L.Rev. 199 (1975).

17j. See New York Law Journal of June 4, 1984, p. 1.

17k. The arguments in favor of legislation such as New York's statute and Rules are eloquently stated by W. R. Slomanson, California Becomes Latest State to Consider "Foreign Legal Consultants", 80 Am.J. Int.L. 197 (1986). See also id., supra n. 17i.

than the French to equate New York with the United States—they insisted on strict state-by-state reciprocity.[17m] The pressure thus put on jurisdictions other than New York had the effect that in 1985 and 1986 Michigan, Hawaii and the District of Columbia adopted statutes or Rules similar to New York's.[17n] In California the Board of Governors of the State Bar in late 1986 requested the Supreme Court of the State to adopt a Rule "relating to registered foreign legal consultants"; the proposed Rule is substantially similar to the New York scheme, but somewhat more restrictive in defining the kinds of legal matters on which the registered consultant may give advice.

It is reasonable to assume that additional American jurisdictions will follow the example of those I have mentioned.

Edge: If you do not mind, I should like for a moment to return from the Pacific rim to France. Did the French reform of 1972 abrogate the traditional freedom of unlicensed persons to give legal advice and to prepare legal instruments not required to be in notarial form?

Comparovich: In principle, that freedom still exists for nationals of France and other Common Market countries; but some salutary restrictions have been imposed. An unlicensed person may no longer use the title of *conseil juridique* or any similar designation pointing to law or the legal profession. And there is now some provision (which prior to 1972 was sadly lacking) for keeping felons and disbarred attorneys from acting as legal advisers.

Smooth: The French system, it seems to me, could fairly be described as one of a fragmented legal profession. Is that system followed in the majority of civil-law countries?

Comparovich: No. Even the countries whose laws in other respects bear the mark of French influence, by and large have failed to adopt this fragmentized system. Italy, for instance, has not followed the French example.[18] In the German-speaking countries, the *Rechtsanwalt* performs the combined functions of the French *avocat, avoué*

17m. As a result of the discussions mentioned in the text, the Japanese Diet on March 23, 1986, promulgated the "Special Measures Law Concerning the Handling of Legal Business by Foreign Lawyers" (Law No. 66 of 1986). Effective April 1, 1987, this statute makes it possible for American lawyers under certain conditions to be licensed as foreign legal consultants, but subject to state-by-state reciprocity. Thus lawyers from New York or the District of Columbia receive more favorable treatment than American lawyers from jurisdictions that do not provide reciprocity for Japanese lawyers.

17n. Massachusetts is another jurisdiction which apparently is regarded by the

Japanese as meeting their reciprocity requirement. The Commonwealth has not adopted special legislation concerning foreign legal consultants; but a foreign lawyer who has practiced for five years in his own country (regardless of whether or not it is a common-law country) may upon motion be admitted as a full-fledged member of the Massachusetts Bar. In addition to meeting character and residency requirements, the candidate must pass the Multistate Professional Responsibility Examination; but there is no other examination requirement. See Cone, supra n. 17d, at 22.

18. See Perillo, The Legal Professions of Italy, 18 J.Legal Ed. 274, 279–84 (1966).

and *conseil juridique.*[19] The French *agent d'affaires* (unlicensed legal adviser) has virtually no counterpart in Germany where a non-member of the Bar may not practice law without a license, which is granted only in exceptional cases.[20]

Smooth: Does the *Rechtsanwalt* also perform the functions of a Notary? [21]

Comparovich: In this respect the picture is not uniform, sometimes not even within a single country;[22] but the trend has been toward separating the two functions.[23]

Smooth: Would it be accurate to say that much of the counseling and drafting of documents which is done by an attorney here, would be within the province of the civil-law Notary, and that the latter, in most of the civil-law countries, is not at the same time an attorney?

Comparovich: That is an accurate statement.[24] It should be noted, however, that in at least one civil-law country (The Netherlands) ". . . enterprising attorneys and notaries have formed amalgamated firms, which provide substantially all the services of a large U.S. law firm." [24a]

19. See E. J. Cohn, The German Attorney—Experiences with a Unified Profession, 9 Int. & Comp.L.Q. 580 (1960) and 10 id. 103 (1961).

Technically, the statement in the text is true even with respect to the German Democratic Republic (East Germany). But there, as in all other communist countries recognizing Soviet leadership, the Bar has lost much of its former independence and prestige. See Law on the Collegia of Advocates of the German Democratic Republic of Dec. 17, 1980, reproduced in English in "Law and Legislation in the German Democratic Republic", vol. 1–2/1981, pp. 23 ff.; H. H. Bruhn, Die Rechtsanwaltschaft in der DDR (1972). See also supra pp. 185–187. In most Peoples' Democracies, lawyers have been regimented into collectives, and the work of each member of a law-office collective is subject to a good deal of official supervision. For discussions of the Russian prototype of the system, see the interesting opinion in Matter of Mitzkel, 36 Misc.2d 671, 233 N.Y.S.2d 519 (Surr.Ct. Kings Co. 1962); W. E. Butler, Soviet Law 78–89 (1983); D. Kaminskaja, Final Judgment: My Life as a Soviet Defense Attorney (1982); E. Huskey, Russian Lawyers and the Soviet State 215–28 (1986); S. Pipko & R. Pipko, Inside the Soviet Bar: A View from the Outside, 21 Int.Lawyer 853 (1987).

The article by W. Gray, Legal Education in the Soviet Union and Eastern Europe, 5 Int. Lawyer 738 (1971), contains interesting observations collected during its author's stay in Moscow, Budapest and Prague.

20. Rechtsberatungsgesetz of Dec. 13, 1935 (RGBl. I 1478), as amended. Moreover, in civil litigation before a court of general jurisdiction or an appellate court the attorneys admitted to practice before the particular court enjoy a complete monopoly (system of so-called *Anwaltszwang*); this monopoly covers the oral arguments as well as the paper work, and excludes not only unauthorized representatives but also the parties themselves from handling the litigation.

Foreign (e.g., American) attorneys seeking to practice law in Germany sometimes receive a license under the statute just cited. The license usually contains restrictions limiting the type of practice the applicant may engage in. For details see U. Schultz & P. Koessler, The Practicing Lawyer in the Federal Republic of Germany, 14 Int. Lawyer 531, 541–43 (1980).

21. Concerning the status and functions of notaries in civil-law countries, see supra pp. 18–20.

22. In some Swiss cantons, and in some parts of West Germany, as well as in Guatemala, the same individual may function as *Rechtsanwalt* and as Notary.

23. See Schlesinger, The Notary and the Formal Contract in Civil Law, 1941 Report of the New York Law Revision Commission 403, 408.

24. See supra nn. 21 and 23.

24a. E. E. Murphy, Jr., A Guide to Foreign Law Source Materials and Foreign Counsel, 19 Int. Lawyer 39, at 46 (1985).

Smooth: To come back to the facts of our case, are you implying that before we approached H, we should have found out whether the drafting of the papers required for the reorganization of a corporation is not properly the function of a Notary in Ruritania?

Comparovich: A stockholders' resolution amending the charter of a corporation usually requires the form of a notarial protocol in civil-law countries. Possibly, it may not become effective until the notarial protocol has been submitted to, and entered in, the Register of Commerce.

Smooth: I suppose it would have been smarter if we had contacted a Ruritanian Notary rather than Mr. H?

Comparovich: Most probably, you would have needed the services of a Notary in any event if you had gone through with the reorganization. Nevertheless, H might have been useful to you in giving tax advice and in transmitting and explaining your instructions to the Notary; [24b] but the limited nature of his functions should have been reflected in the fee arrangements.

Smooth: Of course, this is where we made our biggest mistake. Although it may be doubtful whether H's claim for remuneration is governed by Ruritanian law, we should not have approached him without having educated ourselves regarding the civil-law system of lawyers' fees.

B. LAWYERS' FEES

Comparovich: There is no uniform "civil-law system" in this regard. In France, the fees of *avoués* and notaries are regulated by official tariffs (see supra). The honorarium paid to an *avocat*, however, traditionally was thought of as a voluntary and spontaneous token of the client's gratitude.[25] In the course of the 19th and 20th centuries, it has become recognized that the *avocat* has a legally enforceable right to compensation, the amount of which, unless fixed by agreement, is determined in accordance with principles similar to our notion of quantum meruit. A statute passed on December 31, 1957, has expressly recognized this right and has provided a special procedure for its enforcement.[26] Nevertheless, it remains customary for an *avocat* to

---

24b. "In the Netherlands Antilles, the more imaginative notaries have launched into tax planning and business law advice as well as the traditional documentary functions of a notary." Ibid. But in most civil-law countries a client seeking tax-planning advice will do better by turning to a lawyer other than a notary, perhaps one specializing in tax law.

25. The long history of this tradition, which originated in ancient Rome, is discussed by Pound, The Lawyer From Antiquity to Modern Times 51–55 (1953). As recently as 1885 the Bâtonnier (President)

of the Paris Bar stated in a treatise: "The avocat does not discuss any money question with his client. He requests nothing from him either before or after the case." Quoted by Lepaulle, Law Practice in France, 50 Colum.L.Rev. 945, 949–50 (1950).

26. In order to understand the statutory procedure, one has to know that in every district the *avocats* are organized in the form of an integrated local bar association (*barreau*) which has disciplinary powers over its members. The head of a *barreau* has the title of *Bâtonnier*.

protect his interests in the traditional manner, i.e., by asking that the client pay at least a portion of the anticipated fee in advance.[27]

Smooth: What about contingent fees?

Comparovich: Our colleagues in the civil-law world traditionally use a Latin term when they speak of an agreement made in advance pursuant to which the lawyer's compensation is to be a percentage of the amount recovered. The term is *pactum de quota litis.* For a French *avocat* to enter into such a *pactum,* would be both unethical and unlawful; an agreement of this kind would be absolutely void, and the offending *avocat* would be subject to severe disciplinary sanctions.[28] The same prohibition applies to *conseils juridiques.*[28a] This traditional and deeply ingrained attitude of hostility toward the contingent fee is shared by most civil-law countries.[29]

Edge: But if lawyers cannot accept retainers on a contingent basis, how can indigent litigants, or even middle-class litigants of moderate means, ever enforce their rights?

Comparovich: To begin with, one should not assume that litigation costs are everywhere as high as they are here. For a number of reasons,[29a] the level of such costs traditionally has been modest in most civil-law countries. In recent years, however, there has been a marked increase (though not as explosive as here) in civil-law countries as well.

The cost-risk of a party who is not poor but of moderate means, can be quite severe in a civil-law country. This is due, not only to the

As amended by decrees of 1972 and 1974, the statute provides that when the question of compensation becomes the subject of controversy between the *avocat* and his client, the first procedural step has to be the initiation of a conciliation proceeding before the *Bâtonnier* of the local *barreau.* It appears that in practice two-thirds of the controversies are settled as a result of such conciliation efforts. If conciliation fails, the *Bâtonnier* can render a decision which settles the dispute and is enforceable like a judgment, but subject to an appeal to be taken to the President of the court of first instance and ultimately to the President of the intermediate appellate court. See J. Vincent, Procédure Civile 264–65 (18th ed., 1976).

27. In the courts of first instance, the *avoué*-functions and the *avocat*-functions are now performed by the same individual. See supra. That individual is entitled (a) to statutory fees for his work as *avoué,* and (b) to quantum meruit compensation as *avocat.*

28. See Crémieu, Traité de la Profession d'Avocat (2d ed. 1954) 239–40; J. Lemaire, Les règles de profession d'avocat et les usages du barreau de Paris, Sec. 471 (1975). This traditional rule is, moreover,

statutorily confirmed by Art. 10 of Law No. 71–1130 of December 31, 1971.

28a. See T. T. T. Trai Le, Professional Independence and the Associate in a Law Firm: A French Case Study, 29 Am.J. Comp.L. 647, 655 (1981).

29. See infra pp. 702 ff. and 857 ff. The reader should not assume, however, that the rule is completely uniform throughout the civil-law world. In Japan, for instance, contingent fees are lawful and are said to be frequently resorted to. See T. Kojima & Y. Taniguchi, Access to Justice in Japan, in 1 M. Cappelletti, Access to Justice 689, 704–05 (1978). And in Brazil it appears to be permissible, and indeed customary, for lawyers to enter into fee arrangements with their clients that provide for a fixed fee *plus* a contingent fee; but "Fee arrangements totally contingent upon the success of litigation are not used" and would be regarded as unethical. K. S. Rosenn, Civil Procedure in Brazil, 34 Am.J. Comp.L. 487, 519 (1986).

29a. Some of the reasons are set forth by R. B. Schlesinger, The German Alternative: A Legal Aid System of Equal Access to the Private Attorney, 10 Cornell Int.L.J. 213, at 215–16 (1977).

absence of the contingent fee, but also to the fact that the prevailing civil-law rule—like the English rule, and unlike the basic rule in our country—permits the victorious party to recover his attorneys' fees from the loser, as part of the recoverable "costs".[29b] In addition to court costs, the loser thus has to pay the fees of the attorneys for both sides. Quite often, this can be a ruinous burden. In some European countries, however, this problem has been successfully alleviated by commercially marketed legal-expense insurance.[29c]

To deal with the plight of the litigant or would-be litigant of insufficient means, most civil-law countries have long recognized Legal Aid as a public function to be regulated by law.[30] Statutory schemes—differing in their details from country to country, but ordinarily uniform within each country—make sure that in civil as well as criminal cases a party of insufficient means will be represented by competent counsel.

Edge: In order to obtain such assistance, does the applicant have to show that he has a meritorious claim or defense?

Comparovich: Under the German system,[30a] which in this respect is fairly typical, he merely has to show that his claim or defense "has a

---

29b. For details and references see infra, Section C of the present Dialogue, where this point will be further pursued.

29c. See R. A. Riegert, Empirical Research About Law: The German Picture, 2 Dickinson Int.L.Annual 1, 38–40 (1983); W. Pfennigstorf & S. L. Kimball, Aspects of Legal Expense Insurance: A Review of Four New Publications, 1983 A.B.F. Research J. 251; W. Pfennigstorf, Legal Expense Insurance: The European Experience in Financing Legal Services (1975).

Our contingent fee system offers only a partial substitute for such insurance. See the last-cited work, at 31–39. It is not surprising, therefore, that American insurance companies have attempted to market "Legal Services Insurance Plans"; but how successful these attempts will be, remains to be seen. Cf. W. Pfennigstorf & S. L. Kimball, Legal Service Plans: A Typology, 1976 ABA Research J. 411, 412 (1976).

30. The reader who seeks comprehensive information on legal aid in civil-law and other foreign countries, has two book-length comparative treatments at his disposal: F. H. Zemans (Ed.), Perspectives on Legal Aid: An International Survey (1979), and M. Cappelletti, J. Gordley & E. Johnson, Jr., Toward Equal Justice: A Comparative Study of Legal Aid in Modern Societies (1975). See also the monumental Directory of Legal Aid and Advice Facilities Available Throughout the World, published by the International Legal Aid Association (2 vols., 1966, loose-leaf). Much

relevant material of a comparative nature is contained, furthermore, in International Legal Center (Committee on Legal Services to the Poor in the Developing Countries), Legal Aid and World Poverty: A Survey of Asia, Africa and Latin America (1974), and in the multi-volume work by M. Cappelletti (Gen.Ed.), Access to Justice (1978/79).

There are, in addition, many useful law review articles, such as M. Cappelletti and J. Gordley, Legal Aid: Modern Themes and Variations, 24 Stan.L.Rev. 347 (1972); R. B. Ginsburg, J. L. Kagele, J. F. Murphy, R. E. Lee, R. C. Benitez et al., Symposium on "The Availability of Legal Services to Poor People and People of Limited Means in Foreign Systems," 6 Int.Lawyer 128 (1972) (covers England, India, Italy, Japan, Latin America, The Netherlands and Scotland); P. Herzog and B. E. Herzog, The Reform of the Legal Professions and of Legal Aid in France, 22 Int. & Comp.L.Q. 462, 483–90 (1973). Perhaps the most advanced system today is the Swedish one, as revised by a Law of July 1973. It is described and discussed, from a comparative point of view, by P. S. Muther, The Reform of Legal Aid in Sweden, 9 Int.Lawyer 475 (1975).

30a. For a description of the German system, as amended in 1980, see W. B. Fisch, Recent Developments in West German Civil Procedure, 6 Hastings Int. & Comp.L.Rev. 221, 272–75 (1983). Older discussions, still valid in some (but not all) respects, can be found in K. A. Klauser &

sufficient prospect of success and is not frivolously asserted."[30b] The courts have interpreted this to mean that an application for assistance should be denied only if the applicant's action or defense is hopeless or frivolous.[30c] It was argued that this rule, though quite favorable to the litigant seeking assistance, nevertheless violates the Equal Protection clause of the West German Constitution, because a wealthy party would be free to initiate even a hopeless action; but the Federal Constitutional Court rejected the argument and upheld the rule.[30d]

Edge: What showing does a German applicant have to make concerning his or her financial circumstances?

Comparovich: Until 1980, only a "poor" person was able to obtain legal aid in litigation. But a 1980 amendment of the German Code of Civil Procedure eliminated all references to "poverty" or "poor" litigants. Under the new provisions,[30e] assistance is to be granted to any party who in the light of his or her "personal economic circumstances" is wholly or partly unable to bear the costs of the litigation in question. This means that a party of moderate means, although not poor, may have court costs and the fees of his attorney wholly or partially paid out of public funds;[30f] but to the extent that he has income or assets in excess of certain specified amounts, he may have to use such excess to repay, perhaps in installments, the public treasury's outlay. Assistance to an applicant who is not truly indigent thus can be partial rather than total; and it may take the form of a mere advance, which eventually has to be repaid. Compared to the pre-1980 provisions, which authorized assistance only to "poor" litigants, this new scheme considerably expands the group of people who may receive some form of public assistance with respect to litigation expenses. At least in cases involving large claims (and correspondingly substantial litigation expenses, see infra), members of the middle class may be among the beneficiaries of the revised scheme.

Edge: Suppose an applicant meets all the requirements you mentioned. What is the procedure by which a lawyer is appointed to represent him or her in a civil case?

Comparovich: The answer to this question varies somewhat from country to country. In Germany (and a number of countries following the German example) the party seeking assistance must apply to the

---

R. A. Riegert, Legal Assistance in the Federal Republic of Germany, 20 Buff.L.Rev. 582 (1971); R. B. Schlesinger, supra n. 29a.

For a case illustrating the operation of the German system see infra pp. 608 ff.

30b. See German Code of Civil Procedure § 114.

30c. For details see Baumbach-Lauterbach-Albers-Hartmann, Zivilprozessordnung, § 114, Anno. 2B (42nd ed., 1984).

The proscription of "frivolous" as well as "hopeless" actions is not redundant. An action can be frivolous even though it is

not hopeless. An example frequently mentioned is an action seeking monetary recovery from a defendant who is, and is expected to remain, totally judgment-proof.

30d. The case is cited and discussed by W. B. Fisch, Recent Reforms in German Civil Procedure: The Constitutional Dimension, 1 Civil Justice Q. 33, 39–40 (1982).

30e. For details see Fisch, supra n. 30a.

30f. In Germany, public funds are available for that purpose; but this is not true of all civil-law countries. See infra.

court.[31] Upon finding that the applicant meets the requirements we have discussed, the court appoints a lawyer to represent him in the projected or pending proceeding. If the applicant has indicated a preference for a particular lawyer, and the chosen lawyer is willing to handle the case, the applicant's choice must be honored.[31a] Needless to say, defendants as well as plaintiffs (provided they meet the above-mentioned requirements) may utilize this procedure.

In France, the allegedly indigent party must first apply to a "Legal Aid Bureau", an independent commission composed of representatives of the Government, the judiciary and the organized Bar. If the application is approved, an *avocat* and (in cases where it is still necessary) an *avoué* have to be designated to assist the applicant; ordinarily, these designations are to be made by the heads of the respective professional organizations.[32]

Edge: Will the lawyer or lawyers thus appointed receive compensation from public funds?

Comparovich: In some countries, such as Italy,[33] the answer is No. As a result, members of the profession are not particularly anxious to obtain such assignments, and in practice the task of representing the poor is largely left to the younger and less experienced lawyers. The official legal aid scheme thus acquires a well-deserved poor reputation, with the further consequence that little use is made of it. Private organizations sometimes try to fill the gap; in Italy, for instance, it seems that to a considerable extent the function of providing legal aid has been taken over by the labor unions.[34]

Constitutional attacks on the system of unpaid appointed counsel were unsuccessful in Italy[35] but met with success in Austria.[35a]

31. The procedure is illustrated by the German case reproduced infra pp. 608 ff. See also the editorial footnotes appended to that case.

31a. Code of Civil Procedure § 121. In practice, the application is ordinarily prepared and filed by the applicant's lawyer, who thus automatically qualifies as the chosen lawyer. Even if the party seeking assistance applies *in propria persona* (which he may do), he has a right to designate the attorney whom the court will appoint to represent him.

Prior to the 1980 amendment of the German Code of Civil Procedure (see supra), the court was not legally bound, although in practice it was customary, to appoint the lawyer of the applicant's choice.

32. For details see Herzog & Herzog, supra n. 30; Lemaire, supra n. 28, at pp. 229–51.

33. See the report by V. Vigoriti, in Zemans, supra n. 30, at 177 ff. Only in cases involving labor disputes or actions for social security benefits can a lawyer appointed to represent an indigent party be compensated out of public funds. See G. L. Certoma, The Italian Legal System 50–51 (1985).

34. The labor unions regard their position in the legal aid field as a source of power, and for this reason apparently have failed to support recent attempts to bring about statutory improvements in Italy's *official* legal aid scheme. See Vigoriti, supra n. 33.

35. See supra n. 33.

35a. An English translation of the decision of the Austrian Constitutional Court (the Gussenbauer decision handed down on December 19, 1972) appears in Cappelletti, Gordley & Johnson, supra n. 30, at 721–26. Strange to relate, the Court based its decision on the lawyer's rather than the client's constitutional rights.

In the 1983 case of Van der Mussele v. Belgium the European Human Rights Court held that an apprentice-lawyer who had been appointed by a Belgian criminal court to defend an accused without com-

→ Jn France

In France, it was the rule until 1972 that lawyers appointed to represent indigent litigants had to serve without compensation, with the result that such cases usually had to be handled by inexperienced *avocats stagiaires.* Under the 1972 reform legislation, repeatedly amended since then, compensation is now paid out of public funds in civil as well as criminal cases; [35b] but the rates of such compensation are exceedingly modest.[35c]

In Germany, on the other hand, a system of compensating the court-appointed lawyers of financially handicapped litigants, and of paying such compensation out of public funds, has been in operation for a long time. On the whole, the system seems to meet with the approval of the general public as well as the Bar; [35d] and as a result of the 1980 amendment which I have mentioned previously, the German system now benefits not only litigants who are outright poor, but all those who are financially unable to bear the cost of the particular litigation.

Smooth: A German colleague once told me that the rates at which attorneys were compensated in such legal aid cases were lower than the ordinary statutory fee schedule, and were known as "paupers' rates". Is that still the case today?

Comparovich: As I mentioned before, the 1980 amendment has eliminated all terms such as "pauper" and "poor person" from the relevant provisions of the German Code of Civil Procedure. Thus one speaks no longer of "paupers' rates". But the schedule determining the amounts payable to the court-appointed lawyers of assisted litigants is still not identical with the ordinary statutory schedule of fees to which retained lawyers are entitled. In relatively small matters, there is no significant difference between the two schedules; but as the amounts involved in the litigation become larger, the fees payable by unassisted clients under the ordinary schedule can rise to very substantial amounts (see infra), while the progression under the legal aid schedule is much less steep.[35e] Thus in a really big case the fee paid to a court-appointed lawyer out of public funds will be considerably less than

---

pensation and without reimbursement of expenses, had no remedy under the European Human Rights Convention. In particular, it was held that his appointment did not amount to "forced and compulsory labor" within the meaning of the Convention. See A. Drzemczewski, The European Convention on Human Rights, 3 [1983] Yearbook of Eur. Law 439, 445–47 (1984).

35b. See Herzog & Herzog, supra n. 30.

35c. A contested divorce would entitle a French lawyer to a legal aid payment equivalent to about $250. Decree No. 84–1218 of December 28, 1984, reproduced in 1985 D.L. 67. In a criminal case, a lawyer appointed to defend a client against a felony charge normally receives less than $150 for his work prior to and during the trial. Decree No. 83–154 of February 28, 1983,

reproduced in 1983 D.L. 159, and Decree No. 84–1218, supra.

Despite the modesty of these rates, the post-1972 scheme has resulted in better representation of the indigent. It also provides needed income for the younger lawyers who, at least in simpler cases, still handle much of the legal aid work. Nevertheless, the new scheme is a matter of concern for many members of the Bar, who fear that they may lose their prized independence by becoming too dependent on government funds. Whether these fears are justified in the light of German experience, gathered over a much longer period (see infra), is another question.

35d. See Schlesinger, supra n. 29a.

35e. For details see Fisch, supra n. 30a.

what he would receive from an unassisted client. Yet the rates under the legal aid schedule, though not overly generous, are by no means negligible, with the result that court appointments to represent assisted litigants are sought after by many lawyers, including some of the more experienced ones.

Edge: Does the lawyer appointed to represent an assisted client remain uncompensated, or compensated at lower-than-ordinary rates, even if he wins his client's case?

Comparovich: You have to remember that pursuant to a virtually universal rule the "costs" of a lawsuit can be taxed against the loser. In most civil-law countries, as I have mentioned a minute ago, these taxable costs include the fees of the victor's attorney, and such fees will be taxed at the ordinary statutory rate rather than the legal aid rate, even in a case in which the winning party is assisted by an appointed lawyer.

Edge: Thus an Italian lawyer appointed to represent an indigent party gets nothing if he loses, but recovers regular statutory fees if he wins; and a German lawyer in the same situation is paid at the legal aid rate if unsuccessful, but recovers statutory fees (at the higher regular rate) in case of success. Is this a correct deduction from what you have told us?

Comparovich: It is.[35f]

Edge: Does this not inject a "contingent" element into the compensation of a lawyer appointed to represent an assisted litigant?

Comparovich: You have a point here; [36] but it remains true that an *agreement* between attorney and client, providing for compensation expressed in terms of a percentage of the expected recovery, is unethical and void in most civil-law countries.

Edge: I should like to bring up a broader parenthetical question. Are the civilians' systems of legal assistance not far better than ours; and should we not seek to learn from their superior efforts?

Comparovich: In order to answer your question properly, one has to recognize that by almost universal consent the subject of legal aid and assistance, like Caesar's Gaul, must be divided into three parts: (1)

35f. Unless he is completely judgment-proof, even a loser who is himself financially weak will have to pay the fees to which the victor's attorney is entitled in accordance with the ordinary statutory fee schedule. Under German law, the public treasury helps the assisted litigant by paying his own attorney (and court costs); but the legal aid scheme does not protect him, if he turns out to be the loser, from having to pay the regular fees of his opponent's attorney.

36. In France, the *avocat*-fees (as distinguished from the *avoué*-fees) of the victori-ous indigent party's lawyer are not always recoverable from the vanquished opponent. (See infra, section C of this Dialogue). But occasionally a French *avocat* representing a poor litigant may in another way obtain "contingent" compensation if he wins: where the client's recovery is so large that he is no longer indigent, the client himself must pay a reasonable amount of compensation to the *avocat*, although the latter was originally appointed rather than retained. See Lemaire, supra n. 28, at Sec. 232.

defense of indigent persons accused of crime;[36a] (2) assistance to poor parties in civil litigation; and (3) situations in which, without any immediate thought of actual or contemplated litigation, an impecunious person wishes to obtain legal advice or the help of a person skilled in the drafting of documents.[37] Our discussion has dealt only with the second of these three areas.

Edge: All right—how will you answer my previous question if I limit it to the area of civil litigation?

Comparovich: Your question raises a point which in recent years has become quite controversial in this country. The civil-law systems, by ordinarily relying on the private Bar for the delivery of legal services to the poor, in effect adhere to what we call the "judicare" system of delivering such services. In the United States, on the other hand, the presently prevailing system is that of delivering such services through staff attorneys who are employed by a variety of local legal assistance organizations and paid from a number of private and public sources, including federal funds administered by the Legal Services Corporation. There has been much debate on the relative merits of "judicare" and staff-attorney systems.[38] Until now, the latter type of system has been consistently favored in the expenditure of federal funds; but the statute creating the Legal Services Corporation imposes upon the Corporation the duty to experiment with other systems of delivery, including "judicare";[39] and a number of such experiments are presently in progress.

If you are interested in the "judicare versus staff attorney" controversy, and especially in the contribution which foreign experience can make to the debate, you have a huge literature at your disposal.[39a]

36a. In this area, dramatic advances have been made in the United States since the Supreme Court handed down its famous decision in Gideon v. Wainwright, 372 U.S. 335, 83 S.Ct. 792 (1963). The civil-law countries, in some of which there is still no compensation for assigned defense counsel, no longer are ahead of the United States in their handling of this particular problem.

37. Regarding legal aid in non-litigated matters, Germany has instituted an interesting experiment. Along with the other legal aid reforms mentioned above, a new Law Concerning Consultative Legal Assistance (B.G.Bl. 1980 I 689) was enacted on June 18, 1980, eff. Jan. 1, 1981. Under this Law, an impecunious party may obtain legal advice from, or have a document drafted by, a lawyer of his choice; the lawyer will be compensated by the public treasury by means of a voucher system. For details see G. Greissinger, Beratungshilfe—eine Zwischenbilanz, 1985 NJW 1671.

For an instructive, partly statistical comparison of the German scheme with legal aid in The Netherlands and Great Britain, see E. Blankenburg, Subventionen fuer die Rechtsberatung im Rechtsvergleich, 19 Zeitschrift fuer Rechtspolitik 108 (1986).

38. See, e.g., S. J. Brakel, Styles of Delivery of Legal Services to the Poor: A Review Article, 1977 American Bar Foundation Research J. 217; M. Cappelletti & E. Johnson, Jr., Toward Equal Justice Revisited, 2 The Common Law Lawyer No. 6, pp. 2 ff. (1977); S. J. Brakel, Surrebuttal: Further Comments on Styles of Delivery of Legal Services to the Poor, 3 The Common Law Lawyer No. 1, pp. 2 ff. (1978). Cf. P. L. Brantingham, The Burnaby, British Columbia Experimental Public Defender Project: An Evaluation Report, publ. by the Canadian Ministry of Justice (1981).

39. See 42 U.S.C.A. § 2996f(g) (1986 Supp.).

39a. See supra ns. 30 and 38. See also the symposium entitled International Comparison of Legal Services for the Poor, 10

Edge: Do you personally favor the judicare system or the staff attorney system?

Comparovich: Your question implies that those who make public policy should choose between the two systems. I disagree. The choice should be left to the individual consumer of legal services, i.e., the client. To provide such a choice for the client, the judicare system and the staff attorney system should function side by side, not excluding each other, but competing with each other.[39b]

Edge: Have any foreign countries experimented with such a two-track approach?

Comparovich: Yes.[39c] To mention just a few examples, both in Sweden [39d] and in some of the Canadian provinces [39e] the client is given a choice between the services of a private lawyer selected by him and paid out of public funds, and those of a staff attorney employed by a legal assistance organization.

Edge: That sounds like a good idea. In this country, we seem to be very far from such a fair solution. The reason for our backwardness, it seems to me, is that according to the view prevailing here the indigent civil litigant—in contrast to the indigent criminal defendant—is not thought to be entitled to the assistance of counsel as a matter of right.

Comparovich: In civil cases (except those that have a quasi-criminal flavor, such as paternity or child neglect cases), our courts indeed do not recognize any right of an indigent litigant to the assistance of counsel, paid or unpaid. Some courts, it is true, have the power in their discretion to appoint counsel for an indigent party;[40] but in civil cases they are reluctant to make use of that power, knowing that in such a case an attorney thus appointed normally would have to serve without compensation.[41] Some courts have brought about a slight

---

Cornell Int.L.J. 205 (1977). Foreign experience would seem to indicate that a properly structured judicare system is not necessarily over-expensive. See the interesting German, Dutch and British cost figures given by Blankenburg, supra n. 37. The German experience is particularly instructive. As a result of (a) the 1980 liberalization of the German legal aid scheme (see supra, text at ns. 30e and 30f) and (b) an increase in the number of divorce cases, which constitute the largest portion of legal aid matters, the cost of the German scheme increased ten-fold from 1977 to 1984. Nevertheless, as shown by Blankenburg, ibid., the *per capita* cost of legal aid in Germany is still very moderate.

39b. See Schlesinger, supra n. 29a.

39c. Id., at 217–18.

39d. See P. H. Lindblom, Procedure, in S. Strömholm (Ed.), An Introduction to Swedish Law 95, at 127–29 (1981); Muther, supra n. 30.

39e. See Zemans, supra n. 30, at 93 ff.

40. The federal courts certainly have that power, not only in civil rights cases, 42 U.S.C.A. § 2000e–5(f)(1), but in other cases as well, 28 U.S.C.A. § 1915(d). See Anno., 69 ALR Fed 666 (1984).

41. See Dreyer v. Jalet, 349 F.Supp. 452, at 486–87 (S.D.Texas, 1972), where several ingenious theories in support of compensation are discussed but in effect rejected.

The courts are split on the issue whether they have inherent power to order that court-appointed attorneys be compensated by the appropriate local government unit. Even courts claiming such power tend to exercise it only in exceptional circumstances. See Note, 81 Colum.L.Rev. 366, 368–69 (1981).

In certain types of civil actions (but only in those) the indigent party's attorney may, if he wins, recover counsel fees from

improvement of this regrettable situation by the adoption of local Rules authorizing the clerk of the court to maintain an official list of attorneys willing to handle *pro bono* cases.[41a] Another glimmer of hope for the future perhaps can be seen in the fact that in some recent cases the trial court's discretionary refusal to appoint counsel for an indigent civil litigant has been reversed on appeal.[41b] On the whole, however, our courts continue to cling to the archaic view that a civil litigant has absolutely no *right* to the assistance of counsel.[41c]

By their refusal to recognize the existence of such a right, our courts and legislatures make the words Due Process and Equal Protection of the Laws sound rather hollow for the impecunious litigant who loses a meritorious cause of action or defense because of his inability to obtain the assistance of competent counsel.[41d] With greater wisdom and justice, the West German Federal Constitutional Court has recognized that an indigent party to a civil action has a constitutional right to be represented by a member of the Bar.[42]

✻ mentioned

the opponent. See infra, section C of this Dialogue.

41a. See, e.g., General Order No. 25, Rules for Appointment of Counsel in Civil Cases, of the U.S. District Court for the Northern District of California, dated October 13, 1982.

It has been reported, moreover, that one court, the U.S. Court of Appeals for the Tenth Circuit, has adopted the practice of compensating appointed attorneys in certain cases up to $500, to be paid from the court's trust fund. See L. M. Swygert, Should Indigent Civil Litigants in the Federal Courts Have a Right to Appointed Counsel?, 39 Wash. & Lee L.Rev. 1267, 1291 (1982).

41b. See, e.g., Bradshaw v. Zoological Society of San Diego, 662 F.2d 1301, 1318–20 (9th Cir. 1981); Branch v. Cole, 686 F.2d 264, 266–67 (5th Cir. 1982).

41c. See, e.g., Lassiter v. Department of Social Services, 452 U.S. 18, 101 S.Ct. 2153 (1981). Only in dissent have Justices of the U.S. Supreme Court supported the notion that an indigent civil litigant is constitutionally entitled to the assistance of counsel. See Meltzer v. C. Buck LeCraw & Co., 402 U.S. 954, 91 S.Ct. 1624 (1971) (Black and Douglas, JJ., dissenting); Hackin v. Arizona, 389 U.S. 143, 89 S.Ct. 325 (Douglas, J., dissenting, 1967). See also the dissent of Douglas and Fortas, JJ., in Sandoval v. Rattikin, infra n. 41d. An imprisoned indigent who is a party to a civil action, may have a better chance (than a party who is poor but free!) to obtain the services of a lawyer as a matter of constitutional right. This somewhat ironical result was reached in Payne v.

Superior Court, 17 Cal.3d 908, 132 Cal. Rptr. 405, 553 P.2d 565 (1976).

For more comprehensive discussions, and further references, see Swygert, supra n. 41a, and D. L. Shapiro, The Enigma of the Lawyer's Duty to Serve, 55 N.Y.U.L.Rev. 735 (1980).

41d. Cf. Sandoval v. Rattikin, 395 S.W.2d 889 (Tex.Civ.App.1965), cert. denied 385 U.S. 901, 87 S.Ct. 199 (1966).

42. Decision of June 6, 1967, BVerfGE 22, 83. In this case the poor party, having lost in the court of first instance, did not have a lawyer who was admitted to practice before the intermediate appellate court. Before the expiration of his time for an appeal, the indigent party filed an application with the intermediate appellate court, asking for permission to appeal *in forma pauperis* and for appointment of an attorney to represent him before the appellate court. The application was granted, but only after the time for an appeal had run out. The lawyer designated as the indigent party's appellate counsel filed a notice of appeal immediately upon his appointment; but the appeal was dismissed as untimely. The Federal Constitutional Court, ordering a reversal, directed that the appeal be treated as timely. The Court reasoned that a wealthy appellant, under the same circumstances, could and would have retained a lawyer to file the notice of appeal in time. Consequently, the Court held, it would be a violation of the Equal Protection Clause of the West German Constitution to deny a like effect to the comparable procedural steps of the indigent appellant. The delay which had occurred in the implementation of the ap-

Edge: The question occurs to me whether, with respect to the constitutional issue, the situation in the United States is truly comparable with that in Germany. Under German procedure, as you have told us,[43] it is legally impossible for a person, whether poor or not, to litigate in a court of general jurisdiction or an appellate court without being represented by an attorney admitted to practice before the particular court. In view of this, could one not argue that the indigent litigant's need for a lawyer is stronger in Germany than here?

Comparovich: In a German court of general or appellate jurisdiction, it is *legally* impossible for a litigant to represent himself. In our courts, it is *practically* impossible. I do not think that this difference is decisive.[43a] In both countries, an indigent litigant is at a serious disadvantage for the simple reason that he is unable to afford the services of counsel. It seems to me, therefore, that the Equal Protection argument in favor of a right to counsel—in civil as well as criminal matters—is as persuasive here as in Germany.

Edge: But—to come back to the starting point of our discussion of legal aid—is it not true that in this country the needs of the poor litigant are met by the contingent fee system?

Comparovich: Only in part. The contingent fee system works only in a case in which the indigent person as plaintiff seeks a monetary recovery. It does not work, for obvious legal and practical reasons, in matrimonial matters, which constitute a fairly large part of the legal needs of the poor. Nor does the contingent fee system provide counsel for the millions of indigent people who are defendants in actions brought by lenders, landlords or installment sellers.

Smooth: Gentlemen, I hate to be abrupt in changing the subject. But I must say that from the standpoint of our corporate client we are not making the most efficient use of our time in discussing the problems of indigent litigants.

Comparovich: You may meet them as opponents, though.

---

pellant's constitutional right to the appointment of competent counsel, was not due to the appellant's own fault (he had made his application in time), but to the intermediate appellate court's failure to act more speedily in granting the application.

Cf. OLG Frankfurt, Oct. 8, 1965, 19 NJW 838 (1966): similar holding in a case in which a poor plaintiff had made his application (for the appointment of an attorney to represent him) before the expiration of the rather short statutory limitation period, but the court granted the application after the period had run out.

Note that the constitutional right recognized by these German cases is that of the *client.* Concerning the related issue of the appointed *attorney's* constitutional right to compensation, see supra ns. 35, 35a and 41.

43. See supra n. 20.

43a. The statement in the text is supported by the relevant provisions of the German Code of Civil Procedure. Section 121 of the Code requires appointment of an attorney for a financially handicapped litigant not only (a) in courts of general jurisdiction, where a litigant *must* be represented by counsel, but also (b) in inferior courts (where legally a litigant may represent himself) if the opponent is represented by an attorney or if for other reasons the appointment of counsel for the financially handicapped party appears indicated. Thus it is clear that the German legislator sees no decisive difference between a case where representation by counsel is *legally* necessary and a situation where such representation is *practically* indicated.

Smooth: Maybe; but to steer the conversation back to H's alleged cause of action, I should like to hear from you, Professor, what the Ruritanian rules are concerning attorneys' fees.

Comparovich: In Ruritania, as in most civil-law countries, such fees are governed by a statutory tariff unless the parties agree otherwise.[44] In some countries, it is unethical for a lawyer to agree to a fee which is below the statutory rate. Agreements for a higher fee, on the other hand, are sometimes subjected to stringent form requirements, probably in order to protect clients from unwittingly assuming exorbitant obligations.[45] An excessive fee, moreover, even if specified in an agreement, may be reduced by the court.[46]

Smooth: But in the absence of express agreement, the statutory tariff prevails (except in France with respect to compensation for *avocat*-functions)?

Comparovich: By and large, yes.

Edge: American lawyers are not wholly unfamiliar with that system. Since colonial days, we have had statutes fixing or limiting fees.[47]

Comparovich: Our position, nevertheless, is very different from the statutory tariff system prevailing in many civil-law countries. In the first place, the various state and federal statutes regulating attorneys' fees do not constitute a system; these statutes are exceptional and always limited to specified types of cases, such as workmen's compensation, social security, pension claims, war claims, alien property claims, Indian claims, or tort claims against the United States.[48] Secondly, statutes of this kind usually do not establish a tariff, but only a ceiling; subject to the ceiling, our law still treats the fee as governed by agreement or quantum meruit.[49] Keeping these points of difference in mind, one must conclude that an American lawyer may find himself in

44. Such schedules differ from country to country "with respect to the scope of services covered, the criteria used for measuring individual fees, and the degree of flexibility left for possible [contractual] deviations." W. Pfennigstorf, Legal Expense Insurance—the European Experience in Financing Legal Services 36 (1975). In some countries, such schedules are embodied in national or local statutes; in others, they have been promulgated by the organized Bar. For detailed information on the fee schedules of a number of continental countries, see id. at 37.

45. See, e.g., Sec. 3 subd. 1 of the German Federal Law Concerning Attorneys' Fees of July 26, 1957:

"An agreement providing for compensation in an amount higher than the statutory tariff cannot be enforced by the attorney unless the client's promise is in writing; such promise may not be con-

tained in a power of attorney or in a printed document which in addition includes other terms. If, however, the client has voluntarily and without reservation performed the agreement, he cannot obtain restitution on the ground that his promise failed to comply with the form requirements of the preceding sentence."

46. See, e.g., Sec. 3 subd. 3 of the German statute cited in the last footnote. As to France, see Crémieu, op. cit. supra n. 28, at 250.

47. See Pound, The Lawyer from Antiquity to Modern Times 137–8 (1953).

48. For a discussion of these statutes, see S. B. Jacoby, The 89th Congress and Government Litigation, 67 Colum.L.Rev. 1212, at 1220–21 (1967).

49. Cf. Hopkins v. Cohen, 390 U.S. 530, 88 S.Ct. 1146 (1968).

a completely unaccustomed environment when he has to deal with problems involving the fees of local counsel in civil-law countries.

Smooth: Could you give us some information concerning the general nature of the statutory tariffs which in the absence of agreement are apt to govern the fees of local counsel in those countries?

Comparovich: The most elaborate is the German one, which has exercised a measure of influence in other countries, including Ruritania. The German statute [50] lists and defines, in minute detail, every conceivable type of litigating or counseling activity, and provides that for every activity so defined the attorney shall receive one "basic fee", or a multiple or fraction thereof. For instance, three "basic fees" constitute the normal compensation for conducting a lawsuit from the commencement of the action to the entry of judgment by the court of first instance. Traditionally, the German fee schedule has been modest by American standards; but recent statutory amendments have raised the amounts of the "basic fees". This raise, together with the deterioration of the value of the Dollar vis-à-vis the German Mark, has had the effect that (from our point of view) litigation in Germany is no longer as inexpensive as it used to be. Similar observations could be made with regard to litigation costs in other continental countries.

Edge: How much is the "basic fee" under the German statute?

Comparovich: That is the trick. In most civil matters the basic fee is simply a percentage of the *Gegenstandswert*, i.e., of the amount involved in the dispute or other matter handled by the lawyer.[51]

Smooth: You mean to say that under the German statutory tariff the amount and difficulty of the work done by the lawyer, his standing and experience, the results achieved by him, the client's ability to pay and all the other well-known factors determining a fair and reasonable fee are disregarded, and that the only factor to be considered is the amount involved?

Comparovich: Yes, as a rule that is so.

Smooth: The effect of this system must be that in a case involving a small *Gegenstandswert* but lots of work, the lawyer's compensation is

---

50. Federal Law Concerning Attorneys' Fees of July 26, 1957 (BGBl 1957 I 907), as amended.

51. The German schedule of basic fees shows that the percentage is retrogressive; it is relatively high when the *Gegenstandswert* is low. For a *Gegenstandswert* of DM 100 the basic fee is DM 30, or 30%. But when the *Gegenstandswert* is DM 100,000, the basic fee is DM 1,585, barely more than 1½%. And when the amount in dispute climbs into tens or hundreds of millions, the percentage determining the basic fee goes down to .3%. Nevertheless, when the *Gegenstandswert* is very high, the basic fee may be substantial. For instance, in the case of a dispute involving a hundred million DM, the basic fee is in the neighborhood of DM 300,000. For handling a case in the court of first instance, a lawyer normally is entitled to three basic fees. Thus, in the hundred-million-DM case, he would be entitled to DM 900,000. If the case goes to the intermediate appellate court and the court of last resort, this figure may be quadrupled, because on appeal the basic fee is increased by substantial percentages. (Note that the foregoing figures do not reflect a very slight increase that went into effect Jan. 1, 1987).

Under the loser-pays-all rule, the risk of losing a big case in Germany thus may well run into millions.

inadequate, while a combination of little work and a fancy *Gegenstandswert* may occasionally (as in the case of our dealings with H) lead to an excessive windfall of a fee.[52]

Comparovich: That is true; but parties who are familiar with the system usually can protect themselves by substituting a contractual fee for the statutory one.[52a]

Smooth: Well, we were certainly unfamiliar with the system when we negotiated with H.

Edge: H asked us about the net worth of the Ruritanian subsidiary, without disclosing the true point of his question, and we pure souls told him that it was between 15 and 20 million dollars.

Comparovich: Given a *Gegenstandswert* of that magnitude, it is not surprising that under the Ruritanian fee schedule (if it is applicable) Mr. H would have been entitled to $95,000 for just conferring with you.

Smooth: Regardless of the Ruritanian schedule, however, it is clear that under our standards a $95,000 fee for less than one day's work is excessive. This raises an interesting—though fortunately hypothetical—question: If H had obtained a $95,000 judgment in his Ruritanian action, would a court in this country have enforced that judgment, or refused enforcement on the ground that the recovery of such an excessive fee is against public policy?

Comparovich: Assuming that the jurisdictional and other general requirements for the enforcement of such a judgment are met, it would be enforced; the fact that the foreign court determined the fee by criteria alien to our law, and that the fee thus computed is excessive by our standards, is not a sufficient "public policy" ground for refusing enforcement.[52b] Therefore, even if your company had not had substantial assets in Ruritania at the time of H's action, you would have had to take that action seriously.

C. RECOVERY OF ATTORNEYS' FEES BY THE VICTORIOUS PARTY

Smooth: Your advice concerning fee arrangements to be made with foreign lawyers will be of great benefit to us in the future. Is it not true, however, that when we are threatened with litigation abroad, the

---

52. In an interesting New York case the plaintiff, an Argentine lawyer, asserted that under the law of his country he was entitled to a fee in the amount of $16,000,000. See Haines v. Cook Electric Co., 20 A.D.2d 517, 244 N.Y.S. 483 (1st Dep't 1963); a later phase of the case is reported in 53 Misc.2d 178, 278 N.Y.S.2d 357 (Sp.T.N.Y.Co. 1967).

52a. Moreover, many (if not most) civil-law systems have no rule against the splitting of a cause of action. Where the dispute involves a large amount of money, it is thus possible for the plaintiff drastically to reduce the prospective costs by the simple device of suing for part of the amount in controversy (usually an amount just sufficient to appeal, if necessary, to the court of last resort, see infra p. 463). Whether or not the parties have agreed in advance to abide by the result of the test suit, its outcome will, as a practical matter, usually settle the dispute.

52b. Ackermann v. Levine, 788 F.2d 830 (2d Cir. 1986).

fees of our own local counsel are only a part of the total cost-risk to be considered?

Comparovich: Your point is well taken. If at the end of the litigation you turn out to be the loser, then in civil-law as well as common-law countries you have to pay the "costs" of the action. Concerning the nature and amount of "costs", there are great differences among legal systems:

First, in civil-law countries, where (as we shall see later) there is virtually no discovery, the "costs" do not include the massive amounts of money which we often spend for stenographers' services in connection with discovery. This tends to reduce "costs" in civil-law countries compared to American jurisdictions. Nevertheless, the total amount of the "costs" to be paid by the loser tends to be much larger abroad than here, because of a second, even more important factor to which I now turn.

Second, and this is a point of cardinal significance in transnational litigation, legal systems differ drastically in their answers to the weighty question whether the attorneys' fees expended by the victorious party should be included in the "costs" to be reimbursed by the loser. In contrast to the so-called "American rule", the overwhelming majority of foreign countries [52c] permit the victor to recover his attorneys' fees from the losing party, regardless of whether it is the plaintiff or the defendant who wins the case.[52d] This "loser-pays-all" rule

52c. Although very few jurisdictions outside of the United States are in agreement with the "American rule" on the subject, it is not quite accurate to say that on this point there is a split between the United States, on the one hand, and the rest of the world, on the other. Japanese law, for instance, is in the same camp as the "American rule" and rejects recovery of attorneys' fees, except that in tort cases a prevailing plaintiff may recover his attorneys' fees as an item of damages. See T. Kojima & Y. Taniguchi, Access to Justice in Japan, in 1 M. Cappelletti (Ed.), Access to Justice 689, 705 (1978); T. Hattori & D. F. Henderson, Civil Procedure in Japan, § 10.1 (1985).

52d. The enormously important practical consequences which flow from the fact that most foreign countries adhere to the "loser-pays-all" rule, are underscored and further enhanced by the following factors:

(a) An American party who unsuccessfully litigates in a foreign court and is ordered by the foreign court to pay "costs" (including his opponent's attorney's fees), normally will find that our courts enforce such foreign judgments for "costs." A number of cases to this effect are collected by C. H. Peterson, Foreign Country Judgments and the Second Restatement of Conflict of Laws, 72 Colum.L.Rev. 220, 254 (1972).

(b) Suppose an action is brought in an American court, not on a foreign judgment, but on a foreign cause of action. Even then the foreign country's "loser pays all" rule may assert itself. In Cutler v. Bank of America Nat'l Trust and Sav. Ass'n, 441 F.Supp. 863 (N.D.Cal. 1977) Judge Renfrew held that the question of recovery of attorneys' fees is substantive not only for *Erie* purposes but for choice-of-law purposes as well. It follows, according to Judge Renfrew, that where a plaintiff in our courts successfully asserts a cause of action governed by the laws of country X, and he shows that under X law he is entitled to the recovery of his attorneys' fees, he may recover them here as part of his damages. A recent case holds that even a defendant may recover attorneys' fees from the vanquished plaintiff, if the latter's unsuccessful claim was based on the law of a foreign country allowing such recovery. See DeRoburt v. Gannett Co., 13 Med.L.Rptr. 1025 (D. Hawaii 1986).

(c) In connection with the planning of litigation to be instituted in a foreign court, it should be kept in mind that the question of the amount of recoverable

prevails in most civil-law countries as well as in England and many other parts of the British Commonwealth.[52e]

Smooth: I take it that the effect of the "loser-pays-all" rule is mitigated or modified where the winning party's victory is only a partial one.

Comparovich: Correct.[52f]

Smooth: The French, as you have told us a short while ago, still distinguish between *avoué*-fees and *avocat*-fees, even though in the courts of first instance the same individual now performs both functions. This raises a question in my mind: Does the "loser-pays-all" rule apply to both kinds of fees?

Comparovich: Until the enactment of the new Code of Civil Procedure,[52g] the French rule was that the winning party could recover the fees of his *avoué*, but not the honorarium of his *avocat*. The new Code still adheres to the traditional principle that only that part of the winning attorney's compensation which constitutes a fee for his *avoué*-functions can be recovered from the loser as of right. But by an innovative provision (new Art. 700) the Code now empowers the court, "when it appears inequitable" to let the victorious party bear the burden of compensating his own *avocat*, to order that the loser pay the victor "a sum which the judge determines." Thus the present French rule is that recovery of the victor's *avoué*-fees is a matter of right, while (total or partial) recovery of his *avocat*'s compensation rests in the court's discretion. This rule applies regardless of whether the *avoué*-functions and the *avocat*-functions are performed by different individuals (as would be the case on appeal) or by the same person (in the court of first instance).

Needless to say, such two-track refinements are to be found only in France and a few other civil-law countries which have, or once had, a divided Bar.[52h] In the majority of civil-law countries the "loser-pays-all" rule is simpler and, as a consequence, may be even more drastic in its effect on the vanquished party.

"costs" (and especially the question whether attorneys' fees are to be included in such "costs") may become of immediate practical importance long before the end of a lawsuit; it may indeed present itself right at the outset. In the great majority of jurisdictions, civil-law as well as common-law, a non-resident plaintiff may be compelled, at the very beginning of the action, to deposit security for "costs." For a survey of the relevant provisions in many countries, and of international treaties which sometimes bear on this question, see F. G. Dawson and I. L. Head, International Law, National Tribunals and the Rights of Aliens 135–49 (1971).

52e. Details—especially concerning the amount of attorneys' fees that is recoverable, and the procedure for determining such amount—vary from country to country. For an excellent comparative discussion see W. Pfennigstorf, The European Experience with Attorney Fee Shifting, 47 Law & Contemp. Problems 37 (1984).

court costs may include substantial attorney fees

52f. See id., at 46.

52g. See supra, text at ns. 4 and 5.

52h. Pfennigstorf, supra n. 52e, in this connection mentions Belgium and The Netherlands, in addition to France.

Edge: The "American rule", while in principle rejecting the loser-pays-all approach,[52i] has become riddled with so many statutory [52j] and judge-made [52k] exceptions that in numerous "exceptional" situations our own courts today permit the victor to recover attorneys' fees from the losing party. That being so, is there still such a dramatic difference between the majority civil-law rule and our own solution of this problem?

Comparovich: If one compares our approach to the problem of fee-shifting with that of the civilians, one is struck, first of all, by a tremendous difference in legal method. While the civilians favor the across-the-board application of broad, general rules and principles, our courts and legislators (and also our lobbyists and advocates of special interests) are more apt to think in terms of narrower categories—categories that reflect common interests and functionally related fact situations. When providing for recovery of attorneys' fees, our deci-sionmakers thus have not favored a broad and abstract grouping such as "all victorious litigants"; rather, they have used, and probably will continue to use, the powerful weapon of fee-shifting only for the benefit of pragmatically defined political constituencies such as *plaintiffs* in certain *types* of actions. It is no accident, therefore, that our "rule" is shot through with hundreds of widely scattered exceptions—exceptions which, reflecting political cross-currents, of course are by no means uniform in all American jurisdictions.

Edge: True, the *form* of our approach differs from the relatively clear-cut "loser-pays-all" rule of the civil-law majority. But if one focuses on *substance* and *policy thrust* rather than form, one might well argue that our "exceptions" have narrowed the gap between our approach and that of the civilians.

Comparovich: I disagree. Your argument overlooks the fact that in the civil-law countries and the British Commonwealth the "loser-pays-all" rule is applied routinely and regardless of whether the victori-ous party is the plaintiff or the defendant. In the United States, on the other hand, the general rule is that there shall be no recovery of counsel fees; and in the exceptional instances in which such recovery is authorized by statute or judge-made law, a closer look very often shows

---

52i. For wide-ranging discussions of the "American rule" and of the numerous ex-ceptions to it, see Symposium, Attorney Fee Shifting, 47 Law & Contemp. Problems 1–354 (1984).

52j. For massive citations of such stat-utes, federal and state, see Anno., 73 ALR3d 515 (1976); 1 ALR Digest, Attor-neys' Fees, § 28 (1985). On the federal level, the most widely known statute of this kind is 42 U.S.C.A. § 1988, as amended by the Civil Rights Attorney's Fees Awards Act of 1976.

52k. Such judge-made exceptions usual-ly are based on the "bad faith" theory, the "common fund" theory, the "substantial benefit" theory or the "private attorney general" theory. Some of these theories are controversial. The "private attorney general" theory, for instance, has been re-jected insofar as the federal courts are concerned. Alyeska Pipeline Service Co. v. Wilderness Society, 421 U.S. 240, 95 S.Ct. 1612 (1975). The effect of that decision was only partially undone by the 1976 stat-ute cited in the preceding footnote.

that only a successful *plaintiff* may recover such fees.[52m] The constitutionality of these unilateral statutes has often been attacked, but has been upheld by the majority of the courts passing on the issue.[52n] Even under a statute which in terms authorizes recovery of attorneys' fees by any victorious party, it has been held that such fees should be routinely awarded to a successful plaintiff, but only under exceptional circumstances (when the plaintiff's action "was frivolous, unreasonable or without foundation") to a victorious defendant.[52o]

In terms of policy, the thrust of our approach thus is to permit recovery of counsel fees *by the plaintiff* in many (though not all) situations, while such recovery *against the plaintiff* is almost never allowed. This is quite consistent with the rationale underlying the "American rule" which was announced by our highest Court: that a general loser-pays-all system would "be too great a movement in the direction of some systems of jurisprudence, that are willing, if not indeed anxious, to allow litigation costs so high as to discourage litigants from bringing lawsuits, no matter how meritorious they might in good faith believe their claims to be".[52p]

By allowing many victorious plaintiffs to recover counsel fees from the losing defendant, we do not "discourage litigants from bringing lawsuits"; our unilateral exceptions, therefore, are completely in line with the Supreme Court's formulation of the rationale underlying the "American rule" itself.

The "American rule", especially when combined with a contingent fee arrangement, totally shields the plaintiff from any risk of having to pay either his own or his opponent's attorney a single penny in case the suit is lost. Moreover, the many pro-plaintiff exceptions to the "American rule", again in conjunction with the contingent fee, make it attractive for counsel to represent plaintiffs, i.e., to start lawsuits.

Smooth: I am beginning to see your point, Professor. By the combined effect of all the pro-plaintiff devices you have mentioned, we have built an unbelievably powerful engine for the encouragement of litigation.

The policy thrust of the civil-law majority's bilateral "loser-pays-all" rule goes essentially in the opposite direction. A plaintiff who cannot retain a lawyer on a contingent fee basis, and who is faced with the risk of having to pay his opponent's attorneys if the case goes the wrong way, normally [52q] will think twice before he initiates litigation.

52m. See supra n. 52j.

52n. See the ALR Anno. cited supra n. 52j.

52o. Christiansburg Garment Co. v. Equal Employment Opportunity Comm., 434 U.S. 412, 98 S.Ct. 694 (1978).

52p. See the dictum of Mr. Justice Black, speaking for the Court in Farmer v. Arabian American Oil Co., 379 U.S. 227, 235, 85 S.Ct. 411, 416 (1964). See also Mr.

Justice Goldberg's concurring opinion in the same case. Needless to say, many other rationales assertedly supporting the "American rule" have been offered. See supra, n. 52i. It would seem, however, that the rationale quoted in the text, supra, is the one coming from the most authoritative source.

52q. In certain instances (e.g., where the plaintiff feels that he cannot possibly

Except to the extent that this (possibly very large) expense risk can be covered by insurance,[52r] the system of the civil-law majority must have a severely restraining effect upon those who are contemplating litigation.[52s]

Comparovich: Quite so. I could not have put it much better myself. We deal here with a sharp split among legal systems which is of crucial importance in practice and raises fascinating issues of social policy. The debate concerning those issues probably will never end.[52t]

Smooth: We should leave the resolution of those issues to the policymakers of each country, and continue the discussion of our case.

D. ORGANIZATION OF COURTS

Comparovich: What happened after H sent you a $95,000 bill for one day's work?

Edge: We refused to pay him anything, mainly on the ground that we had not definitely retained him. About two years later, after the change of political conditions in Ruritania, he returned to that country, and then brought an action there.

Comparovich: Before the Civil Chamber of the Tribunal of First Instance?

Smooth: Yes; but I have never understood how that particular court, or "chamber", fits into the judicial institutions of Ruritania.

Comparovich: I shall try to answer that question as briefly as I can.[53] The first point to be made is that in most civil-law countries the subject-matter jurisdiction of an ordinary court, such as the Ruritanian Tribunal of First Instance, is much more limited than in a common-law system. The reason is that in civil-law countries the determination of several important types of disputes, which under our system would be

lose, or where he is judgment-proof) the "loser-pays-all" rule may encourage rather than discourage a plaintiff contemplating the institution of a lawsuit. But such instances are exceptional.

52r. See supra n. 29c.

52s. The strength of that restraining effect will, of course, depend on plaintiff's financial condition. Potential plaintiffs who are either super-rich or judgment-proof may pay scant attention to the cost risk; but the great majority of individual and corporate plaintiffs fall somewhere between those extremes, and their decisions—to sue or not to sue—thus will be substantially influenced by the cost risk.

52t. The plight of the impecunious litigant, which we discussed in section B of this Dialogue, is only one of the factors to be considered. The issue, which affects middle-class as well as indigent litigants, ultimately turns on whether the poli-

cymaker (a) is determined to limit the social cost and psychological trauma of litigation, and consequently seeks to restrain its frequency, or (b) for socio-political purposes or for reasons of professional self-interest favors litigation as a cure of societal ills, and hence desires to encourage it.

To a degree, the policymaker's decision will depend, also, on whether he favors or opposes rapid changes in the law. The "American rule", by encouraging even speculative lawsuits (i.e., lawsuits that can succeed only if plaintiff can persuade the court to adopt a novel theory), clearly favors relatively rapid changes of judge-made law. This is illustrated, inter alia, by the recent development of our law of torts.

53. For details see the materials listed in the text and footnotes supra at nn. 1–6.

For a useful survey covering the whole continent of Europe, see Council of Europe, Judicial Organisation in Europe (1975).

handled by the ordinary courts, normally is entrusted to one or more hierarchies of special courts. Thus there may be special courts for commercial matters [54] and for labor disputes. In the great majority of civil-law systems, moreover, we find one or several special courts dealing with public-law disputes, i.e., matters involving administrative law, taxation, social insurance and the like.[55]

Edge: If I understand you correctly, the jurisdiction of the ordinary courts in a typical civil-law country is essentially limited to (a) criminal prosecutions, and (b) cases involving matters of private law, such as contracts,[56] torts, property rights, matrimonial disputes and controversies over decedents' estates.

Comparovich: You are right. The case brought by H against your company, however, was squarely within the subject-matter jurisdiction of the ordinary courts.

Smooth: No doubt there are several levels of ordinary courts in a typical civil-law country. Could you explain, in rough outline, the basic structure of those courts?

Comparovich: A single-judge inferior court (in criminal cases sometimes sitting with lay assessors) usually has jurisdiction over civil and criminal cases of a relatively minor nature. All other cases—provided they come within the jurisdiction of the ordinary courts rather than some special court—have to be instituted before a court of general jurisdiction, which has different names in different countries, but is always the court of first instance in the more important civil and criminal matters and may, in addition, have jurisdiction to hear appeals from the inferior courts.[56a] The nation or state is divided into judicial districts, and there is such a court of first instance for every district. Under the traditional civil-law system (now modified in some countries, see infra), this court sits in panels, usually called chambers. There are civil chambers and criminal chambers; in those countries where commercial matters are not entrusted to separate commercial courts, a court of first instance may also have commercial chambers, i.e., panels dealing with commercial disputes. The number of chambers differs from court to court, depending on the workload. The court of first instance for a metropolitan district is apt to comprise dozens of chambers, while a similar court in a sparsely populated rural area might conceivably consist of a single civil chamber and one or two criminal chambers.

Smooth: In other words, "the court" that heard our case, was one of the panels of the first-instance court of general jurisdiction?

Comparovich: Yes, a civil panel. I take it that this panel or chamber consisted of one presiding judge and two associate judges?

54. See infra pp. 470–471.

55. See infra p. 499.

56. In some civil-law countries, special courts may have jurisdiction to deal with commercial contracts and labor contracts.

56a. In some countries, however, an appeal from a single-judge inferior court is heard by the intermediate appellate court rather than the first-instance court of general jurisdiction. Such is the situation, for instance, in France.

Smooth: Correct.

Comparovich: That is the classical system in civil-law countries.[57] As a rule, all of the members of the panel are career judges.[58] In civil cases, there is usually no jury [59] or other lay element participating in the work of the court.[60]

Smooth: How about appellate courts?

Comparovich: Appeals from the decisions of the first-instance court of general jurisdiction are heard by an intermediate appellate court, and further appeals may be carried to a court of last resort. These appellate courts, again, normally sit in panels consisting of one presiding judge and an even number (often more than two) of associate judges. Needless to say, the appellate judges belong to the higher or highest echelons of the hierarchic judicial service.

Edge: Is it correct to assume that the typical structure of the ordinary courts, as outlined by you, is more or less uniform throughout the civil-law world?

Comparovich: There are some variations. They are due to a number of factors, of which I shall mention only three. First, additional complexities of course must be expected in those civil-law countries which have a federal structure.[61] Secondly, in developing countries, even though they belong to the civil-law orbit, the scarcity of trained manpower may make it necessary to modify the classical civil-law scheme of judicial organization. In such a country the first-instance court of general jurisdiction sometimes consists of a single law-trained judge, possibly sitting with lay assessors. The reason is that there are not enough professional judges to staff three-member panels of the kind envisaged by the classical scheme.[62]

57. The scarcity of trained manpower in developing nations, and the explosive recent increase of litigation in some of the highly developed countries, have brought about variations of the classical system. See infra at nn. 62 to 62h.

58. See supra pp. 180–182. There are exceptions, however. In Switzerland, the federal judges are elected by the national legislature, while cantonal judges are elected either by the people or by the legislature of the particular canton.

59. The civil jury, however, was introduced into a number of legal systems originally belonging to the civil-law orbit, when for one reason or another those systems were exposed to common-law influence. Concerning the somewhat paradoxical situation in Scotland, where many personal injury actions are tried before a jury (while in England the same cases would be tried without a jury), see Hardin, An American Lawyer Looks at Civil Jury Trial in Scotland, 111 U.Pa.L.Rev. 739 (1963); T. B. Smith, Civil Jury Trial: A Scottish Assess-

ment, 50 Val.L.Rev. 1076 (1964). The latter article, at 1081–82, contains interesting comparative references to the experience in other "mixed" legal systems.

Concerning lay assessors in the civil as well as criminal courts of the socialist countries, see infra n. 62i.

60. It should be noted, however, that commercial chambers, where they exist, typically consist of a career judge, who presides, and two merchants serving (part-time of course) as associate judges.

61. See W. J. Wagner, Federal States and Their Judiciary (1959); Riesenfeld and Hazard, Federal Courts in Foreign Systems, 13 Law & Contemp.Prob. 29 (1948).

62. See, e.g., Farnsworth, Law Reform in a Developing Country: A New Code of Obligations for Senegal, 8 J.Afr.L. 6, at 16 (1964).

Most of the Latin American countries do not suffer from a shortage of trained manpower today. Nevertheless, the pre-independence system of the single-judge court

Thirdly—and this is a recent development—, the increasing pressure of crowded dockets is forcing some of the highly developed civil-law countries to modify the traditional organization of ordinary courts.

Edge: I suppose that in civil-law countries (similarly to what we observe here) there is a tendency to raise the monetary limits on the jurisdiction of the single-judge inferior court in civil matters?

Comparovich: Yes, by raising monetary limits, and in other ways, the jurisdiction of the single-judge courts is being expanded. Moreover, even in courts of general jurisdiction it is now less certain than heretofore that the decision will be rendered by a three-judge panel. Both of these tendencies are illustrated by recent developments in Germany.

Smooth: I take it that, subject to these recent modifications, Germany adheres to the classical civil-law system of judicial organization?

Comparovich: Yes. The single-judge inferior court is called *Amtsgericht*, while the first-instance court of general jurisdiction, which normally sits in three-judge panels, is named *Landgericht*.

The recent developments to which I have referred, are the following:

(a) A 1976 statute, which went into effect on July 1, 1977,[62a] transferred jurisdiction in matrimonial matters, including disputes as to matrimonial property, alimony and custody, from the *Landgericht* to a newly created single-judge Family Court, which organizationally is part of the *Amtsgericht*. It is interesting to note, however, that the decisions of the Family Court can be appealed to a three-judge panel of the *Oberlandesgericht*, i.e., to the same intermediate appellate court which normally hears appeals from the *Landgericht*.[62b] The procedure before the *Oberlandesgericht* is essentially the equivalent of a trial *de novo*.[62c] Thus, even in Family Court matters it remains true that the court that has the last word on issues of fact consists of more than one judge.

(b) The other recent innovation relates to the composition of the *Landgericht* itself. Traditionally, each case coming before that court of course is decided by a three-judge "chamber". Even before the recent reform, a civil case could be referred to a single member of such a panel; but such reference was only for the purpose of having the single judge interrogate witnesses and perform other judicial acts preparatory to a final decision. Once the case was thought ready for such decision, the single judge had to refer it back to the full "chamber", which then decided the case.[62d] A drastic modification of this procedure was brought about by a 1974

---

of first instance has generally been preserved in that region.

62a. BGB*l* 1976 I 1421.

62b. On points of law, a second appeal may be possible from the *Oberlandesgericht*

to the court of last resort. See infra pp. 460–469.

62c. See infra pp. 457–460.

62d. This type of reference, by which a single member of the panel is authorized to

amendment of the German Code of Civil Procedure.[62e] As amended, the Code now provides that, unless the case is one of particular difficulty, or of major importance reaching beyond the parties to the action, any civil case may be referred by the civil chamber to one of its members. In contrast to the old law, this reference now is *for decision*; after such reference, the single judge today normally has the power and duty to hear *and determine* the case.[62f] This innovation, like the even more recent introduction of the one-judge Family Court (see supra), marks an important breach in the traditional principle—regarded as fundamental by many civilians—that major disputes should not be determined by a single judge. Again, however, we must keep in mind that decisions of the *Landgericht*, whether rendered by a panel or by a single judge, are appealable to the *Oberlandesgericht*, where issues of fact as well as law will be reviewed, and in effect tried *de novo*. The *Oberlandesgericht* can refer the case to one of its members only for preparatory measures, but *not for decision* (unless both parties agree).[62g] Thus, again we find that in the court which has the final say on the facts,[62h] the principle of three-judge determination is maintained.

Smooth: Is it fair to assume that, subject to the kinds of recent modifications you have mentioned, the classical pattern of judicial organization is still dominant in the civil-law world?

Comparovich: Yes. By and large, and in spite of local variations (which, for the reasons discussed by us, may have become more pronounced in recent years), the classical pattern still can be said to prevail throughout the civil-law world.[62i] In some countries, it was copied from the judicial organization instituted in post-revolutionary France, while in others, it would seem, national legislators independently found this scheme of judicial organization to be the simplest, clearest and most efficient to be devised.

do much or all of the preparatory work, but not to make a final decision in the case, has become fairly common in the civil-law world during the last 50 years. See infra p. 434.

62e. See Law of December 20, 1974 (BGBl I 3651, eff. January 1, 1975), amending § 348 of the Code of Civil Procedure.

62f. Note, however, that the power to refer the case to a single judge is discretionary. The degree to which courts make use of the power varies greatly from one locality to another; this may reflect differences in attitudes as well as caseloads.

62g. See German Code of Civil Procedure § 524, as amended by the 1974 statute cited supra n. 62e.

62h. Occasionally, the *Oberlandesgericht* may have the final word even on the law. See infra p. 463.

62i. In the socialist countries of Europe, on the other hand, the standard type of a first-instance court in civil as well as criminal cases is the so-called mixed tribunal. Such a tribunal ordinarily is composed of one professional judge and two lay assessors. In some of the socialist countries (e.g., Poland), however, a panel of three professional judges can be substituted for the mixed bench if in the judgment of the President of the court the case is of overwhelming factual or legal complexity. See Comment, Lay Judges in the Polish Criminal Courts: A Legal and Empirical Description, 7 Case West.Res.J.Int.L. 198, 199–200 (1975), where further references can be found.

Smooth: Before we return to the vicissitudes of the action brought against us by Mr. H, I should like to ask one further question that goes to the fundamental powers and functions of the judiciary in a civil-law country. You have given us some information concerning the structure of civil-law courts. Which ones (if any) of those courts have the power to declare a statute unconstitutional?

Comparovich: The civil-law orbit, like the common-law world, is divided on the issue of judicial review. In some civil-law countries, the constitutionality of statutes can be judicially reviewed; in others, it cannot.[62j]

Austria, Germany and Italy come to mind as civil-law countries where comprehensive judicial review was introduced (or re-introduced) immediately after World War II. Portugal, Spain and a number of other civil-law countries in Europe and the Middle East followed suit more recently. But the system of judicial review adopted by most of those countries differs from ours in one important respect: Under their system, the power to declare a statute unconstitutional is entrusted exclusively to a separate Constitutional Court, which stands outside of, and in a sense above, all the other courts.

Edge: Under that system, how does a case reach the Constitutional Court?

Comparovich: A full answer to this question would require more time than we have today. Using Germany as my example,[62k] and somewhat oversimplifying the relevant German rules,[62m] I can say that there are three principal avenues for bringing the issue of the constitutionality of a statute before the Constitutional Court:

62j. See generally M. Cappelletti, Judicial Review in the Contemporary World (1971); id., The "Mighty Problem" of Judicial Review and the Contribution of Comparative Analysis, 53 So.Cal.L.Rev. 409 (1980); id., General Report, in L. Favoreu & J. A. Jolowicz (Eds.), Le Controle Juridictionnel des Lois (1984); id., Repudiating Montesquieu? The Expansion and Legitimacy of "Constitutional Justice", 35 Catholic U.L.Rev. 1 (1985); W. K. Geck, Judicial Review of Statutes: A Comparative Survey of Present Institutions and Practices, 51 Cornell L.Q. 250 (1966). See also supra p. 331.

62k. The German example is fairly typical, even though the procedures used in other civil-law countries tend to be somewhat less elaborate. For an interesting comparison between the German Constitutional Court and its counterparts in Austria, Italy and Spain, see M. Lovik, The Constitutional Court Reviews the Early Dissolution of the West German Parliament, 7 Hastings Int. & Comp.L.Rev. 79, at 97–104 (1983). As to Italy, see T. Ritterspach, Constitutional Review in Italy, 4 Human Rights L.J. 179 (1983); A. Pizzorusso, V. Vigoriti & G. L. Certoma, The Constitutional Review of Legislation in Italy, 56 Temple L.Q. 503 (1983). See also infra n. 62n.

62m. For more extensive information on the powers and the procedure of the (West) German Federal Constitutional Court, see H. G. Rupp, The Federal Constitutional Court and the Constitution of the Federal Republic of Germany, 16 St. Louis U.L.J. 359 (1972); id. The Federal Constitutional Court in Germany: Scope of Its Jurisdiction and Procedure, 44 Notre Dame Law. 548 (1969); id., Judicial Review in the Federal Republic of Germany, 9 Am.J. Comp.L. 29 (1960); E. Benda, Constitutional Jurisdiction in West Germany, 19 Colum.J.Transn.L. 1 (1981); M. Lovik, supra n. 62k. By way of comparison with its counterparts in the common-law world, the German Federal Constitutional Court is extensively discussed in the recent book by E. McWhinney, Supreme Courts and Judicial Law-Making: Constitutional Tribunals and Constitutional Review (1986).

First, even though there is no "case or controversy" (as we would say), the Court must determine the constitutionality of a statute upon the request of the federal government, of a state government, or of a specified number of legislators.

Edge: In other words, the Court is empowered to render advisory opinions.

Comparovich: Yes, if you wish to use our terminology. The Germans speak of "abstract examination of norms". In any event, the opinion the Court thus renders is binding. The number of matters which reach the Court in this way, is not large; but some of them are highly controversial and of great public concern.

The second avenue by which a constitutional issue may reach the Court, is that of judicial referral. When a case is pending in any other court of the land, whether it be a court of first instance or an appellate court, and a constitutional issue arises, that court is not completely precluded from dealing with the issue. If the court concludes that the statute in question is constitutional, it will apply the statute (provided it is relevant) and decide the case. The only thing a court (other than the Constitutional Court) may not do, is to declare or treat a statute as unconstitutional. Therefore, if a court (other than the Constitutional Court) feels that a statute relevant to its decision is unconstitutional, it must refer the issue of that statute's constitutionality to the Constitutional Court. The latter Court determines only that issue. Having done so, it returns the record to the referring court, which then deals with all of the other issues.

The third way of bringing a constitutional issue before the Court, is the constitutional complaint (*Verfassungsbeschwerde*).[62n] This remedy, which accounts for over 90% of the Court's caseload,[62o] may be invoked by any person who feels aggrieved by unconstitutional official action. Before filing a constitutional complaint, however, the complainant must have exhausted other available judicial remedies.

Edge: Does this mean, in effect, that a litigant must have fought his way through a first-instance court, an intermediate appellate court and a court of last resort before he may file a constitutional complaint with the Constitutional Court?

Comparovich: Yes, normally that is so. You have to keep in mind, however, that the referral procedure and the constitutional complaint procedure interact. Let me illustrate that by a simple example. Sup-

62n. In some of the other civil-law countries that have created Constitutional Courts, there is no equivalent of the German *Verfassungsbeschwerde*. This is true, e.g., of Italy, where the referral method is the most frequently used avenue by which cases reach the Constitutional Court. See the articles cited supra n. 62k.

62o. In order not to be engulfed by the enormous number of constitutional complaints filed, the Court uses a screening procedure. As part of that procedure, a committee of 3 judges determines whether the complaint is either unauthorized or "clearly unfounded", and summarily rejects it upon a unanimous finding to that effect. It appears that 97% of all constitutional complaints are disposed of in this way. See W. B. Fisch, Recent Reforms in German Civil Procedure: The Constitutional Dimension, 1 Civil Justice Q. 33, 45 (1982).

pose in a criminal case the defendant (D) is prosecuted under a recent statute. In the trial court, D attacks the constitutionality of that statute. If the trial court agrees with D's contention that the statute is unconstitutional, it must refer the constitutional issue to the Constitutional Court. If, on the other hand, the trial court regards the statute as valid (on its face and as applied to D), it will apply the statute, and the result may be a judgment of conviction. Upon D's appeal, the same situation arises in the intermediate appellate court and, if that court affirms the conviction and D takes a further appeal, in the highest court for civil and criminal matters. In other words, if any one of the three regular courts (trial court, intermediate appellate court, or highest court) agrees with D's constitutional argument, the constitutional issue will reach the Constitutional Court by referral. If, on the other hand, all three of the courts in the regular judicial hierarchy treat the statute as constitutional and apply it in the case, in that event D may ultimately bring the constitutional issue—and only that issue—before the Constitutional Court by way of a constitutional complaint.

Smooth: A neatly constructed system; but it may compel D to fight his way through a hierarchic succession of *four* courts in order to get a constitutional issue definitively determined.

Comparovich: You are right. I suppose that some complexity and unwieldiness are bound to result whenever an attempt is made, in litigation before regular courts, to single out one issue and to have that issue determined by a special court.[62p] The framers of the German Constitution, in providing for a separate Constitutional Court, obviously felt that these disadvantages are outweighed by other considerations.[62q]

Smooth: Does France have a similar system of judicial review?

Comparovich: Not at all. Until the 1950s, France was always cited as the classical example of a civil-law country lacking judicial review. The traditional French attitude of opposing judicial review probably can be explained by pre-revolutionary judicial abuses,[62r] which after the Revolution led to distrust of the judiciary and to a rigid interpretation and application of the doctrine of separation of powers.

In 1958, the Constitution of the Fifth Republic introduced a modicum of judicial review. A Constitutional Council was created, composed of the former Presidents of the Republic and nine appointed members. Of the latter, three are appointed by the President of the Republic, and three each by the presiding officers of the two houses of Parliament. When a statute has been passed by Parliament, certain

---

62p. For another example of such a procedure, see Art. 177 of the Treaty Establishing the European Economic Community.

A comparable phenomenon in our law is the procedure by which federal courts, including the U.S. Supreme Court, occasionally certify an issue of state law to the highest court of the respective state. Cf.

Aldrich v. Aldrich, 375 U.S. 75, 84 S.Ct. 184 and 375 U.S. 249, 84 S.Ct. 305 (1963).

62q. For the reasons why Germany and other continental countries have entrusted judicial review to separate constitutional courts, see infra p. 516.

62r. See supra p. 266.

representatives of the executive or the legislative branch may, before promulgation of the statute (i.e., within a very brief time limit), submit the issue of its constitutionality to the Constitutional Council.[62s] If the Council holds the statute to be unconstitutional, it is ineffective and may not be promulgated.[62t] In a sense, therefore, this procedure can be called judicial review.

Edge: What happens if no representative of the executive or the legislative branch of the government makes a timely submission to the Constitutional Council?

Comparovich: In that event, the statute is promulgated and becomes law, and its constitutionality cannot be questioned by anybody in any court. Thus, under French law—in contrast to German law and our law—the individual citizen still has no right to seek judicial review of the constitutionality of a statute enacted by duly elected legislators.

Edge: In other words, under the French system, judicial review of a statute can be sought only before promulgation, and only by certain political leaders or political groups.

Comparovich: If you wish to characterize the system in political terms, your observation is correct.[62u] One of the consequences of the ordinary French citizen's continuing inability to attack the constitutionality of a statute is that in France such attacks are much less frequent than in Germany or the United States. The politicians who under the French system have the exclusive power to institute a proceeding before the Constitutional Council, tend to attack only very controversial statutes that have a high degree of visibility in the media, with the result that on average no more than ten cases are brought before the Council in a year.[63] Compare that with the thousands of cases per year in which review of the constitutionality of statutes is

62s. Originally, the only officials authorized to make such a submission to the Constitutional Council were the President of the Republic, the Prime Minister, and the presiding officers of the Chamber of Deputies and the Senate. But in 1974, the system was importantly strengthened. Law No. 74–904, of October 29, 1974, now provides that such a submission can be made, also, by 60 members of the Chamber or the Senate. Thus, the right to attack the constitutionality of a statute is no longer monopolized by leaders of the party in power; it can be exercised, also, by the political opposition. For further details, see G. D. Haimbaugh, Jr., Was It France's Marbury v. Madison?, 35 Ohio St.L.J. 910 (1974); J. E. Beardsley, The Constitutional Council and Constitutional Liberties in France, 20 Am.J.Comp.L. 431 (1972); B. Nicholas, Loi, Règlement and Judicial Review in the Fifth Republic, 1970 Public Law 251; id., Fundamental Rights and Judicial Review in France, 1978 Public Law

85 ff., 155 ff.; L. Favoreu, La Décision de Constitutionnalité, 38 Rev. de Droit Comparé 611 (1986).

62t. The Constitutional Council has refused, however, to rule on the question whether a statute is compatible with a Treaty ratified by France. Whether the courts can invalidate a statute on the ground that it is inconsistent with a Treaty, is an issue that has generated much controversy. See G. A. Bermann, French Treaties and French Courts: Two Problems in Supremacy, 28 Int. & Comp.L.Q. 458 (1979).

62u. For an interesting discussion of the political history and significance of the Constitutional Council, see O. Duhamel, L'histoire extravagante du Conseil constitutionnel, L'Express (Int. Ed.) of July 4, 1986, pp. 50 ff.

63. See ibid. Before the 1974 reform mentioned in n. 62s, supra, the number was even smaller.

sought by individual and corporate litigants in German or American courts.[64]

Edge: The French, it seems to me, have taken only half a step toward espousing the idea of judicial review of legislation.

Comparovich: Before you jump to conclusions, you have to consider that under the French Constitution of 1958 the power to legislate is divided between Parliament and the Executive.[65] In its Article 34 the Constitution enumerates a fairly large number of subjects on which Parliament, and only Parliament, can legislate. Article 37 vests in the executive branch of the Government the exclusive power to legislate (by decree) on all subjects not enumerated in Article 34.

Among the non-enumerated subjects one finds some rather significant ones, such as Civil Procedure.[66] Thus, in the area of Civil Procedure, as in all other areas relating to non-enumerated subjects, French legislation today takes the form of governmental decrees rather than that of statutes passed by Parliament.[67]

Smooth: Are you about to tell us that this division of legislative power has an impact on the problem of judicial review?

Comparivich: You are correctly anticipating my next point. Statutes and decrees are treated differently for purposes of judicial review.

Statutes, as we have seen, are subject only to restricted constitutional review (by the Constitutional Council).

A decree, on the other hand, though legislative in nature and having the force of law, is still regarded as an administrative act. It follows, according to French legal tradition, that every interested party, by way of a so-called *recours pour excès de pouvoir*, may ask the Conseil d'État, the country's highest administrative tribunal,[68] to annul a decree that is incompatible with constitutionally recognized principles.[69]

Example: Certain provisions of the 1975 Code of Civil Procedure, which was promulgated by decree, were interpreted as authorizing

---

64. As to Germany, the reader will remember that in that country both "politicians" and ordinary citizens may attack the constitutionality of a statute. As in France, attacks by "politicians" (i.e., petitions for advisory opinions) are relatively rare and limited to highly controversial statutes; in the overwhelming majority of the cases coming before the German Federal Constitutional Court the constitutional point has been raised by an ordinary litigant.

65. For references see supra p. 332, n. 105.

66. There are also some subjects, such as labor law and the law of obligations, as to which Parliament is authorized to enact "fundamental principles", while the details are to be filled in by decree. Note that the power of the executive branch to fill in such details (or to legislate freely on non-enumerated subjects) is not a delegated power; it is derived from the Constitution and cannot be taken away by Parliament.

67. The reader will recall that the new French Code of Civil Procedure was enacted by decrees. See supra, text preceding n. 5. Had a statute been necessary, the enactment of the new Code might have taken much longer.

68. For a more extensive treatment of the functions of the Conseil d'État, see infra pp. 499–500.

69. See J. Boulouis, Droit Administratif, in 2 R. David (Ed.), Le Droit Français 365, 380 (1960).

the court to decide a case on the basis of a legal theory not put
forward by any party, but thought up by the court and not
discussed with the parties prior to the announcement of the court's
final decision.   In a proceeding brought by several Bar Associations,[70] the Conseil d'État annulled those provisions (as thus interpreted) on the ground that they violated the parties' constitutional
right to be heard.[71]

Edge: I think I am getting the point. The written law of France
today consists of statutes and decrees. From what you have told us, I
conclude that the constitutionality of statutes can be attacked only
before promulgation, and only by "politicians". But any interested
party can at any time seek judicial review of the constitutionality of a
decree.[72]

Comparovich: Your conclusion is correct.

E. "JURISDICTION"—SOME TRADITIONAL (BUT GRADUALLY DISAPPEARING) DIFFERENCES BETWEEN CIVILIAN AND COMMON LAW THINKING *

Smooth: Let us return to our struggle with Mr. H. Your explanations have made it clear that under Ruritanian law the Tribunal of

70. The Conseil d'État is very liberal in
determining who has a sufficient "interest" to attack an administrative act in the
administrative courts.   See J. Boulouis,
ibid.

71. Decision of Oct. 12, 1979, reported
in 1979 Rec. Dalloz 606. This decision was
followed by an amendatory decree recognizing the parties' right to be heard on a
point of law thought up by the court. Under the amended provision, the court, before deciding the case on a theory not put
forth by either party, must give the parties
an opportunity to discuss such theory. See
infra pp. 420–421.

72. The attack on the validity of a decree may be based (a) on the ground that
the decree deals with a subject enumerated
in Article 34 of the Constitution and thus
reserved for parliamentary legislation, or
(b) on the assertion that (as in the above
Example) the terms of the decree, as written or as interpreted, violate recognized
constitutional rights.

* In perusing the materials in this section, the reader should keep the following
point in mind:

It is of course fundamental in civil-law
as well as common-law thinking that when
an action is brought in F–1, and the F–1
court examines the question whether it has
power to adjudicate the case, the court will
determine that question in accordance
with F–1 law. If recognition or enforce-

ment of the F–1 judgment is later sought
in F–2, the latter court (even assuming
that the judgment is valid under F–1 law)
probably will refuse to recognize or enforce
it unless the F–2 court is persuaded that
the F–1 court had "jurisdiction"; and under the view that strongly predominates in
civil-law as well as common-law countries,
the F–2 court, in thus examining the "jurisdiction" of the F–1 court, will apply the
jurisdictional rules of F–2.

Thus, whether the issue of the F–1
court's adjudicatory power arises in F–1 or
in F–2, that issue normally will be decided
in accordance with the *national law* of one
of those two countries. This, however, is
subject to an important qualification: If
there is an applicable treaty, then *international or supra-national law* may become
the rule of decision both in F–1 and in F–2.

The impact of supra-national law on this
subject is particularly heavy in Europe,
where the member nations of the Common
Market have entered into a Convention
dealing with judicial jurisdiction and the
mutual recognition and enforcement of
judgments. Some features of that Convention (which for the EEC performs a function similar to that of our own rules of
constitutional law concerning state court
jurisdiction and Full Faith and Credit) will
be discussed in the second half of this
section. But even before we reach that
discussion, the reader should realize that

First Instance, being a court of general jurisdiction, had subject-matter competence to deal with our case. But I find it hard to understand how the court, from the standpoint of any civilized legal system, was able to act as if it had obtained personal jurisdiction over the defendant corporation.

Edge: The action was not against our Ruritanian subsidiary, with which H had not had any dealings, but against International Dulci-Cola Corporation, a Delaware corporation having its main office in this State. The plaintiff did not attach any property in Ruritania belonging to the defendant. The action was purely in personam. Several methods of service were successively used by plaintiff.

Comparovich: We shall come back to the method of service at a later point. But so long as the topic of our discussion is personal jurisdiction, the method of service is irrelevant from a civilian point of view.

Smooth: That sounds fantastic. I can understand that where the basis of jurisdiction is domicile, consent, or the doing of an act (long-arm), the function of service of process is merely to give notice to the defendant; in these cases, therefore, the method of service can be neatly separated from the basis of jurisdiction. But in cases in which jurisdiction is based on defendant's "presence",[72a] personal delivery of the summons to the defendant traditionally has been thought to serve two functions, namely (a) to give notice, *and* (b) by a kind of symbolic arrest, which historically may be a remnant of more drastic methods of

in the EEC the rules regarding judicial jurisdiction and enforcement of foreign-country judgments today are derived partly from national laws, and partly from supra-national or European law.

Like the national laws of the original six EEC members, the above-mentioned Convention has a distinctly civilian bent. Therefore, much of what Professor Comparovich tells us about basic "civilian" approaches to jurisdictional problems, is true of the supra-national as well as the national rules on the subject in the civilian EEC countries. Indeed, at some points in the discussion the relevant provisions of the Convention will be cited as typifying the civil-law approach.

The Convention's official title is "Convention on Jurisdiction and the Enforcement of Judgments in Civil and Commercial Matters". Its text can be found in CCH Common Market Reporter ¶6003 ff. Originally signed in 1968, it became effective in the six original member countries in 1973. The Convention has been ratified, also, by Denmark and the United Kingdom (the latter eff. January 1, 1987). In the other member countries the Convention will become effective upon ratification, which is expected in the near future.

For informative discussions see F. K. Juenger, Judicial Jurisdiction in the United States and in the European Communities: A Comparison, 82 Mich.L.Rev. 1195, especially 1206–12 (1984); E. Jayme & C. Kohler, Zum Stand des internationalen Privat- und Verfahrensrechts der Europaeischen Gemeinschaft, 5 IPRax 65 (1985); and, with special reference to the United Kingdom, I. K. Mathers, The Brussels Convention of 1968: Its Implementation in the United Kingdom, 3 [1983] Yearbook of Eur. L. 49 (1984).

The cumbersome official title of the Convention will not be used in the discussion which follows; references will be to "the Convention" or "the European Convention".

72a. See Restatement, Second, Conflict of Laws § 28 (1971). Following Professor Ehrenzweig's terminology, many courts and scholars now use the phrase "transient jurisdiction" when they refer to cases in which the court's power over an individual defendant is based solely on the fact that process was personally served upon him within the forum state. See Ehrenzweig, The Transient Rule of Personal Jurisdiction: The "Power" Myth and Forum Conveniens, 65 Yale L.J. 289 (1956).

physical compulsion used in former days,[72b] to establish the very basis
of the court's power over the defendant. For this reason, I fail to see
how anybody can say that service of process is completely irrelevant
when we deal with the bases of jurisdiction.

Comparovich: You are merely restating the traditional American
view on the subject. Lawyers brought up in the civil law, however,
emphatically reject the idea that a forum having no pre-existing contacts with the parties or the transaction can create personal jurisdiction
for itself by the mere act of handing the summons to a non-resident
defendant who may be in transit through, or perhaps flying over, the
territory of the forum state.[72c] The proposition that such service of
process, without more, is sufficient to give a court personal jurisdiction,
recently has become questionable even under our law.[72d] Our civilian
brethren, in any event, have long rejected that proposition as barbarous.[72e] In their view, jurisdiction is never based on a mere procedural
step, such as service of a summons. It is invariably based on a
relationship, or contact, which connects the parties or their acts with
the forum.

Smooth: What are the relationships, or contacts, which they regard
as sufficient bases of jurisdiction?

72b. There is much controversy concerning the history of the rule of transient
jurisdiction. Scholars have disagreed, in
particular, as to whether the rule is of
ancient and respectable common law origin, or whether it is a 19th century cuck-
oo's egg laid into the nest of the common
law. Compare Beale, The Jurisdiction of
Courts Over Foreigners, 26 Harv.L.Rev.
193, 283 (1913) with Ehrenzweig, Treatise
on the Conflict of Laws 104–107 (1962) and
G. C. Hazard, A General Theory of State-
Court Jurisdiction, 1965 Sup.Ct.Rev. 241,
at 252–62. For an instructive discussion
examining the historical evidence, see N.
Levy, Jr., Mesne Process in Personal Actions at Common Law and the Power Doctrine, 78 Yale L.J. 52 (1968).

This dispute is certainly of interest to
legal historians; but it does not have much
bearing on the policy question whether the
rule of transient jurisdiction should remain
a part of our law. One of the authors of
this casebook has argued that in our day
and age the rule is a senseless and indeed
vicious atavism, and that it should be abolished, regardless of whether it is 700 or
only 100 years old. See Schlesinger, Methods of Progress in Conflict of Laws, 9
J.Pub.L. 313, especially at 317–18 (1960).

72c. See, e.g., Grace v. MacArthur, 170
F.Supp. 442 (E.D.Ark.1959) (jurisdiction obtained by service effected in an airplane
while in flight over the territory of the
forum State).

It should be kept in mind, however, that
in most American jurisdictions the effect of
the rule of transient jurisdiction is mitigated by the doctrine of *forum non conveniens.*

72d. Dicta in Shaffer v. Heitner, 433
U.S. 186, 97 S.Ct. 2569 (1977), appear to
require a "reasonable" basis for any exercise of state court jurisdiction. Whether
transient jurisdiction meets that requirement, may well be doubted. See, e.g., R. B.
Schlesinger, Jurisdictional Clauses in Consumer Transactions: A Multifaceted Problem of Jurisdiction and Full Faith and
Credit, 29 Hast.L.J. 967, at 974–75 (1978).

72e. See Pillet, Jurisdiction in Actions
Between Foreigners, 18 Harv.L.Rev. 325,
335 (1905): "In France (as formerly in
Rome) one asks first if the French courts
have jurisdiction; this primary question
out of the way, the law gives the complainant a way of summoning his opponent before the tribunal which is to judge him. In
England and in America the process is
reversed; one seeks first to find out if the
writ of summons (*l'assignation*) can be legally delivered to the person wanted (personal service) or something equivalent
done (substituted service). Then, once it is
established that the writ can be regularly
served, the jurisdiction of the English
courts naturally follows. In France we
should call that putting the cart before the
horse."

> → civil law countries

Comparovich: Apart from "presence" (which they reject as a basis of jurisdiction), they use largely the same bases of personal jurisdiction which today [72f] are recognized in our law.[72g]

Smooth: Perhaps it would be instructive to run through the most important bases of personal jurisdiction one by one. To begin with the obvious, I suppose the civilians agree that an individual defendant can be sued at his domicile?) — *as basis of jurisdiction*

Comparovich: They do.[72h] Under many civil-law systems the defendant can be sued, also, at the place of his residence. Moreover, most of the civil-law countries provide, either generally or with respect to certain types of cases, that a defendant can be sued in the country of his nationality, even though he may be domiciled elsewhere.[72j]

Edge: That is not surprising. In our law, too, the nationality of the defendant has been treated as a proper basis of judicial jurisdiction.[72k]

Comparovich: You are right; but there is a difference, at least in degree, between our law and the position of the civilians on this point. In our view, nationality is not a common law basis of jurisdiction. It follows that a statute—in fact a federal statute— [72m] is necessary in order to give a court personal jurisdiction over a defendant on the basis

72f. In former days, before "long-arm" jurisdiction was recognized in the United States, the difference between American and civilian notions concerning the proper bases of jurisdiction was much more pronounced.

72g. The statement in the text, supra, relates only to the regular bases of jurisdiction. Concerning the occasional use of "exorbitant" bases of jurisdiction, see infra, at nn. 84 ff.

72h. Switzerland has gone so far as to make it a principle of constitutional law, embodied in Art. 59 of the Federal Constitution, that a personal action against a Swiss domiciliary ordinarily can be brought *only* in the canton in which the defendant is domiciled. The principle, however, is subject to some exceptions. In automobile accident cases, for instance, the action may be brought at the place of the accident. See Fleiner-Giacometti, Schweizerisches Bundesstaatsrecht 861 (1949, reprinted 1965); M. Guldener, Schweizerisches Zivilprozessrecht 59–60, 83–84 (2d ed., 1958). By way of another exception, it is recognized that the protection of Art. 59 may be waived, either by a stipulation made in advance of litigation or by a general appearance in the litigation itself. Usually the waiver will take the form of a prorogation clause (see infra at nn. 73–80).

Such a clause, however, will be sustained by the courts only if it is not hidden in a mass of small print, and if it is phrased in language which a person of the defendant's

education and experience can readily understand. This is exemplified by a case in which the defendant, a Swiss musician domiciled in Geneva, had signed a prorogation clause which was contained in the "General Conditions" of a Swiss bank and which (strangely and for unexplained reasons) was in English. The clause read: "For the present contract Swiss law is applicable. Venue is Zurich, Switzerland". Switzerland's highest court held the clause invalid. Federal Court Jan. 20, 1965, BGE 91 I 11.

If on the basis of a similar prorogation clause a foreign court rendered a judgment against a Swiss domiciliary, such judgment would not be recognized or enforced in Switzerland. See Fleiner-Giacometti, id. at 858.

72j. Concerning the nationality *of the plaintiff* as a possible basis of jurisdiction, see infra at n. 84, and also infra pp. 852–856.

72k. Blackmer v. United States, 284 U.S. 421, 52 S.Ct. 252 (1932); Restatement, Second, Conflict of Laws § 31 (1971).

72m. When a State asserts jurisdiction over its absent "citizens", the assertion can always be explained on the ground that the defendant has maintained his domicile in the State. It is very questionable, therefore, whether State "citizenship" (as distinguished from U.S. citizenship) can be treated as an independent basis of jurisdiction, i.e., a basis independent of domicile.

of the latter's U.S. citizenship; and Congress has enacted such statutes only for the purpose of enforcing, in exceptional situations, a particular duty of loyalty owed by the defendant citizen to the United States. In most civil-law countries, on the other hand, the defendant's nationality constitutes a routine basis of jurisdiction in ordinary private litigation.[72n] Some countries permit the use of this jurisdictional basis in every type of action, including an ordinary suit for a sum of money; others limit its use to certain types of litigation, such as matrimonial matters and other actions involving a person's status. In proceedings involving an estate, the nationality of the decedent is not infrequently viewed as a proper basis of jurisdiction.

Smooth: How about the domicile of a corporation?

Comparovich: Strictly speaking, a corporation does not have a domicile. Under the law of most civil-law countries, however, a corporation can be sued at its "seat". The term "seat" is a technical one. Concerning its precise definition, there is much controversy.[72o] For present purposes, and without aspiring to a high degree of accuracy, I would say that "seat" means something like headquarters or principal place of business. At its "seat", a corporation can be sued on any cause of action. In addition, most civil-law countries provide that if a corporation maintains a "branch" or "establishment" in a locality other than its "seat", it can be sued at the place of the "branch" or "establishment"; but in this case jurisdiction tends to be limited to causes of action arising from the activities of the "branch" or "establishment".[72p]

Edge: Before we leave the subject of an individual's domicile or a corporation's "seat" as a basis of personal jurisdiction, I should like to bring up a case which was mentioned in a legal journal and which thoroughly confused me. In that case, it seems, a Swiss Bank sued two defendants in a French court. One of the defendants was a French corporation; the other was an individual U.S. citizen domiciled in New York. To my utter amazement, the French court apparently exercised personal jurisdiction over both defendants, although admittedly there was no long-arm or other basis of jurisdiction over the American defendant. If the latter had been the sole defendant, the action would have failed on jurisdictional grounds; the French court conceded that. Nevertheless, it was held that the French court's undoubted jurisdiction

72n. Note, however, that the European Convention, although in general it reflects civilian thinking, is opposed to the use of nationality as an independent basis of personal jurisdiction in all cases where the defendant is domiciled in one of the Common Market countries.

72o. For an interesting, partly comparative discussion of the definition of "seat", see Bayerisches Oberstes Landesgericht, decision of July 18, 1985, 6 IPRax 161 (1986).

72p. In this country, it is thought that under certain circumstances a State's judi-

cial power over a foreign corporation doing business within its territory extends to causes of action that do *not* arise from such local business. See, e.g., J. H. Friedenthal, M. K. Kane & A. R. Miller, Civil Procedure 127–28 (1985). In the view of the civilians, this extension of jurisdiction over foreign corporations is as barbarous as our assertion of personal jurisdiction over transiently "present" individuals. See B. M. Carl, Relevance to Texas Practitioners of Recent Conventions on International Conflict of Laws, 35 Texas Bar J. 425 (1972).

over the French defendant in some way extended to the American co-defendant. This is a puzzling case. Are we to infer from it that a civil-law court, once it obtains proper jurisdiction over one of the defendants, will automatically assert jurisdiction over all co-defendants, regardless of whether or not there is any valid basis of jurisdiction as against the latter?

Comparovich: Concerning this question, which is important in practice, the civil-law systems do not speak with a single voice. In a number of civil-law countries, of which Germany is typical, the answer is essentially the same as under our law: that the issue of personal jurisdiction must be separately and independently examined with respect to each defendant. But in France and some other countries following its example the rule is that when several parties are properly joined as co-defendants, and one of them has his domicile (or its "seat") in the forum country, the court has personal jurisdiction over all of them.[72q]

Edge: This is an odd rule. It makes jurisdiction dependent on whether the joinder was proper.

Comparovich: On this ground, and also for reasons of fairness, the French rule has been criticized. The relative merits of the French rule of "jurisdiction by joinder" and of the opposite German rule were intensively debated at the time when the European Convention was in the drafting stage. In the end, the French view prevailed. As a result, the Convention provides in Art. 6, subd. 1, that a defendant who is domiciled (or has its "seat") in a signatory country, can be sued not only at his or its own domicile or "seat", but also at the domicile or "seat", within a signatory country, of any co-defendant.[72r]

Smooth: To turn to the next alternative basis of personal jurisdiction: What is the civilians' attitude toward the notion that defendant's consent is a proper basis of jurisdiction?

Comparovich: In the civil-law systems this notion has an older tradition, and is even more firmly established, than in our law. The civilians agree with us that the defendant's consent, i.e., his voluntary submission to the jurisdiction of a particular forum, can either (a) take the form of what we would call a general appearance, or, (b) be declared in advance, usually in a contract clause.

72q. See the new French Code of Civil Procedure, Arts. 42 and 43. These provisions of the 1975 Code do not constitute an innovation, but essentially restate the traditional French rule. See P. Herzog, Civil Procedure in France 193–94 (1967). For a comparative discussion see U. Spellenberg, Oertliche Zustaendigkeit kraft Sachzusammenhangs, 79 Z.f.Vergl. Rechtsw. 102 (1980).

72r. Note that this affects only defendants having their domicile or "seat" in a signatory country. Under the French rule, on the other hand, any non-resident co-defendant, when sued together with a French-domiciled defendant, may become the target of "jurisdiction by joinder". *Quaere*, however, whether an American court would enforce a French judgment against an American defendant who was hauled into the French court solely through the device of "jurisdiction by joinder".

Edge: I have read somewhere that the civilians use the term "prorogation" when they refer to such a forum-selecting agreement.

Comparovich: You are right. The term has an interesting history. Although the idea was derived from Roman law, it seems that the words *prorogatio fori* were first used in canon law to signify a stipulation by which the parties themselves choose a forum.[72s]

Smooth: What is the effect of a prorogation agreement according to the civilian view? [73]

Comparovich: With respect to the intended effect of such an agreement, it is necessary to draw an important distinction. Some prorogation clauses merely purport to *confer* jurisdiction on the courts of forum F, without attempting to interfere with the concurrent jurisdiction of other forums where jurisdiction may exist on the basis, for instance, of the defendant's domicile or nationality. On the other hand, there are choice-of-forum clauses which go further and purport, not only to confer jurisdiction on the courts of F, but also to *oust* all other courts (i.e., all courts other than those of F) of jurisdiction. Viewed from the standpoint of a forum thus sought to be deprived of jurisdiction, a clause of the latter kind is sometimes called a "derogation" agreement.

Smooth: The terms "prorogation" and "derogation" are a bit too erudite for me. Could we not distinguish, quite simply, between non-exclusive and exclusive forum-selecting clauses?

Comparovich: Yes, that would be possible. It might be even more fruitful, however, to look at all such clauses (a) from the standpoint of the chosen forum, and (b) from the standpoint of a forum sought to be ousted. To the chosen forum, it will not make much difference whether the clause is exclusive or non-exclusive; the question here is simply whether the law of the chosen forum holds the parties to their agreement and whether the courts will accept the jurisdiction sought to be conferred upon them by such agreement. The courts of an "ousted" forum, on the other hand, may have to face the question (which arises only in the case of an exclusive forum-selecting clause) whether their otherwise existing jurisdiction is impaired by the clause.

[72s]. See Lenhoff, The Parties' Choice of Forum: "Prorogation Agreements", 15 Rutgers L.Rev. 414, at 415–16 (1961).

[73]. In practice, a prorogation clause sometimes takes the form that the parties "elect domicile" in a named locality; or the draftsman may achieve the same result indirectly, by stipulating that all obligations arising from the contract be performed at a given place. Concerning the jurisdictional significance of the place of performance see infra, text at n. 83.

Very frequently, a prorogation clause is combined, perhaps in the same sentence, with a choice-of-law clause. E.g.: "Any

disputes arising from, or in connection with, this contract are to be determined by the courts of Ruritania City in accordance with the substantive law of Ruritania." Needless to say, in analyzing a clause of this kind, one must distinguish between choice of forum and choice of law, even though the draftsman has dealt with both issues in the same breath.

For an extensive comparative treatment of choice-of-forum clauses, see 1 Delaume, Transnational Contracts—Applicable Law and Settlement of Disputes, Ch. 6 (Rev.Ed., 1986).

Smooth: I accept your analysis; but let us take it in easy steps. The first question, then, would be how a forum-selecting clause is treated by the courts of the chosen forum.

Comparovich: The rule is that the courts of the chosen forum should give effect to the forum-selecting agreement of the parties. On this point, the civil-law authorities appear to be virtually unanimous.[74] The rule, however, has always been subject to some exceptions,[75] and the more progressive civil-law countries have added an important new exception in recent years.

Edge: I think I can guess what the new exception is. European legislators, like their counterparts in this country,[75a] probably seek to protect consumers against contract clauses selecting a forum favorable to the creditor.

Comparovich: You are right. Both in France [75b] and in Germany,[75c] recent enactments provide that a forum-selecting clause in a contract is invalid unless all parties to the contract are merchants.[75d] In a similar vein, the European Convention proscribes forum-selecting clauses which favor the creditor in a consumer transaction.[76]

Smooth: Our interest centers mainly on transactions among business entities. Am I correct in assuming that when dealing with such a transaction, a civil-law court normally will give effect to the parties' choice of forum?

Comparovich: Yes.

---

74. See Riezler, Internationales Zivilprozessrecht 306–13 (1949).

Note, however, that many countries require written form for forum-selecting agreements.

75. If the litigation involves, e.g., matters of personal status, or title to land situated in another country, the courts of the chosen forum may refuse to give effect to the choice-of-forum clause.

75a. See R. B. Schlesinger, Jurisdictional Clauses in Consumer Transactions: A Multifaceted Problem of Jurisdiction and Full Faith and Credit, 29 Hast.L.J. 967 (1978).

75b. See the new French Code of Civil Procedure, Art. 48.

75c. See § 38, par. 2, of the German Code of Civil Procedure, as amended in 1974; E. von Hippel, Verbraucherschutz 157–58 (3rd ed., 1986). It should be noted, however, that under German law the prohibition against choice-of-forum clauses in contracts with a non-merchant applies only when all parties are domiciled in Germany. A written choice-of-forum agreement between a party in Germany and a party outside of Germany is valid regardless of whether the parties are merchants. Using

our terminology, one could say that with respect to a contract with a non-merchant German law prohibits *venue* agreements, but not agreements concerning *jurisdiction.* (But note that where the defendant is domiciled in a Common Market country, a German court cannot apply the German rule; instead, it must apply the more protective rule of the European Convention, see infra n. 76).

If all parties to the contract are merchants, the forum-selecting clause as a rule is valid, even though it is contained in a printed standard contract form. See Baumbach-Lauterbach-Albers-Hartmann, Zivilprozessordnung, § 38, Anno. 2 B (45th ed., 1987).

75d. The commercial codes of civilian countries usually contain elaborate definitions of the term "merchant". See infra pp. 590–596. Civilian legislators, when dealing with consumer problems, thus often find it unnecessary to use and to define the term "consumer"; they simply speak of the consumer as a non-merchant.

76. See Art. 15 of the Convention. Similarly, Art. 12 invalidates most jurisdictional clauses in insurance policies if they favor the insurer.

Edge: Our law is quite similar in that respect.[77]

Smooth: Up to now, we have looked at the problem from the standpoint of the chosen forum. Let us now turn to the second step in your analysis, Professor. Will civil-law judges, when they find themselves in the role of the "ousted" court, give effect to a choice-of-forum clause purporting to be exclusive?

Comparovich: In the majority of civil-law countries—including France, Germany and Switzerland—the answer is Yes, at least in principle.[78] Even under the majority view, however, an oppressive or unreasonable clause can be invalidated as being *contra bonos mores*,[79] or disregarded on some other theory.[80] If the clause is contained in a contract of adhesion, it may be particularly vulnerable under statutes recently passed in some of the civil-law countries.[80a]

Edge: Suppose a contractual choice-of-forum clause is reasonable at the time the contract is made, but becomes unreasonable or oppressive due to a subsequent change of circumstances. Will civil-law courts enforce the clause in such a situation?

Comparovich: If this were a law school class, I would answer your question by referring you to a fairly recent case:

> *Example:* Plaintiff, a citizen of West Germany, was employed as a pilot by defendant Lebanese corporation. The written employment contract provided for the exclusive jurisdiction of the courts of Lebanon in any and all disputes arising in connection with such contract. When civil war subsequently erupted in Lebanon, the

---

77. See, e.g., Restatement, Second, Conflict of Laws §§ 32 and 43 (1971). See also supra n. 75a.

78. See M. Pryles, Comparative Aspects of Prorogation and Arbitration Agreements, 25 Int. & Comp.L.Q. 543 (1976); Lenhoff, supra n. 72s; J. M. Perillo, Selected Forum Agreements in Western Europe, 13 Am.J.Comp.L. 162 (1964); M. A. Schwind, Derogation Clauses in Latin-American Law, 13 Am.J.Comp.L. 167 (1964). These articles indicate that Spanish courts refuse to be "ousted", and that in Italy, too, a rather restrictive rule prevails. See also McCusker, The Italian Rules of Conflict of Laws, 25 Tul.L.Rev. 70, 87 (1950).

Concerning attempts to bring about international unification with respect to the recognition and enforcement of prorogation clauses, see K. H. Nadelmann, The Hague Conference on Private International Law and the Validity of Forum Selecting Clauses, 13 Am.J.Comp.L. 157 (1964); id., Choice-of-Court Clauses in the United States: The Road to Zapata, 21 Am.J. Comp.L. 124 (1973).

When a choice-of-forum clause is invoked in a court in F, but the contract containing the clause has its center of gravity in X, difficult choice-of-law problems may arise as to whether the validity of the clause is governed by the law of F or of X. These problems, which are beyond the scope of the present discussion, are thoroughly discussed by Delaume, supra n. 73, and by O. Kahn-Freund, Jurisdiction Agreements: Some Reflections, 26 Int. & Comp.L.Q. 825 (1977). From the standpoint of American law, these choice-of-law questions are discussed also in the article cited supra n. 75a.

79. See infra pp. 702–731.

80. For a recent example see n. 72h supra. See also L. O. Lagerman, Choice-of-Forum Clauses in International Contracts: What is Unjust and Unreasonable?, 12 Int. Lawyer 779, 793–94 (1978); P. Gottwald, Grenzen internationaler Gerichtsstandsvereinbarungen, in D. Henrich & B. von Hoffmann (Eds.), Festschrift fuer Karl Firsching 89 (1985).

80a. See infra pp. 723–725. Note, however, that in cases governed by the European Convention such national laws may be pre-empted. See Gottwald, supra n. 80.

plane piloted by plaintiff was shot at and hit while flying over that country. Plaintiff thereupon refused to make further flights over Lebanese territory. Defendant considered such refusal unjustified and fired the plaintiff.

Plaintiff's action for wrongful dismissal was brought in a German labor court. That court concededly would have had personal jurisdiction over defendant corporation if the contract had not contained a choice-of-forum clause. Defendant, however, in proper and timely fashion objected to the jurisdiction of the court, arguing that the German courts had been "ousted" of jurisdiction by the contract clause. In response to this objection, plaintiff alleged and proved that at the time of his action the Lebanese courts had ceased to function.

This jurisdictional dispute was ultimately resolved by the *Bundesarbeitsgericht*, the highest German court in labor matters.* The court held that the jurisdictional clause in the contract was originally valid, and that under normal circumstances the clause would give defendant the right successfully to attack the jurisdiction of any non-Lebanese court. But, the court further held, defendant in this case was guilty of *abusing that right* ** by insisting on the exclusive jurisdiction of the Lebanese courts at a time when those courts were closed. Plaintiff's action (which had not yet been determined on the merits) thus was permitted to proceed in the German courts.

ruling

Edge: Using our terminology, we might say that the German court held the defendant to be estopped from invoking the (originally valid) choice-of-forum clause. I think the case stands for the proposition that such a clause should not be enforced if it was unreasonable or oppressive at the time it was written into the contract, *or* if in the light of subsequent events it has become unreasonable or oppressive to invoke it.

Smooth: But when business entities, in a freely negotiated contract, have agreed on the exclusive jurisdiction of the courts of country A, and one of the parties—in violation of that agreement—then brings an action in civil-law country B, is it not reasonable to assume that ordinarily the courts of B will throw out the action?

Comparovich: If B belongs to the majority group of civil-law countries, that is a reasonable assumption.

Edge: In recent years, our own law has moved in the same direction.[80b]

---

* The decision is reported in 32 NJW 1120 (1979).

** The case illustrates the wide use made by civil-law courts of the doctrine of *abuse of rights*. For an extensive discussion of that doctrine see infra pp. 740–766.

80b. See M/S Bremen v. Zapata Off-Shore Co, 407 U.S. 1, 92 S.Ct. 1907 (1972).

For comments on this important case see F. K. Juenger, Supreme Court Validation of Forum Selection Clauses, 19 Wayne L.Rev. 49 (1972); G. R. Delaume, Choice of Forum Clauses and the American Forum Patriae, 4 J. Maritime Law & Commerce 297 (1973); K. H. Nadelmann, Choice-of-Court Clauses in the United States—The

Comparovich: Yes. This is an instance of what is often referred to as convergence. The majority of the civil-law systems started with the rule that B, although otherwise it would have jurisdiction, is deprived of such jurisdiction by the parties' advance agreement conferring exclusive jurisdiction on the courts of A. In time, however, it was found necessary to qualify this rule in order to protect parties of inferior bargaining power. Thus, unreasonable and oppressive forum-selection agreements (especially when they are contained in contracts of adhesion) were invalidated. American courts, in sharp contrast to the majority of the civilians, started out by holding that the parties have no power by their agreement to "oust" a court of jurisdiction. In time, however, it became recognized that the "ousted" court, even though it was not deprived of jurisdiction, might still refuse to exercise its jurisdiction, and in this way might, and indeed should, give effect to the parties' agreement, provided such agreement is not unreasonable or oppressive. Thus, although coming from the opposite starting point, our courts ultimately have reached a position which basically is quite similar to the approach presently prevailing in the majority of civil-law systems.[80c]

Smooth: Almost every time we negotiate an international deal, the question of inserting a choice-of-forum clause into the contract comes up. I am glad you have given us a better understanding of the civilians' attitude toward party autonomy in matters of jurisdiction. But let us move on. One important basis of jurisdiction remains to be discussed: What about the "long-arm" of courts in civil-law countries?

Comparovich: In the civil-law world, the long-arm notion is much older than in the United States, and older even than in England, where this basis of jurisdiction (though not the term) has been used since the enactment, in 1852, of the Common Law Procedure Act.[81] Thus in tort cases, most civil law countries adhere to the rule that the courts of the *locus delicti commissi* have jurisdiction.

Edge: Our rule is essentially the same; but it causes headaches (and not only for first-year law students) in the many situations where the defendant, acting in state or country A, has caused an injury occurring in state or country B. How do the civilians deal with those situations?

Road to Zapata, 21 Am.J.Comp.L. 124 (1973). For an interesting comparison of American and German law in this area, see F. K. Juenger, Vereinbarungen ueber den Gerichtsstand nach amerikanischem Recht, 35 Rabels Zeitschrift 284 (1971). See also supra n. 80.

It should be noted that M/S Bremen v. Zapata, a federal admiralty decision, is not binding on state courts in non-maritime cases. But state courts tend to be influenced by the persuasive force of the Zapata opinion. See, e.g., Smith, Valentino &

Smith, Inc. v. Superior Court, 17 Cal.3d 491, 131 Cal.Rptr. 374, 551 P.2d 1206 (1976).

80c. As the course progresses, the reader will discern many further examples of convergence between civil-law and common-law approaches. The phenomenon of convergence is observable in substantive as well as procedural contexts.

81. 15 & 16 Vict. c. 76, especially §§ 18 and 19.

Comparovich: The civil-law systems are not unanimous on this point. The German courts have developed the view that in such a situation the plaintiff, at his option, may sue either in A or in B. This view has found a following in other civil-law countries. By now, one may perhaps call it the prevailing view, because it was adopted, also, by the Court of Justice of the EEC when that court had to construe the Convention's ambiguous provision dealing with long-arm jurisdiction in tort cases. The case which brought this problem before the Court of Justice of the EEC, was an interesting one:

Example: Defendant corporation, as the owner and operator of a chemical plant located in France, discharged waste materials into the Rhine. Downstream, these materials caused damage to plaintiff's land and horticultural operations in the Netherlands. When plaintiff sued for damages in a Dutch court, defendant objected to the court's jurisdiction on the ground that pursuant to Art. 5, subd. 3, of the Convention the action (if not brought at defendant's "seat") had to be instituted at the *locus delicti commissi*, and that the alleged tort had been committed in France. As the issue thus raised involved a doubtful question of interpretation of the Convention, the Dutch appellate courts had to refer that question to the Court of Justice of the EEC. The latter court, adopting the above-mentioned German theory, held that plaintiff, at his option, could sue either in France or in The Netherlands. Defendant's objection to the Dutch court's jurisdiction was overruled.[82]

Smooth: In this case it was apparently found as a fact that defendant's act, though done in France, had *caused* an injury which occurred in The Netherlands. Were there additional findings to the effect that defendant had "purposefully availed" itself of business opportunities in The Netherlands and on that basis had reason to expect that it would be hauled into a Dutch court?

Comparovich: No, there were no such additional findings. The only relevant factual finding was that defendant's act had *caused* an injury in The Netherlands. That finding, by itself, was held to be sufficient to sustain the jurisdiction of the Dutch court.

Smooth: Compared to the pronouncements of the U.S. Supreme Court, especially *World-Wide Volkswagen Corp. v. Woodson*, 444 U.S. 286, 100 S.Ct. 559 (1980), the rule laid down by the European Court is not only more pro-plaintiff, but also very much simpler.

Comparovich: I agree. Yet even the simpler "European" rule can lead to doubts and difficulties, especially in situations where the defendant has acted in country A, and as a result the plaintiff has suffered injuries and damages in *several* other countries, e.g., in country B *and* country C.

---

82. See Handelswerkerij G. J. Bier B. V. v. Mines de Potasse d'Alsace S.A., Case No. 21/76, Decision of November 30, 1976, C.C.H. Common Market Reporter ¶8378.

Edge: Are you referring to cases of defamation by mass media, i.e., fact situations similar to *Keeton v. Hustler Magazine, Inc.*, 465 U.S. 770, 104 S.Ct. 1473 (1984)?

Comparovich: Precisely. I thought you might be interested in a recent French defamation case which presented a novel question of long-arm jurisdiction under Art. 5, subd. 3, of the Convention, and in which the facts were virtually identical with those of *Keeton*:

> *Example:* Suing for defamation in a French court, Princess Caroline of Monaco brought this action against the publisher of "Bunte", an illustrated tabloid published in Germany but having a substantial circulation in France as well. As in *Keeton*, it appeared that defendant had acted only at its home base; but plaintiff had suffered injuries to her reputation, and resulting damages, in France as well as in Germany. Applying Art. 5, subd. 3, of the European Convention, as interpreted by the European Court of Justice (see supra), the French court held that Princess Caroline's action was properly brought in France, since some of the injuries caused by the defamatory article had occurred in France. But the French court, in accordance with lower-court precedents, also held that in a French court the Princess could recover only that part of her damages that was caused by the publication of the libel *in France*.[82a]

The second part of the court's holding, restricting French jurisdiction to the damages suffered in France, does not seem to be compelled by the rather general language of Art. 5, subd. 3, of the Convention, and has been criticized by European legal writers.[82b] Those writers, without citing *Keeton*, apparently prefer the result reached by the U.S. Supreme Court: that the courts of a state or country where any substantial part of plaintiff's injuries occurred, should have jurisdiction to deal with the plaintiff's entire claim for all damages caused by a multi-state or multi-country defamation.

Smooth: Problems of long-arm jurisdiction in tort cases are always fascinating. But from a practical point of view it is even more important for us to know how the civilians apply the long-arm doctrine in contract cases.

Comparovich: According to traditional civil-law thinking, jurisdiction in a contract action is predicated either on the place where the contract was made, or on the place where it is to be performed.[82c] While some civil-law countries favor the place of making, it seems that

---

82a. This decision, which was rendered by an intermediate appellate court, is reported and thoroughly discussed in the article by B. Reinmüller, Gesamtschaden und internationale Deliktszuständigkeit nach dem EuGVU, 5 IPRax 233 (1985).

82b. See ibid.

82c. See M. Weser, Bases of Judicial Jurisdiction in the Common Market Countries, 10 Am.J.Comp.L. 323, 331–32 (1961); B. Kulzer, Some Aspects of Enforceability of Foreign Judgments: A Comparative Summary, 16 Buff.L.Rev. 84, 93 (1966); H. Smit, Common and Civil Law Rules of In Personam Adjudicatory Authority: An Analysis of Underlying Policies, 21 Int. & Comp.L.Q. 335, 348–50 (1972).

the majority view prefers the place of performance. The European Convention, adopting and somewhat streamlining the majority position, provides in Art. 5, subd. 1, that long-arm jurisdiction in contract cases is predicated on "the place of performance of the obligation in question," i.e., the place where *the defendant* has to perform the particular obligation the enforcement of which is sought by the plaintiff.[82d]

Edge: A similar rule, predicated solely on place of performance or place of making, was adopted in some of the earlier and less sophisticated American long-arm statutes. But any single-factor rule of this kind strikes me as unduly rigid. By way of contrast, our truly modern long-arm statutes speak in much more flexible terms—such as "transacting business"—and thus make it possible for the court to consider not only the place of making and the place of performance, but all the factors (and only the factors) which genuinely connect the contract with the forum.[83]

Comparovich: There is no doubt that the most advanced of our American long-arm statutes, as applied to contract actions, are more flexible than the typical civil-law rule. Of course, flexibility has its price. The more flexible the rule, the less predictable the result will be in many situations. On the other hand, to base jurisdiction exclusively on "place of making" or "place of performance", as most of the civil-law countries do, makes the result dependent on highly technical factors; on factors, moreover, which easily can be manipulated by a clever draftsman.

Edge: It seems that they can be manipulated, also, by a liar. In our case, for instance, H's complaint mendaciously alleged an oral agreement for professional services which by its express terms was to be performed by both sides in Ruritania.

Comparovich: Under Ruritanian conflict-of-laws rules, this allegation probably served the dual purpose of establishing a basis of jurisdiction for the Ruritanian courts, and of supplying an argument in favor of the application of the internal substantive law of Ruritania. Whatever its purpose, however, the allegation had to be proved by H. Did he ever attempt to do so?

Smooth: In order to answer this question, I must continue with our story. H made various attempts to serve summons and complaint upon the defendant. For the time being, I shall skip the details of these attempts, since you have indicated that you prefer to devote a separate part of our discussion to service of process. In any event, there came a

---

82d. The Convention, however, does not define "place of performance". The Court of Justice of the EEC has refused to adopt an "autonomous" definition of the term, with the unfortunate result that the forum must first, by using its own national choice-of-law rules, decide what country's law governs the contract, and then, applying the substantive law of that country, determine the place of performance. See

A. Lüderitz, Fremdbestimmte internationale Zuständigkeit?, in H. Bernstein, U. Drobnig & H. Kötz (Eds.), Festschrift für Konrad Zweigert 233, especially 235–36 (1981).

83. See, e.g., Longines-Wittnauer Watch Co. v. Barnes & Reinecke, Inc., 15 N.Y.2d 443, at 456–58, 261 N.Y.S.2d 8, at 17–19, 209 N.E.2d 68, at 75–76 (1965).

time when we received a copy of the complaint. At that point, we retained Dr. Lavocatich (L), a Ruritanian lawyer (of the right kind) who had been recommended to us by our subsidiary there. In our first letter to L, we pointed out that there was not a shred of truth to H's allegation concerning the agreed-upon place of performance, and that, consequently, we might well be successful in contesting the jurisdictional basis asserted by H. The reply we received from L left us completely bewildered. He wrote that it was immaterial whether the contract was in fact performable in Ruritania, because the Ruritanian court would in any event affirm its own jurisdiction on a different and undeniable ground: i.e., on the ground that the defendant corporation owned property in Ruritania. We immediately wrote back to L, pointing out that the plaintiff had not attached any property of the defendant, so that no question of *quasi in rem* jurisdiction could possibly arise in the case. The further correspondence between L and us indicated that he simply did not understand the point. He seemed to be obsessed by the insane notion that the defendant corporation, by virtue of its ownership of Ruritanian property, was subject to the unlimited personal jurisdiction of the Ruritanian courts. To this day, I have been unable to understand how this absurd idea got into the head of L, who otherwise turned out to be a competent lawyer.

Comparovich: L's advice to you was neither insane nor absurd. In fact, it was entirely correct. But in order to explain the theory behind L's advice, I have to acquaint you with some bases of personal jurisdiction which, although unknown in common-law countries, play a considerable role in the civil-law world.

Smooth: I thought we had pretty well covered the various bases of jurisdiction of which a plaintiff may avail himself in a civil-law forum.

Comparovich: Insofar as the regular bases of jurisdiction are concerned, we have touched on the more important ones in our discussion a minute ago.[83a] I have not previously mentioned, however, that civil-law countries occasionally resort to other, much more objectionable grounds on which they subject a non-resident defendant to the jurisdiction of their courts. Scholars often refer to these grounds as improper or exorbitant bases of jurisdiction.[84] One of the exorbitant bases is the nationality (and sometimes the domicile or residence) of the plaintiff.

Smooth: H was a citizen of Ruritania. At the time of the commencement of the action, moreover, he had resumed his Ruritanian domicile. But L never mentioned the possibility that the jurisdiction of the Ruritanian court might be bottomed on H's nationality or domicile.

Comparovich: This basis of jurisdiction is used mainly in France and in some of the French-influenced countries.[85] Apparently it is not

---

83a. For more extensive surveys, and a wealth of further references, see the articles cited supra n. 82c.

84. See K. H. Nadelmann, Jurisdictionally Improper Fora, in the volume "Twentieth Century Comparative and Conflicts Law—Legal Essays in Honor of Hessel E. Yntema" 321 ff. (1961).

85. Ibid. See also infra pp. 852–856.

used in Ruritania. There is, however, a second type of exorbitant jurisdictional rule, which, first developed in Germany, has spread to a number of other civil-law countries. This latter rule, which evidently has been adopted by Ruritania, is to the effect that a defendant who owns any property—however insignificant—in the forum country, thereby becomes subject to the personal jurisdiction of the courts of that country.[86] No attachment is necessary,[87] and although the jurisdiction of the court depends on a finding that the defendant owns some specified property located within the country, the effect of the judgment ultimately rendered by the court is not limited to such property.[87a] In other words, the court, having found that defendant owns a piece of local property worth $300, may render a *personal* judgment against the defendant in the amount of five million Dollars.[87b]

Smooth: Now I understand what L had in mind. I owe him an apology for having accused him of temporary insanity. But I must say that the bases of jurisdiction which you just outlined for us, strike me as being not only improper and exorbitant, but as totally uncivilized.

Comparovich: Just as uncivilized as our assertion that a contactless forum can obtain personal jurisdiction over a transiently "present" defendant on the sole ground that he was ambushed by a seedy-looking process server.

Edge: The situation, it seems to me, really cries out for international conventions or other forms of international cooperation. We should give up our claim that we can obtain jurisdiction over transient defendants by merely catching them here. As their part of the bargain,

86. See DeVries and Lowenfeld, Jurisdiction in Personal Actions—A Comparison of Civil Law Views, 44 Iowa L.Rev. 306, 330 ff. (1959); R. W. Millar, Jurisdiction Over Absent Defendants, 14 La.L.Rev. 321 (1954). The historical evolution of this jurisdictional theory is explained in the article by K. H. Nadelmann, Jurisdictionally Improper Fora in Treaties on Recognition of Judgments: The Common Market Draft, 67 Colum.L.Rev. 995, at 1006–11 (1967).

87. The notion of *quasi in rem* jurisdiction, founded upon an attachment and limited in its effect to the attached res, is unknown in the present-day law of most civil-law countries. It is only in Switzerland and a small number of other civil-law countries that an attachment serves to obtain jurisdiction over a non-resident defendant owning local assets. See K. H. Nadelmann, ibid., especially at nn. 63, 69.

87a. In the early part of 1968 it was reported that in a paternity suit brought against the well-known French skier, Jean-Claude Killy, an Austrian court based its jurisdiction on the fact that when departing from Austria, he had left a piece of underwear behind. This report inspired a well-known American law teacher to ex-

press his feelings in poetry. See D. D. Siegel, Pack up Your Troubles—Carefully, New York Law Journal of March 19, 1968.

87b. The statement in the text, supra, is true with respect to most of the countries which have adopted this form of exorbitant jurisdiction. But there is a minority view, to the effect that equitable considerations should not be disregarded in such cases. In Japan, for instance, although the relevant section of the Japanese Code of Civil Procedure is a replica of its German model, the courts do not apply that section as rigorously as is done in Germany. Where the defendant's property in Japan is insignificant, and unconnected with plaintiff's claim, the Japanese courts (invoking "justice and fairness") may refuse to regard the presence of such property as a sufficient basis for the exercise of personal jurisdiction over the defendant in an action involving a large amount. See the decision cited and quoted by Y. Fujita, Procedural Fairness to Foreign Litigants As Stressed by Japanese Courts, 12 Int.Lawyer 795, at 798–99 (1978). Cf. T. Hattori & D. F. Henderson, Civil Procedure in Japan, § 4.07[2] (1985).

the civil-law countries should eliminate the exorbitant bases of jurisdiction now used by them.

Comparovich: I agree that such a bargain would be desirable. But there are many difficulties standing in the way of a multilateral treaty (or even bilateral treaties) embodying a bargain of this kind. So far as the Common Market countries in Europe are concerned, they have in advance strengthened their bargaining position by entering into a Convention among themselves.[87c] Under the terms of that Convention, they (a) forego the use of exorbitant bases of jurisdiction as against defendants domiciled in the Common Market area,[88] but (b) strengthen exorbitant jurisdiction as against all other non-resident defendants (including defendants domiciled in the United States) by agreeing that each of the signatories will recognize and enforce the judgments which other Common Market countries, using a regular or an exorbitant basis of jurisdiction, in the future will render against such defendants.

Smooth: Does the Convention, in naked words, spell out this blatantly discriminatory approach?

Comparovich: The terms of the Convention, which generally applies to "civil and commercial matters", are quite clear in this respect. Art. 3 provides that a defendant "domiciled in a Contracting State" can be sued at a place other than his domicile "only by virtue of the rules set out in Sections 2 to 6 of this Title." These Sections deal only with jurisdiction based on long-arm or consent, i.e., with regular bases of jurisdiction. To make assurance doubly sure, the second paragraph of Art. 3 enumerates all the exorbitant bases of jurisdiction that exist under national laws of the various member countries,[88a] and explicitly prohibits the use of those exorbitant bases against a defendant domiciled in a Common Market country. By way of contrast, Art. 4 provides that when a defendant domiciled outside of the Common Market area is sued in a court of one of the Common Market countries, the jurisdiction of the court is determined by the law of the forum country (including, of course, the exorbitant provisions of that law).

87c. For references see the * footnote at the beginning of this section, supra p. 380. A brief but instructive discussion of the impact of the Convention, and of attempts to deal with the problems created by it, can be found in the article by B. M. Carl, The Common Market Judgments Convention—Its Threat and Challenge to Americans, 8 Int.Lawyer 446 (1974).

Even before it was signed, successive drafts of the Convention had occasioned much scholarly discussion. See (also for further references) P. Hay, The Common Market Preliminary Draft Convention on the Recognition and Enforcement of Judgments, 16 Am.J.Comp.L. 149 (1968); K. H. Nadelmann, The Common Market Judgments Convention and a Hague Conference Recommendation: What Steps Next?, 82 Harv.L.Rev. 1282 (1969). See also the ear-

lier articles by Professor Nadelmann, cited supra nn. 84, 86.

88. Pursuant to Art. 53 of the Convention, a corporate defendant is treated as having its domicile at the place of its "seat".

88a. This enumeration has always included both the nationality of the plaintiff and the local presence of defendant's property as bases of personal jurisdiction.

After the United Kingdom became a member of the Common Market, some common-law bases of jurisdiction were added to the catalogue of bases regarded as exorbitant; interestingly, these include presence as a basis of personal jurisdiction, and (subject to some qualifications) attachment as a basis of quasi-in-rem jurisdiction.

Edge: If I understand you correctly, this means that in civil and commercial matters each of the countries that are signatories of the Convention has two separate sets of jurisdictional rules: One set, embodied in the Convention, for cases in which the defendant is a domiciliary of one of the Common Market countries; and an entirely different set (this one including exorbitant rules) which is derived from the forum country's national law and applied to defendants who are domiciled outside of the Common Market area.

Comparovich: You have understood me correctly, and have stated the position very well. As an example, let me present to you a recent case decided by a Dutch court of first instance:

BV ALGEMENE INDUSTRIËLE MINERAAL-EN ERTSMAATSCHAPPIJ (A.I.M.E.) v. MACINA MINERALE SpA

Decision of January 13, 1978, Arrondissementsrechtbank Rotterdam, European Commercial Cases, Vol. 1, Part 3, p. 382.*

Facts

By statement of claim of 29 January 1976 the plaintiff, a Dutch private company established in Amsterdam, asked the District Court of Rotterdam to order the defendant, a body corporate under Italian law, established in Milan, to pay against quittance the sum of A$225,000 a converted into Dutch currency at the rate of exchange prevailing on the day of delivery of zircon sand purchased by the defendant and in addition to pay the compound interest on the moneys borrowed by the plaintiff from the bank to finance this transaction, as well as the statutory interest as from the date of the writ of summons.

The plaintiff alleged that it had sold to the defendant verbally on 22 October 1974 approximately 500 tons of zircon sand at the price of A$450 per 1,000 kgs. to be paid in Milan, which it had confirmed in writing on 6 November 1974.

The defendant submitted that the court had no jurisdiction to take cognisance of the case under the EEC Full Faith and Credit Convention 1968; alternatively, if the court had jurisdiction, it asked that the court should dismiss the plaintiff's claim on the ground that the alleged sales agreement had not been concluded.

Subsequently the plaintiff amended its claim to ask the court to dissolve the alleged sales agreement on the ground that the defendant had failed to fulfil its obligation to take delivery of the sand and to order the defendant to pay the sum of 486,000 fl. by way of damages and, in addition, compound interest at 8 per cent. per annum over two years as well as statutory interest as from 15 April 1977, the date of the amended claim.

The defendant opposed the amendment of the claim and maintained its previous defence of non-jurisdiction of the court.

---

* Reproduced by permission of European Law Centre Ltd., the publisher of European Commercial Cases.

a. Australian Dollars.

Judgment

[In the first paragraph of this part of the decision, the court rejects defendant's objection to plaintiff's amendment of his claim. Thus it is clear that the court has to deal with the claim as amended.]

In so far as it is material at present, the plaintiff bases its amended claim on the premises that it sold on 22 October 1974 approximately 500 tons of zircon sand at A$450 per 1,000 kilograms to the defendant, and that the latter has defaulted by not taking delivery of this sand. Furthermore, the plaintiff bases its claim for damages on the fact that the market price of this sand and the exchange rate of the Australian dollar have fallen in the meantime to such an extent that the damages amount to 972 fl. per ton of sand. Finally, the plaintiff advances in support of its claim for compound interest that it had to operate with bank credits in order to finance the transaction in issue by moneys borrowed from the bank.

The defendant opposes these claims, with the submission that this court has no jurisdiction to hear the case by virtue of the provisions of Article 3 of the EEC Full Faith and Credit Convention 1968 (hereinafter called the Convention).[b] Furthermore, the defendant disputes the correctness of the plaintiff's submissions although it does not contest that it did not take delivery of the sand.

The plaintiff replies to this argument that this court has jurisdiction as the court of the place where the obligation has to be fulfilled (special jurisdiction within the meaning of Art. 5(1) of the Convention).[c]

If it could not be established in these proceedings that the alleged sales agreement has been concluded between the parties there would be no question of an obligation within the meaning of Article 5(1) of the Convention and this court would certainly not have jurisdiction to take cognisance of the matter by virtue of the provisions of Article 3 of the Convention since the defendant is established in Italy.[d] Neither do any

---

b. In its first paragraph, Art. 3 of the Convention provides:

> Persons domiciled in a Contracting State may be sued in the courts of another Contracting State only by virtue of the rules set out in Sections 2 to 6 of this Title.

c. Art. 5(1) of the Convention provides:

> A person domiciled in a Contracting State may, in another Contracting State, be sued:
>
> 1. in matters relating to a contract, in the courts for the place of performance of the obligation in question;. . . .

For a discussion of other cases dealing with this article of the Convention, see P. Herzog, The Common Market Convention on Jurisdiction and the Enforcement of Judgments: An Interim Update, 17 Va.J. Int.L. 417, 428–29 (1977).

d. When, as in this case, jurisdiction is predicated on the place of performance of a contract, the existence of the contract is a jurisdictional fact. Under the national

laws of France and The Netherlands, such a jurisdictional fact must be *proved* by the plaintiff, while under the view prevailing in Germany it is sufficient, for jurisdictional purposes, if the plaintiff has *alleged* the fact.

In the present case, the issue was governed, not by the national law of any country, but by the Convention. The terms of the Convention are silent on the issue, and the Dutch court, without even discussing the issue, obviously followed the French-Dutch view. This part of the opinion, however, is now overruled by a later decision of the European Court of Justice, in which that Court adopted the German view and held that a forum has jurisdiction under Art. 5, subd. 1, of the Convention if the plaintiff has *alleged* facts giving rise to such jurisdiction, and that defendant's denial of such facts (i.e., of the existence of the contract) does not deprive the court of the power to make a decision *on the merits* concerning all substantive issues relating to the contract, including the issue wheth-

of the other provisions of the Convention apply from which this court could derive special jurisdiction.

If it were established that the alleged agreement had been concluded between the parties the jurisdiction of this court would indeed depend on the place where the obligation had to be fulfilled (Art. 5(1) of the Convention). Where the plaintiff claims damages and seeks the rescission of the agreement at the expense of the defendant, the obligation referred to in Article 5(1) of the Convention is the obligation whose non-fulfilment has been alleged in justification of the claim instituted.

Although the plaintiff expressly submits, as has been set out above, in its amended claim that 'it concerns here the non-fulfilment of the obligation to take delivery in Rotterdam', in essence the amended claim is based on non-payment of the alleged purchase price. The starting point of the statement of damages is in fact the allegedly stipulated purchase price. Moreover, the plaintiff itself has stated that it does not wish to amend the initially submitted factual grounds—clearly meaning non-payment.

Since it has not been disputed between the parties that payment of the purchase price—if indeed due—was to take place in Milan, the court has likewise no jurisdiction in the matter if it were established in these proceedings that the alleged sales agreement had indeed been concluded. Consequently, the court has no jurisdiction in this matter in any event. . . .

Action dismissed with costs, for lack of jurisdiction.[88e]

Comparovich (continuing): This case illustrates the treatment of a defendant who is domiciled within the Common Market. You will have noticed that in dealing with the jurisdictional issue the court made no reference whatever to Dutch law. It relied exclusively on the provisions of the Convention, under which the only arguable basis of personal jurisdiction over the defendant was predicated on the theory that the defendant's contractual obligation (which the plaintiff sought to enforce in this action) was to be performed in The Netherlands. The court rejected that theory, and that was the end of the case.

er such contract was validly concluded. Decision of March 4, 1982, reported in CCH Common Market Reporter, Transfer Binder (Court Decisions 1981–83) 8820, noted by P. Gottwald in 3 IPRax 13 (1983). See also J. C. Schultsz, Zwischenbilanz des Europäischen Gerichtsstands-und Vollstreckungs-Übereinkommens, 3 IPRax 97, 100–101 (1983).

If the Dutch court in the present case had correctly anticipated the ruling of the European Court of Justice, it would nevertheless have reached the same result, for the reason stated in the last three paragraphs of the opinion.

88e. If an appeal were taken from this decision, the intermediate appellate court could, and the Dutch court of last resort would have to, request the Court of Justice of the EEC to give a preliminary ruling on any relevant question of interpretation of the Convention. See Protocol on the Interpretation by the Court of Justice of the Convention of September 27, 1968, C.C.H. Common Market Reporter ¶6081. The significance of the Protocol is interestingly discussed in the article by Schultsz, supra n. 88d.

In this way, the uniform interpretation of the Convention is assured. Needless to say, this suggests a comparison with our own Supreme Court's power authoritatively to lay down jurisdictional and Full Faith and Credit rules derived from the United States Constitution and hence uniformly binding throughout the United States.

Edge: What would have been the outcome of the case if (all other facts being unchanged) the defendant had been domiciled in the United States?

Comparovich: In that event, the court would have derived the applicable jurisdictional rules, not from the Convention, but from Dutch law. Under Dutch law, the court would have had jurisdiction over the non-resident defendant because of a code provision, universally decried as exorbitant, which gives Dutch courts jurisdiction over such defendants if the plaintiff is domiciled in The Netherlands.[88f]

Edge: I take it that in the actual case, the defendant being domiciled within the Common Market, that exorbitant provision of Dutch law could not be invoked because the Convention does not tolerate the use of exorbitant bases of jurisdiction against such a defendant.

Comparovich: That is correct.

Edge: Does this not constitute blatant discrimination?

Comparovich: Indeed it does. The Convention not only perpetuates the use of exorbitant bases of jurisdiction against defendants domiciled outside the Common Market; it also increases the impact of a judgment rendered on such a basis.

Edge: How come?

Comparovich: Suppose Ruritania were a member of the Common Market and a party to the Convention. Suppose further that on the exorbitant jurisdictional basis invoked in your case a default judgment had been entered against your company by the Ruritanian court. That judgment would be enforceable not only in Ruritania, but—by virtue of the full-faith-and-credit provisions of the Convention—in every country adhering to the Convention.[89]

Even if Ruritania is not a member of the Common Market, the chances are that the Ruritanian judgment will be recognized and enforced in Germany and in other civil-law countries which, like

---

88f. See D. C. Fokkema, J. M. J. Chorus, E. H. Hondius & E. Ch. Lisser, Introduction to Dutch Law for Foreign Lawyers 280 (1978). Unlike its French counterpart (see infra p. 853), the Dutch provision is predicated solely on plaintiff's domicile, and not on his nationality. There can be little doubt, however, that any assertion of jurisdiction based on *plaintiff's* personal status (whether nationality or domicile) is unfair.

89. Similarly, an Arkansas judgment against a French defendant, rendered on the basis solely of transient jurisdiction, is enforceable in every other State under the Full Faith and Credit Clause of the U.S. Constitution. Thus we, too, spread the effect of an exorbitantly obtained judgment

over the whole area of a "common market"; but we do not practice the kind of *discrimination* (against defendants domiciled outside of the area) which marks the Common Market Convention.

Note, however, that quasi-in-rem jurisdiction based on footnote 37 of the Supreme Court's majority opinion in Shaffer v. Heitner, 433 U.S. 186, 97 S.Ct. 2569 (1977), discriminates against non-residents of the United States, if the words "no other forum" in that footnote are construed to mean "no other forum in the United States". If that construction were to prevail, we would be guilty of a discriminatory practice rather similar to that instituted by the European Convention.

Ruritania, have adopted the German type of exorbitant jurisdiction.[90] Moreover, if the defendant, in order to protect his property there, defends the Ruritanian action on the merits, the Ruritanian court thereby acquires unquestionable jurisdiction, and its judgment is likely to be enforced in most other countries, including our own.

Smooth: This is a bad situation. Perhaps Congress should bring a little counter-pressure to bear on foreign countries that use exorbitant bases of jurisdiction against American defendants.[91]

Comparovich: I am skeptical concerning the wisdom of retaliatory measures, especially when those measures would have to be directed against nations who are our allies and our principal trading partners.[91a] It must be remembered, moreover, that we are ourselves guilty of invoking exorbitant jurisdiction against transient defendants. A truly constructive solution of the problems created by the widespread assertion of exorbitant bases of jurisdiction will require international cooperation—the kind of cooperation that is brought about by enlightened self-interest rather than by coercion. Interested business groups should press their respective governments to seek such cooperation.

The European Convention contains a provision authorizing its signatories to enter into bilateral treaties with outsiders by which the rendition and recognition of judgments based on exorbitant jurisdiction would be outlawed as between the parties to such a treaty.[91b] Making use of this provision, the Governments of the United Kingdom and the United States engaged in prolonged negotiations looking toward the conclusion of a bilateral treaty concerning the reciprocal recognition and enforcement of judgments in civil matters. If these negotiations, which were reflected in the publication of an interesting draft,[91c] had ultimately succeeded, the resulting treaty would have made it impossible for courts in the United Kingdom to invoke an exorbitant basis of jurisdiction against an American defendant, or, as against such a defendant, to enforce a judgment rendered elsewhere (and especially in another Common Market country) that has an exorbitant jurisdictional basis.[92] Thus the U.S.-U.K. treaty, it it had entered into force, would

---

90. See Baumbach, Kommentar zur Zivilprozessordnung, § 328, Anno. 2 (45th ed., 1987). A German court, when asked to recognize or enforce a foreign judgment, determines the jurisdictional validity of that judgment pursuant to German rules of judicial jurisdiction. Ibid.

91. Cf. H. Smit, The Proposed United States—United Kingdom Convention on Recognition and Enforcement of Judgments: A Prototype for the Future?, 17 Va. J.Int.L. 443, 468; Nadelmann, loc. cit. supra n. 87c, at 1289. For a general statement of the U.S. Government's approach to controversial assertions of jurisdiction, see the address by Secretary Shultz on Trade, Interdependence and Conflicts of Jurisdiction of May 5, 1984, U.S. Department of State, Bureau of Public Affairs, Current Policy Series No. 573 (1984).

91a. It should be kept in mind, also, that many American corporations have subsidiaries within the Common Market area. Having its "seat" in a Common Market country, such a subsidiary is treated as a domiciliary of that country, and thus may be a beneficiary of the Convention's discriminatory provisions.

91b. See Art. 59, as amended by the 1978 Convention on Accession. This provision is discussed in G. Delaume, Transnational Contracts, Ch. VIII, Sec. 8.31 (1986).

91c. 16 Int'l Leg. Mat. 71 (1977).

92. See P. Hay & R. J. Walker, The Proposed Recognition-of-Judgments Con-

have reduced the discriminatory effect of the European Convention, and might have served as a model for similar treaties to be negotiated in the future with other members of the Common Market.[93]   But, alas, the U.S.-U.K. negotiations hit a snag,[93a] due at least in part to British concerns engendered by the high level of damage awards in the United States.[93b]

Edge: Let us hope that in spite of this setback the vexing problem of exorbitant bases of jurisdiction will ultimately be eliminated by some form of international cooperation.   If that happens, the remaining problems of jurisdiction will no longer hold much terror for the international practitioner.   This for the reason that, insofar as the regular bases of jurisdiction are concerned, common-law and civil-law approaches seem to have become fairly similar during the last half-century.

Comparovich: Such convergence has indeed occurred to a remarkable degree.[94]   Yet, even apart from the problem of exorbitant bases of jurisdiction, there remain some basic differences between civil law and common law with respect to jurisdictional matters.[95]   An American lawyer who is unaware of these differences, is apt to misunderstand the relevant civil-law rules.

Edge: Could you give us some examples?

vention Between the United States and the United Kingdom, 11 Tex.Int.L.J. 421 (1976); H. Smit, supra n. 91; P. Hay & R. J. Walker, The Proposed U.S.-U.K. Recognition of Judgments Convention: Another Perspective, 18 Va.J.Int.L. 753 (1978).

In contrast to the United States, which until now has been reluctant to enter into treaties concerning the recognition and enforcement of foreign judgments, European nations have long favored such treaties. The presently existing treaties of this kind are conveniently collected and reproduced in Council of Europe, The Practical Guide to the Recognition and Enforcement of Foreign Judicial Decisions in Civil and Commercial Law (1975).

93. Prior to the conclusion of the European Convention, the Hague Conference on Private International Law had done considerable spadework in preparing a *multilateral* convention on recognition and enforcement of judgments. But these efforts suffered a setback as a result of the adoption of the European Convention, with its discrimination against outsiders. See, in addition to the articles cited supra n. 87c, R. H. Graveson, The Tenth Session of the Hague Conference of Private International Law, 14 Int. & Comp.L.Q. 528 (1965); B. Kulzer, loc. cit. supra n. 82c, at 106–08.

93a. See A. T. Von Mehren, Recognition and Enforcement of Sister-State Judgments: Reflections on General Theory and

Current Practice in the European Economic Community and the United States, 81 Colum.L.Rev. 1044, at 1060 (1981).

93b. See I. K. Mathers, The Brussels Convention of 1968: Its Implementation in the United Kingdom, 3 [1983] Yearbook of Eur. Law 49, 73 (1984), referring to a debate in the House of Lords.

94. See R. B. Ginsburg, The Competent Court in Private International Law, 20 Rutgers L.Rev. 89 (1965).

95. See id. at 91–92, where it is pointed out that in the United States, due to the interplay of U.S. Constitution, State Constitutions and other (statutory and decisional) rules bearing on the subject, the structure of the pertinent norms is highly complex, more complex than in the continental systems (with the possible exception of Switzerland). In spite of the relative simplicity of their structure, however, the jurisdictional rules of continental countries are not easy to ascertain and to understand. In most of those countries (with the notable exception of Italy) there is no separate set, or only an incomplete set, of statutory provisions dealing with jurisdictional questions. Jurisdictional rules thus must often be derived, by way of analogy, from code provisions regulating the distribution of judicial power within the country, i.e., from provisions which in our parlance would be spoken of as venue statutes.

Comparovich: The civilians' views drastically differ from ours with respect to *the effect* (a) of the existence and (b) of the lack of jurisdiction.

Let us first deal with the effect of the existence of jurisdiction. When an American court affirms its own jurisdiction, that does not necessarily mean that the court will adjudicate the case on the merits. Depending on a number of factors, the court, although having jurisdiction, in its discretion may refuse to exercise such jurisdiction under the doctrine of forum non conveniens. In civil-law countries, on the other hand, that doctrine generally is not recognized,[95a] with the result that a court, once it affirms its jurisdiction, *must* decide the case on the merits.

Edge: Let me put before you the following

Hypothetical Case: Suppose our company has a dispute with a customer in Ruritania, a country that is not a member of the European Common Market. Knowing that the customer has a bank account in Germany, we invoke German rules of exorbitant jurisdiction and start an in-personam action against the Ruritanian defendant in a German court. Would that court be *compelled* to adjudicate the case on the merits, even though both parties are non-residents of Germany, all of the evidence is outside of Germany, and the substantive law applicable to the issues in the case is "foreign law" from the standpoint of a German court?

Comparovich: The answer to your question is unequivocally in the affirmative.[95b] Your hypothetical case furnishes a dramatic illustration of the practical consequences of the civilians' failure to use the doctrine of forum non conveniens. Experienced international practitioners are increasingly aware of the fact that by a combination of exorbitant jurisdiction and the absence of forum non conveniens some civil-law countries have become litigation havens.[95c] Clever plaintiffs' lawyers are quick to make use of such havens when they look for a forum that is both surprising and inconvenient for the defendant.

Smooth: In what way do the civilians' views differ from ours with respect to the *effect of lack of jurisdiction?*

Comparovich: Ever since Pennoyer v. Neff,[96] American lawyers have taken it for granted that if a court lacks jurisdiction, the judgment

95a. See, e.g., P. Schlosser, Forum Non Conveniens wegen Inaktivität der Prozessbeteiligten?, 3 IPRax 285 (1983); B. Löber, Forum Shopping, forum non conveniens oder schlicht: Justizgewährungsanspruch, 6 IPRax 283, 284 (1986).

95b. For a recent holding by a German court explicitly rejecting the suggestion to introduce forum non conveniens into German law, see L. G. München I, decision of November 25, 1982, 4 IPRax 318 (1984), aff'd, O. L. G. München, decision of June 22, 1983, 4 IPRax 319 (1984).

German writers have even argued that it would be unconstitutional to introduce the doctrine of forum non conveniens into German law. See the articles cited supra n. 95a.

95c. German practitioners have exhibited no signs of regret in observing that this adds to the volume of their litigation business. See Löber, supra n. 95a.

96. 95 U.S. (5 Otto) 714 (1877).

— Don't take default judgment if member of European Convention is a country under convention; full faith and credit goes to judgment and is recognized by all member states; and no collateral attacks —

404   *COMMON LAW AND CIVIL LAW*

No collateral attack in civil law countries

of such court is open to collateral attack even in the State or country where it was rendered. This is hard to understand for civilian lawyers. They agree with us that the judgment of a court not having jurisdiction may be refused recognition and enforcement in other countries;[97] but in the rendering country, they feel, such a judgment is final and not subject to collateral attack once the time for an appeal (or, in the case of a default judgment, the time for a motion to re-open the default) has run out.[98]

Edge: In other words, if we had defaulted in the Ruritanian action brought by H, and if the court had entered a default judgment against us, that judgment would not have been open to collateral attack in Ruritania; thus, with respect to our Ruritanian assets, we would have been stuck with the judgment even if at a later time we could have demonstrated that the court had misapplied Ruritania's own jurisdictional rules when it exercised jurisdiction over the defendant.

No collateral attack by member countries

Comparovich: That is correct. Moreover, if Ruritania were a member of the Common Market, the European Convention would make the Ruritanian judgment enforceable not only in Ruritania, but throughout the Common Market area.

Edge: But even on the assumption that Ruritania has joined the Common Market and acceded to the Convention, another Common Market country, such as France, surely would not enforce the judgment of a Ruritanian court lacking jurisdiction?

Comparovich: You are looking at the problem through American eyes. In this country, we take it for granted that when F-1 lacks jurisdiction, then the F-1 judgment (unless saved by the so-called bootstrap doctrine) is invalid even in F-1, and hence necessarily invalid everywhere. The civilians, as I just explained, do not share this view. Once the time for a direct attack on the F-1 judgment has expired, they treat that judgment as valid in F-1, even though the F-1 court lacked jurisdiction. Since a collateral attack on the judgment is thus precluded in F-1, it is quite logical for civilian lawyers to feel that (as between countries that owe each others' judgments full faith and credit) such a collateral attack is equally precluded in F-2. And that is precisely the position adopted in the European Convention, which states in the third paragraph of Art. 28 that normally the jurisdiction of F-1 "may not be reviewed" in F-2.[99]

97. See supra n. 90. Note, however, that a treaty between F-1 and F-2 may deprive F-2 of the power to re-examine the question whether F-1 had jurisdiction. Concerning the relevant provisions of the European Convention, see infra, text at n. 99.

98. See, e.g., P. Herzog, Civil Procedure in France 175 (1967).

For a comparative discussion of the subject of collateral attack on judgments, see Baade, Nullity and Avoidance in Public International Law, 39 Ind.L.J. 497, 548–53 (1964).

99. The ramifications of this provision are interestingly discussed in the article by G. H. Roth, Zulässiges forum shopping?, 4 IPRax 183 (1984). Even in a case where the F-1 defendant was domiciled in F-2 (another Common Market country) and the jurisdiction of the F-1 court thus was governed by the Convention, it was held that F-2, when asked by the plaintiff to enforce the F-1 default judgment, could not ex-

Edge: This means that, insofar as judgments in civil and commercial matters are concerned, the obligation of F–2 to give full faith and credit to an F–1 judgment is carried further in the European Community than in the United States.

Comparovich: You have a point here. The same observation has been made by a noted European scholar.[100]

Smooth: There is a practical lesson to be drawn from this. Suppose a defendant against whom an action has been brought in F–1 (a Common Market country), is advised by counsel that F–1 has no jurisdiction. If defendant has assets anywhere in the Common Market area, he would be foolish to default in F–1. Even if the F–1 court's lack of jurisdiction is crystal-clear, the defendant would be well-advised to *raise his jurisdictional objection in F–1.*

Comparovich: I agree.

Smooth: In actuality, Ruritania is not a Common Market country. Nevertheless, in the light of everything you have told us, and considering that the defendant corporation had large assets in Ruritania, we were wise not to default in the action instituted by Mr. H.

Comparovich: You were.

F. SERVICE OF PROCESS (AND A FIRST GLIMPSE AT INTERNATIONAL JUDICIAL COOPERATION)

Smooth: By now, the time seems to have come to discuss service of process. Although service, and even personal service within the forum's territory, never creates jurisdiction according to the view of the civilians, I take it that their codes of civil procedure contain rules on the subject.

Comparovich: Naturally, they do; and these rules are of great practical importance, especially in case the defendant defaults. In such a case the court, ex officio, must examine whether service was properly made. If it was not, no default judgment can be entered.

amine the question of the F–1 court's jurisdiction. See the decision of the Supreme Court of Luxembourg, dated March 5, 1974, in Mamer v. Brand Ladenbau K. G., 2 C.M.L.R. 407.

Note, however, that the rule stated in the text, supra, is subject to some exceptions. For instance, the rule does not apply if the F–1 court has asserted jurisdiction in violation of the Convention's special provisions concerning insurance and consumer transactions.

100. See P. Bonassies, La Frontière Normative et le Marché Commun, in Faculté de Droit et de Science Politique, Etudes Offertes à Alfred Jauffret 99, 111 (1977).

While the F–2 court normally may not review the *jurisdiction* of the F–1 court, the Convention provides, and the European Court of Justice has held, that F–2 may refuse enforcement of the F–1 judgment if it finds that in the F–1 action the defendant did not receive proper *notice*. See Decision of July 15, 1982, CCH Common Market Reporter, Transfer Binder (Court Decisions 1981–1983), ¶8854; F. K. Juenger, Judicial Jurisdiction in the United States and in the European Communities: A Comparison, 82 Mich.L.Rev. 1195, at 1209 (1984).

Regarding the question whether F–2 may refuse to enforce the F–1 judgment on the ground that it violates the public policy of F–2, see infra p. 866.

How did H effect service on your corporation?

Edge: At first, he obtained from the Ruritanian court so-called letters rogatory[1] requesting the Superior Court of this State to direct service on the defendant of the summons and complaint issuing out of the Civil Chamber of the Ruritanian Tribunal of First Instance.[2]

Comparovich: The laws of a number of civil-law countries provide for this method of service on a non-resident defendant.[3]

Edge: Our Superior Court, however, refused to comply with the Ruritanian court's request, citing a precedent that seemed to be squarely in point:

In re Letters Rogatory out of First Civil Court of Mexico, 261 Fed. 652 (D.C.S.D.N.Y., 1919; Augustus N. Hand, D.J.): "This is a motion to vacate an order directing the service of a summons within this district upon a resident to answer to a suit brought against him in the republic of Mexico for the payment of rent and redelivery of certain property which is claimed by virtue of a contract of lease made in the city of Mexico for the term of one year, from June, 1914, to June, 1915. The process was accompanied by a request from the judge of the court having jurisdiction in the city of Mexico that process of that court be served upon defendant in New York. This judicial request is said to come within the definition of letters rogatory in the civil law, is addressed to any one who may be a judge having jurisdiction over a civil case in the city of New York, and, as translated, reads as follows:

" 'In order that such decisions may be accomplished in the name of the national sovereignty existing between the two nations, allow me the honor of sending this requisitorial letter, begging that, when you get it, do me the favor of deciding to accomplish it in its terms, and, when it is made, send it back to this court, assuring you my reciprocity in similar cases at your request.' "

"I am referred to the following articles of the Civil Code of Mexico * deemed to be applicable to the situation:

" 'Art. 25.　Both Mexicans and foreigners residing in the federal district or in (Lower) California may be sued in the courts of this country, on obligations contracted with Mexicans or foreigners within or without the republic.

" 'Art. 26.　They may also be sued in said courts, even though they do not reside in said places, if they have property which is affected by

1. For a definition of "letters rogatory" see 22 CFR § 92.54 (1986).

2. Concerning the transmission of letters rogatory, see 28 U.S.C.A. § 1781, as amended in 1964. For a discussion of the history and significance of this statute see H. Smit, International Litigation Under the United States Code, 65 Colum.L.Rev. 1015, at 1019–22 (1965).

3. See H. L. Jones, International Judicial Assistance, 62 Yale L.J. 515, 543–45 (1953).

* The Civil Code of 1884, to which the Court referred, was subsequently (Oct. 1, 1932) replaced by a new Code. The quoted provisions, however, regardless of whether they still accurately state present-day Mexican law, will not appear surprising to the reader who, in perusing the preceding pages, has familiarized himself with civil-law thinking on the subject of jurisdiction. For an introduction to the pertinent Mexican provisions presently in effect, see S. A. Bayitch and J. L. Siqueiros, Conflict of Laws: Mexico and the United States 224–25 (1968).

any obligations contracted or if the same are to be performed in said places.' "

"By reason of the foregoing provisions, it is apparently possible through the aid of this court to render the person sought to be served subject to a personal judgment in Mexico, because the contract sued upon was to be performed there. Such a result is contrary to our own system of jurisprudence, which treats the legal jurisdiction of a court as limited to persons and property within its territorial jurisdiction. Pennoyer v. Neff, 95 U.S. 714, 24 L.Ed. 565. It is undesirable, in my opinion, to aid a process which may require residents of this district to submit to the burden of defending foreign suits brought in distant countries, where they have no property, or as an alternative to suffer a personal judgment by default, which will be enforceable against them personally whenever they may enter the foreign territory. As a matter of policy, the matter would be quite different, if the effect of the service would only be a judgment enforceable against property of the defendant in Mexico.

"While this court has power to execute letters rogatory in the sense in which the term is used in the American and English law, neither it nor, so far as I can discover from the reported decisions, any other American or English court, has by an order directing the service of process aided a foreign tribunal to acquire jurisdiction over a party within the United States. Letters rogatory have been so long familiar to our courts, and so exclusively limited by understanding and in practice to proceedings in the nature of commissions to take depositions of witnesses at the request of a foreign court, that I should hardly feel inclined to assume such a novel jurisdiction as is proposed without statutory authority, even if I regarded the case as one where, as a matter of sound policy, aid should be given to the foreign tribunal.

"The New York Supreme Court reached a similar conclusion to the one I have arrived at, for much the same reasons that I have given, in the Matter of Romero, 56 Misc.Rep. 319, 107 N.Y.Supp. 621. . . .

"The motion to vacate the order is granted, both on the ground that the judicial aid invoked is without precedent, and also because it is contrary to the ideas of American courts as to the limits of judicial jurisdiction."

Comparovich: I am surprised to hear that the courts of your State still follow this old case. Even in 1919, when it was decided, its reasoning was questionable. More recently, the holding of the case has been overruled by statute, insofar as the practice in the federal courts is concerned.[4] Federal courts now are expressly authorized to honor a request, coming from a foreign or international tribunal, to aid in the service of a summons or other judicial document; the statute makes it clear, however, that such service, although effected with the help of a United States court, "does not, of itself, require the recognition or enforcement in the United States" of the judgment ultimately rendered by the foreign court.[4a] The Uniform Interstate and International

---

4. 28 U.S.C.A. § 1696, added in 1964. The history of the statute, and the practice under it, are extensively discussed in B. Ristau, International Judicial Assistance, Vol. I, Part II, Ch. 1 (1984).

4a. The importance of this statutory proviso is illustrated by Sprague & Rhodes Commodity Corp. v. Instituto Mexicano Del Cafe, 566 F.2d 861 (2d Cir. 1977).

Procedure Act proposes substantially the same rule for the state courts.[5]

Smooth: Our State, however, has not adopted this proposed Uniform Act.

Comparovich: Even in the absence of a pertinent statute, it seems hardly justifiable today to refuse such judicial assistance to a foreign court which asserts jurisdiction on grounds very similar to our own "long-arm" principles.[6]

Edge: H commenced his action against us after the 1964 federal statute had gone into effect. It seems, therefore, that the request of the Ruritanian court probably would have been honored if it had been directed to the U.S. District Court for our district rather than to the State court.

Comparovich: You are right. So long as it remains uncertain whether such a request will be honored by the courts of a given State, it is always wiser, from the standpoint of the plaintiff and of the foreign tribunal, to send the letters rogatory to the federal court. I suppose that H (or his American counsel) was unfamiliar with the federal statute, and thus failed to call the attention of the Ruritanian court to the availability of federal judicial assistance.

Edge: Well, our friend H missed that trick; but he was not discouraged. A little later, the defendant received the Ruritanian summons and complaint by registered mail, in an envelope sent by the Ruritanian Consulate.[6a] There was a rubber-stamped notation on the documents which indicated that a few weeks previously they had been served upon a high official in the Ruritanian Ministry of Justice. That rubber-stamped notation caused considerable puzzlement in our office.

Comparovich: The explanation probably is that in this respect Ruritania, like many other civil-law countries, follows the traditional French practice of *notification au parquet*. This means that in actions against non-residents the summons is served at the "*parquet*", the office of the local district attorney or of his superior in the Ministry of Justice. The official thus served normally attempts, perhaps through diplomatic or consular channels, to effect actual delivery of the documents to the defendant.[7] The important point is, however, that (according to the view which formerly prevailed in France, and which still prevails in some civil-law countries) the effectiveness of the service does not depend on whether the attempt to notify the defendant is success-

---

5. 13 U.L.A. 459 ff., § 2.04 (1980, and 1986 Supp.).

6. See the remarks by Judge Maris and by Professor Schlesinger in the symposium entitled "Service and Evidence Abroad Under English Procedure", 29 Geo.Wash.L. Rev. 495, at 528–34 (1961). Cf. Cherun v. Frishman, 236 F.Supp. 292 (D.D.C. 1964); Bank of Montreal v. Kough, 430 F.Supp. 1243 (N.D.Cal. 1977).

6a. The United States permits foreign consuls to serve process in this country, in actions originating in the sending state. See Restatement (Revised), Foreign Relations Law, Tent. Dr. No. 5, § 481, Reporter's Note 2 (1984).

7. The former French practice in this regard is exemplified by the facts of Schibsby v. Westenholz, (1870) L.R. 6 Q.B. 155.

ful, or whether such attempt is undertaken in the first place. In those countries in which the system of *notification au parquet* prevails, the service is deemed to have been effectively completed as soon as the documents are served upon the official. When in case of non-appearance of the defendant the court examines the propriety of service, the examination may be limited to the question whether *the official* was duly served; if he was, a default judgment can be entered.[8]

Edge: This practice must lead to many default judgments against non-resident defendants who have never received actual notice of the litigation.

Comparovich: Experience shows that this is so. Frequently, the hardship inflicted upon the defendant is enhanced by the fact that the jurisdiction of the court is invoked upon an exorbitant basis (such as nationality of the plaintiff); in such a case, the defendant probably has not anticipated any litigation in the forum chosen by the plaintiff. To make things worse, the default judgment will be served in the same manner as the summons; the defendant thus may not receive actual notice of the judgment even after it has been entered. If for that reason, or for any other reason, he is unable to make a timely motion for the reopening of his default, the judgment will be treated as valid and enforceable in the forum country, and will not be subject to collateral attack, even if under the forum's own jurisdictional rules the court lacked any semblance of jurisdiction.

Edge: Do such outrageous practices prevail in all civil-law countries?

Comparovich: No, but in some of them.

Edge: Is this not, again, a problem that should be resolved by some form of international cooperation?

Comparovich: European nations have long been in the habit of dealing with problems of this kind by way of bilateral or multilateral treaties. The United States, somewhat belatedly, in 1964 evinced its desire to join in these cooperative efforts by becoming a member of The Hague Conference on Private International Law.[9] Membership in the Conference is not universal; but most of our important trading partners, including those belonging to the civil-law orbit, are among the members. Thus the Conference serves as a useful vehicle for studies and negotiations looking toward improvements in international judicial cooperation.

Edge: What exactly do you mean when you speak of international judicial cooperation?

Comparovich: Broadly speaking, the term "international judicial cooperation" refers to mutual assistance which sovereign nations ren-

---

8. For details see P. Herzog and H. Smit, International Co-operation in Litigation: France, in the vol. "International Cooperation in Litigation: Europe" (H. Smit, Ed.) 119, at 122–29 (1965). Although recently this practice was changed in France (see infra at n. 18), it still prevails in some other countries.

9. 22 U.S.C.A. § 269g (1979).

der to each other in matters such as (a) service abroad of process and
other judicial documents; (b) taking of testimony abroad, and obtaining
documentary and other tangible evidence abroad, for use in domestic
litigation; (c) proof, in domestic litigation, of foreign law and foreign
official records; (d) recognition and enforcement of foreign judgments.
Needless to say, a nation can extend such cooperation unilaterally and
voluntarily, without being bound by an international treaty. I am
proud to say that our own country, as a result of the work done in the
late 1950's and early 1960's by the U.S. Commission and Advisory
Committee on International Rules of Judicial Procedure and by the
Project on International Procedure of the Columbia University School
of Law, has set an example in this respect.[10] For some purposes,
however, it is not enough to improve one's own practices; if one needs
the cooperation of other nations, a treaty approach may be indicated.[11]

Edge: Do consular conventions contain relevant provisions?

Comparovich: They never deal with international judicial cooperation in a systematic and comprehensive manner; but many of them do
authorize consular officials to take depositions, and some of the consular conventions add the further authority to serve judicial documents,
on behalf of the courts of the sending nation, upon persons in the host
nation.

Edge: Would a consul not have the authority to take these harmless and non-compulsory steps even in the absence of a pertinent
treaty?

Comparovich: In the first place, there is always the question
whether the service regulations issued by the sending nation give the
consul the requisite power;[12] even when he has that power pursuant to
the laws and regulations of his own country, the consul cannot perform
any act of this kind if it would be unlawful for him to do so under the
law of the host country.

Edge: Are there any host countries which in the absence of a
pertinent treaty make it illegal for the consular officials of other
nations to assist (without using any compulsion) in matters such as the
taking of depositions or the serving of documents?

Comparovich: In this respect, a rather fundamental difference in
attitude exists between common-law and civil-law countries. According
to the common-law view of civil litigation, the court performs only the
limited and essentially passive function of an umpire. It follows that
most of the procedural steps by which the litigation is actively moved
forward—such as service of process and other papers, or the summoning and examining of witnesses, to mention but a few examples—are

10. The actual changes in federal statutes and Rules, and the proposed Uniform
Act, that resulted from the efforts mentioned in the text, are conveniently set
forth in the volume cited supra n. 8, at 409
ff. See also the Introduction by H. Smit,
id. at 1–15.

11. See Schlesinger, loc. cit. supra n. 6.

12. Cf., insofar as U.S. consuls are concerned, 22 CFR §§ 92.49 to 92.95 (1986).

regarded as acts of the parties or their counsel. Even if performed in furtherance of litigation pending abroad, such acts are private in nature and hence do not run afoul of the prerogatives of the state. Adhering to this view, the nations of the common law orbit usually do not object when foreign consuls, or other persons acting on behalf of the parties, take non-compulsory procedural steps in connection with litigation pending before the courts of another country.[12a]

In the civilian systems, on the other hand, the court plays a much more active role in a lawsuit. Many procedural acts which under a common-law system would be performed by counsel, are carried out or directed, and perhaps even initiated, by judges or other officials. Thus it is natural for a lawyer brought up in the civil law to think of many procedural steps, such as the service of judicial documents or the examination of witnesses, as official acts. Many civil-law nations, therefore, regard it as an infringement of their sovereignty if such official acts are performed within their territory by anybody other than their own judges and other officials.

Edge: If that is the attitude of civil-law countries, we might run into great difficulties in connection with cases that are litigated here. Suppose in such a case the defendant lives in civil-law country X, and the plaintiff asks a lawyer or other private person in X to serve summons and complaint upon the defendant. Would such service be illegal from the standpoint of X?

Comparovich: In some civil-law countries, it would be.[13] There may be even greater difficulties when, for purposes of litigation here, an attempt is made to examine witnesses in X, or to obtain other kinds of evidence located there, without the help of the local judiciary.[14]

Edge: I am beginning to see why it is necessary for this country, through negotiations with our friends in the civil-law orbit, to obtain the benefit of conventions specifically aimed at the improvement of international judicial cooperation.

12a. See supra n. 6a.

13. See, e.g., A. R. Miller, International Cooperation in Litigation Between the United States and Switzerland, 49 Minn.L. Rev. 1069, 1075–79 (1965).

Many civil-law countries require that service of process be effected by a local public official. In practice, the monopoly thus bestowed on certain minor officials may lend itself to abuse. In some of the civil-law countries, especially non-European ones, such a public official often plays a delaying game (particularly unpleasant when there is danger of the statute of limitations running out) until he receives some unofficial payment over and above the regular fee, which ordinarily is fixed by statute. See F. G. Dawson & I. L. Head,

International Law, National Tribunals and the Rights of Aliens 106 (1971). The United States Congress took notice of the existence of such practices when it enacted the Foreign Corrupt Practices Act of 1977, 15 U.S.C.A. § 78dd–2 (1981, and 1986 Supp.). The Act exempts from its prohibitions the payment of a bribe to a foreign official having "essentially ministerial or clerical" functions. Thus Americans litigating in foreign courts, and their lawyers, will not become subject to federal prosecution if they continue to grease the official process-serving machinery of certain foreign countries.

14. See Jones, supra n. 3, at 519–29. This point will be taken up in more detail infra pp. 443–448.

Comparovich: Both common-law and civil-law nations have a great deal to gain by entering into such conventions. In many of the civil-law countries the feeling prevails that litigation pending before their courts often requires official acts which, if they are to be effected on our territory, can be performed only with the active assistance of our judges and other public officials. So far as we are concerned, we are less interested in their active judicial assistance (except when it comes to dealing with recalcitrant witnesses). The concessions we seek to obtain from our civil-law friends consist mainly of (a) their adherence to what we regard as minimal standards of due process (by abandoning, for instance, the practice of *notification au parquet*), and (b) their permission to perform, within their territory, certain acts in aid of litigation here—acts which we regard as private but which they might treat as infringing on their sovereignty unless they have, in the form of a treaty, granted a partial waiver of their sovereign rights. These different desires and attitudes can be accommodated only by the give-and-take of intelligently negotiated conventions.

Insofar as service of process is concerned,[15] real progress has been achieved by the wide-spread adoption of the multilateral Convention on Service Abroad of Judicial and Extra-judicial Documents in Civil and Commercial Matters. This convention, to which the United States is a party and which has been in effect since 1969, provides for a new method of transmission and service, through a Central Authority established in each of the signatory nations.[16]

Edge: Thus, if H brought his action today, and if Ruritania were a party to the Convention, summons and complaint could be served by this new method?

Comparovich: Yes.[16a] This, however, is not the only important effect of the Convention. It also contains strong safeguards for the defendant, by providing that no default judgment may be entered by

---

15. Concerning the range of problems arising under this heading, see the materials cited supra nn. 2–14.

16. For the text of the Convention, see 16 Int'l Legal Materials 1339 (1977). On the part of the United States, the Assistant Attorney General in charge of the Civil Division of the U.S. Department of Justice has been designated as the "Central Authority". See 28 CFR § 0.49 (1986).

The Service Convention was the first multilateral treaty ratified by the United States that was specifically and exclusively aimed at the improvement of international judicial cooperation. It was followed, a few years later, by the Evidence Convention, discussed infra pp. 443–448.

For a list of the countries that are parties to the Service Convention, and a most instructive discussion of its operation, see Ristau, supra n. 4, Part IV and Appendices A, B and D.

16a. The Convention also permits alternate methods of service, including service by mail, "provided the state of destination does not object." Art. 10(a). Neither the U.S. nor Japan has objected to service by mail; but Germany has. See, e.g., Harris v. Browning-Ferris Ind. Chem. Serv., Inc., 100 F.R.D. 775 (D.La. 1984); Dr. Ing. H.C.F. Porsche A. G. v. Superior Court for Sacramento County, 123 Cal.App.3d 755, 177 Cal.Rptr. 155 (1981). For a complete list of the countries which have objected, see Ristau, supra n. 4, at 169.

If the country of destination has not objected to service by mail, then (as between countries adhering to the Convention) such service is sufficient regardless of whether it is authorized by the local law of either country. See Ackermann v. Levine, 788 F.2d 830 (2d Cir. 1986).

the courts of any signatory nation against a defendant to be served within the territory of another signatory, unless the defendant's actual receipt of notice of the litigation has been reasonably assured by one of several alternative methods of service specified in the Convention.[16b]

Edge: Does this mean that in the future American defendants in civil-law courts will be protected against the scandalous device of service by *notification au parquet?*

Comparovich: Yes, to the extent that civil-law countries which in the past have used that device, become parties to the Convention. Even in countries which for one reason or another do not adhere to it, the Convention may serve as a model for internal legislation, in much the same manner as a model statute or uniform act.[17] This "educational" effect of the Convention is illustrated by what happened in France. The Convention was ratified by France in 1972; but several years prior to that, at a time when France was not yet a party to the Convention, French domestic legislation already had adopted some of the Convention's important features, eliminating most of the objectionable aspects of *notification au parquet.*[18] Since this method of service originated in France, it is to be hoped that other countries, which at the present time still use it, will follow suit, either by becoming parties to the Convention or by treating it as a model for internal reform.[19]

G. ABATEMENT BECAUSE OF PENDENCY OF ANOTHER ACTION

Comparovich: There is one other point that should be touched upon before we move on to pleadings and evidence. In cases of transnational disputes it has become very frequent that the parties—each of them striving to select the forum considered most favorable to it—litigate the same claim by way of several actions successively brought in different countries. This often leads to difficult procedural problems.

16b. See Arts. 15 and 16, discussed by Ristau, supra n. 4, at 172–74. For a comparative survey of many countries' national laws relating to default judgments, see J. B. Elkind, Non-Appearance Before the International Court of Justice—Functional and Comparative Analysis 1–30 (1984).

17. Cf. L. Kos-Rabcewicz-Zubkowski, The Possibilities for Treaties on Private International Law to Serve as Model Laws, 26 Revue du Barreau 229 (1966).

18. See P. Amram, A Revolutionary Change in Service of Process Abroad in French Civil Procedure, 2 Int.Lawyer 650 (1968).

At the present time, the French rules concerning *notification au parquet* are embodied in Arts. 683–687 of the new Code of Civil Procedure. It is now made the duty of the official making the service, not only to deliver a copy of the document to the Attorney General or his local deputy (the so-called *Parquet*), but on the same day to mail another copy to the defendant by registered mail; moreover, in cases where the proof of service does not establish that the defendant received actual and timely notice, the court may order additional measures of notification, including service by letters rogatory.

19. Ideally, both methods (adoption of the Convention *and* internal reform) should be used. The Convention makes sure that proper notice will be given to defendants residing in countries adhering to the Convention. Internal reform is necessary in order to extend similar protection to defendants who reside in other countries.

Before H sued your company in Ruritania, had he brought an action on his alleged claim in this country? Or had you brought an action against him here, seeking a judicial declaration of the non-existence of his claim?

Smooth: No, there was never any litigation in this country between H and our company. But the point you are raising is an important one; we have encountered it in other cases. Let us discuss it for a minute.

We are, of course, familiar with the general rule that Action No. 2 must be abated if it is shown that another action (Action No. 1), involving the same parties and the same claim, has been previously instituted and is still pending in a court of the same jurisdiction. Will Action No. 2 be similarly abated if Action No. 1 is pending in the court of a foreign country?

Comparovich: The various legal systems give conflicting answers to your question. When Action No. 2 is brought in a federal court in the United States, that court has discretionary power to abate the action if defendant shows that another action (Action No. 1), involving the same parties and the same claim, is pending in the courts of another country.[20]

Smooth: I take it that the factors which the court considers in making its discretionary decision, are similar to those that influence the outcome of a forum non conveniens motion; but the fact of the prior pendency of foreign Action No. 1 furnishes an additional weight on the scale, in favor of staying or dismissing Action No. 2.

Comparovich: That is a correct understanding of the federal rule. Many state courts appear to follow a similar rule.[21]

Smooth: If Action No. 2 is brought in a civil-law court, how will such a court approach the problem?

Comparovich: The civil-law systems are opposed to making the issue a discretionary one, and tend to approach the problem by announcing a clear-cut, non-discretionary rule. But there is no agreement among them as to what the thrust of the rule should be.

The German rule, probably representing a minority point of view, is to the effect that the later Action No. 2 will be dismissed if it can be expected that a subsequent judgment in Action No. 1 will be recognized in the country where Action No. 2 has been brought.[22] But if Action No. 2 is brought in a majority civil-law country, such as France or Italy,

---

20. See Continental Time Corp. v. Swiss Credit Bank, 543 F.Supp. 408 (S.D.N.Y. 1982) and authorities there cited. Note, however, that when the defendant in the U.S. action moves to dismiss or stay that action, the plaintiff sometimes will counter with a motion to enjoin the action instituted abroad. See Anno., 78 ALR Fed. 831 (1986).

21. See A. A. Ehrenzweig, Conflict of Laws 127–29 (1962); Restatement Second, Conflict of Laws, § 86 and Reporter's Note (1971).

22. See 1 A. Bülow & K.-H. Böckstiegel, Internationaler Rechtsverkehr in Zivil- und Handelssachen 606–169 (1985); Baumbach-Lauterbach-Albers-Hartmann, Zivilprozessordnung, § 261, Anno. 2B (45th ed., 1987).

the general rule is that an action (Action No. 1) previously instituted in another country will be disregarded, with the result that both actions can simultaneously proceed to a determination of the merits.[23]

Smooth: Under the majority civil-law rule, each party will seek to expedite the action in the forum it considers more favorable. The first party which obtains a final judgment (in either forum) will then try to use that judgment as res judicata in the other forum. Thus you get what one might describe as a race to judgment. The German rule, on the other hand, encourages a race to the court-house door at the very beginning of the litigation process.

Comparovich: Your observation shows that you have had experience in transnational litigation.

Edge: I assume that when Action No. 2 as well as Action No. 1 is brought in a country adhering to the European Convention, the issue of abatement of the later action is governed, not by the national law of either country, but by the Convention. Is that a correct assumption?

Comparovich: It is. Art. 21 of the Convention, essentially adopting the German view, provides that if both actions involve the same parties and the same claim, the later action must be dismissed in such a case.[24]

Edge: What if Action No. 1 was brought in a non-Convention country, such as the U.S., and Action No. 2 is brought in a Convention country?

Comparovich: In that event the Convention rule does not apply, and the court in which Action No. 2 is pending will have to determine the abatement issue in accordance with its national law.

Smooth: I am glad you have explained these complexities to us. In future cases, I hope, this will enhance our gamesmanship as forum-shoppers.

H. PLEADINGS AND FORMATION OF ISSUES

Comparovich: What happened next in Mr. H's action?

Edge: Upon L's advice, we authorized him to appear for the defendant. He filed an answer, which, like the complaint, contained some discussion of legal points as well as a prayer for relief and, of course, factual denials and allegations. In essence, the answer raised the following issues:

23. See P. Herzog, Civil Procedure in France § 4.31 (1967); M. Cappelletti & J. M. Perillo, Civil Procedure in Italy § 4.10 (1965). The effect of the rule is often modified by treaty. See ibid.

24. This seemingly simple rule is sometimes difficult to apply. Which is the "later" action in a case where one of the two complaints was filed in March and served in August, while the other was filed and served in May of the same year? The European Court of Justice gave a complex answer to this question in its Decision of June 7, 1984, CCH Common Market Reporter, Transfer Binder (Court Decisions 1983–85) ¶14102.

(1) Although realizing that this was a weak point, we denied the jurisdictional facts alleged by H, and expressly objected to the court's jurisdiction.[1]

(2) Concerning the merits, defendant

    (a) denied that a definite contract had been made;

    (b) argued as a matter of law that H's fee, even if the alleged contract had been made, would not be governed by Ruritanian law;

    (c) pointed out that according to H's own assertions the alleged oral contract was made in this State, and that according to the law of this State the contract is illegal because H engaged in the unauthorized practice of law.[2]

Smooth: You will note that point (2)(b) raises a question of law. The complaint was expressly and exclusively based on the Ruritanian statutory tariff. Hence the complaint was bad on its face, if under the applicable choice of law rule that retainer was not governed by Ruritanian law.[3] I pointed this out to L, and asked him to file a demurrer on this ground; but from L's reply to my letter I gathered that he simply did not get my point.

Comparovich: That is understandable. Demurrers and their counterparts in our present-day procedure, like many of our pre-trial motions, serve the purpose of neatly separating issues of law from issues of fact, so that in the end a few clearly formulated, material issues of fact can be submitted to the jury.[4] In the civil-law countries, where no jury participates in the decision of civil cases, such early separation of

1. In the majority of civil-law countries, a special appearance is neither necessary nor permissible. It is generally held in those countries that a defendant does not waive his jurisdictional objection by joining it (in his answer) with defenses going to the merits. See O. Sandrock, Die Prorogation der internationalen Zuständigkeit eines Gerichts durch hilfsweise Sacheinlassung des Beklagten, 78 Z. für Vergleichende Rechtswissenschaft 177, 181–82 (1979), and authorities there cited. Art. 18 of the European Convention, as interpreted by the European Court of Justice, is to the same effect. See F. K. Juenger, Judicial Jurisdiction in the United States and in the European Communities: A Comparison, 82 Mich.L.Rev. 1195, at 1209 (1984); Baumbach-Lauterbach-Albers-Hartmann, Zivilprozessordnung 2450 (45th ed., 1987).

2. Cf. In re Roel, 3 N.Y.2d 224, 165 N.Y.S.2d 31, 144 N.E.2d 24 (1957).

3. Mr. Smooth seems to assume that under Ruritanian procedure the plaintiff, having invoked a certain theory of law in his pleading, may not recover on any other theory. This used to be, but no longer is,

the prevailing view in the United States. See Clark on Code Pleading, Sec. 43 (1947); Field, Kaplan & Clermont, Materials for a Basic Course in Civil Procedure 408–411 (5th ed., 1984). In civilian procedure, it is in keeping with the generally more active role of the judge that the court should not be confined to the legal theories espoused by the parties. This is the German view. See Zöller-Stephan, Zivilprozessordnung, § 253, Anno. 12 (14th ed., 1984). But the civilians are not unanimous concerning this question. See, e.g., Millar, The Formative Principles of Civil Procedure, 18 Ill.L. Rev. 1, 94, at 113 (1923); id., Civil Pleading in Scotland, 30 Mich.L.Rev. 545, at 562, 736 (1931). As will be seen later, the court in the instant case followed the German view. For purposes of the present discussion in the text, however, Mr. Smooth's assumption may be treated as correct.

4. In non-jury cases, this rationale does not hold; but the procedural merger of law and equity is thought to compel us to employ the same procedural devices in both kinds of cases.

factual and legal issues is unnecessary. Hence no demurrers or motions to dismiss for insufficiency, and no other motions addressed to the pleadings.[5]

Smooth: Without such motions, and in view of the general informality of their pleadings, how do they narrow and formulate the issues?

Comparovich: The Romano-Canonistic system, which dominated procedural thinking on the continent from the 13th to the 18th century, had two outstanding characteristics: First, the proceedings, including the examination of witnesses, were largely conducted *in secret*. Secondly, the task of hearing the parties, the witnesses, and even the lawyers, was often left to subordinate officials who had to reduce everything to *writing*; the judges then based their decisions exclusively on the written record.[6] The modern procedural codes of the civilians reflect a violent reaction, and indeed a revolt, against this medieval system.[7] They stress that all proceedings shall be *oral* and *public* throughout. Consequently, they de-emphasize the written pleadings,[8] and treat them as merely preparatory to a hearing in open court at which the attorneys orally present their clients' allegations, arguments and prayers for relief.[9] At the same time, or subsequently at an adjourned hearing, they make offers of proof concerning disputed issues of fact. In many

5. A civil-law court, of course, *may* dismiss a complaint which is bad on its face. But there is no procedural device by which the defendant can *compel* the court to decide a doubtful point of law before the defendant has to take a position on the plaintiff's factual allegations. The defendant's response to the complaint, therefore, always has to take the form of an answer, in which the defendant, unless he wishes to admit the allegations of the complaint, must raise factual as well as legal issues. Thereupon, the court may well (although in theory it should not) proceed to try the factual issues without too much previous study of their materiality as a matter of law. In order to minimize the danger of a reversal, the court may prefer to decide the case on the facts rather than on a difficult point of law.

6. See Engelmann-Millar, A History of Continental Civil Procedure 457–8 (1927); Cappelletti and Perillo, Civil Procedure in Italy 36 (1965). For the fundamental differences between this "Romano-Canonistic" system, which was developed during the middle ages, and classical Roman procedure, see id., at 26–31.

7. The statement in the text is true of most civil-law systems; but there are differences among them as to (a) the exact time of that revolt, (b) its abruptness or gradualness, and (c) the thoroughness with which the Romano-Canonistic features were eliminated. Id., at 37–46. In Spain,

and even more in the Spanish-speaking countries of Latin America, the process of reforming the Romano-Canonistic features of civil procedure has been especially timid and slow—so much so that the discussion which follows is frequently subject to some qualification as applied to Spanish-speaking countries. The reader who is interested in those countries' civil procedure, is referred to International Encyclopedia of Comparative Law, Vol. XVI (Civil Procedure, M. Cappelletti, Ed.), Ch. 6, Part VI (by E. Vescovi) (1984).

8. See Millar, Some Comparative Aspects of Civil Pleading Under Anglo-American and Continental Systems, 12 A.B.A.J. 401 (1926).

9. This, at least, is the theory. In practice, the presiding judge of a busy court sometimes will cut the hearing so short that the attorneys' "oral" presentation may amount to little more than a reference to their "preparatory" pleadings previously filed. There are differences in this respect from country to country, and in fact from locality to locality, depending on the work-load of each court and the temperament of the President of each "chamber".

Recently, some attempts have been made to re-emphasize the principle of orality, and to enforce it in practice. See the discussion of the so-called Stuttgart Model, infra pp. 437 ff.

Section 139

civil-law countries, the presiding judge is under a duty, if necessary, to make the parties clarify their demands, allegations and offers of proof. Section 139 of the German Code of Civil Procedure, for instance, provides as follows:

> The presiding judge has to see to it that the parties make completely clear their respective positions concerning all material facts and that they request the proper relief; in particular, he has to see to it that they supplement insufficient statements of alleged facts, and that they designate the means of proof. For this purpose, so far as is necessary, the presiding judge has to discuss with the parties [10] the factual and legal aspects of the controversy, and has to ask questions.
>
>   . . . The presiding judge has to permit every member of the court, upon his request, to ask questions.

Smooth: This makes it possible for the court to inject new legal and factual issues into the case, and thus in effect to help a dumb lawyer who did not think of those issues.

Comparovich: Quite so. But it seems to me that you have pointed to a virtue rather than a vice of the German provision. Lawsuits should be decided on their merits, and not necessarily in favor of the party who can find (and afford) the shrewdest lawyer.

Section 139 of the German Code has been called the Magna Charta of fair procedure, for the very reason that it effectively reduces (although it cannot wholly eliminate) the impact of the relative ability of counsel upon the outcome of litigation, and increases the probability of an ultimate decision that is legally and factually correct.

Let me illustrate this by the following

Example: Plaintiff, who was injured in a traffic accident, first sued the individual tortfeasor T, and obtained a judgment against him; but T apparently failed to satisfy the judgment. In the present action, based on the German "direct action" statute (see infra p. 555), plaintiff seeks to recover from T's liability insurer. Under the German statute, which is similar to "direct action" statutes in this country, plaintiff can recover from the insurance company only if he alleges and proves facts giving rise to liability on the part of the insured (T). Plaintiff in this case alleged no such facts, but merely asserted that he had obtained a *judgment* against T holding the latter liable for a certain amount of damages.

The court of first instance dismissed the action against the insurance company, pointing out that the latter had not been a party to plaintiff's prior action against T, and hence was not bound by the judgment against T.[10a]   Under these circumstances, the

---

10. In practice, the discussion is usually with the attorneys.

10a. The reader should assume that under German law the court of first instance was correct with respect to this res judicata point. The reasons for this will become clearer infra pp. 454–456. Under our law, the result might be different if the insurance company financed and controlled T's conduct of the prior action. Cf.

court of first instance held, the plaintiff's reference to the judgment was not a proper substitute for the necessary allegation of facts creating liability on the part of T. The court of first instance thus held the complaint to be insufficient.

On plaintiff's appeal, the intermediate appellate court reversed and remanded. In the higher court's view, the court of first instance should have noticed that plaintiff's lawyer was mistaken in believing that defendant insurance company was bound by the judgment in the prior action. By asking proper questions pursuant to § 139 of the Code of Civil Procedure, the lower court should have called the lawyer's attention to this mistake, and thus should have made it clear to the lawyer that it was necessary for him to allege, and offer to prove, the facts underlying T's liability. This failure of the lower court to comply with the mandate of § 139 was held to be reversible error.[10b] In reversing, the appellate court criticized the lower court for having sacrificed justice to speed.

Edge: Suppose the facts of a case suggest the possibility that the defendant might win on the basis of an affirmative defense; but the defendant's lawyer has failed to interpose such defense. For instance, the facts show that plaintiff's claim is stale, but defendant has not invoked the statute of limitations. Does a German court, in order to comply with § 139, have to educate the defendant's lawyer in such a situation?

Comparovich: This is such a good question that I was about to bring it up myself. Among German courts and writers, a big controversy rages concerning this question. According to the view which until recently was the prevailing one, a distinction must be drawn. If defendant's lawyer, though not explicitly invoking the statute of limitations, in some way has pointed to the staleness of plaintiff's claim, or to the difficulty of defending the action after years of inaction on plaintiff's part, § 139 clearly requires the court to seek clarification of the defendant's opaque hints, and such clarification can be attained only by asking whether or not the defendant wishes to assert the statute of limitations. Where, on the other hand, the defendant has totally failed to assert, or even to hint, that the action is time-barred, the court under this view was not compelled, and not even authorized, to alert the defendant (and especially a defendant represented by counsel) to the availability of an affirmative defense such as the statute of limitations. According to most of the courts and writers holding this view, it follows that a judge who in the latter case nevertheless asks a question alerting the defendant, can be forced by the plaintiff to recuse himself.[10c]

Restatement Second, Judgments, § 39 (1982).

10b. OLG Düsseldorf, Decision of July 25, 1974, DRZ 1974, 327. For a similar holding, in a slightly more complicated factual setting, see OLG München, Decision of July 14, 1973, OLGZ 1973, 362.

10c. For references see E. Peters, Richterliche Hinweispflichten und Beweisinitiativen im Zivilprozess 89–90, 99–100, 135–38 (1983); E. Schneider, Richterlicher Hinweis auf Verjährungsablauf, 39 NJW 1316 (1986); V. Hermisson, Richterlicher Hinweis auf Einrede- und Gestaltungsmöglichkeiten, 38 NJW 2558

The contrary view, which appears to be in the ascendancy among lower courts as well as legal authors, is to the effect that even a defendant who is represented by counsel and who has totally neglected to assert an affirmative defense such as the statute of limitations, must be alerted by a question asked pursuant to § 139, if the circumstances of the case suggest the possible availability of such a defense.[10d]

Edge: With respect to affirmative defenses which serve the cause of justice, this may be a sound view. But the statute of limitations defense does not serve that cause. Therefore, the policy behind § 139 does not apply in this instance.

Comparovich: A German legal writer has expressed a similar argument.[10e] It is true that the statute of limitations serves peace rather than justice; but *quaere* whether in our scale of values the postulate of peace should be treated as inferior to that of justice.

Smooth: Whichever way this controversy regarding affirmative defenses is ultimately resolved, it is plain that § 139 modifies the adversary nature of the process and gives the court broad powers, not only to influence the formulation of the issues, but even to inject into the lawsuit important issues not brought up by the parties. Have other civil-law countries adopted provisions similar to the Germans' § 139?

Comparovich: Yes. The trend in the more advanced civil-law systems clearly goes in that direction. To mention but two examples: The Japanese Code of Civil Procedure, in its Art. 127, has followed in the footsteps of German § 139; and, more recently, France has adopted a similar rule in Arts. 8, 13 and 442 of its new (1975) Code.

I should mention, however, that there is one important difference between the German provision, on the one hand, and its Japanese and French counterparts, on the other. The German Code casts the rule in mandatory terms, with the result that it is clearly reversible error for the court not to ask a clarifying question when such a question is indicated.[10f] Under the French and Japanese provisions, the court "may" ask clarifying questions. In a long line of vacillating and often criticized decisions, the Japanese Supreme Court has struggled with the question under what circumstances the lower courts' failure to ask questions should be treated as reversible error.[10g] The new French provisions may well give rise to similar difficulties.

Smooth: It appears from our discussion that a provision of this kind, whether cast in mandatory or in permissive terms, greatly adds to the court's power to direct the course, and to influence the outcome, of the litigation. But to this point, it seems to me, there is a counterpoint.

(1985). The reasons given for the formerly prevailing view usually were derived from the "principle of adversariness" or the "nature of an affirmative defense". These are, of course, question-begging arguments.

10d. See ibid.

10e. See Hermisson, supra n. 10c, at 2561.

10f. See supra n. 10b. For further references see Baumbach-Lauterbach-Albers-Hartmann, Zivilprozessordnung, § 139, Anno. 2 E (45th ed., 1987).

10g. See T. Hattori & D. F. Henderson, Civil Procedure in Japan, § 7.02[10] (1985).

Whether the bench in U.S. should be obligated to remind
absent minded attorney of proper procedure instead of
deferring right is waived

PROCEDURE IN CIVIL LAW COUNTRIES 421

These provisions also deprive the court of the power (a power that appears to exist under our law) to dream up a new legal theory, i.e. a theory not presented by either party, and to decide the case on that surprise theory without having given the parties an opportunity to discuss it.

Comparovich: You are absolutely right. Both the German Code and the new French Code make this crystal-clear.[11] Keep in mind, moreover, that this negative aspect of the rule—i.e., the prohibition against deciding a case on a point not previously discussed with the parties—is clear-cut and non-discretionary in France as well as in Germany.

> *Example:* D, as employee of a garage owned by one X, had sold a car to P. When it turned out that the car had a defect that was not apparent to P at the time of purchase, P sued D for breach of an implied warranty. The court of first instance dismissed the action on the ground that D had acted only as agent for X, and thus was not himself a party to the contract for the sale of the car. On P's appeal, the intermediate appellate court agreed with the lower court that D was not liable for breach of warranty. But of its own motion, and without discussing this aspect of the case with the parties, the intermediate appellate court held D liable in tort and on this basis, reversing the court of first instance, entered judgment for the plaintiff. On defendant's appeal from that judgment, the Court of Cassation reversed and remanded, holding that it was error for the intermediate appellate court to decide the case on a legal theory injected into the case by the court, without first discussing it with the parties and giving the defendant an opportunity to meet the new theory by additional offers of proof.[11a]

Edge: Contrast this enlightened civil-law rule with the deplorable situation existing in this country, where trial as well as appellate courts routinely decide cases on legal theories thought up by the judges

compare

11. In Germany, the relevant provision is Code of Civil Procedure, § 278, subd. 3, as amended in 1976, which supplements § 139. It is recognized that at least to some extent this provision reflects a constitutional mandate. See Baumbach-Lauterbach-Albers-Hartmann, § 278, Anno. 5A (45th ed., 1987). An example is presented by the German case cited supra p. 72, where the lower court's surprise reliance on foreign law led to reversal. The reason for the reversal was the lower court's failure to discuss the foreign law aspect of the case with the parties before rendering a decision based on foreign law.

As to France, see arts. 12 and 16 of the new Code of Civil Procedure. The reader will recall that an earlier version of these provisions (which arguably authorized the court to decide a case on a legal theory

thought up by the court and not previously discussed with the parties) was struck down as unconstitutional. See supra p. 380. Thereafter, Art. 16 was clarified, and rendered clearly constitutional, by the addition of a new third paragraph, which reads as follows:

> "He [the judge] may not base his decision upon points of law brought up by him ex officio without previously having invited the parties to submit their observations."

11a. Decision of the French Cour de Cassation of November 4, 1974, Bull. Civ. 1974 IV 226, No. 275. If a similar case came before the Cour de Cassation today, the result would be the same—*a fortiori*—under the Code provision quoted in the preceding footnote.

and never discussed with the parties.[11b] This makes the words "Due Process" ring hollow.

Comparovich: Your point is well taken. But you may derive a little consolation from the fact that when courts commit abuses of this kind too patently and too frequently, their power to render such surprise decisions may at least in part be curtailed by the legislature.[11c]

Smooth: To come back to the normal course of a lawsuit in a civil-law country: What happens after the parties have presented their allegations and offers of proof, and have responded to such clarifying questions as the court may have put to them?

Comparovich: The next step is a decision by the court. In rare instances, when there are no factual issues in the case, that decision may be a final judgment. Much more frequently, the decision will take the form of an *interlocutory order for the taking of evidence.* On the basis of the parties' offers of proof, but in the words of the court,[12] that order will specify the precise propositions on which evidence is to be taken, and also the means of proof, e.g., the names of the witnesses [13] to be examined.[14]

Smooth: This leaves me flabbergasted. Do you mean to say that under civil-law procedure I could never introduce a witness unless his name and the propositions to be proved by his testimony have been previously notified to my opponent, and have been incorporated into an interlocutory order of the court?

Comparovich: This is precisely what I mean. There is no such thing as a surprise witness under that system.[15]

Edge: To me, this does not seem so striking. Our own practice, at least in those jurisdictions which are past the stone-age, is moving in the same direction, by way of pre-trial hearings and discovery devices.

Smooth: I dissent. Even under the liberal discovery provisions of the Federal Rules we still distinguish between (a) asking one's opponent for the names of witnesses who have knowledge of the transaction, and (b) asking him what persons he intends to call as his witnesses at the

---

11b. The Supreme Court of the United States sets a bad example in this respect. When deciding a case on the basis of a "plain error" not briefed by the parties but noticed by the Court ex officio under its Rule 34.1(a), the Justices ordinarily announce their decision without first inviting the parties to submit comments or observations.

11c. See Cal. Government Code § 68081, added by L. 1986, Ch. 1098.

12. In most civil-law countries, orders and judgments are formulated by the court, and not by the attorneys.

13. In some civil-law countries, the order does not name the witnesses, but di-rects the party who has made the offer of proof to furnish the witnesses' names and addresses at a stated time, i.e. at a time well in advance of the actual examination of such witnesses.

14. If the court is composed of three judges, the order may provide that during the proof-taking stage of the litigation the three-judge panel be represented by one of its members. See infra at n. 49.

15. Except in proceedings involving temporary injunctions or other provisional remedies, in which there is no time for interlocutory orders.

trial. Discovery of type (a) is generally permitted today;[16] but the majority of our courts, even of the federal courts, will not stand for (b).[17] Our courts, in other words, have not adopted the civil-law practice of compelling advance disclosure of the witnesses' names, and of the points to be proved by each of them.[18] In this, our courts have shown considerable wisdom. What the civilians do, must be an invitation to tamper with the witnesses.

Comparovich: No. The civilian lawyer usually regards it as his client's job to dig out the facts. The lawyer rarely engages in factual investigation. Normally, he will not have much contact with witnesses outside of the courtroom; thus, there is little opportunity for coaching witnesses, or for "tampering" with them. In some continental countries, moreover, there are canons of ethics prohibiting an attorney from discussing the facts of a case with a prospective witness.[19]

Edge: This is an important point, which we shall have to keep in mind in our dealings with local counsel abroad.[20]

I. EVIDENCE *

Smooth: To come back to our case, the court in fact issued an interlocutory order of the kind we are talking about.[21] That order had

16. See 8 Wright & Miller, Federal Practice and Procedure § 2013 (1970 and 1986 Supp.).

17. See Anno., 19 A.L.R.3d 1114 (1968); Wright & Miller, supra n. 16.

18. Note, however, that the names of expert witnesses whom a party intends to call are discoverable under FRCP Rule 26(b)(4)(A), as amended, and that in a proper case a court occasionally will use a pre-trial conference to require disclosure of the names of all witnesses (even of ordinary witnesses) whom the parties propose to call at trial. See Wright & Miller, supra n. 16. In some U.S. District Courts, the latter requirement is routinized by local Rules insisting on the filing of pre-trial statements in which the parties must disclose (inter alia) the names of the witnesses to be called at trial. The practice of some of our courts thus reflects a measure of convergence with the civil-law rule precluding the use of surprise witnesses. Mr. Smooth's statement in the text, supra, nevertheless remains correct in a number of American jurisdictions. See, e.g., City of Long Beach v. Superior Court, 134 Cal. Rptr. 468 (1976) and authorities there cited.

19. See, e.g., von Büren, Zur Praxis der Zürcherischen Aufsichtskommission über die Rechtsanwälte, 45 Schweizerische Juristen-Zeitung 102 (1949). In Germany, the prohibition was dropped in the 1963 revision of the Canons of Ethics (Richtlinien für die Ausübung des Rechtsanwaltberufs, §§ 4 and 58); but it is still in force in other civil-law countries. See Int. Encyclopedia of Comp. L., Vol. XVI, Ch. 6, § 446 (1984).

20. Cf. Becker v. Webster, 171 F.2d 762, 765 (2d Cir. 1949), where Judge L. Hand remarked that the custom of interviewing one's witnesses before trial and reducing their proposed testimony to writing is "universal", and that it would be a "fantastic extreme" to consider such custom unprofessional for an attorney in any country. With deference, it is submitted that this strikingly erroneous remark of the eminent jurist proves only one thing: the hazards inherent in uncritically assuming that one's own domestic practices are "universal".

* For a comparative treatment of the law of evidence see H. Nagel, Die Grundzüge des Beweisrechts im europäischen Zivilprozess (1967). For comprehensive discussions of the manner in which facts are proved in civil cases under German and French law, see also J. H. Langbein, The German Advantage in Civil Procedure, 52 U.Chi.L.Rev. 823 (1985), and J. Beardsley, Proof of Fact in French Civil Procedure, 34 Am.J.Comp.L. 459 (1986).

21. For the form of such an order see 2 E. J. Cohn, Manual of German Law 193–94 (2d ed., 1971).

several features which baffled me. In the first place, it did not contain a word concerning the documentary evidence, especially the correspondence we had with H both before and after his visit here.

Comparovich: I assume the correspondence had been attached to the pleadings, or in some other way had been placed into the court's *dossier?*

Smooth: Yes; but wasn't it still necessary to introduce it in evidence?

Comparovich: No. The civilian view is that a document, unless its authenticity is specifically challenged,[22] proves its own existence, and that it is unnecessary to waste time by formally introducing it in evidence.[22a] Hence a party is permitted to submit documents (i.e., documents in his possession)[23] in an informal way, provided he notifies the opponent and gives him an opportunity for inspection.

Smooth: But in this way the court's *dossier* will be cluttered with irrelevant documents.

Comparovich: As a matter of self-interest, the parties will not provoke the judges' anger by submitting totally irrelevant stuff, and the court, sitting without a jury, will be able to appraise the evidentiary value of each document.

Smooth: The documents may contain hearsay or opinion.[24]

Comparovich: So what? Except for matters of privilege and of personal incompetence to testify (based on reasons such as kinship, tender age or prior felony convictions),[25] civilian codes contain *no*

---

22. Such challenge is rendered particularly difficult in the case of notarial protocols and other "public documents". See Schlesinger, The Notary and the Formal Contract in Civil Law, 1941 Report of the New York Law Revision Commission 403, 413.

22a. For an able discussion of the contrary (and unnecessarily cumbersome) rule traditionally prevailing in this country, see J. W. Strong, Liberalizing the Authentication of Private Writings, 52 Cornell L.Q. 284 (1967). Even under modern liberalizing enactments such as Rules 901 and 902 of the Federal Rules of Evidence, our practice generally is far more time-consuming and cumbersome than that of the civil-law countries. Only a few types of documents can be introduced in our courts with a degree of informality reminiscent of civil-law procedure. See UCC § 1–202 and Federal Rules of Evidence, Rule 902(9).

23. As to documents in the possession of the opponent or of a third party, see the discussion of discovery, infra. One important point, however, should be noted immediately: Specific documents as well as entire files of documents in the possession of some public office—including another court—normally can be sent for, and attached to the court's *dossier*, without much formality. This practice (*Aktenbeiziehung* in German terminology) is of particular importance in personal injury litigation, where the entire record of an earlier criminal action thus can be globally incorporated into the *dossier* of the court dealing with a subsequent civil suit.

24. The reader will note that even under our law a document executed by a party normally can be introduced against such party; and third-party documents frequently will be admissible under one of the many exceptions to the hearsay rule.

25. As to competence to testify and to take an oath, the rules in civil-law countries often contain more restrictions than one finds in our law. See H. Silving, The Oath, 68 Yale L.J. 1329, 1527, at 1543–51 (1959). Regarding testimonial privileges, see M. Pieck, Privilege Against Self-Incrimination in The Civil Law, 5 Villanova L.Rev. 375 (1960).

exclusionary rules of evidence,[25a] and particularly no hearsay or opinion rule.[26]

Most of the grounds which under our law serve to preclude the admission of evidence, according to the civilians merely affect its weight;[26a] and they consider the weight to be accorded to each item of documentary or other evidence to be a matter for the court's *free evaluation.*[27]

Edge: By a process of gradual erosion of the hearsay rule, our law is moving toward the civil-law approach. Would it not simplify and improve our law if the hearsay and opinion rules were thrown out altogether?

Comparovich: There is no doubt that such a reform would simplify our law and bring cheer to the hearts of future bar examination candidates. Whether total elimination of the exclusionary rules of evidence would improve the fact-finding process, is less certain. Perhaps one should draw a distinction between jury and non-jury cases. With respect to the latter, the arguments in favor of adopting the civilian approach are strong;[28] but even on this point the experts are divided.[29]

25a. Although modern civil-law systems generally reject exclusionary rules of evidence, there are some recent German cases excluding evidence obtained in violation of a constitutionally protected right of privacy. In contrast to the majority of our courts, the German courts have applied this new (and intelligently limited) exclusionary rule in civil as well as criminal actions, and regardless of whether the evidence was obtained by police officers or by private individuals. See H. W. Baade, Illegally Obtained Evidence in Criminal and Civil Cases: A Comparative Study of a Classic Mismatch, 51 Texas L.Rev. 1325 (1973) and 52 id. 621 (1974), especially 52 id. at 621–24; M. Cappelletti, Fundamental Guarantees of the Parties in Civil Litigation: Comparative Constitutional, International and Social Trends, 25 Stan.L.Rev. 651, 707–11 (1973).

26. A witness may, of course, be asked to state the source of his knowledge; and if a witness or a document points to a named individual as such source, the court may call that individual as a witness, or direct the parties to call him. See Hammelmann, Hearsay Evidence—A Comparison, 67 L.Q.Rev. 67 (1951).

26a. Civilians often refuse to understand, or to comply with, our technical rules regarding admissibility of evidence. A striking example is reported by F. H. Thomann, Recent Developments in Swiss International Law, 14 Int. Lawyer 525, 527 (1980).

27. In Romano-Canonistic procedure there existed a complex system of mechani-

cal rules precisely determining the number and quality of witnesses necessary to prove an event or to overcome other evidence. The codes' repudiation of this system resulted in the principle of free evaluation of evidence. Civilians regard the latter principle—coupled with the absence of exclusionary rules—as the cornerstone of their treatment of evidentiary problems. Among the exceptions to the principle, which ordinarily are few in number, the following should be noted: (a) certain documents, and especially public documents, may in some respects have a conclusive effect, which cannot be overcome by other evidence; (b) in some civil-law countries, an attack upon the genuineness of certain documents is made relatively difficult by special procedural and evidentiary requirements (see supra n. 22); (c) the ancient relic of the "decisory oath", infra at nn. 36 and 37, still survives in a few jurisdictions.

28. See, e.g., J. Weinstein, Probative Force of Hearsay, 46 Iowa L.Rev. 331 (1961).

One might well ask why observance of the hearsay and opinion rules should be more necessary in civil non-jury cases than in administrative proceedings. In proceedings of the latter kind these rules have long been held to be inapplicable. See Opp Cotton Mills v. Administrator, 312 U.S. 126, 155, 61 S.Ct. 524, 537 (1941); Richardson v. Perales, 402 U.S. 389, 407–08, 91 S.Ct. 1420, 1430 (1971). See also the relevant provisions of the Administrative Procedure Act, 5 U.S.C.A. § 556(d).

29. See F. E. Booker and R. Morton, The Hearsay Rule, The St. George Plays

Smooth: Let us come back to the interlocutory order issued by the court. The first paragraph of the order called for the personal appearance of H before the court, so that he could be examined concerning the conversations we had with him during his visit here. This puzzled me for a number of reasons. First of all, it seemed to me that before H testified in court, we should have been given an opportunity for a pre-trial examination.

Comparovich: Working without a jury, the civilians do not have to divide a civil lawsuit into (a) the pre-trial phase and (b) the "trial". A "trial", in the sense of a single, dramatic, concentrated and uninterrupted presentation of everything that bears on the dispute, is unknown to them.[30] Their traditional practice is to develop a case through a series of successive hearings,[30a] at some of which evidence is taken.[31] It follows that in their procedure there is no room for a "pretrial" examination. Once Mr. H's testimony is taken at one of the successive hearings, it automatically becomes part of the record. Note, moreover, that in your case his testimony was taken primarily to give him an opportunity to tell the court his side of the story. Any use you might make of his examination for *discovery* purposes, would be merely incidental, and probably not too effective.

Edge: You have left me a bit confused, Professor. Is there no discovery in civil-law procedure?

Comparovich: In the civil-law systems, discovery is much weaker than under Rules 26 ff. of the Federal Rules of Civil Procedure and their counterparts in the procedural Rules and codes of our states. This is so for two reasons. First, the devices used by the civilians to extract information or documents from an unwilling opponent or third party are not as strong and as sweeping as they are here.[32] Secondly,

and The Road to the Year Twenty-Fifty, 44 Notre Dame Law. 7 (1968).

30. The statement in the text refers to civil procedure. In criminal matters, whether or not heard by a jury, the civilians do require a "trial" in the sense in which we understand the term. See infra p. 477.

Concerning recent attempts of German reformers to introduce the notion of a single, concentrated trial into *civil* procedure, see the discussion of the "Stuttgart Model", infra pp. 437 ff.

30a. Clearly, this is an important difference between civil-law and common-law procedure. For an attempt to explain this difference, and to put it into the context of a broader comparison of the two systems in terms of political history, see M. Damaska, The Faces of Justice and State Authority 51–52 (1986).

31. In non-jury cases, piecemeal trials are not entirely unknown in the United States, although we regard them as un-

usual. In the Philippines, where an American-derived system of civil procedure (but without a jury) has long prevailed, piecemeal trials seem to be the rule rather than the exception. See G. W. Pugh, Aspects of the Administration of Justice in the Philippines, 26 La.L.Rev. 1, at 21–22 (1965).

32. The situation in France may be taken as fairly typical. French law, prior to the recent procedural reform, knew only weak discovery devices. See P. Herzog, Civil Procedure in France 233–34, 239 (1967). In spite of the high-sounding programmatic announcement in Art. 10 of the Civil Code (as amended by Law 72–626 of July 5, 1972), that "Everyone must cooperate with the judiciary (*la justice*) in order that truth may prevail," the recent revision of French civil procedure does not seem to have brought about a radical change in this respect. Some discovery devices, it is true, have been introduced by a Decree of September 9, 1971, and are now embodied in the new Code of Civil Procedure. Articles 138 to 142 of that

in the civil-law systems the process of discovery is not separated from the process of introducing evidence into the record. In this country, a party who has conducted discovery and by such discovery has elicited depositions or documents from his opponent or a third party, very often cannot use such depositions or documents as evidence at the subsequent trial.[32a] Even in situations where our law would permit him to use the fruits of discovery as trial evidence, he is not compelled to do so, and may choose to use such depositions and documents only for his own information rather than to put them into the record as evidence.[32b] No such freedom of choice exists in civil-law procedure. Any testimony or document elicited from an opponent or a third party automatically becomes part of the record. Thus, if such testimony or document turns out to be unfavorable to the side which asked the court to elicit it, that side may be sorry, because it finds itself in the position of having placed unfavorable evidence into the record.[33]

compare

Edge: These relative weaknesses of "discovery" in the civil-law systems must play a large role in the strategic planning of lawyers who are contemplating transnational litigation and find that they have a choice between a forum in the United States and a civil-law forum.[33a]

Comparovich: You bet your sweet life that that is so. Of course, there are many factors (including differences in substantive law and choice-of-law rules; location of witnesses; ease of enforcement; amount and recoverability of costs; and many others) which determine a

Code provide for some discovery of documents in the possession of an adverse party or of a third person; a judicial order for such discovery is enforceable by a fine (*astreinte*). Pursuant to Arts. 184 to 198, a party can be ordered to appear personally before the court, in order to answer questions. But the interrogation will be conducted by the court rather than by counsel, and will not be under oath. All of these measures of discovery, moreover, take place only if ordered by the court, which has much discretion in the matter. In this connection, it must be remembered that effective discovery in civil litigation runs counter to a French tradition of long standing. Such a tradition does not die overnight; it continues to influence the exercise of judicial discretion. See J. Beardsley, Proof of Fact in French Civil Procedure, 34 Am.J.Comp.L. 459 (1986).

Under German law, discovery is similarly restricted, and with respect to documents in the custody of the opponent or of a non-party even more restricted than in France. See the comprehensive discussion by D. J. Gerber, Extraterritorial Discovery and the Conflict of Procedural Systems: Germany and the United States, 34 Am.J. Comp.L. 745, especially at 757–67 (1986).

In general, see Millar, The Mechanism of Fact Discovery: A Study in Comparative Civil Procedure, 32 Ill.L.Rev. 261 et seq., 424 et seq. (1937); A. Homburger, Functions of Orality in Austrian and American Law, 20 Buff.L.Rev. 9, 19–32 (1970).

32a. This is due to our rules of evidence, and also to specific provisions such as FRCP Rule 32.

32b. Of course, under certain conditions his opponent sometimes may be able to introduce such depositions or documents into evidence; but again, this is by no means automatic.

33. See the articles cited in the last paragraph of n. 32, supra.

33a. American courts have taken cognizance of the relative weakness of discovery in civil-law countries. See, e.g., Pain v. United Technologies Corp., 637 F.2d 775, 789 (D.C. Cir. 1981), cert. denied 454 U.S. 1128, 102 S.Ct. 980 (1981).

Such weakness may be a factor militating against forum non conveniens dismissal of an action brought in an American court, if the allegedly more convenient alternative forum is a civil-law jurisdiction. See, e.g., Mobil Tankers Co., S.A. v. Mene Grande Oil Co., 363 F.2d 611 (3d Cir. 1966).

lawyer's choice in such a case; [33b] but my experience has been that the differences in the conduct of discovery loom larger than all the other factors. Sometimes, a plaintiff engaged in litigation in a civil-law country will go so far as to institute a second action here, without intending to bring the case to trial in our courts, but merely for the purpose of obtaining the advantage of American-style discovery.[33c]

Smooth: To come back to our case, there was a second reason for my puzzlement regarding the court's order calling for the personal appearance of H. I had always thought that in civil-law countries the parties were incompetent to testify.[34]

Comparovich: The civilians still hold to the idea that a party cannot be a "witness"; but their codes of civil procedure, at least the more modern ones, do provide for judicial examination of the parties so that they may clarify their contentions and assist the court in finding the truth. Normally, the statements made by a party in the course of such judicial examination are unsworn.

Edge: Yet, as I gathered by reading Surrogate Foley's interesting opinion in Matter of Rutherfurd's Estate,[35] a party may be put under oath in civil-law countries.

Comparovich: In order to understand the civilians' practice in this regard, one must distinguish between two groups of civil-law systems. The countries belonging to the first group, of which France and Italy are typical, have retained the archaic device described in Surrogate Foley's opinion: the decisory oath.[36] The gist of it is that a party, being

---

33b. Some of the factors determining the choice between a civil-law and a common-law forum are interestingly discussed in the Court's opinion in Piper Aircraft Co. v. Reyno, 454 U.S. 235, 102 S.Ct. 252, 263–64 (especially footn. 18) (1981), citing an earlier edition of this book.

33c. If in such a case the defendant moves to dismiss or stay the American action on forum non conveniens grounds, and the court concludes that the case could more conveniently be tried abroad, the court can relegate the plaintiff to a trial in the foreign tribunal, and yet let him have the benefit of American-style discovery. Several techniques are available to accomplish this. The court may (a) defer a ruling on the forum non conveniens motion until after discovery is completed, see Omnium Lyonnais v. Dow Chemical Co., 73 F.R.D. 114 (C.D.Cal. 1977), or (b) "dismiss subject to the condition that defendant corporations agree to provide the records relevant to the plaintiff's claims." Piper Aircraft Co. v. Reyno, supra n. 33b, at Court's footn. 25.

34. At common law—at least since the 16th century—, parties were not competent to testify as witnesses. But throughout the common-law world, this rule has been changed by statutes enacted since the middle of the 19th century.

35. 182 Misc. 1019, 46 N.Y.S.2d 871 (1944).

36. The history of the decisory oath reaches back to Roman days. See H. Silving, supra n. 25, at 1338–40; L. Wenger, Institutes of the Roman Law of Procedure 297–8 (1940).

Whether or not stemming from the same original source as the Roman decisory oath, there is a similar device in Islamic and in Jewish law. See, as to the latter, Hellman v. Wolbrom, 31 A.D.2d 477, 479, 298 N.Y.S.2d 540 (1st Dept. 1969). Concerning Islamic law, see H. J. Liebesny, Comparative Legal History: Its Role in the Analysis of Islamic and Modern Near Eastern Legal Institutions, 20 Am.J.Comp.L. 38, 46–51 (1972).

Parenthetically, it should be noted that the historical interest of the decisory oath is greater than its present-day practical significance. Insofar as Western legal systems are concerned, it appears that even where procedural codes have preserved the decisory oath, it is not frequently used.

unable to prove a disputed fact (let us call it fact X) in any other way, may "defer an oath" to his opponent, provided the truth concerning fact X can be assumed to be within the latter's personal knowledge. This is done by asking the opponent to affirm, under oath, the proposition that X is untrue.[37] The court then fixes a time and place for the taking of the oath. If the party to whom the oath has been deferred, refuses or fails to take the oath at the time and place thus fixed, the truth of fact X is deemed conclusively established. If, on the other hand, he duly takes the oath, this is treated as conclusive proof of the untruth of fact X. There is no issue of credibility for the court to determine, and judgment will be entered accordingly. If fact X, although denied by way of a decisory oath, later on should turn out to be true, the only remedy is a criminal prosecution for perjury. Even after a perjury conviction, the judgment entered upon the decisory oath cannot be set aside; but the perjurer may be sued for damages.

The legal systems of the French-Italian group also have preserved a variant of the decisory oath which is called supplemental oath. The latter is not "deferred" by a party, but authorized by the court on its own motion. The court can do this when there is some evidence tending to prove fact Y, but the evidence is not quite sufficient. In such a case the court may permit the party asserting Y to affirm his assertion by a supplemental oath. As to whether the supplemental oath has the same conclusive effect as the decisory oath, there is disagreement within the French-Italian group.

Edge: As I mentioned a minute ago, I had read a New York case that explained the institution of the decisory oath. When we were engaged in our litigation with Mr. H, it occurred to me that it might embarrass H if he were forced to affirm his mendacious allegations under oath. We, therefore, wrote to our lawyer in Ruritania and asked him to consider whether a decisory oath should be deferred to H. The lawyer answered that Ruritania had abolished the decisory oath almost half a century ago.

Comparovich: This shows that concerning the point in question Ruritania does not belong to the French-Italian group, but to the second group.

The second group consists of the German and numerous other civil-law systems which, following a pattern first developed in Austria, have abolished the decisory oath and attempted to substitute a modernized form of party examination. Adapting certain aspects of the old supplemental oath, and combining them with some features consciously borrowed from the deposition procedure developed in English Chancery practice,[38] the Austrian reformers have created a system under which

---

37. The opponent may, if he chooses, "refer" the oath back to the party who originally "deferred" it, thus asking the latter to affirm, under oath, that X is true. The further procedure, in case the oath is "referred", is the same as that about to be described in the text, except that the roles of the parties are reversed.

38. See E. J. Cohn, New Regulations in the German Code of Civil Procedure, 17 J.Comp.Leg. & Int.L. (3d ser.) 73, 79–80 (1935); Pekelis, Legal Techniques and Po-

the court has broad discretionary power to order the personal appearance of the parties and to interrogate them. No oath is administered to a party *before* he is interrogated; but *after* the interrogation of the parties the court, acting in the light of their demeanor and of all the other evidence in the record, may in its discretion give one of them an opportunity to affirm his testimony by an oath.[39] This oath is not conclusive, but subject to free evaluation of the affiant's credibility. However, since the party admitted to the oath normally will be the one whose version of the facts appeared more plausible to the court in the first place, the chances are that in practice the party oath thus administered will determine the outcome of the case.[40]

Edge: This second group of civil-law systems seems to have emerged from the Neanderthal period. But I wonder what happens if the court decides to put neither party under oath. Do the unsworn testimonial statements elicited from the parties have any effect in that event?

Comparovich: Any statement made by a party which is unfavorable to the deponent's cause, may be used as an admission. Beyond that, it is recognized that even when the interrogated party makes only self-serving statements, the effect of such statements is governed by the principle of free evaluation.[41] In evaluating the (as yet) unsworn testimony of a party, the court can choose between three possibilities: It may reject the testimony as not credible. At the other extreme, it

litical Ideologies: A Comparative Study, 41 Mich.L.Rev. 665, 679 (1943). The wheel thus turned full cycle. The chancery practice of party interrogation had in turn been borrowed from continental, Romano-Canonistic procedure. See Hickman v. Taylor, 329 U.S. 495, at 515, 67 S.Ct. 385, at 395 (1947); (concurring opinion by Jackson, J.); Ragland, Discovery Before Trial 13–16 (1932); Coing, English Equity and the Denunciatio Evangelica of the Canon Law, 71 L.Q.Rev. 223, at 237–8 (1955). See also supra pp. 286–287. In spite of these mutual influences and borrowings, however, it remains true that discovery devices in modern civil law are much weaker than in the United States. See supra at nn. 32 through 33c.

39. The court is not permitted to put both parties under oath. One of the policies underlying this system is to avoid the spectacle of conflicting partisan oaths. See H. Silving, supra n. 25, at 1532. In some countries, this policy is extended, and a similar rule of selective admission to the oath is applied, to interested witnesses.

40. In the recent past, the countries of the first group (which have retained the decisory oath) have tended to adopt a similar system of informal party interrogation, and thus in effect to superimpose that modern system on the old institution of the

decisory oath. The new French Code of Civil Procedure, for instance, treats informal party interrogation in Arts. 184 to 198, systematically remote from the provisions concerning the decisory oath, which are found in Arts. 317 to 322 (and partly in the Civil Code). As the provisions concerning informal interrogation are thus separated from those dealing with party oaths, it is not surprising to find that informal party interrogation is never under oath in a French court. Theoretically, it would seem that a French court has the same power as a German court: to end the informal interrogation of the parties by permitting one of them to affirm his version of the facts by an oath. Under French law, this result could be accomplished by first informally interrogating the parties under Arts. 184 ff., and then administering a "supplemental oath" to one of them pursuant to Arts. 317 ff. But it appears that French courts in practice hardly ever make use of this possibility; the reason probably is that they do not view the old supplemental oath and the new system of informal party interrogation as parts of an integrated whole.

41. The German Code of Civil Procedure is explicit on this point. See § 453. Art. 198 of the new French Code of Civil Procedure is similar in its effect.

may credit the testimony even though it is and remains unsworn; in this case, there is no need for an oath.[42] Or, as an in-between solution, the court may proceed, as I indicated a moment ago, to put the party under oath. This last alternative will recommend itself when the court is not sufficiently convinced by the unsworn testimony, but feels that the testimony should be believed if reaffirmed under oath.[43]

Smooth: I am beginning to understand the civilians' methods of examining parties.[43a] Yet, there is another point that puzzles me in connection with the court's order directing the examination of H. Doesn't the civil law require a writing for every contract involving more than a trifling sum?

Comparovich (taking a book out of his briefcase): I suppose you are referring to Arts. 1341 ff. of the French Civil Code, which read as follows:

FRENCH CIVIL CODE

Art. 1341 (as amended in 1980). It is necessary to execute an instrument drawn up in the presence of notaries or made under private signature in all matters exceeding a sum or value fixed by Decree [presently 5,000 French Francs, equivalent to appr. $800],[a] even for voluntary bailments, and no proof by witnesses against or outside of the contents of an instrument, nor as to what is alleged to have been said previously, at the time of or since it was drawn up shall be allowed, even if the sum or value involved is less:[b]

---

42. Normally there will be corroborating evidence in the record. Cases in which the court is asked to rely solely on the uncorroborated testimony of a party, are relatively rare in civil-law courts, where the absence of exclusionary rules usually makes it possible to adduce some other evidence.

43. See, e.g., German Code of Civil Procedure § 452. Concerning French law, see supra n. 40.

43a. These civilian methods—in theory always based on the notion that a party or party representative cannot be a "witness"—also tend to influence the practice of international arbitration tribunals, whenever the arbitrators, or a majority of them, have been brought up in the civil law. See, e.g., M. Straus, The Practice of the Iran-U.S. Claims Tribunal in Receiving Evidence from Parties and from Experts, 3 J.Int.Arbitration 57 (1986).

a. The amount of 5,000 Francs has been fixed by Decree No. 80–533 of July 15, 1980. Prior to the 1980 amendment of Art. 1341, the amount was fixed in the Code itself (at 50 Francs).

b. Subject to special provisions requiring notarial form for certain types of transactions (see supra p. 18), Art. 1341 gives the parties a choice between the rather solemn and expensive form of a notarial document and a simple private writing. But note that the latter has to be signed. Thus an illiterate party may be able to satisfy the requirement of Art. 1341 only by availing himself of the services of a notary. In 1804, when the Code was enacted, this strict form requirement probably was thought to provide proper and needed protection for illiterate parties.

Today, the problem of illiteracy is no longer a significant one in France; but it plays an important role in developing countries, many of which have a legal system based on, or modeled after, the French codes. Some of them have found it necessary to modify the requirement of notarial form for the transactions of illiterates, because notarial services are not easily available in their rural areas. See, e.g., Farnsworth, Law Reform in a Developing Country: A New Code of Obligations for Senegal, 8 J.Afr.L. 6 (1964).

All of which is without prejudice to what is specified in the laws relating to commerce.[c]

Art. 1346. All actions whatever, which are not entirely substantiated by writings, shall be joined in the same proceedings; after which the other actions which are not substantiated by written proofs shall not be maintainable.[d]

Art. 1347. The above rules are subject to exceptions, when there is a commencement of written proof.

This term includes any written instrument which emanates from the person against whom the action is brought, or from the person he represents, and which tends to make the alleged fact probable.

Declarations made by a party at the time of his personal appearance in court [informal interrogation], his refusal to answer or his failure to appear [for interrogation by the court] may be considered by the court as the equivalent of commencement of written proof. [This paragraph was added by Law No. 75–596 of July 9, 1975, by way of implementing the relatively recent introduction of informal party interrogation into French civil procedure.]

Art. 1348 (as amended in 1980). The above rules are subject to further exceptions when the obligation arises from a quasi-contract or from a delict or quasi-delict (tort), or when it was physically or morally impossible for a party to obtain documentary proof of a jural act, or when a party has lost the documentary evidence as a result of an accident or of vis major.[e] . . .

Comparovich (continuing): If the Ruritanian code contained similar provisions, the court would have been faced with an interesting conflict of laws question.[44]

c. The Code de commerce permits oral testimony for the proof of commercial transactions. Art. 1341 thus applies only to "civil" but not to "commercial" transactions. This illustrates the importance of the distinction, which will be discussed infra pp. 590–596.

d. The purpose of this somewhat cryptic provision is to prevent the splitting of one action for more than 5,000 Francs into a number of successive actions, each involving less than that sum. Most civil-law countries have no *general* rule against the splitting of causes of action. Therefore, a special rule against the splitting of actions based on *oral contracts* is necessary to prevent evasion of Art. 1341. Other conceivable methods of evading Art. 1341 are outlawed by Arts. 1342 to 1345.

e. The former version of Art. 1348, which in essence was not very different from the present one, was interestingly discussed in Lenn v. Riche, 331 Mass. 104, 117 N.E.2d 129 (1954).

44. The French courts in a celebrated case enforced an oral contract made in England which, had it been made in France, would have come under Art. 1341. See Benton c. Horeau, decided by the French Cour de Cassation on August 24, 1880, Dalloz 1880. 1. 447, discussed by Judge Coleman in Mandelbaum v. Silberfeld, 77 N.Y.S.2d 465, 469 (City Ct. 1944), and by Lorenzen, The Statute of Frauds and the Conflict of Laws, 32 Yale L.J. 311, 318–20 (1923).

Concerning the converse question, whether an oral contract made in France may be enforced in a jurisdiction which does not have a statute of frauds similar to Art. 1341, compare Mandelbaum v. Silberfeld, supra, with the German case discussed by Moses, International Legal Practice, 4 Ford.L.Rev. 244, 259–60 (1935). A more recent German decision, BGH July 30, 1954, 10 Juristenzeitung 702 (1955, with Annotation by Gamillscheg), 45 Revue Critique de Droit International Privé 58 (1956, with Annotation by Mezger) arrives at the same result as the Mandelbaum case: that the French proof requirement is "procedural".

Similarly, in a recent case involving a contract made in Brazil, a federal court sitting in New York and applying New York choice-of-law rules declined to apply a Brazilian code provision modeled after Art. 1341 of the French Civil Code. See

Edge: Even assuming that Ruritania had copied Arts. 1341 ff. of the French Code, and further assuming that the Ruritanian court would apply these provisions to a contract made and performable in the United States, this might not have helped us. After all, the correspondence showed that there were serious negotiations looking toward a contract. Didn't this constitute "a commencement of written proof" within the meaning of Art. 1347?

Comparovich: Perhaps. Whether the correspondence "makes the alleged fact probable" within the meaning of that article, is a question of fact.[45] However, all this is purely academic, because Ruritania has not adopted any general restriction on oral proof of contracts involving more than a certain amount.[46] Of course, Ruritania, like all civil-law countries, subjects certain *types* of transactions to the requirement of a simple writing or of a notarial document; but it does not have a sweeping, *general* rule comparable to Art. 1341.

Smooth: The interlocutory order further provided that Mr. Edge and I should testify concerning our conversation with H.

Comparovich: Aren't you officers of the defendant corporation?

Smooth: I am a Vice-President; but Mr. Edge is not a corporate officer. I suppose this was the reason why the order designated only Mr. Edge as a witness; with respect to me, it directed that "defendant corporation appear personally by its legal representative, Mr. Malcolm Smooth", and be examined in the same manner as the plaintiff.

Comparovich: This is merely a logical application of the civilian view that the two concepts, "party" and "witness", are mutually exclusive.[47] Was your testimony taken here, by way of letters rogatory? [48]

Smooth: No. We did not object to being examined in Ruritania, because we had some other business to which we had to attend in that part of the world.

Edge: What struck us, however, was that under the terms of the interlocutory order the examination of Mr. Smooth and myself was to take place, not in the presence of the whole three-judge court, but before a single member of that court. *Noted*

Kristinus v. H. Stern Com. E Ind. S.A., 463 F.Supp. 1263 (S.D.N.Y. 1979).

45. See Planiol-Ripert, Treatise on the Civil Law (11th ed. 1939), Translation by the Louisiana State Law Institute, Vol. 2, Part 1, Sec. 1124 (1959).

46. Such general restrictions exist mainly in countries where French influence is predominant. They do not exist, e.g., in Germany, Switzerland and Austria. The Italian Civil Code of 1942 (Art. 2721), while in principle adhering to the French rule, granted the court discretionary power to admit testimonial evidence of contracts, "having regard to the character of the par-ties, the nature of the contract and any other circumstances."

For an interesting comparative discussion of form requirements, see J. M. Perillo, The Statute of Frauds in the Light of the Functions and Dysfunctions of Form, 43 Fordh.L.Rev. 39 (1974).

47. Under our law, a party may be a witness; but the testimony of a party, or of an officer of a corporate party, is in some respects treated differently from the testimony of other witnesses. See, e.g., FRCP Rule 32(a).

48. Cf. 28 U.S.C.A. § 1782, as amended in 1964.

Comparovich: Such is the practice in many civil-law countries.[49]

Smooth: That means that factual issues ultimately must be decided by three judges, only one of whom has seen and heard the witnesses.

Comparovich: Quite so. This is the feature of present-day continental procedure which has been most strenuously criticized.[50] It violates the "principle of immediacy" advocated by most leading scholars, and especially by Franz Klein, the famous Austrian proceduralist of the late 19th century.[51] On the other hand, there is a practical problem of economy and of limited judicial manpower, even though in most civil-law countries the number of judges is greater than here.

Edge: When we travelled to Ruritania, we looked forward to being confronted with H, and to seeing him squirm under vigorous cross-examination.

Comparovich: I am sure you were disappointed. There is nothing in the civilian codes that compels the court, or the single judge conducting an interrogation, to hear all of the witnesses (or parties) at the same time.

Edge: We found that out. As H had a professional engagement on the day set for our examination, the judge interrogated us but adjourned H's examination to a date two weeks later.

As to cross-examination, we learned that it does not exist. All the questioning is done by the judge, who starts by telling you the general subject of the examination, and then asks you to give your story in your own words. After you have responded to that, he may ask some specific questions. Further questions might be suggested by counsel; but it is the judge who asks these questions, and not necessarily in the form proposed by the attorneys.[51a]

---

49. See H. Nagel, Die Grundzüge des Beweisrechts im europäischen Zivilprozess 62–66 (1967).

In some civil-law countries, the single judge charged with preparing the case for the court's final decision has power to issue as well as to execute the interlocutory orders for the taking of proof. Once the case is ripe for a final decision, however, it goes back to the full three-judge chamber. This, at least, is the practice prevailing in most civil-law countries, and in some of them it is required that there be a final hearing before the full chamber. Concerning the more radical innovation recently adopted in Germany, which makes it possible to transfer a case to a single member of the chamber for proof-taking *and final determination*, see supra p. 374.

50. See, e.g., 1 Cappelletti, La testimonianza della parte nel sistema dell'oralitá 149 ff. (1962).

51. See Lenhoff, The Law of Evidence: A Comparative Study Based Essentially on Austrian and New York Law, 3 Am.J. Comp.L. 313, 318 (1954).

Our law furnishes many comparable examples of procedural arrangements under which issues of fact may be determined by a judge who has never personally seen or heard the witnesses. See, e.g., FRCP Rule 53(c). Due Process attacks on such arrangements, which in civil-law parlance violate the "principle of immediacy", have been rejected. See Razatos v. The Colorado Supreme Court, 549 F.Supp. 798 (D. Colo. 1982), and cases there cited.

51a. Concerning the method of examining witnesses, the contrast between civil-law and common-law attitudes is very pronounced. How totally opposed the common-law tradition is to the civil-law practice of judicial interrogation of witnesses, is neatly illustrated by the English case of Ali v. London Spinning Co., Ltd., a decision of the Court of Appeal handed down April 29, 1971, reported in The Times of April 30, 1971, p. 9. Their Lordships reversed

Comparovich: In some civil-law countries, the court may permit counsel to address direct questions to the witnesses, usually after interrogation by the court;[52] but anything approaching a real cross-examination is rare in civil-law countries,[53] partly because the lawyers do not master the technique, and partly because of the overriding position of the judge, who may even order an adjournment if a witness declares himself unable to answer a question right away.[54]

Smooth: I think their system is an invitation to mendacity.

Comparovich: Civilians, on the other hand, sometimes argue that the spontaneous narrative of an uncoached [55] witness is preferable to an artificial and (so far as direct examination is concerned) often pre-arranged series of questions put by counsel.[56]

Smooth: This argument leaves me cold.

Comparovich: Personally, and speaking on the basis of practical experience under both systems, I share your belief that our method of examining witnesses results in a more vigorous and, as a rule, a more effective search for truth.[57] But the point is highly controversial; and even the admirers of our method must recognize that the common-law system of examination by counsel contributes to the inordinate expensiveness of litigation in this country and in England,[58] a condition

the decision of the trial judge on the ground that he had too actively participated in the questioning of witnesses. The appellate court noted, in a most critical vein, that the judge had asked 334 questions—more than both counsel had asked. American appellate courts, while equally critical of trial judges who usurp the role of counsel, do not treat such usurpation as reversible error unless the trial judge acted in an unfair or biased way, or his conduct had the effect of conveying to the jury that he had reached certain conclusions concerning issues of fact. See People v. Rigney, 55 Cal.2d 236, 10 Cal.Rptr. 625, 359 P.2d 23, 98 A.L.R.2d 186 (1961); (op. by Traynor, J.); Ratton v. Busby, 230 Ark. 667, 326 S.W.2d 889, 76 A.L.R.2d 751 (1959); Anno., 6 A.L.R.4th 951 (1981).

52. In Germany, such permission must be granted upon counsel's express demand. Code of Civil Procedure, § 397.

53. The situation is different in Sweden. See Ginsburg and Bruzelius, Civil Procedure in Sweden 288 (1965).

54. In most civil-law countries, moreover, the witness' testimony is not taken down verbatim, but the judge dictates his own résumé of the testimony to the clerk. Thus, only the résumé becomes part of the record.

This practice has not escaped criticism. There may be some danger that in formulating the summary of the testimony given

by the witness, the judge will—unwittingly or otherwise—alter its meaning. See W. G. Weyrauch, Zum Gesellschaftsbild des Juristen 253–57 (1970).

55. See supra at n. 19.

56. See, e.g., Hartung, Einführung des englisch-amerikanischen Strafverfahrensrechts in Deutschland?, 5 N.J.W. 201 (1952).

The debate between protagonists of the common-law method and their civilian counterparts raises the question whether and how the relative merits of the adversary and the inquisitorial method of examining witnesses can be determined by scientific tests employing some of the techniques of experimental psychology. For a discussion of this question (focused mainly on criminal proceedings), see M. Damaska, Presentation of Evidence and Fact-Finding Precision, 123 U.Pa.L.Rev. 1083 (1975).

57. The remark in the text is limited to civil proceedings. In a criminal case, where the presiding judge of a civil-law court, in interrogating the defendant and the witnesses, has the benefit of a thorough official investigation conducted prior to the trial, the situation is quite different. See infra pp. 477–478.

58. Amos, A Day in Court at Home and Abroad, 2 Camb.L.J. 340, 348–9 (1926): "A foreigner would be likely to say that in the

which is further aggravated by the fact that in so many cases we go over the same ground twice, first in pre-trial examinations and then again at the trial.

Edge: Apart from the merits and demerits of the two systems, it seems to me that the differences between civil-law and common-law methods of examining witnesses may lead to practical problems in litigation pending before our own courts. If in such a case the deposition of a witness has been taken in a civil-law country and in accordance with civil-law methods, the question may arise whether such deposition will be admissible at the trial.[59]

Comparovich: For the federal courts, this troublesome question has been largely resolved by the last sentence of FRCP Rule 28(b), as amended in 1963.[60] But in state courts (except in states that have adopted the Uniform Interstate and International Procedure Act)[61] the answer may be more doubtful.[62]

Edge: It is interesting, also, to consider the converse situation. What if the Ruritanian court, in an action pending there, addresses a letter rogatory to an American court, requesting that the testimony of a witness residing here be taken in accordance with Ruritanian methods of interrogation?

Comparovich: The U.S. District Courts are expressly authorized to comply with such a request.[63] Thus it may happen that in a case of this kind the civil-law methods of interrogation are practiced in an American courtroom.[64]

Smooth: Gentlemen, let us come back to our case. The examination of Mr. Edge and of myself, and two weeks later the examination of H, produced no surprises. Each side stuck to its guns. After these

---

pursuit of technical perfection we have thrown too great a share of the task of bringing out the truth upon the parties themselves or their professional advisers and representatives. The day in court puts a great premium upon forensic skill; and its necessary corollary, an adequate system of preparation, makes considerable demands upon the judgment and experience of solicitors and counsel . . .".

59. See H. Smit, International Aspects of Federal Court Procedure, 61 Colum.L. Rev. 1031, 1058–59 (1961).

The difficulties mentioned in the text, supra, may be even more severe in criminal cases. See United States v. Hay, 376 F.Supp. 264 (D.Colo. 1974), aff'd 527 F.2d 990 (10 Cir. 1975), cert. denied 425 U.S. 935, 96 S.Ct. 1666 (1976).

60. "Evidence obtained in response to a letter rogatory need not be excluded merely for the reason that it is not a verbatim transcript or that the testimony was not taken under oath or for any similar departure from the requirements for depositions taken within the United States under these rules." See also the Advisory Committee's Note accompanying the 1963 amendments of Rule 28(b).

61. Sec. 3.01, subs. (b) of that Act contains the same language as the part of the federal Rule quoted in n. 60 supra.

62. See, e.g., 3 Weinstein, Korn & Miller, New York Civil Practice ¶3108.08 (Loose-Leaf ed.); Note, Obtaining Testimony Outside the United States: Problem for the California Practitioner, 29 Hast.L.J. 1237, 1250 (1978).

63. 28 U.S.C.A. § 1782, as amended in 1964. See also the discussion of the Evidence Convention, infra pp. 443–448.

64. In practice, this task is apt to be performed by a magistrate rather than a district judge. See 28 U.S.C.A. § 636(b), as amended in 1976.

hearings, L asked us whether we had any further evidence to offer. This amazed me. I thought the trial was over.

Comparovich: As I said before, there is no such thing as a "trial" in continental civil procedure. Unless the court suspects you of dilatory tactics, you may always offer new evidence after some evidence has been taken. Sometimes, it is only through the examination of one witness that a new witness is discovered, or a new field of inquiry is opened up.

Smooth: Is this not a piecemeal method of trying cases?

Comparovich: Indeed it is. But such a method has certain advantages. The testimony of a witness can always take an unexpected turn.[64a] In that event, the piecemeal system gives the parties a chance to study such testimony, to conduct new investigations, and then, in the light of such investigations (and of what the witness has said), to make further offers of proof.

Edge: Under our system, a similar function is served by discovery, which lets the parties take an advance look at what the witness is likely to say at the trial.

Comparovich: True—but note that our system is more wasteful, in that almost every witness has to testify twice, first by way of pretrial examination and a second time at the trial. Under the civil-law system, each witness normally testifies only once. The possibility exists that if and when the case is tried *de novo* before the intermediate appellate court,[64b] the same witness will be interrogated again; but in practice this is rare. Through the piecemeal system, the civilians thus manage (a) as a rule, to interrogate each witness only once, but (b) nevertheless to afford the parties an opportunity to meet the witness' (perhaps unexpected, and possibly untruthful) testimony by suitable counter-evidence.

The critics of the piecemeal system tend to emphasize its potential for delay. The efficiency with which a case is steered through a smaller or larger number of successive hearings, varies not only from country to country, but even within a single country from one locality to another. Much depends on the personality of the presiding judge.

One particularly efficient German judge, sitting at Stuttgart, in the late 1960s and early 1970s persuaded his local colleagues to experiment with a novel calendar practice which has become known as the "Stuttgart Model." In 2 E. J. Cohn, Manual of German Law 201–02 (2d ed. 1971), the essence of this experiment is described as follows: "[Upon receipt of the complaint and the answer] the court deliberates on the measures to be taken in preparation for the trial. These may consist in demanding from the parties supplementation of the factual allegations

---

64a. The danger of such surprise developments is, of course, enhanced by the civilian rules and practices discouraging lawyers from interviewing witnesses in advance. See supra, text at n. 19.

64b. See the discussion of appeals, infra.

Stuttgart Model

contained in the pleadings, outlining the court's prima facie attitude to the legal problems involved and inviting comments thereon, requiring the submission of documents, etc. When the parties have complied with this order the case is set down for an oral hearing to which the personal appearance of the parties and all witnesses whose testimony appears relevant is ordered. At the oral hearing, which—in complete distinction from the habits of most German courts—is conceived as the one and only hearing, the court discusses the matter with the attorneys and parties and then examines the witnesses, after complying with the rules of the Code by making the prescribed 'order for evidence.'" When the taking of evidence is completed, the court retires and deliberates, and then announces its tentative conclusions to the parties and their counsel. This is followed by the final arguments of counsel—arguments which of course will be focused on the points revealed as crucial by the court's previous statement of its tentative conclusions. The final decision of the court is rendered within a week after the hearing.[64c]

This experimental system was tried out not only at Stuttgart, but in some other localities as well. It is claimed that on average about 85–90% of civil proceedings employing the Stuttgart Model were disposed of—whether by settlement or judgment—in one hearing. Thus the use of the piecemeal method remained necessary only in 10 to 15% of the cases (probably the more complicated ones).

Smooth: In this way there is a real "trial", in our sense of the term, in the majority of cases. Sounds like a good idea to me.

Comparovich: The German legislators were of the same opinion. In 1976, after the Stuttgart Model experiment had gone on for almost 10 years, a statute was passed which strongly encourages all German courts to adopt some of the Stuttgart Model practices.[64d] The key provision of this important statutory reform is Section 272 of the Code of Civil Procedure, which, as amended by the 1976 statute, now postulates that "As a rule, the case should be disposed of in a single, comprehensively prepared oral hearing (trial)." [64e]

The words "as a rule," which qualify the mandate of Section 272, still vest much discretion in the presiding judge of each court. Judges accustomed to the formerly prevailing system of piecemeal prooftaking in successive hearings sometimes use that discretionary power to "fall

---

64c. For a comprehensive description and discussion of the Stuttgart Model experiment, by the judge who initiated it, see R. Bender, The Stuttgart Model, in Vol. II, Book 2, of M. Cappelletti (Gen.Ed.), Access to Justice, at pp. 431–75 (1979).

64d. The statute, called "Simplification Amendment" of the Code of Civil Procedure (BGBl 1976 I 3281), went into effect on July 1, 1977. For comprehensive descriptions of the reformed procedure see P. Gottwald, Simplified Civil Procedure in West Germany, 31 Am.J.Comp.L. 687 (1983), and W. B. Fisch, Recent Developments in West German Civil Procedure, 6 Hastings Int. & Comp.L.Rev. 221 (1983).

64e. It is interesting to observe that until the 1976 amendment the term "trial" (in German: *Haupttermin* or *Hauptverhandlung*) had been used by the German legislator only in the Code of Criminal Procedure, but not at all in the Code of Civil Procedure.

back into the old trot." [64f] On the whole, however, it appears that the 1976 reform has had a measure of success in expediting civil litigation.[64g]

Smooth: Assuming that the majority of German courts attempt to comply with Section 272 and to dispose of a large percentage of their cases in a single trial, how do they implement the mandate of that provision that such trial must be "comprehensively prepared"?

Comparovich: The court does not conduct an ex officio investigation. It is a basic principle of civil procedure, in Germany as well as in other countries of the civil-law as well as the common-law world, that the parties—and not the court—determine the parameters of the litigation by their allegations. Equally fundamental, though subject to some limited exceptions,[64h] is the further principle that the court, in determining what evidence should be heard, is limited to such evidence as has been offered by the parties. These basic principles have not been altered by the German reform of 1976. Thus, in directing the court to "prepare" the trial, the draftsmen of Section 272 were principally interested in making sure that well before the date of the trial the court will elicit all the proper allegations and offers of proof *from the parties.*

Edge: This fits in with the issue-clarifying functions and duties of a German court, which we touched upon a few minutes ago in discussing Section 139 of the Code (see supra, text at ns. 10–10g).

Comparovich: You are absolutely right.

Smooth: It seems clear from what you have told us that the German Code requires the court, before trial, to exchange communications—probably repeated communications—with the parties or their lawyers. Is this done in writing or by way of a preliminary hearing?

Comparovich: In the discretion of the presiding judge, either method may be used.

Regardless of which method of communicating is chosen, the real problem is to force the parties, and especially the defendant, to submit all their allegations and offers of proof so speedily that the decisive hearing (which is now called a trial) can be held within a few months after the filing of the complaint, and that no further subsequent hearings will be necessary. Addressing this problem, the Code authorizes the court to fix deadlines for the submission of allegations and offers of proof. If a party delays the proceeding by failing to meet such a deadline, the sanction is drastic: a belatedly submitted allegation or

---

64f. Baumbach - Lauterbach - Albers-Hartmann, Zivilprozessordnung, Anno. 4 preceding § 272 (45th ed., 1987).

64g. See Gottwald, supra n. 64d, at 700.

64h. Pursuant to § 273 of the German Code of Civil Procedure, the court may ex officio procure certain types of evidence. For instance, the court may obtain public records, order the personal appearance of the parties, and appoint experts—all this without waiting for any offer of proof coming from the parties. Note, however, that the court cannot ex officio subpoena non-expert witnesses who have not been named by the parties.

offer of proof will be rejected, unless the lateness is "sufficiently excused." [64j] Moreover, even if no deadline has been set, the parties are under a duty to submit all their allegations and offers of proof expeditiously, and if a party causes delay by violating that duty in a grossly negligent manner, such party will be hit by the same drastic sanction: preclusion of the assertions dilatorily presented.

Smooth: Do the German courts make frequent use of this formidable power to preclude?

Comparovich: An affirmative answer to your question seems to be indicated by the large number of reported cases involving such preclusion.

Edge: This large number of reported cases also reveals something else: that judges and lawyers spend much of their time on fights over the preclusion issue rather than on the resolution of the parties' substantive disputes.[64k]

Comparovich: Good point. You have put your finger on the neuralgic spot of the 1976 reform. Nevertheless, as I have mentioned already, the reform has succeeded in reducing the average duration of lawsuits. Although some judges have been criticized as "hyper-active" and "hyper-speedy",[64m] the majority of observers seem to feel that the reform has expedited the litigation process without unduly sacrificing substantive justice.[64n] In any event, there is no doubt that the Stuttgart Model and the subsequent German reform legislation have injected some new ideas into the traditional civilian approach to the handling of civil litigation.

Smooth: Some of those new ideas may deserve being studied even in non-civilian countries struggling with the—apparently worldwide— phenomenon referred to as the litigation explosion.

Edge: Have other countries taken notice of this bold German experiment?

Comparovich: As comparative legal studies are on the increase everywhere, I have no doubt that reformers and legislators in other civil-law countries will pay some attention to these German develop-

64j. German Code of Civil Procedure, § 296. For a more detailed description of the German courts' power to preclude belated or dilatory assertions of the parties, see Fisch, supra n. 64d, at 243–54.

64k. The intensity and duration of squabbles over preclusion of allegedly belated submissions are enhanced by the fact that an unjustified order of preclusion violates not only the Code of Civil Procedure, but at least in the more serious instances also violates the precluded party's constitutional (due process) rights. Frequently, therefore, such squabbles go through two successive appeals in the hierarchy of ordinary courts, and in addition have to be dealt with by the—already overburdened— Constitutional Court. See the interesting decision of the Constitutional Court dated April 14, 1987, reported in 40 NJW 2003 (1987), where references to many of the earlier decisions in point can be found.

64m. See H.-J. Birk, Wer führt den Zivilprozess—der Anwalt oder der Richter?, 38 NJW 1489 (1985).

64n. See the articles by Gottwald and Fisch, supra n. 64d, and (with some reservations) Baumbach-Lauterbach-Albers-Hartmann, supra n. 64f, where further references can be found.

ments. At the present time, however, the piecemeal system still prevails in most civil-law countries.

Smooth: How does a lawsuit ever end under that system?

Comparovich: Evidence which could and should have been offered in the first round may be rejected if offered later on. Hence, the later offers ordinarily deal with new points suggested by the evidence previously taken, or by colloquy between court and counsel. After two or three rounds of this, new points are not likely to arise any more. In this connection you must remember, also, that at every stage of the proceeding the court (or the single judge) has taken an active part in clarifying the issues and in asking the parties to offer evidence on the points regarded as crucial.[65] Although ordinarily it is for the parties to allege and prove the facts, there are certain types of evidence, especially expert opinions, which the court may even obtain on its own motion.[66]

noted

Smooth: This is what happened in our case. After H and we had been interrogated, a new interlocutory order was entered, advising the parties that the court would ask the Ruritanian Institute of Comparative Law [67] for an opinion on the following question: "Assuming H was retained by the defendant for legal work in connection with the reorganization of defendant's Ruritanian subsidiary, and assuming further that the question of H's compensation is governed by American law, what statutory tariff or other rule would determine the amount of such compensation?" [68]

Comparovich: This method chosen by the court for informing itself on a point of foreign law is not the only one used in civil-law countries; [69] but where it is available (as, e.g., in Germany), the courts usually prefer it to all other methods.[70]

Edge: It worked all right in our case. After about a month the Institute rendered its opinion, saying that in dealing with "American" contract law it is necessary to consult state law rather than federal law;

---

65. During the last half-century, most civil-law countries have amended their procedure codes so as to strengthen the power of the court (or the single judge) to speed up the litigation. To what extent these reforms have been successful, is a matter of considerable debate. For comparative discussions, see W. J. Habscheid, Richtermacht oder Parteifreiheit, 81 ZZP 175 (1968); J. Jacob, Accelerating the Process of Law, in M. Storme & H. Casman (Eds.), Towards a Justice with a Human Face 303 ff. (1978).

66. For references see Habscheid, supra n. 65, at 176. See also supra n. 64h.

67. See supra p. 225.

68. Note that H had predicated his complaint exclusively on Ruritanian law, and had not pleaded any foreign law. Nev-

ertheless, the duty of the court to ascertain the applicable rule of foreign law (see supra p. 225) came into existence when the court concluded that foreign ("American") law governed the retainer.

69. See supra pp. 224 ff.

70. Perhaps it is not an accident that use of an academic Institute as an expert is particularly widespread in Germany, where the practice of *Aktenversendung* (i.e., the judicial practice of asking the law faculty of a University for advice on how to decide a pending case, see supra pp. 158–159) retained its great practical importance well into the 19th century. See I. Zajtay, Le traitement du droit étranger dans le procès civil, 1968 Rivista di Diritto Internazionale Privato e Processuale 233, 253.

that under applicable state law there is no tariff; and that in the absence of express agreement the attorney is entitled to a "fair and reasonable" fee. They added that in the United States the question of what is "fair and reasonable" would be determined by a jury, and that in any event it was not a question of law. They refused, therefore, to express an opinion on the amount of the fee, and suggested that such amount be determined by an expert familiar with the actual practice in the United States.

Comparovich: This sounds like a sensible opinion.

Smooth: We thought so too. We informed L that we had hired the President of our local Bar Association to testify as our expert; but L wrote back that the court would appoint somebody from its permanent official list of experts.

Comparovich: This is the general practice in civil-law countries.[71] Who was appointed as expert?

Smooth: It turned out that no expert on American fees was on their permanent list. Therefore, the court wrote to the Ruritanian Bar Association, and on the latter's recommendation the court appointed as expert an elderly, retired lawyer from Cleveland who had settled down in sunny Ruritania.

Comparovich: Theoretically, you could have offered the testimony of your own expert in addition to that of the official expert; but as a practical matter, the court usually follows the opinion of the official expert.[71a]

Smooth: This is one feature of their system that I admire. It avoids the battle of partisan experts which has become such a sorry part of our practice.

Comparovich: Your enthusiasm for the official expert is shared by many eminent scholars and reformers in this country,[72] including some of my best friends; but lawyers who have practiced under the continen-

---

71. For a comparative survey—principally of French, German, Italian, British and American procedures employed in presenting expert testimony—see G. M. White, The Use of Experts by International Tribunals 15–33 (1965), reviewed by S. B. Jacoby in 26 Fed.Bar J. 255 (1966).

In some of the continental countries the expert may, in effect, have the status of an auxiliary officer of the court. He may have the power to conduct certain investigations, and even to examine witnesses. See, e.g., Arts. 242, 243, 266, 268, 275, 278 and 279 of the new French Code of Civil Procedure. See also E. J. Cohn, The Rules of Arbitration of the UN Economic Commission for Europe, 16 Int. & Comp.L.Q. 946, at 968 (1967), where further references can be found.

71a. In Germany, empirical studies have shown that the court-appointed ex-

pert's view is followed by the court in 95% of the cases. See the penetrating article by H. Sendler, Richter und Sachverständige, 39 NJW 2907 (especially at 2909) (1986), where this heavy judicial dependence on the official expert is critically discussed.

72. The efforts of those who favor the official expert, and the inroads which these efforts have made upon our traditional practice, are interestingly discussed in the Advisory Committee's Note accompanying Rule 706 of the Federal Rules of Evidence, where further references can be found. For a discussion of English and American practice with respect to court-appointed experts, see J. Basten, The Court Expert in Civil Trials—A Comparative Appraisal, 40 Mod.L.Rev. 174 (1977). See also supra pp. 221 ff.

tal system, are apt to be more skeptical. The official expert may owe his appointment to "connections"; [73] he may be incompetent, or worse.[74] Nevertheless, his opinion is almost invariably followed by the court.[75] The effect of his incompetence or corruption is even more deleterious than that of similar weaknesses on the part of a judge, who under the civil-law system (if the case is heard by a court of general jurisdiction) is only one of three members of a panel. Moreover, judicial error can be corrected on appeal, while the expert's erroneous or corrupt opinion will poison the record in the appellate as well as in the lower court.

Smooth: I shall have to give this matter additional thought. In our case, however, the continental system worked well. The expert testified [76] that $950 would be a fair and reasonable fee for the work which H alleged to have done.

Edge: Notice the subtle humor? That was exactly 1% of what H demanded.

J. DISCOVERY AND GATHERING OF EVIDENCE ABROAD (A FURTHER LOOK AT "INTERNATIONAL JUDICIAL COOPERATION")

Comparovich: In our brief survey of the civilians' approach to the gathering and production of evidence in a lawsuit, we have found that their approach is basically different from ours. While we regard the entire pre-decision course of a lawsuit, including the collection and presentation of evidence, as an essentially private matter to be handled by the parties and their attorneys, the civil-law tradition has stamped the word "official" on these matters, with the result that—although offers of proof ordinarily have to come from the parties—the process of proof-taking is dominated by the court. As I have mentioned before (see supra, text at ns. 59–64), this basic difference between civil-law and

---

73. See Ploscowe, The Expert Witness in Criminal Cases in France, Germany and Italy, 2 Law & Contemp.Prob. 504, 508–9 (1935).

74. See, e.g., Jacobson v. Frachon, 138 L.T.R., N.S., 386 (C.A.1927).

Although listed in the official roster of experts, a particular individual will obtain actual judicial appointments only occasionally. The bulk of his income will have to come from other sources. Thus it is only natural that most of the "official" experts are persons engaged in some kind of private business or profession. By establishing business or professional contacts with the expert (contacts which of course are technically unconnected with the case at hand), unscrupulous litigants frequently attempt subtly to corrupt the impartiality of the "official" expert.

Practitioners in civil-law countries are well aware of these dangers. See E. Pause, Der "unabhängige" Sachverständige, 38 NJW 2576, 2577 (1985).

75. See supra n. 71a. See also Hammelmann, Expert Evidence, 10 Mod.L.Rev. 32, 38 (1947), with reference to French practice.

76. In most civil-law countries the expert, instead of being examined orally, will (or at least may) be asked by the court to render a written report; but in some jurisdictions the rule prevails that after the report has been filed, upon the demand of either party, the expert must be examined in open court, so that he can be questioned on specific points. In Germany, for instance, the Bundesgerichtshof has consistently imposed this rule on the lower courts. See E. Ankermann, Das Recht auf mündliche Befragung des Sachverständigen: Keine Wende, 38 NJW 1204 (1985).

Mentioned issue

common-law attitudes can lead to thorny problems in the many situations where an action is brought in one country but an item of evidence to be used in that action is located in another country. If in such a case one of the two countries is a civil-law jurisdiction, while the other belongs to the common-law orbit, very difficult problems are apt to arise.

I suggest that, in order to deal with these problems, we digress for a few minutes from your case against Mr. H.

Smooth: That is agreeable. We frequently face problems of this kind, especially when, for purposes of litigation in this country, we try to obtain evidence that is located abroad.

Example: A number of years ago, we needed the testimony of witnesses A and B in a case that was litigated here. Both A and B lived in civil-law country X. When we tried, in accordance with our procedure, to obtain a commission for the taking of the witnesses' depositions in X, we were told that X does not permit such a procedure, and that nobody except a judge duly appointed in X may examine a witness within the territory of that country.[77]

Comparovich: This rule, which prevails in the majority of civil-law countries, is the logical outgrowth of their fundamental notion that the taking of evidence in a lawsuit is not a private matter, but a function of the state, i.e., a function that may be performed only by judges or other officials deriving their authority from the local sovereign.

Edge: Is this not an archaic notion unworthy of the 20th century?

Comparovich: Even today, policy arguments can be adduced in support of that notion. Where judges rather than aggressive party representatives are in charge of evidence-taking, the privacy and other interests of witnesses are apt to be better protected.

Of course, from the standpoint of the litigants, the civil-law approach has its drawbacks, because it forces them to use the more cumbersome and often more expensive method of letters rogatory, i.e., of a request directed to a court in X, when a witness residing in X is to be deposed.

Smooth: Such a letter rogatory for the taking of the depositions of A and B was issued in the case I just mentioned. Witness A voluntarily appeared and testified before a court in X. He was interrogated by the judge. His testimony was not recorded verbatim; but a summary of such testimony was dictated by the judge. When, at the subsequent trial here, we tried to introduce that summary into evidence, our opponent objected to it as hearsay, and there was quite a squabble over its admissibility.[78]

77. Some civil-law countries make it a criminal offense for a private person (i.e., for any person who is not a local judge) to take depositions. In Switzerland, for instance, foreign lawyers have been jailed for attempting to do so. See H. L. Jones, International Judicial Assistance, 62 Yale L.J. 515, at 520, 528–29 (1953).

78. For a brief discussion of this issue of admissibility see supra, text at ns. 60–62.

Witness B, although duly notified, failed to appear before the court in X. When we petitioned that court to enforce B's duty to appear and testify, our petition was rejected, on the ground that there was no judicial cooperation treaty between X and the United States. In the absence of such a treaty, the X court pointed out, it had no authority under X law to compel a witness to appear and testify for purposes of litigation pending in another country.[79]

Comparovich: Regrettably, this is the law in some civil-law countries. But as between the United States and the majority of its most important trading partners, this difficulty has been overcome by the Evidence Convention,[80] which in Article 10 explicitly provides that in such a case a court executing a Letter of Request (letter rogatory) "shall apply the appropriate measures of compulsion" against the witness.

Many of the problems in this area that formerly plagued us as a result of the divergencies between civil law and common law, have been resolved or alleviated by the Evidence Convention.[81] Using your Example: If X adhered to the Convention, witness B could be compelled to appear and testify, and if the Letter of Request issued by the American court contains an appropriate suggestion, the court in X ordinarily would permit an American-style examination of witnesses A and B, i.e., an examination in which the questions are asked by counsel and the witnesses' answers are recorded verbatim.[82]

Unfortunately, time does not permit a comprehensive discussion of the many other improvements in transnational evidence-taking brought about by the Evidence Convention; but I strongly suggest that you familiarize yourselves with its provisions.

Edge: Can the Evidence Convention be used to obtain documentary evidence?

Comparovich: In principle, yes. But the fear of some of the signatories that the Convention mechanism might be used for American-style "fishing expeditions", led to the inclusion, in the text of the Convention, of the following ambiguous language:

> Art. 23. A Contracting State may at the time of signature, ratification or accession, declare that it will not execute Letters of Request issued for the purpose of obtaining pre-trial discovery of documents as known in Common Law countries.

79. In the converse case, i.e. when a deposition is to be taken here for purposes of litigation pending in another country, our courts are authorized to use measures of compulsion against a recalcitrant witness. 28 U.S.C.A. § 1782, as amended in 1964.

80. Convention on the Taking of Evidence Abroad in Civil and Commercial Matters, done at The Hague March 18, 1970; entered into force for the United States October 7, 1972, TIAS 7444. The text of the Convention, and a list of the countries adhering to it, can conveniently be found in 7 Martindale-Hubbell, Law Directory, Part VII (1986). For a comprehensive analysis of the Convention, see B. Ristau, International Judicial Assistance, Vol. I, Part V (1984).

81. An obvious point, however, should be kept in mind: The Convention applies only as between countries that are parties to it.

82. See Art. 9, par. 2, of the Convention.

The majority of the nations that are parties to the Convention have made declarations under Art. 23.[83]

Smooth: This seems to indicate that many other countries resent American-style discovery when it is used by litigants (including the U.S. Government as a litigant) for extraterritorial information-gathering.

Comparovich: Correct. This resentment, moreover, is intensified when American litigants (again including the U.S. Government) seek to extract information from foreign nationals and domiciliaries who have been brought into our courts only by expansive and perhaps exorbitant theories of jurisdiction. Motivated by such resentment, a number of other countries, including some of our closest friends and allies, have adopted so-called "blocking" statutes, prohibiting compliance with discovery orders of American courts.[84] France has gone so far as to make it a criminal offense, punishable by fines and imprisonment, even to *ask* for "documents or information of an economic, commercial, industrial, financial or technical nature that may constitute proof with a view to legal or administrative proceedings in another country." [85]

Edge: Litigants and witnesses caught in the cross-fire of American discovery orders and such foreign "blocking" legislation are not to be envied.

Comparovich: These cross-fire situations have become very frequent and are burdening our courts with problems of unusual difficulty. Let me acquaint you with a recent

Example: Defendants, French corporations engaged in manufacturing aircraft in France, advertise and sell their products in the United States. In 1980, a "short take-off and landing" aircraft manufactured by defendants was involved in an accident in Iowa. Plaintiffs, who are citizens and residents of the United States, claimed to have suffered injuries as a result of that accident, and sued defendants in the U.S. District Court for the Southern District of Iowa, alleging that the accident was caused by defects of the said aircraft.

Invoking Rules 26 ff. of the Federal Rules of Civil Procedure, plaintiffs sought discovery by way of interrogatories, requests for admission, and requests for production of documents. Most of the documents and other items of information requested were in the custody of the defendants, who in the ordinary course of business kept such documents and other information in France. Denying defendants' motion for a protective order, the District Court [86]

---

83. For details see Ristau, supra n. 80, § 5–35; Amicus Brief for the United States in Societe Nationale Industrielle Aerospatiale v. United States District Court, at 27–28, reprinted in 25 Int. Legal Materials 1504, 1517–18 (1986).

84. Such legislation has been enacted, e.g., in Canada, France, The Netherlands, Sweden and the United Kingdom.

85. Law No. 80–538 of July 18, 1980. Information-gathering activities authorized by an international treaty to which France is a party (e.g., the Evidence Convention) are exempt from the prohibition of the statute.

86. Actually, the ruling was made by a Magistrate to whom the matter had been

ordered defendants to comply with plaintiffs' discovery requests. The Court of Appeals for the Eighth Circuit granted review by mandamus, in view of the novelty of the questions presented, but on the merits agreed with the lower court (thus letting the discovery order stand).[87]

Defendants, supported by the U.S. Government and a number of foreign governments as Amici Curiae,[88] sought further review in the Supreme Court of the United States.[89] They derived separate but interconnected arguments from (a) the Evidence Convention, (b) the French "blocking" statute, and (c) general notions of international comity.

Edge: Concerning the Evidence Convention, the first question is whether by its terms it applies at all to the facts of this case. If the documents and other items of information requested were in the hands of a non-party residing in France, resort to the Convention, and through the Convention machinery to a French court, would be necessary in order to force such non-party to furnish the information. But in this case the information is in the custody of a party to the action, a party over whom the American court clearly has personal jurisdiction. That party can be compelled to produce the information *in Iowa*. No judicial assistance by any French court is needed. Thus, it seems to me, the Evidence Convention is not applicable.

Comparovich: That was the position taken by the lower courts, not only in this case, but in a number of similar cases as well. Under this interpretation, the effect of the Evidence Convention would be limited to information in the hands of persons who are not parties to the action.

Smooth: Even assuming, arguendo, that this interpretation is too narrow, and that the Evidence Convention does apply to the facts of this case, could the plaintiffs not argue that they may, at their option, seek the information *either* through Convention channels *or* in accordance with Rules 26 through 37?

Comparovich: You are suggesting, in other words, that the Convention is non-exclusive, and does not prevent an American court from using information-gathering methods based on our own law.[90] This is indeed what the plaintiffs argued. Even if this argument is accepted, however, the question remains whether principles of international comity do not impel an American court, either as a rule or under the circumstances of a particular case, to try to obtain the information through Convention channels before resorting to the more drastic unilateral methods provided by our own discovery provisions.

referred in accordance with 28 U.S.C.A. § 636(c)(1).

87. In re Societe Nationale Industrielle Aerospatiale, 782 F.2d 120 (8th Cir. 1986).

88. The Amicus briefs as well as the other briefs in the case are reprinted in 25 Int. Legal Materials 1475–1586 (1986).

89. cert. granted ___ U.S. ___, 106 S.Ct. 2888 (1986).

90. Art. 27 of the Convention appears to support the argument for non-exclusivity.

Edge: In the context of comity, the French "blocking" statute may have to be considered as well. An American court, presumably, will not allow such a foreign statute automatically to thwart the court's discovery processes; [91] but it may try, by use or first-use of the Convention, to obviate a direct clash between our discovery procedures and the French statute.

Comparovich: You are getting into the fine points of the case. It would be fascinating to continue this exchange of refined arguments; but for practical purposes, the arguments have been settled by the U.S. Supreme Court.[92] I recommend that you study the Court's decision with care.

Smooth: This, I suppose, brings us to the end of our interesting digression into the subject of international judicial cooperation. We should now resume the discussion of our case against Mr. H.

K. THE COURT'S DECISION

Comparovich: What happened next in that case?

Smooth: After a further exchange of briefs, and after a final hearing at which the case, in the light of the evidence received, was argued by counsel before the full bench,[1] the court handed down its final decision. Consisting of a single document, it contained

(a) the dispositive provisions of the decision, concisely formulated and similar to what we could call a "judgment"; and

(b) a supporting statement that sounded somewhat like a combination of findings of fact, conclusions of law, and an opinion.

Edge: The form of the supporting statement did not strike me as strange. In non-jury cases, even our courts can include their findings of fact and conclusions of law in a reasoned opinion.[2]

Comparovich: Regarding length and style of judicial opinions, there is no uniformity in the civil-law world.[3] A comparative study of

---

91. Cf. Societe Internationale Pour Participations Industrielles et Commerciales, S.A. v. Rogers, 357 U.S. 197, 78 S.Ct. 1087 (1958).

92. Societe Nationale Industrielle Aerospatiale v. United States District Court for the Southern District of Iowa, ___ U.S. ___, 107 S.Ct. 2542 (1987).

1. In France and French-influenced countries, this final hearing (*audience*) tends to give the *avocats* an opportunity for a thorough (and frequently eloquent) discussion of the evidence that has accumulated in the *dossier*, and of the relevant issues of law. In other civil-law countries, depending on the workload of the court and the personal views of the presiding judge, the final hearing may be more informal and perhaps rather brief.

2. FRCP Rule 52(a).

3. The practice of appellate as well as trial courts differs from country to country, as can be seen by comparing the opinions of the various foreign courts reprinted in this book. See also J. G. Wetter, The Styles of Appellate Judicial Opinions (1960), and infra pp. 649–650.

For an enlightening discussion of the traditional German technique of preparing and formulating judicial decisions, see W. O. Weyrauch, The Art of Drafting Judgments: A Modified German Case Method, 9 J.Legal Ed. 311 (1956). In the Appendix to that article (at 330–31) the reader will find an instructive sample. For further sample decisions see 2 E. J. Cohn, Manual of German Law 196–97 (2d ed., 1971) and (reflecting Austrian practice) Appendix D

the style of judicial decisions shows, nevertheless, that there are some points on which the civil-law systems, with virtual unanimity, have adopted a practice differing from ours:

The first point, illustrated by the case at hand, is that civil-law courts combine judgment and opinion in a single document.

Secondly, the whole document, and every part of it, is prepared by the court, and not by counsel.[4]

Thirdly, and most importantly, civil-law countries generally adhere to the rule that every final judgment *must* be accompanied by an opinion, and that the opinion must show the position of the court on every issue. Non-compliance with this requirement, which the civilians regard as an essential safeguard against judicial arbitrariness, would be reversible error.[5]

Smooth: The opinion did not disclose the name of its author.

Comparovich: In this respect, the practice of the various civil-law countries is not quite uniform. In France and Germany, however, and in a large number of jurisdictions following their example, every opinion (usually combined with the judgment in one document) is issued *per curiam*; this is true even of the opinions of most of the courts of last resort. Under this system, neither the precise number nor the identity of the judges who voted for the decision is revealed. This is thought to be part of the judges' deliberations, the secret of which is closely guarded.[6] Dissenting opinions are, of course, unknown in the countries where this system is maintained without qualification.[7]

of the article by F. R. Lacy, "Civilizing" Nonjury Trials, 19 Vand.L.Rev. 73, 121–28 (1965).

4. Under prevailing American practice, the court's "opinion" (if one is filed) must be prepared by the court itself. See Chicopee Mfg. Corp. v. Kendall Co., 288 F.2d 719, 724–25 (4th Cir. 1961), cert. denied 368 U.S. 825, 82 S.Ct. 44 (1961). Cf. Westside Property Owners v. Schlesinger, 597 F.2d 1214, 1216 (9th Cir. 1979). But counsel commonly are expected to prepare "orders" and "judgments" for the court's signature. As to the proper authorship of findings of fact and conclusions of law, see the interesting opinion of Judge Wisdom in Railex Corp. v. Speed Check Co., 457 F.2d 1040, 1041–42 (5th Cir. 1972), cert. denied 409 U.S. 876, 93 S.Ct. 125 (1972).

5. Concerning the history of this important rule see T. Sauvel, Histoire du jugement motivé, 61 Revue du Droit Public et de la Science Politique 5 (1955).

6. In many countries, there are *statutory* provisions to this effect. A change of the system thus may require *legislative* action.

In France, the statute imposing secrecy is occasionally circumvented by a judge who has remained in the minority. He can do this by publishing, in a legal periodical, a critical comment on the decision of his own court. Without in terms disclosing that its author voted against the decision, the comment will leave no doubt on this point in the minds of knowledgeable readers.

In Switzerland and Norway the deliberations of the highest court are conducted in public. Thus, in this small minority of countries the public (which includes the parties and their counsel) is informed of the position taken by each member of the court, regardless of whether formal dissenting opinions are written and published.

7. The fascinating subject of dissenting opinions has given rise to a voluminous literature, much of it of a comparative nature. See, e.g., K. H. Nadelmann, The Judicial Dissent—Publication vs. Secrecy, 8 Am.J.Comp.L. 415 (1959); J. Federer, Die Bekanntgabe der abweichenden Meinung des überstimmten Richters, 23 JZ 511 (1968), where many of the other relevant writings are cited. See also K. H. Nadelmann, Non-Disclosure of Dissents in Constitutional Courts: Italy and West Germany, 13 Am.J.Comp.L. 268 (1964);

Edge: Does this spineless system reflect the status and the attitude of a civil service judiciary? [8]

Comparovich: A German sociologist has intimated that his compatriots' traditional resistance to the publication of judicial dissents can be ascribed to a general tendency to suppress conflicts, and to a yearning for painless synthesis.[9] *Quaere,* however, whether this theory can explain the fact that publication of dissents is prohibited also in France, a country whose citizens can hardly be characterized as conformists and indeed are known to cultivate a tradition of contentiousness and of healthy skepticism.

Edge: How, then, can it be explained that the majority of common-law systems authorize the publication of dissenting opinions, while the majority of civil-law systems do not? [9a]

Comparovich: A well-known Italian scholar has suggested a very interesting explanation which, in abbreviated and over-simplified form, comes to this: [10] At common law, judicial decision-making occurs in the form of several distinct steps. In a jury case, ordinarily there is a verdict, followed by a judgment and perhaps by an opinion accompanying the disposition of motions. In a non-jury case, findings of fact take the place of the verdict, but traditionally there is the same multiplicity of steps as in a jury case; and even in appellate proceedings the separation between judgment and opinion is maintained. That part of the decision-making process which consists of a judicial statement of legal reasoning, used to be (and in some English courts still is) part of the oral colloquy between court and counsel.[10a] Where the court consists of several judges, such a system makes it necessary for them to state their views seriatim, and the open disclosure of disagreements among the members of the court has developed as a natural consequence of this traditional procedure.

In civil-law systems, on the other hand, a judicial decision normally is handed down by way of a single step; it is wholly in writing and embodied in a single document which, since it contains the judgment as

---

Anand, The Role of Individual and Dissenting Opinions in International Adjudication, 14 Int.Comp.L.Q. 788 (1965); A. Tunc, La Cour Suprême Idéale (concluding part of a comparative symposium on Courts of Last Resort), 30 Revue Internationale de Droit Comparé 433, 456–59 (1978).

8. See supra pp. 180–182.

9. See Dahrendorf, Gesellschaft und Demokratie in Deutschland 234–42, 268–71 (1965).

9a. The civilian tradition of not allowing publication of dissents is followed by the European Court of Justice. See L. N. Brown & F. G. Jacobs, The Court of Justice of the European Communities 206 (2d ed. 1983). The European Court of Human Rights, on the other hand, does

publish dissenting and concurring opinions.

10. See Gorla, La struttura della decisione giudiziale in diritto italiano e nella "Common Law": Riflessi di tale struttura sull'interpretazione della sentenza, sui "Reports" e sul "Dissenting", 1965 Giurisprudenza Italiana (Disp. 9a, parte I, sez. la) 23 ff.; id., "Dissenting Opinions" und italienische Entscheidungen, 28 Rabels Z. 801 (1964).

10a. The English-style colloquy between court and counsel, as well as the practice of the judges' seriatim statement of their views, is described by B. Rudden, Courts and Codes in England, France and Soviet Russia, 48 Tul.L.Rev. 1010, 1014–16 (1974).

well as the supporting opinion, must speak in the name of the court, i.e., *per curiam*. Under such a system, separate statement of every judge's individual reasoning is not a natural concomitant of the procedure by which the court's decision is reached and announced.

Edge: This may be true. Yet it does not seem impossible for a legislator, while preserving the basic civil-law structure of judicial decisions, to permit that dissenting opinions be filed and published (with or without identification of the dissenting judges).

Comparovich: Quite so. Professor Gorla does not deny that; and the fact is that a few civil-law systems do authorize the publication of dissenting votes or even of dissenting opinions.[11] Still it seems that the difference between common-law and civil-law systems, to which Professor Gorla has called attention, is a significant one: while in common-law systems the dissenting opinion is simply the natural result of routine procedures followed since medieval days, a modern civil-law country usually can introduce the dissenting opinion only by a conscious policy decision of the legislator.

Smooth: Once they face this policy question, however, it should not take them long to recognize that the "unanimity" of their *per curiam* decisions is a sham, and that the enforced anonymity of judicial decisions must kill the judges' sense of individual responsibility.

Comparovich: These are forceful arguments. Moreover, as was said by the late Judge Wiltraut Rupp-von Brünneck, the "great dissenter" of the German Federal Constitutional Court, "it is of the very essence of a pluralistic democracy that nobody may claim to have a lease on the absolute truth or correctness of his views." [11a] Published dissents constantly remind us that the members of the court's majority are not infallible, and such a reminder may be an important contribution to the openness of our society.

Nevertheless, we must expect that in countries where the judges are career civil servants, and where respect for the judiciary is not as deeply ingrained as it is here, some counter-points are apt to be raised.[12] It is said, for instance, that in such countries the anonymity of the *per curiam* decision may be necessary (a) to protect the individual judges from improper pressures, and (b) to add more dignity and force to their

---

11. See Nadelmann, supra n. 7. Apparently it was through Romano-Canonistic procedure that the principle of judicial anonymity—a principle opposed to the Germanic tradition—was brought to the continental legal systems. Historical research has shown, nevertheless, that even in the centuries immediately following the reception of Roman law and of Romano-Canonistic procedure some continental systems permitted the publication of dissenting opinions. See Federer, supra n. 7; G. Gorla & L. Moccia, A "Revisiting" of the Comparison Between "Continental Law" and "English Law" (16th–19th Century), 2 J.Leg.Hist. 143, 151 (1981).

11a. Quoted in the interesting article by W. Hill, Die Stimme der Minderheit, 18 Zeitschrift für Rechtspolitik 15, 17 (1985).

12. Those who take the negative side of the argument, do not always make it clear whether their reasoning is intended to militate against (i) the publication of the fact of a split vote, or (ii) the publication of dissenting opinions, or (iii) merely against identifying the dissenters.

judgments by keeping judicial disagreements from the eyes of the public.

It is arguable, moreover, that the need for dissenting opinions is greater in common-law than in civil-law systems. In common-law jurisdictions, dissents often mark the controversial and developing areas of the law. We all know that, at least in those areas, today's dissent frequently foreshadows tomorrow's majority position. The dissent, by reminding the profession of the possibility of future change, thus becomes an element of flexibility that tends to mitigate whatever rigidity may still be inherent in the principle of stare decisis. It might be argued that the civil-law systems, which have not adopted that principle,[12a] correspondingly have less need for the mitigating device.[12b]

In this connection, it is interesting to observe that even in Germany, where in general the law reflects the civilians' traditional anti-dissent attitude, recent legislation now permits the publication of dissenting opinions in the only court whose decisions have a binding effect in future cases: the Constitutional Court.[12c]

Edge: Has the traditional system of anonymous *per curiam* decisions been retained for all other German courts?

Comparovich: Yes. During the 1960s, the German legal profession engaged in a great debate concerning the question whether and to what extent the traditional system should be modified.[13] The upshot was that the status quo was left undisturbed with respect to all courts other than the Constitutional Court. Concerning the practice in the Federal Constitutional Court, the great debate resulted in statutory change;[14] but even in that Court the old principle of anonymity was not completely eradicated. Under the new practice, the reader of a decision of the Federal Constitutional Court is always told whether the decision was unanimous and, if not, how many judges voted for and against it. Moreover, if dissenting opinions have been written by one or more of the dissenting judges, those opinions are published together with the majority opinion. Nevertheless, there remain many cases in which the

---

12a. See infra pp. 597–657.

12b. From a functional point of view, it is perhaps not too far-fetched to see a civil-law analogue of the dissent in the power of (civilian) lower courts occasionally to deviate from, and even to disregard, a precedent set by the highest court in a previous case. See infra pp. 646–647. True, this power is sparingly exercised, but

"It is no accident that those parts of the private law in which the lower courts of France and the USSR most frequently diverge from the decisions of the Supreme Courts—in the field of automobile and industrial injuries—are precisely those in which the House of Lords is likely to be divided 3–2." B. Rudden, Courts and Codes in England, France

and Soviet Russia, 48 Tul.L.Rev. 1010, 1016 (1974).

12c. Concerning the binding effect of decisions of the German Federal Constitutional Court, see infra p. 598.

13. See, e.g., M. Heidenhain, Der 47. Deutsche Juristentag, 23 JZ 755, 757 (1968). See also supra n. 7.

14. See § 30 of the Law Concerning the Federal Constitutional Court (Bundesverfassungsgerichtsgesetz), as amended in 1971.

Even before this change in the federal law, the constitutional courts of some of the *Laender* were authorized to, and did, publish dissenting opinions.

identity of majority and minority judges is not revealed;[14a] and the names of the authors of the various opinions normally remain undisclosed.[14b]

But let us come back to our case. What was said in the decision of the Ruritanian Tribunal of First Instance?

Smooth: In one respect the decision was disappointing for us. Concerning the facts, the court completely swallowed H's story, which they found to be corroborated by the correspondence. They even believed H's assertion that the contract, by its express terms, was performable in Ruritania. On that basis, the opinion overruled our objection to the court's jurisdiction.[14c]

Following the factual finding that H had been retained by us, the opinion rejected our defense of illegality, and then proceeded to discuss the choice of law question whether the retainer, and H's compensation under it, should be governed by the law of the place of performance, or the law of the place where the contract was made. The opinion espoused the latter view as being in accordance with the presumed intention of the parties.[15] Referring to the opinions of the Institute and

14a. The judges who join in a dissenting *opinion*, are identified by name. Thus, if all of the judges who voted against the majority decision join in a dissenting opinion, the reader in effect knows the identity of all of the judges who voted for as well as against the decision. It is possible for a judge, however, to vote against the majority decision without joining in a dissenting opinion. If no dissenting opinion is written, in that event the names of the dissenters are not published. Even when a dissenting opinion is written and published, it may happen that one or several of the judges who voted against the majority and thus in effect dissented, refused to join in the dissenting opinion. Suppose, for instance, that the vote was 5 to 3. It may happen that 2 of the 3 dissenters join in a published dissenting opinion; the names of these 2 judges will be published. The name of the 3rd dissenter, however, will not be published, because he did not join in a dissenting *opinion*. In this latter event, the reader cannot be sure who the 3rd dissenter is; nor can the reader be certain of the identity of the 5 majority judges.

The system in effect appears to amount to this: A judge who casts a dissenting vote may choose between publicity and anonymity. If he writes, or joins in, a dissenting opinion, he makes his position public; but if he abstains from writing or supporting an opinion, he can remain anonymous, with the further consequence that the majority judges, also, to some extent retain their anonymity.

14b. Under the practice of the German Federal Constitutional Court, the authorship of an opinion, whether it be a majority or a dissenting opinion, is not disclosed. Thus every majority opinion in effect is rendered "Per Curiam"; and a dissenting opinion, if concurred in by more than one judge, also must be taken as the expression of a group position rather than the voice of an individual judge.

14c. Note that the court thus affirmed its own jurisdiction on what we would call a long-arm basis. This made it unnecessary for the court to examine the further question whether it had jurisdiction, also, on the (exorbitant) basis of the presence in Ruritania of some of defendant's property.

15. In cases which fit into the routine pattern of attorney-client relationships, both civil-law and common-law courts tend to apply the law of the place where the attorney has his office. Cf. Gonzalez Y Barredo v. Schenck, 287 F.Supp. 505, 526 (S.D.N.Y. 1968), rev'd on other grounds 428 F.2d 971 (2d Cir. 1970); Ehrenzweig, Conflict of Laws 532 (1962); 3 Rabel, The Conflict of Laws 201–02 (2d ed., 1964). Cf. also the German case, infra p. 857. The principal case, however, was unusual in that H, although consulted in his capacity as a Ruritanian lawyer, had no office in Ruritania, and did not reside there, at the time when the alleged contract was made. Moreover, even if the contract contained a term which (with respect to some contractual duties) named Ruritania as the "place of performance", the fact remains that H

of the expert, the court further found that under the law of the place where the contract was made, H was entitled to a fee of $950.

At the end of the opinion, it was explained that H, having recovered only a minute fraction of his demand, must in effect be treated as the losing party. The ordering part of the judgment, therefore, after directing the defendant to pay $950 (or the Ruritanian equivalent thereof) to the plaintiff, further provided that the plaintiff should bear all costs and should reimburse the defendant for the latter's attorneys' fees. Our bill of costs (including attorneys' fees) was substantial, because the amount involved in the litigation ($95,000) was relatively high. At any rate, it came to more than $950, so that on balance Mr. H owed us money. This outcome greatly increased my respect for the Ruritanian courts.

Edge: Suppose H had not taken a timely appeal from this decision. In that event, would Ruritanian law have precluded him from bringing a new action for his fee against the same defendant?

Comparovich: Yes, he would have been precluded.

Edge: Does this mean that the civil-law systems recognize the same rules of res judicata which we apply here?

Comparovich: It has been said that "The doctrine of res judicata is a principle of universal jurisprudence forming part of the legal systems of all civilized nations." [16] This, however, is true only insofar as the basic principle is concerned; regarding the detailed rules of res judicata, there is considerable diversity among legal systems.[17]

Smooth: Don't all legal systems, or virtually all of them, agree that once an action has been judicially determined on the merits, a second action between the same parties is precluded if it involves the same cause of action? [18]

Comparovich: They do; but this is an instance of what in my writings I have called mere acoustic agreement among legal systems: all of them utter identical or similar sounds, but they do not necessarily reach the same results. With respect to the "universal" rule to which your question refers, the catch is that there is no agreement whatever concerning the definition and the dimensions of a cause of action.

Edge: Even within our own country, this is a very controversial matter.

---

did not render any services in that country. The choice of law question faced by the Ruritanian court thus was not a simple one.

16. Gates v. Mortgage Loan & Ins. Agency, 200 Ark. 276, at 284, 139 S.W.2d 19, at 23 (1940).

17. See W. J. Habscheid, Rechtsvergleichende Bemerkungen zum Problem der materiellen Rechtskraft des Zivilurteils, published as a separate reprint from Offer-

ings in Honor of C. N. Fragistas (Thessaloniki 1967); A. Zeuner, Rechtsvergleichende Bemerkungen zur objektiven Begrenzung der Rechtskraft im Zivilprozess, in H. Bernstein, U. Drobnig and H. Kötz, Festschrift für Konrad Zweigert 603 (1981).

18. Similar terms, e.g., "claim" or "demand", sometimes are used instead of "cause of action".

Comparovich: On a multi-national scale, there is an even wider variety of views on this point. In this connection, it is important to remember (see supra p. 365) that most civil-law countries do not have a rule against splitting a cause of action. Suppose a plaintiff, although he claims that defendant owes him $500,000, in his complaint asks for a judgment in the amount of $20,000 only.[18a] A judgment in that action, whether in plaintiff's or defendant's favor, under the majority civil-law rule will have no claim-preclusion effect with respect to the $480,000 balance of plaintiff's claim.[19]

As we move from claim preclusion (also known as total res judicata, or doctrine of bar and merger) to issue preclusion (usually referred to as collateral estoppel or partial res judicata), the disagreement becomes even more intense. With respect to issue preclusion, there is not even acoustic agreement among legal systems; they are in open conflict as to whether and to what extent the findings and conclusions underlying the prior judgment have any binding effect in a second action brought on a different "cause of action".[20]

Edge: Are the civil-law countries in agreement among each other?

Comparovich: Only to this extent: none of them will go as far as we do in extending the doctrine of collateral estoppel. Most civil-law systems either reject the doctrine, or limit it severely, e.g., by applying it only to the "over-riding issue" of fact or law determined in the first action.[21]

18a. In civil-law countries, a plaintiff may be prompted by cost-saving considerations to sue for less that the full amount of his claim. See supra p. 365.

19. Whether as a practical matter a party who lost in the first action will find it promising to engage in new litigation concerning the balance, is another question. Even in the absence of an applicable rule of claim preclusion (or issue preclusion, see infra), the parties generally will expect that on the issues determined in the first action the court will reach the same conclusions in the second suit. But in exceptional situations (e.g., discovery of previously unknown evidence, or a new turn in the decisions of the highest court) it may occasionally be promising, even as a practical matter, to relitigate. Note, however, that with respect to the $20,000 portion of plaintiff's claim that was involved in the first action, claim preclusion will prevent relitigation in any legal system.

20. See supra n. 17; R. W. Millar, The Premises of the Judgment as Res Judicata in Continental and Anglo-American Law, 39 Mich.L.Rev. 1 ff., 238 ff. (1940).

For an unusually interesting case that turned on the precise limits of the doctrine of collateral estoppel under Dutch law, and on the non-recognition of the doctrine in

Swiss law, see Bata v. Bata, 39 Del.Ch. 258, 163 A.2d 493, especially at 502–11 (1960). The relevant Swiss rule is even more extensively discussed, and Swiss authorities are quoted, in In re Zietz' Estates, 207 Misc. 22, 135 N.Y.S.2d 573, 578–9 (Surr.Ct. 1954), aff'd 285 App.Div. 1147, 143 N.Y.S.2d 602 (1st Dept. 1955), motion for leave to appeal dismissed 1 N.Y.2d 748, 152 N.Y.S.2d 295, 135 N.E.2d 49 (1956).

There are many other American cases in which a judgment rendered in a civil law country (F–1) was invoked as the basis of collateral estoppel in an American F–2 court. The difficult conflict of laws issues arising (and not always recognized) in those cases are extensively discussed in the interesting articles by R. C. Casad, Issue Preclusion and Foreign Country Judgments: Whose Law?, 70 Iowa L.Rev. 53 (1984), and by C. H. Peterson, Foreign Country Judgments and the Second Restatement of Conflict of Laws, 72 Colum.L. Rev. 220, 263 (1972).

21. See the authorities cited supra n. 20, especially the discussion of Dutch law in the Bata decision and the article by Casad, at 62–70, where the reader will find some material on the law of issue preclusion in France, Germany, Japan and several Latin American countries.

Edge: Might this stem from a feeling, on the part of the civilians, that in their systems—due to the absence of effective discovery devices, and the relatively weak role played by counsel in the unearthing and presenting of evidence—the fact-finding process in the first action is unreliable? [22]

Comparovich: It is, of course, true that where the decision in the first action is the result of slipshod fact-finding, the injustice thus inflicted on the loser grows in direct proportion to the expansion of the preclusionary effect upon claims and issues which a legal system accords to that decision. I doubt, however, whether the civilians' relative caution in dealing with res judicata, and especially with issue preclusion, is due to any conscious lack of confidence in their own fact-finding processes.

Edge: What, then, is the reason for that cautious attitude?

Comparovich: For a civil-law court it is usually possible to make effective use of the findings made in a previous action, even though the doctrine of collateral estoppel may be non-existent in the particular legal system or inapplicable to the case at hand. This is so because, as I mentioned before,[23] the absence of exclusionary rules of evidence enables a civil-law court simply to send for the *dossier* of the prior proceeding and to use the contents of that *dossier*, including the decision and the findings recorded therein, as evidence in the new action. Thus the civilians are not faced with the hard choice which an American court normally must make in cases of this kind: either to treat the findings made in the prior case as binding (which often leads to harsh results), or completely to disregard those findings, not even admitting them as evidence (which may be unrealistic and wasteful).[24] This all-or-nothing approach of the common law has been criticized by Bentham and others.[25] The civilians, by rejecting or restricting the doctrine of collateral estoppel, while at the same time treating the earlier findings as evidence, in effect have adopted the intermediate view advocated by these critics.[26]

L. APPEALS

Edge: Actually, H did appeal to the Intermediate Appellate Court.

---

22. A somewhat similar thought has been suggested in the interesting article by Toyohisa Isobe, Civil Procedure, in 15 Japan Annual of Law and Politics 77, 81 (1967), referring to a paper by Tōichirō Kikawa.

23. Supra p. 424.

24. Under our law, the former judgment is treated as hearsay. Thus, as a rule (though subject to exceptions) it is not admissible evidence in later litigation. For a thorough and critical discussion of the rule and the exceptions, see H. Motomura, Using Judgments as Evidence, 70 Minn.L. Rev. 979 (1986). See also infra p. 493.

25. See 7 Works of Jeremy Bentham 171 (Bowring ed., 1843).

26. Occasionally there are situations where a party finds it particularly important to have an issue of fact or law judicially determined in such a way that the determination will be *binding* in future litigation between the same parties; some civil-law systems provide a special form of declaratory judgment action for this purpose. See Millar, supra n. 20.

Smooth: Upon L's advice, we filed a cross-appeal. L asked us again whether we had any further evidence, and, in particular, whether anybody, in addition to Mr. Edge and myself, had overheard the conversation with H. This idea of new evidence on appeal amazed us.[26a]

Comparovich: In most civil-law countries, the first appeal is on the law and the facts. The original record (nothing is printed) of the court of first instance is sent to the appellate court, which determines factual issues on the basis of that record and of such additional evidence as it orders to be taken.[27] — *As opposed to U.S. courts where appeal is on the law (on facts only if clearly erroneous).*

Edge: When an offer of proof is made for the first time on appeal, does the appellate court have the power to reject such offer if it appears that the party making the offer was dilatory?

Comparovich: Yes. In most civil-law countries it is the traditional practice of appellate courts to use that power sparingly. But in Germany the tough preclusion rules introduced by the 1976 reform (see supra pp. 439–440) are carried over into the procedure of the intermediate appellate court (*Oberlandesgericht*).[27a]

Smooth: In our case, neither party offered any new evidence concerning our conversation with H. The plaintiff, of course, was completely satisfied with the factual findings made below, and appealed only on the law. We asked the appellate court to draw different factual inferences from the evidence in the record, and, in particular, to disbelieve H's testimony, although we had no new evidence to disprove

26a. To American lawyers, this system is not as alien as it might seem at first blush. In equity and other nonjury cases, appeals on the facts are commonplace even though a reversal on the facts may require a showing that the findings of the trial court were "clearly" or "manifestly" erroneous. In some states, moreover, there are explicit statutory provisions which in nonjury cases confer upon appellate courts the power—sparingly exercised, to be sure—to permit the introduction of new evidence on appeal. See, e.g., Cal.Code Civ.Pro., § 909. See also R. W. Millar, New Allegation and Proof on Appeal in Anglo-American Civil Procedure, 47 N.W.U.L.Rev. 427 (1952).

27. In Louisiana, this traditional civil-law approach has had a strong impact on the practice of the courts, even in jury cases. Art. VII Section 29 of the Louisiana Constitution preserves the civil-law rule under which the appeal to the intermediate appellate court is on the facts as well as the law. Since 1805, Louisiana has had jury trials in civil cases; but the constitutionally protected power of the intermediate appellate court, to review factual findings of the court below, extends to all civil cases, including those in which the factual findings made at the trial level are those of

a jury. Although Louisiana appellate courts pretend to reverse only "manifestly erroneous" findings of fact, it is no secret that jury verdicts in tort cases often are overturned on appeal for no reason other than that the appellate court weighs the evidence differently. The constitutionality of this practice, which finds more favor with insurance companies than with plaintiffs, was upheld, against an attack based on the U.S. Constitution, in Melancon v. McKeithen, 345 F.Supp. 1025 (Three-judge court) (E.D.La., 1972), aff'd mem. sub nom. Hill v. McKeithen, 409 U.S. 943, 93 S.Ct. 290 (1972). The opinion in that case (at 1027) contains the following remark:

"Many Louisiana lawyers consider that appellate scrutiny of the facts offsets the advantages of sympathy or pooled intuition associated with jury trials. As a consequence, civil jury trials are a rarity in Louisiana. A related rarity is a long queue of litigants, often found in other states, waiting for many months or years for their actions to be tried."

27a. See German Code of Civil Procedure, §§ 527 and 528. These provisions are discussed in the articles cited supra p. 438, n. 64d.

his version of the alleged agreement. We also assigned as error the rejection of our defense of illegality.

Comparovich: In order to be consistent, the lower court should have determined this defense in accordance with the law of the place where the contract was made.

Smooth: The Presiding Justice of the appellate court, who obviously had studied the record with care, pointed this out at the first hearing. Upon L's suggestion, the court right then and there issued an interlocutory order requesting a new opinion from the Institute of Comparative Law, concerning the following question: "Under applicable American law, did H's acceptance of the retainer constitute unauthorized and illegal practice of the law?" Thereupon the hearing was adjourned.

Comparovich: What did the Institute say?

Smooth: They said that the retainer agreement was illegal if H dealt with officers or agents of defendant corporation who were not members of the Bar of our State; but that H was not guilty of unauthorized practice of the law if he was retained by or through duly licensed attorneys. The Institute concluded, therefore, that the answer to the question depended on a factual issue: whether Mr. Edge and I, at the time of our negotiations with H, were members of the Bar of our State.

Comparovich: It seems the Institute was familiar with the *Roel* case.[28]

Smooth: At the next hearing, the Presiding Justice stated that according to the testimony given by Mr. Edge and myself, we were members of the Bar at the time of such testimony. He asked whether we had been admitted to the Bar prior to our negotiations with H. Defendant's counsel had to answer this question in the affirmative.

The court reserved decision, and three weeks later handed down a judgment and opinion, combined in one document, in all respects affirming the lower court and imposing the costs of the appeal and the cross-appeal on the respective appellants.

Excerpts from this decision were subsequently published in a Ruritanian law journal, together with a learned annotation authored by a professor who criticized the court's views on the choice of law question.

Comparovich: As regards the reporting of judicial decisions, there is no uniformity among civil-law systems.[28a] Decisions of intermediate

---

28. In re Roel, 3 N.Y.2d 224, 165 N.Y.S.2d 31, 144 N.E.2d 24 (1957).

28a. For details see C. Szladits & C. M. Germain, Guide to Foreign Legal Materials: French (2d ed., 1985) and the other volumes published in the same series under the auspices of the Parker School of Foreign and Comparative Law.

One noteworthy point on which there is lack of uniformity among civil-law systems, relates to the important question whether the names of the parties should be disclosed. In some countries (e.g., Germany) official as well as unofficial reports of judicial decisions omit the names of the parties. The German cases reproduced in later parts of this book reflect that practice.

appellate courts as a rule are not officially reported. Even with respect to the decisions of courts of last resort, most of those countries leave the reporter's task wholly or partly to private enterprise; where official reports exist, they may be selective or limited to abstract, headnote-like summaries of the court's legal reasoning.[29] The upshot of this situation is that in many civil-law countries the function of bringing judicial decisions to the attention of the profession must to some extent be performed by legal periodicals. In the civil-law world, the usual practice of these periodicals is to publish the text of selected important decisions, either in full or in excerpt;[30] an annotation prepared by an expert frequently follows the decision itself. The author of the annotation may have looked at the record or at unpublished parts of the decision, and thus may be in a position not only to comment on the legal points involved, but also to enhance the reader's understanding of the facts and the procedural history of the case.

Decisions published in legal periodicals, plus the annotations thereto, thus constitute indispensable sources for anyone engaged in legal research concerning the law of civilian countries.

Edge: I am somewhat surprised that legal periodicals in civil-law countries bother to publish decisions of intermediate appellate courts. Since these courts pass on issues of fact as well as law, it is clear that much of what they say in their single-document decisions deals with factual matters and thus is of no general interest for purposes of legal research.[31]

Comparovich: You are putting your finger on a significant and often neglected problem. Although this problem can arise in any legal system where intermediate appellate courts have the power to review factual findings,[32] it is of particular importance in civil-law systems.[33] In some types of cases, especially negligence cases, it may often be

---

Needless to say, such a practice protects the privacy of the parties; but it has the disadvantage that cases cannot be remembered or cited by name and must always be referred to, somewhat awkwardly, by volume and page number.

In other civil-law countries, such as France and Switzerland, the names of the parties normally are indicated in reported decisions. This practice (like our own) of course raises privacy issues. The well-known French law journal *La Gazette du Palais* once was sued for having published the name of a respondent in a provincial divorce action. See Le Monde of November 12, 1971, p. 19.

29. See, e.g., Gorla, Some Comments on the Italian Legal System, in 1 Schlesinger (Gen.Ed.), Formation of Contracts—A Study of the Common Core of Legal Systems 297, 298 (1968).

30. Where, as in the instant case, the decision is still subject to a further appeal,

an editorial note ordinarily will so inform the reader.

31. Regarding the general question of the force of judicial precedents in a civil-law system, see infra pp. 597–657.

32. See D. W. Robertson, The Precedent Value of Conclusions of Fact in Civil Cases in England and Louisiana, 29 La.L.Rev. 78 (1968).

33. In common-law jurisdictions, the problem (a) does not arise in jury cases; and (b) even in non-jury cases may lose some of its poignancy as a result of statutory provisions which in the event of a reversal or modification require the intermediate appellate court to specify whether its determination is on the law, or on the facts, or both. See, e.g., NYCPLR § 5712, subd. (c). Cf. FRCP Rule 52(a). Such provisions reflect the attitude of lawyers brought up in the common-law jury system, to whom it has become second nature, even when dealing with a non-jury case, to

difficult to determine, in reading the opinion of a court which has power to pass on factual as well as legal issues, whether the court announced a rule of law or merely resolved an issue of fact.[34] Nevertheless, it is generally assumed in the civil-law world that when an opinion of an intermediate appellate court is cited as an alleged precedent, it is both necessary and possible by careful analysis of the opinion to separate its legal reasoning (which may have some precedential value) from the discussion of factual issues (which has no such value).[35]

Not infrequently, American courts are faced with this problem in foreign-law cases. Suppose a tort action governed by French law is brought in New York. The French law expert for one of the parties relies on a decision—squarely in point—in which a French intermediate appellate court (*Cour d'Appel*) held certain conduct to be negligent. In order not to be over-impressed by this decision, the New York court will have to keep in mind that a French *Cour d'Appel* examines questions of fact as well as law. Only careful analysis of the French court's decision, based on sufficient background knowledge of French law, can show to what extent that court's finding of negligence in the case before it expressed or necessarily implied a particular view of the law, and to what extent it was a mere factual finding that would not be reviewable by the French court of last resort. Insofar as it is shown to constitute a factual finding, it has no precedential value—no more than a jury verdict rendered in a common-law court.

Smooth: From the decision of the Intermediate Appellate Court, H took a further appeal to the highest court of Ruritania, the Court of Cassation. Before the appeal was argued, settlement negotiations were initiated. As an argument in favor of settlement, L pointed to some complexities and uncertainties inherent in Ruritanian appellate procedure; he talked about the possibility of a decision by 43 judges sitting en banc, and of successive remands to the Intermediate Appellate Court, all of which had us totally bewildered.

Comparovich: To clear up the bewilderment, we shall have to go into some of the intricacies of the civilians' rules concerning appeals to the court of last resort.

Edge: Excuse me for interrupting you, Professor. It seems to me the very term "court of last resort" may require some explanation in reference to countries such as Germany and Italy, where, in addition to the court at the apex of the hierarchy of ordinary courts, there exists a separate Constitutional Court. As you have told us in an earlier part of our discussion, the Constitutional Court in such countries normally has

keep the law-fact dichotomy constantly before their eyes.

34. See Robertson, supra n. 32.

35. Cf. Employers' Liability Assur. Corp. v. Madden, 219 F.2d 205 (5th Cir. 1955); Wright v. Paramount-Richards Theatres, 198 F.2d 303 (5th Cir. 1952); Gillen v. Phoenix Indemnity Co., 198 F.2d 147 (5th Cir. 1952).

the last word on issues of constitutional law, and in that sense may be regarded as the highest court of the land.[36]

Comparovich: Good point. It should be noted, in addition, that a party's right to what we call "due process" occasionally may receive not only constitutional but also international protection. This is true especially in Europe, where 21 nations have ratified the European Convention on Human Rights. Under the terms of that Convention, complaints concerning violations of human rights, including fundamental procedural rights, may be lodged with the European Commission of Human Rights, and (depending on the Commission's determination) with the European Court of Human Rights.[36a]

The significance of such constitutional and international guarantees is greater in administrative and criminal proceedings than in civil ones. But even in civil actions, as we have seen already, it can happen that for the reasons just mentioned by you and by me the court at the apex of the ordinary court system will not really have the last word.[36b]

Smooth: This is interesting. But let us be practical about it. I suggest that in our discussion here, unless otherwise indicated, the terms "court of last resort" or "highest court" be taken as referring to the court at the summit of the hierarchy of ordinary courts, i.e., the court which in civil and criminal cases hears appeals from the decisions of intermediate appellate courts.[36c]

Comparovich: This is an excellent suggestion.

36. See supra p. 375. When the Constitutional Court upholds the constitutionality of a statute, but at the same time requires a particular construction of the statute in order to make it constitutional, the question arises whether the ordinary courts are then bound to adopt that construction. In Italy, the Constitutional Court and the Court of Cassation have given conflicting answers to that question. See J. H. Merryman & V. Vigoriti, When Courts Collide: Constitution and Cassation in Italy, 15 Am.J.Comp.L. 665 (1966–67).

36a. See M. Cappelletti, Fundamental Guarantees of the Parties in Civil Litigation: Comparative Constitutional, International and Social Trends, 25 Stan.L.Rev. 651 (1973); S. A. Cohn, International Adjudication of Human Rights and the European Court of Human Rights: A Survey of Its Procedural and Some of Its Substantive Holdings, 7 Ga.J.Int. & Comp.L. 315 (1977); W. K. Geck, Individual Freedoms in Today's World: Laws and Reality, 1 Hastings Int. & Comp.L.Rev. 235 (1978).

The possibility of such an ultimate appeal to a supra-national forum may be the most important effect of the Convention; but it is not the only one. Its protective provisions frequently can be invoked while a case is still pending in the national courts of a signatory country. The majority of the signatories recognize the Convention not merely as creating international governmental obligations, but also as a source of domestic law. See A. Z. Drcemczewski, European Human Rights Convention in Domestic Law, passim and especially 189–91 (1983); J. Robert, La France et la protection transnationale des Droits de l'Homme, 38 Rev.Int. de Droit Comparé 635, 637–47 (1986). Austria has gone a step further and has given the Convention the force of domestic constitutional law. See ibid.

36b. Moreover, as the reader will recall, the highest courts of Common Market countries may have to refer questions of Community law, including questions arising under the Convention dealing with jurisdiction and enforcement of judgments, to the Court of Justice of the European Community.

36c. In the great majority of cases (i.e., in all cases not involving constitutionally or internationally protected rights) that court does indeed have the last word.

In one respect the civilians' treatment of appeals to the court of last resort [36d] is similar to our law: such appeals are exclusively on the law and cannot raise issues of fact. But on several significant points of appellate practice the rules governing the highest courts in civil-law systems (or at least in some of them) differ sharply from those familiar to a common-law lawyer. These differences relate to the following three questions:

(a) Can an appeal to the court of last resort be taken as of right, or merely by permission or upon a grant of certiorari?

(b) What disposition should the highest court make of the case if it concludes that the decision below rests on reversible error?

(c) Since the highest court of a civil-law country, like the lower courts, normally sits in panels or divisions, the further question arises: how can inconsistencies and contradictions between the decisions of various panels be avoided?

Concerning question (a), I should emphasize, first of all, that it does not involve a mere technicality; the answer to that question is of the greatest significance for the development of the law in a given jurisdiction.

Smooth: I quite agree. A court of last resort which does not control its own calendar, must be in danger of becoming so flooded with enormous numbers of (in large part unimportant) cases that it can devote only insufficient time and energy to the truly novel and important issues of law coming before it. The real mission of the highest court—to keep the law straight, up-to-date and uniform—can hardly be accomplished if the court does not have the power to select the cases it considers worthy of thorough review.

Comparovich: You have eloquently stated the argument in favor of the principle of selectivity that has been adopted in the majority of common-law jurisdictions.

The traditional civil-law rule is to the effect that the party who lost in the intermediate appellate court may as of right seek review by the highest court.[36e] As applied to the civil-law world, your argument in favor of selectivity is somewhat weakened by the fact that the highest courts of civil-law countries—consisting as they do of a number of civil and criminal panels—can distribute the workload among a larger corps of judges.[36f] Nevertheless, civilian scholars have criticized the tradi-

36d. For an excellent comparative symposium on the structure and procedure of courts of last resort in a number of leading civil-law and common-law countries, see A. Tunc (Ed.), La Cour Judiciaire Suprême: Une Enquête Comparative, 30 Revue Internationale de Droit Comparé 1 ff. (1978).

36e. In some civil-law countries it is provided that in certain matters an appeal to the court of last resort may not be taken if it involves less than a specified minimum amount.

36f. Both in France and in West Germany, the court at the apex of the hierarchy of ordinary courts consists of more than 100 judges. For details see the study cited supra n. 36d.

tional civil-law rule of non-selectivity on policy grounds very similar to those stated by you.[36g]

Smooth: It seems that in most countries the last few decades have witnessed an explosive increase in the workload of courts, and especially of appellate courts. Has this not forced the legislators of civil-law countries to modify their system of non-selectivity?

Comparovich: In a few civil-law countries the traditional system has indeed been modified. In West Germany, for instance, the present rule is that an appeal to the court of last resort can be taken as of right only if the matter is "patrimonial" (i.e., if it involves financial or property interests) and if the amount in dispute exceeds DM 40,000. In cases where the amount in dispute is less than that, or the matter is non-patrimonial (e.g., in divorce actions), an appeal to the highest court can be taken only if the intermediate appellate court has permitted it. Such permission is granted if the case presents a question of "fundamental importance", or if the intermediate appellate court's decision in the case deviates from a prior decision of the highest court.[37]

A further restriction was introduced in 1975. Section 554b of the Code of Civil Procedure, which was added in that year, provides that appeals taken as of right (i.e., appeals in patrimonial matters where the amount in dispute exceeds DM 40,000) can be summarily dismissed by the highest court if a two-thirds majority of the panel in charge of the case concludes that the matter is without "fundamental significance".[37a]

Edge: Does this provision confer upon the German court of last resort the same unfettered discretionary power which the U.S. Supreme Court enjoys in selecting cases for full review?

Comparovich: The *Bundesgerichtshof* (the German court of last resort in civil and criminal matters) at first thought so. But in 1980 the Constitutional Court held, en banc, that in order to render § 554b constitutionally valid, it must be construed as authorizing summary dismissal only of appeals which appear to be without merit.[37b] It follows that in considering a summary dismissal the *Bundesgerichtshof* may not pay any attention to a factor—such as the workload of the court—that is unconnected with the merits.[37c] In support of its holding, the Constitutional Court pointed out that to keep the law straight and uniform, is only one of the functions of the court of last resort; the

36g. See M. Cappelletti, The Doctrine of Stare Decisis and the Civil Law: A Fundamental Difference—or No Difference at All?, in H. Bernstein, U. Drobnig & H. Koetz, Festschrift fuer Konrad Zweigert 381, 385–87 (1981), and authorities there cited.

37. West German Code of Civil Procedure § 546.

37a. A somewhat similar statute enacted in Japan in 1950 was thought of as a temporary emergency measure; by its terms, the statute remained in force only

for 4 years. In 1954, Japan returned to the non-selectivity system, which since then has remained in effect. See T. Hattori & D. F. Henderson, Civil Procedure in Japan, §§ 8.03[1] and 8.06 (1985).

37b. Decision of June 11, 1980, BVerfGE 54, 277.

37c. For a more detailed discussion of the decision see W. B. Fisch, Recent Reforms in German Civil Procedure: The Constitutional Dimension, 1 Civil Justice Q. 33, 41–45 (1982).

other—equally important—function is to do justice between the parties. Therefore, the Constitutional Court added, the label "insignicant" can never be applied to a case in which the appellant's rights have been violated by an incorrect decision of the lower court.[37d]

Edge: As limited by the Constitutional Court, does § 554b of the German Code still perform a substantial screening function?

Comparovich: Yes. It has been reported that about one-third of the appeals taken as of right are treated as meritless and summarily dismissed by the highest court.[37e]

Edge: The German example thus seems to indicate that a modicum of screening is possible even though the principle of non-selectivity is not entirely discarded, and only meritless appeals are "selected out".

Comparovich: Partly influenced by the German experience, the French by recent legislation have adopted a somewhat similar screening system.[37f] Under the French system, a three-judge committee of the Court of Cassation panel handling the case may summarily dismiss the *pourvoi* (appeal) if the committee unanimously finds it to be "manifestly without merit." It is interesting to note that the French statute, by its clear wording, adopted the same standard which was read into the more ambiguous German provision by the German Constitutional Court.

Smooth: Let us turn to question (b), involving the highest court's disposition of the case upon reversal.

Comparovich: On this question the civil-law countries are divided. Some follow the German system of "revision", while others have adopted the French system of "cassation". Under the German system, the highest court may, if it finds reversible error in the judgment appealed from, either (1) reverse and remand to the intermediate appellate court, or (2) reverse or modify the judgment below and itself enter such judgment as corresponds to its view of the case.

Edge: This is similar to our system.

Comparovich: Correct. But the French system of cassation is quite different, and this is the system which seems to prevail in Ruritania, as indicated by the name of that country's highest court. Under that system, the highest court traditionally has only the power to "*casser*", i.e. to break, the judgment below, and upon doing so *must* remand the case to an intermediate appellate court.[38] As a rule, the latter court

---

37d. The Constitutional Court, however, left open the question whether a different standard might apply if the statute, instead of authorizing the summary dismissal of an appeal already taken, provided that the highest court's permission must be obtained *before* an appeal may be filed. A statute of the latter type had been proposed, but was rejected, at the time § 554b was enacted.

37e. See Fisch, supra n. 37c.

37f. Code de l'Organisation Judiciaire, Art. 131–6, as amended in 1979 and 1981.

38. The French Cour de Cassation, in reversing the decision of a Cour d'Appel, formerly always remanded the case to another (usually neighboring) Cour d'Appel. This practice is exemplified by the case which appears infra p. 749. But Art. 626 of the new Code of Civil Procedure, as amended in 1979, now authorizes the Court of Cassation, at its option, to remand either

will then decide the case in accordance with the views expressed by the highest court. But it may happen, and it has happened, that upon such remand the intermediate appellate court refuses to follow the opinion of the Court of Cassation. Under the traditional French doctrine, the intermediate appellate court does not violate any rule of law by adopting this course, because it is not bound by decisions of the highest tribunal, not even by a decision rendered in the same case. Of course, if the intermediate appellate court hands down a judgment defying the view previously expressed by the highest court in the same case, the losing party will again bring the matter before the Court of Cassation by a new appeal. This time, the appeal is heard by the *assemblée plénière* [39], a super-panel of the highest court consisting of 25 judges.[39a] If this large judicial body takes the same view of the case as the much smaller "chamber" which previously entered the highest court's first judgment of reversal and remand, there will be a second reversal. This time, however, the decision of the Court of Cassation has a greater degree of finality. If the *assemblée plénière* remands a case to an intermediate appellate court,[39b] the latter court is bound to follow the views expressed in the judgment of reversal.[39c]

Smooth: I am beginning to see the complexities and uncertainties of which L sought to warn us.[39d]

Comparovich: One has to understand the reasons for this excessive complexity of the French system of "cassation". Remembering judicial abuses committed during the *ancien régime*, post-revolutionary France was unwilling to entrust the country's highest court with much power. As time went on, and the practical problems created by the non-finality of decisions of the Court of Cassation became intolerable, the legislator gradually and grudgingly accorded binding effect to some decisions of that Court, but only to those rendered by a super-panel. The enormous complexity of the system which thus evolved over the years is not too surprising.

to a different Cour d'Appel or to the same Cour d'Appel (composed of different judges) from which the case came originally.

39. The resolution of a conflict between the Court of Cassation and an intermediate appellate court (see text, supra) is not the only function of the super-panel called *assemblée plénière*. Appeals can be referred to it also in other cases involving a "question of principle", especially when there is a conflict on a point of law among several intermediate appellate courts. See Code de l'Organisation Judiciaire, Art. 131–2, as amended in 1979.

39a. Before this super-panel was instituted in 1967, cases of this kind had to be decided by the so-called *chambres réunies*, a body which consisted of an even larger number of judges and resembled a true en-banc sitting of the (approximately one hun-

dred) members of the court. See P. Herzog, Civil Procedure in France 163 (1967).

39b. See supra n. 38.

39c. This binding effect is now given to all decisions of the *assemblée plénière*, not only to those rendered upon a second appeal to the Court of Cassation. See Code de l'Organisation Judiciaire, Art. 131–4, as amended in 1979.

39d. The danger of such complexities, especially the danger that upon the first reversal and remand by the Court of Cassation the intermediate appellate court will defy the views of the highest court, is not merely theoretical. On average, the *assemblée plénière* has to be called together five times a year to deal with such situations.

In the recent past, the French have made an attempt—albeit a somewhat halfhearted one—to modify the classical system of pure "cassation". Art. 627 of the new Code of Civil Procedure authorizes the Court of Cassation,[39e] in its discretion, to "reverse without remand", and to enter a final judgment, if further proceedings before a court having fact-finding powers appear unnecessary. At first blush, this seems to confer upon the Court of Cassation the kind of power that is possessed by an American or German court of last resort, i.e., in case of a reversal freely to choose between remand and final decision. But the highest court of France is still called the "Court of Cassation", and in the light of its tradition may be expected to make only occasional use of its new power to "reverse without remand".[39f] Moreover, when you have to deal with the system of "cassation" in another country, such as Ruritania, you have to remember that such a country originally may have taken over the classical French model of "cassation", but that perhaps it has not adopted the modifications more recently enacted in France. It is quite possible, therefore, that the Ruritanian Court of Cassation, when it reverses a judgment of the intermediate appellate court, is forced to remand the case to the latter court.

Smooth: Let us now turn to what you called question (c), the question dealing with the internal functioning of a court of last resort.

Comparovich: As I have mentioned before, the courts of civil-law countries, including the highest courts, sit in panels. Some of these panels deal with civil cases, and others with criminal matters. In the German *Bundesgerichtshof*, a case is heard by five judges.[40] In the French *Cour de Cassation*, where until recently a quorum of seven judges was required to hear a case, the number is now reduced to five;[40a] and whenever the President of the *Cour de Cassation* or the President of the "*Chambre*" in question considers a case a simple one, he can refer it to a "*formation restreinte*" consisting of only three judges.[40b]

Although all cases relating to a given field of the law (e.g., divorce, or corporation law) normally are referred to the same panel,[40c] it is

---

39e. As amended in 1979, Art. 627 of the Code of Civil Procedure confers this power not only upon the *assemblée plénière*, but upon the Court's regular panels as well. Before 1967, this power did not exist at all. Between 1967 and 1979, it was given only to the *assemblée plénière*.

39f. See R. Lindon, De certaines récentes modifications de la procédure devant la Cour de Cassation, 1980 J.C.P. I 2967; P. Hébraud, "Aggiornamento" de la Cour de Cassation, 1979 D.Chr. 205, 210–12.

40. Each panel of the highest court is called a "*Senat*" in Germany, a "*Chambre*" in France. The total membership of a panel is apt to be larger than five; the statements in the text, supra, refer to the number of judges who will hear a given case (sometimes called the quorum), and not to the total number of members of a panel.

40a. Code d'Organisation Judiciaire, Art. 131–6, as amended in 1981.

40b. Ibid. See also J. Boré, La Loi du 6 août 1981 et la réforme de la Cour de Cassation, 1981 D.Chr. 299.

40c. This system of specialization is particularly refined in Germany. For a detailed description see D. J. Meador, Appellate Subject Matter Organization: The German Design from an American Perspective, 5 Hastings Int. & Comp.L.Rev. 27 (1981).

inevitable that occasional conflicts arise between the decisions of various panels, especially in connection with general problems which cut across diverse areas of the law.

Edge: This problem is by no means unknown in our country. It arises, for instance, in the practice of the United States Courts of Appeals, which ordinarily sit in panels.[41]

Comparovich: You are right; but the problem is not quite as serious as it is in the civil-law countries, because the United States Courts of Appeals are not courts of last resort. If a conflict develops between two panels of a Court of Appeals,[41a] and such conflict is not resolved by that court sitting *en banc*,[41b] the Supreme Court ultimately may determine the disputed question.[42]

The problem is more acute in countries where the highest court itself sits in panels.[43] The Germans sought to solve the problem by providing that any panel wishing to deviate from a prior decision of another panel had to submit the question to a plenary session. If both panels involved were civil panels, the plenary session would be attended by all the judges of the civil panels; but if a civil panel wanted to deviate from a previous decision of a criminal panel, the plenary session would become a true "Plenum", and would consist of at least two-thirds of all of the members of the court, i.e. (in the case of the former German *Reichsgericht*, the predecessor of the *Bundesgerichtshof*) about fifty persons.[44] Understandably, the judges were reluctant to employ this cumbersome procedure. Therefore, they developed an

41. 28 U.S.C.A. § 46, as amended; Fed. Rules of App.Pro. Rule 35. Concerning similar problems arising in the practice of the U.S. Court of Claims, see the 1966 amendments of 28 U.S.C.A. § 175, discussed by S. B. Jacoby, Recent Legislation Affecting the Court of Claims, 55 Geo.L.J. 397, 398–402 (1966).

41a. According to a large body of authority, a panel of a U.S. Court of Appeals is bound to follow a precedential decision previously handed down by another panel of the same court, at least until the matter is reconsidered *en banc.* See, e.g., United States v. Olivares-Vega, 495 F.2d 827 (2d Cir. 1974); United States v. Hernandez, 580 F.2d 188 (5th Cir. 1978). See also Anno., 37 A.L.R.Fed. 274 (1978). Nevertheless, experience shows that intra-circuit conflicts are quite frequent. See A. B. Rubin, Views from the Lower Court, 23 U.C.L.A.L.Rev. 448, 452 (1976).

41b. See Fed.Rules of App.Pro. Rule 35.

It is interesting to note that pursuant to 28 U.S.C.A. § 46, as amended in 1978, the larger circuits now are permitted to hold "*en banc*" hearings attended by less than all of the circuit judges. See, e.g., Rule 25 of the Rules of the United States Court of Appeals for the Ninth Circuit. Thus the super-panel, so beloved by the civilians, has come to our country as well.

42. Moreover, when confronted with an intra-circuit conflict, the Supreme Court may remand a case, suggesting—and in effect directing—an *en banc* hearing before the judges of the Court of Appeals. See United States ex rel. Robinson v. Johnston, 316 U.S. 649, 62 S.Ct. 1301 (1942).

43. The problem, of course, is intimately connected with the broader question of the force of precedents, which will be discussed in detail, infra pp. 597 ff. At this point, the reader may assume, subject to the more elaborate explanation which will follow in the subsequent materials just mentioned, that a "court" (including the highest "court") in a civilian country is not bound by a stringent rule of *stare decisis*, and has the power to overrule its own prior decisions. But there remains the question whether in a matter as grave as the overruling of a precedent a single panel may speak for the "court", and whether Panel A may overrule a previous decision by Panel B. The discussion in the text is directed to these procedural issues.

44. For details and for interesting comparative observations see E. J. Cohn,

attitude known in Germany as "*horror pleni*", making strenuous and often ingenious efforts to distinguish previous decisions in order to avoid the open admission of a conflict which would necessitate submission of the case to the Plenum. More recently, this unwieldy system was modified by the creation of super-panels, consisting of at least nine judges where the conflict is between two civil panels, and of at least seventeen judges where it is between a civil and a criminal panel.[45] These super-panels now wield the powers formerly exercised by plenary sessions.[45a] The size of the group of judges who must assemble in order to resolve a conflict between panels, has been reduced by this reform; and although it seems that the "*horror pleni*", i.e. the reluctance of individual panels to invoke the conflict-resolving procedure, has not been entirely eliminated, the revised system is a workable one.

Until 1947, the French had no similar machinery for avoiding conflicts among panels of the Court of Cassation. This was explained as reflecting the strength of "French opinion opposed to the theory of the binding force of judicial decisions." [46] But when in 1947 the Court of Cassation was reorganized, and the number of civil panels increased, the French adopted the German system of a plenary session for the prevention of intra-court conflicts; and more recently (again following the German example) they replaced that plenary session with a super-panel called *chambre mixte*, consisting of a number of judges that varies between 13 and 25, depending on the number of panels involved in the conflict. French law thus provides for two different types of super-panels of the Court of Cassation. The *assemblée plénière* determines conflicts between the Court of Cassation and a lower court which upon remand refuses to follow the views expressed by the highest court in the same case, while the *chambre mixte* resolves conflicts among panels of the highest court itself.[47]

Smooth: L also mentioned another peculiar feature of Court of Cassation practice. He pointed out that arguments would be presented to the Court not only by counsel for the parties but also by the Government. This baffled me, because I could not see any reason why the Government of Ruritania would wish to become an amicus curiae in this purely private dispute.

Comparovich: In France and a number of other civil-law countries (not including Germany), government attorneys appearing for the

Precedents in Continental Law, 5 Camb. L.J. 366 (1935).

45. See Gerichtsverfassungsgesetz (Law Concerning the Organization of Courts), §§ 132 and 136.

45a. Even in the absence of an intra-court conflict, any panel of the Court can refer a case of "fundamental importance" to a super-panel. Gerichtsverfassungsgesetz, § 137. It remains true, nevertheless, that the main function of the super-panels is to resolve conflicts among several panels of the Court.

46. See Cohn, supra n. 44, at 370.

47. Formerly, the super-panel determining intra-court conflicts was called *assemblée plénière*, and the reader may find this designation in older texts. The French legislator, by giving one of the two types of super-panels the name formerly used for the other type of super-panel, has made it easy for the outside observer to become confused.

ministère public and forming the so-called *parquet* of each court serve a dual function: (1) They prosecute criminal proceedings and some of the other types of actions to which the Government is a party. (2) They can intervene in *any* litigation to represent the public interest; [47a] this power exists even though the Government is not a party to the particular case and may have no financial interest in its outcome. In the lower civil courts, the power is used sparingly. Every case reaching the highest court, however, is thought so strongly to affect the public interest in the sound development of the law that the views of the *ministère public* must be presented.[48] These views do not bind the court in any way; but often brilliantly expressed, they may prove highly persuasive.[48a]

Edge: I suppose that a case sometimes takes a striking turn in the Court of Cassation, perhaps due in part to a new argument injected by government counsel?

Comparovich: I have heard of instances where this happened.

Smooth: In view of everything you have told us about the Court of Cassation, it seems that we did the smart thing when we settled our case while it was pending before that Court.

Comparovich: How much did you pay?

47a. By considering this function of the *Parquet* in civil proceedings, we are led to a broader question: Who does, and who should, represent the public interest in civil litigation? A public office, like the French *Parquet*, or a "private attorney general" such as the typical plaintiff in class-actions and similar kinds of litigation in the U.S.? For thought-provoking comparative discussions, see M. Cappelletti, Governmental and Private Advocates for the Public Interest in Civil Litigation, 75 Mich.L.Rev. 794 (1975); H. Koetz and A. Homburger, Klagen Privater im oeffentlichen Interesse (Vol. 68 of Arbeiten zur Rechtsvergleichung, 1975); M. Cappelletti & J. A. Jolowicz, Public Interest Parties and the Active Role of the Judge in Civil Litigation (1975); M. Cappelletti & B. Garth, The Worldwide Movement To Make Rights Effective: A General Report, in 1 Cappelletti (Gen.Ed.), Access to Justice 3, at 35–48 (1978); W. B. Fisch, European Analogues to the Class Action: Group Action in France and Germany, 27 Am.J. Comp.L. 51 (1979).

For an interesting judicial discussion of some of the differences between a consumer-protection action brought by a public official and a private class-action instituted for the same purpose, see People v. Pacific Land Research Co., 20 Cal.3d 10, 141 Cal. Rptr. 20, 569 P.2d 125 (1977).

48. See Deák and Rheinstein, The Machinery of Law Administration in France and Germany, 84 U.Pa.L.Rev. 846, 857–58 (1936); Herzog, supra n. 39a, at 122, 165–66.

Under our practice, the Attorney General has the power to present amicus curiae briefs to the courts, and especially to the highest courts. See Fed.Rules of App.Pro., Rule 29, and U.S. Supreme Court Rule 36.4. But, in contrast to the French practice described in the text, supra, that power is sparingly exercised in this country.

48a. In France and in other countries following the French example, the representative of the *ministère public* is present during the court's secret deliberations, from which private parties and their counsel are rigorously excluded. This practice seems rather objectionable, especially in criminal cases where the government is not merely a defender of the public interest, but a party to the proceeding. Yet, in a much-criticized decision, the European Court of Human Rights has rejected a due process attack on this practice. See the Court's January 17, 1970, decision in the Delcourt case, [1970] Y.B. Eur.Conv. on Human Rights 1100. See also K. H. Nadelmann, Due Process of Law Before the European Court of Human Rights: The Secret Deliberation, 66 Am.J.Int.L. 509 (1972).

Smooth: We paid the plaintiff $1,350, and waived our right to reimbursement of costs and attorneys' fees, in exchange for a general release.

Comparovich: Considering that the case involved a conflict of laws question which was not entirely free from doubt, and that the outcome in the Court of Cassation was uncertain, you made a wise decision.

Smooth: Thus ended the Haifisch case,[49] which we now understand much better in the light of your post-mortem comments. Let us adjourn until after lunch.

2. THE PLACE OF "CIVIL" LITIGATION IN A CIVILIAN SYSTEM—LINES OF DEMARCATION

A. COMMERCIAL COURTS *

The Dialogue Continued

Smooth: As we have completed our chronological discussion of the Haifisch case, we should like to ask you, Professor, whether there are any general comments or qualifications which you would care to add?

Comparovich: The case gave us an opportunity for discussing some important civilian notions of procedure in "civil" cases, i.e., in cases coming up before a civil chamber of a tribunal of first instance. In continental terminology, "civil" matters must be distinguished not only from criminal and administrative, but also from commercial cases.

Edge: Are there "commercial chambers", in addition to the civil and criminal chambers of the courts?

---

49. The Haifisch case typifies ordinary adversary litigation. It should be pointed out that in many civil-law countries there exists, in addition, another type of proceeding—governed either by special provisions in the Code of Civil Procedure or by a separate statute—, which usually is conducted in a simpler, more informal manner. Proceedings of the latter type are referred to as *voluntary or non-contentious proceedings.* They deal with matters such as guardianship, adoption, probate of Wills and the administration of decedents' estates; in some countries the courts having jurisdiction in non-contentious matters also operate or supervise the land register, the commercial register and the many other official registers which play such an important role in civil-law systems.

The term "non-contentious" proceedings is not quite accurate, because in many instances these proceedings are in fact contested; but issues of title to property, or of the validity of a Will, ultimately must be settled by way of ordinary litigation in the regular courts rather than in a "non-contentious" proceeding. See Neitzel, Non-Contentious Jurisdiction in Germany, 21 Harv.L.Rev. 476 (1908); Cappelletti and Perillo, Civil Procedure in Italy 352–59 (1965); Herzog, supra n. 39a, at 494–99; J. Jodlowski, La procédure civile non-contentieuse, in Acta Instituti Upsaliensis Jurisprudentiae Comparativae, Vol. IX, Rapports Généraux au VIIe Congrès International de Droit Comparé (Stockholm 1968), p. 189. For cases illustrating the effect here of a non-contentious proceeding conducted in Germany, see Estate of Bellmer, 144 Misc. 462, 258 N.Y.S. 964 (Surr.Ct. 1932); Estate of Hahnel, 88 Misc. 2d 524, 389 N.Y.S.2d 970 (Surr.Ct., 1976), aff'd 58 A.D.2d 531, 395 N.Y.S.2d 395 (1st Dept. 1977).

* Concerning the historical reasons for the dichotomy between "civil" and "commercial" law in the civilian orbit, see supra pp. 301–304. The difficult definitional problem of what is a "commercial" matter, will be discussed infra pp. 590–596.

Comparovich: We can observe three different systems, each of which has a substantial following in the civil-law world. Under the German system, a court of first instance has three types of chambers—criminal, civil and commercial. The civil chambers are composed exclusively of professional judges; but a commercial chamber consists of a legally trained, professional judge as P.J., and two merchants as associate judges.[1] The procedure before a commercial chamber is essentially the same as before a civil chamber,[2] and appeals from its decisions are heard by the same courts (sitting without lay judges) which determine appeals from judgments of a civil chamber.

Under the French system, the Commercial Court is a separate court, and not a mere chamber of the ordinary tribunal of first instance. It is entirely composed of merchant judges, elected—indirectly—by their fellow merchants; and its procedure, partly governed by provisions of the Commercial Code, is simpler and speedier than that of the ordinary courts.[3] On the appellate level, however, the French system is much like the German, in that the intermediate appellate court and the Court of Cassation, even when they hear appeals from the Commercial Court, are composed exclusively of professional judges.

There is also a third system—adopted by a minority of civil-law countries of which Italy is typical—, under which separate commercial courts and commercial chambers have been abolished, with the result that commercial as well as civil cases come before the civil chambers of the ordinary tribunals of first instance. The idea behind this minority system is that the separate treatment of commercial matters, though deeply rooted in the civilian tradition, is no longer necessary or even desirable in this age.[4]

B. ARBITRATION [1]

Edge: In commercial matters, we often avoid the necessity of coping with foreign law and foreign procedure, by inserting arbitration clauses into our international contracts.

Comparovich: This practice of yours is in accord with a worldwide trend among business concerns increasingly to choose arbitration as the method by which disputes arising in international trade transactions should be settled. I must dissent, however, from your statement that

1. The merchant judges are appointed upon recommendation of local or regional Chambers of Commerce and Industry.

2. The two merchant judges are judges, not jurors. Issues of law as well as fact are determined by a majority of the three judges. Their decisions are announced per curiam, even though as a practical matter they are always prepared by the P.J.

3. The case-load in the French commercial courts is heavy. It is reported that before the recent increase in automobile tort litigation the civil chambers of the ordinary tribunals of first instance handled fewer cases than the commercial courts. See P. Herzog, Civil Procedure in France 146 (1967).

4. Of course, the basic problem—whether the separate system of rules for commercial transactions should be continued—arises with respect to substantive law as well as with respect to jurisdiction and procedure. It is a difficult and controversial problem, which has given rise to much debate throughout the civil-law world. See infra p. 542.

1. This section contains only a few—very brief—practical suggestions. The reader who is interested in studying arbitration, and especially international commercial arbitration, has many extensive treatments of the subject at his disposal. See, e.g., 2 G. R. Delaume, Transnational Contracts—Applicable Law and Settlement of Disputes, Ch. 13 (Rev.Ed., 1986); L. Kanowitz, Alternative Dispute Resolution—Cases and Materials (1986).

the use of arbitration makes it unnecessary to study foreign law and procedure.

In spite of current efforts aiming at increased uniformity in this field, there is still a great deal of diversity among the arbitration laws of the various legal systems. If arbitration is to take place abroad, say in Ruritania, you have to know whether the Ruritanian courts would recognize the validity of the arbitration agreement,[2] and will lend their aid (a) negatively, by refusing to entertain a court action brought in violation of the agreement to arbitrate, and (b) affirmatively, e.g. by appointing arbitrators, by compelling witnesses to testify before the arbitral tribunal, and by confirming the award.[3]

In addition, you have to keep in mind that if under the terms of the arbitration clause the arbitration is anchored in Ruritania, it is Ruritanian law which (subject to applicable treaties) guides the arbitrators in determining questions of procedure and of choice of law.

Edge: Of course, if we provide for arbitration in Ruritania, we must consult Ruritanian law on all these points. I have heard, however, that when parties in different countries provide for arbitration of present or future disputes, they now increasingly tend to adopt contract clauses intended to denationalize the arbitration, e.g., a provision to the effect that the arbitrators shall apply "the general principles of law recognized by civilized nations".[4]

Comparovich: Even the adoption of such a denationalizing clause does not render it unnecessary to study the law of the country where the arbitration is anchored. Validity and effect of the clause depend on that law.[5]

The parties to an arbitration agreement have the tremendous advantage that they can choose the country where the arbitration will be anchored. But as a practical matter this advantage is lost unless the draftsman, after having compared the arbitration laws of various countries, selects one that (a) assuredly gives effect to the terms of the

2. Unless the question is controlled by an applicable international treaty (see infra), this will involve, inter alia, a problem of (Ruritanian) conflict of laws.

3. The laws of the various nations (except as affected and unified by treaties) differ widely concerning the grounds on which judicial confirmation of an award may be refused. In some countries, such as Italy and several Latin American nations, the foreign citizenship of an arbitrator may justify such refusal. See Cappelletti and Perillo, Civil Procedure in Italy 362, 365 (1965); Bayitch, Treaty Law of Private Arbitration, 10 Arb.J. 188, 192 (1955). There are many countries, also, where confirmation can be refused on the ground that the arbitrators did not state the reasons for their award. See M. Domke, Arbitral Awards Without Written Opinions: Comparative Aspects of International Commercial Arbitration, in the volume "Twentieth Century Comparative and Conflicts Law—Legal Essays in Honor of Hessel E. Yntema" 249 (1961); P. Sanders, Procedures and Practices Under the UNCI-TRAL Rules, 27 Am.J.Comp.L. 453, 455 (1979).

In the codes of civil-law countries one is apt to find not only specific rules of the kind just mentioned, but also catch-all provisions directing the courts to refuse confirmation if the award violates the principles of "good morals" or "the public order". Such formulations are typical of the legislative technique of civil-law codifiers. This technique will be discussed infra pp. 702–766.

4. See 1 Schlesinger, Formation of Contracts—A Study of the Common Core of Legal Systems 13–16 (1968), where further references can be found.

5. See Schlesinger and Gündisch, Allgemeine Rechtsgrundsäze als Sachnormen in Schiedsgerichtsverfahren, 28 Rabels Z. 4 (1964). For references to recent cases see V. Danilowicz, The Choice of Applicable Law in International Arbitration, 9 Hastings Int. & Comp.L.Rev. 235 (1986).

agreement, and (b) provides for a fair procedure expeditiously leading to an enforceable award.[5a]

Edge: Generally it is our practice to provide for arbitration in New York, because both federal law and New York law favor the enforcement of arbitration agreements.

Comparovich: If the other party to the agreement is in Ruritania, and if you have property there, you would still have to study the law of Ruritania (including applicable treaties to which Ruritania is a party) in order to know whether the arbitration clause will effectively prevent the other party from suing you in a Ruritanian court.[6]

Moreover, assuming you obtain an award, and a judgment confirming it, in New York, you may have to go to Ruritania for its enforcement.[7] This again will require a hard look at Ruritanian law and practice,[8] and at multilateral [9] as well as bilateral [10] treaties that may be applicable.

C. CRIMINAL PROCEDURE

Smooth: You will be surprised to learn that quite frequently this office runs into problems of criminal procedure, in connection with automobile accidents and extracurricular activities of our staff members abroad. For this reason, Mr. Edge and I are interested in familiarizing ourselves with the fundamentals of the criminal process in civil-law countries.

Comparovich: There is a further reason why you and I, and indeed all American lawyers, should be interested in that subject. Our own system of criminal justice has been so signally unsuccessful that every attempt should be made to study, and to learn from, the relevant experience of other nations.

5a. See the instructive article by N. C. Ulmer, Drafting the International Arbitration Clause, 20 Int. Lawyer 1335 (1986).

6. Needless to say, the draftsman must examine not only the relevant domestic and conflict-of-laws rules of Ruritania, but also applicable treaties. See infra nn. 9 and 10. Moreover, if an arbitral institution is named in the agreement, the draftsman has to be familiar with the Rules of that institution.

7. See M. Domke, American Arbitral Awards: Enforcement in Foreign Countries, 1965 Ill.L. Forum 399. This informative article also appears in W. R. LaFave and P. Hay, International Trade, Investment and Organization, at 65ff. (1967).

8. If Ruritanian law should require "reciprocity", it is important to remember that New York liberally enforces foreign awards and judgments entered thereon. Gilbert v. Burnstine, 255 N.Y. 348, 174 N.E. 706 (1931); further cases are cited by E. F. Scoles & P. Hay, Conflict of Laws, § 24.47 (1982, and 1986 Supp.).

9. The 1958 U.N. Convention on the Recognition and Enforcement of Foreign Arbitral Awards has been adopted by the United States and by over 55 other nations. See P. Sanders, A Twenty Years' Review of the Convention on the Recognition and Enforcement of Foreign Arbitral Awards, 13 Int.Lawyer 269 (1979); H. Harnik, Recognition and Enforcement of Foreign Arbitral Awards, 31 Am.J.Comp.L. 703 (1983); A. J. van den Berg, The New York Arbitration Convention of 1958—Towards a Uniform Judicial Interpretation (1981).

The United States, along with a very large and still growing number of other nations, also is a party to the Convention on the Settlement of Investment Disputes Between States and Nationals of Other States. See P. C. Szasz, A Practical Guide to the Convention on Settlement of Investment Disputes, 1 Cornell Int.L.J. 1 (1968); D. T. Wilson, International Business Transactions 409–11 (2d ed., 1984).

10. Treaties of Friendship and Commerce often contain relevant provisions. See Bayitch, supra n. 3.

Edge: I quite agree with you. Is it not true, moreover, that some of our military lawyers, as a matter of their daily practice, have to immerse themselves in the criminal procedure of civil-law countries?

Comparovich: Yes. This is due to the fact that every year, under traditional rules of international law and under the terms of Status of Forces Agreements, thousands of our military people stationed abroad become subject to prosecution in the courts of "receiving states",[1] most of which belong to the civil-law orbit.[2] The ratification of the first of these treaties by the U.S. Senate was coupled with an important statement of "the sense of the Senate",[3] which, among other things, directed the military services to undertake thorough studies of the criminal procedure of the countries where our men are stationed. This legislative request has been called "the first instance of the study of comparative law being required by a legislative body of the United States".[4] Implemented by a directive of the Department of Defense,[4a] it resulted in valuable "country studies" of the criminal procedure of various civil-law countries.[5]

Edge: A lawyer friend of mine, who as a Captain in the J.A.G. Division of the U.S. Army is presently serving abroad (in a civil-law country), tells me that he spends most of his time observing trials of U.S. servicemen that take place in the local courts, and writing reports to higher authority in which he has to comment on (a) the adequacy of defense counsel,[6] (b) the adequacy of the interpreter retained for the accused, and (c) the fairness of the trial.[7] Many other military lawyers seem to be engaged in similar work throughout the many foreign countries where U.S. troops are stationed.

1. For some interesting statistics, showing the large number of cases in which U.S. servicemen become subject to the jurisdiction of the courts of civil-law host countries, see S. Riesenfeld, Book Review, 67 Am.J.Int.L. 377 (1973). See also Dept. of Defense, Report of Statistics on the Exercise of Criminal Jurisdiction by Foreign Tribunals Over U.S. Personnel 1 December 1977–30 November 1978.

2. The first and most important of the SOF Agreements mentioned in the text was Article VII of the North Atlantic Treaty, Status of Forces, (1953) 4 U.S. Treaties and Other International Agreements 1792. For scholarly treatment of the subject see J. M. Snee and K. A. Pye, Status of Forces Agreements and Criminal Jurisdiction (1957); R. Heath, Jr., Status of Forces Agreements As a Basis for U.S. Custody of an Accused, 49 Mil.L.Rev. 45 (1970); G. C. Coleman, Custody Provisions of Status of Forces Agreements As Authority to Confine U.S. Military Personnel Abroad, 17 Mil.L. & Law of War Rev. 441 (1978); J. H. Williams, An American's Trial in a Foreign Court: The Role of the Military's Trial Observer, 34 Mil.L.Rev. 1 (1966). The latter article contains a wealth of further references and (as an Appendix) a list of the relevant treaties. See also R. J. Stanger, Criminal Jurisdiction Over Visiting Armed Forces (1965); J. M. Snee, NATO Agreements on Status: Travaux Préparatoires (1966) (vols. 52 & 54 of the

International Law Studies published by the U.S. Naval War College); Anno., Criminal Jurisdiction of Courts of Foreign Nations Over American Armed Forces Stationed Abroad, 17 ALR Fed. 725 (1973). The constitutional problems arising in this context are highlighted in Holmes v. Laird, 459 F.2d 1211 (D.C.Cir. 1972), cert. denied 409 U.S. 869, 93 S.Ct. 197 (1972).

3. 4 U.S. Treaties and Other International Agreements 1828–29.

4. Schwenk, Highlights of a Comparative Study of the Common and Civil Law Systems, 33 N.C.L.Rev. 382, 397–8 (1955).

4a. Department of Defense Directive No. 5525.1 of August 7, 1979.

5. The military services' interest in the subject has produced, also, many other comparative studies dealing with criminal procedure. Some of these are unpublished (though not necessarily classified); but many of them have been published in the Military Law Review and elsewhere.

6. When necessary, the local judge advocate office assists the accused serviceman in obtaining local counsel. In certain instances the U.S. Government pays the fees of such counsel. See Williams, supra n. 2, at 25. For details see Departments of the Army, Navy and Air Force, (Joint) Regulations of 1 December 1978.

7. Id. at 41–42.

Comparovich: This trial observer system, mandated by the same Senate Resolution that I just mentioned, has the effect that many young American lawyers become quite familiar with the criminal procedure of civil-law countries.[8]

Smooth: Neither Mr. Edge nor I have ever been military lawyers, and we are badly in need of information on the basic differences between civilian systems of criminal procedure and ours. Can you give us this information in a nutshell?

Comparovich: The best "nutshell" I can think of is a law review article, written by a very good friend of mine, which in a concise (and perhaps overly condensed) manner first presents a thumbnail sketch of a typical criminal proceeding in one of the more enlightened civil-law countries, and then proceeds to elaborate on some—though not all—of the significant differences between the civilians' approach and ours. I brought a couple of reprints of that article. My suggestion is that you quickly read the article, and that we resume our discussion when you have finished.

R. B. SCHLESINGER, COMPARATIVE CRIMINAL PROCEDURE: A PLEA FOR UTILIZING FOREIGN EXPERIENCE

26 Buffalo L.Rev. 361 (1977).[*]

. . .

I. Outline of the Course of a Criminal Proceeding in a Continental Country [1]

In the civilian systems, as in our own, the policeman [2] normally is the first public official to arrive at the scene of an alleged crime, or to

---

8. When these lawyers come back home, their experience is never utilized by those who profess to be interested in reforming the administration of criminal law in our own country. This regrettable state of affairs will not change unless and until our criminal law reformers overcome their traditional attitude of narcissistic provincialism. See W. J. Wagner, Crime and the Law: Sociologico-Legal Observations, 20 Cath. Lawyer 177, 199–201 (1974). See also supra p. 23.

* What follows is a revised excerpt from the article, which is the printed version of the 1976 James McCormick Mitchell Lecture presented by the author to the Faculty of Law and Jurisprudence, State University of New York at Buffalo, on October 14, 1976.

Most of the footnotes are omitted. The ones reproduced here have been renumbered and revised.

1. The reader who seeks more comprehensive information on the structural and procedural differences between our criminal process and that of the civil-law (and socialist) countries, is referred to a series of articles by Professor Damaska. See Damaska, Evidentiary Barriers to Conviction and Two Models of Criminal Procedure: A Comparative Study, 121 U.Pa.L. Rev. 506 (1973) [hereinafter cited as Damaska, Barriers]; Damaska, Structures of Authority and Comparative Criminal Procedure, 84 Yale L.J. 480 (1975) [hereinafter cited as Damaska, Structures]; Damaska, Comparative Reflections on Reading the Amended Yugoslav Code: Interrogation of Defendants in Yugoslav Criminal Procedure, 61 J.Crim.L.C. & P.S. 168 (1970) [hereinafter cited as Damaska, Reflections].

There are many valuable comparative discussions of the subject in the English language. Only some of them can be mentioned here. See, e.g., J. A. Coutts (Ed.), The Accused—A Comparative Study (1966); G. O. W. Mueller and F. Le Poole-Griffiths, Comparative Criminal Procedure (1969); Rosett, Trial and Discretion in Dutch Criminal Justice, 19 U.C.L.A.L.Rev. 353 (1972); G. W. Pugh, Administration of Criminal Justice in France: An Introductory Analysis, 23 La.L.Rev. 1 (1962); A. V. Sheehan, Criminal Procedure in Scotland and

---

2. See note 2 on page 476.

receive a report concerning it. He may conduct an informal investigation; but his power to arrest the suspect without judicial warrant, or to proceed to warrantless searches and seizures, is seriously limited. Thus, whenever measures are contemplated by the police that affect the freedom of the suspect, it becomes necessary at a very early stage of the investigation to involve the prosecutor and the court.

There is no grand jury. The official phase of the pretrial investigation is in the hands of a judge—whom the French call *juge d'instruction* (investigating judge)—or of the prosecutor.[3] Both the judge and the prosecutor are essentially civil servants.[3a] The judge enjoys the usual guarantees of judicial independence. The prosecutor typically does not; he may be a link in a hierarchical chain of command, often leading up to the Minister of Justice. Nevertheless, except perhaps in cases having strong political overtones, the civil-servant prosecutor operating in a continental system can be expected to be reasonably impartial. He does not have to run for re-election; and his promotion within the civil service hierarchy may depend as much on his efficiency in sorting out and dropping investigations mistakenly commenced against innocent suspects as it does on his record of procuring convictions of the guilty.[4]

The magistrate or prosecutor conducting the investigation will build up an impressive dossier by interrogating all available witnesses, including those named by the suspect, and collecting other relevant evidence. The suspect himself will be interrogated, and in the most progressive continental countries such interrogation will take place in

France (1972); J. Langbein, Comparative Criminal Procedure: Germany (1977). Several instructive papers on German Criminal Procedure were presented to a conference held at De Paul University College of Law in Chicago on April 12, 1980. The proceedings of that conference were published by the Association Internationale de Droit Pénal under the title "The Criminal Justice System of the Federal Republic of Germany" (1981).

For historical antecedents of criminal procedure in civil-law countries, see Esmain, History of Continental Criminal Procedure (1913); Ploscowe, The Development of Present-Day Criminal Procedures in Europe and America, 48 Harv.L.Rev. 433 (1935); Langbein, Torture and the Law of Proof (1976).

2. It is important not to equate a French or German policeman with his American counterpart. In the more advanced continental countries, most of the police officers engaged in criminal work are highly professionalized members of a non-local, tightly-knit organization and are subject to strict organizational discipline which by and large assures their adherence to legal rules circumscribing their investigatory powers. See J. H. Langbein &

L. L. Weinreb, Continental Criminal Procedure: "Myth" and Reality, 87 Yale L.J. 1549, 1555–56, 1560–61 (1978).

3. According to formal statements of the law, informal police inquiries should proceed only to the point necessary to avoid the disappearance of evidence. In practice, however, the police usually conduct extensive inquiries prior to forwarding the findings to the prosecutor or the judge. For Germany, see The Criminal Justice System of the Federal Republic of Germany, supra n. 1, at 36.

3a. See supra pp. 180–182.

4. An excellent discussion of these problems can be found in C. Guarnieri, Pubblico Ministero e Sistema Politico (1984). Observe also that in many of the continental systems the discretionary powers of the prosecutor are much more narrowly circumscribed than in this country. See, e.g., Hermann, The Rule of Compulsory Prosecution and the Scope of Prosecutorial Discretion in Germany, 41 U.Chi.L.Rev. 468 (1974). Concerning prosecutorial discretion *not* to prosecute, see Damaska, The Reality of Prosecutorial Discretion, 29 Am. J.Comp.L. 119 (1981).

the presence of his counsel. In many civil law countries the law expressly provides that the suspect has a right to remain silent and that he must be informed of this right. Of course, there is no physical compulsion to make him talk. Experience in continental countries shows, nevertheless, that in the preliminary investigation as well as at the trial itself the defendant usually does talk. The reasons for this will be explored below.

At the conclusion of the official investigation, the prosecutor (or, in some countries, the investigating magistrate) must decide whether in his judgment the evidence is strong enough to warrant the bringing of formal charges against the suspect. If charges are brought, the accused still does not necessarily have to stand trial. Under the traditional civil-law practice, the dossier now goes to a three-judge panel—on a higher level of the judicial hierarchy. Only if this panel, having studied the dossier and having given defense counsel an opportunity to submit arguments and to suggest the taking of additional evidence, determines that there exists what we would call "reasonable cause," will the accused have to stand trial. (It should be noted here how misleading it can be to call the continental procedure "inquisitorial" and to contrast it with our allegedly "adversary" process. Under continental procedure, the accused has a two-fold opportunity to be heard—first in the course of the preliminary investigation, and again when the three-judge panel examines the dossier—*before* any decision is made whether he has to stand trial. This should be compared with the completely nonadversary grand jury proceeding by which in the overwhelming majority of American jurisdictions a prosecutor can obtain an indictment.)

In every civil-law country, counsel for the accused has the absolute right to inspect the whole dossier. This will be discussed later.

At the trial, the bench normally (though not uniformly) will consist of one or three professional judges and a number of lay assessors. The jury system, which was introduced in continental Europe in the wake of the French Revolution, more recently was replaced in most continental countries by the system of the mixed bench.[5] Under this system, the professional judges and the lay assessors together form the court, which as a single body passes on issues of law as well as fact, and determines both guilt and sentence. Thus, the trial does not have to be bifurcated into a first hearing devoted solely to the issue of guilt, and a subsequent second hearing dealing with the sentence.[6] The issue of guilt and the

---

5. See Damaska, Structures, at 492–93. For a thorough study of the system of the mixed bench, see Casper & Zeisel, Lay Judges in the German Criminal Courts, 1 J.Leg.Stud. 135 (1972). Cf. Z. Krystufek, The Function of the Lay Judge in Czechoslovakia, in L. M. Friedman & M. Rehbinder (Eds.), Zur Soziologie des Gerichtsverfahrens (Vol. 4 of Jahrbuch für Rechtssoziologie und Rechtstheorie), at 301 (1976).

6. The participation of lay judges (historically a derivative of the civilians' jury trial, see supra) has the further effect that the trial has to be a continuous session without substantial interruptions or adjournments. Thus, in contrast to the successive, chopped-up hearings which characterize the civilians' *civil* proceedings, a *criminal* trial conducted under their system has the quality of a single, concen-

measure of punishment are determined simultaneously and by the same body of adjudicators.[6a]

The dossier, reflecting the pretrial investigation, plays a role during the trial as well. Three of the *dramatis personae* at this point are thoroughly conversant with its contents: the prosecutor, the defendant's counsel, and the Presiding Justice. The Presiding Justice has the dossier in front of him during the trial. On the other hand, the lay judges, and often the professional judges other than the Presiding Justice of the court, are unfamiliar with the dossier. Consequently, only the evidence received in open court (as distinguished from the contents of the dossier) may be considered in reaching a decision.[6b]

After a reading of the charges, the Presiding Justice normally will call upon the defendant to give his name and occupation and to make a statement concerning his general background. Then, after a warning that he has the right, at his option, to remain silent concerning the charges against him, the defendant will be asked what (if anything) he wishes to say about the charges.[7] The defendant, who is not put under oath, at this point has the opportunity to tell his side of the story by way of a coherent statement. This will be followed by questions addressed to the defendant. In practice most of the questioning will be done by the Presiding Justice, who is well prepared for this task by previous study of the dossier in his hands. Prosecution and defense counsel may suggest, or be permitted to ask, additional questions.

Not by counsel

Frequently, the defendant's response to such questioning will be a confession. But regardless of whether he confesses before or during the trial, trial proceedings must go on, and the court must satisfy itself of the defendant's guilt by means of evidence corroborating his confession. In other words, the defendant cannot waive his right to trial by "pleading guilty" (or nolo contendere).

After this interrogation of the defendant, the witnesses will be examined in similar fashion. Normally, the witnesses will be the same individuals whose preliminary testimony is recorded in the dossier; but additional witnesses, not discovered in the course of the pretrial investigation, may be subpoenaed by the defense or may appear voluntarily at the trial. Nontestimonial evidence, especially physical evidence, also may be produced, and the court may inspect the place of the crime.

Rules leading to the exclusion of relevant evidence are less numerous than in this country, and much less capable of impeding the factfinding process. Counterparts to our "exclusionary rule" exist in

trated and dramatic event; it is truly a "trial" in our sense of the word.

6a. On the possibility of transplanting the mixed bench to America, see J. Langbein, Mixed Court and Jury Court: Could the Continental Alternative Fill the American Need?, 1981 American Bar Foundation Research Journal 195.

6b. But see infra p. 484 regarding exceptional situations in which portions of the dossier may be read at the trial.

7. The trial described in this and the following three paragraphs of the text reflects the applicable code provisions. In practice, many of the steps outlined in the text can be omitted or condensed in cases where a confession has been obtained, that is, in the great majority of routine cases.

few civil law countries; even where they exist (as in Germany), their practical impact is much less significant than here.[7a]

After closing arguments by prosecution and defense, and after the defendant has been accorded the last word, the court retires to deliberate. The lay judges, whose vote in most (but not all) continental countries carries the same weight as that of their professional colleagues, may outnumber the latter.[8] In the great majority of civil-law countries, the judgment does not have to be unanimous; and the fact that it is not unanimous will not be disclosed. Unless the judgment is one of acquittal, it will pronounce conviction and sentence. It will say, for example, that defendant is found guilty of armed robbery and for such crime is sentenced to four years in the reformatory.

As a rule, the judgment of the court of first instance is subject to an appeal on both the law and the facts.[9] New evidence may be presented to the appellate court, and the proceedings before that court, which has power to review the sentence as well as the determination of guilt or innocence, may amount to a trial de novo. The decision of the appellate court normally can be attacked by a second appeal to a court of last resort, but in this last court only questions of law will be reviewed. The right to appeal is given not only to the defendant but to the prosecutor as well.[10]

In concluding this brief overview, I should like to stress that it is too highly abbreviated to be totally accurate, and that it does not make sufficient allowance for the considerable differences that exist among the various civil-law systems of criminal procedure. My hope is that despite such over-generalization I have been able to highlight some of

---

7a. Reasons for the weak practical implementation of existing exclusionary rules in the civil-law systems are discussed in Damaska, Barriers at 523–524. See also C. M. Bradley, The Exclusionary Rule in Germany, 96 Harv.L.Rev. 1032, 1063 (1983).

8. It has been argued, however, that the purposes of lay participation—to keep the professional judges from performing their tasks too routinely, and to increase popular confidence in the administration of justice—can be attained without having the lay members of the panel outnumber (and conceivably outvote) the professional judges. This argument, coupled with the further consideration that historically the inclusion of a lay element in criminal tribunals is but a surviving remnant of the 19th-century transplantation of the English jury trial into the continental systems, recently led the West German Legislature to adopt an important change in the law. Until 1974, the trial court that dealt with the gravest crimes consisted of three professional judges and six lay assessors, but a 1974 amendment, now embodied in Gerichtsverfassungsgesetz [GVG] § 76, as re-

promulgated by Law of May 9, 1975, [1975] BGBl I 1077 (W. Ger.), reduced the number of lay assessors to two. See 1 Loewe-Rosenberg, Die Strafprozessordnung und das Gerichtsverfassungsgesetz, Introduction, ch. 15, annos. 6–9 (23d ed. 1976) [hereinafter cited as Loewe-Rosenberg (23d ed.)]. The statement in the text is still correct with respect to other continental countries.

9. In some continental countries, there are exceptions to this rule: the decisions of the courts dealing with the gravest crimes sometimes are subject to an appeal only on points of law. See Mueller & Le Poole-Griffiths, supra note 1, at 210. These presently illogical exceptions can be explained only on historical grounds. They date back to the 19th-century period when an English-style system of jury trials (which of course precluded appellate review of the jury's express or implied factual findings) prevailed on the continent.

10. The reader will recall that in the Palko case Mr. Justice Cardozo called attention to this civil-law practice. See supra p. 7.

the important features that are common to a number of the civil-law systems and set them apart from our procedure.

II.   Arrest and Pretrial Detention in Civil-Law Countries

With the above comments as a background, let me now turn to a discussion of some of the procedural devices and arrangements to be found in civil-law countries that might provide American reformers with food for thought.

The first two items—treated together because they are so closely connected—are arrest and pretrial detention.

In this country, it is still the general rule that criminal proceedings routinely "start with the harsh, and in itself degrading, measure of physical arrest."[11]   In the federal courts, and in less than one-half of the states, this brutal and (as a rule) unnecessary routine has been modified by statutory provisions that in certain situations authorize the issuance of a summons in lieu of arrest.   But these modifications are halfhearted; frequently they are limited to cases of minor violations, and most of the relevant provisions leave it to the discretion of the police or the prosecutor whether a summons should take the place of physical arrest.

The civil-law countries, on the other hand, unanimously recognize that the initiation of a judicial proceeding, whether civil or criminal, never requires the defendant's physical arrest.   It follows, according to civilian thinking, that the necessary notification of the defendant is to be effected by a summons, in criminal as well as civil proceedings, and that it is unthinkable to use physical arrest as a routine measure against a suspect who has not yet been tried and who, consequently, must be presumed innocent.

The question whether a suspect should be detained pending trial is, in the civilians' view, completely separate and distinct from the routine of initiating the proceeding.   Except in carefully defined emergency situations, a judicial order is required to detain the suspect before trial. The requirements for the issuance of such an order are strict.   In West Germany, for instance, it can be issued only if the court, by definite findings of fact, determines that the following three elements exist: First, there must be strong reasons for believing that the suspect has committed the crime.[11a]   Second, the evidence before the court must show a specific, rational ground for pretrial detention, such as danger of flight or danger of tampering with the evidence.[12]   Third, such detention must meet the requirement of proportionality; that is, it will not be ordered if the hardship caused by it is disproportionate to the

---

11.   S. A. Cohn, "Criminal Records"—A Comparative Approach, 4 Ga.J.Int.Comp.L. 116 (1974).

11a.   Strictly speaking, this is a ground supporting the initiation of proceedings, rather than justifying detention as such.

12.   In homicide cases, this requirement is eliminated.   In cases involving certain other types of very serious crimes the requirement can be met by a finding that the suspect would be likely to commit similar offenses if he were released.

gravity of the offense.[13] The order, which must state the grounds on which each of these requirements is thought to be met, is subject to immediate appeal.[14]

Compare this rational design of pretrial detention with our traditional law of arrest and bail. Probable cause that the suspect has committed the crime, a ground merely supporting the initiation of prosecution, suffices for arrest. Once arrested, the suspect's release depends on his capacity to post bail. Under procedures still prevailing in many states, an indigent defendant can thus be kept in jail despite the absence of any rational justification for detaining him, while the wealthy suspect may be released even though he is likely to flee or to intimidate witnesses. It is true that recently, through the Federal Bail Reform Act and similar legislation in a minority of states, we made progress in this area. But note that the provisions of the federal Act as well as those of state statutes authorizing so-called "Own Recognizance" (O.R.) releases become operative only *after* the suspect has been subjected to the (frequently unnecessary) indignity of the initial arrest. There is a further contrast to continental practice: in many states (but not under the federal Act) an application for "O.R." release may be denied without any statement of reasons, and in some jurisdictions the burden is upon the arrestee to show good cause why he should be released. It follows, I submit, that even in our most liberal jurisdictions something might yet be gained by comparative study of the subject of arrest and pretrial detention.[14a]

III. The Prosecutor's and the Defendant's Contribution to the Search for Truth

The two remaining topics I should like to discuss have one feature in common: both of them bear, directly and importantly, upon the central function of the criminal process, the ascertainment of truth.

A. Discovery

The first of these two related topics comes under the heading of "discovery." The continental systems invariably provide that at an early stage of the proceedings, and in any event well before the trial, the defendant and his counsel acquire an absolute and unlimited right to inspect the entire dossier, that is, all of the evidence collected by the prosecution and the investigating magistrate.[15] Thus it is simply im-

---

13. Moreover, pretrial detention is precluded in most of the cases in which the maximum sentence does not exceed six months.

14. The detainee also has the right at any time to demand a judicial inquiry regarding the continuing existence of all the requirements for detention.

14a. For a case showing that (with respect to pretrial detention) even the most liberal American jurisdictions still do not accord the defendant the same legal safeguards he would normally enjoy in one of the more enlightened civil-law countries, see Van Atta v. Scott, 27 Cal.3d 424, 166 Cal.Rptr. 149, 613 P.2d 210 (1980).

15. See Damaska, Barriers, at 533–34. A good example of a code provision spelling out the details of this right of inspection is § 147 of the German Code of Criminal Procedure (Strafprozessordnung).

possible to obtain a conviction by a strategy of surprise.[16] It must be remembered, moreover, that in most cases there can be a trial de novo on appeal, which, of course, acts as a second barrier against the successful use of surprise evidence.

To facilitate inspection of the dossier by defense counsel, German law provides that upon his request he should normally be allowed to take the dossier to his office or home for thorough and unhurried study.

Concerning this latter point, and generally concerning details of inspection procedure, other continental systems may not go quite so far as the German Code. But defense counsel's basic right to timely inspection of the entire dossier has become an article of faith throughout the civil law world—and, indeed, in the socialist orbit as well. This is well illustrated by an incident that occurred during World War II, when representatives of the United States, Great Britain, France and Soviet Russia met in London to prepare the Charter of the International Tribunal which later tried the principal war criminals at Nuremberg. Among other issues of procedure, the question of discovery came up for discussion. Mr. Justice Jackson, who attended the meeting as the representative of the United States, later reported that at that point

> the Soviet Delegation objected to our practice on the ground that it is not fair to defendants. Under the Soviet system when an indictment is filed every document and the statement of every witness which is expected to be used against the defendant must be filed with the court and made known to the defense. It was objected that under our system the accused does not know the statements of accusing witnesses nor the documents that may be used against him, that such evidence is first made known to him at the trial, too late to prepare a defense, and that this tends to make the trial something of a game instead of a real inquest into guilt. It must be admitted that there is a great deal of truth in the criticism.[17]

So far as the Nuremberg trial was concerned, the problem was overcome by a compromise between the common-law and civil-law positions. What seems significant beyond the immediate context, however, is the fact that Mr. Justice Jackson had to listen to, and did not have much of an answer for, this lecture on due process delivered by his Soviet counterpart.[17a]

The prosecutor must include in the dossier every document that contains any information relating to the investigation; nothing except purely internal instructions and communications among members of the prosecutorial staff may be kept from the defendant. See 1 Loewe-Rosenberg, Die Strafprozessordnung und das Gerichtsverfassungsgesetz § 147, anno. 2 (22d ed. 1973) [hereinafter cited as Loewe-Rosenberg (22d ed.)].

16. See, e.g., Murray, A Survey of Criminal Procedure in Spain and Some Comparisons with Criminal Procedure in the United States, 40 N.D.L.Rev. 7, 9, 13 (1964).

17. Quoted by Bull, Nuremberg Trial, 7 F.R.D. 175, at 178 (1948).

17a. However, as we shall soon see, fair comparison requires that the problems of criminal discovery be placed in a larger context. The continental defendant acquires an unlimited right to discovery only

In its aversion to unlimited pretrial discovery in criminal proceedings, the American legal system today stands virtually alone. In England, the older common law tradition of trial by surprise has long been abandoned, and present English practice, by a combination of procedural devices and informal arrangements, permits defense counsel, well before the trial, to become fully familiar with every element of the facts known to the prosecution.

In this country, although we are ahead of the rest of the world with respect to discovery in civil procedure, we have been remarkably slow in taking the blindfolds from the eyes of the criminal defendant. Many states have not even begun to devise effective tools for criminal discovery.[18]

The hope that broad criminal discovery would be forced on the states by the Supreme Court, has not been fulfilled. The contours of the limited constitutional right recognized in cases such as Brady v. Maryland [19] are quite indistinct, with the result that this constitutional doctrine supplies reliable guidelines only in cases of outrageously suppressive tactics employed by the prosecution.

A few jurisdictions, including the federal courts,[20] have progressed beyond the Neanderthal stage. But under the Federal Rules the defendant is still precluded from getting a pretrial look at the most vital materials—the statements made by government witnesses or prospective government witnesses. With very few exceptions,[21] state

---

after pretrial investigators had ample opportunity to "discover" information from him. This opportunity is unparalleled in American criminal prosecutions. See infra p. 484, text following note 23, and especially pp. 486–487.

18. The preliminary hearing, in its American form (as distinguished from the English version), is not an effective discovery device. See Goldstein, The State and the Accused: Balance of Advantage in Criminal Procedure, 69 Yale L.J. 1149, 1183 (1960); cf. Adams v. Illinois, 405 U.S. 278, 282, 92 S.Ct. 916, 919 (1972), id. at 292 (Douglas, J., dissenting). Moreover, in most of those American jurisdictions that have not abolished grand juries the prosecutor can cut off the defendant's right to a preliminary hearing by securing an indictment. See A.L.I., A Model Code of Pre-Arraignment Procedure 592 (1975), and authorities cited therein. But cf. Hawkins v. Superior Court, 22 Cal.3d 584, 150 Cal. Rptr. 435, 586 P.2d 916 (1978).

Nor is the motion to inspect grand-jury minutes a viable discovery tool. See, e.g., Proskin v. County Court of Albany County, 30 N.Y.2d 15, 330 N.Y.S.2d 44, 280 N.E.2d 875 (1972).

19. 373 U.S. 83, 83 S.Ct. 1194 (1963). See also Brown v. Chaney, 469 U.S. 1090,

105 S.Ct. 601 (1984) (Burger, C.J., and White and Rehnquist, JJ. dissenting from denial of cert.); United States v. Agurs, 427 U.S. 97, 96 S.Ct. 2392 (1976). It must be emphasized that Brady and cognate cases usually do no more than require disclosure at trial, when disclosure is of limited usefulness.

20. See Fed.R.Crim.P. 16.

21. The most notable exception is California's liberal discovery law. See D. Louisell & B. Wally, Modern California Discovery, para. 14.03 (2d ed., 1972, Cum. Supp. 1978 and Supp. 1979). California's lead was followed by New Jersey. See N.J. Rules Governing Criminal Practice 3:13–3(a)8, as amended in 1973. A recent Utah provision also provides for wide discovery. See Utah Code Ann. 1953, para. 77–35–16 (1982). Note, however, that the absence of broad discovery rights is sometimes compensated by informal discovery arrangements: in many jurisdictions prosecutors have adopted an "open file" policy for most cases. Strict formal rules are applied only to cases where reasons exist to fear for the safety of a witness or the security of evidence. See S. H. Kadish (Ed.), Encyclopedia of Crime and Justice, Vol. 2 at 619 (1984).

discovery practice in the so-called liberal states is subject to similar limitations, and in many American jurisdictions, including the federal system, even the names of the People's witnesses cannot be obtained as of right before trial.

In no American jurisdiction does the defendant have a right to continental-style inspection, to discovery routinely obtained and unlimited in scope.[22]

I submit that experience gained under the continental systems could be exceedingly useful in dealing with the classical anti-discovery arguments that continue to mold the attitude of our courts and legislators. Let us look, first of all, at the "abuse" argument, which is born of the fear that the defendant, once he is apprised of the State's evidence, will be enabled to prepare perjured testimony and to bribe or intimidate, or perhaps even eliminate, the witnesses for the prosecution. It must be conceded that in many situations, and especially in cases involving organized crime, this danger is real. American advocates of discovery have replied that the danger can be minimized by giving the court discretionary power to issue protective orders.[23] *Quaere*, however, whether it is a satisfactory solution to leave everything to the court's discretion. The civil law has a better answer to the "abuse" argument. Under the continental systems—and I shall soon explain this more thoroughly—the defendant normally will have stated his own version of the facts in considerable detail at a very early stage of the proceedings. Thus, at the time when he or his counsel inspects the dossier, his position has assumed a sufficiently firm shape so that it can no longer be effectively improved by fabrications.[24] The further danger, that prosecution witnesses might be bribed or intimidated, usually is neutralized in the civil-law systems by the sensible rule that if at the trial the witness suddenly suffers a loss of memory or seeks to contradict his prior statements, his previous testimony can be used not only to assist his power of recall but even as substantive evidence. A slight modernization of our antediluvian rules of evidence (including the rule against impeaching one's own witness) would permit our courts to reach the same result.[25]

---

22. See Damaska, Barriers, at 534.

23. The Federal Rules already authorize such protective orders. See Fed.R. Crim.P. 16(d)(1).

24. It must be remembered that in a continental country the judge presiding at the trial has the dossier in his hands and is thoroughly familiar with its contents. Thus, if at the trial the defendant should present a recently fabricated story, the Presiding Justice may remind him of any contradictions between that story and his previous testimony, or of the fact that he failed to mention the point when he previously talked with investigating officials. Should the defendant deny the accuracy or completeness of the portions of the dossier

to which the Presiding Justice refers, the officials who recorded the previous statements of the accused may be called as witnesses. See Loewe-Rosenberg (22d ed.) § 254, anno. 6. Thus, any attempt to change his original position may well hurt rather than help the defendant, unless the change is satisfactorily explained. Where the change is a fabrication, it is unlikely that such an explanation can be presented.

25. Under the Federal and Revised Uniform Rules of Evidence the prior inconsistent statement can be used for impeachment purposes (Rule 607); but under Rule 801(d)(1), as a House-Senate Conference Committee phrased it after long and bitter controversy, it is admissible as substantive

To kill or incapacitate a prosecution witness before the trial, again will not help the defendant at all in a civil-law country; the previous testimony of the witness is recorded in the dossier, and if the witness in the meantime has become unavailable, this particular portion of the dossier may be read at the trial.

In our system, the problem of utilizing pretrial depositions is somewhat more difficult because of the constitutional confrontation requirement. But the Supreme Court's 1970 decision in California v. Green [26] makes it clear that, subject to certain safeguards, the deposition of an unavailable witness may be used at the trial even under our system. In some situations such use now is authorized by the Federal Rules.[27]

It follows, I submit, that the answers by which the civilians have neutralized the "abuse" argument against effective discovery, are relevant in our system as well.

The only other respectable argument against unlimited discovery is that of prosecutors crying "one-way-street." Even if one is free from prosecutorial bias, one must wonder why, in an allegedly adversary system, one party should have to play with completely open cards, while the other party—the party who presumably has the most intimate knowledge of the facts—has the right to sit back and in effect to limit his utterances to two taunting words: "Prove it." Some writers have attempted to answer this question within the framework of our system, but their answers have largely failed to persuade our courts and legislators. As a practical matter, it does not seem likely that unlimited discovery—the hallmark of civilized criminal procedure—will be widely and effectively introduced into our system unless the "one-way-street" argument can be laid to rest.[28] To do that, one must take a

evidence only if originally made under oath. Thus a prior inconsistent statement, contained in unsworn testimony given to the police by a witness (before he was intimidated or bribed), cannot be used as substantive evidence under the Federal and Revised Uniform Rules of Evidence.

The state courts are split on whether the witness' prior inconsistent statement can be used as substantive evidence. The view that it can be so used is gaining ground, but may still be the minority position. See Anno., 30 ALR4th 414 (1984); McCormick on Evidence §§ 38, 39, 251 (3d ed. E. Cleary 1984).

26. 399 U.S. 149, 90 S.Ct. 1930 (1970).

27. Fed.R.Crim.P. 15(e). Note, however, that this rule, although liberal by comparison with our traditional approach, is more restrictive than the practice in continental countries, where even unsworn statements made by the witness to the police or the prosecutor can be read at the trial if the witness in the meantime has died or if for other reasons his testimony has become difficult to obtain.

The restrictions built into Rule 15(e) reflect the Supreme Court's interpretation of the due process and confrontation clauses. See California v. Green, 399 U.S. 149, 90 S.Ct. 1930 (1970). Keeping in mind, however, the need for the protection of witnesses who are willing to testify against powerful and ruthless criminals, a strong argument can be made in favor of the less restrictive German rule.

28. The basis of the argument against "one-way-street" discovery is plain enough. If a criminal proceeding is regarded as essentially a sporting contest between opposing counsel, it follows that no greater burden of making pretrial disclosures should be imposed on the prosecution than is imposed on the defense. If, on the other hand, the ascertainment of truth is perceived as the major and essential objective of such a proceeding, then it is clear that defendant's silence is at least as inimical to

fresh look, aided by comparison, at the whole problem of the defendant's contribution to the ascertainment of the true facts. This brings me to the final topic of the present discussion.

B. *The Accused as a Source of Information*

The role of the accused as a source of information in the truthfinding process is an important and thorny topic in any system of criminal procedure. It is also the topic concerning which—upon superficial inspection—the gap between common law and civil law appears most unbridgeable.

Closer analysis, however, shows that the rock-bottom principle that is the foundation of all specific rules in this area of the law today is shared by virtually all civilized legal systems: no physical compulsion may be used to make the suspect talk. In this sense, almost all civilized legal systems give the suspect, even before he becomes the defendant, the right to remain silent.[29] The more enlightened legal systems, whether of the common-law or the civil-law variety, also are in agreement today on the principle that from the very beginning of the investigation the accused is entitled to the assistance of counsel. It follows that when the suspect, at any stage of the proceedings, is called upon to exercise his all-important option—to talk or not to talk—at least the more enlightened legal systems will make it possible for him to be guided by counsel's advice.

Up to this point, I repeat, there is a large measure of agreement among civilized and enlightened legal systems, regardless of whether they belong to the common-law or the civil-law orbit. Crucial differences, however, come to light when we ask the next question: Which course will counsel advise the defendant to take? Under our system, "any lawyer worth his salt will tell the suspect in no uncertain terms to make no statement to police under any circumstances."[30] Quite often, counsel will keep his client equally silent at the trial; indeed, in the many cases where the client has a criminal record, our majority rule permitting the prosecution to unearth such record on cross-examination makes it almost impossible for counsel to let the defendant take the stand. In its perverse striving to keep the defendant silent, our law, furthermore, seeks to assure the defendant and his counsel that legal rules can repeal the laws of logic, and that by legal rules the jury can be induced not to draw the natural inferences from defendant's silence.

the attainment of that objective as lack of discovery, because "[m]any offenses are of such a character that the only persons capable of giving useful testimony are those implicated in the crime." Kastigar v. United States, 406 U.S. 441, 92 S.Ct. 1653 (1972), quoted with approval in United States v. Mandujano, 425 U.S. 564, 96 S.Ct. 1768, 1775 (1976).

29. See Pieck, The Accused's Privilege Against Self-Incrimination in the Civil Law, 11 Am.J.Comp.L. 585 (1962).

30. Watts v. Indiana, 338 U.S. 49, 59, 69 S.Ct. 1347, 1358 (1949) (Jackson, J., concurring and dissenting). Note that the prosecution cannot impeach a defendant's testimony at trial by pointing to his post-arrest silence. This prohibition extends to remarks in a prosecutor's closing argument. See Doyle v. Ohio, 426 U.S. 610, 96 S.Ct. 2240 (1976); Cleveland v. Pulley, 551 F.Supp. 476, 478 (N.D.Cal. 1982).

In Griffin v. California [31] the Warren Court—over a powerful dissent by Mr. Justice Stewart—held that no state may permit any judicial comment (no matter how fair and reasonable) upon defendant's failure to testify.[31a]

In thus encouraging the accused to remain silent, our legal system stands virtually alone. In England, defendants rarely opt for silence, because English law differs from ours in two crucial respects. If the accused takes the stand, the English rule is to the effect that he cannot by reason of that alone be cross-examined as to previous convictions. And if he remains silent, the judge is authorized by English law to suggest to the jury that it draw an adverse inference from the defendant's failure to explain away the evidence against him.[32]

Implementing a similar policy by partly different techniques, the continental systems likewise discourage the accused from standing mute. In many (though not all) of those systems the defendant's silence may serve as corroborating evidence of guilt. Even where, as in West Germany, this traditional rule has been modified, a defendant generally is not well advised to remain silent. At the very outset of the trial, he has to stand in front of the judges, to be questioned by the Presiding Justice of the court. True, he may refuse to answer any questions relating to the charges against him; but he must announce such refusal in open court and cannot simply, as he might under a common law system, remove himself from the questioning process by deciding not to take the stand.[33] Moreover, only in the event of a *total* refusal by the defendant to answer any questions relating to the charges does German law prohibit the drawing of inferences from his

31. 380 U.S. 609, 85 S.Ct. 1229 (1965). The arguments against this holding are cogently stated in Justice Stewart's dissent, id. at 617, and even more elaborately in Chief Justice Traynor's opinion in People v. Modesto, 62 Cal.2d 436, 42 Cal.Rptr. 417, 398 P.2d 753 (1965). For an exchange on the Griffin rule, see D. B. Ayer, The Fifth Amendment and the Inference of Guilt from Silence: Griffin v. California after Fifteen Years, 78 Mich.L.Rev. 841 (1980); C. M. Bradley, Griffin v. California: Still Viable After All These Years, 79 Mich.L.Rev. 1290 (1981).

31a. After Griffin, the Supreme Court has created yet another incentive for defendants to stay off the stand at trial: if they testify, they can be impeached by an otherwise inadmissible confession. See Harris v. New York, 401 U.S. 222, 91 S.Ct. 643 (1971).

32. There are some restrictions on the phrasing of such judicial comment. The prevailing view is that the judge is not permitted to say that the defendant's silence adds weight to the prosecution's case, but only that his silence casts doubt on

what has been said in his favor. See Gernstein, The Self-Incrimination Debate in Great Britain, 27 Am.J.Comp.L. 81, 107–108 (1979). In most cases, of course, this technical distinction makes no difference in terms of the comment's impact on the jury.

On differences between the American and the English approach, see M. H. Graham, Tightening the Reins of Justice in America: A Comparative Analysis of the Criminal Jury Trial in England and the United States (1984), reviewed by G. Hughes in the New York Review of Books, March 14, 1985, at 17–18. The reviewer, though critical of the book, agrees with the author's attack on Griffin v. California. See now also the British Police and Criminal Evidence Act of 1984, in force since January 1986. With emphasis on pre-trial interrogation, English and American practices are thoroughly compared in the recent article by G. Van Kessel, The Suspect as a Source of Testimonial Evidence: A Comparison of the English and American Approaches, 38 Hastings L.J. 1 (1986).

33. See Damaska, Barriers, at 527–30.

silence. If he answers any of such questions, but then refuses to answer others, the court may draw logical inferences from his refusal. Thus, selective silence is strongly discouraged. Total silence of the defendant (although in theory under the present German rule it does not support adverse inferences) will occur only rarely in a German court because it carries with it a grave disadvantage for the defendant: since there will be no separate hearing regarding the sentence,[34] a totally silent defendant may forfeit the opportunity to present facts tending to mitigate his punishment.[35]

The continental systems, moreover, reject our dysfunctional rule that previous convictions of the defendant can be proved if, but only if, he takes the stand. The rules developed in those systems regarding admissibility of previous convictions are neither simple nor uniform, but they exhibit unanimity on the crucial point: the admissibility of previous convictions *never* hinges on whether or not the defendant testifies.[36] Thus he will never be dissuaded from testifying by the fear that his decision to do so will open the door to evidence of his criminal record.

Nor does a defendant who decides to testify before a continental court have to dread that a prosecution for perjury might arise out of such testimony. What he says in his defense is not under oath.[37]

34. See supra, part I.

As to whether a unitary system of guilt-determination and sentencing would be constitutionally permissible under our law, the authorities appear to be in conflict. See D. B. Ayer, supra n. 31, at 859; McCormick on Evidence, supra n. 25, at 319.

35. Under German law the questioning of the defendant at the trial is divided into two phases. The first deals with his personal history and general circumstances, while the second phase centers on the charges against him. His right to remain silent comes into play only when the second phase is reached. It follows that those mitigating facts that relate to defendant's personal history and general circumstances (for example, poverty or lack of education) can always be mentioned by him during the first phase. But mitigating facts connected with the crime itself (for example, that he was only a minor participant; that he tried to persuade his accomplices not to hurt the victim; that he is remorseful) cannot be brought out by his testimony if he decides to remain completely silent during the second phase of the questioning, the phase dealing with the charges against him.

The disadvantage thus suffered by a silent defendant is further accentuated if a confession in itself is treated as a mitigating circumstance. Under German law a confession should lead to mitigation only if it is indicative of sincere repentance; but many courts nevertheless tend to accord a confession an automatic mitigating effect. See H. H. Jescheck, Lehrbuch des Strafrechts 714 (3d ed, 1978); Damaska, Barriers, at 528 n. 44. In the Far East the role of a confession as a mitigating circumstance is especially pronounced. See the Japanese Criminal Code § 42; Korean Criminal Code § 52.

36. See Damaska, Barriers, at 518. The Federal Rules of Evidence now provide for some limitations on the use of prior convictions to impeach the defendant who takes the stand. See McCormick, supra n. 25, § 43.

37. In their free evaluation of the evidence the triers of the facts must weigh the accused's statement along with all other items of proof; and no adverse inference can be drawn from the fact that the statement is unsworn, because the accused is not eligible to be put under oath.

There is a fine comparative discussion of the point in an appendix forming part of the late Judge Jerome Frank's dissenting opinion in United States v. Grunewald, 233 F.2d 556, 587–92 (2d Cir. 1956). Judge Frank's dissent ultimately prevailed: the decision of the majority of the court of appeals was unanimously reversed by the Supreme Court, 353 U.S. 391, 77 S.Ct. 963 (1957).

Thus the inducement to speak, and not to stand mute, is very strong in the civil-law systems. Experience shows that "almost all continental defendants choose to testify" at the trial.[38] This being so, the accused normally has little to lose and much to gain by presenting his side of the story not only at the trial, but also in the earlier phases of the proceeding.[39] If the accused is innocent, this may lead to an early dismissal of the charges. In any event, the combination of a talking defendant and unlimited discovery will clarify the issues well before trial and make the trial both shorter and more informative— much to the benefit of an innocent defendant.

In cases where the accused is clearly guilty, the same combination of factors will prove equally potent. Through active colloquies between the accused and the investigator, combined with inspection of the dossier, such an accused and his counsel are apt to become persuaded that a denial of guilt simply will not stand up. The usual result is a confession, followed by an attempt to present evidence of mitigating circumstances.[40]

Thus, by combining unlimited discovery for the benefit of the defense with rules making it advantageous for the accused to talk, the continental systems have fashioned a highly efficient vehicle for the ascertainment of truth. If the accused is in fact innocent, unlimited

---

38. Damaska, Barriers, at 527.

39. It should be remembered that in some of the continental countries the pretrial investigation is conducted by a judge, and that the same judge may have the power to determine whether the accused should be detained (and remain detained) pending trial. Thus, at least from the subjective standpoint of the accused, it may well appear unwise to incur the judge's displeasure by a stubborn refusal to help in clearing up the facts. The investigating judge is apt to be quite impartial, in the sense that it makes no difference to him whether the facts he unearths ultimately will show guilt or innocence. But he does have a personal and professional interest in clearing up the case as expeditiously as possible and may become irritated when he sees his investigation obstructed.

40. Because defendants in civil-law systems cannot waive trials by entering a plea of guilty, there can be no plea-bargaining in the strict sense of the term. It is true that defendants can contribute to the shortening of trials by fully confessing, but agreements between the prosecution and the defense, granting sentencing and other concessions in return for a confession, remain illegal and are almost generally repudiated. As a result, the hope offered to the defendant that his confession will be treated by the sentencing court as a mitigating circumstance, is the most important and

widespread incentive to the defendant to cooperate with law enforcement authorities. See supra n. 35.

Of late, reports have appeared in some civil-law countries about covert arrangements between the prosecution and the defense concerning concessions in exchange for confessions, waiver of appeals and similar cooperative behavior on the part of the defendant. For West Germany see Schmidt-Hieber, Verständigung im Strafverfahren (1986); "Die Zeit" of May 1, 1987 p. 5. Sporadically, certain forms of such agreements are defended. See J. Baumann, Von der Grauzone zur rechtsstaatlichen Regelung, 7 Neue Zeitschrift für Strafrecht 157–162 (1987). However, it remains the dominant view that even the most informal arrangements between parties to a criminal proceeding are inappropriate, and indeed repugnant. It is only in the area of petty crime that some mild forms of negotiation between the prosecution and the defense are permitted. For West Germany, see *J. Langbein*, Land Without Plea Bargaining: How the Germans Do it, 78 Mich.L.Rev. 204, 224 (1979). See also infra n. 41.

Thus, no matter how brief the trial following a confession may be, the continental court's decision still reflects its own independent factfinding, its own characterization of the crime, and its own notions of justice and mercy.

pretrial discovery will give him the best possible chance—a much better chance than he would have under a system of trial by surprise—to meet whatever evidence there may be against him. And if he is guilty, the unavailability of silence as a viable strategy will make his conviction more probable and less time-consuming.[41]

. . .

[The last part of the article, not reproduced here, deals with The Teachings of Foreign Experience, i.e., the lessons which reformers of our own system of criminal justice might derive from a study of comparable civil-law institutions.]

The Dialogue Continued

Edge: During my vacation last year, I attended some criminal trials both in France and in Germany. The atmosphere is very different from that in an American courtroom.[1] I was struck, especially, by the fact that the examination of the accused and of the witnesses is primarily conducted by the presiding judge.[2]

41. See supra n. 40. In the case of petty offenses, German law has long used a special speed-up device known as an order of punishment (*Strafbefehl*). The essence of this device is that when the preliminary investigation shows the defendant to be guilty, the court can, without a previous hearing, send the defendant an "order of punishment," i.e. an order to pay a specified fine. If the defendant within 30 days objects to this order, a hearing must be held in accordance with regular procedure; in that event, the "order of punishment" performs merely the function of notifying the defendant of the charge against him. On the other hand, if the defendant does not file a timely objection, then the "order of punishment" acquires the force of a judgment convicting and sentencing the defendant.

It should be noted that even this summary practice which in German law is provided for dealing with petty offenses (and which, in 1972, was adopted by France as well), does not involve a bargain between prosecutor and defense counsel. The *Strafbefehl* simply gives a choice to the defendant: either to accept the tentative sentence by which the court has imposed a fine, or to demand a regular trial. Experience shows that in the majority of cases the fine is paid and no trial is demanded.

There are, of course, some similarities between the *Strafbefehl* and the type of traffic ticket used in some American jurisdictions; but the *Strafbefehl* can be used in the case of any petty offense, whether or not it involves a traffic violation.

1. For poignant comparative descriptions, by an observing and sensitive non-lawyer, of the atmosphere in the criminal courts of various nations, see Sybille Bedford, The Faces of Justice (1961). With emphasis on the difference between Soviet-style trials and those in non-socialist countries, atmospheric elements are interestingly discussed also in the Article by J. N. Hazard, Furniture Arrangement as a Symbol of Judicial Roles, 19 ETC.: Review of General Semantics 181 (1962).

2. As we have seen, nothing may be used against the defendant that is not brought out in open court during the trial. The *dossier* compiled during the preliminary investigation is not evidence. The presiding judge, however, is thoroughly familiar with the contents of the *dossier*, and usually has it in his hands during the trial. His interrogation of the accused and of the witnesses thus becomes thorough and searching. From this, uninformed observers have occasionally inferred that there is no presumption of innocence in civil-law countries.

The inference is, of course, nonsensical. See Esmein, History of Continental Criminal Procedure 46 (1913); Schwenk, Comparative Study of the Law of Criminal Procedure in NATO Countries, 35 N.C.L.Rev. 358, 373–74 (1957); Mirelli v. Switzerland, European Court of Human Rights, Judgment of March 25, 1983, 4 HRLJ 215 (1983).

Reasons for the civilians' reluctance to abandon "unilateral examination" by an impartial official are discussed in Damas-

Smooth: To my mind, this is an objectionable system, in criminal cases even more than in civil cases.[3]

Comparovich: I agree with you that this feature of their procedure lends itself to abuse if the President of the court is a "hanging judge"; but the effect, under our system, of clever and unfair cross-examination by a skillful prosecutor may be worse, because we subject the accused, if he takes the stand, to the additional psychological torture of having to testify under oath.[4]

Smooth: If you were an accused, Professor, wouldn't you rather be tried under the common-law than under a civil-law system?

Comparovich: My preference would depend on many factors, some of which might require a lengthy discussion.[5] But let me give you a rough answer that covers most of the cases I can readily imagine. If I were guilty, I would prefer a system under which I can obtain sentencing and other concessions in exchange for a plea of guilty, and under which, if my case comes to trial, I can stand mute, and effectively object to incriminating evidence on technical grounds. But if I were innocent, I would prefer a system under which I have a right to discover all of the incriminating evidence, and to challenge it, before it is decided whether I have to stand trial. And if there is a trial, then (as an innocent defendant) I would much rather be tried under a system which makes it impossible for the prosecution to spring surprises at the trial; which enables me to present evidence without regard to technicalities, and to utilize all of the exculpating evidence unearthed by the official investigation; and which does not subject me to the difficult choice between standing silent and testifying under oath. Moreover, if acquitted, I would prefer a system that makes the state pay my counsel's fee.[6]

ka, Presentation of Evidence and Factfinding Precision, 123 U.Pa.L.Rev. 1083, 1093 (1975).

3. Cf. Holtzoff, Book Review, 52 A.B.A.J. 1055, at 1056–7 (1966): "Our concept of the privilege against self-incrimination is unknown in France. One might well ask, perhaps naively, why it is not sensible to question the defendant in court, since he probably knows more about the facts than anyone else. It is in the nature of man, however, to be hidebound by history and tradition, and it is this factor which would prevent us from even thinking of adopting the French practice."

4. An argument has been made that the accused's interrogation under oath is a *tortura spiritualis.* See H. Silving, The Oath, 68 Yale L.J. 1329, 1527 passim (1959). In practice, however, the fear of an independent perjury prosecution does not loom too large among the factors that make the accused's decision to testify a difficult one.

5. For example, incriminating evidence of various degrees of strength may point to an accused person's guilt, even though in fact he is innocent. His choice between the two systems of prosecution could be affected by this factor. For some other considerations, see the suggestions in Langbein, Comparative Criminal Procedure: Germany 150 (1977).

6. In contrast to our system, most other countries have adopted indemnity schemes under which the accused, if acquitted, is reimbursed for his counsel's fee. For Germany, see Code of Crim. Procedure § 467(I). Thus an innocent defendant, even though he does not qualify for legal aid, does not have to fear that his successful defense will involve a crushing financial burden. Compare this with the situation in the United States, where an innocent defendant sometimes is forced to plead guilty (perhaps to a lesser charge) in order to avoid the prohibitive expense of a trial.

D. PROCEDURAL TREATMENT OF CONCURRENT
CRIMINAL AND CIVIL LIABILITY

Smooth: In practice we often encounter cases in which one and the same wrongful act entails both criminal and civil liability. In such a situation, it seems, many civil-law jurisdictions give the injured party a right of election: he may bring an independent civil action, or he may intervene in the criminal action and become a co-plaintiff together with the public prosecutor.

Comparovich: That is correct. If the victim chooses the latter method, which often will be speedier and less expensive, the criminal court has jurisdiction to include in the sentence a provision for damages to be paid by the defendant to the injured plaintiff, who is referred to as the *"partie civile"*.[1]

The practical significance of this procedure is enhanced by the fact that in many civil-law countries it is a crime negligently to cause bodily injury to another; this has the effect that automobile accidents frequently are followed by criminal prosecution, even when there was no violation of traffic regulations or of other penal statutes specifically dealing with the operation of automobiles.[2]

Edge: In talking with our lawyer friends abroad, I gained the impression that intervention (in the criminal proceeding) by the *"partie civile"* is of great practical importance in some civil-law countries, but not in others.

Comparovich: Correct. In theory, most civil-law countries provide for some form of such intervention. As a practical matter, it seems that in France and Italy many victims of traffic accidents prosecute

1. For details, see Larguier, The Civil Action for Damages in French Criminal Procedure, 39 Tul.L.Rev. 687 (1965); P. Campbell, A Comparative Study of Victim Compensation Procedures in France and in the United States: A Modest Proposal, 3 Hast.Int. and Comp.L.Rev. 321 (1980); A. V. Sheehan, Criminal Procedure in Scotland and France 20–23 (1975); E. Lobedanz, Schadensausgleich bei Straftaten in Spanien und Lateinamerika (1972), interestingly reviewed by J. G. Fleming in 21 Am.J.Comp.L. 615 (1973). For a broad comparative discussion of the subject, see J. A. Jolowicz, Civil Remedies in Criminal Courts, in Vol. XI, Ch. 13 of the International Encyclopedia of Comp. Law, especially pp. 4–15 (1972). The "partie civile" procedure in the context of mass injuries and mass claims is discussed in W. B. Fisch, European Analogues to the Class Action: Group Action in France and Germany, 27 Am.J.Comp.L. 51, 60–68, 71–74 (1979).

In this country, state statutes often provide for restitution as one of the conditions of probation. See, e.g., N.Y. Penal Law § 65.10, subd. 2(g). From the victim's standpoint, however, this provides much weaker protection than the civilian "partie

civile" procedure. Restitution as a condition of probation is an informal adjunct to sentencing rather than a civil remedy obtainable in a criminal proceeding. The victim has no procedural rights (e.g., no right to appeal, and no right to enforce the order providing for restitution). See In re Button, 8 Bankr. Reporter 692, 694 (D.C. W.D.N.Y., 1981). The broadly based victims' movement of recent years led to the adoption in 1982 of the Federal Victim and Witness Protection Act. Public Law 97–291, 97th Cong., Oct. 14 1982, 96 Stat. 1248. Under its section 5(a), restitution need no longer be a mere condition of probation, but can be *ordered* in the sentencing judgment in addition to, or in lieu of, any other penalty. See 18 U.S.C.A. § 3579(a)(1). In the federal system, then, restitution has been transformed from an adjunct to sentencing (involving judicial discretion) to an independent avenue of relief for the victim.

2. The *"partie civile"* procedure can be of significance also in defamation cases, because in France (and many other civil-law countries) defamation constitutes a crime as well as a tort. See B. S. Markesinis, The Not So Dissimilar Tort and Delict, 93 L.Q.Rev. 78, 103–07 (1977).

their damage claims in this way;[2a] but in Germany the victims rarely seek to recover their damages in the criminal proceeding, probably because of jurisdictional and procedural restrictions which until recently rendered it unattractive from the standpoint of the injured person to proceed in this manner.[3]

Edge: Suppose the injured person prefers to pursue his claim for damages by way of an independent civil action. In that event, I take it, the criminal proceeding normally will end before the civil one, and the whole criminal *dossier*—including the pre-trial investigation, the evidence introduced at the trial, and the decision of the court—can be used as evidence in the civil action. I believe this follows from what you have told us before.[4]

Comparovich: Your observation is correct.[5] Thus, whichever method the injured person chooses for the assertion of his damage claim, one thing is certain: The fact-finding process involved in the determination of that claim is greatly strengthened by the parties'

2a. In the courts of Paris, approximately 20% of criminal actions have a civil action joined to it. See Sheehan, supra n. 1, at p. 21.

3. The German legislator has recently abolished limitations on the amount recoverable by the victim, as well as several other restrictions on the intervenor's claim. See the new §§ 403 subs. I, 404 subs. V and 406 subs. I of the Code of Criminal Procedure. The intent of these recent legislative changes, in effect since April 1, 1987, was to counteract the decline of victims' intervention in criminal proceedings. Whether the changes will produce the desired practical effect, remains to be seen.

4. See supra pp. 424, 456.

5. Under rules of evidence prevailing in common-law countries, many obstacles would stand in the way of an attempt globally to introduce the criminal "dossier" as evidence in a subsequent civil action.

As to police reports, see Anno. 31 ALR4th 913 (1984). If the officer was under a duty to make the report, his own observations, as recorded in the report, usually are held admissible evidence under the official records exception to the hearsay rule. But statements of other witnesses, even though recorded by the officer on the scene, normally are excluded. Generally, that part of the *dossier* which consists of the testimony of witnesses, is inadmissible as hearsay. See Healy v. Rennert, 9 N.Y.2d 202, 213 N.Y.S.2d 44, 173 N.E.2d 777 (1961) (witness' sworn testimony given at prior criminal trial only exceptionally admissible in subsequent civil action). Even in modern jurisdictions, such hearsay would be admissible only under the extraordinary circumstances envisaged, e.g.,

by Fed.R.Evid., Rule 804(b)(1) or Rule 803(24).

As to the admissibility of the criminal judgment itself, there is much controversy in the common-law world. Even in jurisdictions which are not totally opposed to the admissibility of such a judgment (see supra p. 456, n. 24), fine distinctions have been drawn depending on (a) whether the judgment is one of conviction or of acquittal; (b) whether it was entered after trial or upon a plea of guilty or nolo contendere; and (c) whether the criminal proceeding involved a real crime or a mere traffic violation. See McCormick on Evidence, Chapt. 32, § 318 (3d ed., 1984). Compare Fed.R.Evid., Rule 803(22) and Cal. Evid. Code § 1300 with Wheelock v. Eyl, 393 Mich. 74, 223 N.W.2d 276 (1974). Even where a statute seemingly authorizes the admission of a criminal judgment in a subsequent civil case, the trial court may have discretionary power to reject it. See, e.g., Clemmer v. Hartford Ins. Co., 22 Cal.3d 865, 879, 151 Cal.Rptr. 285, 292, 587 P.2d 1098, 1105 (1978).

The injured person's lawyer (who may have looked at the police report as part of his own investigation) normally will be able, under American law, to take depositions of the persons who testified in the previous criminal proceeding, and to call them as witnesses at the civil trial. But this will consume much more time and effort than the civil-law methods mentioned in the text. Moreover, where the criminal record consists of grand jury testimony followed by a plea, the plaintiff in a subsequent civil action may have difficulty in gaining access to such testimony. See R. M. Buxbaum, Public Participation in the Enforcement of the Antitrust Laws, 59 Calif.L.Rev. 1113, 1140 (1971).

ability to utilize the *dossier* of the criminal proceeding, i.e. of a proceeding in which as a rule much more vigorous discovery methods have been used than would be permitted under continental civil procedure.[6]

Edge: The civil law thus strengthens the position of the victim. But all this hinges on an important condition: that a criminal proceeding be initiated in the first place. What if the prosecutor decides not to initiate such a proceeding?

Comparovich: Even in this situation the victim is by no means deprived of the advantages he can derive from a criminal proceeding; but his remedies vary from country to country.

In one group of civil-law countries, led by France, it is provided that in such a case the victim himself can initiate a criminal proceeding, with details of the procedure depending on whether more or less serious offenses are involved. While the prosecutor remains technically responsible for the conduct of such victim-initiated proceedings, in practice he normally leaves it to the victim to prosecute the case. The victim's procedural rights are substantially (though not in every detail) the same as those of the prosecutor.[7]

In Germany, and the countries following its example, the basic approach to the problem is somewhat different. Under the German doctrine, known as the "legality principle", the prosecutor has no discretionary power to forego prosecution of a serious offense; if there is reasonable cause to believe that such an offense has been committed, and that D is the perpetrator, the prosecutor *must* bring charges against D.[8] If he refuses, the victim can appeal to the intermediate appellate court, and if that court, after studying the dossier and (when indicated) making additional investigations, decides that there is probable cause, it orders the prosecutor to bring charges. Needless to say, this order is binding on the prosecutor.[9]

---

6. American readers will note that the reverse problem arises under their legal system, which liberally grants discovery in civil actions but puts severe restrictions upon fact-gathering in criminal proceedings. In the United States the parties to a criminal proceeding often attempt to use (or abuse) the discovery devices available in a civil suit in order to obtain information or evidence that is wanted mainly for purposes of a concurrent criminal proceeding, but could not be secured under rules governing a proceeding of the latter kind. Cf. United States v. Kordel, 397 U.S. 1, 90 S.Ct. 763 (1970). See also the 1977 decision of the House of Lords in In re Westinghouse El. Corp. Uranium Contract Litigation, [1978] 2 W.L.R. 81, 17 Int.Legal Materials 38 (1978).

7. See Sheehan, supra n. 1, at 21–22. Under the French system the victim need not seek damages in order to cause institution of proceedings in cases where the public prosecutor refuses to act. It suffices for the victim to show that he has the right to seek damages "in principle". See R. Merle and A. Vitu, Traité de Droit Criminel, Vol. 2 Procédure Pénale 67–68 (2d ed., 1973).

For the Austrian variant of the system, espoused also by Yugoslavia, see Foregger and Serini, Die österreichiche Strafprozessordnung, § 48, anno. I (2d ed., 1976).

8. See references supra p. 476 n. 4.

9. See German Code of Criminal Procedure §§ 172–175. For details of this *Klageerzwingungsverfahren* (i.e., a mandamus proceeding against the prosecutor), see Langbein, Comparative Criminal Procedure: Germany 113–114 (1977).

Under our law, mandamus (against the D.A., to compel him to prosecute) does not lie, because his decision to prosecute or not to prosecute is generally regarded as discretionary. For arguments in favor of limiting that discretion, see A. Goldstein, The Passive Judiciary: Prosecutorial Discretion and the Guilty Plea 9–11 (1981).

The French method—i.e., to let the victim do the prosecuting when the public prosecutor refuses to do so—may be equally unworkable here, even in a state such as California where some statutes on their face seem to give the victim the power to commence a criminal proceeding by simply filing a complaint with the appropriate

There are a few exceptions to the German rule just stated. Perhaps the most important exception is the one that relates to the crime of negligently causing bodily harm—the crime most frequently committed by careless drivers of motor vehicles. A criminal proceeding involving this particular crime has to be instituted by the public prosecutor only if he finds that such official prosecution is necessary by reason of the public interest. In other words, when dealing with this particular kind of crime, the prosecutor (exceptionally) does have a measure of discretion. But if, in the exercise of that discretion, he decides that an official prosecution is not warranted in the case at hand, then the victim, as private prosecutor, can institute a criminal proceeding.[10]

Edge: In other words, even though in general the victim's remedy under German law is very different from what it would be in France, the two systems substantially agree on the remedy which the victim *of an automobile accident* has in case the prosecutor refuses to initiate criminal proceedings against the allegedly guilty driver: the victim himself can institute criminal proceedings in such a case.

Comparovich: Correct. But you have to keep in mind that in France this result flows directly from a general rule, i.e., a rule applicable to the victim of any crime, while in Germany the same result is reached by virtue of an exception—an exception applicable to victims of the crime of negligently inflicting bodily harm. If a different kind of crime were involved (e.g., robbery or arson), the victim's remedy under German law would be quite different, as I have explained.

Smooth: From what you have told us, it seems to me that the civilian systems give the victim a much stronger position in criminal proceedings than he has under our law.

Comparovich: You are right. It is worth noting, moreover, that this stronger position is accorded not solely to those victims who seek damages in the criminal proceeding. In contrast to our system, where the public prosecutor enjoys a monopoly of prosecution, many civilian jurisdictions allow private prosecution by the victim, either generally (as in France), or at least exceptionally in certain important instances of frequently committed misdemeanors.[11] In addition, victims are often entitled to intervene in a criminal proceeding brought by the public prosecutor, even though they do not seek to recover damages in that proceeding. Until recently, this right of intervention was somewhat restricted in Germany; it existed primarily in those cases where the public prosecutor had been judicially compelled to prosecute.[12] In 1987,

court. Constitutional considerations, both of separation of powers and of due process, lead the courts to postulate (perhaps erroneously, see A. Goldstein, infra n. 14) that no criminal proceeding can be commenced without the participation, or at least the approval, of the public prosecutor. See People v. Municipal Court (Pellegrino), 27 Cal.App.3d 193, 103 Cal.Rptr. 645 (1972). Cf. United States v. Cox, 342 F.2d 167 (5th Cir. 1965) (upholding the requirement of Rule 7(c)(1) of Fed. R. Crim. Pro. that the U.S. attorney sign the indictment, and holding that he may, in his discretion, abort a prosecution by failing to sign).

For further (and in part conflicting) authority on this point, see Anno., 24 ALR4th 316 (1983).

10. See supra n. 8.

11. Concerning Germany, this possibility was illustrated above by the example of negligently causing bodily harm (see text supra at n. 10); but German law allows private prosecution for several other misdemeanours as well. In some European countries a narrow class of misdemeanours can be prosecuted *only* by the victim.

12. Supra, text at *ns.* 8–9. Where the public prosecutor instituted proceedings on his own initiative, there was only one prac-

however, amendments to the Code of Criminal Procedure greatly expanded the victim's right to intervene, and today that right no longer depends on whether the prosecutor was judicially compelled to act.[12a] Moreover, in many other European countries the victim's right of intervention exists in *every* criminal case, even when the public prosecutor has instituted the proceeding on his own initiative.[13] As intervenor, the victim has important procedural rights: he can, for example, call witnesses, ask questions of them, make closing arguments, and (in some countries) recover his attorney's fees from a convicted defendant. These rights reflect recognition of the fact that the victim has a strong interest in the outcome of the criminal process.

Edge: In this country, too, the influence of the victim on the course of the criminal proceeding seems to be increasing. In many states, victims are now entitled to be heard before the sentencing court or the Parole Board makes a decision. Recent federal legislation requires public prosecutors to consult with victims at critical stages of the proceeding, and "victim impact statements" must sometimes be prepared.[14] Yet, even the most dramatic reforms stop short of enabling the victim to participate as of right in the entire criminal process, and especially in its trial phase.

Comparovich: There are many reasons for this difference between our law and the civilian systems, and we have no time to discuss them extensively. Observe, however, that where the trial is organized, as it is here, as a contest of two parties before a jury and an essentially passive judge, any intervention by a third party, including the victim, would create problems unparalleled in civil-law systems where the active conduct of the trial is in the hands of the presiding judge.[15]

Edge: The interaction between the criminal proceeding and the victim's civil claim gives rise to yet another question. If the injured person asserts his claim as intervenor in the criminal proceeding, then the criminal judgment and the decision involving the civil claim are handed down by the same court; thus, I assume, they are apt to be consistent with each other. How do the civilians handle the consistency problem in cases where the victim chooses to bring an independent civil action?

Comparovich: The criminal *dossier* being admissible as evidence in the civil action, an inconsistency between the results reached in the two proceedings will not occur too frequently. In what is probably a

---

tically important case of permissible intervention—that of the relatives of victims of homicide.

12a. The right of intervention is now conferred upon the victims of all those offences that attack "highly personal values" (e.g., sex offences, offences against freedom or honor and most offences against life and limb.) See § 395 subs. I of the Code of Criminal Procedure, in effect since April 1, 1987.

13. Such intervention is possible also in many Eastern European countries, including the Soviet Union. See Code of Criminal Procedure of the RSFSR art. 53.

14. See Victim and Witness Protection Act, supra n. 1. The victims' movement and its effects on criminal justice reform are perceptively discussed in A. Goldstein, Defining the Role of the Victim in Criminal Prosecution, 52 Miss.L.J. 515 (1982).

15. It is widely feared that under our system, if the victim were given the procedural rights of an intervenor, every witness would become subject to examination and cross-examination by defense counsel, prosecutor *and counsel for each victim*, and that this might lead to much disruption and delay. *Quaere*, however, whether this potential difficulty could not be avoided by a legislator who is willing to consider intelligent and innovative compromise solutions.

majority of civil-law systems, this slight danger of inconsistent results is regarded with equanimity.[16]

A minority group led by France, however, has adopted the principle that a criminal judgment is absolutely conclusive and binds the whole world (including, of course, the injured party).[17] Strangely, this absolute res judicata effect is accorded not only to judgments of conviction, but to acquittals as well. In practice, the rule is rendered bearable only by limiting the conclusive effect of the criminal judgment to what we would call the court's precise "holding". The cases seeking to stake out a line of demarcation between binding holdings and non-binding dicta— especially with respect to acquittals in traffic accident cases—are numerous and often difficult to reconcile. One important rule, however, seems to be well established: When it is possible for the victim of an automobile accident to recover from the driver or owner of the car on a theory of absolute or quasi-absolute liability,[18] he may be successful in his civil action even though the driver has been acquitted of a charge of criminal negligence.[19]

16. In some of the majority countries, e.g., The Netherlands, the danger of inconsistency is further reduced by the rule that the civil court must treat the criminal judgment as presumptively correct; the presumption, however, is rebuttable. See n. 17 infra.

In most American jurisdictions, on the other hand, the consistency problem would be taken very seriously and would be treated under the heading of collateral estoppel. See supra p. 456. An acquittal in the criminal proceeding would have no collateral estoppel effect in the subsequent civil action. Whether a criminal judgment of conviction after trial has such an effect, depends largely on the attitude which a particular jurisdiction adopts concerning the question of "mutuality". See R. C. Casad, Res Judicata in a Nutshell, § 5–73 (1976).

17. See the brief but interesting discussion by E. L. Johnson, Res Judicata: A Comparative Study of the Effect of Convictions and Acquittals in Subsequent Civil Proceedings, 18 Current Legal Problems 81 (1965).

There is, however, an important exception to the French rule that a criminal judgment is res judicata as against the whole world. As the reader will recall (see supra p. 490, n. 41), the French in 1972 adopted the German *Strafbefehl* procedure.

See Law No. 72–5 of January 3, 1972 (Rec. Dalloz Hebd.1972, p. 58). If the defendant does not file a timely objection, such a *Strafbefehl* acquires the force of a judgment convicting and sentencing the defendant. However, Art. 528–1 of the French Code of Criminal Procedure, as amended by the above-mentioned Law of 1972, expressly provides that the *Strafbefehl*, even if it acquires the force of a judgment, shall not have any res judicata effect in a subsequent civil action that might be brought against the defendant for damages caused by his infraction. Thus, in the case of a petty offense the res judicata effect of a French criminal judgment will depend on whether the criminal proceeding was instituted in the regular manner or by way of the new *Strafbefehl* procedure.

18. See infra pp. 556–559.

19. See P. Herzog, Civil Procedure in France 138 (1967) and authorities there cited.

It should be remembered, also, that in the criminal proceeding the driver usually is charged with a specific negligent act, such as speeding, going through a red light, or the like. Acquittal of that specific charge does not prevent the civil court from imposing liability on the basis of some other (actual or presumed) act of negligence.

See Supp 136

E. PUBLIC–LAW DISPUTES *

(AA) THE CIVILIANS' DICHOTOMY BETWEEN PRIVATE-LAW AND PUBLIC-LAW LITIGATION

Smooth: In many countries, we sell our products by vending machines installed in public places, or from specially equipped small trucks in the streets. Ordinarily, this requires an official license of some kind. If the issuance of such a license is refused, or if a license is revoked by the administrative authorities, we often get into litigation. In our system, of course, such cases would be handled by ordinary courts under writs of certiorari, mandamus or prohibition, or some statutory version of these ancient writs. We noticed, however, that in continental countries such cases are not considered by the ordinary courts about which we have been talking, but by administrative tribunals.

Comparovich: Apart from criminal matters, the jurisdiction of the ordinary courts in most civil-law countries is essentially limited to "private law" disputes.[1] A controversy involving the validity or propriety of an administrative act (such as the refusal or revocation of a business license), involves issues of public law and under their system will be determined by a separate hierarchy of administrative tribunals.[1a]

---

* The materials in this section deal with *judicial* remedies available to a party who feels aggrieved by an act of the governmental bureaucracy. The reader should keep in mind, however, that judicial remedies are not the only possible ones, and that in many countries there are less formal, non-judicial channels through which a citizen can seek redress against official arbitrariness. A comparative study of these channels (which may exist in addition to, or in lieu of, judicial remedies) is of great interest. The classical work is W. Gellhorn, Ombudsmen and Others: Citizens' Protectors in Nine Countries (1966). For more recent contributions, see, e.g., G. E. Caiden (Ed.), International Handbook of the Ombudsman (1983); J. C. Juergensmeyer & A. Burzynski, Parliamentary and Extra-Administrative Forms of Protection of Citizens' Rights (1979) (covers Poland, East Germany, West Germany, Sweden, U.S.A., U.S.S.R., and Yugoslavia); M. Wierzbowski, Administrative Procedure in Eastern Europe, 1 Comp.L. Yearbook 211 (1977–78); D. Rowat, The Ombudsman Plan: Essays on the Worldwide Spread of an Idea (1973); L. N. Brown & P. Lavirotte, The Mediator: A French Ombudsman?, 90 L.Q.Rev. 211 (1974).

On American counterparts, see S. V. Anderson, Ombudsman Papers: American Experience and Proposals (1969); A. J. Wyner

(Ed.), Executive Ombudsmen in the United States (1973).

1. Concerning the historical reasons for the sharp distinction between "private law" and "public law" in continental countries, see supra pp. 300–301.

1a. For a comprehensive comparative treatment of the subject, see Max-Planck-Institut für ausländisches öffentliches Recht und Völkerrecht, Judicial Protection against the Executive (H. Mosler, Ed., 1971), especially Vol. 3.

The civilian tradition of separate administrative courts is seldom followed in socialist countries of Eastern Europe. In some (USSR, Czechoslovakia, East Germany) there is virtually no judicial review of administrative acts. In others (Bulgaria, Hungary, Roumania, Yugoslavia) a more or less wide range of administrative acts is reviewable in ordinary courts, or in special sections of supreme courts. In 1980, Poland reintroduced a special administrative court of the traditional continental genre. This court has broad jurisdiction to set aside administrative acts that violate the law; but certain acts, such as the expulsion of an alien, or denial of a passport, are exempted from the court's jurisdiction. The impact of this reintroduced system of administrative adjudication seems to be considerable. For a survey of Eastern Eu-

Edge: It thus appears that under their system the respective subject-matter jurisdiction of ordinary courts and administrative courts depends on whether the dispute belongs to the realm of private law or that of public law. As a consequence, the distinction between private law and public law must be of much greater practical significance in civil-law systems than under our law.

Comparovich: You are basically right. But this difference between the civilians and us should not be exaggerated: we also assign practical importance to the distinction between private and "public rights" disputes, although for a more limited purpose. The legislative branch of the federal government has the power (not infrequently exercised) to have cases involving public rights—i.e., cases ordinarily involving a dispute between the Government and a non-governmental party— adjudicated by special legislative courts or by administrative agencies. The latters' decision may be subject to review by ordinary courts, but such review can be limited to issues of law, in much the same manner as the reviewing court's scope of review is limited in jury cases. On the other hand, Congress has no similar power to assign cases involving purely private rights to legislative courts or administrative agencies.[1b]

But let me return to continental administrative tribunals. Their members usually have a high degree of expertise in administrative matters; but ordinarily they are independent of the Executive and of the administrators over whose acts they sit in judgment.[2] They are judges in every sense of the word.

In Germany, where a high value is placed on specialized judicial expertise, there are several separate hierarchies of tribunals dealing exclusively with public law disputes: tax courts, social security courts, and "administrative" courts.[3] The latter deal with all public law disputes not involving tax or social security matters.

In France, jurisdiction over public law disputes is less fragmented. In particular, there is no separate hierarchy of tax courts, with the result that tax controversies normally come before the regular administrative tribunals.[4] The advantages of judicial specialization, however, are not necessarily lost under the French system. The Conseil d'Etat, the administrative court of last resort,[4a] normally sits in panels, called

ropean systems (save Yugoslavia), see M. Wierzbowsky and S. C. McCaffrey, Judicial Control of Administrative Authorities: A New Development in Eastern Europe, 18 Int. Lawyer 645 (1984).

1b. See, e.g., Northern Pipeline Construction Co. v. Marathon Pipeline Co., 458 U.S. 50, 67, 69, 102 S.Ct. 2858, 2869, 2870 (1982). Nor can Congress, when dealing with actions at law that involve *private* disputes, take the fact-finding function away from the jury. See Atlas Roofing Co., Inc. v. Occupational Safety and Health Review Commission, 430 U.S. 442, 450, 97 S.Ct. 1261 (1977).

2. See, e.g., R. Drago, Some Recent Reforms of the French Conseil d'Etat, 13 Int. & Comp.L.Q. 1282, 1287 (1964).

3. Altogether, Germany has five separate judicial hierarchies: ordinary courts,

labor courts, tax courts, social security courts, and administrative courts. Each of these hierarchies includes tribunals of first instance, intermediate appellate courts and a court of last resort. In addition, there is the Federal Constitutional Court (see supra pp. 375–377). For a description of the entire system, see H. G. Rupp, Judicial Review in the Federal Republic of Germany, 9 Am.J.Comp.L. 29 (1960).

4. The statement in the text, supra, should be understood as referring to direct taxes. There are some peculiarities with respect to indirect taxes. For details see 1 Auby and Drago, Traité de Contentieux Administratif, §§ 569–71, 623–30 (3d ed., 1984).

4a. It should be noted that not all of the business of the Conseil d'État is judicial. Of its five Sections, only one, the

sous-sections; matters requiring specialized knowledge, such as tax cases, always are referred to particular panels.[5]

Edge: Do civil-law systems generally provide for a hierarchy of administrative courts, distinct from the hierarchy of ordinary courts?

Comparovich: A few of the developing countries, though otherwise influenced by French legal thinking, declined to adopt or retain the continental system of separate administrative courts. They made this policy decision on the ground that because of scarcity of trained judicial manpower it would be undesirable for them to maintain several hierarchies of tribunals. In the Republic of Senegal, for instance, "the courts of first instance have jurisdiction over administrative as well as civil matters, and the Supreme Court performs the functions of both the French *Cour de Cassation* and the *Conseil d'État*, although they are performed by separate sections of the Court." [6]

Subject to this observation concerning some of the developing nations, and subject also to certain reservations with respect to Latin America,[7] the answer to your question is in the affirmative: In the overwhelming majority of civil-law countries the administrative courts form a judicial hierarchy separate and distinct from that of the ordinary courts. This, indeed, can be regarded as one of the earmarks distinguishing civil-law from common-law systems.[8]

Edge: I have familiarized myself with the main features of the French system of administrative law and administrative courts, which is described in a large number of English-language books and articles.[9]

Section du Contentieux, has judicial functions. What is said in the text about the Conseil d'État as the highest administrative court of France, refers entirely to the work of its *Section du Contentieux*. The work of the four non-judicial Sections is discussed by L. N. Brown, The Participation of the French Conseil d'État in Legislation, 48 Tul.L.Rev. 796 (1974). This article is particularly instructive because its author was "privileged to witness in person the functioning of the Conseil d'État in its less publicized role of legal consultant to the French government and its Ministers."

5. See S. Grevisse, France: Le Conseil D'État, in A. Tunc (Ed.), La Cour Judiciaire Suprême—Enquête Comparative, 30 Revue Internationale de Droit Comparé 1, at 217, 223 (1978).

6. E. A. Farnsworth, Law Reform in a Developing Country: A New Code of Obligations for Senegal, 8 J.Afr.L. 6, 11 (1964).

7. The attitude of Latin-American countries toward the jurisdictional separation of "private law" and "public law" disputes is somewhat wavering. These countries, it will be remembered (see supra p. 315), belong to the civil-law orbit with respect to their private law; but in the area of public law, the United States model has exercised considerable influence. It is not too surprising, therefore, to find that the Latin-American legal systems are almost evenly

divided on the issue whether public law disputes should be determined by the ordinary courts, as in this country, or by administrative tribunals of the continental type. See H. Clagett, Administration of Justice in Latin America 61 ff. (1952). See also Note, The Writ of Amparo: A Remedy To Protect Constitutional Rights in Argentina, 31 Ohio St.L.J. 831 (1970); P. P. Camargo, The Claim of "Amparo" in Mexico: Constitutional Protection of Human Rights, 6 Cal.West.L.Rev. 201 (1970); C. E. Schwarz, Rights and Remedies in the Federal District Courts of Mexico and the United States, 4 Hastings Const.L.Q. 67 (1977).

8. For a suggestion that the civil-law approach be adopted here, see C. H. Fulda, A Proposed "Administrative Court" for Ohio, 22 Ohio St.L.J. 734 (1961).

9. E.g., L. N. Brown and J. F. Garner, French Administrative Law (2d ed., 1973); C. E. Freedeman, The Conseil d'Etat in Modern France (1961); B. Schwartz, French Administrative Law and the Common Law World (1954); C. J. Hamson, Executive Discretion and Judicial Control (1954); Letourneur and Drago, The Rule of Law As Understood in France, 7 Am.J. Comp.L. 147 (1958); M. J. Remington, The Tribunaux Administratifs: Protectors of the French Citizen, 51 Tul.L.Rev. 33 (1976).

Is it safe to assume that in most other civil-law countries the French model is followed?

Comparovich: There is considerable diversity as to many points of jurisdiction, procedure and substantive law; almost every civil-law system presents some unique features in its administrative law.[10] It seems, nevertheless, that most civilians share a basic approach to the subject and readily understand each others' systems. This is clearly demonstrated by the experience of the European Communities.[11]

The two systems of administrative law and administrative courts which have been most influential throughout the civil-law world, are the French [12] and, to a lesser degree, the German.[13] Before we go into the differences between them, let me briefly point out some of the important aspects in which they are similar to each other:

(1) Both in France and in Germany, virtually *every* administrative act is subject to review by the administrative courts, and may be *annulled* in case of unlawfulness or abuse of discretion.[14]

(2) In both countries, the administrative courts ordinarily have power to annul the administrator's action for errors of fact as well as law.

(3) The procedure of the administrative courts is informal, inexpensive and largely inquisitorial.[15] The court can direct the administrator

A short but helpful introductory discussion can be found in H. J. Abraham, The Judicial Process 277–82 (5th ed., 1986). For a masterful brief description of the workings of the Conseil d'Etat, written by an insider but containing some comparative sideglances at similar institutions in other countries, see M. Lagrange, The French Council of State, 43 Tul.L.Rev. 46 (1968).

10. See, e.g., G. Treves, Judicial Review in Italian Administrative Law, 26 U.Chi.L. Rev. 419 (1959); R. Parker, Administrative Law Through Foreign Glasses: The Austrian Experience, 15 Rutgers L.Rev. 551 (1961).

For a comparative survey of the administrative courts of the six original member nations of the Common Market, see J.-M. Auby & M. Fromont, Les recours contre les actes administratifs dans les pays de la Communauté économique européenne (1971).

11. See E. Stein, P. Hay & M. Waelbroeck, European Community Law and Institutions in Perspective: Text, Cases and Readings 109–71 (2d ed., 1976 and Supp. 1985 at 33–44).

12. The French system of administrative courts and administrative law is said to have served as model in The Netherlands, Belgium, Luxembourg, Spain, Turkey, Egypt, and a number of other countries. See Lagrange, supra n. 9, at 57.

13. English-language literature on German administrative law is less voluminous

than that dealing with the French system. There are, however, some useful accounts. See Bachof, German Administrative Law With Special Reference to the Latest Developments in the System of Legal Protection, 2 Int. & Comp.L.Q. 368 (1953); W. Feld, The German Administrative Courts, 36 Tul.L.Rev. 495 (1962), where further references can be found.

For an interesting comparison of the French and German systems, see H. G. Crossland, Rights of the Individual to Challenge Administrative Action Before Administrative Courts in France and Germany, 24 Int. & Comp.L.Q. 707 (1975).

14. If the challenged act is a negative one (e.g., a refusal to issue a license or a passport), its annullation may in effect amount to an affirmative command, not unlike an order of mandamus.

15. The inexpensiveness of proceedings in continental administrative courts is emphasized by K. C. Davis, Discretionary Justice: A Preliminary Inquiry 156 (1971). According to Professor Davis, one of the reasons for the inexpensiveness of those proceedings is that the party suing the Government is not only legally but also practically able to proceed without the help of a lawyer, because "Clerks or lawyers attached to the court help parties to prepare their written complaints." Moreover, if the citizen-litigant has an attorney, and if his action is successful, German law permits him to recover counsel fees from

to submit his entire *dossier* relating to the matter at hand. In addition, parties are given an opportunity to introduce, or suggest the taking of, new evidence which was not before the administrative agency. Arguments of counsel for both sides usually are presented in writing and orally in open court. The administrative courts in both countries have a high reputation for impartiality and efficiency, and their operation is regarded as essential to the maintenance of the rule of law.

(4) Neither German nor French administrative law has been systematically codified. In both countries there are relevant statutes, especially on matters of procedure; [15a] but the bulk of the rules determining the legality and propriety of administrative acts is judge-made.[16] When we speak of the civil-law orbit as a world of codes, we must always remember that the statement requires qualification with respect to public law.

(5) Both French and German lawyers are plagued by the difficulty of defining the line of demarcation between the jurisdiction of the ordinary courts and that of the administrative courts.

Edge: How do they draw the line?

Comparovich: Concerning this point, the French system and the German system are very different from each other.

In the first place, they use different procedures for resolving a conflict of jurisdiction.[17] The French submit such a conflict to a special "Tribunal of Conflicts", composed of judges drawn from the *Cour de Cassation* and the *Conseil d'État*.[18] Under the present German system, both the ordinary and the administrative courts have power to determine their own jurisdiction. If an ordinary or administrative court, in a decision no longer subject to appeal, has affirmed or denied its own jurisdiction, such decision is res judicata in all subsequent proceedings

the defeated Government. See ibid. Compare 28 U.S.C.A. § 2412 (1978 and Supps.).

15a. In Germany, the procedure of administrative courts is governed by an elaborate and systematic federal statute, the *Verwaltungsgerichtsordnung* of 1960, as amended. In its organization and terminology, the *Verwaltungsgerichtsordnung* is patterned after the Code of Civil Procedure. This makes the procedure before the administrative courts comparable, and in some respects similar, to ordinary court procedure. But the greater simplicity of administrative court procedure has been preserved.

While the *Verwaltungsgerichtsordnung* regulates the procedure of administrative courts, the practice of the administrative agencies themselves is governed by a more recent statute, the *Verwaltungsverfahrensgesetz* of 1976.

16. This is especially true of France, where a single central institution, the Conseil d'État, during the last 150 years has *created* a modern body of administrative law, in much the same way in which the common law courts created the law of England.

In Germany, the situation is somewhat different. Administrative law is partly state law. Moreover, it was only after World War II that a federal administrative court of last resort was created. Until then, no appeal to a federal court could be taken from the decisions of the various states' highest administrative tribunals. Thus no single court was able to acquire a position of nation-wide importance and prestige comparable to that of the French Conseil d'État. Therefore (and again, comparable developments in earlier periods of history easily suggest themselves), academic influence on German administrative law has been strong, much stronger than in France.

17. Such a conflict may be "positive", if both the ordinary and the administrative courts *claim* jurisdiction; or it may be "negative", in a case in which both *decline* jurisdiction.

18. For an interesting and typical example of a case decided by the Tribunal of Conflicts see Note, 67 L.Q.Rev. 44 (1951).

that may be brought concerning the same matter in the same or any other court (even if the other court belongs to a different judicial hierarchy).[19] A court which considers itself incompetent on the ground that the case should have been brought before a court belonging to a different judicial hierarachy, may upon plaintiff's motion transfer the case to the latter court; the decision to transfer, unless it is reversed on appeal, is binding on the transferee court.[20]

Edge: It seems to me that by their method the Germans aim to *avoid* head-on conflicts between ordinary and administrative courts, while the French provide machinery to *resolve* such conflicts.[21]

Comparovich: If you like pithy generalizations, you might put it that way.[21a] From a policy point of view, good arguments can be made for and against either method. Certain it is, however, that any legal system that creates several separate judicial hierarchies, must provide some method by which jurisdictional conflicts can be avoided or resolved.

Edge: Do the French and the Germans agree on the criteria by which they seek to distinguish between private and public disputes?

19. See Gerichtsverfassungsgesetz § 17; Verwaltungsgerichtsordnung §§ 40, 41. See also infra n. 73.

Similar problems of conflicts of jurisdiction can arise in our law, e.g. between a Workmen's Compensation Board and an ordinary court. Our solution appears to be similar to the German one: Each set of tribunals has the power to determine its own jurisdiction, and such determination, once it becomes final, is binding on the parties, with the result that the judgment, even if erroneous on the jurisdictional point, cannot be collaterally attacked on the ground of lack of subject-matter jurisdiction. See, e.g., Murray v. New York, 43 N.Y.2d 400, 407, 401 N.Y.S.2d 773, 776, 372 N.E.2d 560, 563 (1977); Scott v. Industrial Accident Comm., 46 Cal.2d 76, 293 P.2d 18 (1956). Cf. Doney v. Tambouratgis, 23 Cal. 3d 91, 151 Cal.Rptr. 347, 587 P.2d 1160 (1979).

20. There is controversy concerning the extent to which the transferee court is bound. According to most of the commentators, the transferee court *must* take jurisdiction. E.g., if an administrative court has transferred to an ordinary court, then the latter court, in the opinion of the commentators, *must* proceed to determine the case on the merits. Many courts have held, however, that in such a situation the ordinary court is bound only to the extent that it may not dismiss or transfer the case on the ground that the administrative court has jurisdiction; under this view, it would still be open to the transferee court (the ordinary court in our example) to hold that the case is not justiciable at all, or that a tribunal belonging to a third hierarchy, e.g., a tax court, has jurisdiction, and

to dismiss or again transfer accordingly. See Baumbach-Lauterbach-Albers-Hartmann, Zivilprozessordnung, GVG § 17, Anno. 3B (45th ed., 1987) and authorities there cited. Such complexities (and this is not the only one) are part of the price which the German system must pay for its multiplicity of judicial hierarchies and for the advantage of operating without a separate Tribunal of Conflicts superimposed upon them.

21. It should be noted, however, that the German statute (Gerichtsverfassungsgesetz § 17a) authorizes the states to create special tribunals similar to the French Tribunal of Conflicts. It seems that at present such a Tribunal exists in Bavaria, but that otherwise this sytem is not widely used in Germany. Whether the powers of the Bavarian Tribunal of Conflicts can be invoked in a case in which a court, of whatever hierarchy, already has made a final (i.e., no longer appealable) jurisdictional determination, is a question which, again, has caused much doubt and controversy.

21a. Mr. Edge's generalization, although it captures the traditional spirit of the two methods, is no longer quite accurate. Pursuant to a Decree of 1960, a ruling of the French Tribunal of Conflicts can now be obtained even though no actual ("positive" or "negative") conflict between an ordinary and an administrative court has as yet arisen. The Decree authorizes the Tribunal of Conflicts to issue a preliminary ruling on where the action *should be* brought; and this, it seems, is now the most common procedure. See Crossland, supra n. 13, at 715.

504   COMMON LAW AND CIVIL LAW

Comparovich: No, on this subject, again, there is a great deal of disagreement between them. Relatively little difficulty arises under either system in cases in which the plaintiff seeks to have an administrative act annulled; ordinarily there is little doubt that this is a matter of public law, regardless of whether the administrative act to be reviewed is an act of the police [21b] or of any other public authority.[21c] Really tough problems of demarcation, however, are encountered in the innumerable cases—of contracts, of torts, and of eminent domain—in which the redress sought by the individual is a money judgment against the State or one of its subdivisions. Are such disputes private or public? On this point, the French and the Germans part company.

Smooth: We have run into this problem repeatedly. Both in France and in Germany our trucks have been damaged in one-vehicle accidents caused by bumps and potholes that were the result of negligent maintenance of public roads. We found that we had to sue the French Government in the administrative courts, while in Germany such an action must be brought before the Civil Chamber of the ordinary court of first instance.[22] What is the reason for this difference?

21b. The statement in the text must be qualified with respect to police activities in the course of formal criminal proceedings, which are subject to the jurisdiction and supervision of ordinary rather than administrative courts. In West Germany, a distinction is drawn between informal police inquiries and those that have turned—following the intervention of the Public Prosecutor's Office—into formal criminal proceedings. With respect to the former, administrative courts have jurisdiction. In a series of decisions these courts have held, for example, that a person under informal police investigation can, by a proceeding before an administrative court, obtain information from police files, or may even compel the police to destroy the relevant records and discontinue further inquiries. See, e.g., the decision of the VGH München of 9–27–1983, Neue Juristische Wochenschrift 1984, p. 2235. The line of demarcation between formal and informal criminal proceedings can be difficult to draw, leading to uncertainties as to whether administrative or ordinary courts have jurisdiction. For an interesting article, critical of the above-cited decision, see A. Schoreit, Verwaltungsstreit um Kriminalakten, Neue Juristische Wochenschrift 1985, p. 169.

In France, a distinction is drawn between the *police judiciaire* (which deals with criminal cases and whose acts are, at least to some extent, subject to the control of the prosecutor and the criminal courts), and the *police administrative* (which deals with non-criminal matters and whose acts can be reviewed by the administrative courts). See L. H. Levinson, Enforcement of Administrative Decisions in the United States and in France, 23 Emory L.J. 11, at 13–15, 90 (1974); C. L. Blakesley, Conditional Liberation (Parole) in France, 39 La. L.Rev. 1, at 16–17 (1978).

But there are troublesome border areas. When the public authorities act in such a border area, the affected citizen may well be in doubt as to whether he should turn to the ordinary or the administrative courts for review. A good example is incarceration for "vagrancy". See the fascinating and highly instructive Vagrancy Cases decided by the European Court of Human Rights in 1971 and extensively discussed by S. A. Cohn, International Adjudication of Human Rights and the European Court of Human Rights: A Survey of Its Procedural and Some of Its Substantive Holdings, 7 Ga.J.Int.Comp.L. 315, at 377–408 (1977).

21c. Difficult questions arise in connection with the activities of nationalized enterprises and of other public corporations. For a comparative treatment of the important question of judicial control (by ordinary or administrative courts) over the activities of such corporations, see W. Friedmann (Ed.), The Public Corporation, passim (1954).

22. Frequently these jurisdictional problems are treated incidentally in books and articles primarily dealing with the substantive aspects of tort liability for the acts of public officials and employees. The most extensive comparative treatment to date is the 1964 Colloquium on "Liability of the State for Illegal Conduct of Its Organs" published by the Max-Planck-Institut für Ausländisches Offentliches Recht und Völkerrecht (1967). For comparative discussions in the English language see,

noted ✳

Comparovich: The French tried to draw a distinction along functional lines. If the damage is caused by some malfunctioning of the public service (including human failure of the State's agents, high or low), the State is liable, and must be sued in the administrative courts. If the official or employee who caused the damage, is personally at fault, he is liable as an individual, and his liability can be enforced in the ordinary courts.

Edge: I suppose such personal fault will be found where an official has maliciously caused defendant's injury or loss.

Comparovich: Yes, but the notion of personal fault, upon which the jurisdiction of the ordinary court as well as the official's personal liability is bottomed, is not limited to cases of malice. A policeman who in arresting a person commits hideous and unnecessary acts of brutality, can be personally sued in the ordinary courts, regardless of whether he was motivated by personal hatred of his victim or by an excess of zeal in the performance of his duties. Even a non-intentional but grossly negligent act can constitute personal fault.[23] Some of the cases so holding involved careless use of firearms by soldiers or policemen.[24]

Smooth: Are the situations in which the State is liable, and those in which the official is individually liable for his intentional or negligent wrongdoing, mutually exclusive?

Comparovich: They were under the older doctrine, which prevailed until the beginning of this century. But since then, and with ever-growing liberality, the French courts have recognized that there are countless situations in which the State's servant is sufficiently blameworthy to be subjected to personal liability, and in which, at the same time, the damage is so closely connected with the public service that the State, also, should be held liable.

Smooth: This is similar to our doctrine of respondeat superior. In cases to which that doctrine applies, you can sue the servant *and* the master.[24a]

---

e.g., H. Street, Governmental Liability (1953); Z. Szirmai (Ed.), Governmental Tort Liability in the Soviet Union, Bulgaria, Czechoslovakia, Hungary, Poland, Roumania and Yugoslavia (1970), reviewed by H. R. Hink in 21 Am.J.Comp.L. 616 (1973); S. B. Jacoby, Federal Tort Claims Act and French Law of Governmental Liability, 7 Vand.L.Rev. 246 (1954); K. Kautzor-Schroeder, Public Tort Liability Under the Treaty Constituting the European Coal and Steel Community Compared With the Federal Tort Claims Act, 4 Vill.L.Rev. 198 (1958–9); R. Braband, Liability in Tort of the Government and Its Employees: A Comparative Analysis With Emphasis on German Law, 33 N.Y.U.L.Rev. 18 (1958); H. R. Hink, Service-Connected Versus Personal Fault in the French Law of Government Tort Liability, 18 Rutgers L.Rev. 17 (1963); id., The German Law of Governmental Tort Liability, 18 Rutgers L.Rev. 1069 (1964).

Under German law (as in the United States under the Federal Tort Claims Act),

the substantive aspects of the State's tort liability are essentially governed by general tort principles, i.e., by private law. See infra n. 45. In France, on the other hand, it was held that the provisions of the Civil Code are not applicable to governmental liability, which is governed by principles peculiar to public law. This divergence of the relevant sources also leads to substantive differences between French and German law with respect to governmental tort liability. For an example, see infra n. 27. Cf. K. Lipstein, The Law of the European Economic Community 323 (1974); id., Some Practical Comparative Law: The Interpretation of Multi-Lingual Treaties with Special Regard to the EEC Treaties, 48 Tul.L. Rev. 907, 913–14 (1974).

23. See A. de Laubadère, Traité de droit administratif, §§ 1193–94 (8th ed., 1980).

24. Ibid. For further examples see Hink, supra n. 22, at 27.

24a. This is the general rule. For a statutory exception see infra at n. 34.

Comparovich: Correct; but with respect to governmental liability, the French have gone further. "Cumulative liability" of the official and of the Government often exists in French law even though in terms of our phraseology the wrongdoing official has not acted within the scope of his employment.[25] As examples one can cite a number of cases in which the plaintiff's injury or loss was caused solely [26] by what we would call a "frolic" of the official; in these cases the Government as well as the individual official was held liable under French law, on the ground that the wrongdoing functionary had acted on the occasion of an official function or had used an instrumentality entrusted to him by the Government. In one such case a high official, while inspecting a police station, had engaged in target practice and negligently wounded a person who happened to pass by. Although it was clear that the shooting exercise had been purely for fun and had nothing whatever to do with the wrongdoer's official duties, this was held to be a case of cumulative liability, on the ground that the official had acted on the occasion of his inspection visit and had used one of the service guns kept at the police station.[27]

Smooth: I take it that in cases of this kind, in which both the State and the individual public servant are liable, both can be sued in the same court?

Comparovich: No, even in these cases the public authority must be sued in the administrative courts, while an action against the individual is within the jurisdiction of the ordinary courts.[28] As a matter of practice, plaintiffs prefer to sue in the administrative courts, out of fear that the individual tortfeasor may be judgment-proof, although the administrative courts have the reputation of being conservative in determining the amount of damages to be awarded.

25. See de Laubadère, op. cit. supra n. 23, at §§ 1202–08.

26. In cases in which the damage is caused (a) by the wrongdoing official's personal fault *and* (b) by some malfunctioning of the public service that is separable from the conduct of the primary wrongdoer (e.g., failure of higher officials properly to supervise the malefactor), it was even less difficult for the French courts to justify the imposition of cumulative liability. See ibid.

27. See M. Waline, Droit Administratif, Sec. 1458 (9th ed.1963), where the reader also will find further references to relevant cases.

In Germany, where governmental tort liability is controlled by private law (see supra n. 22), a more restricted rule has been adopted. Under relevant principles of private law, which in this respect are somewhat similar to our notion of "scope of employment", the German courts have declined to hold the State liable in situations where, as in the French case mentioned in the text, the accident was caused by a frolic involving misuse of firearms kept for official purposes. See RGZ 105, 230 (1922).

The fact that the frolicking functionary acted on the occasion of an official activity, and that he used a service gun or other State-owned instrumentality, in the German view is insufficient to support governmental liability in such cases. See Palandt, Bürgerliches Gesetzbuch, § 839, Anno. 2Ac(bb) (43rd ed., 1984), and cases there cited. See also infra at nn. 44–46.

For further substantive details of the French and German doctrines of governmental tort liability, the reader is referred to the books and articles cited supra n. 22. The aim of the present discussion is merely to throw some light on the jurisdictional demarcation lines between the business of the ordinary and of the administrative courts.

28. The general jurisdictional principles discussed in the text, supra, no longer apply to those actions against the State or its subdivisions in which the plaintiff seeks recovery for personal injury or property damage caused by a "vehicle". The question of jurisdiction over such actions now is governed by a special statute of relatively recent vintage. See infra, at nn. 32–40.

Smooth: Having satisfied the judgment of the administrative court, can the public authority recover indemnity or contribution from the negligent functionary?

Comparovich: Yes. Overruling older decisions to the contrary, the highest administrative court held in 1951 that the public authority *in its own right* is entitled to such recovery.[29] In addition, it seems to be the practice of the administrative courts, in the action brought by the victim against the public authority, to condition an award in favor of the victim upon the latter's *assigning* to the public authority his tort cause of action against the official who was guilty of "personal fault". The public authority usually does not collect the assigned claim. The purpose of the assignment is to prevent the victim from suing the official rather than to have the public treasury reimbursed. This practice has been criticized on the ground that in effect it relieves the guilty individual of civil responsibility.[30]

Smooth: If the public authority chooses to sue its negligent functionary, must the suit be brought in the administrative or the ordinary court?

Comparovich: Cute question. I can see you're getting into the spirit of these refinements. It seems that the public authority, if it sues as the assignee or subrogee of the victim (which is rarely done), stands in the shoes of the victim, and hence must sue in the ordinary court. Where, however, the public authority in its own right seeks contribution or indemnity, the administrative courts have jurisdiction, according to a much-criticized decision of the Tribunal of Conflicts.[31]

Smooth: These rules of French law must cause grave difficulties in automobile accident cases when one of the vehicles involved is owned by the State or one of its subdivisions. In such a case, it would follow from the rules just discussed that the plaintiff is unable to join the driver and the owner of the government vehicle as defendants in the same action. Moreover, in cases of collisions between private cars and government vehicles, when multiple parties assert criss-crossing claims based on tort, indemnity, contribution and subrogation, the resulting jurisdictional problems must be staggering.

Comparovich: They used to be staggering indeed; but in 1957 the legislator came to the rescue.[32] The statute of December 31, 1957, addressing itself to this specific problem, provides that—regardless of the involvement of the government or some other public authority—all actions seeking recovery for injury or damage caused by "a vehicle" shall be governed by principles of private law and must be brought in

29. See Waline, supra n. 27, Sec. 1617; Laubadère, supra n. 23, Sec. 1213.

Compare United States v. Gilman, 347 U.S. 507, 74 S.Ct. 695 (1954). It is interesting to observe that in dealing with this important question the French Conseil d'État and the U.S. Supreme Court, both acting at about the same time, effected radical changes—in opposite directions.

30. See Waline, supra n. 27, Sec. 1615. It should be noted, however, that today (i.e., since 1951, see supra at n. 29) this criticism is justified only if the State enforces neither the assigned claim nor the reimbursement claim which it has in its own right. The reported cases (see infra nn. 31, 37 and 38) show that at least in some instances the State's own reimbursement claim in fact has been enforced.

31. Id., Sec. 1617.

32. For the text of the 1957 statute, and an instructive discussion of its provisions, see 1 Auby and Drago, supra n. 4, §§ 563–65.

the ordinary courts.[33] The statute further contains a provision, comparable to a section of our Federal Tort Claims Act,[34] which in effect deprives the victim of any cause of action against the driver of the vehicle, thus rendering the public authority exclusively liable in cases of this kind.

Edge: Does this create an exception to the general French rule, explained by you a minute ago,[35] that the public authority, having satisfied the injured person's claim, can obtain reimbursement from the derelict functionary?

Comparovich: No, the statute renders the public authority's liability exclusive only insofar as the victim is concerned. With respect to the guilty functionary's duty to reimburse the public authority, the vehicular accident cases are governed by the general rule. Thus, if it so chooses, the public authority can obtain total or partial [36] reimbursement from the negligent driver.[37]

Edge: Am I correct in assuming that in this situation, where a vehicular accident covered by the 1957 statute is involved, the public authority's reimbursement claim against its agent (even though the public authority asserts the claim in its own right) has to be pursued in the ordinary courts?

Comparovich: No. In a 1965 decision—of questionable soundness—the Tribunal of Conflicts has held that even though the injured party had recovered from the State by way of an action in the ordinary court under the 1957 statute, the State must proceed in the administrative court in order to obtain reimbursement from the negligent driver.[38]

Edge: The legislator's obvious aim—to subject all of the legal consequences of vehicular accidents to the jurisdiction of the ordinary courts—thus is partly thwarted.

Comparovich: I tend to agree with you on this point. Moreover, there are other rough edges which indicate that even in the limited subject-area of vehicular accidents the statute did not overcome all of the doubts and super-refinements stemming from the jurisdictional dichotomy.

Though a vehicle is damaged, or a person riding in a vehicle is injured, the 1957 statute by its terms does not apply unless the damage

---

33. The statute applies regardless of whether the "vehicle" travels on land, in the water, or in the air. Nor does it make any difference whether the vehicle serves military or civilian purposes. If the vehicle is used by a public servant for purposes of the public service, the statute applies even though the public servant rather than the State or its subdivision owns the vehicle. Tribunal of Conflicts, November 20, 1961, D.1962, 265.

34. 28 U.S.C.A. § 2679(b), as amended in 1961 and 1966. For a discussion of this statute, see Anno., 16 A.L.R.3d 1394 (1967). See also the removal provision in 28 U.S.C.A. § 2679(d), discussed in Anno., 41 A.L.R.Fed. 288 (1979).

Prior to the enactment of these statutory provisions, the driver of a U.S. Government vehicle could be sued in a state court,

and sometimes only in a state court, while the Government was suable only in a federal court. This created difficulties somewhat similar to those experienced by the French before 1957. See, e.g., Falk v. United States, 264 F.2d 238 (6 Cir. 1959).

35. See supra at n. 29.

36. In determining the amount of such reimbursement, the court takes into account the extent to which the victim's damage has been caused (a) by the driver's "personal fault", and (b) by some malfunctioning of the public service not attributable to him personally.

37. 1 Auby and Drago, supra n. 4, § 564.

38. Tribunal of Conflicts, November 22, 1965, Préfet de la Seine-Maritime, D.S.1966, 195.

or injury is "caused *by* a vehicle" (emphasis added). Thus the one-vehicle accidents caused by holes in the road, to which Mr. Smooth referred a while ago, are not covered by the statute; the action against the public authority responsible for road maintenance must still be brought in the administrative court.

There remain tricky borderline problems, exemplified by the following two cases:

Case No. 1: Two private cars collided on a narrow bridge. Access to the bridge was controlled by a traffic light at one end, and by a traffic-directing officer at the other. The car coming from the direction of the traffic light entered the bridge because the light was green. The driver of the other car entered because the officer, without paying sufficient attention to the light at the other end, had waved him on. Clearly, for any resulting litigation among the owners and drivers of the two cars, the ordinary courts had jurisdiction. But what of an action against the governmental unit responsible for the act of the officer? Before 1957, such an action doubtless had to be brought in the administrative court. Did the 1957 statute effect a change in this regard?

Case No. 2: An official of the State's Bureau of Mines was engaged in checking the brakes of a truck belonging to a private mining company. He was not himself in the truck, but directed the driver to engage in certain go-and-stop maneuvers. One of these maneuvers, a sudden stop ordered by the official, caused an accident. Here again, an action of the victim against the owner or driver of the truck (an action of doubtful chances) would have to be brought in the ordinary courts. But what court has jurisdiction over the victim's suit against the State?

Smooth: In my opinion the two cases are indistinguishable from each other. In both situations the public official, while not actually driving the vehicle, had assumed control over its movements. Thus in both cases the vehicles were in effect operated by an official, and the 1957 statute should be applied.

Comparovich: Your reasoning is of Gallic finesse; but the Tribunal of Conflicts has cut it even more finely. It held that in Case No. 2 the official was "associated with the operation" of the truck, with the result that the 1957 statute applied and that the State could be sued in the ordinary court.[39] But Case No. 1 was held to be distinguishable on the ground that the officer directing traffic did not really control the movements of the car, and that by his single, momentary act of letting the car pass, the officer did not become "associated with the operation" of the vehicle. Therefore, in this case the statute was not applicable, and the public authority had to be sued in the administrative court.[40]

Smooth: I realize that the jurisdictional problems arising in cases of torts committed by public officials are rarely simple. Even in our legal system, we encounter some difficulties in this respect, because suits against the State may have to be brought in a special court (Court of Claims), while actions against private persons, though arising from the same occurrence, must be instituted in the ordinary courts.[41]

39. Tribunal of Conflicts, March 5, 1962, Dame Boule et Cie. d'Assurances "La France" c. Etat, J.C.P. 62, II, 12593.

40. Tribunal of Conflicts, June 28, 1965, Del Carlo c. Laurent, Req.N.1866, J.C.A. Fasc. 710.

41. The difficulties to which Mr. Smooth refers are illustrated by cases such

Perhaps the subject is inherently complex; but the French approach, it seems to me, compounds the difficulty. Is the German solution any simpler? [42]

Comparovich: Perhaps a little. Basically, the German solution is not radically different from the French. The Germans, also, must draw a line between those acts which are purely personal wrongs of the employee (e.g., the driver of a mail truck intentionally runs down a bicyclist whom he suspects of illicit relations with his wife), and those acts for which the State should be liable; [43] but according to the German view, liability of the State, where it exists, completely supplants the liability of the individual official or employee. [44]

Smooth: Does the victim of the tort bring his action in the ordinary or the administrative court?

Comparovich: An action against the individual naturally must be brought in the civil courts. Contrary to the French rule, moreover, positive provisions of the German Constitution and of the German Civil Code confer upon the ordinary courts jurisdiction over tort actions against the State or its subdivisions. [45]

as Horoch v. State of New York, 286 App. Div. 303, 143 N.Y.S.2d 327 (3d Dep't, 1955); Smith-Cairns Motor Sales Co. v. State, 45 Misc.2d 770, 258 N.Y.S.2d 51 (Ct.Cl. 1965). See also J. J. McNamara, The Court of Claims: Its Development and Present Role in the Unified Court System, 40 St. John's L.Rev. 1, 24–25 (1965).

In cases where jointly or concurrently with a private tortfeasor the Federal Government is liable, it is sometimes—but not always—possible to join or implead all parties in a U.S. District Court. An example is Ayala v. United States, where the Government was sued for injuries sustained in an explosion of Government-owned box-cars, and plaintiffs attempted to join the manufacturer of the box-cars as defendant. Some of the plaintiffs were diverse, some non-diverse. The latters' claims against the manufacturer were dismissed, the court holding that there was no "pendent party" jurisdiction. 550 F.2d 1196 (9th Cir. 1977), cert. dism. 435 U.S. 982, 98 S.Ct. 1635 (1978). But there seems to be some District Court authority *contra.* See J. Cound, J. H. Friedenthal, A. R. Miller & J. E. Sexton, Civil Procedure—Cases and Materials 268 (4th ed., 1985).

42. In speaking of "German" law, the text refers to the law of the West German Federal Republic. In East Germany, as in other socialist countries, judicial remedies against wrongdoing functionaries and against the State itself tend to be more restricted. See §§ 11, 330 and 331 of the 1975 Civil Code of the German Democratic Republic; Szirmai, supra n. 22; W. Gray, Soviet Tort Law: The New Principles Annotated, 1964 U.Ill.L.F. 180, 193–96.

43. See infra n. 45. For an example, see infra p. 608.

44. This is a general rule, not limited to vehicular accident cases. The existence of governmental liability constitutes a complete defense in an action by the victim against the individual official or employee. For an exceptional case, in which the assertion of this defense was held to constitute an abuse of rights, see infra p. 752.

The government, having satisfied a claim for damages, may recover indemnity from the official or employee who caused the damage intentionally or by gross negligence; see infra n. 45. As in France, however, it cannot be taken for granted that in practice such indemnity will always be collected.

For a comparative discussion, see G. A. Bermann, Integrating Governmental and Officer Tort Liability, 77 Colum.L.Rev. 1175 (1977).

45. See Art. 34 of the Basic Law of the German Federal Republic: "If any person, in exercising the duties of a public office entrusted to him, violates his official obligation towards a third party, liability shall in principle rest with the state or his employing authority. If such person has acted wilfully or with gross negligence, the [state's] right of recourse [against him] shall be reserved. In respect to the claim for damages and in respect to the right of recourse, the jurisdiction of the ordinary courts must not be excluded."

Sect. 839 of the Civil Code (which went into effect January 1, 1900) originally provided that the public servant should be personally liable in such a case. In subse-

Smooth: I prefer the German system to the French. The latter—in addition to the other difficulties to which we have alluded already—must produce very doubtful cases whenever a public servant commits a tort of a kind (such as assault and battery) which has only a slight or problematic connection with his official duties.[46] The plaintiff may have to choose at his peril, not only between possible defendants, but also between two different tribunals—unless as a matter of precaution he brings two actions in two different courts.

Comparovich: Yes, an enormous amount of lawyers' time and clients' money is spent to resolve such doubts. Dichotomies in the law always lead to such wasted effort. Our dichotomy between law and equity illustrates the same point.

Smooth: The German system seems to avoid some of these difficulties.

Comparovich: That is true. The French, on the other hand, will argue that the German system requires two actions, one in the administrative and the other in the ordinary court, if the aggrieved individual desires to annul an administrative act *and* to recover damages in tort.[47]

---

quent statutes, in Art. 131 of the Weimar Constitution, and again in Art. 34 of the Basic Law of 1949, the State assumed this liability of its servants; but the essentially private nature of the liability was not changed (see supra n. 22), and the ordinary courts retained their jurisdiction. A 1981 federal statute created a new type of *direct* state liability. See the Staatshaftungs-gesetz of June 26, 1981 (B.G.Bl. I 553). But this statute was declared unconstitutional by the Federal Constitutional Court, which, in its decision, strongly emphasized the private-law character of the existing system of state liability. See Decision of Oct. 19, 1982, BVerfGE 61, 149, NJW 1983, p. 25.

In this connection, it must be remembered that German administrative law is largely state law, and that until recently there was no federal administrative court of broad jurisdiction. Private law, on the other hand, was essentially unified and federalized by the enactment of the Civil Code; the civil court hierarchy has had a single federal court of last resort at its apex since 1879. Therefore, to allocate governmental tort liability to the sphere of "private" law, has had the effect (a) of federalizing and unifying the applicable substantive rules, and (b) of entrusting their development to a single federal court of last resort.

In the United States, where private law is not nationally unified, the adoption of ordinary (private) tort law principles in the Federal Tort Claims Act has had the opposite effect: to preserve the motley variety of state laws even with respect to claims against the Federal Government.

46. Under the German system, too, these borderline cases may produce doubts as to whether the State or the wrong-doing official is liable; but since both the State and the individual tortfeasor can be sued in the same court, the plaintiff can join both as defendants, even though his action will be successful only against one or the other. The point is somewhat controversial; but according to the better view such alternative joinder of parties is permissible. See Rosenberg-Schwab, Zivilprozess-recht, § 65 IV 3 b (13th ed., 1981).

47. For a case exemplifying this problem, see infra p. 608.

An analogous problem often troubles American courts: Can the petitioner in a certiorari or mandamus proceeding, or in a statutory proceeding of similar nature, obtain *damages* as well as an order directing the doing or undoing of an administrative act? The cases, reflecting a quaint common law rule as well as a variety of pertinent statutes, are numerous and disharmonious. See Anno., 73 A.L.R.2d 903 (1960). The excellent analysis of the problem in Weinstein-Korn-Miller, New York Civil Practice ¶7806.01 (1967 and Supp.), though limited to a discussion of the unfortunate New York statute, carries more general implications. It shows that jurisdictional and procedural difficulties, comparable to those encountered in some of the continental countries, also exist in our law, but that often these difficulties are overshadowed by the niggardliness and obscurity of our substantive rules regarding governmental liability for official wrongdoing.

In France, he can get both kinds of relief in one proceeding before the administrative court.

Edge: Our business involves many contracts with foreign governments.[48] Are such contracts to be enforced in the ordinary or the administrative courts?

Comparovich: Both in France and in Germany, it is recognized that contracts between a private party and a public authority are sometimes enforceable in the administrative courts, and sometimes in the ordinary courts, depending on the public or private nature of the particular contract.[49]

Edge: What criteria are used to attribute a contract to the public or the private sphere?

Comparovich: Here, again, the French and the Germans are not in agreement. In general, one can say that the French extend the jurisdiction of the administrative courts over a much wider range of contracts than the Germans do. In searching for a workable basis of distinction, the French avowedly use a flexible and somewhat casuistic method, while the Germans have tried to develop a single abstract criterion.

The German theory is predicated on the essential nature of the legal relationship between the parties.[50] If that relationship is one which could equally well exist between private individuals or corporations, then any dispute resulting from it is "private". Applying this principle to contractual relationships, the German courts have found that some contracts involve the enforcement or distribution of public burdens, or relate to some other subject with which private parties, by themselves, could not deal under any circumstances;[51] contracts of this kind are "public". Most contracts between the Government and a private party, however, involve transactions which in the abstract (and the German criterion emphasizes the abstract nature and the typical features of the relationship more than the particular facts of the case at hand) could equally well be concluded among private parties. Contracts for the sale or purchase of goods, or involving sales or leases of real property, are the classical examples; such contracts are private and hence enforceable in the ordinary courts, even though one of the contracting parties is the Government.

---

48. For comparative treatments of British, United States and French law dealing with government contracts see Street, Governmental Liability 81 ff. (1953, repr. 1975), and Mitchell, The Contracts of Public Authorities (1954), reviewed by Pasley, 41 Cornell L.Q. 342 (1956). A good comparative survey of administrative (or public law) contracts in various countries of Western Europe can be found in C. C. Turpin, Public Contract, Vol. VII (Contracts in General), International Encyclopedia of Comparative Law, Ch. 4, at pp. 27–31 (1982).

49. The French distinguish between "administrative contracts" and *contrats de droit commun.* The Germans use terms such as "public law contract" and "private law contract".

50. For references, see Baumbach-Lauterbach-Albers-Hartmann, Zivilprozessordnung, GVG § 13, Annos. 3 and 4 (45th ed., 1987).

51. E.g., the owner of a city plot, who desires to build an apartment house but pursuant to the provisions of a statute can get a building permit only on condition of providing a certain number of parking spaces, enters into a contract with the city; under the terms of the contract, the city will issue the permit unconditionally and will itself provide the parking spaces, while the owner will pay the city a specified sum of money. This was held to be a "public law contract", enforceable only in the administrative courts. BGHZ 32, 214 (1960).

Although its precise formulation as well as its application to borderline situations remains somewhat controversial,[52] this German theory seems to furnish a reasonably clear line of demarcation.[53]

Edge: In virtually all cases of what we would call government contract disputes, the effect of the German doctrine must be to bring such disputes before the ordinary courts.

Comparovich: That is correct.

Edge: You told us that the French, in distinguishing between administrative and private contracts, use an approach more flexible than the German. Is the French distinction similar to that which our courts draw between governmental and proprietary functions of municipal corporations? [54]

Comparovich: During the 19th century, the French used a similar formula. Since the beginning of this century, however, they have abandoned the attempt to encapsule the guiding criteria in a formula, and have adopted a pronouncedly pragmatic approach.[55] According to the present French view, the nature of a contract as administrative or private may be determined by statute,[56] by decisional law,[57] or, to a certain extent, by the terms of the contract.

Edge: Do the parties have the power to stipulate in their contract that the administrative courts (or the civil courts) shall have jurisdiction?

Comparovich: No. This stipulation, as such, would have no effect because the parties do not have the power to change the pertinent

---

52. There is some doubt, e.g., concerning contracts which publicly-owned suppliers of water, gas, or electricity conclude with their customers. See E. Eyermann and L. Fröhler, Verwaltungsgerichtsordnung, § 40, Annos. 50–53 (8th ed., 1980).

53. The theory seems to work even in complex situations, e.g., where a statute, as part of a subsidy program, authorizes the Government to make loans to private persons for the construction of low-rent housing or for similar social purposes. When an application for such a loan has been denied, it is clear that judicial review of the denial must be sought in the administrative court. But once a contractor has obtained such a loan, the relationship between him and the Government is the ordinary one of debtor and creditor, with the result that the Government's action for repayment of the loan must be brought in the ordinary court. In spite of doubts expressed by some authors, this rule has been generally recognized in judicial practice. See the cases cited by Eyermann-Fröhler, supra n. 52, § 40, Anno. 46.

54. Cf. Langrod, Administrative Contracts—A Comparative Study, 4 Am.J. Comp.L. 325, 328 (1955).

A comparable distinction (between acts *jure gestionis* and acts *jure imperii*) is drawn by the courts of many countries in applying the international law doctrine of sovereign immunity. See, e.g., H. G. Maier, Sovereign Immunity and Act of State: Correlative or Conflicting Policies?, 35 U.Cin.L.Rev. 556, 561 ff. (1966). See also 28 U.S.C.A. §§ 1602 to 1605, added in 1976.

55. 1 De Laubadère, Moderne and Devolvé, Traité des Contrats Administratifs 126–28 (2d ed., 1984).

56. A statute, for instance, provides that contracts for public works are administrative. But a seller who merely furnishes paving stones to a public authority, without participating in the work of paving, can sue in the ordinary courts. So can the financier whose loan enables a municipality to carry out such a project. Id., at 265–66.

57. The rules have grown in casuistic fashion, and the distinctions are as subtle as any to be found in the common law. Sales of movables to a municipal or other local authority are "private" unless the contract contains an "exorbitant" element (see n. 58 infra). In the case of the sale of movables to the central government, however, the opposite presumption applies: such a contract is administrative unless its terms or certain circumstances external to the contract show that the government intended to subject itself to the principles of private law. Id., at 148, 270–71.

→ generally not in a b/t two private parties

jurisdictional rules. But the entire contract will be scrutinized for indications of so-called *"clauses exorbitantes"*, i.e. terms which are unusual in, and perhaps inconsistent with the nature of, a contract between private parties. In this connection, an express stipulation providing for jurisdiction of the administrative court may assume some significance. Much more frequently, however, a *"clause exorbitante"* will be found in contract terms which give the public authority far-reaching powers of supervision, direction and unilateral cancellation.[58] The presence of a *"clause exorbitante"* will as a rule mark the contract as an administrative one,[59] while its absence (in cases not governed by a special statute) is at least a strong indication of the private nature of the agreement.[60]

    Smooth: At this moment, one of our subsidiaries is about to sue the French Government in order to obtain payment for two million bottles of Dulci-Cola delivered to military canteens. It seems that soft drinks have met with a measure of customer resistance; the French Government now claims the merchandise was unfit for human consumption. According to what you said, I take it that we have to bring the action in a civil court?

    Comparovich: Was there an elaborate, formal contract?

    Smooth: No. Our subsidiary received an informal, routine order.

    Comparovich: In that event, the action has to be brought in the civil court. It was so held in a very similar case.[61]

---

58. The criteria of what constitutes a "clause exorbitante" are not wholly clear and in part controversial. Id., at 213–29. However, the practical significance of the clause seems to be declining. Currently, the distinction between public and private contracts turns less on "exorbitant" elements introduced into the contract by the parties, than on elements external to the contract that render contractual relationships "exorbitant" (e.g., the impact of governmental regulations). Id., at 131. On the evolving distinction between the "régime exorbitant" and the "clause exorbitante" within the larger notion of "éléments exorbitants", see id., at 159, 183, 229–35.

59. This rule, which is well-established as to actions against the domestic Government, has an interesting side-effect in cases where a foreign government is sued in a French court. The point is illustrated by the decision of February 7, 1962, rendered by the Court d'Appel of Paris in the case of Perignon c. Etats Unis d'Amérique, 89 Journal du Droit International 1016 (1962) (noted ibid., in French and English, by J. B. Sialelli), aff'd on December 8, 1964, by the Cour de Cassation, 92 id. 416 (1965) (again noted by J. B. Sialelli). In that case, the U.S. Government was sued by a French contractor who had done construction work on buildings (near Paris) intended to house U.S. Government personnel dealing with foreign aid. Defendant's claim of immuni-

ty was sustained on the ground that its contract with the plaintiff contained the dispute settlement clause ordinarily used in U.S. Government contracts as well as other terms which in the French view constituted "clauses exorbitantes". Read together with earlier cases (referred to ibid.), the decision seems to indicate that in the absence of any "clauses exorbitantes" the court would have been more inclined to treat the U.S. Government as having entered into a purely private transaction and as having waived its immunity in this way. The doctrine of "clauses exorbitantes" thus radiates into the field of international law.

60. For examples and discussion, see Auby and Drago, supra n. 4, at 466–69, and 590–93; De Laubadère, supra n. 23, § 576.

There is a further and somewhat controversial refinement. In spite of the absence of a "clause exorbitante", the contract may be treated as an administrative one where the State has delegated the performance of inherently governmental functions or duties to the private party (e.g., to provide food for refugees confined by the Government in a "repatriation center"). See the cases cited by De Laubadère, Traité élémentaire de droit administratif, Sec. 527 (4th ed., 1967).

61. See 1 De Laubadère, Traité Théorique et Pratique des Contrats Administratifs 30–31 (1956). Even though the contract may have been made with the central

Smooth: It is getting late, and we should not keep our distinguished visitor much longer. Before we adjourn, however, I would like to raise a more general question which has bothered me throughout our discussion of public law disputes.

Where you have two separate judicial hierarchies, as in France, (or five, as in Germany), each with its own court of last resort, it must happen—perhaps not too infrequently—that on some point of law the several courts of last resort take conflicting positions. When that occurs, how is the citizen or his legal adviser to know what "the law" is?

Comparovich: This is an important and difficult question. Before I attempt to answer it, let me point out, by way of a caveat, that when the Cour de Cassation and the Conseil d'État deal with what seems to be the same problem, their respective solutions sometimes can differ from each other without actually being in conflict. For example, in connection with administrative as well as private contracts the question may arise whether a radical and unforeseeable change of circumstances, which has occurred after the formation but before the complete performance of the contract and has rendered such performance unduly burdensome for one party, gives such party a right to demand cancellation or modification of the contract. Over the last half-century, the Conseil d'Etat has developed an elaborate body of rules (the so-called doctrine of *imprévision*) pursuant to which the administrative court has broad powers [62] to adjust the parties' rights and duties under an administrative contract in such a case.[63] The Cour de Cassation, in dealing with private contracts, has declined to follow this doctrine; by and large, it has adhered to the view that, unless performance has become literally impossible, the contract should be enforced no matter how painfully the parties' expectations have been frustrated by virtue of a change of circumstances.[64] Thus we find that on this important point of contract law the position of the Cour de Cassation differs drastically from that of the Conseil d'Etat. Yet it would be misleading, in my opinion, to call this a "conflict". It merely means that there is one rule for private contracts, and a very different one for administrative contracts. It is not difficult to present policy arguments supporting this difference in the treatment of the two types of contracts; and regardless of what one may think of the strength of these arguments, it is clear that we deal here with an attempted distinction rather than an outright conflict.

Smooth: There must be cases, however, in which the several courts of last resort take truly conflicting positions.

government, the presumption mentioned supra n. 57, would be overcome by the absence of a "clause exorbitante", or other exorbitant elements, and by the businesslike manner in which the transaction was concluded and carried out.

62. In observing the resourcefulness with which the Conseil d'Etat has fashioned remedies in cases of this kind, a lawyer brought up in the common law is strongly reminded of the powers and the practice of courts of equity.

63. See De Laubadère, supra n. 55, §§ 637–39.

64. See Amos and Walton's Introduction to French Law 165 (3d ed. by F. H. Lawson, A. E. Anton and L. N. Brown, 1967); 2 K. Zweigert & H. Kötz, An Introduction to Comparative Law 195–98 (1977); De Laubadère, supra n. 23, at 392. With respect to private contracts, the French position on this point is more conservative than that of most other legal systems in the civil-law as well as the common-law orbit. See P. Hay, Frustration and its Solution in German Law, 10 Am.J.Comp.L. 345, especially at 346–56 (1961). See also infra pp. 731–740.

Comparovich: Yes, cases of such inter-hierarchy conflicts do occur in civil-law countries.[64a]

Theoretically such a conflict could arise, first of all, with respect to a question of constitutional law. It appears, however, that in the great majority of those civil-law countries which provide for judicial review of the constitutionality of statutes,[65] such review is entrusted to a separate Constitutional Court, which stands outside of, and in a sense above, the top courts of the several judicial hierarchies.[66] If the power of constitutional review were not thus concentrated in a single court, it might easily happen in a civil-law country that the same statute is upheld by the highest administrative court but declared invalid by the ordinary court of last resort (or vice versa). The necessity of obviating this kind of inter-hierarchy conflict was one of the most potent reasons for the creation—by Austria, Germany, Italy, and other civil-law countries—of a single separate super-court dealing only with constitutional matters.[67] By adopting that system, they have avoided such conflicts with respect to the most fundamental issues—those of constitutional law.[67a]

Outside of the constitutional area, true conflicts can arise when the top courts of several judicial hierarchies take inconsistent positions on the same issue of substantive law. A French case, which at the time caused some flurry in the daily press, may serve as an

Example: [68] The mayor of Lyon had issued an ordinance which reserved certain parking spaces, near the city's Produce Market, for the trucks of vendors of vegetables. An automobilist not belonging to the privileged class, who had parked in one of the reserved spaces and was criminally prosecuted and fined for this violation of the ordinance, carried his case all the way to the Cour de Cassation, where his conviction was reversed on

---

64a. For a general discussion of the interaction of administrative decisions and decisions of the ordinary courts in France, see L. H. Levinson, Enforcement of Administrative Decisions in the United States and in France, 23 Emory L.J. 11, at 47–79, 102 (1974).

65. See supra p. 375.

66. Ibid.

67. Even though the Constitutional Court always has the last word on questions of constitutional law, it is not entirely impossible that a conflict might arise between the Constitutional Court and one of the other top courts. Suppose, for instance, that the Constitutional Court, in upholding the constitutionality of a statute, gives it a particular construction. In Italy, it seems, the Court of Cassation has not considered itself bound by such construction. See J. H. Merryman and V. Vigoriti, When Courts Collide: Constitution and Cassation in Italy, 15 Am.J.Comp. L. 665 (1967); G. Bognetti, The Political Role of the Italian Constitutional Court, 49 Notre Dame Law. 981, 995–99 (1974). Conflicts of this type seem to be rare, however; they can be avoided by a properly drawn constitutional or statutory provision. Cf.

German Bundesverfassungsgerichtsgesetz § 31.

67a. In Greece, the system of judicial review is similar to ours in the sense that every trial or appellate court that is called upon to apply a given statute, has the power to examine the constitutionality of that statute and in a proper case to declare it unconstitutional. At the same time, as a typical civil-law country, Greece has several judicial hierarchies, each of which has its own court of last resort. It is possible, therefore, that the several courts of last resort differ on the question whether a particular statute is unconstitutional. In that event, the question is submitted to a Special Highest Court, consisting of eleven judges drawn from the courts of last resort of several hierarchies, and of two law professors. The decision of this special court is binding on all courts. See E. Spiliotopoulos, Judicial Review of Legislative Acts in Greece, 56 Temple L.Q. 463, 496–501 (1983).

68. Le Monde, Dec. 6, 1962, p. 14. Additional examples can be found in G. A. Bermann, French Treaties and French Courts: Two Problems in Supremacy, 28 Int. and Comp. L.Q. 458, 477 (1979).

the ground that there was no proper statutory authority for the mayor's ordinance.[68a] In another case, the Conseil d'Etat refused to nullify the mayor's ordinance (the very same ordinance involved in the case before the Cour de Cassation), holding that it was valid and duly supported by an authorizing statute.

Here we observe a direct clash of conflicting decisions.

Edge: Can this conflict be resolved by the Tribunal of Conflicts?

Comparovich: No. That Tribunal resolves only jurisdictional conflicts. It does not deal with cases where the Cour de Cassation and the Conseil d'Etat, each clearly acting within its jurisdiction, reach inconsistent results on a point of substantive law.

Edge: What machinery does the French system provide for the resolution of conflicts of the latter kind?

Comparovich: None whatsoever, unless the legislator acts to resolve the disputed question.[69]

Edge: As a practical matter, then, it would seem that the ordinary court's view will prevail in the end. It is true that after the mayor has won his case in the highest administrative court, nobody can force him to withdraw the ordinance, or to discontinue his attempts to enforce it. Yet everybody who has heard of the—probably much-publicized—decision of the Cour de Cassation, will merrily park in the reserved spaces; and to prosecute violators will be a hopeless undertaking, since the lower criminal courts know that no conviction would survive an ultimate appeal to the Cour de Cassation.

Comparovich: On the other hand, if the mayor orders the police to erect a physical barrier preventing access to the reserved spaces, and to lift the barrier only to admit vegetable trucks, the public authority may have the last laugh. Any legal action challenging the use of the barrier would have to be brought in the administrative court, with predictable results.

Edge: How does the German legal system deal with this problem?

Comparovich: In an entirely different way. The parliament of the German Federal Republic, implementing a constitutional mandate,[70] has enacted a statute setting up machinery for the resolution of conflicts between courts of last resort.[71] The statute is based on the

68a. There is no doubt under French law that a criminal court in which the defendant is charged with violation of an *ordinance*, has the power and duty to examine the validity of such ordinance (even though the court could not review the constitutionality of a *statute*). See L. H. Levinson, Presidential Self-Regulation through Rulemaking: Comparative Comments on Structuring the Chief Executive's Constitutional Powers, 10 Vand.J.Transn.L. 1, at 17–18 (1977).

69. In a pre-1957 automobile accident case the victim of a collision between a private and a government vehicle was denied relief in the civil courts on the ground that the accident had been caused by the governmental car; the administrative courts also denied relief, holding that the driver of the private vehicle was to blame for the accident. In this instance the legislator intervened, conferring power on the Tribunal of Conflicts to resolve a conflict of this kind (even though the conflict is a substantive rather than a jurisdictional one). But this statute has lost much of its significance due to the enactment of the 1957 statute mentioned supra at n. 32. See P. Herzog, Civil Procedure in France 117–18 (1967).

70. Basic Law, Art. 95, par. 3, as amended in 1968.

71. Law of June 19, 1968, BGBl I 661. The provisions of the statute are reproduced and discussed in Baumbach-Lauter-

idea that conflicts among the top courts of the several judicial hierarchies should be treated in a similar manner as conflicts between several panels of a single court of last resort.[72] Both types of conflicts are to be resolved by a super-panel of judges; the only difference is that in the case of an inter-hierarchy conflict the super-panel is composed of judges representing all five hierarchies, i.e., the presidents of the five top courts plus four additional judges (two from each of the hierarchies involved in the particular dispute).

Edge: I take it that if a case like that of the Lyon parking imbroglio occurred in Germany, and the highest administrative court found itself unable to agree with the position taken by the ordinary (criminal) court of last resort, it would have to certify the controversial question of law to the super-panel.

Comparovich: Precisely.[72a] It should be noted, moreover, that in Germany the same machinery can be utilized to resolve inter-hierarchy conflicts on questions of jurisdiction.[73]

Smooth: In bringing this discussion to a close, I should like to thank you, Professor, for having enhanced our understanding of foreign and—seen from where I sit—rather strange institutions and approaches. In the area of public law disputes, in particular, there appears to be a real chasm between civil law and common law.

Comparovich: If you view them in a broader perspective, you may find that the differences reflected in this "chasm", although they are remarkable and of great significance in legal practice, relate only to matters of technique. The fundamental social problem to be resolved is everywhere the same: to strike a balance between the interests of individuals and of voluntary associations, on the one hand, and those of the community, on the other; and to do so in an era of accelerating industrialization and urbanization, necessarily accompanied by the constant growth and proliferation of the tentacles by which various public authorities reach into our lives. The responses to this problem that have been fashioned by civil-law and common-law systems, do not seem to be basically dissimilar. In both types of systems it has been recognized that strengthened judicial protection of the individual against an increasingly powerful and ubiquitous government plays a central role in the required balancing of interests. To the extent that

bach-Albers-Hartmann, Zivilprozessordnung, Appendix following § 140 GVG (45th ed., 1987).

72. See supra pp. 466–468.

72a. It has been held that certification to the super-panel is necessary even though the prior decision of the other court (from which the certifying court desires to deviate) was rendered prior to the enactment of the 1968 statute creating the super-panel procedure. See Baumbach, supra n. 71.

73. The reader will recall (see supra, at nn. 19–21) that in Germany the resolution of inter-hierarchy jurisdictional conflicts as a rule is not entrusted to a Tribunal of Conflicts, and that generally the jurisdictional question can be determined, in binding fashion, by the court—of whatever hierarchy—in which the action has been brought. But the binding effect of the jurisdictional determination thus made is limited to the case at hand. For example, if in case A the administrative court of last resort affirms the jurisdiction of its hierarchy, that is the end of the matter insofar as case A is concerned; but if subsequently case B, involving identical facts and issues, is instituted by another party in an ordinary court, the decision rendered in case A is not binding on the latter court. Thus the jurisdictional question may again be litigated up to the highest court—this time the ordinary court of last resort. If that court, in dealing with case B, wishes to deviate from the position taken in case A by the highest administrative court, it must submit the question to the super-panel.

there remains a measure of disagreement on this fundamental point, the dissenters are to be found in some of the socialist systems rather than in the civil-law or common-law orbit.[74]

(BB) THE DICHOTOMY (BETWEEN PRIVATE-LAW AND PUBLIC-LAW LITIGATION) IN INTERNATIONAL CONTEXTS

Smooth: There may be a good deal of truth in what you just said; but on the technical level—which is the level on which we spend most of our working hours—it seems unavoidable that the difference between civil law and common law as to the nature and treatment of "public-law disputes" will lead to endless misunderstandings and difficulties. For instance, when we speak of a "civil" action, we include in that category all judicial proceedings other than criminal ones. Thus in our view, a proceeding to enforce or to set aside an administrative determination is a civil proceeding, to be brought in an ordinary court and governed by the procedural Code or Rules which we apply in civil litigation. But our civilian colleagues, I gather from our discussion here, surely would not classify such a proceeding as a civil one. What a golden opportunity for misunderstandings among lawyers from different countries seeking to communicate with each other!

Comparovich: Such misunderstandings have indeed occurred on a large scale, and sophisticated international practitioners are beginning to become aware of them.[74a] Let me conclude our discussion by giving you a few examples:

(A) An Unreported Recent Case

I was consulted by a lawyer whose client had the unfortunate experience of having his driver's license revoked by the Department of Motor Vehicles of his State. The lawyer sought judicial review of the Department's action. In the judicial proceeding thus instituted, an issue arose as to whether the client had caused an accident in France, and whether he had left the scene of that accident.[74b] Almost all of the

74. See the broad-based comparative study by V. Bolgár, The Public Interest, 12 J.Pub.L. 13 (1963). For further references see supra n. 1a.

74a. Even within the civil-law world, the international practitioner may encounter difficulties caused by the different ways in which various countries draw the line between private and public law litigation. A telling example is provided by the decision of the Court of Justice of the European Communities in the matter of The Netherlands v. Rüffer. The decision, dated Dec. 16, 1980, RS 814/79, appears in the 1982 Common Market Reporter, Transfer Binder § 8702, p. 8388. In this case, the Dutch Ministry of Transport sued a West German shipowner in an ordinary court at The Hague. The action sought reimbursement for the cost of removing the wreck of defendant's ship which had sunk in waters belonging to Germany but administered by Dutch authorities. A reimbursement claim of this kind is treated as private

under Dutch law, while the other original members of the Common Market would regard it as a public-law dispute. The European Court, applying its own independent criteria, held that this was not a "civil or commercial" matter, and that consequently the Dutch court's jurisdiction was not governed by the Brussels Convention of 1968. At first blush, this may look like a victory of the Dutch Ministry of Transport, which may now pursue the case in a Dutch court under Dutch rules of jurisdiction (permitting an action against a non-resident to be brought at the domicile of the plaintiff). But, the case not being covered by the Convention, *quaere* whether the German courts (which regard the matter as "public") will enforce the judgment of the Dutch court?

74b. Under the law of the State in question, the Department's findings concerning this issue were subject to de novo review by the court.

witnesses were in France, and the taking of their depositions would have been greatly facilitated if the provisions of the Hague Convention on the Taking of Evidence Abroad [75] could have been brought to bear on the case. But that Convention, like the equally important Convention on the Service Abroad of Judicial and Extrajudicial Documents,[76] by its terms applies only in "civil and commercial matters." While in common-law countries the proceeding in the case at hand would be classified as a "civil" one, it is clear that from the civilians' standpoint we were engaged in "administrative" or "public-law" litigation, and not in civil litigation, so that from their point of view the Convention was not applicable.[77]

How, then, could the French authorities be persuaded to lend their co-operation under the terms of the Convention which, according to their view, did not cover our case? We argued that, inasmuch as the definition of "civil" is not the same in all of the signatory countries, there should be a clear-cut rule (somewhat in the nature of a choice-of-law rule) determining the question *whose* definition should prevail in a given case; and that the simplest and most sensible rule would be to apply the definition of the country where the proceeding is pending and where the request for co-operation originates. The French, while not agreeing that this is a binding rule, have indicated that as a matter of courtesy they will co-operate in cases of this kind, i.e., in cases which in the requesting country (though not in France) would be classified as "civil".[78] Consequently, there is at least some hope that in the case at hand (which is still pending) the depositions can be taken in France in accordance with the Convention. Nevertheless, the case illustrates the doubts and difficulties arising from the fact that the civilians' treatment of public-law disputes is so fundamentally different from ours.[78a]

(B) The Case of König v. Federal Republic of Germany [79]

Stated in over-simplified form,[80] the facts of this very complex case were as follows: Dr. Eberhard König (K), a national and domiciliary of Germany, was a licensed physician. He also had the necessary governmental authorization to run a clinic, and in fact ran and managed a clinic where he performed medical services, especially plastic surgery. On the basis of a number of charges of professional misconduct, his authorization to run the clinic was revoked by the competent administrative office in 1967; and in 1971 his licence to practice medicine was likewise revoked. He promptly sought review of both of these adminis-

[handwritten margin note: Noted I / Revocation of physicians / license to / practice & / run clinic]

---

75. See supra p. 445.

76. See supra p. 412.

77. See the Hague Conference Reports in 17 Int.Legal Materials at 315–16, 320–21, 1417–19, 1426–27 (1978).

78. See ibid. In tax cases, however, the attitude of the civilian signatories of the Convention is somewhat less accommodating. Id., at 1419. Concerning French, German and British practice in cases where the request emanates from an administrative agency or tribunal (or a party to a proceeding before such agency or tribunal) in the U.S., see also Restatement (Revised), Foreign Relations Law, § 481, com. f, and § 483, com. c (T.D. 1984).

78a. For other illustrations, and further references, see H. Koch, Zur Praxis der Rechtshilfe im amerikanisch—deutschen Prozessrecht—Ergebnisse einer Umfrage zu den Haager Zustellungs—und Beweisuebereinkommen, 5 IPRax 245, at 246–47 (1985).

79. European Court of Human Rights, decision of June 28, 1978, 17 Int.Legal Materials 1151 (1978).

80. The Court's opinion is lengthy; but the patient reader will find it rewarding to peruse it in full.

trative acts in the administrative court of first instance; but (at least with respect to the revocation of the medical licence) the effectiveness of the administrative act was not suspended pending judicial review.[81] Thus, in spite of the pendency of the judicial proceedings, he was effectively barred from practicing medicine after mid-1971. The judicial proceedings moved very slowly. In mid-1978, both proceedings (one involving the authorization to run the clinic, and the other the licence to practice medicine) were still pending in various stages of the appellate process. In part, but only in small part, the delays were attributable to K's own maneuvers, especially to his frequent change of attorneys. In the main, however, the administrative court and the administrators were responsible for the inordinately long duration of the two proceedings—11 years in one case, and 7 years in the other.

Without awaiting the final outcome of the proceedings in the German administrative courts, K brought the matter before the European Commission of Human Rights and (with the Commission's endorsement) before the European Court of Human Rights. K claimed that, regardless of the merits of the case, his due process rights under Art. 6 Section 1 of the European Human Rights Convention had been violated by the dilatory manner in which the German courts had handled the two proceedings. He sought a declaratory judgment to that effect, and also asked for damages.

In its pertinent part, Art. 6 Section 1 of the Convention reads as follows:

> "In the determination of his *civil rights and obligations* or of any criminal charge against him, everyone is entitled to a fair and public hearing *within a reasonable time* by an independent and impartial tribunal established by law." (emphasis added)

After analyzing the complicated procedural history of the two proceedings, the Court had no difficulty in concluding that K's right to a reasonably speedy determination had been violated by the German courts. The big issue in the case, however, was whether administrative court proceedings of the kind here involved are covered by the terms of the above-quoted provision of the Convention. The German Government, as respondent, argued that proceedings before an administrative court deal with *public-law* disputes, and hence by definition do not involve "*civil rights and obligations*" within the meaning of the Convention. From a civil-law point of view, this was a strong argument. In the Court's opinion, however, it is emphasized that the terms used in the Convention "cannot be interpreted solely by reference to the domestic law of the respondent State," and that the Court, as an international tribunal, has to use an "autonomous" method in construing such terms. Turning, then, to the task of "autonomously" construing the term "civil rights and obligations", the Court said the following:

> Whilst the Court thus concludes that the concept of "civil rights and obligations" is autonomous, it nevertheless does not consider that, in this context, the legislation of the State concerned is without importance. Whether or not a right is to be regarded as civil within the meaning of this expression in

---

81. Under German law, the effectiveness of an administrative act normally is suspended while a proceeding for judicial review of that act is pending in an administrative court. But the administrator whose act is involved, may by a written and reasoned decision give it immediate effect in spite of the pendency of a review proceeding, and this had been done in the instant case.

the Convention must be determined by reference to the substantive content and effects of the right—and not its legal classification—under the domestic law of the State concerned. In the exercise of its supervisory functions, the Court must also take account of the object and purpose of the Convention and of the national legal systems of the other Contracting States. . . .

The Government submit that Article 6 § 1 covers private-law disputes in the traditional sense, that is disputes between individuals or between an individual and the State to the extent that the latter had been acting as a private person, subject to private law; amongst other things, disputes between an individual and the State acting in its sovereign capacity would be excluded from the ambit of that Article.

As regards the field of application of Article 6 § 1, the Court held in its Ringeisen judgment of 16 July 1971 that "for Article 6 § 1 to be applicable to a case ('*contestation*') it is not necessary that both parties to the proceedings should be private persons. . . . The wording of Article 6 § 1 is far wider; the French expression '*contestations sur (des) droits et obligations de caractère civil*' covers all proceedings the result of which is decisive for private rights and obligations. The English text, 'determination of . . . civil rights and obligations', confirms this interpretation. The character of the legislation which governs how the matter is to be determined . . . and that of the authority which is invested with jurisdiction in the matter . . . are therefore of little consequence" (Series A no. 13, p. 39, § 94).*

If the case concerns a dispute between an individual and a public authority, whether the latter had acted as a private person or in its sovereign capacity is therefore not conclusive.

Accordingly, in ascertaining whether a case ("*contestation*") concerns the determination of a civil right, only the character of the right at issue is relevant.

The Court recalls firstly that the applicant's appeals before the German administrative courts do not concern the right to be authorised to run a clinic and to be authorised to exercise the medical profession . . .; in challenging the withdrawal of his authorisations ordered by the competent authorities, Dr. König is claiming the right to continue his professional activities for which he had obtained the necessary authorisations. If the proceedings before the administrative courts were successful, the applicant would not be granted new authorisations: the court would simply annul the withdrawal decisions taken by the *Regierungspräsidenten* in Wiesbaden and Darmstadt. . . .

Therefore, it remains to be ascertained whether Dr. König's right to continue to run a private clinic and his right to continue to exercise the medical profession are civil rights within the meaning of Article 6 § 1.

* For a discussion of this point, see also L. B. Sohn & T. Buergenthal, International Protection of Human Rights 1194–95 (1973), where further references can be found.

The Court notes that, in the Federal Republic of Germany, the running of a private clinic is in certain respects a commercial activity carried on with a view to profit, classified by German law as a "*Gewerbe*". This activity is carried on in the private sector through the conclusion of contracts between the clinic and its patients and resembles the exercise of a private right in some ways akin to the right of property. Private clinics are certainly subject to supervision effected by the authorities in the public interest in order, *inter alia*, to protect health; supervision in the public interest, which moreover exists as a general rule for all private professional activities in the member States of the Council of Europe, cannot of itself lead to the conclusion that the running of a private clinic is a public-law activity. An activity presenting, under the law of the State concerned, the character of a private activity cannot automatically be converted into a public-law activity by reason of the fact that it is subject to administrative authorisations and supervision, including if appropriate the withdrawal of authorisations, provided for by law in the interests of public order and public health. . . .

The medical profession counts, in the Federal Republic of Germany, among the traditional liberal professions; . . . Even under the national health scheme, the medical profession is not a public service: once authorised, the doctor is free to practise or not, and he provides treatment for his patients on the basis of a contract made with them. Of course, besides treating his patients, the medical practitioner, in the words of the [applicable German statute], "has the care of the health of the community as a whole". This responsibility, which the medical profession bears towards society at large, does not, however, alter the private character of the medical practitioner's activity: whilst of great importance from the social point of view, that responsibility is accessory to his activity and its equivalent is to be found in other professions whose nature is undeniably private.

In these conditions, it is of little consequence that here the cases concern administrative measures taken by the competent bodies in the exercise of public authority. Neither does it appear pertinent that, under the law of the State concerned, it is for administrative courts to give the decision on these cases and to do so in proceedings which leave to the court the responsibility for the investigation and for the conduct of the trial. All that is relevant under Article 6 § 1 of the Convention is the fact that the object of the cases in question is the determination of rights of a private nature.

Since it thus considers the rights affected by the withdrawal decisions and forming the object of the cases before the administrative courts to be private rights, the Court concludes that Article 6 § 1 is applicable, without it being necessary in the present case to decide whether the concept of "civil rights and obligations" within the meaning of that provision extends beyond those rights which have a private nature.

On the basis of this reasoning, the court held that the Convention's guarantee of a reasonably speedy proceeding applied in the case at hand, and that this guarantee had been violated. Subsequently, Dr. König was awarded DM 40,000 as "just satisfaction" under Art. 50 of the Convention.[82]

Edge: I am bewildered, especially by the Court's emphasis on the fact that the case involved the revocation rather than the denial of a licence. Does this mean that the *denial* of a medical licence does not affect the applicant's "civil rights and obligations", and that in a judicial proceeding instituted to obtain review of such *denial* there would be no guarantee of a speedy hearing?

Comparovich: I am as puzzled as you are. An even more doubtful case would be that of a student seeking administrative-court review of a University's refusal to admit him. Is the right which the student seeks to enforce a private one as conceived by the Court? If not, the litigation might not be regarded as affecting the student's "civil rights and obligations" as that term was defined by the Court, and the due process guarantees of Art. 6 Section 1 of the Convention might not apply.[82a]

Edge: It seems to me that these doubts and difficulties arise because the Court, although it disclaims any intention of adopting the *German* distinction between public-law and private-law disputes, in the end cannot completely tear itself away from the general *civilian* notion that there is a necessary contrast between "civil rights and obligations", on the one hand, and rights flowing from public law, on the other.

Comparovich: You have a point here. For a common-law lawyer, there would be nothing startling in the proposition that even rights and obligations created by public law and belonging wholly to the public sphere can be termed "civil rights and obligations".

The civilian view, which treats private-law disputes and public-law disputes as mutually exclusive categories, seems to have been carried by the Court into the interpretation of the Convention. Dr. König won his case only because the Court, in a somewhat strained fashion, treated the doctor's asserted rights as "private". The clear implication

---

82. Judgment of March 10, 1980, Series A no. 36, cited by W. J. Ganshof van der Meersch, Reliance, in the Case-Law of the European Court of Human Rights, on the Domestic Law of the States, 1 Human Rights Law Journal 13, at 35 (1980).

In 1981 the court decided another case in which the petitioner claimed that German courts had violated their duty under Art. 6, § 1 to adjudicate his case within a "reasonable time": five years had elapsed between commencement of his action in the hierarchy of labor courts and the rejection of his constitutional complaint by the Federal Constitutional Court. The Human Rights Court chose to consider only delays that occurred in the German labor courts, but not the period of time consumed by proceedings before the Constitutional Court, on the theory that only the litigation before the labor courts involved "civil rights

and obligations" within the meaning of Art. 6 § 1. On this theory, then, a citizen's attempt to secure rights protected by his country's national Constitution is an assertion of rights created by public law and consequently falls outside the ambit of the due process guarantees of the Human Rights Convention. See the Decision of May 6, 1981 (the Buchholz case) reported in 2 Human Rights Law Journal 176 (1981).

For some other cases in which the Court had to deal with the claim that official delay constituted a violation of Art. 6, § 1, see the Judgment of July 13, 1983, Zimmerman and Steiner v. Switzerland, reported in 4 Human Rights Law Journal 363 (1983), and cases cited therein.

82a. Cf. the Buchholz case discussed in the preceding footnote.

is that, unless the Court adopts a much broader view in the future,[83] all proceedings involving the protection of "public" rights are excluded from the due process guarantees of the Human Rights Convention. The civilian dichotomy between "private-law" disputes and "public-law" disputes thus has been introduced into the area of international protection of human rights, with the result that grave doubts have been thrown on the protective scope of the European counterpart of our Due Process Clause.

3. COMPARATIVE CIVIL PROCEDURE—SOME QUESTIONS AND OBSERVATIONS

QUESTIONS

(1) What are the basic similarities between common-law and civil-law procedure? Do these similarities reflect agreement on the values underlying, and inherent in, the rule of law? Do they include adherence, by both systems, to the fundamental principles of rationality, objectivity and impartiality? Do they go beyond these fundamentals?

(2) What are the essential differences between common-law and civil-law procedure? Can all of these differences ultimately be traced to the different *roles* played by the various actors in the drama of litigation? Consider, in this connection, that common law and civil law clearly differ as to the distribution of functions (a) between professional and lay adjudicators; (b) between parties and their lawyers (especially in the investigative phase of litigation); and (c) between court and counsel.

What are the historical roots of the essential differences between common-law and civil-law procedure?

Do these differences, even though rooted in tradition, indicate any basic schism between the common-law and civil-law orbits concerning moral, political or social values relevant to the problems of our generation?[1] The question is important; to the extent that it is answered in the negative, it would follow that these differences have been produced by historical factors which are accidental and irrelevant in terms of the problems and values moving us today. It would follow, further, that there is no intrinsic virtue in keeping the civil law "pure" from

---

83. Note that in the last paragraph of the above-quoted opinion the Court left that possibility open.

In a recent decision, however, the Court again held that a physician's right to continue his *private* practice is a "civil right" within the meaning of Art. 6(1) of the Convention. It follows, according to the Court, that in a disciplinary proceeding that may lead to the revocation of his licence a *private medical practitioner* is entitled to a public hearing. Four judges dissented, and one of the dissenters criticized the majority for bestowing the benefits of Art. 6(1) on private practitioners while apparently withholding them from a doctor who exercises the medical profession as a civil servant or a salaried employee. See A. Drzemczewski, The European Convention on Human Rights, 3 (1983) Yearbook of European Law 439, 441 (1984). The Court thus seems to persist in fashioning a contrast between "civil" and "public" matters, and in narrowing the scope of the European Due Process clause.

1. Is it true that our procedural arrangements and institutions reflect our antipathy to governmental intervention, while the civilian attitude is more "etatist"? Cf. J. B. Board, Jr., Legal Culture and the Environmental Protection Issue, 37 Albany L.Rev. 603, at 609–10 (1973).

common-law influences, or in our continuing refusal even to experiment with procedural institutions of a civilian bent.[1a]

(3) If we attempt not only to compare but also to evaluate procedural institutions, what standards and criteria should we use? At the outset, can we agree that the aim of a sound system of procedure is "the just, speedy and inexpensive determination" of every justiciable dispute? [2]

Assuming that we find common-law procedure superior in some respects, and civil-law procedure in others, to what extent is it possible to combine the best features of both?

The two Notes which follow are not intended to provide complete answers to these difficult questions,[3] but merely to start off the discussion with a few data and suggestions.

NOTE ON THE SWEDISH CODE OF JUDICIAL PROCEDURE [4]

This modern Code, which went into effect January 1, 1948, shows an interesting combination of continental and Anglo-American features. It divides civil proceedings into two stages: (a) the preparatory proceeding in which the parties file informal pleadings and offers of proof and then appear before a single judge for the purpose of clarifying the issues and for other purposes inherent in the nature of a pre-trial hearing; (b) the main hearing, which is concentrated into one "day in court" before the full bench.[5]

Although the witnesses may be interrogated by the court, in practice their examination and cross-examination ordinarily is left to counsel. This, combined with the Code's insistence that all of the evidence be produced at the main hearing, i.e., in the course of a single, virtually uninterrupted session, creates an atmosphere not unlike that

---

1a. It is true, of course, that in some respects (e.g., jurisdiction over non-resident defendants; prevention of surprise), our law has moved in the direction of civil-law solutions. But this has come about haphazardly, and not as the result of a systematic effort to learn from the experience of others.

For some suggestions concerning the use of the comparative method for purposes of procedural reform, see infra, Note on Procedural Reform. See also R. B. Schlesinger, Comparative Criminal Procedure: A Plea for Utilizing Foreign Experience, 26 Buff.L.Rev. 361, at 382–85 (1977); J. Langbein, The German Advantage in Civil Procedure, 52 U.Chi.L.Rev. 823 (1985).

2. Cf. Rule 1 of the Federal Rules of Civil Procedure.

3. For a broad and challenging attack on procedural traditionalism, with special emphasis on legal aid, representation of diffuse interests, and alternatives to traditional forms of civil litigation, see the multi-volume comparative study by M. Cappel-

letti (Ed.), Access to Justice (1978–79), especially the General Report (by M. Cappelletti & B. Garth) at the beginning of the first volume.

4. A thorough and incisive treatment of the subject can be found in R. B. Ginsburg and A. Bruzelius, Civil Procedure in Sweden (1965). For concise discussions see P. H. Lindblom, Procedure, in 1 S. Strömholm (Ed.), An Introduction to Swedish Law 95 ff. (1981); L. B. Orfield, The Growth of Scandinavian Law 284–90 (1953); P. O. Ekelöf, Das schwedische Untergerichtsverfahren in Zivil-und Strafsachen, Vol. 82 of the Schriftenreihe der Juristischen Studiengesellschaft Karlsruhe (1967).

5. Concerning the composition of the full bench the Code (as amended) provides that in criminal cases and in civil cases involving family matters the professional judges sit together with lay assessors. In civil cases not involving family matters the full bench is composed, civil-law style, of professional judges only. See Lindblom, supra n. 4, at 108–111.

perhaps
something
for us,
to copy

of an English or American trial. On the other hand, "in marked contrast to proceedings in the United States, the witness is permitted to commence his testimony by relating all he knows about the matter under investigation in narrative form and without undue interruption." [6] Only after the witness has told his story in his own words, questions are put to him by counsel and perhaps by the court. The Swedish Code follows the modern continental view also in permitting the introduction of any evidence which is relevant and not privileged, and in providing for free evaluation by the court of the factual assertions and proofs presented at the trial.[7]

NOTE ON PROCEDURAL REFORM

The reformer who seeks to utilize foreign experience, will at the outset meet the challenging question to what extent rules of procedure which seem to work well in one country, can be transplanted into another country governed by a different legal system. At first blush, he will feel that provincialism, which is particularly entrenched in the procedural subjects, should be overcome, and that common-law lawyers as well as civilians should profit by the other side's ideas and experiences. Further analysis, however, shows that the matter is more complicated. The numerous differences in procedural concepts and techniques which exist between the common-law and the civil-law worlds, cannot be reduced to a common denominator, because these differences fall into two distinct categories.

On the one hand, we observe differences which, however accidental their historical origin may be, relate to matters of genuine popular interest and feeling—matters, moreover, which under our system may be insulated from easy legislative reform by constitutional provisions. The question of lay participation in the administration of justice is the prime example, but not the only one. The elevated status of judges in common-law countries, and the corresponding paucity of judicial manpower, as distinguished from the usual civil-law system of a more numerous civil service judiciary,[1] constitutes another tradition of such long standing that it may be beyond the reformer's reach. It follows that continental practices which are inconsistent with (a) the jury system, or (b) the traditional status and organization of our judiciary, could not be duplicated here in the foreseeable future, even were the legal profession desirous of doing so. So long as the civil jury remains

---

6. See Ginsburg and Bruzelius, supra n. 4, at 288.

7. Id. at 295–98.

1. West Germany, for instance, has many times the number of judges sitting in England, although as to size of population there is only a small difference between the two countries. The pertinent figures are set forth by F. A. Mann, Fusion of the Legal Professions?, 93 L.Q.Rev. 367, 371–72 (1977); id., Die deutsche Justizreform im Licht englischer Erfahrung 4–5 (Heft 63 der Schriftenreihe der Juristischen Studiengesellschaft Karlsruhe, 1965). Recent figures for West Germany show

16,429 state and 493 federal judges (federal judges functioning only at the level of highest courts). See Statistisches Jahrbuch für die B.R. Deutschland 338 (1984).

P. Calamandrei, with his usual insight (though perhaps a trifle hyperbolically), made a similar point in Procedure and Democracy, at 83 (1956): "The same judicial function that some 6000 career judges are unable to perform effectively in Italy is accomplished successfully and with considerably greater rapidity in England by not more than 100 judges!"

with us, it will always be necessary to introduce all the evidence in *one* concentrated trial which then becomes the focus of the whole proceeding, as distinguished from the successive hearings and enquêtes which in civil-law procedure serve to build up the all-important dossier.[1a] Our extreme economy in the number of judicial positions compels us to preserve the system of one-man trial courts and the somewhat lopsided division of labor between Bench and Bar, by which we burden counsel with many of the chores which the civil law imposes upon the court.

On the other hand, there are large areas of the law of procedure where the existing institutions are not so strongly underpinned by cherished traditions and hence are less resistant to change. It is in these areas that the reformer is most likely to derive practical benefit from comparison.[1b] As a prime example one might mention the litigation problems of the poor, and of parties of limited means.[1c] Here we are no longer paralyzed by an obsolete tradition; on the contrary, there is today a near-consensus among American lawyers that in the past we unforgivably neglected the problems of the impecunious litigant, and that much further progress needs to be made, especially with respect to civil litigation. Yet in our frantic rush to right old wrongs, we have paid too little attention to the large store of relevant experience accumulated in foreign countries, including those of the civil-law orbit.[2]

Foreign experience can be utilized even more easily when we deal with matters which today are entirely non-political and generally conceded to be of a technical nature, such as the question whether issues should be formulated by formal written pleadings or orally in open court, and the related question whether and to what extent the court should be able to influence such formulation. Modern pre-trial procedure, as exemplified by Rule 16 of the Federal Rules of Civil Procedure, shows that with respect to this question we are slowly (perhaps too slowly) moving toward the continental idea. The same is true of the question whether a party should be permitted to keep its evidence from the other side until the moment when such evidence is actually produced.[3] The civilians, on the other hand, might profitably

---

1a. On the other hand, it should be kept in mind that in criminal cases the civilian as well as the common-law systems utilize lay adjudicators and espouse the idea of a single concentrated trial. With respect to criminal procedure, therefore, it would seem that we might well be able to benefit from civil-law experience without having to change any cherished institutional arrangements. Going a step further, Professor Langbein has suggested that without giving up the essential values and purposes of the jury system we could introduce some of the beneficial features of the civilian "mixed bench". J. Langbein, Mixed Court and Jury Court: Could the Continental Alternative Fill the American Need?, 1981 Am. Bar Found. Research Journal at 195–219.

1b. For some interesting remarks concerning the extent to which a study of civil-law procedure can bear fruit for purposes of procedural reform in a common-law country, see Going to Law—A Critique of English Civil Procedure (a Justice Report, 1974) at 28–29.

1c. Further examples are furnished by procedural problems that typically arise in environmental and consumer protection lawsuits, as well as in litigation that involves a multiplicity of parties and issues. In such cases American judges, at least in the federal system, feel an increasing need to assert greater control in the pretrial process and to play a more "managerial role". Continental experience in dealing with the same problems can be a useful source of inspiration for reformers. See M. Cappelletti and B. Garth, A Comparative Conclusion, in International Encyclopedia of Comparative Law, Vol. XVI (Civil Procedure) Chapt. 6 (Ordinary Proceedings in First Instance) (1984); J. Langbein, supra n. 1a.

2. See supra pp. 354–362.

3. Another example is presented by our practice, traditionally prevalent in trial

more difficult to dismiss case on summary judgment type motion in U.S.

study, for instance, the benefits and costs of our more efficient discovery procedures (originally of civilian provenience), and the potentialities, in the search for truth, of vigorous examination and cross-examination by counsel.

Of particular interest is a comparative look at the law of evidence. To continental lawyers it is a cause of pride that they have essentially freed their courts from the fetters of artificial restrictions on the admission of relevant evidence. In common-law countries, on the other hand, many of these restrictions have survived to this day, although there is controversy concerning their basis in history, policy and logic. Some scholars assert that our rules of evidence are a by-product of the jury system, and are necessary for a proper functioning of that system.[4] If that is the true and only justification for exclusionary rules of evidence, then we should follow the example of our civilian brethren, and (much more radically than we have done heretofore) discard such rules in all non-jury proceedings.

Other scholars, however, have attempted to justify the hearsay rule [5] on the ground that the testimony of a witness not having first-hand knowledge is inherently unreliable and hence dangerous to the integrity of the fact-finding process, no matter who may be the trier of the facts.[6] The soundness of this view, which would tend to preserve at least some of the present exclusionary rules in non-jury as well as jury cases, is hotly disputed.[7] Thorough scrutiny of the civilians' experience may well be the most promising step toward resolving the dispute.[8]

A comparative approach to matters of procedure becomes an immediate practical necessity in the ever-growing number of cases in which litigation cuts across national boundaries. Many of the problems arising in such litigation can be resolved only by international judicial

courts staffed by more than one judge, to have successive motions decided by different judges, and to have yet another judge, who is unfamiliar with the case, preside at the trial. The author remembers a case in New York County in which seven different judges of the same court successively had to study the complicated issues of the same litigation. This kind of waste (not only of the judges' time, but also of the efforts of counsel who have to produce avalanches of affidavits and briefs in order to explain the issues to each successive judge), is virtually unthinkable under the civil-law system of assigning each case to a three-judge panel which then handles it from beginning to end. Our courts, unwilling to learn from civil-law experience, had to re-invent the wheel. During the last two decades, the pressure of overcrowded dockets, and the demands of certain types of mammoth litigation, forced them to experiment with the "individual assignment" method, under which a case is assigned to a particular judge for all purposes. These experiments, which have found favor with many federal courts and some state courts, in effect amount to the re-invention of an obviously salutary procedural device employed by the civilians for more than a century.

4. This is the well-known Thayer thesis. J. B. Thayer, A Preliminary Treatise on Evidence at the Common Law 266 (1898). Lately, this widely accepted thesis has been subject to criticism. See, e.g., J. H. Langbein, The Criminal Trial Before the Lawyers, 45 U.Chi.L.Rev. 263, 306 (1978).

5. Similar arguments might conceivably be made in support of other exclusionary rules.

6. See F. E. Booker and R. Morton, The Hearsay Rule, The St. George Plays and the Road to the Year Twenty-Fifty, 44 Notre Dame Law. 7 (1968).

7. See McCormick on Evidence § 60,327 (3rd ed., by E. W. Clearly et al., 1984); A. L. Levin and H. K. Cohen, The Exclusionary Rules in Nonjury Criminal Cases, 119 U.Pa.L.Rev. 905 (1971). For a particularly effective presentation of the case against the present state of the law, see J. B. Weinstein, Probative Force of Hearsay, 46 Iowa L.Rev. 331 (1961). But see R. Lempert and S. Saltzburg, A Modern Approach to Evidence 519–532 (2d ed., 1982).

8. Cf. Weinstein, supra n. 7 at 347.

cooperation (see supra, pp. 409–413, 443–448). To bring about such cooperation, is one of the objectives of intelligent procedural reform. In the United States this specific subject of reform was badly neglected until the late 1950's. Since then, however, rapid progress has been made, first by a highly successful program of unilateral revision of American procedures for providing and obtaining international judicial assistance,[9] and since 1964 by active participation in the treaty-writing work of the Hague Conference on Private International Law.[10] Thus, as has been shown in the preceding materials,[11] some of the difficulties caused by differences between civil-law and common-law procedure have been overcome or mitigated during the last three decades. The task, however, is far from completed.[12]

III. SUBSTANTIVE LAW

1. SYSTEM AND ORGANIZATION OF THE CODES

INTRODUCTORY NOTE

The materials which follow deal with the codes, especially the civil and commercial codes, of leading civil-law countries. In studying these materials, the reader should keep in mind that in each of the countries in question the enactment of the codes constituted (a) the culmination of a long historical evolution, and (b) the starting point of new, code-oriented (and presently continuing) developments in the national legal system. Thus it goes without saying that the materials which follow must be placed into the historical context outlined supra, pp. 245–310.

9. See Fourth Annual Report of the Commission on International Rules of Judicial Procedure (1963) (the Commission and its Advisory Committee had been created by Congress in 1958, 72 Stat. 1743); H. Smit (Ed.), International Cooperation in Litigation: Europe 1–15, 409–64 (1965).

10. See supra pp. 409, 412, 445. After each session of the Hague Conference, the drafts prepared at such session usually are published (and commented on) in the American Journal of Comparative Law. For general discussions of the work of the Conference, and of American participation therein, see R. D. Kearney, Progress Report—International Unification of Private Law, 23 The Record 220 (1968); P. H. Pfund, United States Participation in International Unification of Private Law, 19 Int. Lawyer 505 (1985).

11. See supra pp. 412–13, 445.

12. This is shown most dramatically by the continuing imbroglio regarding the use of American-style discovery in transnational litigation. See supra pp. 445–448.

[handwritten annotations:]

Categories

Persons
Family Law
Marital property
Property
Successions
Relations : torts, contracts

FRENCH CIVIL CODE—TABLE OF CONTENTS [a]

PRELIMINARY TITLE: Publication, Effects and Application of Laws in General

Book I. Of Persons [b]

Book II. Of Property and of Different Kinds of Ownership

Book III. Of the Different Ways of Acquiring Property

a. This is a summary table of contents. For a more elaborate one, indicating the headings of chapters and sections as well as titles, see J. H. Crabb, The French Civil Code IX–XX (1977).

b. Book one of the Code was subjected to very heavy revision beginning in 1965. See the discussion infra at pp. 548–549 and B. Audit, Recent Revisions of the French Civil Code, 38 La.L.Rev. 747 (1978). The headings given here reflect these revisions.

c. In French legal terminology, the expression "civil rights" (*droits civils*) does not quite have the same connotation as in American legal usage. In a matter raising the same issue as the *König* case mentioned supra pp. 520–524, for instance, the French Conseil d'Etat ruled that proceedings to determine conscientious objector status, handled by a special commission set up for that purpose, did not involve "civil rights" within the meaning of the Europe-an Convention on Human Rights. Mr. V., Cons. d'Etat, Dec. 21, 1979, 1981 Y.B.Eur. Conv.Hum. Rights 512.

Title I, as originally enacted, contained in particular rules as to the acquisition and loss of French nationality. These rules were later incorporated in a special, often modified statute, now called the Code of French Nationality (*Code de la Nationalité française*). The modern tendency in civil-law countries is to treat citizenship as a public-law subject, not to be covered in a civil code. Nevertheless, because in France nationality has a significant impact on the jurisdiction of courts (see supra p. 394–395) and, to some extent, on choice of law, French textbooks on conflict of laws usually contain extensive discussions of the rules relating to the acquisition and loss of French citizenship, and commercial publishers of the Civil Code tend to include excerpts from the Nationality Code.

Title

NOTES AND QUESTIONS

(1) The organizational scheme of the French Civil Code is similar to that of Gaius' *Institutiones*. See supra p. 274 n. 19. Whether this similarity is accidental or due to the Roman law learning of the Code's draftsmen is somewhat controversial.[1]

(2) Compare the organization of the French Civil Code of 1804 with that (a) of the Spanish Code of 1889, supra, pp. 238–240, and (b) of the German Civil Code, reproduced below.[2]

d. For instructive discussions, in English, of the drastic revisions which this title underwent in 1965, see I. Soubbotich, Recent Important Reforms in the French Matrimonial Regime, 12 N.Y.Law Forum 245 (1966); L. N. Brown, The Reform of French Matrimonial Property Law, 14 Am. J.Comp.L. 308 (1965); M. A. Glendon, State, Law and Family: Family Law in Transition in the United States and Western Europe 143–47 (1977).

In the last-cited work, and in the same author's previous article, Matrimonial Property: A Comparative Study of Law and Social Change, 49 Tul.L.Rev. 21 (1974), the French reforms of 1965 are compared with developments in Germany, England and the United States. For a more comprehensive comparative treatment (covering Belgium, England, France, Germany, Italy and the Netherlands), see A. Kiralfy (ed.), Comparative Law of Matrimonial Property (1972).

e. In civil-law systems, a lease (even of immovable property) generally is treated as a type of *contract* rather than as an estate in land. This accounts for the fact that leases are dealt with in Book III, and not in Book II of the French Civil Code.

f. This title was added by a 1971 amendment.

g. This title was drastically revised in 1978.

h. This title was added in 1976.

i. This title was added in 1972. Former Title XVI, which dealt mainly with imprisonment for debt, had been abrogated in 1867.

1. See S. Herman, The Uses and Abuses of Roman Law, 29 Am.J.Comp.L. 671, 686–87 (1981).

2. Much comparative material on organization of codes can be found in general discussions of law as a system and of its

Do you find, in the French and Spanish Codes, anything resembling the German Code's "General Part"? [3]

GERMAN CIVIL CODE—DETAILED SYNOPSIS [a]
(Translation by Forrester, Goren, and Ilgen). [*]

Book One. General Part §§ 1–240 [b]

division and classification. See 5 R. Pound, Jurisprudence, sec. 131 (1959).

3. The historical roots of the "General Part" have been traced in an earlier chapter of this book. For a more extensive discussion of the "General Part", from a comparative and historical point of view, see F. Schmidt, The German Abstract Approach to Law—Comments on the System of the Bürgerliches Gesetzbuch, 9 Scandinavian Studies in Law 131 (1965).

The basic organizational differences between the French and German Civil Codes, and the recurrent French debates concerning the desirability of a "General Part", are discussed by I. Zajtay, Rechtsvergleichende Bemerkungen über den Code civil und das Bürgerliche Gesetzbuch, 157 Arch.Civ.Pr. 479, especially 483–86 (1959).

a. Enacted in 1896 and effective as of January 1, 1900, this Civil Code (as amended) remains the law of the German Federal Republic (West Germany). In the German Democratic Republic (East Germany) the bulk of the provisions of the 1896 Code remained in force until 1975. But on June 19, 1975, East Germany adopted a new socialist Civil Code, which in style and

organization as well as in substance differs from the "capitalist" Code of 1896. For the text of the East German Code, and an instructive introduction, see H. Roggemann, Zivilgesetzbuch und Zivilprozessordnung der DDR mit Nebengesetzen (1976).

For an up-to-date text of the 1896 (West German) Civil Code, see, e.g., Schoenfelder, Deutsche Gesetze (loose-leaf ed.).

Throughout this book, except where otherwise indicated, all references to the German Civil Code should be understood as pointing to the 1896 (West German) Code, as amended.

[*] By permission of the publisher, Fred B. Rothman & Co., this translation is reproduced from I. S. Forrester, S. L. Goren & H. M. Ilgen, The German Civil Code V–IX (1975), with some changes reflecting recent legislative modifications.

b. The organization of Book One and Book Two of the Code is helpfully discussed by R. A. Riegert, The West German Civil Code, Its Origin and Its Contract Provisions, 45 Tul.L.Rev. 48, 54–67 (1970).

c. The German term is "Rechtsgeschaeft", which has been translated, also, as "jural act". The concept of "Rechtsgeschaeft" cuts across all fields of law; it "embraces all the elements common to contracts, wills, negotiable instruments . . ., and one-sided declarations such as notices and renunciations." Parker, Book Review, 42 Cornell L.Q. 448 (1957).

On the definition of *"Rechtsgeschaeft"* see also infra n. d, and F. H. Lawson, Notes on Some General Problems of Terminology, 17 Netherlands Int.L.Rev. 237 (1970).

d. Roughly speaking, the German term "Willenserklaerung", literally "declaration of will", covers any declaration of a party which is intended to be transactional.

The relationship between the two terms, *Rechtsgeschaeft* and *Willenserklaerung*, is explained by a leading commentator as follows: "A legal transaction (Rechtsgeschaeft) consists of one or several declarations of intention (Willenserklaerungen), which by themselves or in conjunction with other elements [e.g., a necessary governmental authorization] produce an intended legal effect." Palandt, Bürgerliches Gesetzbuch, Introduction preceding § 104, Anno. 1b (45th ed., 1986).

e. A "deposit" of this kind is somewhat comparable to our institution of payment into court.

f. This is the German version of "negotiorum gestio". See supra p. 5.

g. This title deals with duties to "produce", i.e., to exhibit, or to permit inspection of, a document or other thing. The reader will recall that under German law there can be no discovery of a document or other thing in the custody of the opponent or of a third party unless it can be shown that the person from whom discovery is sought is under a substantive-law duty to produce such document or other thing. Whether or not such a substantive-law duty exists, is usually determined by §§ 809 to 811 of the Civil Code.

h. Condominium-type ownership of apartments was not satisfactorily regulated, and in effect discouraged, by the Code. When the acute shortage of dwellings resulting from World War II made it necessary to employ large amounts of tenants' savings in building and rebuilding operations, it was thought desirable to create a firm legal foundation for arrangements by which the suppliers of such funds could become *owners* of their respective apartments, and *co-owners* of the common portions of the buildings. This was done by a separate statute (Wohnungseigentumsgesetz) of March 15, 1951, rather than by amending the Code. See also infra p. 684.

i. All provisions which were inconsistent with the constitutional principle that "Men and women shall have equal rights", became ineffective on March 31, 1953. See Basic Law of the German Federal Republic, Arts. 3 and 117. By the Equal Rights Law of June 18, 1957 (BGB*l* I 609), the Fourth Book of the Civil Code was extensively revised in order to make its provisions consistent with the constitutional command; the changes became effective July 1, 1958. See Leyser, "Equality of the Spouses" Under the New German Law, 7 Am.J.Comp.L. 276 (1958); W. Müller-Freienfels, Equality of Husband and Wife in Family Law, 8 Int. & Comp.L.Q. 249 (1959); id., Family Law and the Law of Succession, 16 Int. & Comp.L.Q. 409 (1967).

k. The Second, Third, Fourth and Seventh Titles were repealed by the Marriage Law of 1938 (based on Nazi racial principles), which in turn was replaced by the Marriage Law of 1946. The provisions of the latter Law, insofar as they deal with the validity of marriages, are still in force, and §§ 1303 through 1352 of the Civil Code remain repealed; but those provisions of the Marriage Law which deal with divorce, have been reincorporated into the Civil Code in 1977. Thus (as was the case before

1938) the provisions concerning divorce can again be found in §§ 1564 to 1587 of the Civil Code; but the new provisions, which reflect the no-fault principle, in their substance are very different from the pre-1938 ones. See G. Beitzke, Les Causes de Divorce Dans le Nouveau Droit Allemand, 29 Annales de la Faculté de Droit et des Sciences Politiques et de l'Institut de Recherches Juridiques, Politiques et Sociales de Strasbourg 33 (1979).

l. Sections 1408 to 1518 of the Code make it possible for the parties to adopt, by notarial contract, certain types of matrimonial property regimes. Sections 1363 to 1390, on the other hand, spell out the details of the so-called legal regime, i.e., the regime that prevails in the very frequent event that the parties have not regulated their matrimonial property regime by a notarial contract.

Formerly, the "legal regime" gave to the husband the management of, and the income from, the wife's property. The Equal Rights Law of 1957 (see supra) now provides, again subject to notarial agreement substituting another regime, that each spouse shall separately own and manage his or her property, and shall be entitled to one-half of the amount by which the net value of the other spouse's property increases during coverture; the mutual claims thus arising are to be settled upon dissolution of the marriage. The details, which vary depending on whether the marriage has been dissolved by death or otherwise, are exceedingly complicated. See E. J. Cohn, Manual of German Law, Vol. I, pp. 234–41 (2d ed. 1968); E. D. Graue, German Law, in A. Kiralfy, Comparative Law of Matrimonial Property 114 ff. (1972).

m. See supra n. k.

n. Using our terminology, this heading would read Parents and Children.

INTRODUCTORY ACT

[promulgated together with the Civil Code]

o. This Title was repealed, and its provisions superseded, by the Testament Law of July 31, 1938 (RGB*l* I 973). By a Law of March 5, 1953 (BGB*l* I 33), however, the revised provisions of the Testament Law were reincorporated into the Civil Code.

p. The term "compulsory portion" or "obligatory portion" (Pflichtteil) refers to that portion of the decedent's estate which, by cogent provisions of the Code, is set aside for the benefit of his surviving spouse and children. These provisions thus limit freedom of testation.

a. The conflict of laws provisions of the Introductory Act were substantially revised by a statute approved in June, 1986. For a discussion, see infra pp. 847–848.

GERMAN COMMERCIAL CODE—TABLE OF CONTENTS

Book I. Commercial Status

Book II.

[The second Book deals essentially with partnerships and limited partnerships. Formerly, it also dealt with stock corporations.[c]]

Book III. Commercial Bookkeeping

[Subheadings omitted. Book III, inserted by a Law of December 19, 1985 (BGB*l* I page 2355) deals with the books and records to be kept by merchants and especially covers the rules, including the publicity rules, governing the balance sheets and profit and loss statements of corporations.]

Book IV. Commercial Transactions

Book V. Maritime Commerce

[Subheadings omitted. The provisions of Book V (Sections 474–905) deal with the subject of maritime law. By several amendments, and by a partial revision carried out in 1937 and 1940, German maritime law was largely adapted to Anglo-American ideas in this field, especially to those which are reflected in the Hague Rules.[d]]

---

b. Substantially revised by Law of August 6, 1953 (BGB*l* I 771). No reliance may be placed on the text of these provisions as it appears in older editions.

c. See infra pp. 793 ff.

d. See 2 E. J. Cohn, Manual of German Law 3, 44 (2nd ed., 1971).

VARIANTS OF CODE ORGANIZATION

(1) *Variants in the Civil-Law World.* As the reader will have observed, the Civil Codes of France and Germany—the two most influential seminal Codes of the civil-law world—differ from each other in their basic organization. But there is agreement between the French and German systems, and among the many followers of both, on a very important point: that the total area of substantive private law should be divided into (a) non-commercial ("civil") law and (b) commercial law, and that this division should be reflected in the enactment of two separate codes, a Civil Code and a Commercial Code. The historical reasons for this dualism have been mentioned supra pp. 301–304.

In the course of the present century, this traditional dualist system of private-law codification has come under attack, and a unitary system of private law (and especially of the law of obligations) has been advocated by a number of scholars.[1] Among other points, it has been argued by the unitarists that in a highly developed modern society, with adequate education available to all, there is no longer any need for a separate body of law governing the transactions of the sophisticated class, i.e., of the merchants. It has been said, moreover, that in a democracy there should be no class legislation, and that for this reason, also, no separate commercial code (or merchants' code) should be enacted.[2]

Responding to these arguments, the Swiss legislator chose a scheme of code organization quite different from the French and German ones. In Switzerland, the law of obligations (including the law of contracts) is not treated in the Civil Code at all.[3] A separate *Code of Obligations* covers both the law of contracts and most of those subjects which in other civil-law countries (such as Germany, see supra) are treated in the Commercial Code. The Swiss legislator thus deals with commercial and non-commercial contracts in the same Code, abolishing, at least on the face of the codes, the traditional civilian dichotomy between "civil" and commercial law. A similar trend away from the dualism of "civil" and commercial law, can be observed in some (thus far a distinct minority) of the other continental countries.[4]

1. The present state of the controversy between the dualists and the unitarists is reflected in the excellent collection of essays appearing in M. Rotondi (Ed.), The Unity of the Law of Obligations (1974). For policy arguments in favor of the dualist approach, interestingly presented by an American observer, see J. M. Steadman, Book Review, 120 U.Pa.L.Rev. 1013, 1015 (1972).

2. In the civil-law world, a Commercial Code generally is regarded as establishing separate and special rules for the transactions of merchants. This is true regardless of definitional details (see infra p. 590 ff.). The concept of our own Uniform Commercial Code is, of course, quite different. The coverage of the UCC (which is not as broad as that of a civilian Commercial Code) is based on the nature of the transaction, and not on the merchant status of the partici-

pants. Only relatively few provisions of the UCC turn on such status. See R. B. Schlesinger, The Uniform Commercial Code in the Light of Comparative Law, 1 Inter-Am.L.Rev. 11, 42–44, 48–51 (1959); B. H. Greene, Commercial Law in the United States, in Rotondi, supra n. 1, at 159; W. Gray, Civil and Commercial Law in the United States, id. at 151. The last-mentioned article, at 155, contains a helpful discussion of the UCC provisions which refer to a special merchant status. See also UCC § 2–104, Official Comment 2.

3. For the table of contents of the Swiss Civil Code see p. XXXV ff. of the translation by Shick (Boston 1915).

4. The Italian Civil Code of 1942, different in this respect from its 19th century predecessor, contains both civil and commercial law. The separate Commercial

(2) *The Two Great Debates Among Modern Civilian Codifiers.* Any 20th century law-giver who undertakes to codify his country's substantive private law, faces two basic problems of code organization:

(i) Whether, in addition to the Civil Code, there should be a separate Commercial Code; and

(ii) Whether the Civil Code, following the German example (and in contrast to the French model), should contain a "General Part", i.e., a separate division which serves as a reservoir of rules and principles of such abstractness and generality that they pervade all of the—functionally quite diverse—areas of law covered by the Code.[5]

In part (1) of this Note, some comments have been offered on the first of these great debates. We now turn to the second, the one involving the desirability of a "General Part".

To insert into a code some abstract and pervasive provisions, which are potentially applicable to all of its subdivisions, has some obvious advantages: it promotes economy of words and gives the courts a tool for the resolution of problems not foreseen by the code's drafters. But abstractness and pervasiveness also create complications, as shown in the following examples:

(a) Section 164 of the German Civil Code clearly implies that *any jural act* of a person may come into existence either by that person's own declaration or by a declaration of his duly authorized agent. The draftsmen, however, were aware that the broad rule permitting any jural act to be done by an agent had to be qualified by exceptions; some types of jural acts are of such a personal nature that action by the principal himself should be required. The execution of a testament comes to mind as an obvious example, and the German Civil Code in § 2064 indeed requires, by way of a specific exception engrafted upon the general rule, that a testament be personally executed by the testator. In book IV and book V of the German Code (dealing with family law and decedents' estates) one finds more than a dozen other provisions which, by way of similar exceptions, require personal declarations and thus preclude the use of an agent for the specified types of jural acts.[5a] It follows that the broad and pervasive rule announced in the General Part, while elegant in its abstractness,[5b] can be used with confidence only after one has familiarized oneself with the exceptions that are dispersed through various parts of the Code.

Code was abolished at the same time. See M. Cappelletti, J. H. Merryman and J. M. Perillo, The Italian Legal System 225–27 (1967); M. Rotondi, Entstehung und Niedergang des autonomen Handelsrechts in Italien, 167 Archiv für die civilistische Praxis 29 (1967).

5. The rules and principles stated in the General Part are so abstract and general that at least in theory (and subject to specific exceptions and qualifications) they are applicable in every area of private law, including contracts, property law, corporation law, family law and decedents' estates.

An example is provided by the famous Section 138 of the German Civil Code, invalidating every "jural act" that is immoral. Later on, we shall encounter several illustrations showing how this provision operates in practice.

5a. See Palandt, Buergerliches Gesetzbuch, Introduction preceding § 164, Anno. 1(d) (45th ed., 1986).

5b. Compare the unsystematic and unhelpful provision of Restatement (Second), Agency, § 20 and comment (d), which seems to be aimed at the same problem.

(b) German Civil Code § 158 indicates that any "jural act" can be subjected to conditions precedent or conditions subsequent. In many instances this is a salutary rule, permitting flexibility in transactional dealings. But with respect to some types of jural acts, certainty is more important than flexibility, and where this is so, conditions perhaps should not be tolerated. The draftsmen of the German Civil Code recognized that, and—by way of specific exceptions to the rule of § 158—provided that certain jural acts cannot be subjected to conditions. Perhaps the best-known examples are marriage (Marriage Law § 13) and transferring real property inter vivos (Civil Code § 925). So far, the legal researcher does not face any great difficulty; he merely has to be aware (i) of the rule stated in the General Part of the Code and (ii) of the explicit statutory exceptions appearing in subsequent parts of the Code itself and in other statutes.

What is more troublesome is that German courts and legal writers have found certain types of jural acts to be resistant to conditions and hence exempt from the rule of § 158, even though the written law does not grant such an exemption. Thus it has been held that the jural act of rescinding or terminating a contract is valid only if the rescission or termination is unconditionally declared.[5c] In cases of this kind, a mere reading of the Code and other statutory materials would mislead the researcher. The reason for this somewhat unsatisfying effect of a supposedly comprehensive Code lies in the enormous breadth and generality of provisions such as § 158. The draftsmen apparently realized that there were some jural acts as to which the rule of § 158 had to be qualified by specific exceptions; but understandably they were unable to think of all instances of this kind.

It is not surprising, therefore, that in the civil-law world these matters of code technique have given rise to "great debates". These debates, as we have seen, focus on the desirability of (i) a separate Commercial Code, and (ii) a German-style General Part. In the Netherlands—the only continental country where a complete overhaul of private-law codes is presently in progress—[6] both of these problems were thoroughly studied and interestingly resolved. Concerning the first problem, the traditional dualist approach was discarded. Following the Italian example,[7] the new Dutch Code will be a unitary one, covering not only the traditional Civil Code subjects, but also the topics traditionally assigned to a separate commercial code.[8] Thus, to mention but one example, the law of commercial partnerships and of stock corporations will be dealt with in the new Civil Code. And, of course, there will no longer be a separate Commercial Code once all parts of the new Civil Code will have become effective.

5c. For authorities see Palandt, supra n. 5a, Introduction preceding § 158, Anno. 6.

6. See infra p. 548.

7. See supra n. 4.

8. See A. S. Hartkamp, Civil Code Revision in the Netherlands: A Survey of Its System and Contents, and Its Influence on Dutch Legal Practice, 35 La.L.Rev. 1059 (1975); H. Drion, Introduction to the Unofficial Translation of Book 6 of the Draft of a New Netherlands Civil Code, 17 Netherlands Int.L.Rev. 225 (1970–71); I. Kisch, Structure of the Netherlands Civil Code, in D. C. Fokkema, J. M. J. Chorus, E. H. Hondius & E. Ch. Lisser, Introduction to Dutch Law for Foreign Lawyers 39–41 (1978).

The "General Part" problem was resolved by the draftsmen of the new Dutch Code in an interesting and innovative way. They decided to include a "General Part" in their Code, but to limit its effect to those areas of the law which deal with "patrimony", i.e., with rights having a money value.[9] Thus, purely personal rights, especially in the area of family law, are not affected by the rules and principles stated in the General Part of the new Netherlands Code.

(3) *Variants in the Socialist Orbit.* The reader will recall that the legal systems of Europe's socialist countries, in spite of their different ideology, are greatly influenced by the civil law insofar as terminology, code structure and other legal techniques are concerned. Yet, in some respects the socialist codes show significant structural differences when compared to the codes of the civil-law orbit.[10] The tendency in most of the socialist countries is to abolish or downgrade the Commercial Code, without, however, necessarily adopting the Swiss-Italian-Dutch solution of dealing with all commercial as well as non-commercial transactions in a unitary Civil Code or Code of Obligations. For instance, in East Germany (as in some of the other socialist countries) the subject of Contracts has been divided into three systematically separate parts:

(a) Contracts among socialist (usually state-owned) enterprises, i.e., the economically most important transactions, are governed by a special code, which in East Germany is called Vertragsgesetz (Contract Law). The emphasis here is on fulfillment of the Plan, and disputes arising in connection with such contracts are determined, not by the ordinary courts, but by special arbitration boards.[11]

(b) Retail transactions and contracts among individuals— which, in a socialist society, tend to be of limited economic significance—are governed by provisions of the Civil Code, provisions which are not dramatically different from their counterparts in the "capitalist" civil law countries.

(c) Separate treatment is often accorded to international transactions. East Germany, for instance, has enacted a separate Law Concerning International Business Contracts, which governs contracts concluded by East German enterprises with foreign parties, regardless of whether the foreign party is located in a socialist or a capitalist country. The Law applies whenever, by virtue of a choice-of-law clause or of applicable legal rules of choice of law, such a contract is subject to East German law.[12] The provisions of

9. For details, see Hartkamp, supra n. 8, at 1065–67; Drion, supra n. 8, at 230.

10. Generalizations are difficult, because with respect to code organization the socialist countries differ *inter sese.*

11. Even in those socialist countries (e.g., Poland) where contracts among units of the socialized economy are treated in the Civil Code rather than in a separate statute, such contracts are differentiated from other contracts. See D. Lasok, Codification of Polish Civil Law, in D. D. Barry, F. J. M. Feldbrugge & D. Lasok (Eds.), Codification in the Communist World 185, 203–05 (1975); W. J. Wagner, Some Comments on the Polish Legal System with Particular Reference to the Law of Contracts, in 1 R. B. Schlesinger (Gen.Ed.), Formation of Contracts—A Study of the Common Core of Legal Systems 311, 312–16 (1968).

12. See F. K. Juenger, The Conflicts Statute of the German Democratic Republic: An Introduction and Translation, 25 Am.J.Comp.L. 332 (1977).

the Law, like the contract provisions of the Civil Code, essentially reflect traditional civil-law notions.[13]

NOTE ON CODE FAMILIES

Common law much more difficult to export

In an earlier part of this book (pp. 8–17), there was some reference to the general processes of migration and reception of legal ideas. Code law, it seems, is particularly suitable for export from one country to another, because of its systematic, compact and almost package-like form.[1] Such export may be the result of military conquest, of a conscious effort to establish cultural links, or simply of the inspiration which radiates from a great intellectual accomplishment.

Although the worldwide picture of these criss-crossing influences is complex, one can discern a pattern. There is almost no private-law-code in force in any civilian country today which is not substantially copied from, or in its structure or some of its provisions directly or indirectly influenced by, the codes of France, Germany or Switzerland.[2] The German Civil Code of 1896 (effective date Jan. 1, 1900) was in turn somewhat, although not too strongly, influenced by provisions of the French Code; and the Swiss Code of 1907, while largely based on existing local institutions and on original thinking of its distinguished draftsman, Professor Eugen Huber, did not escape the influence of the German and French codes.

Depending on the predominance of French, German or Swiss influence, it is possible to divide the civil-law countries into "Code families".[3] Many of the principal members of these "families" have been identified in our earlier discussion.[4] But it should be kept in mind that the draftsmen of a code often prefer not to follow a single pattern but to skim what they consider the best features from all existing codes.[5]

---

13. See F. Enderlein, Das Gesetz ueber internationale Wirtschaftsvertraege der DDR vom 5. Februar 1976, 140 Zeitschrift fuer Handelsrecht 442 (1976); 1 Schlesinger, Formation of Contracts—A Study of the Common Core of Legal Systems 22–29 (1968).

1. See Andreas B. Schwarz, Das schweizerische Zivilgesetzbuch in der auslaendischen Rechtsentwicklung 2 (1950).

2. The sweeping statement in the text requires one (and perhaps only one) qualification: the Austrian General Civil Code of 1811 was a work of great originality. It exercised considerable influence throughout Eastern and Southeastern Europe; but outside of Austria itself this influence is now greatly reduced, as a result of the expansion, after World War II, of the communist orbit. See supra pp. 328–329. (The influence of the Austrian Code of Civil Procedure has been more widespread and more lasting, as pointed out earlier in the discussion of Procedure in Civil Law Countries.)

3. For an excellent discussion of the history and significance of "code families", see Schwarz, supra n. 1.

4. See supra pp. 315–330. For further details, see J. Limpens, Territorial Expansion of the Code, in B. Schwartz (Ed.), The Code Napoleon and the Common Law World, at 92 ff. (1956); A. B. Schwarz, supra n. 1, passim; 1 Schnitzer, Vergleichende Rechtslehre 195–243 (2d ed. 1961); Association Henri Capitant pour la culture juridique française et Société de législation comparée, Travaux de la semaine internationale de droit, Paris, 1950: L'influence du Code civil dans le monde (1954); F. H. Lawson, The Comparison (Vol. 2 of Selected Essays) 13–15 (1977).

5. The Greek Civil Code of 1946 is one of the outstanding examples of a code based on painstaking comparative research. While its structure largely follows the German pattern, various other sources (including the Swiss and French models) have contributed to shaping the method and the substance of the Greek Code. See P. J. Zepos, Greek Law 72, 77 ff. (1949); id., The Historical and Comparative Back-

Moreover, a given country may follow one example in its civil law, and other examples in its commercial, criminal or procedural law. Turkey, for instance, adopted this eclectic method,[6] and so did many, if not most, Latin-American countries.

Even if a given code of Nation X has been literally copied by Nation Y, the two codes may not in all respects be uniformly interpreted by the courts of both countries.[7] Divergencies in the application of the same text are particularly apt to arise if the two nations are at different stages of cultural, economic and social development.[8]

CHANGE AND GROWTH OF THE LAW IN A CODE SYSTEM

(1) *Revision of Codes.*[1] Most of the codes of the civil-law orbit have proved exceedingly resistant to large-scale revision. The task of rewriting a comprehensive code is so staggering, the number of issues and of affected groups and interests so great, that overall revision often yields to the more pressing daily demands upon the legislators' time. Even violent upheavals, such as war, revolution or political dismemberment of a nation, do not always lead to substantial changes in the text of established codes.[2]

ground of the Greek Civil Code, 3 Inter-American L.Rev. 285 (1961).

6. See supra p. 323.

7. For instances in which the same code provisions were differently interpreted by French and Belgian courts, see Piret, Le Code Napoléon en Belgique de 1804 à 1954, 6 Revue Internationale de Droit Comparé 753 (1954).

Another illuminating example is provided by Art. 1384 of the French Civil Code and its counterpart in the present (not the newly projected) Dutch Code. Art. 1384 deals with the tort liability of the custodian of a thing. From its rather general provisions, the French courts, as will be seen infra, have distilled an elaborate body of rules of quasi-absolute liability in automobile and various other accident cases. Although the wording of the equivalent Dutch provision is the same as that of French Art. 1384, the Dutch courts refused to follow the French case law on the subject, thus in effect compelling the Dutch legislator to seek a statutory solution dealing specifically with tortious liability for automobile accidents. See D. C. Fokkema, J. M. J. Chorus, E. H. Hondius & E. Ch. Lisser, Introduction to Dutch Law for Foreign Lawyers 139–40 (1978).

A further example: The Turkish Civil Code has literally copied the tort liability provisions of the Swiss Civil Code; but these provisions have been differently interpreted by the courts of the two countries. See R. Rodière, Introduction au Droit Comparé 111 (1979), citing an article

by S. Kaneti in 24 Rev.Int.Dr.Comp. 629 (1972).

8. For a striking example—involving an outdated provision of the French Civil Code, which has long been disregarded by the French courts but still has a strong effect upon the legal systems of certain developing nations—see infra p. 651.

For further examples see P. H. Sand, Die Reform des äthiopischen Erbrechts—Problematik einer synthetischen Rezeption, 33 Rabels Z. 413 (1969); K. H. Neumayer, Fremdes Recht aus Büchern, fremde Rechtswirklichkeit und die funktionelle Dimension in den Methoden der Rechtsvergleichung, 34 Rabels Z. 411, 418–19 (1970).

1. This section of the present Note is based in part on Prof. Schlesinger's paper, The Uniform Commercial Code in the Light of Comparative Law, 1 Inter-American L.Rev. 11, 33–35 (1959), where further references can be found.

2. With only minor textual changes (except in the Fourth Book, see supra) the German Civil Code of 1896 has served the Empire, the Weimar Republic, the Nazi Reich, the democratic West German Bundesrepublik, and (until 1975) the communist regime of East Germany. It may be dangerous, however, to draw too general a conclusion from the German experience. The Mexican revolutionary movements which began in 1910, did result—even though somewhat belatedly—in a new Civil Code for the Federal District which went into effect in 1932, and has since been

Two great revision projects were launched in western Europe shortly after the Second World War. They were aimed at the French Civil Code of 1804,[3] and its descendant, the Netherlands Code of 1838. The Netherlands project, on which work has been in progress since 1947, is likely to come to fruition. Several parts of the new Code have been promulgated and put into effect, and the remaining parts are in advanced stages of the drafting and parliamentary process.[4]

In France, the Civil Code Reform Commission has produced valuable scholarly studies, which contribute to our understanding of the technique of code revision and of the basic substantive issues involved in codifying or re-codifying the private law of a modern nation.[5] The Commission also found, and called attention to, a number of specific and particularly disturbing defects in the existing law, and some of these findings led to the enactment of amendments. But the plan of a total revision of the Civil and Commercial Codes was not successful and was abandoned in the 1950's.[6] The idea of Code reform was revived a decade later, though on a more modest scale. By that time, many of France's more pressing problems had been solved and greater governmental support was forthcoming for the project. It did not hurt that a law professor interested in reform, Jean Foyer, became Minister of Justice at about the same period. In addition, the French Constitution of 1958 had made it much easier for the executive branch to obtain the enactment of legislation.[7] Furthermore, portions of the Code, particularly in the family law area, were now even less in tune with changes in societal attitudes and in the economy than had been true during the post-1945 reform attempts. This time, however, the changes were not

adopted, with little or no change, by the majority of the 31 States of the Mexican Union. Italy, also, repealed its old codes, especially its Civil Code of 1865, and enacted a new set of codes around 1940. These latter codes, which after the War were purged of racialism and other Fascist aberrations, are still in force.

3. See Pascal, A Report On the French Civil Code Revision Project, 11 La.L.Rev. 261 (1951); Houin, Reform of the French Civil Code and the Code of Commerce, 4 Am.J.Comp.L. 485 (1955); Julliot de la Morandière (transl. by Dainow), Preliminary Report of the Civil Code Reform Commission of France, 16 La.L.Rev. 1 (1955); id., Report to the Minister of Justice— Second Report of the Civil Code Reform Commission of France, 23 La.L.Rev. 506 (1963).

4. See A. S. Hartkamp, Civil Code Revision in the Netherlands: A Survey of Its System and Contents, and Its Influence on Dutch Legal Practice, 35 La.L.Rev. 1059, 1061-65 (1975); I. Kisch, Structure of the Netherlands Civil Code, in D. C. Fokkema, J. M. J. Chorus, E. H. Hondius & E. Ch. Lisser, Introduction to Dutch Law for Foreign Lawyers 39-41 (1978).

5. See supra n. 3.

6. See R. Houin, The Revision of the French Civil Code, in A. N. Yiannopoulos

(ed.), Civil Law in the Modern World 192, 195 (1965).

7. The 1958 French Constitution, in its article 37, gave the executive autonomous authority to enact, in a wide variety of areas, decrees of an essentially legislative nature. This authority is in no way dependent on a delegation of legislative powers by parliament. To mention but one example, the new Code of Civil Procedure, mentioned supra p. 339, was adopted in that way. For most matters coming within the ambit of the Civil Code, article 34 of the Constitution still requires true legislation, though detailed implementing provisions may be enacted by decrees. However, the 1958 Constitution also provided, in Articles 39-49, for a number of changes in legislative procedure that made passage of bills backed by the executive a much less tedious and uncertain process. It should be noted, also, that this time the final drafting of reform proposals was entrusted to a single draftsman, Dean Carbonnier. The process of Code reform is helpfully discussed in two valuable articles: B. Audit, Recent Revisions of the French Civil Code, 38 La.L.Rev. 747 (1978) and D. Tallon, Reforming the Code in a Civil Law Country, 15 J.Soc.Publ. Teachers of the Law 33 (1980).

to be effectuated all at once, but by groups of Code provisions. Drastic changes were made in the rules concerning the relations of spouses, divorce, adoption, illegitimacy, minority, guardianship, etc., leading to an almost complete revision of book I of the Code dealing with family law. In addition, the provisions on matrimonial property regimes, contained in book III, were also completely changed.[8] Two parts of the code not related to family law received major revisions, the provisions on partnerships (companies-*sociétés*)[9] and those on proof of legal instruments.[10] There were, moreover, numerous changes in individual articles of the Code, often on the occasion of the enactment of a statute dealing with a different but related matter.

One significant recent attempt at civil code revision occurred in Quebec. An Office of Civil Code Revision was created in 1955 to revise what was then officially called the Civil Code of Lower Canada. Prof. Crépeau became the chief draftsman for the project. A draft of a proposed "Civil Code of Quebec" was presented to the Quebec legislature in 1978, but it was decided to submit, for the moment, only book II of the draft, dealing with family law, to parliamentary debate. The provisions of the revised Code concerning that topic were, in fact, enacted in 1980.[11]

Too long a delay in the overall rejuvenation of a code will, of course, generate pressures for piecemeal amendments. One recent example of a limited, "piecemeal" amendment due to a current problem is provided by the 1979 statute that added sections 651a through 651k, dealing with contracts between travellers and tour operators, to the

---

8. See note d on page 532 for references.

9. The French term *société* refers, in its narrow meaning, to partnerships, but may refer to business organizations generally. Thus an expression specifying the type of organization intended will normally be appended to the word *société*. While the Code provisions mentioned in the text deal primarily with partnerships, they do also contain a general part applicable to all forms of business organizations unless the specialized statutes (discussed infra p. 794) governing them provide otherwise. See French Civil Code art. 1834. Under a law adopted in 1985 amending French Civil Code art. 1832, in a few limited instances it is possible to have a *société* having only one member. See also infra p. 831.

10. See supra pp. 431–432. In addition, occasionally articles were added to deal with specific modern problems, such as real estate promotions.

11. L.Q. 1980, ch. 39. The provisions went partially into effect in 1981 and 1982. On Code revision in Quebec, see C. L'Heureux-Dubé, The Quebec Experience: Codification of Family Law and a Proposal for the Creation of a Family Court System, 44 La.L.Rev. 1575 (1984); Mac Donald, Civil Law-Quebec-New Draft Code in Preparation, 58 Can.B.Rev. 185 (1980); P. A. Crépeau, Les lendemains de la réforme du Code Civil, 59 Can.B.Rev. 625 (1981)

The Louisiana Civil Code also was subjected to major, though only partial, revisions beginning in 1976, when its Book II (Property) was revised by 1976 La. Acts 321, 1977 La. Acts 612, 629, 1309, 1978 La. Acts 1900; its provisions on matrimonial property were revised by 1979 La. Acts 1857 and 1886, its provisions on partnerships (Book III, title III) were revised by 1980 La. Acts 346 and the provisions on prescription (Book III, title XXIV) by 1982 La. Acts 518. This was followed by a complete revision of the Code's rules on obligations by 1984 La. Acts 331 (effective January 1, 1985). Interestingly, in the revision of the obligation portion of the Code, many civil-law rules, in addition to those contained in the French Code, were considered, as well as common law rules. Particular attention was given the Code revision efforts in Quebec because of the many similarities in the legal background. See M. S. Herman, Obligations Symposium: Introduction, 32 Loyola L.Rev. 5, 9–10 (1986) and, for a discussion of substantive changes, the balance of the Symposium.

A revision of the family law provisions of the Swiss Civil Code has been approved by the Swiss legislature, eff. January 1, 1988.

German Civil Code.[12]   In many civil law countries, however, the great codes are regarded as national symbols; they are venerable texts, and there is a certain reluctance to tamper with their language.[13]   When particular provisions or omissions of a code, reflecting the views of a past generation, become obnoxious to an influential group, the situation is sometimes remedied by the adoption of auxiliary statutes (see infra). In many instances, also, reform is brought about by decisional law which re-interprets or supersedes out-moded provisions of the code. Thus, there may be important changes and developments outside of the code, with the result that the text of the code no longer reflects the latest state of the law and may mislead the uninitiated.

(2) *Auxiliary Statutes.*   From the tables of contents of typical civilian codes, which are reprinted above, the reader will have gathered that the coverage of such codes is exceedingly broad.   Carrying the civilian concept of codification to its logical extreme, one might imagine a code system in which the civil code and the commercial code (or the civil code alone, if there is no separate commercial code) cover the whole area of substantive private law.   In actuality, however, such all-embracing integration has not been achieved anywhere.   In every civil-law country, there exist so-called auxiliary statutes (*Nebengesetze*), i.e., statutes which, although pertaining to the general subject matter of a code, have been separately enacted and have not been incorporated into the code itself.

Such a statute may antedate the code; the codifiers may have decided for some reason to leave the older enactment intact and not to incorporate its provisions into the code.   The German Law Concerning Damages For Deaths and Personal Injuries Caused in the Operation of Railroads, Mines and Similar Enterprises of June 7, 1871, for example, which imposes on such enterprises a tort liability not dependent on proof of negligence or other culpability, could have been made a part of the last Title ("Delicts", see supra p. 536) of the Second Book, Section VII, of the Civil Code, dealing with tort law; but this was not done, and the Law of 1871, as amended, is still in force as a separate statute.[14]

More frequently, auxiliary statutes come into existence subsequent to codification, in response to new social or technological developments

---

12.   Note that in this case it was relatively easy to fit the change into the organizational scheme of the German Civil Code.   The legislator merely added one more type of contract to the types specifically mentioned in Section VII of Book Two (see pp. 535–536).   Technically, this was done by changing the heading of Title VII to "Contracts for Work and Similar Contracts" and subdividing the Title into (I) Contracts for Work and (II) Travel Contracts.   No changes in other parts of the Code were necessary to accommodate this particular reform.   It is relatively rare that drastic substantive changes can be fitted into the system of a code in such a simple and painless way.   For a good discussion of the way in which this was done in connection with the various changes in the French Civil Code, see B. Audit, supra note 7.

13.   Both in France and in Germany a majority of the provisions of the Civil Code are still in effect in their original form. See J. H. Crabb, The French Civil Code 13 (1977); I. S. Forrester, S. L. Goren & H.-M. Ilgen, The German Civil Code XXV–XXX-VII (1975).   There are, of course, important amendments, some of which are mentioned above or in the footnotes appended to the tables of contents of the two Codes, supra; but if one considers the age of the two Codes (especially the French one), and the intensity of the technological and social changes that have occurred since their enactment, one marvels at the tenacity with which so much of the Codes' orginal language has survived.

14.   Re-enacted in somewhat revised form in 1978, this auxiliary statute is now known under the shortened and simplified title of Haftpflichtgesetz (Liability Law).

not anticipated by the codifiers. This, indeed, is one of the recognized methods by which a codified legal system can deal with changed conditions.[15] Sometimes this can be accomplished, as in the case of the German statute concerning liability for automobile accidents (see infra), without any change in the language of the code, by the enactment of a separate statute creating a new cause of action unknown to the Code. On other occasions, legislators abrogated a segment of a code, and substituted a separate statute for the repealed provisions.[16]

In the area of commercial law, auxiliary statutes are particularly prevalent. By examining the table of contents of the German Commercial Code, for instance, the reader will have found that the Code fails to cover a number of subjects traditionally treated as commercial in the civilian world: e.g., insurance, negotiable instruments, limited responsibility companies,[17] and stock corporations.[18] All of these subjects are treated in separate statutes.[19]

The trend to replace provisions of the Commercial Code with separate statutes has been particularly strong in France, where, as a result of a gradual process of what one might call decodification, most "commercial" matters are now covered by separate statutes. It has been said that, as a result, the French Commercial Code today is not much more than an "empty shell".[20] When the number of "auxiliary" statutes in a field becomes quite substantial, they may become the object of a new code. This has been significant in France, where the extensive legislative powers of the executive facilitate the process.

15. Land reform in developing countries is an example of a social problem usually tackled (if at all) by way of special enactments outside the framework of the traditional codes, which are apt to enshrine the status quo. See J. R. Thome, The Process of Land Reform in Latin America, 1968 Wis.L.Rev. 9. The interaction between the Civil Code and the reform legislation may, however, cause thorny problems in practice. See id. at 20, and K. A. Manaster, The Problem of Urban Squatters in Developing Countries: Peru, 1968 Wis.L.Rev. 23; K. A. Manaster, Squatters and the Law: The Relevance of the United States Experience to Current Problems in Developing Countries, 43 Tul.L.Rev. 94 (1968).

16. As examples, one might mention the German Marriage Law, which was substituted for certain sections of the Civil Code, and the German Corporation Law which replaced a division of the Commercial Code. See text infra. Sometimes, as in the case of the German Testament Law of 1938 (see supra), the auxiliary statute is later reintegrated into the code. Sweeping code revisions (as to which see supra) sometimes are undertaken for the specific purpose, among others, of effecting such reintegration of auxiliary statutes.

17. See infra pp. 829–833.

18. The provisions dealing with stock corporations were eliminated from the Code in 1937, when a separate Corporation Law was enacted. A revised Corporation Law, again separate from the Commercial Code, was adopted in 1965. For an excellent English translation of the 1965 Law, with a helpful introduction, see F. K. Juenger and L. Schmidt, German Stock Corporation Act (1967).

Many of the cases decided under former §§ 178–334 of the Commercial Code (before these sections were replaced, first by the Corporation Law of 1937, and later by the Corporation Law of 1965) are still of importance for the interpretation of identical or similar language in the present Law. The case immediately following these Notes illustrates the point.

19. The Turkish Commercial Code of 1956 (eff. Jan. 1, 1957), while otherwise strongly German-influenced, covers all of these subjects within the four corners of the Code itself. The Turkish Code thus is not only one of the newest, but probably the most integrated of all existing commercial codes.

20. See D. Tallon, supra note 7 at 35. Prof. Tallon titles the section of his article in which he discusses developments concerning the Commercial Code "The Slow Death of the Commercial Code". See ibid. at 34.

Thus, in addition to the basic old codes, one finds in France a Labor Code, a Social Security Code, a General Tax Code, an Insurance Code, a Code of Court Organisation, etc.[21]

It follows that for purposes of research on questions arising under a civil-law system, it is not sufficient to peruse the basic codes. Just as the student of our law must be on the lookout for statutes that may change a common law rule or supplant the common law's silence, the civilian has to search for auxiliary enactments which may have a comparable impact upon the provisions, or the silence, of his codes.[22]

The relationship which in a civil-law country exists between basic codes and auxiliary enactments, may generally be compared with the interaction, familiar to us, of common law and statutes. Quantitatively, the growth of auxiliary enactments in civil-law countries, and of statutory law in most common-law jurisdictions, has been enormous—a fact never to be forgotten by one undertaking research on a concrete point of law. Nevertheless, the basic codes remain to the civilian, as the common law remains to us, the very core of the legal order, containing not only rules but also the general principles which give life and systematic direction to every positive norm, and to which we must turn, in particular, when we are faced with a novel or doubtful case.

(3) *Example: The Code Systems' Shift from the Fault Principle to Risk Allocation in Some Areas of the Law of Torts.* In a code system, as we have seen, four different methods are available to adjust the law to changed conditions: over-all revision of the code; piecemeal amendments; auxiliary statutes; and case law.[1] The choice of one or the other method can have important consequences. This is illustrated by the different responses of the German, French and Dutch code systems to the advent of the age of automobiles and automobile accidents and to products liability.

---

21. See id., at 38–39. These so-called "administrative codifications" in France do, however, differ from the Civil and the other "true" Codes since they represent essentially a compilation of existing statutes in logical and updated fashion, and not a true rethinking of a whole major area of the law. Thus, they bear some resemblance to the individual titles of the United States Code. Furthermore, since in many of the areas covered by these codes the executive may adopt detailed implementing rules by decree, they usually consist of two series of articles, a first series with articles having the prefix L (for legislation), which results from the compilation of statutes, and a second series with the prefix R (for regulation) where the implementing decrees are compiled.

Concerning the "administrative codifications" see also the interesting Circular of the Prime Minister of June 15, 1987, published in 1987 D.L. 230.

22. Study of the codes alone, without regard to the "Nebengesetze", may often lead to incorrect results. This danger is great if a code translation is used, because such translated editions rarely contain adequate references to materials outside the code. In the code countries themselves, most of the better editions of codes, whether annotated or not, contain some Appendix or footnote references calling attention to special statutes which affect the operation of code provisions.

1. In a civil-law country, where in theory only the written law is recognized as "law", the phenomenon of case law raises special problems, which will be taken up infra at pp. 597–657. At this point, the reader should assume (subject to the more thorough later discussion of the point) that to varying degrees the civil-law systems in practice have developed certain bodies of case law, not only in the area of public law (where case law tends to predominate), but also in some fields of their (generally codified) private law.

I. Automobile Accidents

(a) *Germany:* The German Civil Code devotes only two sections to the general principles of tort liability:

Section 823

(1) A person who, intentionally or negligently, by an unlawful act injures the life, body, health, freedom, property or some other right of another, is bound to compensate the latter for any damage arising from such injury.

(2) The same obligation is imposed upon one who violates a statute intended to protect another person [i.e., the plaintiff]. If under its terms such statute can be violated even by one acting without fault, the duty to make compensation [nevertheless] arises only in the event of fault [on the part of the defendant].[1a]

Section 826

One who intentionally damages another in a manner which violates the commands of morality is bound to compensate the other for any damage thus caused.

As applied to automobile accidents, § 823 clearly makes the defendant's liability dependent on proof of negligence, while § 826 does not cover such cases at all. In 1896, when the Code was promulgated, the automobile was still a *rara avis*, and the draftsmen of the above provisions surely did not anticipate the social and legal problems arising from widespread use of the automobile and the resultant slaughter on the highways. But within a decade after the date (January 1, 1900) when the Code went into effect, the frequency of motor vehicle accidents in Germany increased quite dramatically, and it became apparent that the above Code provisions, embodying the fault principle, were not adequate to deal with the new problem.[1b]

In a relatively quick response to that new problem, the German legislature enacted an auxiliary statute dealing with liability for motor vehicle accidents.[2] The statute makes *the driver* liable for deaths, personal injuries and property damage unless he proves that he was not at fault.[2a] At the same time, the statute imposes

---

1a. Another provision of the Code (§ 276) makes it clear that there can be no "fault" unless the defendant's act is either intentional or negligent.

For a general comparative discussion of the development of tort law, beginning with the Roman period, see F. H. Lawson and B. S. Markesinis, Tortious Liability for Unintentional Harm in the Common Law and the Civil Law (1982) (2 vols; vol. 1 text, vol. 2 sources).

1b. Unlike their American confrères, the civilians cannot rely on juries to correct hardships and inequities created by legal rules. In a civil-law country, therefore, it is often more clearly apparent than

under our system that the rules themselves must be changed if they have become inadequate in the light of new social or technological developments.

2. Motor Vehicle Traffic Act of 1909 (re-enacted in 1952 under the title of Road Traffic Act), as amended.

In 1922, a similar auxiliary statute extended the principle of liability without proof of negligence to the operation of aircraft. See Air Traffic Law of 1922 (re-enacted in 1968).

2a. The same technique (of changing the burden of proof so that the defendant has to prove absence of fault on his part) is

an even more stringent liability upon the so-called "*Halter*", i.e., the person (usually the owner) who at the time of the accident was entitled to the use and control of the vehicle.[3] The latter can avoid liability only if he proves that the injury or damage was due to an unavoidable event which was not connected with any defect in the condition of the vehicle or a failure of its mechanical parts. This heavy burden of proof can be met by the "Halter" only in exceptional cases, e.g., when he can show that the accident was caused *exclusively* by the victim,[4] by a third party or by an animal, and that both "Halter" and driver used every reasonably possible precaution to avoid the accident.

Where the vehicle has been used without the "Halter's" consent, e.g. by a thief, the statute provides that in principle the "Halter" is not liable, unless by failure to remove the ignition key or by similar negligence he facilitated the unauthorized use of the car. There is, however, an important exception to this principle of non-liability for unauthorized trips. Pursuant to a 1939 amendment of the statute, the "Halter" is responsible for every accident caused by an employee to whom he has entrusted the custody of the vehicle. This responsibility exists even though the particular trip, in the course of which the accident occurred, was totally unauthorized and not within the scope of employment (e.g., a drunken joyride of the employee and his girlfriend).

Liability *under the statute* is restricted to compensation for pecuniary losses, such as medical expenses and lost earnings; the statute does not authorize any recovery for pain and suffering. Liability *under the statute*, moreover, is limited in amount. The aggregate of claims arising from deaths and personal injuries caused by a single accident may not exceed a statutory maximum.[4a] The amount of that maximum, which has been raised repeatedly since the original enactment of the statute, now stands at DM 500,000 if there is only a single victim, and at DM 750,000 if there are several victims of the same accident.[4b]

It should be kept in mind, however, that the statute does not preclude the victim from pursuing a cause of action *under the general tort provisions of the Civil Code*, pursuant to which an unlimited amount of damages, including an adequate compensation for pain and suffering, can be recovered if the plaintiff proves that his injury (or the death of his provider) was caused by the negli-

---

used even more broadly in modern Soviet law. See W. Gray, Soviet Tort Law: The New Principles Annotated, 1964 U.Ill.L.F. 180, 183–86.

"comparative causation" principle (somewhat similar to our comparative negligence statutes) embodied in § 254 of the German Civil Code.

3. As a practical matter, every person "to whose house or business the car belongs", is apt to be treated as a "Halter". See 1 E. J. Cohn, Manual of German Law 165 (2d ed. 1968).

4a. It is interesting to note that the original German statute embodying this scheme was enacted in 1909, more than 50 years before the idea of no-fault liability was born (or reborn) in the United States.

4. In cases where the victim's negligence is a contributing but not the exclusive cause of the accident, the amount of his recovery may be reduced, under the

4b. The maximum amounts mentioned in the text are those for death and personal injury claims. The maximum amount for property damage is considerably lower.

gence of the defendant or of a person for whose fault the defendant is liable under the Code's general principles of vicarious liability.[5]

Where the victim is a passenger who gratuitously was given a ride in the vehicle, the liability provisions of the 1909 statute do not apply at all. Such a victim thus can recover solely on the basis of the Civil Code, i.e. only if he can prove negligence.[6]

By way of additional auxiliary enactments—again outside of the Civil Code—Germany has adopted a system of compulsory liability insurance and a direct action statute.[7]

(contrast Germany w/ France)

(b) *France.* The tort provisions of the French Civil Code are even less detailed than their German counterparts. The basic principles of tort liability are covered in the following articles of the French Code:

| Art. 1382 |

Foundation for tort liability under French civil code

Every act of a person which causes damage to another obliges the person through whose fault the damage occurred to repair it.

(negligence, not strict liability)

Art. 1383

Everyone is responsible for the damage which he has caused not only by his own act, but also by his negligence or lack of prudence.

5. Sec. 831, a much-criticized provision of the German Civil Code, in many cases makes it possible for the principal to escape liability for his agent's tort by proving that he (the principal) exercised due diligence in selecting and supervising the agent. This unfortunate provision, found among the tort sections of the Code, weakens the principle of respondeat superior in German law (unless plaintiff can bring his case under the 1909 statute, holding the defendant liable as "Halter" rather than as employer). With respect to automobile accidents, however, the German courts have mitigated this defect of the Code by requiring proof of a high degree of diligence in selecting and supervising any employee entrusted with the operation of a potentially murderous machine such as an automobile. See Palandt, Bürgerliches Gestzbuch, § 831, Anno. 6A (45th ed., 1986).

6. For a more extensive discussion of the German scheme, based on a typical case, see Comment, Tort Liability for Negligent Operation of a Motor Vehicle in Germany and the United States, 1960 Duke L.J. 579. Another very helpful description of the German scheme can be found in the report by W. Pfennigstorf which appears in U.S. Department of Transportation (Automobile Insurance and Compensation Study), Comparative Studies in Automobile Accident Compensation 33

(1970). For a discussion of the whole series of German auxiliary statutes providing for strict liability in certain situations, see M. Will, Quellen erhoehter Gefahr 2–39 (1980).

7. See Pflichtversicherungsgesetz (Compulsory Insurance Law) of 1939, as re-enacted in 1965. The direct action provision appears in § 3 of that Law.

Subsequently, compulsory insurance for automobile accidents became mandatory in all countries which are members of the European Economic Community. This was effectuated by the Council Directive of April 24, 1972, 1972 O.J. No. L 103, p. 1, amended by Council Directives of December 19, 1972, 1972 O.J. No. L 291, p. 162 and December 30, 1983, 1984 O.J. No. L 8, p. 17. The 1983 Directive also required the establishment of a scheme for uninsured motorist coverage. Under a system partly based on these Directives and partly on a Convention sponsored by the Council of Europe, an accident victim can obtain compensation from a central agency in the State where the accident occurred, even if the accident was caused by a car registered and insured elsewhere. For a case showing the working of this scheme, see, e.g., Bureau Central Français v. Fonds de Garantie Automobile, Case No. 64/83, February 9, 1984, 1984 E.C.R. 689.

Art. 1384

Everyone is responsible not only for the damage caused by his own acts, but also for damage caused by the acts of persons for whom he must answer or by [objects in his custody. . . .

These basic provisions are followed by a few additional ones, dealing with vicarious liability (especially for acts of children, employees and pupils) and with liability for damage caused by animals or by disintegrating buildings.

For many decades after the advent of the automobile as a popular means of transportation, the French legislature, unlike its German counterpart, did not enact an auxiliary statute dealing with liability for automobile accidents. Victims of such accidents thus had to seek relief on the sole basis of the above Code provisions. Under articles 1382 and 1383, the victim clearly cannot recover except by showing some negligence on the part of the defendant or (under a provision of Article 1384 not reproduced here), the defendant's employer. Nor did the first paragraph of Article 1384 initially promise much help. During most of the 19th century, it had been thought that it served merely as a kind of catchline for the more specific rules on liability that follow. In 1896, however, the Cour de Cassation held, in a case involving an employee killed by the explosion of a boiler, that the employer, who was in control of the boiler, was liable on the basis of the first paragraph of article 1384 in the absence of any showing that the accident was due to an act of God or some outside force. The employer could not defend by showing that the explosion was due to the fault of the manufacturer or the hidden nature of the defect which caused it.[8] The case, which seemed to create a presumption of liability if an object under the control of the defendant caused some harm, was not, at first, useful to victims of automobile accidents, however, since it implied liability by the person in control of an object only in instances in which something inherent in the object had caused the harm, while most automobile accidents were the result of human action or inaction. But in 1930, in *Jand'heur*, one of the most famous cases decided by it, the Cour de Cassation, sitting *en banc*, ruled that it was immaterial, for the purpose of applying the presumption of liability provided in the first paragraph of article 1384, that the object causing the harm was directly controlled by a human being. The owner of a truck that had hit the plaintiff while being operated by the owner's servant could thus be held liable to the plaintiff without any showing of fault.[9] An exception existed only if the accident was the sole fault of the victim, or the result of an act of God, or of some unforeseeable external force. This produced a fairly satisfactory solution to the problem of compensation for automobile and, indeed, many other accidents, since the quasi-strict liability imposed by article 1384(1) was applied in all instances in which a person had control (*la garde*) over the object which caused the harm.[10] The automobile accident victim's position was further

---

8. Guissez v. Teffaine, Cass. civ., June 16, 1896, 1897 D.I. 433.

9. Jand'heur v. Les Galeries Belfortaises, Cass. ch. réunies, February 13, 1930, 1930 D.I. 37.

10. See the report by A. Tunc on the French Auto Accident Compensation System, in U.S. Department of Transportation, supra n. 6.

enhanced by the existence of an uninsured motorist fund since 1952, and compulsory automobile liability insurance a few years later, which was rendered even more effective by the right to sue the insurer directly.[11] However, the Cour de Cassation was never able to make up its mind on the point whether article 1384(1) was essentially but a kind of presumption of negligence and thus remained within the ambit of the fault principle enunciated by articles 1382 and 1383, or whether it imposed strict liability. In borderline situations its case-law thus wavered somewhat.[12] It was definitely influenced by the fault principle in its long-continued holding that the contributory (partial) fault of the victim reduced the victim's recovery proportionately, in line with the rule prevailing in cases based on article 1382.[13]

[handwritten margin note: perhaps, not pure strict liability]

Expressing dissatisfaction with this situation, Prof. Tunc urged, some twenty years ago, the adoption of a no-fault type statute for automobile accidents.[14] His proposals encountered strong opposition from the organized Bar even when, after the electoral victory of the socialist party in 1981, the idea found favor with the then Minister of Justice, Mr. Badinter, who appointed a high-level commission to report on it.[15] However, in 1982, in a decision usually referred to as the *Desmares* case, the second civil panel of the Cour de Cassation reversed its case-law on the effect of the contributory fault of the accident victim. It ruled that the victim's fault could not reduce damages although, in line with previous decisions, the victim was entitled to no compensation if his fault was the *sole* cause of the accident.[16] The case led to an enormous amount of comment.[17] Many lower courts disliked it and continued to apply the principle of a reduction of damages in cases

[handwritten margin note: No comparative negligence]

---

11. The applicable provisions are now principally contained in Code des Assurances arts. L 124–3 (claim of victim against insurer), 211–1 (compulsory insurance) and 420–1 (uninsured motorists). The family of the driver, formerly not covered by this insurance, has been included since an amendment of art. 211–1 adopted in 1981. The provisions are in conformity with the European Community Directives mentioned supra n. 7.

12. This led to over 2000 tort cases being brought to the Cour de Cassation for review annually. See R. Rodière, note to Cozette v. Régnier, Cass. civ. 2d., April 23, 1971, 1972 D.J. 613. Professor Rodière stated that the Cour de Cassation performed a kind of high-wire act when applying art. 1384; it was being pulled in one direction by the fault principle and in the other by strict liability. Thus, it held until 1969 that gratuitous guests were not covered by art. 1384, but reversed itself at that time. Y. Lambert-Faivre, Le transport bénévole, 1969 D.Chr. 91.

13. For a general discussion of the French system of liability based on article 1384, see e.g. 2 J. Flour & J.-L. Aubert, Les Obligations 263; Walton & Amos, Introduction to French Law 205–06, 233–37 (3d

ed. by F. H. Lawson, A. E. Anton & L. N. Brown 1967).

14. E.g. A. Tunc, La sécurité routière (1965); A. Tunc, Traffic Accident Compensation in France: The Present Law and a Controversial Proposal, 73 Harv.L.Rev. 1409 (1966); A. Tunc, Accidents de la circulation, faute ou risque, 1982 D.Chr. 103, translated as A. Tunc, Traffic Accidents, Fault or Risk, 15 Seton Hall L.Rev. 831 (1985); A. Tunc, The French Law of Traffic Victim Compensation: The Present and the Possible, 31 Am.J.Comp.L. 489 (1983).

15. The Commission was presided over by Mr. Bellet, a retired presiding judge of the Cour de Cassation and, subsequently, one of the neutral members of the U.S.-Iran claims tribunal at the Hague.

16. La mutualité industrielle v. Epoux Charles, Cass. civ. 2d, July 21, 1982, 1982 D.J. 449, (reprinted with the submissions of *avocat général* Charbonnier and a note by Prof. Ch. Larroumet). *Desmares* was the name of the owner of the vehicle involved in the accident.

17. E.g. G. Viney, L'indemnisation des victimes de dommages causés par le "fait d'une chose" après l'arrêt de la Cour de cassation (2e Ch. civ.) du 21 juillet 1982,

New statute?
Strict liability?

of contributory negligence on the part of the victim. Though the
Desmares case was not limited to automobile accidents, the resulting legal uncertainty was felt most severely in the event of such
accidents and gave new impetus to the proposals for the enactment
of legislation,[18] which was finally adopted in July, 1985.[19] Unlike
the German Road Traffic Act [20], the French statute does not establish an alternative form of liability, in addition to that provided in
the civil code; nor does it limit the amount of damages, though
such limitations were contained in the earlier proposals mentioned.
It retains the liability based on article 1384(1) but eliminates most
defenses available under the former case-law. In particular, victims of motor vehicle accidents, other than drivers, may recover for
personal injuries even if the accident was due to an act of God or of
a third party, or the fault of the victim, unless the fault of the
victim was the sole cause of the accident. Even that exclusion is
inapplicable to minors under 16 years, the aged over 70 years and
the severely handicapped. The fault of the driver reduces the
driver's recovery, or excludes it (if the sole cause of the accident),
but drivers too can recover from the person "in control" of a
vehicle if the accident was caused by an act of God or the act of a
third party. Persons who have brought harm upon themselves
intentionally are excluded from recovery.[21] At the same time the
rules on compulsory insurance were amended to require that motor
vehicle liability insurance cover also the liability of persons whose
control of the vehicle was not authorized. When no other insurance is applicable, coverage must be provided by the uninsured

---

1982 D.Chr. 201; Y. Lambert-Faivre, Aspects juridiques, moraux et économiques de
l'indemnisation des victimes fautives, 1982
D.Chr. 207; J.-L. Aubert, l'arrêt Desmares,
une provocation à quelles réformes? 1983
D.Chr. 1.

18. Thus, following the *Desmares* case,
the intermediate appellate court in Rennes
permitted full recovery for victims even
when they were substantially at fault
themselves, while, not too far away, the
appellate court at Angers continued to reduce damages in the event of the victim's
fault. Ch. Larher-Loyer, Le sort des victimes d'accidents de la circulation après la
loi du 5 juillet 1985, 1986 D.Chr. 205. For
a discussion of these developments, see G.
Viney, Vers la Construction d'un Droit
Européen de la Responsabilité Civile 7–13
(Vorträge, Reden und Berichte aus dem
Europa-Institut der Universität des Saar-
landes No. 59, 1986).

19. Law No. 85–677 of July 5, 1985 concerning the improvement of the condition
of traffic accident victims and the speeding
up of the procedures for their indemnification, J.O. July 6, 1985, p. 7584, 1985 D.L.
371.

20. Supra, n. 2.

21. Law No. 85–677, supra note 19,
arts. 1–6. The new law also appears to

resolve another problem which arose formerly under article 1384(1), namely whether the article could be used when the object
under the "control" of the defendant
played a purely passive role in the accident, as when the operator of a motorcycle,
who had made a turn too rapidly, was
precipitated against a lawfully parked automobile. Under article 1 of the new law,
liability is to be imposed whenever a motor
vehicle is "implicated" in an accident.
This would not seem to require an "active"
role of the object. While the language
cited does not explicitly mandate the construction advanced here, that construction
appears in line with legislative history and
has been adopted by the cases so far applying the provision. Ch. Larher-Loyer, supra
note 18 at 206–07.

The opinion, mentioned in the text, that
the new law is merely ancillary to the
existing rules which it simply modifies, but
that it has not created an independent
basis of liability, is not universally shared.
For an argument in favor of the view that
the new law establishes a new and independent liability (a minority position), see
G. Wiederkehr, De la loi du 5 juillet 1985
et de son caractére autonome, 1986 D.Chr.
255.

motorist fund.[22] The liability insurer of the vehicle implicated in the accident must offer to settle claims made by victims no later than eight months after the accident. If the offer of settlement is not timely, interest is payable at double the legal rate. In the event litigation ensues, the judge may impose a penalty on the insurance company, payable into the uninsured motorist fund, and award additional damages and interest to the plaintiff, if he finds that the settlement offered was "manifestly insufficient".[23] In line with previous French practice, victims cannot recover for medical expenses which have, in fact, been paid by a health insurance organization under the French laws on social security, nor for wages which their employers have paid during their absence from work. But these organizations and employers have subrogation rights.[24] Interestingly, the new law also contains a provision applicable to all tort cases: it amends the Civil Code by establishing, for tort cases generally, a limitation period of ten years from the time of the "manifestation" of the harm.[25] The new law has been criticized as inconsistent because it has not completely adopted no-fault principles, while at the same time not fully maintaining a system based on fault.[26] It is too early to predict what the practical effects of the new law will be. In any event, while it may have solved some of the problems which had arisen under the previous rules, it has created a number of doubts and uncertainties of its own.[27]

22. Law No. 85–677, supra note 19, arts. 7–11.

23. Law No. 85–667, supra note 19, arts. 12–27.

24. Law No. 85–677, supra note 19, arts. 28–34. At times, insurers governed by the social security laws may also have a direct claim (not based on subrogation) against persons having caused injuries to their insured. Association générale des institutions de retraite des cadres v. Cie Le Lloyd Continental, Cass. ass. plén., May 23, 1986, 1986 D.J. 341.

25. Code Civil art. 2270–1, as added by Law No. 85–677, supra note 19. The previous limitation period, applicable to most tort and contract actions, was 30 years. Code Civil art. 2262. It remains in effect in non-tort cases.

26. There have been numerous comments on the new law, e.g. Ph. Bihr, La grande illusion, 1985 D.Chr. 63; Ch. Larroumet, L'indemnisation des victimes d'accidents de la circulation: amalgame de la responsabilité civile et de l'indemnisation automatique, 1985 D.Chr. 237; G. Viney, supra note 18.

27. For instance, it is now necessary to define who is a "driver", not a legal issue until the new law came into effect. For an assessment of the new law in the light of the relatively numerous cases decided so far (article 46 of the law gave it retroactive application to pending suits and claims less

than three years old not yet presented to a court at the time of its adoption), see G. Viney, Réflexions après quelques mois d'application des articles 1er à 6 de la loi du 5 juillet 1985 modifiant le droit à indemnisation des victimes d'accidents de la circulation, 1986 D.Chr. 209.

Article 1054(1) of the Civil Code of Lower Canada (Quebec) is almost identical to art. 1384 of the French Civil Code, and it received an interpretation that was somewhat similar. See G. Castel, The Civil Law System of the Province of Quebec 448–76 (1962). Nevertheless, in 1961, Quebec adopted a statute providing for strict liability in automobile accident cases, but without a limitation of damages. S.Q. 1960–61, c. 65. That system was eventually abandoned in favor of a scheme under which automobile accident victims receive their compensation directly from an official insurance agency (*Régie*). Quebec Automobile Insurance Act, Quebec Revised Statutes 1977, ch. A–25 (effective 1978).

On the interpretation of the Louisiana Civil Code tort rules, which are rather similar to the French rules, see Simon v. Ford Motor Co., 282 So.2d 126 (La. 1973) and W. Malone, Ruminations on Liability for the Act of Things, 42 La.L.Rev. 979 (1982). For recent attempts to square common-law notions of liability with Code provisions, see Bell v. Jet Wheel Blast, 462 So.2d 166 (La. 1985); Halphen v. Johns Manville Sales Corp., 484 So.2d 110 (La. 1986). Cf.

(c) *The Netherlands.* As has been mentioned before, the language of Art. 1403 of the Dutch Civil Code is a replica of Art. 1384 of the French Code. But the Dutch courts refused to follow the interpretation which the French courts since 1930 have placed on Art. 1384. In The Netherlands, therefore, the fault principle would have continued to control the treatment of automobile accident cases if the legislator had not intervened. In 1935, however, the legislator did intervene by enacting special liability provisions which are incorporated into the Road Traffic Act. Not surprisingly, these provisions are substantially similar to those of the German statute,[28] but with one notable exception: Under the terms of the Dutch statute, the recovery of a plaintiff who has suffered personal injury is not limited to a maximum amount, even though his action is based on the Road Traffic Act rather than the general tort provisions of the Civil Code.[29] The Dutch Road Traffic Act sets an artificial monetary limit only for the recovery of property damage.[30]

Upon enactment of the relevant portion of the proposed new Civil Code (see supra p. 548), all provisions dealing with liability for motor vehicle accidents possibly will be re-integrated into the Code, with the result that the Code itself in terms will provide for a considerable measure of liability not based on fault.[31]

II.   Products Liability

Under German law, an injured consumer having no direct link with the manufacturer can sue the latter only in tort, that is, on the basis of § 823 of the Civil Code, which clearly requires fault. Some younger German scholars who had become familiar with American notions of products liability during stays in the United States, appear to have been particularly active in pointing out how unsatisfactory it was to adhere to the fault principle in this type of situation. [32] This time, however, change came from the courts, not through a special statute.[33] In the famous "Chicken Pest" case [34], the *Bundesgerichtshof* held that once the plaintiff has proved that the defect which caused the damage arose within the manufacturer's sphere of interest,

A. Tunc, Louisiana Tort Law at the Crossroads, 48 Tul.L.Rev. 1111 (1974).

28. See D. C. Fokkema, J. M. J. Chorus, E. H. Hondius & E. Ch. Lisser, Introduction to Dutch Law for Foreign Lawyers 139–40 (1978); W. Pfennigstorf, Compensation of Auto Accident Victims in Europe 69–70 (1972).

Like its German model, the Dutch statute cannot be invoked by a non-paying passenger who was injured while riding in defendant's car. Such a passenger, therefore, can recover from that defendant only on the basis of the general tort provisions of the Civil Code, i.e., upon proof of negligence.

29. See Pfennigstorf, supra n. 28.

30. The limit is the value of defendant's car, with a modest minimum fixed by law.

31. See Pfennigstorf, supra n. 28.

32. M. Will, Asides on the Nonharmonization of Products Liability Laws in Europe, in P. Herzog (ed.), Harmonization of Laws in the European Communities 28–29 (1983).

33. See W. Lorenz, Some Comparative Aspects of the European Unification of the Law of Products Liability, 60 Cornell L.Rev. 1005, 1011–12 (1975).

34. Decision of November 26, 1968, 51 BGHZ 91; 22 N.J.W. 269 (1969). Interestingly, in a part of the opinion not translated here, the court uses the expression "strict liability" *in English*—some indication of American influence on the development of German products liability law.

"then the manufacturer is closer to the facts and he must clarify them. . . . He knows the circumstances of production, he determines and organizes the manufacturing process and the inspections when the finished products are delivered. The size of the plant, complexities in the organization caused by division of labor, and complicated technical, chemical or biological processes often render it impossible for the victim to find the cause of the defect which resulted in damage. [Note that this point is of particular significance in a country such as Germany where discovery devices are weak.] He is therefore not able to explain the facts to the court in such a way that a court can judge whether the management should be blamed for an omission. . . . [Consequently,] if somebody uses an industrial product in accordance with the expected use and suffers damage with respect to one of the interests specified in § 823 par. 1,. . . . it is for the manufacturer to elucidate the events which caused the defect in the goods and to prove that they did not involve fault on his part."

The case thus reversed the burden of proof and required the manufacturer to show he was *not* at fault. Subsequent cases show that this burden is difficult to carry. While liability is still formally based on fault, it comes close to strict liability.[35]

In France, too, a form of strict liability has been developed in products liability cases without amendment of pertinent Code provisions; this result has been based in part on art. 1641 of the French Civil Code, under which, in any sale, there is an implied warranty against hidden defects. Not only the original purchaser, but any subsequent owner may rely on that provision.[36] Under art. 1645 of the Code, the vendor is liable for any harm caused if he was aware of the defects; but art. 1646 requires only return of purchase price and repayment of expenses caused by the sale if the seller was not aware of the defect. This might have eliminated consequential damages, but the French courts eventually came to hold that a seller in the business of selling goods of the kind involved in the case *must* know all defects and hence is always liable for consequential damages. Of course, the plaintiff must show that

35. W. Lorenz, supra n. 33. See also H.-V. von Hülsen, Products Liability in 3 B. Rüster (ed.), Business Transactions in Germany (FRG), ch. 38 (with further references on German and comparative aspects of products liability); cf. G. Brueggemeier, Perspectives on the Law of "Contorts": A Discussion of the Dominant Trends in West German Tort Law, 6 Hastings Int. & Comp. L.Rev. 221 (1983). For further examples, see also Palandt, Bürgerliches Gesetzbuch, § 823, Anno. 16 (45th ed. 1986).

Additionally, liability may be based on the violation of a protective statute, for instance requiring manufacturers to produce only safe machinery for use at work. The Drug Law (*Arzneimittelgesetz*) of August 24, 1976, 1976 BGBl 2445, amended by a law of February 24, 1983, 1983 BGBl 169, imposes, in its section 84, strict liability on

the manufacturers of drugs. Liability is limited to an amount of 500000 German Marks per person, with total liability arising out of incidents concerning the same drug limited to 200 Million Marks.

Japanese courts, operating under a Code provision akin to § 823 of the German Civil Code, similarly have shifted the burden of proof. D. F. Henderson, Japanese Regulation of Recombinant DNA Activities, 12 U. of Toledo L.Rev. 891, 899 (1981). For a brief comparative discussion of products liability law, see also Mr. Justice Marshall's opinion in Piper Aircraft Co. v. Reyno, 424 U.S. 235 at 252 n. 19 (1981).

36. See B. S. Markesinis, The Not so Dissimilar Tort and Delict, 93 L.Q.Rev. 78 (1977).

[handwritten margin note: production costs higher in strict liability states, lower in proof of fault states.]

the defect was in the product at the time it left the defendant's premises. If the person harmed due to a defective product is neither a direct nor a remote purchaser, the warranty for hidden defects may not be used as a basis for liability. Instead, liability must then be predicated on the fault-based art. 1382. However, the courts have consistently held that a manufacturer is under a duty to know the problems inherent in his products and is consequently at fault if he puts a defective product on the market. There is thus not much difference in result, regardless of whether liability is based on article 1641 or on Article 1382. Because of the requirement of control, article 1384 has been used relatively rarely in products liability cases, except when it could be said that control had been retained by the manufacturer to some extent.[37]

[handwritten margin note: integrated market, unified product law]

In other European countries, products liability law is less favorable to the consumer. In Italy, for instance, there is a Code provision reversing the burden of proof in the event of harm caused by dangerous activities;[38] but, in spite of some scholarly opinion favoring its use in products liability cases, it has generally not been applied in that context.[39] Fault is the basis for liability in a number of other countries as well. Variations in European law are thus substantial.[40] Feeling that this state of affairs impeded the free flow of goods across national borders and distorted conditions of competition by giving manufacturers in low-liability countries an unfair advantage, the Commission of the European Communities proposed a Directive in 1976 for the harmonization of product liability law among the Member States.[41] The original proposal provided for strict liability for personal and property damage, subject to certain maximum limitations. Even harm not foresee-

[handwritten margin note: Now in effect]

---

37. There is, however, a difference between articles 1382 and 1641 as far as limitation periods are concerned: under art. 1648, liability based on art. 1641 must be asserted within a reasonably short period of time after discovery of the defect (under case law not more than two years); for actions under article 1382 the normal tort limitation period, now ten years, applies. Any warranty given by the manufacturer must state that the implied warranty against hidden defects remains in full effect. Decree No. 78 464 of March 24, 1978, art. 4. In the more recent cases, defects in design, defective packaging, etc., when leading to harm, have usually been treated in a way similar to hidden defects. For discussions of the French law of products liability, see B. Herzog, The French Law of Products Liability, A Creature of the Courts, in P. Herzog (ed.), Harmonization of Laws in the European Communities 3 (1983); Ph. Malinvaud, Redhibitory Defects and Their Importance in Contemporary Society, 50 Tulane L.Rev. 517 (1976); F. Orban, Product Liability, a Comparative Legal Restatement-Foreign National Law and the EEC Directive, 8 Ga.J. Int'l & Comp.L. 342, 346–50 (1978). In French see, C. Gavalda (ed.), La Responsibilité des fabricants et distributeurs (1975) and, for the most recent developments, the note by G. Huet appended to Union des Assurances de Paris c. Dame Duvelle, 1985 D.J. 485, and Viney, Vers la Construction d'un Droit Européen de la responsabilité Civile—Les Apports du Droit Français 19–31 (1986).

38. Italian Civil Code art. 2050.

39. M. Will, supra n. 6, at 189.

40. The draft of the new Netherlands Civil Code would reverse the burden of proof, and this seems to have had some influence on current cases. For comparative discussions of products liability see H. Duintjer Tebbens, International Products Liability (1980); Association Européenne d'Etudes Juridiques et Fiscales, Product Liability in Europe (1975); W. C. Tower, the Issue of Product Liability in American and European Law, 1 Comp.L. Yearbook 35 (1977–78), F. F. Stone, Liability for Damage caused by Things, in Vol. XI, Ch. 5 of the International Encyclopedia of Comparative Law 72–80 (1970). See also the works cited supra ns. 32–39.

41. For the original proposal, see 1976 O.J. No. C 241, p. 9; 1976 E.C.Bull.Supp. No. 11.

able by the manufacturer at the time of manufacture (called by the Europeans the manufacturer's "development risk") would have been included. The proposal produced extensive comments [42]; its provision for limitations on liability led to objections from consumer groups, the inclusion of "development risks" to objections by industry. Craftsmen and farmers wished to be completely excluded.[43] The Directive, when finally enacted, maintained the principle of strict liability for product defects causing personal injury, or death, or property damage to non-commercially used property. It puts the burden on the manufacturer to show that the defect which caused the harm occurred after the product had left his premises. Non-commercial sales are not covered, nor are sales of unprocessed agricultural goods. The Directive does not mandate liability for "development risks", but the Member States may impose such liability. It does not contain a maximum limit of recovery for individual plaintiffs, nor any global limitation; but Member States are authorized to impose a global limitation of 70 Million European Currency Units (ECU) for personal injuries and death due to the same defect in the same kind of product. Property damage (to the extent covered at all) is compensable only if it exceeds 500 ECU. Suits must be brought within three years of discovery of harm and cause, subject to a ten year statute of repose.[44] The Directive must be implemented by national legislation by July 30, 1988. By that time, appropriate modifications in all of the national products liability rules mentioned above will have to be made. However, national rules concerning matters not covered by the Directive remain in effect. The Council of Europe has proposed a European Convention on Products Liability containing somewhat similar terms.[45] Its wide ratification would lead to—at least partial—harmonization of product liability law in Europe beyond the boundaries of the European Economic Community.

(d) *Some Comparative Questions and Observations.* (aa) Does the information set forth above lead to any conclusions concerning the relative merits of code revision, auxiliary statutes and case law as vehicles of reform? [45a]

42. For a listing of many of the relevant writings, see 3 H. Smit & P. Herzog, The Law of the European Economic Community, Preliminary Observations on Articles 100–102, No. 8(VII).

43. Some of these criticisms are reflected in the opinions of the Community's Economic and Social Committee, 1979 O.J. No. C 114, p. 15, and of the European Parliament, 1979 O.J. No. C 127, p. 61, and were partially reflected in an amended proposal by the Commission at 1979 O.J. No. C 271, p. 3, which did not, however, eliminate the liability for "development risks."

44. For the text of the Directive see 1985 O.J. No. L 210, p. 29. See also J. R. Maddox, Products Liability Law in Europe: Towards a Régime of Strict Liability, 19 J. World Tr.L. 508 (1985); K. M. Nilles, Defining the Limits of Liability: A Legal and Political Analysis of the European Community Products Liability Directive, 25 Va J.

Int'l L. 729 (1985); H. C. Taschner, Die künftige Produzentenhaftung in Deutschland, 39 N.J.W. 611 (1986). The European Currency Unit mentioned in the text is a composite of the currencies of the Member States of the European Communities. Its value tends to fluctuate between $0.75 and $1.35.

45. Opened for signature, January 27, 1977, 1977 Europ.T.S. No. 91, 16 I.L.M. 7 (1977). See B. Hanotiau, The Council of Europe Convention on Products Liability, 8 Ga.J.Int. & Comp.L. 325 (1978); A. C. Evans, Council of Europe: Consumer Protection Initiatives, 14 J. World Tr.L. 454 (1980).

45a. As demonstrated by the above materials, it is clear that in many countries, especially those belonging to the European Economic Community, measures of law reform today are sometimes sparked by supra-national agreements and institu-

(i) The reader will have noticed that in some respects the French case law regarding the "custodian's" presumptive liability for motor vehicle accidents is strikingly similar to the rules laid down in the German auxiliary statute.[46] But the French courts, which until 1985 lacked the aid of the legislator, did not adopt (and clearly were unable to adopt by decisional law) the most refined feature of the German solution: unlimited recovery of all damages from the defendant when negligence can be proven; and amount-limitation as well as restriction to pecuniary damages in those cases in which the judgment against the defendant is based exclusively on the more modern doctrine of quasi-absolute liability for the risks created by the operation of the vehicle.

Similarly, given the broad language of article 1384, the French courts could hardly have developed a special system of quasi-strict liability for motor vehicles only, excluding other accidents due to arguably less dangerous objects. Being based on a broadly-worded Code provision referring to "things" generally, rather than on a special statute, the judge-made rule of quasi-strict liability logically had to be applied to all things, of whatever nature, in defendant's custody. The German auxiliary statute, on the other hand, is clearly limited to motor vehicle accidents. The German statute thus contains a number of qualifications and limitations which could not easily be duplicated in a judge-made rule.

(ii) Even the brief outline of the relevant French case law which has been presented above demonstrates that the unsteady and vacillating course of the courts' decisions has had an adverse effect on certainty and predictability of French law in this area. It has been observed that "In France, automobile accidents seem to result in litigation more often than in other European countries, due largely to the complexity and uncertainty of the case law." [47]

Is complexity and uncertainty an inherent feature of decisional law, or might it be said that the instability of French case law is to some extent due to peculiarities of French legal method, especially the non-communicative way in which the decisions of the French Court of Cassation are reported (see infra pp. 649–650)?

(bb) It is tempting to speculate why neither France nor Germany used Code revision to solve the problems of traffic accidents or products liability, why France adopted a special statute concerning traffic accidents only three quarters of a century after Germany had done so, and why in both countries products liability law remained primarily a matter for case-law development.

That neither country used the technique of Code revision was presumably due to the (already noted) reluctance to tamper with Code language. Revision of a Code is generally undertaken only when a major portion of it is no longer in conformity with prevail-

---

tions. It is only for the sake of focusing the discussion on our present topic (structure and evolution of code systems) that the question formulated in the text has been limited to methods of change within the context of national systems only.

46. For comprehensive comparative treatment of the subject, see A. Tunc, Traf-

fic Accident Compensation: Law and Proposals, Int.Enc.Comp.L. XI Torts, ch. 14 (1983).

47. Pfennigstorf, supra n. 28, at 16. For some striking figures bearing out the statement in the text, see n. 12 supra and the article by A. Tunc, supra n. 10, at p. 4.

Noted

ing social norms.[48]   As a consequence, recent major Code revisions   *Noted* have occurred primarily in the area of family law.[49]   Even limited changes in a Code are more likely to be made in order to implement broad principles rather than to tamper with specific rules.[50] For problems concerning narrow fact situations, auxiliary statutes are, generally, the preferred tool.   Thus it is not surprising that automobile accidents eventually became the subject of such statutes in both countries.[51]   That the French statute was adopted so much later than the German one, may have been due to both historical and political factors.   When automobile accidents began to become a significant problem, the German Civil Code was still quite new.   Its language had been carefully drafted and its tort provisions were clearly based on the fault principle.   The previous significant departure from that principle, the Liability Law of 1871, had not even been incorporated into the Code.[52]   Consequently, it would have been difficult for the German courts to impose strict liability for motor vehicle accidents by an audacious interpretation of the Code, and the enactment of a special statute seemed a plausible solution, especially given the precedent of the Liability Law.[53]   In France, on the other hand, the Code was over one hundred years old at that time.   Article 1384 had already received an expansive interpretation and its extension to automobile accidents in the *Jand'heur* case, while a significant departure, was not an extraordinary feat of judicial activism.[54]   Following *Jand'heur*, there seemed to be no great social need for the enactment of special legislation dealing with automobile accidents.   Indeed, legislation along German lines, with its limitations on liability, might have been perceived as regressive.   On the other hand, the volume of automobile litigation in France was, as already noted, quite high.[55]

48.   See C. L'Heureux-Dubé, The Quebec Experience: Codification of Family Law and a Proposal for the Creation of a Family Court System, 44 La.L.Rev. 1575 (1984). Of course, Code revision also becomes necessary when a portion of the Code suffers from a constitutional infirmity as was true of the German provisions on matrimonial property, completely revised in 1957, as noted in note 1 on p. 537 supra; the revision of the German conflict of laws rules, discussed infra p. 847 has likewise been due in substantial part to constitutional reasons.   Code revisions may also become necessary as a result of international agreements or enactments.   Thus, the European Convention on Human Rights has led to some changes in certain codes of criminal procedure and art. 1844–5 of the French Civil Code was amended in 1981 to comply with the European Community Directives on company law.

49.   See supra, pages 548–549.

50.   Thus a French Law No. 70–643 of July 17, 1970 added a new article 9 to the Civil Code, providing broadly for a right of privacy (which to some extent had previously been recognized by case law).   *But see* the relatively narrow rules on contracts

with tour operators mentioned supra p. 549, which were recently added to the German Civil Code.

51.   The Italian Civil Code, in art. 2054, has a specific provision dealing with motor vehicle accidents, but the provision has been part of that relatively recent Code since its enactment in 1942.

52.   See the discussion and materials on p. 550, supra

53.   At about the same time the German statute was enacted, similar statutes were adopted in Austria and in the Scandinavian countries.   See A. Tunc, Limitation on Codification—A Separate Law of Traffic Accidents, 44 Tul.L.Rev. 757, 759 (1970).

54.   See supra pp. 556–559.

55.   See supra n. 47 and accompanying text.   In addition to the uncertainties created by the courts' somewhat wavering case-law, two other factors may have contributed.   In France, the public health insurance agencies have traditionally joined with the accident victims in suing tortfeasors in order to assert their subrogation rights, thus splitting legal expenses on the plaintiff's side.   In addition, the "loser pays all" rule applies only with limitations

This type of litigation was thus a substantial source of income for the Bar, and the Bar reacted on the whole unfavorably when the enactment of no-fault legislation was proposed. Reform legislation thus had a chance for enactment only after the socialist electoral victory of 1981 put a person with a substantial interest in law reform in that particular area at the head of the Ministry of Justice. Moreover, the confusion due to the refusal of many lower courts to follow the *Desmares* case had resulted in widespread dissatisfaction with the relevant case law. Even so, the French legislation was only a limited modification of existing law, especially if one compares it with a much more radical statute enacted in Quebec in 1977 against a quite similar Code background.[56] That the long-delayed and relatively modest character of French law reform in the automobile accident area has been due to factors other than opposition to strict liability based on legal principle, may also be seen from the fact that in certain areas, such as the liability of aircraft operators, operators of cable cars and of nuclear installations, statutes providing for strict liability were enacted.[57] But the volume of actual litigation in all these areas was relatively small.

As to products liability, on the other hand, we have previously seen that that problem began to be regarded as requiring special solutions only during the third quarter of this century, after European scholars had studied strict liability rules developed in the United States. The problem was not difficult for the French courts, which had become used to interpret many provisions of their (by then quite old) Code with great liberality. They solved it by imposing a rather far-reaching liability on manufacturers, in part on a contractual, in part on a tort basis. Furthermore, by that time—more than fifty years after the enactment of their Civil Code—the German courts had become bolder in interpreting the Code, and probably more receptive to the idea of using the law of torts as a risk-spreading device. Thus the courts, acting on the basis of § 823 of the Code, were able to devise a reasonable solution of the problem of products liability, and to do so rather promptly once the social significance of the problem was recognized. This made it unnecessary for the legislature to tackle the politically sensitive task of formulating a broad rule of products liability applicable to all industrial processes.[58]

(cc) Law reform in any highly-developed society of the industrial or post-industrial era is a complex process. The relative merits of code revision, auxiliary statutes and case law as vehicles of such reform in a civil-law country depend on so many historical, social

---

in France, see supra p. 367, thus further reducing the financial risk of litigation. It appears that the French health insurance agencies have, recently, concluded an arrangement with the automobile liability insurers providing for lump sum payments. This may have an impact on future litigation frequency.

56. For a discussion of French developments see supra, text at ns. 8–27; for a reference to the Quebec statute, see supra n. 27.

57. See B. Starck, the Foundation of Delictual Liability in Contemporary French Law: An Evaluation and a Proposal, 48 Tul.L.Rev. 1043, 1046–47 (1974).

58. Note, however, that in the near future both France and Germany will have to enact legislation modifying the existing case law on products liability, in order to comply with the Common Market Directive mentioned supra, text at ns. 41–44.

and political factors that it becomes hazardous to generalize on the reasons why, in bringing about a particular type of reform, one of those techniques should be, or in fact is, preferred over the others.

One generalization, however, may be ventured. Whatever technique is used to adjust the private law of a codified legal system to changed conditions, the pertinent provisions of the Code always remain the all-important point of departure. When decisional law is used as the vehicle of reform, such law can be developed only by way of interpreting the language of the Code. And when reform is accomplished by way of an auxiliary statute, such statute must be fitted into the system of the Code; and close attention must be paid (and usually is paid, as shown by the example of the German statute of 1909) to the interaction between the Code and the auxiliary statute.

NOTE

In the preceding discussion, our focus was mainly on the dynamics of a code system. In analyzing the cases which follow, the reader again may encounter occasional questions relating to the ways in which such a system reacts to social and technological changes; but the emphasis will shift to other systematic aspects of code law.

Corporation Question

PROCESS + METHODS OF JUDICIAL REASONING

OPINION OF THE GERMAN REICHSGERICHT IN THE MATTER OF S. S. v. M. E. CORP.

2nd Civil Division, January 22, 1935, RGZ 146, 385.

same as present German S.C.

[Defendant corporation has a capital of one million Reichsmarks, divided into 1000 bearer shares, each with a par value of RM 1000. Plaintiff has been a substantial minority shareholder since 1919. The majority of the shares are held by one M. W. and members of his family. M. W. has been an officer and shareholder since the corporation was organized. At a shareholders' meeting on Nov. 30, 1932, a vote was taken on a resolution approving the conduct of the corporation's affairs by the management during the fiscal year 1931–32. The vote was 498 for approval and 416 against, a total of 914 votes. Of the 498 approving votes, 486 were cast by J. W., the son of the officer, M. W. The 416 votes against approval were cast by plaintiff and his attorney. Plaintiff then sued to set aside the resolution approving the management's conduct, on the ground that J. W. was only the ostensible holder of the shares voted by him, and that the real owner was M. W. who was disqualified from voting. By a judgment of the Landgericht Muenchen, dated May 7, 1933, the resolution was set aside, on the theory that the voting prohibition contained in the Commercial Code, § 252, subd. 3, had been violated. This section in substance provides that no shareholder may vote on the question of approval of his own acts as officer or director of the corporation.[a] No appeal was taken from this judgment of May 7, 1933.

Meanwhile, on Dec. 17, 1932, defendant corporation had called a new shareholders' meeting for Jan. 10, 1933. The public notice of this meeting stated that the agenda would include the question of re-scinding the Nov. 30 resolution and of adopting a new resolution approving the acts of the management. Any shareholder desiring to vote in the Jan. 10 meeting had to deposit his shares not later than Jan. 6, 1933.]

By notarial document of Jan. 5, 1933, M. W. and J. W. and their wives set up a limited liability company (Gesellschaft mit beschraenkter Haftung, GmbH)[b] with a capital of RM 500,000, designating as the object of the new company the investment of its funds in industrial and other enterprises of every description. Of the capital, M. W. subscribed RM 300,000, his wife 100,000, J. W. 70,000 and his wife 30,000; the subscribers paid up their subscriptions by transferring their shares of stock of the defendant corporation to the new company. M. W. was given the right during his life to appoint and remove the officers of the new company, and as the first officers he appointed himself and J. W. . . . On the same day on which it was set up, the new company was registered in the register of commerce. On Jan. 6, it deposited shares of stock of the defendant corporation having a par value of RM 528,000 and announced that it would participate in the Jan. 10 shareholders' meeting with 528 votes.

In the meeting of Jan. 10, 1933, shares of a total par value of RM 953,000 were represented by four shareholders or representatives of shareholders. The plaintiff and his attorney, Dr. E., represented shares of a par value of RM 416,000, with 416 votes. The B.V. Bank represent-

a. In Germany and in many other countries it is customary (and often pre-scribed by law) that the stockholders at their regular annual meeting vote on the question whether to grant *Entlastung* (in French, *décharge*; meaning release from responsibility, or approval of management conduct), to the members of the manage-ment group. At the time of the principal case, such a vote of approval, unless set aside by the court, had the effect of releas-ing any cause of action for mismanage-ment which the corporation might other-wise have against the officers in question. The Corporation Laws of 1937 and 1965 somewhat weakened the effect of a resolu-tion granting *Entlastung*. See B. von Falkenhausen and E. C. Steefel, Sharehold-ers' Rights in German Corporations, 10 Am.J.Comp.L. 407, 415 (1961). But it is still an important corporate act, for the reason, among others, that a resolution refusing *Entlastung* to a particular officer would be a vote of no-confidence, which ordinarily would constitute "cause" for the

dismissal of that officer. See § 84, subs. 3, of the present Corporation Law.

Under Swiss law, as under pre-1937 Ger-man law, a *décharge* given to members of the management group still constitutes a waiver of liability for negligent conduct of corporate affairs; but the waiver affects only those matters of which all of the shareholders approving the *décharge* had been informed. See decision of the Swiss Federal Court of November 18, 1969, 95 BGE II 320.

b. For present purposes, it is sufficient to note that a German GmbH is a close corporation. It must be distinguished from a stock corporation (Aktiengesellschaft, ab-br. AG), such as the M. E. Corporation in the principal case, which may issue shares to the public. The GmbH form of organi-zation, which will be discussed infra pp. 829–833, is suitable for many purposes, in-cluding—as the principal case shows—that of a family holding company.

ed shares of RM 9,000 par value with 9 votes and the new GmbH, for which Justizrat D. (an attorney) appeared on the basis of a proxy executed by J. W., represented shares of a par value of RM 528,000 with 528 votes.

[Prior to the voting Dr. E. moved in his own name and in the name of the plaintiff to have the conduct of the management examined by auditors. There was no objection to the addition of this point to the agenda.]

The meeting resolved with 537 votes, that is the 528 votes of the GmbH and the 9 votes of the Bank, against the 416 votes of the plaintiff and of Dr. E., to approve the officers' conduct of the corporate affairs. By the same ratio of votes the motion to appoint auditors was voted down. The notarial protocol shows that plaintiff and Dr. E. promptly declared their opposition to both resolutions.

On Jan. 11, 1933, J. W. was registered in the register of commerce as an additional officer of defendant.

[Plaintiff promptly brought this action to set aside the two resolutions of the meeting of Jan. 10, 1933.] Plaintiff contends that both resolutions are void because of the violation, by the participation of the GmbH in the voting, of the voting prohibitions of the Commercial Code . . ., and because of the immoral purpose of such participation, such invalidity allegedly flowing from §§ 134 and 138 of the Civil Code.[c] In any event, plaintiff contends, the resolutions are subject to being set aside pursuant to Sec. 271 of the Commercial Code.[d]

The Landgericht declared the said two resolutions of the meeting of Jan. 10, 1933, to be invalid. The Oberlandesgericht reversed and dismissed the complaint. The further appeal of the plaintiff [to the Reichsgericht] leads to reversal and remand.

Reasons: 1. The intermediate appellate court is correct in holding that on the basis of plaintiff's allegations the case involves no question

c. Civil Code, Sec. 134: "A jural act which is contrary to a statutory prohibition is void, unless a contrary intention appears from the statute."

Sec. 138: "A jural act which is contra bonos mores (violative of the commands of morality) is void. . . ."

d. Commercial Code, Sec. 271: "A resolution of a shareholders' meeting may be attacked by an action to set it aside if it violates the law or the articles of association. Such action must be brought within a month. Every shareholder who has been present at the meeting may bring the action provided he has entered his opposition in the protocol. . . ." The substance of this provision is now to be found in §§ 243–46 of the Corporation Law of 1965.

The action to set aside a stockholders' resolution, while relatively infrequent

here, is by no means unknown in our law. Statutes in many states provide for a summary proceeding to set aside an election. See 5 Fletcher, Cyclopedia Corporations, Section 273 (Perm.Ed.1967, and Supps.); N.Y.Bus.Corp.L. Section 619. Resolutions other than elections can be attacked, on procedural or substantive grounds, by way of a plenary suit in equity. For an example of such an action to set aside a stockholders' resolution see Davison v. Parke, Austin & Lipscomb Inc., 165 Misc. 32, 299 N.Y.S. 960 (Sup.Ct., N.Y.Co., 1937), modified, 256 App.Div. 1071, 128 N.Y.S.2d 358. See also Goldfield Corp. v. General Host Corp., 29 N.Y.2d 264, 267–68, 327 N.Y.S.2d 330, 332–33, 297 N.E.2d 387, 389–390 (1971).

of the absolute invalidity of the resolutions of Jan. 10, 1933, but only a question of setting them aside, because judged by their contents the resolutions are not contra bonos mores: the alleged violation of the standards of boni mores is based only on the manner in which the said resolutions came about [citing cases supporting the proposition that only those resolutions are absolutely invalid the terms or contents of which are contra bonos mores.] Therefore, this court reviews only the question whether the action to set aside (Commercial Code, Sec. 271) was properly decided.[e] . . .

2. . . . One whose managerial conduct is to be approved by a shareholders' resolution is deprived of the right to vote on such resolution by virtue of Section 252, subd. 3 of the Commercial Code; nor may he in such case exercise the right to vote for another shareholder.[f] Section 266, subd. 1, second sentence, of the Commercial Code, as amended . . ., provides that where the subject of a shareholders' resolution is the appointment of auditors for the examination of certain events connected with the organization or management of the corporation, those shareholders who are directors or officers may not vote, if the examination is to extend to events which have a bearing on the approval of such directors' or officers' conduct of the management, or on the question of the institution by the corporation of an action against such directors or officers.[g]

The voting prohibitions in Sections 252 and 266 of the Commercial Code thus affect the shares of a member of the management if such member's conduct is to be approved or the appointment of auditors for the examination of his conduct is in question. Therefore, the prohibition applies only if the member in question is a shareholder of the corporation. . . .

There is no doubt that as an officer of defendant, M. W., if he himself had been a shareholder, would have had no right to participate in the vote on the two resolutions which have been attacked in this action. However, at the time of the resolutions he was no longer a

---

e. In the principal case it makes no practical difference to the plaintiff whether the resolutions are declared to be "void" pursuant to Sections 134 and 138 of the Civil Code, or whether they are "set aside" pursuant to Section 271 of the Commercial Code. But in a case in which for some reason (e.g., because he failed to bring the action within a month) the plaintiff cannot successfully sue under the latter provision, it becomes crucial for him to know whether he can nevertheless attack the resolution of the stockholders as a "jural act" which is contra bonos mores and hence absolutely void under the broad terms of the above-mentioned sections of the Civil Code.

The criterion by which the court distinguishes void and voidable resolutions, originally was developed by case law. Today,

the same criterion appears in § 241, subd. 4 of the Corporation Law of 1965.

f. The corresponding provision of the German Corporation Law of 1965 is to be found in § 136.

American legislators tend to be more reluctant to prohibit shareholders (as distinguished from directors) from voting on matters in which they have a personal interest. But such voting prohibitions are not unknown in our law. See H. G. Henn & J. R. Alexander, Laws of Corporations § 238 (3rd ed., 1983, and 1986 Supp.). See also § 310(a)(1) of the present California Corporations Code (eff. Jan. 1, 1977), introducing a voting prohibition that did not exist under former § 820.

g. The German Corporation Law of 1965 contains a similar provision in § 142.

shareholder. The shares with which Justizrat D. exercised the voting rights, . . . had at that time been validly transferred to a properly organized family corporation, and had thus become the property of the latter. The mere fact that its officer M. W. was also an officer of the defendant corporation and that the approval or examination of his managerial conduct was the subject of the resolutions, would not have deprived the GmbH of its right to vote. The GmbH being a separate legal entity with independent juristic personality, such extensive interpretation of the voting prohibitions is out of the question. These prohibitions are directed solely against a shareholder; but the officer of a GmbH, that is, of a separate legal entity, cannot be regarded as the owner of shares belonging to the GmbH.

This Division of the Court, overruling prior decisions,[h] has decided in the opinion reported on p. 71 of this volume that the voting prohibition of Section 266, subd. 1, second sentence, of the Commercial Code extends to shares owned by a *partnership*, if a member of the management of the corporation is one of the partners of the partnership, and if the resolution [to be voted on by the shareholders' meeting] involves the question whether a damage action for improper conduct of the corporate affairs should be brought by the corporation against the members of its management. This holding, however, was based on the view that according to the prevailing opinion the assets of a partnership are jointly owned by the partners, that shares belonging to a partnership constitute part of these [jointly owned] partnership assets and that the partners are thus "shareholders" within the meaning of the said provisions of law. A general analogous extension of these principles to the GmbH is, however, impossible inasmuch as the shareholders of a GmbH are not co-owners of the GmbH's assets.

3. Nevertheless, under the special circumstances of this case, the exercise of the voting right with respect to the shares belonging to the GmbH was prohibited by Sections 252, 266 . . . of the Commercial Code. This conclusion follows directly from the rationale and purpose of the said provisions. Rationale and purpose are these: If the resolution of the shareholders' meeting involves approval of the acts of a member of the management, or the appointment of auditors for the examination of such acts with the aim of instituting damages actions against such member on the basis of the audit, then the members of the management shall not be the judges in their own cases, which they would be if they participated in the formation of the corporate will relating to these matters.[i] They would be their own judges if they voted with their own shares; and the same would be true if a vote were

---

h. The prior decisions had been rendered by the same Division, or panel, of the Court. Therefore, as the reader knows, the panel was able to overrule these prior decisions without submitting the issue to a super-panel.

i. This statement has been cited many times. See K. Schmidt, Rechtsschutz des Minderheitsgesellschafters gegen rechtswidrige ablehnende Beschlüsse, 39 N.J.W. 2018, 2019 (1986). It is now recognized that voting prohibitions come into play (a) in case of self-dealing and (b) in situations in which a shareholder, were he permitted to vote, would be a judge in his own cause. Ibid.

carried by shares which are legally controlled by a member of the management, because in the latter case, too, a free and independent exercise of the voting right solely in the best interest of the corporation is not assured, in view of the conflicting interests of the officer or director in question. . . . The officer or director who controls the shareholdings of a juristic person and determines the latter's exercise of its voting right, must be treated like a shareholder within the meaning of the said provisions of law. Such identification of a juristic person with the individual behind it, who legally is in complete control of its doings, has been recognized in prior decisions of this Court dealing with other fact situations [citing cases].

Such identification of the corporate owner of shares with the individual who by law and charter dominates it, will be unavoidable especially in the case of a one-man GmbH, that is of a company whose every legal act depends upon the will of this one individual. The case at bar presents a situation of this kind, in view of the way in which according to the factual findings of the court below the new GmbH (to which the W. family transferred its shares) was organized.

[The court then discusses the facts found below, and comes to the conclusion that as matter of law the GmbH was completely controlled by M. W., and that the proxy used in the shareholders' meeting of Jan. 10, 1933, although formally executed by J. W. as an officer of the GmbH, must nevertheless, like every other jural act of the GmbH, be considered a jural act of M. W.]

The courts below discussed the question, answered affirmatively by the Landgericht and negatively by the intermediate appellate court, whether because of the purpose of *evading* the statutory voting prohibitions the formation of, and the transfer of the shares to, the GmbH was contra bonos mores and void;[j] but this is not the decisive question. The said voting prohibitions were here *directly* applicable, because the GmbH was merely the form in which M. W. exercised the voting rights with respect to the shares which the W. family had transferred to the GmbH.[k]

4. The foregoing, however, has to be qualified: The voting prohibition was not in all respects applicable to the resolution by which the motion for appointment of auditors was voted down.

---

j. Plaintiff made two distinct arguments, both based on Sections 134 and 138 of the Civil Code, quoted supra: (a) that the *resolutions* adopted at the meeting of Jan. 10, 1933 were absolutely void (this argument was rejected in part "1" of the court's reasons), and (b) that the *transfer* of the shares from M. W. to the family holding company was void. At this point, the court deals with the latter argument.

k. In part 3 of its opinion the German court obviously applies the doctrine of "dis-regarding the corporate entity" or "piercing the corporate veil". For an interesting comparative discussion of that doctrine, which in essence seems to be almost universally recognized, see Justice O'Connor's majority opinion in First National City Bank v. Banco Para El Commercio Exterior De Cuba, 462 U.S. 611, 103 S.Ct. 2591, at 2601–02 (1983).

[The Court then points out that pursuant to Section 266 of the Commercial Code the shareholders' meeting has power to direct an auditors' examination of certain "events" in the corporate management, but that, according to the prevailing view,[1] the shareholders' meeting has no power to order an audit of "the whole conduct of the corporate affairs". The motion which plaintiff's attorney had made in the meeting of Jan. 10, 1933, was in two parts. The first part demanded a general audit of corporate affairs, whereas the second specified certain "events" to be examined by the auditors. The Court holds that the first part of this motion proposed a general audit which as a matter of law the shareholders' meeting was unauthorized to direct, and that, since this proposal had to be rejected as unauthorized, it was immaterial whether the resolution embodying such rejection had been adopted in a proper manner. As to the second part of plaintiff's motion, the Court holds that further factual clarification is necessary before it can determine whether in this part of the motion the "events" to be examined were sufficiently specified. For the purpose of such clarification the Court remands the matter to the intermediate appellate court.

The Reichsgericht then turns to the question whether, in the event that the second part of plaintiff's motion should be found to have been sufficiently specific, and the resolution rejecting that part of the motion should correspondingly be found invalid, such invalidity would affect that part of the resolution which rejected the first (unauthorized) part of plaintiff's motion.]

. . . In this respect it is material whether this was a so-called composite resolution which pursuant to the will of the shareholders' meeting was to form a united whole, and whether, consequently, by way of at least analogous application of Section 139 of the Civil Code [m] invalidity of a part of the resolution made the whole resolution invalid (see Hueck, Voidable and Void Resolutions of Corporate Stockholders, pp. 221, 222); or whether in the instant case a different rule should prevail in view of the fact that with respect to that part of the resolution which is not in itself invalid the opposite resolution—adoption instead of rejection of the motion—could not have been made because of the lack of legal authorization [that is, because the shareholders' meeting has no power to order a general audit of corporate affairs without specification of the "events" to be investigated.][n]

1. As evidence of the "prevailing view", the court cites two older decisions of intermediate appellate courts, one monograph and one well-known commentary.

m. "If part of a jural act is void, the whole jural act shall be void, unless it appears that it would have come into being even without the void part."

This section, like the above-quoted sections 134 and 138, is contained in the First Book (General Part) of the German Civil Code. Note that the applicability of the three sections is not limited to contracts, not even to obligations; they apply to all "jural acts".

n. Even if all parts of the resolution (including the rejection of the motion for a general audit) are invalid, it is clear that a new resolution ordering a *general* audit could not effectively be adopted. What, then, is the practical importance of the discussion in this paragraph of the opinion? Consider in this connection that in Germany, as in most other civil-law jurisdictions, the victorious party is entitled to recover costs and attorneys' fees from the

5. According to the above, at least some of the resolutions . . . were adopted in violation of the voting prohibitions of §§ 252, 266 . . . of the Commercial Code. Nevertheless, the Court is not yet in a position to make a final disposition of this part of the case by setting aside the resolutions to the extent indicated, because no sufficient consideration has yet been given to defendant's contention that under the special circumstances of this case plaintiff's action to set aside constituted an improper exercise of rights, an abuse of rights.

Defendant had alleged and offered to prove that the plaintiff, who had been active in other stock corporations as a professional opposition-ist bent on obtaining personal rather than corporate benefits, was here engaged in the same kind of practice; that ever since he failed of reelection as a director in the shareholders' meeting of Nov. 15, 1926, he carried on obstruction solely for the purpose of acquiring the shares of the W. family at a cheap price and to compel either his election as a director or the distribution of a higher dividend; and that the present action, again, was to serve plaintiff's own selfish rather than corporate purposes. The legal relevance of these allegations should not have been denied.

True, according to the decisions of this Court which we reaffirm, it is recognized that the right of action conferred upon a shareholder by § 271 of the Commercial Code does not depend upon a special need for legal protection within the meaning of § 256 of the Code of Civil Procedure [o], the statutory scheme shows that the shareholder's special need for legal protection results from the sole fact of his membership in the corporation, of his ownership of a share of the capital, by virtue of which, for the preservation of order in corporate affairs, he is given the right to attack those resolutions of the corporation which are inconsistent with law or charter, even though they may cause no detriment to him personally. [Citing a case.] But this right has its limits where it conflicts with the duty of faithfulness which the shareholder owes the corporation and which permeates all rules of corporation law.[p] . . .

loser (see supra pp. 366–370), but that this right may be curtailed or defeated if the victory is a partial one only (German Code of Civil Procedure, Sections 91, 92).

o. Section 256 of the German Code of Civil Procedure deals with declaratory judgment actions, and permits such actions only if the plaintiff "has a legal interest in having the legal relation . . . immediately determined by judicial decision." See Borchard, Declaratory Judgments 101–03 (1941). An action to set aside a shareholders' resolution is not an action for a declaratory judgment. Nevertheless, some legal writers and lower courts took the position that the general principle announced in Section 256 of the Code of Civil Procedure (i.e., the requirement of a special need for legal protection) should be analogously applied to actions brought under Section 271

of the Commercial Code. The Reichsgericht, as shown by the statement in the text, rejected that position.

p. By way of criticism of the principal case, it has been argued that the right to bring an action to set aside a stockholders' resolution (as distinguished from other rights of a stockholder, such as the right to vote) may be exercised not only for corporate but also for individual and even selfish purposes. See Fischer, Die Grenzen bei der Ausuebung gesellschaftlicher Mitgliedschaftsrechte, 7 Neue Juristische Wochenschrift 777, 779 (1954). Do the code provisions set forth in the opinion and in the footnotes, supra, support this classification of stockholders' rights? Even if certain rights are given to a minority stockholder for his own rather than the corporation's benefit, does it follow that the exercise of

In all steps he takes, the shareholder has to consider himself a member of the collective body to which he belongs, and he is bound to make this duty of faithfulness the supreme standard of his actions. If a shareholder exercises the right of action conferred upon him by Section 271 of the Commercial Code for such purposes as here alleged and offered to be proved, that is for the purpose of selfishly and extortionately subjugating the corporation to his will rather than for corporate purposes, then he violates the duty of faithfulness so grossly that the exercise of his right becomes an *abuse* which cannot be tolerated by the legal order. The idea of the impropriety of an abuse of rights has found statutory recognition in the prohibition, contained in Section 226 of the Civil Code,[q] of a purely spiteful exercise of legal rights. Beyond the confines of that provision, however, the same principle must apply whenever the exercise of a right constitutes a gross violation of the maxim dominating the entire field of private law, the maxim of *bona fides.* This thought has repeatedly been recognized in court decisions; see, for instance, the doctrine of laches in the field of revaluation.[r] In legal literature the same thought has recently been elaborated in the monograph by Siebert, Laches and Abuse of Rights, especially pp. 60 et seq. Decisions of this Court have repeatedly recognized that the principle of bona fides contained in Section 242 of the Civil Code[s] constitutes a general limitation upon the exercise of rights also in the law of stock corporations and of limited liability companies. [Citing several Reichsgericht cases and the comment upon one of them by Hachenburg, at that time the leading German authority on the law of limited liability companies, as well as another article in a legal periodical]. . . .

such rights is subject to no restraint whatever? Concerning the latter question, the reader may wish to suspend judgment until the important doctrine of *abuse of rights*, invoked by the court in the principal case, is taken up in more detail. See infra pp. 740–766.

q. "The exercise of a right is improper if it cannot have any purpose other than that of harming another."

r. In the process of the disastrous inflation following the First World War, old "Marks" became completely worthless. In November, 1923, the new "Rentenmark" or "Reichsmark" (abbr. RM) was created. The subject of "revaluation" covers the statutory and decisional rules by which it was attempted to find a fair basis for the conversion of old "Mark" obligations into RM. For details see the excellent study by Dawson, Effects of Inflation on Private Contracts: Germany, 1914–1924, 33 Mich. L.Rev. 171 (1934), and also Rashba, Debts in Collapsed Foreign Currencies, 54 Yale L.J. 1, 9–14 (1944). The 1948 currency reform in Western Germany, which in turn abolished the RM currency and substituted a new "Deutsche Mark" (DM) currency, raised similar problems. See Eisner v. United States, 127 Ct.Cl. 323, 117 F.Supp. 197 (1954). This time, however, the problems were met by comprehensive legislation which left little room for decisional law applying the general principles of bona fides and abuse of rights. See Enneccerus-Lehmann, Recht der Schuldverhaeltnisse 48–51 (1958).

s. "The obligor is bound to perform the obligation in such a way as is required by the principles of bona fides with due regard to existing usage."

Note the similarity between Section 242 of the German Civil Code and UCC Section 1–203. Quaere, however, whether an American court would, by way of analogical application of Section 1–203, declare a plaintiff unfit to bring a stockholders' suit. If it wished to reach such a result, an American court probably would employ different reasoning.

Of course, in each case in which abuse or improper exercise of rights is alleged, particular caution will be indicated. Ordinarily it can be assumed that the shareholder upon whom the law confers the right to sue for cancellation of a resolution, is entitled to make use of such right. The burden of proving that in the particular case the exercise of this right constitutes an abuse, is fully upon the defendant; he has to prove beyond doubt that the exercise of the right under the given circumstances amounts to a gross violation of the principles of bona fides, of the duty of faithfulness incumbent upon the shareholder. In the case at bar such gross violation would exist if defendant succeeded in proving that plaintiff uses the remedy for the purpose of selfishly imposing his will upon the corporation rather than for the purpose of protecting the real interests of the corporation.[t] But the question whether in fact there was no real justification for bringing the action, will have to be examined with particular care. In this connection consideration will have to be given to the contention of the plaintiff . . . : that the resolutions were not justified by the real interest of the corporation, and that they came about by the majority, contra bonos mores, beating down the minority. . . . From the standpoint of substantive law, the discussion of this contention of the plaintiff by the court below is not free from error, in that the court below limits the examination of the real justification [reasonableness] of the attacked resolutions to the question whether the officers, especially M. W., *intentionally* violated their duties as such officers. It has been overlooked that pursuant to Section 241 of the Commercial Code[u] the officers of a stock corporation are liable also for the damage the corporation incurs as a result of their *negligence*. If the possibility cannot be excluded that plaintiff at least believed that the officers became liable to the corporation for a violation, even if only a negligent violation, of their duties as such officers, then it will be hardly possible for the defendant to meet its burden of proving that the action was exclusively brought for noncorporate purposes, and that it therefore constitutes an abuse of legal rights.

t. In Matter of Ochs v. Washington Heights Federal Savings & Loan Association, 17 N.Y.2d 82, 268 N.Y.S.2d 294, 215 N.E.2d 485 (1966), where the plaintiff sought an order permitting him to inspect defendant's membership list, the Court said, at 88: ". . . the desire of a stockholder to become a member of the board of directors does not constitute bad faith. . . . We need not even conjecture here whether a design to remove a director motivated by personal malice would preclude the exercise of a right to inspection. However, it is clear that the institution of such a proceeding as this for the sole purpose of harassment, not motivated by any interest in the association but rather by personal gain completely apart from any benefit to the association, would constitute *mala fides* which the courts of this State are loath to protect. Our case law has uniformly and without hesitation required a bona fide intention on the part of him who seeks such common-law relief."

Compare, also, Clarke v. Greenberg, 296 N.Y. 146, 71 N.E.2d 443 (1947), discussed in American Law Institute, Principles of Corporate Governance § 7.14 (Tent. Draft No. 6, 1986), regarding the fiduciary duties of a minority stockholder who is plaintiff in a derivative action.

u. Sec. 93 of the German Corporation Law of 1965 is to the same effect.

QUESTIONS

What conclusions can be drawn from the principal case regarding a German court's use of authorities? Regarding its methods of reasoning and of developing the law? [v] Regarding the differences between a code and an isolated statute? Regarding the interdependence of the civil, commercial and procedural codes in the German legal system? [w]

Can a code provision express a *principle* as well as a *rule*? The Notes which follow contain some observations bearing on this question.

THE USE OF ANALOGY: NOTES AND ILLUSTRATIONS

(1) *Filling Gaps in the Codes.* The problem of the casus omissus—a fact situation not anticipated by the legislator, and hence not covered in the Code or other written law—is a troublesome one for the civilians. According to their traditional theory, only the written law is authoritative, and there exists no common law.[1] How, then, can a court reach a decision when faced with a case not provided for in the written law?

Two principal techniques have been developed by civilian codifiers to meet this difficulty:

(a) Most of the 19th and 20th century codes contain some provisions of enormous breadth and generality. We have encountered several examples of such provisions (sometimes referred to as "general clauses" of the codes) in the German decision immediately preceding these Notes. More extensive materials dealing with the "general clauses" will be presented infra pp. 702–766.

As each of the "general clauses" covers a wide variety of fact situations, including fact situations which perhaps were not in the minds of the Code's draftsmen, it is clear that by the use of this technique the codifiers can reduce the number of instances in which the written law is found to be silent.

(b) To deal with those cases in which neither a specific provision of the Code nor one of its "general clauses" is applicable, civilian codifiers developed the further technique of inserting so-called directory provisions into their codes. These provisions, although their terms differ from code to code,[2] invariably express a command addressed to the courts, telling the courts what methods

---

v. In this connection, consider the difference between the German conception of a code and the use made of "codes" in common-law jurisdictions (e.g., California). See supra pp. 291–295.

w. The principal case also throws light on some specific problems in the area of corporation law. With reference to these problems, the case appears again infra, p. 834.

1. To a somewhat uncertain degree, traditional civilian theory makes allowance for customary law; but the practical importance of ancient customary law is insignificant in most of the continental legal systems. Concerning a new type of

"customary law", which in reality is decisional law, see infra pp. 620 ff.

In the course of the present century, the traditional theory referred to in the text, supra, has been somewhat liberalized. See infra n. 8 and pp. 597–619, infra. Yet it still remains true that at least in the areas of private law, criminal law and procedural law the civilians think of non-legislated sources of law as something highly exceptional. Cf. D. P. Kirchhof, Richterliche Rechtsfindung gebunden an Gesetz und Recht, 39 N.J.W. 2275 (1986).

2. In previous parts of this book, we have already encountered several examples of such directory provisions. See su-

noted

and sources to use (or not to use) when they encounter an ambiguity or a gap in the written law. Since such a directory provision is contained in the Code itself, it is possible to maintain, at least in theory, that a court using the (possibly extracodal) methods and sources thus prescribed is following the Code's own command, and hence is staying within the confines of the written law.

(2) *Analogy as a Gap-Filling Technique.* As we have seen in studying the *Shoop* case, supra, the Spanish Civil Code contains a directory provision which, inter alia, refers a court to the "general principles of law," i.e., the principles which by the use of analogy can be distilled from positive provisions of the Code itself and of other written laws.

A somewhat comparable directory provision was proposed by the draftsmen of the German Civil Code. The first draft of that Code contained the following Section 1:

> "Questions for which the Code contains no provision are to be answered by analogous application of the provisions referring to legally similar questions. In the absence of such provisions, the principles derived from the spirit of the legal order shall be determinative."

In later drafts of the German Code this provision was deleted as unnecessary.[3] It was felt that even in the absence of such a code provision the courts, when faced with a gap in the written law, could not help but to resort to analogy. This expectation turned out to be well-founded. A recent study, based in part on quantitative analysis, has shown that since the enactment of the Code the German courts have used analogical reasoning in a very large number of decisions, including many important decisions of the court of last resort.[4]

The above-quoted provision in the first draft of the German Civil Code appears to draw a distinction between two kinds of analogy. The first sentence of the draft provision refers to so-called "statutory analogy," i.e. the derivation of a principle from a single provision, or a group of closely connected provisions, to be found in the Code or some other statute. The second sentence of the draft provision speaks of an even bolder use of analogical reasoning, to which German legal writers refer as "analogy of law." It means the distillation of a principle from several, and not necessarily inter-connected, provisions of written law, which may be contained in a number of diverse codes and statutes.[5] In practice, the distinction between these two kinds of analogy has not proved to be of great significance.

The distinction between interpretation and analogy, on the other hand, is important in practice as well as in theory. In a codified legal system, no case can be decided without interpreting and applying one or several provisions of the Code or other statutes. On the other hand, it is clear that resort to analogy, although not infrequent, is justified only in the exceptional cases in which the written law furnishes no

---

pra pp. 73, 235. For further examples and explanations, see infra pp. 651–653.

3. See Staudinger-Riezler, Commentary on the German Civil Code, Vol. I, Introduction, pp. 34–35 (10th ed., 1936). Due to the deletion of § 1 of the first Draft, the German Civil Code (in contrast to the great majority of comparable civilian codes) contains no express directory provisions.

4. See E. Bund, Die Analogie als Begründungsmethode im deutschen Recht der Gegenwart, 77 Z. für Vergleichende Rechtswissenschaft 115 (1978).

5. See Staudinger-Riezler, supra n. 3.

answer to the issue at hand.[5a] Interpretation, however bold and extensive, "means that the judge applies a norm to the facts because the norm still covers such facts; by way of analogy, he applies the norm to the facts although he finds that the norm does not cover the facts." [6]

Suppose that fact situations A, B and C are covered by one or several Code provisions, establishing the same rule for all three of these situations. If a court, confronted by fact situation D, holds that the language of these Code provisions, though not explicit on the point, can be stretched to cover D, the court uses the method of extensive interpretation. But if the court, while admitting that the rule expressed in the code provisions cannot be stretched to cover D, finds that these provisions reflect a principle broader than the explicitly stated rule, and if the court then uses that broader principle to determine case D, the decision is made by way of analogical reasoning.

The use of such reasoning, however, requires caution. The Code provisions dealing with the expressly defined and enumerated fact situations A, B and C may imply that *only* those fact situations are intended to be covered by the rule, and that other fact situations (including D) thus are to be treated differently. This latter kind of argumentation is known as *argumentum a contrario*. There is no rule of thumb telling the courts of a civil-law country how to choose between the two conflicting approaches of analogical reasoning and *argumentum a contrario*. Whenever such a conflict arises, the court will have to be guided by legislative history as well as policy considerations.[7]

(3) *The Limits of Analogy*. It has been suggested by German legal authors that occasionally the courts are confronted with problems to the solution of which the written law has contributed absolutely nothing, not even a starting point for analogical reasoning.[8] In such a case, these authors propose, a German court should act as if Art. 1 of the Swiss Civil Code [9] were in force in Germany; i.e., after examining potentially helpful ideas developed in other legal systems, the judge should creatively fashion a solution as if he were the legislator.[10] As an example of a solution which the courts, unaided by written law, thus have independently developed, the said authors cite the 1953 decision of the German Supreme Court discussed in Note (4) below.[11] *Quaere*,

---

5a. In the area of criminal law, moreover, the meting out of punishment for an offense not previously defined by the written law is proscribed by constitutional or statutory provisions in most civilized countries. This principle of *nulla poena sine lege* precludes the use of analogy to the detriment of the accused.

6. Staudinger-Riezler, supra n. 3.

7. See Palandt, Bürgerliches Gesetzbuch, Introduction preceding § 1, Anno. VI 3 (45th ed. 1986).

In later parts of this book, the reader will find several cases in which a (civilian) court was required to make a reasoned choice between analogy and *argumentum e contrario*.

8. See Staudinger-Brändl-Coing, Commentary on the German Civil Code, Vol. I, Introduction, p. 41 (11th ed., 1957).

Concerning the jurisprudential roots of these suggestions, see E. Bodenheimer, Significant Developments in German Legal Philosophy Since 1945, 3 Am.J.Comp.L. 379 (1954).

9. See infra p. 653.

10. This point—which, coming from a civilian, at first blush may appear startling—will be discussed more extensively in the next-following chapter.

11. Other—and perhaps better—examples of cases in which German courts engaged in creative law-making without the aid of analogical reasoning, will be found in the next-following chapter. See also Palandt, Bürgerliches Gesetzbuch, Introduction preceding § 1, Anno. VI 4 (45th ed. 1986).

however, whether that was not a classical case of analogy, i.e., a case in which the written law did furnish the guiding appraisal of values or policies, even though such appraisal may have been expressed in provisions which in terms did not cover the case at hand.

(4) *Decision of the German Bundesgerichtshof* of February 19, 1953, BGHZ 9, 83: Plaintiff, who was vaccinated as a child pursuant to a compulsory vaccination statute, suffered permanent injuries to her health as a result of post-vaccinal encephalitis. The vaccination statute then in force contained no provision for the payment of damages or compensation in such a case. Plaintiff was unable to prove that the vaccination had been negligently performed. She sued the State on the theory that in submitting to the public duty created by the compulsory vaccination statute, she had been compelled to sacrifice her health in the public interest, and that for this loss she should receive adequate compensation from the community.

Both plaintiff and defendant found some support in previous decisions. Plaintiff relied on a line of cases in which the former Reichsgericht, on the basis of statutes providing for just compensation in certain well-defined instances of expropriation (eminent domain), had evolved the general principle that even in the absence of an applicable compensation statute an individual is entitled to damages if he has to sacrifice a private right in the public interest, and that this claim for damages comes into existence regardless of whether or not the detriment suffered by him is due to negligence or any other fault of an official. The defendant, on the other hand, pointed to a 1937 decision rendered by a super-panel[12] of the former Reichsgericht (RGZ 156, 305), holding that this so-called theory of sacrifice should be limited to cases of property losses, and denying recovery in a fact situation indistinguishable from that of the principal case.

In its 1953 decision the Bundesgerichtshof overruled the last-mentioned case [13] and permitted the plaintiff to recover. The court referred to the principle recognized in the Basic Law of the German Federal Republic, which provides compensation for an individual whose property is expropriated and who thus has to sacrifice his property for the common good. *A fortiori*, the court reasoned, the community owes compensation to one who was forced to make a special sacrifice—i.e., a sacrifice not exacted from other persons in the same class—involving loss of life or health.

The specific holding of the court, allowing recovery in cases of disease caused by compulsory vaccination, subsequently has been confirmed by a statute, which also regulates the amount of compensation in some detail.[14] But the general principle recognized and broadened in the 1953 case retains its great significance; it is, of course, applicable to many fact situations which do not involve vaccination and thus are not covered by the new statute.[15]

---

12. See supra p. 468.

13. It was not necessary for the court again to refer the question to a super-panel, because technically the new Bundesgerichtshof, created in the German Federal Republic after World War II and having its seat at Karlsruhe, is not identical with the former Reichsgericht, which was physically and institutionally obliter-ated when Leipzig, the seat of that court, was conquered by the Soviet Army in 1945.

14. Bundesseuchengesetz (Federal Law Concerning Infectious Diseases) of July 18, 1961, §§ 51 ff.

15. The principle has been applied, e.g., to the case of an innocent bystander who was injured when the police (lawfully) opened fire to prevent a felon from fleeing.

A similarly broad principle of compensation for special sacrifices exacted from an individual in the public interest has been developed by the French administrative courts. As in Germany, a plaintiff may recover on this theory even though he can show no fault on the part of a public official.[16] One of the cases in which the French courts allowed recovery on this theory, was factually identical with the German vaccination case of 1953.[17]

(5) *Some Comparative Observations.* Reasoning by analogy—i.e., the application "in consimili casu" of a general principle which is derived from rules developed in a different factual context—is a tool employed by judges in the common-law as well as the civil-law orbit.[18] There is, however, a perceptible difference in the way the tool is put to work.

The usual starting point for the civilian's reasoning by analogy or by induction will be a provision, or a number of provisions, of the code or codes. The German case involving a stockholder's action, supra, furnishes an illustration. As was said by Wisdom, J., in Shelp v. National Surety Corp., 333 F.2d 431, at 435 (5 Cir.1964):

> . . . in Louisiana, as in all civilian jurisdictions, the Civil Code is more than an ordinary legislative act. The Code, doctrinally, constitutes the whole body of private law. A statute, on the other hand, is small in scope, narrow in its objective and . . . is intended to deal with a specific mischief or a specific need. The relation between a code and a statute in the field of private law may be analogized to the relation between the common law and a statute in derogation of the common law.

Quoting from a law review article,[19] the opinion continues:

> The very nature of a code requires that analogies be drawn from its express provisions in deciding cases for which no exact rule can be found in the code. . . .

Under our system, a general principle ordinarily will be extracted from case law.[20] Even where a "code" exists, our judges traditionally fill the gaps in the written law by falling back on the common law,

The plaintiff was permitted to recover from the State without having to prove negligence on the part of the police officers. See Palandt, Bürgerliches Gesetzbuch, Introduction preceding § 903, Anno. 3b (45th ed., 1986), where many additional judicial decisions applying the same principle are cited.

16. See the decision of the Conseil d'Etat of November 6, 1968 in the case of Minister of National Education v. Dame Saulze, reported in the article by L. G. Weeramantry, Judicial Application of the Rule of Law, 1 Rev. of the Int. Commission of Jurists 43 (1969). In that case, the State was held liable to pay compensation to a school teacher whose child suffered from a birth defect caused by German measles which the plaintiff, then pregnant, had contracted when performing her teaching duties.

17. Decision of the Administrative Tribunal of Lyon, reported in La Dépêche du Midi of July 26, 1965, p. 2. For a comparative discussion of the "doctrine of sacrifice" (covering French, German and U.S. law), see Comment, 24 U.Chi.L.Rev. 513 (1957).

18. See J. Stone, Legal System and Lawyers' Reasonings 312–16 (1964); E. H. Levi, An Introduction to Legal Reasoning, 15 Un. of Chi.L.Rev. 501 (1948); B. H. Levy, Cardozo and Frontiers of Legal Thinking 51, 56 (rev.ed. 1969).

19. G. Dreyfous, Partial Defacement of Olographic Wills, 15 Tul.L.Rev. 272 (1941).

20. See H. W. Goldschmidt, English Law from the Foreign Standpoint 32–33 (1937).

rather than by extending, or analogizing from, the provisions of the "code".[21] But this tradition is becoming weaker; in the United States there is a growing modern trend toward using a statute, or a complex of statutes, as a basis for analogical reasoning.[22] With respect to the Uniform Commercial Code, one of the draftsmen's own comments to § 1–102 invites the use of Code provisions as starting points for such reasoning.[23] Our mental processes thus become more similar to those of the civilians.[24]

Yet this convergence of civil-law and common-law approaches has gone only part of the way.[25] The very language, e.g., of § 1–103 of the UCC makes it clear that lawyers brought up in the common-law tradition still do not treat a "code" the way the civilians do. That section provides that "Unless displaced by the particular provisions of this Act, the principles of law and equity, including the law merchant and the law relative to capacity to contract, principal and agent, estoppel, fraud, misrepresentation, duress, coercion, mistake, bankruptcy, or other validating or invalidating cause shall supplement its provisions." In a civilian code system, in which each code is intended to constitute a complete statement of authoritative rules and to displace all of the pre-existing law on the subject, such a reference to the supplemental role of "principles of law and equity" would be unthinkable.

supra 164
Statutory analogy

NOTE

For a proper understanding of the next case it is necessary to consider the following sections of the German Commercial Code:

Sec. 66

The employment contract between [a commercial enterprise] and a clerk, if entered into for an indefinite period, can

---

21. Cf. Strand Imp. Co. v. Long Beach, 173 Cal. 765, 161 P. 975 (1916).

22. See National City Bank v. Republic of China, 348 U.S. 356, 360, 75 S.Ct. 423, 426, 427 (1955); United States v. American Trucking Associations, Inc., 310 U.S. 534, 542–5, 60 S.Ct. 1059 (1940); South & Central American Commercial Co., Inc. v. Panama R.R. Co., 237 N.Y. 287, 142 N.E. 666 (1923); H. F. Stone, The Common Law in the United States, 50 Harv.L.Rev. 4, 13–16 (1936); R. J. Traynor, Statutes Revolving in Common-Law Orbits, 17 Cath.U.L.Rev. 401 (1968).

23. See I. R. Macneil and R. B. Schlesinger, Some Comments on the Legal System of the United States, With Particular Reference to the Law of Contracts, in 1 Schlesinger (Gen.Ed.), Formation of Contracts—A Study of the Common Core of Legal Systems 194–95 (1968), where further references can be found.

It should be noted, however, that our courts have been somewhat slow in re-

sponding to this invitation of the UCC draftsmen. In 1978, it was observed by an American scholar that while the UCC occasionally has been used by analogy, "this is a technique generally undeveloped in American law." J. Sweet, Book Review, 26 Am.J.Comp.L. 482, 492 (1978).

24. See J. Frank, Civil Law Influences on the Common Law, 104 U.Pa.L.Rev. 887, 890 (1956).

English courts are said to be more reluctant to treat a statute "as a source of public policy in cases not within its expressed terms." D. Lloyd, Public Policy 8 (1953). See also Lord Lloyd of Hampstead & M. D. A. Freeman, Lloyd's Introduction to Jurisprudence 1143 (5th ed., 1985). But see R. Cross, Precedent in English Law 168–70 (3rd ed., 1977), where it is asserted that English courts do reason from statutes by analogy.

25. See supra n. 24.

be terminated by either party by giving six weeks' notice, such notice to become effective at the end of any calendar quarter.[a]

Sec. 67

If a longer or shorter notice period is agreed upon, it must be the same for both parties, and in any event such notice period may not be less than one month.

A "month" means a calendar month.

The provisions of the first paragraph are applicable in a case where an employment contract has been entered into for a fixed period, with a stipulation that the contract shall be automatically renewed unless notice of termination is given before the end of such period.

Any agreement contrary to these provisions is null and void.

Sec. 68

The provisions of Sec. 67 are not applicable when the salary of the clerk is more than 5000 Marks per year. . . .[b]

Sec. 69

If a clerk is hired temporarily, the provisions of Sec. 67 are not applicable, unless the duration of service exceeds three months. The notice period must in such a case be the same for both parties.[c]

---

a. Note that these provisions, which to an American reader may seem to reflect a high degree of social protectiveness, were enacted long before World War I.

In present-day German law, as in the law of most civil-law countries, the protection of employees against arbitrary termination of their employment is carried very much further. The Kündigungsschutzgesetz, a relatively recent auxiliary statute supplementing the pertinent provisions of the Civil Code and the Commercial Code, now provides that an employer who regularly employs more than five employees may (even if he complies with the Code's notice requirements) terminate the employment of an employee who has served more than 6 months only if such termination is "socially justified". See Baumbach-Duden-Hopt, Handelsgesetzbuch, § 59, Anno. 9D (26th ed., 1985). American employers operating in foreign countries often suffer an acute case of shock when they are confronted with statutory provisions of this kind.

Note, however, that provisions of this kind are a disincentive to new employment, especially at times of slow economic growth. The recent period of substantial unemployment in Europe has thus seen a weakening of some of these rules. See, e.g., the German Beschäftigungsförderungsgesetz (Law for the Promotion of Employment) of April 26, 1985, 1985 BGBl 710. In a similar vein, the French rules requiring administrative approval for the dismissal of personnel (see R. P. Sokol, Termination of French Labor Contracts, 14 Int. Lawyer 267 (1980)) were largely eliminated in 1986. Law No. 86–797 of July 3, 1986 on the Elimination of the Administrative Authorization for the Dismissal of Employees, J.O. July 4, 1986, p. 8302, 1986 D.L. 395.

b. At the time when this Code provision was enacted, a salary level of more than 5000 Marks per annum normally indicated that the employee in question was at least a junior executive.

c. In 1969, these provisions were taken out of the Commercial Code and (with some modifications) incorporated into § 622 of the Civil Code, which is part of the Title dealing with contracts of employment. See Baumbach-Duden-Hopt, supra n. a, Anno. following § 65.

OPINION OF THE GERMAN REICHSGERICHT IN THE MATTER OF NORDFR. BANK, DEFENDANT–APPELLANT, v. P., PLAINTIFF–RESPONDENT

3rd Civil Division, May 1, 1908, RGZ 68, 317.

[In May, 1906, the parties entered into a written contract by which the defendant Bank employed the plaintiff as assistant manager of one of its branches. The agreed-upon salary was less than 5,000 Marks per year. The contract was for 10 years; but plaintiff was to have the privilege, after the end of the first 3 years, to terminate the contract by giving 6 months' notice. In December, 1906, the defendant notified the plaintiff that the employment would come to an end on April 1, 1907. Plaintiff thereupon brought this action. One of the grounds upon which defendant relied in order to justify the termination of plaintiff's employment as of April 1, 1907, was the contention that the contractual provisions concerning the duration of the contract, not being equal for both sides, were void because they violated Section 67 of the Commercial Code, and that therefore the right of either party to terminate the contract was governed by Section 66, with which Section defendant had complied. The intermediate appellate court overruled this contention of the defendant and the Reichsgericht affirmed.]

Reasons: . . . [The Court first discusses the terms of the contract, and concludes that in fact defendant was bound for 10 years, whereas plaintiff was bound only for 3 or 3½ years.]

The provisions of Section 67 must be read together with Section 66 of the Commercial Code, and if so read they appear to refer only to ordinary "notice", i.e., the right of either party to terminate the employment without cause, by a unilateral declaration. Such right to give notice is, under the terms of this contract of employment, not given to either party, and for the first 3 years not even to the plaintiff. For these 3 years the contract is not subject to termination; to this extent it is a contract for a definite term. Sections 66, 67 do not cover contracts of this kind. The present action involves only the question whether the notice given on Dec. 28, 1906, that is *within the first 3 years*, has terminated the contract as of April 1, 1907; during the first 3 years, however, the contract was one for a definite term and was thus unaffected by the provisions of Section 67. Those provisions in Section 67 which limit the parties' freedom of contract, are therefore presently irrelevant. Only concerning the later period may a question arise as to whether the difference in the right to give notice invalidates the provisions in Par. 4 of the contract. This question must be answered in the negative.

The intermediate appellate court is incorrect in assuming that Section 67 does not apply in cases of unequal rights to give notice in which one party cannot give *any* notice, while the other party is privileged to terminate the contract by giving, say, six months' notice. In such cases, the court below holds, no unequal *periods of notice* are involved. In reality such agreement does constitute the stipulation of unequal periods. The notice period of the one who during a certain length of time may not give any notice, is, as compared to the right of the other party, just so much longer. Cf. Staub, Commercial Code, 8th ed., Section 67, Ann. 1. . . .

On the other hand, however, the court below is right in holding that the invalidity of unequal agreements, which is provided in Section 67, subd. 4, affects only agreements in favor of the employer. True, by its terms the Code prescribes that the period of notice "must be the same for both parties", and that "Any agreement contrary to these provisions is null and void." Seemingly, it makes no difference whether the contrary agreement is favorable or unfavorable to the clerk. Therefore, it is the view of several textwriters that no such differentiation should be indulged in. See Goldmann, Commercial Code, Section 67, Ann. 1, subd. II 1; Horrwitz, The Law of Commercial Clerks, 2nd ed., p. 120; Lotmar, The Labor Contract, Vol. 1, p. 593 [titles translated].

This interpretation, however, is inconsistent with the legislative purpose as expressed in the legislative history and in the Code itself.

The provisions of Section 67 were enacted in order to correct frequently encountered evils which became apparent in connection with commercial employments, which evils resulted from the unlimited freedom of the parties to make contracts unfavorable to the commercial clerks. [The Court then discusses the history of the bill which embodied the provision in question, and quotes from a Memorandum of the Reich Ministry of Justice which was submitted to the Reichstag together with the draft of Sections 66, 67 and the other 1897/98 amendments of the Commercial Code:] [a] "The provisions of the [old] Commercial Code relative to commercial clerks are no longer adequate under present conditions; especially, they are insufficient to protect such clerks against inequitable contract clauses imposed upon them at the time of their employment. The principle of absolute freedom of contract, upon which the [old] Commercial Code is based, has therefore been abandoned in the draft; in particular, agreements concerning periods of notice and promises not to compete have been subjected to certain restrictions in the interest of the clerks. . . ." [b] . . .

a. The quality of the materials that make up the legislative history of a code or statute, depends on the manner in which legislation is drafted and processed under the governmental system of the country in question. See F. Schmidt, Construction of Statutes, in 1 Scandinavian Studies in Law 155, 168–71 (1957). Where, as in most civil-law countries, important bills are carefully prepared by the Ministry of Justice or some other governmental agency possessing considerable expertise, the quality of the explanatory materials produced during the legislative process is apt to be high. See supra p. 294.

Some of the codes of the civil-law world contain express provisions concerning the extent to which the legislative history of a statute may be used in interpreting it. See, e.g., Art. 9 of the Civil Code of Panama, quoted in Compania de Aguaceros S.A. v. First National City Bank, supra p. 72.

b. Would similar use of the legislative history of a statute be made by an American court? By an English court? See A. W. Murphy, Old Maxims Never Die: The "Plain-Meaning Rule" and Statutory Interpretation in the "Modern" Federal Courts, 75 ColumL.Rev. 1299 (1975); H. W. Jones,

Not only its history, but also the law itself shows that Section 67 was enacted solely in the interest of the commercial clerks. Section 67 restricts freedom of contract; but Section 68 exempts from this restriction those commercial clerks who receive an annual salary of at least 5,000 Marks. . . . The law thus drops the restriction (placed upon freedom of contract) in cases involving a class of commercial clerks whose economic and social position renders special protection unnecessary. From this it follows that the restriction upon freedom of contract in Section 67 itself, in spite of the general language, is to serve only the interests of the commercial clerks whose economic position, it was believed, was too weak for unlimited freedom of contract. At the same time, Section 68 indicates that a contrary interpretation would lead to a result which could not be characterized as satisfactory: that the economically strong commercial clerk would as a matter of law be able to obtain more favorable periods of notice than he grants to his employer, whereas a like privilege would be denied to the economically weaker commercial clerk.

For these reasons we prefer an interpretation of Section 67, subd. 4, which invalidates contrary agreements only if they make the position of the clerk less favorable than that of the employer. Cf. Staub, Commercial Code, 8th ed., Section 67, Ann. 7; Dueringer-Hachenburg, Commercial Code, Section 67, Ann. III.

Inasmuch as the provisions concerning termination and notice in the instant contract favor the plaintiff as compared to the defendant, defendant as employer may not invoke Section 67, subd. 4. The contract provisions are valid.

NOTES AND QUESTIONS

See pg 73

(1) What are the mental processes by which the court in the principal case reaches the result that a notice period which is longer in case of termination by the employer than in case of termination by the employee, is valid in spite of the legal requirement that the notice period "*must be the same* for both parties"?

It is interesting to compare these mental processes with those reflected in J. H. Holding Co. v. Wooten, 291 N.Y. 427, 52 N.E.2d 934 (1943), where the New York Court of Appeals reached a strikingly similar result in construing a comparable statute.[1]

The Plain Meaning Rule and Extrinsic Aids in the Interpretation of Federal Statutes, 25 Wash.Un.L.Q. 2 (1939); Gutteridge, A Comparative View of the Interpretation of Statute Law, 8 Tulane L.Rev. 1, 5–11 (1933); W. Dale, Legislative Drafting: A New Approach 296–97, 311–12 (1977); Lord Lloyd of Hampstead & M. D. A. Freeman, Lloyd's Introduction to Jurisprudence 1142–56 (5th ed., 1985).

1. The statute involved in the New York case—old § 230 of the Real Property Law, which meanwhile has been transferred to § 5–905 of the Gen.Obl.Law—also dealt with the subject of notice periods in the context of a long-term legal relationship (landlord-tenant) between parties of unequal economic strength.

More refined draftsmanship can, of course, avoid the problem of interpretation presented both by the principal case and by the New York case cited in the text, supra. Thus the last paragraph of the present § 622 of the Civil Code provides that an individual contract may never impose a longer notice period on the employee than on the employer. In essence, this new wording codifies the holding of the

(2) In every legal system the courts must face up to the question whether and under what circumstances the interpretation of a written norm may deviate from its literal meaning.[1a] In civilian codes, one often finds an explicit directory provision intended to guide the courts in answering this question.[1b] But the German Civil Code, as the reader knows, differs from the majority of civil-law codes in that it contains no directory provisions. The German courts, nevertheless, found some helpful guidance in the Code itself. Among the provisions of the First Book which deal with "jural acts" and "declarations of intention" (see supra p. 534), one encounters § 133, which reads as follows:

> In interpreting a declaration of intention the true intention shall be explored, and the literal meaning of the expression [by which such intention has been declared] is not necessarily determinative.

In terms, this provision governs the interpretation of contracts, deeds, corporate resolutions and other jural acts, but not of codes and statutes. German courts and legal writers, however, are virtually unanimous in recognizing that § 133 should be analogously applied in interpreting the written law.[2] It follows, as the principal case demonstrates, that legislative history and considerations of policy can be resorted to, not only to resolve a doubt arising from an ambiguity in the written law, but even to create a doubt concerning the true meaning of a statute or code provision which, if taken literally, would be clear and unambiguous.

In other civil-law countries, directory provisions of the Civil Code are to the effect that legislative history and other interpretive aids can be used only to resolve a doubt, but not to create one.[2a] Without further study, however, it cannot be taken for granted that such directory provisions will always be obeyed by the courts.

(3) In civilian terminology, a distinction is drawn between cogent rules (*ius cogens*), which cannot be abrogated by the parties and render all contrary agreements null and void, and yielding rules (*ius dispositivum*), which are subject to the autonomy of the parties in the sense that the parties have the power to make agreements contrary to the rule.[3] A rule of the latter type is mere gap-filling law; it comes into play only to the extent that the parties have failed to cover the point in their agreement or other transaction.[4]

principal case. See also § 624, providing that employment contracts for life or for more than five years may, in any event, be terminated by the employee after five years, upon six months' notice.

1a. For references, see the footnotes accompanying the principal case.

1b. See, e.g., Art. 9 of the Civil Code of Panama, quoted supra p. 73.

2. See Palandt, Bürgerliches Gesetzbuch Introduction preceding § 1, Anno. VI 3 (41st ed., 1982).

2a. See supra n. 1b.

3. See Lenhoff, Optional Terms (Ius Dispositivum) and Required Terms (Ius Cogens) in the Law of Contracts, 45 Mich. L.Rev. 39 (1946).

Lawyers brought up in the common law, while familiar with the distinction between *ius cogens* and *ius dispositivum* in the law of contracts, use somewhat different terminology. In referring to those rules which the civilians characterize as *ius dispositivum*, the UCC uses the term "subject to agreement otherwise".

4. In dealing with particular types of contracts, the civil and commercial codes of civil-law countries tend to lay down many rules of *ius dispositivum*. Specifics with which the parties (intentionally or otherwise) have not dealt in the terms of the contract, thus are supplied by the code.

It has been observed that the civilians' frequent use of non-cogent *rules* of contract law marks a contrast to the common-law

Section 67, subd. 4 of the German Commercial Code, supra, expressly provides that any agreement contrary to the rule of subd. 1 (as construed by the courts) would be "null and void." To a German lawyer the provision of subd. 4 will appear unnecessary and repetitious, because subd. 1 already provides that the period "must" be the same for both parties. The draftsmen of the German codes aimed at accuracy and consistency in the use of terms. Those construing the codes, therefore, have to take the words "must" and "cannot" as conclusive indication of the cogent nature of a code provision, while the terms "may" and "shall" are held to characterize yielding rules.[5]

This rigorous, systematic use of terminological technique is peculiar to the German Code. The Civil Codes of France and Switzerland do not employ this method, and thus leave more room for judicial interpretation when a question arises concerning the cogent or yielding nature of a code provision.[6]

(4) The reader will recall our discussion (supra pp. 301–304) of the historical reasons which led most civil-law countries to adopt two separate codes of substantive private law—a civil code and a commercial code.[7] We have now seen such codes in action, and we know that provisions of both codes, by their terms, may be applicable in the same case. In what logical relationship do the two codes stand to each other? The practical examples given in the article which immediately follows, should help in answering this question.

---

habit of attempting "to derive all the consequences of a contract from the will of those who made it (or at least ostensibly to do so . . .)". See B. Nicholas, Rules and Terms—Civil Law and Common Law, 48 Tul.L.Rev. 946, 948 (1974). Professor Nicholas interestingly explains the historical reasons for this difference between the two systems. In recent times, however, this contrast has become less pronounced. As common-law countries subject more and more types of contracts (e.g., contracts for sale, transportation, insurance, etc.) to statutory regulation, they become increasingly civilian in their use of constructive terms which are derived, no longer from judicial analysis of the particular contract before the court, but from legislative imposition of *rules* (albeit rules subject to agreement otherwise) upon certain types of contracts.

5. See Schuster, The Principles of German Civil Law 9–10 (1907).

6. See Morrison, Legislative Technique and the Problem of Suppletive and Constructive Laws, 9 Tulane L.Rev. 544 (1935).

The problem whether and in what way the cogent or yielding nature of code provisions should be made clear in the code itself, must be faced by the draftsman of every code dealing with transactional subjects. Compare the German technique with the method employed in Sec. 1–102(3) and (4) of the Uniform Commercial Code. See also the comments on the latter provision in N.Y.Leg.Doc. (1955) No. 65(B) pp. 29–30, 1955 Report of the New York Law Revision Commission 155–6 (analysis by Professor Fulda); and Franklin, On the Legal Method of the Uniform Commercial Code, 16 Law & Contemp.Prob. 330, 332 (1951).

7. The reader will recall, also, that in the majority of civil-law countries (i.e., the countries which have preserved a separate Commercial Code) the function and coverage of the Commercial Code is quite different from that of our own UCC. See supra p. 541.

FRITZ MOSES, INTERNATIONAL LEGAL PRACTICE
4 Fordham L.Rev. 244 (1935).

[Footnotes renumbered.]

. . . We want to find whether an oral guaranty of a merchant is valid under French or German law.[a]

The answer as to the French law can be found only by a circuitous route. There is in the Code Civil a chapter entitled "On the Proof of Obligations and that of Payments" and therein a section "On Proof by Witnesses." Art. 1341 I of that section provides that no agreements involving more than [5000] Francs can be proven unless in writing.[b] But the second paragraph of Art. 1341 states that its first paragraph does not apply if something different is provided in the laws referring to commerce. Thus we examine the Code de Commerce. There we find under the title "Purchases and Sales" an article (109) stating that sales contracts can be proven, in addition to various other means, by witnesses, providing the court deems such evidence admissible. Nothing is said about guaranties. Nevertheless, this article is [1] generally interpreted to apply to all commercial transactions. And thus the final answer to our question as to French law is: An oral guaranty is valid, but enforcible only if involving not more than [5000] Francs, or—regardless of the amount—if given by a merchant in the course of his business.[2]

. . . In the section of the German Civil Code, dealing with guaranties, it is expressly provided that the promise to answer for the debt of another must be in writing in order to be valid,[3] and this is so regardless of the amount involved. As to the guaranty of a merchant no reference such as in Art. 1341 of the French Civil Code is made in the German Civil Code to the Code of Commerce. No chapter in the German Commercial Code deals with guaranties. But among the "General Provisions" of the book "Commercial Transactions" in the Code of Commerce we find a provision [4] according to which the Civil Code provision dealing with the written form does not apply to a

a. For a broader treatment of the question see E. J. Cohn, The Form of Contracts of Guarantee in Comparative Law, 54 L.Q. Rev. 220 (1938).

b. See supra p. 431 for the present, slightly revised version of Art. 1341.

1. Lyon-Caen & Renault, Manuel de droit commercial (14th ed. 1924) § 385: "The Code of Commerce (art. 109) refers expressly to the most usual commercial contract, the sale; but it follows from the Civil Code that the same rule applies in a general manner in matters of commerce."

2. Planiol et Ripert, Traité pratique de droit civil franҫais, Vol. XI, Contrats Civils (1932) § 1528.

[In other words, the specific provisions of Art. 109 of the Commercial Code were extended to cover all commercial transactions, even those outside the terms of the Article. This was clearly an instance, not of interpretation in the technical sense, but of bold analogical reasoning. In 1980, as part of the reform of the rules on documentary evidence, Art. 109 was amended to state expressly what it had traditionally been interpreted to mean: that as to merchants, the written form was unnecessary for commercial transactions except when required by an express statutory provision. Ed.]

3. Par. 766 German Civil Code.

4. Par. 350 German Commercial Code.

guaranty, provided it is given as a commercial transaction. Thus, under German law the oral guaranty of a merchant is valid. . . .

NOTES ON "CIVIL" AND "COMMERCIAL" LAW [a]

(1) *Divergencies Between the Civil Code and the Commercial Code.* Every Commercial Code enacted in a civilian country contains numerous provisions which are at odds with the provisions of the same country's Civil Code. Generally speaking, commercial law favors the easy and informal conclusion of transactions as well as their speedy consummation and rigorous enforcement. The Civil Code, on the other hand, may place a lesser value on speed and efficiency than on the protection (e.g., by form requirements) of the weak, the ignorant and the imprudent.[b] We just encountered an important example of this difference in attitude when we found that the German and French Civil Codes subject guarantees to a form requirement, but that under the Commercial Codes of both nations the oral guarantee of a merchant is valid and enforceable. The following are further examples, all taken from German law, of tough provisions embodied in the Commercial Code which are at variance with what the Civil Code provides:

(a) Contractual penalties are valid, but ordinarily may be reduced by the court (Civil Code § 343); there can be no such reduction, however, if the promisor is a merchant (Commercial Code § 348).[1]

(b) The rate of legal interest is higher in "commercial" than in "civil" matters. Compare Civil Code § 246 and Commercial Code § 352.

(c) In a commercial sales transaction the buyer is deemed to have waived his right to complain of any discoverable defects of the goods unless he examines them immediately upon arrival, and promptly notifies the seller of the defect (Commercial Code § 377). There is no such requirement in the case of a "civil" sale governed exclusively by the Civil Code.

(d) Among merchants, silence is more easily construed as acceptance of an offer than in non-commercial transactions.[2]

(e) Only a merchant can issue a promissory note as a negotiable one (Commercial Code §§ 363–365). If the issuer is not a

---

a. These Notes are partly based on Professor Schlesinger's study, The Uniform Commercial Code in the Light of Comparative Law, 1 Inter-Am.L.Rev. 11 (1959).

b. For an excellent discussion of the basic attitudinal difference between "civil" and commercial law, and of the continuous interaction between these two bodies of law, see B. Kozolchyk, The Commercialization of Civil Law and the Civilization of Commercial Law, 40 La.L.Rev. 3 (1979).

1. For further discussion of contractual penalties in civilian systems, see infra pp. 671–684. Under the Standard Terms Act of 1976, discussed infra p. 723, a penalty clause contained in a standard contract

may be void even as to a merchant if it is excessively burdensome.

2. See W. Lorenz, Acceptance by Silence (Report on Austrian, German and Swiss Law), in 2 Schlesinger (Gen.Ed.), Formation of Contracts—A Study of the Common Core of Legal Systems 1152 ff. (1968). One of the relevant provisions of the German Commercial Code is § 362, which provides that a merchant whose business involves the performance of services for others is under a duty to reply without delay if he receives an offer concerning the performance of such services from one with whom he maintains business relations; his silence is treated as acceptance of the offer.

merchant, then the note, even though purporting to be payable to the payee's order, can be transferred only by way of an ordinary assignment, with the result that defenses which would defeat the assignor are equally available as against the assignee.[2a]

These German examples could easily be multiplied, and similar examples could be given under the law of most other civil-law countries.[3]

(2) *Which of the Two Code Applies?* Suppose a French or German lawyer is asked to draft a contract of sale, of bailment, of carriage, or of guarantee; or to deal with a problem involving a partnership or an agency relationship. Will he find the applicable rules in the Civil Code or in the Commercial Code? The answer is seemingly simple: If the matter at hand is not commercial, the Civil Code alone (perhaps in conjunction with some auxiliary statute) will govern, and there is no need for consulting the Commercial Code. If the matter is commercial, then the Civil Code controls only with respect to points not covered by provisions of the Commercial Code, the latter provisions being treated as *lex specialis*.[4]

It follows that in the countless instances in which the positive provisions of the two codes differ from each other, the Civil Code provision must be applied if the matter is "civil" (i.e., non-commercial), while the Commercial Code prevails in commercial matters. The outcome of many cases thus turns on whether the transaction in question is classified as "commercial". In addition, as the reader will remember (see supra pp. 470–471), many civil-law countries provide

2a. Suppose a consumer (C), who has purchased goods from seller S, has issued a promissory note, or a series of such notes, for the purchase price. Suppose further that these notes are in negotiable form. If S endorses these notes to finance company F, and the law recognizes the negotiability of the notes, C is apt to find himself in a most unenviable position. Although the goods are defective, C may have no defense when he is sued on the notes by F, because F is likely to be regarded as a "holder in due course". Thus F will recover from C, and whether C can ever enforce his claim against S (who may have absconded or gone bankrupt), is most uncertain.

Note the elegant simplicity of the device by which German law protects the consumer from this "holder in due course" racket. Under German law, a non-merchant's promissory note cannot be made negotiable. Thus, regardless of the terms of the notes, F cannot acquire the status of a holder in due course; he is a mere assignee, and as such he is exposed to all defenses which C could interpose if he were sued by the assignor, i.e., by S.

Contrast the simplicity and effectiveness of the German solution with the complexities which have been created in our law by the manifold attempts of state courts, state legislatures and (most recently) federal regulators to overcome the "holder in due course" racket. For an instructive discus-

sion of these complexities, see J. J. White & R. S. Summers, Uniform Commercial Code § 14–8 and Appendix at pp. 1137 ff. (2d ed., 1980).

3. A further example from French law is provided by French Civil Code art. 1843 under which persons who have acted in the name of a company in the process of being formed are liable for the obligations thus created in a joint and several manner if the company has been formed under commercial law, but only ratably if the company has been formed under civil law. This is in line with the general proposition that "commercial" obligations are normally joint and several but that "civil" obligations are not. See infra p. 622.

For a Mexican example, see infra, text under (3). More generally, concerning the transplantation to Latin America of the classical civilian dichotomy between civil and commercial law, see R. Batiza, The Unity of Private Law in Latin America Under the Spanish Rule, 4 Inter-Am.L.Rev. 139, 155 (1962); id., Teaching Commercial Law in Latin America, Foreign Exchange Bulletin, Vol. V, Issue No. 2, p. 3 (1964).

4. See Art. 2 of the Introductory Law to the German Commercial Code: "Commercial matters are governed by the provisions of the Civil Code only insofar as the Commercial Code . . . does not establish different rules. . . ."

that "commercial" actions be brought before special commercial courts, or before commercial divisions of courts of general jurisdiction.[5] Procedure in "commercial" matters usually is simpler and speedier than in ordinary "civil" litigation.

Demarcation of what is "commercial" thus becomes a matter of central importance in most civilian systems. Some types of transactions, such as contracts made in the ordinary course of the banking or insurance business, and dealings which involve negotiable instruments, often are regarded as commercial *per se*. Many other transactions, however, of which contracts of sale, bailment and carriage as well as partnership agreements may be mentioned as examples, are sometimes "civil" and sometimes "commercial". Criteria are sought to be derived either from the parties' status as "merchants," or from the nature of the transaction as a "mercantile act."

Some civil-law jurisdictions, especially the German-speaking ones, stress the *subjective* element, i.e., the quality of the parties as "merchants" or "mercantile enterprises." [5a] The definition of "merchant" may be predicated on (a) the nature and object of the activities carried on,[6] or (b) the existence of a permanent business organization, or (c) the legal form of the organization (some jurisdictions provide that a business corporation is *per se* a merchant), or (d) certain formalities, such as registration in the *Register of Commerce*, or (e) a combination of these factors.

In other countries, especially in those influenced by French legal culture, the *objective* criterion of the "mercantile act" is emphasized. Code definitions of "mercantile acts" usually consist of lengthy and unsystematic enumerations.[7] Even within the French-influenced fami-

---

5. Separate commercial courts (or commercial divisions) may exist even in countries which in their substantive law do not have a separate Commercial Code. This is the case, for instance, in some of the Swiss cantons (jurisdiction and procedure being cantonal matters, while substantive private law is essentially covered by federal law, i.e. the Civil Code and the Code of Obligations). See 1 Guldener, Schweizerisches Zivilprozessrecht 19–21, 104–08 (2nd ed., 1958). Thus, although the structure of the Swiss code system (see supra p. 542) deemphasizes the distinction between civil and commercial matters in the area of substantive law, a Swiss lawyer still may have to struggle with the distinction in order to choose the proper court.

In a small minority of civil-law jurisdictions, commercial courts have been abolished, for instance in Italy (which no longer has a separate Commercial Code) and in the Netherlands (where a Commercial Code still exists but where its merger into the revised Civil Code is contemplated).

5a. In the more recent Latin American commercial codes, also, the trend seems to be to emphasize the subjective element. It

is predicated, however, on the notion of "enterprise" rather than on an individual's status as "merchant". See S. A. Bayitch, Empresa in Latin American Law: Recent Developments, 4 Lawyer of the Americas 1, at 5–6 (1972).

6. Some codes stress the *nature* of the activities (e.g., buying and selling), while in other codes the profit-making *object* of the activities is made the primary touchstone. Extractive and even agricultural activities may become "commercial" under a code emphasizing the latter point, especially if the enterprise is of such size as to require a commercial organization.

Doubts may arise, also, with respect to the "merchant" status of non-profit-making organizations engaged in large-scale activities which by their nature (as distinguished from their object) could be considered commercial.

7. See, e.g., Amos and Walton's Introduction to French Law 341–42 (3rd ed. by F. H. Lawson, A. E. Anton and L. N. Brown, 1967), where the relevant provisions of the French Commercial Code are discussed.

ly of codes, there are vast differences with respect to inclusion or exclusion of manufacturing, mining and agricultural activities.[8]

The two concepts, "merchant" and "mercantile act", are interrelated in complex ways. A person's status as "merchant" may depend on whether he makes it his business to engage in mercantile acts.[9] The nature of a transaction as a "mercantile act", on the other hand, may be predicated on whether the parties entering into it are business enterprises permanently engaged in, and organized for, a business involving transactions of the same kind. The resulting confusion is confounded by the circumstance that occasionally a transaction is treated as "commercial" for jurisdictional and procedural but not for substantive purposes.

Both legislative and doctrinal attempts to establish a demarcation line between "commercial" and "civil" transactions, have led to obscurity and excessive refinement. The draftsmen of most of the European and Latin-American commercial codes have attempted to blend the subjective and the objective criteria. The resulting mixed systems, however, differ greatly from each other.[9a] Even within a single jurisdiction, there is apt to be doubt and ambiguity, reflected in controversies among text-writers and in conflicting judicial decisions.[10]

The practical difficulties arising from these doubts, however, are greatly reduced by an institution founded on old tradition and anchored in the commercial codes and statutes of almost all civil law countries: *the Commercial Register*.[11] This Register, operated by a judicial or other public officer, usually is open to public inspection. It facilitates the demarcation between merchants and non-merchants. As has been mentioned before, entry in the Register, or the lack of it, is one of the factors determining a person's status as a merchant. Some codes go further and provide that an individual, partnership or corporation [12]

8. Historically and philosophically, it is easy to understand why the French legislator of 1807 preferred the objective criterion of "mercantile act" or "act of commerce" over the older subjective test predicated on a person's quality as "merchant". In keeping with the spirit of the period, this choice extolled contract over status. In practice, however, the objective criterion has not worked well, and there have been proposals to abandon it. See Houin, Reform of the French Civil Code and the Code of Commerce, 4 Am.J.Comp.L. 485, 502 (1955).

9. See, e.g., § 1 of the German Commercial Code.

9a. The reader who is interested in a particular country's detailed rules concerning the demarcation line between "civil" and "commercial" transactions, is referred to the Digest of Commercial Laws of the World, published under the auspices of The National Association of Credit Management, Inc. As an example, see T. Ansay, The Commercial Laws of Turkey 3–8 (1979).

10. Counsel's effort and clients' money often are spent on litigating a single issue:

the "civil" or "commercial" nature of the case. For an example which happens to be available in the English language, see Compania Agricola v. Reyes, 4 Phil. 2 (1904), commented on by Lobingier, Codification in the Philippines: Uniting the Civil and Commercial Codes, 10 Jour. of Comp. Leg., N.S., 239, 240 (1910).

11. The Commercial Register exists even in countries which do not have a separate Commercial Code. See, e.g., Swiss Code of Obligations Arts. 927–943.

The reader should note, also, that the Commercial Register can be found in many of the countries (e.g., Islamic countries) which have adopted only some features of the civil law. See, e.g., T. W. Hill, The Commercial Legal System of the Sultanate of Oman, 17 Int. Lawyer 507, 516 (1983).

12. In many countries, a corporation does not acquire juristic personality (i.e., does not become a legal entity) until it is registered; and it may automatically lose its juristic personality upon cancellation of its registration. See the Swiss case infra, pp. 762–765.

listed in the Register is deemed to be a merchant, at least for the benefit of other persons dealing with him, who in good faith have relied on the entry in the Register.[13] Moreover, if a person or firm is in fact a merchant under the definition prevailing in his country, the official in charge of the Register normally has the power to compel registration. In practice, therefore, the Register as a rule will furnish reliable information as to whether a given person or organization may be regarded as a "merchant".[14]

(3) *Unilaterally Commercial Transactions.* Special difficulties arise in cases of so-called "mixed" transactions, i.e., of transactions which are "commercial" for one party but not for the other. The opera singer who buys securities from or through a brokerage house, is a favorite classroom example. More importantly, most retail sales are "mixed", because ordinarily the seller is a merchant and for him the sale is a mercantile transaction, while the consumer-buyer normally is neither a merchant nor engaged in a mercantile act.

The Commercial Codes of some countries contain reasonably clear provisions concerning the treatment of "mixed" transactions. The German Commercial Code, for instance, in § 345 lays down the rule that "except as otherwise provided, the provisions concerning commercial transactions apply to a transaction which is commercial for either of the parties." The clause "except as otherwise provided" is of great significance. To avoid hardship, many exceptions to the general rule of § 345 have been spelled out in other Code provisions; e.g., § 350 of the Commercial Code, repeatedly mentioned above, provides that a guarantee is exempt from the Civil Code's requirement of a writing only if *the guarantor* is a merchant.

There are other countries, however, especially in Latin America, where the Commercial Code, by provisions that are either unwarrantedly broad or lacking in clarity, extends its coverage so as to bring too many of the "mixed" transactions within its sweep.[14a] Often this results in frustrating the protective purpose of a Civil Code provision, and in oppression of the weaker party, as is shown by the following

> *Example:* [15] *B*, a Mexican farmer who has no business experience, purchases a television set from *S*, a Mexican corporation engaged in the retail distribution of such sets. The price is

In France, where the commercial register has been renamed the Commercial and Company Register, even partnerships can have legal personality, but only if they are registered. Civil Code, Arts. 1842 and 1871. (Note, however, that in the case of partnerships such legal personality does not imply limited liability under French law).

13. The evidentiary and estoppel effect of the Register will be the subject of more detailed discussion in a later part of this book. See infra pp. 696–702.

14. Indirectly, the Register will be helpful, also, in determining whether (in a jurisdiction adhering to the objective theory) a given transaction is a "mercantile act", because, as we have seen, the latter issue may largely depend on whether the contracting parties are merchants.

14a. Art. 7 of the Argentine Code of Commerce reads: "When a transaction is commercial for one of the parties, all parties involved shall be subject to commercial law." In contrast to German law, the law of Argentina apparently does not modify the broad sweep of this rule by proper exceptions. The situation seems to be similar in many, if not most, of the other Latin American countries. See R. Batiza, The Civilian Codes of Commerce and the U.C.C., 5 Int. Lawyer 308, 310 (1971).

15. This example is based on information appearing in the article by W. D. Warren, Mexican Retail Installment Sales Law: A Comparative Study, 10 UCLA L.Rev. 15, especially at 53–57 (1962).

almost twice the going market price for sets of the same kind; interest charges on the unpaid part of the 24 monthly installments amount to 70% per annum; and the contract virtually negatives any warranty. Another contract clause provides that in case any installment is not paid when due, the whole balance shall become payable at once. When eight months after delivery the picture tube fails, *B* refuses to make any further payments, and *S* sues for the balance due under the contract.

B's lawyer may attempt to base his defense on the Mexican Consumer Protection statute.[15a] However, no relief may be available under that statute. It contains no general provision prohibiting unconscionable contracts. The contract involved here appears to comply with its various mandatory rules, e.g. on legible print. The warranty provisions of the statute cannot be used any longer since they are limited to a period of two (or sometimes six) months from the date of sale. The extent to which the statute would invalidate the acceleration clause is unclear. Hence B's lawyer would probably have to rely on Art. 17 of the Mexican Civil Code,[16] which reads as follows:

> "When any person, taking advantage of the supreme ignorance, notorious inexperience or extreme poverty of another, obtains an excessive profit which is evidently disproportionate to the obligations assumed by him, the person damaged has the right to demand the rescission of the contract, and if this be impossible, an equitable reduction in his obligation." [17]

S's lawyer, on the other hand, will point to Art. 385 of the Mexican Commercial Code (a federal statute), which in effect provides that in transactions governed by the latter Code, the rule of Art. 17 of the Civil Code does not apply. The outcome of the case thus will hinge on whether the "mixed" transaction between *S* and *B* is governed by the Commercial Code. This question is a difficult and debatable one. At first blush, one might think that *B* can derive some comfort from Art. 1050 of the Commercial Code, the only provision expressly dealing with mixed transactions, which reads as follows:

15a. In 1975, Mexico adopted a federal statute for the protection of consumers. See D. J. Kaye, Ley Federal de Protection al Consumidor, comentada y concordada (2d ed. 1981). The Law creates a federal consumer procuracy which must study consumer problems and suggest solutions; it may also act as a mediator for consumer complaints. In addition, the law imposes some minimum requirements on consumer contracts—they must be in writing, must inform the consumer as to cash price and interest, etc.

16. This is the Civil Code for the Federal District, which has been the model for the Civil Codes adopted in the majority of the States.

17. This article, to be compared with the German provision invoked in the *Neuergasthof* case, infra p. 615, embodies a modern version of the civil-law doctrine of *lésion*, which has a long history reaching back to Roman law. See the classical study by J. P. Dawson, Economic Duress and Fair Exchange in French and German Law, 11 Tul.L.Rev. 345, especially 364–76 (1937) and 12 Tul.L.Rev. 42 (1937). For more recent comparative discussions of *lésion*, see B. Kozolchyk, The Commercialization of Civil Law and the Civilization of Commercial Law, 40 La.L.Rev. 3, at 9–12 (1979); A. T. Von Mehren, The French Doctrine of Lesion in the Sale of Immovable Property, 49 Tul.L.Rev. 321 (1975); A. Watson, The Doctrine of Enorm Lesion, 2 J. Legal Hist. 186 (1981).

"Whenever . . . of the two parties who enter into a contract, one effects an act of commerce and the other an act purely civil, and such contract gives rise to litigation, it shall be prosecuted in conformity with the provisions of *this Book*, if the party who effected the commercial act is the defendant; in the other case the act shall be prosecuted in conformity with the rules of civil law." (Emphasis supplied.)

Closer scrutiny shows that "this Book", to which Art. 1050 refers, is Book Five of the Commercial Code, which deals with procedure in commercial matters. Thus, although *B* is the defendant, Art. 1050 negatives the application of the Commercial Code only insofar as *procedure* is concerned. Regarding the question whether *substantively* this installment sale should be governed by the Commercial Code, Art. 1050 leaves us in the dark. Thus the Mexican court is likely to turn for guidance to the most prestigious scholarly writings, and these seem to favor indiscriminate application of the Commercial Code to "mixed" transactions. Under this view, the protection of Art. 17 of the Civil Code is withdrawn from the weaker party in the very cases when it is most needed, i.e. when he deals with an expert; [18] but since the Code provisions are not clear regarding the substantive treatment of "mixed" transactions, there is a real danger that the court, influenced by authoritative treatises, will declare Art. 17 inapplicable and hold *B* liable in accordance with the terms of the contract. [19]

---

18. See B. Kozolchyk, Fairness in Anglo and Latin American Commercial Adjudication, 2 B.C.Int. & Comp.L.Rev. 219, 227–29 (1979).

19. See Warren, supra n. 15. See also supra n. 14a. Compare the Uniform Commercial Code's technique of dealing with "mixed" transactions. As a rule, the UCC applies to retail sales; but its § 2–302 *strengthens* consumer protection. See the interesting—and partly comparative—discussion of the relevant cases in J. J. White & R. S. Summers, Uniform Commercial Code 155–60 (2d ed. 1980). For a more recent discussion of the situation in the United States, see Ph.I. Blumberg, Consumer Protection in the United States: Control of Unfair or Unconscionable Practices, 34 (Supp.) Am.J.Comp.L. 99 (1986).

In continental Europe, code provisions as well as auxiliary statutes aiming at consumer protection usually are applicable regardless of whether or not the transaction is "commercial"; sound results can thus be reached in fact situations which are similar to the Mexican example in the text. On the German statute on standard contract terms, which protects consumers, but is not limited to consumer protection, see infra pp. 723–724. For a recent case declaring a stipulation for excessive interest in a consumer loan void on the basis of German Civil Code § 138, which is similar to Mexican Civil Code art. 17, see BGH, July 10, 1986, 39 N.J.W. 2564 (1986). In France, the implied warranty against hidden defects (with a limitation period running from the discovery of the defect, not from the sale) cannot be excluded in a consumer contract. Decree No. 78–464 of March 24, 1978, arts. 2, 4. In Austria, § 1 of the *Wuchergesetz* (Law on "usury", i.e. grossly unfair contracts) of 1949, as amended, 1949 Austrian BGBl 1271, 1974 BGBl 1422, 1979 BGBl 1410, which also is quite similar to art. 17 of the Mexican Civil Code, clearly applies to such transactions. On European law see also Consumer Redress, 1985 E.C. Bull Supp. No. 2.

2. JUDICIAL INTERPRETATION OF CODES—THE FORCE OF PRECEDENTS IN A CODE SYSTEM

IN RE SHOOP

Supreme Court of the Philippine Islands, 1920.
41 Phil. 213.

Reported ante, p. 229.

NOTES AND QUESTIONS ON THE "BINDING" FORCE OF PRECEDENTS

(1) In a common-law system, judicial decisions constitute "the law." Therefore, without a doctrine of stare decisis, "the law" would be uncertain.[1] In a code system, codes and auxiliary statutes are "the law." In theory, the courts merely "apply" and "interpret" the law. As the written law is thought to provide the necessary element of certainty, judicial decisions need not, and generally do not, have binding force under such a system.[2]

As a general proposition, therefore, and as a convenient starting point for discussion, it is correct to state that in common-law jurisdictions judicial decisions are binding on subordinate courts, and in some measure on co-ordinate courts and on the deciding court itself, while the civil-law world does not regard judicial pronouncements as binding in subsequent cases.[3] But the statement needs to be qualified. First of all, we must allow for the great variations which exist within the common-law world. We know, for instance, that in this country the doctrine of stare decisis is applied less rigidly than in England.[4] Sec-

1. Once the doctrine is established, common-law courts tend to apply it, also, to precedents which merely interpret a statute; see infra p. 603. This may not be too logical, but a contrary view would lead to practical difficulties in the many instances in which a single decision is based partly on statutes and partly on common law.

2. Resorting to exaggeration in order to drive home the point, one might say that in a common-law system the case law, made binding by the doctrine of stare decisis, represents an element of stability, and that change is brought about mainly by statutory law. In the civil law, on the other hand, the codes provide some certainty (at least verbal certainty) and structural stability, while judicial "interpretation", unfettered by a formal rule of stare decisis, constitutes an element of flexibility.

3. Until he has read all of the materials in this chapter, the reader should suspend judgment as to what *practical* difference it makes whether judicial precedents are formally binding or not. At this point, atten-

tion should be focused on the basic difference between common-law and civil-law *theory*. The reader already is familiar with some of the historical reasons for this difference. See supra pp. 245–310. For further light on the historical and doctrinal roots of the difference, see Lipstein, The Doctrine of Precedent in Continental Law With Special Reference to French and German Law, 28 J.Comp.Leg. & Int.L. (3rd ser.) 34 (1946).

4. See Goodhart, Case Law in England and America, 15 Cornell L.Q. 173 (1930); C. M. Schmitthoff, Law Reform in England, 1965 J.Bus.L. 219, at 228–31.

The statement in the text is still true today, even though the English version of the doctrine of stare decisis has been slightly relaxed by the famous statement of the House of Lords of July 26, 1966. For a discussion of that statement, see J. Stone, 1966 and All That! Loosing the Chains of Precedent, 69 Colum.L.Rev. 1162 (1969); R. Cross, Precedent in English Law 107–22 (3rd ed., 1977).

ondly, to the broad assertion that in the whole civil-law world the courts are never bound by precedents, we must hasten to add at least the following qualifications:

(a) Under German and French procedure, which we have studied earlier (supra p. 466ff.), an *en banc* or super-panel decision is required in certain cases in which a division of the highest court desires to deviate from a prior ruling of the court.

(b) Some civil-law countries, especially in the Spanish-speaking world, have constitutional or statutory provisions to the effect that a certain number of successive decisions, all of which express the same view on the same point of law, shall have the force of a controlling precedent.[5] In Mexico, for instance, five decisions of the highest court in certain constitutional and other federal matters will have such force.[6] The Spanish rules concerning "*doctrina legal*" (supra p. 236), although not specifying the required number of successive decisions, have a similar effect.[6a]

In Brazil, the official headnotes of certain appellate decisions—either rendered *en banc* or sufficiently repetitive to reflect the weight of authority—can be inscribed in a collection called the *Súmula*; they then acquire a "de facto stare decisis" effect.[6b]

(c) In Germany and Italy, and also in other civil-law countries which have a separate Constitutional Court, it is provided that certain decisions of that Court shall have the force of law.[7]

(d) Most civil-law systems recognize "customary law" as a subsidiary source of law, i.e., a source that can be used to fill gaps in the written law. In general, the practical importance of this source of law tends to be limited (see infra pp. 621–622). There are occasional instances, however, in which a particular line of decisions of the highest court is said to have created a rule of "customary law". See the German cases infra pp. 615–641. Needless to say, by thus being converted into "customary law", certain judicial decisions are given the force of law and acquire the status of binding precedents.

---

5. See H. L. Clagett, The Administration of Justice in Latin America 125 (1952); K. L. Karst, Latin American Legal Institutions 106–08 (1966); K. L. Karst & K. S. Rosenn, Law and Development in Latin America 137–38 (1975); G. Ireland, Precedents' Place in Latin Law, 40 W.Va.L.Q. 115, 127–28 (1934).

6. See B. Kozolchyk, Mexican Law of Damages for Automobile Accidents: Damages or Restitution?, 1 Ariz.J.Int. & Comp. L. 189, at 194 (1982); W. J. Wagner, Federal States and Their Judiciary 118 (1959); R. C. Maxwell and M. G. Goldman, Mexican Legal Education, 16 J.Legal Ed. 155, 162 (1963); S. A. Bayitch and J. Luis Siqueiros, Conflict of Laws: Mexico and the United States 17–19, 23 (1968). An English translation of the relevant Mexican provisions will be found in Karst, supra n. 5, at 626–27 (1966).

6a. The Spanish rule mentioned in the text, supra, is not unique. A similar provision is contained in Art. 303 of the Argentine Code of Civil and Commercial Procedure. See G. R. Carrió, Judge Made Law Under a Civil Code, 41 La.L.Rev. 993, 1002 (1981).

6b. K. S. Rosenn, Civil Procedure in Brazil, 34 Am.J.Comp.L. 487, 513–14 (1986).

7. In Germany, this is true of most decisions of the Federal Constitutional Court which involve the constitutionality of a statute. See § 31 of the Gesetz über das Bundesverfassungsgericht (Law Concerning the Federal Constitutional Court), re-enacted on Feb. 3, 1971. In Italy, Art. 136 of the Constitution provides that "When the Court declares that a provision of law . . . is unconstitutional, the provision shall cease to have effect from the day following the publication of the decision."

Though subject to these exceptions and qualifications, it remains true that the civilians do not accord formally binding force to judicial precedents. Many scholars believe that, at least in theory, this creates a gulf between civilian thinking and ours.[8] Much has been written on the subject, under the heading of Jurisprudence as well as Comparative Law. Some writers go so far as to regard a given jurisdiction's attitude toward stare decisis as the principal touchstone determining whether it is a common-law or a civil-law jurisdiction. The treatment of precedents by Louisiana courts, for instance, has played a major part in the scholarly controversy concerning the question whether that State is still a civil-law jurisdiction.[9]

(2) A judicial decision rendered in a civil-law country, and not constituting a binding precedent in such country, may become binding elsewhere by a strange process of transplantation. In Puerto Rico, for instance, it was held that the Insular Legislature, when it enacted a Civil Code almost entirely copied from that of Spain, adopted not only the provisions of the Code but also the interpretations previously placed upon them by the highest court of Spain. See Olivieri v. Biaggi, 17 P.R.R. 676 (1911); Marchan v. Eguen, 44 P.R.R. 396 (1933). Spanish decisions, which under the civil-law doctrine may have had no binding force in Spain, and which were not binding in Puerto Rico when it was a Spanish possession, thus became binding precedents under American rule. Is this the necessary result of reenactment of a civil-law-inspired statute or code? Or is the well-known rule, that by reenacting a statute the legislature presumably adopts prior judicial interpretations of the statutory language, itself an outgrowth of common-law thinking? If so, is it sound to apply this rule of statutory interpretation to a civilian code, reenacted by legislators who were not necessarily thinking in common-law terms?

BREEDLOVE v. TURNER

Supreme Court of Louisiana, 1821.
9 Mart. (Old Ser.) 353.

PORTER, J. The plaintiffs allege that they employed the defendant, an attorney and counsellor at law, to commence a suit by attachment, against Thos. H. Fletcher, a citizen of Tennessee, on a claim arising from his endorsement of a protested bill of exchange, drawn by C. Stump, of Nashville, on Stump, Eastland & Cox, New Orleans, for $8200, for which sum, together with the interest and damages, amounting in the whole to $10,500, he, Fletcher, was indebted to them. That for a reasonable fee and reward, by them to be paid, the defendant agreed to conduct said suit skilfully, faithfully and diligently. But that, not regarding his previous agreement, he had unfaithfully

---

8. See, e.g., Pound, The Theory of Judicial Decision, 36 Harv.L.Rev. 641, 645–9 (1923).

9. For conflicting answers to this question, see, on the one hand, Ireland, Louisiana's Legal System Reappraised, 11 Tulane L.Rev. 585, 591–2 (1937) and Comment, 7 Tulane L.Rev. 100 (1932); but see, on the other hand, Daggett, Dainow, Hebert and McMahon, A Reappraisal Appraised: A

Brief for the Civil Law of Louisiana, 12 Tulane L.Rev. 12, 17–24 (1937) and Note, 17 Geo.Wash.L.Rev. 186, 192–3 (1949).

When studying the Louisiana case immediately following these Notes, and the subsequent materials, the reader will be able to judge for himself whether the attitude toward precedents exhibited (at various times) by the highest court of Louisiana reflects common-law or civil-law notions.

and negligently commenced it in the parish court of the parish of New Orleans, which had not authority to take cognizance of the same; when he ought to have brought it in the district court, for the first judicial district, which had jurisdiction of the matters and things thereunto appertaining; that the cause of action, on said bill of exchange, arose out of the limits of New Orleans; that the supreme court of this state had decided, long before the commencing of this suit, that the parish court had no jurisdiction of such cases, and that the defendant had due notice thereof.

They further aver, that by reason of the unskilfulness, mismanagement and gross neglect of said Turner, they have lost their lien on the property attached, and with it, the debt aforesaid; have been obliged to stop payment, and have suffered damage to the amount of twenty thousand dollars, for which sum they pray judgment.

The defendant, in his answer, denied all these allegations; the plaintiffs produced in evidence the record in the case of Breedlove & Bradford v. Fletcher, the case of Delille v. Gaines, decided in the supreme court, March, 1817. That of Dunwoodie v. Johnson, and Smith v. Flower, both decided in the same court in January term, 1819.

. . . records of seventy-seven cases brought in the parish court were introduced for the purpose of showing that it was customary to institute suits in that court, on contracts originating out of the parish, since the decision in the suit of Delille v. Gaines.

It was admitted that Judge Derbigny dissented from the opinion delivered by the supreme court, in the case of Breedlove & Bradford v. Fletcher.

The letter from the plaintiffs to the defendant, employing him as attorney, to bring suit against Fletcher, and have his property attached, was also produced. It was dated on Saturday evening, and requested that everything might be prepared by Monday morning.

To rebut the presumption arising from the practice of bringing suits in the parish court, the plaintiffs examined Isaac T. Preston, Alfred Hennen, and Levi Pierce, attorneys, practising in the courts of this city.

The two first named gentlemen severally declared that from the time the decision of the supreme court in the case of Delille v. Gaines came to their knowledge, they had considered the parish court not to have jurisdiction in cases originating out of the parish. L. Pierce stated that his opinion as to the jurisdiction which he had before doubted, was fixed by the decision in the case of Dunwoodie v. Johnson.

The cause on this evidence was submitted to a special jury, who found for the defendant.

The novelty of the present action, the large amount involved in its decision, and the circumstance that the judgment which has to be pronounced, must eventuate in a total loss to the party cast, has given

Attorney's defenses →

to this case a degree of interest which rarely occurs from the discussion of mere legal rights.

1. Various grounds of defence have been taken; the first is, that the decisions of the supreme court, in the cases of Delille v. Gaines, Smith v. Flower, and Dunwoodie v. Johnson, were wrong; that notwithstanding the opinions pronounced then, the defendant had a right to disregard them, and bring his action in the parish court of the parish of New Orleans; and that there was error here in dismissing this case, for want of jurisdiction in that court.

2. That lawyers practising in this state are not under any obligation to notice the opinions which this court may pronounce, and that a difference of opinion between the court and the advocate, cannot make the latter responsible in damages. *Noted*

3. That if the jurisdiction of the parish court was doubtful, this tribunal had no authority to decide the question, but should have referred it to the legislature, such being the practice in Spain.

4. That the law cited by the plaintiffs as to fault and negligence, applies only to attorneys; and that gentlemen at our bar, practising both as counsellors and attorneys, are not responsible in the latter capacity, because they act under the advice of themselves as counsellors, and they are not responsible as counsellors for errors of judgment in giving that advice.

5. That the defendant can only be made responsible for fault or negligence; that there was no *fault*, because that implies an act of the will, an intention to do wrong, of which it is not pretended the defendant can be accused; and that there was no *negligence*, because that consists not in doing a thing incorrectly, but in failing to do it at all.

6. That at most, the defendant only committed an error of judgment, for which he is not responsible. That in that error, he was supported by the opinion and practice of many of his brethren, as the evidence proves that a learned and able judge, then on the supreme bench, dissented from the decision in the cause of Breedlove & Bradford v. Fletcher.

And lastly, that the plaintiffs have not produced legal evidence that the cause of action in the case of Breedlove & Bradford v. Fletcher, arose out of the parish of New Orleans.

. . . First, as to the correctness of the decision of this court, in the case of Breedlove & Bradford v. Fletcher, 8 Martin 69.

In ordinary cases, I should deem it unnecessary after a subject has been so frequently agitated, and so often prounounced on, to say anything more than refer to the decisions of this court, by which the law had been settled. But as there has been a change in some of the members of this tribunal since the decision complained of, and as a contrary doctrine has been urged with a zeal which excited attention, it has been thought proper to examine the question again, and with an anxiety to correct the error into which the court might have fallen, if we could be satisfied it was one. [The Court then discusses the statute defining the jurisdiction of the parish court.]

I conclude, therefore, that the parish court had not jurisdiction of cases arising out of the parish of New Orleans, and that, therefore, the first ground of defence fails.

The next objection, that the lawyers practising in this state are not under any necessity of noticing the judgments given by the supreme court, has, certainly, the merit of novelty, to justify an examination of its correctness.

In support of this position, a great deal of time was occupied in showing, that the decisions were not law; that nothing could be properly called so, but those acts passed by that branch of our government, in whom the power of legislation is vested by the constitution.[a] This is true, and we never before supposed that they were so considered. But as we are obliged, by our duty, to decide on every question that is brought before us,[b] and, as many of these questions turn on ascertaining the true meaning of the lawmaker, when the expressions used are ambiguous, whether that ambiguity be considered in relation to the language used in the act, or the applicability of the provision to particular cases; I had supposed it not doubted, that the decisions of this tribunal were to be regarded as the interpretation of the legislative will; as an exposition of its meaning and intention. And that, until the legislative authority, by subsequent acts, chose to make different provisions on the subject, that it is an acquiescence on their part, that the court fairly understood their meaning, and wisely and faithfully expounded it. There is, also, a variety of questions presented for decision, where positive law is silent, and where recourse must be had to legal analogies, to arrive at truth. Are not the decisions which this court makes, amid the frequent conflicting opinions of foreign jurists, to be received as determining which doctrine is in force here? We are told not; that recourse must be had to the law itself, and that law is found where? In some obscure commentator, who lived, perhaps, some centuries ago, and who is quoted, triumphantly, as better evidence of what is a rule of action for the people of Louisiana, than the decisions of men, who, whatever in other respects be their abilities, have, at least, the advantage of using the knowledge and the learning that latter times have produced—who enjoy the light of the age in which they live, and who have the aid of able counsel, discussing every subject on which they are called to pronounce an opinion.

This, then, is the fair extent to which the authority of the decisions of this tribunal may be carried. They are evidence of what the law is,

---

a. Civil Code of Louisiana, Art. 1: "Law is a solemn expression of legislative will." Prior to the 1825 revision of the Code this Article read: "Law is a solemn expression of legislative will upon a subject of general interest and interior regulation."

b. Cf. Art. 4 of the French Civil Code: "A judge who refuses to adjudicate a case, under the pretext that the law is silent, obscure or insufficient, can be prosecuted as being guilty of a denial of justice."

A lawyer should recognize obvious precedents; failure to do = malpractice, but here cases were not printed so no malpractice

SUBSTANTIVE LAW . 603

under such circumstances, as has been just stated, and as it is the duty of the court to see that they are correct, and that they are uniform; so, also, is it important, that society should know, that we feel ourselves bound by them, unless we are clearly, and beyond doubt, satisfied that they are contrary to law or the constitution, and that we never can consider it a proper discharge of duty in any member of the bar, who pursues his profession with an avowed determination to disregard them.

Noted

It is no answer to this reasoning, to say that the law is different from the decision of the court, for that is begging the question, and taking for granted, the very point which the court has otherwise decided.

On this view of the subject, I need not examine the difference between the authority to which decisions under our law are entitled, and those of the courts in England; many of the latter, as was truly stated, turn on the common law, many of them, however, grow out of the expressions used in their statutes, and are given in expounding them. Cases of the latter description are delivered under circumstances similar to those in which this court pronounces here, and have, in that country, the same weight which I have just stated, the decisions of this tribunal should enjoy in this.[c]

Nor do I find, that the opinion or practice of other countries is different on this head. In France, where the science of jurisprudence has been carried to great perfection, the decisions of their courts of last resort are referred to by the most eminent writers on the laws of that country, by D'Aguesseau, by Denisart, by Merlin, by Paillet, by Duguien, by Pothier, by the jurists who have published a late edition of the last mentioned author's works.[d]

c. This sentence of the opinion cannot, or at least no longer, be said to be correct. Insofar as the application of the modern English doctrine of stare decisis is concerned, it makes no difference whether the precedent announces a rule of common law or interprets a statute. See H. W. Goldschmidt, English Law from the Foreign Standpoint 43 (1937); H. C. Gutteridge, A Comparative View of the Interpretation of Statute Law, 8 Tul.L.Rev. 1, 16 (1933). Slowly, however, some inroads have been made on the rigidity of the whole doctrine. See supra p. 597.

d. This observation by the Court is entirely correct. Recent research, conducted by Professor Gorla and others, has shown that during the 17th and 18th centuries the reported decisions of judicial tribunals became noticeably influential throughout the civil-law world. See supra p. 297, and also G. Gorla, La "Communis Opinio Totius Orbis" et la réception jurisprudentielle du droit au cours des XVIe, XVIIe et XVIIIe siècles dans la "Civil Law" et la "Common Law", in M. Cappelletti (Ed.,), New Perspectives for a Common Law of Europe 45 (1978), where further references can be found. As to France, see also R. David, French Law 8–9 (1972). Whether during the period just mentioned the influence of reported decisions actually became greater than that of professorial writings, is a difficult and somewhat controversial question, the answer to which will have to be found through further research, and probably will vary from country to country. Certain it is, however, that during the centuries which immediately preceded the date of the Court's decision in this case, voluminous collections of judicial decisions were published in Italy, France and other civil-law countries, and that legal writers as well as practitioners made ample use of such collections.

Since the enactment of the different codes, under the reign of Napoleon, an immense number of the reports of the decisions of their court of cassation, and other tribunals of appeal, have been collected and published with the utmost care, see Jurisprudence du Code Civil, 22 vols., Sirey, Recueil général des Lois et des Arreêts, 16 vols., Journal des audiences de la Cour de cassation, 14 vols., by Denevers. If, as contended here, decisions of courts, under the civil law, were only evidence of the law between the parties litigating, why all this care in collecting and preserving them, and does not the simple fact of their publication, their rapid and extensive circulation, and the frequent reference to them, completely answer all that we have heard on this subject?

In Spain, also, the decisions of their courts are quoted to the same purpose. Febrero Addicionado, pa. 2, lib. 3, cap. 3, sec. 2, n. 178, and many other passages in that author's works.

Nor is there any assumption of power in giving the decisions of this court the authority just spoken of. The tribunals of the last resort, in every state of the union, hold the same doctrine, each in relation to their own judgments. They are acquiesced in, without objection, by the citizens of those states; men not unacquainted with their rights, or slow to perceive or check any usurpation of them. Congress appropriates annually a sum of money to ensure a publication of the decisions of the supreme court of the federal government; and here in Louisiana the representatives of the people have expressed the same sense of their utility, by ordering the purchase of the decisions of this court, and directing their distribution through the state.

I confess, therefore, that I have been unable to feel the force of what has been said in the argument of this cause, respecting the impropriety of considering the decisions of the court as anything more than declaring the law between the parties. They, who in their zeal for their client, so eloquently urge this doctrine, would do well to reflect to what it leads. That its tendency is not to take power from this court, but to give it. That if we were under no obligation to follow that which we had decided ourselves, or what was declared law by our predecessors, we would possess an authority dangerous to the citizen, and, in the exercise of which, this tribunal would become at once feared and hated.

I conclude, therefore, that the second ground of defence fails.

The third ground of defence, which denies our right to decide in doubtful cases, and requires us to refer them to the legislature, is easily disposed of. Under our constitution and law, we have no such authority, and, instead of referring doubtful cases, I think they are the very class of causes that it is most necessary we should decide.

The fourth, which contends for an exemption from all liability, because the defendant acted both as attorney and counsellor, is equally untenable. Persons may increase their responsibility by acting in a two-fold capacity, but cannot diminish it.

The fifth point made is, that fault or negligence can alone charge the defendant; that neither is proved here, as the first means an intention to do wrong, and the second a total neglect to perform an act, not performing it erroneously.

By the Partida, 3, 5, 26, sec. 26,[e] attorneys are made responsible for fraud and fault. If we construe the word fault, as insisted on by the defendant, it would be synonymous with fraud; for if the intention must combine with the act in doing wrong, then the agent acts fraudulently. We presume, therefore, that something else is intended; but it is unnecessary to decide that, as our statute, 1 Martin's Dig. 528, has made attorneys responsible for any neglect by which their clients may suffer damage.

I think that neglect may exist as well in the careless manner of doing an act, as in not doing it. . . .

This ground of defence also fails.

It is still, however, insisted, that the act complained of was nothing more than a mere error of judgment, and we have given to this point as serious consideration as we are able to bestow on any subject.

From the moment the cause was opened in argument, we were all of opinion that attorneys are not responsible for an error in judgment.

But the doubt was, whether more had not been proved here.

Whether, after the repeated judgments of this court on the subject of the jurisdiction of the parish court, there was a necessity for at all exercising the judgment in selecting a tribunal.

That, admitting the decisions of this tribunal to be neither law, nor evidence of law, still, as they were evidence of the opinion on this subject, of those who had to pronounce on the cause, in the last resort. [sic] Whether it was ordinary diligence to bring an action in a court whose authority they had decided against, when there was another tribunal open, whose jurisdiction was not disputed.

Whether ordinary diligence might not have enabled the defendant to become acquainted with these decisions, and whether not knowing them was not ordinary neglect.

But these considerations have been outweighed by reasons, which may be fairly urged on behalf of the defendant.

The decisions in the cases of Smith v. Flower, and Dunwoodie v. Johnson, 6 Martin 9 and 12, had not been published at the time the suit of Breedlove & Bradford v. Fletcher, was commenced, and all that can be required of any gentleman of the bar, is, that he should make himself acquainted with the decisions after publication.

e. Concerning the influence of the Siete Partidas in the Western Hemisphere in general, and in Louisiana in particular, see supra pp. 14, 236.

Even technically, the Siete Partidas (except to the extent that the Civil Code of 1808 changed or abrogated particular provisions thereof) remained part of the law of Louisiana until the adoption of the Civil Code of 1825. See Williams v. Employers Liability Assur. Corp., 296 F.2d 569, 575–77 (5 Cir., 1961).

That in Delille v. Gaines, it is true, had been printed long before the suit was brought [sic]; but the point, as it respects the jurisdiction, was not decided there; it is only said, that the authority of the parish court, to take cognizance of the case, might be doubted.

What was said in that case, it is evident, did not settle the question. It was not so considered. It appears not to have been noticed by many members of the bar; as it has been proved, that a number of gentlemen still continued to bring suits of a similar description in that court.

If that decision be left out of view, the jurisdiction was doubtful, and one, regarding which, men might fairly differ in opinion. Nay, with that decision, and after this court had intimated in the case of Smith v. Flower, the same view of the question, and in that of Dunwoodie v. Johnson, expressly decided it; a learned judge, then on the bench, dissented from the opinion of the majority, and held, that the defendant had properly brought the action.[f]

No man is supposed to know any branch of the law perfectly, particularly when called on to act at once, and without time for reflection. The knowledge which we use the utmost industry to acquire, is often forgotten at the moment when most needed. The science is a most extensive and difficult one. Cases frequently occur, when learned men differ, after the greatest pains is taken to arrive at a correct result. No one, therefore, would dare to pursue the profession, if he was held responsible for the consequences of a casual failure of his memory, or a mistaken course of reasoning.

I do not wish to be understood to say, that cases may not arise, in which ignorance of the common and plain principles of the law and practice in our courts, or negligence in not properly using the knowledge the party possesses, will not make an attorney responsible. But here the parish court decided it had jurisdiction.

A learned judge of this court, which is composed only of three individuals, held, that that opinion was right.

Many members of the bar, and some of them gentlemen of much experience, pursued the same course. Under such circumstances, to make the defendant pay damages for error, is carrying the doctrine of responsibility further than, we think, the law will authorize, or than justice demands.

.   .   .

The judgment of the district court ought therefore to be affirmed with costs. . . .

f. Whenever a lawyer is sued on the ground that he was negligent in taking a certain position on a point of law, his defense is apt to be greatly strengthened by a showing that his position was approved or shared *by a judge* (e.g., a lower court judge), even though the latter's opinion did not prevail in the end. For a discussion of this point, with many examples taken from German malpractice cases, see F. Scheffler, Darf man vom Anwalt mehr erwarten, als das Kollegialgericht leistet?, 13 NJW 265 (1960).

NOTE

For a more recent Louisiana decision dealing with the force of precedents, see *Johnson v. St. Paul Mercury Ins. Co.*, 256 La. 289, 236 So.2d 216 (1970). In that case the intermediate appellate court, deviating from the old *lex loci* rule, had applied Louisiana substantive law to an Arkansas accident; both parties were domiciled in Louisiana. The Louisiana Supreme Court, in reversing the lower court decision and announcing its continued adherence to *lex loci*, used the following strong language (at 217–18):

"So far as we can ascertain, this is the first case in the history of the jurisprudence of this state in which a Louisiana court has applied Louisiana law to a foreign tort. . . . What is unique here is that this departure from the settled jurisprudence should be undertaken by an intermediate court. The action involves, at least, a failure by the Second Circuit to recognize its obligation to follow the settled law of this State.[a] For, since the question is not regulated by statute, the law is what this court has announced it to be. . . .

"Fundamental and elementary principles recognize that certainty and constancy of the law are indispensable to orderly social intercourse, a sound economic climate and a stable government. Certainty is a supreme value in the civil law system to which we are heirs. Merryman, The Civil Law Tradition 50 (1969). In Louisiana, courts are not bound by the doctrine of *stare decisis*, but there is a recognition in this State of the doctrine of *jurisprudence constante*. Unlike *stare decisis*, this latter doctrine does not contemplate adherence to a principle of law announced and applied on a single occasion in the past.

"However, when by repeated decisions in a long line of cases, a rule of law has been accepted and applied by the courts, these adjudications assume the dignity of *jurisprudence constante*; and the rule of law upon which they are based is entitled to great weight in subsequent decisions."

Perhaps the reader will be a trifle surprised to learn that, exactly three years after these ringing words were pronounced in the Johnson case, that case was overruled by the same court in Jagers v. Royal Indemnity Co., 276 So.2d 309 (La.1973).

A superficial observer might think that the Johnson and Jagers cases can be reconciled; that the former decision makes the *jurisprudence constante* of the highest court binding *upon the intermediate appellate courts and all lower courts*, while the later case exemplifies the power *of the highest court itself* to overrule its prior holdings if they are regarded as obsolete. Closer scrutiny, however, shows that this is not a sufficient explanation, and that during the three years that elapsed between the Johnson and Jagers decisions, the Louisiana Supreme Court's attitude concerning the force of precedents underwent a real change.

a. Would such an "obligation" exist in a civil-law country? Compare the situation in France, where the intermediate appellate court, even after reversal and remand by one of the panels of the Cour de Cassation, may take a position contra to that of the highest court. See supra p. 465.

In appraising Louisiana's post-Jagers approach to the problem of the force of precedents, we are aided by a most interesting law review article, the author of which was a member of the Jagers majority.[1] From that article we learn that the Jagers overruling, which according to some eminent scholars "surprised everyone",[2] perhaps was not all that surprising.[3] The Johnson majority, although using French terminology, in effect had taken a (slightly modified) common-law approach towards the question of the binding nature of judicial precedents. The Jagers overruling was the natural, and perhaps predictable, result of the fact that, after some changes in the personnel of the Court, and apparently after vigorous debate, the new majority adopted a civil-law approach towards that question.[4]

County had to endure groundless lawsuits by indigent indiv. who had free appeal help.

OPINION OF THE GERMAN REICHSGERICHT IN THE MATTER OF COUNTY OF G., PLAINTIFF–APPELLANT v. STATE OF PRUSSIA, DEFENDANT–RESPONDENT

3rd Civil Division, January 26, 1932, RGZ 135, 110.

[On June 29, 1927, a police officer in County G ordered the preliminary closing of the restaurant of one H, on the ground that H was "unreliable." At the same time, the police officer brought an administrative action against H before the County Commission of G (an administrative court of first instance), asking the Commission to revoke H's liquor license and to confirm the closing of the restaurant. By a temporary order of the President of the Commission, it was decreed on July 7, 1927, that the restaurant remain closed. Upon H's appeal, this temporary order was first reversed, but (by reversal of the reversal) subsequently affirmed by a higher administrative court. At the same time, on October 14, 1927, the higher court remanded the whole case to the County Commission, on the ground that procedural errors had been committed, and ordered a hearing before the County Commission. No such hearing took place, however, because in the meantime the *Landrat* (the highest administrative official in the County, and the superior of the police officer whose action had started the whole matter)

---

1. See A. Tate, Jr., The Role of the Judge in Mixed Jurisdictions: The Louisiana Experience, 20 Loyola L.Rev. 231 (1974). A somewhat amplified version of that article, along with papers by other prominent authors dealing with related topics, appears in J. Dainow (Ed.), The Role of Judicial Decisions and Doctrine in Civil Law and Mixed Jurisdictions (1974).

2. R. C. Cramton, D. P. Currie & H. H. Kay, Conflict of Laws 739 (3rd Ed., 1981).

3. See Tate, supra n. 1, at 239. Note especially the last paragraph on that page, and the footnotes accompanying it.

4. If this explanation is correct, could the Court in the future adhere to the John-son holding that intermediate appellate courts and lower courts are *bound* by the highest court's *jurisprudence constante*? In trying to answer this question, the reader perhaps will recall our prior discussion (see supra p. 236) of the Spanish *doctrina legal*. But it should be remembered that in Spain the *doctrina legal* rule has an explicit statutory basis, and that in the absence of such a statutory provision the intermediate appellate courts and lower courts in civil-law countries are not bound by the decisions (and not even by repeated decisions) of the highest court.

had looked into the case, and, by way of amicable settlement with H, apparently had permitted the latter to reopen his restaurant.

The restaurant had been closed from June 29th until some time in October. Subsequently, H decided to bring an action for the damages which he had suffered as a result of such closing. He was advised by his lawyer to bring a tort action against County G, on the theory that both the police officer and the President of the County Commission had violated their official duties,[a] the former by the unjustified closing of the restaurant, and the latter by failure to permit reopening as well as by dilatory handling of the whole matter, and by wrongly advising H concerning appellate procedure.[b] In February, 1928, H applied to the Landgericht (court of first instance) in Breslau for permission to sue as a poor person.[c] The Landgericht denied the application on the ground that H's case was hopeless,[d] because he had failed to show an intentional or negligent violation of official duty, and because his amicable settlement with the Landrat implied a waiver of his right to damages. Upon H's appeal from this decision, the Oberlandesgericht (intermediate appellate court) reversed, and granted H's application to sue as a poor person, holding that the intended action was not entirely hopeless insofar as it was predicated on the alleged dilatory conduct of the administrative proceeding.

Thereupon, the Landgericht appointed a lawyer to represent H,[e] and on December 10, 1928 that lawyer commenced an action for damages against County G. The latter denied its liability on the ground, among others, that the (acting) President of the County Commission, upon whose alleged violation of official duty the action was based, was an official of the State, and not of the County, and that the plaintiff, consequently, had sued the wrong defendant. The County argued that for this reason plaintiff's action was hopeless, and moved to vacate the order by which plaintiff had been granted permission to sue as a poor person. This motion was denied by the Landgericht. Shortly thereafter, however, the Landgericht entered a judgment dismissing the

a. The German doctrine concerning liability of the State and its subdivisions for the misconduct of officials is briefly explained supra pp. 510–511.

In some American jurisdictions, the action against the County might well be hopeless on the ground that the closing of the restaurant was a quasi-judicial determination. See Restatement, Second, Torts § 895B, com. c, and § 895C, com. g (1979). In Germany, however, where the State often can be held liable for *judicial* negligence (see infra, footn. f), the liability of the State or its subdivision clearly is not precluded by the *quasi-judicial* nature of the official's wrongful act.

b. In most continental countries, administrative officials and administrative courts, when deciding a controversy, have to advise the losing party as to his right to appeal and the procedure to be followed.

c. If such application is granted, the applicant is temporarily relieved of the payment of filing fees and other costs, and the court, in addition, appoints an attorney to represent him. The attorney will be paid from public funds. See supra, p. 357.

d. The reader will recall that even today such an application can be denied if the court concludes that the applicant's case is hopeless. See supra p. 355.

e. Under present law, the court in appointing a lawyer must honor the applicant's choice. Even in 1928 it was the prevailing practice to do so. See supra p. 356.

complaint on the merits, for the reason that defendant County was not liable for any violation of official duty which might have been committed by the Acting President of the County Commission, but that such liability, if any, would fall upon the State.

Plaintiff applied to the Oberlandesgericht for permission to appeal as a poor person. This application was granted and an attorney was appointed to represent the plaintiff on appeal. In the appellate court, again, the dispute centered on the question whether the Acting President of the County Commission had to be regarded as an official of the County or of the State, and which of the two bodies had to bear the liability for his violation of official duty. The Oberlandesgericht affirmed the decision and the reasoning of the lower court, and no further appeal was taken from that judgment of affirmance.]

In the present action, County G seeks to hold the State of Prussia liable for the negligence of the judges of the Landgericht and of the Oberlandesgericht. Plaintiff argues that the judges negligently violated an official duty which they owed the County, by their improvident order granting H's application for permission to sue as a poor person in the prior litigation, and by their failure to vacate such order after the County had demonstrated the hopelessness of H's action.[f] As a result, plaintiff County argues, it was compelled to incur expenses in defending H's action, which expenses, in the amount of RM 707.62, plaintiff was unable to collect from H, the latter being judgment-proof. Plaintiff,

---

f. Sect. 839 of the German Civil Code, which in conjunction with other constitutional and statutory provisions (see supra, pp. 510–511) establishes the State's liability for a public officer's culpable violation of official duty, contains a proviso to the effect that the State is not liable if such violation is committed by a judge "in giving judgment in an action." But the preliminary order (sometimes issued ex parte), by which an application for permission to sue as a poor person is granted, is not regarded as a judgment in an action. Therefore, the defendant State cannot defeat the present suit by simply pointing to the judicial nature of the allegedly negligent acts. *If* the judges, in passing on H's application for permission to sue as a poor person, owed an official duty of due care to County G, and *if* they negligently violated that duty, the State would be liable for damages proximately caused by such violation.

It is interesting to compare this German rule with our own, much more restrictive rules concerning governmental and personal liability for judicial negligence. See Stump v. Sparkman, 435 U.S. 349, 98 S.Ct. 1099 (1978), where the older authorities are thoroughly reviewed. See also Murray

v. Brancato, 290 N.Y. 52, 48 N.E.2d 257 (Lehman, Ch.J., 1943); Restatement, Second, Torts §§ 895B to 895D (1979); Annos., 64 A.L.R.3d 1251 (1975) and 55 L.Ed.2d 850 (1979). For comparative treatment of the subject, see M. Cappelletti, Who Watches the Watchmen ?, A Comparative Study on Judicial Responsibility, 31 Am.J.Comp.L. 1 (1983), reprinted (in revised form) in S. Shetreet & J. Deschênes (eds.), Judicial Independence: The Comtemporary Debate 550 (1985).

Could the differences between German and American rules concerning judicial immunity perhaps be explained on the ground that judge-made rules on the subject tend to be more protective than legislated rules?

With respect to our law, it should be noted, furthermore, that even apart from the question of immunity it is doubtful whether judges are "employees" within the meaning of the Federal Tort Claims Act. Compare Cromelin v. United States, 177 F.2d 275 (5th Cir. 1949) and Foster v. MacBride, 521 F.2d 1304 (9th Cir. 1975) with United States v. Lepatourel 593 F.2d 827 (8th Cir. 1979). Cf. Tomalewski v. United States, 493 F.Supp. 673 (W.D. Pa. 1980).

therefore, seeks damages in the amount just mentioned, plus interest. . . .

Having lost below, plaintiff . . . appeals to this court; but the appeal cannot succeed.

Reasons: [At the outset, the court points out that in passing on an application for permission to sue as a poor person, the judges owed no duty of due care *to the* applicant's *opponent.* In this connection, the court refers to provisions in the Code of Civil Procedure (see infra n. k) which make it clear that such an application may be granted by an ex parte order, from which the opponent cannot appeal (while the denial of permission to sue as a poor person, as we have seen, is appealable). These provisions of the Code show that in handling such applications, the judges owe a duty to the applicant, but not to the opponent.

In the second part of the opinion the court develops the view that plaintiff must lose even if it be assumed that the judges owed an official duty to plaintiff (i.e., to the County, who is the plaintiff in the present action). This for the reason that the judges did not act negligently. The issue in the lawsuit between H and the County was whether the County or the State was liable for a tort committed by one W, the Acting President of the County Commission. W was at all times on the payroll of the State; but the function in the performance of which he had damaged H's interests, arguably was a County function. This posed an intricate problem: Which governmental unit was liable for W's official tort? The unit which had employed him and paid his salary, or the unit the powers and functions of which he exercised at the time?[g] The Reichsgericht had indicated in two cases decided in 1920 and 1925 that ordinarily the State is liable for the consequences of unlawful acts of officials in the position of W. As plaintiff in the present action, the County argued that in granting H's application for permission to sue as a poor person, the judges in the prior action had disregarded these two decisions of the Reichsgericht and thus had acted negligently.]

It was repeatedly pointed out by this court [citations] that a judge acts culpably if he interprets a written law[h] in a manifestly incorrect manner. But it is not possible to blame him if he incorrectly applies

g. This question was long controversial in Germany. The two opposing views became known as the "employment theory" and the "function theory." Ultimately, the employment theory gained a complete victory; but in the 1920s, although the Reichsgericht had rendered a few decisions which in principle favored the employment theory, the point was not yet completely clarified. The history of the controversy is traced by H. R. Hink, The German Law of Governmental Tort Liability, 18 Rutgers L.Rev. 1069, at 1134–37 (1964).

Comparable doubts and problems have arisen under the Federal Tort Claims Act.

If one tried, in German fashion, to capsulize the relevant decisions of our federal courts in terms of a "theory", one would have to conclude that they follow neither the "employment theory" nor the "function theory", but rather have developed a "control theory". See Logue v. United States, 412 U.S. 521, 93 S.Ct. 2215 (1973), where many other authorities are cited.

h. The German term is *Gesetz* (Latin *lex*, Fr. *loi*), meaning written or statutory law. This must be distinguished from the broader term *Recht (ius, droit)* which in its objective sense denotes law, i.e., every legal norm, whatever its source.

statutory provisions of doubtful interpretation and unclear wording the meaning of which has not yet been clarified by a decision of the highest court. [The court then goes on to explain that the two above-mentioned decisions of 1920 and 1925 had clarified the general principles governing the question at issue in the case of H against the County, but that the application of these principles to the facts of that case might still give rise to doubts.] It may have been impossible, and it was in any event unnecessary, to resolve these doubts in the purely preliminary proceeding concerning the question whether H should be permitted to sue as a poor person.

In passing on the responsibility of judges for their decisions in granting or denying permission to sue as a poor person—especially in granting such permission—it should not be overlooked, moreover, that this involves an area of judicial discretion. Often it is a matter of personal attitude and of judicial discretion . . . to determine whether the applicant has met the burden of showing that the intended action . . . is neither wanton nor hopeless. In this connection, the judges passing on such an application must consider whether the poor party should receive an opportunity to litigate his claims—even seemingly weak claims—in an orderly adversary action, and thus to obtain a judgment and opinion exhaustively examining all of the disputed issues, or whether by a brief order denying the application, perhaps unaccompanied by a thorough opinion,[i] the presentation of the poor party's rights should be cut off with practical finality. A somewhat liberal attitude may be indicated, particularly when—as in the case of H against the County—a citizen claims that his rights were impaired by a public body. [The court points out that it has dismissed many actions based on the alleged negligence of nonjudicial officials, where the official involved had acted within the limits of discretionary power, and that abuse of discretion must be shown in such a case to justify recovery.[j] Judicial discretion should not be more narrowly circumscribed than the discretion of administrative officials. It follows that the plaintiff in the present action can prevail only if it can show that the judges abused their discretion.] The facts before us in the instant case show no such abuse of discretion. . . . During the whole proceeding concerning H's application for permission to sue as a poor person, and until such permission was granted by the Oberlandesgericht, nobody mentioned the question whether the County was the right

i. When an application for assistance is denied, the reasons for the denial should be explained to the applicant. See Baumbach-Lauterbach-Albers-Hartmann, Zivilprozessordnung, § 127, Anno. 4 (45th ed., 1987). But the explanation can be very brief, in contrast to the elaborate opinion which *must* accompany a final judgment in a regular action (see supra, p. 449).

j. Compare the provisions of the Federal Tort Claims Act, especially 28 U.S.C.A. § 2680(a), immunizing the government from claims based upon "the exercise or performance or the failure to exercise or perform a discretionary function or duty on the part of a federal agency or an employee of the Government, whether or not the discretion involved be abused." This exemption has been applied in cases in which the plaintiff claimed to have been the victim of official arbitrariness or negligence in the administration of justice. See the cases cited in Anno., 99 ALR2d 1016, especially 1037–40 (1965).

defendant, and no attention was paid to the position, and the nature of the functions, of the official involved. The County, in particular, failed to raise these points, although it was given an opportunity to file papers in opposition to H's application.[k] It should be observed, furthermore, that the Oberlandesgericht . . . granted H's application for permission to sue as a poor person only insofar as he sought damages for the dilatory conduct of the administrative proceeding concerning the closing of his restaurant. It is conceivable, therefore, that the Oberlandesgericht—apart from the alleged negligence of W—considered the possibility of negligence on the part of other officials, for whom the County might be responsible. In view of this possibility, it must be held, also, that the judges of the Oberlandesgericht were not necessarily guilty of negligence when after the dismissal of H's action by the Landgericht they permitted H to appeal as a poor person. There remains only the final question whether the judges of the Landgericht acted negligently when they refused to vacate the permission to sue as a poor person, a permission which had just been granted to H by the appellate court. This question, clearly, must be answered in the negative. . . .

[handwritten: Judge's mistake could only go to stat. law not to interpretation of case law]

NOTES

(1) *Decision of the German Reichsgericht of November 14, 1922, RGZ 105, 356:* According to § 288 of the German Civil Code, a debtor in "default" is liable to pay interest. The notion of "default" is a technical one; it will be discussed infra pp. 666–667. For present purposes, it suffices to know that a debtor who has reasonable doubts concerning the existence of the debt has been held not to be in "default"; thus he does not have to pay interest for the period up to the commencement of an action against him. The debtor's reasonable doubt may relate to a point of fact or of law.

In the present case, however, the Court held that a doubt concerning a point of law is never reasonable if that point has been adversely determined by "decisions of the highest court". The reader will note that the Court spoke of "decisions" rather than "a decision". But whether this use of the plural was intentional, is not certain. If plainly faced with the problem, the German courts may well hold that even a single precedential decision of the highest court can remove the possibility of a reasonable doubt.

(2) *Decision of Landgericht Braunschweig, dated Nov. 28, 1984, reported in 38 N.J.W. 1171 (1985):* By a notarial act, P and two other individuals formed a close corporation (GmbH). Under German law, such a corporation does not come into existence until it is registered in the Commercial Register. Before this particular corporation was so

[handwritten: Noted]

---

k. At the time in question, the court was not required to hear the applicant's opponent before granting permission to sue as a poor person; it was proper to grant the application ex parte. But the court had the power, if it saw fit, to serve a copy of the application on the opponent, and to afford the latter an informal opportunity to be heard. By a more recent amendment, which did not affect the principal case, it is now provided that before granting the application, the court "shall" give the opponent an opportunity to file a statement, unless this appears inexpedient in the particular case. Code of Civil Procedure, § 118. Even today, however, the opponent has no right to appeal from an order granting the application. Id., § 127.

registered, P on the corporation's behalf entered into a contract with X. Under the terms of the contract, X leased a piece of machinery to the corporation, at a monthly rental of about $400.00. Subsequently, the corporation was registered and used the leased machine for several months; but no payments were ever made to X, and after some time the corporation went bankrupt. X then sued P for the accrued rental installments. P retained lawyer D to represent him in the action brought by X. In the court of first instance, X prevailed; in September 1981 he obtained a judgment against P for the full amount of the accrued rental installments, plus interest and costs (including the fees of X's attorneys). No appeal was taken from that judgment.

In the present action, P sues D for malpractice, asserting that D was negligent in failing to recommend an appeal from the judgment obtained by X. Under the German statute relating to this type of corporation (GmbH Gesetz, § 11, subs. 2), it is clear that incorporators who on the corporation's behalf—but prior to its registration in the Commercial Register—enter into a contract with another party, become personally liable to such party. The statute, however, is silent on the question whether this personal liability of the incorporators continues after the corporation has been registered and thus has become a legal entity. The judgment obtained by X against P was obviously based on the assumption that the correct answer to this question is in the affirmative. Such an assumption might have been reasonable in the light of pre-1981 German authorities.[1] But in three cases decided during 1981 and 1982, Germany's highest court in civil and criminal matters, the *Bundesgerichtshof* (BGH) decided that

(a) at the time of its becoming registered, the corporation automatically acquires all rights and assumes all obligations flowing from a contract which prior to such registration was concluded by the incorporators on behalf of the corporation, and that

(b) the personal liability of the incorporators arising from such a contract ceases at the time when the corporation itself assumes the liability, i.e., at the time the corporation is registered.

Under the rule established by these decisions of the highest court, the judgment obtained by X against P was clearly incorrect.

In P's malpractice action against D, the court found that the time for an appeal from the judgment obtained by X ran out in October 1981. The last of the above-mentioned three decisions of the BGH was handed down in 1982; thus D could not possibly be familiar with that decision when in September/October 1981 he had to determine whether he should advise his client to appeal. But the situation was different with respect to the first two BGH decisions. The first one, which already spelled out the holding summarized above, was rendered on March 9, 1981, and on June 16, 1981, was reported in an issue of *Neue Juristische Wochenschrift* (NJW), a well-known and widely circulated legal periodical that is published under Bar Association auspices. The second

---

1. In our law, it is still the prevailing view that the incorporators' liability under pre-incorporation contracts normally continues after incorporation unless the corporation, by a new contract with the third party, assumes exclusive liability. See H. G. Henn & J. R. Alexander, Hornbook on the Laws of Corporations §§ 111–114 (3d ed., 1983, and 1986 Supp.).

decision, which repeated the same holding, was rendered on March 16, 1981, and similarly reported in the June 30, 1981, issue of NJW.

Clearly, if D had been familiar with these decisions, he would have recommended an appeal from the judgment obtained by X. In the malpractice action, the court held that inasmuch as two of the relevant BGH decisions were rendered in March 1981 and reported in June 1981, it was negligent on the part of D not to have familiarized himself with the decisions before the time when (in September/October 1981) he had to consider the advisability of an appeal to be taken by his client. Hence D was held to be liable for the full amount of the incorrect—but by now unappealable—judgment obtained by X.

[handwritten margin notes: "attorney should have taken notice of case... thus liable pursued"]

OPINION OF THE GERMAN REICHSGERICHT IN THE MATTER OF NEUERGASTHOF G.M.B.H. ET AL., DEFENDANTS v. K., PLAINTIFF

2nd Civil Division, December 14, 1928, RGZ 123, 102.

The plaintiff is the principal subscriber of the shares of the Neuergasthof G.m.b.H., which was organized and registered in the register of commerce in May, 1923. In payment of her subscription, plaintiff transferred a piece of realty to the said new corporation; the latter was recorded as owner of that realty in June, 1923. In July, 1923, the said realty was mortgaged in favor of the other shareholder, the M Corporation, as mortgagee. The amount of the mortgage was 179.2 kg. of gold. In this action plaintiff seeks a declaration, as against the G.m.b.H. [the first defendant], to the effect that plaintiff's subscription of shares of said defendant and the transfer of the realty to said defendant are invalid. As against her co-shareholder, the M Corporation [second defendant], plaintiff demands cancellation of the mortgage. . . . Plaintiff contends that at the time of the organization of the G.m.b.H. she was insane, and, therefore, incompetent, such insanity resulting from the fact that she was then suffering from the after-effects of a venereal disease and particularly from syphilis of the brain. She further contends that her mental inferiority was exploited by the second defendant in a usurious manner.[a]

a. Subdivision 1 of Section 138 of the German Civil Code invalidates every jural act which is contra bonos mores. See supra, p. 569. Subdivision 2 of the same section in its original version provided as follows: "In particular a jural act is void whereby a person exploiting the difficulties, indiscretion, or inexperience of another, causes to be promised or granted to himself or to a third party for a consideration, pecuniary advantages which exceed the value of the consideration to such an extent that, having regard to the circumstances, the disproportion is obvious." The Germans, who do not use the Latin-derived word *lésion* (supra p. 595), refer to all transactions covered by this subdivision 2 as *"usurious"*, no matter whether the disproportion is caused by a promise of excessive interest or by other elements.

In 1976, long after the principal case was decided, the wording (though not the basic thrust) of the second subdivision of Section 138 was modified by an amendment. It now reads as follows: "In particular, a jural act is void whereby a person, exploiting the oppressed situation, inexperience, lack of judgment or essential weakness of willpower of another, causes to be promised or granted to himself or to a third party for a consideration, pecuniary advantages which plainly exceed the consideration."

The Landgericht dismissed the complaint. The Oberlandesgericht rendered a judgment declaring that plaintiff's subscription of shares of defendant G.m.b.H. was invalid. It further granted plaintiff's prayer that the first defendant be compelled to re-transfer the realty to the plaintiff. As against the second defendant the intermediate appellate court held that such defendant was under a duty to cancel the mortgage of record. . . . Upon the further appeal of the first defendant the judgment of the Oberlandesgericht was reversed insofar as it affected the first defendant, and the judgment of the Landgericht dismissing the complaint against the first defendant was reinstated.

Reasons: The plaintiff demands a declaration of the invalidity of her jural act by which she subscribed to shares of the Neuergasthof G.m.b.H., and also re-transfer of the realty to her. She is not entitled to such re-transfer unless her subscription, and the contract by which she transferred the realty to the G.m.b.H. in payment of the subscription, are to be treated as invalid. Such subscription and such contract, however, cannot be declared invalid. The first defendant, that is the G.m.b.H., was registered in the register of commerce on May 7, 1923. The question whether as against the *registered* G.m.b.H. plaintiff can still derive any legal consequences from the fact that one of her co-incorporators was guilty of immoral conduct in connection with the incorporation of the G.m.b.H., is to be answered in the negative. Without legal error the intermediate appellate court finds as a fact that the co-incorporator, the M Corporation, immorally exploited the mental inferiority of the plaintiff and usuriously overreached her. Thus, both subdivisions of Section 138 of the Civil Code are applicable pursuant to their terms. But according to the "customary law" which has been developed by a consistent and—during many decades—constant course of judicial decision, the plaintiff cannot assert the invalidity of her subscription as against the registered G.m.b.H. She can only bring a tort action for damages against her co-incorporator, the M Corporation (Section 826 of the Civil Code.)[b] This norm of customary law has for its purpose the preservation of the capital basis of the G.m.b.H. It is further based on the consideration that the subscription is meant to be relied on by the public. [Plaintiff argued that this rule should be limited to cases where the subscription is sought to be rescinded on the ground of mistake, fraud or duress; and that it should not apply where the subscription, being immoral and usurious within the meaning of § 138, is absolutely void and not merely voidable.] True, the decision of this Division in RGZ Vol. 82, page 375, which is cited by the appellant, merely held that after the registration of a G.m.b.H. in the register of

The purpose of the amendment was to correlate this provision of the Civil Code with § 302a of the Penal Code, which subjects "usury", as thus defined, to criminal sanctions. It has been observed that as a result of the amendment it is now perhaps a little easier for a court to invalidate a transaction as "usurious". See Palandt,

Buergerliches Gesetzbuch, § 138, Anno. 4a (41st ed., 1982).

b. German Civil Code, Section 826: "One who intentionally injures another in a manner violating the moral precepts, is liable to the other for the damages resulting from such injury."

commerce a subscription to its capital can no longer be rescinded on the ground of mistake or fraud.[c]

. . . It is true that the Code provides different remedies for mistake, fraud, etc. (Section 119 et seq.), on the one hand, and for a violation of the precepts of good morals, especially usury (Section 138, subdivisions 1 and 2 of the Civil Code), on the other. In cases of the former kind the Code leaves it to the injured party himself to protect his interests by permitting him under certain conditions to rescind the transaction and thus to annihilate his jural act. On the other hand, it is not left to the discretion of the injured party whether he wishes to assert the invalidity of a jural act if such invalidity flows from Section 138 of the Civil Code; such invalidity is automatic and independent of the will of the injured party. If the facts are such that they are covered by Section 138, the judge is under a duty ex officio to apply this provision. . . .

However, this difference in the remedy provided in different cases of defective jural acts [that is, the difference in the remedy for deceit, on the one hand, and for usury, on the other] . . . is of no importance for the issue at hand. The provision of Section 138 [Subdivision 2] is a positive norm. Whether it properly serves its purpose, has been doubted, and not without reason [citing a well-known text-book on the General Part of the Swiss Civil Code]. True, usurious exploitation of the other party may be immoral, but this is equally true where one party intentionally deceives the other. The important point in either case is that the effect of such immoral conduct is limited to the narrow circle of the parties; it does not affect the public. Therefore, our Civil Code might reasonably have made the same provision which we find in Article 21 of the Swiss Code of Obligations. The latter article provides that in cases of usury the injured party may within one year disaffirm the contract and demand restitution of his performance. The similarity of usury and deceit is particularly apparent in cases in which, as in the instant case, the inexperience of one of the parties has been exploited. Actually, the plaintiff was intentionally deceived concerning the value of the M shares. [Although the opinion does not state this, it

---

c. "According to the German system, followed in Austria and Switzerland, the *subscriber* of shares (as distinguished from a buyer) induced to subscribe by mistake, fraud or duress, generally cannot invoke a rescission against the corporation although this denial of a remedy departs from the principles governing ordinary contracts. . . . The advocates of the rule lay stress on the theory that the subscription of stock is not only a contract between the corporation and the subscriber . . ., but is also a public declaration of intention to be unconditionally liable up to the amount subscribed, a declaration upon which the public can rely. In the last analysis this argument rests upon the theory that the capital stock of a corporation is a trust fund for the benefit of the creditors of the corporation, from which it follows that the capital stock cannot be diminished by allowing rescission of the subscription." Kessler, The American Securities Act and its Foreign Counterparts: A Comparative Study, 44 Yale L.J. 1133, 1156–7 (1935).

Concerning the common-law approach to the problem of rescission of stock subscriptions, compare MacNamee v. Bankers' Union for Foreign Commerce & Finance, 25 F.2d 614 (2d Cir. 1928); In re Morris Bros., 293 Fed. 294 (9th Cir. 1923); Stevens on Corporations 405–12 (2d ed., 1949); H. G. Henn & J. R. Alexander, Hornbook on Laws of Corporations, § 169 (3d ed., 1983, and 1986 Supp.).

is reasonable to assume that either plaintiff or the G.m.b.H. received M shares as part of the deal.]

In addition, we have to consider that pursuant to the provisions of the Civil Code the effect upon the position of the innocent purchaser is the same whether his predecessor in title had acquired title by way of a transaction which is void under Section 138, or by way of a transaction which is only voidable [because of mistake or fraud]. This is true, for instance, concerning the second purchaser of a piece of real property. The provisions of Sections 891, 892 of the Civil Code [d], which protect the purchaser acquiring a piece of real property from a transferor whose name [as owner] appears in the land register, also cover the case in which the transferor had acquired the property by way of a usurious or otherwise immoral transaction. In the law of negotiable instruments the defense of usury and the defense based on subdivision 1 of Section 138 have equally no effect "in rem." [e] The effect of invalidity because of usury or immorality is in this respect no different from the effect of mistake or fraud which would have made the transferor's purchase voidable rather than void. The public interest in the annihilation of usurious or otherwise immoral transactions and the interest of the victim have to yield to the necessity of protecting those members of the public who become holders in due course. . . .

The text writers do not occupy themselves with the question here involved, whether the subscriber-shareholder of a G.m.b.H. may, as against the G.m.b.H., invoke Section 138 of the Civil Code, after the G.m.b.H. has been registered in the register of commerce. The Reichsgericht has not yet decided this precise question. The numerous decisions concerning the legal consequences of mistake, fraud, or similar elements affecting the contract by which a stock corporation, a cooperative, or a G.m.b.H. is set up, treat only the question whether, after registration of the company in the register of commerce, the subscriber may still *rescind* his participation in the new venture and his subscription to the capital [citing cases].

These decisions denied such right of rescission. They were based upon the ground that after registration of a corporation or cooperative the subscriptions of the original subscribers constitute the capital basis

---

d. Quoted infra pp. 685–686.

e. This means that under German law these defenses are not available against a holder in due course, even though the original issuance of the instrument was absolutely "void" pursuant to the first or second subdivision of § 138 of the Civil Code.

Our law treats this question differently. UCC § 3–305(2)(b) permits the assertion, even against a holder in due course, of "such . . . illegality of the transaction, as renders the obligation of the party a nullity." Whether a particular type of transaction, e.g. a usurious one (in our sense of the word), is a nullity, is not determined by the UCC but by local law. "If under that law the effect of . . . the illegality is to make the obligation entirely null and void, the defense may be asserted against a holder in due course. Otherwise it is cut off." (§ 3–305, Comment 6). Thus under the UCC the ultimate criterion is whether the defense renders the defendant's obligation "void" or merely voidable. German law, as the Reichsgericht points out, rejects that criterion, and protects innocent third-party members of the public (in this instance the holder in due course) even though the transaction between the defendant and his immediate transferee was "void".

of the new corporation, which will immediately establish contacts with the public generally. From this point of view the subscription is addressed to the public. It means that the subscriber will be absolutely liable for the amount subscribed as soon as the corporation has been registered in the register of commerce. The interest of those who, relying upon the capital basis thus created, have established or are going to establish legal relationships with the new enterprise, requires that this capital basis be preserved undiminished.[f] This principle of protection of creditors precludes any rescission of the subscription as against the newly registered corporation, if such rescission is sought for reasons which lie in the relations between the subscriber, on the one hand, and the co-subscribers or third persons on the other. But this is not the full range of the principle. Consistently applied, the same principle also makes it impossible for any subscriber to invoke Section 138 of the Civil Code if he seeks to do so on the ground of an immorality which pervades his relations with co-subscribers or third persons. . . .

So long as the defect of the subscription has its roots in the relationship between the subscriber on the one hand and a co-subscriber or third person on the other, it cannot make any difference whether such defect makes the subscription void or only voidable. [In either event, the court holds, the creditor interest in seeing the capital basis of the company maintained is worthier of protection than the desire of the subscriber to be relieved from the consequences of his subscription which was induced by improper means].

[f]. Note that the court does not stop to inquire whether the G.m.b.H. *actually* has any creditors. The protection of *potential* creditors, and others who might do business with the G.m.b.H., is thought so important that the subscription may not be invalidated. Why is the solution found by common-law courts (see, e.g., the *MacNamee* and *Morris* cases, cited supra n. c.), so much more refined than the German one? Is this a result of the common-law method, which tends to lead to fine distinctions? Consider, also, that the dichotomy between law and equity is unknown to the civilians, and that the German codes purport exhaustively to specify the types of relief which a court can grant. See Zöller, Zivilprozessordnung, Anno. 2 preceding § 253 (14th ed., 1984). See also supra pp. 291 ff.. It follows that a German court does not have the same freedom in fashioning remedies which a court of equity would have in a common-law jurisdiction. The court in the principal case, which did not involve an action for dissolution of the GmbH, thus could not adopt a solution (such as subordination of the victimized subscriber's refund claim to the claims of ordinary creditors) which for its procedural implementation requires an equitable receivership or some other flexible remedy not specified in the Code of Civil Procedure.

Another point to be considered is the fact that the total amount of all subscriptions has been publicly registered in the *Register of Commerce*. The entry in the Register, on which the public may rely (see infra pp. 696–702), would become misleading if plaintiff were allowed to withdraw the capital subscribed and contributed by her, unless such withdrawal were properly publicized in the Register as a reduction of the previously registered capital of the GmbH. Again, a common-law lawyer might feel that (except in a case in which the withdrawal reduces the capital of the company below the statutory minimum) this poses no insuperable problem, because the court could order the appropriate corrective entry in the Register. But in the mind of one who is not accustomed to the Chancellor's creativeness in fashioning remedies, this procedural difficulty will loom much larger.

NOTE ON "CUSTOMARY LAW" AND "JURISPRUDENCE"

(1) The use which the *Reichsgericht* (the predecessor of the *Bundesgerichtshof*) makes of "customary law" may appear rather startling to one who has been taught that there is no decisional law in civil-law countries, and that in any event decisional law could never abrogate a provision of the written law. The method employed by the Reichsgericht is supported by the leading German textbooks, in which it is frankly recognized that judicial decisions may create a rule of customary law, even *contra legem*, i.e., by a line of cases erroneously construing the written text.[1]

For the sake of proper perspective, however, the following points should be kept in mind:

(a) Even in the German-speaking countries, the instances of such purely judge-made "customary law" are few and far between. Normally, the broad general clauses of the codes themselves enable the judges to avoid undesirable results which might seem to flow from the more specific provisions applicable to a given case; and it is only in exceptional cases, in which no amount of "interpreting" the Code will suffice to reach a desired result, that resort will be had to the open announcement of "creation of law" by the courts. In the foregoing case, the difficulty was caused, not by a specific provision, but by the "general clause" of Section 138, which, if literally applied, would render the stock subscription absolutely *invalid*. The Court considered this result undesirable and inconsistent with the principles expressed in the law of vendor and purchaser and in the law of negotiable instruments. Inasmuch as the "general clause" was itself the source of the difficulty, that clause could not be used for the purpose of rationalizing the desired result, and the Court was thus driven to an open avowal of its use of "customary law".[1a]

(b) German legal writers draw a sharp distinction between (i) the countless instances, exemplified by almost every German case in this book, of highly persuasive but not formally binding

---

1. See 1 Enneccerus-Nipperdey, Allgemeiner Teil des Buergerlichen Rechts § 40 (1959), with comparative references; 1 Cosack-Mitteis, Lehrbuch des Buergerlichen Rechts 16–18 (8th ed. 1927); Palandt, Bürgerliches Gesetzbuch, Introduction, Anno. V 1 e (41st ed., 1982).

A similar view prevails in Switzerland, where Art. 1 of the Civil Code (see infra p. 653) contains an express reference to customary law. See H. Deschenaux, in 2 M. Gutzwiller et al. (Eds.), Schweizerisches Privatrecht 105–06 (1967).

There is another side of the same coin. According to the German doctrine, the formation of customary law (as distinguished from usage) requires (a) inveterate custom, and (b) *opinio necessitatis*. The latter, i.e. the recognition of the custom *as law*, normally is supplied by the courts, and in

practice it is never safe to rely on the normative nature of a custom unless *the courts* have recognized it as customary law. See 1 Enneccerus-Nipperdey, id. at § 39; 4 W. Fikentscher, Methoden des Rechts 318–20 (1977).

In a common-law system, the problem of "customary law" poses itself somewhat differently; the law-creating force of judicial decisions is taken for granted, and questions similar to those debated by the civilians arise only with respect to customs of non-judicial origin. See Note, Custom and Trade Usage: Its Application to Commercial Dealings and the Common Law, 55 Colum.L.Rev. 1192, 1206 (1955).

1a. Although not too numerous, other examples of such "contra legem" judge-made customary law do exist. See Fikentscher, supra n. 1, at 317.

decisions, most of which interpret, or analogize from, one or several provisions of the written law, and (ii) the rare and exceptional instances (exemplified by the *Neuergasthof* case, supra) in which a line of judicial decisions, by being labelled "customary law", has been declared—sometimes in the teeth of a contrary code provision—to be the source of formally binding "law".[1b]

(c) In recent years, constitutional attacks have been launched against the notion that courts can create binding "customary law" and thus in effect modify or repeal provisions of written law. As a result of these attacks (which we shall soon survey in detail, see infra pp. 627–642), the courts' power to create such "customary law" has been restricted.

(2) As the reader will recall from our discussion of the Shoop case (supra p. 229), the Spanish Code of Civil Procedure provides that a repeated holding of the highest court is regarded as a *doctrina legal*, and that by ignoring or disregarding such a *doctrina legal* a lower court commits reversible error. This provision of the Code of Civil Procedure, which in effect makes repeated holdings of the Supreme Court binding on the lower courts, is of great importance in practice. Spanish legal scholars, however, have always found it difficult to reconcile the *doctrina legal* with the Civil Code's general theory of sources of law. As originally enacted, the Civil Code in Art. 6 (quoted in the Shoop case, supra p. 235) recognized only three sources of "law": written law, custom [1c] and general principles of law. Judicial decisions were not included in this enumeration. In 1974, the entire Preliminary Title of the Civil Code was revised, and the wording of old Art. 6, now renumbered as Art. 1, was considerably amplified.[1d] The new version, an English translation of which appears infra p. 652, does mention the *doctrina legal*, calling it "the doctrine which the Supreme Court establishes in a reiterated manner", but does not recognize it as one of the sources of law.

1b. See, e.g., Palandt, supra n. 1; 3 Fikentscher, op. cit. supra n. 1, at 697–99 (1976). For an English-language discussion of the German notion of judge-made customary law, see R. David, Sources of Law, in International Encyclopedia of Comparative Law, Vol. II, Ch. 3, § 185 (1984); but that discussion fails to deal with the distinction emphasized in the text, supra.

1c. The Spanish word is *costumbre*. A party who invokes a *costumbre*, bears the burden of proving an actual usage (either local or general) that is inveterate, reasonable and recognized as binding. To meet this burden is extremely difficult, and in practice *costumbre* is not often used as a source of law. In contrast to their German colleagues, Spanish judges have not claimed the power to create a *costumbre* by judicial decisions alone.

Costumbre must be distinguished from *fueros* (supra p. 236). The latter originated in medieval customary law, usually of a local or regional nature; from the 15th century on, these local and regional customs were everywhere reduced to writing and thus became a species of local or regional *written law*. While other European countries generally repealed those local and regional laws when they enacted national codes, Spain preserved a number of the regional *fueros*, which continue to play an important role in the Spanish legal system. See supra p. 236. The reader should keep in mind, however, that whatever their historical origin may be, these regional *fueros* today do not constitute customary law; they are *written* regional law, in effect a form of regional statutes.

1d. The Spanish-language literature discussing the new Preliminary Title is vast. For an introduction in French, see J. M. Castan-Vasquez, La Réforme du Titre Préliminaire du Code Civil Espagnol, 26 Rev.Int. de Droit Comparé 835 (1974).

The precise nature and status of the *doctrina legal* thus remains in doubt. The Spanish legislator, although fashioning a sound practical solution, apparently was still too steeped in the civilian tradition to allow itself an open admission of the fact that judges make law.

(3) In France, it is generally taught that a custom may supplement but not abrogate a rule of written law.[2] But the line between supplementation and abrogation sometimes is a shadowy one. For example, Art. 1202 of the Code Civil prescribes that as a rule each of several co-obligors is presumed to be liable only for his ratable share, and not jointly and severally. Under ordinary principles, this rule would govern commercial as well as civil contracts since the Code de Commerce contains no relevant provision. But in reliance on "usage",[3] the courts have held that Art. 1202 does not apply to commercial obligations, and that the latter, contrary to the plain language of the Code, are presumed to create a "solidary" (i.e., joint and several) liability on the part of the co-obligors.[4] It is true, of course, that Art. 1202 is a *loi supplétive*, i.e., a provision which permits the parties to agree otherwise (see supra p. 587). In the cases just referred to, however, no actual intention of the parties was shown, nor an actual trade usage which could be read into the agreement of the parties. The rule was created by judicial rather than commercial "usage".

Instances such as this, in which French courts may be said to have *changed* a rule of code law by a judge-made "custom", are quite rare. But judge-made customary law *supplementing* the written law, which French authors often lump together with case law of the nonbinding, merely persuasive kind, is of great importance in France. The French refer to it as *jurisprudence*. A leading textbook defines that term as follows:

> "Jurisprudence is the aggregate of the decisions rendered by the courts, from which one can extract general rules enabling him to foresee the solution of future similar disputes. Each decision determines only *a particular case*, but the *repetition of similar decisions* permits the conclusion that the courts recognize the existence of a rule governing the solution and will follow it in the future. Hence it becomes necessary to take that rule into account in the conduct of one's affairs." [5]

Instances of rules and indeed of whole institutions which owe their existence to judicial "repetition of similar decisions" (*jurisprudence constante*) are without number in French law. The reader already is familiar with some pertinent data: That French administrative law is in large measure the creation of the Conseil d'Etat, and that the rules relating to tort liability for automobile accidents until recently were

---

2. See Loussouarn, The Relative Importance of Legislation, Custom, Doctrine, and Precedent in French Law, 18 La.L.Rev. 235, 250–54 (1958); 1 Planiol-Ripert, Traité Elémentaire de Droit Civil 50–52 (1948); Enneccerus-Nipperdey, supra n. 1.

For a somewhat different analysis see R. David, French Law 170–78 (M. Kindred, Transl., 1972). A comparative discussion of French and other civil-law theories regarding judge-made "customary law" can

be found in J. P. Dawson, The Oracles of the Law 416–31, 498–99 (1968).

3. See 1 Escarra, Manuel de droit commercial 24, 40 (1947).

4. Cass.Req. 20 Oct. 1920, S. 1922, 1.201, note Hamel; 7 Jan. 1946, D. 1946 J. 132, S. 1947, 1.32. See also David, supra n. 2, at 177.

5. Planiol-Ripert, supra n. 2.

fashioned, on the basis of code provisions of almost meaningless generality, by the *jurisprudence* of the Cour de Cassation.[6]

The French codes deal with some subjects in specific detail, while other matters (e.g., the whole law of torts) are covered by broad provisions which merely announce a general principle.[7] The practitioner knows that only case law can give concrete meaning to provisions of the latter type. Some further illustrations will be found in a later chapter of this book (infra p. 702 ff.), which deals more specifically with the code technique of "general clauses".[8]

POUND: THE SPIRIT OF THE COMMON LAW

1921. Pp. 170–181.*

. . . As a critic has put it, the theory of the codes in Continental Europe in the last century made of the court a sort of judicial slot machine. The necessary machinery had been provided in advance by legislation or by received legal principles and one had but to put in the facts above and take out the decision below. True, this critic says, the facts do not always fit the machinery, and hence we may have to thump and joggle the machinery a bit in order to get anything out. But even in extreme cases of this departure from the purely automatic, the decision is attributed, not at all to the thumping and joggling process, but solely to the machine. . . .

It was not always the Roman doctrine that law was made only by a legislative act or authentic interpretation by the sovereign. On the contrary in Cicero's time precedents were enumerated among the forms of the law. At the end of the second century a jurist could lay down, on the authority of a rescript, that the authority of cases adjudged to the same effect had the force of law. But Roman case law was made by jurisconsults rather than by judges. For whereas we entrust judicial power to a permanent judge learned in the law but bid him take the facts from a lay jury, the classical Roman polity put the judicial power in the hands of a lay *iudex* chosen for the case in hand and bade him take his law from a duly licensed jurisconsult. Where jurisconsults differed he had to decide what opinion he would adopt. Yet his decision, as that of a layman acting only for the one case, had no particular weight and was not preserved. What was significant was the answer of the learned jurisconsult whose opinion had been sought, and the most enduring part of the Roman law was made up of such

6. See supra pp. 555–558. For further examples see David, supra n. 2.

7. The reader, who has seen an English translation of the French Civil Code's principal tort provisions (supra p. 555), is familiar with the broad sweep of those provisions.

8. For other examples of judicial lawmaking by way of "interpretation" of the code, see Razi, Guided Tour in a Civil Law Library, 56 Mich.L.Rev. 375, 387–8 (1958); Amos, The Code Napoleon and the Modern World, 10 J.Comp.Leg. & Int.L., 3d Ser., 222, 231–3 (1928); Gutteridge and David, The Doctrine of Unjustified Enrichment, 5 Camb.L.J. 204 (1934); Ancel, Case Law in France, 16 J.Comp.Leg. & Int.L., 3d Ser., Part I, p. 1 (1934).

* Reprinted by permission of Marshall Jones Company, Francestown, N.H.

opinions. As a permanent judicial magistracy grew up under the empire the function of the jurisconsult waned and it is not unlikely that judicial decisions would have established themselves as a form of law had not the union of all powers, legislative, administrative and judicial, in the emperors after Diocletian led to the doctrine which Justinian handed down to the modern world with the authoritative stamp of his compilation—the doctrine that the judge can do no more than decide the particular case for the purposes of that case, and that only the sovereign by a legislative act is competent to make a binding rule which shall govern in other cases than that in which it was used as the ground of a decision.* In the Middle Ages it was enough that this doctrine had behind it the unassailable authority of Justinian. But when Roman law was first applied by lay judges advised as to the law by learned doctors of the law from the universities, a practice which the trial in Shakespeare's Merchant of Venice may serve to illustrate, it was not to be expected in any event that the decisions of such magistrates could acquire the force of law. The doctrinal writer who furnished the materials for decision was the real voice of the law.

Thus a conception of the judicial office arose on the Continent which persisted after permanent courts learned in the law had been set up,** since it appeared to accord with the theory of the separation of powers and was in line with the political theory which developed in the seventeenth and eighteenth centuries. It was in line also with the eighteenth-century doctrine of a complete code deduced from the principles of natural law. Through the influence of the latter doctrine it became a favorite notion of legislators that the finding of law for the purposes of judicial decision might be reduced to a simple matter of genuine interpretation; that a body of enacted rules might be made so complete and so perfect that the judge would have only to select the one made in advance for the case in hand, find what the law giver intended thereby through application of fixed canons of genuine interpretation and proceed to apply it. The code of Frederick the Great was drawn up on this theory. The intention was that "all contingencies should be provided for with such careful minuteness that no possible doubt could arise at any future time. The judges were not to have any discretion as

---

* The idea that only the legislating sovereign, and not the judge, may create law, is traced by Dean Pound to Byzantine absolutism. As a matter of continental legal history, this is undoubtedly correct. It should not be forgotten, however, that the 18th century produced theories which might justify the same idea on democratic principles: in a society in which the "legislator" is a popularly elected parliament, an extreme application of the doctrine of separation of powers may lead to the postulate that judges should only "apply" but not "develop" or "interpret" the laws. This is why the prohibition of judicial interpretation which was written into the French Civil Code (see text, infra), was consistent with Napoleonic as well as Revolutionary philosophy. See Maier-Hayoz, Die Bedeutung der Materialien fuer die Gesetzesanwendung, 48 Schweizerische Juristenzeitung 213, 214–5 (1952).

** Recent research has shown that at least in some parts of 17th and 18th century Europe the decisions of the courts were of somewhat greater importance for the development of the law than Dean Pound appears to have assumed. See supra p. 297. But even if his statement in the text, supra, is overbroad, it still contributes to our understanding of civilian theories which equate law with written law.

regards interpretation but were to consult a royal commission as to any doubtful points and to be absolutely bound by its answer." "This stereotyping of the law," says Schuster, "was in accordance with the doctrines of the law of nature, according to which a perfect system might be imagined, for which no changes would ever become necessary, and which could, therefore, be laid down once for all, so as to be available for any possible combination of circumstances." . . . It is as clear as legal history can make it that interpretation apart from judicial application is impracticable; that it is futile to attempt to separate the functions of finding the law, interpreting the law and applying the law. For example, the plan of interpretation by a royal commission, tried in the code of Frederick the Great, failed utterly. It soon appeared that there was no reason for supposing that the executive commission would have more foresight than the legislature. Experience quickly taught that the most which might be achieved in advance was to lay down a premise or a guiding principle and that the details of application must be the product of judicial experiment and judicial experience.

Nevertheless the Byzantine doctrine dies hard. In the nineteenth century certainty was sought not by a complete body of rules covering every case in advance but by a complete body of principles and a complete system of logical exposition and application of those principles. All the nineteenth-century codes in Continental Europe, except the German Civil Code of 1896, go upon the theory that judicial decisions shall have no authority beyond the cases in which they are rendered and that there can be no authoritative interpretation by anyone except the legislature itself. If the codes left anything open, the judges were directed * where to turn in order to decide the case. But the next judge was not to look upon the decision of his predecessor as establishing anything. He was to repeat the process independently. An excellent example may be found in *article 5 of the French Civil Code.* That article reads as follows: *"Judges are forbidden, when giving judgment in the cases which are brought before them, to lay down general rules of conduct. . . ."* ** [Italics added.] Its purpose was, as we are told by an authoritative commentator, to prevent the judges from forming a body of case law which should govern the courts and to prevent them from "correcting by judicial interpretations the mistakes made in the [enacted] law." Before fifty years had passed legislation

---

* I.e., directed by a provision of the code itself. Dean Pound is alluding to the express provisions contained in most civil codes (but not in the German Code) which deal with the sources of law to which a court should turn in case the written law is silent. We have previously encountered some examples of such directory provisions. For some further examples see infra pp. 651–653.

** A judge who violates this prohibition is, theoretically, guilty of a criminal of-

fense. French Penal Code, Art. 127. According to the intention of its draftsmen, the prohibition means that a court may not decide a case by holding it is governed by a previous decision; by so holding the court would convert the previous decision into a "general rule of conduct".

Concerning the historical reasons for French hostility against judicial lawmaking, see supra, p. 266.

was required to compel the lower courts to follow the solemn decision of the highest court of France *** and now, after a century of experience, French jurists are conceding that the article in question has failed of effect. Today elementary books from which law is taught to the French students, in the face of the code and of the received Roman tradition, do not hesitate to say that the course of judicial decision is a form of law. . . .

NOTES

(1) Did Art. 5 of the French Civil Code express the true intention of the draftsmen, or did its language present a mere political gesture which the draftsmen themselves did not expect to have any lasting effect?

The reader will recall (see supra p. 277) that Napoleon commissioned four eminent lawyers to prepare a draft of the Code, and that Portalis was the most influential member of that group. Thus it is rewarding to study the pertinent statements made by Portalis. Fortunately, many of these statements have been preserved, and excerpts from them have been translated into English.[1]

In perusing Portalis' own comments, the reader will find that he castigated the foolishness of the idea (embodied in the Prussian Code of Frederick the Great) of depriving the courts of the power to *interpret* ambiguous or obscure code provisions. He said: "A Code, however complete it may seem, is hardly finished before a thousand unexpected issues come to face the judge." At the same time, Portalis rejected the notion of *authoritative* judicial interpretation. But his position on this point was less clear, because almost in the same breath he stressed the necessity of case law, which by utilizing experience would "gradually . . . fill up the gaps we leave." On the vital point of the precedential force of judicial decisions, one can find certain contradictions in Portalis' elegant formulations. Perhaps he had to pay lip service to the revolutionary postulate rejecting all *règlements* and *dispositions générales*,[2] while at the same time he also wished to express his personal opinion that as a practical matter it was necessary for the courts to develop, and ultimately to be guided by, a stable case law based on experience.

(2) In a country where the civil-law version of the principle of separation of powers is anchored in the Constitution, and where the constitutionality of statutes and other legal norms is subject to judicial review, one can expect a great deal of debate concerning the question whether and under what circumstances *the Constitution* permits the

---

*** Dean Pound apparently refers to the Law of April, 1837 (meanwhile repeatedly amended and re-enacted). That Law first introduced the system, described in detail supra pp. 465–466, under which the second reversal pronounced in the same case by the Cour de Cassation (this time sitting en banc or as a super-panel) is binding on the intermediate appellate court to which the case is remanded. The latter court, however, is "bound" only in the case at hand, and not in future cases presenting the same question of law.

1. See M. S. Herman, Excerpts from a Discourse on the Code Napoleon by Portalis, 18 Loyola L.Rev. 23 (1972); A. Levasseur, Code Napoleon or Code Portalis?, 43 Tul.L.Rev. 762, 767–74 (1969).

2. I.e., the kinds of usurpation of law-making power for which certain pre-revolutionary French courts were strongly criticized by the revolutionaries and their successors.

creation of judge-made law. Such a debate is not always academic. The case which follows will demonstrate that substantial rights and obligations of real-life parties may hinge on the outcome of that debate.

[handwritten: Example of court's changing their interpretation of a statute over time]

[handwritten: Soraya Case]

OPINION OF THE GERMAN FEDERAL CONSTITUTIONAL COURT IN THE PROCEEDING CONCERNING THE CONSTITUTIONAL COMPLAINT OF PUBLISHING COMPANY "DIE WELT" AND MR. K.–H. V.

[handwritten: see § pg 634]
[handwritten: Strong argument for judicial activism]

First Panel,* February 14, 1973.
BVerfGE 34, 269, also reported in NJW 1973, 1221.

[The plaintiff is Princess Soraya, the ex-wife of the Shah of Iran. At the time in question, after her divorce from the Shah, the plaintiff resided in Germany. The defendants are the publisher and chief-editor of an illustrated weekly paper which is distributed throughout Germany and known to specialize in sensational society stories.

In April 1961, defendants' paper carried a front-page story purporting to be the transcript of an interview with the plaintiff. The interview, which appeared to reveal much of plaintiff's private and very private life, was wholly fictitious, i.e., it was totally and freely invented by its author, a free-lance journalist. Defendants published the story without investigating whether the interview had actually taken place. In July, 1961, defendants' paper carried another story dealing with Princess Soraya, and as a part of that new story the defendants published a brief statement by the Princess to the effect that the alleged April interview had not taken place.

In the present action, plaintiff seeks damages for "violation of her personality rights." The Landgericht as court of first instance awarded her D.M. 15,000. The Oberlandesgericht (intermediate appellate court) and the Bundesgerichtshof (court of last resort in civil and criminal matters, abbr. BGH) affirmed, and the defendants brought the case before the Federal Constitutional Court by way of a constitutional complaint.[a]

In order to understand the thrust of defendants' constitutional arguments, we must take a brief look at the development and present status of the rules of substantive law which the plaintiff successfully invoked in the courts below.

Apart from a section protecting a person's right to his name, the German Civil Code contains no specific provisions concerning the subjects which we would label as defamation or invasion of privacy. In Germany, as in France, defamation traditionally has been thought of as

---

* A case coming before the Federal Constitutional Court, unless summarily disposed of (see supra p. 376), is heard by one of the two eight-judge panels. In the instant case, the decision of the panel was unanimous.

a. For an explanation of this procedure see supra p. 376.

a crime rather than a tort.[b]   Under this traditional view, defamation actions normally have to be brought in the criminal courts, even though such an action ordinarily has to be prosecuted by the victim rather than the public prosecutor.[c]   If the defendant is convicted in such a criminal proceeding, he will be fined, or (in a very serious case) subjected to a jail sentence; but the victim cannot recover substantial damages in that proceeding.[d]

Until after World War II, attempts to bring *civil* actions for defamation or invasion of privacy found little favor with the German courts.   The first paragraph of § 823 of the Civil Code [e] authorizes tort recovery only if the plaintiff can show injury to his "life, body, health, freedom, property, or some other (similar) right."   In order to bring cases of defamation or invasion of privacy within the ambit of this code provision, plaintiffs often argued that a person's interest in his reputation and privacy should be regarded as his "personality right" and should be protected as one of the "other rights" mentioned in § 823. But throughout the periods of the Empire, the Weimar Republic and the Third Reich, the courts essentially rejected that argument.[f]

A different judicial approach to the problem emerged after World War II, and after the adoption of the new West German Constitution, which contains the following provisions:

> Art. 1.   The dignity of man is inviolable.   Every state authority is duty-bound to respect and protect it . . .

> Art. 2.   Everyone is entitled to the free development of his personality insofar as he does not violate the rights of others or offend the constitutional order or the rules of morality. . . .

b. See B. S. Markesinis, The Not So Dissimilar Tort and Delict, 93 L.Q.Rev. 78, 103–05 (1977); J. F. Murphy, An International Convention on Invasion of Privacy, 8 N.Y.U.J.Int.L. & Pol. 387, 422–23 (1976).

c. See German Code of Criminal Procedure, §§ 374, 376. See also supra p. 495. The public prosecutor brings such an action only if this is required in the public interest.

The reader will recall that German law generally vests the prosecutor with little or no discretion, and obligates him to prosecute whenever there is reasonable cause to believe that the defendant has committed a crime. This general rule, however, is subject to exceptions in the case of certain relatively minor offenses, such as defamation.

d. Apart from other difficulties, German law until recently imposed a relatively low ceiling on the amount which the victim can recover in a criminal proceeding. See supra p. 493.

e. For a translation of that provision see supra p. 553.

f. For details, see Markesinis, supra n. b, at 105–06.

It is interesting to note that in France the courts began much earlier than in Germany to employ tort remedies for the protection of privacy interests. The reason may be that Art. 1382 of the French Civil Code (see supra p. 555), in contrast to German § 823, is of such generality that a French court, when granting a tort recovery, could always claim to act on the authority of that Code provision. See W. J. Wagner, The Development of the Theory of the Right to Privacy in France, 1971 Wash. U.L.Q. 45, 49ff. Since 1970, moreover, tort remedies for invasion of privacy are explicitly authorized by the French Civil Code, Art. 9 (added by Law No. 70–643 of July 17, 1970).

During the 1950s the BGH, explicitly invoking these constitutional *court made law* provisions, gave up the former narrow interpretation of § 823 of the Civil Code and repeatedly held that a plaintiff's "personality right" is one of the "other rights" which are protected by § 823 against intentional or negligent infringement. This was an important development. It meant that—in contrast to prior law—the German courts now were treating injuries to a person's reputation or privacy as actionable torts.

Even after this judicial breakthrough, however, a difficult issue remained to be resolved regarding the kind of damages for which recovery could be allowed under German law in cases of injury to the plaintiff's "personality right." The difficulty was caused by one of the Civil Code's provisions dealing with damages. These provisions, insofar as they are relevant to the present discussion, read as follows:

§ 249. A person who is liable to make compensation, has to bring about the condition which would exist if the circumstances making him liable had not occurred.[g] If the liability exists for injury to a person or damage to tangible property, then the obligee [at his election] may demand, instead of restitution in kind, the sum of money necessary to effect such restitution.

§ 251. Insofar as restitution in kind is impossible or is insufficient to compensate the obligee, the obligor has to compensate the obligee by the payment of money damages. . . .

§ 253. *For an injury which is not an injury to patrimony [i.e., to interests having a pecuniary value], compensation in money can be demanded only in the cases provided by (written) law.*[h] (emphasis supplied)

There are a few limited and narrowly defined cases in which an express provision of written law (within the meaning of § 253) permits the victim of a tort to recover money damages for an injury to non-pecuniary interests; the prime example is the case of personal injury, with respect to which § 847 of the German Civil Code explicitly authorizes the recovery of money damages for pain and suffering. The draftsmen of the Civil Code clearly regarded this provision of § 847 as an exception to the general rule laid down in § 253: that no money damages can be recovered for an injury to non-pecuniary interests.[i]

Neither the Civil Code nor any auxiliary statute provides for the recovery of non-pecuniary damages by a person whose "right of personality" has been injured. Thus when the tort of injury to a person's

g. This means that as a rule, subject to the exceptions listed in the second sentence of § 249 and in the subsequent sections, the obligor is bound to make restitution in kind rather than to pay money damages.

h. The German text makes it clear that a victim whose non-pecuniary interests have been injured, can demand money damages only in the cases provided by

"Gesetz". As distinguished from *Recht*, which in its objective sense means law (regardless of its source), the word *"Gesetz"* denotes a statute or other written law.

i. See Palandt, Bürgerliches Gesetzbuch, § 847, Anno. 1a (41st ed., 1982). Some additional exceptions are provided for in auxiliary statutes. See ibid.

"personality right" was first developed by the German courts, it was initially thought that a plaintiff, while perhaps entitled to the publication of a retraction or to similar non-monetary relief under § 249, could not recover money damages without proof of what we would call "special damage", i.e., loss of his job, loss of customers, or the like.[j] The plain language of § 253 indeed appears to preclude the plaintiff in such a case from recovering "general" damages for his soiled reputation and injured feelings.

In 1958, however, the German courts broke away from this restriction seemingly imposed by § 253. The occasion was the so-called *Herrenreiter* case (the case of the gentleman horse-back rider).[k] That case involved a picture of the plaintiff, a well-known equestrian, elegantly positioned on horse-back while jumping over a hurdle. Without plaintiff's authorization, the picture was publicly and widely disseminated by the defendant as part of an advertisement promoting a sexual stimulant. The plaintiff's "personality right" was seriously injured by this advertisement, not only because it conveyed the impression that the plaintiff had sought to commercialize his great reputation as a sportsman, but also because it implied that he needed and used sexual stimulants.

The lower courts awarded the plaintiff a substantial sum of money as damages for the injury to his reputation and feelings. The BGH affirmed, essentially on the ground that § 847 of the Civil Code should be extended by analogy to cover the case at hand. This analogy argument was questionable, because the word "only" in § 253 explicitly prohibits an analogical extension of provisions, such as § 847, which engraft exceptions upon the general rule of § 253. Recognizing this, the BGH subsequently abandoned the analogy argument; but the result reached in the *Herrenreiter* case was reaffirmed in later cases, on the ground that in many situations the tort of injury to a person's "personality right"—a tort developed in response to value judgments expressed in the Constitution—would be without an adequate remedy if the victim of such a tort could not recover money damages for the violation of his non-monetary interests.

The BGH limited the breadth of these rulings by further holding that such a cause of action for money damages should be recognized only if (a) the injury to the plaintiff's "personality right" is substantial, and (b) the defendant's act is sufficiently culpable to justify the rendition of a money judgment in a sizeable amount. According to the BGH, both conditions, (a) and (b), are clearly satisfied in a case in which a defendant, by way of large-scale promotion of his own commercial interests, has wantonly violated the plaintiff's "personality right." The repetition of such intolerable conduct, the BGH held, should be prevent-

j. See Markesinis, supra n. b, at 105–07.

k. Decision of February 14, 1958, BGHZ 26, 349.

ed by announcing a rule of tort law which makes it clear to would-be violators that such conduct is costly for them.

In the decisions dealing with this question, the BGH also pointed to the drastic technological and social changes that have taken place since the enactment of the Civil Code. The development of mass media, hardly predictable in 1900, makes the protection of an individual's personality right more important and more difficult in our day. Therefore, the BGH held, a court which takes the value system of the Constitution seriously can no longer feel bound by § 253 of the Civil Code insofar as that provision denies recovery for non-pecuniary damages even in cases of grave injuries to an individual's personality right.

The lower courts, after some initial reluctance on the part of some of them, generally followed these holdings of the BGH, which were approved, also, by the majority of the commentators. In the instant case, both the lower courts and the BGH itself based their decision on those previous holdings.

The defendants' constitutional complaint was based mainly on the following provisions of the German Federal Constitution:

> Art. 5. . . . Freedom of the press and freedom of reporting by broadcast and film are guaranteed. . . .

> These rights are limited by the provisions of general (written) laws,[1] by statutory measures for the protection of juveniles, and by the right of personal honor. . . .

> Art. 20. . . .

> All of the State's power originates with the People. Such power can be exercised by the People through elections and ballots, and by special organs of the legislative, executive and judicial branches of the government.

> The legislature is bound by the constitutional order. The executive and the judiciary are bound by statute and law.[m]
> . . .

In particular, the defendants argued that the substantive rule pursuant to which the lower courts ordered them to pay money damages to the plaintiff, had been created by the courts in violation of the principle of separation of powers laid down in Art. 20 of the Constitution. The BGH, they argued, had acted *contra legem* when it developed the right to money damages for violation of an individual's "personality right." This, it was contended, was a usurpation by the courts of legislative power.

---

l. The German term is *"allgemeine Gesetze"*. As to the meaning of the word *"Gesetz"*, see supra n. h.

m. The German term is *"Gesetz und Recht"*. The words *"Gesetz"* and *"Recht"* are not synonymous. See supra n. h.

Literally, this provision of the Constitution means that the executive and the judiciary are bound by written law and by other law.

The defendants did not question the constitutionality of the view that the personality right of a person is one of the "other rights" mentioned in the first paragraph of § 823 of the Civil Code. Their attack was directed only against the decisional rule which—contrary to the language of § 253 of the Civil Code—permits a plaintiff whose personality right has been gravely injured, to recover a money judgment for non-monetary damages.

The defendants did not deny that the recognition of plaintiff's personality right as one of the "other rights" protected by § 823 of the Civil Code was in part dictated by Arts. 1 and 2 of the Constitution. But they argued that the rights derived from Arts. 1 and 2, like other human rights protected by the Constitution, are essentially defensive in nature. For this reason, the defendants contended, it is not possible to treat those constitutional provisions as the direct foundation of a cause of action for money damages.

In addition, the defendants argued, the money judgment rendered by the courts below violated the constitutional principle of freedom of the press. In the defendants' view, the money damage rule developed by the courts and applied in this case did not constitute the kind of "general (written) law" which pursuant to Art. 5 of the Constitution may be used by the law-giver to limit the freedom of the press.]

The constitutional complaint is unfounded.

I

The litigation which gave rise to the judgment under attack, was a civil proceeding, to be determined in accordance with the principles and rules of private law. The Federal Constitutional Court does not review the interpretation and application of private law as such. However, the value system reflected in the Constitution's guarantees of fundamental rights has an impact upon all areas of law, including that of private law. To make sure that this "radiation effect" of the Constitution be properly observed, is one of the functions of the Constitutional Court. Our Court, therefore, must examine whether the decisions of the civil courts are based on a basically incorrect view of the scope and effect of a fundamental constitutional right, or whether the result of such a decision itself violates fundamental constitutional rights of one of the parties. [citations] [n]

In the instant case the complainants [i.e., the defendants, who have filed the constitutional complaint] not only oppose the result reached by the civil courts; they object above all to the manner in which those courts have reached such result. The complainants argue that an ordinary court is bound to obey the written law, and hence is not permitted to award monetary damages in cases of this kind. This argument compels us to reflect upon the nature and limits of the

n. For other German cases showing how this "radiation effect" of constitutional principles can affect the interpretation and application of provisions of the Civil Code, see infra pp. 729–731.

judicial function as outlined in the Constitution. We must examine the question whether decisions such as those rendered by the courts below, can be arrived at by way of judicial application of the law. A judge may not proceed in an arbitrary manner when he seeks to implement the value concepts of the Constitution in his decisions. He would likewise violate the Constitution if he reached a result in accord with the value concepts of the Constitution but did so by employing a method exceeding or disregarding the constitutional limits imposed upon the exercise of the judicial function. The Federal Constitutional Court would have to review, and object to, a decision thus reached.

The plaintiff's claim in the present action was based on the first paragraph of § 823 of the Civil Code. The BGH includes the "general right of personality" among the rights protected by that provision, citing a line of earlier decisions [going back to the early 1950s]. The BGH regards the conduct of the defendants in the instant case as violating that right. It is not the task of the Federal Constitutional Court to examine the "correctness" of this line of decisions so long as their reasoning and development remain within the area of private law. Suffice it to state that the general right of personality—which at the time of the enactment of the Civil Code was still rejected by the codifiers—has successfully asserted itself in the course of scholarly discussions extending over several decades, and, following its recognition by the BGH [in the early 1950s], has now become a formally recognized part of the system of private law [citing several leading textbooks and commentaries].

The Federal Constitutional Court sees no reason why this line of decisions of the BGH should be questioned on constitutional grounds. The personality and dignity of an individual, to be freely enjoyed and developed within a societal and communal framework, stand at the very center of the value system reflected in the fundamental rights protected by the Constitution. Thus, an individual's interest in his personality and dignity must be respected, and must be protected by all organs of the State (see Arts. 1 and 2 of the Constitution). Such protection should be extended, above all, to a person's private sphere, i.e., the sphere in which he desires to be left alone, to make (and to be responsible for) his own decisions, and to remain free from any outside interference [citation]. Within the area of private law, such protection is provided, inter alia, by the legal rules relating to the general right of personality. . . . The Federal Constitutional Court has never questioned the recognition by the civil courts of a general right of personality [citations].

The first paragraph of § 823 of the Civil Code is a "general written law" within the meaning of Art. 5 of the Constitution. [The Court then points out that under the terms of Art. 5 the freedom of the press can be limited by an "allgemeines Gesetz", or "general written law". As the protection of a person's personality right is derived from § 823 of the Civil Code (clearly a "general written law"), it is plain that the courts did not violate Art. 5 when they recognized that injury to a person's personality right may constitute a tort.] . . .

II

When a "general written law" potentially limits the freedom of the press, the question arises how such limitation is to be made effective; this question must be answered exclusively in accordance with the terms of such written law. If follows that only the sanctions authorized by such written law may be used against the press to limit its freedom. This is where the argument of the complainants comes in: they contend that there is no "general written law" authorizing a money judgment to compensate for non-monetary damages suffered as a result of injury to the plaintiff's personality right. Section 253 of the Civil Code, they argue, explicitly precludes such a money judgment. Complainants further assert that by granting such money judgments the courts have exceeded the boundaries within which they are permitted by the Constitution to limit the freedom of the press. . . .

The Federal Constitutional Court can examine only the constitutional aspects of these decisions [i.e., of the decisions which permitted recovery for money damages in cases of injury to a plaintiff's personality right]. From the standpoint of constitutional law, there are two questions: first, whether the substantive result brought about by that line of decisions violates the fundamental right of freedom of the press; and secondly, whether it is consistent with the Constitution to reach that result through judicial decisions in spite of the lack of an unequivocal basis in the written law. . . .

III

[In this part of the opinion, the Court addresses the first of the two questions just formulated. It calls attention, first of all, to the fact that money judgments for violation of a plaintiff's personality right can be entered, and have been entered, not only against the press, but against other defendants as well. The line of decisions in question thus does not in any way discriminate against the press.

The Court further refers to the fact that the imposition of monetary damages for injury to non-monetary interests is not a sanction alien to the German legal system. This is shown by § 847 of the Civil Code. A substantive rule extending this sanction to cases of injury to the plaintiff's "personality right" is not unconstitutional, provided the rule is subject to proper safeguards. The rule developed by the BGH does contain the necessary safeguards. It applies only where remedies other than a money judgment, (e.g., an injunction or a judgment ordering the defendant to publish a retraction) are impossible or inadequate. Furthermore, the rule developed by the BGH subjects the defendant to a duty to pay money damages only in cases where the injury to plaintiff's reputation and feelings is a grave one, and where the defendants' conduct can be characterized as seriously culpable. For these reasons, the Court concludes that the limitations which the BGH decisions (in allowing money damages for injuries to plaintiff's reputation and feelings) have imposed upon the freedom of the press, must be regarded as reasonable.

The opinion contains a hint to the effect that Art. 5 of the Constitution might be violated if in cases of this kind the courts permitted the recovery of excessively large amounts of damages. There is, however, no indication that the German courts are excessively generous in assessing such damages. In the instant case, in any event, the amount awarded to the plaintiff is distinctly modest.

The second of the two questions formulated by the Court at the end of Part II of its opinion relates not only to Art. 5 of the Constitution (freedom of the press), but equally to Art. 20 (separation of powers). The Court turns to that question—the crucial question in the case—in Part IV of its opinion.]

IV

The judge is traditionally bound by the *Gesetz* (written law). This is an inherent element of the principle of separation of powers, and thus of the rule of law. Our Constitution, however, in Art. 20 has somewhat changed the traditional formulation by providing that the judge is bound by "*Gesetz und Recht*" [i.e., written law and (other) law]. According to the generally prevailing view, this implies the rejection of a narrow positivistic approach predicated solely upon the written law. The formulation chosen in Art. 20 keeps us aware of the fact that although *Gesetz* and *Recht* in general are co-extensive, this is not necessarily always the case. The legal order is not identical with the aggregate of the written laws. Under certain circumstances there can be law beyond the positive norms enacted by the State—law which has its source in the constitutional legal order as a meaningful, all-embracing system, and which functions as a corrective of the written norms. To find this law, and to make it a reality through their decisions, is the task of the courts. The Constitution does not confine the judge to the function of applying the language of legislative mandates to the particular case before him. Such a concept [of the judicial function] would presuppose that there are no gaps in the positive [written] legal order— a condition which in the interest of legal certainty might be postulated as desirable, but which in practice is unattainable. The judge's task is not confined to the ascertainment and implementation of decisions made by the legislator; he may be called upon, through an act in the nature of a value judgment (an act which necessarily has volitional elements), to bring to light and to realize in his decisions those value concepts which are immanent in the constitutional legal order, but which are not, or not adequately, expressed in the language of the written laws. In performing this task, the judge must guard against arbitrariness; his decision must be based upon rational argumentation. He must make it clear that the written law fails to perform its function

Sounds like common law

of providing a just solution for the legal problem at hand. Where this
is so, the gap thus found is filled by the judge's decision in accordance
with practical reason and "the community's established general concepts of justice" [citation].   *i.e. public policy*

In principle, this duty and power of the judge to render "creative
decisions" has never been questioned since the adoption of our present
Constitution [citations]. The courts at the apex of our judicial hierarchies have claimed such power from the beginning [citations]. It has
always been recognized by the Federal Constitutional Court [citations].
The legislator himself bestowed upon the highest courts [i.e., the courts
at the apex of each of the five judicial hierarchies] the task of "further
development of the law" (see § 137 of the Law on the Organization of
Courts).⁰ In some areas of the law, such as labor law, this task has
become particularly important, because legislation has not kept up with
the rapid flow of social development.

There remains only the question of the limits which have to be
imposed upon such creative [judicial] decision-making, keeping in mind
the principle that the judge is bound by the written law, a principle
that cannot be abandoned if the rule of law is to be maintained. Those
limits cannot be capsulized in a formula equally applicable to all areas
of the law and to all legal relationships created or controlled by the law
within those areas.

For purposes of the present decision, the question just posed can be
confined to the area of private law. In that area, the judge confronts a
great codification, the Civil Code, which has been in force for over 70
years. This has a dual significance: in the first place, the freedom of
the judge creatively to develop the law surely grows with the "aging of
codifications" [citation], with the increased distance in time between
the enactment of the legislative mandate and the judge's decision of an
individual case. The interpretation of a written norm cannot always,
for an unlimited period of time, remain tied to the meaning which the
norm has been given at the time of its enactment. One has to explore
what reasonable function such norm might have at the time of its
application. The norm remains always in the context of the social
conditions and of the socio-political views with which it is intended to
interact; as these conditions and views change, the thrust of the norm
can, and under certain circumstances must, be adjusted to such change.
This is true especially when between the time of the enactment of a
written law and the time of its application the conditions of life and
peoples' views on matters of law have changed as radically as they have
in the present century. The judge cannot, by simply pointing to the
unchanged language of the written law, avoid the conflict that has

o. The Court here refers to the functions of the super-panels of the BGH and
the other highest courts. The super-panels
can be called upon to decide a case (a)
when there is a conflict or potential conflict between two regular panels (see supra
p. 468), or (b) when the regular panel (to
which the case has been assigned) concludes that, because of the fundamental
importance of the issue presented, a super-
panel decision is required in the interest of
"the further development of the law". See
§ 137 of the German law on the Organization of Courts.

arisen between the norm [as written] and the substantive notions of justice of a changed society. If he is not to be derelict in his duty to hand down decisions based on "law," he is forced to manipulate the legal norms more freely. Secondly, as experience demonstrates, legislative reforms encounter particularly great difficulties and obstacles when they are intended to revise a great codification, such as the Civil Code covering our private law, which has put its stamp on the system and character of the whole legal order.[p]

The question dealt with by the decisions presently under attack [i.e., the question of recoverability of money damages for injury to a non-monetary interest] was controversial already at the time when the preparatory work on the draft of the Civil Code was in progress [citations]. The solution chosen by the legislator immediately ran into criticism—criticism which at that time did not yet involve any constitutional arguments. That criticism has never ceased. The critics were able to point to the development of the law in other countries of the Western world, where a more liberal approach has been taken toward the possibility of recovering money damages for injuries to non-monetary interests. [The Court here cites extensive comparative studies]. It was pointed out that only in Germany, and nowhere else in the Western world, could one observe large numbers of cases in which an unlawful act—causing "merely" non-monetary damages—remained without any civil sanction. The rule which permits the recovery of money damages for injury to non-monetary interests only in a few enumerated special cases—which special cases, moreover, were selected without much logic—was characterized as a "legislative failure" [citations]. Criticism became even sharper after the courts, under the influence of "the Constitution's force of shaping private law" [citation], had taken the step of recognizing the general right of personality. The gap that existed in the remedies available for a violation of that right, thus became visible. This problem, the importance of which could not be perceived at the time when the Civil Code was drafted, now urgently demanded a solution responsive to a changed awareness of legal rights and to the value concepts of a new Constitution. Such a solution could not be deduced from the enumeration requirement of § 253.[q]

The courts were faced with the question whether to close this gap by the methods at their disposal, or whether to wait for the intervention of the legislator. When the courts chose the first alternative, they

p. The Court here emphasizes the special difficulty of *legislative* revision of a comprehensive, integrated code. The reader is familiar with this point. See supra p. 547. The implication is, of course, that when reform becomes necessary, and *legislative* revision cannot be brought about, the need for *judicial* development of the law increases.

q. The expression "enumeration requirement" may call for some explanation. Section 253 of the Civil Code does not itself enumerate the instances in which a money judgment for injury to non-monetary interests is recoverable. But, using a method which might be described as enumeration by reference, that section provides that such a money judgment can be recovered only in the cases provided for (or enumerated) in other code sections or statutes. German courts and legal writers, therefore, often speak of the "enumeration requirement" or "enumeration principle" embodied in § 253.

were able to refer to the writings of influential legal authors who previously had advocated that course [citation]. From the beginning, the relevant [innovative] decisions of the BGH and of other courts were widely approved by legal scholars [citations]. This shows that these decisions were in accord with generally recognized concepts of justice, and were not regarded as intolerable restrictions upon freedom of opinion or freedom of the press. . . . Insofar as there was criticism of these decisions, such criticism was directed less against the result reached by the BGH than against the methodological and doctrinal considerations invoked by the courts to justify the new approach. To the extent that this involves methodological questions in the area of private law, it is not within the province of the Federal Constitutional Court to determine the validity of the objections raised by the critics. But it should not be overlooked that the majority of the authors who are specialists in the area of private law, apparently regard the reasoning of the courts as dogmatically unobjectionable [citations]. Moreover, the discussions of the Private Law Section of the Society for Comparative Law, at its 1971 meeting in Mannheim, demonstrate that the position which the BGH has taken concerning this question, is largely in harmony with the course of the law in other countries [citations]. From the standpoint of the Constitution, one cannot object to a result which was reached in a manner at least arguably acceptable in the private law area, and which does not (or at least not obviously) run counter to the rules of interpretation developed in that area; this is particularly true when, as here, that result serves to implement and effectively to protect an interest which the Constitution itself regards as central to its value system. Such a result is "law" in the sense of Art. 20 of the Constitution. It does not contradict, but supplements and develops, the written law.

The other alternative, to wait for legislative regulation, under the circumstance cannot be regarded as constitutionally mandated. It is true that the Federal Government has tried twice to bring about a legislative solution of the problem of private law protection of an individual's personality right. But the bills drafted in 1959 and 1967 died early in the legislative process, even though there was no indication of any legislative intention to perpetuate the status quo. The judge, who is compelled to decide every case submitted to him, thus cannot be blamed if he becomes convinced that he should not, in reliance upon a wholly uncertain future intervention of the legislator, adhere to the literal meaning of the existing written law in a case in which such adherence would to a large extent sacrifice justice.

The method by which the BGH reached the decisions in question, is constitutionally unobjectionable also for a further reason: this method deviated from the written law only to the extent that such deviation was absolutely necessary in order to resolve the legal problem presented by the concrete case at hand. The BGH has not regarded § 253 in its entirety as no longer binding. Nor has it treated that provision as unconstitutional. . . . The BGH has left intact the principle of enumeration [r] expressed in § 253, and has merely added one situation to the legislator's own enumeration of situations in which money damages can be recovered for injury to non-monetary interests; this one addition appeared to the BGH to be compellingly justified by the evolution of social conditions, and also by a new law of higher rank, to wit, Arts. 1 and 2 of the Constitution. The BGH and other courts which followed its holdings, thus have not abandoned the system of the legal order, and have not exhibited an intention to go their own way in making policy; they have merely taken a further step in developing and concretizing basic ideas that are inherent in the legal order molded by the Constitution, and they have done so by means which remain within the system [citations]. The legal rule thus found is, therefore, a legitimate part of the legal order; and as a "general Gesetz" within the meaning of Art. 5 of the Constitution it limits the freedom of the press.[s] The purpose of that rule is to fashion and guarantee, by the methods of private law, an effective protection of the individual's personality and dignity—i.e., of interests that stand at the center of the constitutional ordering of values—, and thus, within a particular area of the law, to strengthen the effect of constitutionally protected fundamental rights. For these reasons, the constitutional arguments of the complainants must fail. . . .

QUESTION

The reader will recall that in the *Neuergasthof* case, supra, and in other decisions antedating the case of Princess Soraya, German courts of last resort had claimed the power to give binding effect to a line of decisions—even to a line of decisions in conflict with a code provision or other statute—by calling it "customary law." Was that power enlarged or diminished by the Constitutional Court's holding and reasoning in the *Soraya* case?

Careful reading of the *Soraya* opinion will supply a plausible answer to this question. The more recent case which follows makes the answer completely clear.

OPINION OF THE GERMAN FEDERAL CONSTITUTIONAL COURT CONCERNING THE CONSTITUTIONAL COMPLAINTS OF TWO TRUSTEES IN BANKRUPTCY

Second Panel, October 18, 1983.
BVerfGE 65, 182, also reported in NJW 1984, 475.

[On the basis of statutory provisions contained in the *Betriebsverfassungsgesetz* (Enterprise Organization Law), employees who lose their jobs because of the closing of a business or plant frequently acquire claims for severance pay. The said statute is silent on the

---

r. See supra n. q.

s. Concerning the meaning of the word "*Gesetz*", see supra n. h. Does the Court explain why it treats a judge-made rule as a "*Gesetz*" within the meaning of Art. 5?

Note that such a difficulty does not arise with respect to Art. 20 of the Constitution, which speaks of "*Gesetz und Recht*". See supra n. m. But the wording of Art. 5 presents a tougher nut to crack. Did the Court successfully crack it?

important and much-litigated question of the priority (if any) that should be accorded to such claims in the employer's bankruptcy. The issue of priorities, i.e., of the rank order in which claims are to be satisfied, is, however, explicitly and comprehensively addressed in Section 61 of the German Bankruptcy Law. Stated in somewhat simplified form, the rank order established by Section 61 is as follows:

Class I: Claims of employees for wages earned during the last year before bankruptcy.

Class II: Tax claims of enumerated government units.

Class III: Claims of School Districts and other public institutions not enumerated in Class II.

Class IV: Claims of physicians and hospitals for services rendered during the last year.

Class V: Claims of the bankrupt's children and wards that arise out of the management (by the bankrupt) of claimants' property.

Class VI: All other claims.[a]

The statutory claims of employees for severance pay are not claims for wages earned during the last year and hence do not come within Class I.[b] Section 61 of the German Bankruptcy Law thus relegates claims for severance pay to Class VI.[c] Whether as a matter of social policy this should be regarded as a desirable result, became a hotly debated question. In numerous cases coming before the labor courts, employees and their lawyers developed various legal theories that were aimed at taking severance pay claims out of Class VI and giving them a higher priority. After much conflict and turmoil, the court at the apex of the labor court hierarchy, the *Bundesarbeitsgericht* (BAG) by way of a super-panel decision finally held in 1978 that claims for severance pay were entitled to a rank ahead of all classes of claims described in Section 61, i.e., ahead of Class I.[d] To justify this holding, the BAG invoked reasons of social policy and a vague provision of the German Constitution referring to social justice. Although the holding was unabashedly in conflict with the scheme of Section 61 of the Bankruptcy Law, it was consistently followed in subsequent decisions of the BAG.

In the instant case the Labor Court as court of first instance, following the said decisions of the BAG, held that the employees' claims for severance pay ranked ahead of Class I. Affirming that holding on appeal, the intermediate appellate court and the BAG equally accorded super-priority to those claims. The Constitutional Court unanimously and unhesitatingly *reversed.*

---

a. The comparable provision of our own Bankruptcy Act appears in 11 U.S.C.A. § 507 (1979, and 1986 Supp. Pamphlet).

b. In our law, claims for severance pay are equated with wage claims for purposes of bankruptcy priority. See subd. (a)(3) of § 507, supra n. a.

c. Experience shows that Class VI creditors in most cases receive nothing or very little.

d. BAG (Super-Panel), decision of Dec. 13, 1978, NJW 1979, p. 774.

The Constitutional Court pointed out that the subject of bankruptcy priorities is regulated by Section 61 of the Bankruptcy Law, which sets forth a clear and exhaustive scheme of classification and rank order. [In the opinion of the Constitutional Court, there was no justification whatever for the BAG's attempt to alter that statutory scheme by judge-made law. The Constitution's reference to social justice is so vague and indefinite that it must be regarded as a mere exhortation addressed to the legislator and not as a mandate or authorization for the judiciary.]

In contrast to the so-called *Soraya* case . . . the present case does not involve the protection of the general right of personality, which in view of Articles 1 and 2 of the Basic Law occupies a central place in the value system of our basic rights. In *Soraya* the BGH dealt with cases of grave violations of an absolute right already recognized by the legal order, and merely added a further sanction, i.e., the awarding of monetary damages for non-physical injuries. The decisions of the BAG, on the other hand, which interfere with the statutory order of bankruptcy priorities in favor of one group of creditors, gravely disadvantage all other groups of creditors. . . . Unlike the BGH in the *Soraya* case, the BAG could, finally, not assert that its judge-made rule is supported by a generally prevailing legal opinion. . . . This is shown by the divided reception which its ruling has encountered in the [legal] literature.

NOTES ON THE TWO PRECEDING CASES

(1) Neither of the two preceding opinions of the German Federal Constitutional Court throws any doubt on the proposition that, even in a legal system heavily emphasizing the primacy of the written law, the courts may and indeed must play a creative law-making role (a) in deriving concrete results from code provisions of utmost generality, and (b) in dealing with gaps in the written law. The two opinions focus on a relatively narrow problem: whether and under what conditions an unambiguous mandate of the written law may be modified or bent by judge-made "customary" law or by some other form of decisional law.

(2) In the *Soraya* case, the Constitutional Court put its stamp of approval on a rule of judge-made law although that rule was concededly *contra legem*. In the bankruptcy case, the same Court struck down a rule of decisional law modifying a statutory scheme. It is obvious, therefore, that the Court is trying to draw a line. On one side of the line, but not on the other, will the courts of the various judicial hierarchies be permitted to create judge-made law *contra legem*.

(3) German legal writers have criticized the Constitutional Court for not etching that line with sufficient clarity.[1] A truly careful reading of the *Soraya* opinion, however, shows that in that case the Constitutional Court upheld the judge-made rule fashioned by the BGH only because it met all of the following conditions:

1. See, e.g., J.-H. Bauer & C. Moench, Sozialplanabfindungen im Konkurs, 37 NJW 468, 469 (1984).

(a) According to the overwhelmingly prevailing view of German judges, lawyers and legal authors—a view strongly fortified by comparative research—, a provision contained in an old Code had become unbearable in the light of social developments and changed attitudes.

(b) The old Code provision, if literally applied, would come into conflict with value judgments *clearly* expressed in the Constitution.

(c) Over a long period of time it had turned out that legislative reform could not be expected.

(d) The judicially imposed reform did not go further than absolutely necessary.

In the bankruptcy case, on the other hand, it would have been absurd to argue that the BAG's rule of decisional law met all of these conditions. Thus it should not be difficult to see the distinction between the two cases.[2]

(4) It should be noted that while the *Soraya* case involved freedom of the press as well as separation of powers, the Constitutional Court's decision in the bankruptcy case rested exclusively on the separation of powers provision of the Basic Law.

More recently, the Constitutional Court has invoked the Equal Protection clause of the German Basic Law in order to strike down judge-made rules improperly modifying provisions of written law. The most recent case of this kind involved a provision of the German Income Tax Law which grants the benefit of a reduced tax rate to a certain group of taxpayers. Without any basis in the statute, the *Bundesfinanzhof* (BFH), the highest court in tax matters, in a line of decisions had excluded a particular sub-group of that group from the benefit of the said provision. The Constitutional Court disapproved that line of decisions, holding that the courts violate the Equal Protection clause of the Basic Law by according unequal treatment to different members of a group all of whom are treated equally by the written law.[3] *Quaere* whether this holding, if pressed to its ultimate logical consequences, will not convert an undue number of issues going to the scope of a statute into constitutional issues? [4]

2. A further reason for striking down the judge-made rule in the bankruptcy case may have been that the complexity and multiplicity of the interests involved in that case required a balanced and fine-tuned solution of the kind the courts are ill-equipped to fashion. See T. Raiser, Richterrecht heute, Zeitschrift fuer Rechtspolitik 1985, pp. 111 ff., especially at 117.

3. Federal Constitutional Court, Decision of January 14, 1986, reported in 39 NJW 2242 (1986). To the same effect see BVerfGE 66,331, also reported in 37 NJW 2346 (1984). In the income tax case the Constitutional Court apparently assumed that *the Legislature*, without violating the Equal Protection clause of the Basic Law, could have deprived the sub-group of the benefits bestowed on other members of the group. But *the courts* were held to have violated the Equal Protection clause by disregarding the statutory command to treat all members of the entire group alike. Would the U.S. Supreme Court, in dealing with a state statute, go to similar lengths?

4. The query posed in the text, supra, is by no means academic. The reader will recall that under German law, if an issue is thus "constitutionalized", the jurisdiction of the Constitutional Court is brought into play.

See supp 172
R oku Reports

NOTES ON "CASE LAW" IN CIVIL–LAW JURISDICTIONS

(1) *Civilian Theory and Civilian Practice.* The classical civilian doctrine, that the judge can never create law, has broken down in practice. This fact is recognized by everybody, even though the text-writers have found it difficult to fit the actual existence of case law into the framework of civilian theory.[1]

What has caused the breakdown of the "Byzantine Doctrine"? The reasons, no doubt, are numerous and complex; but some factors can be identified:

(a) It has been said that "a principle of mental economy leads judges to follow the opinions of their predecessors rather than to develop their own views, untrammelled by authority."[2]

(b) Certainty and predictability of the law, a postulate basic to western culture and a conditio sine qua non of the proper functioning of a complex modern economy, surely would suffer if judges were in the habit of disregarding their prior pronouncements.

(c) Equality, perhaps the most basic element of justice, would give way to arbitrariness if, without compelling reasons justifying an exception, unequal decisions were made upon identical facts.

(d) A subordinate court, moreover, will follow the decisions of a higher court for the simple reason that judges do not like to be reversed. This seems to be a world-wide phenomenon; but the fear of reversal is, of course, particularly strong in countries in which the judge is a civil servant whose promotion may be adversely affected if too many of his decisions are reversed.[3] In civil-law countries, most of which have a civil service judiciary, this may create a special pressure for lower court conformance with precedents—a pressure which occasionally may be as strong as the impact of the doctrine of stare decisis upon the more independent nisi prius judges of the common-law world.

Reasons courts follow precedent

1. The difficulty stems in part from the impossibility of drawing a sharp line between "making" and "applying" law, and from a wide-spread failure to recognize that the two functions are not only complementary but interrelated and interacting in exceedingly complex ways. For a thorough comparative study of this problem, with emphasis on its jurisprudential aspects, see Esser, Grundsatz und Norm in der richterlichen Fortbildung des Privatrechts (1956).

2. K. Lipstein, The Doctrine of Precedent in Continental Law with Special Reference to French and German Law, 28 J.Comp.Leg. & Int.L. (3d Ser.) 34, at 36 (1946).

From the standpoint of a judge, especially one who does not suffer from illusions of infallibility, there are additional considerations pointing in the same direction as that mentioned in the text, supra. Modesty and self-restraint will lead judges everywhere to the "humbling assumption, often true, that no particular court as it is then constituted possesses a wisdom surpassing that of its predecessors." People v. Hobson, 39 N.Y.2d 479, 488, 384 N.Y.S.2d 419, 425, 348 N.E.2d 894, 900 (Breitel, Ch.J., 1976). See also Baden v. Staples, 45 N.Y.2d 889, 892, 410 N.Y.S.2d 808, 809, 383 N.E.2d 110, 111 (1978).

3. In some civil-law countries, every affirmance or reversal of a lower court opinion is reported to the Ministry of Justice and noted in the personnel file of the judge who wrote the opinion below. See, e.g., Karlen and Arsel, Civil Litigation in Turkey 76 (1957).

In Peru, the performance of all lower-court judges is periodically reviewed by the members of the highest court sitting as a "jury." Substantial numbers of lower-court judges are discharged as a result of such review. This procedure tends to increase the respect of lower courts for the decisions of the court of last resort. See D. B. Furnish, The Hierarchy of Peruvian Laws: Context for Law and Development, 19 Am.J.Comp.L. 91, 101–02 (1971).

This enumeration of factors, though far from exhaustive, may serve to explain and to emphasize the undeniable fact that decisional law is playing an ever-growing role in the civil-law world. If we further consider that in the common-law orbit, and especially in the United States, the doctrine of stare decisis has lost much of its seeming rigidity, the conclusion is clear that civil-law and common-law attitudes toward the judicial function are slowly converging.[4]

(2) *Civilian Practice and Common-Law Practice.* Not all differences between common-law and civilian methods in the treatment of precedents have disappeared. Some of the remaining differences are clearly observable; others are more elusive and controversial.

(a) Clearly, the two systems differ concerning the question of the relative weight to be accorded to judicial authority and to the authority of legal writers. The very term "secondary authority", by which we deprecate the scholar's interpretation of the law, as distinguished from "the law" laid down by the judges, does not exist in the civilians' vocabulary.

Civilian textwriters are much bolder in their criticism of judicial opinions, while courts in civil-law countries show more respect for the scholar's view than is customary in the common-law world.[5] Overwhelming disapproval of a rule of case law by the academic commentators often induces a civil-law court to reexamine its holding (for an example see infra p. 704).

As an experienced observer of both systems has remarked, the average practitioner in a civil-law country

> "can quickly obtain information in a systematic form on any subject of the law through monographs and commentaries, large or little; and this refers also to new important statutes, on which commentaries appear often immediately after their enactment and before the courts have had occasion to interpret them.[6]

> With this literature the lawyer must be familiar. For lawyers, when working on a case, first reach for the commentaries, not for the reports; and in briefs the literature is quoted at least as often as court decisions. When a lawyer in a 'civil law' country has a legal problem which is not definitely settled by statute he may be satisfied to solve it without reference to decisions, but never without the literature." [7]

---

4. See Esser, supra, n. 1, especially at 221 ff.; A. F. M. Plötzgen, Präjudizienrecht im angelsächsischen Rechtskreis 11 (1979).

At the same time, the civilians have joined their common-law brethren in paying increasing attention to the political aspects of the matter, and especially to the vexing question whether excessive lawmaking by judges (who ordinarily are not accountable to the People) perhaps injects an undemocratic and indeed antidemocratic element into the political process. See, e.g., T. Koopmans, Legislature and Judiciary—Present Trends, in M. Cappelletti (Ed.), New Perspectives for a Common Law of Europe 309 ff. (and the Editor's comment in his Introduction, at 18–19) (1978).

5. Concerning the historical reasons for this attitude, see supra, pp. 245–310. See also Angelesco, La technique législative en matière de codification civile 445 ff. (1930). For a history of code interpretation by textwriters, see Gaudemet, L'Interprétation du code civil en France (1935).

6. As there are generally no citators or similar mechanical tools in civil-law countries, a commentary or textbook also will serve as the practitioner's efficient and time-saving guide to the cases in point.

7. Moses, International Legal Practice, 4 Fordh.L.Rev. 244, 266 (1935). To the same effect see Razi, Guided Tour in a

No wonder, then, that doctrinal influence on the development of the law is strong in civil-law countries.[8] Some of the modern codes, especially the Swiss Civil Code (see infra p. 653) recognize this influence by expressly reminding the judges that in deciding novel or doubtful questions they should consult "approved legal doctrine" as well as "judicial tradition".[8a]

In common-law countries, the trend seems to be in the same direction; but there is still a discernible difference of degree.

(b) In some civil-law countries, the courts are reluctant to rely on a single precedent, even though it may be in point, and are much more easily persuaded by a line of decisions.[9] This is in direct contrast to the English doctrine of stare decisis,[10] while in the United States the courts occasionally indicate that there may be a difference of degree between the binding force of a single precedent and that of a line of cases.[11]

(c) Civilians as a rule seem to be disinclined to draw fine distinctions between holding and dictum. Occasionally, however, a German court of last resort, when driven by its *horror pleni* (see supra p. 468), will excuse its disregard of a rule announced in a prior case by explaining that the result reached in the former case did not "rest upon" such rule.

A civilian often displays a lack of interest in the precise facts of the former case on which he relies—an attitude shocking to the common-law mind. The abstract proposition which can be distilled from a precedent or a line of precedents is more likely to impress itself on a civilian's memory than the factual setting in which that proposition was applied.[12]

Civil Law Library, 56 Mich.L.Rev. 375 (1958).

8. Occasionally this influence transcends national frontiers. In Latin America, especially, textbooks of French, Italian and occasionally German origin are much in use, sometimes in the form of Spanish translations. It may be expected, however, that this foreign influence will decline as a result of the growing productiveness of native and immigrant scholars in Latin America.

8a. In those civil-law countries whose law has remained uncodified, the influence of certain authors is even greater. In Scotland, for instance, "there is no doubt that opinions expressed in works of certain authors referred to as the 'institutional writers' enjoy a special authority—an authority which Lord Normand set as just inferior to that of a House of Lords decision." T. B. Smith, Authors and Authority, 12 (N.S.) J.Soc.Pub.T. of L. 3, 7–8 (1972). Concerning the similar situation in South Africa, see supra p. 252.

9. In the most advanced civil-law countries, however, this attitude is changing. In France, for instance, there used to be a well-known saying that "The student weighs the precedents; the practitioner counts them." 1 Planiol-Ripert, Traité élé-

mentaire de droit civil 56 (1948). This reflected the view that in practice only a "*jurisprudence constante*" could fix the state of the law. More recently, however, this view has been called obsolete and erroneous by Professor Tunc, who asserts that at least so far as decisions of the Cour de Cassation are concerned, a single precedent in point "pratiquement" establishes the law. See A. and S. Tunc, Le droit des Etats-Unis d'Amérique—sources et techniques 179–81 (1955). It must be remembered, moreover, that in France and Germany a panel of the court of last resort may not deviate from a decision—even a single decision—of another panel without submitting the matter to a super-panel.

The reader should keep in mind that the statement in the text refers only to *some* (probably the more old-fashioned) of the civil-law systems.

10. See Goodhart, Precedent in English and Continental Law, 50 L.Q.Rev. 40 (1934).

11. See, e.g., Kimball v. Grantsville City, 19 Utah 368, 57 P. 1 (1899); St. Germain v. Lapp, 72 R.I. 42, 48 A.2d 181 (1946).

12. In some of the civil-law countries, this way of looking at judicial decisions is

(d) In a common-law system, where judges openly avow that they are making and not merely "discovering" law,[12a] little theoretical difficulty is encountered in holding that the courts, like legislators, in principle have the power to give a newly announced rule of case law either prospective or retroactive effect.[12b] But where, as in the civil-law systems, the law-making power of the judiciary is in theory denied, or recognized only in exceptional circumstances, it becomes much harder to justify a judicial decision laying down a new rule for the future only, i.e. a decision which admits that the law *was* otherwise but *is being changed by the court.* If it is assumed that the court does not make law but only finds what always has been the law, it is difficult to escape the conclusion that today's holding, although perhaps overruling prior decisions, merely "finds" a rule which (at least in a non-existential and rather transcendental form) has been in force since the enactment of the code section or statute which the court purports to "interpret". It is probably due to these conceptual difficulties that most civil-law courts thus far have failed to avail themselves of the technique of prospective overruling of prior decisions. Even in Germany, where the Bundesgerichtshof in recent years has discussed and occasionally used the technique,[12c] the court found it necessary to justify this step by resort to complex and unrealistic notions of changes in "customary law".[12d]

(e) From the theoretical premise that judges do not make law, it also follows that (subject to exceptions and qualifications we have previously noted) judicial decisions are not binding in other similar cases that may subsequently arise. The judges before whom these other cases are brought, in civil-law theory are free from any constraint of stare decisis. In practice, this freedom is seldom used; but occasionally it is asserted, with the result that even lower courts sometimes display a rather independent attitude, especially where controversial issues or borderline questions are involved.[13] Particularly in instances

reflected in, and in turn reinforced by, the form of the law reports, which may fail to contain an accurate statement of the facts, or even (as in Italy) be limited to what we would call headnotes. See infra, text at nn. 20–27.

12a. See U.S. ex rel. Durocher v. Lavallee, 330 F.2d 303, 312 (2d Cir. 1964), cert. denied 377 U.S. 988, 84 S.Ct. 1921 (1964), and authorities there cited.

12b. See ibid. and the numerous further authorities cited in Adams v. Carlson, 488 F.2d 619, 625–26 (7th Cir. 1973), on remand 368 F.Supp. 1050 (E.D.Ill. 1973). For comparisons between the American and the more hesitant English approach see W. Friedmann, Limits of Judicial Lawmaking and Prospective Overruling, 29 Mod.L.Rev. 593, 602–05 (1966); R. J. Traynor, Quo Vadis, Prospective Overruling: A Question of Judicial Responsibility, 28 Hast.L.J. 533 (1977). Even more extended comparative horizons are opened in the interesting study by G. Tedeschi, Prospective Revision of Precedent, 8 Israel L.Rev. 173 (1973).

12c. See C. H. Fulda, Prospective Overruling of Court Decisions in Germany and the United States, 13 Am.J.Comp.L. 438 (1964). The Court of Justice of the European Communities also has on occasion made its decisions applicable prospectively.

12d. See the decisions of July 8, 1955, BGHZ 18, 81, and especially of June 19, 1962, BGHZ 37, 219.

Quaere whether the theory of these decisions should now be modified in the light of the opinion of the Federal Constitutional Court in the *Soraya* case, supra.

13. See Goodhart, supra n. 10. For a fascinating example (involving the lower courts' refusal to go along with the Cour de Cassation when the latter court permitted the enforcement of outrageous contractual penalty clauses), see J. Beardsley, Compelling Contract Performance in France, 1 Hast.Int. & Comp.L.Rev. 93, 104–07 (Inaugural Issue, 1977).

in which decisions of the highest court have been subjected to criticism by the more prominent legal writers, such independence of intermediate or lower courts may assert itself rather forcefully.[13a]

It must be remembered, in this connection, that one of the principal reasons for the lower courts' adherence to precedent is fear of reversal. In the many cases which cannot be appealed to the highest court,[14] the lower courts make ample use of their freedom from binding precedents.

(f) Precedents affect only the "law" to be applied to a case, and not the "facts". Therefore, in a comparative appraisal of the effect of precedents, we must ask ourselves whether civil law and common law are in agreement as to where to draw the line between "law" and "facts." The answer is in the negative. In the law of torts, in particular, the civilians treat many issues as factual which to us are issues of law.[15] This, of course, tends to increase, in the civil-law orbit, the lower courts' area of freedom from precedents.

(3) *The Mortal Danger of Generalization.* Much that has been written on the subject (including, perhaps, some of the preceding remarks) suffers from the defects which necessarily attend the use of too wide a brush.

We have seen that the significance of case law, and the method of its use, vary *from time to time.* It is no less important to remember that such variations can be observed also (a) *from subject to subject* and (b) *from country to country.*

(a) It has been pointed out above, but the point bears repeating, that the substantive codes and auxiliary statutes which were passed by civilian legislators during the 19th and 20th centuries, embody provisions of two different kinds:

(aa) With respect to certain subject matters, the legislator consciously refrained from laying down any detailed rules, and limited himself to the formulation of a broad and sweeping principle. The greater part of the German law of unfair competition, for example, is governed by the sole provision that any competitive act which is contra bonos mores is illegal. (Section 1 of the German Law Against Unfair Competition). Such "blank norms" have been construed as express legislative authorization for the creation of

---

13a. It has been remarked above, in part 2(a) of these Notes, that vigorous criticism by leading scholars, directed at a decision or line of decisions of the highest court, may induce that court to re-examine its position. A fortiori, a re-examination may be forced upon the court of last resort in instances where a number of intermediate appellate courts and other lower courts—perhaps influenced by scholarly writings—refuse to accept the view previously expressed by the highest court. For an interesting example, see E. Wahl & H. Soell, Ersatzansprüche wegen Unfruchtbarmachung auf Grund unrichtiger Entscheidung des Erbgesundheitsgerichts, 167 Arch.Civ.Pr. 1, at 28 (1967).

14. E.g., actions originally brought in an inferior court. Ordinarily, an appeal can be taken from the inferior court's judgment to the lowest or the intermediate layer of the hierarchy of courts of general jurisdiction; but many legal systems do not permit a further appeal to the highest court in such a case.

15. See supra p. 460. In the law of contracts, also, some civil-law systems (especially the French) tend to treat as factual, and governed by "the intention of the parties", many questions which in our view are questions of law. In these civil-law systems, an intermediate appellate court's finding concerning such a question is (a) not reviewable by the court of last resort, and (b) of no precedential value. See 1 Schlesinger, Formation of Contracts—A Study of the Common Core of Legal Systems 56 (1968).

decisional law, and in the fields governed by norms of this type the courts have consciously set about to build up a body of case law which has almost all the earmarks of a "common law".

Similar developments occur whenever political or economic upheavals make existing law unbearably obsolete, and the legislative machinery proves too slow to keep pace with events. The collapse of the German currency in the early twenties resulted in such an upheaval. Legislation afforded only belated and partial relief. In this situation, the courts, taking the general clauses of the Civil Code as their verbal starting point, sought to master the ensuing problems by creating a body of decisional "revaluation" law which any American or English lawyer would recognize as case law in every sense of the word.[16]

Working in such an area of the law, where he is fettered neither by explicit code provisions nor by "binding" precedents, the civil-law judge may well have more creative freedom than his common-law colleague.

(bb) Other subject matters, however, such as mortgages, the matrimonial property regimes, wills and intestate succession, negotiable instruments, corporation law, and many others, usually are treated in the codes in specific detail. Doubts and ambiguities may occur even in those areas, but only with respect to the more extraordinary situations; the bulk of positive rules is found in the written law itself.[17]

In their criminal law, non-totalitarian civil-law countries adhere to the principle *nulla poena sine lege*. This means that nobody may be subjected to punishment except for an act which at the time it was committed was declared criminal by a *lex*, i.e., a rule of *written law*.

Procedure is another area in which, as the reader will remember (see supra p. 291ff.), the more modern civilian codes are so complete and, on the whole, so specific as to leave relatively little scope for the development of case law. Code provisions, of course, may require interpretation; but decisional law fashioning new procedural devices and remedies, without the aid of specific code provisions, is rarely encountered in civil-law countries today.[18]

---

16. See supra p. 575. Inflation has given rise to similar developments in other civil-law countries as well. The example of Argentina is discussed in the article by G. R. Carrió, Judge Made Law Under a Civil Code, 41 La.L.Rev. 993 (1981).

17. Not infrequently, we find that specific provisions and general clauses interact (see, e.g., the German case, supra, p. 567), in much the same way in which law and equity interact under our system. In such instances, the specific code rules play the same role as our "law", while case law based on the broad doctrines of boni mores, bona fides and abuse of rights develops "equitable" causes of action and defenses. By such case law, the civilians usually reach results very similar to those encountered in our courts of equity. See, e.g., the examples of civilian counterparts of estop-

pel and laches, infra, pp. 754–755. But note that the civilians' ability to match the accomplishments of equity seems to be limited to the area of substantive law; the flexibility of equity in fashioning procedural remedies has no parallel in the civil law. See infra, text at n. 18.

18. There is one celebrated example of a procedural device originally fashioned by case law: the French *astreinte* (see infra p. 669). This example has been played up by writers on comparative law, for the very reason that innovative judicial law-making in the area of procedural devices and remedies is exceptional in civil-law systems. Recently, however, the *astreinte* has been given a statutory basis. See Arts. 5–8 of Law 72–626 of July 5, 1972, as amended by Law 75–596 of July 9, 1975. See also infra p. 669.

(b) From a practical point of view, it seems obvious that decisional law, in the sense in which we know it, is most likely to develop in a jurisdiction where opinions, especially appellate opinions, are reported fully, that is with a full statement of the facts as well as the reasons and authorities relied on. Such full reports of appellate opinions are available in some but not all of the civil-law countries.[19]

All of the German-speaking countries have such reports, as is shown by the many examples of German and Swiss cases in this book.

The opinions of the French Cour de Cassation,[20] on the other hand, are of utmost brevity.[21] Trying to describe them in American terms, one might say that they are comparable to one-paragraph *per Curiam* opinions of American appellate courts.[22] Where this system of opinion-writing and of reporting prevails, it is impossible to use a precedent in the typical common-law manner; if the facts of the former case are not fully reported, then the judge deciding a later case cannot determine whether the two cases are "on all fours", and he cannot apply the familiar common-law technique of probing for factual differences which may form the possible basis for a distinction. The difficulty of discerning the court's precise holding in a decision of the Cour de Cassation is further increased by the fact that the court's opinions do not cite any previous cases.[23] Often this makes it impossible for the reader of the opinion accurately to reconstruct the grounds on which the holdings of prior cases have been extended or distinguished by the court.[23a]

19. For an extensive comparative study of the style of reported opinions see J. G. Wetter, The Styles of Appellate Judicial Opinions (1960).

In F. Schmidt, The Ratio Decidendi—A Comparative Study of a French, a German and an American Supreme Court Decision (publ. as vol. VI of the Acta Instituti Upsaliensis Iurisprudentiae Comparativae, 1965), the reader will find a brief but highly instructive analysis of the three different techniques of opinion-writing, based on three decisions, all dealing with the same problem, which are set forth (in English) in an Appendix.

See also the general discussion, supra pp. 448–452, of the style of "decisions" in civil law countries.

20. For examples, see infra pp. 745–751, and F. Schmidt, supra n. 19.

21. For the reasons, largely historical, which explain this style of opinion-writing, see T. Sauvel, Histoire du jugement motivé, 61 Revue du Droit Public et de la Science Politique 5 (1955); I. Zajtay, Begriff, System and Präjudiz in den kontinentalen Rechten und im Common Law, 165 Arch.Civ.Pr. 97, 105 (1965); M. Lupoi, Cenni storici introduttivi allo studio delle fonti del diritto francese, 1968 Rivista Trimestrale di Diritto e Procedura Civile 1253; J. L. Goutal, Characteristics of Judicial Style in France, Britain and the U.S.A., 24 Am.J.Comp.L. 43, 60–65 (1976).

22. In the Cour de Cassation each case is assigned to one of the associate judges, the so-called *Rapporteur*, who submits a full report to the court. This report, although technically not part of the court's decision, often would reveal much of the reasoning behind it; but it is *not published*, except in rare cases such as some of those decided by a superpanel.

23. For an explanation of the reasons for this—to us—rather strange practice see Zajtay, supra n. 21.

23a. Cf. Bata v. Bata, 39 Del.Ch. 258, 163 A.2d 493, 507 (1960): "The apparent absence of citations of decided cases in continental opinions may well create especial difficulty in determining, first, the scope of the foreign determination, and second, the effect that would be later given to it by the foreign courts."

Even among French lawyers and legal scholars, there is no lack of critics of the over-abbreviated style in which the decisions of the Cour de Cassation are written and reported. See A. Tunc, Conclusions: La Cour Suprême Idéale, 30 Revue Internationale de Droit Comparé 433, 460–70 (1978). Professor Tunc's article, which forms part of a comparative symposium on courts of last resort, contains a wealth of further references.

Illustrations of the uncertainty and lack of precision resulting from the peculiar style of the published reports of the French

Publications of decision, an annotated version written by the judge, not the scholar

The lower courts in France do cite previous decisions in their opinions; but in doing so, they are apt to refer to a presumed step in the abstract reasoning rather than to the facts of the previous case (the facts, perhaps, being largely unreported). In this connection it should be remembered that French and other continental cases are often reported in unofficial collections or periodicals, where an *annotation* by a learned author is published together with the decision itself.[24] In referring to the reasoning of a previous decision, a court is, therefore, likely to adopt the reasons read into the former case by a learned annotator, and not necessarily the (insufficiently stated) reasons which actually prompted the prior decision.

In other countries, again, the technique of opinion-writing and reporting is somewhere between the extremes exemplified by Germany and France.[25] In Italy, for instance, the Court of Cassation writes rather elaborate opinions, which ordinarily disclose the facts as well as the various steps in the reasoning of the court. As a rule, however, these full opinions are not published. The published report consists only of a so-called *massima* which "may be roughly described as a rule or head-note. . . . In many cases it contains very abstract and general propositions, often including mere *obiter dicta*. This increases the difficulty of understanding the real significance of a *massima*."[26] The lawyers representing the parties in the case receive copies of the complete opinion of the court. Other lawyers and legal scholars also can obtain such copies from the clerk of the court against payment of a moderate fee. Thus, it is not quite impossible for one engaged in legal research to inform himself fully and authentically concerning the true holding of a decision of the Court of Cassation; but the method is cumbersome, and in practice Italian lawyers ordinarily limit their study of the case law to the published *massime*.[27]

The age of a code is another factor affecting the significance of case law. With the years, the judicial and doctrinal gloss growing around a code and filling its gaps becomes as much a part of the legal tradition of a nation as the terms of the code itself. As new social and technologi-

Cour de Cassation, can be found in many areas of the law. For an example drawn mainly from the law of torts, see W. J. Wagner, The Development of the Theory of the Right to Privacy in France, 1971 Wash. U.L.Q. 45. Another example, relating to the law of contracts, is discussed in 1 Schlesinger, Formation of Contracts—A Study of the Common Core of Legal Systems 54–55 (1968).

24. Occasionally, the annotator turns out to have been a member of the *chambre* of the court which decided the case, or perhaps the *Rapporteur*. In any event, the annotator may have examined the report of the *Rapporteur*. Thus he may be in a position to convey more information concerning the facts of the case and the probable reasoning of the court than a mere reading of the opinion would reveal.

25. Concerning Latin America, see Clagett, Administration of Justice in Latin America 125–6 (1952); Ireland, The Use of Decisions by United States Students of Civ-

il Law, 8 Tulane L.Rev. 358 (1934); Ireland, Precedents' Place in Latin Law, 40 W.Va.L.Q. 115 (1934). For many examples (in English translation) of reported opinions of Latin American courts, see K. L. Karst, Latin American Legal Institutions: Problems for Comparative Study (1966).

26. G. Gorla, Some Comments on the Italian Legal System, With Particular Reference to the Law of Contracts, in 1 Schlesinger, Formation of Contracts—A Study of the Common Core of Legal Systems 297, at 298 (1968), where further references can be found.

The "scanty, abstract" nature of the *massime* was the subject of comment by an American court in Instituto Per Lo Sviluppo Economico v. Sperti Products, Inc., 323 F.Supp. 630, at 636 (S.D.N.Y.1971).

27. For severe and detailed criticism of the system, see G. Gorla, Lo studio interno e comparativo della giurisprudenza, 1964 Foro Italiano, Part V, pp. 73 ff.

cal conditions arise which were unknown to the codifiers' generation, the text of the code may become inadequate, and in the absence of legislative revision the courts must fashion answers to the new questions as best they can.[27a] The importance of this factor varies from country to country, depending on the age of each country's codes, and the speed of social developments.

Another element of variety in the civil-law systems' attitude toward case law stems from express provisions in the codes themselves. Almost all of the civil codes, with the notable exception of Germany (see supra p. 578), contain express directions to the judges as to (i) what may be considered proper sources of law, and (ii) what may not be so considered.[28] These provisions, some of which are reprinted immediately following this Note, range all the way from the express *prohibition* of case law in the Code Napoleon [29] to emphatic *recognition of* the possibility of deriving guidance from precedents.[30]

CODE PROVISIONS RELATING TO SOURCES OF LAW

AUSTRIAN GENERAL CIVIL CODE (1811)

Sec. 7: Where a case cannot be decided either according to the literal text or the plain meaning of a statute, regard shall be had to the statutory provisions concerning similar cases and to the principles which underlie other laws regarding similar matters. If the case is still doubtful, it shall be decided according to the principles of natural justice, after careful research and consideration of all the individual circumstances.*

27a. The reader will recall that the significance of a code's age was commented on, also, by the German Constitutional Court in the *Soraya* case, supra.

28. For collections of code provisions of this kind, see Cheng, General Principles of Law As Applied by International Courts and Tribunals 400–408 (1953); A. P. Blaustein, Legislative Interpretation and the Foreign Codes, 16 J.Leg.Ed. 317 (1964); Ireland, supra n. 25.

29. The provision expressly prohibiting the development of case law, which is contained in Art. 5 of the French Civil Code (quoted supra p. 625), has been copied, more or less literally, in a number of Latin American codes. See B. Kozolchyk, Law and the Credit Structure in Latin America 41 (publ. 1966 as Memorandum RM 4918–RC by the Rand Corp.); Ireland, supra n. 25, 40 W.Va.L.Q. at 123–24. While in France this provision has long been recognized as a dead letter which cannot prevent the courts from filling gaps in the codes and from developing the law, its Latin American counterparts continue to be taken seriously and to impede the exercise of a creative and modernizing judicial func-

tion. According to Kozolchyk, ibid., this is one of the significant obstacles standing in the way of adjusting Latin American legal systems to present-day needs and conditions.

30. The list, in the text, of elements of variety differentiating the various civil-law countries' attitudes towards case law, is not exhaustive. It should be noted, moreover, that within a single country the various factors listed (and others not listed) may pull in different directions. In France, for instance, the provision of Art. 5 of the Civil Code, and the uncommunicative form of reported decisions, probably were factors retarding the development and recognition of case law; these factors, however, were overcome by others, especially the sweeping generality of some of the code provisions, and the growing inadequacy of the text of a Code enacted in 1804.

* This provision must be read together with Sec. 12 of the same Code, which expressly states that a decision is not the source of law, and that its effect is not suitable for being extended to other cases. See Lenhoff, On Interpretative Theories: A

SPANISH CIVIL CODE (1889)

PRELIMINARY TITLE: LEGAL NORMS, THEIR APPLICATION AND EFFECT [a]

Article 1.

(1) The sources of the Spanish legal system are the [written] law, custom and the general principles of law.[b]

(2) Any norm that contravenes another norm of a higher order shall be void.

(3) Custom [c] shall govern in the absence of applicable [written] law, provided it is not contrary to morals or to the public order, and provided it is proved. . . .

(4) The general principles of law shall apply in the absence of [written] law or custom, without prejudice to their informative function [d] in the legal system.

(5) Legal norms contained in international treaties shall have no direct application in Spain until they have become part of the domestic legal system by being published in the Official Gazette.

(6) Judicial decisions shall complement the legal order with such doctrine (*doctrina*) as the Supreme Court shall repeatedly establish in interpreting and applying the written law, custom, and the general principles of law.[e]

Comparative Study in Legislation, 27 Tex. L.Rev. 312, 321 (1949).

The much-discussed provision of Art. 21 of the Louisiana Civil Code is similar to the directory provision of the Austrian Code set forth in the text, supra. The Louisiana provision was copied from an article contained in a *draft* of the French Civil Code; but in France that provision, including its reference to "natural law", was eliminated from the final version of the Code. This last-minute change was preceded by a fascinating debate, recounted by M. Franklin, Equity in Louisiana: The Role of Article 21, 9 Tul.L.Rev. 485, at 495–97 (1935).

a. As the reader will recall from our discussion of the Shoop case, supra, the preliminary title of the Spanish Civil Code was revised in 1974. The present Art. 1, reproduced in the text, supra, is the new version of former Art. 6, quoted by the court in the Shoop case. The new version is more elaborate, but does not substantially change the hierarchy of sources of law established in old Art. 6.

b. While the Austrian Code speaks of "principles of natural justice", the Spanish Code uses the expression "general principles of law". The two phrases are not synonymous. During the 19th century, the

disciples of positivism and of the historical school insisted that "general principles of law" could be derived only from the *positive* norms of a given *national* system, thus sharply differentiating the "general principles" from natural law. It was only in the relatively recent past that a broader view of the notion of "general principles of law" became predominant, partly in consequence of the fact that the same notion has been used in Art. 38 of the Statute of the International Court of Justice. See Schlesinger, The Nature of General Principles of Law, in Rapports Généraux au VIe Congrès international de droit comparé 235, 269 (publ. 1964 by the Belgian Centre Interuniversitaire de Droit Comparé).

c. The Spanish word is *costumbre*. As explained supra p. 621, *costumbre* must be distinguished from *fueros*, which today are written sources of law in certain regions of Spain.

d. Where there is an applicable written law, general principles of law cannot be invoked as sources of law; but such principles might still provide "information" concerning the meaning of the written law.

e. This provision appears to be an attempt to fit the notion of *doctrina legal* (with which the reader is familiar) into the

(7) In resolving the matters submitted to them, judges and courts always have the absolute duty to abide by the established system of sources.

SWISS CIVIL CODE (1907)

Art. 1: The Code governs all questions of law which come within the letter or the spirit of any of its provisions.

If the Code does not furnish an applicable provision, the judge shall decide in accordance with customary law, and failing that, according to the rule which he would establish as legislator.

In this he shall be guided by approved legal doctrine and judicial tradition.*

CIVIL CODE OF IRAQ (1951, EFF. 1953)

Reprinted ante, pp. 325–326.

USATORRE v. THE VICTORIA
United States Court of Appeals, Second Circuit, 1949.
172 F.2d 434.

[The Victoria was an Argentine tank vessel, flying the Argentine flag, and owned by the appellant, an Argentine corporation. Five of the crew were Spaniards, three Portuguese and the others Argentineans. They all signed articles at Buenos Aires for a voyage to Edgewater, New Jersey, and return. At about 6:50 P.M. on April 17, 1942, when 360 miles from New York and 300 miles off the coast, the Victoria was struck by a torpedo which tore a hole about 25 feet in width and 25 feet in height under the water line on her port side near the bow, opening up tanks 1 and 2. The captain ordered the life-boats to be made ready for use and ordered the chief officer and some members of the crew to board life-boat No. 1, which was launched and made fast to the Victoria.

system of sources of law. Whatever its precise nature may be, a *doctrina legal* in theory does not have the same rank as the three "sources" enumerated in subd. (1) of Art. 1, and subd. (7) exhorts the judges to keep that in mind.

* Concerning the doctrinal antecedents of this famous article of the Swiss Code, see J. Mayda, Gény's Méthode After 60 Years (Introduction to the English translation of Gény, Method of Interpretation and Sources of Private Positive Law (2d ed. 1963) passim, especially XLII ff.

The Swiss courts have shown restraint in using the broad powers conferred upon them by Art. 1. See A. E. von Overbeck, Some Observations on the Role of the Judge Under the Swiss Civil Code, 37 La.L. Rev. 681 (1977). On the (not overly numerous) occasions when Switzerland's highest court relied on Art. 1 to fill gaps in the written law, it repeatedly engaged in comparative research and referred to relevant solutions in other countries, especially in Germany and France. See I. Zajtay, Beiträge zur Rechtsvergleichung 60 (1976). See also id., Aims and Methods of Comparative Law, 7 Comp. & Int.L.J. of Southern Africa 321 (1974).

At about 8 P.M. she was struck again by a second torpedo, which tore another hole about 25 feet wide and 25 feet high under her water line near her stern, opening up tanks No. 6 and No. 7. The captain thereupon ordered the ship to be abandoned and he and the seventeen remaining members of the crew left in life-boat No. 2.

Thereafter the life-boats were rowed or sailed away until they lost sight of the vessel and each other. Shortly after 2 A.M., April 18, 1942, the United States destroyer Owl sighted the Victoria. At about 8 A.M. she went alongside the drifting derelict and placed aboard eight men who got her under way for a short distance. At about 7 A.M. April 19, the Owl picked up life-boat No. 1, transferred the crew to the Victoria and returned the eight men to the Owl, leaving the Victoria in command of her chief officer. At about 11 A.M., the Victoria, escorted by the Owl, got under way for New York under her own power. At 6 P.M., Arpil 19, the U.S. destroyer Nicholson picked up life-boat No. 2 and transfered her crew to the Victoria. At about 10 A.M., April 20, the Owl was relieved by the Navy tug, Sagamore, which continued to escort the Victoria until port was reached.

Some of the crew libeled the Victoria for salvage claims, and the action was tried in the District Court for the Southern District of New York, where the libellants were successful.[a] The trial court held that the jus gentium applied, and not the law of Argentina, and that under the jus gentium the bona fide abandonment of the ship by the master and crew without any hope or intention of returning terminated the voyage and the contractual services of the seamen. The court reasoned that, although ordinarily seamen are not entitled to salvage awards for saving their own ship, because that service is part of their duty, yet they do become entitled thereto when their ship has been abandoned in good faith without any hope of recovery.[b] The court awarded each crew member $500. The shipowner appeals.]

Before L. HAND, Chief Judge, and CHASE and FRANK, Circuit Judges.

FRANK, Circuit Judge.[c]   1. If, as the trial judge held, the jus gentium applies, then, regarding the decisions of our courts as reflecting it, libellants would seem clearly to be salvors. According to those decisions, abandonment by the master, in the face of what he deems a disaster, without expectation of returning, severs the crew's employment contract even if, subsequently, the vessel turns out to be safe and the crew then returns. That rule would apply here.

. . .

2. But while the district court had discretion to take jurisdiction, and that discretion has been said to be justified "because salvage is a question arising under the jus gentium and does not ordinarily depend

---

a. The prior history of this litigation is discussed in Note, 28 Corn.L.Qu. 69 (1942).

b. On the question of salvage by the vessel's own crew, see Robinson on Admi-

ralty 724 (1939); Gilmore and Black, The Law of Admiralty 541–43 (2d ed., 1975).

c. The Court's footnotes are omitted.

on the municipal laws of particular countries," we think that whether on the facts as found, the crew were "released from any obligation to exert themselves for the benefit of the vessel," must be determined as a matter of the "internal economy" of the ship, by the Argentine law, the "law of the flag."

3. For us, Argentine law is a fact. With respect to that fact, defendant introduced the testimony of an expert witness. He is an American and a member of the New York Bar, and of the Bars of Cuba and Puerto-Rico. He studied civil law for forty years. He has a degree of Doctor of Civil Laws from the University of Havana. He was a judge in Puerto Rico for seven years, and a member for two years of a commission that drafted new legislation for Cuba. He has studied Argentine law, and is the author of a digest of that law appearing in the Martindale-Hubbell Law Directory. He has not practiced admiralty or maritime law anywhere, but has "occasionally given advice on maritime law" in Latin-American countries. He is authorized to practice in no Latin-American countries except Cuba, but can give advice in other such countries.

He testified that Article 929 of the Argentine Code of Commerce reads: "A captain is forbidden to abandon his ship, whatever may be the danger, except in case of shipwreck." He also said that the pertinent portions of the Code relating to termination of the employment contract between seamen and their ship are contained in Articles which provide that the contract is terminated in the case of "any disaster happening to the vessel which absolutely renders it incapable of navigation." According to the expert witness, this means that the captain's judgment that the vessel is in such condition is not conclusive, but that the sole test is the actual objective fact as to the ship's condition. ("The final decision is the fact of whether the vessel remained fitted for navigation.") It was the witness' opinion that, on the facts here, under Argentine law the libellants' contract was not ended when the captain ordered them to abandon the ship, although the men were obliged to obey that order.

According to this witness, Latin-American courts pay little attention to court decisions as precedents. He had found "practically nothing" by way of decisions of the Supreme Court of the Argentine bearing on the Code provisions in question, in part because of the difficulty of finding such decisions since they are "badly indexed" or "digested." [d] He relied, as, he said, Argentine lawyers do, on the "commentators," especially including the French commentators because, he said, the Argentine Code of Commerce is based on the French law. Where there was a difference of opinion between commentators, he had made a

---

d. A North-American scholar familiar with the law of Argentina recently remarked: "Of all the Hispano-American countries, Argentina has the best developed system of reporting, publishing and indexing case decisions." R. C. Casad, Unjust Enrichment in Argentina: Common Law in a Civil Law System, 22 Am.J.Comp. L. 757, at 783 (1974). This observation perhaps throws doubt on some of the statements made by the expert in the principal case; but note that Professor Casad's article was written in 1974, while the principal case was litigated in the 1940s.

choice. In his testimony, he cited no commentators, but merely gave his interpretation of uncited commentators' interpretations of the Code.

The judge is not bound to accept the testimony of a witness concerning the meaning of the laws of a foreign country, especially when, as here, the witness had never practiced in that country. Moreover, as defendant says in its brief, this witness "relied strictly upon the Code provisions." As already noted, he gave little or no attention to Argentine decisional material. We have no knowledge of Argentine "law," nor more than a vague acquaintance with the judicial methods there prevailing. But casual readings of readily available material clearly indicate that, in all civil-law countries, despite conventional protestations to the contrary, much law is judge-made, and the courts are by no means unaffected by judicial precedents or "case law" (which the civilians call "jurisprudence," as distinguished from the interpretation of text-writers or commentators, called "doctrine"). Recaséns Siches, a widely respected professor of law in Spain for many years, now in Mexico, recently wrote: "Now jurisprudence, that is, the decisions of the courts, has had the part of greatest protagonist in the formation of the law; and, although in much less volume, it continues today of great importance." "Both the slavish obedience of [civilian] judges to codes, and their freedom from precedent are largely a myth", writes Friedmann. "In truth, while there is greater freedom towards the provisions of codes, there is also much greater respect for judicial authority than imagined by most Anglo-American lawyers." A recent treatise by Cossio, a distinguished Argentine lawyer, shows that this attitude prevails in the Argentine.[e]

The expert witness' adherence to the literal words of the code may have caused the trial judge to question his conclusions. For, we are told, the civilians, influenced by an interpretative theory which derives from Aristotle (and which has affected Anglo-American practice as well) are accustomed to interpret their statutory enactments "equitably," i.e., to fill in gaps, arising necessarily from the generalized terms of many statutes, by asking how the legislature would have dealt with the "unprovided case." In civil-law countries, "there are countless examples of judicial interpretation of statutes . . . which gave the statutory interpretation a meaning either not foreseen by or openly antagonistic to the opinions prevailing at the time of the Code, but in accordance with modern social developments or trends of public opinion. This attitude finds expression in Art. I of the Swiss Civil Code [of 1907] which directs the judge to decide as if he were a legislator, when he finds himself faced with a definite gap in the statute."[f]

In a colloquy which occurred after the judge had filed his opinion, he expressed himself as in disagreement with the witness' interpretation of the Code. But doubtless because the judge thought the jus

e. Cf. Suzuki v. Central Argentine Railway Ltd., 27 F.2d 795, 800 (C.C.A.2, 1928).

f. Quotation from Friedmann, Legal Theory 294 (1944). In the 1967 edition of Friedmann's book the relevant material appears on pp. 533–35.

gentium governed, he did not make a finding as to Argentine law. We must therefore reverse and remand for such a finding. Perhaps it can be made without further testimony on the subject. It may be that, if he considers it desirable, some arrangement will be agreed upon which will enable the judge to summon an expert of his own choosing.[g] . . .

Reversed and remanded.[h]

QUESTIONS

(1) In the light of the materials previously studied, do you share the District Court's and the appellate court's skepticism concerning the correctness of the expert's opinion? If so, does your skepticism spring from the same reasons as Judge Frank's?

(2) Concerning the reasons which Judge Frank gives for his doubts as to the expert's testimony, the following questions, among others, suggest themselves:

(a) Is it permissible to cite Art. 1 of the Swiss Civil Code as indicative of the spirit permeating a Latin-American code largely modelled upon the French? Even though the court was unwilling (and at that time perhaps powerless) to take judicial notice of specific rules of Argentine law, should it not have noticed that the Argentine Civil Code contains general directions relating to methods and sources of law,[1] and that these directions are quite inconsistent with Art. 1 of the much more modern Swiss Code?

(b) Should civil-law theories of interpretation which grew up principally in connection with the codes' ["general clauses"] and with gaps in the written law, be resorted to in applying code provisions as specific as those involved in the Usatorre case?

3. POLITICAL, SOCIAL AND MORAL ELEMENTS IN THE PRINCIPAL CODES

INTRODUCTORY NOTE

Codification is a *method*—a method which in itself is politically colorless.[1] It was used by Napoleon and by the Soviet rulers, but also

g. Concerning court-appointed experts see also supra, pp. 221–224.

h. It seems that following this reversal and remand the libellants discontinued the action. See Nussbaum, Proving the Law of Foreign Countries, 3 Am.J.Comp.L. 60, 64 (1954). Perhaps they had received discouraging advice from an expert on Argentine law. More likely, they gave up because of their financial inability to procure the necessary trial testimony of such an expert.

If the case came up today, would FRCP Rule 44.1 make it possible (a) to avoid a reversal and remand, or (b) in case the Court of Appeals reverses and remands, then to present foreign law materials to the District Court in an informal and less expensive manner?

1. See Ireland, Precedents' Place in Latin Law, 40 W.Va.L.Q. 115, 130–34 (1934); A. P. Blaustein, Legislative Interpretation and the Foreign Codes, 16 J.Leg. Ed. 317, at 318 (1964).

1. See Patterson and Schlesinger, Problems of Codification of Commercial Law, N.Y.Leg.Doc. (1955) No. 65A, pp. 50–51, 57–

by the democratically elected parliaments of countries such as Switzerland and (at that time) Uruguay. The rules embodied in a code may be liberal, paternalistic or socialistic; or they may represent any other brand or mixture of political and economic views. In each instance, these views are the product of a particular time and a particular place.

To make a thorough comparison of all codes, or even of the most important present-day codes of the civil-law world, with reference to the moral and socio-political views underlying them, would be a monumental task. In this chapter no more is proposed to be done than to show, by a few examples,

(a) how the value judgments of the legislator or legislators are reflected in the positive provisions of a code, and

(b) how code provisions, though their language may remain unaltered, change their meaning with the rise of new regimes and new political and social philosophies.

In the process, we shall compare law not only in space but also in time. The Code provisions and other materials of which the examples will consist, are in part of recent vintage; but others go back more than 150 years. This calls for a caveat concerning their comparability. It will be found that the social changes which took place in the wake of the French Revolution, are clearly and dramatically spelled out in the Code Napoleon. That code, as we know, legalized the demise of feudalism and ratified the triumph of the *tiers état*. It did so, mainly, by the use of two concepts: *freedom of contract* and a redefinition of *ownership* in terms of an absolute right, unfettered and unfetterable by entailment, freely alienable, and strongly, almost fiercely, protected against any public or private interference.[2] These two concepts, revolutionary as they were 180 years ago, belong to the sphere of *private law*, and, consequently, appear clearly on the face of the Code civil. The economic and social changes which have taken place during the present century, on the other hand, mostly are reflected in the growth of such *public law* fields as administrative law, labor law, social security, taxation, nationalization and public corporations.[3] Many of these changes, therefore, are only faintly reflected on the face of the modern private law codes.[4] While the moral, political and social spirit of the early 19th century is unmistakably imprinted upon the provisions of the Code Napoleon, we must often dig more deeply, and draw subtler inferences, if we seek to find indications of 20th century social develop-

61, 1955 Report of the New York Law Revision Commission at pp. 80–81, 87–91.

2. It has been said, and often repeated, that the French Civil Code of 1804 is "the code of the employer, of the creditor and of the property owner." Charmont, Le droit et l'esprit démocratique 54 (1908). See Ripert, Le régime démocratique et le droit civil moderne 17–18 (1948); Pound, The French Civil Code and the Spirit of 19th Century Law, 35 B.U.L.Rev. 77 (1955).

3. In the free world, there has been no atrophy of private law in spite of this enormous growth of public law. On the contrary, the constant increase in the mobility of men, goods and ideas, and in the total volume and frequency of business transactions, has further enhanced the importance of private law. By way of over-simplification, one might say that in the communist world public law has to some extent displaced private law, while in the free world the modern institutions of public law merely add a new dimension of complexity to a vigorously surviving system of private law.

4. The statement in the text is subject to at least one qualification: the changed status of women does appear on the face of many of the civil codes. See, e.g., supra pp. 532, 537–8.

ments in private law codes and private law decisions of the last two generations.[5]

A. THE CODES AND ECONOMIC FREEDOM

(AA) THE PARTIES' FREEDOM TO SHAPE THEIR CONTRACTS AND OTHER TRANSACTIONS

FRENCH CIVIL CODE

Art. 1134. Contracts lawfully entered into have the force of law for those who have made them.

They can be rescinded only by mutual consent or for causes allowed by law.

They must be performed in good faith.[a]

SWISS CODE OF OBLIGATIONS

Art. 19. Within the limits of the law, the parties may determine the terms of their contract as they please.

Contract terms at variance with provisions of law are permissible unless they are inconsistent with a cogent provision,[b] contra bonos mores or violative of the public order or the right of personality.[c]

SWISS CIVIL CODE [d]

Art. 11. Every man is capable of rights. For all men, therefore, within the bounds of the law's regulation the same capacity exists to have rights and duties.

Art. 27. . . . No one can renounce his freedom or restrict himself in its use in a degree offensive to law or morality.

5. See F. Wieacker, Das Sozialmodell der klassischen Privatrechtsgesetzbücher und die Entwicklung der modernen Gesellschaft (Heft 3 of the Schriftenreihe der Juristischen Studiengesellschaft Karlsruhe, 1953) and the 3-volume work by J. Savatier, Les métamorphoses économiques et sociales du droit civil d'aujourd'hui, especially the first volume entitled Panorama des mutations (3rd ed. 1964).

a. The reader will recall that the historical roots of the sweeping principle announced in Art. 1134 have been traced in an earlier part of this book.

b. Concerning the distinction between ius cogens and ius dispositivum, see supra p. 587.

c. The meaning of the expression "right of personality", as used in the Swiss Code of Obligations, will become clearer by reading Art. 27 of the Civil Code, infra.

d. Transl. by Shick, and reprinted by permission of the American Bar Association.

CIVIL CODE FOR THE FEDERAL DISTRICT OF MEXICO [e]

Art. 6. The will of private persons cannot exempt from the observance of the law, nor alter it nor modify it. Private rights which do not directly affect the public interest may be waived only when the waiver does not impair rights of third parties.

Art. 7. The waiver authorized in the foregoing article produces no effect if it is not made in clear and precise terms, so that there is no doubt as to the right which is waived.[f]

NOTES AND QUESTIONS

(1) As we have seen in a previous chapter (see supra pp. 280–281), some of the civilian codes provide that an offer, though not supported by any consideration,[1] normally is irrevocable for the period specified in the offer itself, or for a reasonable period. In this way the principle of transactional autonomy of private parties is carried a step beyond freedom of "contract"; even the mere offer, a unilateral jural act, is made binding. It is mainly in the more modern codes (e.g. the German and Swiss) that this extension of the principle of the parties' transactional autonomy can be observed.[1a]

(2) On the whole, however, the tendency of the modern codes is to restrict the scope of the parties' transactional freedom more severely than was thought desirable at the beginning of the 19th century. To be sure, even the Code Napoleon invalidates contracts that are illegal or immoral.[2] But the notion of *lésion*, although well known in pre-code civil law, was consciously rejected by the draftsmen of that Code as a

e. Transl. by Schoenrich (Baker, Voorhis & Co., Inc., 1950). The Code was adopted by the majority of the States of the Mexican Union.

f. The Mexican Constitution, the Civil Code and other statutes contain elaborate provisions for the protection of employees, rural tenants and other classes of persons thought to be in need of protection. See, e.g., Gillies v. Aeronaves De Mexico S.A., 468 F.2d 281 (5th Cir. 1972). Consider the effect of Arts. 6 and 7 upon the waivability of the rights of such persons.

1. The doctrine of consideration is peculiar to the common law and is not recognized in the civil-law systems, which use different criteria in order to determine whether an agreement should be enforced as a contract. See, e.g., A. G. Chloros, The Doctrine of Consideration and the Reform of the Law of Contract, 17 Int. & Comp. L.Q. 137 (1968); Lorenzen, Causa and Consideration in the Law of Contracts, 28 Yale L.J. 621 (1919); Mason, the Utility of Consideration, 41 Colum.L.Rev. 825 (1941). Even an agreement by which one party promises to make an outright gift to the other, is enforceable as a contract in most

civil-law countries, provided that it is made in proper notarial form. See, e.g., In re Estate of Danz, 444 Pa. 411, 283 A.2d 282 (1971). In France and in a few countries following the French example, even the requirement of notarizing can be avoided if the promise is made in the form—though it may be a mere simulation—of an exchange contract. See J. P. Dawson, Gifts and Promises, 74–83 (1980).

Inasmuch as a *contract* does not require consideration in the civil-law systems, it stands to reason that the revocability of an *offer* does not depend on the presence or absence of consideration. But an offer inviting a contract for which the law prescribes written or notarial form, normally will have to comply with such form requirement.

1a. For an extensive comparative treatment of the problem of revocability or irrevocability of offers, see 1 Schlesinger, Formation of Contracts—A Study of the Common Core of Legal Systems 109–11, 745–91 (1968).

2. See Arts. 1131 and 1133, quoted infra p. 747.

general principle; only in certain instances of well-defined particular transactions (e.g. sale of immovables, where the seller has been victimized) will the French Civil Code authorize the setting aside of a transaction on the ground of a gross disproportion between value given and value received.[3] By way of contrast, we have observed (see supra pp. 595, 615) that under the heading of "lésion" or "usury" some of the more modern codes provide the courts with potent weapons for invalidating one-sided bargains concluded by parties of flagrantly unequal mental or economic strength.[4]

(3) If the principle of freedom of contract, embodied in Art. 19 of the Swiss Code of Obligations, were carried to its ultimate logical consequence, a person would be free to make himself unfree by entering into a contract to that effect. Art. 27 of the Swiss Civil Code makes it clear, however, that the principle of freedom of the personality is of a higher order than the principle of freedom of contract. Contracts which go too far in restricting an individual's personal or economic freedom are declared invalid. The question of exactly where the line should be drawn is left to the courts by one of those "general clauses" which are typical of modern civil-law codes. Many different types of contracts may be affected by the provision.

A promise to change or not to change one's religion, or to become or remain a member of a certain religious or political association, clearly would be considered an illicit restriction of the promisor's personal freedom.[5] The same would be true of a clause (as is sometimes found in the employment contract of an airline hostess) amounting to a promise not to marry during a period of substantial duration.[6] A promise to make a will, or to include a certain provision in the promisor's will, likewise would be void under Art. 27 of the Swiss Civil Code.[7]

Even contracts which are predominantly business bargains, sometimes are struck down as unduly interfering with the personal freedom of one of the parties. Thus Art. 27 would invalidate a promise not to compete, made by the seller of a business, if such promise were so broad in its terms as to preclude the promisor from any future use of his skills

---

3. See Amos and Walton's Introduction to French Law 163–64 (3rd ed. by F. H. Lawson, A. E. Anton and L. N. Brown, 1967). See also supra p. 595.

4. The reader will recall that we have previously studied the relevant provisions in the Civil Codes of Germany and Mexico (see supra pp. 595, 615). The differences *inter sese* of the German and Mexican solutions are not without interest. The Mexican Code, although described as a "socialist" one, provides considerably less protection for the weaker party than the older German Code, which was originally drafted during the unquestionably "capitalist" era of Bismarck's Reich and was not substantially changed by a recent amendment of its wording. The point may not be of earth-shaking significance; it is important only insofar as it underscores the necessity for caution in the use of (and reliance upon) generalizing labels.

5. See J. M. Grossen in 2 M. Gutzwiller et al. (Eds.), Schweizerisches Privatrecht 297–98 (1967), and authorities there cited.

6. Ibid.

7. Such a promise is void in most civil-law countries. The German Civil Code (Sec. 2302) contains a specific provision to this effect. In France and Switzerland the same result is reached in the absence of a specific prohibition; the Swiss courts derive the invalidity of such promises from Art. 27 of the Civil Code. See 1 Egger, Kommentar zum Schweizerischen Zivilgesetzbuch, Art. 27, Ann. 13 (1930).

Such promises must be distinguished from agreements of inheritance, which are duly executed testamentary dispositions in contractual form, and are valid in some of the civil-law countries.

and experience.[8] An assignment of future wage claims violates Art. 27 at least insofar as the wages are necessary to provide a livelihood for the assignor and his family.[9]

(4) Do the provisions of the Mexican Civil Code, reproduced above, limit or enhance freedom of contract? Do they, standing by themselves, tend to support the statement that "The new Code reflects the agrarian and socialistic tendencies of the revolutionary leaders, their desire to subordinate the interests of the individual to those of the community, while leaving him the fullest freedom of action consistent with such subordination . . ."?[10]

(5) Even in the civil codes of Marxian socialist countries one can find provisions to the effect that citizens may conclude contracts of any kind, and that the parties are free to determine the terms of their contracts. See, e.g., §§ 6, 8 and 45 of the new (1975) Civil Code of the German Democratic Republic. Such provisions, however, must be read in the light of the manifold legal and factual restrictions to which this "freedom of contract" is subject in the planned economy of a socialist state.[11] Moreover, other provisions of the same Code impose upon each citizen the duty, in concluding and performing contracts and other transactions, "to be guided by socialist morality and by the necessity of reconciling individual and collective interests with the requirements of society."[12] All rights granted by the Code (and this includes the right to enter into contracts and to fix their terms) must be exercised "in accordance with their social essence and purpose";[13] the exercise of a right is improper, if such exercise serves purposes that are illegal or "contrary to the principles of socialist morality."[14]

8. See the comparative study by A. Kuttler, Vertragliche Konkurrenzverbote 47 ff. (1955). Promises not to compete which are contained in employment contracts are governed, not by the "general clause" of Art. 27 of the Civil Code, but by specific (and stricter) provisions of the Code of Obligations.

9. Bundesgericht, decision of Jan. 21, 1959, BGE 85 I 17, at 30–31.

In several of the fact situations covered by the Swiss Code provision, our courts might reach the same result on grounds of "public policy"; but in our law the result in each case would depend on much narrower considerations peculiar to the particular type of contract involved in the case. Even when we use statutes to deal with problems of this kind, we draft them in narrow, specific terms. Cf. Cal. Labor Code § 2855, a provision of great significance for the entertainment industry.

10. Schoenrich, The Civil Code of Mexico, p. VII (1950). See also supra n. 4.

11. See V. Peter, Vergleich einiger grundlegender Rechtsinstitute des Zivilgesetzbuches der DDR und des Bürgerlichen Gesetzbuchs, 77 Z. für Vergleichende Rechtswissenschaft 207, especially at 225–29 (1978).

In Yugoslavia, whose economy is not subject to an all-encompassing plan, provisions on contractual freedom, resembling those of Art. 19 of the Swiss Code of Obligations, must be read in light of various restrictions on that freedom—restrictions that stem from "self-managing compacts". See Arts. 4–13 of the 1978 Yugoslav Statute on Obligations (in effect since 1980).

12. Civil Code of the German Democratic Republic, § 14.

13. Id., § 15.

14. Ibid.

(BB) ENFORCEMENT OF CONTRACTS

VAZQUEZ v. SUPERIOR COURT (SAN MIGUEL Y CIA., INTERVENOR)

Supreme Court of Puerto Rico, 1955.
78 P.R.R. 707.

passed over quickly

[*Some of court's footnotes omitted; others renumbered.*]

Mr. Chief Justice SNYDER delivered the opinion of the Court.

San Miguel & Cía., Inc., and Julián Vázquez Olmedo executed a contract whereby they agreed to organize a corporation in which each of them would own $100,000 worth of stock and of which Vázquez would be General Manager. San Miguel & Cía., Inc., sued Vázquez for performance of the contract and damages. We granted certiorari to review the order of the Superior Court denying the defendant's motion to strike the paragraph of the prayer asking for performance of the contract. . . .

The contract, which is made part of the complaint, provides that the parties have agreed to organize a domestic corporation to engage in commerce in electrical, fluid gas, and refrigeration products, with the principal office in San Juan. The contract contains [elaborate details concerning the manner in which the corporation is to be organized]. . . .

By his motion to strike a portion of the prayer . . . the defendant sought a ruling that the plaintiff is not entitled to the remedy of performance of the contract, as distinguished from damages.[1] Rule 12(*f*) of the Rules of Civil Procedure provides that only ". . . redundant, immaterial, impertinent, or scandalous matter . . ." may be stricken from a pleading. Motions to strike are not favored. Matter will not be stricken ". . . unless it is clear that it can have no possible bearing upon the subject matter of the litigation. If there is any doubt as to whether under any contingency the matter may raise an issue, the motion should be denied." [Citations.]

We therefore turn to the question of whether the allegations of the complaint, including the prayer, could by any possible contingency entitle the plaintiff to performance of the contract. Under the civil law—contrary to the common law—the fact that a plaintiff who alleges a breach of contract has an adequate remedy by way of damages does not bar him from seeking performance of the contract. The plaintiff ". . . may choose between exacting the fulfilment of the obligation or

---

1. We put to one side the contention of the plaintiff that the motion to strike a portion of the prayer should have been denied without further ado, in view of the fact that the prayer is not generally considered as part of the complaint. We assume we would make an exception in this case in view of the brief and general allegations of the body of the complaint. Cf. People v. Henneman, 60 P.R.R. 58, 66. [It should be noted that while the *substantive* private law of Puerto Rico is based on the Spanish-derived Civil Code, the *procedural* Rules of the Commonwealth are patterned after FRCP. Ed.]

its rescission, with indemnity for damages . . .". Section 1077, Civil Code, 1930 ed., 31 L.P.R.A. § 3052; § 1340 of the Civil Code, 31 L.P.R.A. § 3747; Szladits, The Concept of Specific Performance in Civil Law, IV Am.J.Comp.L. 208; Jackson, Specific Performance of Contracts in Louisiana, 24 Tulane L.Rev. 400. But although the adequacy of the remedy of damages plays no role under our law, §§ 1077 and 1340 of the Civil Code do not create an automatic and absolute right to performance of a contract in all cases. For example, this remedy does not lie where the contract is impossible to perform or with rare exceptions where personal services are required. See Szladits, supra; Nuñez v. Soto Nussa, District Judge, 14 P.R.R. 190; Annotation, 135 A.L.R. 279; 5 Williston on Contracts, Rev.Ed., § 1422, p. 3973; id., § 1423A, p. 3983. In the same way, in view of the special nature of a corporation and of some of the provisions of our Corporation Law—Act No. 30, Laws of Puerto Rico, 1911, as amended, 14 L.P.R.A. §§ 52 et seq.—there may be factors and circumstances involved in a particular contract to organize a corporation which would prevent our courts from ordering performance of the contract.

Section 6 of our Corporation Act—14 L.P.R.A. § 81—provides for three or more incorporators. The defendant and three other persons are named in the contract as incorporators. Since the three other persons did not sign the contract, they are not obliged to act as incorporators. The defendant therefore argues that it is impossible for the trial court to compel performance of the contract in view of the possibility that two of these three other persons might refuse to serve as incorporators.

The plaintiff might perhaps argue that the identity of the incorporators is a somewhat formal matter and that new incorporators may be readily secured to replace those who refuse to serve. But incorporators—in addition to subscribing to stock of the proposed corporation—perform important functions in connection with the organization of a corporation. See paragraph 7 of § 7 of the Corporation Act, 14 L.P.R.A. § 82, par. 7. There is therefore considerable force in the contention of the defendant that the failure to obtain three incorporators from the list of four found in the contract would defeat the right of the plaintiff to performance of the contract. However, the case is not ripe for the determination of this question. The willingness of three incorporators to serve is a matter for proof by way of affidavits on a motion for summary judgment or of testimony at the trial, and not for speculation in passing on a motion to strike. For the same reason we can not speculate, as the defendant asks us to do, that it might not be possible to obtain acceptance from three of the persons listed in the Sixth clause of the contract to serve as directors as required by § 9 of the Corporation Act, 14 L.P.R.A. § 85. All these matters may be raised by the defendant at a later stage of the case. We cannot pass on them on a motion to strike.[2]

---

2. The defendant cannot be compelled to serve as a director or as Vice-President and General Manager. *Nuñez v. Soto Nussa, District Judge,* supra. *Quaere,* whether

The President of a corporation must be selected from among the directors, who must be bona fide stockholders. Section 11 of the Corporation Act, 14 L.P.R.A. § 87. The contract provides that Marcelino San Miguel shall be a director and President, but no provision is made for him to be a stockholder. The defendant therefore argues that this will prevent performance of the contract. Here again we cannot assume in considering a motion to strike that the plaintiff will not be able to show that San Miguel is in a position to obtain a qualifying share from the plaintiff corporation. Once more consideration of this matter must be postponed until definite information is before the court on it. . . .

. . . We cannot say on the record before us—a complaint and a motion to strike—that there is no possible contingency on which the plaintiff would be entitled to performance of the contract. The trial court therefore did not err in denying the motion to strike.[*]

NOTES AND QUESTIONS ON SPECIFIC PERFORMANCE

(1) The "civil law" doctrine stated by the court in the principal case is not peculiar to Spanish-derived codes such as the Puerto Rican one. The principle that obligations, especially contractual obligations, as a rule can be specifically enforced, and that ordinarily it is for the obligee and not for the court to choose between specific performance and a non-specific remedy, has been adopted in the overwhelming majority of civil-law systems.[1] The German Civil Code in § 241 tersely announces the principle: "On the strength of the obligation, the obligee is entitled to demand that the obligor render the performance owed." Other codes, especially the Code Napoleon, on their face express themselves less clearly;[2] but this has not prevented the French and other civilian courts from adhering to the same principle.

this plus other factors would prevent a judgment for performance of the contract since it is impossible to order performance of all the terms of the contract. . . .

[*] To similar effect, see Felix A. Rodriguez, Inc. v. Bristol-Myers Company, 281 F.Supp. 643 (D.Puerto Rico, 1968).

1. In addition to the authorities cited by the court in the principal case, see J. P. Dawson, Specific Performance in France and Germany, 57 Mich.L.Rev. 495 (1959), where the historic development as well as the modern shape of the civil-law doctrine is discussed, and 2 K. Zweigert & H. Kötz, An Introduction to Comparative Law § 12 (Transl. by T. Weir, 1977).

The principle that contractual obligations can be specifically enforced has been adopted also in socialist legal systems. Somewhat different rules evolved for contracts concluded between state enterprises and those that fall outside the sphere of the national economic plan. See O. Ioffe and P. Maggs, Soviet Law in Theory and Practice 210–12 (1983).

A voluminous literature has appeared in recent years on the question of whether specific performance or a non-specific remedy is more desirable in terms of economic efficiency, i.e., the effort to ensure that resources be allocated to their best use. On the basis of economic analysis it has been argued that—subject to the existence of special circumstances—non-specific relief better advances efficient resource allocation (at least in the setting of a market economy). See A. Kronman, Specific Performance 45 U.Chi.L.Rev. 351 (1978). For a different view see A. Schwartz, The Case for Specific Performance, 89 Yale L.J. 271, 279 (1979). A thoughtful treatment of the economic perspective on contract law can be found in A. Von Mehren, A General View of Contract in VII International Encyclopedia of Comp. Law (Contracts in General), Ch. 1, at 88 and 104 (1982).

2. The French Civil Code and, following it, the codes of many other civil-law countries distinguish between obligations "to give" and obligations "to do" or "not to do". Although the Code Napoleon con-

(2) As the principal case shows, the civilians' recognition of the obligee's right to specific performance (so long as such performance is not shown to be actually impossible) stands in marked contrast to the common law's preference for non-specific remedies. This divergence between civil law and common law would not exist if the civil-law systems had adopted the old Roman rule which was similar to the common-law rule providing for money damages as the primary remedy for breach of contract.[2a] Virtually all of the modern civilian codes, however, have rejected this Roman rule and have adopted the opposite principle stated above in Note (1).[2b]

(3) The essence of the modern civilian doctrine is that mere unexcused failure to perform at the proper time (i.e., a "breach" in our sense of the word) ordinarily gives rise only to a claim *for performance.*[3] An action for damages,[4] rescission or restitution will lie only if the obligor is in "default".[5] In the absence of a contract term which expressly makes time of the essence, "default" (in the civilian sense) does not occur automatically as a result of the obligor's failure to render due and timely performance, even though such failure is unexcused; it further requires a "putting in default", i.e., a warning or admonition to perform, to be given to the obligor by the obligee, unless the obligor, by express refusal or prevention of performance, has made it clear that such putting in default would be a futile gesture.

tains a provision which tends to create some doubt with respect to the obligee's right to demand specific performance of obligations "to do" or "not to do", much of the doubt has been cleared up by the courts. For references see n. 1 supra and 2 S. Litvinoff, Obligations § 162 (1975).

2a. This was the rule during the classical period of Roman law. See Buckland and McNair, Roman Law and Common Law 412–13 (2d ed. by F. H. Lawson, 1952); Lee, An Introduction to Roman-Dutch Law 265–66 (5th ed. 1953). It seems that toward the end of that period the Roman Praetor, like the English Chancellor many centuries later, granted specific performance in certain situations. See Jackson, Specific Performance of Contracts in Louisiana, 24 Tulane L.Rev. 401, 410–12 (1950).

Modern notions of specific performance, in the civil law as well as the common law, in part are traceable to canon law influence. See H. Coing, English Equity and the Denunciatio Evangelica of the Canon Law, 71 L.Q.Rev. 223 (1955).

2b. See Szladits, The Concept of Specific Performance in Civil Law, 4 Am.J.Comp. L. 208 (1955); 6 Williston on Contracts 677–78 (3rd ed. by W. H. E. Jaeger, 1962); G. H. Treitel, Remedies for Breach of Contract 8–17, 22, in Vol. VII, Ch. 16 of the International Encyclopedia of Comparative Law (1975).

3. See, e.g., Sections 241, 242, 284, 320 ff. of the German Civil Code. Pertinent provisions of the codes of other civil-law countries are referred to, and in part quoted (in English translation), in the article by Szladits, Discharge of Contract by Breach in Civil Law, 2 Am.J.Comp.L. 334 (1953), and in the same author's article cited supra n. 2b.

4. The statement in the text refers to damages for non-performance, which must be distinguished from damages for delayed performance. Damages of the latter kind (sometimes consisting merely of legal interest) may be recovered in addition to the performance itself, while specific performance and damages for non-performance are mutually exclusive remedies, at least in the simple case of an indivisible performance.

5. For a thorough discussion of the civil-law doctrine, especially as it applies to the more complex case of a bilateral contract that is still executory on both sides, see 6 Williston, op. cit. supra n. 2b, §§ 893–98, where further authorities are cited.

In French law, the requirement that the obligor be put in default has given rise to some difficulties and doubts; in principle, however, the requirement appears to be recognized by the prevailing view. See Litvinoff, supra n. 2, §§ 212–15, 274–76; P. Bonassies, Cours de Droit Civil 154–58 (mim. 1967).

An action for performance, moreover, will lie in every case of unexcused non-performance (unless the contract provides otherwise), while the availability of the other remedies may depend on the gravity of the breach and on additional factors. The result is that, contrary to common-law notions, a judgment ordering specific performance, i.e., performance in accordance with the terms of the contract, is the normal, primary remedy for non-performance in most civil-law countries.[6]

The idea that *performance* of a contract in accordance with its terms is the desirable solution, and that damages, rescission and restitution constitute at best a second-class substitute for performance, strongly prevails in modern civil-law systems; so strongly, indeed, that even after being "put in default", and even during the pendency of an action seeking restitution or damages for non-performance, the obligor ordinarily may defeat such action by tendering performance, together with interest (or other damages for the delay) and costs.[7]

(4) On the basis of the rule stated in the principal case, civil-law courts tend to grant *decrees* of specific performance more readily than common-law courts. It is clear, however, that the obligee who has obtained such a decree has won a hollow victory unless he can actually enforce it. Therefore, before we can judge the effectiveness of the remedy of specific performance in civil-law systems, we must take a look at the post-judgment procedures available under those systems. This is the purpose of the materials which follow.

GERMAN CODE OF CIVIL PROCEDURE [a]

Sec. 883. If the judgment debtor has to deliver a chattel or a number of specified chattels, the sheriff shall take them and hand them to the judgment creditor.

If the chattel to be delivered is not found, then the judgment debtor, upon motion of the judgment creditor, must affirm under oath that he does not have the chattel in his possession and that he does not know where it is.

The court can change the wording of the affirmation so as to adapt it to the circumstances of the case.

. . .

6. See supra n. 2b.

7. Concerning the French rule, see 6 Williston, op. cit. supra n. 2b, at 689. The Italian rule is discussed in the interesting case of Transamerica General Corp. v. Zunino, 82 N.Y.S.2d 595, 605 (Sup.Ct.N.Y. Co., 1948). See also Schlesinger, Book Review, 3 Utah L.Rev. 147, 151–2 (1952). In the case of reciprocal promises, the rule is subject to additional qualifications. See supra nn. 2b and 5.

a. The provisions set forth hereunder appear in the Code's 8th Book, entitled "Execution".

The substance of these provisions has remained unchanged for a long time; but the limitations upon the amount of fines that can be imposed under §§ 888 and 890 were introduced by amendments of 1970 and 1974. Prior to those amendments, the Code did not put a ceiling upon the amount of such fines. The 1974 amendment also reduced the maximum duration of imprisonment that can be imposed pursuant to § 888.

For references to cases applying these provisions, see the articles cited in the preceding Notes.

Sec. 884. If the judgment debtor has to deliver a definite quantity of fungible chattels or securities, the provisions of the first paragraph of § 883 are applicable.

Sec. 885. If the judgment debtor has to turn over, surrender or vacate a parcel of immovable property . . ., the sheriff has to dispossess him and give possession to the judgment creditor.[b]

Sec. 887. If the judgment debtor fails to perform an obligation to do an act which could be performed by a third person, then the court of first instance shall authorize the judgment creditor, upon the latter's motion, to have the act done at the expense of the judgment debtor.

The judgment creditor may at the same time move that the court order the judgment debtor to advance the expenses [of such substituted performance], without prejudice to the judgment creditor's right to demand payment of the balance in case the doing of the act occasions expenses in an amount exceeding the advance payment. . . .

Sec. 888. If an act cannot be performed by a third party, and if such act depends exclusively upon the will of the judgment debtor, then the court of first instance, upon motion, shall order that the judgment debtor be compelled to perform the act. For the purpose of such compulsion, the court may impose either (a) monetary fines, and imprisonment in case such fines are not collectible, or (b) imprisonment. A single monetary fine may not exceed DM 50,000. [By way of a cross-reference to another section, the maximum duration of imprisonment under this section is fixed at six months.]

This provision is inapplicable where the judgment orders the judgment debtor to enter into a marriage, to resume marital relations, or to perform services pursuant to a contract for services.[c]

Sec. 890. If the judgment debtor violates a duty to refrain from doing, or to tolerate, a certain act, then upon motion of the judgment creditor the court of first instance shall impose upon the judgment debtor either (a) a monetary fine, and imprisonment in case such fine is not collectible, or (b) imprisonment of up to six months [for each contravention]. A single monetary fine may not exceed DM 500,000. The total maximum duration of imprisonment [for all contraventions] is two years.

---

b. This section enables the judgment creditor to obtain *possession* of the premises. If under the terms of the judgment, the judgment debtor has to transfer *title* to the judgment creditor, § 894 (see infra) is applicable. Under § 894, the judgment replaces the deed as well as the transferor's consent which normally would be necessary in order to bring about the registration of the transfer in the land register. (Such registration is required in order to bring about a change in title, see infra p. 685.)

c. The exception stated in the second paragraph is not as broad as the rule of the first paragraph. For instance, cases in which the defendant has been directed to render an account, to supply certain information, or to issue a specified document (e.g. a letter of reference) needed by the plaintiff, normally would be covered by the rule of the first paragraph without coming under the exception.

[The second and third paragraphs of this section provide that the judgment debtor must receive an appropriate warning before he can be condemned to a fine or imprisonment, and that upon the judgment creditor's motion the debtor may be forced to give security for any damage that may arise from further violations on his part.]

Sec. 892. [This section specifies the methods by which the authorities must break any resistance of the judgment debtor against enforcement measures taken pursuant to §§ 887 and 890.]

Sec. 894. If the judgment directs the judgment debtor to make a declaration of intention, such declaration is deemed to have been made as soon as the judgment has become res judicata.[d]

NOTES

(1) French law contains no statutory provisions comparable to the foregoing sections of the German Code of Civil Procedure. Thus on the face of the French codes the position of an obligee who has obtained a decree of specific performance, would seem to be a difficult one. Over the past century, however, the French courts, without the help of a written text, have developed a remedy: the so-called *astreinte*.[1] In essence, an *astreinte* is an order of the court threatening the judgment debtor with the imposition of a monetary penalty if he fails to comply with the judgment. Should the threat fail to produce compliance, then the court (perhaps after having modified the amount) authorizes the obligee to collect the penalty. Until about thirty years ago, the effectiveness of the *astreinte* was questionable, and indeed was questioned by many legal writers inside and outside of France, because ordinarily the penalty was fixed at the approximate amount of the plaintiff's damages, or was reduced to that amount before it became due to be collected. Thus a recalcitrant defendant could, in effect, force the plaintiff to accept damages in lieu of specific performance. More recently, however, the Cour de Cassation has changed its position and has developed the rule that, depending on all the circumstances of the case and especially on the gravity and obstinacy of the defendant's refusal to perform, the penalty may be fixed *and collected* in an amount exceeding the plaintiff's actual damages.[2] This has rendered the *astreinte* considerably more effective, especially since in many cases the courts are willing to fix the penalty in terms of a certain amount for each day of non-performance or for each act of disobedience.[2a]

Noted

specific performance

d. This section of the German Code of Civil Procedure will remind the reader of a somewhat similar institution of our law: the power of a court of equity to enforce the promise of a vendor of real property by ordering that a document in the nature of a sheriff's deed be delivered to the purchaser. Note, however, that the German provision is not limited to the enforcement of contracts for the sale of real property; it covers every case in which the defendant has been ordered to execute a document or in some other way to effect a transfer or transaction of any kind.

1. The development of the *astreinte* is instructively discussed by J. Beardsley, Compelling Contract Performance in France, 1 Hast.Int. & Comp.L.Rev. 93, 95–102 (Inaugural Issue, 1977). See also P. Herzog, Civil Procedure in France 560–64 (1967); Amos and Walton's Introduction to French Law 180–82 (3rd ed. by F. H. Lawson, A. E. Anton, and L. N. Brown, 1967).

2. The 1959 decision of the Cour de Cassation which brought about this change can be found, in English translation, in B. Rudden, Courts and Codes in England, France and Soviet Russia, 48 Tul.L.Rev. 1010, 1025 (1974).

2a. By Law No. 80–539 of July 16, 1980, the *astreinte* procedure was made availa-

The solution worked out by the French courts (which, as noted previously, received legislative approval in 1972) thus has become more similar to the German scheme; but there are still some notable differences:

(a) In cases in which enforcement of the judgment requires pressure "in personam", the French courts utilize only monetary penalties, while the German provisions make it possible, in addition, to resort to imprisonment of the recalcitrant defendant.[3]

(b) Under German law, a fine imposed upon the defendant is payable to the State; it flows into the public treasury. In France, on the other hand, a monetary penalty exacted from the judgment debtor is payable to, and may be kept by, the judgment creditor. Where the penalty has been fixed in an amount exceeding the damages suffered by the latter, this may lead to a windfall; but if one considers that the real loss suffered by the obligee as a result of the obligor's non-performance may be much higher than the "damages" that are legally recoverable and provable, it becomes clear that at least in some situations such a "windfall" may well serve the ends of justice.

(2) There are some civil-law systems which have adopted French-influenced codes but have not imported the *astreinte* procedure fashioned by the French courts. Under such a system there may be serious difficulties in enforcing a decree of specific performance.

Even in a legal system where there are highly developed provisions for the rendition and enforcement of decrees of specific performance, situations can arise in which this remedy lacks practical usefulness. The complexity or the personal (and perhaps artistic or otherwise creative) nature of the promised acts of performance may make it impractical for a court to formulate and enforce an appropriate decree of specific performance. Moreover, in the many cases in which the promisee is vitally interested in receiving *timely* performance, specific performance often is a useless remedy for the reason that it is impossi-

ble, also, for the enforcement, by the Conseil d'Etat, of administrative court decisions against a governmental unit. Prior to the enactment of that Law, it happened with some frequency that governmental units simply ignored adverse decisions of administrative courts, and this had become something of a scandal. The 1980 statute, enacted in response to that scandal, provides not only for *astreintes* against units of government, but also for fines to be imposed on, and to be paid personally by, recalcitrant officials.

3. The historical and socio-political reasons for the reluctance of French courts (as well as the courts in some other "Latin" countries) vigorously to enforce private obligations, are interestingly discussed by A. Pekelis, Legal Techniques and Legal Ideologies, 41 Mich.L.Rev. 665 (1943). However, the stark contrast between the potency of common-law and the weakness of civil-law enforcement mechanisms which was em-

phasized by Pekelis almost 50 years ago, has been attenuated in recent years. See A. Blomeyer, Types of Relief Available in XVI International Encyclopedia of Comp. Law (Civil Procedure) Ch. 4, at pp. 32–33 (1982).

Interestingly enough, Soviet law preserves the traditional reluctance of some of the civil-law systems to enforce civil judgments in those situations where the enforcement requires pressure against the person of the judgment debtor; only fines (up to a total of 300 rubles) can be imposed on contumacious defendants. See Code of Civil Procedure of the RSFSR, art. 406. For an example of the failure of this enforcement mechanism to secure compliance by two American reporters with a Soviet court's order to publish a retraction of an article the reporters had written, see The New York Times of August 5, 1978, sec. I.

ble to obtain a judicial decree before the date for which the performance has been promised.

A promisee who is vitally interested in obtaining actual and timely performance, and who at the negotiating stage foresees the possibility that for legal or practical reasons the projected contract may not be specifically enforceable, will wish to know whether under the law governing the contract he can effectively protect himself by inserting a drastic penalty clause into the contract itself.

FRENCH CIVIL CODE (PRE–1975)

Art. 1226. A penalty is a clause by which a person, in order to insure the performance of an agreement, promises something in case such agreement is not performed [by him].*

Art. 1152. When an agreement provides that the party who fails to perform it shall pay a certain amount as damages, no larger or smaller amount may be awarded to the other party.

Art. 1231. The penalty can be modified by the Judge if the principal obligation has been partially performed. [This provision must be read together with Art. 1244 which states that ordinarily the obligor cannot compel the obligee to accept part performance. Moreover, prior to 1975 the French courts held that the protection of Art. 1231 could be stipulated away by the obligor.]

NOTES

(1) As shown by the materials immediately following these Notes, the above provisions of the original Code Napoleon were drastically revised by the French legislator in 1975. The pre-1975 provisions, however, retain more than a mere historical interest. It must be remembered that many countries have copied, or virtually copied, the Code Napoleon. It is very likely, therefore, that the older version of the French provisions remains in force in a number of legal systems, even though the seminal Code has been changed on this point.

(2) Referring to the pre-1975 penalty clause provisions of the French Civil Code, a noted English scholar commented as follows: [1]

* Depending on the terms of the contract, the penalty may be forfeited in case of (a) non-performance, or (b) delayed performance (e.g., $500 for each day of delay.) The penalty for delay may be recovered together with specific performance. But as between specific performance and a penalty for non-performance, the obligee must elect (Art. 1228), and he may not recover damages for nonperformance in excess of the stipulated penalty (Art. 1229). For a critical discussion of the latter provision, and of its Louisiana counterpart, see Thayer, Penal Clauses in Contracts, 9 Tul.L. Rev. 191 (1935).

Although the Code does not say so, it seems to be recognized that the promisor does not have to pay the penalty if his nonperformance was not due to any fault of his. But this is subject to agreement otherwise; even if he is faultless, the promisor is liable for the penalty if his non-performance is due to an event, even a wholly fortuitous event, the risk of which he has assumed. See Planiol's Treatise on the Civil Law, Vol. 2, Part 1, Sec. 255 (English transl. by Louisiana State Law Institute 1959).

1. N. S. Marsh, Penal Clauses in Contracts: A Comparative Study, 32 J.Com. Leg. & Int.L. (3rd Ser.) 66 (1950).

In striking contrast to the majority of previous juristic opinion, the makers of the Code Civil refused to allow the court to reduce a penalty agreed between the parties. In the *Exposé des Motifs* of contracts and conventional obligations in general (Livre III, Titre II, Procès-Verbaux du Conseil d'Etat, tome iv, p. 195) Bigot-Préameneu [a] stated this principle in uncompromising terms:

> "La peine stipulée par les contractants fait la loi entre eux. Le créancier ne doit pas être admis à dire que cette peine est insuffisante, ni le débiteur à prétendre qu'elle est excessive. Quel serait le juge, qui mieux que les parties, pourrait connaître les circonstances et les intérêts respectifs qui ont déterminé la fixation de la peine?" [b]

It is remarkable that this insistence on the sanctity of contracts with regard to penal stipulations which is to be found or implied from articles 1226, 1134,[c] and 1152 of the Code Civil has persisted up to the present day, and especially in a period when, in general, the theory of contract as the expression of the will of the party is on the decline. Even as recent as 1940 we find the Chambre Civile [of the Cour de Cassation] (D.H. 1940, 161) quashing a decision which in the name of justice and equity had allowed a sum less than that fixed by a penal clause to be recovered, the court emphasizing that, in the words of article 1134, "Les conventions légalement formées tiennent lieu de loi à ceux qui les ont faites."

The policy thus pursued by the French courts is not without its dangers, especially where there is a great disparity of power between the contracting parties. This may arise either when the penalty fixed is much larger than any damage which may result or when the penalty is excessively small in relation to the damage.

FRENCH CIVIL CODE (1975 REVISION) *

By Law 75–597 of July 9, 1975, the following second paragraph was added to Art. 1152:

"Nevertheless, the Judge may reduce or increase the agreed-upon penalty if it is manifestly excessive or ridiculously small. Any contrary stipulation will be considered not written."

a. One of the members of the Council of State who helped to prepare the Code and to hammer out its final form in long day-and-night sessions under Napoleon's active chairmanship. For the names of the other members of the Council who made the most important contributions, see Cassin, Codification and National Unity, in Schwartz (Ed.), The Code Napoleon and the Common-Law World 46, 48 (1956).

b. "The penalty stipulated by the parties has, as between them, the force of law. The creditor may not afterward complain that the penalty is inadequate; nor may the debtor argue that it is excessive. Where would one find a judge who knows, better than the parties themselves, the circumstances and the respective interests which have determined the fixing of the penalty?"

c. See supra p. 659.

* For an interesting discussion of the developments which led to this revision of the Code, see J. Beardsley, Compelling Contract Performance in France, 1 Hast. Int. & Comp.L.Rev. 93, 103–07 (Inaugural Issue, 1977).

The 1975 Law also amended Art. 1231 to read as follows:

"When the engagement has been performed in part, the agreed-upon penalty may be diminished by the Judge in proportion to what the creditor obtained through the partial performance, without prejudice to the application of Article 1152. Any contrary stipulation will be considered not written."

NOTES ON THE NEW FRENCH PROVISIONS CONCERNING CONTRACTUAL PENALTY CLAUSES

The 1975 revision of the French Civil Code has led to an avalanche of litigation. Faced by numerous demands for judicial reduction of allegedly excessive contractual penalties, the French courts have found that the new provisions call not only for the wise exercise of discretion, but also for the resolution of some difficult questions of law.

(1) May the penalty be reduced to the amount of actual damages suffered by the obligee?

The French commentators seem to be virtually unanimous in espousing the view that, even after reduction, the amount of the penalty normally should remain higher than the obligee's actual damages.[1] This view is supported by the legislative history of the 1975 Law, which makes it clear that the legislators intended to preserve the "salutary value of the penalty as a threat," i.e., its function of inducing the obligor to render actual performance rather than to relegate the obligee to the recovery of damages. The very language of the statute, moreover, is said to militate against a result which would limit the obligee's recovery to the amount of the damages suffered by him; if he recovered no more than such damages, then the penalty itself—as distinguished from damages—would be wiped out and not merely "reduced."

(2) A French trial court's decision concerning modification of a penalty is in all respects subject to review by the intermediate appellate court. See supra p. 457. But how about review by the court of last resort?

In France, this question has given rise to a great deal of debate. Two issues must be distinguished:

(a) As we have seen in an earlier part of the course (see supra p. 449), it is a basic tenet of procedural law in civil-law countries that every judgment of a court must be supported by a statement of reasons. To avoid reversal by a reviewing court, such statement must cover every issue of fact or law duly raised by the parties. It follows that where the issue of judicial reduction of a penalty has been raised, the court of first instance and the intermediate appellate court must deal with that issue in their opinions (i.e., the opinion-part of their decisions). In a recent French case,[2] the intermediate appellate court had reduced the penalty to one-third of the stipulated amount; as its reason, that court had merely announced that the stipulated amount was "a little high," but without any clear indication of the circumstances which in the

---

1. See the Annotation by Professor Vasseur in 1977 Rec. Dalloz Sirey, Jur. 264.

2. Cour de Cassation, Chambre Mixte, 20 Jan. 1978, D.1978 I.R. 229.

court's opinion rendered the penalty manifestly excessive. The
Court of Cassation, speaking through one of its super-panels,[3]
reversed on the ground that the intermediate appellate court had
failed to state any proper reason for the reduction.

Three months later, the Court of Cassation had to deal with a
case in which the intermediate appellate court, in refusing to
reduce the penalty involved in that action, had said no more than
that it "did not find in the case any elements which would enable
the court to treat the stipulated penalty as excessive." The Court
of Cassation, distinguishing this case from the one decided three
months earlier, held that the quoted sentence advanced a sufficient
reason for refusing to reduce the penalty, and affirmed the decision
below.[4]

The up-shot of these two decisions seems to be that in France
the lower courts have to state somewhat more specific reasons for
the reduction of a penalty than for a refusal to reduce. It might be
interesting to speculate as to whether this will have an effect on
the lower courts' eagerness to reduce penalties.

(b) The more important issue is the second one: Assuming that
the intermediate appellate court in its opinion has used a verbal
formula which satisfies the procedural requirement of stating reasons, will the highest court *as a matter of substantive law* review
the question whether and to what extent a penalty should be
reduced? Or will this be treated as a question of fact not reviewable in the court of last resort?

In Germany, where § 343 of the Civil Code (see infra) raises
the same issue, the court of last resort has consistently claimed the
power to examine whether the lower courts, in reducing a penalty
or in refusing to do so, have been guided by "legally correct
considerations." [5] In other words, even though the lower courts
are accorded a measure of discretionary power, the German court
of last resort reviews the "correctness" of the reasons for reduction
or nonreduction which are stated in the opinion of the intermediate
appellate court.

In France, the highest court's position on this question is less
clear.[5a] The commentators are not unanimous;[6] but most of them

---

3. Concerning the functions and composition of such super-panels, see supra pp.
467–468.

4. Cour de Cassation, 3rd Civil Chamber, 28 April 1978, Rec. Dalloz Sirey 1978,
Jur. 349.

5. See Palandt, Bürgerliches
Gesetzbuch, § 343, Anno. 1 c (41st ed.,
1982).

5a. In its decision of January 3, 1985,
the Court of Cassation dealt with a case in
which the intermediate appellate court
had reduced a penalty from ffrs. 150,000 to
ffrs. 12,000, and had justified the reduction
by finding that plaintiff had not proved
any actual damages. Plaintiff-appellant
argued that this was an erroneous reason
for reduction, because the true purpose of a
penalty clause is not the contractual fixa-

tion of the amount of damages but the
creation of pressure leading to actual performance. The highest court affirmed,
pointing out that a penalty clause can
serve either or both of these purposes and
that the intermediate appellate court's reasoning, therefore, was not erroneous.

The fact that in this case the Court of
Cassation discussed, and thus in effect substantively reviewed, the lower court's reasoning, may indicate that the highest court
reserves for itself the power to "break" a
decision of an intermediate appellate court
if the latter court, in reducing a penalty (or
in refusing to reduce) states a criterion of
excessiveness which on its face is plainly
irrelevant or absurd. This, however, will

---

6. See note 6 on page 675.

apparently expect that the Court will treat the question as one of fact. The result of such an approach would be that the intermediate appellate court—provided it has stated sufficient "reasons"—would always have the last word on the issue of judicial modification of a penalty. This, however, can lead to problems in today's world of mass transactions and of standard contract forms used on a national scale. *Example:* A French finance company, which apparently does business in many parts of France, in extending loans at a 10½% interest rate, used a standard clause to the effect that in case of default the borrower had to pay a penalty, consisting of a one-time payment in the amount of 4% of the balance, plus 17½% per annum for the period from the beginning of the default to the repayment of the loan. In several parts of France, defaulting debtors of the company litigated the question whether this standard penalty was manifestly excessive. Some intermediate appellate courts held that it was, and substantially reduced the penalty, while other intermediate appellate courts reached the opposite result, even though the same standard contract of the same finance company was involved in all of these cases.[7]

Is there a need for a nationally uniform solution in such a case?[8] Or could it be argued that the personal circumstances of each debtor should be taken into consideration; that a given penalty may be "manifestly excessive" in the case of one debtor but tolerable in the case of another; and that, consequently, even a standard penalty clause used throughout the nation does not necessarily call for a nationally uniform rule as to what is "manifestly excessive"? There are, as yet, no firm answers to these questions insofar as French law is concerned.

GERMAN CIVIL CODE

Sec. 339. If the obligor promises to pay a sum of money as a penalty in the event that he should fail to perform his obligation, or that he should not perform it in a proper manner, such penalty shall be forfeited upon the obligor's default.[a] If the obligation to be performed

---

occur only exceptionally. So long as the criterion stated by the Cour d' Appel is not erroneous on its face, the Court of Cassation may well treat the criterion's application to the circumstances of the case as a non-reviewable issue of fact. For the decision discussed above, see Bulletin des Arrêts de la Cour de Cassation, Chambres Civiles, Janvier 1985, Première Partie at 4.

6. See Vasseur, supra n. 1.

7. Ibid.

8. In this particular instance, a nationally uniform solution was ultimately achieved, not by the Court of Cassation, but by the legislator. A statute and Decree issued in 1978 now specify the exact percentage of the overdue balance which may be exacted by the creditor as a penalty for the debtor's default in small-loan

contracts and certain other types of consumer transactions. See Law 78–22 of 10 Jan. 1978, Arts. 20–22, Rec. Dalloz Sirey 1978, Leg. 84; Decree 78–373 of 17 March 1978, Rec. Dalloz Sirey 1978, Leg. 200.

Nevertheless, the broader question raised in the text, supra, remains important for many other types of contracts and contract clauses.

a. "Default" is a technical term. See supra, pp. 666–667. Ordinarily, the obligor will be in default only if (a) he has received an express warning or admonition to perform, and (b) his non-performance is not excused. It would be excused, for instance, by impossibility not due to the obligor's fault, or, in the case of a bilateral contract, by the obligee's own default. See Secs. 275 to 285, 320 to 326 of the Civil Code. (Note

consists of an omission [i.e., a duty to refrain from doing certain acts], then the forfeiture takes place as soon as an act contravening the obligation is committed.[b]

Sec. 340. . . . If the obligee is entitled to damages for nonperformance, he shall receive the forfeited penalty as the minimum amount of damages. The recovery of further damages is not excluded.[c]

Sec. 343. If a forfeited penalty is disproportionately high, the court may upon the obligor's request[d] reduce it to an appropriate amount. In determining the question of what is appropriate, every rightful interest of the obligee, not only his monetary interest, has to be considered. . . .

———

GERMAN COMMERCIAL CODE

Sec. 348. A contractual penalty promised by a merchant in the course of his business cannot be reduced under the provisions of § 343 of the Civil Code.

———

SWISS CODE OF OBLIGATIONS

Art. 161. The forfeited penalty may be recovered even though the obligee has suffered no damage.[e]

If the damage suffered exceeds the amount of the penalty, the obligee may recover the excess only in so far as he proves fault [i.e., a fault of the obligor which caused the non-performance.]

Art. 163. The amount of the contractual penalty can be fixed by the parties as they please.

The penalty cannot be recovered if it is intended to secure the performance of an unlawful or immoral promise.[f] Unless the parties

the drafting technique typical for this Code: the single word "default" is in effect a cross-reference to a whole galaxy of other interacting provisions.)

The requirement of "default" is subject to agreement otherwise. Thus by express agreement the parties can provide (as under French law) that the penalty is payable even though the promisor's non-performance is due to a fortuitous event. See Kommentar von Reichsgerichtsraeten und Bundesrichtern zum Buergerlichen Gesetzbuch, Sec. 339, Anno. 7 (1960); Palandt, Buergerliches Gesetzbuch, § 339, Anno. 2 (45th ed., 1986).

b. I.e., in this case no "default" is necessary, but only a simple breach of the obligation, roughly in the sense in which we understand the latter term. The courts have held, however, that this sentence is

ius dispositivum, so that the parties, even in the case of a duty not to do, may agree that the penalty shall not be forfeited if the promisor is faultless.

c. Compare this with Art. 1152 of the French Civil Code.

d. Such request may be made by action, or by interposing an affirmative defense in the obligee's action for recovery of the penalty.

e. No action can be brought, however, to recover a penalty stipulated to secure the performance of a promise to marry. Swiss Civil Code, Art. 91. To the same effect see German Civil Code, Sec. 1297.

f. Concerning the point covered in this first sentence of the paragraph, French and German law would be to the same effect.

agree otherwise, the penalty cannot be recovered if performance has become impossible due to no fault of the obligor.[g]

An excessively high penalty has to be reduced by the court, in its discretion.

SOME OBSERVATIONS SUGGESTED BY COMPARING THE FRENCH, GERMAN AND SWISS PROVISIONS

(1) By giving the court the power to *reduce* an excessive penalty, and by providing that this judicial power can never be stipulated away, the French legislators of 1975 modified the original codifiers' fanatical adherence to the principle of freedom of contract. The 1975 revision is in line with the position of most of the modern Codes. This rapprochement between French law and the law of other major civil-law countries no doubt was welcomed by the scholars in charge of the Council of Europe study aimed at harmonizing the member states' laws on the subject of penalty clauses. The outcome of that study was a resolution adopted by the Committee of Ministers of the Council of Europe recommending that courts of the member states be empowered to reduce the sum stipulated in penal clauses where such sum is "manifestly excessive". See Resolution on Penal Clauses in Civil Law (78)3 of January 20, 1978, art. 7.

It should be noted that the revised French provisions apply regardless of whether the promisor is a merchant. This is in line with Swiss law, but different from German law. Whether in the future this difference between French and German law will be eliminated as a result of the harmonizing efforts of the Council of Europe, remains to be seen.

(2) By authorizing the court to *increase* the amount of a ridiculously low penalty, the French legislator has adopted a rule which at first blush seems to diverge sharply from German and Swiss law, and indeed to be quite novel.

One must remember, however, that under German and Swiss law the obligee can recover damages in excess of the agreed-upon penalty if the obligor is responsible for his failure to perform. This obviates the need for judicial augmentation of the penalty. All the obligee has to do in such a case, is to prove that he has suffered damages in excess of the amount of the penalty. Under German or Swiss law, he can then recover the excess. In contrast, the French Civil Code in Article 1152 provides that when the contract contains a clause fixing a penalty, "no larger or smaller amount can be awarded" as damages. Depending on which side has superior bargaining power, this provision can be used and misused by the obligor as well as the obligee. In drafting construction contracts, for instance, it was customary in France until 1975 to provide for a minimal penalty to be forfeited in case of the obligor's (contractor's) non-performance or delayed performance. Such a contract clause, in conjunction with Article 1152 of the Code Civil, deprived the other party of any right to substantial damages. The 1975 revision, while adding the above-quoted second paragraph, did not change the original language of Article 1152 which precludes the

g. In its substance, the Swiss rule stated in the second sentence of this paragraph is similar to both French and German law. But note the strikingly different stylistic manner in which each of the three codes expresses (or implies) the rule.

recovery of damages in excess of the penalty; but when the penalty is "ridiculously small," the court is now authorized by the new second paragraph to increase the amount and in this way, one may assume, to bring it more closely into line with the damages actually suffered by the obligee.

Compared to the German and Swiss provisions, the new French solution may appear complicated. Note, however, that the French court's power to increase an inadequate penalty cannot be stipulated away by the parties. On the other hand, the German-Swiss rule—that excess damages, if proved, can be recovered as such—appears to be subject to agreement otherwise. See Palandt, Buergerliches Gesetzbuch, Section 340, Anno. 1 (45th ed., 1986). An obligee who is in an inferior bargaining position thus is more effectively protected by the new French provisions than by the German-Swiss rule.

(3) Experience gathered under the new French provisions has shown already that reduction of contractual penalties is sought much more frequently than augmentation. In the exceedingly numerous cases in which judicial reduction of a penalty is asked for, the 1975 revision of the French Code confronts the French courts with many of the questions which the German and Swiss courts have faced for almost a century. One might expect, therefore, that the French courts and commentators would try to benefit from the wealth of experience gathered by the German and Swiss courts in applying their older but rather similar provisions for the reduction of excessive penalties. But such is not the case. French textbooks and articles in legal periodicals have devoted many hundreds of pages to discussing the numerous issues raised by the 1975 amendment; but the French readers are never told that—perhaps only a few kilometers away—the German and Swiss courts have struggled with the same issues for nearly 100 years, and perhaps have reached some arguably sound solutions.

For one who is interested in the broader aspects of comparative law, it is not without interest to observe this extreme example of what in an earlier chapter of this book has been referred to as "the intellectual isolation of each national system which resulted from the codifications." [1]

Suppose the legislature of one of our states were to enact a new statute similar to one which for a long time has been on the books, and frequently applied by the courts, in a sister state or in some other common-law country. Would our courts and commentators, when wrestling with problems created by the new statute, likewise ignore the relevant experience—including, of course, the judicial decisions—accumulated in the other jurisdiction?

ILLUSTRATIONS *

(1) A undertakes to deliver to B in a year's time 100 tons of a certain commodity at $1,000 per ton. The penalty for non-delivery is to be $200 per ton. A fails to deliver 50 tons; but by the time the year has expired the market price of the commodity has fallen to $500 per ton so that B has in fact saved $500 per ton on the 50 tons which A has failed to deliver. Under pre-1975 French law it seems clear that B can

1. See supra p. 306.

* The first of these Illustrations is largely taken from the interesting article by N.

S. Marsh, Penal Clauses in Contracts: A Comparative Study, 32 J.Comp.Leg. & Int. L. (3rd ser.) 66, 72–73 (1950).

recover the penalty of 50 × \$200 or \$10,000.[1] As revised in 1975, the French provisions authorize judicial reduction in such a case; but, as noted supra, a French court (even today) probably could not reduce the penalty to zero. In German law, if A is a merchant he may have to pay the \$10,000 unless it can be said that insistence on payment would be contra bonos mores, or contrary to principles of good faith.[2] Any other party in German law might apply to the Court to reduce the penalty on the ground that it was excessive in relation to the actual loss incurred; indeed it would seem that no loss has been incurred and therefore there might be no penalty at all.[3] In English law, on the other hand, the question would turn on whether, when the contract was made, \$200 per ton was a reasonable bona fide pre-estimate by the parties of the loss which would be incurred a year ahead on failure to deliver the commodity. If it was such a reasonable pre-estimate, the \$10,000 would be recoverable, otherwise it would be a penalty in the strict sense and not recoverable.[4]

(2) The highest court of Switzerland, in its decision of February 25, 1915, BGE 41 II 138, had to deal with the following facts: The defendant, a Swiss inventor, and the plaintiff, a German businessman, had concluded a contract for the joint exploitation of an invention made by the defendant. Under the terms of the contract, the proceeds of patent licensing agreements and of options were to be divided fifty-fifty; to secure this division, all such proceeds were to be deposited with a named Notary in Berlin. A party violating this latter provision was to incur a penalty in the amount of M 10,000. In fact, very substantial amounts were received from patent licensees, and were deposited with the Notary in accordance with the contract. Only in one instance, when the relatively small amount of M 1,000 was received by him from a Japanese optionee on June 23, 1913, defendant inadvertently forgot to deposit the money with the Notary. A short time later, however, defendant informed plaintiff of the receipt of the M 1,000. In Novem-

---

1. At first blush, this conclusion may seem doubtful, because A has performed in part. But the court's power to apportion the penalty pursuant to old Art. 1231 does not exist if the parties have agreed otherwise; hence that power cannot come into play where, as here, the parties themselves have specified the precise amount of penalty (\$200 *per ton*) payable in case of partial non-performance.

2. See §§ 138 and 242 of the German Civil Code, set forth supra pp. 569, 575.

Section 138 of the German Civil Code does not authorize reduction of a contractual penalty; but in an extreme case, i.e., where the penalty clause of the contract is "immoral", it would invalidate such clause. The German courts, however, appear to be very reluctant to use the sharp weapon of § 138 to invalidate *a merchant's* promise of a penalty. The same attitude has been exhibited by the Japanese courts, operating under similar, German-derived code provisions. For example, "a penalty clause in a sales contract was held not to offend Japanese public policy, and the Japanese

seller was ordered to pay the agreed amount of \$15,000 to the Filipino buyer, when the amount of actual damages was not more than \$4,000." Y. Fujita, Procedural Fairness to Foreign Litigants As Stressed by Japanese Courts, 12 Int.Law. 795 (1978).

3. The matter rests in the discretion of the court. All of the circumstances of the case (as of the time when the court is requested to reduce the penalty) have to be considered. If the obligee can show that for some peculiar reason he had an interest in the delivery of the goods in spite of the price decline, the court might let him recover the penalty in whole or in part. See Kommentar von Reichsgerichtsraeten und Bundesrichtern zum Buergerlichen Gesetzbuch, Sec. 343, Anno. 8 (1960).

4. Concerning the American rule, compare UCC § 2–718(1). For an analysis of the American law on the subject, see I. R. Macneil, Power of Contract and Agreed Remedies, 47 Cornell L.Q. 495 (1962). See also the Notes following these Illustrations.

ber, 1913, defendant actually remitted frs.500 to the Notary for the account of the plaintiff. Apparently the defendant had intended to remit M 500; but through a mistake of his office personnel the remittance was in the amount of frs.500, which at that time was the equivalent of about M 410.

Plaintiff sued for the full amount of the penalty, i.e., frs.12,380 (the equivalent of M 10,000). The lower court reduced the penalty to frs. 1,000, and the plaintiff appealed. The court of last resort assumed that under German law (§ 348 of the German Commercial Code) the penalty could not be reduced, and that, consequently, the decision of the case hinged on whether Swiss or German law was to be applied. Turning to the conflict-of-laws question thus raised, the court said that under ordinary rules of private international law the contract would be governed by German law since it was made and performable in Germany; but, in the view of the court, the Swiss rule authorizing reduction of the penalty was so clearly based upon fundamental principles of morality underlying the Swiss social order that to apply a contrary foreign rule would be inconsistent with the Swiss *ordre public*.[5] For this reason, the highest court affirmed the lower court decision by which the penalty had been reduced in accordance with Swiss law.

Was the court correct in assuming that, as applied to the facts of the case, German law differed from Swiss law and that under German law the penalty could not be reduced?[6]

(3) Staccato is a dachshund whose market value is only $75, but whose owner, Professor P, is extremely devoted to him. P, leaving town to attend a meeting of the Association of American Law Schools, entrusts custody of Staccato to D, the owner of a kennel, for 5 days at the rate of $9.00 per day. P and D agree that Staccato is to have a daily portion of one-half pound of Filet Mignon, and D promises a penalty of $1,000 for every day on which Staccato should fail to receive the stipulated food. Thinking that P will never find out, D gives Staccato nothing but scraps; but a disgruntled employee of D informs P, who sues D for $5,000. What result under former French law? Under present French law? Under German law? Under Swiss law? Under English or U.S. law?

Which legal system offers the most desirable solution? In this connection, it should be remembered that dog-lovers are not the only persons who enter into contracts for the purpose of protecting nonmonetary interests, or interests which are difficult to evaluate in terms of provable damages. Esthetic and environmental interests, for instance, often are sought to be protected by contractual stipulations involving a penalty. Under our law, such stipulations normally are unenforceable, even when the promisee is a governmental agency.[7] The promisee thus is relegated to seeking either specific performance or damages. Neither remedy provides reliable protection for environmen-

---

5. Concerning this conflict of laws point, see infra pp. 849–851.

6. Who bears the burden of proof, under German law, as to the existence of the facts upon which the applicability of § 348 of the German Commercial Code depends? In this connection, it should be noted that—except for the bare statement that defendant was an inventor—the opinion of

the Swiss court contains no information whatever concerning defendant's occupation.

7. See City of Rye v. Public Service Mutual Ins. Co., 34 N.Y.2d 470, 358 N.Y.S.2d 391, 315 N.E.2d 458 (1974). See also the Notes immediately following these Illustrations.

tal or other non-pecuniary interests. The equitable remedy of specific performance is uncertain because of its discretionary nature, and the assessment of damages for injuries to environmental and other non-pecuniary interests has proved to be extremely difficult.[8] Under these circumstances, does the solution offered by the modern civilian codes not appear to be preferable? [9]

U.S. invalidates all penalties which do not qualify as liquidated damages.

NOTES AND QUESTIONS

(1) In comparing civil-law and common-law approaches to the legal devices by which actual performance of a contract can be secured, one is tempted to formulate some broad conclusions. Would it be correct, for instance, to say that the principle of freedom of contract is carried further by the civilian codes than in the common-law systems? Or that the civil-law systems tend to let *the parties* decide whether the promisor should be forced to perform the contract in accordance with its terms, while the common law always gives to *the court* the power to make an ultimate—and often discretionary—decision on this point?

In the United States, one encounters increasing skepticism concerning the soundness of the common-law (and UCC) rule invalidating all contractual penalties which do not qualify as liquidated damages.[1] California has recently undertaken a statutory revision of its rules relating to liquidated damages.[1a] Although far from radical in their

---

8. See Note, Assessment of Civil Monetary Penalties for Water Pollution, 30 Hast.L.J. 651 (1979).

9. See also the Notes which immediately follow these Illustrations.

1. See C. J. Goetz & R. E. Scott, Liquidated Damages, Penalties and the Just Compensation Principle: Some Notes on an Enforcement Model and a Theory of Efficient Breach, 77 Colum.L.Rev. 554 (1977).

The unpredictability of results under the common-law rule is illustrated by numerous cases discussed in Anno., Contractual Provisions for Per Diem Payments for Delay in Performance as Ones for Liquidated Damages or Penalty, 12 ALR 4th 891 (1982).

Note that both systems, civil law and common law, inject an element of uncertainty into the calculations of a promisor who considers the probable cost of a contemplated breach. In a common-law jurisdiction, such a promisor often will not know in advance whether the contractual clause ultimately will be treated by the court as valid or invalid. In the majority of modern civil-law jurisdictions, the promisor in such a situation will wonder whether and to what extent the court will reduce the stipulated amount. Yet there is a real difference between the two systems. Under the common-law rule the promisor, al-

though often he cannot be sure, may well hope to have the contract clause declared a penalty, and thus to defeat it completely. In a civil-law country, he knows that at best he can obtain only a *reduction* of the stipulated amount of penalty. The difference between the common-law and the civil-law approaches will make itself felt especially in cases where the stipulated amount is high and clearly intended to pressure the promisor into rendering actual and timely performance. In many cases of this kind a promisor acting under the common-law rule will be encouraged to breach, because his lawyer will tell him that, if it comes to litigation, the contractual clause probably will be held invalid. Under modern civil law, on the other hand, a promisor contemplating breach will be informed by his lawyer that it is uncertain whether and by how much the court will reduce the stipulated penalty, and that in any event— if the promisor decides to breach—he will probably have to pay more, and perhaps substantially more, than provable damages. Thus the two systems differ considerably in their impact on the promisor's decision to breach or not to breach.

1a. See Cal. Civil Code § 1671 and Cal. Public Contract Code § 10226. This statutory revision was based on a recommendation of the California Law Revision Commission. See 13 Cal.L.Rev.Comm'n Reports 2139 (1976). That recommenda-

departures from the traditional common-law approach, the new California provisions somewhat enlarge the parties' freedom to determine the consequences of a breach, and thus take a hesitant (and still rather timid) step in the direction of civil-law solutions.

(2) Specific performance and the penalty clause are functionally related devices. Their possible interaction should be kept in mind. A legal system which discards or excessively weakens either of the two devices, thereby will become more dependent on the other.[1b] Conversely, it might be argued that the more a legal system strengthens one of the two devices, e.g. specific performance, the less need there will be for rigorous application of the other.

It should be kept in mind, however, that the two devices, though related, are not interchangeable. As has been pointed out (supra pp. 670–671), there are many situations where no legal system can resort to specific enforcement of a promise, and where actual and timely performance can be assured, if at all, only by a penalty clause. On the other hand, it is obvious (at least in a free-enterprise system) that the device of the penalty clause can be used only when the negotiating situation is such that both parties are willing to assent to such a clause. Thus it makes sense for a legal system to employ both devices, making sure at the same time that neither of them will be used in an oppressive manner.

(3) In socialist systems, where the attention of lawyers and economists centers primarily on contracts among state-owned enterprises,[2] "the penalty is in practice the most important remedy for breach of contract."[3] Insertion of penalty clauses into all contracts concluded among state-owned enterprises is obligatory in communist countries.[3a] When an enterprise has to pay a certain amount as a penalty, such amount is charged to a fund which is the source of bonus payments and fringe benefits accruing to managers and workers. Since the penalty sanction results in a reduction of that fund, it is felt by every employee of the enterprise.[4] Thus the penalty not only enables the promisee to obtain compensation without having to prove damages;[5] more impor-

---

tion, in turn, relied heavily on the study by J. Sweet, Liquidated Damages in California, 60 Cal.L.Rev. 84 (1972), reprinted in 11 Cal.L.Rev.Comm'n Reports 1229 (1973).

1b. The point made in the text is illustrated by the Palestinian case of The Syndics in the Bankruptcy of Khoury v. Slavousky, 5 P.L.R. 378; 1938, 1 A.L.R. 387. The case is interestingly discussed by U. Yadin, Reception and Rejection of English Law in Israel, 11 Int. & Comp.L.Q. 59, 63–65 (1962).

2. See 1 Schlesinger, Formation of Contracts—A Study of the Common Core of Legal Systems 22–29 (1968).

3. B. Grossfeld, Money Sanctions for Breach of Contract in a Communist Economy, 72 Yale L.J. 1326, 1341 (1963); to the some effect, see O. Ioffe and P. Maggs, Soviet Law in Theory and Practice 210–12 (1983).

3a. Indirectly, this practice also affects contracts between Western businessmen and state-owned enterprises in socialist countries. Soviet foreign trade organizations, when dealing with trading partners in other countries, ordinarily use forms that provide for penalties payable in the event of non-performance or late performance. See A. J. Heath, Sales of Industrial Goods to the U.S.S.R.—An Analysis of Standard Russian Forms of Agreement, 17 Harv.Int.L.J. 71, 84–86 (1976).

In Yugoslavia the insertion of penalty clauses is not mandatory. See Art. 270 of the 1978 statute on obligations.

4. See R. Krevet, Das Vertragsrecht in der mitteldeutschen Industrie 56–57 (1965); Z. M. Mihaly, The Role of Civil Law Institutions in the Management of Communist Economies: The Hungarian Experience, 8 Am.J.Comp.L. 310, 322 (1959).

5. To fix the amount of damages without reference to a market (which at least in theory does not exist in a socialist economy), may sometimes cause special prob-

tantly, it performs an educational function and serves to ensure actual performance of the contract and, at least indirectly, of the Plan.[5a]

The principal legal problems arising in connection with penalty clauses are the same in socialist as in non-socialist systems: Should the penalty be payable even though the non-performance is due to no fault on the part of the promisor?[6] Should the arbitration board (which has jurisdiction over disputes among socialist enterprises) have power to reduce the penalty? These questions are much debated in communist legal literature. The legislative solutions have not been completely uniform throughout the communist world. In recent years, perhaps as a result of de-stalinization, the general tendency has been away from an overly brutal and toward a more flexible enforcement of penalty clauses.[6a] The relevant articles in the 1964 Civil Code of the Russian Soviet Federated Socialist Republic[7] are similar, in substance as well as style, to the German and Swiss provisions set forth above.

Art. 187 of the Russian Code provides that "A creditor may not demand payment of . . . a penalty if the debtor is not responsible for the nonperformance or improper performance of an obligation"; this must be read together with Art. 222 which makes it clear that the debtor is responsible for his non-performance only if it is due to his fault, but that (a) this requirement of fault—just as in German, French and Swiss law—can be stipulated away, and that (b) in any event the burden of proving absence of fault on his part is borne by the debtor. Art. 190 provides that penalties promised in ordinary contracts among citizens (as distinguished from enterprises) can be reduced by the court, and that "in exceptional cases" an arbitration board dealing with contracts among socialist enterprises may do the same.[8]

These provisions undoubtedly reflect a tendency to make the implementation of penalty clauses more flexible and more humane. The similarity with the trend of the modern "capitalist" codes in civil-law countries is evident. It should not be forgotten, however, that in a country where in principle the parties are free to shape their contracts, the whip of the penalty clause can be used only against a promisor who has assented to its use; in the socialist systems, on the other hand,

---

lems, over and above the evidentiary difficulties which a plaintiff suing for damages encounters even in a "capitalist" system.

5a. This point of "contractual discipline" is strongly emphasized by socialist authors. See G. Eörsi, Contractual Remedies in Socialist Legal Systems, in International Encyclopedia of Comparative Law, Vol. VII, Ch. 16, pp. 153 ff., especially at 166-81 (1975).

6. A related question—of great importance in a socialist economy—is whether the promisor is excused if its own non-performance is due to the "fault" of another state-owned enterprise which should have, but did not, supply the promisor with necessary raw materials, machinery, power or transport. For references see nn. 3, 3a and 4, supra.

6a. See Eörsi, supra n. 5a.

7. See English translation by W. Gray and R. Stults (1965).

8. These provisions of the Russian Code are fairly typical of the recent trend in communist countries. See Eörsi, supra n. 5a, at 167-73. But the East German Law Concerning the Contract System in the Socialist Economy of 1965 (regulating contracts among "enterprises", as distinguished from private contracts among citizens, which are governed by the Civil Code) is somewhat tougher. It authorizes the contracting enterprises to provide not only for "penalties", which are subject to the "fault" principle and in exceptional cases can be reduced by the arbitration board, but also for so-called "price sanctions" (Preissanktionen). The latter are, in reality, additional penalties for nonperformance; but they become payable regardless of the promisor's fault (§ 105) and apparently cannot be reduced. See Krevet, supra n. 4, at 58; W. Seiffert, Wirtschaftsrecht der DDR 36, 450, 453 (1982).

penalty clauses are mandatorily inserted into economic contracts, without the consent of those who ultimately will feel the pressure and bear the burden of the penalty.

B. THE CODES AND SECURITY OF TRANSACTIONS

(AA) THE PRINCIPLE OF PUBLICITY IN THE TRANSFER OF LAND

INTRODUCTORY NOTE

The Code Napoleon and all the other 19th century codes in varying degrees reflect the desire to break the power and privileges of the landed aristocracy, and to make land as freely marketable as possible, "the result expected being that every piece of land would always be in the ablest and fittest hands." [1]

To carry out these aims, the concept of private property was divorced from the owner's status and public office. Under the influence of the theory that property was a natural right, not granted by the sovereign but at most limited by him, the right of ownership was redefined in absolute terms, negating any idea of an overlord's reversionary interest.[2] Most forms of future interests, being of feudal origin, were radically abolished. In general, the codes of the civil-law world make it possible for several persons to own a piece of realty in common or jointly, and modern legislation in many civil law countries also authorizes horizontal division of buildings and separate ownership of apartments.[3] Subject to limited and carefully defined exceptions, however, the right of ownership cannot be split into successive estates, and of course not into "legal" and "equitable" interests.[4]

1. Rheinstein, Some Fundamental Differences in Real Property Ideas of the "Civil Law" and the Common Law Systems, 3 U.Chi.L.Rev. 624, 625 (1936).

2. Cf. French Civil Code, Article 544: "Ownership is the right to enjoy and dispose of things in the most absolute manner, provided they are not used in a way prohibited by law or regulations."

Article 545: "No one can be compelled to give up his property, except for public use and against a just compensation payable in advance."

3. See, e.g., the reference to the German Law of 1951, supra p. 536. For comparative discussions of the subject, which is of tremendous practical importance in today's urbanized world, see 1 A. Ferrer and K. Stecher, Law of Condominium 14–127 (1967); A. N. Yiannopoulos, Property 295–298 (Vol. 2 of Louisiana Civil Law Treatise, 2d ed. 1980); Leyser, The Ownership of Flats—A Comparative Study, 7 Int. & Comp.L.Q. 31 (1958).

It is interesting to note that the first American jurisdiction which passed legislation authorizing "condominium" ownership of apartments was Puerto Rico. How this civilian institution spread from Puerto Rico to most of the States, is interestingly explained by W. K. Kerr, Condominium—Statutory Implementation, 38 St. John's L.Rev. 1 (1963). See also C. J. Berger, Condominium: Shelter on a Statutory Foundation, 63 Colum.L.Rev. 987 (1963).

4. Under the heading of "usufruct", most civil-law systems make it possible, by inter vivos transaction or by testament, to create an interest in rem which is limited in time. See A. N. Yiannopoulos, Usufruct: General Principles—Louisiana and Comparative Law, 27 La.L.Rev. 369 (1967); id., Rights of the Usufructuary: Louisiana and Comparative Law, 27 La.L.Rev. 668 (1967); J. H. Merryman, Ownership and Estate (Variations on a Theme by Lawson), 48 Tul.L.Rev. 916, 930–32 (1974). The practical significance of this institution varies from country to country, partly as a

All other rights in rem (i.e., rights other than full ownership) are thought of as mere restrictions or encumbrances upon the title of the owner. In many civil-law countries, the principle of the so-called *numerus clausus* of rights in rem has been adopted. This means that the code contains an exhaustive catalogue of permissible restrictions and encumbrances and that other rights in rem cannot validly be created.[4a] Hypothecas (roughly equivalent to mortgages) and servitudes (similar to easements) usually are the most important of the rights so catalogued.[5]

The resulting simplicity of the substantive law of real property greatly contributes to the speed and security of land transactions. In some civil-law countries, notably in Germany, Switzerland and Austria, the marketability of real property is further enhanced by a highly efficient registration system.[6] The materials which follow deal with some aspects of that system.

GERMAN CIVIL CODE

Sec. 873. For any transfer [meaning transfer by transaction inter vivos] of title to land, for the creation of any right in rem encumbering the owner's title, and also for transferring or encumbering such a right in rem, it is necessary, except as otherwise provided by law, that the proper parties agree on the change to be effected, and that the same be registered in the land register.

Sec. 891. If in the land register a right has been registered in the name of a person, it is presumed that the right exists and belongs to such person. [This presumption is rebuttable.]

If a registered right has been canceled in the land register, it is presumed that the right does not exist. [This presumption is rebuttable.]

Sec. 892. For the benefit of a person who by a jural act [i.e., his own jural act, as distinguished from an acquisition by inheritance or by

result of differences in tax laws. In some countries, usufruct arrangements are frequent, while in other civil-law systems the elaborate code provisions dealing with usufruct are virtually a dead letter.

Apart from the usufruct device, it is possible in some (but not all) civil-law countries to create certain forms of future interests in a decedent's entire estate (as distinguished from future interests in individual pieces of property). See Merryman, id. at 932–34; Rheinstein, supra n. 1. For a case in which an American court had to deal with such a civil-law-type future interest, see Hedwig Zietz, 34 T.C. 351 (1961), discussed by O. C. Sommerich and B. Busch, The German First Heir: Owner or Life Tenant?, 11 Am.J.Comp.L. 92 (1962).

4a. For in-depth analysis, see B. Rudden, Economic Theory v. Property Law:

The *Numerus Clausus* Problem, in J. Eekelaar & J. Bell, Eds., Oxford Essays in Jurisprudence 239 (Third Series, 1987).

5. For the catalogue of rights in rem permitted by German law, see 1 Cohn, Manual of German Law 206 (2d ed. 1968). Leases are not mentioned in the catalogue. In Germany, as in the majority of civil-law countries, a lease constitutes a mere contract, and as a rule does not create rights in rem.

6. For a detailed comparative discussion of land registration systems in continental countries (with emphasis on the law of Denmark) see the second volume of Kruse, The Right of Property, transl. by David Philipp (1953).

operation of law] acquires an in rem right with respect to a parcel of land, or an in rem right with respect to such right, the entries in the land register are deemed to be correct, unless an objection against the correctness [of a particular entry] has been registered, or unless the incorrectness [of the entry] is known to the acquirer. If the [registered] holder of a right registered in the land register is subject to a restriction of his power to dispose of such right, and if such restriction exists for the benefit of a particular person,[a] the restriction is not effective as against the acquirer unless it appears in the land register or is known to the acquirer. . . .

SWISS CIVIL CODE

Art. 656. For the acquisition of title to immovable property, an entry [of the transfer] in the land register is necessary.[b]

When, however, title is acquired by . . . inheritance, expropriation, execution or judicial decree, the purchaser becomes the owner already before he is registered as such; but he can dispose of the property only when the registration has occurred.

Art. 973. Whoever in good faith has relied upon an entry in the land register, and thereby acquired property or other real rights, is to be protected in such acquisition.[c]

E. J. COHN (ASSISTED BY W. ZDZIEBLO): MANUAL OF GERMAN LAW *
2nd ed. 1968, Vol. 1, pp. 186–89.

Dispositions regarding immovable property are valid only if the effect which the disposition purports to have is noted in the land register (*Grundbuch*) either by way of an entry or by a cancellation of an existing entry. In addition to the entry or cancellation the parties must conclude an agreement to the effect that the disposition is to come into force. This agreement may be replaced by some other fact such as, e.g., a judgment of a court of law, prescription etc.

a. *Example:* During bankruptcy, the bankrupt is restricted in his power to dispose of assets. This restriction exists "for the benefit" of a particular person, to wit, the trustee in bankruptcy. Suppose X, the owner of Blackacre, goes into bankruptcy. Thereafter, but before the fact of bankruptcy is registered in the land register, X sells and transfers Blackacre to bona fide purchaser Y. Pursuant to the second sentence of § 892 quoted in the text, supra, Y acquires good title.

b. . . . tapu sicilinde kayit şarttir (Turkish Civil Code, sec. 633). Did that make sense in Turkey in 1926, and does it now? (Tapu sicili = land register; there was none in 1926.)

c. The careful reader will have noticed that these two articles of the Swiss Code in substance lay down the same rules as are contained in §§ 873 and 892 of the German Code, supra. But note the striking difference in style!

* Reprinted by permission of The British Institute of International and Comparative Law.

No entry is required where rights are transferred by law as, e.g., in case of succession.

> *Example:* A, the owner of Redacre, dies. B is his successor. In this case B becomes owner of Redacre at the time of A's death, even though this has not been entered in the *Grundbuch*. The contents of the *Grundbuch* have therefore become inaccurate and B may apply for a correction.

Only dispositions, i.e., the creation, transfer, encumbrance and cancellation of absolute rights in respect of immovable property, require registration and are capable of it. Contractual rights cannot and must not be registered.[d]

> *Example:* (*a*) A sells Redacre to B. This is merely a contract. As such it cannot be registered.
>
> (*b*) A complies with his obligations under the contract of sale and transfers Redacre to B. This can and must be registered. Without registration the transfer is not valid. /

The *Grundbuch* is not a register of deeds. It is a register of titles showing the legal situation of the immovable property to which it refers. . . .

If a right has been registered in the *Grundbuch* in the name of any person, it is presumed that the right exists and belongs to that person. Similarly if a right registered in the *Grundbuch* has been cancelled, it is presumed that the right does not exist (see section 891 *BGB*). These presumptions are rebuttable.

> *Example:* If A, who is registered as owner of Redacre in the *Grundbuch*, sues B, the possessor of Redacre, in order to obtain a judgment of eviction, he need not prove that he is the owner, but B may prove that A is not the owner.

In favour of a person who acquires a right in respect of immovable property by way of a transaction *inter vivos*, the entries in the *Grundbuch* are deemed to be correct, unless the transferee knows of their incorrectness. Sec. 892 *BGB*. This is often referred to as the rule of public faith (*öffentlicher Glaube*) of the *Grundbuch*. It should, however, be noted that it does not require any reliance on the part of the transferee upon the contents of the *Grundbuch*. The transferee is protected in any case in which he did not positively know that the contents of the *Grundbuch* were incorrect. It does not matter whether his ignorance was due to lack of care. It does not even matter whether he ever consulted the *Grundbuch*. Even if he did not know the actual contents of the *Grundbuch* the latter are treated as if they were correct.

> *Example:* A, who is registered as owner of Redacre sells and transfers Redacre to B who is not aware of the fact that C is the true owner of Redacre, A having been registered by a

---

d. It should be noted, however, that a *Vormerkung* (preliminary notation) can be registered for the purpose of securing the future performance of a registree's promise to grant, transfer, alter or cancel a registrable right. See 1 Cohn, id. at 198.

clerical mistake as owner of Redacre, instead of as owner of Slumhouse, which adjoins Redacre. B acquires the ownership of Redacre in consequence of the transfer. C loses it and has only a claim against A on the ground of delict or unjust enrichment, sections 892, 823(1), 816 *BGB*, or against the official at the land register office or the state employing him for damages. . .

ILLUSTRATIONS

(1) *A*, the registered owner of Greenacre, executed a notarial agreement with *B* by which Greenacre was to be sold and transferred to *B*. The notary before whom this agreement was made, normally would see to it that without delay *B* will be registered as the new owner. In the instant case, however, one of the parties to the notarial agreement, being unable to appear in person before the notary, was represented by an attorney-in-fact, and the latter's power of attorney had not been executed in proper form; therefore, before submitting the documents for registration, the notary had to wait for a properly executed power of attorney. In the meantime, while the registration of the transfer to *B* is thus delayed, *A* is approached by *C* who offers to purchase Greenacre from *A*. The facts of the pending transaction between *A* and *B* are known to *C*; but *C*, who is anxious to acquire Greenacre and also has a grudge against *B*, by the offer of a higher price and of immediate cash payment persuades *A* to "forget about *B*". In order to carry out their scheme, *A* and *C* go to a different notary (i.e., a notary other than the one who recorded the transaction between *A* and *B*) and tell him that *A* wishes to sell and transfer Greenacre to *C*. The notary routinely checks the register and finds that *A* is registered as the owner; the register, at this point, does not indicate anything concerning the transaction between *A* and *B*. Thus the notary will not hesitate to record the contract between *A* and *C* and the transfer from *A* to *C*. These documents then are promptly submitted to the registration office, and *C* is registered as the new owner.

What are *B's* rights and remedies under German law?

At first blush, *B* appears to be in a difficult position. The plain language of § 873 of the German Civil Code indicates that *C*, since he was the first to obtain registration, obtained good title to Greenacre, regardless of whether he acted in good or bad faith. Thus, on the face of the Code provision, one might conclude that *B* has lost his chance of acquiring Greenacre, and that he is relegated to an action seeking to recover damages for breach of contract from *A* (who may be judgment-proof, if he has managed quickly to dispose of the cash payment received from *C*).

A German court, however, would be able to reach a more equitable result by resorting to one of the "general clauses" of the Civil Code. Sec. 826 of that Code provides that

"One who intentionally damages another in a manner which is contra bonos mores, is liable to the other for restoration of the damage thus caused."

A German court probably would have no difficulty in finding that C as well as A is liable under this section;[1] but there remains the question whether B can recover the property itself, as distinguished from money damages. Sec. 826 appears in that part of the Code which deals with torts, and a lawyer brought up in the common law might think that it permits only the recovery of money damages. A reader familiar with the earlier parts of this book, however, will recall another code provision which must be considered at this point: the restitution-in-kind rule embodied in § 249. As the reader knows, that section (which appears in the first part of the Second Book and thus deals with all "obligations", whether based on contract, quasi-contract or tort) provides as follows:

> "He who is liable in damages, has to bring about the condition which would exist if the circumstances making him liable had not occurred. If the liability exists for injury to a person or damage to tangible property, then the obligee [at his election] may demand, instead of restitution in kind, the sum of money necessary to effect such restitution."

Specific performance

Under this provision it is possible for B, in a tort action, to obtain a judgment against C for the recovery of Greenacre.[2] The result thus reached derives additional strength from the doctrine of abuse of rights (see infra pp. 740 ff.).

It is interesting to compare the German treatment of this rather common problem with our own approach. The common-law rule gave priority to the first transferee, regardless of the good or bad faith of the later transferee.[3] This rule proved to be a serious obstacle to real estate transactions, because no purchaser could ever be quite sure that his vendor had not executed an effective prior conveyance. To overcome this defect of the law, a recording system was necessary, and such a system could be introduced only by legislation. In England and in some of the American colonies, recording statutes were enacted at an early date. Today, recording or registration acts exist in virtually all common-law jurisdictions. In the United States, the predominant type of recording statute, exemplified by § 291 of the New York Real Property Law, is the so-called "notice-race-statute".[4] Under such a statute, the later transferee prevails if he is the first to have his purchase duly recorded, and if he has acquired his interest in good faith and for a valuable consideration.

1st recorded not 1st purchaser

Contrast this with the German system. Under that system, the basic rule is that among multiple transferees the one first registered will prevail.[5] In other words, the German rule is the exact opposite of the common-law rule. But just as the common-law rule had to be altered in favor of a subsequent *bona fide* transferee who is the first to record, the seemingly unqualified command of § 873 of the German Civil Code has to be modified so as to withhold the benefits of the

---

1. See Palandt, Bürgerliches Gesetzbuch, § 826, Anno. 8 q (45th ed., 1986).

2. See Decision of the Reichsgericht of Dec. 9, 1905, RGZ 62, 137; Kommentar von Reichsgerichtsräten und Bundesrichtern zum Bürgerlichen Gesetzbuch, Sec. 873, Anno. 105 (1959).

3. See Powell on Real Property, Vol. 6A, ¶912 (1979 Revision by P. J. Rohan).

4. See id. at § 913.

5. In the United States, a similar result is reached in the very few states having a "race-type" recording statute. See ibid.

section from a later transferee who becomes the first to be registered but who has acted *in bad faith*.

This is a fine example of the phenomenon of convergence so often observed in comparative law. Although the starting points of the two systems—i.e. of the common-law system, on the one hand, and the system of the German and German-inspired codes, on the other—were diametrically opposed to each other, rather similar solutions have emerged in the end. Today it seems to be the law, both under an American recording statute of the predominant type and under the German and German-influenced codes, that in cases of multiple transfers the transferee first recorded or registered as a rule will prevail, provided he did not act with knowledge of a prior (though as yet unrecorded or unregistered) transfer.

Thus, by a process of convergence, a large area of agreement among seemingly diverse legal systems has come into existence. Yet, the agreement is not complete. The remaining differences in the starting point or in theory are apt to make themselves felt on occasion, especially in somewhat exceptional fact situations, such as that presented in the next Illustration.

(2) In proper notarial form, X (the registered owner) has sold and deeded Redacre first to Y, a purchaser for value, and later to Z. The latter is a donee, i.e., he has neither promised nor paid value; but he does not know, and has no reason to know of the previous transaction between X and Y. If in this case Z is the one who first obtains recordation or registration, he will acquire title and prevail over Y under § 873 of the German Civil Code; Y will be relegated to an action for damages against X, and will have no cause of action against Z, who acted in perfectly good faith and whose conduct, consequently, was not tortious.[6] Under most of the American recording statutes, on the other hand, it would seem that Y prevails over Z in this case, because Z is not a purchaser for value.[7] In such a situation, Z is not protected by the statute, and Y's common-law priority thus becomes decisive under our law.

(3) A, the registered owner of Blackacre, is judicially declared incompetent because of insanity. Without the consent of his committee, he sells and transfers Blackacre to B. As A succeeds in concealing his incompetency from B, from the officiating notary and from the land register official, the transaction is registered, and B is entered as the new owner. Upon discovering the transaction, A's committee sues B for retransfer of the property to A.

Under German law, B loses. If A had been declared bankrupt, his power to dispose of Blackacre would have become restricted, and within the meaning of § 892 such restriction would have existed "for the benefit" of a particular person, i.e., the trustee in bankruptcy. Such a limitation is registrable, and in the absence of an appropriate entry in

---

6. A German lawyer representing Y would examine the question whether his client might have a cause of action against Z on the theory of unjust enrichment (Civil Code §§ 812 ff., especially 816, 822); but since X, from whom Z acquired his title, at the time of the transfer to Z was not only registered as owner, but actually *was the owner*, the theory of unjust enrichment probably would be no more successful than the tort theory.

7. The term "purchaser" implies this requirement in our law. See Powell, supra n. 3, at ¶915. Moreover, some statutes, such as McKinney's N.Y. Real Property Law § 291, contain express language spelling out the requirement.

the register, *B* would be protected in his bona fide belief that *A* is not bankrupt. But lack of capacity due to incompetency is a different matter; it need not, and indeed cannot, be registered in the land register,[8] because a person's lack of capacity is not a restriction (upon his power of disposal) which exists "for the benefit of a particular person." Therefore, Sec. 892 does not apply by its terms. It is true that one who relies on an entry in the Grundbuch, or the lack of an entry therein, is protected by the principle of "public faith"; but this does not apply to non-registrable matters such as lack of capacity.

(4) Same facts as above; but before being sued by *A*'s committee, *B* sells and transfers Blackacre to *C*. *A*'s committee now sues *C*.

C wins. He acquired the property from a person who, though not the owner, was registered as such. Therefore, *A* has lost his title to *C*, unless *A*'s committee can prove that *C* actually knew of *B*'s lack of title.

C would be equally protected if the transfer from *A* to *B* (or any previous transfer of the same property) had suffered from any other kind of defect. It follows that *C*, before purchasing Blackacre, did not have to search the title back to Charlemagne or Friedrich Barbarossa; all he or his legal adviser had to do was to inspect the land register—a task which, except in unusually complicated cases, will not take more than five or ten minutes of an experienced person's time.[9]

C has not only saved time; but his title, also, is much more secure than under a system which subjects his rights to virtually undiscoverable hazards, such as the title of an adverse possessor, or the many types of conditions, limitations, defects and equities that may lurk somewhere in the chain of deeds upon which his own title depends.[10]

(5) In a case decided by the West German Supreme Court on July 11, 1952, BGHZ 7, 64, the facts were as follows: Plaintiff *P* was the owner, and registered as the owner, of a stately villa in Berlin. At the end of April, 1945, Berlin was conquered by the Russian army, and a Russian colonel by the name of *S* became military commandant of the part of the city where the villa was situated. In June, 1945, *S* decided to donate the villa to Mrs. *K*, a

---

8. See F. Baur, Sachenrecht, § 15 (13th ed. 1985). The only interests and limitations which are permanently registrable are the following: (a) the title of the owner or owners; (b) any rights of other persons (within the catalogue established by the Code) which encumber or restrict the owner's title, especially mortgages and servitudes; (c) transfers of, or encumbrances upon, the rights listed under (b), such as an assignment or pledge of a mortgage; and (d) restrictions upon the power of alienation of a person who has a right registered pursuant to (a), (b) or (c), provided that the restriction operates "for the benefit of a particular person."

9. Tax liens and other encumbrances created by public law are not registrable under the German system. Such liens and encumbrances, therefore, are not covered by § 892, and can be asserted even against a purchaser who had no knowledge of their existence. The notary recording the transaction, however, is under a duty to warn the purchaser of the possible existence of tax liens and the like; and since the public agencies and authorities who conceivably might be the lienees of such liens, are known and not too numerous, the purchaser or his attorney usually can make the necessary inquiries within a short time, even if he is not satisfied with the receipts or other documents submitted to him by the vendor. Moreover, in practice the problem often is solved by an escrow arrangement; the notary, serving as escrow agent, will hold a certain part of the purchase price and pay it over to the vendor only after he has convinced himself that certain tax liens or other public-law encumbrances are non-existent or have been removed.

10. E.g., forgeries, matters of heirship, reversionary interests, marriage and divorce, infancy, insanity, etc.

local resident who had no connection with *P*, but presumably had managed to endear herself to *S*. There was no sale or transfer from *P* to Mrs. *K*; but *S* and Mrs. *K* "persuaded" the German mayor to issue an official document certifying that *S* had "donated" the villa to Mrs. *K*. Through an attorney, Mrs. *K* submitted this document to the officials in charge of the land register, and asked to be registered as the new owner. As the document on its face was most irregular, the officials at first hesitated to register the transfer of title from *P* to Mrs. *K*; but they were told that unless such transfer were registered within 24 hours, they would be summarily executed or sent to Siberia. Under the circumstances then prevailing in Berlin, the credibility of this threat could not reasonably be doubted, and the officials—with the blessing of their superiors, who had been hurriedly consulted—registered Mrs. *K* as owner. In November, 1945, Mrs. *K* by notarial document sold and transferred the villa to defendant *D*, who paid a substantial price, and on Dec. 1, 1945, *D* was registered as owner.

Subsequently, *P* brought an action against *D* for the recovery of the villa. As *P* was unable to offer any evidence of bad faith on the part of *D*, the latter had to be treated as a bona fide purchaser. Pointing this out, and applying § 892 of the Civil Code, the court of first instance dismissed *P*'s action. The intermediate appellate court and the Supreme Court, however, held in favor of *P*. The reasoning of the highest court can be summarized as follows: As a matter of international law as well as German law, it is clear that Mrs. *K* never acquired title. Nevertheless, since *D* was not shown to have had any knowledge of Mrs. *K*'s lack of title, the plain language of § 892 would mandate a decision in *D*'s favor were it not for the unprecedented circumstances under which Mrs. *K* became registered as owner. The registration system is a facility organized and operated by the State. Ordinarily every entry in the land register is an official act, and it is this official quality of the entry upon which its "public faith"—ordained by § 892— is necessarily based. An entry, however, that has been brought about by physical threats against the officials in charge of the register, cannot be recognized as an official act.[11] Thus the essential reason for giving the entry its normal effect, as provided in § 892, is lacking here.

The German Supreme Court probably was right in feeling that there is a limit beyond which the principle of the register's "public faith" should not be carried, and that this limit is reached when under the impact of war-connected events the very foundation of the registration system—the independent power and responsibility of the officials in charge—has broken down. It is important to note, however, that the fact situation which gave rise to this decision was most extraordinary and indeed unique in the annals of the German land registration system. On the whole, it must be said that in spite of repeated political and economic upheavals that system has operated smoothly and efficiently since the beginning of the present century.

---

11. In this context, the court referred to the elaborate body of principles which has been developed by German scholars and administrative courts concerning "*fehlerhafte Staatsakte*" (defective official acts). Such acts may be either "voidable", i.e. susceptible of being set aside through appeals or other regular remedies, or absolutely void. In the principal case, the entry in the land register concerning the transfer to Mrs. *K* was held to be void.

NOTE

As the preceding Illustrations have shown, the proper working of a German-style land registration system depends on the competence and incorruptibility of the notaries and registrars who operate the system.

Little imagination is required to conjure up fact situations involving the following elements: (a) Goldacre is owned by X, and X is properly registered as owner. (b) Y, a crook, in some way—due to negligence or corruption on the part of notary or registrar—manages to have a transfer of Goldacre from X to Y registered in the land register. (c) This transfer was never consented to by X; indeed until much later X knows nothing of the whole transaction, which has been brought about by criminal methods (e.g., by forging X's signature, or by a co-conspirator of Y impersonating X). (d) As soon as he is registered as owner, Y sells and transfers Goldacre to Z, and absconds with the proceeds. Z is a bona fide purchaser, i.e., a person whose bad faith cannot be proved. In a situation like this, it is clear that under a provision such as § 892 of the German Civil Code poor X has lost Goldacre, i.e., his title to that property.

In Germany, where notaries and land register officials are apt to be highly competent and incorruptible, situations of this kind arise infrequently. When they do arise, it is possible for the victim (as the reader knows) to invoke the State's liability for negligent or intentional wrongdoing of its officials,[1] or to recover from the notary who always carries liability insurance.

It goes without saying, however, that it may be dangerous to export the German land registration system to a country—e.g., a developing country—where competence and incorruptibility of notaries and registrars are not as assured as in Germany. If the principle of "public faith" is applied in such a country, large numbers of owners might lose their properties as the result of crooked machinations. In order to avoid these dire consequences, the courts in such a country perhaps will modify the system, e.g., by holding that a purchaser who fails carefully to examine the vendor's whole chain of title, is not acting in good faith.[2] Such a holding, however, although it may protect innocent victims of corrupt schemes, destroys the efficiency of the system as a cheap and expeditious mechanism for land transfers.[3]

---

1. Pursuant to constitutional and statutory provisions with which the reader is familiar, the State is liable for the registrar's negligence. Insofar as notaries are concerned, a specific enactment (§ 19 of the Bundesnotarordnung) provides, by way of an exception to the general rule of state liability for the wrongdoing of officials, that the notary himself must respond for his torts, and that there is no state liability. From the standpoint of the victim, however, this does not make too much difference; in effect he can still sue a "deep pocket", because the notary's liability is always covered by insurance.

2. Apparently, this is what has happened in Mexico. See the exceedingly interesting article by B. Kozolchyk, The Mexican Land Registry: A Critical Evaluation, 12 Ariz.L.Rev. 308 (1970), where the Mexican case law is analyzed.

3. See ibid.

COMPARISON WITH OUR LAW—SOME
QUESTIONS OF POLICY [4]

Many common-law jurisdictions have adopted the so-called Torrens system of registration of title, as distinguished from mere recordation of muniments of title. Although historically independent of the continental system, the Torrens method is similar in its practical effect.[5] In the United States, it has been adopted in a minority of jurisdictions; but even in those jurisdictions it is generally optional with the owner whether he wishes to register his title. It seems that, except in a few communities, registration has been sought for only a small fraction of all titles.[6]

The question whether title registration should be made compulsory, as it is in Germany and Switzerland, is highly controversial in the United States. Up to now the proponents of compulsory registration have been beaten in every state; but the controversy is not yet settled. The following questions, therefore, are not wholly academic:

Do we subscribe to the basic policy considerations which underlie the German and Swiss provisions quoted above? Do the tendencies of the modern welfare state, especially in matters of urban development, make the unimpeded marketability of real estate less important, or more important, as compared to the days of 19th century laissez faire?

Does recording of deeds, in combination with title insurance, afford the purchaser or mortgagee the same degree of protection which he enjoys in Germany or Switzerland, or under the Torrens system?

Does the necessity of title search and title insurance slow down transfers, and add to their cost? On the other hand, how expensive is the initial setting up of a registration system? [7]

4. For a more extended discussion of some of the questions raised in this Note, and for ample references, see 6A Powell on Real Property ¶¶919–23 (1979 Revision by P. J. Rohan). For comparative treatments see the monograph by K. von Metzler, Das anglo-amerikanische Grundbuchwesen (1966) and the article by Rheinstein, Some Fundamental Differences in Real Property Ideas of the "Civil Law" and the Common Law Systems, 3 U.Chi.L.Rev. 624, 633–35 (1936).

5. For a brief description of the operation of the Torrens system, see United States v. Ryan, 124 F.Supp. 1 (D.C.D.Minn., 3rd Div., 1954). For more extensive treatment, see B. C. Schick & I. H. Plotkin, Torrens in the United States (1978).

With respect to the underlying theory, American registration statutes differ from the German system. Under our statutes, unregistered interests are eliminated by the combined operation of the doctrines of "jurisdiction in rem" and "res judicata". Therefore, a judicial proceeding is indispensable; but upon successful completion of the proceeding the title of the first registered owner (and not only that of bona fide transferees purchasing from him) becomes indefeasible. The German system, on the other hand, is based on the principle of protecting the bona fide purchaser; under that system, an indefeasible title is acquired, not by the first person to be registered as owner, but only by his first bona fide transferee. The initial registration was effected in Germany by way of a simpler and less expensive judicial proceeding than under our registration statutes.

Concerning a third possible theory justifying the elimination of unrecorded interests (time limitation), see infra n. 9.

6. In England, on the other hand, there has been a "rapid expansion of registered title in post-war years." L. N. Brown, Book Review, 95 L.Q.Rev. 157, at 159 (1979). Common lands and village greens, too, have now been registered. See A. Samuels, Common Land and Rights of Common: How the Commons Registration Act 1965 has Worked Out, 49 Conv. & Prop. Lawyer 24 (1985).

7. A study conducted by an economist has shown that—even allowing for the cost of the initial registration procedure—a reg-

In Germany and Switzerland (and in Puerto Rico) the public servants in charge of the land register are judges or other well-qualified officials. In addition, most of the documents necessary for registration must be prepared by, or executed before, a highly trained Notary (see supra p. 18). Are continental United States institutions equally suitable for the efficient operation of a registration system?

Can a compulsory registration system work efficiently in a jurisdiction where the substantive law of real property is complex, and where the number of registrable transactions presumably would be swelled (as compared to Germany) by the inclusion of leases, at least of long-term leases?

The German system has been used, and occasionally abused, for fiscal and regulatory purposes. The system makes it easy to decree that certain transactions may not be registered unless payment of transfer taxes is proved, or unless some administrative permit is obtained and exhibited to the registrar. Can a system of recording deeds be used or abused in the same way?

The compulsory registration system has been adopted in some civilian code jurisdictions and in some common-law jurisdictions. It has been rejected or long delayed both in civil-law [8] and common-law jurisdictions. Thus, as usual in difficult matters, we do not deal with a simple civil-law—common-law dichotomy. What are the forces which bring about, or successfully oppose, the adoption of the system? Is it a question of weighing opposing arguments? Of initial expense vs. continuing social cost? Of rationality vs. tradition? Of title insurance companies and other vested interests vs. the one group which is rarely aided by lobbyists: the general public?

If as a matter of practical politics we must conclude that in this country a workable compulsory registration system is presently unobtainable, can we secure some of the benefits of such a system by other methods, such as Marketable Title Acts or similar attempts to use time limitations for the purpose of extinguishing old interests lurking in the chain of title? [9]

As between the sharply conflicting answers which have been given to each of these questions[10] the reader will have to make his own choice,

istration system is considerably less expensive, and thus less of a burden on real estate transfers, than our traditional recording system. See J. T. Janczyk, An Economic Analysis of the Land Title Systems for Transferring Real Property, 6 J. Legal Studies 213 (1977). See also D. Whitman, Home Transfer Costs: An Economic and Legal Analysis, 62 Geo.L.J. 1311 (1974). The Puerto Rican registration system, which follows the Spanish model, is painstakingly described by H. M. Brau del Toro, Apuntes para un curso sobre el estado del Derecho Inmobiliario Registral Puertorriqueño, bajo la Ley Hipotecaria de 1893, 48 Rev.Jur.U.P.R. 111–495 (1979).

8. The French system, reformed in 1955, in its essential features is more similar to an American recording statute than to the German Grundbuch. See 2 M. Ferid

& H. J. Sonnenberger, Das franzoesische Zivilrecht 599–600 (2d ed., 1986). For a comparison of the French and German systems see F. Sturm, Bringt die französische Bodenregisterreform eine Annäherung an das deutsche Grundbuchrecht?, in M. Ferid (Ed.), Festschrift für Hans G. Ficker 459 (1967).

9. For references see Powell, op. cit. supra n. 4, at ¶923; P. E. Basye, Clearing Land Titles §§ 171–189 (2d ed., 1970 and 1985 Supp.). The relevant constitutional issues are highlighted by Board of Education of Central School Dist. No. 1 v. Miles, 15 N.Y.2d 364, 259 N.Y.S.2d 129, 207 N.E.2d 181 (1965).

10. For references see the writings cited supra n. 4.

keeping in mind that technological advances in the storage and retrieval of data are rapidly adding a new dimension to the old controversies.[11]

(BB) THE PRINCIPLE OF PUBLICITY IN TRANSACTIONS
NOT RELATING TO LAND

INTRODUCTORY NOTE

One brought up in the common law, even if he favors the Torrens system, is apt to think of it purely in terms of the problem at hand, i.e., of improving the method by which real property is conveyed. To the civilian lawyer, whose tradition leads him to develop broader, more abstractly formulated propositions, the *Grundbuch* is merely one application of a pervasive principle: the *principle of publicity*.[1] The essence of this principle is that all rights and legal relations which may harm or trap an innocent purchaser, or otherwise interfere with the reasonable expectations of persons entering into ordinary every-day transactions, must be made public in some form recognizable to purchasers and other participants in such transactions. With respect to chattels, the principle leads to the postulate that ownership should be publicized by possession; the innocent purchaser may assume that the possessor is the owner, and if he purchases from the possessor, he will ordinarily acquire good title, even though it turns out that the possessor was a faithless bailee.[2]

There are, however, many types of rights and legal relations which cannot be adequately publicized by possession. In those instances, the principle of publicity usually leads to a requirement of registration in a public register. The land register is one example. Another type of register which is in use in some civil-law countries, is the register of matrimonial property rights, designed to publicize the restrictions upon the capacity and the power of alienation of married women, or of their husbands, due to community property or other matrimonial arrangements.[3]

In a typical civil-law country, one encounters a number of public registers thus devoted to the implementation of the principle of publicity.[4] For the businessman, the most important of these is the Register

---

11. Computerization of the Grundbuch, with terminals in the offices of notaries, banks and other institutions, has been effected or proposed in several countries, such as Austria and Sweden; but some privacy concerns have been raised. As to Germany, see H. Geiger, Rechtsfregen um das Computer-Grundbuch, 1974 JZ 250.

1. See, e.g., Weiser, Trusts on the Continent of Europe 9–14 (1936).

2. This is the rule in the majority of civil-law systems. Normally the bona fide purchaser is not protected, however, if the possessor turns out to be a thief who has acquired possession without the owner's consent. See infra pp. 818–819. Concerning the history of these rules see supra pp. 283–285.

3. See, e.g., Art. 248 of the Swiss Civil Code:

"The conditions as to property rights, based upon a marriage contract or judicial decree, as well as the juridical acts by the couple concerning the property contributed by the wife, or the common property, require for legal force as against third persons that they shall be entered upon the register of property rights and be published.

"Heirs of the deceased spouse shall not be considered third persons."

4. The reader may be surprised, however, to learn that a public register of non-possessory security interests in movable property—i.e., the kind of public record

of Commerce, already familiar to the reader (supra p. 593). The way in which it implements the principle of publicity, is exemplified by the code provisions which follow.[5]

GERMAN COMMERCIAL CODE

see problem 7 on pp 700

Sec. 5. Once a firm [a] is registered in the Register of Commerce, it is not permissible to deny, as against a party invoking the registration, that the business conducted by such firm is a commercial business.

. . .

see Note 1 pq 699

Sec. 15. If a fact which ought to be registered in the Register of Commerce,[b] is not registered and published, the person concerning whose affairs the fact should have been registered cannot avail himself of such fact as against a third party, unless such party was aware of the fact.

If the fact has been registered and published, such fact can be relied upon as against a third party. This rule [i.e., the rule stated in the preceding sentence] does not apply to transactions taking place

which Art. 9 of the UCC has so successfully established in our law—does *not yet* exist in civil-law countries. The result is that in some of those countries, such as Germany, one encounters unpublicized non-possessory security interests. These are hard to reconcile with the principle of publicity, and often constitute a trap for unwary creditors; but the German courts have recognized their validity. See N. Horn, H. Koetz & H. G. Leser (transl. by T. Weir), German Private and Commercial Law: An Introduction 185–88 (1982); 1 E. J. Cohn, Manual of German Law §§ 256 and 354 (2d ed., 1968). In other civil-law countries, legislators and courts have taken the opposite view: that in the absence of a register in which non-possessory security interests could be recorded, security interests in personal property as a rule cannot be created without delivery of possession.

Both of these conflicting approaches are widely recognized as inferior to the solution provided by Art. 9 of the UCC. In a number of civil-law countries, Art. 9 has been, and is being, carefully studied with a view to the eventual adoption of a similar solution.

5. Both in France and in Germany, the substance of these provisions has been on the books for a long time. As to a few details, however, both countries have amended those provisions in the recent past in order to comply with the compulsory disclosure requirements contained in the First Directive on Company Law

Harmonisation issued by the EEC Council of Ministers on March 9, 1968. The text of that Directive (in English) is reproduced in Stein, Hay & Waelbroeck, European Community Law and Institutions in Perspective 610 ff. (2d ed., 1976).

The code provisions which follow in the text, supra, reflect these recent amendments. It may be worth noting that the amendments, while unimportant in themselves, exemplify the (often indirect) ways in which Community law increasingly tends to infiltrate the legal systems, and to affect every-day legal practice, in EEC member countries.

a. German Commercial Code Sec. 17: "The firm of a merchant is the name under which he conducts his business and signs business documents. A merchant may sue and be sued under his firm name."

b. Among others, the following data must be registered: The legal form under which a business is conducted; all facts pertaining to its ownership; appointment and removal of agents exercising managerial functions, as well as limitations upon, and revocation of, their powers; in the case of a partnership, the names of the general partners, and the names and liability limits of limited partners; in the case of a corporation, the amount of its capital as well as appointment and removal of officers, and limitations upon, and revocation of, their powers.

within fifteen days after publication, if the third party proves that he neither knew nor reasonably should have known such fact. . . .

If a registrable fact has been incorrectly published, in that event a third party can avail himself of such fact as published, against the person concerning whose affairs the fact was to be registered, unless the third party was aware of the incorrectness. . . .

———

FRENCH DECREE CONCERNING THE REGISTER OF COMMERCE
DECREE NO. 84–406 OF MAY 30, 1984 [c]

Art. 64. Entry of a natural person into the Register creates the presumption that he has the quality [i.e., status] of a merchant. Nevertheless, this presumption is inoperative as against third [private] parties and governmental agencies who submit proof to the contrary. Third parties and administrative agencies cannot avail themselves of the presumption if they knew that the person registered was not a merchant.[d]

Art. 65. A person who is required to be registered and has not requested registration within fifteen days from the beginning of his commercial activity, cannot avail himself of [the advantages of] his quality of being a merchant until registration, neither with respect to third parties nor with respect to governmental agencies. Nevertheless, he may not invoke his failure to register for the purpose of avoiding responsibilities and obligations inherent in such quality. . . .

Art. 66. In pursuing his activity, the person required to be registered cannot, as against third parties or governmental agencies, avail himself of registrable facts and acts which have not been published in the Register; but such third parties and governmental agencies may nevertheless avail themselves of such facts and acts [against the person who failed to have them registered]. . . .[e]

c. The articles of the Decree which are set forth hereunder constitute a slightly modified version of provisions of the Decree No. 62–237 of March 23, 1967. The latter abrogated Articles 61–64 of the French Commercial Code. Observe that Art. 64 of the 1984 Decree deals solely with individuals (natural persons) rather than with juridical persons. However, entry of corporations and other juridical persons in the Register produces essentially the same effects as the entry of individuals. See J. P. LeGall, Droit Commercial, 64–65, 91 (10th ed., 1985).

d. Compare this with the even stricter rule of the German Commercial Code, § 5. See infra, Illustration (5).

e. Former Art. 64 of the Commercial Code contained an elaborate enumeration of the facts and acts covered by the provision quoted in the text. Among the facts and acts so covered were, inter alia, "The cessation or revocation of the powers of any person who has been authorized to enter into engagements on behalf of a merchant, a partnership, a corporation, or a public enterprise." In the present version of the relevant provisions, this enumeration has been omitted as unnecessary. There is no doubt, however, that the cessation or revocation of the powers of individuals authorized to act on behalf of a commercial firm continue to be treated as "acts or facts" required to be registered.

. . . . The provisions in the preceding paragraphs are applicable to facts and acts required to be registered [in the Register of Commerce], even if they have been made public pursuant to some other legal requirement of publicity. These provisions cannot be invoked by third persons and governmental agencies who had personal knowledge of the relevant facts and acts.

M not liable

ILLUSTRATIONS

Noted

M not liable

(1) M, who is a merchant and is registered as such, appoints X as general manager of his jewelry store and causes this appointment to be registered. On September 15, M fires X and revokes his authority. This latter fact is registered on September 28. On September 26, X purporting to act for M, purchases jewelry from S, the purchase price of $100,000 to be payable on October 1. S, who did not know that X had been fired, delivered the jewelry to X on September 26. X promptly absconded, taking the jewelry with him. On October 2, S sues M for $100,000. What result under German law? Under French law?[1]

pg 697

M liable

(2) Same facts, except that M is a corporation, and that X was appointed, and later removed, as a corporate officer. Same result?

(3) In 1960, A, B and C formed and registered a partnership, under the firm of A & Co. In 1972 C withdrew from the partnership, but his withdrawal was never registered. In April 1979, A & Co. (now consisting of A and B) bought, upon credit, merchandise from S at the agreed price of $25,000. In June 1979, A & Co. became insolvent. Shortly thereafter, S sued C for $25,000. What result in France? In Germany?[2]

(4) A is a merchant, but he is not registered. His business friend X buys merchandise priced at $75,000 from Y, upon credit; A *orally* promises Y that he (A) will satisfy X's obligation in case X should default. X defaults. Y sues A.

Y wins under French + German law — oral obligation of merchant binds

Y wins under German as well as French law. This result flows, not from the principle of publicity, but simply from the fact that A *is* a merchant. As we know, the oral guarantee of a merchant is enforceable in Germany and in France. See supra p. 589. The fact that A is not registered, may prevent him from enjoying the advantages of his status; but it does not protect him from the disadvantages. The latter point is explicitly spelled out in the French provisions, while in German law it is taken for granted.

(5) B, who operates as a theatrical manager, but who is not a merchant, upon the erroneous advice of his lawyer applied for registration in the Register of Commerce, and was registered as a merchant. His friend X, a television entertainer, hired Y, a famous star, for five appearances on X's show, Y's fee of $40,000 to be payable after the last appearance. B *orally* guaranteed X's obligation to pay Y's fee. Y duly

---

1. In comparing the French and German solutions with our own law, the reader should ask himself under what system it is more likely that disputed and possibly difficult issues of fact will arise.

2. Compare § 35 of the Uniform Partnership Act, discussed in J. A. Crane and A. R. Bromberg On Partnership, § 81 (1968), as well as §§ 36 and 37 of the English Partnership Act.

performed, but X defaulted. Y sues B for $40,000. What result under German law? Under French law?

 (6) B, the same person as in Illustration 5, has made a contract with P, and under the terms of that contract has forfeited a contractual penalty in the amount of $500,000. The actual damages suffered by P amount to $750, and B feels that the penalty is excessive. Would a German court have power to reduce the penalty? [3]

(7) X Bank agrees to loan $5,000,000 to Y Corp. (a New York corporation) and Z A.G. (a German corporation), upon a note on which Y and Z will be jointly and severally liable. Before consummating the transaction, the Bank naturally has to be convinced, by reliable documentary evidence, that the individuals who will sign the note on behalf of Y and Z, respectively, have power to bind the debtor corporations. How much trouble is it to produce such evidence (a) for Y, and (b) for Z? [4]

NOTE

In most civil-law countries it is required that a commercial enterprise be registered not only at its principal place of business, but also at every place where it maintains a branch. See, e.g., Sections 13 ff. of the German Commercial Code. In the case of a company doing business in several countries, this requirement often creates problems for the company's lawyers.

Suppose a company incorporated and having its principal place of business in country A seeks to do business in country B. The laws of the latter country are apt to require that the company observe certain formalities in order to "qualify" (to use our terminology) for the doing of business in B. If B is a civil-law country, this process of qualification normally will include registration in B's register of commerce. In cases where A also is a civil-law country, the facts to be registered in B (such as the valid existence and precise legal nature of the registree corporation) normally can be shown quite simply by submitting to the registrar in B a certified copy of the corporation's original registration in A. But if A is a country like the United States, where there is no commercial

---

3. As to the rules of German law concerning reduction of penalties, see supra p. 676. The penalty promised by B cannot be reduced. The wording of § 5 makes it clear that the merchant status of a registree is irrebuttable, and that (contrary to the rule prevailing in situations coming under § 15) it does not even make a difference whether P knew of the incorrectness of the registration. See Baumbach-Duden-Hopt, Handelsgesetzbuch, § 5, Anno. 1A (26th ed., 1985).

4. From the German viewpoint the question is interestingly discussed by K. Jacob-Steinorth, Die Vertretungsmacht bei den wichtigsten amerikanischen Handelsgesellschaften, 1958 Deutsche Notar-Zeitschrift 361. For further references see H. H. Schippel and H. Schippel, Lateinisches Notariat, 5 Juristen-Jahrbuch 78, 80 (1964/65).

The individuals purporting to represent Y Corp. will need stacks of documents, certified by the secretary of the corporation, in order to prove that they have been duly appointed and that they have the power to represent the corporation in the transaction at hand. If these documents raise the faintest doubt concerning an issue of law, the Bank probably will, in addition, require an opinion letter to be issued by a law firm. This, of course, adds to the costs of the transaction. It has been observed by experienced international practitioners that in this country the absence of a commercial register often creates a need for lawyers' opinion letters in situations where no such need would exist in a civil-law country. See K. H. Jander & R. Du Mesnil de Rochemont, Die Legal Opinion im Rechtsverkehr mit den USA, 6 Recht der Internationalen Wirtschaft 332, 333 (1976).

register, then the facts to be registered in B will have to be proved in other ways, and it will be more difficult to satisfy the official in charge of the register in B, with the result that the whole process of obtaining registration (and thus "qualifying") in B will require considerably more time and effort.[1]

OPINION OF THE GERMAN REICHSGERICHT IN THE MATTER OF NEUERGASTHOF G.M.B.H. ET AL., DEFENDANTS v. K., PLAINTIFF

2nd Civil Division, December 14, 1928, RGZ 123, 102.

[Reported ante, p. 615.]

OPINION OF THE SWISS FEDERAL COURT IN THE MATTER OF BOEHLER–BIERI, PLAINTIFF–APPELLANT v. BUCHER, DEFENDANT–RESPONDENT

March 9, 1912. BGE 38 II 103.

[Reported post, p. 775.]

FURTHER ILLUSTRATIONS: SOME PROBLEMS ARISING UNDER SECTION 15 OF THE GERMAN COMMERCIAL CODE

(1) A, a sole trader, sells and transfers his entire business to B; the transfer is completed on March 10, but is not registered until June 20. On May 25, C is injured by a truck belonging to B's (formerly A's) business. Is A liable to C?

A literal reading of § 15 might suggest an affirmative answer. But according to the view strongly prevailing among German courts and commentators, the correct answer is that A is not liable to C.[1] The reason is that even if C had had knowledge of the fact to be registered (i.e., the transfer from A to B), such knowledge could not possibly have had any influence upon his conduct which brought him into contact with the business now owned by B.[2]

In other words, the effect of § 15 is limited to business transactions, and only a person entering into a *business* transaction with the registree can invoke the protection which that section provides.

(2) A and B are general partners of a partnership doing business as "A & Co." They are registered as such. On February 20, they ask the registrar to register the fact that X has joined the partnership as its third general partner. By inadvertence, the official in charge registers

---

1. See E. C. Stiefel, "As They See Us": Typische Rechtsprobleme bei amerikanischen Investitionen in Deutschland, in Festschrift fuer Reimer Schmidt 237, at 243 (1976).

1. See RGZ 93, 238 (1918); G. Bandasch, Kommentar zum Handelsgesetzbuch, § 15, Anno. 1 (1973); 1 Gessler-Hefermehl-Hildebrand-Schröder, Handelsgesetzbuch, § 15, Anno. 13 (1973).

2. See K. Ballerstedt, Discussion of an Examination Case in Commercial Law, in 1965 JuS 272, at 277–78.

Y, and not X, as a new general partner, and this incorrect entry is made public. The mistake is not corrected until April 10.

(a) On March 16, Y, purporting to act on behalf of the partnership, sells merchandise to Z, who does not know that Y was registered by mistake. Is this transaction binding on the partnership, i.e., the actual partners?

An affirmative answer is suggested not only by the clear wording of the third paragraph of § 15, but also by the protective policy behind that provision.[3] The partnership, however, may have a claim for indemnification against the State, if the registrar can be shown to have acted negligently.[4]

(b) On March 29, the partnership (represented by A) borrows $200,000 from creditor C. If the partnership and its actual partners turn out to be unable to repay this loan, is Y liable for it?

The answer is No—unless Y either caused the mistake of the official or, after having learned of the mistaken entry and publication, failed to have it corrected within a reasonable time. The reason for this negative answer can be found in the language of the first paragraph of § 15. The estoppel which § 15 creates for the protection of innocent third parties, can be invoked only against "the person concerning whose affairs the fact should have been registered," i.e., only against the true owner or owners of the business.[5]

C. THE CODES AND THE IDEA OF JUSTICE: BONI MORES, BONA FIDES AND ABUS DES DROITS—NO SEPARATION OF LAW AND EQUITY

OPINION OF THE GERMAN REICHSGERICHT IN THE MATTER OF G., PLAINTIFF–APPELLANT v. F., DEFENDANT–RESPONDENT

3rd Civil Division, October 20, 1933, RGZ 142, 70.

[Plaintiff, an attorney, sues the defendant, his former client, upon a contract providing for contingent remuneration.[a]

Defendant was the lessee of a large hotel property in Berlin. The lease, entered into in 1928, provided for an annual rental of RM 240,000. During the ensuing depression defendant became unable to meet the stipulated rent payments, and around the beginning of 1931 he retained the plaintiff for the purpose of seeking a reduction of rent.

From the beginning of 1931 the defendant paid to his lessor only one half of the monthly rent installments, whereupon the lessor instituted four actions for the recovery of the balance of four rent installments. On the other hand, defendant, represented by the plaintiff, brought an action against the lessor for refund of alleged overpay-

---

3. See Gessler-Hefermehl-Hildebrand-Schröder, supra n. 1, at Anno. 26a.

4. Id., at Anno. 28.

5. Id., at Anno. 26a.

a. For background information concerning attorneys' fees in Germany and other civil-law countries, see supra pp. 352–365.

ments. All these actions were settled in December, 1931. This settlement reduced the annual rental payable by defendant to his lessor from RM 240,000 to RM 165,000.

Concerning plaintiff's fees, the parties entered into an agreement which under date of February 16, 1931 was confirmed by plaintiff as follows:

". . . in addition to my statutory fees you will pay to me ten percent (10%) of those amounts which for the duration of the lease you will save as compared to the originally stipulated rental. You will make these payments to me regardless of whether or not you obtain these benefits directly or indirectly through my activities . . . You will not enter into any settlement without my cooperation."

On the following day this agreement was supplemented by an additional letter agreement which provided that the ten percent should be reduced to five percent (5%) if it should become necessary for defendant to retain another attorney.

Under date of August 5, 1931, the parties entered into a new supplemental agreement which plaintiff confirmed by letter as follows:

"You have recognized that my claim for fees is justified on the basis of the agreement existing between us. You have contended, however, that prior to entering into the said agreement you did not realize what amounts would become payable thereunder. For this reason you have requested that the stipulated fee be reduced. We have agreed that my percentage participation . . . be reduced to five percent. You guarantee that I shall receive a minimum of RM 30,000 out of this participation. In all other respects our former agreement remains unchanged. We have expressly agreed that my participation extends over the whole duration of your tenancy."

Defendant concedes that through the settlement which he made with his lessor in December, 1931, he obtained considerable savings of rent, as compared with the previous terms of the lease. Plaintiff claims that his 5% share of these savings, for the period prior to the commencement of the action, amounts to RM 13,000. Plaintiff is suing for this amount plus interest. Defendant denies the validity of the said agreements. He claims that such participation of a lawyer in the benefits obtained by him for his client is not only professionally unethical but contra bonos mores and hence void.

The court of first instance granted the relief prayed for by the plaintiff. The intermediate Appellate Court reversed and dismissed the complaint. Plaintiff's further appeal to the Reichsgericht was unsuccessful.]

Reasons: . . . The contract sued upon is characterized by the feature that defendant did not promise a fixed sum payable in case of successful termination of the matter for which plaintiff was retained, but that plaintiff was to participate in the benefits which his activities were to procure for the defendant by way of legal action or settlement. Defendant promised to plaintiff a specified percentage of these benefits. Plaintiff himself calls this a "savings percentage". The stipulation of such a "savings percentage" is, however, contra bonos mores and hence void, especially if one considers the collateral terms of the agreement. The intermediate Appellate Court was rightly guided by the principles which this Division, in accordance with its prior decisions, had developed in the opinion reported in RGZ 115, 141. As is there pointed out, an attorney, being an organ of the administration of justice, may in his capacity as helper and adviser of his client not be guided by any considerations other than those dictated by the nature of the matter entrusted to him. For this purpose he must retain the necessary freedom as against his client. This position is jeopardized and deprecated if the attorney amalgamates the interest which he has in an adequate remuneration, with the interests of his client, by making his remuneration depend upon the success of the action. A lawyer who enters into such an agreement, violates the principles of professional ethics. Only exceptionally may a different conclusion be warranted by the special circumstances of the case.

This court realizes that legal writers have vigorously attacked the foregoing view, and that this view has not been followed by some of the intermediate Appellate Courts. Nevertheless, this view cannot be abandoned. . . . The unethical nature of an agreement by which a lawyer obtains a part of the product of his activities as his remuneration, can be denied only by those who think the individual lawyer should enjoy complete freedom with respect to the economic side of his professional life. But in view of the position which the legislature has conferred upon the legal profession, this is impossible. True, the lawyer, as distinguished from the public official, belongs to a free profession. Nevertheless he does not enjoy the freedom of a private individual whose economic activities are limited only by the general laws. The status of the lawyer is ordered by statute. Special privileges have been bestowed upon him. The legal profession has special importance for the administration of justice and for the public life of the nation. From all this it follows that every individual lawyer is subject to special duties. Section 28 of the Lawyers' Code summarizes these duties by providing that every lawyer is bound to use due diligence in the exercise of his profession and by his professional conduct to prove himself worthy of the respect which his profession requires. This diligence in the exercise of the profession, however, is no longer absolutely assured if the lawyer completely allies himself with the economic interests of his client by making the client promise him a part of the benefits which the client hopes to obtain through the work of the lawyer. In such event, the lawyer's own interest in the matter becomes so great that his legally imposed status as protector of the legal order becomes jeopardized. The lawyer who causes such jeopardy, will as a rule violate the canons of professional ethics.

[handwritten margin note: Why contingency fee not allowed]

The very case at hand demonstrates that these are not imaginary dangers, but that a lawyer who through a percentage agreement is strongly interested in the outcome of a matter entrusted to him, will more easily resort to improper methods than a lawyer not thus personally interested. While the settlement negotiations with the lessor of the hotel were pending, the defendant sought to obtain more favorable terms by painting his financial condition in the drabbest colors. Therefore, on November 12, 1931, he wrote a letter which was addressed to the plaintiff but which, as plaintiff knew, was meant to be forwarded to the adversary. In this letter defendant pointed out that for financial reasons he was not in a position to accept the offers of settlement previously made by the lessor. Plaintiff states in one of his briefs in the present action that this letter as originally drafted by defendant did not seem to him completely suitable for the purpose for which it was written. Therefore, plaintiff improved the letter, had it re-typed and had defendant approve the new version. Then he sent the letter to the attorney for the lessor, as if it were an original letter of the defendant. The plaintiff himself says concerning this incident . . . that it was intended by the use of that letter "to bluff the adversary". . . . That plaintiff's participation in these deceptive machinations of his client constitutes a grave violation of his professional duties, is too plain for argument. There is at least some ground for assuming that plaintiff acted that way only for the reason that he was to derive immediate personal benefits from a more favorable settlement. Of course, our conclusion that the fee arrangement between the parties was contra bonos mores, is not based upon the subsequent conduct of the plaintiff. Such conduct merely justifies the suspicion that because of the amalgamation of his own interests with those of his client the plaintiff was no longer able to live up to his professional duties. . . .

The views of this Court concerning the participation of an attorney in the economic products of his work are in complete agreement with the views of the National Honor Court for Attorneys [b]. . . .

The view opposing the strictness of this Court in matters of this kind is in the last analysis traceable to a different conception of the nature of the legal profession. This conception, which emphasizes the economic factors, does not sufficiently consider the public law character of the legal profession and the professional duties flowing therefrom. This philosophy was favored by certain general tendencies of recent years. Nevertheless, especially in view of the decisions of the National Honor Court for Attorneys, it cannot be said that that philosophy has ever gained controlling influence. To let this philosophy become victo-

---

b. At the time of the principal case, the National Honor Court for Attorneys was the court of last resort in disbarment and other disciplinary proceedings against attorneys. Under the present, somewhat modified system, such disciplinary matters are handled by a three-tiered hierarchy of honor courts. The court of first instance consists of members of the Bar, while the intermediate appellate court and the court of last resort (a special panel of the Bundesgerichtshof) are composed of professional judges and attorneys. For details see Bundesrechtsanwaltsordnung (Federal Law Concerning Attorneys) of August 1, 1959, as amended, §§ 92–161.

rious at this time, is entirely out of the question, since the national resurrection has generally re-established a more moral conception of law.[c] One of the characteristics of this conception of law is the emphasis upon duties rather than rights, especially as regards those who are incorporated into the public legal order. The legal sentiment of today more than of any other period commands us not to loosen, but on the contrary to maintain, the rules preventing the selfish exercise of the legal profession. . . .

Even the presently prevailing philosophy does not make it impossible that exceptionally, under special circumstances, an agreement of the said kind between an attorney and his client may not be considered unethical. The present case, however, does not belong to that exceptional category. On the contrary, the intermediate Appellate Court was correct in holding that the details of the arrangement made by the parties reveal particularly objectionable features.

In this connection the intermediate Appellate Court rightly emphasizes the length of the period for which the defendant promised to make payments to the plaintiff. . . . It is absolutely improper for an attorney to stipulate for such payments which his client is to make for an indefinite period, and at least for a period of almost ten years.

It is true that by the supplemental agreement of August 5, 1931, the plaintiff reduced his participation in the savings obtained by defendant from ten percent to five percent. For this concession, however, plaintiff received ample consideration in the form of a guaranteed minimum of RM 30,000. . . .

The agreements of the parties also contain other stipulations which the intermediate Appellate Court rightly considered as factors militating against the contentions of the plaintiff. Plaintiff was to be entitled to the stipulated remuneration regardless of whether and to what extent defendant's benefits were directly or indirectly caused by plaintiff's work . . . Furthermore, in case it should become necessary for the defendant to retain another lawyer in lieu of the plaintiff, plaintiff was to remain entitled to five percent of the savings. Settlements were not to be entered into without plaintiff's consent and cooperation.[d] Plaintiff believes that all these stipulations can be justified on the ground that their purpose was merely to secure the rightful claim for the so-called savings percentage; plaintiff says it was his purpose to prevent defendant from evading his obligations. It might be that

c. Note that this decision was rendered about eight months after the Nazis had come into power. Yet, the sentence in the text, supra, should not lead the reader to exaggerated conclusions as to the judges' espousal of Nazi ideology. The court, it should be remembered, in this decision reaffirms a view which it had consistently held during the days of Bismarck's Reich and the Weimar Republic—a view, in other words, that had nothing whatsoever to do with Nazism. The reference to "the national resurrection", while not exactly an indication of judicial fortitude, thus may have been mere lip service.

d. Note that this particular clause might render the agreement invalid in many jurisdictions in the United States. See F. B. MacKinnon, Contingent Fees for Legal Services 74–77 (1964); 14 Williston on Contracts § 1712 (3rd ed. by W. H. E. Jaeger, 1972).

plaintiff had this aim in mind. His argument overlooks, however, that the contingent fee arrangement as such was highly objectionable and that it became only more objectionable by security measures intended to tie up the client even more firmly. A creditor may be permitted to secure an *unobjectionable* claim in this manner. Where according to the standards of professional ethics and general morals the claim itself is objectionable, such security measures can only lead to even stronger condemnation . . .

In the above-mentioned decision of this Division, RGZ 115, at 143, certain conditions are stated under which the stipulation of a percentage fee would not violate the standards of professional ethics. It is there said:

> "If the facts were such that defendant *could not* have undertaken the payment of compensation in any other form, . . . then the contingent nature of the promise would not in itself constitute a violation of the lawyer's professional duties."

Appellant relies upon this statement and argues that the present case . . . is covered by the principles there stated. This is incorrect.

In the first place, the intermediate Appellate Court was right in holding that it was irrelevant whether the plaintiff, as he claims, originally demanded a contingent fee in a fixed amount, and that only upon request of the defendant he agreed to a percentage participation. An attorney is himself responsible for his professional honor, and he has to protect his honor particularly as against improper requests of his client. Plaintiff further argues that defendant refused to promise a straight extra-fee; that defendant sought to justify this refusal by pointing out that the current lease would ruin him unless the rentals were reduced, so that he would be unable to pay more than the statutory fee unless he were to obtain considerable relief through the activity of the plaintiff. In such a situation it may perhaps be possible to justify a fee in a fixed amount, contingent upon success; but it does not follow that a percentage participation is permissible. . . .

It is thus clear that in entering into said arrangement the plaintiff has disregarded his professional duties. But to be invalid pursuant to Section 138, Subdivision 1, of the Civil Code,[e] the agreement must be not only professionally unethical but also generally immoral. The intermediate Appellate Court has been correct in so holding, and has correctly analyzed the logical relation between a violation of professional honor and a violation of the precepts of morality. Not every violation of the former is at the same time a violation of the latter. . . .

. . . On the other hand, we decidedly reject the argument that fee arrangements between attorney and client should be subject only to the principles of professional ethics and should be taken out of the reach of Section 138 of the Civil Code. . . .

e. Quoted supra p. 569.

test [handwritten]
compare to 717 [handwritten]
x 726 [handwritten]

As in other cases, it is thus necessary in the instant case to examine whether the violation of professional honor, of which the plaintiff has been guilty, is so grave that persons whose views are just and equitable would consider it morally objectionable.[f] This question has been answered in the affirmative by the intermediate Appellate Court, and rightly so. The applicable standard cannot be based upon the philosophy of those persons who think only in economic terms and who have no understanding of the special legal status which the statute provides for attorneys. If this special status is taken into consideration, the conclusion is clear: in making the arrangement with the defendant, the plaintiff did not live up to the moral standard which an attorney should never relinquish. He pursued his personal advantage so unscrupulously that his conduct, far from being in accord with justice and equity, must be characterized as morally objectionable.

NOTES

(1) In 1944, subsequent to the principal case, an express provision outlawing all contingent fees was incorporated into a statute. See infra p. 860. But when the statute was re-enacted as Sec. 3 of the Federal Law Concerning Attorneys' Fees of July 26, 1957 (BGBl 1957 I 907), the provision expressly prohibiting contingent fees was omitted. The legislative intention behind this omission was to restore the law as it stood at the time of the principal case, i.e., to leave it again to the courts to derive a solution of the contingent fee problem from the broad principle of Sec. 138 of the Civil Code. In several more recent decisions the Bundesgerichtshof has accordingly re-established the rule—and the very limited exceptions—stated in the principal case.[1] The court thus has preserved the distinction between (a) percentage or *"quota litis"* agreements, which as a practical matter are always invalid, and (b) agreements providing for a *fixed amount* of compensation or extra-compensation payable in the event of success, which under exceptional circumstances may be upheld.[2]

(2) If the lawyer who has made an invalid contingent fee agreement, loses the case entrusted to him, he often cannot even recover the statutory fee. The German courts reached this result by way of the following reasoning: The client was justified in relying on the validity of the agreement, and presumably arranged his affairs accordingly. The lawyer, therefore, would violate the principles of *bona fides* (Civil Code Sec. 242, supra p. 575) by sending a bill for the statutory fee; the client, relying on the terms of the agreement, had no reason to expect such a bill.[3] The lawyer who has entered into an invalid contingent fee

---

f. The same phrase has been used by German courts innumerable times, in an attempt to define the kind of conduct which is contra bonos mores within the meaning of Secs. 138 and 826 of the Civil Code. This definitional point will be taken up infra, pp. 725–731.

1. See, e.g., Decisions of Dec. 15, 1960, BGHZ 34, 64, and of Feb. 28, 1963, 16 NJW 1147 (1963).

2. The same approach is reflected in §§ 40 and 41 of the Guidelines for the

Exercise of the Legal Profession, the German equivalent of the Canons of Ethics. See F. Schmitz, Anwaltliches Standesrecht, insbesondere die neuen Richtlinien für die Ausübung des Rechtsanwaltsberufs, 16 NJW 1284, 1288 (1963).

3. Bundesgerichtshof, Decision of Oct. 26, 1955, BGHZ 18, 340, reported also in 8 NJW 1921 (1955).

agreement, thus finds himself in an unenviable position. He is estopped from recovering any amount which is not due under the terms of the (invalid) agreement; and under no circumstances, even if he is entirely successful, will he recover more than the statutory fee.[4]

(3) The common law does not speak with a single voice concerning the question whether contingent fee agreements are lawful. In England, they are illegal.[5] In the United States, contingent fees have been disapproved, or severely restricted, in certain branches of law practice, such as divorce matters, lobbying activities, and criminal cases.[6] The courts, moreover, always have power to strike down a fee arrangement if it contains objectionable terms or if the fee is excessive.[7] In principle, however, "contingent fees are generally allowed in the United States because of their practical value in enabling a poor man with a meritorious cause of action to obtain competent counsel".[8] In some

But not England permits (92) some contingent fee arrangements

Noted → same idea of German court in case on p. 702

4. Does the common law permit a lawyer who has made an illegal fee agreement to recover in quantum meruit? See 14 Williston on Contracts § 1713 (3rd ed. by W. H. E. Jaeger, 1972). In Gonzalez Y Barredo v. Schenck, 428 F.2d 971 (2d Cir. 1970) the court read the New York authorities, and the authorities generally, as basically permitting quantum meruit recovery by a lawyer who has made a champertous retainer agreement; but the possibility is left open that in certain fact situations the result might be different, especially when the "vitiating element . . . goes to the essence of the service." This phrase comes from the opinion of Cardozo, Ch.J., in Matter of Gilman's Estate, 251 N.Y. 265, 272, 167 N.E. 437, 440 (1929).

5. See F. B. MacKinnon, Contingent Fees for Legal Services 38 (1964), where further references are given. But where an English court was asked to enjoin a tort victim from suing the tortfeasor in a U.S. court, the House of Lords held that the contingent nature of the compensation payable to the attorneys representing the victim in *the American court* was not a relevant factor in determining whether the injunction should be granted by the English court. Castanho v. Brown and Root (U.K.) Ltd., [1981] All. E.R. 143, 152. Generally, concerning the choice-of-law questions that arise in connection with the compensation of attorneys in transnational litigation, see Restatement Second, Conflict of Laws, § 196 (1971); A. Ehrenzweig, Conflict of Laws 532 (1962); see also the German case, BGHZ 22, 162, reproduced infra pp. 857–863.

6. In criminal cases defense counsel may not accept contingent compensation, mainly on the ground that legal services in criminal cases do not produce a *res* with which to pay the fee. ABA's Code of Professional Responsibility, Ethical Consideration 2–20. In the case of lawyers working for the prosecution, the reason for the rejection of contingent compensation is that they should seek justice rather than a "successful" outcome, and that they should not have a personal interest in the case.

Even in certain types of civil cases—especially those of quasi-criminal nature such as actions for the abatement of a public nuisance—the lawyer representing a governmental unit must be neutral and hence may not accept a contingent fee. See People ex rel. Clancy v. Superior Court (Ebel), Sup. Ct. of Cal., 218 Cal.Rptr. 24 (1985). For disapproved contingent fees in other branches of law practice, see MacKinnon, supra n. 5, at 45–53.

7. The judicial determination whether a given fee is excessive ordinarily is made in litigation between the parties to a particular fee agreement. But such determination may be made also in advance of individual litigation and in more general terms; a court having disciplinary power over attorneys may issue Rules indicating that contingent fees in excess of certain stated percentages will not be tolerated. Gair v. Peck, 6 N.Y.2d 97, 188 N.Y.S.2d 491, 160 N.E.2d 43 (5:2 decision) (1959); American Trial Lawyers Ass'n v. New Jersey Supreme Court, 66 N.J. 258, 330 A.2d 350 (1974). But cf. In the Matter of the Florida Bar, 349 So.2d 630 (Fla.1977).

8. Gair v. Peck, supra n. 7, 6 N.Y.2d at 103.

The argument based on the client's poverty becomes somewhat questionable in cases in which the client is wealthy enough to pay a non-contingent fee. See Comment, 20 Ohio State L.J. 329 (1959). For more general criticism of the contingent fee, duplicating some of the arguments used in the civil-law world, see K. M. Clermont & J. D. Currivan, Improving on the Contingent Fee, 63 Cornell L.Rev. 529 (1978). [Cont'd on next page]

states, the contingent fee tradition is further fortified by statute. Sec. 474 of the New York Judiciary Law, for instance, provides that "The compensation of an attorney or counselor for his services is governed by agreement, express or implied, which is not restrained by law, except that" the amount of the fee must be judicially approved where the client is an infant.[9]

OPINION OF THE SWISS FEDERAL COURT IN THE MATTER OF DR. HAASS, DEFENDANT–APPELLANT v. LEOPOLD WYLER, PLAINTIFF–RESPONDENT

1st Civil Division, July 3, 1915, BGE 41 II 474.

[Defendant's wife was interested in two estates, in both instances as one of several co-legatees. One of the other co-legatees, Gustav Reber, was managing both estates as fiduciary. Defendant, suspecting that Reber had been guilty of improper management, retained plaintiff, an attorney, requesting him to look after the interests of his (defendant's) wife in the matter. Plaintiff thereupon negotiated with Reber, and both sides seemed inclined in principle to accept a settlement by which Reber would buy out the shares of defendant's wife in both estates. There was, however, considerable bargaining concerning the purchase price to be paid by Reber. While this bargaining went on, plaintiff and defendant agreed in writing that, in lieu of statutory fees to which he was entitled as an attorney, the plaintiff should receive a brokerage commission if he succeeded in selling Mrs. Haass' share in the estates to Reber. The amount of the brokerage fee payable to plaintiff in that event was fixed at fifty percent (50%) of the excess of the purchase price over Fr. 300,000. Shortly after this agreement concerning a brokerage fee had been entered into between the parties, plaintiff succeeded in bringing about a settlement with Reber pursuant to which Reber was to purchase Mrs. Haass' share in the two estates for Fr. 409,000. Reber immediately paid Fr. 155,000 on account, and on the same day defendant paid Fr. 30,000 to plaintiff who issued a receipt "on account of brokerage commission." A few months later Reber paid the balance of Fr. 254,000. Plaintiff then demanded the balance of his brokerage commission in the amount of about Fr. 24,000, but defendant refused payment of this balance.

It is arguable, however, that regardless of the client's financial condition both he and the lawyer are best served by a system which recognizes the infinite variety of clients' interests and of lawyers' services by leaving them free, within reasonable limits, contractually to determine the conditions and the amount of the fee. In any event, whether persuaded by this or by other arguments, all American jurisdictions are now unanimous in recognizing that as a rule a contingent fee arrangement is valid. Writing in 1964, MacKin-non (supra n. 5, at 39) stated that "In this country only Maine retains a complete prohibition against contingent fees". But a year later the Maine statute containing the prohibition (17 Rev.Stat.Ann. § 801) was amended so as to bring the law of Maine into line with the other American jurisdictions.

9. For a multi-national comparative survey concerning the propriety of contingent fees, see W. Kalsbach, Les barreaux dans le monde 156 (1959).

Plaintiff thereupon sued for Fr. 24,000 plus interest. By way of counterclaim defendant demanded refund of the Fr. 30,000 paid on account, on the ground that the whole "brokerage commission" agreement was invalid.

While the action was pending, there was a disciplinary proceeding against the plaintiff. In the latter proceeding plaintiff was censured for having, as an attorney, illegally stipulated for compensation in excess of the statutory fee.

In the instant (civil) action the tribunal of first instance of the Canton of Berne dismissed the complaint on the ground that the contract sued upon was invalid. The counterclaim also was dismissed, on the ground that the parties were *in pari turpitudine.*[a] Upon defendant's appeal the Federal Court, as court of last resort in civil cases, reversed the judgment below in so far as it dismissed the counterclaim, and granted defendant's prayer for a judgment against the plaintiff in the amount of Fr. 30,000.]

Reasons: The decision appealed from holds that the agreement between the parties is invalid. Plaintiff argues that said agreement is a brokerage contract, and not a contract by which plaintiff as an attorney stipulated for a fee in the form of a commission dependent upon the result of the controversy. . . . The question arises whether federal or cantonal law governs. . . . The relationship between the attorney and his client is under Swiss law ordinarily that of a mandate[b] [citing a commentary, a monograph, and a thesis]. Exceptionally it may be an employment contract. In any event it is a contractual relationship, belonging to the sphere of private law and generally covered by the federal Code of Obligations.[c] The attorney promises to perform certain work, whereas the client promises to pay for the work performed. If the performance of the attorney is defective, he may, pursuant to ordinary principles of private law, be sued for damages. On the other hand, he may sue a client for his fee in an ordinary civil action [citing cases]. This does not mean, however, that the cantons are precluded from any influence upon that legal relationship. To the

a. Swiss Code of Obligations, Article 62: "He who unjustly obtains a benefit from another, has to make restitution of the enrichment.

"Such obligation exists especially in a case in which a person has obtained something of value without legal causa, or on the basis of an anticipated causa which did not come into existence, or on the basis of a causa which has subsequently ceased to exist."

Article 63: "He who voluntarily pays a non-existing debt, can demand restitution only if he proves that he mistakenly believed in the existence of the debt.

"No claim can be made for restitution, if the payment was made for a debt barred by the Statute of Limitations, or if the payment was made in performance of a moral duty. . . ."

Article 66: "What has been paid or delivered with the intention of producing an illegal or immoral result, cannot be demanded back".

b. See infra, pp. 768 ff.

c. In Switzerland, most subjects belonging to the sphere of private law, including commercial law, are governed by the federal Civil Code and the federal Code of Obligations. Many subjects of public law, on the other hand, are governed by the laws of the cantons.

extent that they control the administration of justice as a province of public law,[d] they may regulate the affairs of attorneys, especially with respect to fees. In the latter respect, it has been recognized by the consistent practice of this Court that the cantons may provide for official supervision of attorneys' bills [citing cases] and may subject attorneys' fees to a statutory tariff [citing cases]. It follows that the cantons also must have power to determine the *kind* of remuneration to which the attorney is entitled for his services, and especially to prohibit fees measured by the result of such services. . . . Such cantonal regulations are justified by the legal and factual monopoly of the attorneys. There is also the additional consideration that a percentage participation in the result of a dispute involves a speculation, and that the attorney, who due to his knowledge of the law is in a better position to weigh the chances, occupies a superior position in this connection.

It follows further that the cantons must have the power to determine *which acts* of attorneys should, with respect to the question of remuneration, be considered as connected with the *administration of justice*. Of course the cantons may not treat those services as belonging to the administration of justice which are not covered by this term as generally understood. If they did, they would improperly invade the area of private law which governs the contractual relations between attorney and client; that area is completely and absolutely preempted by federal codes, to the exclusion of the public law of the cantons.

[The Court then points out that in the present case the services rendered by plaintiff were not, or at least not exclusively, the services of a broker, and that, consequently, they were services rendered by the plaintiff as an attorney and as an organ of the administration of justice. That being so, the Court concludes that the Canton of Berne had power to regulate the fees to be exacted by plaintiff for such services. The Court then refers to a Berne statute of 1840, pursuant to which a percentage agreement between attorney and client (*pactum de quota litis*) is illegal. Such, at any rate, had been the construction of the Berne statute by the court below, and the federal court is bound by the construction which a cantonal court places upon a statute of its own canton. The present agreement is thus illegal as violating a valid Berne statute.]

Federal law, however, determines what should be the *effect of such illegality* of the agreement in question. . . . Even though the prohi-

---

d. Many of the civilians think of procedure, including civil procedure, as a *public law* subject, on the theory that procedural law regulates the functioning of the courts, and that the courts are a branch of the *government*.

With the exception of the Federal Court at Lausanne, the ordinary Swiss courts are cantonal courts, and their procedure is governed by the Codes of Civil Procedure of the various cantons. Cases which have run through the hierarchy of cantonal courts, may be appealed to the Federal Court; the latter Court can reverse the decision below only if it is based on a violation or misapplication of federal law. It must be remembered, however, that the Civil Code and the Code of Obligations are federal laws, so that the Federal Court has the last word on most questions of substantive law which arise in private law cases. See Riesenfeld and Hazard, Federal Courts in Foreign Systems, 13 Law & Contemp. Prob. 29, 56–58 (1948).

bition violated by the agreement is not a federal but a cantonal statute, the question of the effect of such violation is one of federal law.[e] . [The Court then points out that Article 20 of the Swiss Code of Obligations [f], in the same way as Section 134 of the German Civil Code [g], invalidates illegal contracts.]

The invalidity of the contingent fee agreement further leads to the conclusion that the counterclaim is well founded and that defendant is entitled to demand restitution of the amount of Fr. 30,000 paid on account. By paying this sum to the plaintiff in performance of his promise, defendant has voluntarily paid a non-existing debt within the meaning of Article 63 of the Code of Obligations. He was mistaken concerning the existence of his obligation, being of the opinion that he was paying pursuant to the terms of a contract which was binding upon him and did not incorporate illegal provisions. This must be considered proved, because no other motive appears which might have induced the defendant to make the partial payment in question. . . . Such mistake of law is sufficient to justify restitution pursuant to Article 63 [citing a case] . . . The court below erred in holding that the dismissal of the counterclaim could be based upon Article 66 of the Code of Obligations. The defendant did not pay "with the intention of producing an illegal or immoral result". He paid in the mistaken belief that he was performing a valid and legal contract. Moreover, the result of the performance was illegal, and perhaps immoral, only in so far as the person and the mentality of the plaintiff as payee was involved. There was no illegality or immorality on the part of the defendant as payor. On the contrary, it is the client-payor's interest which was sought to be protected by the statute condemning contingent fees. The principle "in pari turpitudine melior est causa possidentis," [h] applied by the court below in reliance upon the distinguishable case of [citation], is not applicable to the case at bar.[i]

[handwritten: Broad Statement]

e. In our legal system, where state law generally predominates in the area of private law, the converse question sometimes presents itself: If a transaction is invalidated by a federal statute, are the consequences, including the restitutionary consequences, of such invalidity determined by state or federal law? Cf. Francis v. Southern Pacific Co., 333 U.S. 445, 68 S.Ct. 611 (1948); H. J. Friendly, In Praise of Erie— and of the New Federal Common Law, 19 The Record 64, 88 (1964).

Similarly, in the European Common Market it has become apparent that where national courts enforce new substantive rights created by Community Law, they face the thorny question whether the remedies used to implement such rights are to be derived from Community or national law. See N. Green, The Treaty of Rome, National Courts, and English Common Law, 48 Rabels Z. 509 (1984).

f. Swiss Code of Obligations, Art. 20: "A contract the object of which is impossible, illegal or immoral, is invalid. . . ."

g. See supra p. 569.

h. Freely translated, this Roman maxim means that, where both parties are guilty of equal turpitude, the law will not help one against the other. In varying phraseology, most of the modern civil-law codes have incorporated the maxim into their provisions dealing with unjust enrichment. See, e.g., Art. 66 of the Swiss Code of Obligations (supra, p. 711), which is the basis of the Court's discussion of the point.

i. If German law had been applicable, the plaintiff attorney, having been successful, could have recovered the amount of his statutory fee. See Notes preceding the principal case. The Swiss Federal Court, by directing that plaintiff repay the *entire* sum he had received on account, in effect determined that he should obtain no com-

COMMON LAW AND CIVIL LAW

A rule invalidating contingent fee agreements naturally raises questions concerning the plight of impecunious litigants. The foregoing cases, therefore, should be considered in the light of the materials on *legal aid* in civil-law countries (supra pp. 353–362).

A closely related problem is that of *recovery of counsel fees* from a vanquished opponent (supra pp. 365–370). This may be an appropriate time, therefore, to review the whole subject of litigation expenses previously discussed in this book, and to compare American and civilian approaches to that problem.

INTRODUCTORY NOTE ON DISCLAIMER CLAUSES IN STANDARDIZED CONTRACTS

Courts and legislators throughout the world are confronted with problems created by unilaterally drafted, standardized contract conditions. These problems become particularly acute when the standardized contract contains one-sided clauses grossly favoring the side that drafted the document. The materials which follow illustrate the treatment which some of these problems have received in Germany and in other civil-law systems. The interest of a comparative examination of the topic is enhanced, in this instance, by the fact that the most important recent development in the American law on the subject (UCC § 2–302) may well be regarded as German-inspired.[1]

The discussion which follows will center on the question of the *validity* of standardized disclaimer clauses. The reader should realize, however, that cases involving standard contracts, and especially adhesion contracts, also may raise other issues. These issues, which frequently have to be determined before one even reaches the question of the validity of a particular clause, cannot be examined here in detail; but two of them should be briefly mentioned:

    (a) The first of these issues comes under the heading of Formation of Contracts. How does the printed standard form of an enterprise—e.g., of a carrier, bank or insurance company—become part of a particular contract which the enterprise concludes with a customer, especially in cases in which the enterprise is the offeree?[2] The German courts have held that, even though the offer contains no reference to the standard form, the terms embodied in the form must be read into the contract if the customer (i) knows or should know of the existence of the standard form used by the enterprise, or (ii) knows or should know as a matter of general experience that an enterprise such as the one with which he is dealing normally does business only on the basis of its own standard conditions.[3]

pensation whatever. It is possible, however, that plaintiff—consistently with his contention that he had earned a broker's commission rather than a professional fee—had not raised the point concerning his statutory fee.

1. See supra p. 16.

2. For comparative discussions of this question see O. Lando, Standard Con-

tracts—A Proposal and a Perspective, 10 Scandinavian Studies in Law 127, at 130–33 (1966); 2 Schlesinger (Gen.Ed.), Formation of Contracts—A Study of the Common Core of Legal Systems 953–1001 (1968).

3. The German Standard Terms Act of 1976 (which will be discussed in more detail below) has adopted a more protective rule for consumer transactions; but for

(b) How are standard contracts to be interpreted? In some legal systems there is a tendency to interpret ambiguous provisions of such a contract *contra proferentem*, i.e. against the party responsible for their formulation.[4] The Italian Civil Code (Art. 1370) explicitly adopted this approach as a rule of interpretation.[4a] (The materials which follow, however, deal with situations where the validity rather than the interpretation of a particular clause was at issue.)

OPINION OF THE GERMAN REICHSGERICHT IN THE MATTER OF G., DEFENDANT–APPELLANT v. ST., PLAINTIFF–RESPONDENT

1st Civil Division, October 26, 1921, RGZ 103, 82.

Also relies on sec 138, as in attorney fees case

[Plaintiff's agent at Mannheim delivered 17 cases of cigars to defendant, a forwarder and carrier, requesting defendant to send them to plaintiff by express freight. Only 16 cases were delivered to plaintiff by defendant, and plaintiff sues for M 5,166, the value of the missing case. Defendant demands that the complaint be dismissed, on the ground that its liability as a forwarder is limited to M 60. By previous public announcements, all Mannheim forwarders had limited their liability to a maximum of M 60 for each shipment.]

The court of first instance granted the relief prayed for by the plaintiff. The intermediate Appellate Court affirmed. Upon the further appeal taken by the defendant, the Reichsgericht affirmed the decisions below.

Reasons: The intermediate Appellate Court holds that the general Announcements of the Mannheim Forwarders became part of the contract between the parties, because the agent of the plaintiff was a merchant residing at Mannheim, who presumably took notice of such announcements in the daily press. The intermediate Appellate Court further points out that contractual exemption from liability is not necessarily contra bonos mores, even though the exemption may cover cases of negligence on the part of employees of the forwarder. But, the court below further says, it is improper and immoral for *all* the Mannheim forwarders to exploit their monopolistic position for the purpose of exempting themselves from liability for their own negli-

contracts among merchants, the rules stated in the text, supra, are still in force. See O. Sandrock, The Standard Terms Act 1976 of West Germany, 26 Am.J.Comp.L. 551, 558–60 (1978).

For a comparative discussion of the special problems which arise when offeror and offeree both seek to incorporate their own standardized conditions into the contract, see P. H. Schlechtriem, The Battle of the Forms Under German Law, 23 Bus.Law. 655 (1968).

4. See V. Bolgár, The Contract of Adhesion: A Comparison of Theory and Practice, 20 Am.J.Comp.L. 53, 76–77 (1972).

4a. A similar provision appears in § 5 of the German statute of 1976 which will be discussed infra. That provision reads as follows: "Any uncertainty concerning the interpretation of standard contract terms is resolved against the party responsible for the use of such terms."

gence.[a] The court below found that in the case at bar there was
negligence on the part of defendant itself, in that on October 16, 1919,
the day on which the missing merchandise was stolen, defendant failed
to send a second man along with its driver [the idea apparently being
that a second man was necessary in order to keep an eye on the trailer
while the driver was in his cab].

Appellant argues that under the provisions of Section 276, Subdivision 2 of the Civil Code [b] contractual exemption from liability is
improper only in so far as liability for intentional acts is concerned.
Therefore, appellant argues, a clause exempting the forwarder from
liability for its own negligence is quite proper; it is further said that
there cannot be any question of immoral exploitation, inasmuch as the
shipper can take out transportation insurance.

These views of the appellant cannot be approved. . . .

. . . The concerted action of all carriers and forwarders residing
at Mannheim constituted an immoral exploitation of their actual monopoly, in so far as they attempted to exempt themselves from liability
even in case of the forwarder's own negligence. . . . Section 276,
Subdivision 2 of the Civil Code does not prohibit the contractual
exemption from, or limitation of, liability for any case of negligence.
Nevertheless such an agreement is a rare exception in business life,
especially where its coverage is intended to be so broad that one of the
parties is thereby exempted from liability for its own negligence. The
statutory scheme concerning the legal position of commission merchants, forwarders, warehouses and carriers is that in principle such
firms are liable for lost or damaged goods and that they can avoid such
liability only by proving that the exercise of due care could not have
averted the damage (Commercial Code, Sections 390, 407, 417, 429).
This state of the law, which was intended by the legislature and is
generally regarded as equitable, is completely reversed if the forwarder
or carrier exempts himself from liability even for its own fault. If such

a. At the time of this case, agreements
in restraint of trade, as such, were not
illegal in Germany. See I. E. Schwartz,
Antitrust Legislation and Policy in Germany, 105 U.Pa.L.Rev. 617, 625–41 (1957).
After World War II, the Occupation Authorities introduced antitrust laws, which
are now replaced by the Law Against Restraint of Competition of July 27, 1957
(BGBl 1957 I 1081) (for an English translation of the Law as amended in 1980 see
Mueller, Heidenhain and Schneider, German Antitrust Law 148 (3rd ed., 1984)).
Pursuant to that Law, it is still lawful for
competitors to agree on standardized contract terms (not relating to prices); but
such terms must be filed with the Cartel
Authority, and the Authority may order
the participating enterprises to desist from
the use of the form contracts, or to change
them, insofar as their terms "constitute a
misuse" of the market position of such
enterprises. Only the transportation industry is exempt from general provisions
prohibiting price fixing (Sec. 99). In 1982,
the Cartel Authority has in fact approved
an agreement limiting carriers' liability
and providing instead for transportation
insurance. See Notification No. 19/82 of
Feb. 2, 1982, BAnz. No. 47.

The fact, however, that a given form
contract has been filed with the Cartel
Authority and that the Authority has
failed to object to any of its terms, would
not deprive the courts of the power, in a
lawsuit between the enterprise using the
form and one of its customers, to examine
the validity of a particular term contained
in such form. See Ulmer, Brandner and
Hensen, AGB-Kommentar, § 9 Anno. 43
(4th ed., 1982); Löwe-Graf von Westphalen-
Trinkner, Kommentar zum AGB-Gesetz,
Introduction to §§ 8–11, Anno. 45 (1977).

b. "An obligor cannot be exempted in
advance from liability for intentional acts"
[i.e., from liability for intentional violation
of his duty to perform the obligation in
good faith.]

exemption comes about other than by way of a completely free agreement, and if a whole group of entrepreneurs within a certain district by exploiting their actual monopoly forces such exemption upon those who are dependent upon the services of forwarders and carriers, then such conduct is grossly violative of the moral standards of those people whose thinking is just and equitable. Thus it is contra bonos mores within the meaning of Section 138 of the Civil Code. . . .

Noted compared to p9 708

OPINION OF THE GERMAN REICHSGERICHT IN THE MATTER OF SUEDD. TRANSP. VERS. A.G., PLAINTIFF–APPELLANT v. W., DEFENDANT–RESPONDENT

1st Civil Division, March 21, 1923, RGZ 106, 386.

[Plaintiff as assignee of the shipper sues defendant forwarder for the full value of goods stolen while in defendant's custody. Plaintiff's assignor had apparently signed defendant's "General Terms and Conditions of Forwarders", a form drafted by the Association of Berlin Forwarders and used by all members of the Association. Section 8 of the form contract provided: "If the value of the goods is stated in the accompanying papers, then the forwarder will insure such goods against local risks for the account of the shipper, at premium rates to be fixed from time to time by the Association of Berlin Forwarders. If no value is stated, or no insurance is desired, then the liability of the forwarder is limited to a maximum of M 1.20 [a] for each kilogram gross weight."]

The intermediate appellate court has assumed . . . that the interests of the shipper are fully protected by the willingness of the forwarder to take out insurance if the value of the goods is stated. . . . The court below reasons that inasmuch as the insurance premium would be small in relation to the protection gained, the clause [Section 8] amounts ultimately to nothing but an increase in the freight rate. Therefore, it is said, there is here no immoral exploitation of a monopolistic position.

Plaintiff-appellant [who had lost in both courts below] argues that this reasoning is inconsistent with the decisions of this Court, and especially with RGZ 103, 82.[b] This argument must be regarded as justified.

. . . In most cases the interests of the shipper are not really protected if he is relegated to a money claim against an insurer, and can no longer dispose of the goods. As a rule he is interested in the goods, and not in a cause of action for damages. Therefore he is entitled to insist that the forwarder take the measures required by the circumstances in order to protect the goods from damage or loss. It is the duty of the forwarder so to proceed. From such duty he cannot

---

a. In view of the inflation then prevailing in Germany, this was tantamount to zero.

b. Reported ante, p. 715.

exempt either himself or his executive employees, by offering to take out insurance. This fundamental principle of law cannot be shaken by the consideration that the shipper, in case the forwarder has violated his duty, is again relegated to a money claim for damages against the latter. In the first place, this claim may be considerably broader than a claim against the insurer.[c] Furthermore, although it may be true that as a rule a claim for damages will be a money claim, it does not follow that the forwarder should have an option to substitute a claim against an insurance company for the performance of his duty of due care—a duty imposed by fundamental and generally recognized principles of law.

———

OPINION OF THE GERMAN BUNDESGERICHTSHOF IN THE MATTER OF E. Gu. (DEFENDANT) v. K. B. (PLAINTIFF)

2nd Civil Division, February 7, 1964, BGHZ 41, 151.

The defendant had stored furniture and household effects in plaintiff's warehouse. In this action, plaintiff sued for the balance of the storage fees allegedly owed by defendant. The latter . . . counterclaimed for damages, asserting that some of the stored articles had been damaged, and that others had been stolen. In the intermediate appellate court, plaintiff's action was successful and defendant's counterclaim was dismissed. Upon defendant's further appeal, the judgment below is reversed and the case remanded.

Reasons: . . . It is true that pursuant to § 1 of the Storage Conditions the owner of the warehouse is liable only if he or one of his agents is chargeable with fault. Thus, contrary to the provisions of § 417 par. 1 and § 390 par. 1 of the Commercial Code[a] . . ., the burden of proof is placed upon the bailor in all those cases in which the property is lost or damaged in storage. Such a clause, if contained in standardized contract conditions,[b] is irreconcilable with the principles of good faith (Civil Code § 242).[c]

c. Although not citing any specific provision in support of this statement, the Court probably refers to the principle of restitution in kind. That principle, which is embodied in § 249 of the German Civil Code (quoted supra p. 689), assumes special importance in a period of inflation.

Even when the lost article cannot be returned in specie, the principle of restitution in kind asserts itself, because it follows from the principle that the value of the article must be determined as of the time of the court's decision rather than the (possibly much earlier) time of the loss. See Palandt, Bürgerliches Gesetzbuch, Comments preceding § 249, Anno. 9 (41st ed., 1982), and cases there cited. Our rule concerning this point is less clear. See cases collected in 8 Am.Jur.2d, Bailments, §§ 332 and 333 (1963 and Supps.).

a. The substance of these code provisions is stated in the last paragraph of the decision of Oct. 26, 1921, RGZ 103, 82, reproduced ante p. 715 at p. 716.

b. The opinion obviously implies that the "Storage Conditions" involved in this case constituted standardized contract conditions or standard terms (allgemeine Geschäftsbedingungen).

c. For an English translation of § 242 of the German Civil Code, see supra p. 575.

[The court points out that the above-cited provisions of the Commercial Code expressly deal with the question of the burden of proof in cases in which an article of personal property is lost or damaged during storage in a warehouse. The Code provisions make it clear that in such a case the warehouseman can avoid liability only if *he* proves that the loss or damage resulted from circumstances which could not have been averted by the exercise of due care.] It is true that these provisions of the Commercial Code constitute *ius dispositivum* [d] . . .; thus these provisions yield to a contrary agreement of the parties. . . . [The court then points out that although in principle the parties have the power to modify the Commercial Code's rule as to the burden of proof, the question remains whether the particular contract clause here in question must be recognized as valid.] With respect to individually negotiated contracts one can say that in general—unless examination of the particular circumstances of a case dictates a different result—there is no objection against contractual terms which allocate the burden of proof in a manner differing from the dispositive provisions of the written law.[e] A different rule, however, applies to standardized contract conditions, which are intended to perform a function similar to that of statutes in affecting the legal process. When one party imposes standard conditions upon the other, true freedom of contract does not exist; standardized contract conditions thus derive their effectiveness, not from the parties' private autonomy, but only from the submission of the other party. Therefore, recognition must be denied to those terms of such standard conditions which for an indefinite number of future cases establish a rule inconsistent with the principles of good faith.

Insofar as dispositive provisions of law were enacted, not for reasons of expediency, but in response to a plain postulate of justice, the effect of such provisions may be modified by standardized contract conditions only if there are sufficient reasons justifying such modification. To be sufficient, the reasons must throw doubt on the postulate of justice underlying the rule of dispositive law, and must indicate that the modified solution [i.e. the solution adopted in the standard conditions] is consistent with justice and equity. The elements of justice which are inherent in the provisions of dispositive law enacted by the legislator are not always of the same strength. The stronger they are, the stricter must be the standard of good faith to which any modification (by way of a clause in a form contract) of such provisions of dispositive law must be held.

[The court refers to a previous case, in which these principles were applied to a warranty disclaimer in a contract of sale.]

d. See supra p. 587.

e. The expression "dispositive provision" (admittedly a teutonism) is a literal translation of the German term "dispositive Vorschrift" or "Dispositivnorm". The term, which is a term of art, is derived from the Latin *ius dispositivum*, which is the opposite of *ius cogens*. See supra p.

587. Freely translated, the German term could be rendered as "provision of a code or other statute which is subject to agreement otherwise". For the sake of brevity, however, the literal rather than the free translation is used wherever the term appears in this opinion.

A provision in a standard contract which in effect changes the legal rule with respect to the burden of proof cannot be regarded as equitable if the party who submits to the standardized conditions thereby is made to bear the burden of proof as to circumstances that lie within the sphere of responsibility of the party imposing such conditions. The outcome of many lawsuits of this kind depends on the burden of proof. The bailor whose goods have been damaged often would be remediless if, having proved the delivery of the goods to the bailee, he had to show, in addition, what the circumstances were under which the stored goods were damaged . . ., and had to prove furthermore that these circumstances involved some fault on the part of the bailee. Standard contract conditions, if they are to remain consistent with the requirements of honest dealing in business, cannot change the rule that the risk of failure to ascertain the cause of the damage must be borne by the bailee who has taken undamaged goods into his custody, and that even when the cause has been ascertained, he must prove lack of fault on his part. It is unfair, by subjecting the bailor to standardized contract conditions, to place upon him the burden of proof as to circumstances which are outside of his sphere of influence and which lie within the bailee's area of responsibility. [The court refers to some of its own previous decisions, and to the fact that in the General Contract Conditions of German Freight Forwarders—a standard contract form drafted with the cooperation of trade associations representing shippers as well as freight forwarders and carriers—the burden of proof question was resolved more favorably to the bailor than in the standard contract involved in the instant case.] It follows that § 1 of the Storage Conditions involved in this case is ineffective insofar as it places upon the bailor the entire burden of proving that a fault of the bailee caused the damage to, or the loss of, the stored property. The provisions of §§ 390 and 417 of the Commercial Code must be applied in lieu of the invalid terms of the Storage Conditions.

[Apparently there was some indication that in part the damage was caused by an attempt forcibly to open a cupboard, a desk and other stored articles belonging to the defendant. Thus pilferage was suspected. In this connection, the court refers to § 3 of the Storage Conditions, pursuant to which the warehouseman is not liable for losses caused by burglary or robbery. The court seems to assume that § 3 is valid, but points out that the burden of proving burglary or robbery rests on plaintiff. The damaged articles, and the nature of the damage, must be specified by the defendant (who, if necessary, may inspect the damaged articles which are still in plaintiff's custody); but the burden of explaining and proving the cause of the damage must be borne by plaintiff. Since the lower court erroneously imposed the burden on the defendant bailor, and dismissed his counterclaim when he was unable to meet the burden, the decision below is reversed, and the case remanded for further proceedings not inconsistent with the opinion of the highest court.]

Fraud
Duress
undue influence   } *American Concepts*
                         compare to

used in
contra
bonos
doctrine and has now
shifted to
good
faith

NOTES AND QUESTIONS

(1) In analyzing the three preceding cases, it is interesting to compare the two older decisions with the most recent one. Has there been a shift between the 1920's and the 1960's (a) as to the Code provision cited by the court as the basis for its decision, and (b) more importantly, as to the substance of the rule?

↓

(2) The traditional German approach to the whole problem of one-sided standard contracts is characterized by the sweeping nature of the rules which the German courts have developed.[1] Since these rules are based on Code provisions of utmost generality, they can be employed to strike down *any* one-sided clause in a standard contract which the court considers objectionable, regardless of the type of contract, or the type of business, in which it is used.[1a]

immoral
vi,
unfair

Our statutes and decisions, on the other hand, traditionally deal in casuistic manner with specific types of clauses in specific types of contracts.[2] As to the validity of disclaimer clauses, separate and often unconnected bodies of law, both statutory and decisional, have grown up for public service corporations, railroads, housing authorities, banks, landlords, bailees, building contractors, innkeepers, and other types of business enterprises.[3]

With respect to disclaimer clauses in contracts for the transportation of goods, the casuistic bent of our method is particularly extreme. We start with the general proposition that a common carrier may not exempt itself from liability for its own or its servants' negligence and that a contractual limitation on the amount of the carrier's liability is valid only if a choice of rates is offered.[4] But the rule is subject to qualification by numerous provisions of the Interstate Commerce Act, the Carriage of Goods by Sea Act, and other federal and state statutes.[5] These statutes have the effect that one and the same limitation of value

U.S. position
on contractual
limitations on
liability

---

1. The German courts' use of the general provisions of their Civil Code for the purpose of invalidating oppressive contracts and contract clauses is enlighteningly discussed by J. P. Dawson, Unconscionable Coercion: The German Version, 89 Harv.L.Rev. 1041 (1976). Professor Dawson's article deals with (although it is not limited to) German cases involving exemption clauses in standard contracts. Note, however, that the Dawson article was written before the adoption of the new German statute mentioned below in the text.

For an excellent comparative discussion of the pertinent case law see E. von Hippel, The Control of Exemption Clauses: A Comparative Study, 16 Int. & Comp.L.Q. 591 (1967).

1a. It is true that in German law one can find also some specific statutory provisions invalidating certain contract clauses, especially disclaimer clauses, in particular types of contracts. See, e.g., Eisenbahnverkehrsordnung § 83; Binnenschiffahrtsgesetz § 59; Güterkraftverkehrsgesetz § 26. However, in view of the

sweeping—and often stricter—rules derived by the courts from the general provisions of the Civil Code, these specific enactments have lost some of their practical importance with respect to those disclaimer clauses which are contained in standardized contract conditions.

Concerning the recent German statute dealing generally with standard terms, see part (3) of these Notes and Questions.

2. See Schlesinger, The Uniform Commercial Code in the Light of Comparative Law, 1 Inter-Am.L.Rev. 11, 32–33 (1959).

3. See the cases collected in Anno., 175 ALR 8 (1948). For further examples illustrating the extreme casuistry of our decisional and statutory rules dealing with standardized contracts, see J. Sweet, Liquidated Damages in California, 60 Calif.L. Rev. 84, 85–86 (1972).

4. See 6A Corbin On Contracts, § 1472 (1962 and Supps.). The essence of this rule has been taken over into UCC § 7–309.

5. See UCC § 7–103.

clause is sometimes valid and sometimes invalid, depending on whether the transportation takes place by railroad, truck, boat or airplane, and whether it is in international, interstate or intrastate commerce.[6]

The Uniform Commercial Code has used a variety of techniques in dealing with one-sided contract terms, especially disclaimer clauses. Some of the relevant sections are fairly specific in their language and apply only to particular types of contracts;[7] but the Code also contains a provision of almost civilian sweep, applicable to all transactions governed by the Code, which broadly announces that "the obligations of good faith, diligence, reasonableness and care prescribed by this Act may not be disclaimed by agreement, but the parties may by agreement determine the standards by which the performance of such obligations is to be measured if such standards are not manifestly unreasonable."[8]

Even more civilian in style is § 2–302, which deals with "unconscionable" contracts and contract clauses.[9] By virtue of its extraordinary breadth and elasticity,[10] this provision is quite reminiscent of §§ 138 and 242 of the German Civil Code.[11] It must be remembered, however, that in contrast to the German provisions, which are applicable to all "jural acts" or all "obligations", § 2–302 in terms applies only to contracts for the sale of goods. Whether in this country (in states other then California [11a]) § 2–302 will play a pervasive role comparable to that of the "general clauses" of the civilian codes, thus depends on the

---

6. See 10 Williston On Contracts, § 1071 (3rd ed. by W. H. E. Jaeger, 1967).

7. See, e.g., §§ 4–103, 7–204, 7–309.

8. Sec. 1–102(3).

9. See R. S. Summers, "Good Faith" in General Contract Law and the Sales Provisions of the Uniform Commercial Code, 54 Va.L.Rev. 195, 230–32 (1968); A. A. Leff, Unconscionability and the Code—The Emperor's New Clause, 115 U.Pa.L.Rev. 485 (1967); M. P. Ellinghaus, In Defense of Unconscionability, 78 Yale L.J. 757 (1969); S. Deutch, Unfair Contracts: The Doctrine of Unconscionability (1977). For a partly comparative discussion of § 2–302 see Comment, 109 U.Pa.L.Rev. 401 (1961).

For a provision similar to UCC § 2–302 but broader in coverage, see Cal.Civil Code § 1670.5, added by L.1979, Ch. 819, eff. September 19, 1979.

10. The possible argument, that a provision of such breadth would give too much uncontrollable leeway to the jury and therefore could not work satisfactorily in the context of the American legal system, was neatly side-stepped by the draftsmen, who made it clear that § 2–302 becomes operative only "if the court as a matter of law finds the contract or any clause of the contract to have been unconscionable . . . .". It is further provided in subs. (2) that the parties may submit evidence bearing on the unconscionability of a contract or contract clause; but such evidence, as is pointed out in Official Comment 3, "is for the court's consideration, not the jury's".

11. The draftsmen of the UCC seem to have thought in terms of the *older* German rule, i.e., the rule applied in the cases which appear supra at pp. 715 and 717. Apparently they considered the much more far-reaching approach subsequently adopted by the German Bundesgerichtshof (see supra p. 718), but rejected it. See Section 2–302, Official Comment 1, where the following statement appears: "The principle is one of the prevention of oppression and unfair surprise . . . and not of disturbance of allocation of risks because of superior bargaining power."

Many illustrations of the use of Section 2–302 to invalidate warranty and damages limitation clauses can be found in Anno., 38 ALR4th 25 (1985).

With the German case that appears supra at p. 718 one might compare A & M Produce Co. v. FMC Corp., 135 Cal.App.3d 473, 186 Cal.Rptr. 114 (1982), striking down as "unconscionable" a warranty disclaimer and consequential damages exclusion clause in a sales contract. At one point (fn. 14 at 126) the California court comes close to the reasoning of the German court. But in general, the approach of the former is much more cumbersome; it lays down a rule that makes for less predictability of results and creates many more issues of fact than the German rule. Cf. Perdue v. Crocker Nat. Bk., 141 Cal.App.3d 200, 190 Cal.Rptr. 204 (1983).

11a. As to California, see supra n. 9.

extent to which our courts will be inclined to resort to analogy and to extend the sweep of the section to other types of transactions.

The traditional German method of dealing with disclaimer clauses and other one-sided terms in standardized contracts was evolved by the courts' imaginative and innovative use of some of the Civil Code's very general provisions. What are the advantages and disadvantages of that method, as compared to ours? Which of the two methods can more truly be called a case law method?

(3) Despite the boldness which the German courts had displayed in dealing with standardized contracts,[12] there was considerable agitation during recent decades in favor of a broad legislative attack on the problem. The end result of that agitation, and of a great deal of solid preparatory work, was the *Gesetz zur Regelung des Rechts der allgemeinen Geschäftsbedingungen* (Standard Terms Act) of December 9, 1976, which went into effect on April 1, 1977.[13] Although legislation on this topic has been passed in many countries during recent years, it is fair to say that the German statute constitutes the most thorough treatment of the subject. What follows is a highly condensed outline of the substantive and procedural safeguards which the statute provides:[14]

On the substantive side, there is a lengthy catalogue of forbidden clauses, i.e. clauses which, while permissible in individually negotiated contracts, are no longer tolerated in standardized consumer contracts. In connection with the case on p. 718, supra, it is worth noting that clauses changing the burden of proof are listed in this catalogue. The catalogue is supplemented by a catch-all provision of sweeping breadth. The latter provision, which is not limited to consumer transactions but applies to all preformulated standardized contracts of adhesion, invalidates any terms in such contracts which in violation of the dictates of good faith put the other party at an unfair disadvantage. Inspired by previous judicial decisions of which the case at p. 718, supra, is typical, the catch-all section of the statute further provides that a clause in a preformulated adhesion contract is always invalid if it is inconsistent with the essential policy thrust of a statutory rule, even though such statutory rule may be one the effect of which could be changed by the parties in an individually negotiated contract.

As to procedure, the new Law provides that consumer organizations as well as trade associations may sue to enjoin the use of standardized contracts or contract clauses which are substantively unlawful. An official public register will be kept of all pending actions of this kind, and of all judgments rendered in such actions. An injunction obtained in such an action can be enforced in accordance with Section 890 of the German Code of Civil Procedure (see supra pp. 668–669). The new statute further contains an innovative provision to the effect that if in spite of such an injunction the use of the enjoined contract or clause is continued, the injunction decree can be invoked as binding (res judicata) by a private party such as a consumer in subse-

12. For some comparative observations concerning the boldness of judicial law-making in Germany and the United States, see R. B. Schlesinger, Book Review, 15 Am. J.Comp.L. 576, 577–78 (1967).

13. BGBl 1976 I 3317. An English translation of the German Standard Contracts Act appears in the Appendix volume of B. Rüster (Ed.), Business Transactions in Germany (1983), as Appendix 8.

14. For a more extensive and exceedingly interesting discussion of the statute see O. Sandrock, The Standard Terms Act 1976 of West Germany, 26 Am.J.Comp.L. 551 (1978).

quent litigation. Thus the danger of conflicting court decisions concerning the effectiveness of the same clause is considerably diminished, and the individual customer no longer bears the main burden of attacking objectionable form contracts or clauses.[15]

(4) It has been correctly observed by a German scholar that in its substantive provisions the German statute of 1976 has largely "codified, clarified, extended or restricted the rules which were part of the former judge-made law. To this extent it is more or less a concretization of the law that had already been in effect before 1977." [16]   And another European scholar perceptively remarked that "Without the rich experience of the German case law, which was based on general clauses in the Civil Code, the new Standard Contracts Law could hardly have been written." [17]

This raises an interesting point of legal method. The reader will recall our previous discussion (supra pp. 552–567) of the techniques by which social and technological changes can be accommodated in a codified legal system. That discussion focused on code revision, auxiliary statutes and case law as the main methods of adjustment. The example of the German Standard Terms Act of 1976 teaches us that even though in a given situation a choice has been made among those three methods, such choice is not necessarily final. Sometimes, and especially in the face of difficult and multifaceted problems, the slow and groping process of judicial law-making (on the basis of the Code's "general clauses") may be necessary in order to develop a body of experience. Once sufficient experience has been gathered, however, the legislator may feel that by codifying the case law he can enhance its certainty and predictability, and at the same time introduce new refinements. A civilian legislator, in particular, is apt to favor such a *return to the written law.*

The reader may wonder why in this particular case the German legislator's return to the written law took the form of a new auxiliary statute rather than that of amending the contract provisions of the Civil Code. The reason probably is that in addition to its substantive provisions the 1976 statute announces important procedural rules, which do not fit into a Civil Code. Some German commentators, however, seem to expect that ultimately, if and when an over-all revision of the Civil Code occurs, the substantive part of the 1976 statute will be integrated into the Code.[18]

15. Earlier drafts of the new statute had provided for the creation of an official Consumer Protection Agency. There were various proposals to the effect that preformulated standardized contract clauses could be used only if approved by the Agency, or that the Agency (as well as consumer organizations) be authorized to bring actions to enjoin the use of unlawful contracts or contract clauses. As finally enacted after much debate and preparatory work, the German statute did not follow these proposals, and did not set up an official body of this nature. A recent Swedish law, on the other hand, provides for the office of Consumer Ombudsman; the official holding that post, either upon his own motion or acting upon an outside suggestion, can apply to the Market Court for an order enjoining the use of terms in a standard form contract that are thought unfair to consumers. See J. E. Sheldon, Consumer Protection and Standard Contracts: The Swedish Experiment in Administrative Control, 22 Am.J.Comp.L. 17 (1974).

16. Sandrock, supra n. 14, at 553.

17. O. Lando, Unfair Contract Clauses and A European Uniform Commercial Code, in M. Cappelletti (Ed.), New Perspectives for a Common Law of Europe 267, at 279 (1978).

18. See Löwe-Graf von Westphalen-Trinkner, Kommentar zum AGB-Gesetz, Introduction, Anno. 22 (1977).

(5) Not only Germany and Sweden, but also many other countries have attempted in recent years to find legislative solutions of the problems created by one-sided clauses in standardized contracts.[19] Some of the innovative ideas reflected in those solutions differ considerably from the German approach,[20] and from our own. For an excellent overview, see E. H. Hondius, Unfair Contract Terms: New Control Systems, 26 Am.J.Comp.L. 525 (1978).

———

OBERLANDESGERICHT CELLE, OPINION OF DECEMBER 5, 1947

Reported in 2 Monatsschrift fuer Deutsches Recht 174 (1948).

The plaintiff is over fifty years old. She used to be a gardener and formerly lived in East Prussia. In the fall of 1944, the eastern front moved closer to her home town. Because of the threat of Russian invasion the evacuation of that town was ordered, and the plaintiff fled from East Prussia on October 29, 1944. She was permitted to stay in Goettingen with a family whom she had known previously.

[The defendants, husband and wife, are horticulturists residing in Goettingen. Shortly after her arrival at Goettingen, the plaintiff paid a visit to the defendants whom she had met before. Defendants asked the plaintiff about conditions in East Prussia. Plaintiff gave a truthful report of the unfavorable conditions there. She mentioned that fear of the Russians had induced many people there to commit suicide.] In the course of the conversation the plaintiff said: "Nobody in East Prussia believes in Adolf Hitler any more." Both defendants were present when this remark was made. . . . A few days later the first defendant (the husband) made a written report to the Gestapo concerning the remarks made by the plaintiff. The second defendant (the wife) saw the report after the first defendant had written it. She did not sign the report, but she did not object to its dispatch. A few days later a Gestapo official interrogated both defendants in their apartment . . . The second defendant then made a truthful statement of the conversation with the plaintiff. Upon the denunciation of the first defendant the plaintiff was arrested by the Gestapo. After her arrest the Gestapo telephoned to the first defendant and asked him whether he considered the matter very serious. He answered that it was up to the Gestapo to determine that. He did not retract his denunciation. In the meantime a judicial warrant of arrest was issued againt the plaintiff, and she was

19. A legislative solution of less recent vintage, but of continuing interest, is offered by Art. 1341 of the Italian Civil Code, which enumerates certain types of one-sided clauses (including disclaimer clauses) and provides that if such a clause appears in a standardized contract, it has no effect unless it is "specifically approved in writing." See G. Gorla, Standard Conditions and Form Contracts in Italian Law, 11 Am. J.Comp.L. 1 (1962). The effect of Art. 1341 is that although the customer may have signed the contract as a whole, the one-sided clause is not effective unless he has indicated his approval of the clause by a separate, additional signature. Compare UCC §§ 2–205 (last half-sentence), 2–209(2), 2–316(2).

20. See Sandrock, supra n. 14, at 554–55; E. von Hippel, Verbraucherschutz 118–39 (3d ed., 1986).

transferred to the jail of the tribunal of first instance in Goettingen. There she experienced two air attacks . . ., by which the jail was damaged. For reasons of security she and other prisoners were subsequently transferred to the Insane Asylum in Goettingen and a few days later to the jail of the tribunal of first instance in Hildesheim. There she was discharged on August [sic [a]] 25, 1945, shortly before the arrival of the Americans.

. . . The plaintiff contends that as a consequence of her long imprisonment and the mental anguish occasioned thereby, she suffered a serious impairment of her health. She demands damages from the defendants pursuant to Section 826 of the Civil Code.[b] *—see pg 688*

The tribunal of first instance entered an interlocutory judgment determining the issue of liability in favor of plaintiff and against both defendants, and limiting the further proceedings to the issue of the amount of damages.

Upon defendants' appeal from this interlocutory judgment, the Oberlandesgericht affirmed the judgment against the first defendant, but reversed the judgment against the second defendant and dismissed the complaint against her.

Reasons: . . . The first defendant has intentionally injured the plaintiff in a manner violating the moral precepts. Therefore he is liable under Section 826 of the Civil Code. It can be assumed that the report made by him against the plaintiff was true. But this is immaterial. So long as it can be anticipated that a person reported to the competent authorities will be treated in an orderly proceeding, governed by humane principles, such denunciation would not be contra bonos mores, at least not in the absence of improper motives. Such orderly proceeding would have been the rule in former times. There was no Gestapo. There were no Gestapo methods. . . .

But things were entirely different at a time when the most trivial political denunciation was sufficient to deliver the denounced person to the whims of so arbitrary an institution as the Gestapo [citing two recent decisions of the Oberlandesgericht Frankfurt].

The question of immorality is to be determined pursuant to the views of those persons whose thinking is just and equitable. There is controversy among text writers and among judicial decisions whether this refers to the views prevailing at the time of the allegedly tortious act or to the views prevailing at the time when liability is sought to be enforced by legal proceedings. It is not necessary to decide this question here. In the fall of 1944, it was already generally known with what arbitrariness the Gestapo proceeded, and reasonable men could no longer ignore the irresponsibility with which a government now recognized as criminal continued the hopelessly lost war. The course and outcome of the war could not be affected by the fact that the plaintiff communicated her sad impressions and her correct conclusions to a

---

a. This date seems to be erroneous. The correct date was probably April, 1945.   **b.** For a translation of that section of the German Civil Code, see supra p. 688.

larger or smaller circle of persons. . . . When the first defendant denounced the plaintiff in order, as he himself expresses it, to render her harmless, he made himself a tool of the Gestapo. . . . The argument that he was motivated by an honest conviction would help the first defendant only if the inhuman consequences of such denunciation had been unknown to him. [The Court then points out that the first defendant admittedly was an ardent reader of National-socialist newspapers and magazines, which at that time contained frequent references to the drastic punishment meted out to persons criticizing the regime and its acts. Therefore, the Court concludes, the first defendant undoubtedly knew what consequences his denunciation would have for the plaintiff.] It follows that even under the views prevailing at that time the defendant committed an immoral act.

Held

The first defendant tries in vain to deny his responsibility for the consequences of the denunciation on the ground that the injury occurred only after issuance of the judicial warrant of arrest, and that therefore the causal connection was interrupted. Defendant's purpose was to render the plaintiff harmless, that is, to deprive her of her liberty. For this purpose it did not matter whether the imprisonment was imposed by the Gestapo or by the court. It may be true, as the witness B. testifies, that the judicial warrant of arrest was issued only in order to remove the plaintiff from the control of the Gestapo. This Court takes judicial notice of the fact that this was a practice frequently applied. It is thus clear that without the previous arrest by the Gestapo a judicial warrant of arrest would never have been issued. Even if the judicial warrant of arrest was not specifically issued for this purpose, it was in any event a consequence of the denunciation filed with the Gestapo.

It follows that the first defendant is liable for the damages caused by the imprisonment which was brought about by his denunciation.

With respect to the second defendant a different decision is called for . . . [The Court points out that the second defendant did not take part in the denunciation written and filed by the first defendant]. The mere fact that the second defendant, when interrogated by the Gestapo, truthfully reported the facts involved in the denunciation, is not a sufficient basis for the imposition of liability.

NOTES AND QUESTIONS

(1) In a subsequent case, which reached the West German Federal Supreme Court,[1] the facts were basically similar. During World War II, plaintiff had made defeatist, anti-Hitler remarks in front of soldiers, and defendant had denounced her to the Gestapo. As compared to the principal case, however, events took a somewhat different turn in that upon her arrest the plaintiff was put before the "People's Court",[2] and was tried for "subversion of the armed services." Plaintiff was convict-

1. Bundesgerichtshof, Decision of May 25, 1955, 8 Neue Juristische Wochenschrift 1274 (1955).

2. Only rabid Nazis could become members of this court, which was not a part of the regular judicial system. Its

ed and sentenced to 3 years of hard labor. In this case, therefore, plaintiff's imprisonment was authorized by the judgment of a court.

The Supreme Court held that the denunciation was an act *contra bonos mores*, because "persons whose views are just and equitable would consider it morally objectionable. Sec. 826 of the Civil Code serves to implement a law of higher order and permits the Court to consider the postulates of true justice not dependent on positive laws." Law of such higher order, the Court held, must prevail over any legislative, administrative or judicial act.

In view of the fact, however, that plaintiff's imprisonment had been authorized by a judicial sentence, the Supreme Court further held that plaintiff could recover damages only if it were shown that the judgment convicting and sentencing her was so unjust that it must be treated as a nullity.[3] Such might be the case if the judgment of the People's Court was based

(a) on a Nazi-tinged and unjust law,[4] or

(b) on an unjust interpretation or application of that law by the People's Court, or

(c) on a sentencing practice of that court so brutal as to be inconsistent with law of a higher order.

For clarification of the question whether the judgment of the People's Court suffered from any of the defects mentioned under (b) or (c), the Supreme Court remanded the case.[5]

(2) Note that the *"contra bonos mores"* concept is used in the Code for two purposes: (a) as a restriction on freedom of contract and other

sentences—very frequently death sentences—were unappealable. The procedure was summary, but the accused did receive the semblance of a trial, and occasionally a defendant was acquitted. See Loewenstein, Justice, in Litchfield, Governing Post-War Germany 236, 249 (1953); Marsh, Some Aspects of the German Legal System Under National Socialism, 62 L.Q. Rev. 366, 372 (1946); G. Gribbohm, Der Volksgerichtshof, 1969 JuS 55; D. Schwab, Literaturschau: Die Rechtsentwicklung im Dritten Reich, 1976 JuS 132, 134 (1976).

3. Cf. Brandt v. Winchell, 3 N.Y.2d 628, 170 N.Y.S.2d 828, 148 N.E.2d 160 (1958).

4. The statute under which plaintiff had been convicted by the People's Court, was directed against "subversion" of the armed services in wartime. The Supreme Court observed that this statute, although passed by the Nazi government, was similar to laws enacted in other unquestionably civilized countries, and held that the statute was not unjust on its face, not even from the standpoint of a "higher law."

5. The cautious (perhaps overly cautious) attitude of the Supreme Court may have been due to the consideration that *if* the judgment of the People's Court is treated as "unjust" and hence as a nullity, the informer may be subject to criminal as

well as civil liability. In a case in which an "unjust" death sentence of the People's Court was foreseen by the informer (the victim's brother), whose volunteered testimony was responsible for the conviction, the informer was held guilty of intentional homicide. Bundesgerichtshof, Nov. 6, 1952, 6 Neue Juristische Wochenschrift 793 (1953). For discussion of similar criminal cases, see W. Friedmann, Legal Theory 350–56 (1967), where many further references can be found.

The Supreme Court failed to examine whether the notorious People's Court was not, as an institution, so tainted with the spirit of totalitarian lawlessness that *every* judgment of that "court" must be considered unjust. By a Resolution dated Jan. 24, 1985, the *Bundestag* declared that the so-called "Volksgerichtshof" (People's Court) was not a court in the traditional sense of the word, but "an instrument of terror used to implement the arbitrary policies of the National-Socialist regime." See Editorial, Bericht aus Bonn, 18 Zeitschrift für Rechtspolitik 93, at 94 (1985); B. R. Sonnen, Die Beurteilung des "Volksgerichtshofs" und seiner Entscheidungen durch den Deutschen Bundestag, 38 NJW 1065 (1985).

transactions, and (b) in the definition of a tort. The concept thus serves both as a shield and as a sword.

(3) By what standard should a court determine whether a given act is *contra bonos mores*? Is the question one of law, with the result that the judges are presumed to know the answer? Or can it be treated as one of fact, as to which the parties may introduce evidence (e.g., experts' testimony on properly tested community attitudes)? [5a] Compare the German courts' formula, which is predicated on the supposed feelings of "persons whose views are just and equitable",[6] with similar attempts of United States courts to determine the meaning of the terms "good moral character" and "moral turpitude" as used in the immigration laws. Cf. Johnson v. United States, 186 F.2d 588 (2d Cir. 1951); [7] Ablett v. Brownell, 240 F.2d 625 (D.C.Cir. 1957); Forbes v. Brownell, 149 F.Supp. 848 (D.D.C. 1957).[8]

(4) The judicial determination of what is *contra bonos mores* within the meaning of the Civil Code, sometimes is affected by value judgments inherent in provisions of the Constitution.[8a] It was so held by the German Federal Constitutional Court in the famous Lüth case (Decision of Jan. 15, 1958, BVerfGE 7, 198). The plaintiff in that case was the producer of the 1950 film "Immortal Beloved". The director of that film was an individual of international fame, who had become notorious by lending his unquestioned artistic talents to the production, during the Nazi period, of base antisemitic propaganda. The defendant Lüth, a high official of the State of Hamburg, was concerned that the reputation of post-war Germany and of its film industry would suffer if a film directed by that notorious individual were shown in Germany and other countries. Therefore, he publicly criticized the plaintiff for having chosen such a tainted individual as the director of "Immortal Beloved" (which in itself was an unobjectionable film), and by such public criticism admittedly sought to discourage the owners of film

---

5a. Cf. Judge Frank's provocative dissenting opinion in Repouille v. United States, 165 F.2d 152, 154–55 (2 Cir. 1947).

6. Except in the case of members of certain professions (e.g., lawyers, physicians) who are held to higher ethical standards, this formula is thought to refer to the *average* morality of decent people. See 2 Enneccerus-Nipperdey, Allgemeiner Teil des Buergerlichen Rechts, § 191 I 2 (1960). Palandt, Bürgerliches Gesetzbuch, § 826, Anno. 2 (41st ed., 1982).

7. Judge Learned Hand's fascinating opinion in the Johnson case deals with the question whether and under what circumstances an adulterer can be regarded as a person of good moral character within the meaning of the naturalization laws. As a matter of legal method, it is interesting to note that subsequent to the Johnson decision Congress sought to take this specific question out of the hands of the judiciary and to resolve it by statute. It is doubtful, however, whether the statute (as interpreted by the courts) has changed the standards laid down in the previous case law, especially in the Johnson decision. For a

survey of the somewhat conflicting decisions, see Anno., 33 A.L.R.Fed. 120 (1977).

8. For a discussion of these and similar cases see M. Shapiro, Morals and the Courts: The Reluctant Crusaders, 45 Minn. L.Rev. 897 (1961), where references to the relevant writings of many other authors can be found.

8a. Some fundamental rights provided by the German Constitution are viewed not only as safeguards against the state but also as "ordering principles" for social life in general. Accordingly, these rights are not only binding on public authority, but can also exercise an effect (Drittwirkung) on private-law relationships. This effect of fundamental rights has repeatedly been acknowledged in decisions of the Federal Supreme Court and the Federal Labor Court. See K. Hesse, Grundzüge des Verfassungsrechts der Bundesrepublik Deutschland 139–43 (14th ed., 1984). The text that follows focuses on the attitude of the Federal Constitutional Court toward this "radiation" effect of the Constitution. See also the "Die Welt" case, *supra* p. 627.

theaters from exhibiting that film. The court of first instance at Hamburg held that by this attempt to bring about a boycott of the film the defendant had violated § 826 of the Civil Code. Upon direct appeal (which in exceptional cases may be permitted) the Federal Constitutional Court reversed the judgment for the plaintiff which the court of first instance had entered. After a painstaking review of the record, the highest Court concluded that if in balancing the public and private interests involved in this case the court of first instance had accorded the proper weight to the protection of defendant's freedom of speech (and especially of political speech), it would not have found defendant guilty of "immoral" conduct within the meaning of § 826 of the Civil Code.[8b] The highest Court did not attempt to produce a capsulated verbal formula for the decision of future cases in which constitutional guarantees might affect the application of the Code's tort provisions, and especially of § 826. It merely held that, in applying § 826, the values reflected in constitutional provisions must be *considered*.[9] The most important consequence of this holding is that in proper cases the Federal Constitutional Court can review the question whether the ordinary courts, in deciding a purely private dispute seemingly governed by a provision of the Civil Code, have given sufficient weight to those postulates and values which have received constitutional recognition.

In subsequent cases, the Constitutional Court emphasized that it was not trying to usurp the function of reviewing the ordinary courts' interpretation and application of the provisions of the Civil Code, and that it would interfere only where the ordinary courts, in applying provisions such as § 826, had given insufficient weight to freedom of speech or other constitutionally protected values. While admitting that the problem of where to draw the line is a disturbing one, the Court indicated that in general it would not overturn a tort judgment for the plaintiff rendered by an ordinary court where defendant's conduct amounted to more than speech,[10] or where the ordinary courts

---

8b. Note that the Lüth case deals with incitement to boycott rather than with defamation. In defamation cases the German courts seem to have been somewhat slower than the U.S. Supreme Court to recognize the "radiation effect" of constitutional provisions protecting freedom of speach. Until the late seventies, the German law of libel was virtually unaffected by such provisions: liability attached if plaintiff succeeded in proving mere negligence. In 1977, however, the Federal Supreme Court extended the constitutional protection to cover libelous statements concerning questions of political relevance; with respect to such matters liability now attaches only if reckless disregard of standards of "journalistic diligence" can be established. See Palandt, Bürgerliches Gesetzbuch, § 823, Anno. 15 (45th ed., 1986). For a comparison of German and American law on this point, see J. Scherer, Pressefreiheit zwischen Wahrheitspflicht und Wahrheitsfindung, 7 Europäische Grundrechte-Zeitschrift 49 (1980).

9. Such a radiation effect can emanate not only from provisions of a country's national instruments such as the European Human Rights Convention. In Germany and in several other European countries, the provisions of the Convention have been cited by the courts in deciding disputes among private parties, e.g., disputes involving the question whether a particular contractual provision violates the public order or prevailing principles of morality. For examples and references, see A. Z. Drzemczewski, European Human Rights Convention in Domestic Law 199–218 (1983).

In a broader context, the problem of the case is interestingly discussed by K. M. Lewan, The Significance of Constitutional Rights for Private Law: Theory and Practice in West Germany, 17 Int. & Comp.L.Q. 571 (1968).

10. See, e.g., the *Blinkfüer* case, BVerfGE 25, 256 (1969) (defendant, in addition to "speaking", had put economic pressure on its dealers to boycott the plaintiff's publications). An English-language summary of this interesting case appears in the instructive article by H. G. Rupp. The

had treated defendant's utterance as tortious on account of its form rather than its substance.[11]

See pg 184 supp

_____

OPINION OF THE SWISS FEDERAL COURT IN THE MATTER OF ROGENMOSER AGAINST TIEFENGRUND A.G.

1st Civil Division, October 10, 1933, BGE 59 II 372.

[In May, 1929, the plaintiff as lessee and the defendant as lessor entered into a lease contract involving the Exchange Restaurant at Zurich. Defendant let the space in question to plaintiff for fifteen (15) years beginning July 1, 1930. The annual rentals were to be progressive and were to rise from an initial annual amount of Fr. 150,000 to Fr. 198,000 annually for the last three years of the contract period.

In June, 1931, plaintiff requested that defendant consent to the reduction of the stipulated rentals, on the asserted ground that plaintiff had been hard hit by the depression. When defendant refused to give such consent, plaintiff brought this action.

He demands primarily judicial modification of the lease contract, either by substituting contingent rentals (contingent upon plaintiff's gross receipts) for the stipulated fixed rentals, or by an outright reduction of the fixed rentals. In the alternative, plaintiff asks for a declaration that he is entitled to rescind the contract of lease.

The Commercial Court of the Canton of Zurich dismissed the complaint.

Upon plaintiff's appeal, this judgment was affirmed by the Federal Court.]

Reasons: . . . Pursuant to Articles 254 and 255 of the Code of Obligations, which deal with the contract of lease, a reduction of rentals or a rescission of the lease contract is possible only if the leased property, at the time when the lessee takes possession or subsequently, is in such a condition that it cannot be used in accordance with the contract of lease. This is not the case here, as appears from plaintiff's own contentions. . . .

Thus there remains, as the only possible basis of the action, plaintiff's contention that the lease contract in question contains as an implied condition a clausula rebus sic stantibus.[a] . . .

stitution of the Federal Republic of Germany, 16 St. Louis U.L.J. 359, at 369 (1972).

11. Decision of the Federal Constitutional Court of May 11, 1976, N.J.W. 1976, 1677 (in defendant's publication the plaintiff's publication had been called a "right-radical demagogic muckraking sheet"). In this case the Court held that the form of an utterance enjoys less constitutional protection than its substance. Since the ordinary courts' condemnation of defendant's utterance in this case was based exclusively on its form, the Constitutional Court did

At the same time, the Court indicated that if defendant had expressed the same criticism of plaintiff's publication in a less offensive form, the Constitution would protect defendant from liability in tort.

a. Generally speaking, this Latin phrase, as used by the civilians, means that contracts are made upon the tacit assumption that an existing factual situation having an important bearing on the contract will remain basically stable during the life of the contract. A court applying the doctrine will read into the contract

In Romanist doctrine the view was taken that the so-called clausula rebus sic stantibus constitutes a general limitation on the continued existence of a contractual obligation. Like the other modern codifications, the positive law of Switzerland has not adopted this view. Nevertheless, this Court has recognized that a promisor must be discharged if extraordinary and unforeseeable circumstances render his duty to perform the promise so onerous that insistence upon such performance would cause his economic ruin [citing cases]. However, at the outset there arises the question whether the remedy may consist in judicial adjustment of the terms of the contract, or whether the remedy must be limited to complete termination of the contract. Applied to the instant case, this raises the question whether plaintiff's primary demand for reduction of the rentals should not be denied for this reason alone. . . . The German Reichsgericht declared it permissible for the court to grant the demand of one of the contracting parties, who had already performed, for an increase of the consideration promised by the other party, and thus to adjust the contract to changed conditions which had been brought about by a rise in the price of raw materials (RGZ 100, page 130). Some legal writers have criticized this decision as a "messing around" of the judge in the terms of binding contracts [citing a monograph by Professor Reichel]. From the standpoint of Swiss law, however, there is no decisive objection against permitting judicial modification of a contract in lieu of its termination. It should be pointed out in the first place that, if termination only is permitted, and modification is not, such termination can, in certain cases, be declared only for the future. In such event the termination has no retroactive effect. . . . Such prospective termination of the contract, having effect only for the future, is in the last analysis equivalent to judicial adjustment of the contract. Furthermore, it should be considered that the law itself (Code of Obligations Article 373, Subdivision 2), dealing with service contracts of independent contractors, provides for judicial modification of contractual duties. The criticism directed against Article 373, Subdivision 2, of the Code of Obligations [again citing Professor Reichel's book] is without importance here because it presents an argument which can only be addressed to the legislature. [The Court then points out that in a previous decision the principle expressed in Art. 373, subd. 2, was analogously applied and an adjustment of the terms of the contract granted, although the case did not involve a contract of the kind covered by the terms of that Article of the Code.] . . . If the opponent of the party invoking the clausula rebus sic stantibus should prefer termination of the contract to the adjustment demanded, the court will as a rule decree termination

tion or termination of the contract in case of a substantial change of circumstances.

Treaties among nations give rise to analogous problems in international law. For discussion of these problems, and for further references, see Restatement, Second, Foreign Relations Law of the United States § 153 (1965); H. J. Steiner & D. F. Vagts, Transnational Legal Problems 334 (3d ed., 1986).

rather than adjustment, in view of the principle contained in Art. 20, subd. 2, of the Code of Obligations.[b] . . .

[Having determined that adjustment of the terms of the contract would be a proper remedy *if* the clausula rebus sic stantibus applies, the Court now turns to the question under what circumstances the clausula can be invoked.]

. . . At the bottom of the doctrine of the clausula rebus sic stantibus there is the consideration that even the principle imposing the duty to perform one's contractual obligations is limited by the higher principle of good faith. This is indicated by Art. 24, subd. 4, of the Code of Obligations.[c] If a contract may be rescinded in case of a mistake concerning its necessary original basis, then there must be some relief also in case such basis is subsequently changed in an intolerable degree. . . .

In applying the clausula, this Court has repeatedly used the criterion whether the duty of performance has become so onerous for the obligor that insistence upon his performance would be equivalent to his economic ruin. . . . Upon renewed examination, we cannot adhere to this criterion without qualification. If the principle of bona fides is the yardstick for the application of the clausula, then the decision cannot be made to depend solely upon the effect which the change of circumstances has had upon the *obligor's* duty to perform. The effect of the change on the entire legal relationship must be examined. The criterion of the threatened ruin of the obligor would in the last analysis depend upon his subjective ability to perform. . . . [The court points out that this subjective criterion would be inconsistent with the provision of the Code which prescribes that only objective but not subjective impossibility shall excuse performance.]

The disturbance, through change of circumstances, of the balance between performance and counterperformance must be recognized as a ground for termination or adjustment if such disturbance is great, obvious, excessive. . . . There must be an obvious disproportion. Inasmuch as Art. 21 of the Code of Obligations uses this latter term, we may look to that Article for some indication of what is meant.[e] The

b. The first subdivision of Art. 20 was referred to in Haass v. Wyler, supra. The whole Article reads as follows:

"A contract the contents of which is impossible, illegal or immoral, is invalid.

"If the defect affects only some parts of the contract then only such parts are invalid, unless it appears that without the invalid part the contract would not have been made at all."

Compare subd. 2 of this Article with Section 139 of the German Civil Code, supra, p. 573.

c. Art. 23 declares a contract to be not binding on a party who in entering into such contract was prompted by a material mistake. Art. 24 declares the mistake to be material if . . .

"4. It concerned a factual situation which such party regarded as a necessary basis of the contract under the principles of good faith as generally practiced in business."

d. Compare Sec. 242 of the German Civil Code, supra, p. 575.

e. Art. 21 is the Swiss "usury" provision which the German Reichsgericht (supra, p. 617) thought superior to the German rule embodied in Section 138, subd. 2, of the German Civil Code. Art. 21 of the Swiss Code of Obligations reads as follows:

question of disproportion is to be determined by the objective value of the performances [rendered or promised] as of the time when the issue of the clausula is before the court. [Citing a textbook and a commentary]. . . .

Even such obvious disproportion, however, is not sufficient to justify termination or adjustment of a contract . . . There must be, in addition, the subjective factor that the obligee's insistence upon the terms of the contract amounts to an exploitation of the obligor's emergency, in other words that the conduct of the obligee is usurious and predatory. . . . The decisive question of the instant case, as correctly formulated by the court below, is thus whether defendant's insistence on the original terms of the contract must be characterized as usurious exploitation of an obvious disproportion, caused by the change of conditions, between performance and counterperformance.[f]

It is true that with respect to the making of a contract a predatory intention of one party and an obvious disproportion of performance and counterperformance are not sufficient to give the victim the option to declare the contract not binding. Pursuant to Art. 21 of the Code of Obligations there must be the additional element of distress, lightmindedness or inexperience on the part of the victim. . . . The question arises whether it is not inconsistent to terminate a contract merely because of subsequent change of circumstances and exploitation of an obvious disproportion, that is, on the basis of factors which, if they had been present at the time of the making of the contract, would under the rule of Art. 21 not have sufficed to vitiate the contract. But in reality there is no inconsistency. The legislator may assume that a party entering into a contract will know the relative values of his own promise or performance, on the one hand, and of the counterpromise or counterperformance, on the other. It is thus understandable that the legislator assists the obligor only if such obligor, at the time the contract was made, was afflicted with a special weakness (distress, lightmindedness, inexperience). The subsequent disproportion, however, results from a change of circumstances which is not caused by either party, and for which the party who has to suffer from such change bears no responsibility—otherwise he is entitled to no relief. Therefore, it is not necessary to insist on a subjective requirement insofar as the victim is concerned [i.e., the requirement of distress, lightmindedness or inexperience]. Moreover, in a case of such subsequent substantial disturbance of the balance between performance and counterperformance, there will always be distress on the part of one party, and the ultimate ground for termination or modification of the

"If an obvious disproportion between performance and counterperformance results from a contract the conclusion of which one party has induced by exploiting the distress, lightmindedness or inexperience of the other, then the victimized party may declare within a year from the making of the contract that he is not bound by the contract, and may demand restitution of any performance already rendered."

f. Would this be a workable rule in a jurisdiction where questions of fact are for the jury?

contract lies in the very fact that the other party is exploiting such distress. . . .

[The Court then takes up the contention of the plaintiff that during the crisis years 1931 and 1932 the receipts of his restaurant decreased substantially] . . . The contract of lease was entered into for not less than 15 years. This long duration contained a speculative element, at least on the part of the plaintiff. Also the nature and the size of the premises rendered it clear from the beginning that the contractual risk was a substantial one. Contracts of this kind should not be lightly terminated or modified. Where a contract is made for a long period of time, each party must count on substantial fluctuations of the general level of prosperity [citing a decision of a Zurich court] . . . This does not mean that the clausula rebus sic stantibus is never applicable to contracts of lease. But in the case of such slightly speculative contracts it makes no difference whether the subsequent change of conditions was actually foreseen, or whether it was merely foreseeable. Otherwise the clausula would put a premium on rashness and lightmindedness, to the detriment of the other party. . . . In the instant case, moreover, it was the plaintiff who repeatedly and insistently urged the defendant to enter into the contract, by picturing various advantages. Particularly in his letter of December 9, 1929,[g] plaintiff referred to the income from his other restaurant, the "Paradise", which he put at Fr. 80–90,000 annually, and with respect to which he said: "This financial reserve may be an attraction also from your point of view." The court below rightly inferred from this that plaintiff was conscious of the possibility of bad years, and that he tried to impress the defendant with his ability to cover any losses from the restaurant in the instant premises by the use of his other revenues. Consequently, plaintiff cannot now contend that defendant, by demanding that plaintiff actually use that "financial reserve", is exploiting a disproportion between performance and counterperformance. . . . Moreover, plaintiff has not even alleged that the objective rental value of the leased premises has fallen since the time when the contract was made, or that similar space in Zurich would today be available for a substantially lesser rental.

Affirmed.

NOTES AND QUESTIONS

(1) After the principal case had been decided by the highest court, the tenant gave notice of termination pursuant to Art. 269 of the Code of Obligations, which provides that a contract of lease, even before it is terminated or terminable by its terms, shall come to an end at the close of any half-year period if either party, "for reasons of weight which make . . . the continuation of the lease intolerable for him," gives three months' notice of termination; to be effective, such notice must

g. This date is possibly a misprint. Although supplementary agreements between the parties were made in 1930, it appears that the principal contract of lease was made on May 10, 1929.

contain an offer of "full compensation" for the damages which the other party suffers by reason of the premature termination of the lease.

This notice of termination was followed by new litigation, and the matter, again, came before the highest court. On May 29, 1934, the Federal Court *held* in Rogenmoser v. Tiefengrund A. G., 60 BGE II 205, that the lease was effectively terminated pursuant to Art. 269 of the Code of Obligations, and remanded the case to the lower court for determination of the amount payable by the tenant as "full compensation."

Upon remand, the lower court fixed the amount of damages at sfrs. 400,000. The tenant appealed again, and the Federal Court, in its third decision dealing with this dispute, *held* on October 29, 1935 (Rogenmoser v. Tiefengrund A. G., 61 BGE II 259) that this amount should be reduced to sfrs. 200,000. The evidence showed that the premises could be re-let by the landlord only for a substantially lesser rental, and that, consequently, the landlord would suffer an annual loss of revenue of sfrs. 100,000 for the remaining term of the lease, that is, for 11 years. The Court reasoned that under these circumstances, if the tenant had been guilty of a *breach* of the lease contract, the damages would amount to sfrs. 1,100,000; but that in case of a *termination* authorized by Art. 269 the amount so computed is subject to a reduction "*ex aequo et bono.*" The Court took the view that the following considerations justified the drastic reduction (from sfrs. 1,100,000 to sfrs. 200,000):

(a) The tenant was not guilty of fraud or negligence.

(b) The economic crisis was foreseeable not only for the tenant but also for the landlord.

(c) The damages were caused in part by the landlord's stubborn insistence upon payment of a rental which was unbearably high.

(d) If the tenant had to pay the amount of sfrs. 400,000 fixed by the lower court, he would be exposed to misery.

(e) A certain discount must be deducted from rentals payable in future years.

(f) A portion of the premises might be used for purposes other than a restaurant.

Are the 1934 and 1935 decisions of the Federal Court consistent with the principal case? Can you explain why the tenant did not invoke Art. 269 in the principal case?

It is recognized in Switzerland that Art. 269 of the Code of Obligations constitutes a specific application of the general principle of the clausula rebus sic stantibus to the law of landlord and tenant. See Oser-Schoenenberger, Das Obligationenrecht, Art. 269, Ann. 1 (1936). That being so, could it not be argued that in the law of landlord and tenant the general principle should be invoked only within the limits specified by Art. 269? Is this the view taken by the Court in the principal case? What conclusions can you draw from the principal case concerning the breadth and pervasiveness of general principles and "general clauses", as distinguished from specific provisions of the codes?

(2) Compare the following case, also decided by a Swiss court: In 1930, at which time plaintiff was an officer and director of defendant corporation, the parties entered into an employment contract which

contained a provision whereby defendant promised to pay plaintiff 1000 francs per month from his retirement until the end of his life. Subsequently, it was agreed between the parties that plaintiff's retirement should begin in 1934. The promised monthly payments were made until 1945. In the latter year, defendant reduced the monthly payments to 40% of the promised amount, invoking the clausula rebus sic stantibus on the ground that its business had suffered a severe setback due to conditions then prevailing in Europe. Plaintiff sued for the balance of the promised payments, and was successful in the court of first instance. Upon defendant's appeal to the Appellate Court of the Canton of Basel, *held*, affirmed. The risk of a deterioration of its business was assumed by defendant, as shown by the contract as a whole, and especially by a clause therein dealing with plaintiff's rights in case of defendant's liquidation. [No such liquidation had occurred.] Hence, the deterioration of defendant's business was not an unforeseen event, but a contingency which was, at least implicitly, covered by the terms of the contract. Appellationsgericht Basel-Stadt, February 7, 1947, reported in 45 Schweizerische Juristenzeitung 42 (1949).

(3) The Greek Civil Code of 1946, one of the most modern and most carefully drafted civil-law codifications, has recognized the clausula rebus sic stantibus doctrine in the text of the Code itself. Its Art. 388 reads as follows:

> "If the circumstances in which the parties, having regard to the rules of good faith and to business practice, decided to conclude a synallagmatic contract,[1] subsequently change, for extraordinary reasons which it was impossible to foresee, and if, as a result of this change, fulfilment of the obligations, taking into account the counter-obligations, becomes inordinately burdensome for the obligor, the latter may request the judge to reduce the obligations at his discretion to a suitable extent, or to rescind the whole of the contract or the part not carried out."

In the Alsing case, an arbitration proceeding brought by a subsidiary of the Swedish Match Company against the Government of Greece, the plaintiff asked the arbitrator, on the basis of the foregoing provision, to extend the duration of the contract between the parties; but the arbitrator (the then President of the Swiss Federal Tribunal) held that the frustration of the expectations of the parties was not so profound as to merit judicial intervention. He expressed doubt whether, even if the circumstances of the case justified some judicial tampering with the terms of the contract, it would be proper to prolong its agreed-upon duration.[2]

(4) For enlightening comparative discussions of the problems raised by the principal case see J. P. Dawson, Judicial Revision of Frustrated Contracts: Germany, 63 B.U.L.Rev. 1039 (1983); P. Hay, Frustration and Its Solution in German Law, 10 Am.J.Comp.L. 345 (1961); H. Smit,

---

1. In civil-law terminology, the expression "synallagmatic" refers to contracts in which both parties make mutually dependent promises. Very roughly, one could equate synallagmatic contracts with bilateral contracts; but with respect to the term "bilateral" there are subtle differences between common-law and civil-law terminology. See 1 Schlesinger (Gen.Ed.), Formation of Contracts—A Study of the Common Core of Legal Systems 92–93 (1968).

2. The important parts of the arbitrator's opinion are set forth in the article by S. M. Schwebel, The Alsing Case, 8 Int. & Comp.L.Q. 320 (1959). See especially at 341 ff.

Frustration of Contract: A Comparative Attempt at Consolidation, 58 Colum.L.Rev. 287 (1958).[2a]

Common-law courts ordinarily will not use the Latin terms *bona fides* and *clausula rebus sic stantibus*; but by invoking "implied conditions", "impossibility" or "frustration of purpose" they often reach comparable results. See Patterson, Constructive Conditions in Contracts, 42 Colum.L.Rev. 903, 943 ff. (1942); Farnsworth, Contracts 670 ff. (1982).[3]

There remains, however, an important difference between the civil-law and the common-law approach to the problem. This difference is illustrated by the dictum in the principal case, to the effect that if the tenant's factual showing had been sufficiently strong, the Swiss court would have had the power (in lieu of terminating the contract) to let the tenant stay in the rented premises for the balance of the agreed-upon period, but at a judicially reduced rent. Common-law courts—although occasionally they show some boldness in "interpreting" the terms of an agreement—rarely assert such a sweeping power to adjust the terms of a contract to changed circumstances.[3a] Perhaps there is more need for the exercise of this broad judicial power in the civil-law systems, where a contract, so long as its performance is physically possible, as a rule can be specifically enforced.[3b] In the common-law systems, in which the normal remedy for a breach of contract is an action for damages, the necessary adjustment frequently can be brought about by rules permitting a reasonable determination of the amount of damages (see also infra, text at n. 5).

Both common law and civil law thus have developed methods of adjustment which can be employed in order to reach equitable results in the cases, or at least in some of the cases, in which the contractual

2a. See also 2 K. Zweigert & H. Kötz, An Introduction to Comparative Law 187 ff. (1977), where a wealth of further references can be found. For a recent discussion of the clausula rebus sic stantibus in German law, see H. Korbion, The Effects of Changed Conditions on the Contractor's Remuneration According to German Construction Law, in P. Gauch and J. Sweet, Selected Problems of Construction Law: International Approach 187 ff. (1983).

3. Common-law courts, indeed, have been criticized for having adopted too sweeping and too "civilian" an approach in dealing with the problem of frustration of contracts. See H. J. Berman, Excuse for Nonperformance in the Light of Contract Practices in International Trade, 63 Colum.L.Rev. 1413 (1963), where it is argued that our courts should return to the true common-law method of deriving a solution in each case from discriminating analysis of the particular contract or type of contract before the court. See also supra p. 587, n. 4.

3a. Even under the liberal rule of UCC § 2–615, commercial impracticability caused by unforeseen circumstances merely "excuses a seller from timely delivery of goods". Official Comment 1. There is no judicial rewriting of the terms of the contract. But the Restatement Second takes a step in the direction of the civil-law approach: for both impracticability (§ 261) and frustration (§ 265) it gives the court the power "to grant relief on such terms as justice requires", including protection of the parties' reliance interests, if this is necessary to avoid "injustice" (§ 272). However, until now few courts have engaged in such equitable adjustment of contractual relationships. See Farnsworth, Contracts 705 (1982). For an elaborate and judicious discussion of the adjustment problem in American law, see S. W. Halpern, Application of the Doctrine of Commercial Impracticability: Searching for "the Wisdom of Solomon", 135 U.Pa.L.Rev. 1123 (1987).

3b. For discussion of a German case in which the court in effect rewrote the terms of a contract the enforcement of which would have been highly inequitable because of drastically changed circumstances, see E. A. Farnsworth, Disputes Over Omission in Contracts, 68 Colum.L.Rev. 860, at 883–84 (1968).

relationship has been disturbed by an unanticipated and radical change of circumstances. The difference between common-law and civil-law methods of adjustment is significant mainly in situations involving a long-term contract. Here the extraordinary (and sparingly exercised) power of the courts of some civil-law countries—to let the contractual relationship continue but to modify the terms of the contract—has hardly any counterpart in the common law.[3c]

(5) Note the subtlety displayed by the Swiss Federal Court in the Rogenmoser cases. In the first case, the Court refused to employ the sweeping clausula doctrine for the purpose of modifying the contract or releasing the tenant from his contractual obligations. In the second case, however, the Court held that pursuant to a specific provision of the Code, the tenant had the right to terminate the contract, provided he would hold the landlord harmless.[4] The third decision of the Court fixed a very moderate amount of damages.

With no less subtlety, our courts sometimes manage to refuse application of the frustration doctrine, and yet to avoid a "pound of flesh" result. They do so by (a) equity's discretionary refusal to order specific performance,[5] combined with (b) the law court's reliance on the good sense of a jury which, in fixing the amount of damages in a situation like that presented by the principal case, might well arrive at a practical result similar to that ultimately reached in the Swiss litigation.

The foregoing, however, requires some qualification. In situations in which the creditor can bring a legal action in debt, our law may be less flexible, and more conducive to "pound of flesh" results, than the civilian codes. Similarly, in a situation in which, as in the principal case, a tenant is forced by economic circumstances to abandon the leased property,[6] an action for the full stipulated amount of rent may lie under our law, and not merely an action for damages.[7]

3c. For a rare case where a court did tamper with the terms of a long-term contract, see Miller v. Campello Co-Op Bank, 344 Mass. 76, 181 N.E.2d 345 (1962); note, however, that the court in that case failed to discuss the relevant issues of law. Other "aberrational" cases of this kind are discussed by Halpern, supra n. 3a.

4. Modern codes frequently contain provisions authorizing unilateral termination for cause (for "reasons of weight") of long-term agreements, such as leases, partnership agreements and employment contracts. Such termination for cause is possible before the end of the agreed-upon term, but sometimes it is conditioned upon payment of damages.

Code provisions of this kind ordinarily refer to particular types of contracts. In some civil-law countries, however, the courts have used such code provisions as starting points for analogical reasoning and thus have developed a broad principle to the effect that all long-term contractual relationships may be terminated by either party before the end of the agreed-upon period of the contract, if reasons of weight justifying such premature termination can be shown.

5. See 407 East 61st Garage, Inc. v. Savoy Fifth Avenue Corp., 23 N.Y.2d 275, 283, 296 N.Y.S.2d 338, 244 N.E.2d 37, 42 (1968); Note, Equitable Contract Remedies—Denial of Both Specific Performance and Rescission, 32 Mich.L.Rev. 518 (1934).

6. In the landlord-tenant cases, a common-law court encounters the additional difficulty that basically a lease is an estate and not a "contract", and that there is doubt concerning the extent to which contract principles may be applied at all. See Wright v. Baumann, 239 Or. 410, 398 P.2d 119, at 120–21 (1965). On special problems concerning the application of the doctrine of frustration to lease cases, see Farnsworth, supra n. 3a, at 693–94.

As to the contractual nature of a lease in most civil-law countries, see supra p. 685. The difference between common-law and civil-law thinking regarding the nature of a lease is discussed at length in Viterbo v.

7. See note 7 on page 740.

What is the reason for this occasional inflexibility of our law? Could it be connected with the fact that the *forms of action*, although buried and emphatically "abolished" in most jurisdictions, still rule us from their graves, and that, in particular, the distinction between debt and assumpsit is still with us? Perhaps, we are dealing here with one of the areas in which our courts must slowly, step by step, free themselves of the grip of the forms of action [8]—a problem from which civil-law courts have been saved by the strength of their scholars' systematizing influence and by the codifiers' break with the past.

See supr. p 185

H. C. GUTTERIDGE, ABUSE OF RIGHTS
5 Cambridge Law Journal 22, 32–39 (1933).[*]

[Most of the author's footnotes omitted.]

. . . [The] operation of the theory of abuse in practice may be illustrated by reference to three of the leading French cases.

Chronologically the first of these is a decision of the Court of Appeal of Colmar given in the year 1855. The owner of a house erected a tall dummy chimney on his roof for the sole purpose of annoying a neighbouring householder by depriving him of the access of light to certain of his rooms. Art. 552 of the Code Civil states that the owner of land can plant or build on it whatever he thinks proper, subject only to certain exceptions which are irrelevant for our present purpose.[a] It was argued that the defendant was merely doing what he had an absolute right to do, and that the motive of his act must be disregarded, but it was held by the Court that this was no answer to the claim. Although the defendant was exercising a right given to him by the law he was acting with spiteful intent, and had no serious and legitimate interest in what he was doing. His act must, therefore, be treated as wrongful.

Friedlander, 120 U.S. 707, 7 S.Ct. 962 (1887).

7. In the majority of American jurisdictions it has been held that the landlord, unless he has accepted the tenant's surrender of the leasehold, can sue for rent rather than damages, and that the landlord's claim for rent is not defeated or diminished by virtue of his failure, or even his outright refusal, to look for another tenant or to take any other steps tending to mitigate damages. See the cases collected in M. Friedman on Leases, Vol. II, pp. 842–43 (2d ed., 1983). The lower New York courts have recently drawn a distinction between residential and other leases and now impose a mitigation requirement if the lease is of the former kind. See, e.g., Forty Exchange Co. v. Cohen, 125 Misc.2d 475, 479 N.Y.S.2d 628 (Civ. Ct. 1984).

8. Cf. Wright v. Baumann, supra n. 6, and authorities there cited.

[*] Reprinted by permission of Cambridge Law Journal.

a. Article 552 of the French Civil Code still reads as quoted by Prof. Gutteridge. But it must now be read in conjunction with Code de l'Urbanisme art. L 112–1, which provides: "The right to build is part of the ownership of the land. It is exercised subject to the rules contained in the statutes and administrative regulations relating to the use of land." Rules on land use control, building permits, etc. are contained in the Code de l'Urbanisme and in the Code de la Construction et de l'Habitation. To-day, the owners of the two "spite" structures mentioned by Prof. Gutteridge would not, presumably, have received a building permit.

A year later a decision to the same effect was given by the Court of Appeal of Lyons, only in this case the question turned not on the erection of a structure, but on the excavation of the subsoil, the circumstances being much the same as those in Mayor of Bradford v. Pickles.[42] There was a number of adjacent springs yielding the famous St. Galmier mineral water, and the proprietor of one of the springs installed a powerful pump with the result that the yield of an adjoining spring belonging to another owner was diminished by two-thirds. There does not seem to have been any direct evidence of spite in this case, but it was inferred that the owner of the pump was inspired solely by a desire to inflict harm because he merely wasted the additional supply of water which he had obtained in this way. Reliance was placed by the defendant on Art. 544 of the Code Civil which states that "ownership is the right of enjoying and disposing of a thing in the most unlimited manner provided that it is not utilized in a manner forbidden by law." It was decided in terms that where an act is done with the sole and deliberate intention of inflicting harm it is wrongful and cannot be justified by pleading a proprietary right.[b]

The third case which is of a curious and interesting description was decided many years later [1917] by the Court of Cassation. It is the most famous of all the decisions which have been given on this question and it is one of the few French cases which is referred to by name, i.e. as the "*affaire Clément-Bayard.*" The Clément-Bayard Company were the owners of certain hangars in which they housed airships which were being built to the order of the French Government. Friction arose between the company and the owner of the adjoining site, who was piqued by the failure of negotiations for the purchase by the company of his land at a high valuation. He erected within his own boundaries a number of wooden scaffolds of a considerable height fitted with projections bristling with spikes. The intention was, of course, to bring pressure to bear on the company by making it impossible or difficult to launch the airships, and in fact on one occasion an airship collided with one of these structures and was severely damaged. In an action brought by the Clément-Bayard Company for damages and an order for the removal of the obstructions, it was pleaded by the defendant that he

---

42. [1895] A.C. 587. [That case is still good law in England; but its effect has been greatly weakened by a recent statute. See Megarry and Wade, The Law of Real Property 72 (4th ed., 1975). In the United States the majority of jurisdictions, rejecting the rule of Mayor of Bradford v. Pickles and adopting the doctrine of reasonable use, have reached a result comparable to that of the French decisions. See 5 R. R. Powell, The Law of Real Property, ¶696 (Recompilation by P. J. Rohan, 1986); Pound, The French Civil Code and the Spirit of 19th Century Law, 35 B.U.L.Rev. 87, 95 (1955). For a case which on its facts is similar to the French *St. Galmier* case,

see Hathorn v. Natural Carbonic Gas Co., 194 N.Y. 326, 87 N.E. 504 (1909). Ed.]

b. This decision was reached although the defendant was able to point, not only to the general definition of property rights in Art. 544, but also to the specific language of Art. 641 which then read: "The owner of land on which a spring rises is entitled to make such use of it as he pleases." See Amos, The Code Napoleon and the Modern World, 10 J.Comp.Leg. & Int.L. (3rd Ser.) 222, 232 (1928). More than 40 years after the St. Galmier case, Art. 641 (renumbered 642) was amended by the addition of the words "within the limits and for the purposes of his property".

was merely exercising a right given to him by the provisions of the Code Civil which have been just cited. It was held successively by the Civil Tribunal of Compiégne, the Court of Appeal of Amiens and the Court of Cassation that the defendant was liable. The case is important because the defendant was in a sense animated by more than one motive. His primary intention seems to have been to force the Clément-Bayard Company to buy him out, but he also intended, if necessary, to wreck their airships for this purpose. It was held that the dominant motive must be taken to have been the infliction of harm, since the circumstances showed that the defendant hoped to secure his ends by the threat of injury to the airships of the plaintiff company. He could not, therefore, be permitted to shelter himself behind the plea that, whereas one of his motives was the deliberate infliction of harm, the other was not.[c]

It seems to be beyond doubt that the French Courts will invariably repress any spiteful exercise of a proprietary right. But the principle of abuse has also been extended so as to cover a much wider area. . . . Thus it has been held to be abusive for an employer to refuse to employ trade unionists where his motive is to damage the trade union, and likewise for a trade union to blacklist an employer from a vindictive motive.[d] Dramatic criticism of an unfavourable character is abusive if it is prompted solely by a desire to harm the author of a play. The malicious institution of legal proceedings also comes under this heading; in fact an English lawyer will find that many matters which we regard as separate wrongs have been swept up by the French Courts into the net of the abuse of rights. Planiol attributes this to the popularity of the word "abuse" ("l'expression a fait fortune") and he holds the opinion, which is supported by other writers, that the concept has been exaggerated and overworked.

. . . [Turning to German law], Art. 226[e] (the famous "*Schikaneverbot*") runs as follows: *"The exercise of a right is forbidden if it can have no other purpose than to harm some other person."* . . . A close examination of the words employed in Art. 226 shows that its operation is limited to cases in which it is possible to establish that a right has been exercised *solely* for the purpose of harming some other person. As I have already pointed out, this is a matter which it is

c. Faced with a fact situation remarkably similar to that presented in the French *Clément-Bayard* case, an American court reached the same result, but without invoking a theory as pervasive as "abuse of rights". See Commonwealth v. Von Bestecki, 30 Pa.D. & C. 137 (1937). Compare also Schork v. Epperson, 74 Wyo. 286, 287 P.2d 467 (1955).

d. For a discussion of the doctrine of abuse of rights in the context of French labor law, see Lenhoff, Compulsory Unionism in Europe, 5 Am.J.Comp.L. 18, 37–38 (1956).

Code du Travail art. 412–2 now prohibits employers from discriminating against workers on account of their participation in a union, and Code du Travail art. 481–3 penalizes such conduct. There is thus no more need for employees to rely on the doctrine of abuse of rights in such a case. For a somewhat analogous, but much broader rule under German law, see Betriebsverfassungsgesetz (Law on the Organization of Enterprises) § 75.

e. The reference is to Section 226 of the German Civil Code; see supra, p. 575.

extremely difficult to prove in a great many cases. The German courts have realized this, and they have accordingly adopted an objective test of intention by which an *animus vicini nocendi* can be inferred from the circumstances. Even so, the difficulties of proof are often such as to render Art. 226 inoperative.[57] But it has been found to be useful in the case of the spiteful exercise of proprietary rights, and the experience of German lawyers is that it has not been accompanied by any undesirable restrictions on the liberties of individuals. . . . It has been held to be abusive for a father to refuse, for purely personal reasons, to allow his son to visit his mother's tomb, situated on land belonging to the father.[59] It is clear, however, that the tendency is to place a strict interpretation on the provisions of Art. 226, and that the role which it plays in checking abuses of legal rights is correspondingly restricted.

The German law of civil wrongs does not recognize any general duty to refrain from inflicting harm on others, but it is much more supple and adaptable in this respect than our law of torts. This is due to the operation of two of the articles of the Civil Code (Arts. 138 [f] and 826 [g]) which have as their object the repression of acts which are against *Sittlichkeit* ("boni mores"). . . . The standard of boni mores must obviously vary from tribunal to tribunal, but it is a real and potent force in the development of German law, and it has conferred praetorian powers on the German judges. So far as the theory of abuse is concerned it is difficult to conceive of any case in which the malevolent exercise of a right could not be checked by the application of the principle of *boni mores.*

. . . Mention must also be made of another concept of German law which plays its part in curbing the abuse of legal rights. Where the enforcement of a business contract is in question the Civil Code by virtue of Arts. 157 [h] and 242 [i] requires that the parties shall act in accordance with *Treu und Glauben.* This again is a term which defies accurate translation, but it means that the parties must act in accordance with good faith as understood by men of affairs. In such cases as commercial sales, for example, this is a principle which may often be invoked to restrain an abusive exercise of a contractual right. . . .

57. It may be observed that this is perhaps due, to some extent, to the fact that the parties to an action do not, normally, give evidence in Germany, and are not cross-examined. [The court may, however, order that a party be examined, usually by a member of the court, and sometimes under oath. Professor Gutteridge is nevertheless right in implying that in Germany as in most civil-law countries the procedural devices for extracting information from an unwilling adversary are weaker than in common-law jurisdictions. See supra, pp. 426–428. Ed.]

59. . . . Art. 226 has also been employed as a check to prevent the rejection of goods by a buyer for some trivial fault. [citation], and cf. Jackson v. Rotax Motor Co. [1910], 2 K.B. 937. It is also available as a remedy against the malicious institution of legal proceedings. [citation]

f. See supra p. 569.

g. See supra p. 688.

h. "Contracts must be interpreted in accordance with the principles of good faith, with due regard to usage."

i. See supra p. 575.

The Swiss law deals with abuses of rights . . . [in] Art. 2 of the Civil Code [, which] provides that *"every person is bound to exercise his rights and to fulfil his obligations according to the principles of good faith. The law does not protect the manifest abuse of a right."* It will be observed that nothing is said about intention to harm one's neighbour; the Code goes straight to the point and condemns an abuse of rights in so many words without defining the phrase in any way. . . .

This is one of the instances of the policy adopted by the framers of the Swiss Codes in abandoning certain questions entirely to the judges. Art. 4 of the Civil Code states that where the law expressly leaves a question to the discretion of a judge he must base his decision on principles of justice and equity, a provision which is supplementary to Art. 1 of the Code [j] which directs the judge to apply the spirit as well as the letter of the law. . . .

NOTE ON "ABUS DES DROITS"

For an understanding of the French doctrine of abus des droits it is important to realize that the doctrine is sometimes used as a basis for a *cause of action*, and sometimes as a basis for a *defense*. Where a cause of action is based on defendant's abuse of a right, it is technically supported by the famous Article 1382 of the French Civil Code (supra p. 555) which in broad terms imposes liability upon anybody who "causes damage to another." The counterclaim for damages in the case of Kirsch v. Davoust, infra, can be so supported.

In those cases, however, in which abus des droits is interposed as a defense against an action based on a technically well-founded right, many French authors have felt that the tort provision of the Code, broad as it is, cannot be the true basis supporting the defense. Therefore, under the leadership of Josserand,[1] they substitute for the older tort theory of abus des droits the modern theory that every Code article or other statute creating a right must be *interpreted* as limiting the exercise of such right to the object for which it was created.[2] It goes without saying that in the hands of judges holding strong progressive convictions this theory of the relativity of rights could become a potent instrument of social reform. Contrary to the expectations of some theorists, however, the French courts have not attempted to use the doctrine for such a purpose.[3] In France as elsewhere, the modern welfare state has been inaugurated by legislative and administrative measures of *dirigisme*, and not by judicial expansion of the concept of abus des droits.

The preliminary draft prepared in the 1950s by the Civil Code Reform Commission contained an express provision (Art. 147) dealing with abuse of rights:[4]

j. See supra p. 653.

1. Josserand, supported by the writings of Duguit, Saleilles and Charmont, wrote the classical treatise on the subject, entitled De l'Abus des Droits (1905, second ed. 1927).

2. See Walton, Motive as an Element in Torts in the Common and in the Civil Law, 22 Harv.L.Rev. 501 (1909).

3. See Ripert, Le Régime Démocratique et le Droit Civil Moderne 219 (1948).

4. See Julliot de la Morandière (transl. by Dainow), Preliminary Report of the Civil Code Reform Commission of France, 16 La.L.Rev. 1, 27–28 (1955).

"Every act or every fact which, by the intention of its author, by its object or by the circumstances in which it occurred, manifestly exceeds the normal exercise of a right, is not protected by the law and makes its author responsible.

"This provision does not apply to rights which by their nature or by virtue of the law can be exercised in a discretionary manner".[5]

No innovation would be brought about by the enactment of this provision which, by the requirement that the act *manifestly* exceed the *normal* exercise of the right in question, carefully steers away from the more radical terms in which some authors had asserted the "relativity" of all individual rights.[6] The formulation chosen by the draftsmen seems to be intended merely to restate, briefly and abstractly, the doctrine as it now exists in decisional law.[7]

DECISION OF THE FRENCH COUR DE CASSATION IN THE MATTER OF KIRSCH c. DAVOUST

Req. June 21, 1926, S.[a] 1926 1.294.

The Court. . . . Considering that the spouses Kirsch have sought to have nullified, as lacking in the necessary requirements of form and substance, the holographic testament dated December 20, 1918, by which Mme. Redenbach disinherited her sister, Mme. Kirsch, and made Davoust her universal heir; that after the taking of oral

5. The notion that there are certain rights which are discretionary or absolute, with the result that the exercise of such rights can never constitute an "abuse of rights", was by no means a novel idea of the Reform Commission. On the contrary, the notion is well established in existing French case law. The number of such absolute rights (which in effect are exempted from the operation of the doctrine of abuse of rights) is not large. Examples are: the right to refuse to contract (even though the right is subject to statutory exceptions, as in the case of public services); the right of parents to consent to the marriage of a minor child, or to refuse such consent; the right to make a will and to disinherit one's statutory distributees (within the limits drawn by code provisions concerning the rights which the decedent's spouse and children have as compulsory heirs); the right to enforce a contractual penalty clause (subject, however, since 1975, to judicial modification of the amount of the penalty); the right of the majority shareholders of a corporation to remove a member of the board of directors. See Dainow, supra n. 4; P. Bonassies, Die Ermessensfreiheit des Richters und die Rolle der Billigkeit im französischen Recht, in J. Esser (Ed.), Ermessensfreiheit und Billigkeitsspielraum des Zivilrichters 72 (1964).

6. For a discussion of the conflicting doctrinal views, see Ripert, supra n. 3, at 209–228.

7. For more extensive discussions of the French doctrine of abuse of rights, see P. Catala and J. A. Weir, Delict and Torts: A Study in Parallel, 38 Tul.L.Rev. 221 (1964); J. H. Crabb, The French Concept of Abuse of Rights, 6 Inter-Am.L.Rev. 1 (1964); A. Mayrand, Abuse of Rights in France and Quebec, 34 La.L.Rev. 993 (1974); V. Bolgár, Abuse of Rights in France, Germany and Switzerland: A Survey of a Recent Chapter in Legal Doctrine, 35 La.L.Rev. 1015 (1975).

For a thorough discussion of the operation of the abuse of rights doctrine in a particular area of social concern, see Z. L. Zile, Judicial Control of Land Use in France, 45 Cornell L.Q. 288 (1960). In reading that article, one must, however, bear the large amount of subsequent enactments in mind.

a. This abbreviation stands for Recueil général des lois et des arrêts, fondé par J.-B. Sirey.

testimony the trial judges decided that the testament was duly made and executed by the testatrix, and dismissed the action of the spouses Kirsch, decreeing that they should pay damages in the amount of Fr. 500 in favor of Davoust;

Considering that according to the contention of the appellants that imposition of damages was unlawful, on the ground that the pursuit of legal remedies cannot constitute a wrong unless accompanied by acts of malice or bad faith, which acts were not found by the court; but

Considering that it appears from the findings of the court below that the spouses Kirsch, who had charged that Mme. Redenbach had made no testament at all, neither on December 20, 1918, nor on any subsequent day until her death, have not produced any evidence at the hearing; that they did not hesitate to assert as true a fact of which they were not sure; that they have attributed sentiments to the deceased which were inconsistent with her real sentiments as proved at the hearing; that they have thus altered the truth for the manifest purpose of influencing the judges in favor of their position; that by the protracted proceedings wantonly initiated and pursued by them they have caused Davoust not only trouble but also expenses over and above taxable costs and fees; [b]

Considering that from these dominant findings the court could infer that the spouses Kirsch did not limit themselves to the legitimate pursuit of their legal remedies, but have committed a tort to the prejudice of Davoust, and that the order [of the court below] is thus found to be legally justified, . . .

Rejects the appeal taken against the order of the court at Bourges dated February 25, 1925.

[The omitted part of the opinion shows that Davoust was the lover of the testatrix and that the latter, although not legally married to him, signed the testament as "Mme Davoust". The spouses Kirsch thus might have had an arguable point in seeking to have the will declared

---

b. It should be remembered that in France, although in principle the "loser pays all" rule is followed, a distinction must be drawn between the fees of the victorious party's *avoué*, and the fees of his *avocat*. Prior to the recent procedural reforms which established a more refined rule (see supra p. 367), only the victorious *avoué's* fees could be recovered from the loser as costs, but not the fees paid by the winning party to his *avocat*. See P. Herzog, Civil Procedure in France 542–43 (1967). The lower court, therefore, was unquestionably right in finding that Davoust incurred legal expenses over and above taxable costs.

Article 700 of the new Code of Civil Procedure now gives the court discretionary power to award costs not normally recoverable if it seems equitable to do so. See supra p. 367. Moreover, new Code of Civil Procedure art. 32–1 now provides that he who proceeds in court in an abusive or dilatory manner may be fined, in addition to being subject to liability for damages. Similar provisions have been inserted into the Code in connection with a number of more specific procedures to prevent their "abuse". See new Code of Civil Procedure art. 581. But so as not to discourage the bringing of meritorious claims or the raising of meritorious defenses, French courts apply fairly strict criteria before finding an abuse. The party concerned will normally have to have acted with malice or with a recklessness that may be equated with malice. See J. Vincent & S. Guichard, Procédure Civile at No. 20 (20th ed. 1981).

invalid under Articles 1131 and 1133 of the French Civil Code.[c] These Articles, although in terms applicable only to "obligations", are generally held to apply by analogy to other kinds of jural acts, including testaments. If this had been the principal contention of the spouses Kirsch, then it would perhaps be hard to understand why the Court regarded their attack against the validity of the will as "wanton." It appears, however, that the spouses Kirsch put the main emphasis of their attack upon the baseless contention that no will had ever been duly executed by the deceased.]

NOTES AND QUESTIONS

(1) Would an American court permit Davoust to recover on the theory of malicious prosecution? If so, could he recover by way of a counterclaim in the very action that was maliciously brought against him?[1]

c. Article 1131: "An obligation without cause, or with a wrongful or illicit cause, can have no effect."

Article 1133: "A cause is illicit when it is prohibited by law, or when it is contrary to good morals or to public order."

With respect to liberalities in favor of the donor's or testator's concubine, the French courts have drawn some fine distinctions. Where the purpose of the gift is to induce or preserve the illicit relationship, it is held to have an immoral causa; but a different result is reached in cases where the donor's main object is to assure the future livelihood of the donee, or where the liberality is prompted by the memory of a relationship no longer in existence. The burden of proving the motives and circumstances making the liberality an illicit one is always imposed on the party attacking it. For an excellent comparison of the French, German and Swiss decisions on the subject, see W. Müller-Freienfels, Zur Rechtsprechung beim sogenannten "Mätressen-Testament", 23 JZ 441 (1968).

In American law, one observes a remarkable contrast between (a) cases dealing with wills in favor of the testator's concubine—see 1 Page On Wills § 3.14 (1960 and Supps.) and Anno., 76 ALR3d 743 (1977)—and (b) cases which involve a promise to make a will in favor of such a person. As to the latter, see 1 Williston On Contracts § 148 (3d Ed. by Jaeger, 1957 and 1977 Supp.); 15 Williston on Contracts § 1745 (3rd ed. by Jaeger, 1972 and Supp.). The inconsistency between these two lines of cases may reflect a dislike for the kind of broad, pervasive, and consistently applied principles of which the civilians are so fond.

1. ". . . it is well settled that a claim in the nature of malicious prosecution, which arises out of the main action, generally cannot be asserted as a compulsory or a permissive counterclaim, since such a claim is premature prior to the determination of the main action. 3 Moore's Federal Practice ¶13.13, at 13–308 (2d ed. 1974)." Harris v. Steinem, 571 F.2d 119, 124 (2 Cir., 1978).

For a recent study discussing the insufficiencies of the current action for malicious prosecution and suggesting some improvements, see Recommendation of the [New York] Law Revision Commission to the 1984 Legislature Relating to Malicious Prosecution Actions, N.Y. Leg. Doc. (1984) No. 65[G]. While the Commission suggested some changes, it advised against the right to interpose a malicious prosecution claim as a counterclaim, fearing such a counterclaim would then become routine in all suits.

Another way to combat abusive litigation tactics is by the imposition of costs not otherwise payable. See now Fed. R. Civ. Pro. R 11 (as amended in 1983), under which attorneys' fees caused by frivolous litigation may be recoverable. Cf. Note, Plausible Pleadings, Developing Standards for Rule 11 Sanctions, 100 Harv.L.Rev. 630 (1987). Consider the similarity with provisions of the new French Code of Civil Procedure, discussed supra p. 746 n. b. For a comparative discussion stressing the Commonwealth countries, see Kolilinye, Setting in Motion Malicious Prosecutions: The Commonwealth Experience, 36 Int. & Comp.L.Q. 157 (1987).

French
Abuse of
Rights

(2) Under French law, the right to prosecute an action is not the only procedural right that is susceptible of being "abused". Liability can be incurred also by one who abuses the right to defend an action (e.g., if he interposes frivolous defenses or resorts to dilatory tactics),[2] or who pursues an appeal although the decision below is so clearly correct that he cannot reasonably expect ultimate success.[3]

U.S. comparison

In our law, the absence of a pervasive principle makes itself felt rather sharply in cases of this kind. "There is a paucity of precedent, if any exist, for plenary remedies for abusive or malicious use of defensive maneuvers in litigation." [4] Even in a shocking case of harassing and frivolous tactics on the part of a husband-defendant, who had boasted that he would keep the litigation alive forever, "like the hundred years' war", a New York court found it impossible to hold the defendant liable in tort, because the case did not fit into any of the established tort categories.[5]

Because of the absence of a rational and pervasive principle, our courts have reached absurd results in cases where a defendant, without probable cause, alleges fabricated facts as a basis both of an affirmative defense and of a counterclaim. According to the overwhelmingly prevailing view, the malicious interposition of a spurious defense is not a tort.[6] But by using the same spurious allegations in a counterclaim (which, it should be remembered, is contained in the same answer as the affirmative defense), the defendant commits the tort of malicious prosecution! [7] This approach makes the result turn exclusively on whether the defendant's act can be fitted into the pigeonhole of "malicious prosecution". For a civilian, who thinks in terms of the broad and pervasive notion of abuse of rights, it is difficult to understand such a pigeonhole distinction, which is supportable, if at all, only on historical grounds having little present-day relevance.[8]

---

2. The French refer to such conduct as *résistance abusive*. When a French judgment allowing the recovery of damages for such *résistance abusive* was sought to be enforced in England, the defendant argued that the judgment violated English public policy, and for this reason should be denied enforcement. This argument was rejected by the Court of Appeal. See decision of July 4, 1977, The Times of July 7, 1977, p. 27.

3. See the comparative study by K. Hopt, Schadensersatz aus unberechtigter Verfahrenseinleitung 102–09 (1968), where the numerous French cases on the subject are collected and analyzed.

4. Wolf v. Wolf, 26 A.D.2d 529, 530, 271 N.Y.S.2d 155, 157 (1st Dept. 1966), reversing 47 Misc.2d 756, 263 N.Y.S.2d 195 (Sp. T.N.Y.Co. 1965). In a situation very similar to that in the case just cited, a California court imposed a $10,000.—penalty on the husband for prosecuting an appeal merely for purposes of delay. However, this result was reached on the basis of a specific statutory provision (California Code of Civil Procedure § 907) enacted to

discourage frivolous appeals, and not on the basis of a general doctrine of abuse of rights. In re Marriage of Stich, 167 Cal. App.3d 226, 213 Cal.Rptr. 344, 352–53 (Ct. of Appeal, 1st Dist. 1985).

5. See the Wolf case, supra n. 4. In order fully to appreciate the facts of the case, one has to read the opinion of Special Term as well as that of the Appellate Division.

6. See, e.g., Eastin v. Bank of Stockton, 66 Cal. 123, 4 P. 1106 (1884). For further references, see Anno., 66 A.L.R.3d 901 (1975).

7. See Bertero v. National General Corp., 13 Cal.3d 43, 118 Cal.Rptr. 184, 529 P.2d 608 (1974), discussed by M. A. Levinson, Bertero v. National General Corp.: Drawing the Line Between an Aggressive Defense and Malicious Prosecution, 4 Hast. Const.L.Q. 739 (1977).

8. Proposals for the creation of a tort of malicious defense have recently increased. See Van Patten & Willard, The Limits of Advocacy; A Proposal for the Tort of Mali-

DECISION OF THE FRENCH COUR DE CASSATION IN THE MATTER OF DUVAL c. CHEDOT

First Civil Chamber, Decision of June 17, 1969. J.C.P. 1970. II. 16162.

[As usual (see supra p. 649), the facts are not adequately stated in the opinion of the Cour de Cassation. It so happens, however, that in this case the opinion of the court of first instance has been published.[a] Thus the detailed statement of facts appearing in the lower court opinion is easily accessible. The next two paragraphs present a condensed version of the facts as stated by the court of first instance.

Plaintiff Chedot, the owner of a garage business, for several years had been a client of defendant Duval, a certified public accountant. The latter did all of the bookkeeping and accounting work that became necessary in plaintiff's business, and prepared plaintiff's tax returns. Apparently dissatisfied with defendant's services, plaintiff discharged him in June 1964, and retained another accounting firm. Defendant sent plaintiff a bill in the amount of frs. 2,200 (appr. $500) for services rendered prior to June 1964; but the bill remained unpaid, apparently for the reason (although this is not entirely clear) that plaintiff believed to have a larger claim against defendant for malpractice. Shortly after June 1964, the tax authorities notified plaintiff that they were about to audit his returns for the years 1961–1963. Most of plaintiff's books, ledgers and other documents that were needed for the audit were still in the possession of defendant, who asserted a "right of retention", i.e., the right to retain these documents until payment of his bill.[b] Plaintiff, therefore, asked defendant to let the tax officials see the documents, pointing out that the returns which were the subject of the audit had been prepared by defendant, and that he (plaintiff) would get into serious difficulties if the tax officials were not given access to the books and documents supporting the returns. The defendant, however, refused to make the books and documents available to the tax officials. The officials, who thus were unable to verify the figures in plaintiff's tax returns, then proceeded—apparently in accordance with French tax law—to estimate the pertinent figures. On the basis of this estimate, they assessed about frs. 16,000 (appr. $2,750) in additional taxes and frs. 23,000 (appr. $4,000) in penalties against plaintiff.

In early 1965, plaintiff brought this action, seeking to hold defendant liable in damages for the amounts thus assessed. Defendant prayed for dismissal of the action, and counterclaimed (a) for his fees in

cious Defense in Civil Litigation, 35 Hastings L.J. 891 (1984).

a. J.C.P. 1967. II. 14935.

b. The *ius retentionis*, recognized in most civil-law systems, is based on the simple theory that when A and B have mutual claims and obligations arising from the same legal relationship, each of them can refuse to perform until the other performs.

Although more broadly conceived, the civilian right of retention in its nature and effect is comparable to the so-called retaining lien of an attorney, which is recognized in our law. See 7 Am.Jur.2d, Attorneys at Law, §§ 315–323 (1980 and Supps.)

the amount of frs. 2,200, and (b) for a judicial declaration that he could retain the documents in his possession until payment of such fees. On April 26, 1965 the court of first instance at Caen (i) ordered the taking of evidence concerning plaintiff's claim, and (ii) on defendant's counter-claim entered judgment in accordance with defendant's prayer for relief.[c] No appeal was taken from this decision. After evidence had been taken, the court of first instance on June 20, 1966 entered a judgment permitting plaintiff to recover damages in the amount of frs. 25,000 from the defendant. Upon appeal from the judgment of June 20, 1966, the Court of Appeal at Caen, as intermediate appellate court, reduced the amount of damages, but otherwise affirmed. It is this judgment of affirmance, dated April 10, 1967, that Duval seeks to have reviewed by the Cour de Cassation.]

The Court. . . . Taking note of the principles governing the right of retention;

Considering that the creditor exercising the right of retention is entitled, absent a contrary statutory provision, until full payment of his claim to refuse giving up possession of the things and documents lawfully retained;

Considering that the findings made below show that garage-owner Chedot confided the keeping of his books to Duval, a certified public accountant; that the latter, as determined in a judicial decision no longer subject to appeal,[d] was entitled to retain the books and docu-ments belonging to Chedot as security for the payment of his fees; that the tax authorities assessed penalties against Chedot after Duval, who had been notified by his former client, had declined to furnish the authorities with data in his possession; that Chedot, believing the additional taxes and penalties to be the consequence of Duval's tortious failure [to furnish such data], demanded payment of damages;

Considering that the Court of Appeal has in part upheld this demand on the theory that Duval "has abused his right of retention"; that in so holding—on the asserted ground that Duval should have made the accounting documents retained by him or the data contained

c. The procedure adopted by the French court is not difficult to understand. An American court could bring about the same procedural effect by entering summa-ry judgment in favor of the defendant on the latter's counterclaim, while letting the plaintiff's claim go to trial.

d. It should not be assumed that by this reference to a prior decision (apparently the decision of the court of first instance of April 26, 1965) the Cour de Cassation in-tends to invoke the doctrine of res judicata, or of the law of the case. With respect to defendant's right of retention the decision of April 26, 1965 merely confirmed the *existence* of that right, which in any event seems to have been undisputed. The issue now before the Court, which goes to the

limits and the alleged *abuse* of defendant's right of retention, was not determined in the decision of April 26, 1965. On the contrary: the fact that, simultaneously with its judgment upholding the counter-claim, the court of first instance directed the taking of evidence concerning plain-tiff's tort claim against defendant, makes it crystal-clear that the court of first instance in rendering that judgment did not intend to pass upon, or preclude, any of the issues involved in plaintiff's tort claim.

Under these circumstances, the highest Court's reference to the decision of April 26, 1965 appears to serve no purpose other than that of emphasizing that the exis-tence of defendant's right of retention can-not be doubted.

therein available to the tax authorities, since it is incumbent upon the retaining creditor to preserve the property of his debtor—the intermediate appellate court has violated the above-mentioned principles;

For these reasons . . . reverses and annuls the judgment rendered herein on April 10, 1967 by the Court of Appeal at Caen,[e] and remands the case to the Court of Appeal at Rouen.[f]

NOTE

Under German Law, the garage owner in the principal case could have defeated the accountant's right of retention by posting security for the latter's claim. German Civil Code § 273 III. In addition, the "abuse of right" argument would have had a better chance. German Civil Code § 273 I authorizes a right of retention only if a different result does not follow from the obligation [meaning the obligation owed by the debtor to the creditor]. The courts have interpreted this language to mean that the right of retention may be defeated either by a clause to that effect in the contract between the parties or by the nature of the parties' relationship. On that basis, one German court seems to have held that there is no right to retain items on which the other party must base its bookkeeping. See Palandt, Bürgerliches Gesetzbuch, § 273, Anno. 5(c) (45th ed., 1986), citing Oberlandesgericht Düsseldorf, 1977 N.J.W. 1201. See also the German Rechtsanwaltsordnung [Code on Attorneys] § 50 I, under which, in contrast to the rule announced by the French Cour de Cassation, the exercise of the right of retention to compel payment of a small claim is considered an abuse of right. The French court, on the other hand, seems to have felt that where the amount involved is small, there can be no hardship, and hence no abuse, in compelling its payment.

compare to French decision

e. In an annotation appended to the report of this case (J.C.P.1970. II. 16162) Professor N. Catala-Franjou expresses approval of the result reached by the Cour de Cassation. She points out that by virtue of the right of retention the creditor has no power to sell his debtor's res, but only to retain it. Therefore, Professor Catala-Franjou argues, the right of retention is exclusively negative in nature, and it is of the very essence of the right to cause the debtor inconvenience and embarrassment. The more urgently the debtor needs the retained res, the more likely he is to pay his debt in order to regain possession. It follows that a creditor who exerts pressure by invoking his right of retention, employs his right in a normal rather than an abusive manner. Half a century ago, an American court used a very similar argument in a case involving an attorney's retaining lien. See Bulk Oil Transports v. Robins Dry Dock & Repair Co., 277 F. 25, 30–31 (2d Cir. 1921), cert. denied 257 U.S. 657, 42 S.Ct. 184 (1922). For a collection of further English and American cases in point, see Anno., 111 A.L.R. 487, 489–91 (1937). See also supra n. b.

Professor Catala-Franjou apparently would treat the right of retention as one of these exceptional rights (see supra p. 745) which are absolute and not subject to abuse. Are there not possible fact situations (involving, e.g., a physician's right of retention of medical records, exercised at a time of medical emergency) in which this view would lead to overly harsh results? Is the decision of the Court of Cassation not explainable on the simple ground that Chedot could have obtained possession of the books by paying the small amount of frs. 2,200? Such payment would not have precluded him from pursuing his malpractice claim against Duval by way of an independent action.

f. Upon inquiry, the clerk of the Court of Appeal (intermediate appellate court) at Rouen indicated in 1977 that no further proceedings took place upon remand. Perhaps the case was settled after the Court of Cassation had spoken. In any event, the above decision of that Court seems to have constituted the final chapter in this litigation.

NOTES AND QUESTIONS REGARDING THE GERMAN
DOCTRINE OF ABUSE OF RIGHTS

(1) The German scheme for dealing with "abusive" exercise of rights is as comprehensive as the French. The *tort* provision of Sec. 826 of the Civil Code (supra, p. 553) imposes liability on him who intentionally harms another in a manner violating the precepts of boni mores. Sec. 138 (supra p. 569) invalidates *contracts* and other *transactional acts* which are contra bonos mores. From these provisions, and from Sects. 157, 242 which prescribe that all transactions (or "*jural acts*") should be *construed and carried out in good faith*, German theorists and judges inferred the existence of a general principle as broad as that explicitly stated in the famous Art. 2 of the Swiss Civil Code.[1]

(2) An illustrative German case dealt with facts which, in somewhat simplified form, may be stated as follows:[2] Plaintiff's husband and her 19-year-old son had deserted from the German army a few weeks before the final collapse of the Nazi government in 1945; they were kept in hiding by plaintiff. Defendant, as the local deputy of the Reich Defense Commissar, was in charge, locally, of a last-ditch drive against "deserters and defeatists." Having heard, through an informer, of the whereabouts of plaintiff's husband and son, defendant had both of them arrested and summarily killed. The husband was shot to death in plaintiff's presence. The killings, a detailed description of which seems unnecessary, were in violation even of the positive "laws" then in existence, which required a trial, however perfunctory, before a drumhead court-martial.

Defendant argued that he had acted as an official of the Reich, in the exercise of a public function, and that pursuant to clear provisions of law (supra p. 510) only the Reich and not the individual official could be held liable for a tort committed under such circumstances. Technically, this was correct. At the time, however, when the plaintiff brought her action, the Reich was defunct, and the new German Federal Republic refused to assume the liabilities of the Reich. Hence, plaintiff's cause of action against the former Reich was, as a practical matter, unenforceable and valueless. *Held:* for plaintiff. On their face, applicable provisions of law support defendant's argument that the liability of the Reich for defendant's tort is exclusive. But defendant is abusing his right to invoke that defense. In cases of torts committed by public officials, the exclusive liability of the public body that employed the official has been established by law for two reasons: (1) to protect officials from the threat of civil action, because such threat might inhibit their initiative, and (2) to assist the victim by enabling him to obtain a judgment against a judgment-debtor of unquestionable solvency. In the case at bar the second reason does not hold, the Reich being defunct; and the first reason cannot apply to an act so bestial as to deserve no encouragement whatever. Therefore, the reasons for the principle of the Reich's exclusive liability being absent here, the defendant may not invoke the provisions, however plainly apposite, embodying that principle.

1. Art. 2 of the Swiss Civil Code is quoted by Gutteridge, supra, p. 744.

2. Bundesgerichtshof, July 12, 1951, BGHZ 3, 94.

American Estoppel
Fraud: American answers to abuse of rights

(3) Suppose M, who is unmarried, gives birth to a child C. As co-plaintiffs, M and C's guardian sue D, alleging that he is the father of C. M falsely testifies that she had intercourse with D during the period in question. Her testimony is not under oath, but the court seems inclined to believe her and to put her under oath at the next hearing. Thinking that his case is hopeless, D does not appear at that hearing, and the court enters a default judgment against him (a) in favor of M, for $700 hospital expenses, (b) in favor of C, for alimony in the amount of $120 per month until C reaches the age of 16. D pays M $700, and pays C's alimony for two years. He then finds out that during the last year before C's birth, M lived with a man named X. Blood tests are thereupon taken, which establish with certainty that D is not the father of C. Faced with the true facts, M admits that her former testimony was false. D now sues M for repayment of $700. At the same time, he sues C for repayment of alimony paid, and asks for a declaratory judgment declaring that he is not liable for further alimony. The action is based on Sec. 826 of the German Civil Code.[3]

A German court would have no difficulty whatever in letting D recover from M. Relief against judgments has been granted under the broad provision of Sec. 826 not only in cases in which the judgment was obtained by fraud,[4] but also in other cases in which the following three factors are present: (a) the judgment must be incorrect; (b) such incorrectness must be known to the judgment-creditor at the time when he enforces the judgment; and (c) there must be "special circumstances" (not necessarily amounting to fraud in procuring the judgment) which render such enforcement immoral.[5] In the case at hand, there can be no doubt as to the first two factors, and the third would be found in M's false testimony and the concealment of her relationship with X. The res judicata effect of the former judgment is disregarded on the ground that even though the policy implemented by the rule of res judicata is an important one, the principle of morality and justice reflected in Sec. 826 is of a higher order.[6]

3. There are specific provisions for setting aside a judgment obtained by false testimony. German Code of Civil Procedure § 580. But these provisions are not applicable here because the judgment, being a default judgment, technically was not based on M's testimony.

4. It makes no difference whether the fraud was committed for the purpose of obtaining service by publication, or to influence the court's decision on the merits. See BGHZ 50, 115 (1968) and the further cases cited by Stein-Jonas-Pohle, Kommentar zur Zivilprozessordnung, § 322, Anno. XI 4 (19th ed., 1972).

The American majority rule distinguishes between "extrinsic" and "intrinsic" fraud and thus is considerably more restrictive. See, e.g., R. C. Casad, Res Judicata in A Nutshell 275–76 (1976). There is, however, a minority view that permits an equitable attack on a judgment on the ground of intrinsic fraud. This minority view, which in its effect comes close to the position of the German courts, has been espoused by the Restatement, Second, Judgments, §§ 68 and 70 (1982); see especially § 70, Comment c, and Reporter's Note.

5. See Bundesgerichtshof, Decision of June 21, 1951, 4 NJW 759 (1951), cited with approval in BGHZ 50, 115, at 117 (1968); Palandt, Bürgerliches Gesetzbuch, § 826, Anno. 8o (46th ed., 1987).

6. Ibid. A similar result was reached by the Japanese Supreme Court, which based its decision (in a very dramatic factual setting) on the express prohibition of "abuse of rights" in § 1 of the Japanese Civil Code, as amended in 1947. See Professor Toru Ikuyo's report on Civil Law, 12 The Japan Annual of Law and Politics 33 (1964).

Concerning our law's approach to the problem, see the authorities cited supra n. 4.

As to whether D would prevail against C, the cases are in conflict.[7] It has been held that a party such as C's guardian, who did nothing improper in the prior litigation and was unaware at that time of the falsity of M's testimony, may continue to enforce the judgment even if subsequently he learns of the true facts;[8] but there is authority also for the opposite view: that the element of immorality on the part of C's guardian is supplied by his attempt to exploit, *after* he has acquired full knowledge of the facts, a default judgment which the judgment-debtor permitted to be entered because he was the victim of a fraud.[9]

(4) Numerous other German cases applying the doctrine of abuse of rights rely on the principle of good faith announced in Sec. 242 of the Civil Code (supra, p. 575) rather than on the concept of boni mores embodied in Sec. 138 and in the tort provision of Sec. 826. It was held, for example, that a party to a contract who had advised the other party that the contract could be validly entered into without any formality, was prevented by the principle of good faith from later interposing a defense based on the Statute of Frauds.[10] Similarly, the defense of the Statute of Limitations was disallowed if interposed by one who, by settlement negotiations conducted in bad faith, had caused the plaintiff to refrain from the timely commencement of an action.[11]

It was further held that a party to a contract may not suddenly avail himself of a right of rescission which by the terms of the contract he may exercise in the event of certain contingencies, if in prior similar situations he failed to exercise the right and thus led the other party to believe that he did not insist on rigorous enforcement of the contract clause in question.

In numerous other cases it was decided that even before the expiration of the statutory period of limitation the exercise of a right may be violative of the principles of good faith and hence improper, if the plaintiff has been silent during a long period of time, and if defendant has changed his position in reliance upon plaintiff's continued inaction.[12]

---

7. See Reinicke, Die Kollision zwischen Rechtsfrieden und Gerechtigkeit, 5 NJW 3 (1952). The title of this article means "The Conflict between Legal Peace and Justice". Some authors, commenting on the cases mentioned here, note that in trying to do justice, German courts may have weakened the principle, embodied in the notion of *res judicata*, that the law must eventually provide an end to litigation in order to give the litigants peace. See Palandt, supra note 5; Baumbach-Lauterbach-Albers-Hartmann, Zivilprozessordnung, Introduction before §§ 322–327, Anno. 6(B) (45th ed., 1987).

8. RGZ 163, 287 (1940).

9. Oberlandesgericht Duesseldorf, Juristische Wochenschrift 1939, p. 417.

10. See the decision of the Bundesgerichtshof reported in 1959 Versicherungsrecht 145, 147, where the German court cited and followed the similar holding of the Swiss Federal Court in BGE 72 II 39 (1946). See also Kommentar von Reichs-

gerichtsräten und Bundesrichtern zum Bürgerlichen Gesetzbuch, § 242, Annos. 161–63 (1960).

11. Id. at Anno. 164. In our law, the doctrine of equitable estoppel generally leads to similar results; but, again, our rules may be more restrictive because equitable estoppel has been held not to operate where the time limitation involved is a "built-in" one, such as the time limitation typically found in wrongful death statutes. See Annos., 24 ALR2d 1413, 1418–20 (1952) and 3 L.Ed.2d 1886, at 1888 (1959), where further references are given. Fortunately, some recent decisions have broken away from this unjustifiable restriction. Ibid.

12. See Palandt, supra n. 5, at § 242, Anno. 9d, and cases cited.

Swiss law is to the same effect. See the excellent article by F. von Steiger, Unzulaessige Rechtsausuebung, insbesondere die Verwirkung, 75 Zeitschrift fuer Schweizerisches Recht (N.F.) 13 (1956). The article also surveys similar developments in

(5) In recent years, German legal authors have gone even further and have postulated that non-performance of a contract should be excused under principles of *bona fides* whenever such non-performance serves interests or values which are of a higher order than those promoted by the contract. The famous singer who at the last minute refuses to honor her engagement because her child suddenly has become gravely ill and she feels that she must not leave the child's bedside, furnishes a fine textbook example.[13]

It has been argued, moreover, that the principle of freedom of conscience, expressly recognized in Art. 4 of the West German Constitution, further expands the doctrine of *bona fides* stated in § 242 of the Civil Code.[14] The hypothetical (or perhaps not entirely hypothetical) case of the atomic scientist, who breaks his long-term contract of employment because he has developed conscientious scruples with respect to the purposes for which the results of his research might be used, has caused considerable discussion among German legal scholars.[15]

Recently, some German courts have begun to follow the lead of the scholars in recognizing the doctrine that conscientious scruples on the part of the promisor, if they reflect deeply-felt moral or socio-political convictions, may excuse the non-performance of a valid contractual obligation.[16]

How would an American court deal with problems of this kind? Would it make a difference whether the promisee sues at law or in equity, and whether he pursues a performance, reliance or restitutionary interest?

EXPRESS CODE PROVISIONS EMBODYING THE PRINCIPLE OF ABUSE OF RIGHTS

In developing the far-reaching doctrines discussed above, the French and German courts did not have the benefit of any code provision expressly phrased in terms of "abuse of rights".[1] Many of the more recent codes, however, influenced by the famous Art. 2 of the

other European countries, in comparison with the English doctrines of estoppel and laches.

13. See 1 K. Larenz, Lehrbuch des Schuldrechts, § 10c (1970).

14. For references see Palandt, supra n. 5, at § 242, Anno. 1d. See also Heinrichs in 2 Münchener Kommentar zum BGB, § 242, Annos. 224–248 (2d ed., 1985).

15. See Larenz, supra n. 13, where further references can be found. Professor Larenz suggests that the scientist's employer is not entitled to damages measured by his performance interest; but if in reliance upon the scientist's promise the employer has incurred expenses or obligations (e.g., by hiring an assistant who cannot be discharged immediately but whose services become worthless when the scientist

leaves), Professor Larenz would let the employer recover reliance damages.

16. See H. W. Baade, Hoggan's History, 16 Am.J.Comp.L. 391 (1968), where a highly controversial German case of this kind is presented and analyzed.

1. A number of other civil-law jurisdictions have followed the French and German examples, and have adopted the abuse of rights doctrine despite the absence from their codes of any express language dealing with the exercise of rights. For comparative discussions, in addition to those previously cited, see J. Cueto-Rua, Abuse of Rights, 35 La.L.Rev. 965 (1975), and, with specific reference to environmental nuisance litigation, A. N. Yiannopoulos, Violations of the Obligations of Vicinage, 34 La. L.Rev. 475, 504 ff. (1974).

Swiss Civil Code (quoted supra p. 744),[1a] contain explicit provisions of this kind.

(1) In the Greek Civil Code of 1946, we find two relevant provisions. Art. 288, which is part of the Second Book ("Obligations"), is practically identical with the *bona fides* provision (§ 242) of the German Code. Its importance, however, has been eclipsed by Art. 281 (in the last chapter of the First Book, the "General Part"), which reads as follows:

> "The exercise of a right is improper if it evidently exceeds the limits drawn by bona fides, boni mores, or by the social or economic purpose of such right."

During the early years after the enactment of the 1946 Code, the highest court of Greece approached this provision very cautiously and treated it as inapplicable to the exercise (a) of contractual rights and (b) of rights created by cogent rules of law.[2]

(a) The first of these judge-made exceptions was given up by the court in a case in which a tenant sought to avail himself of a contractual right to demand a 20-year renewal of the lease at a rental fixed in the original contract. Because of inflation, that rental had become wholly inadequate at the time of the attempted renewal, and in view of this fact the court held the tenant's exercise of his option right to be improper and ineffective.[3]

(b) The second of the exceptions engrafted upon Art. 281, however, seems to be more resistant to change. This exception is of particular importance in cases where a party seeks to avoid a transaction on the ground that it fails to comply with a legal form requirement. Such form requirements are matters of "cogent" law. Therefore, on the basis of the exception mentioned above under (b), the highest court of Greece has held that Art. 281 is inapplicable in such a case, even though the party invoking the lack of the legally required (written or notarial) form is acting in bad faith. In other words, according to the view espoused by the highest court the right to invoke the lack of a legal form requirement is absolute, and the exercise of such right cannot be treated as improper under any circumstances.[4] This formalistic view—surely a strange one in the country which by its ancient notion of *epieikeia* paved the way for the more modern concepts of estoppel and abuse of rights—has been opposed by some of the lower courts; but the highest court seems to be slow in changing its attitude.[5]

1a. An illustrative Swiss case, in which Art. 2 as well as Art. 1 of the Civil Code was invoked by the court in support of the result reached, appears infra pp. 762–765.

For a discussion of Art. 2 and of the cases implementing it see V. Bolgár, Abuse of Rights in France, Germany and Switzerland: A Survey of a Recent Chapter in Legal Doctrine, 35 La.L.Rev. 1015, 1030–36 (1975).

2. See K. I. Simantiras, Das griechische Zivilgesetzbuch und moderne Rechtsprobleme 12–16 (1967).

3. Id., at 13. See also N. A. Deloukas, Der Rechtsmissbrauch im griechischen

Privatrecht, in M. Rotondi, L'Abus de Droit 55, at 62 (1979).

4. Note the contrast with the more liberal German doctrine mentioned supra p. 754.

5. See Simantiras, op. cit. supra n. 2, at 14–16. In its more recent decisions, the highest court appears to weigh the factors of honesty and decency protected by Art. 281 against the policies supporting the legal provisions the abuse of which is asserted. See Deloukas, supra n. 3, at 71–72.

The outside observer, who is not truly familiar with the Greek legal system, can but speculate on the reasons why in Greece, where the Code itself expressly and solemnly consecrates the doctrine of abuse of rights, the courts were so much more hesitant in extending the scope of that doctrine than the courts, e.g., of France and Germany, where "abuse" or "improper exercise" of rights is not explicitly mentioned in the written law. Does the explanation lie in the language of Art. 281 of the Greek Code, especially the word "evidently"? Should one conclude that in the end the presence or absence of an express code provision embodying the doctrine of abuse of rights is less important than the judges' willingness to play a creative role in the development of the law?

(2) Recent developments in the Netherlands, on the other hand, seem to indicate that a *well-drafted* code provision expressly dealing with exercise of rights can have a truly liberalizing influence on the attitude of the courts.[6]

In the course of the preparation of the new Dutch Civil Code (see supra p. 548), a rather sophisticated abuse of rights provision has been proposed. It reads as follows: [7]

(i) The abuse of a right is prohibited.

(ii) A right is abused, when it is used either for the exclusive purpose of harming others, or for a purpose different from that for which it has been granted, or when it is exercised in circumstances in which, taking into account the interests served and those which are harmed, no reasonable person would have decided to exercise it.

(iii) A right cannot be abused, if its exercise is left completely to the discretion of the person who has it.[8]

Although the part of the new Code containing this provision has not yet become law, the Dutch courts have been noticeably influenced by the draft provision.[9] Under its impact the highest court of the Netherlands abandoned an older line of decisions which in essence had restricted the application of the abuse of rights doctrine to cases of proven malice, and adopted a more liberal test substantially conforming to the second paragraph of the draft provision.[10]

(3) In Japan, the doctrine of abuse of rights, originally developed by the courts under European influence, was expressly incorporated into the Civil Code by a 1947 amendment. But it has been said that "The number of cases wherein the doctrine is applied did not notably increase after incorporation into the Code." K. Sono & Y. Fujioka, The

---

6. See C. J. H. Brunner, Abuse of Rights in Dutch Law, 37 La.L.Rev. 729 (1977).

7. See id., at 738.

8. This paragraph of the Dutch draft provision, which deals with absolute or discretionary rights, is similar to the preliminary draft which, by way of codifying French case law, was prepared by the now-defunct French Civil Code Reform Commission. See supra p. 745.

9. As has been mentioned previously, the Dutch courts generally treat the pro-

posed new Code (i.e., those parts of the draft Code that have not yet been finally enacted) as persuasive authority. For several examples of such "anticipating interpretation", see A. S. Hartkamp, Civil Code Revision in the Netherlands: A Survey of Its System and Contents, and Its Influence on Dutch Legal Practice, 35 La.L.Rev. 1059, 1085–89 (1975).

10. See id., at 1089, and Brunner, supra n. 7, at 738–39.

Role of the Abuse of Rights Doctrine in Japan, 35 La.L.Rev. 1037, 1044 (1975). It may be true that its codification did not, by itself, have a great impact on the treatment of the abuse of rights doctrine by the Japanese courts. But, whether under the influence of the 1947 Code amendment or not, the Japanese courts have been remarkably creative in developing this doctrine. Two aspects of Japanese case-law, both discussed in M. K. Young, Judicial Review of Administrative Guidance: Governmentally Encouraged Consensual Dispute Resolution in Japan, 84 Colum.L.Rev. 923, 970–73 (1984), are particularly interesting:

a) The Japanese courts have, independently, arrived at formulations surprisingly similar to the last clause of subsection (ii) of the Dutch draft provision, reproduced above; on the basis of such formulations, they make the success of abuse of rights arguments dependent on a social cost-benefit calculus.

b) The Japanese courts also have made imaginative use of the abuse of rights doctrine in public-law litigation. Professor Young, in his article, provides this example: The Japanese, as is well known, believe strongly in cooperation between governmental bodies and private business enterprises. Accordingly, the competent governmental bodies often issue some form of "guidance" to private firms, even in the absence of statutory authority. Municipalities, for instance, often use such "guidance" to persuade developers to reach an amicable accord with adjoining property owners concerned with the impact of the proposed project on their enjoyment of sunlight, air, etc. The aim obviously is to have the relative rights of developer and adjoining property owners determined by negotiation, not litigation. This is in conformity with the general Japanese attitude towards law and the legal process (see supra pp. 332–334). While, presumably, negotiations based on official "guidance" are normally successful, litigation ensued in one instance (see Young, supra, 84 Colum.L.Rev. at 971) because the municipality involved, feeling that the failure of the negotiations was due to the developer's insufficient compliance with official "guidance", refused to supply water to the building erected by the developer. The latter than sued the municipality, asking the Tokyo District court to compel it, by injunction, to provide water. While the developer technically had a right to have his building connected to the water supply, the court did not grant the injunction as a matter of course but first examined carefully whether the developer had made a reasonable effort to reach an agreement with his neighbors concerning their demands for more access to sunlight and air. Only after concluding that such an effort had taken place, was the injunction issued. The case thus stands for the proposition that though a developer may have a formal right to obtain water from a municipality, he abuses that right, and thus will be defeated in any suit seeking to assert it, if he has failed to negotiate in good faith with his neighbors. The municipality's public-law obligation to supply water is thus qualified by the doctrine of abuse of rights, which enables the court, through the use of a cost-benefit analysis, to determine whether the positions taken by the developer and the efforts made by him in the negotiations with the neighbors, were reasonable. Pressure is thus put on the developer to base his relations with his neighbors on reasonable compromise rather than the vindication of legal rights. And even if, exceptionally, compromise is not attained and litigation ensues, it is determined not on the basis of technical legal rights, but on the basis of the court's assessment of the question whether the developer acted reasonably in his negotiations with his neighbors.

(4) The civil codes of the socialist orbit generally contain explicit provisions to the effect that the exercise of any legal right is improper if the purpose for which it is exercised is not consistent with "socialist morality" or similarly defined postulates of Marxist ideology. For an example of such provisions, see supra p. 662.[11]

Most important note in the book

SOME PROBLEMS OF COMPARISON

With respect to each of the German and French cases reproduced or synopsized in the foregoing materials, the reader will ask himself whether an American court would have reached the same *result*. In many instances, the answer will be in the affirmative.

Note, however, the difference in the *methods* by which the results, even identical results, are reached. The American or English lawyer cannot point to a recognized general concept of abuse of rights, i.e., to a single doctrine so pervasive that it will serve, sometimes as a basis for a cause of action and sometimes as a defense or reply, in cases involving such diverse matters as contracts, judgments, family relations, exercise of property rights, and tortious interference with every conceivable type of interest. Therefore, he has to invoke numerous, seemingly unconnected doctrines in dealing with the vast array of cases which his German, French and Swiss colleagues subsume under *Rechtsmissbrauch* or *abus des droits*.

In which of the cases mentioned above would an Anglo-American lawyer resort to equitable doctrines, such as estoppel and laches? In which of them would he argue for the application of one of our specific, compartmentalized tort doctrines, such as false imprisonment, malicious prosecution, abuse of process and the like? Which of the cases could, in our law, be brought under the prima facie theory of tort?[2]

---

11. See also section 6 of the "Principles of Civil Legislation of the USSR", provisions analogous to which are contained in the codes of all the constituent units of the USSR: "Civil rights are protected by law except where they are enforced in a manner which would be inconsistent with the purpose of such rights in a socialist society during the period of establishment of communism." 6 Law in Eastern Europe 263 (R. Kiralfy, tr., 1962).

1. Voices are not lacking in the common-law world, demanding that in our analysis of tort law we should think "in terms of general principles rather than compartments." See Ward, The Tort Cause of Action, 42 Cornell L.Q. 28, 38 (1956). It seems, however, that in deciding tort cases of a somewhat unusual nature many of our courts continue to think in compartmentalized terms. See R. F. Dole, Jr., Merchant and Consumer Protection: The New York Approach to the Regulation of Deceptive Trade Practices, 53 Cornell

L.Rev. 749, 780–83 (1968); J. E. Brown, The Rise and Threatened Demise of the Prima Facie Tort Principle, 54 N.W.U.L. Rev. 563 (1959). For massive further references to law review articles as well as cases see Anno., 16 A.L.R.3d 1191 (1967). See also n. 2 infra.

Even when a new tort is recognized by statute or case law, courts and commentators brought up in the common-law method immediately proceed to splinter it into numerous (and more or less traditional) categories. This tendency to create rigid new compartments has been decried by E. J. Bloustein, Privacy as an Aspect of Human Dignity: An Answer to Dean Prosser, 39 N.Y.U.L.Rev. 962 (1964).

2. For an interesting discussion of the origin and purpose of the prima facie tort theory, see Nees v. Hocks, 272 Or. 210, 536 P.2d 512 (1975).

Many of our courts apply that theory only in cases in which it was the sole or at

The absence from our law of a broad, unifying theory of abuse of rights is particularly apparent in cases of spiteful or otherwise anti-social exercise of proprietary rights. To a common-law court dealing with a spite fence problem, it will not easily occur to look for enlighten-ment in an earlier case involving percolating waters, even though, judging by results, the same principle seems to govern both situations.[3] Statutes of narrow coverage limited to such specific problems as spite fences or spite structures,[4] further reinforce the casuistic character of our method.

In our law of contracts, also, one can observe the lack of a unifying principle concerning the improper exercise of rights, especially in cases where brutal unilateral termination of a contract or lease, though consistent with the terms of the agreement, causes undue hardship or loss.[5] Should such termination be treated as ineffective at least in those instances in which it can be shown that its true purpose was to intimidate the other party, or to punish him for the exercise of an unquestioned statutory or constitutional right? Our courts, unable to invoke an established formula such as "abuse of rights", thus far have failed to agree on a principled answer to this question.[6]

Lest one exaggerate the importance of the difference between civil-law and common-law methods, it is well to keep in mind that the civil-law judge, even though he uses a general principle as his guide, still has to determine, from case to case, whether and in what way the principle

least the primary purpose of defendant's act to harm the plaintiff. See, e.g., Rein-force, Inc. v. Birney, 308 N.Y. 164, 124 N.E. 2d 104 (1954) and other cases cited by M. D. Forkosch, An Analysis of the "Prima Facie" Tort Cause of Action, 42 Cornell L.Q. 465, 476–80 (1957). See also the arti-cles cited supra n. 1. The prima facie tort thus becomes just another narrow pigeon-hole, as has been shown by the case of Drago v. Buonagurio, 46 N.Y.2d 778, 413 N.Y.S.2d 910, 386 N.E.2d 821 (1978).

Under German law, an argument could be made for a similarly restrictive rule, by reading Sec. 226 of the Civil Code (supra, p. 742) into the broad "boni mores" standard of Sec. 826; but German courts and writers have rejected this argument. See Ennec-cerus-Lehmann, Recht der Schuld-verhaeltnisse, § 236 II 2 (1958), and cases there cited.

3. Compare Hathorn v. Natural Car-bonic Gas Co., 194 N.Y. 326, 87 N.E. 504 (1909) with Schorck v. Epperson, 74 Wyo. 286, 287 P.2d 467 (1955).

4. See, e.g., 3 Tiffany, The Law of Real Property, Sec. 716 (1939, and 1979 Supp.).

5. Employing the casuistic method which in common-law countries usually permeates the statutory as well as the deci-sional law, Congress has dealt with a nar-row and specific part of this problem in the Automobile Dealer Franchise Act of 1956, 15 U.S.C.A. §§ 1221–1225. See C. H. Fulda and W. F. Schwartz, Cases and Materials

on the Regulation of International Trade and Investment 782–83 (1970) and authori-ties there cited. There is also an increas-ing number of state statutes restricting the termination of contracts with distributors. See, e.g., the Puerto Rican statute involved in Southern Int'l Sales Co. v. Potter & Broomfield Div., 410 F.Supp. 1339 (S.D. N.Y. 1976).

6. In our law, the pertinent rules ap-pear to be enshrined in separate, seeming-ly air-tight compartments. In one com-partment, we find the rules governing retaliatory evictions. See Anno., 40 A.L.R.3d 753 (1971); 9 A.L.R.4th 329 (1981). Cases in which an employee, serv-ing under an employment contract termi-nable at will, has been discharged for rep-rehensible reasons, are treated and collected in an entirely different compart-ment. See Anno., 62 A.L.R.3d 271 (1975). See also Mt. Healthy City Bd. of Educ. v. Doyle, 429 U.S. 274, 283–84, 97 S.Ct. 568, 574 (1977). The rules developed within these compartments are not remembered when cases arise that involve yet other types of contracts, and the absence of a unifying principle may lead to inconsistent results. Compare House of Materials, Inc. v. Simplicity Pattern Co., 298 F.2d 867, 871–73 (2d Cir. 1962) (no relief for retalia-tory termination of supplier-customer rela-tionship) with L'Orange v. Medical Protec-tive Co., 394 F.2d 57 (6th Cir. 1968) (relief granted in a case of retaliatory termina-tion of medical malpractice insurance).

should be applied. In addition, once it has been generally recognized that a particular social problem exists, the case-law solution based on a general principle, such as abuse of rights, may eventually be replaced by a specific statutory provision [7]. When that is the case, the temptation is strong to think, henceforth, only in terms of the new regulatory provision, rather than in terms of the broad principle. Thus it has been held that the 1978 French statute on abusive clauses in consumer contracts, which authorizes the executive to enact decrees listing prohibited clauses, must be interpreted to mean that only clauses specifically listed in the implementing decree are illegal.[8] To some extent, as the mass of specific legislation increases, there is thus a narrowing of approaches. Nevertheless, broad categories do not lose their significance, because they may furnish the basis for appropriate court action in the novel situations, not yet covered by legislation, that always arise in a changing society.[9]

The common-law judge, on the other hand, who has no verbalized general concept of abuse of rights as a starting point, and who has to find the pertinent authorities under the most disparate headings, may almost subconsciously sense the existence of the underlying general principle. The fact remains, nevertheless, that the civilian thinks in terms of more abstract, considerably broader categories than his common-law brother. This is not without practical significance.[10] When a case arises which does not fit into any of our narrower mental compartments, a common-law court must either refuse relief, or take the difficult, seemingly revolutionary step of expanding or exploding the existing compartments. In the same situation, a civil-law court may find it easier to innovate, because it can rationalize the result as the mere "application" of an established general principle.[11]

---

7. Abusive terminations of employment contracts, for instance, are now prohibited in France by Code du Travail art. 122–14–4. Cf. Soc. An. Loury-Thezelais v. Thezelais, Cass. soc., June 5, 1986, 1986 D.J. 558 (with an annotation by Prof. Karaquillo). See also the provisions on abusive utilization of legal procedure now contained in the French Code of Civil Procedure, mentioned supra p. 746 note b.

8. Mongibeau v. Deschamps, Cour d'appel Paris, May 22, 1986, 1986 D.J. 563 (with note by Prof. Delebecque); cf. Société Rayconile v. Bodier, Cass. civ., April 15, 1986, 1986 D.I.R. 393 (with a note by Prof. Aubert).

9. Thus the French courts have, in the recent past, created a principle of "abuse of a minority position in a corporation" when minority stockholders, who enjoy a blocking position, refuse to go along with majority proposals deemed to be necessary for the good of the company. Consorts Palthey c. Crepet, Cour d'appel Lyon, December 20, 1984, 1986 D.J. 506 (with a note by Prof. Reinhard).

It has also been said that the new legislation, enacted after the conservative election

ral victory in March, 1986, which eliminated most price controls and made other laws regulating business (such as the one prohibiting refusals to sell) more flexible, would increase the use of broad principles, such as "abus de droit". Fourgaux & Marchi, Réflexions sur la nouvelle réglementation de la concurrence, 107 Gaz. Pal. [Jan. 15, 1987] p. 2.

10. The law of privacy furnishes interesting illustrations of the point. See J. K. Weeks, Comparative Law of Privacy, 12 Cleveland Marshall L.Rev. 484, especially at 502–03 (1963). But note that seven years after Professor Weeks' article, the right of privacy received a statutory sanction in France. See French Civil Code art. 9.

11. With his usual perceptiveness, the late Judge Jerome Frank in two of his opinions emphasized the great influence which a convenient generalization may have on the development of the law. See Guiseppi v. Walling, 144 F.2d 608, 618–19 (2d Cir. 1944); Granz v. Harris, 198 F.2d 585, 590–91 (2d Cir. 1952). Perusal of these brilliant opinions is strongly recommended.

assign rights okay — delegating duty is not always

OPINION OF THE SWISS FEDERAL COURT IN THE MATTER OF WEBER, HUBER & CIE., DEFENDANT-APPELLANT, AGAINST "RIMBA", PLAINTIFF-RESPONDENT

1st Civil Division, November 4, 1931, BGE 57 II 528.

On November 4, 1930, the M Corporation and defendant entered into a contract of sale under the terms of which M Corporation bound itself to sell, and defendant bound itself to buy, 200 tons of Polish mineral oil, at a price of $1.46 per 100 kilograms, payable 14 days after shipment.

On December 22, 1930, M Corporation and J Corporation made an agreement by which the latter took over all of the assets and liabilities of the former, and changed its firm name to Rimba Corporation. The excess of the value of the assets of M Corporation over the amount of its liabilities was Fr. 118,266.42 as of December 31, 1930, and this amount was paid to the shareholders of M Corporation by way of transfer to them of sixty-two (62) fully paid shares of J Corporation [now Rimba Corporation]. The President of M Corporation was elected a member of the Board of Directors of Rimba. On Jan. 7, 1931, the registration of M Corporation in the Register of Commerce was cancelled, on the basis of a resolution of the Shareholders' Meeting of December 23, 1930, and of the above-mentioned agreement of December 22, 1930. About the middle of January 1931, the defendant was advised by a circular letter that the assets and liabilities of M Corporation had been taken over by Rimba. Immediately upon receipt of this letter the defendant answered that it could not consent to the transfer to, or assumption by, Rimba of rights and obligations under the contract of November 4, 1930, and that it regarded said contract as annulled. Rimba thereupon insisted that the contract be carried out.

On May 5, 1931, Rimba brought the present action for a declaratory judgment against the defendant, praying for a declaration to the effect that

(1) The contract of November 4, 1930 was validly taken over by the plaintiff and

(2) The defendant is bound to accept two hundred (200) tons of Polish mineral oil from the plaintiff . . . and to pay the purchase price of Fr. 15,184 plus interest. . . .

On July 16, 1931 the Commercial Court of the Canton of St. Gallen entered judgment granting the relief demanded by the plaintiff. . . .

[Upon defendant's appeal, the Federal Court affirmed.]

Reasons: 1. If the transaction entered into by M Corporation and J Corporation had constituted a merger in the technical sense of the term, the defendant would have had no choice but to accept the merged corporation as the new obligor of the obligation to deliver the oil. In other words, the consent of the defendant to such change of the person of the obligor would have been unnecessary in that event. It is just for this reason [because the creditors have no choice] that article 669 of the Code of Obligations provides for certain measures of protection in favor of the creditors of merged corporations.[a] . . . But it is questionable whether in the present case there was a merger in the proper sense of the word.

[The Court then points out that according to the view taken by the more recent commentators, two requirements must be met if a transaction is to be treated as a merger in the technical sense of the word: (a) the shareholders of the dissolved corporation must receive payment in the form of shares of the receiving corporation, and (b) the shares of the receiving corporation thus given to the former shareholders of the dissolved corporation must be simultaneously created by an increase in the capital of the receiving corporation. In the present case the first requirement was met; but the second was not, because the sixty-two shares issued to the former shareholders of M Corporation had previously been in the portfolio of J Corporation (as treasury stock), and were *not* authorized by way of a capital increase immediately preceding such issuance.

The Court holds, however, that the court below was correct in leaving open the question whether or not there was a merger in the technical sense of the word; even if there was no merger, plaintiff must win.

The Court takes as its starting point the general rule that one obligor cannot be substituted for another without the consent of the obligee, and that ordinarily this rule must apply even in cases where a whole business, with all its assets and liabilities, is taken over by a purchaser.]

It must be considered, however, that the obligor [of the obligation to sell and deliver the oil] was a corporation. In view of the constant change of economic conditions . . . ., a person dealing with a corporation must always contemplate the possibility of a merger or of a sale of the whole business of the corporation. For this reason, and because there may always be shifts in the membership of the corporation and in the personnel of its management, the court below correctly held that dealings with a corporation have an impersonal character . . . The more modern school of thought among the writers on commercial law emphasizes the concept of the enterprise and of its continuity. Wieland, Commercial Law, Volume 1, page 295. In accordance with this school of thought we hold that where the obligor is a corporation, and such corporation transfers all of its assets and liabilities, the obligee should ordinarily be compelled to accept the transferee as his new obligor unless he can show that there are weighty reasons in the person of the transferee which would make such a result unjust under the

a. Article 669 (now renumbered 748) of the Swiss Code of Obligations provides that in case of merger the assets of the dissolved company are to be kept separate from the assets of the receiving company until the creditors of the former are satisfied or secured.

particular circumstances of the case. This rule may not apply to all types of contractual relationships; but it does apply, among others, to the contract of sale, which is essentially impersonal in character. In the case at bar the defendant has not adduced any weighty reasons why the transferee should not be acceptable as new obligor. . . . It is true that this result cannot be based on Article 181 of the Code of Obligations.[b] That provision does not deal with the problem presented by a case in which [as in the instant case] the joint and several liability which Article 181 prescribes for a period of two years is impossible because the registration of the original obligor in the Register of Commerce has been cancelled. [What the Court means is apparently this: Article 181 deals with the assumption of liabilities in case A sells his whole business to B. The article provides that during a two year period A and B shall be jointly and severally liable for the obligations of the business which had been incurred prior to the time of its sale. This provision, of course, presupposes that during such two-year period both A and B are in existence as natural or juristic persons. In the present case that is not so, because M Corporation, having divested itself of all of its assets and having caused its registration in the Register of Commerce to be cancelled, has ceased to exist.[c] The joint and several liability of transferor and transferee, which is contemplated by Article 181 for a period of two years, is therefore impossible. It follows that Article 181 fails to provide a solution for the problem of the instant case.] Therefore, and because there is also no customary law governing this case, we were faced with a gap in the statutory law which had to be filled pursuant to Article 1 of the Civil Code.[d]

b. Art. 181 of the Swiss Code of Obligations reads as follows:

"He who takes over . . . a business including assets and liabilities, becomes automatically obligated to the creditors of debts connected therewith, as soon as he has advised the creditors of such taking over or has made a public announcement thereof.

"The old debtor remains liable, severally and jointly, . . . with the new one, for two years. . . ."

For instructive comparative studies of the rights of creditors in cases of this kind, see Bayitch, Transfer of Business, 6 Am.J. Comp.L. 284 (1957); id., Empresa in Latin American Law: Recent Developments, 4 Lawyer of the Americas 1, at 7–12 (1972).

c. The Court assumes that dissolution plus deregistration results in the complete death of a Swiss stock corporation. The common-law rule was similar. It is true that in equity, and under the terms of certain statutes, a different rule prevails in a number of American jurisdictions. See 16A Fletcher, Cyclopedia of the Law of Private Corporations, Sec. 8113 (1962 and Supp.) But in some of our states there are

statutes which are quite different and mark a partial return to the common-law rule, by providing that a dissolved corporation may no longer be suable after the expiration of a specified period (which period may begin to run either at the time of dissolution or at the time of publication of notice to creditors). See F. K. Juenger and S. H. Schulman, Assets Sales and Products Liability, 22 Wayne L.Rev. 39, 41 (1975). Thus a situation analogous to that in the principal case—i.e., a situation in which the original promisor is no longer suable— can easily arise in an American setting.

d. For a translation of Art. 1 of the Swiss Civil Code, see supra p. 653. Other cases in which the Swiss courts have utilized the broad authorization expressed in Art. 1, are helpfully discussed by A. E. von Overbeck, Some Observations on the Role of the Judge Under the Swiss Civil Code, 37 La.L.Rev. 681 (1977).

The present case is somewhat extraordinary in that it brings both Art. 1 and Art. 2 into play. Should the Court not have discussed the applicability of Art. 2 *before* it exercised its subsidiary law-making power under Art. 1?

2. Even if one did not wish to go quite so far [meaning: not quite so far as to create a new rule of law by way of judicial lawmaking pursuant to Article 1 of the Civil Code], the question would present itself whether defendant's refusal to accept the plaintiff as its obligor was not an abuse of rights. As to this point, the defendant has merely denied that the precipitous decline in the price of oil constituted the reason for such refusal; but defendant has not indicated any other reason. [The Court then points out that the principle of Article 2, paragraph 2, of the Civil Code [e] is broad enough to cover the present case. Normally, where one party to a bilateral contract has sought to transfer his rights and obligations to a third person, the other party has a right of election: he may accept the transferee as the obligor of the promises made to him, or he may refuse to do so and insist that the contract be performed by the one who made it. But in the present case defendant has abused this right of election. Defendant has pointed to no factual reason why Rimba should be a less desirable seller than M Corporation. It would seem, therefore, that defendant objects to the substitution of a new obligor merely for the reason that, marketwise, the contract has turned out to be disadvantageous from defendant's point of view.]. . .

QUESTIONS

(1) After having read the foregoing opinion, try to retrace the steps in the reasoning of the Court (a) on the theory of Article 1, and (b) on the theory of Article 2 of the Swiss Civil Code.

With respect to Article 2: What was the right which defendant abused? For what purpose was that right given? For what purpose did defendant seek to use the right? As to its actual purpose, does defendant carry the burden of proof? A burden of explanation? For further examples applying article 2, see P. Tuor, Das schweizerische Zivilgesetzbuch 51–54 (9th ed., B. Schnyder ed., 1975).

(2) How would a common-law court analyze the problem?[1] In British Waggon Co. v. Lea, 5 Q.B.D. 149 (1879), the Parkgate Waggon Co. had agreed to let a number of railway cars to the defendants and to keep them in repair. The Parkgate Co. went into liquidation and assigned its rights and duties under the agreement to the British Waggon Co. The defendants contended that the contract was at an end, and refused to accept the services of the British Waggon Co. In holding for the plaintiff, on the ground that the defendants could not have attached special importance to the repairs being done by the Parkgate Co., the court said: *So long as the Parkgate Co. continues to exist,* and, through the British Co., continues to fulfill its obligation to keep the waggons in repair, the defendants cannot, in our opinion, be heard to say that the former company is not entitled to performance by them." (Italics added)[2] What if the Parkgate Co. did *not continue to*

---

e. For a translation of this provision, see the Gutteridge article, supra p. 744.

1. See Fulda, An Examination in Comparative Law, 9 J.Legal Ed. 536, 537–9 (1957).

2. The case is discussed in G. H. Treitel, The Law of Contract 526–28 (4th ed., 1975). For a comparable American decision, which also places great emphasis on the continued existence of the assignor corporation, see Matter of Ehrlich, Inc. (Unit

exist? This question, which common-law courts have found a difficult one to answer, is discussed in 4 Corbin On Contracts §§ 865–869 (1951, see especially at pp. 437–38, and Supps.).[3] See also E. A. Farnsworth, Contracts 796 (1982), suggesting that in such a case the customer may be discharged because he has no effective remedy against his promisor.

If an American court today had to deal with a fact situation like that in the "Rimba" case, would the doubts existing under the common law be resolved by § 2–210 of the Uniform Commercial Code?

Frame Corp.), 5 N.Y.2d 275, 184 N.Y.S.2d 334, 157 N.E.2d 495 (1959).

3. Cf. Restatement, Second, Contracts § 262 (1981).

C. A TOPICAL APPROACH TO THE CIVIL LAW: SOME ILLUSTRATIVE SUBJECTS

INTRODUCTORY NOTE

Up to this point, the emphasis has been on method and system of the civil law, rather than on specific subjects or detailed rules. As illustrations, however, positive rules of German, Swiss and French law have been used, and the careful reader will have noticed that the choice of illustrations has not been entirely fortuitous. They were selected with a two-fold object in mind. Primarily, they served to exemplify and to explain the workings of codified law; the historical developments and socio-political ideas reflected in the codes; the civilians' mental processes, and the categories in which they think. Only secondarily, the same illustrations were designed (a) to highlight some of the institutional differences between the common law and the civil law; (b) to outline the basic elements of civil-law procedure; and (c) to familiarize the reader with some of the important civil-law doctrines in the area of substantive private law, with special emphasis on the law of Obligations. The latter term, in civilian terminology, includes Contracts, Quasi-Contracts,[1] and Torts. Though all three of these subjects were represented, there was a predominance of illustrations relating to the area of contracts,[2] in order to lay the groundwork for a study of other segments of the law of business transactions.

From this point on, the emphasis will be somewhat different. To supplement the systematic and in part theoretical study of civil-law *methods*, a few selected *topics* will be studied as such.

This topical approach will provide additional opportunities for observing (this time from a different angle) how civil-law methods operate in concrete situations. Three subject areas, Agency, Corporations and Conflict of Laws, have furnished all of the topics to be studied. The choice of the subject areas and of the particular topics has been guided by considerations based (a) on their great importance in international legal practice,[3] and (b) on their close connection with the matters previously covered in the method-oriented part of the course.

---

1. Quasi-Contracts, in turn, ordinarily is subdivided into negotiorum gestio (supra p. 5) and unjust enrichment (supra pp. 711–713).

2. The reader who wishes to review the contract materials as such, is referred to the following, supra: freedom of contract (pp. 659–662); limitations on that freedom, and doctrines invalidating certain types of contracts (pp. 582–585, 594–596, 615–619, 702–725); offer and acceptance (pp. 245–253, 279–281, 660–661); consideration and form requirements (pp. 17–22, 280, 431–433, 589–591); change of circumstances as a ground for termination of a contract, or even for judicial adjustment of its terms (pp. 731–740); non-performance ("default") (pp. 666–667); excuses for non-performance (pp. 754–755, 762–766); and remedies for non-performance (pp. 511–515, 663–684).

3. The subject of Conflict of Laws, or International Private Law as our civil-law brethren would call it, necessarily impinges upon every transaction across international boundaries; and the appointment of agents as well as the choice of a form of business organization is a threshold problem unavoidably facing every lawyer whose clients engage in foreign business.

I. AGENCY

1. THE "ABSTRACT NATURE" OF THE AGENT'S POWER

R. W. LEE: THE ELEMENTS OF ROMAN LAW *
1956. Pp. 334–336.

[Author's footnotes omitted.]

. . . Mandate is a contract whereby one person (mandator) gives another (mandatarius) a commission to do something for him without reward, and the other accepts the commission. It is imperfectly bilateral . . ., because, though it may give rise to reciprocal rights and duties, the duty of the mandatarius arises immediately upon the acceptance of the commission, while the duty of the mandator, *viz.* to indemnify the mandatarius against loss and liability, is merely contingent. . . .

The object of the contract must be lawful. It may consist either in general management (procuratio omnium bonorum) or in the doing of a specific act (procuratio unius rei). It may, but does not necessarily, imply entering into legal relations with a third party. . . .

The mandatarius was bound:—1. to execute the mandate, subject to the right of renouncing it re adhoc integra, i.e., while he can do so without prejudice to the mandator . . .; 2. not to exceed the mandate; 3. to exercise exacta diligentia. In the classical law he was liable only for dolus; 4. to render accounts; 5. to make over to the mandator all benefits accruing from the mandate including rights of action against third parties. . . .

The duties of the mandator were principally: 1. to indemnify the mandatarius against expense, loss and liability incurred in the execution of the mandate; 2. not to revoke the mandate to his prejudice. . . .

We are apt to think of mandatum in terms of agency, and the word agency is sometimes employed to translate the word mandatum. But this is incorrect. In the law of contract agency implies a contractual relation established between one person termed the principal and a third party by another person termed the agent, who acts as intermediary. In English Law, at least, the topic "Principal and Agent" is mainly concerned with this relation, though also with the relation of Principal and Agent *inter se*. But mandate is essentially a contract of employment [a] and its rules are concerned only with the reciprocal

---

* Reprinted by permission of Sweet & Maxwell, Ltd.

a. Modern civilian codes draw a sharper distinction between employment con-

rights and duties of the mandator on the one hand and the mandatarius on the other. . . .

BASIC CIVIL LAW CONCEPTS IN THE LAW OF AGENCY

(1) The officials and lawyers who were responsible for the development of classical Roman law, like their common-law brethren many centuries later, were slow in recognizing that a contract or other transaction entered into by X could or should create rights and duties directly and exclusively for Y. After a period of vacillation, it was finally recognized in the Justinian and Post-Justinian period that such a situation could exist.[1] The power by virtue of which X was able to create direct legal consequences on behalf of Y, was called *procuratio*. But the distinction between *mandatum* and *procuratio*, though discernible in the Digests and recognized in medieval canon law as well as (much later) in the writings of natural law scholars, did not become firmly established until the second half of the 19th century.[2] In the codifications dating from the early 19th century the distinction is hopelessly blurred. The French Civil Code, in its Article 1984, uses the terms "mandat ou procuration" as synonymous and interchangeable. This method of treating the agent's *power* (to create rights and duties directly for the principal) merely as a by-product of the contractual relationship existing between principal and agent, has been severely criticized as unsystematic. Planiol, one of the leading French authors, has been among the critics. In spite of all theoretical objections, however, this method of jumbling mandatum and procuratio was taken over by many of the French-influenced 19th century codes.[3]

It was only a little over a hundred years ago that German scholars—drawing inspiration not only from Roman, canonistic and Germanic sources, but, more importantly, from the law merchant and from the writings of Grotius and other natural law scholars—clearly formulated the distinction between mandatum and procuratio, and convincingly demonstrated the practical usefulness as well as the inherent logic of

tracts, on the one hand, and contracts of mandate, on the other. An agent operating under a contract of the latter kind (even though he may receive compensation) normally is more independent, and less subject to the principal's control, than an employee. For an interesting discussion of this distinction, with specific reference to the law of Colombia, see Curtis v. Beatrice Foods Co., 481 F.Supp. 1275, 1288 (S.D.N.Y. 1980).

In countries where the employment contract is subject to extensive regulation, such as in France, it is, in fact, largely governed by rules contained in a special labor code (e.g. the French Code du Travail), while the rules concerning "mandate" remain part of the civil code.

1. In the old Quiritary law, which was the law of an agricultural society, the concept of agency was unknown. The commercial exigencies of the Imperial period, however, led to its recognition, partly by a process of Praetorian law-making akin to equity's correction of the rigidities of the common law, and partly by way of importation of Greek and Hellenistic ideas. See Riccobono, Reception of Forms of Agency in Roman Law, 9 N.Y.U.L.Q.Rev. 271 (1932). For further references see Pound, Readings in Roman Law 62 et seq. (1914). See also Holmes, The Common Law 16, 228–33 (1881).

2. See the important article by W. Müller-Freienfels, Legal Relations in the Law of Agency: Power of Agency and Commercial Certainty, 13 Am.J.Comp.L. 193, 341 (1964).

3. See W. Müller-Freienfels, Law of Agency, 6 Am.J.Comp.L. 165, 171 (1957).

separating the two concepts.[3a] The draftsmen of the German Civil Code of 1896 enthusiastically adopted the distinction and the principle behind it: that for the third party dealing with the agent it should not be necessary to inquire into the details of the legal relationship existing between the principal and the agent, and that for the purpose of proper protection of the third party it is important to make the agent's *power* of representation largely independent of the existence of a valid contract of mandate or employment between principal and agent. Consequently, the German Code treats the agent's "power of representation" (Stellvertretung) in the General Part (§§ 164–181). The general rules dealing with the "power of representation" are applicable to powers granted by law as well as to powers created by a jural act of the principal. A power of representation created by an act of the principal is called "Vollmacht." It is to be noted, however, that Vollmacht denotes merely the *power* of the agent (to create legal consequences directly as between principal and third party), and that it must be strictly distinguished from the mandate, employment or other contractual relationship determining the *rights and duties* of principal and agent inter sese. The internal relationship between principal and agent, which ordinarily will be a contract of mandate or employment, is, in the system of the German Civil Code (supra, p. 533), widely separated from the power of representation. While the latter, as we have seen, is dealt with in the First Book (General Part), we find the provisions concerning contracts of mandate and employment in that part of the Second Book (Obligations) which regulates particular types of contracts (§§ 611 et seq., 662 et seq.).

The German system of making the agent's *power* independent of the contractual relationship between principal and agent and of emphasizing this independence in the very system of the Code,[4] has greatly influenced the thinking of legal scholars in all civil-law countries. With some modifications, it has been taken over into the Swiss Civil Code and, significantly, into the new Italian Civil Code.[5] The former Italian Code had followed the French example in this respect. The new Italian Code, however, sharply emphasizes the difference between "procura" and "mandato", and treats the two institutions in different chapters (Articles 1387–1400, 1703–30). Article 1704 of the Italian

---

3a. See W. Müller-Freienfels, Agency (Law of), in Encyclopaedia Britannica (15th ed., 1974). See also id., Die Abstraktion der Vollmachtserteilung im 19. Jahrhundert, in H. Coing & W. Wilhelm (Eds.), Wissenschaft und Kodifikation des Privatrechts im 19. Jahrhundert (Vol. 2: Die rechtliche Verselbständigung der Austauschverhältnisse vor dem Hintergrund der wirtschaftlichen Entwicklung und Doktrin) 144–212 (1977), where the historical development of the agent's "abstract" power (see text, infra) is extensively discussed.

Note, however, that modern technological developments have somewhat changed the context in which agency relationships exist, especially when complex negotiations are involved. Since even lengthy documents can now be transmitted around the globe within seconds through the use of telecopying machines and similar devices,

agents are likely to receive closer supervision when substantial matters are at stake. See R. De Quenaudon, Quelques remarques sur les conflits de lois en matière de représentation volontaire, 73 Rev.cr.d.i.p. 413, n. 1 (1984), citing U. Spellenberg, Geschäftsstatut und Vollmacht im Internationalen Privatrecht 19 (1979).

4. In continental legal literature, this principle of independence is often referred to as the "abstract nature" of the Vollmacht.

5. For a complete list of the countries which have adopted the German system, see Müller-Freienfels, supra n. 2, at 199–200; P. Hay & W. Müller-Freienfels, Agency in the Conflict of Laws and the 1978 Hague Convention, 27 Am.J.Comp.L. 1, 5 (1979).

Code expressly recognizes that a mandatory may or may not have power to act in the name of the principal, and provides that where he has such power, the chapter dealing with power of representation (Articles 1387–1400) shall govern that aspect of the matter. In France itself, the Civil Code Reform Commission [6] recommended to separate the treatment of the subject of "power of representation" from that of the contract of mandate.[7]

(2) The independent or "abstract" nature of the agent's power, as recognized in the codes of Germany and of many other civil-law countries, is an important legal device for the protection of a third party with whom the agent, acting on behalf of the principal, has concluded a contract. This protective device is of particular significance in situations where for some reason the contractual relationship between principal and agent is legally defective. The late Professor E. J. Cohn, in his well-known Manual of German Law (Vol. 1, at p. 88, 2d ed. 1968) gave the following

> *Example:* A employs B, a minor, as his servant without the service agreement having been approved by B's guardian. The service agreement is therefore invalid. This, however, does not affect the validity of a power granted expressly or impliedly by A to B to purchase goods for A's household or to book seats for him at a theatre.[7a]

Let us assume that the person from whom B bought household goods (on credit) on behalf of A, is the merchant T. *If T had been notified by A* of B's authority to purchase household goods for A, in that event T would be protected by the doctrine of apparent authority, which prevails in German law as well as our law.[8] In all likelihood, however, A did not issue such a notification to T. The chances are that T was never notified of B's authority to act for A, or that he was notified only by B; in either event, T derives no protection from the doctrine of apparent authority. But, as pointed out in Professor Cohn's

---

6. See supra, p. 548.

7. See Oftinger, Die Revision des Code Civil Français, 44 Schweizerische Juristenzeitung 307, 308 (1948).

Even under existing law, French courts and legal writers recognize that viable solutions often cannot be derived from the jumbled provision of Art. 1984 of the Code Napoleon. See A. N. Yiannopoulos, Brokerage, Mandate and Agency in Louisiana: Civilian Tradition and Modern Practice, 19 La.L.Rev. 777, 784 (1959).

7a. The same result would now be reached in France. Pursuant to an amendment of Civil Code art. 1990, adopted in 1965, a non-emancipated minor may be made an agent, but the *principal* has a cause of action against his minor agent only in accordance with the general rules applicable to the obligations of minors. Note, however, the narrow scope of this amended code provision, which stands in marked contrast to the broad sweep of the German doctrine discussed in the text, supra.

8. In German law, this doctrine is based on the "good faith" principle expressed in § 242 of the Civil Code. A principal who has brought the agent's authority to the attention of a third party, or who has knowingly tolerated a situation in which the agent has acted as if he had such authority, is thought to violate the principles of good faith if he denies the existence of the agent's power after the third party, in reliance upon it, has dealt with the agent. See, e.g., Bundesgerichtshof, decision of March 10, 1953, 7 MDR 345 (1953). See also Bundesgerichtshof, Decision of March 12, 1981, 34 N.J.W. 1727 (1981).

The theory of apparent authority is recognized not only in Germany, but in other civil-law systems as well. See e.g., M. J. Bonell, The 1983 Geneva Convention on Agency in the International Sale of Goods, 32 Am.J.Comp.L. 717, 739–40 (1984). For French law, see Cour de Casation, Assemblée plén., Dec. 12, 1962, 1963 D.J. 277.

Example, T *is* protected under German law because of the "abstract" nature of B's power. Even though the *contract* between A and B is invalid, the *power* granted by A to B is valid. Hence B had *real authority* to buy household goods for A, and thus T is protected regardless of whether or not the doctrine of apparent authority applies.[8a]

(3) It is possible, and indeed usual in practice, that the contract between principal and agent, and the agent's authority to act for the principal, come into existence simultaneously and through the same act or document. Nevertheless, under the law of Germany and of the other civil-law countries recognizing the "abstract" nature of the agent's authority, the agent's *power* is legally independent of the effectiveness of the *contract* between principal and agent.

Under German law, no form is required for the authorization creating the agent's power.[9] But the contract between principal and agent may under certain circumstances require written or notarial form. A contract concluded in violation of such a form requirement is invalid; but the *power* which has been given to the agent as part of the same transaction, is nevertheless valid, because its "abstract" nature makes its validity independent of the effectiveness of the contract between principal and agent.[10]

(4) Both aspects of the principal-agent relationship, the agent's power as well as the internal relationship between principal and agent, are in most civil-law countries governed by the *civil* code. In cases in which no merchant and no commercial transaction is involved, the civil code is apt to be the exclusive source of the applicable rules. In cases involving merchants or commercial transactions, however, these rules may be qualified by the commercial code and its auxiliary statutes.[11] The agent may be a commercial clerk or a commercial broker, and in

---

8a. It should be noted, however, that the German Civil Code, while strongly consecrating the principle of the independent or abstract nature of the agent's authority, contains one express exception to that principle: pursuant to § 168, the Vollmacht terminates when the underlying contract or other legal relationship between principal and agent comes to an end. Where, as usual, the underlying contract is one of mandate or employment, both contract and Vollmacht are terminated by the death of the agent, but ordinarily not by the death of the principal. See Palandt, Bürgerliches Gesetzbuch, § 168, Anno. 1 (46th ed., 1987). See also infra p. 784.

9. See id., § 167, Anno. 1.

10. Under German law, as in any other legal system, two separate questions must be distinguished in dealing with the subject of the form required for the authorization which the agent receives from his principal: (a) If the contract between principal and agent, i.e., the contract underlying the authorization, is subject to a form requirement, does the authorization as such require the same form? (b) Does the authorization require the same form as the

transaction with a third party which the agent is authorized to conclude?

As shown in the text, supra, the answer given in German law to question (a) is in the negative. This follows from the "abstract" nature of the authorization. By an express provision in the second paragraph of § 167, the German Civil Code also answers question (b) in the negative; but the rule may be different where the parties are trying to use an unnotarized Vollmacht, especially an irrevocable one, for the purpose of *evading* the requirement of notarization, for instance with respect to real estate transactions. See, e.g., Bundesgerichtshof, July 11, 1952, 5 NJW 1210 (1952).

As to the rules of other civil-law countries with respect to the form required for powers-of-attorney, see infra pp. 778–779.

11. A point of great practical importance, previously mentioned in this book, should be re-emphasized here. During the last decades, many civil-law countries have enacted code amendments or auxiliary statutes strongly protecting commercial agents (distributors and other more or less independent agents as well as clerks and traveling salesmen) against arbitrary dis-

that event the commercial code will have an impact on the contractual relations between principal and agent.[12] Moreover, the scope of the agent's power of representation, that is of his power to create legal consequences directly between the principal and a third party, may be governed by special provisions of the commercial code, especially by the provisions (with which the reader is quite familiar, see supra pp. 697–702) which require registration of such power in the Register of Commerce and regulate the effect of such registration. See infra, Opinion of the Swiss Federal Court in the Matter of Boehler-Bieri v. Bucher, and the Notes following that opinion.

The civil-law theorist will classify the partner's power to bind the partnership and the corporate officer's power to bind the corporation as "powers of representation", and these powers, too, may be subject to special provisions of the commercial code and its auxiliary statutes. Where the commercial code is silent, however, the same method is used which has been seen in operation in many other instances: the applicable provisions of the civil code must be resorted to as subsidiary rules.

---

missal. American and English businessmen, not accustomed to social legislation of this particular kind, often experience a sense of shock when they discover how difficult and costly it can be under some of the civil-law systems to fire an agent, even when the attempt to terminate the relationship appears consistent with the terms of the contract. For an early example of such social legislation, see the provisions of the German Commercial Code involved in the case supra pp. 584–586. The modern statutes enacted in many civil-law countries go much further and often provide for substantial severance pay or in other ways seek to compensate the agent for losses incurred by him as a result of the termination of the relationship. Typically, the provisions of these statutes are not subject to a contrary agreement in favor of the principal. For references and examples see C. H. Fulda and W. F. Schwartz, Cases and Materials on the Regulation of International Trade and Investment 782–90 (1970). See also M. Dobson & R. Gaudenzi, Agency and Distributorship Laws in Italy: Guidelines for the Foreign Principal, 20 Int'l Law. 997 (1986); H. T. King, Legal Aspects of Appointment and Termination of Foreign Distributors and Representatives, 17 Case Western Res.J. Int'l L. 91 (1985); Puelinckx and Tielemans, The Termination of Agency and Distributorship Agreements, A Comparative Survey, 3 Nw. J. Int'l L. 452 (1981); J. Salès, Termination of Sales Agents and Distributors in France, 17 Int'l Law. 741 (1983); T. W. Simons, Jr., Termination of Sales Agents and Distributors in Belgium, 17 Int'l Law. 752 (1983).

Cf. G. Vorbrugg, Agency and Distributorship Agreements under German Law, 19 Int'l Law. 607 (1985).

In EEC countries, the rules just mentioned will have to be coordinated during the next few years, as a result of the Council Directive of December 18, 1986, on Self-Employed Commercial Agents, 1986 O.J. No. L 382, p. 17.

12. Most commercial codes also contain a title or chapter dealing with the law of commission merchants; but inasmuch as the commission merchant deals with third parties in his own name, and not in the name of his principal, civilians do not consider him an agent. Civil-law jurisdictions are virtually unanimous in refusing, at least in principle, to extend rules of agency (Stellvertretung) to cases of agents acting for undisclosed principals. See Müller-Freienfels, Comparative Aspects of Undisclosed Agency, 18 Mod.L.Rev. 33 (1955).

In order to overcome this difference between the common-law and the civil-law approach to the problem of the undisclosed agent at least in one important area, a Diplomatic Conference held in Geneva in 1983 has proposed a Convention on Agency in the International Sale of Goods. See the article by Bonell, cited supra n. 8. In France, the law on undisclosed principals may have been changed as a result of a recent case. Soc. Dead Sea Bromine v. Crédit commercial de France, Cass Com., April 26, 1982; Cour d'appel Chambéry, October 15, 1984, 1986 D.J. 233 (with an annotation by D. Rambure).

ILLUSTRATIONS

(1) Farmer P employs A as assistant farm manager and authorizes him to sell cattle. Acting on behalf of P, A sells 30 head of cattle to T. A is an alien. It is provided by statute that no alien may be employed without governmental permission.[1] P applies for such permission, but the application is denied. The employment contract between P and A is, therefore, invalid under the provisions of the statute. The contract for the sale of the 30 head of cattle is nevertheless clearly effective under German law. A's *power to make that* contract is, as a German lawyer would put it, of an "abstract nature"; it is independent of the *contract* of employment. Under German law, this result would be reached on the ground that A had real authority. It is immaterial, therefore, whether P informed T of A's authority and thus, in addition, created the appearance of authority.

Would the result, and the reasoning, be the same under our law? Cf. W. A. Seavey, Handbook of the Law of Agency, § 3A (1964); M. Ferson, Principles of Agency, § 293 (1954); H. G. Reuschlein & W. H. Gregory, Handbook on the Law of Agency and Partnership 31–37 (1979, and 1981 Supp.); Restatement, Second, Agency § 1, Comment b, and §§ 15, 16 (1958).

(2) S, as president of P Corporation, was authorized by its by-laws to "perform all duties incident to the office of president which are authorized and required by law." He also was president of X Corporation. When P Corporation received a $15,000 check, S appropriated it in the following manner: He endorsed the check to X Corporation, signing the endorsement as president of P Corporation; this endorsement was co-signed by his son, who signed as secretary of P Corporation, although in fact he was not the secretary and had no authority whatever. Then, acting as President of X Corporation, the endorsee, S deposited the check in X Corporation's account with defendant bank. Defendant collected the check and credited the proceeds to X Corporation. S then withdrew the money from the account of X Corporation and never accounted for it to P Corporation. P Corporation sues defendant bank on the theory that S's endorsement was unauthorized and could not transfer title to the check. Consequently, plaintiff argues, defendant is liable for conversion of the check.

In a case presenting these facts,[1a] an American court held for the plaintiff. According to the opinion of Judge (later Chief Judge) Lehman, writing for the majority, S had no actual authority to endorse the check on behalf of P Corporation, because he "was not acting in behalf of his principal but was stealing its property." [2] Nor was there apparent authority, in the view of the court, because S, who had the endorsement co-signed by his son, did not invoke any apparent power, singly, to sign for P Corporation.[3]

---

1. This hypothetical statute is not a pure product of professorial fancy. A similar statute was involved, and was upheld against constitutional attack, in DeCanas v. Bica, 424 U.S. 351, 96 S.Ct. 933 (1976).

1a. Wen Kroy Realty Co., Inc. v. Public National Bank & Trust Co. of New York, 260 N.Y. 84, 183 N.E. 73 (1932).

2. Note that the majority achieves a result favorable to the principal by reading into the unqualified *powers* of the agent certain limitations flowing from his *duties*.

3. The majority opinion in the *Wen Kroy* case apparently is still regarded as good law in New York. See Maber, Inc. v. Factor Cab Corp., 19 A.D.2d 500, 503, 244

The dissenting opinion points out that S's power to "perform all duties incident to the office of president which are authorized and required by law", concededly included the power to endorse and transfer negotiable paper. It follows, according to the dissent, that S, while violating his *duty*, acted within the confines of his *power*, and that P Corporation is bound by the endorsement. The dissenting opinion, without making any reference to the civil law, in effect states and applies a doctrine identical with the German theory of the abstract nature of the agent's authority.[4] Pursuant to that theory, S's *power* to endorse checks on behalf of P Corporation, as distinguished from his contractual *right* to do so, was unlimited; therefore, he had *real authority*, and not merely apparent authority to negotiate the check.

Under German law, moreover, the defendant bank probably would win on the additional ground that it is protected by the principle of publicity (supra pp. 696–702). As the officer of a German corporation, S would be listed in the Register of Commerce, and unless a limitation upon his power to act for the corporation appears in the Register itself, the corporation is bound by his act.[5]

What are the criteria by which you can determine whether, as a matter of policy, the German rule or the American (New York) rule is preferable?

2. THE INTERACTION OF CIVIL CODES AND COMMERCIAL CODES IN THE LAW OF AGENCY—APPLICATION OF THE PRINCIPLE OF PUBLICITY

OPINION OF THE SWISS FEDERAL COURT IN THE MATTER OF BOEHLER–BIERI, PLAINTIFF–APPELLANT, v. BUCHER, DEFENDANT–RESPONDENT

March 9, 1912, BGE 38 II 103.

[In this action, which is similar to a declaratory judgment action, the plaintiff, Mrs. Boehler-Bieri, demands in effect a declaration that she does not owe the amount of Fr. 2500 which defendant Bucher contends she owes him. The courts below dismissed the complaint, holding that plaintiff is indebted to defendant Bucher in the said

N.Y.S.2d 768 (1st Dept. 1963). See also *Sunshine v. Bankers Trust Co.,* 34 N.Y.2d 404, 358 N.Y.S.2d 113, 314 N.E.2d 860 (1974), and *Scientific Holding Co., Ltd. v. Plessy Inc.,* 510 F.2d 15, 24 (2d Cir. 1974), where *Wen Kroy* was cited with apparent approval. Concerning present New York law, see also McKinney's New York Laws Annotated, Uniform Commercial Code § 3–304(7) and Banking Law § 9. Relevant cases in other jurisdictions are collected in Anno., 100 A.L.R.2d 670 (1965).

4. Even under the German rule, plaintiff might win if mere inspection of the check disclosed a *manifest* abuse of the agent's power. See infra pp. 788–789. But this was not so in the instant case. The endorsement to X Corporation, on its face, did not indicate any impropriety. The fact that S's signature appeared twice on the back of the check (in the endorsement *to* X Corporation and in the endorsement *by* X Corporation), was not manifestly suspicious.

5. This point is further developed in the next-following case.

amount. Upon plaintiff's further appeal to the Federal Court, the decisions below were affirmed.]

Reasons: The plaintiff, Mrs. Boehler-Bieri, is registered in the Register of Commerce as the sole owner of a firm engaged in the purchase and sale of real estate. Her husband is registered as *Prokurist* of her firm.[a] The real estate broker, Max Schlesinger,[b] maintains his office in the same building as the plaintiff. The firm of Sponi & Picci had obtained a judgment against Schlesinger in the amount of Fr. 10,034.15. On November 30, 1909, an agreement was entered into by which the firms of Max Schlesinger and of Boehler-Bieri [the latter as guarantor] promised to pay Fr. 2500 to Sponi & Picci in full settlement of the latter's claims against Schlesinger. This agreement was signed by the husband Boehler, as Prokurist, on behalf of the firm of Boehler-Bieri. The claim for payment of the Fr. 2500 was subsequently assigned to the defendant Bucher, an attorney. . . . Plaintiff contends . . . that the making of the agreement by her husband was not within the scope of his agency.

. . . Plaintiff thus contends, in effect, that she is not bound by the contract which her husband signed in her name as guarantor [of Schlesinger's obligation]. Therefore, it must be examined whether the guaranty involved herein is one of the jural acts which within the meaning of Article 423 of the Code of Obligations (as numbered prior to its revision) "can serve the purpose of the calling or business of the principal." [c]

This definition of the authority of a registered Prokurist—which is identical with the authority of the general partner of a partnership (Article 561 of the unrevised Code of Obligations)—makes it irrelevant whether in the particular case the jural act was in the interest of the principal. It is equally irrelevant whether the operation of the business usually involves jural acts of that kind. The authority exists for every jural act which may *possibly* be within the scope of the purpose of the business. Consequently the authority exists for every jural act which is not *excluded* by the purpose of the business. . . . It must be held to be at least *possible* that a guaranty of the kind here involved

---

a. Only a merchant can appoint a "Prokurist". The latter is an agent possessing broad managerial powers. The extent of these powers is discussed in the opinion. The term "Prokurist" is essentially limited to the German and Swiss code families; but agents performing similar functions can be appointed by a merchant, and must be registered in the Register of Commerce, in most of the other civil-law countries as well. See H. Würdinger, Prokura, in 5 F. Schlegelberger, Rechtsvergleichendes Handwörterbuch für das Zivil- und Handelsrecht 669–77 (1936).

b. Not related to the co-author of this book.

c. Swiss Code of Obligations, Article 459 (formerly 423):

"In dealing with a third party who acts in good faith, the Prokurist [holder of a power of procuration] is deemed to be authorized to sign bills of exchange on behalf of the principal, and to enter, in the latter's name, into any and all transactions which can serve the purpose of the calling or business of the principal."

[Subd. 2 requires express authorization for transactions transferring or encumbering land.]

The principal carries the burden of proof if he contends that the third party did not act in good faith. Swiss Civil Code, Art. 3.

may be in the interest of a business such as that of the plaintiff. The plaintiff is in the business of buying and selling real estate. This object of her business may well make it necessary or desirable to intervene in favor of third parties with whom there are business relationships; for instance for the purpose of protecting such third parties from eager creditors. This may sometimes be a proper way of protecting the normal operations or the credit of plaintiff's own business.

Plaintiff's contention that she had no knowledge of the agreement is irrelevant. Inasmuch as her husband, pursuant to Article 423, had power to enter into the agreement, it is clear that the plaintiff became automatically bound to perform all obligations flowing from such agreement, and that no ratification by her personally was necessary. Nor is it contended by the plaintiff that she limited the statutory scope of her husband's agency by excluding therefrom the power to make guaranties. [The Court points out that even such express limitation, by the principal, of the statutory scope of the agent's power would be unavailing as a defense against a third party unless the principal could show that such limitation was either known to the third party or made a matter of public record in the *Register of Commerce*]. . . .

NOTES AND QUESTIONS

(1) In many commercial codes it is provided that the Register of Commerce shall disclose the names of those agents of a commercial enterprise who possess managerial powers, and that, in addition, all such agents deposit specimen signatures with the Register, where the signatures are open to public inspection. The same rule prevails in many civil-law countries with respect to signatures of general partners of partnerships and officers of corporations.

(2) At this point, the reader may wish to review the materials (supra pp. 696–702) dealing with the principle of publicity. The code provisions upon which the court in the principal case relies, exemplify and apply that principle.

(3) Did the Swiss court, in deciding the foregoing case, measure the scope of the agent's power by the yardstick, so familiar to common-law lawyers, of the "scope of the agent's employment"?

(4) Where the agent is a registered Prokurist, is the scope of his power under Swiss law determined by the statute or by the expressed will of his principal?

(5) With respect to the problems illustrated by the principal case, Swiss law is very similar to German law. For a most instructive discussion of the powers of a Prokurist under German law (and a comparison with French and Anglo-American law) see W. Müller-Freienfels, Legal Relations in the Law of Agency: Power of Agency and Commercial Certainty, 13 Am.J.Comp.L. 193, 341, especially at 206–15 and 341–43 (1964). The German provisions, like the Swiss, give a broad *statutory* scope to the powers of the Prokurist; the powers thus statutorily defined cannot be limited by the principal unless he publishes the limitation in the Register of Commerce.[a]

a. There are similar provisions regarding the powers of the general partners of a partnership, and of the officers of a corporation.

What about a case in which the third party with whom the Prokurist deals, knows or should know that the Prokurist is acting against the interests of his principal, or in violation of the latter's instructions? Can the principal in such a case invoke the doctrine of "abuse of rights" against the third party in order to escape the harsh consequences which otherwise would flow from the "abstract" nature and the unrestricted scope of the Prokurist's power? This question will be taken up infra at pp. 786–793.

3. POWERS OF ATTORNEY—FORM REQUIREMENTS

NOTE

An observer brought up in the common law who surveys the form requirements for powers of attorney existing in the civil-law world,[1] will be struck by

(a) the eminent importance, in this context as in so many others, of the Notary and the "public document" (see supra pp. 18–20) and

(b) the diversity among the solutions adopted in the codes of the various civil-law countries.

The reader is familiar with the German rule (supra p. 772), which ordinarily does not require any formality.[2] Compare, however, the following French and Italian provisions.

FRENCH CIVIL CODE

Art. 1985. A power of attorney can be given either by a public instrument, or by a writing under private signature, even by letter. It can also be given verbally; but testimonial proof thereof is admitted only in accordance with the title *Of Contracts or Conventional Obligations in General.*[a]

1. The following articles are useful vehicles for such a survey: Eder, Powers of Attorney in International Practice, 98 U.Pa.L.Rev. 840 (1950); H. T. King, Jr., Checklist on Agency Agreements in Latin America, 13 Case Western Res.J. Int'l L. 153 (1981); F. W. Taylor, Jr. and H. O. Weisman, Middle East Agency Law Survey, 14 Int'l Law. 331 (1980). Cf. H. H. Lidgard, C. D. Rohwer and D. Campbell, A Survey of Commercial Agency (1984).

2. As a practical matter, formal execution of a power of attorney often is necessary even in countries adhering to the German system. While under that system a transaction (including a transaction requiring some formality) as a rule may be *validly concluded* by an informally authorized agent, some formal authentication of the agent's power of attorney may be required

in order to have the transaction *registered* in an official register, especially the land register.

a. This reference points to Arts. 1341–1348 of the French Civil Code, supra pp. 431–432.

In addition to the evidentiary requirement spelled out (by the reference to Art. 1341) in Art. 1985, the rule seems to prevail in France that the power of attorney must be executed with the same formality (e.g., notarial form) that is required for the transaction into which the agent is authorized to enter. See 2 Planiol's Treatise on the Civil Law, No. 2243 (English transl. by the Louisiana State Law Institute, 1959). This latter rule does not appear on the face of the Code Napoleon, while the more recent Italian Code is explicit in this respect.

The acceptance of the power may be tacit and result from the fact that the attorney-in-fact has acted thereunder.

ITALIAN CIVIL CODE [b]

Art. 1392.   Form of power of attorney.   An agent's power of attorney has no effect unless it is granted with the formalities prescribed for the contract which is to be entered into by the agent.

Art. 1393.   Verification of powers of agent.   A third party who is contracting with an agent may always demand that the powers of such agent be demonstrated and, if the agency is based on a written document, he may demand display of a copy signed by the agent.

NOTES

(1) The question whether the authorization given by the principal to the agent requires the same form as the transaction which the agent concludes on behalf of the principal, is one of considerable importance in practice; it must be faced by every legal system.   The civil-law systems, as we have seen, announce divergent answers to this question; but in each civil-law country the answer is apt to be given in terms of a general, broadly formulated rule, which in principle applies to all transactions requiring written or notarial form.

Contrast this with the casuistic method used in our own statutes of frauds.   Even within the same state, the statute may for some types of transactions require a memorandum signed by the principal or by his lawful agent "thereunto authorized in writing", while in reference to other types of transactions the quoted words may be missing.   See Restatement, Second, Contracts § 135, Comment b and Reporter's Note (1981).

(2) In Spain and in a number of Latin-American countries, an instrument in "public" (usually notarial) form is prescribed for certain enumerated categories of powers of attorney, especially for those conferring managerial or other "general" authority, and for those which empower an attorney-at-law or other agent to appear in a judicial or administrative proceeding.[1]   Although the wide acceptance, in international private law, of the rule *locus regit actum* tends to mitigate the rigor of these rules,[2] it is clear that international practice in countless cases requires the execution of powers of attorney in notarial form.   A principal residing in the United States often cannot comply with such a requirement except by executing the document before an American notary.   In view, however, of the institutional differences between civil-law and common-law notaries (see supra pp. 18–22), a court or administrative agency in a civil-law country may doubt whether a document acknowledged before an American notary can be treated as a "public document" in the civilian sense.[3]   To alleviate such doubts, some states

b. Military Government translation (1944–45).

1. See Eder, Powers of Attorney in International Practice, 98 U. of Pa.L.Rev. 840, 860–62 (1950); Obregon-Borchard, Latin American Commercial Law 319–21 (1921).

2. See Eder, supra n. 1, at 850–57.

3. See infra pp. 873–875.

have enacted provisions similar to the New York statute set forth hereunder.[4]

NEW YORK EXECUTIVE LAW, SECTION 135

Every notary public duly qualified is hereby authorized and empowered within and throughout the state to administer oaths and affirmations, to take affidavits and depositions, to receive and certify acknowledgments or proof of deeds, mortgages and powers of attorney and other instruments in writing; to demand acceptance or payment of foreign and inland bills of exchange, promissory notes and obligations in writing, and to protest the same for non-acceptance or non-payment, as the case may require; *and, for use in another jurisdiction, to exercise such other powers and duties as by the laws of nations and according to commercial usage, or by the laws of any other government or country may be exercised and performed by notaries public, provided that when exercising such powers he shall set forth the name of such other jurisdiction.* . . . (Italics added.)

4. POWERS OF ATTORNEY—CONSTRUCTION AND SCOPE

FRENCH CIVIL CODE

Art. 1987. It [the power of attorney] is either special and for one matter, or for certain matters only, or general and for all the affairs of the principal.

Art. 1988. A power of attorney made out in general terms covers only acts of management.

If it is intended to sell or mortgage, or to exercise other [similar] rights of ownership, express authority must be given.

Art. 1989. An attorney-in-fact cannot do anything beyond what is expressed in his authorization: the power to compromise does not include the power to submit to arbitration.

NOTE

The rule, contained in Articles 1988 and 1989 of the French Civil Code, that a "general" power of attorney authorizes only acts of management, and that express, specific authority is required for actions going beyond routine management, has been carried to great lengths in some Latin American countries, where powers of attorney must thus be

---

4. It has been forcefully argued that the New York statute "is merely declaratory of the customary law in force at the time of Independence and thereafter." Eder, supra n. 1, at 844. It may be diffi- cult, however, to convince a foreign official that the American notary had the requisite powers, unless the State (in which the notary officiates) has a statute proving the point.

incredibly detailed. A good example is furnished by the provisions of the Argentine Civil Code which follow:

ARGENTINE CIVIL CODE
Book II, Section III.—The Mandate [a]

1880. A power drawn in general terms always covers acts of management only, even if the principal declares that he reserves no authority for himself and that the attorney-in-fact may do whatever he considers appropriate. . . .

1881. A specific power is required:

1. To make payments which are not matters of ordinary management;

2. For novations which extinguish obligations that existed at the time the power was conferred;

3. To settle claims, submit claims to arbitrators, select a specific forum, waive the right to appeal or waive the right to assert the defense of the statute of limitations when it has already run;

4. To make any gratuitous waiver, or to excuse or grant remission of a debt, except in the case of the bankruptcy of the debtor;

5. For entering into a marriage in the name of the principal;

6. For the acknowledgment of illegitimate children;

7. For the making of any kind of contract, whether for a consideration or gratuitous, that has as its purpose the transfer or acquisition of the ownership of real estate; [b]

8. For the making of gifts, except for gifts in modest amounts, to employees or persons in the service of the entity [managed by the agent];

9. To lend money, or borrow it, unless lending and borrowing on interest is the business of the entity [managed by the agent], or unless the loans are a consequence of its management, or unless borrowing money is absolutely essential to preserve the things managed [by the agent];

10. To lease, for more than six years, any real estate in charge of the agent;

11. To accept bailments in the name of the principal, unless the agent's role is to accept bailments or consignments, or unless

a. Translated by P.H. On American law, compare Restatement (Second), Agency §§ 50–76 (1958).

b. It should be remembered that under the system followed in France and in some other countries influenced by French law, the conclusion of a contract may effectuate a transfer of title, even of real estate, and also that in the absence of a requirement of consideration, in civil-law countries it is possible to make a valid promise to make a gift, though such a "contract" may be subject to special form requirements. See supra p. 18.

the bailment is a consequence of the [ordinary] management [by the agent];

12. To create for the principal the obligation to perform some service . . .

13. To set up a company; c

14. To make the principal a surety;

15. To create or transfer rights *in rem* concerning real property;

16. To accept an inheritance; d

17. To admit or acknowledge obligations preceding the [grant of the] power.

1882. A special power authorizing a settlement of a claim does not authorize submitting it to arbitration.

1884. A special power authorizing acts of a specific kind must be limited to the acts for which it has been given and may not be extended to other analogous acts even if they can be considered as a natural consequence of the acts the accomplishment of which the principal has authorized.

NOTES ON GENERAL POWERS OF ATTORNEY

(1) *General Powers of Attorney as Fiduciary Devices.* "General" powers of attorney are of much greater practical importance in civil-law countries than in the common-law world. The reason, or one of the reasons, may be that in civil-law countries broad powers of attorney must serve many functions which under our system would be performed by trusts or powers in trust.

In comparative legal literature, one often encounters the statement that the institution of the trust is unknown to the civil law.[1] Technically, this is true. It stands to reason that a legal system in which there is no duality of law and equity, cannot divide ownership into a legal and an equitable title. Such division would be inconsistent, also, with the civilians' *dominium* concept of property, and with the *numerus clausus* of rights in rem.[2] Nor should we expect to find, in a civil-law

c. The Spanish term is "sociedad"; in its narrower meaning this may refer to a partnership, but more broadly, especially if followed by another expression, to other forms of business associations.

d. Under the civil-law system of "universal succession" the unconditional acceptance of an inheritance transfers the decedent's assets *and liabilities* to the heir. Such an acceptance is thus fraught with some danger. See supra p. 26.

1. The literature on the subject is vast. For references see W. F. Fratcher, Trust, in Vol. VI, Ch. 11 of the International Encyclopedia of Comparative Law, at pp. 84–108, 116–18 (1972); Bolgár, Why No Trusts in the Civil Law?, 2 Am.J.Comp.L. 204 (1953); Hefti, Trusts and Their Treatment in the Civil Law, 5 Am.J.Comp.L. 553 (1956). See also C. De Wulf, The Trust and Corresponding Institutions in the Civil Law 13–23 (1965).

In Japan, Quebec, Liechtenstein and several Latin-American jurisdictions it has been attempted to adopt the institution of the trust by legislation. See the articles by Bolgar and Hefti, supra, and K. W. Ryan, The Reception of the Trust, 10 Int. & Comp.L.Q. 265 (1961); R. Goldschmidt, The Trust in the Countries of Latin America, 3 Inter-Am.L.Rev. 29 (1961); J. Garrigues, Law of Trusts, 2 Am.J.Comp.L. 25, 30–32 (1953).

2. See, Fratcher, supra n. 1, at 89–90.

system, those procedures and remedies which are peculiar to chancery practice, such as the tracing of the trust res into the hands of any transferee who is not a bona fide purchaser for value.[3]

It would be a gross mistake, however, to conclude from the foregoing that fiduciary relationships do not exist in civil-law countries. The need for such relationships exists in every society which recognizes private property and permits a measure of free enterprise. Absent the formal trust device, a fiduciary relationship may be created, even inter vivos,[4] by a number of methods known to the civil law,[5] such as the following:

(a) Absolute title to the property in question may be transferred to the fiduciary, and the latter may bind himself *by contract*, perhaps by a contract for the benefit of a third party, to use such property and its income only for specified purposes, and to reconvey it when the arrangement ends. True, in their basic nature the duties of such a fiduciary are merely contractual;[6] but in some civil-law jurisdictions they are reinforced (i) by severe criminal sanctions in cases of defalca-

In the civil law of the pre-codification period, the property concept was less monolithic, and various forms of division between legal and beneficial title existed from Roman days until the beginning of the 19th century. See Bolgár, supra n. 1. It was the Code Napoleon, and the other codes following its leadership, which established the unitary concept of property in the overwhelming majority of civil-law countries. See supra pp. 684–685.

3. Our law provides for a comprehensive and exceedingly effective scheme of judicial supervision of every phase of trust administration. The court has power to construe the trust instrument, to determine its validity, to give directions to the trustee, to make the trustee account, to approve accounts voluntarily rendered, to remove the trustee for neglect of duty, and to follow the trust res into the hands of transferees. All this can be done by way of special proceedings admirably adapted to their purpose. In the civil law, equivalent remedies are either non-existent, or they have to be pursued (at least in the case of inter vivos trusts) by way of ordinary plenary actions of the kind described supra p. 339. This *procedural* difference is often overlooked by comparatists who seek to explain the Anglo-American trust, and its absence from the civil-law scene, exclusively in terms of contrasting concepts of substantive property rights. It is the combination of the two factors—the procedural and the substantive—which makes the Anglo-American trust truly different from its civil-law substitutes and counterparts, and which renders it difficult to introduce the trust in a civil-law country by a stroke of the legislative pen.

With respect to fiduciary relationships that are created, not by the parties, but by law (as in the case of guardians), the civil-law systems do not basically differ from ours. But even here, the procedural devices for keeping the fiduciary in line are much weaker than under our equity practice and related statutes. It was for that reason that a New York Surrogate's Court refused to let a part of a New York estate be delivered to the German guardian of an infant German beneficiary. See Estate of Manvilles, 76 Misc.2d 419, 351 N.Y.S.2d 93 (Surr.Westch.Co., 1973). The New York court obviously was struck by the relative laxity with which fiduciaries are judicially supervised under German law. It should not be forgotten, however, that a faithless guardian or other fiduciary would incur severe criminal sanctions under the German provisions referred to infra n. 7.

4. In the law of Wills and decedents' estates, civil-law countries always have used trust-like devices, such as the appointment of an executor, testamentary foundations, "charges" upon gifts and legacies, and several others. See Nussbaum, Sociological and Comparative Aspects of the Trust, 38 Colum.L.Rev. 408 (1938).

5. The list of such methods is a long one. See the articles cited in ns. 1 and 4 supra. Concerning Swiss family foundations, see infra p. 800.

6. "By virtue of his real right of property, the fiduciary [can] make valid dispositions even when in so doing he violates his obligation. The grantor [and the beneficiary] retains only a claim for damages against the fiduciary and cannot proceed against a third party." Hefti, supra n. 1, at 559.

tion,[7] and (ii) by statutory or decisional rules protecting the property in question from the creditors of the fiduciary.[8]

(b) In many situations, especially where the main purpose of the fiduciary relationship is to confer power *to manage* real or personal property, civilian lawyers may forego any transfer of title to the fiduciary. Instead, he receives a broad and often *"general" power of attorney*, which may contain a clause to the effect that the power shall not be revoked by the death of the principal. Such clauses are valid, and indeed customary, in many continental countries.[9]

(2) *How to Draft a General Power of Attorney.* A "general" power of attorney in the civil-law sense, i.e., a power which authorizes the agent to do *everything and anything* in the name of the principal which the principal himself could do, is theoretically possible under our law as well as under a civil-law system. As a practical matter, however, such unlimited powers are so rarely given in common-law countries that there are only few cases concerning them and that the authors of the Restatement of the Law of Agency have found it unnecessary to deal with them at all.[10] According to Section 3 of the Restatement "A

7. See, e.g., German Penal Law, Sec. 266: "He who intentionally abuses a power, conferred upon him by law, official commission or private transaction, to dispose of property of another or to incur obligations on behalf of another, or who violates a duty, incumbent upon him by virtue of law, official commission, private transaction or of a fiduciary relationship, to protect property interests of another, and thereby causes damage to the one whose property interests are entrusted to him, is guilty of the crime of faithlessness (*Untreue*) and shall be punished by imprisonment of up to five years, or by the imposition of a fine. In particularly grave cases the punishment shall be imprisonment for a period of one to ten years. . . ."

As this provision shows, the German legislator is aware that there are many situations in which a fiduciary or agent has the *power* validly to transfer property or to make other dispositions, although in doing so he violates his *duty*. Due to the principle of publicity and other devices for the protection of innocent purchasers (see supra pp. 684–702, and infra pp. 786–793), such instances of "excessive legal authority" (i.e., of a power exceeding the underlying right) are very frequent under modern codes. As between the despoiled principal or beneficiary, on the one hand, and the innocent purchaser on the other, these codes tend to protect the latter. For the protection of the interests of the principal or beneficiary, the civilian legislator is apt to rely (more than we do) upon the threat of drastic criminal sanctions.

8. See Nussbaum, supra n. 4, at 414–16.

9. See E. Wolff, Legality of a Provision in a Power of Attorney That It Shall Not

Be Revoked By The Donor's Death, 62 L.Q. Rev. 273, 277 (1946). The author, referring to provisions in the German, Swiss and French codes, adds that even in the absence of such a clause the principal's death does not necessarily terminate the power in civil-law countries. "Many Continental laws contain the provision that the power of attorney continues until the relation in connection with which it was created ceases, and this rule is not departed from in the event of the death of the donor. Many of the relations in connection with which powers of attorney are executed continue after the death of the principal, e.g., mandate, agreement for service in certain circumstances, and others."

10. Under a New York statute enacted in 1948 (Art. 5, Title 15 of the Gen. Obligations Law, formerly Art. 13 of the Gen.Bus. Law) it is possible to confer powers of unlimited scope upon an attorney-in-fact, by the use of a statutory short form which must contain, in bold face or similar type, a warning that "The powers granted by this document are broad and sweeping." The recommendation of the New York Law Revision Commission which led to the enactment of this statute was based upon a study prepared by Professor Richard R. Powell. See New York Law Revision Commission, 1946 Report 653 et seq.; 1947 Report 27 et seq.; 1948 Report 39 et seq. Cf. Cal. Civil Code §§ 2450–2473, as amended.

In the absence of such a statute, foreigners are often unsuccessful in attempting to import into our domestic law the civil-law institution of the "general" power of attorney. See Von Wedel v. McGrath, 180 F.2d 716 (3 Cir. 1950). But see Dockstader v. Brown, 204 S.W.2d 352 (Tex.Civ.App.1947).

general agent is an agent authorized to conduct a series of transactions involving a continuity of service." [10a] Comparison with the above-quoted Article 1987 of the French Civil Code shows that an agent whom the Restatement calls a "general agent", would under French law be a mere special agent "for certain matters". Under the French law, and in the civil law generally, a power of attorney for certain matters or, in the language of the Restatement, for "a series of transactions", is to be sharply distinguished from a truly general power, that is, a power of attorney "for all the affairs of the principal." Powers of attorney which are "general" in this latter sense are not even mentioned in the Restatement. In civil-law countries, on the other hand, general powers are so important that no civil-law treatment of the law of agency would be complete without a discussion of unlimited powers of attorney.

A power of attorney "for all the affairs of the principal" may be a dangerous instrument in the hands of an agent whose standards are not the highest. For the purpose of affording the principal a certain measure of protection against these dangers, the French Civil Code provides in the above-quoted Art. 1988 that a power of attorney phrased in general terms authorizes only acts of management, as distinguished from acts of disposition.[11] Under this rule, which has been followed in the majority of civil-law countries, a broad power of attorney will be restrictively interpreted, and will not be regarded as a true "general" power in the civil-law sense unless it specifies in unambiguous terms every type of dispositive transaction in which the agent may have to engage in conducting "all the affairs of the principal."

The German rule, adopted by a minority of civil-law countries, differs from the French rule. German law, as is shown by the cases immediately following this Note, contains no statutory rule of construction limiting the meaning of general terms used in a power of attorney; the language of such an instrument will be given its natural meaning regardless of whether the power sought to be conferred be special or general.

In practice, the difference between the French system and the German system is somewhat minimized by the use of forms. If a German lawyer is asked to draw up a "general" power of attorney, he will ordinarily, with or without the use of a form book, employ language to the effect that the agent shall have power to do anything and everything which the principal could personally do. Under German law these words will be construed to mean precisely what they say. A French lawyer, if confronted with the same task, will not be content with such a brief instrument couched in general terms, for fear that pursuant to Article 1988 of the French Civil Code it would be construed as a mere power of management. He will, therefore, resort to the use of one of those well-known, and often ridiculed, printed or typewritten forms which by special enumeration, continued page after page, confer upon the agent the power to enter into every type of transaction which has ever been known to be within the range of human imagination or desire.[12] By multitudinous paragraphs of fine print or type the lawyer

10a. The Restatement, Second (1958) has taken over this language without change.

11. Cases involving a similar provision of the Louisiana Civil Code are collected and discussed in Comment, Construction of Powers of Attorney in Louisiana, 23 Tulane L.Rev. 242 (1948).

12. For an example of a power of attorney of this type, see the Cuban document reproduced (in English) in Tabacalera Severiano Jorge, S.A. v. Standard Cigar

in France or in one of the countries following the French rule will thus, in practice, often accomplish the same result which the German lawyer will attain by the use of a short-form "Generalvollmacht".

Nevertheless, the difference between the two systems remains important and should be kept in mind by international practitioners who are called upon to draft powers of attorney for use in civil-law countries.

———

— passed over quickly

OPINION OF THE GERMAN REICHSGERICHT IN THE MATTER OF R., PLAINTIFF–APPELLANT, AGAINST WIDOW A., DEFENDANT–RESPONDENT

6th Civil Division, June 14, 1909, RGZ 71, 219.

The defendant had given a general power of attorney [a] to her son, the merchant G.A. Acting under this power of attorney, and in the name of the defendant, G.A. had on April 5, 1905 executed a document embodying a guaranty, whereby defendant guaranteed the payment of business obligations in the amount of M 5000 owed by G.A. to the plaintiff. Upon this guaranty plaintiff brought the present action against the defendant for payment of the balance of the business obligations of G.A. The court of first instance rendered judgment against the defendant. The intermediate appellate court, upon defendant's appeal, dismissed the complaint. Upon the further appeal of the plaintiff the judgment of the intermediate appellate court was reversed. . . .

Reasons: By the notarial General Power of Attorney of July 21, 1902, defendant authorized her son G.A. "to act effectively in her name and on her behalf in all matters or affairs governed by public law or private law. In particular, the agent shall have authority on behalf and in the name of the principal to conduct litigation, to make settlements, to receive monies, to buy and sell real property, to have mortgages recorded and cancelled of record, to transfer and accept the transfer of real property" etc.: [b] generally he was authorized to engage on behalf and in the name of the principal "in jural acts of every conceivable kind, and such jural acts of the agent shall be regarded as if

Co., 392 F.2d 706, 708 (5th Cir. 1968). See also the elaborate form suggested in 48 Revue du Notariat (Québec) 21–45, Supplement of 1945.

a. It is not always accurate to translate the German word *Vollmacht* as meaning power of attorney. The term "power of attorney" connotes the existence of a formal document embodying the power. As has been seen supra, p. 772, such a document is not strictly necessary under German law, and a Vollmacht (theoretically even a Generalvollmacht) may be given orally by the principal or be inferred from his conduct. Where a Vollmacht is thus

given without a formal writing, it might be misleading to use the English term "power of attorney". In the present case, however, the Vollmacht was in fact embodied in a formal document, so that in the context of this opinion the use of the English term "power of attorney" would seem to be defensible.

b. Under the German rule, which is contrary to the rule stated in Restatement, Second, Agency § 37, the enumeration of such *examples* of powers *included* in the general grant does not have the effect of limiting the latter.

they had been done by the principal herself." The primary issue between the parties is whether on the basis of this general power of attorney, G.A. had power to guarantee, in the name of his mother, an obligation of which he himself was the principal obligor. . . .

Defendant has invoked Section 181 of the Civil Code.[c] Both courts below have correctly held that this provision is inapplicable. The guaranty, pursuant to Sec. 765 of the Civil Code, is a contract between the guarantor and the creditor; the principal debtor is not a party to this contract.

The intermediate appellate court thought, however, that the power of attorney by its terms failed to authorize G.A. to make his mother a surety for his own obligation. The intermediate appellate court reasons as follows: It is true that the power of attorney is a general one. On the other hand it follows from language and contents of the document that it was the purpose of the broad authorization given to G.A. to represent his mother in *her* affairs and *her* interests. The document does not show in any way that G.A. was to have the further power to obligate the principal by a guaranty executed in the conduct of his own business and in his interest. The intermediate appellate court uses the analogy of a guardian, and points out that a guardian, of course, is not authorized in the name of his ward to guarantee his own obligations. . . . By executing the guaranty, the intermediate appellate court states, G.A. exceeded the power of attorney and, irrespective of good or bad faith, failed to use such power in accordance with its terms. The court below adds that if plaintiff read into the power of attorney a broader meaning than it really had, then plaintiff himself would have to bear the consequences of such mistake of law.

Appellant contends that these views of the court below are not free from error. In this, appellant is correct. The judgment below is based upon an erroneous view of the legal effect of a power of attorney. . . . In the first place, the analogy based on the powers of a guardian is untenable. The statutory power of representation of a guardian is defined and limited by the Code itself [citing the applicable sections of the civil code]. The scope of a guardian's powers is determined once and for all, and can ordinarily be recognized by anybody [by anybody who can read the Code]. Purpose and nature of the guardian's power of representation make it clear that his powers are limited by the interests of the ward. The guardian's powers of representation are determined by mandatory rules of law and cannot arbitrarily be modified by the parties. A power of attorney created by the will of the principal, on the other hand, is entirely different. Here, the scope of the agent's

---

c. This section provides that, unless specially authorized to do so, an agent has no power in the name of his principal to enter into a transaction with himself as an individual.

For a comparative discussion of the subject of self-dealing by agents see 1 Schles-inger (Gen.Ed.), Formation of Contracts—A Study of the Common Core of Legal Systems 97–100, 603–44 (1968). See also G. M. Badr, The Agent's Contract with Himself: With Special Reference to Islamic Law, 30 Am.J.Comp.L. 255 (1982).

power is determined by the terms of the particular authorization, by the declared will of the particular principal. Even "general powers of attorney" greatly differ among each other as to the definition and scope of the agent's authority [citing text writers].

It is true that logically a general power of attorney, like every power of attorney, can only refer to affairs of the principal. "Affairs" in this sense, however, are not identical with the interests of the principal. The execution of a guaranty is an . . . affair of the principal; whether the transaction serves his economic interest, is another question. The concept of a power of attorney does not necessarily imply that it must be limited by the interests of the principal. The authorization may be given in the interest of the agent [d] . . . or in the interest of a third party (cf. Planck, Commentary on the Civil Code, Section 167, Annotation 1).

The question whether or not the particular transaction is in the interest of the principal, is of importance only for the *internal* legal relationship between principal and agent. But we must strictly distinguish between (a) this internal relationship, e.g., mandate, and (b) the agent's power to represent the principal in dealings with third parties. The agent may act in violation of his mandate (for instance, in violation of instructions) but nevertheless within the limits of the power conferred upon him. Ordinarily the third party with whom the agent contracts does not have to inquire into the internal relationship between principal and agent; what concerns him is only the question whether the transaction is within the scope of the agent's power. . . . Of course, if in entering into the transaction the agent manifestly abused his power by acting against the interests of the principal, and the other party to the transaction was able to recognize such abuse, then the principal would not be bound by the transaction, or he would at least be entitled to rescind it, or to interpose the defense of fraud in an action based upon such transaction. This would be especially so in a case in which the agent has acted with the intention, known to the other party, of causing harm to his principal. Moreover, in cases in which, because of the extraordinary nature of the transaction, the third party should have recognized that such transaction could not possibly have been in the mind of the principal, the third party could not rely upon the language of the power of attorney, even though such language be unlimited. [Citations.]

[The Court then points out by way of dictum that in the case of a Prokurist, a partner, or a corporate officer, unless a limitation of his power of representation is on record in the Register of Commerce, a third party may rely on such agent's general power of representation, and that the only defense open to the Prokurist's principal, to the partnership or to the corporation as against the third party is the defense of collusion, i.e., of intentional concerted action of the agent

---

d. The Court mentions that the Pandectists referred to such an agent as a procurator in rem suam.

and the third party to the detriment of the principal. The Court explains that in cases of ordinary powers of attorney the rule is not quite so strict; here the principal may defeat an action of the third party by showing that the agent has abused his power and that the third party knew or should have known of such abuse. But the abuse must be a *manifest* one. Inasmuch as the third party is under no duty to inquire into the internal relationship existing between principal and agent, he cannot be chargeable with knowledge of an abuse which is not manifest upon the face of the transaction.]

If the holder of a general power of attorney enters into a transaction in his own interest, and even if the third party knows this, it cannot be said that for this reason alone the transaction constitutes a manifest abuse of the power of attorney. It may be that the interests of the agent are intimately interwoven with those of the principal, and the transaction may, therefore, be in the interest of both. Special relations or agreements of a personal or business character which may exist between principal and agent, may cause the principal to guarantee an obligation of the agent, and this may be in the principal's own interest or in the common interest of both. This is not a rare occurrence, especially in the case of partners, relatives and spouses. It is not incumbent upon the third party, in whose favor the agent executes a guaranty in the name of the principal, to investigate these relationships, because ordinarily it makes no difference to him whether or not the guaranty serves the interests of the principal. It was so held in the decision of this Court of May 1, 1891, [citation] in a case in which a husband, acting under a general power of attorney given him by his wife, had in her name guaranteed his own obligation [further citations].

Where there is doubt concerning the meaning and scope of a power of attorney, the declared intention of the principal must be determined by interpretation. Such interpretation is governed by the general principles of Sections 133, 157 of the Civil Code.[e] . . . In the present case, however, the general power of attorney which G.A. had received from his mother was by its terms an authorization of the most comprehensive kind. In the absence of any recognizable limitation such authorization includes the power to execute a guaranty on behalf of the principal. The intermediate appellate court infers from the formulation and the contents of the document that a guaranty for the agent's own obligations was not included. If this were an interpretation based on a factual finding, it would not be reviewable in this Court. In reality, however, this conclusion of the court below is not based on a factual finding but on the erroneous assumption that such [restrictive] interpretation is required by a rule of law. . . .

It cannot be said that as a matter of good faith the agent of the plaintiff, when he accepted the guaranty, should have recognized that

e. Section 133: "In interpreting a jural act the actual intention is to be ascertained and the literal sense of the expression is not necessarily to be adhered to."

Section 157: "Contracts are to be so interpreted as is required by good faith with due regard to usage."

G.A. abused the power of attorney. . . . The witness U., who was employed by the plaintiff as a traveling salesman, testified that he negotiated with G.A. concerning the guaranty to be executed in the name of the defendant, and that originally he had doubts whether G.A. was authorized by the general power of attorney to execute the guaranty in the name of his mother. But the further factual findings of the court below show that thereupon G.A. told the witness U. that he had the right to sign the guaranty on behalf of his mother, and that the witness was satisfied with this answer. It follows that the agent of the plaintiff or plaintiff himself relied upon the correctness of this statement made by G.A. Certainly it cannot be inferred from this that G.A. exceeded the authorization in a manner which plaintiff knew or could not honestly have ignored.

OPINION OF THE GERMAN BUNDESGERICHTSHOF

7th Civil Division, Feb. 28, 1966, 19 NJW 1911 (1966).

[Plaintiff bank sued defendant bank upon promissory notes in the amount of DM 1,800,000 (approximately $1,000,000). The notes were signed on behalf of the defendant by two individuals, G and M, each of whom was a Prokurist of the defendant, and registered as such. Apparently it was undisputed that G and M had signed the notes as part of a complicated transaction, into which they had entered in their own individual interest, and in violation of the fiduciary duties which they owed the defendant. The intermediate appellate court found, as a fact, that plaintiff did not act in collusion with G and M, and at the time of the transaction did not have actual knowledge of the latters' wrongdoing.

There was considerable evidence, however, tending to show that the circumstances of the transaction were very suspicious and that plaintiff acted unreasonably in failing to make further inquiries. The intermediate appellate court regarded such evidence as irrelevant. In support of this position it cited some previous cases, especially the decision of the Reichsgericht, RGZ 71,219 (which is reproduced above, immediately preceding the present case). Since no collusion and no actual knowledge on plaintiff's part had been shown, the intermediate appellate court permitted plaintiff to recover on the notes.

The Bundesgerichtshof reversed and dismissed the complaint. It pointed out that the decision of the Reichsgericht, RGZ 71,219, had to be regarded as partly superseded by later cases insofar as the question of the agent's misuse of his power was concerned. In order to eliminate any remaining doubt concerning the correct formulation of the rule applicable in such a case, the court proceeded to "summarize" its position as follows:]

As a rule, the principal has to bear the risk of a misuse of the power which he has granted to his agent. In general, the third party is under no special duty to examine whether and to what extent the agent is bound, by his contract with the principal or by the latter's instructions, to make only a limited use of a power which, insofar as the third party is concerned, is unlimited. But as between the principal and the third party the former is protected against a recognizable misuse of the power, not only in cases of intentional collusion between agent and third party, but also in situations in which the agent has employed his power in a manifestly suspicious manner, so that in the mind of the third party there had to arise a reasonable doubt as to whether the agent was not violating his fiduciary duties. This is so especially when under the circumstances of the case it was obviously necessary for the third party to direct an inquiry to the principal before entering into the transaction. Such was the case here. [The court then develops this point, referring to a number of facts which should have aroused the suspicion of the plaintiff.]

It follows that § 242 of the Civil Code precludes the plaintiff from demanding payment of the promissory notes signed by Prokurist G and Prokurist M.

NOTES AND QUESTIONS

(1) The significance of the 1966 decision of the Bundesgerichtshof appears to be twofold:

    (a) The court seems to have given up the view stated by way of dictum in RGZ 71,219 (supra p. 786), that in cases where the agent has misused his power, the mutual rights and obligations of the principal and the third party are governed (i) by one rule if the agent is a Prokurist, partner or corporate officer, and (ii) by a different rule if the misused power is an ordinary power of attorney. The court now seems to have consolidated the two rules into a single one covering both types of situations.

    (b) The new consolidated rule improves the position of the principal. To what extent?

(2) Superficial comparison might lead one to think that the new German rule is similar to our law on the subject. Cf. Restatement, Second, Agency § 165 and Comment c; § 166, Comment c (1958). Indeed, if one looks only at the "misuse" rule, there are striking similarities between the language of the Bundesgerichtshof and that of the Restatement.

It should be noted, however, that from the standpoint of the principal an argument based on the "misuse" rule is only an ultimate and somewhat desperate defense, because (regardless of the precise formulation of the rule) he always bears the heavy burden of proving that the third party knew or should have known of the agent's wrongdoing. Under our law, the principal's primary argument usually will be that the agent's power, if properly *construed*, did not cover the transaction in question. Under our law, which in this respect seems to be similar to French but quite different from German and Swiss law, the courts are always ready *by construction* to cut down the most

Civil law = more of a bias to protect 3rd party
common law = more of a bias to protect principle

sweeping and seemingly unequivocal powers.[1] Especially where the agent acted in violation of his fiduciary duties, an American court will be inclined to say that he "was not acting in behalf of his principal but was stealing its property."[2] When the court *by construction* thus limits the power of the agent, the principal prevails over the third party regardless of the latter's good or bad faith.[3]

In German law, the position is quite different. The agent's power is regarded as completely separate and distinct from the fiduciary duties which he owes his principal; and where the terms of the power are unambiguous, the court will not restrict such terms by reading into them the limitations which, as between principal and agent, the latter should have observed in using his power. This is particularly clear in the case of a Prokurist, partner or corporate officer, whose powers are statutorily defined and cannot be limited, insofar as third parties are concerned, without recording the limitation in the Register of Commerce. The rule is not essentially different, however, with respect to ordinary powers of attorney. These powers will be construed by a German court in accordance with the fair meaning of their terms. When the power is a general one, unqualifiedly authorizing the agent to do everything and anything which the principal could do if he were acting himself, a German court will not attempt to change the plain meaning of the language used by the draftsman of the power.[4] Thus, in a case in which the agent has misused his power, the *only* argument open to the principal under German law is that based on the "misuse" rule—an argument which can prevail only if the principal meets the heavy burden of proof imposed upon him.

It follows that in spite of the seeming similarity between the German and the American "misuse" rule, the position of the third party remains much stronger under the German system than under ours.

(3) Subsequent to its 1966 decision reproduced above, the German Bundesgerichtshof has added yet another wrinkle to the rule, further weakening the position of the principal. In its decision of March 25, 1968[5] the Second Civil Division of the Court dealt with a case in which the defendant bank was sued for a large amount upon bills of exchange signed (on behalf of defendant) by a faithless Prokurist. Except for the fact that bills of exchange rather than promissory notes were involved, the case was similar to that decided by the Seventh Civil Division on February 28, 1966 (see supra p. 790).[6] As in the previous case, the

1. For a particularly striking example, see Commission on Ecumenical Mission v. Roger Gray Ltd., 27 N.Y.2d 457, 318 N.Y.S.2d 726, 267 N.E.2d 467 (1971). See also Michaelsen v. United States Trust Co., 13 Misc.2d 1082, 155 N.Y.S.2d 221 (Sup.Ct. N.Y.Co., 1956).

2. See supra p. 774.

3. Nor is the third party always helped by the doctrine of apparent authority. Especially when the agent's power is embodied in a formal document, and that document has been exhibited to the third party, the scope of the agent's apparent authority ordinarily will not exceed that of his actual authority, as construed by the court.

4. What the Reichsgericht in RGZ 71, 219 (supra p. 786) said concerning the *construction* of a power of attorney, and especially a general power of attorney, is still good law. With respect to the "misuse" rule, both the holding and the dicta of that decision have been partly superseded by subsequent rulings; but there is no indication that the German courts have changed their approach insofar as the *construction* of powers of attorney is concerned.

5. 21 NJW 1379 (1968).

6. Although in accordance with German practice the names of the parties and of the other persons involved in the case are not reported, one can gather from the

court held that the agent had gravely misused his power; that plaintiff had no actual knowledge of the agent's wrongdoing; but that there were highly suspicious circumstances which should have induced the plaintiff to make further inquiries. Thus, on the basis of the rule formulated in the decision of February 28, 1966, one might think that the plaintiff's case was hopeless. But the lawyer who represented the plaintiff in the later case, brought up a novel point. Admitting, for the sake of the argument, that his client had been negligent in failing to make the necessary inquiries, he offered to prove that the defendant, also, had been negligent in not properly supervising its own agent and thereby facilitating the agent's course of wrongful conduct. The highest court held that the proof thus offered was relevant, explaining that in a case in which both the third party and the principal are found negligent, analogous application of the rule of comparative negligence should lead to a division of the loss between these two parties, in proportion to the gravity of the fault attributable to each of them.[7]

(4) Generalizations are always dangerous. Nevertheless, on the basis of a comparison between civil-law and common-law solutions in the field of "Agency", one is driven to the general conclusion that at least some of the civil-law systems [8] tend to value the interests of the third party more highly than those of the principal. For a discussion of the historical, social and intellectual forces which have shaped this value judgment, see W. Müller-Freienfels, Legal Relations in the Law of Agency: Power of Agency and Commercial Certainty, 13 Am.J.Comp.L. 193, 341 (1964).

II. CORPORATIONS

SCOPE NOTE

As a matter of daily routine, many American lawyers are called upon to assist clients who encounter legal problems in establishing and operating business organizations abroad. Normally, one of the lawyer's early steps will be to look for local counsel in the particular foreign country involved; thus his first need, insofar as his own knowledge of foreign law is concerned, is to become familiar with the division of functions within the legal profession, and the law and practices relating to legal fees, prevailing in that country. See supra pp. 341–370.

recital of facts that the 1966 decision and the 1968 decision both dealt with episodes arising out of the same series of defalcations, the total amount of which ran into many millions of dollars. The principal (in both cases) was one of the big German banks, and the faithless agents also seem to have been, at least in part, the same individuals in both cases. But since different plaintiffs and different transactions were involved, each of the two cases had to be determined separately, and the doctrine of res judicata did not come into play.

7. The principle of comparative negligence is embodied in § 254 of the German Civil Code. See supra p. 554.

8. The statement in the text refers particularly to the German and Swiss systems, which have exerted considerable influence also in a number of other countries. It should not be assumed, however, that French law is similar to German and Swiss law in the treatment of the agency problems with which we have dealt. On the contrary, French law is probably closer to our law in this respect than to German and Swiss law. See N. Shilling, Myth and Reality in the German and French Closed Corporation, 6 Harv.Int.L.Club J. 1 (1964), where the reader will find a comparative discussion of the basic principles of agency in German and French law.

Eventually, in order to make his cooperation with foreign counsel more effective, the American lawyer may have to educate himself, also, on the particular foreign country's law of corporations and other business organizations. In doing this, he will have to keep in mind:

(a) There are considerable—though slowly narrowing—differences from country to country; insofar as corporation laws are concerned, it is difficult to divide the civil-law world into "code families" or other convenient groupings.

(b) In many legal systems, especially those of continental Europe, the development of corporation law is in rapid flux. Within the last three decades, the corporation statutes of Germany,[1] France[2] and The Netherlands[2a] have been drastically revised and then subjected to additional subsequent amendments, sometimes accompanied by the enactment of further auxiliary statutes.[3] Efforts at similar reforms are in progress in other continental countries.[4]

(c) In all the twelve Member States of the European Economic Community, further changes have been due to, and more changes will be brought about by, the Community's harmonization efforts in that field. These efforts are based primarily on Article 54(3)(g) of

---

1. Stock Corporation Act of Sept. 6, 1965, eff. Jan. 1, 1966. For an excellent English translation and a very useful explanatory Introduction, see F. K. Juenger and L. Schmidt, German Stock Corporation Act (1967). For another bilingual (German and English) edition of the 1965 statute and of some auxiliary statutes, see R. Mueller & E. G. Galbraith, The German Stock Corporation Law (2d ed., 1976). An introductory discussion will be found in E. C. Steefel and B. von Falkenhausen, The New German Stock Corporation Law, 52 Cornell L.Q. 518 (1967). For comprehensive treatment (in English), see E. W. Ercklentz, Jr., Modern German Corporation Law (2 vols., 1979).

All of the forms of business organization available under German law are outlined in the article by G. Kutschelis, Doing Business in the Federal Republic of Germany, 3 Denver J.Int.L. & Pol. 197, 214–27 (1973).

2. Law No. 66–537 of July 24, 1966, as amended; Décret No. 67–236 of March 23, 1967, as amended. On reform of the civil code rules on "companies" generally, see supra p. 549. See S. N. Frommel & J. H. Thompson, Company Law in Europe 9–10 (1975). For an English translation of the new French company law, and a helpful introduction, see Commerce Clearing House, French Law on Commercial Companies (1971). See also B. N. Rawlings, The French Company Law: Choice of Corporate Form Available to the Foreign Investor, 30 Bus.Law. 1251 (1975).

2a. See J. M. M. Maeijer, A Modern European Company Law System: Com-

mentary on the 1976 Dutch Legislation (1978). Interestingly, the Dutch reform did not take the form of a separate corporation law outside the civil and commercial codes, as in the case of France or Germany. Instead, a new Book II was inserted into the Civil Code; it deals in general with entities having legal personality and then, in separate titles, with the different kinds of such entities, whether or not organized for profit. Former Book II of the Code, dealing with property, was renumbered Book III.

3. The work by Frommel & Thompson, supra n. 2, offers a comparative treatment of European company laws. For a helpful comparative discussion of the French and German laws, see R. M. Kohler, The New Corporation Laws in Germany (1966) and France (1967) and the Trend Towards a Uniform Corporation Law for the Common Market, 43 Tul.L.Rev. 58 (1968). For more recent works, see e.g. R. R. Pennington & F. Wooldridge, Company Law in the European Communities (3d ed. 1982); Belmont European Community Law Office, European Company Law—A Guide to Community and Member State Legislation (1986); K. J. Hopt, Groups of Companies in European Laws (1982). Frequently updated, though summary, information on the laws of many countries, including countries not part of the European Communities, can be found in the "Doing Business in Europe" volume of the CCH Common Market Reporter.

4. See ibid.

the EEC Treaty, requiring the Council of the European Communities, on a proposal of the Communities' Commission, to enact Directives for the approximation of those provisions in the company laws of the Member States which concern the protection of creditors and third parties. As "Directives", the measures involved must be transformed into national law before they are legally binding on individuals and firms. Some countries have been somewhat slow in effectuating the required transformation. The company law Directives have been given numbers in the order in which they have been proposed by the Commission, not in the order in which they have been adopted. Those adopted so far include: the First Directive of March 9, 1968, 1968 O.J. No. L 65, p. 8, which inter alia requires companies to publish various items of information; the Second Directive of December 13, 1976, 1977 O.J. No. L 26, p. 71, which sets minimum capital requirements and requires stated capital to be maintained; the Third Directive of October 9, 1978, 1978 O.J. No. L 295, p. 36 setting up various notice, consultation and other requirements for mergers; the Fourth Directive, of July 25, 1978, 1978 O.J. No. L 222, p. 11 (for an amendment see 1984 O.J. No. L 314, p. 28), establishing accounting and valuation rules, and providing for the auditing and publication of accounts; the Sixth Directive, adopted on December 17, 1982, 1982 O.J. No. L 378, p. 47, which complements the Third by somewhat analogous rules concerning the splitting-up of business firms; the Seventh Directive of June 13, 1983, 1983 O.J. No. L 193, p. 1, which extends the rules of the Fourth Directive by requiring the preparation of consolidated accounts for groups of companies; and the Eighth Directive of April 10, 1984, 1984 O.J. No. L 126, p. 20, which complements the Fourth and Seventh Directives by establishing rules concerning the qualifications of auditors auditing accounts pursuant to those Directives. The coverage of the Directives is not the same in all instances. The Second, Third and Sixth Directive apply only to "public" companies, the others to all companies, but sometimes subject to certain monetary limitations.

The Fifth Directive proposed by the Commission would have established rules for the management structure of public companies and provided for worker participation in the management of larger companies. It encountered strong opposition and, in spite of a softening of the proposal by the Commission (for the revised proposal, see 1983 O.J. No. C 240, p. 83) has not yet been approved. More recent Commission proposals concern the liability of a parent towards subsidiaries, trans-border mergers and branches that are not separately incorporated. In addition, the Council has adopted a series of Directives dealing with the issuance and distribution of securities. See p. 804 note 16 infra. Article 220 of the EEC Treaty also requires the Member States to conclude Conventions on various subjects, including the mutual recognition of corporate personality. Such a Convention has been concluded, but remains unratified.[5]

5. The literature on European harmonization efforts in the field of company law is enormous. For older works, see e.g. E. Stein, Harmonization of European Company Laws—National Reform and Transnational Coordination (1971); C. M. Schmitthoff, The Harmonization of European Company Law (1973); id. European Company Law Texts (1974); J. R. Silkenat, Efforts Towards Harmonization of Business Laws within the European Economic Community, 12 Int'l Lawyer 835 (1978). More re-

At one time, a proposal to permit the incorporation of companies at the Community (rather than national) level received much
attention.[6] It too encountered strong opposition, and the idea
appears to have been dropped, though a much more modest version
of it became law through the enactment of Council Regulation No.
2137/85 of July 25, 1985, 1985 O.J. No. L 199, creating a new form
of organization, the "European Cooperation Grouping". Such an
entity must limit its activities to the support of other (nationally
incorporated) business organizations (e.g. by providing joint
purchasing services) and is not to be independently profit-making.
The pertinent rules, having been adopted by way of a Regulation
rather than a Directive, are directly applicable law in all Member
States and thus require no "transformation".[7]

The practitioner who has to deal with corporate problems arising
under foreign laws, and especially under the laws of civil-law countries,
thus must look for legal writings which contain detailed and completely
current information. Fortunately, such writings are available, many of
them in English,[8] and one can expect that they will be updated or
replaced as new developments occur. The materials which follow are
intended, not to duplicate the detailed and comprehensive information
set forth in those writings, but rather to prepare the reader for their
effective use. Obviously, corporation laws drafted by civilians for
civilians can be understood by an outsider only if he is familiar with (a)
certain general aspects of civil-law methods and institutions, and (b)
some of the special ways in which these methods and institutions
impinge upon the law of corporations.[9] The reader who has been
patient enough to follow the authors' peregrinations up to this point,

cent works include: Commission of the Eu-
ropean Communities, The Fourth Company
Accounts Directive of 1978 and the Accounting Systems of the F.R. of Germany,
France, Italy, the United Kingdom, the
United States and Japan (1986); S. M. Mc-
Kinnon, The Seventh Directive: Consolidated Accounts in the EEC (A.D.H. New-
ham, ed. 1984); K. Böhlhoff & J. Budde,
Company Groups—the EEC Proposal for a
Ninth Directive in the Light of the Legal
Situation in the Federal Republic of Germany, 6 J Comp.Bus. & Capital Market L.
163 (1984); A. F. Conard, The Supervision
of Corporate Management: A Comparison
of Developments in European Community
and United States Law, 82 Mich.L.Rev.
1459 (1984); K. v. Hulle, The EEC Accounting Directives in Perspective: Problems of
Harmonization, 18 Common Mkt L.Rev.
121 (1981); J. Keustermans, Countertrends
in Financial Provisions for the Protection
of Corporate Creditors: The Model Business Corporation Act and the EEC Corporate Directives, 14 Denver J.Int'l L.' Pol.
275 (1986); S. Schneebaum, The Company
Law Harmonization Program of the European Community, 14 Law & Pol. in Int'l
Bus. 293 (1982). For additional references,
including references to materials in languages other than English, see 2 H. Smit &
P. Herzog (eds.), the Law of the EEC, Pre-

liminary Observations on Arts. 52–58, Anno. 5(V) (1976 and Supp.).

6. See, e.g., C. E. Zec, The Societas
Europea—A European Company—and
United States Corporation Law, 1 Comp.L.
Yearbook 285 (1977, publ. 1978); D. Ra-
nier, The Proposed Statute for a European
Company, 10 Tex.Int.L.J. 90 (1975).

7. For a discussion of this entity, derived from the French Groupement
d'intérêt économique, see F. Wooldridge,
The Draft Regulation on the European Economic Interest Grouping, 1985 J.Bus.L.
70.

8. For references, see the books and articles cited in nn. 1–5 supra; see also W. N.
Munyon, Shareholders' Rights in the Common Market: A Comparative Study, 9 Cornell Int.L.J. 191 (1976).

One study which, although no longer
completely up-to-date, should be mentioned
as a classical model of such informative
writings, is the article by A. F. Conard,
Organizing for Business, in 2 E. Stein and
T. L. Nicholson, American Enterprise in
the European Common Market 1–151
(1960); a part of this article has been published also in 59 Mich.L.Rev. 1 (1960).

9. The draftsmen of the recently revised French and German corporation stat-

should have no difficulty with requirement (a). The materials which follow are devoted to point (b); at the same time—more as a by-product than a main objective—they should acquaint the reader with some of those fundamental concepts and devices in the corporation laws of the civil-law systems which, at least upon superficial examination, appear to be without counterpart in our law or practice.

1. CIVIL LAW AND COMMON LAW METHODS IN THE LAW OF CORPORATIONS

PH. J. EDER, COMPANY LAW IN LATIN AMERICA
27 Notre Dame Law. 5, 15–16 (1951).

[Author's footnotes omitted.]

. . . The interesting thing to note about these Portuguese, Spanish and colonial companies [of the 15th to the 18th century] is that, in contrast to the rule laid down by Coke and Blackstone and which is still followed in our law, they did not derive their corporate personality from the sovereign, but only their special monopolistic privileges. The corporate or legal personality came from men associating themselves, under the Law Merchant, into a "company." [a] All "companies," whether formed as a general partnership or a limited partnership (*compania en comandita*) had a legal personality separate and apart from that of the individual members. [b] This separate or corporate personality adhered automatically to this new form of company, the stock company or *anonima* as it was soon to be called. In Spain, as in Portugal, insurance was effected by companies without royal grant, and other companies conducted business without special charter.

This concept was continued in the Spanish Commercial Code of 1829, which did not require governmental approval for a corporation.

utes carefully studied pertinent American laws and practices. See Kohler, supra n. 3. The results of such study are reflected in many of the new French and German provisions. Thus an American lawyer, reading the text of the French and German enactments, will encounter a number of "old acquaintances." Yet the new statutes, like their predecessors, are drafted in civilian terminology; and their underlying assumptions as well as some of their technical details will not be understood by an outsider who thinks exclusively in common-law terms. See Juenger and Schmidt, supra n. 1, at 21–22.

a. In the commercial centers of medieval Italy, especially in Genoa, business corporations came into existence at an even earlier date than in Portugal and Spain. The Bank of San Giorgio, founded in Genoa in 1407, is perhaps the best-known example. Until recently, it was not quite settled whether these medieval Italian corporations, like the ones organized somewhat later in Portugal and Spain, owed their existence to the law merchant. See Goldschmidt, Universalgeschichte des Handelsrechts 254, 290–98 (1891). But a recent study of medieval notarial records has shown that business associations having some of the characteristics of limited partnerships and also exhibiting certain corporate features were developed by private agreement and by the private initiative of merchants (and thus, presumably, on the basis of the law merchant) in 13th century Italy. See T. W. Blomquist, Commercial Association in Thirteenth-Century Lucca, 45 Business Hist.Rev. 157 (1971).

b. Cf. Puerto Rico v. Russell & Co., 288 U.S. 476, 53 S.Ct. 447 (1933).

It did require judicial approval; the articles and by-laws had to be passed upon and approved by the Commercial Court, but this was limited to verifying whether the papers were in conformity with law. The concept that corporate personality emanates from the free will of the parties, not from an act of State, continues to be the underlying theory of the law in Latin America, even in some of the countries where special government authorization is required in order to do business. In others, the creation of a new juristic person is the result of compliance with numerous formalities of which government approval is only one. . . .

There has never been confusion, as there has been in our law, between the business corporation and other corporations—foundations, associations and political entities. The business corporation was an exclusive creation of the Law Merchant. Whatever its remote origins in Roman Law, business company law has been little influenced, except in phraseology, by medieval theories relating to other types of corporations.[c] The codes deal separately with juristic persons, under the general title of persons, and with the *societas* under contracts.

The Spanish Law Merchant like our common law was based on a premise of realism. The stock company is not a creature of sovereign power. It is not the State which gives it life. There is no concession theory. Nor is there any need for a legislative grant of limited liability; it flows automatically, under the Law Merchant, from the association of individuals in a stock company.[d] Contrary to the history of our own law, no legislative authority was required for the limitation; the codes and statutes are merely declaratory of the existing law.

NOTES

(1) *Terminology and Classification.* The very term used to designate commercial corporations, in the languages of the civil law, shows that historically these corporations grew out of partnership arrangements recognized or developed by the law merchant. The Latin word denoting a contract of partnership is *societas*. This word, or its equivalent in modern languages (*société, compania, Gesellschaft,* usually

c. For an explanation of these theories see R. S. Stevens, The New Ohio General Corporation Act, 4 U. of Cin.L.Rev. 419, 428–9 (1930).

d. The theory that the basis of a corporation is contractual, sometimes leads to unexpected consequences. In some Latin-American jurisdictions it is deduced from that theory that a corporation is automatically dissolved when the number of shareholders falls below two, or below some other minimum number fixed by statute. See Alyea, Subsidiary Corporations Under the Civil and Common Law, 66 Harv.L.Rev. 1227 (1953).

For similar reasons, the French law No. 85–697 of July 11, 1985, which permits in some instances, the creation of a company by one person (as is now also possible in Germany for the "private" company or GmbH, see the GmbH-Gesetz § 1, as amended in 1980), has caused some perplexity in French legal circles. The idea that every company is contractual in nature, also expressed in Art. 1832 of the French Civil Code before its amendment in 1978, has led to the further notion in some countries that invalidity of the underlying contract among the incorporators would result in the proposed entity never actually coming into existence. One of the purposes of the First EEC company law Directive, mentioned supra, was largely to eliminate that rule.

translated as company) was adopted by the law merchant, and later by the codes. It still signifies to the civilian every form of voluntary, contractual association for business purposes, including those endowed with juristic personality, such as the stock corporation (to which the codes refer as *"anonymous" company* or "share" company) and the *compania en comandita* of the Spanish-speaking world.[1] The indication that a given entity is a *société, Gesellschaft, società*, without further specification and without indication of the legal system to which it belongs, thus does not permit a conclusion as to 1) whether the entity possesses legal personality, and 2) whether its members enjoy limited liability. To avoid giving the impression that an entity having separate legal personality is necessarily involved, these terms, when not further qualified, are thus often translated by the more general English expression "company", instead of by the word "corporation". (See e.g. art. 58 of the EEC Treaty).

In France the equivalent of an American partnership is (unless unregistered), deemed to have separate legal personality, while that is not the case in Germany.

In countries where there are separate civil and commercial codes, an organization similar to an American partnership may be constituted pursuant to the civil code provisions on partnerships for a business purpose that is not strictly "commercial" in nature (such as the exercise of a profession, if the particular profession may be practiced in that form); or it may be constituted pursuant to the provisions of the commercial code, if the purpose of the partnership is "commercial" in the civil-law sense, See supra pp. 591–596. On the other hand, the business entities most closely resembling American corporations (because they enjoy limited liability) normally are governed by the provisions of the Commercial Code or by auxiliary statutes amplifying or replacing commercial code provisions (see supra p. 551), and are deemed to be "merchants", whatever activity they engage in.[2] As has been noted before, however, the civil code may contain general rules applicable to all forms of companies; these general rules are applicable if the special rules dealing with "commercial" companies are silent on a particular point. In France the civil code rules on *sociétés* are applicable to all forms of business organizations if the more particularized rules are silent.[3]

Continental legal authors also draw a distinction between (a) partnerships and similar entities, whether organized under "civil" or under "commercial" law, in which, supposedly, personal ties are the dominant factor in determining the decision to participate, and which are there-

---

1. Concerning the interesting history of the *commenda*, which was known to the Babylonians and was brought to Greece and Rome by Phoenician traders, see Lobingier, The Natural History of the Private Artificial Person: A Comparative Study in Corporate Origins, 13 Tul.L.Rev. 41, 56–57 (1938). See also infra n. 20.

2. The French *Loi sur les sociétés commerciales* of 1966 covers commercial partnerships as well as business corporations. Thus both of these subjects have been taken out of the Code de Commerce, and the statute of 1966 may itself be regarded as a rather comprehensive codification of the law of business organizations.

3. In this connection it should be noted also that some of the Civil Codes (especially the German and the German-inspired ones) contain general provisions relating to juristic persons. In cases where the Commercial Code and its auxiliary enactments are silent on the point at issue, these Civil Code provisions, as a subsidiary source of law, may become applicable to business corporations. On the even more comprehensive Dutch Code, see supra p. 794, n. 2a.

fore called "personal companies" (*Personengesellschaften, sociétés de personnes*) and (b) those companies as to which the participants' dominant purpose is the investment of capital, and which are therefore called "capital companies" (*Kapitalgesellschaften, sociétés de capitaux*). The latter include primarily those entities that are similar to American business corporations.

(2) *The legal personality of associations for "Business" and "Non-Business" purposes.* The above excerpt from the article by Eder throws some light on the historical reasons for the sharp distinction which is normally made in civil-law countries between entities created for a business purpose (whether subject to the civil or the commercial code or one of their auxiliary statutes), in other words the various forms of *Gesellschaften* or *sociétés* on the one hand, and entities created for a non-business purpose (*Vereine, associations, etc.*), on the other.

(a) With respect to entities created for non-business—e.g., political, charitable or cultural—purposes, it became the prevailing view on the continent as well as in England that a corporation, being a fictitious person, can be created only by the sovereign. This combined fiction and concession theory, a welcome tool of absolutist rulers, was not swept away by the French Revolution. The bourgeois class, strongly individualistic, was suspicious of all collective bodies, some of which (such as the guilds) had exercised too much economic power in the past. This attitude of individualism and economic liberalism, paradoxically combined with Napoleon's and other contemporary rulers' police-state mentality, resulted in a policy admitting freedom of association only for business purposes. The Code Napoleon and the other "Civil" Codes of the period, while championing absolute freedom of contract, were hostile to the idea of general freedom of association and incorporation.[4]

It was only gradually, in the second half of the 19th and in the 20th century, that freedom of association for non-business purposes became recognized in the legal systems of the more progressive countries. Freedom of incorporation evolved even more slowly; and there is still no unanimity today—neither in the civil-law nor in the common-law world—on the question whether associations formed for political or other non-business purposes should be permitted to acquire juristic personality without administrative or judicial approval. In the civil-law world, it is not surprising to find that the principle of freedom of association and of incorporation was most emphatically espoused in Switzerland. The Swiss Civil Code provides:

> "Art. 52. Associations of persons organized into corporations . . . receive the right of personality, by entry in the Commercial Register. Public corporations and institutions, societies not for profit, religious foundations and family foundations[5] require no such entry. Associations or institutions

---

4. Concerning recent developments, see infra n. 8.

5. The creation of family foundations (Swiss Civil Code, Arts. 80 ff.) requires merely "the dedication of property to a special purpose", either by a notarial instrument inter vivos or by testamentary disposition. Differing in this respect from most other civil law systems (cf. Nussbaum, Sociological and Comparative Aspects of the Trust, 38 Colum.L.Rev. 408, 413), Swiss law does not make the organization of a family foundation dependent on any governmental approval (Art. 87). Although a separate legal entity, the Swiss foundation (*Stiftung, fondation*) thus performs some of the functions of the Anglo-American trust. See Estate of Swan v. Commissioner, 24 T.C. 829, 853–60 (1955), mod. on another point 247 F.2d 144 (2d Cir. 1957).

for immoral or unlawful purposes cannot acquire legal personality.

Art. 53. Juristic persons are capable of all rights and duties except those which arise from the natural characteristics of man, such as sex, age or relationship."

These provisions leave no power in the government to object to the organization of any corporate entity, business or non-business, unless its purposes are immoral or unlawful. [6] Book II of the Dutch Civil Code, as promulgated in 1976, similarly provides that no official approval is required for the creation of any corporate entity, including a non-profit corporation.[7] The legislators of many other countries, however, have been slow to enact a comparable charter of freedom for non-business corporations.

Even the basic principle that freedom of association (to say nothing of freedom of incorporation) exists for non-business as well as business purposes, is still far from being universally recognized. In France, that principle did not find unqualified acceptance until a 1971 decision of the Constitutional Council forced such acceptance on the Government and the Legislature.[8]

(b) As to business corporations, consistent adherence to the principles of the law merchant might have led to a system of complete freedom of incorporation. But such was not the course of history. Some of the early 19th century codes adopted the concession theory (which in pre-code days had been applied mainly to non-business entities), and required government permission for the formation of commercial as well as civil corporations. Half a century later, when the number of enterprises seeking incorporation began to multiply, the pendulum swung the other way. Quite generally (although with some important exceptions, especially in Latin America), the requirement of government permission was dropped insofar as commercial corpora-

---

6. Details are governed by the Code of Obligations so far as commercial corporations are concerned. The latter Code specifies the papers which the incorporators of such a corporation must execute and file, and the other requirements which they must meet, in order to obtain registration in the Register of Commerce.

For an English translation of the more important Swiss code provisions relating to corporations, see Swiss-American Chamber of Commerce, Swiss Corporation Law (2d ed., 1977).

7. On the revised Dutch rules see supra p. 794, n. 2a.

In the State of New York it was only in 1961 that freedom of incorporation for non-commercial purposes was recognized with a liberality approximating that of the Swiss and Dutch Civil Codes. See Association for the Preservation of Freedom of Choice v. Shapiro, 9 N.Y.2d 376, 214 N.Y.S.2d 388, 174 N.E.2d 487 (1961). See also § 404 of the (subsequently enacted) N.Y. Not-for-Profit Corporation Law. Cf., in California, the even more liberal Non-

profit Corporation Law, effective January 1, 1980. See Cal. Corp. Code §§ 5120, 7120 & 9120.

8. In France, freedom to create (non-profit) associations with legal personality was first established by a law enacted in 1901. When the French Parliament attempted, in 1971, to amend the 1901 statute by inserting, among other provisions, a requirement of judicial approval of associations which were to have legal personality, that provision was struck down by the French Constitutional Council in its first decision invalidating legislation on substantive civil liberties grounds. The Council held that the 1901 statute had established freedom of association as a "principle of Republican legislation," which the preamble of the Constitution had incorporated into that document. Decision of July 16, 1971, 1972 D.J. 685. See J. E. Beardsley, The Constitutional Council and Constitutional Liberties in France, 20 Am.J.Comp.L. 431 (1972); G. D. Haimbaugh, Jr. Was it France's Marbury v. Madison? 35 Ohio St.L.J. 910 (1974).

tions were concerned, and corporation laws became excessively liberal. The formation of stock corporations was made dependent on mere registration in the Register of Commerce, to be obtained with relative ease by the execution and filing of the articles of incorporation and of other papers specified in the commercial codes or statutes.

Soon, however, abuses developed, and it was felt necessary to take stronger measures for the protection of shareholders and creditors. Beginning in 1884 with an amendment of the German Commercial Code, a movement for "corporate reform" (i.e., for strengthening of the legal devices protecting creditors and shareholders) swept through the whole civil-law world.[9] This movement received renewed impetus during the troubled period following the first World War, and resulted in the adoption by most civil-law countries of protective measures such as the following: A stock corporation must have a substantial minimum capital, all of which must be subscribed, and all or a specified portion of which must be paid in, before the corporation can be registered. Where the capital contribution of a subscriber consists of property other than cash, many codes require that the value of such property be determined by impartial appraisers. Similar requirements must be met in case the capital of the corporation is subsequently increased. Specific protection is provided against issue of stock below par. Any direct or indirect return of capital to shareholders without the publicity and formalities of complete or partial liquidation is prohibited, and many codes require that a certain percentage of earnings be added to a compulsory reserve account. Shareholder approval of the annual balance sheet and of dividend declarations is required in many countries. Minority shareholders usually have the right to contest resolutions of shareholders' meetings which violate law or charter. Most codes contain elaborate provisions for independent audits of corporate books, and a measure of disclosure of corporate affairs is commonly required, especially publication of the annual balance sheet.[10]

One does not find every one of these protective devices adopted in every civil-law country; but the trend has been in this direction. It stands to reason that these stringent provisions, especially the requirements of a substantial minimum capital and of public disclosure of corporate affairs, were meant primarily for big corporations selling their securities to the public. These requirements proved unsuitable for smaller, close corporations. For companies of the latter type, therefore, a new and different form of organization had to be evolved. This need produced the limited responsibility company (infra pp. 829–833), first recognized in a German statute of 1892 and subsequently adopted in the majority of civil-law countries.[11] This form of organiza-

---

9. See Feller, The Movement for Corporate Reform: A World-Wide Phenomenon, 20 A.B.A.J. 347 (1934).

This continental reform movement was in part influenced by, and in turn exercised a strong influence on, the post-Bubble Act statutory developments in England. See Feller, ibid.; Gower, Some Contrasts Between British and American Corporation Law, 69 Harv.L.Rev. 1369 (1956).

10. Complying with the above-mentioned EEC Directives, the Common Mar-

ket countries have strengthened these requirements in recent years.

11. England followed the continental trend by giving statutory recognition to the "private company". But in contrast to the method followed in many civil-law countries, there is no separate statute dealing with private companies. The Companies Act applies to public *and* private companies.

tion has gained tremendous popularity, and wherever it is available, one observes that the use of the more stringently regulated form of the stock corporation becomes substantially confined to large enterprises resorting to the public investment market for their capital needs.

In the United States, the development of business corporations and of their regulation took a somewhat different course. In the first decades of the nation's history, a special act of the Legislature was necessary for the formation of any corporation, including a stock corporation. Early in the 19th century, however, the states began to enact general corporation statutes, permitting formation of stock corporations upon compliance with relatively simple formalities. Competition among the states led to progressive reduction and destruction of all effective curbs upon the controlling group.[12] It became apparent, therefore, that the state statutes, under which corporations are organized, could not afford sufficient protection for shareholders and creditors.[13] Such protection had to be achieved outside of the corporation statutes, by courts of equity imposing fiduciary duties upon management and majority, and by the *federal securities legislation* of the 1930's and 1940's.[14] The result is that, in contrast to the method traditionally followed in the civil-law world, the most important legal devices used in this country for the protection of investors are not built into the corporation statutes themselves, but exist as a separate and independent body of law.[15]

Slowly and gradually, however, our approach and that of the civil-law systems seem to converge. In this country, some states have

12. A few civil-law jurisdictions, especially Liechtenstein, have followed the American example. Feller, supra, n. 6, said of the Liechtenstein law of 1926: "This law was drafted by a number of Swiss lawyers intent on making the little principality of Liechtenstein the Delaware of Europe. It embodies every corporate device which the ingenuity of the American corporation bar has devised, plus a few new ones." Chief among the "new ones", that is, among the devices unknown even to the American corporation bar, is of course that paragon of elusiveness and anonymity: the bearer share (to be discussed infra).

13. This remained true even after the adoption of the so-called Blue Sky Laws. See Stevens On Corporations, Sec. 182 (1949).

14. For a more elaborate comparative discussion, see R. M. Buxbaum, The Formation of Marketable Share Companies, in Vol. XIII, Ch. 3, of the International Encyclopedia of Comparative Law 15–22 (1974).

15. In the United States, the smallest family business ordinarily is incorporated under the same corporation statute as the corporate giant; what distinguishes the two from a legal point of view, is that the large corporation, which offers securities to the investing public, is subject to the regulatory powers of the S.E.C. Under the traditional civil-law system, the large corporation must comply with such regulatory requirements as are built into the general corporation law governing stock corporations, while the small business can be incorporated, as a limited responsibility company, under an entirely different statute or code chapter not containing such requirements. As a matter of policy, both systems tend to impose regulation of varying stringency (reinforced by stock exchange listing requirements) upon corporations the securities of which are offered to the public, and to leave the privately financed enterprise free from such regulation. As a matter of legal technique, however, the two systems are quite different. Under the American system, regulation is aimed at the sale and offering of securities, while under the traditional civil-law system a stock corporation cannot even be incorporated without compliance with certain requirements, designed to protect the prospective investor. Most civil-law countries, consequently, have a tradition, now gradually changing, of entrusting enforcement of their regulatory provisions to the official in charge of the Commercial Register, or to another bureau having the power (among others) to pass on the legality of the incorporation itself. Our system, on the other hand, requires a federal enforcement agency which is not concerned with the (state-governed) incorporation as such.

enacted separate close-corporation statutes. See infra p. 832. On the other hand, several civil-law countries in recent years have adopted American-style securities regulations, i.e., regulations (not always built into the corporation statute) imposing stringent disclosure requirements in connection with the issuance of securities to the public. In Europe, the trend towards the creation of such a body of rules separate from general corporation law, dealing specifically with the issuance and sale of securities to the public, has been accelerated by the enactment of a series of Directives by the Council of the European Communities that stands outside the series of numbered company law Directives mentioned above, and is based in part on the general "harmonization of laws" provisions of the EEC Treaty, rather than on its "company law" provision.[16]

(3) *Civil-Law and Common-Law Methods.* The needs served and the functions performed by the modern business corporation are essentially the same in all highly industrialized countries which have preserved a measure of free enterprise, whether they belong to the civil-law or the common-law orbit. In spite of this fact, and in spite of the complexity of the historical cross-currents (some of which were briefly noted above) which have shaped the pertinent rules of law, it is still possible to observe, even in the area of corporation law, the impact of the methodological, procedural and classificatory differences which generally exist between common law and civil law. For example:

---

16. The EEC Directives on securities include the Directive of March 5, 1979, 179 O.J. No. L 66, p. 21 on the coordination of the conditions for the admission of securities to stock exchange listing, the Directive of March 17, 1980, 1980 O.J. No. L 100, p. 1 concerning the particulars to be published for the admission of securities to stock exchange listing and the Directive of February 15, 1982, 1982 O.J. No. L 48, p. 26 on periodic information to be published by companies whose shares are traded on an exchange. The Commission has adopted a "European Code of Conduct for Transactions in Transferable Securities", July 25, 1977, 1977 O.J. No. L 212, p. 13, but only in the form of a non-binding recommendation. A Directive on information to be published on acquisition or sale of an important part of the capital of a company whose stock is listed on an exchange is in the proposal stage. See Doc. COM(85) 791 final. Other proposals concern investment advisers and insider trading. While the company law Directives contain a number of fairly specific rules, those dealing with securities law tend to be more general. They create no enforcement agency at Community level and leave the Member States a certain leeway as to the medium through which they enforce the Community rules. This can be done through an administrative agency (such as the French Commission des Opérations de la Bourse, whose role was strengthened by the French Law No.

83–1 of January 3, 1983, 1983 J.O. p. 162, 1983 D.L. 89 on the encouragement of investments and the protection of savings), or through a judicial body, or even through some form of supervised self-regulation (apparently contemplated, in conjunction with administrative supervision, by the recent British Financial Services Act). In Germany, moreover, case law seems to have subjected issuers to a liability based on general principles of fair dealing. For a description (not restricted to statute of limitation problems), see R. D. Morgen, Die differenzierende Rechtsprechung des BGH zur Verjährung von Prospekthaftungsansprüchen, 40 N.J.W. 474 (1987).

For discussions of this topic in English, see R. A. Stephens, Reevaluation of Disclosure Requirements for Foreign Issuers: Securities Act of 1933, 45 Geo.Wash.L.Rev. 135, 166–69 (1977) (with many additional references); E. Wymeersch, From Harmonization to Integration in the European Securities Markets, 1981 J.Comp.Corp.L. 1; F. Wooldridge, Some Recent Community Legislation in the Field of Securities Law, 10 European L.Rev. 129 (1985), and for country-by-country studies, E. Wymeersch, Supervision of the Securities Markets in the Member States of the European Economic Community (Part I-Commission of the E.C., Competition Studies-Approximation of Legislation Series No. 32, 1978; Part II. Id. No. 33, 1980).

(a) The absence from the civil law of separate equity courts and of their flexible procedure becomes apparent when we study the remedies available to creditors and minority stockholders (see infra pp. 834–841).

(b) Two institutions which in their civil-law form are unknown to the common-law systems, play a vital role in the corporation laws of all civil-law countries: The Notary and the Commercial Register.

A notarial protocol ordinarily is required, not only for the formation of a corporation, but also for charter amendments, and generally for resolutions and other actions taken by a stockholders' meeting.

As we have seen in cases previously studied, a corporation does not acquire juristic personality, and many of its corporate acts do not become effective, until registration in the Register of Commerce. Deregistration of a corporation, on the other hand, may have the effect of immediate and complete termination of its corporate existence (see the "Rimba" case, supra). The reliance of third parties on entries in the Register is strongly protected, as we have had occasion to observe not only in the materials dealing with the "principle of publicity" and with Agency, but also in the "*Neuergasthof*" case (supra p. 615).

(c) The effect of the civilian dichotomy between civil and commercial law can be seen in the following:

(aa) In the law of commercial companies, which are systematically separate from "civil" entities, many institutions and devices of the law merchant were kept alive by the codifiers. The prime illustration, of course, is the bearer share,[17] which will be discussed in the materials immediately following these Notes.

(bb) In a legal system in which the law of business corporations is closely connected with, and indeed an outgrowth of, the law of commercial partnerships, one might expect that the legal powers of the "partners" (shareholders), as compared to those of the managers, are relatively strong. This is actually the case in the civil-law systems. Many important powers, such as the power to declare dividends, which under our law are held by the Board of Directors, are vested in the shareholders' assembly under the corporation statutes of the civil-law world. In this connection the reader will remember, also, that the civil-law systems normally require the officers and directors to seek annual *décharge*, or approval of their managerial conduct, by the shareholders [18]—a requirement that is not at all surprising if one considers that in a partnership the partners are the natural superiors of hired managers, and that in the history of civilian corporation law the shareholder can trace his ancestry to the partner.

17. The men of affairs who created the law merchant were not easily troubled by problems of theory. Having developed instruments payable "to the bearer" in the law of bills and notes, they did not find it difficult to use the same device in order to expedite the transfer of shareholders' interests.

18. See supra p. 568.

(cc) The close relationship between commercial partnerships and commercial corporations which exists in the civil law, has made it relatively easy for civilian legislators to recognize or develop intermediate forms of business associations which successfully combine characteristcs of a partnership and of a corporation.[19] The *société en commandite* (limited partnership) has been mentioned earlier.[20] In addition, many civil-law countries authorize the formation of a special type of limited partnership, in which the interests of the limited partners are represented by share certificates issued in registered or bearer form (*société en commandite par actions*). The limited partner-shareholder can freely and easily transfer his interest, and if he has fully paid his contribution, he is not subject to any further liability for the obligations of the firm. The latter feature distinguishes this form of organization from the (now practically defunct) joint-stock company which in this country was much in use during the last century,[21] and explains why the *société en commandite par actions* is still a living institution in some of the civil-law countries. Commonly, however, it is subjected to the same stringent safeguards as a stock corporation.[22] Moreover, it remains necessary, both in an ordinary limited partnership and in a *société en commandite par actions*, that at least one person be registered as general partner and thus expose himself to unlimited liability.[23] These difficulties are overcome, at least for enterprises not dependent on public financing, by the most modern form of business organization, the limited responsibility company (infra pp. 829–833).

19. See H. D. Krause, "To Incorporate Abroad . . .", 1965 U.Ill.L.F. 453, 454–55.

20. Our own limited partnership statutes can be traced to the New York statute of 1822, which in turn was substantially copied from the pertinent provisions of the French Code de Commerce of 1806. See Ames v. Downing, 1 Bradf. 321, 329–33 (N.Y.Surr.Ct.1850); Evans v. Galardi, 16 Cal.3d 300, 305, 128 Cal.Rptr. 25, 29, 546 P.2d 313, 317 (1976); J. M. Perillo, Book Review, 37 Fordham L.Rev. 144, 148 (1968).

21. See Stevens On Corporations 20–22 (1949).

American lawyers, on the other hand, sought to accomplish the double purpose of limited liability and free transferability of the investor's interest by utilizing the trust device (which is unknown to the civilians, see supra p. 782), and thus developed the business trust. See id., at 22–24.

22. Like a *société anonyme*, the *société en commandite par actions* often issues securities to the public.

23. In some countries it is possible to circumvent this requirement by making a corporation (usually a limited liability company) the sole general partner of the limited partnership. See, e.g., Baumbach-Duden-Hopt, Handelsgesetzbuch, Appendix following § 177a (26th ed. 1985). In Germany, the firm name of such a partnership includes the words "GmbH & Co." The practical extent to which this dodge is used, is of course largely determined by tax considerations. A few big American corporations are said to have organized their German subsidiaries in this form.

Concerning the possible application of the EEC Directives to the GmbH & Co., see M. Schwierz, Einbeziehung der Kapitalgesellschaften & Co. in die 4. und 7. EG–Richtlinie, 39 Betriebsberater 703 (1984).

American commentators used to refer to the "GmbH & Co." as an exotic device. In recent years, however, it has become increasingly popular in the United States, especially in the oil and gas industry, to set up limited partnerships in which a corporation is the sole general partner. See Note, 24 Southwestern L.J. 285 (1970). See also Larson v. Commissioner, 66 T.C. 159 (1976). Cf. Kitchell Corp. v. Hermansen, 8 Ariz.App. 424, 446 P.2d 934 (1968). Like the limited partnership itself (see supra n. 20), this device appears to have been imported into our practice from the civil-law world.

2. BEARER SHARES

COMMERCIAL COURT OF THE CANTON OF ZURICH
OPINION OF SEPTEMBER 12, 1947
Reported in 44 Schweizerische Juristen-Zeitung 175 (1948).

[This is an action brought by a shareholder against defendant corporation. Plaintiff prays that the court set aside a shareholders' resolution amending the charter [a] of the defendant. Section 706 of the Swiss Code of Obligations provides:

"The management and each shareholder may sue for judicial annulment of shareholders' resolutions which violate the law or the charter. . . .

"If the management brings the action, the court appoints a representative of the corporation.

"The right to sue for annulment terminates unless the action is commenced within two months following the shareholders' meeting in which the resolution was adopted.

"A judgment setting aside a shareholders' resolution is effective for and against all shareholders." [b]

The original charter of defendant corporation provided for the issuance of bearer shares. Plaintiff is the owner of a number of such shares. The shareholders' resolution, which plaintiff seeks to have set aside in this action, embodies a charter amendment providing for the transformation into registered shares of all bearer shares issued by the corporation.]

Plaintiff contends that each shareholder has a vested right to insist upon preservation of the existing nature of his shares . . .; that the transformation of bearer shares into registered shares must be provided for in the original charter; that it cannot be forced upon a shareholder against his will if it is not so provided; that the original charter of December 28, 1928, does not provide for a possible transformation of bearer shares into registered shares; that, therefore, the amendment and the resolution containing such amendment . . . are without effect; that, moreover, no interest of defendant is served by such transformation.

. . . The question whether a change from bearer shares to registered shares can be forced upon a shareholder against his will by a majority resolution subsequently amending the original charter, is

---

a. The German word "Statuten" has been translated as meaning charter. This is not entirely accurate, inasmuch as the "Statuten" of a continental corporation usually constitute the equivalent of both charter and by-laws. In the present con-text, however, this inaccuracy would seem to be harmless.

b. A similar remedy exists under German law. See supra, p. 569.

highly controversial among legal writers. There are no judicial decisions in point; the only reported case, which was decided in 1912
[citation], involves the transformation of registered shares into bearer
shares. Numerous authors of the older school, in Switzerland as well
as in Germany, regard the preservation of the original nature and form
of the shares as a right of which the shareholder may not be deprived
without his consent [citing, among numerous other commentators and
text writers, the 10th Edition of Staub, Commentary on the German
Commercial Code]. Some of the Swiss text writers are of the opinion
that this view is still valid under the provisions of the Revised Code of
Obligations which went into effect on January 1, 1937 [the court cites
the writings of Professors Von Steiger and Wieland]. Reasons supporting this view are usually not adduced. Von Steiger . . . points out
that the shareholder has a vested right to see the particular nature of
his shares preserved, because it must be presumed that his decision to
subscribe or purchase was substantially influenced by the nature of
such shares, especially by their nature as registered or bearer shares.
He argues that the character of the share and the stock certificate has
important legal consequences with respect to the purchase, the transfer, the loss and the exercise of the shareholder's rights. He says that
the transformation of bearer shares into registered shares makes such
securities less easily negotiable. There remains the question, however,
whether this lessening of negotiability is of such grave importance that
it must be prevented by the recognition of a vested right.

More recently, the majority of legal writers have adopted the
opposite view. This is in accordance with the modern tendency which
is opposed to an expansion of the concept of vested rights. . . . It is
significant that Staub, the leading commentator of the German Commercial Code, abandoned his former opinion in the 14th (1933) edition
of his Commentary, that is, even before the 1937 revision of the
German Corporation Law. . . .

One argument which has been adduced by Von Steiger in support
of his view, should be rejected at the outset. He says that the
shareholder can invoke the general rule of Article 970 of the Code of
Obligations, pursuant to which the consent of all persons interested as
obligors and obligees is necessary in order to transform a bearer
security into a security issued to a named holder, or vice-versa. [The
court points out that this rule of Article 970 applies only to bills and
notes, i.e., to securities involving a debtor-creditor relationship. Article
970 thus is an outgrowth of the general principle that a debtor-creditor
relationship cannot be modified without the consent of both parties.
The court says that there is no justification for an analogy extending
this principle to the membership rights of a shareholder which by their
nature are subject to at least some subsequent modifications to which
the individual member may not object.]

In principle, a corporation is free to amend its charter. This
freedom is limited by the cogent provisions of public and private law

and by the vested rights which the shareholders possess pursuant to law and charter. . . . Plaintiff asserts the violation of a vested right. . . . According to Article 646, Subdivision 2 of the Code of Obligations ᶜ those rights of a shareholder are vested rights which pursuant to a provision of the statute or of the charter are immune to resolutions of the shareholders' assembly, or which flow from the shareholder's right to participate in such assembly.

It is undisputed that the original *charter* of the defendant contains no provision assuring the shareholders that the nature of their shares would be forever preserved. The next question is whether there is a cogent *statutory* provision preventing the transformation of the shares. [The court examines the language and legislative history of several sections of the Code of Obligations and concludes that these sections fail to confer upon the shareholder the vested right asserted by plaintiff.]

Inasmuch as neither the Code nor the charter of the defendant prohibits a subsequent charter amendment regarding the nature of the shares, there remains solely the question whether such prohibition must be inferred from the general concept or the statutory examples of shareholders' vested rights. This latter question must be answered in the negative.

It has been held by the Federal Court [citations] that Article 646, subdivision 2, of the Code of Obligations does not attempt to define the concept of vested rights. On the contrary, the judge must determine in each particular case what rights he should declare to be vested rights, i.e., rights which cannot be affected by majority resolutions. It is by no means easy to determine the concept of vested rights . . . In subdivision 3 of Article 646, the Code of Obligations, in lieu of a definition, mentions some examples of these inalienable and fundamental rights and thereby shows the general direction of the criteria to be applied . . . The Code thus mentions as examples of vested rights especially the right of membership, the right to vote, the right to sue for annulment of illegal resolutions, the dividend right and the right to share in the proceeds of liquidation. The right to have the nature of the shares preserved . . . is not among these examples. Whether it has the same rank as the examples expressly mentioned by the Code, must be examined in the light of the importance which a change in the character of the shares has for the rights of the shareholder.

Transformation of a bearer share into a registered share has the effect that such share is no longer a bearer security but a security to the order of the named holder. Where there are restrictive provisions

c. Swiss Code of Obligations, Art. 646: "Vested rights to which the individual shareholders are entitled in their capacity as shareholders, cannot be taken away from them without their consent.

"Those rights are deemed vested rights which, pursuant to a provision of the statute or of the charter, cannot be affected by resolutions of the shareholders' assembly, or which flow from the shareholder's right to participate in such assembly.

"The following, especially, are included among the vested rights: the membership; the right to vote; the right to bring an action for annulment of resolutions of the shareholders' assembly; the right to receive dividends, and the right to share in the proceeds of liquidation."

in the charter, it becomes a non-negotiable security standing in the name of its [registered] holder. The transformation thus changes the manner in which the security can be transferred. In the place of a transfer by mere delivery there is substituted a transfer by endorsement or assignment, coupled with registration of the transfer on the books of the corporation, which [in the case of registered shares] is required pursuant to Article 685 of the Code of Obligations. . . .

Under existing corporation law a shareholder cannot withdraw from the corporation. In lieu of the right to withdraw, the shareholder has the right to transfer his membership to another person by selling his share. It is generally recognized that it would be inconsistent with the nature of a bearer share, which can be transferred by mere delivery, to limit the alienability of such share [citations]. The free alienability of bearer shares can, therefore, be regarded as a vested right of the shareholder [citations]. Those writers who believe that the preservation of the character of the share as a bearer share constitutes a vested right of the shareholder, base their view upon the silent or express . . . assumption that the transformation of bearer shares into registered shares makes the sale of such shares more difficult. From this, they conclude that such transformation into registered shares violates the vested interest of the shareholder in the free alienability of his bearer shares. This, however, is incorrect. In principle, . . . registered shares are as freely transferable as bearer shares. The registration of the purchaser on the books of the corporation can be refused only if this is provided in the charter [citations]. It follows that if there are restrictions upon the free transferability of registered shares, such restrictions do not flow from the nature of such shares, but from special charter provisions concerning the so-called *vinculation* [d] of registered shares. The charter may restrict and even prevent the transfer of registered shares.[e] This has the effect that the shareholder is compelled against his will to remain a member of the corporation. It would be incorrect, however, to regard this as a consequence of the transformation of the shares into registered shares. If the restriction upon the transfer of registered shares is provided in the original charter, then the shareholder cannot object to such restriction because he knew or could have known before his subscription or purchase of

d. The Latin verb *vinculare* means to bind, to fetter. In many civil-law countries, shares of corporate stock are spoken of as "vinculated" if by a provision in the charter their transfer is subjected to restrictions.

e. After World War II many Swiss corporations adopted charter provisions restricting the transfer of shares, because they had found by bitter experience that belligerent countries, and especially the United States, froze and seized assets of "neutral" corporations, and released such assets only upon *proof* of the non-enemy character *of the shareholders.* See, e.g.,

Kaufman v. Société Internationale, 343 U.S. 156, 72 S.Ct. 611 (1952). Cf. Société Internationale v. Rogers, 357 U.S. 197, 78 S.Ct. 1087 (1958). Many Swiss corporations, thus suddenly faced with the problem of having to prove the identity of their shareholders, encountered grave difficulties. In order to obviate similar difficulties in the future, a number of corporations decided to issue all or a substantial portion of their shares only in registered form, and to restrict their transfer. See F. von Steiger, Das Recht der Aktiengesellschaft in der Schweiz 24–26 (3rd ed. 1966), where further references can be found.

shares that he might not be able to withdraw from the corporation. The question whether a vested right of the shareholder is violated, arises only in the event that a vinculation of the registered shares is sought to be incorporated into the charter by way of a subsequent amendment. It stands to reason, however, that even in that event the restriction upon the free alienability of the bearer shares does not result from their transformation into registered shares but from the subsequent vinculation of the latter. It is only this subsequent vinculation which decisively affects the individual rights of the shareholder. . . . The controversial question whether a prohibition or restriction of the free transferability of *registered* shares may subsequently be incorporated into the charter against the will of a minority of shareholders, or whether such resolution would violate a vested right of the non-consenting shareholders, does not have to be determined in the present case, because *the amendment in question* does not provide for any vinculation of the registered shares. The plaintiff thus is unable to sue for the annulment of such a vinculation. [The court points out that *the original charter* of the defendant already contained restrictions upon the transfer of shares, by providing that a shareholder had to offer his shares to the other shareholders before he could sell them to a stranger.] [f] It is irrelevant that this restriction was then unenforceable for the reason that the shares were bearer shares.[g] The plaintiff knew this restriction. As one of the incorporators he is responsible for its insertion into the charter. In fact, contrary to the position taken by the majority of the shareholders, plaintiff claims that there was an agreement concerning the transferability of shares which went even further and allegedly was designed to assure permanent equality among the shareholdings of the incorporators. It would thus be an abuse of rights on the part of the plaintiff if he now objected to a restriction upon the negotiability of these shares. . . .

The transformation of bearer shares into registered shares has the further result of changing the impersonal nature of the shareholdings. But surely it cannot be said that a shareholder has a vested right to withhold knowledge of his name from the corporation. The anonymity of the owner of bearer shares is merely an incident of their negotiability. It is true that in its external relations a stock corporation is an anonymous organization formed by capital contributions. Nevertheless, the personal participation of the shareholders in the affairs of the corporation is not excluded. This follows from the fact that the

f. Under Swiss law, such a restriction, if contained in the original charter, ordinarily is valid with respect to registered shares. It is not effective, however, with respect to bearer shares, which by their nature cannot be subjected to any restrictions upon their transfer. See von Steiger, id., at 154.

g. If (as seems to be the case) all of the shares originally issued by defendant corporation were bearer shares, then the provision in the original charter imposing transfer restrictions—which under Swiss law could apply only to registered shares—was a "sleeper". So long as only bearer shares were outstanding, that provision had no immediate effect; apparently it was intended to assume practical significance only in case *registered* shares of defendant corporation should subsequently come into existence.

member, and even the member holding bearer shares, has a right to vote and participate in the control of the corporation.

[The court, having disposed of the alienability argument and the anonymity argument, then proceeds to examine the question whether there are any other respects in which the transformation of bearer shares into registered shares would be harmful to the interests of the shareholder, and answers this question in the negative.[h] The court thus reaches the result that the resolution providing for such transformation was lawful and that the action seeking annulment of the resolution should be dismissed.]

A POSTSCRIPT

In the preceding case, it will be remembered, the transfer of registered shares was restricted by a provision *in the original charter* of the defendant corporation. The Zurich court left open the question whether the majority of the shareholders may subsequently, e.g. at the time it transforms bearer shares into registered shares, *by charter amendment* subject the registered shares to transfer restrictions. This very question was presented to another Swiss court in a later case,[1] the facts of which were as follows:

Plaintiff, a minority stockholder, owned bearer shares of defendant corporation. At a stockholders' meeting, the majority passed a resolution which, by way of amending the charter, (a) transformed all outstanding bearer shares into registered shares, and (b) provided that registered shares could be transferred only with the consent of the management. The resolution made it clear that such consent could be withheld "without any statement of reasons". This transfer restriction was intended to be applicable to all registered shares, whether previously issued or to be issued in the future. The original charter of defendant corporation had not contained any transfer restriction. Within the two-month period provided by § 706 of the Swiss Code of Obligations, the plaintiff brought an action to set aside part (a) and part (b) of the resolution.

h. Many of the best-known big corporations in Switzerland have issued bearer shares *and* registered shares. The latter usually are subject to severe transfer restrictions, which in practice prevent their acquisition by non-Swiss purchasers. A look at the business section of any Swiss newspaper shows that in several instances both bearer and registered shares of the same corporation are listed and traded on a stock exchange, and that (the two classes of stock otherwise having identical rights) the bearer shares invariably command a considerably higher price. Does this fact militate against the soundness of the court's conclusion?

In a more recent German case the price-differential argument was considered but held not to be decisive. The German court reached the same result as the principal case. L. G. Mannheim, Dec. 15, 1966, reported in 12 Die Aktiengesellschaft 83 (1967). In the German case, however, neither class of shares was subject to transfer restrictions.

1. Appellationsgericht Basel-Stadt, Decision of Feb. 9, 1965, cited by F. von Steiger, Das Recht der Aktiengesellschaft in der Schweiz 26 (3rd ed. 1966).

The court held against plaintiff with respect to part (a) of the resolution. It cited with approval the opinion of the Zurich court set forth above, and adopted its reasoning.

At the same time, the court set aside part (b) of the resolution, holding the transfer restriction to be unreasonable because it was more drastic than was required by the corporation's legitimate interest in preventing the acquisition of its shares by aliens or competitors. The court was especially critical of that feature of part (b) of the resolution which purported to confer upon the management of defendant corporation the power *arbitrarily* to withhold its consent to a proposed transfer.[2] The opinion of the court makes it crystal-clear, however, that a more moderate transfer restriction—i.e., a restriction which reasonably reflects a fair balancing of the individual interests of the shareholder and the collective interests of the corporation—would have been upheld. The rule announced by the court is that a transfer restriction, provided it is reasonable, can be adopted not only in the original charter but also by way of a subsequent charter amendment affecting previously issued shares as well as those to be issued in the future.[3]

QUESTIONS

If one reads the 1965 decision of the Basel court together with the 1947 decision of the Zurich court, is one not compelled to conclude that in contrast to a bearer share, the transfer of which is unrestrictable, a registered share is always susceptible of being subjected to transfer restrictions (at least "reasonable" transfer restrictions) under Swiss law?

In the light of the later decision, did the earlier decision not grossly understate the legal and practical disadvantages which a shareholder suffers when a charter amendment transforms his bearer shares into registered shares?

---

2. The court recognized that a completely arbitrary denial of a requested consent might be attacked by the victimized shareholder as an "abuse of rights". But since the shareholder would bear the burden of proving such abuse, the court felt that the remedy furnished by the "abuse of rights" doctrine would not adequately protect the shareholder. The only fair solution, the court held, was to strike down the unreasonable transfer restriction itself.

3. German law is more favorable to the individual stockholder. Sec. 180 of the German Stock Corporation Act of 1965 requires "the approval of all shareholders affected" for the valid adoption of "a resolution pursuant to which the transfer of registered shares . . . is made dependent on the approval of the company." Even before the new Act was passed, this rule prevailed in Germany according to the view which was predominant among courts and legal writers. See H. Wiedemann, Die nachträgliche Vinkulierung von Aktien und GmbH-Anteilen, 17 NJW 282 (1964). Cf. B. von Falkenhausen, Verfassungsrechtliche Grenzen der Mehrheitsherrschaft nach dem Recht der Kapitalgesellschaften 80–81 (1967).

Concerning American law, compare H. G. Henn & J. R. Alexander, Laws of Corporations, §§ 281, 282 (3d ed., 1983, and 1986 Supp.).

NOTES ON DIFFERENCES BETWEEN REGISTERED
SHARES AND BEARER SHARES

(1) It has been said that as a practical matter there is hardly any difference between a stock certificate [1] issued to the bearer and a certificate standing in the name of the registered holder, since the latter (in the absence of specific transfer restrictions) can make his certificate negotiable by endorsing it in blank or by executing a blank stock power. A similar view seems to underlie the decision of the Swiss court in the principal case. Closer examination of the problem, however, shows the following:

From a practical point of view, the most important rights of a stockholder are the right to vote; the right to receive dividends; the right to receive liquidating dividends in case of dissolution; and the right to transfer his stock. With respect to the exercise of each of these four rights there are significant differences between bearer shares and registered shares.[1a]

(a) The registered holder may be recognized as being entitled to vote, even though he has lost possession of his certificate. See UCC § 8–207.[2] The holder of bearer shares, on the other hand, has to deposit his stock certificates in order to qualify as a shareholder entitled to vote. For him, there is no other way to prove his qualification. All continental corporation laws, although differing among each other as to details, recognize this feature of bearer shares and provide, as a prerequisite to the exercise of the right to vote such shares, that before or during the stockholders' meeting the stock certificates be deposited with the corporation or with a bank, such deposit to be in the name of the person who personally or by proxy will vote the shares represented by such stock certificates. The German case, supra, p. 567, illustrates this practice.

(b) Until presentment for transfer of the duly endorsed certificate, the corporation may safely, i.e. without fear of having to pay a second time, pay all dividends to the *registered* holder. See UCC § 8–207.[3] It is, therefore, universal corporate practice in the United States to send dividend checks to the person registered as owner of the shares. The

---

1. In civil-law terminology, the term "share" or its equivalent stands both for the shareholder's bundle of rights and for the paper embodying these rights. For the sake of clarity, the term "stock certificate" or "certificate" is used in this discussion when reference is made to the paper, although such terminology, as applied to civil-law bearer shares, may not be entirely accurate.

1a. Throughout this discussion, it will be assumed that the shares, whether issued in bearer or registered form, are "certificated" within the meaning of UCC § 8–102, as amended in 1977.

2. Once the owner obtains notice of his loss, he must, in order to avert serious disadvantages, notify the issuer within a reasonable time. UCC § 8–405. But even after such notification, the *registered* owner "may properly rely upon his status as such to assure continuity of dividend . . . and to safeguard any voting rights." C. L. Israels and E. Guttman, Modern Securities Transfers, Sec. 13.07 (Rev.Ed.1971). See also infra n. 4.

3. See also Anno., 21 A.L.R.4th 879 (1983): (Construction and Effect of UCC § 8–207(1) Allowing Issuer of Investment Security to Treat Registered Owner as Entitled to Owner's Rights until Presentment for Registration of Transfer).

Swiss Code of Obligations art. 685 is to the same effect as UCC § 8–207.

latter thus may continue to receive dividends even after he has lost possession of his certificate.[4]

In the case of bearer shares the practice is necessarily different. The bearer-holder's right to dividends is represented by coupons. As distinguished from coupons attached to bonds, these share-coupons do not mature at specified times or in specified amounts. Each share-coupon becomes validated and presentable only by the declaration of a dividend, and in the amount declared. Dividend declarations of corporations which have issued bearer shares, are customarily in the form that such and such amount per share shall be payable against presentation and surrender of, e.g., coupon No. 5. Each stock certificate is accompanied by a set of numbered coupons, and by a so-called talon entitling the holder to receive a new set of coupons after the first set is exhausted. The corporation's first dividend declaration will validate coupon No. 1; the second declaration will validate coupon No. 2, etc. The paper embodying the coupons and the talon is often not even attached to the stock certificate itself, so that, at least as a practical matter, it can be separately negotiated.

It stands to reason, therefore, that the owner of bearer shares who has lost physical possession of the share certificates and coupons, cannot collect any dividends.

(c) Liquidating dividends, like ordinary dividends, may safely be paid to the registered shareholder, even though he does not present his certificate.[5] That the holder of a bearer share, on the other hand, cannot obtain a liquidating dividend without presentation of his certificate or a coupon, is abundantly clear.[5a]

(d) It is only with respect to the fourth and last of a shareholder's substantial rights—the right to transfer his stock—that the position of a registered holder is similar to that of the owner of bearer shares. Neither of them can effect a transfer if he is unable to deliver his certificate.[5b] It is true, moreover, that a registered holder who wishes to facilitate a whole series of transfers, by blank endorsement can make his certificate almost the equal of a bearer share insofar as mobility and negotiability are concerned. Yet even here some vital differences must be noted.

(i) As has been pointed out above, the transferability of registered shares may be restricted by provisions in the charter or by-laws of the corporation. The nature of bearer shares makes it impossible to impose similar restrictions.

---

4. See supra n. 2. It is true that the registered owner may lose his rights to a bona fide purchaser of the certificate, and that in that event he will cease to receive dividends. But if the lost certificate was not endorsed, the owner will be deprived of his rights as against the issuer only if (a) the owner's notification to the issuer is not timely in terms of the owner's discovery of the loss, *and* (b) the issuer has registered a transfer of the shares before receiving the notification. UCC §§ 8–404, 8–405. See Israels and Guttman, op. cit. supra n. 2, at Sec. 13.06.

5. See 16A Fletcher on Corporations, § 8224 (Rev.Ed.1962), citing Bank of Hollis-ter v. Schlichter, 191 N.C. 352, 131 S.E. 732 (1926). Formerly the question was not entirely free from doubt; see Stevens On Corporations 613–14 (1949). It would seem, however, that the doubt has been removed by UCC § 8–207.

5a. See, e.g., Decision of the Swiss Federal Court of Dec. 22, 1962, BGE 88 III 140, where it was held that even after dissolution (in this case brought about by the corporation's bankruptcy) the shareholder's rights remain embodied in the certificate.

5b. See supra n. 1a.

(ii) The negotiability of the bearer share is an inherent feature, not dependent on anything the owner does or fails to do. The owner of a registered share, on the other hand, until the very last minute of his period of ownership is always free to keep his certificate unendorsed, and thus to minimize the danger that (in case possession of the certificate should elude him) he might lose his rights to a bona fide purchaser.[6]

(2) The foregoing discussion will have made it clear that the position of the owner of bearer shares who has lost physical possession of his stock certificates is even more unenviable than the position of a registered holder under similar circumstances.

In order to remedy this unhappy plight of the owner of bearer shares who has lost possession, most civil-law countries have enacted provisions—sometimes as part of their civil or commercial code, sometimes in their code regulating civil procedure—authorizing a cancellation procedure of the kind which was sought to be utilized by the plaintiffs in the next-following case. If in such a proceeding, which is initiated ex parte upon public notice to the "unknown present holder" of the paper, the latter does not appear, and the petitioner convinces the court that he is the rightful owner but has lost possession, the outstanding stock certificate will be declared null and void, and the corporation will be authorized to issue a new stock certificate to the petitioner. Insofar as the issuing corporation is concerned, the final decree in such a proceeding will cut off the rights of the holder of the old certificate even though he may be a holder in due course and may not have received actual notice of the proceeding. In this respect the continental cancellation procedure cuts deeper than the procedure for the issuance of a new certificate authorized by UCC § 8–405, which leaves the rights of a bona fide purchaser of the (duly endorsed) old certificate substantially unaffected.[7]

There is no doubt that the stringent civil-law procedure, by which the rights of an honest holder may be seriously affected in a proceeding commenced upon notice by publication,[8] lends itself to possible abuse. Such abuse, however, would be punishable as perjury and criminal deceit. Moreover, the required notice by publication will usually include publication in some official journal. Bankers and brokers peruse every issue of this journal, and will compare the serial numbers of the securities mentioned in such public notice with the numbers of similar

---

6. Under the Uniform Commercial Code, it is not completely impossible for a purchaser who has received a new, re-issued or re-registered security (the so-called "super-sainted purchaser") to acquire good title even though he has relied on a forged endorsement. UCC §§ 8–311, 8–306(1). See F. Leary, Jr., Security Issues and Transfer Under the Uniform Commercial Code, 2 U.C.C.L.J. 7, 24–26 (1969). But the registered owner of an unendorsed certificate nevertheless will not lose his rights as against the corporation or its transfer agent if he has taken the simple precaution prescribed by § 8–405(1). See supra n. 4.

7. For details see N. Penney, Articles 4 and 8 of the Uniform Commercial Code, 26 La.L.Rev. 259, 271 (1966).

8. Under the rule prevailing in Switzerland and other civil-law countries, the bona fide purchaser of the old (now cancelled) certificate cannot recover any damages or other compensation from the corporation, even though he (or his transferor) may have received no actual notice of the cancellation proceedings. In some jurisdictions, he may possibly have a cause of action against the party who initiated the cancellation proceedings; but in practice such a cause of action may be difficult to enforce, especially after the newly issued shares have come into the hands of a new bona fide purchaser.

securities in their custody.[9] An investor who leaves the custody of his bearer shares to a banking institution is thus protected against losing his title through fraudulently instituted cancellation proceedings. This is one, although a comparatively minor one, of the factors which have contributed to the development of the general continental practice of depositing bearer shares with banks or bankers.[10]

OPINION OF THE SWISS FEDERAL COURT IN THE MATTER OF SELIGMANN–GANS AGAINST CIVIL TRIBUNAL OF THE CANTON OF BASEL–STADT

February 20, 1940, BGE 66 II 37.

On September 12, 1939, the petitioners, the spouses Seligmann-Gans, formerly residents of Frankfurt-on-Main, now residents of Villars s/Ollon (Switzerland), filed an ex parte petition with the Civil Tribunal of the Canton of Basel-Stadt in which they prayed that 712 specifically designated stock certificates representing bearer shares of the I. G. Chemie Corporation (a corporation having its corporate domicil at Basel-Stadt) [a] be cancelled and declared null and void.

Petitioners contend that they are the owners of these securities and that they deposited the same with the Mitteldeutsche Creditbank at Frankfurt-on-Main; that when they left Germany in the Fall of 1938, they had to leave these securities behind, because as non-Aryans they were not permitted to take any of their property along; that on December 3, 1938, the German Government issued a Decree Concerning the Utilization of Jewish Property, pursuant to which all securities belonging to non-Aryans were to be deposited with certain banks and could not be withdrawn without a license; that petitioners were thus deprived of their power to dispose of their shares, which was tantamount to a loss of possession; that petitioners did not have any knowledge as to where and in whose hands the securities were at the time of the petition; that repeated inquiries directed to the bank concerning the whereabouts of the securities remained unanswered; that a bank statement of December 12, 1938, contained the remark "loco Berlin", from which it could only be inferred that at that time the securities were somewhere in Berlin; that this removal of the securities [from Frankfurt-on-Main to Berlin] occurred without the knowledge

9. As a practical matter, bankers and brokers are compelled to do so, because ordinarily they will be deemed not to act in good faith if they purchase any bearer securities the numbers of which have been listed in that journal. Section 367 of the German Commercial Code expressly so provides.

10. This practice is discussed infra, pp. 822.

a. The question of the influence of the former German I. G. Farben concern upon the affairs of the Swiss I. G. Chemie Corporation was bitterly litigated in the courts of the United States. See Société Internationale v. Rogers, 357 U.S. 197, 78 S.Ct. 1087 (1958). The question was never judicially determined, because in the decision just cited the Supreme Court disposed only of procedural points, and ultimately the case was settled. There is no doubt, however, that I. G. Chemie Corporation (now Interhandel A.G.) was incorporated under the laws of Switzerland and registered at Basel, Switzerland, where it also had its principal office.

and consent of the petitioners; that since that time they had lost track of the shares. By these facts, the petitioners contended, they had shown lawful possession and loss within the meaning of [Articles 981 et seq. of the Code of Obligations, wherein it is provided that a person who has lawful possession of bearer securities and "loses" the same, may upon a proper showing of the facts obtain a court order cancelling the "lost" securities and authorizing the issuer to issue new securities in their place.] The petitioners further argued that the German Decree of December 3, 1938, by its discriminatory treatment of a racial group, was contrary to the Swiss public order and should, therefore, be disregarded.

The Civil Tribunal, by a judgment entered on October 20, 1939, denied the petition on the ground that the loss of the securities had not been shown.

The petitioners appealed from that judgment. . . .

The meaning of the term "loss" is not defined in Article 981 of the Code of Obligations. Nor is such definition to be found in other provisions concerning the judicial cancellation of securities. . . . Some criteria can be inferred by analogy from the provision of Article 934 of the Civil Code [b] . . . Under that section the lawful possessor may demand restitution of those things which were stolen from him, which he lost or which otherwise got out of his possession against his will. Obviously, the concept of loss within the meaning of Article 981 of the Code of Obligations must be understood in the same sense.

The mere fact, however, that the securities got out of the hands of the possessor against his will, is not yet sufficient to entitle him to judicial cancellation of such securities. There is the additional requirement that the present holder of the security be *unknown*. This follows, as has been pointed out by the court below, from the purpose of the cancellation procedure. Its purpose is to protect the former holder, who has lost possession of the security against his will, against the present unknown holder. Accordingly, it is expressly provided in

---

[b.] Swiss Civil Code, Article 933: "Whosoever receives a movable thing in good faith as his property, . . . shall be protected in his acquisition even if the transferor was a bailee without authority to transfer title."

Article 934: "If a movable thing has been stolen, or lost by the lawful possessor, or if in some other way it got out of his possession against his will, such possessor can demand it back from any transferee within 5 years. . . ."

Article 935: "Money and bearer securities cannot be recovered from the bona fide transferee, even though they got out of the possessor's control against his will."

The rule as to stolen and "lost" goods (Art. 934) is an exception to the general rule (Art. 933) protecting the bona fide purchaser. By way of an exception to the exception (Art. 935), the bona fide purchaser of money and other bearer securities is protected against the original owner, even though the latter "lost" possession by theft or otherwise against his will. This rule of Swiss law was applied in State of the Netherlands v. Federal Reserve Bank (Archimedes), 99 F.Supp. 655, 669 (D.C.S.D. N.Y., 1951), mod. on another point, but aff'd as to findings on Swiss law, 201 F.2d 455, 459 (2 Cir. 1953).

For a comparative discussion of civil-law rules concerning bona fide purchase of bearer securities and other chattels, and for further references, see supra pp. 283–285.

Article 983 of the Code of Obligations that the court, by public announcement, shall request "the unknown holder" to exhibit the security. In the same way it is provided in Article 1074 that a bill of exchange cannot be cancelled by a judicial proceeding unless the holder of the paper is unknown. If he is known, then there is no room for the cancellation procedure. In that event it is up to the former holder to seek recovery of the paper by bringing a possessory action against the present holder. With respect to bills of exchange this rule is expressly laid down in Article 1073 of the Code of Obligations. [Citing a commentary on the German Civil Code and a Swiss thesis, the Court indicates that by analogy the same rule must apply to other kinds of securities.]

Appellants argue: It is not necessary that the security be in the possession of a new holder; the cancellation procedure may be utilized in a case in which, for instance, the paper was burned or otherwise destroyed. This is certainly true; but it does not follow that, as the appellants believe, the former holder is entitled to the remedy of judicial cancellation in a case in which the new holder is known. . . .

In order to show that they lost the securities, the appellants point to the unanswered inquiries which they directed to the bank, to the remark "loco Berlin" in the bank's statements, and to the German Decree Concerning the Utilization of Jewish Property of December 3, 1938.

In this connection the court below points out that . . . the remark "loco Berlin" in the statement of December 31, 1938, is insufficient evidence of the loss; that in the said statement the shares are still designated as the property of the appellants; that regarding the German Decree of December 3, 1938, the appellants merely made general assertions without proving specific facts concerning the *particular* securities involved *herein*.

According to the conclusion reached by the court below the appellants failed to prove that the shares are no longer subject to their power of disposition, and thus failed to prove that they lost possession thereof. This conclusion is based upon correct premises, as has been pointed out above. Insofar as it is based upon findings of fact and the lower court's view of the evidence, it is not reviewable in this Court. . . .

The result would not be different if appellants were correct in contending that the remark "loco Berlin" in the bank statement, and the German Decree of December 3, 1938, are sufficient to prove that the German Government subjected the shares to the requirement of compulsory deposit and confiscated the same.

Assuming the correctness of this contention, it would follow that the securities are now in the possession of the German Government, either directly or through one of the so-called Devisenbanks with whom the securities of Jewish owners must be deposited pursuant to Section 11 of the said Decree. In that event the new holder of the securities would not be unknown. For this reason, in any event, a judicial cancellation proceeding would not lie. The appellants would have to prosecute their claim for recovery of the securities against the German Government. What procedure they would have to use for this purpose, and what their chances of success would be, does not have to be determined in this action; these questions have nothing to do with the question now before the Court: whether or not the petitioners may bring a proceeding for judicial cancellation of the securities.

Nor can the appellants obtain a more favorable result by invoking the "public order" of Switzerland, on the ground that the German Anti-Jewish legislation is inconsistent with such public order. Assuming there is such inconsistency between our fundamental legal principles and the said German decree, the fact still remains that the shares are presently in the hands of the German Government. Therefore, even if the decree embodying the requirement of compulsory deposit were not binding upon a Swiss court, the present holder would not be unknown within the meaning of Articles 981 et seq. of the Code of Obligations. This would be so even if the requirement of deposit, as appellants contend, were practically tantamount to confiscation.

Affirmed.

NOTES AND QUESTIONS

(1) *Looted Bearer Shares.* At a time of social or political upheaval, the volatility of bearer shares may offer advantages to their owner if in spite of persecution and expulsion from his country he manages to keep the shares in his possession. Frequently, however, it happens that the owner, like the plaintiffs in the principal case, must leave the shares behind when fleeing or being expelled; in that event, the tangible and chattel-like nature of such shares tends to hurt rather than help the owner. Experience has shown that bearer shares, especially those issued by foreign corporations, are a favorite object of spoliation by totalitarian usurpers and invaders.

(a) The principal case is a typical illustration of the difficulties encountered by owners of bearer shares who have been deprived of possession by spoliatory measures. The court's advice to the petitioners "to prosecute their claim for recovery of the securities against the German Government", amounts almost to irony. Obviously, no such action could have been brought in Germany at that time (1940). If the petitioners had attempted to sue the German Government in a Swiss court, they would have been met by the defense of sovereign immunity. If they had sought, by an action in a Swiss court, to recover the securities or their value from the Frankfurt bank, the action probably would have been dismissed on jurisdictional grounds, in spite of the fact that the issuer of the shares was a Swiss corporation. See Appellationsgericht Basel-Stadt, March 14, 1947, reported in 44 Schweizerische Juristen-Zeitung 227 (1948), where it was held that bearer shares of a Swiss corporation do not have a situs in Switzerland sufficient to empower a Swiss court to determine the ownership of such shares in an action against a non-resident defendant, unless the stock certificates are physically located in Switzerland at the time of the action.

The net result of the principal case and the last-cited case was to render the owners of looted Swiss bearer shares remediless,[1] even though Switzerland, as a matter of public policy, refused to recognize the validity of the Nazi decrees under which the spoliation had taken place.

(b) Most restitution laws passed by European Governments or Allied occupation authorities for the purpose of undoing the results of Nazi spoliation in liberated countries and in Germany itself, contain a provision similar to that of the French Ordonnance of April 21, 1945, which exempts from restitution "securities sold on the exchange or through a regular dealer without indication of the vendor." [2]

(c) At the end of World War II, huge amounts of securities were taken by the Red Army from the vaults of Berlin banks. If it had been able to use the voting power of the bearer shares so taken, the Soviet Government would have controlled many of the important industrial corporations of *Western* Germany. However, by a series of statutes (Wertpapierbereinigungsgesetze) the West German legislator provided for cancellation and re-issuance of all securities previously issued by West German issuers. These statutes compelled each issuer to institute an omnibus cancellation proceeding in which holders, upon surrender of their old securities, received new securities if they could show a proper chain of title. In cases in which conflicting claims were filed concerning the same security, the contest had to be judicially determined. The details of the scheme were highly complex. Substantial completion of the herculean task imposed by these enactments on issuers, banks and courts required more than a decade.

Generally speaking, continental experience of the period before, during and immediately after World War II tends to show that in the event of a temporary breakdown of the civil order, on a national or international scale, the restoration of property rights is rendered more difficult by the volatile nature of bearer shares.

(2) *Banking Practice and Exercise of Voting Rights.* (a) Under statutes providing for a judicial proceeding in which stolen or lost securities can be cancelled and the issuer be authorized to issue new certificates or other securities, the petitioner must ordinarily submit proof of his ownership. Where the securities are registered in the name of the petitioner, such proof of ownership will not present any major difficulty. In the case of bearer securities, however, this problem may become a crucial one. In some European countries it is customary for banks to have their clients stipulate, by way of printed "general business terms" or otherwise, that the bank shall become the "owner" of all securities deposited by the client, and that the latter shall have only a *contractual* right to have the same number of securities of the same kind redelivered to him upon demand.[3] The dangerous conse-

---

1. If the petitioners in the principal case, before leaving Nazi Germany, had burned their Swiss stock certificates in the presence of a reliable witness, they would have been more successful. In its opinion, the court made it clear that when the owner can prove *destruction* of his certificates, the corporation will be ordered to issue new ones. It makes no difference whether or not the destruction was accidental.

2. See N. D. Berman, Property Claims Arising from Germany's Wartime Occupations, 9 Federal Bar Journal 169, 187 (1948). See also Art. 21 of Mil.Govt.Law No. 59 for the American-Occupied Zone of Germany, 12 Fed.Reg. 7983, at 7985 (1947).

3. In civil-law terminology, this is referred to as an "irregular deposit". See 40 C.J., Modern Civil Law, Sec. 147. In Germany, Sec. 15 of the Depotgesetz of Feb. 4, 1937 (RGBl I 171) provides that a bank

quences which such transformation of property rights into contractual rights might engender in case the bank becomes insolvent, are sometimes mitigated by a special statute.

If in the foregoing case the petitioners' agreement with the Frankfurt bank had been of this kind, could the decision of the Court be supported upon the ground that the petitioners were not the "owners" of the securities in question?

(b) Under the corporation laws of most civil-law countries, corporate charters of stock corporations (as distinguished from limited responsibility companies) may provide for bearer shares or registered shares or both. As a practical matter, many stock corporations in those countries, and especially big corporations whose shares are listed on stock exchanges, issue only bearer shares.[4] Such bearer shares, naturally, require the same degree of physical protection as cash. Moreover, the shareholders' right to receive dividends is embodied in coupons which have to be detached and presented to the issuer whenever a dividend is declared. All this tends to make it impractical for the individual owner of such securities to keep them in his own custody, and most bearer shares are "deposited" with banks or bankers who assume responsibility for their custody and attend to prompt presentation and collection of the dividend coupons.

As custodians of a large percentage of all publicly-held shares, the banks in the bearer-share countries ordinarily are in a position to exercise the voting rights connected with these shares. Being in possession of the shares, a bank can vote in its own name, unless the law expressly requires—as it seems to do, e.g. in France [5]—that share-

---

may accept securities of a customer for custody in the form of an "irregular deposit" only with the customer's express written authorization, and that the document containing such authorization may not include any other matter. This has made it impossible for German banks to include "irregular deposit" clauses in their "general business terms", and has had the effect of discouraging irregular deposits.

The "irregular deposit" must of course be distinguished from a mere authorization given by the customer to the bank to deposit the shares with a central clearing house (in which event the customer becomes a co-owner of the total mass of securities of the same kind thus deposited). Such clearing-house arrangements, which facilitate rapid (and perhaps electronically effected) transfers, were routinely used in Germany and France long before the central depository system was introduced here in the late 1960s. Concerning the functioning of the French central clearing institution, called SICOVAM, see M. Vasseur, Les Valeurs Mobiliéres en Droit Françis, in W. J. Ganshof van der Meersch (Ed.), The Legal Status of Securities in Europe and the United States, at 246–48 (1970). For a comparative study, see U. Drobnig, Vergleichende und kollisionsrechliche Probleme der Girosammelverwahrung, in

H. Bernstein, U. Drobnig & H. Kötz (eds.), Festschrift für Konrad Zweigert 73 (1981). As to some recent changes in France, see infra p. 826.

4. For a discussion of the prevalence of bearer shares in continental Europe, and the reasons for it, see infra p. 828.

The reader will recall that in Switzerland after World War II a number of corporations, including some big ones, converted some or all of the bearer shares issued by them into registered shares. The reasons for this, however, are peculiar to Switzerland. In the event of a war among other nations, a Swiss corporation derives manifold advantages from Switzerland's neutral status, and it may, therefore, wish to be in a position to prove that it is truly Swiss, not only in terms of its corporate domicile, but also in terms of the domicile and nationality of its stockholders.

In many other continental countries, the bearer share has fully preserved its popularity.

5. Law of July 24, 1966, Arts. 161, 167, 440. See 2 Hamel-Lagarde-Jauffret, Traité de Droit Commercial at No. 688 (2d ed. 1980). See also C. Gavalda & J. Stoufflet, Droit de la Banque 792–93 (1974), where it is emphasized that this French rule differs from German law and practice.

holders' votes must be cast in the name of the true owner of the stock. If a bank cannot, or does not wish to, vote in its own name, it will in any event find it easy to obtain a proxy from its customer.[6]

The nature of the bearer share thus vitally affects the realities of corporate control. Where the shareholders are registered, their names and addresses are known to management, with the result that management usually can obtain their proxies. Unless successfully challenged in a proxy fight, management is able through these proxies to perpetuate itself and to control the corporation. Under a bearer-share system, the situation is quite different. There is no list of stockholders, and management has no way of communicating with the stockholders except through published announcements. The banks, on the other hand, are in constant direct communication with the shareholders of whose shares they have custody. Thus they can, and do, obtain proxies from that large majority of stockholders who do not care to devote their own time and energy to the exercise of their voting rights. In many bearer-share countries, this has led to a predominance of banking influence in the shareholders' meetings of publicly-owned corporations.[7] The economic, social and political consequences of this large measure of bankers' control over large corporations have been profound.[8]

In Germany, the issue of the "bankers' vote" has long been recognized as going to the very core of the general problem of control over big, publicly-held corporations. But although the matter was heatedly debated for generations,[8a] the legislator did not impose any stringent

6. The German Stock Corporation Act of 1965 provides in § 135, subs. 2, that such a proxy may be granted only for a period not exceeding 15 months. The 1937 Act contained a similar provision. Experience has shown that banks do not encounter much difficulty in obtaining the required periodic renewals of their proxy forms.

7. European banks routinely use this power (plus the additional power they may have as creditors) to place their representatives on corporate boards.

In the United States, there is a similar problem. Congressional studies and investigations have revealed that control of our major corporations is, to a considerable extent, concentrated in the hands of financial institutions. See the following publications of the Subcommittee on Reports, Accounting and Management of the Senate Committee on Government Operations: Corporate Ownership and Control (94th Cong., 1st Sess., November 1975); Institutional Investors' Common Stock—Holdings and Voting Rights (94th Cong., 2d Sess., May 1976); Voting Rights in Major Corporations (Staff Study, 95th Cong., 1st Sess., January 1978). It should be noted, however, that (as these studies have demonstrated) American financial institutions must resort to numerous and somewhat diverse levers and methods of control in order to obtain a measure of power in the affairs of

publicly-held corporations. The control which the big banks in some European countries exercise by virtue of the voting power of bearer shares in their custody, is more direct and, it is submitted, more heavily concentrated in very few hands. See the Report of the German Monopolkommission, infra n. 12.

8. With specific reference to Switzerland, this is forcefully demonstrated in the article by J. Meister, Der kleine Aktionär in der grossen Gesellschaft, Finanz und Wirtschaft of July 13, 1977, p. 2. For broad-based comparative discussions, see B. Grossfeld & W. Ebke, Controlling the Modern Corporation: A Comparative View of Corporate Power in the United States and Europe, 26 Am.J.Comp.L. 397 (1978); E. von Hippel, Zur Problematik des Aktionär-Stimmrechts, in 2 von Caemmerer-Mentschikoff-Zweigert (Eds.), Ius Privatum Gentium—Festschrift für Max Rheinstein 1081 (1969).

8a. Since the beginning of this century, there has been a steady stream of writings on the subject; the total volume of these writings is colossal. For a selective bibliography see W. Vallenthin, Die Stimmrechtsvertretung durch Banken 58–60 (1966). Further references can be found in the monograph by H.-P. Schaad, Das Depotstimmrecht der Banken nach schweizerischem und deutschem Recht (1972).

regulations until 1965, when the new Stock Corporation Act was adopted.[8b] That Act contains proxy rules avowedly inspired by those issued under § 14(a) of our Securities Exchange Act.[9] One important (and necessary) difference between the German proxy rules and their American model is that in Germany the duty of sending the proxy materials to the shareholders is imposed on the banks rather than on management.[10] There is no doubt that these new German proxy rules mark an improvement over the previous state of the law;[11] but although they will prevent certain types of abuses, it should not be expected that they will bring about a substantial reduction of the degree of corporate control exercised through the "bankers' vote". Thus the discussion of the more basic questions—whether a high degree of bankers' control over the affairs of publicly-held corporations is desirable, and whether by exercising the voting rights of their customers the banks are exposed to conflicts of interest—is continuing among legal writers.[12] Insofar as existing German law is concerned, however, the 1965 Act has settled the matter. In a mildly regulated form, that Act preserves the "bankers' vote", i.e. the power of the banks, as custodians of bearer shares, in effect to exercise the voting rights of most small investors.[12a]

8b. In the 1937 Act the treatment of the subject was essentially limited to the formal requirement mentioned in n. 6 supra.

9. For a more detailed description and discussion of these German proxy rules, see F. K. Juenger and L. Schmidt, German Stock Corporation Act 19–21 (1967); E. C. Steefel and B. von Falkenhausen, The New German Stock Corporation Law, 52 Cornell L.Q. 518, 542–43 (1967); D. F. Vagts, Reforming the "Modern" Corporation: Perspectives from the German, 80 Harv.L.Rev. 23, 53–58 (1966); International Securities Project, 30 Bus.Law. 585, 667 (1975); 1 E. W. Ercklentz, Jr., Modern German Corporation Law 284–87 (1979).

10. Proxy rules of the German type, that is, addressed to the custodians of the stock certificates rather than to management, are not completely unknown in the United States. There are SEC and New York Stock Exchange proxy rules addressed to brokers for securities held by them "in a street name". Under a recent amendment of the SEC Rules, the broker must disclose to the issuer, upon request, the names and addresses of the persons on whose behalf securities are held by the broker, and the number of such securities. See also Vagts, supra n. 9 at 56–57.

11. In the 2nd (1959) edition of this book, at 440, such reform measures had been suggested and strongly advocated. See also the writings cited in n. 9 supra.

12. See, e.g., Vagts, supra n. 9, at 57–58; Vallenthin, supra n. 8a, at 16–30. See also the 1976/77 Report of the official Monopolkommission, entitled "Fortschreitende

Konzentration bei Grossunternehmen", at pp. 44–47, 286–311.

12a. The desire to check the power of stockholders' representatives appears to have been one of the reasons for European legislators' manifold attempts to create a countervailing power by giving workers' representatives a role in corporate governance. Worker participation has been effectuated in two main ways: (a) In most European countries, bodies of elected workers' representatives (usually referred to as works councils) have received the right to be informed concerning certain matters and to be consulted ahead of time about plans affecting the enterprise. (b) In Germany, and to some extent in the Netherlands, and on a voluntary basis in France, worker representatives participate in the actual managing bodies of large corporations. See H. Schneider & D. J. Kingsman, The German Co-Determination Act 1976 (1976); W. Kolvenbach, Workers' Participation in Europe 19–64 (1977); F. Ritter, A New Constitution for German Big Business: The Co-Determination Act of 1976, 1 Hastings Int. & Comp.L.Rev. 113 (1976); T. R. Ottervanger & R. M. Pais, Employee Participation in Corporate Decision-Making: The Dutch Model, 15 Int.Law. 393 (1981). For comparative discussions, see B. Grossfeld, Management and Control of Marketable Share Companies, in Vol. XIII, Ch. 4 of the International Encyclopedia of Comparative Law at 135–41 (1973); W. Kolvenbach, Industrial Democracy: Legal Developments in Europe 1977–1979, 1 N.Y. Law School J.Int. & Comp.L. 77 (1980); Note, Worker participation: Industrial Democracy and Managerial Prerogative in

(3) *The Future of Bearer Shares.* Bearer shares are elusive. They can be used to evade income and inheritance taxes, and to circumvent many types of regulatory laws.[13] The veil of anonymity which they spread over the shareholders, makes it exceedingly difficult, for instance, to enforce a statute seeking to exclude foreigners or foreign-owned companies from certain pursuits. It is probably for this reason that some Latin American countries have prohibited specified types of corporations (e.g. those engaged in newspaper publishing or radio broadcasting) from issuing bearer shares. In other Latin American jurisdictions, the issuance of such shares has been subjected to a variety of restrictions.[14]

Looking at continental Europe, on the other hand, one observes that attempts to abolish or curb the bearer share have met with decisive success only in a small minority of countries. Anti-bearer-share legislation was adopted in France during World War II, and in Germany (under pressure of the Occupation authorities), shortly after the War; but in both countries this legislation was short-lived. Italy is the only one of the major continental countries where severe wartime restrictions on the issuance of bearer shares have been kept in effect, "presumably for the aid they give to the enforcement of taxes, exchange control, and other legislation."[15]

the Federal Republic of Germany, Sweden and the United States, 8 Hastings Int. & Comp.L.Rev. 93 (1984). On relevant EEC proposals, see R. Blanpain, F. Blanquet & F. Herman, The Vredeling Proposal (1983); Income Data Services, Ltd., London, Vredeling and the Fifth (1984); Note, The Proposed Vredeling Directive: A Modest Proposal or the Exportation of Industrial Democracy? 70 Va.L.Rev. 1469 (1984).

13. See Note, 48 Cornell L.Q. 174 (1962).

The anonymous and elusive nature of bearer shares causes regulatory difficulties not only in the countries of issuance, but elsewhere as well. The United States Government is encountering such difficulties, for instance, in the enforcement of its securities legislation. Acting under a power conferred upon it by § 12(g)(3) of the Securities Exchange Act of 1934, as amended in 1964, 15 U.S.C.A. § 78l(g)(3), the S.E.C. exempted certain foreign issuers from the registration requirements and other provisions of the Act. The exemption, however, applies to a given class of securities only if less than 300 shareholders reside in the United States. In cases where the foreign securities in question are bearer shares, the question arises how the Government (or the issuer, for that matter) can possibly determine the number of shareholders resident in the United States. This question has not yet been resolved. See R. M. Buxbaum, Securities Regulation and the Foreign Issuer Exemption: A Study in the Process of Accommodating Foreign Interests, 54 Cornell L.Rev. 358, 363 (1969); R.

M. Phillips and M. Shipman, An Analysis of the Securities Acts Amendments of 1964, 1964 Duke L.J. 706, 756–57; R. A. Stephens, Reevaluation of Disclosure Requirements for Foreign Issuers: Securities Exchange Act of 1934, 45 Geo.Wash.L.Rev. 494, 533 (1977).

14. See Eder, Company Law in Latin-America, 27 Notre Dame Law. 5, 223, at 231–2 (1952). Some countries provide, also, that in paying dividends upon bearer shares, corporations must withhold a coupon tax at the source.

The Mexican Law to Promote and Regulate Foreign Investments, enacted in 1973, prohibits the use of bearer shares insofar as foreign-owned stock is concerned. This provision applies even to companies that were in existence before the effective date of the new law. See H. A. Inman & A. Ortiz Tirado, A Mexican Dividend: "Las Maquiladoras," 9 Int. Lawyer 431, 437–38 (1975).

15. A. F. Conard, Organizing for Business, in 2 E. Stein and T. L. Nicholson, American Enterprise in the European Common Market 1, at 131 (1960). See also V. G. Venturini, Italian Law of Companies, Labour Enterprise and Organisation—The Italian Civil Code Book Five 132 (1967).

Note, however, that a 1974 statute engrafted an exception upon the general rule prohibiting the issuance of shares in bearer form. Under that statute, an Italian stock corporation may issue so-called savings shares, a kind of non-voting preferred shares, and shares of that kind may be in

An interesting development has occurred in France. On the one hand, as in Latin America, enterprises engaged in the publication of newspapers and other periodicals or in audiovisual communication must, under a recent statute, issue registered stock only.[16] Somewhat earlier legislation provided that shares could be issued to the bearer only if the stock was listed on an exchange or traded on the so-called secondary market, or otherwise subject to substantial trading.[17] In addition, a decree adopted in 1983 has "dematerialized" both types of stock. "Registered" stock now exists only as a book entry on the books of the issuing company (or a firm acting on its behalf); bearer stock only as a book entry on the books of a registered broker. Stock must be traded through registered brokers, using the central clearing system (SICOVAM).[18] In France, differences between registered and bearer stock thus have been narrowed substantially.

Subject to these recent developments, however, it remains true that outside of Italy the bearer share remains the principal vehicle by which European corporations, if they "go public", raise equity capital.

WHY NO BEARER SHARES IN THE UNITED STATES?

It is hard to deny that of all legal devices which have contributed to the anonymity and mobility of property, the bearer share is the neatest trick. At first sight, therefore, it appears surprising that American corporation lawyers, who reputedly lack neither ingenuity nor influence upon state legislatures, have neglected this device. How can such neglect be explained?

The question seems simple enough; but the answer can be found only by considering a number of historical, political, social and economic factors. We must remember, first of all, that the continental Codes of Commerce of the 19th century, by adopting the bearer share along with other traditional institutions of the law merchant, provided a firm statutory basis for the development of this form of security. For reasons previously discussed, the common law was not receptive to this particular creation of the law merchant, and investors and businessmen in common-law countries grew accustomed to shares issued in registered form.

It remained nevertheless possible for legislators in common-law jurisdictions to introduce the bearer share by statute. In fact, under the name of "share warrants", bearer shares may be issued by public companies in England.[1] But although statutory authority for their

bearer form. See P. L. Olivetti, Italy, in S. N. Frommel & J. H. Thompson, Company Law in Europe 285, 306–09 (1975).

16. Law No. 86–897 of August 1, 1986, 1986 J.O. p. 9529, 1986 D.L. 423, arts. 4, 15, 20. Transfer is subject to board approval and ownership by foreigners is restricted.

17. Law No. 81–1160 of December 30, 1981, art. 94–I, as amended by Law No. 83–1179 of December 29, 1983, art. 111. The law also provides a procedure for the conversion of bearer into registered stock.

18. Decree No. 83–359 of May 2, 1983, implementing Law No. 81–1160, supra note 17, art. 194–II. In the terminology of UCC § 8–102(b) French securities would thus be essentially "uncertificated securities". The rules mentioned apply to bonds as well as stock.

1. See Companies Act 1985, § 188. The English "share warrant", which in effect is a bearer share, should not be confused with the corporate "warrants" in the American sense of the term, which are not shares but mere options to acquire shares

issuance has existed in England since 1867,[2] share warrants have never been popular with English companies or investors.[3] In recent times, moreover, the issuance of share warrants has been strongly discouraged by tax and foreign exchange legislation.[4]

Most of the corporation statutes in the United States either flatly prohibit the issuance of bearer shares, or in other ways render the issuance of such shares impossible or impracticable.[5] Only two states, Montana and Connecticut, seem to have experimented with the idea of bearer shares. In 1897, presumably in order to attract European investors, Montana enacted a statute authorizing mining companies to issue this type of security;[6] But the practical effect of the statute seems to have been insignificant, and in the 1960s it was repealed.[7] In Connecticut, a 1961 amendment of the Stock Corporation Act authorizes the issuance of share certificates in bearer form.[8] The statute, however, fails to indicate how a holder of bearer shares can collect dividends or exercise his voting rights. Thus, from a practical standpoint, the Connecticut statute cannot be regarded as an adequate basis for the issuance of such shares. In summary, one must conclude that in spite of the half-hearted experiments in Montana and Connecticut the bearer share has never gained a real foothold in the United States.[9]

The first and most important of the factors which militated against the bearer share in the United States and most other common-law countries, thus appears to have been the absence of any legal tradition or business practice favoring it. In addition, it must be kept in mind that during the last 150 years neither England nor this country has been invaded by a foreign enemy, and that, with the exception of the relatively brief period of the War Between the States, both countries have enjoyed freedom from violent internal upheavals. If this picture of relative tranquility is contrasted with conditions in less fortunate parts of the world, it becomes easy to understand why continental and Latin American investors, forever in fear of invasions, revolutions,

---

upon specified terms. See Stevens On Corporations 93 (1949).

2. See Webb, Hale and Co. v. The Alexandria Water Co., 21 T.L.R. 572 (1905).

3. See Gower's Principles of Modern Company Law 440–42 (4th ed. by L. C. B. Gower, J. B. Cronin, A. J. Easson and Lord Wedderburn of Charlton 1979); S. N. Frommel & J. H. Thompson, Company Law in Europe 563 (1975).

4. See ibid., and also Note, 48 Cornell L.Q. 174, 184–85 (1962).

5. Id. at 176–78.

6. Id. at 178.

7. Mont.Rev.Codes Ann. § 15–22–136 (1967).

8. See Note, supra n. 4, at 181.

9. There is, on the other hand, a firm legal basis in our law for trading in bearer shares issued abroad. See UCC §§ 8–102(1)(a) and (e), 8–301 ff.

It should be noted, however, that foreign issuers planning to sell stock in the United States usually attempt to accommodate American preferences by depositing the number of bearer shares allocated to the United States market with a financial institution, which then issues registered "Depository Certificates" to the individuals wishing to purchase such stock. Conversely, American corporations deposit registered shares destined for the European market with a financial institution, which then issues bearer "Depository Certificates". Cf. articles 7 and 8 of the French Decree No. 83–359, which authorize the French central clearing organization (SICOVAM) to issue actual certificates representing stock recorded on its books for circulation abroad and, conversely, in cooperation with appropriate foreign bodies, to open accounts on its books for foreign securities for which actual certificates have come into existence in the country of issue.

oppressive governments and waves of confiscatory legislation, insist upon the most mobile and most anonymous form of personal property.[10]

Other factors which favored the bearer share in civil-law countries, and worked against it in England and the United States, are connected with the way in which corporations are managed and controlled. In countries in which the formulation of corporate charters, and indeed of corporation statutes, is strongly influenced by corporate management, bearer shares will not flourish. Such shares make it impossible for the corporation to get into touch with its shareholders except through newspaper advertisements. As a matter of experience, this makes it more difficult for management to maintain control through the proxy voting machinery.[11] The management group, as such, thus may well be opposed to bearer shares, while many investors, especially non-resident investors who are interested in anonymity, will prefer them to registered shares.

Finally, a point of practical politics must be considered. In those countries where banks derive both revenue and power from their customary role as custodians of bearer shares, they will exert pressure for the retention of such shares. With reference to the situation in the United States, on the other hand, it may be surmised that no feelings of hospitality toward bearer shares are entertained by banks and trust companies, whose profitable business of functioning as registrars and transfer agents is predicated on the issuance of shares in registered form.[12]

10. Gower, supra n. 3, remarks that bearer securities have always been much in demand by continental investors, and that their quality of transferability "greatly facilitated the task of refugees who wished to smuggle their wealth out of the countries from which they were forced to flee." This is quite true; but those victims of confiscatory measures who did not have the foresight to remove their bearer shares in time, may find that the tangible nature of such shares works against their interests (see the Swiss case, supra), and that even after the fall of the confiscating government the restoration of their property rights may be impeded or frustrated by the volatility of bearer shares. See supra p. 821.

11. See Gower, ibid., and supra p. 827.

12. The increasing availability, in Europe as well as here, of central clearing-houses for the computerized transfer of securities tends somewhat to diminish the practical significance of the differences between bearer shares and registered shares. To the extent that a clearing-house system of stock transfer is used, each transfer can be effected by a mere entry on the books or the computer of the clearing-house, with the result that both physical delivery of a bearer share and change of registration on the books of the corporation (in the case of a registered share) become unnecessary. It should be kept in mind, however, that most of the clearing-house systems presently in existence in civil-law countries (with the exception of the French SICOVAM system, see supra p. 826) are of an optional nature; every share-owner is free, by giving the proper instructions to his bank or broker, to use or not to use the clearing-house as the custodian or registered nominee of his shares. In Germany, where such an optional clearing-house system has been available for a long time, experience has shown that, although the clearing-house may offer some convenience and saving of expense, many shareholders nevertheless decide to stay out of the clearing-house system. It seems reasonable to assume, therefore, that in spite of the availability of such systems the differences between bearer shares and registered shares will remain a subject of considerable interest for a long time to come.

3. LIMITED LIABILITY COMPANIES

GAITHER: HANDBOOK ON MEXICAN MERCANTILE LAW *

1948. Pp. 19–20.

. . . The limited company is [a] true entity distinct from the owners. . . . It is an association of individuals who are entirely exempt from individual responsibility as to third parties, except as to the amount of participation subscribed, and yet who own the stock or shares or portions of the entity which is separate from the owners. It has been defined as an incorporated partnership because it does have a status, as to third parties, of a distinct entity and the relations of the associates inter se have some elements of a partnership. There may or may not be certificates of shares issued. For convenience the members are called shareholders or stockholders.

The members of this company agree to invest certain capital in the enterprise and are responsible as to third parties for the unpaid amount of their agreed contribution.

Their shares are not negotiable, they may not be bearer, and may be sold only under certain conditions. The entity must have a name followed by the words "Sociedad de Responsabilidad Limitada" or its abbreviation "S. de R. L." Without these descriptive words the company becomes a partnership and the members are liable to third parties in case of loss.

. . .

Members may number from two to twenty-five—never less than two and never more than twenty-five. Capitalization may be as low as 5,000 pesos divided equally in 100-peso portions or multiples thereof, all fully subscribed and at least 50 per cent paid in.

This class of company may not be opened to public subscription. To sell an interest in the company or to admit new members, unanimous consent of all members or stockholders is necessary, except that the company charter may provide that consent may be by ¾ majority. In such a sale the remaining stockholders have an option or right to buy the shares offered at the same price and conditions stipulated in the sales contract, effective for 15 days after the sale has been authorized in the meeting of the stockholders. If various members desire to effect such purchase they may buy at the ratio of their respective holdings in the company.

Shares may be transmitted by inheritance unless agreed otherwise in the charter. It may be provided that the remaining stockholders

* Reprinted by permission of the author and of The Academy Press, Oberlin, Ohio.

may purchase the share of a deceased member at a given price or at the book value, or it may be preferred to permit the heirs to carry on as stockholders, or to liquidate the company. The law permits great flexibility in this phase of its organization.

Each stockholder owns one part of the company and may vote his shares, one vote for each 100-pesos participation or share. . . .

NOTES AND QUESTIONS

(1) In most civil-law countries, the safeguards surrounding the formation and operation of stock corporations (see supra p. 802) are of such a nature as to make it too expensive and too cumbersome to incorporate a small business in that form.[1] The legislators of those countries thus thought that they were faced with a choice of three alternatives: (a) to deny the benefits of incorporation to all but the larger groups of capitalists; (b) to relax the standards and safeguards of their stock corporation laws, and thus to open the door to abuses in the formation and management of large, publicly-held corporations;[2] or (c) to create a new type of corporate organization to meet the needs of the small incorporator, while maintaining or even raising the standards imposed upon the large corporations.

Following the leadership of Germany, which enacted the first Law Concerning Limited Liability Companies in 1892,[3] most civil-law countries adopted the last of the three alternatives. The Mexican S. de R.

1. See H. P. DeVries and F. K. Juenger, Limited Liability Contract: The GmbH, 64 Colum.L.Rev. 866, 870–71 (1964); W. R. Haskell, The American Close Corporation and Its West German Counterpart: A Comparative Study, 21 Ala.L.Rev. 287 (1969).

2. It is, of course, possible to create statutory legal devices for the protection of investors without building these devices into the corporation statute itself. This, in fact, is the method used here (see supra pp. 803–804); but outside of the United States, even in countries where our securities legislation has been attentively studied, the method of separating legal safeguards for the protection of the investor (especially the equity investor) from the basic corporation statute has gained friends only recently. See, in addition to the materials on p. 804 supra, N. S. Poser, Securities Regulation in Developing Countries: The Brazilian Experience, 52 Va.L.Rev. 1283, at 1291 (1966).

3. We have encountered German companies of this type in the cases reproduced supra on pp. 567 and 615.

For excellent descriptive and comparative discussions of the German GmbH, see the articles cited supra n. 1 and P. Hay, Four Lectures on the Common Market: Trade Provisions—German and French Company Law—Establishment, 24 U.Pitt. L.Rev. 685, 734–40 (1963). See also H. H.

Winkhaus & G. Stratmann, GmbH: The Close Corporation in Germany—Management and Capitalization Problems for U.S. Controlled Subsidiaries, 28 Bus.Law. 1275 (1973). The two-volume work by E. W. Ercklentz, Jr., Modern German Corporation Law (1979), deals with the GmbH as well as the stock corporation.

For an English translation of the German GmbH law, see R. Müller, B. W. Meister & M. H. Heidenhain, The German GmbH Law (4th ed. 1981). In the Introduction, the authors point out than an over-all revision of the 1892 statute was planned a few years ago, but that the plan was abandoned. Instead, an amendment was adopted dealing with numerous details (e.g. raising the minimum capital from DM 20,000 to DM 50,000), but leaving the basic structure of the statute intact. The Introduction helpfully surveys many of the salient features of this form of business organization. See also B. W. Meister, The Limited Liability Company, in 2 B. Rüster (ed.), Business Transactions in Germany (FRG) at 23 (1983). An Appendix volume includes, as Appendix 6, an English translation of the German statute. For yet another English translation, see M. Oliver, the Private Company in Germany (1986) (published as part of the Kluwer series on International Corporate Law).

L., briefly described in the above excerpt from Gaither's Handbook of Mexican Mercantile Law, illustrates some of the typical features which, with many variations in detail, the laws of most civil-law countries have taken over from the German model.[4] In a significant variation from the Mexican rules just described, both Germany and France have recently authorized the establishment of a limited liability company by one person.[4a]

In Germany and in most countries that have followed its model, the limited liability company (GmbH) is enormously popular. At the end of 1985, Germany had about 320,000 limited liability companies as against about 2,100 stock corporations and 27 limited partnerships on shares.[5] A well-know German author has stated that, as compared to the GmbH, "the stock corporation is the more cumbersome and expensive form, subject to greater disclosure and as a rule chosen only if securities are to be offered to the public." [6]

(2) What is the purpose of the provision of the Mexican law limiting the number of shareholders to a maximum of twenty five?

Note that the shares of a Mexican limited responsibility company *cannot be made negotiable.* The German statute goes even further by requiring notarial form for the transfer of shares of such a company, and for contracts by which one party obligates himself to effect such transfer. The German Bundesgerichtshof has made it clear that the purpose of this form requirement is to assure the nonnegotiability of GmbH shares, and to make their transfer relatively cumbersome. See Decision of March 24, 1954, BGHZ 13, 49. By imposing the form requirement, the legislator effectively excluded GmbH shares not only from stock exchanges, but also from organized over-the-counter markets, which necessarily must insist on quick and easily consummated deals.

A power of attorney authorizing the agent to sell and transfer his principal's GmbH shares ordinarily does not require notarial form under the German rule discussed supra p. 772; but when the name of the purchaser is left blank in the power of attorney, it is evident that by such "stock power" arrangement the requirement of notarial form for each successive transfer is sought to be circumvented, and the German courts treat such a power as invalid.

Concerning the question whether the German requirement of "notarial" form for the transfer of a GmbH share can be met by a document executed before a notary outside of Germany, see infra pp. 873–875.

4. For comparative surveys, see, in addition to the articles cited supra nn. 1 and 3, Ph. J. Eder, Limited Responsibility Firms Abroad, 13 U.Pitt.L.Rev. 193 (1952); M. R. von Sternberg, The Close Corporation's Counterparts in France, Germany and the United Kingdom: A Comparative Study, 5 Hastings Int. & Comp.L.Rev. 291 (1982). The most extensive comparative treatment is De Sola Canizares & Aztiria, Tratado de Sociedades de Responsabilidad Limitada en Derecho Argentino y Comparado (2 vols. 1950–54).

4a. In Germany the one-person limited liability company was authorized as part of the 1980 amendments to the GmbH-law mentioned supra n. 3. See A. Baumbach & A. Hueck, GmbH Gesetz, § 1, Anno. 20 (14th. ed. by G. Hueck, J. Schulze-Osterloh & W. Zöllner 1985). In France, this was made possible by a Law No. 85–697 of July 11, 1985, amending art. 34 of the 1966 French statute on commercial companies.

5. See CCH Common Market Rep., Doing Business in Europe ¶23207 (1987).

6. See U. Drobnig, American-German Private International Law 274 (1972).

(3) As an alternative to the one-man GmbH, Liechtenstein has pioneered, and some Latin American countries have adopted, the idea that a sole trader, without incorporating, may obtain the privilege of limited liability, i.e. of liability limited to the assets of a certain enterprise, by complying with specified statutory requirements. See S. A. Bayitch, Empresa in Latin American Law: Recent Developments, 4 Lawyer of the Americas 1, at 2 and 14–20 (1972); M. Rotondi, Limited Liability of the Individual Trader: One-Man Company or Commercial Foundation?, 48 Tul.L.Rev. 989 (1974). In spite of its apparent attractiveness, especially from a tax point of view, this form of business organization does not seem to find much favor with businessmen.

(4) The GmbH as well as other forms of business organization developed in civil-law systems is used also in socialist countries of Eastern Europe.[7] Although its capital is apt to be owned by the State, such a socialist company is "usually registered in a public firm register[8] which contains details about the stated capital, activities, the signature powers of managers and, possibly, restrictions on their powers to assume liabilities."[9]

(5) In the United States, the draftsmen of corporation statutes were slow to recognize the special needs of close corporations. Until the middle of this century, the same basic form of corporate organization had to be used by a family seeking to incorporate a small hardware store, and by a giant corporation offering its stock to many thousands of shareholders. As the typical corporation laws were responsive to the needs of the big corporations, they failed to address the central problem of the close corporation: to combine the flexibility of a partnership with the advantages of a clearly separate and more permanent entity and of limited liability of all partners, including the managing ones.

During the last few decades, many states have injected more flexibility into their business corporation laws and have made it possible to draft charter provisions by which the organization of a stock corporation can be adapted to the needs of a small business.[10] Even after these salutary reforms, however, there remain some interesting differences between the limited liability company of the civil-law world, on the one hand, and the U.S.-style close corporation, on the other. For example:

(i) In the civil-law orbit, the stock corporation and the limited liability company normally are treated in separate statutes, or at least in entirely separate chapters of a code or similar enactment. In this country, on the other hand, most of the states that provide for special

7. See, e.g., A. Burzynski & J. C. Ju-ergensmeyer, East-West Co-operation: The Polish Example, 1 Loyola of L.A.Int. & Comp.L.Annual 37, 62–63 (1978).

8. The reader will find it interesting to note that our old friend, the commercial register, has survived in the socialist world.

9. R. Dagon, Cooperation Agreements and Joint Ventures with Socialist Business Associations: The Hungarian System, 21 Am.J.Comp.L. 752, 756 (1973).

10. See J.A.C. Hetherington, Special Characteristics, Problems, and Needs of

the Close Corporation, 1969 Ill.L.F. 1; F. Hodge O'Neal and T. D. Magill, California's New Close Corporation Legislation, 23 U.C.L.A.L.Rev. 1155 (1976); R. L. Jordan, The Close Corporation Provisions of the New California General Corporation Law, 23 U.C.L.A.L.Rev. 1094 (1976); Note, Separate Statutory Treatment of the Close Corporation in California: Progress and Problems, 27 Hastings L.J. 433 (1975); F. Hodge O'Neal, Close Corporation Legislation: A Survey and an Evaluation, 1972 Duke L.J. 867.

treatment of close corporations, do so without enacting a separate statute. This choice of legislative technique is not accidental. The authors of a law review article [11] suggest that there are three policy reasons which have persuaded American legislators to reject the civil-law technique of a separate statute: (a) It is difficult to arrive at a satisfactory definition of a "close corporation." (b) There is fear that separate legislation may make it harder for successful, growing close corporations to evolve into public-issue corporations. This fear is somewhat borne out by civil-law experience. In Germany, for instance, it was necessary to enact special (and fairly complex) statutory provisions authorizing the conversion of a G.m.b.H. into a stock corporation. See German Aktiengesetz (Stock Corporation Law) sections 376 to 383. (c) "Some members of the corporation Bar serving as advisors or draftsmen for new corporation statutes may have opposed separate legislative treatment of small incorporated enterprises, since such treatment might isolate the public-issue companies politically (depriving them of their identification with politically potent small business). This isolation might lead to separate and more severe regulation and taxation for the larger corporations." [12]

(ii) In those American corporation laws which contain some special provisions applicable to close corporations, the definition of a close corporation sometimes is predicated, at least in part, on the number of shareholders. In order to qualify as a close corporation, the company may not have more than a specified number of shareholders (e.g. 30 in Delaware and Pennsylvania; 10 in California).

The civil-law countries are divided on this point; some do, and some do not, limit the number of persons who can hold shares in a limited liability company. The principal techniques by which the civilians draw the line between the two types of corporations, are (a) to require a minimum capital, which is much higher in the case of a stock corporation than in that of a limited liability company; (b) to subject the stock corporation to much more stringent formation and disclosure requirements than is done in the case of a limited liability company; and (c) to make sure—e.g., by the requirement of notarial form for transfers—that the shares of a limited liability company cannot be represented by negotiable certificates and cannot be publicly traded.

A version of the last-mentioned technique is used by some of the American legislators as well. In Delaware and Pennsylvania, for example, a corporation cannot qualify as a close corporation unless its charter provides that the corporation shall make no offering of its stock which would constitute a "public offering" within the meaning of the Securities Act of 1933.[13]

11. O'Neal & Magill, supra n. 10.

12. Id., at 1155–56.

13. Id., at 1156.

4. PROTECTION OF CREDITORS AND MINORITY STOCKHOLDERS

A. PRESERVATION OF THE REGISTERED AMOUNT OF CAPITAL

OPINION OF THE GERMAN REICHSGERICHT IN THE MATTER OF NEUERGASTHOF G.M.B.H. ET AL., DEFENDANTS v. K., PLAINTIFF

2nd Civil Division, December 14, 1928, RGZ 123, 102.

Reported ante, p. 615.

NOTES AND QUESTIONS

In many civil-law countries, rather substantial minimum capital requirements must be met by stock corporations. See supra p. 802. The amount required as the minimum capital of a limited responsibility company, on the other hand, is invariably modest. See, e.g., supra p. 830. Even a company of the latter type, however, may have a capital much in excess of the statutory minimum (only very few countries prescribe a maximum). Once the company has registered and published the actual amount of its capital, whatever it may be, the principle of publicity (supra pp. 696–702) demands preservation, so far as possible, of the capital basis thus announced to the public. Repayment of capital to a shareholder is prohibited;[1] violation of this prohibition subjects the managers and all of the shareholders (not only those who benefited from the return of capital) to personal liability.[2]

A further consequence of the same principle is illustrated by the Neuergasthof case. Would a court of equity in a common-law country reach a similar result? See supra p. 619.

B. MINORITY STOCKHOLDERS' "EQUITABLE" REMEDIES

OPINION OF THE GERMAN REICHSGERICHT IN THE MATTER OF S.S. v. M.E. CORP.

2nd Civil Division, January 22, 1935, RGZ 146, 385.

Reported ante, p. 567.

---

1. See, e.g., § 30 of the German Law Concerning Limited Responsibility Companies.

2. Id., § 31. In all the twelve Member States of the European Economic Community, these rules have been strengthened by the Community's Second Directive on company law, mentioned supra p. 795, n. 5. One additional consequence of the principle of the maintenance of the stated capital is a general rule which severely restricts the acquisition by a company of its own stock.

COMMERCIAL COURT OF THE CANTON OF ZURICH
OPINION OF SEPTEMBER 12, 1947

44 Schweizerische Juristen-Zeitung 175 (1948).

Reported ante, p. 807.

NOTES AND QUESTIONS

(1) *Substantive Rights.* Our courts of equity, by imposing fiduciary duties on management and majority stockholders, protect the minority from many types of abuses. In civil-law countries, minority stockholders may, as the principal cases show, derive a measure of similar protection from a combination of

(a) specific statutory provisions, such as voting prohibitions designed to prevent the majority stockholders from voting in favor of transactions which would benefit them as individuals;

(b) recognition of certain shareholders' rights which cannot be destroyed or impaired by majority action, and of which an individual shareholder, however small his investment may be, cannot be deprived without his consent;

(c) the rule, usually embodied in express provisions of the written law, that directors and officers (or their counterparts in the somewhat differently organized corporations of the civil-law world) owe the corporation a duty, not only to refrain from intentional wrongdoing, but affirmatively to exercise due care in promoting the corporation's interests; and

(d) the doctrine that every shareholder owes the corporation a "duty of faithfulness", as the German court put it in one of the principal cases.[1]

The substantive rules invoked in continental countries for the protection of minority stockholders thus have a degree of flexibility which makes them truly comparable to the equitable doctrines by which our courts enforce the fiduciary duties of management and majority.[1a] We now turn to the problem of implementing these rights.

---

1. In the German case, this duty of faithfulness was in fact imposed on a minority stockholder. It follows a fortiori that majority stockholders are subject to the same duty. For interesting examples of cases in which French courts prevented majority abuses by invoking the doctrine of bona fides and abuse of rights, see Micou, Corporate Financing Under Latin-American Law, 22 Cornell L.Q. 490, 508–10 (1937). Professor Goebel argues that "Concepts of fiduciary limits on majority stockholders also exist in other countries in varying degrees", citing, in support, Le Gall, French Company Law 171–76 (1974); Verrucoli, Italian Company Law 142–49 (1977); Würdinger, German Company Law 60–62 (1975). R. J. Goebel, Professional Responsibility Issues in International Law

Practice, 29 Am.J.Comp.L. 1, 10, n. 23 (1981).

In Latin-America, on the other hand, litigants and courts have been relatively slow in resorting to these flexible doctrines developed in Europe. See Ph. J. Eder, Company Law in Latin America, 27 Notre Dame Law. 5, 223, 240–41 (1952); N. S. Poser, Securities Regulation in Developing Countries: The Brazilian Experience, 52 Va.L.Rev. 1283, 1300–02 (1966).

1a. See, e.g., L. B. Warren and C. L. Willard, A Comparative View of the New French Approach to Corporate Conflicts of Interest, 24 Bus.Law. 809 (1969). See also infra n. 2, and the article by Starr, cited infra n. 14.

(2) *Problems of Procedure.* What are the *remedies* by which minority stockholders can enforce the substantive rights listed above?[2] Under our system, a court of equity has almost complete freedom to fashion the appropriate remedy in order to redress a breach of fiduciary duty. Some of the weapons in the Chancellor's armory, such as the equitable receivership, are unknown to the civilians (see supra p. 619); but other "equitable" remedies are recognized by the codes.

(a) The basic principle of the stockholders' derivative action is well known to the civilians. It seems that in most civil-law countries a minority shareholder, or in any event a minority group holding a certain percentage of the outstanding stock, can compel members of the management to indemnify the corporation for damages caused by their wrongful acts or omissions, or can at least compel the corporation to seek such recovery from members of the management. In practice, however, derivative actions do not play a significant role in civil-law countries. This is due to a variety of reasons, some of which relate to general features—studied in earlier parts of this course—of the legal process in civil-law countries:

(i) The "general clauses" of the civil codes tend to encourage the courts, at least in the more progressive civil-law countries, to be bold in developing new substantive rights. The procedural codes, however, do not contain such "general clauses", with the result that the same courts which frequently create new law in order to expand *substantive* rights, are quite reluctant to fashion *procedural* devices not sanctioned by the written law. See supra pp. 291–294.

The flexibility with which the remedial aspects of the derivative action have been molded by our courts of equity, thus has no counterpart in civil-law systems, where the conditions and requirements for bringing the action are necessarily laid down in provisions of a code or other statute.[2a] These provisions tend to be rigid and restrictive. Generally, if the majority of the shareholders declines to bring an action against members of the management, such action can be instituted (or its institution compelled) only by a minority group holding a specified minimum percentage—such as 10% and in some countries more than that—of the total outstanding capital of the corporation. In the case of large corporations, it

2. See M. Koessler, The Stockholder's Suit: A Comparative View, 46 Colum.L. Rev. 238 (1946); D. Eckert, Shareholder and Management: A Comparative View on Some Corporate Problems in the United States and Germany, 46 Iowa L.Rev. 12, 70 ff. (1960); E. C. Steefel and B. von Falkenhausen, The New German Stock Corporation Law, 52 Cornell L.Q. 518, 539–49 (1967); R. R. Dillenbeck, The Shareholder's Suit in Mexican Law, 9 Am.J.Comp.L. 78 (1960); M. R. Sonnenreich, Protecting the United States Minority Shareholder in Joint International Business Ventures in Latin America, 5 Va.J.Int.L. 1 (1964); E. Cazorla, Derivative Actions Under Spanish Corporation Law, 4 Tex.Int.L.F. 359 (1968); Eder, supra n. 1; Keiji Matsumoto, Management Responsibility to Minority Share-holders in Japan: Derivative Suit in West-East Melting Pot, 18 N.Y.L.F. 377 (1972); W. N. Munyon, Shareholders' Rights in the Common Market: A Comparative Study, 9 Cornell Int.L.J. 191 (1976); B. Grossfeld, Management and Control of Marketable Share Companies, in Vol. XIII, Ch. 4, of the International Encyclopedia of Comparative Law, at 107–32 (1973); A. Conard, Fundamental Changes in Marketable Share Companies, in Vol. XIII, Ch. 6 of the same Encyclopedia, at 107–11 (1972).

2a. The relative weakness of discovery devices in civil-law countries (see supra pp. 426–428) also tends to work to the detriment of plaintiffs in derivative stockholders' actions. See Keiji Matsumoto, supra n. 2.

is often practically impossible to assemble a minority group which meets this requirement.

(ii) Considerations of expense tend to discourage stockholders' derivative actions in civil-law countries. The amount in controversy is apt to be large in such an action; therefore, under the statutory tariffs prevailing in most of those countries, the sum total of the litigation expenses may be very considerable. A contingent fee arrangement usually is not possible under a civil-law system.[3] Thus the plaintiff faces the discouraging prospect that if he loses he will have to pay not only taxable costs, but also the—possibly very high—fees of his own attorney. Worse still, under the "loser pays all" rule he will in that event have to shoulder, in addition, the fees of the victorious lawyers for the other side. The total burden thus imposed on an unsuccessful plaintiff may well be ruinous. A conscientious lawyer will so advise the plaintiff before he ventures into a stockholders' suit.

In some civil-law countries, the minority group does not itself bring the action seeking recovery from members of the management; the minority shareholders merely compel the corporation to institute the litigation. Thus the minority shareholders may not be parties to the action. This, however, does not necessarily insulate them from the risk of having to bear the litigation expenses. The German Stock Corporation Act, for example, provides in § 147, subs. 4, that "If a minority has requested the assertion of the claim for damages, and if the company has become liable for payment of the costs of the action because it was wholly or partially defeated in such action, the minority shall be obligated to reimburse the company for these costs.. . . ."

(iii) As has been mentioned previously, the organization of corporations in most civil-law countries is more "democratic" than here, in the sense that many matters require stockholder action which under our law would be decided by the board of directors.[4] As a result, the derivative action often affords no practical remedy because "the rascals" have acted in their capacity as majority stockholders, or as proxies for an anonymous majority, and not as directors or officers.

The effectiveness of the derivative action is further impaired by the fact that under the statutes and corporate practice of most civil-law countries, the annual stockholders' meeting may, and in proper cases must, grant the management so-called *décharge* by adopting a resolution approving the conduct of the management for the past fiscal year (see the German principal case). Such a resolution may be adopted by a simple majority.[4a] Inasmuch as

3. Because of the absence from the civil-law scene of the contingent fee, there is also lacking "the disturbing, but often effective, presence of lawyers specializing in plaintiffs' cases." D. F. Vagts, Reforming the "Modern" Corporation: Perspectives from the German, 80 Harv.L.Rev. 23, at 60 (1966).

4. See the articles cited supra n. 2.

4a. It should be noted that civil-law stock corporation statutes generally con-

tain rules intended to make sure that stockholders have adequate information, not based exclusively on that furnished by management, when voting to approve the annual accounts. Thus provisions for an audit by independent auditors are common. In France, in addition, stockholders representing at least ten percent of the capital, the public prosecutor, the works council and, in the case of corporations with publicly traded securities, the *Com-*

majority stockholders and members of the management usually are in the same camp, the *décharge* is a device by which in effect the controlling group approves its own managerial conduct. Unless set aside or declared invalid by the court, such approval constitutes a waiver of any cause of action which the corporation might have in connection with the conduct of management during the year in question, and thus will establish a good defense in a derivative suit based on such conduct. This, at least, is the traditional rule. Although it has been changed in some civil-law countries,[5] it still prevails in others.[6] As a result, two actions often are required in order to enforce the liability of members of the management for their wrongful acts: First a resolution granting *décharge* may have to be set aside in an action such as the one illustrated by the German principal case, and only if that action is successful, can a direct action against the alleged wrongdoers be brought on behalf of the corporation.

(b) Because of these weaknesses of the derivative action, minority stockholders in civil-law countries tend to rely more heavily on other remedies:

(i) Both of the principal cases illustrate the type of remedy which probably is the most frequently used weapon of minority stockholders in civil-law systems: the action to set aside, or to have declared void, a resolution adopted by the majority.[6a] Any stockholders' resolution may be so attacked, whether it seeks to amend the charter (as in the Swiss case), or to grant *décharge* to the management (as in the German case), or to exercise any other power of the stockholders. The attack will be successful if the resolution, by its terms or by the procedure which led to its adoption, violates the law or the charter. See the statutory provisions quoted in the two principal cases.[7] The "law" violated by a majority resolution may be a code provision embodying a specific

---

mission des Opérations de la Bourse, may ask the court to appoint experts to investigate and report on one or more aspects of the company's operations. If experts are appointed, their report is then annexed to the report of the official auditors which must be presented to the shareholders' annual meeting. See Law No. 66–537 of July 24, 1966, as amended by Law No. 84–148 of March 1, 1984.

5. In Germany, for instance, the Stock Corporation Law now provides that the *décharge* (unless granted unanimously) does not operate as a waiver. See Steefel and von Falkenhausen, supra n. 2, at 548; see also supra pp. 567–568. But if the company involved is a GmbH rather than a stock corporation, the *décharge* still has its traditional waiver effect under German law. See A. Baumbach & A. Hueck, GmbH-Gesetz, § 46, Anno. 26 (14th ed. by G. Hueck, J. Schulze-Osterloh & W. Zöllner 1985).

6. See Eder, supra n. 1, at 233. See also the interesting discussion of Venezuelan law in Hausman v. Buckley, 299 F.2d

696 (2d Cir. 1962), cert. den. 369 U.S. 885, 82 S.Ct. 1157 (1962).

6a. While not unknown in our law (see supra p. 569), this type of action is relatively infrequent here.

7. In France, a similar result formerly was reached in the absence of express statutory provisions. The courts developed the theory that a stockholders' resolution, even though all the requisite formalities have been observed in its adoption, may constitute an *abus des droits* on the part of the majority. In such event, every outvoted minority stockholder formerly could bring an action to have the resolution set aside. See 1 Escarra, Manuel de droit commercial 472 (1947); R. S. Saint, France: Stockholder Protection, 9 Am.J.Comp.L. 693, especially at 698–700 (1960).

The Company Law of July 24, 1966, provides in Art. 360 that a corporate act other than the founding of the company or an amendment of the charter can be annulled only if it violates a *cogent* provision "of this Law" or of the laws relating to contracts. It may be assumed that under the new

rule. As the principal cases show, however, it may also be one of the broad "general clauses" (supra pp. 702–766), and the resolution adopted by the majority will be set aside in an action seasonably brought by a minority stockholder if the court is persuaded that such resolution was prompted by motives, or adopted for purposes, which are inconsistent with the principles of boni mores and bona fides.[8]

In spite of its flexibility and broad scope, the action to annul or set aside a stockholders' resolution is not always effective in remedying corporate abuses. As in the case of the derivative action, many potential plaintiffs are deterred by fear of crushing litigation expenses.[9] If an action is commenced by a courageous plaintiff, it is clear that he carries the heavy burden of proving a violation of law or charter. For instance, in a conflict-of-interest situation of the kind exemplified by the German principal case, the plaintiff must prove the facts which indicate that some of the majority shareholders voted in violation of a statutory voting prohibition. The task of meeting this burden of proof often is rendered difficult, if not impossible, by the veil of anonymity which the bearer share draws over the identity of the true owners of the majority stock.[10] The weakness of the discovery devices available under civil-law procedure (see supra p. 428) may make it a hopeless endeavor to lift that veil. In the end, moreover, even a victorious plaintiff can accomplish no more in this type of action than to have a certain stockholders' resolution annulled. The impact of the remedy, in other words, is essentially negative.[10a] If affirmative relief against

Law a resolution can still be judicially nullified if it is illicit or immoral within the meaning of Art. 1133 of the French Civil Code, an undoubtedly "cogent" provision (see supra p. 747.) But—in contrast to the German and Swiss provisions quoted in the principal cases—the French statute apparently does not authorize a minority shareholder to attack a resolution on the ground that it violates the corporate charter. See Conard, supra n. 2, at 108.

8. For an Italian case illustrating this point, see Note, Minority Challenge of Majority Actions in a Close Corporation in Italy and the United States, 1959 Duke L.J. 116.

Concerning German law, see the detailed discussion by W. Zöllner, Die Schranken mitgliedschaftlicher Stimmrechtsmacht bei den privatrechtlichen Personenverbänden 287–356 (1963). The study retains its value although it was published before the passage of the Stock Corporation Act of 1965.

9. The German Stock Corporation Act in § 247 attempts to make the burden somewhat less formidable in actions to set aside a stockholders' resolution. The complicated provisions of that section in essence give the court discretionary power to

reduce the *Gegenstandswert* (see supra p. 364) in such actions, i.e., to reduce it below the amount fixed by the general statutes establishing a tariff for court costs and attorneys' fees.

10. See Dillenbeck, supra n. 2, at 81.

10a. If the shareholders' resolution under attack is itself purely negative, i.e. if it is a refusal to adopt a motion made by the plaintiff minority shareholder, German courts will permit the plaintiff to ask not only for judicial rescission of the resolution actually passed, but also for a judicial declaration to the effect that the opposite resolution (i.e. the affirmative resolution in favor of plaintiff's motion which would have been adopted had there been no violation of the charter) is deemed to have been passed. See BGHZ 97, 28 (1986); K. Schmidt, Rechtsschutz des Minderheitsgesellschafters gegen rechtswidrige ablehnende Beschlüsse, 39 N.J.W. 2018, 2020 (1986). Concerning an additional case expanding the protection of minority shareholders, see R. M. Buxbaum, Extension of Parent Company Shareholders' Rights to Participate in the Governance of Subsidiaries, 31 Am.J.Comp.L. 511 (1983), discussing BGH, February 25, 1982, 37 J.Z. 602 (1982).

members of the management team is needed, it must be sought in a second action.[10b]

(ii) It may be questionable whether any of the *civil* remedies discussed above will effectively deter a dishonorable management from embarking on a course of wrongdoing. In many civil-law countries, however, there are *penal* provisions, often embodied in the corporation statutes, which are so drastic and of such broad scope that they may well induce some hesitation on the part of the would-be wrongdoers. For example, the French Company Law of July 24, 1966, in a provision substantially copied from the old (1867) statute, threatens with heavy fines and one to five years of imprisonment every member of the top management of a stock corporation who "in bad faith has knowingly used the corporation's property or credit, . . . [or] has knowingly used his own official powers . . . in a manner contrary to the interest of the corporation, for personal ends or in order to favor another company or enterprise in which he is directly or indirectly interested." [11]

In France and in some of the other civil-law countries,[11a] the effectiveness of such penal sanctions is enhanced by the fact that a victimized private party can institute, or join in, the criminal proceeding. See supra pp. 492–497. An illustration is offered by the French case summarized in the next paragraph.

(3) *A French Case.* Tribunal Correctionnel de la Seine, Decision of November 14, 1958, reported in Dalloz 1959.568 (with an annotation by Professor Pierre Bonassies): A minority stockholder had caused the institution of a criminal proceeding (hereafter referred to as the first proceeding) against members of the management, on the alleged ground that the defendants had abused their powers as corporate officers in violation of the broad provisions of the statute quoted above (or rather, to be precise, of the similarly worded predecessor statute). That proceeding, which lasted 12 years, finally culminated in a court order exonerating the defendants and dismissing the information. During the pendency of that first proceeding, in accordance with resolutions adopted at several meetings of the stockholders, the defendants used corporate funds to pay for the substantial legal expenses occasioned by the proceeding. The minority stockholder who had initiated the first proceeding thereupon caused a second criminal proceeding to be instituted, on the ground that the payment of those legal expenses from corporate funds was a new abuse of the defendants' power over corporate property. This second proceeding resulted in a conviction. The court held that the obligations incurred for the services of the lawyers who represented the defendants in the first proceeding, were personal

---

10b. If in the first action (the action to set aside a stockholders' resolution) the plaintiff was able to prove wrongdoing on the part of management, the second action may well be a derivative action seeking to recover damages from the culprits. In some countries, minority shareholders may also be able to bring an action to remove the culpable directors. In Japan, such an action may be coupled with an application for a temporary order appointing "acting directors". See Keiji Matsumoto, supra n. 2, at 391.

11. Art. 437, subds. 3 and 4, of the new Law. These provisions are comprehensively annotated in the work by Constantin, cited infra n. 14.

11a. The relevant criminal penalties appear to have been strengthened in several countries in recent years. For German law, see A. Kmenth, Kapitalanlagebetrug und Börsendelikte im 2. Gesetz zur Bekämpfung der Wirtschaftskriminalität, 40 N.J.W. 28 (1987).

debts of the defendants, and that the latter had no right to pay these individual debts out of the corporate till.

Note that the minority stockholder had not even taken the trouble of bringing a civil action to set aside the stockholders' resolutions by which the majority had approved the payments. The court brushed these resolutions aside by remarking that the payments were illegal, and that a resolution authorizing the management to engage in an illegal act is absolutely void.[12] In his critical annotation, Professor Bonassies disagreed with this last point. In his view, the stockholders' assembly had the power to authorize the payments, with the result that the payments thus authorized could not be treated as illegal.[13]

The court did not impose a prison sentence upon the defendants, probably for the reason that before the institution of the second criminal proceeding they had reimbursed the corporation for the full amount of the legal expenses previously paid by the corporation. This reimbursement, however, could be regarded only as a mitigating circumstance; it did not extinguish the criminal character of the acts committed by the defendants. The latter, therefore, were ordered to pay a substantial fine.[14]

Whether or not one agrees with the court's reasoning in this particular instance, the case clearly shows that at least in those civil-law systems which permit a private victim to become an active party in a criminal proceeding, the criminal process serves some of the functions of an American-style stockholders' suit.[15]

III. CONFLICT OF LAWS

INTRODUCTORY NOTE

Fortunately for the domestic practitioner, comparative legal literature on the subject of conflict of laws is so abundant and of such high quality that even without substantial knowledge of foreign languages

12. Compare the discussion in the German principal case concerning the distinction between void and voidable resolutions.

13. If the case had arisen under the 1966 Law, the provision of Art. 360 of that Law (see supra n. 7) might conceivably furnish an additional argument against the view taken by the court.

As an American reader will readily realize, the same issue has given rise to voluminous discussion, litigation and legislation in this country. See H. G. Henn and J. R. Alexander, Laws of Corporations, §§ 379 and 380 (3d ed., 1983, and 1986 Supp.)

14. The decision of the Tribunal Correctionnel was reversed by the intermediate appellate court in Paris; but this reversal was in turn reversed by the Cour de Cassation, which remanded the case to the intermediate appellate court at Amiens. The latter court affirmed the original decision of the Tribunal Correctionnel. See R. I. Starr, Protection of Stockholders' Rights in the French Société Anonyme, 40 Tul.L.Rev. 57, at 92–93 (1965); L. Constantin, Droit Pénal des Sociétés par Actions 651–52 (1968), where the successive decisions of the appellate courts are cited.

15. It would seem that in general the civil-law codes, drafted against the background of efficient police systems and (in the case of France and French-influenced codes) of active victim-participation in the criminal process, often rely on criminal sanctions when dealing with situations in which our law would resort to civil remedies. For another example, see the discussion of trusts and powers of attorney, supra pp. 783–784.

he can study the pertinent rules of most civil-law countries.[1]   Several works of admirable scholarship offer a convenient starting point for research in this field and an astounding wealth of citations.[2]

Any comprehensive comparative study of conflict of laws would require an entire course.   No more is intended here than to convey a first impression of the typical form and structure of conflicts rules fitted into the framework of a codified legal system, and to study the operation of such rules in relation to two relatively narrow illustrative topics: the problem of nationality as a basis of judicial jurisdiction, and the questions of choice-of-law arising in connection with contingent fee agreements.   These topics have been chosen for two reasons.   Their study, first of all, will add a new dimension to important subjects previously studied in this course.   Secondly, a discussion of these topics will permit a glimpse at two distinctive features of civilian conflicts doctrine: the *nationality theory* and the doctrine of *ordre public*.

Both the nationality theory and the doctrine of ordre public are intimately connected with those historical and methodological aspects of the civil law which have been emphasized in earlier parts of this book.   The nationality theory springs from the same concept of law as one of the unifying symbols and attributes of a nation which lies at the very root of a system of national codes;[3] and the doctrine of ordre public, which qualifies every other rule of conflict of laws, illustrates the civilian codifiers' technique of using broad and pervasive "general clauses".

1. CONFLICTS RULES BUILT INTO A CODE SYSTEM: THEIR FORM AND STRUCTURE

ITALIAN CIVIL CODE OF 1942 (PRELIMINARY DISPOSITIONS) [a]

Art. 17. *Law Governing the Status and Capacity of Persons and Family Relationships.*   The status and capacity of persons and family

1. For bibliographies, see each of the three volumes of the work by Ehrenzweig & Jayme, cited infra n. 2.   For a more recent bibliography, see F. K. Juenger, General Course on Private International Law (1983), 1985[IV] Hague Ac. Coll. Courses 377–87.

2. See the four-volume work by E. Rabel, The Conflict of Laws: A Comparative Study (1st ed. 1945–58; 2d ed. of the first three vols., prepared by U. Drobnig and H. Bernstein, 1958–64) as well as the three-volume work by A. A. Ehrenzweig & E. Jayme, Private International Law (1967–77).   Mention should be made, also, of the multi-volume series entitled "Bilateral Studies in Private International Law", published by Columbia University's Parker School of Foreign and Comparative Law. A further bilateral study, not belonging to that series, is S. A. Bayitch & J. L. Si-

queiros, Conflict of Laws: Mexico and the United States (1968).

A comparative approach is adopted, also, in the recent work by F. K. Juenger, supra n. 1, and on some points in the textbook by E. Scoles & P. Hay, Conflict of Laws (Student Ed. 1982, Lawyers' Ed. 1984, and Supp.).

3. Concerning the history of conflict of laws theories, and the emergence of the nationality doctrine in 19th century Europe, see A. Nussbaum, Rise and Decline of the Law-of-Nations Doctrine in the Conflict of Laws, 42 Colum.L.Rev. 189 (1942).

a. This introductory chapter of the Italian Civil Code is interestingly discussed in the article by McCusker, The Italian Rules of Conflict of Laws, 25 Tulane L.Rev. 70 (1950).   The article also contains translations of the pertinent Code provisions.

relationships are governed by the law of the State to which the persons belong.

However, an alien who performs within the State an act for which he lacks capacity according to his national law, is deemed to have capacity if for such act a citizen has capacity according to Italian law, unless it is a matter of family relationships, of successions "causa mortis," of gifts, or of acts disposing of immovables situated abroad.

Art. 18. *Law Governing Personal Relationships Between Spouses.* Personal relationships between spouses of different citizenships are governed by the last national law which has been theirs in common during the marriage, or, if there were no such common citizenship, by the national law of the husband at the time of celebration of the marriage.[b]

Art. 19. *Law Governing Property Regimes Between Spouses.* Property regimes between spouses are governed by the national law of the husband at the time of celebration of the marriage.

Change of citizenship of the spouses does not affect the property regimes, except for contracts between the spouses based on the new common national law.

Art. 20. *Law Governing the Relationships Between Parents and Children.* Relationships between parents and children are governed by the national law of the father, or by the national law of the mother if only maternity is ascertained or if only the mother has legitimated the child.

Relationships between adopting parent and adopted child are governed by the national law of the adopting parent at the time of adoption.

Art. 21. *Law Governing Guardianship.* Guardianship and other institutions for the protection of incompetents are governed by the national law of the incompetent.

These translations have been used in the text, supra. For a translation of the entire Code, see M. Beltramo, G. E. Longo & J. H. Merryman, The Italian Civil Code (1969, and 1978 Supp.).

b. The majority of recent Italian authors doubt whether the reference to the national law of the husband in articles 18, 19 and 20 is constitutional, since the Italian Constitution contains an "equal protection" clause. See G. Cian & A. Trabucchi, Commentario Breve al Codice Civile, Disp. Prel. art. 18, Anno. 8 (1984). The constitutionality of art. 20 came before the Italian Constitutional Court in 1983 in a case involving several related issues, but the court dismissed the challenge to that article on procedural grounds. It did, however, invalidate provisions of the Italian nationality law, also involved in the case, that made it easier for children to acquire Italian nationality if their father, rather than their mother, was an Italian citizen. This seems a clear indication that the Court will strike down discriminatory rules if they are properly before it. See Corte Costituzionale, Feb. 9, 1983, No. 30, 19 Riv. Dir.Int.Priv. & Proc. 601 (1983).

In 1985, the Italian Minister of Justice appointed a committee, chaired by Prof. R. Monaco, for the purpose of reforming the Italian conflict of laws rules. It will undoubtedly deal with the constitutional issue. See 21 Riv.Dir.Int.Priv. & Proc. 687 (1985). An earlier draft of reformed conflicts provisions, prepared by Prof. E. Vitta in 1984, was published in Consiglio Nazionale del Notariato, Problemi di riforma del diritto internazionale privato italiano (1986).

Art. 22. *Law Governing Possession, Ownership and Other Property Rights.* Possession, ownership and other property rights in movables and immovables are governed by the law of the place in which the movables and immovables are situated.

Art. 23. *Law Governing Successions "Causa Mortis."* Successions "causa mortis" are governed by the law of the State to which the person whose inheritance is in question belonged at the moment of his death, wherever the property may be.

Art. 24. *Law Governing Gifts.* Gifts are governed by the national law of the donor.

Art. 25. *Law Governing Obligations.* Obligations arising from contract are governed by the national law of the contracting parties, if it is common; otherwise by the law of the place in which the contract was concluded. In every case the different intention of the parties controls.

Non-contract obligations are governed by the law of the place where the facts from which they arise took place.

Art. 26. *Law Governing the Form of Acts.* The form of *inter vivos* acts and of acts of last will is governed by the law of the place in which the act is completed or by the law which governs the substance of the act, or by the national law of the transferor or by the national law of the contracting parties, if it is common.

The forms of publication of acts creating, transferring and extinguishing rights in things are governed by the law of the place in which the things themselves are located.

Art. 27. *Law Governing Procedure.* Competence [c] and procedure are governed by the law of the place in which the action is brought.

Art. 28. *Efficacy of Penal and Police Laws.* Penal laws and laws of the police and public security bind all those who are within the territory of the State.

Art. 29. *Stateless Persons.* If a person has no citizenship, the law of the place where he resides is applied in all cases in which, according to the foregoing provisions, the national law should be applied.

Art. 30. *Renvoi to Another Law.* When by the terms of the foregoing Articles, foreign law must be applied, the provisions of the

---

c. In Italian law, a sharp distinction is drawn between questions of "competence", which go to the distribution of judicial business among the various courts of the Italian Republic, and questions of "jurisdiction", which relate to the conditions under which a person may be made a party defendant before the courts of the Republic, as distinguished from the courts of other nations. See M. Cappelletti and J. M. Perillo, Civil Procedure in Italy 80–83 (1965). Although clearly differentiated, both "com-petence" and "jurisdiction" are treated in the Code of Civil Procedure.

The conflicts provisions of the Italian *Civil Code*, set forth in the text, deal only with choice-of-law, and not with jurisdiction. A similar system is followed in many of the other civil-law countries which have relatively modern codes. The older French codes, on the other hand, are less systematically arranged and deal with some jurisdictional problems in the Civil Code, as we shall see below.

law itself are applied without taking into account any provision of that law for renvoi.

Art. 31. Notwithstanding the provisions of the foregoing articles, the laws and acts of a foreign state, the regulations and acts of any institution or entity, or private dispositions and agreements, cannot in any case have any effect within the territory of this State if they are contrary to the public order or contra bonos mores.

NOTES AND QUESTIONS

(1) The French Civil Code of 1804 devoted only one article, art. 3, to general choice-of-law questions. It provided that "police and safety" laws bound all persons, even foreigners, in France; that immovables in France, even those owned by foreigners, were governed by French law; and that questions concerning the capacity and status of French nationals, even those living abroad, were also governed by that law. (The choice-of-law provisions of the Austrian Civil Code of 1811 were not much more detailed). The current French choice-of-law rules are thus basically the work of legal authors and of the courts. Later codifiers tended to include more detailed rules in their code or, frequently, in an Introductory Law promulgated as part of the code. Not infrequently, they followed art. 3 of the French Civil Code in one respect: these rules indicated when forum law was applicable, but not what law was to be applied when forum law was not (so-called "unilateral" rules, prevalent, e.g., in the original Introductory Law of the German Civil Code). Again, creative work by scholars and the courts was necessary to establish, on that basis, a comprehensive choice-of-law system. Even more fully worked out ("bilateral") rules, such as those of the Italian Civil Code, reproduced above, were in need of amplification. The role of scholarly comment and theory, and of judge-made law, has thus been particularly significant in the conflict-of-laws area.[1]

The past decade has seen a trend towards the revision of many of the rules mentioned. There were several reasons for this. In some countries, a number of existing choice-of-law rules, particularly those focusing on the nationality of the husband in family law matters, had been declared unconstitutional because they violated "equal protection" or "protection of the family" provisions of recently enacted constitutions[2]. Some choice-of-law provisions of this kind were so obviously unconstitutional that they had to be changed, though not yet declared unconstitutional by a formal court decision.[3] Also, the shifts in population due first to the Second World War and then to the migration of workers, created large pools of non-citizens in many countries. This made it desirable to attenuate the nationality principle. Furthermore,

1. See generally, 1 Rabel, the Conflict of Laws: A Comparative Study 29–32 (2d ed, by U. Drobnig 1958); A. N. Makarov, Sources, in Vol. III, Ch. 2 of the International Encyclopedia of Comparative Law (1972). Cf. P. H. Neuhaus, Die Grundbegriffe des internationalen Privatrechts (2d. ed. 1976).

2. For Germany, see e.g. BVerfG, Nov. 30, 1982, 2 I.Prax. 88 (1982); December 3, 1985, 39 N.J.W. 655 (1986); cf. BGH, Sept. 17, 1986, 40 N.J.W. 583 (1987).

3. This was the case in Spain, where the enactment of a new constitution after the fall of Generalissimo Franco eventually led to the adoption of a new marriage law with revised conflict of laws provisions. See J. A. Carillo Salcedo, La nouvelle réglementation du mariage dans le droit international privé espagnol, 72 Rev.cr.d.i.p. 1 (1983) (with a translation of the statute at p. 140). See also the Italian developments noted supra, p. 843, n. b.

in 1980, the (then) ten Member States of the European Economic Community signed a Convention concerning the law applicable to contracts.[4] Its ratification is progressing only slowly and it is not yet in effect.[5] But its detailed and innovative provisions have influenced national codifications and led to much scholarly comment.[6] Finally, the "revolution" in American conflicts thinking also had some impact. Though the notion (inherent, e.g., in Prof. Currie's analysis) that conflicts problems could be solved completely without rules, only on the basis of a methodology, did not find favor, the related notion that substantive concerns could not be ignored in a conflicts setting was often viewed sympathetically and had some impact.[7] The extent to which the territorial coverage of a statute could, in some cases, be determined by reference to its own terms, rather than through standard choice-of-law rules, had indeed been the topic of some discussion in Europe even before American theories received detailed attention.[8]

As a result of such considerations, many countries revised their existing statutory conflicts rules, or adopted wholly new ones.[9] In Western Europe, recent revisions of codified choice-of-law rules occurred, e.g., in Austria in 1978 (effective January 1, 1979)[10], in West

4. Convention on the law applicable to contractual obligations, Opened for Signature, Rome, June 19, 1980, 1980 O.J. No. L 266, p. 1.

5. By the end of 1986, only Denmark, Germany, France and Italy had adopted legislation approving its ratification. Ratification by seven countries is necessary for the Convention to go into effect. Since it is not directly based on the EEC Treaty, but merely complementary to it, it does not enjoy the immediate direct applicability of regular EEC law.

6. For the views of the Convention's draftsmen, see the Report by M. Giuliano and P. Lagarde at 1980 O.J. No. C 282, p. 1. For Prof. Lagarde's views, see also P. Lagarde, The EEC Convention on the Law Applicable to Contractual Obligations, in Harmonization of Laws in the European Communities 49 (P. Herzog, ed. 1983). Cf. e.g. I. F. Fletcher, Conflict of Laws and European Community Law (1982); A. J. E. Jaffey, The English Proper Law Doctrine and the EEC Convention, 33 Int. & Comp. L.Q. 531 (1984); F. K. Juenger, The European Convention on the law Applicable to Contractual Obligations: Some Critical Observations, 22 Va.J.Int.L. 123 (1981); P. M. North, The EEC Convention on the Law applicable to Contractual Obligations, 1980 J.Bus.L. 382; R. J. Weintraub, Functional Developments in Choice of Law for Contracts, 1984[IV] Hague Ac. Coll. Courses 239, 278–89.

7. For discussions of the impact of modern American conflicts thinking on European courts, see e.g. G. Kegel, The Crisis of Conflict of Laws, 1964[II] Hague Ac. Coll. Courses 91; F. K. Juenger, Trends in Euro-

pean Conflicts Law, 60 Cornell L.Rev. 969, 970–77 (1975); B. Audit, A Continental Lawyer Looks at Contemporary American Choice-of-Law Principles, 27 Am.J.Comp.L. 589 (1979), with comments by A. T. von Mehren (at 605) and F. K. Juenger (at 609); Symposium, The Influence of Modern American Conflicts Theories on European Law, 30 Am.J.Comp.L. 1 ff. (1982), with contributions by B. Hanotiau, F. K. Juenger, A. Lowenfeld and E. Vitta. Cf. O. Lando, New American Choice of Law Principles and the European Conflict of Laws Convention, 30 Am.J.Comp.L. 19 (1982); E. Vitta, Influenze americane nella convenzione CEE sulle obbligazioni contrattuali, 19 Riv.Dir.Int.Priv. & Proc. 261 (1983). See most recently, B. Audit, Le caractère fonctionnel de la règle de conflit, 1984[III] Hague Ac. Coll. Courses 219; P. Lagarde, Le principe de proximité dans le Droit International Privé Contemporain, 1986[I] Hague Ac. Coll. Courses 9.

8. E.g., Ph. Franceskakis, Quelques précisions sur les lois d'application immédiate, 55 Rev.cr.d.i.p. 11 (1966). Cf. P. Hay, Comments on Self-Limited Rules of Law in Conflicts Methodology, 30 Am.J.Comp.L. 129 (1982).

9. For a critique of the trend, see L. McDougal, Codification of Choice of Law: A Critique of the Recent European Trend, 55 Tul.L.Rev. 114 (1980).

10. See E. Palmer, the Austrian Codification of Conflicts Law, 28 Am.J.Comp.L. 197 (1980) (the statute is reprinted id. at 222). For a recent (brief) treatise on the subject, see M. Schwimann, Grundriss des internationalen Privatrechts mit besonderer Berücksichtigung der Staatsverträge

Germany in 1986 [11], and during the early 1980's in Spain [12]. In France, there has been no comprehensive reform, but whenever portions of the family law provisions of the Civil Code were revised during the last two decades [13], specific conflict of laws rules governing that particular subject matter were often inserted into the Code.[14] Revision is in an advanced stage in Switzerland [15], and proposals for reform have been made in Italy.[16] Denmark adopted new contract choice-of-law rules based on the EEC Convention.[17] Western European developments induced a recent codification of private international law in Turkey.[18] Codifications of private international law have occurred also in some of the socialist countries of Eastern and Central Europe.[19] A summary codification of conflict of laws rules has been undertaken in the Peoples' Republic of China.[20]

(1982); cf. G. Beitzke, Neues österreichisches Kollisionsrecht, 43 Rabels Z. 245 (1979).

11. Statute on the Reform of Private International Law of July 25, 1986, 1986 BGBl. I 1142. The statute has generated a fair amount of discussion. E.g. J. Basedow, Die Neuregelung des Internationalen Privat- und Prozessrechts, 39 N.J.W. 2971 (1986) (errors corrected id. at 3190). The author notes that the new statute (a) recodifies the rules of family law, which had been partially declared unconstitutional, and (b) in dealing with contractual obligations largely incorporates, with some changes, the text of the EEC Convention, supra note 5. See also O. Sandrock, Die Bedeutung des Gesetzes zur Neuordnung des Internationalen Privatrechtes für die Unternehmenspraxis, 32 R.I.W. 841 (1986). The Commission of the European Communities has questioned whether the enactment of the statute amounts to a proper implementation of the EEC Convention. See Commission Recommendation of January 15, 1985, 1985 O.J. No. L 44, p. 42.

German tort choice-of-law rules are to be developed later. On these, see F. K. Juenger, Lessons Comparison Might Teach, 23 Am.J.Comp.L. 742, 747–48 (1975).

For a comment in English on the German statute, see e.g. B. Dickson, The Reform of Private International Law in the Federal Republic of Germany, 34 Int. & Comp.L.Q. 231 (1985). See also F. K. Juenger, Book Review, 34 Am.J.Comp.L. 562 (1986).

12. See supra note 3. Some years earlier, Spain had undertaken a more general reform of its conflict of laws rules, as had Portugal. Cf. D. F. Cavers, Legislative Choice of Law: Some European Examples, 44 So.Cal.L.Rev. 348 (1971).

13. See supra p. 549.

14. E.g. French Civil Code art. 310 (divorce); arts. 311–14, 311–15 (filiation).

15. See S. C. McCaffrey, The Swiss Draft Conflicts Law: An Overview, 28 Am. J.Comp.L. 235 (1980). See also Message No. 82–072 of the Swiss Federal Council concerning a federal private international law statute.

16. See supra, p. 843 note b.

17. See 5 I.Prax. 113 (1985). On the Convention, see supra notes 4–6.

18. Law of May 20, 1982, French translation at 72 Rev.cr.d.i.p. 141 (1983).

For a French translation of the conflict of laws provisions (arts. 1, 10–28) of the December 1985 Code of the United Arab Emirates (by S.A.A. Abu-Sahlieh), see 75 Rev.cr.d.i.p. 390 (1986).

19. On the conflicts statute of the German Democratic Republic see F. K. Juenger, The Conflicts Statute of the German Democratic Republic: An Introduction and Translation, 25 Am.J.Comp.L. 332 (1977) with references (at 333–35) to developments, up to that time, in other socialist countries as well. For a translation of the Hungarian conflicts statute see 55 Tul.L. Rev. 88 (1980). On the Yugoslav law of July 15, 1982, see T. Varady, Some Observations on the new Yugoslav Private International Law Code, 19 Riv.Dir.Int.Priv. & Proc. 69 (1983); for a French translation, see 72 Rev.cr.d.i.p. 353 (1983).

20. In 1986, the Peoples' Republic of China, which had been considering the adoption of a formal civil code, adopted instead "General Principles of Civil Law of the Peoples' Republic of China." See H. R. Zheng, China's New Civil Law, 34 Am.J. Comp.L. 669 (1986), with a translation of the "Principles" (by W. Gray and H. R. Zheng) id. at 715. The conflicts provisions of the "Principles" are commented on by Zhen id. at 700–01. For a more detailed discussion of the conflict of laws provisions, see R. Heuser & H. Zhao, Die Rechtsanwendungsnormen in den "Allgemeinen

(2) The codifications of the last decade [21] differ from the earlier ones in several respects. On the one hand, they tend to be much more detailed. Consider the brief provisions applicable to contracts in articles 25 and 26 of the older Italian statute reproduced above. By way of contrast, the new German statute devotes eleven rather elaborate articles (arts. 27–37 of the Introductory Law to the Civil Code, as revised) to conflict of laws rules governing contractual obligations. In addition, articles 11 and 12 of the revised Introductory Law, contained in the General Part of the statute, which concern the form of legal transactions and the protection of contracting parties when dealing with persons lacking legal capacity, are relevant as well. To the extent a statute contains specific and detailed rules, there is less room for development of the law by scholarly comment and case law. Much learned discussion about, e.g., the scope of "renvoi" comes to an end when a statute indicates with some precision, as the new German law does, when the doctrine is, and is not, to be used. Of course, no codification can attempt to supply an answer to every question. In developing a "general clause" to deal with problems not specifically covered, the recent codifications seem to have been influenced by American experience. Thus the German statute, following in this respect the EEC Convention on which it is partly based, states that if the parties to a contract do not choose the applicable law, the contract is governed by the law with which it is most closely related. If a specific issue is more closely related to a different legal system, the latter may supply the law to be applied to such issue.[22] Provisions of this kind are very common in other recent codifications as well. Article 1 of the Austrian statute [23] goes further and makes the principle of the "closest relationship" the basis for the entire Austrian system of private international law. There would thus seem to be some conscious borrowing from our Restatement.[24] Even these general provisions, however, attempt to give the courts some guidance; they usually contain a list of (rebuttable) presumptions as to the law with which typical contracts normally have the closest connection.[25] Since there is a trend in the United States away from the use of a mere methodology in choice of law and towards a return to rules,[26] one may thus wonder whether the gap between United States and continental approaches is not narrowing. This "narrowing of the gap" may, however, be more significant with respect to results than with respect to methods [27], as is shown by the materials which follow.

Regeln des Zivilrechts der Volksrepublik China," 32 R.I.W. 766 (1986).

21. For an attempt at a complete listing of recent conflicts codifications, see F. Rigaux, La méthode des conflits de lois dans les codifications et projects de codification de la dernière décennie, 74 Rev.cr.d.i.p. 1, 2, n. 1 (1985). Cf. D. F. Cavers, supra n. 12.

22. See art. 28 of the revised Introductory Law to the Civil Code and art. 3 of the EEC Convention.

23. See supra n. 10.

24. See Restatement (Second), Conflict of Laws § 6 (1971). Cf. UCC § 1–105.

25. These presumptions are usually based on the notion that ordinarily a contract has the closest connection with the party that supplies the "typical" or "characteristic" performance, e.g. in a contract for services the one who supplies the services, not the one who pays for them.

26. See e.g. M. Rosenberg, The Comeback of Choice of Law Rules, 81 Colum.L. Rev. 946 (1981).

27. The chief draftsman of the Austrian conflicts statute thought he saw in both approaches a similar overriding purpose: to do justice in the individual case. F. Schwind, Aspect et Sens du Droit Interna-

(3) Note the structure of the choice-of-law provisions contained in the Italian Code. In Arts. 17 through 28 the most important areas of law are listed, and for each area a basic choice-of-law rule is laid down. Arts. 29 through 31, on the other hand, deal with general problems; the provisions of these articles cut across, and qualify, all of the specific rules announced in Arts. 17 through 28.

Art. 31, which imports into the conflicts field the codifiers' well-known technique of "general clauses", deserves special attention. The language and systematic position of Art. 31 make it clear that its provisions may come into play in every case in which the specific choice-of-law rules of Arts. 17 through 28 point to the application of non-Italian law. Art. 31 thus qualifies every other choice-of-law rule. In many situations, it requires a two-step process of reasoning. The first step involves the question what law governs the case or issue at hand under the "ordinary" choice-of-law rules spelled out in Arts. 17 through 28. If the answer to that first question is that foreign law governs,[28] then the court must examine the further, separate question whether the foreign solution thus tentatively chosen should not be rejected as violative of Italy's public order or moral standards. A similar two-step approach to choice-of-law problems can be observed in most civil-law systems.[29] The approach is exemplified by the German cases set forth infra pp. 857 and 864.

The idea underlying Art. 31 of the Italian Code is not unknown in our own conflicts law. Occasionally, our courts will use the same technique as the civilians, and will openly declare that the result reached on the basis of ordinary choice-of-law rules is so unbearable that it must be rejected on grounds of "public policy".[30] Much more frequently, however, American courts (and especially the courts operating under post-Bealian principles) will not resort to the two-step method

tional Privé, 1984[IV] Hague Ac. Coll. Courses 9, 126.

28. In appraising the significance of a provision such as Art. 31, the reader should keep in mind that the "ordinary" choice-of-law rules contained in the Italian Code point to non-forum law much more frequently than do our comparable rules. The reason is that for many purposes the Italian rules refer to the law of the parties' *nationality*, whereas our law in similar situations probably would predicate the choice of the applicable law on their *domicile.* "Since law suits are usually conducted in the domicil of the defendant, there is much less opportunity, under the domicil rule, for the application of foreign law." A. Nussbaum, infra n. 31. For a more elaborate treatment of this point, see D. Lloyd, Public Policy 80–90 (1953).

The frequency with which civil-law courts have to face questions of nonforum law, is enhanced not only by their usual adherence to the nationality principle, but also by the absence, from most of the civilian systems, of any discretionary dismissal rules comparable to our doctrine of forum non conveniens. Under that doctrine, our

courts get rid of many foreign law cases without having to determine any issues going to the merits. Lacking statutory authorization of such discretionary dismissals, the courts of most civil-law countries cannot in this way avoid the determination of difficult foreign law questions.

29. The systematic separation of the "ordre public" question from the "ordinary" choice-of-law rules is reflected, also, in the traditional organization of civilian treatises, textbooks and commentaries on private international law. A researcher who does not keep this in mind, may fail to discover the most pertinent sections of the books he is using.

30. See, e.g., Kilberg v. Northeast Airlines, Inc., 9 N.Y.2d 34, 211 N.Y.S.2d 133, 172 N.E.2d 526 (1961); Zeevi & Sons, Ltd. v. Grindlay's Bank (Uganda) Ltd., 37 N.Y.2d 220, 371 N.Y.S.2d 892, 333 N.E.2d 168 (1975). For a later case discussing, but in the end not applying "public policy", see Schultz v. Boy Scouts of America, Inc., 65 N.Y.2d 189, 491 N.Y.S.2d 90, 480 N.E.2d 679 (1985). Cf. Dolinger, World Public Policy-Real International Public Policy in the Conflict of Laws, 17 Tex.Int.L.J. 167 (1982).

of the civilians, but will so mold the basic choice-of-law rule (or "approach") that such basic rule (or "approach") itself will give effect to the relevant interests and policies of the forum. Sometimes, preference is given to forum law and forum policies by pinning a "procedural" label on matters, such as the statute of limitations, which have little connection with the operational aspects of a lawsuit.[31] Even where that is not possible, important forum policies can always be implemented by fashioning a choice-of-law rule (or "approach") based on choice-influencing considerations, relevant factors,[32] or governmental interest analysis. Thus, policy considerations are apt to be reflected in most choice-of-law decisions; to the extent that they are, it becomes unnecessary to cultivate a separate public policy doctrine qualifying, and superimposed upon, the ordinary choice-of-law rules.[33]

ILLUSTRATION

Decision of the German Reichsgericht of December 19, 1922, RGZ 106, 83: Prior to 1909, D had ordered certain goods from P, at an agreed-upon price, and P had delivered the goods to D. As the latter failed to pay, P brought an action against him in 1909. At the time of the sale and of the subsequent action, both parties were domiciled in Switzerland. The sale thus was a Swiss transaction, of a purely local character, without any transnational aspects, and the action was brought in a Swiss court. Since D did not appear, a default judgment for a sum of Swiss Francs was entered against him. Execution was returned unsatisfied, whereupon P, in accordance with Swiss law, obtained from the Execution Office (which has some of the functions of our Sheriff's Office) a so-called certificate of deficiency. Swiss law provides that a claim embodied in such a certificate is not subject to any statute of limitations so long as the debtor is alive.

In 1920, P brought an action upon the certificate of deficiency. As D in the meantime had moved to Germany, the action was brought in a German court. D's only defense was the statute of limitations. The court reasoned that according to the "ordinary" German conflict of laws rule the problem of limitation was governed by the lex contractus, i.e., by Swiss law. But the notion of a claim which is not subject to *any* time limitation, was held to be contrary to basic principles of German law.[34] The court, therefore, refused to apply the particular Swiss rule which exempts certificates of deficiency from all statutes of limitation.

The traditional common-law view would lead to a similar result, on the ground that the point is "procedural". In fact, many American judges probably would go even further than the German court in giving preponderant effect to local policy, by applying the forum's own statute

31. See A. Nussbaum, Public Policy and the Political Crisis in the Conflict of Laws, 49 Yale L.J. 1027, 1028–29 (1940). See also the Illustration immediately following these Notes.

32. See Restatement, Second, Conflict of Laws § 6, and the Comments and Reporter's Note following the section (1971).

33. See 1 A. A. Ehrenzweig, Private International Law 153 ff. (1967).

34. The court pointed out that in German law every type of obligation is subject to a statutory time limitation. That the German legislator insists on a time limit for the exercise of every right, in the court's view can be inferred, also, from § 225 of the Civil Code, which outlaws any agreement purporting to make a claim unbarrable, or to lengthen the statutory period of limitation.

of limitations, though this attitude is slowly changing.[35] In the German case, the lower courts similarly had applied the German statute of limitations, and on that basis had dismissed the complaint. The Reichsgericht, however, made it clear that only the one provision of Swiss law which made this particular kind of claim absolutely unbarrable, should be rejected as violating the German ordre public. The case was remanded, therefore, with instructions to determine it in accordance with those provisions of the Swiss statute of limitations which would control in the absence of the one rejected provision.[36]

2. ILLUSTRATIVE CONFLICTS RULES DERIVED FROM CIVILIAN CODES

A. NATIONALITY AS A BASIS OF JUDICIAL JURISDICTION (THE NATIONALITY PRINCIPLE IN CONFLICT OF LAWS)

(1) *Nationality as a Basis of Choice-of-Law.* Under the choice-of-law provisions of the Italian Civil Code, set forth above, a person's capacity, his family relations, his estate, and many other legal relationships are governed by the law of the country with which such person is most closely connected (personal law); and the personal law of an individual is determined, not by his domicile as under our system, but by his citizenship. The nationality principle reflected in these provisions was spawned by 19th century nationalism.[1] Even today, it may arguably have some merit from the standpoint of a country of emigration, such as Italy. But for a country of immigration it makes little sense to adopt a principle which until the moment of his naturalization ties an immigrant to the law of the "old country". It is surprising, therefore, that the nationality principle has been adopted in some (though by no means all) of the Latin American countries. On the European continent, where it originated, the nationality principle is no longer universally adhered to; but it strongly predominates.[2] An over-

35. By way of exception to the traditional rule, many courts apply the limitation period of the jurisdiction where the claim arose if that jurisdiction's period was "built into" the statute giving rise to the right asserted; in many jurisdictions, also, so-called "borrowing statutes" provide for the use of the shorter limitation period of the jurisdiction where the claim arose. Cf. R. J. Weintraub, Commentary on the Conflict of Laws 56–59 (3d ed. 1986). Moreover, the traditional rule itself has come under attack. See supra p. 212.

36. Limitation questions have led to "public policy" problems in other countries as well. In a case which, in a way, is the converse of the German decision cited in the text, the French Cour de Cassation held that in the light of the French rule under which limitation periods do not run against minors, the Spanish one-year limitation period for automobile accident claims, which is not tolled on account of minority, violated French public policy and could not be applied to the claim of a minor arising out of an accident in Spain. Antunes v. Dame Bakhayoko, Cass.Civ., March 21, 1979, 70 Rev.cr.d.i. p. 81 (1981). Had it not been for the "public policy" point, the French court would have applied the statute of limitations of the place of the accident, i.e. Spain. The French decision (like the German decision discussed in the text, supra) thus illustrates the civilians' two-step method.

1. For an extensive discussion of the history of the principle, and of its present-day importance, see 1 E. Rabel, The Conflict of Laws: A Comparative Study 109–17, 120–23 (2d ed., prepared by U. Drobnig, 1958).

2. For a list of countries which, as of the time of publication, followed the na-

all survey shows that the countries whose choice-of-law rules are permeated by the nationality principle, clearly constitute a majority of the civil-law systems.[3]

(2) *Nationality as a Basis of Jurisdiction.* Many civil-law countries have adopted the view that judicial jurisdiction can be based on defendant's nationality, so that in any kind of action—with the possible exception of an action involving immovable property situated abroad—a court has jurisdiction if the defendant is a citizen of the forum

tionality principle, see id. at 121–23. Concerning Latin America, see also J. Samtleben, Der Territorialitätsgrundsatz im internationalen Privatrecht Lateinamerikas, 35 Rabels Z. 72 (1971) (English summary at 105–06). For a comparative overview of the nationality principle, see also M. Verwilghen (Ed.), Nationalité et Statut Personnel (Vol. XVI of the "Bibliothèque de la Faculté de Droit de l'Université Catholique de Louvain, 1984). The more recent revisions of conflict of laws rules continue to apply the nationality principle, but in attenuated form. See, e.g. French Civil Code art. 310 (providing i.a. that French law may be applied in divorce cases if both spouses domiciled in France); art. 311–15 (possession of status of legitimate child governed in any event by French law if child and at least one parent reside in France). French courts have, traditionally, applied the law of the situs to the descent of immovables and the law of the decedent's domicile to the descent of movables. See also the Introductory Law to the German Civil Code, as revised in 1986, Art. 13 (capacity to marry based on national law of each prospective spouse, but German law to be applied if one party at least resides in Germany and national law would create unreasonable obstacles to marriage). The Hague Conference on Private International Law has frequently used "habitual residence" instead of nationality in its conventions intended to unify conflicts rules. See D. F. Cavers, Habitual Residence, A Useful Concept? 21 Am. U.L.Rev. 475 (1972).

The nationality principle also permeates the recent codifications of conflicts law in the socialist orbit. See F. K. Juenger, The Conflicts Statute of the German Democratic Republic: An Introduction and Translation, 25 Am.J.Comp.L. 332, 343–44 (1977). Interestingly, the new "Principles" of the Peoples' Republic of China are somewhat different. They provide i.a. that the personal status of a Chinese national domiciled abroad "may" be governed by the law of the domicile and also hold the law of the place of marriage applicable to marriages, that of the domicile to succession questions concerning movables. See supra, p. 847, n. 20.

When determining the law applicable to corporations, most, though not all, civil-law countries rely on the law, not of the country of formal incorporation, but of the country where the corporation has its actual management (i.e. its "seat"). For an interesting case concerned with the definition of "seat" and with the law applicable if that seat is itself located in a country applying the place of incorporation rule, see Comité de défense des actionnaires de la Banque Ottomane v. Banque Ottomane, Cour d'appel Paris, October 30, 1984, 113 Clunet 156 (1986).

3. The nationality principle causes some perplexing problems for civil-law courts when they have to deal with the affairs of Americans or other nationals of countries having a non-unitary legal system. Suppose an Italian court is asked to probate the will and to distribute the estate of an American citizen whose last domicile was in Italy. Pursuant to Art. 23 of its Civil Code, the court must apply "American" law. But as there is no national "American" law on the subject of wills and estates, to what body of law should the court turn? See K. H. Nadelmann, Mancini's Nationality Rule and Non-Unified Legal Systems: Nationality Versus Domicile, 17 Am.J.Comp.L. 418 (1969). In Italy, this question is rendered particularly difficult by Art. 30 of the Civil Code; this provision makes it impossible for an Italian court to utilize the American choice-of-law rule, which (with respect to movable property) would lead to the application of the internal law of the country where the decedent was last domiciled (i.e. Italy).

The problem has sometimes been addressed by recent codifiers. See Article 4(3) of the Introductory Law to the German Civil Code, as revised in 1986 (apply pertinent choice-of-law rules of country referred to by German choice-of-law principles; if that country has no rules indicating which of its jurisdictions shall supply the applicable law, apply law of most closely concerned jurisdiction).

country.[4] We have touched on this doctrine in our general discussion of jurisdiction, supra pp. 383–384.

In France, the theory of nationality-based jurisdiction has been carried even further by code provisions enacted and often interpreted in a spirit of strong nationalism. Through the materials which follow, the reader will become familiar with some of the results derived from those provisions. Fortunately, only few other countries have followed the French example on this point. The problems caused by the jurisdictional notions of the French are, nevertheless, of grave concern to American practitioners; at the present time, this concern is growing, because French judgments, rendered on these jurisdictional bases, are now enforceable in other Common Market countries, if the defendant is domiciled outside the territory of the Common Market (e.g., in the United States).[5]

FRENCH CIVIL CODE *

Art. 14. An alien, even if not residing in France, may be summoned before the French Courts, for the fulfilment of obligations contracted by him in France towards a French person; he may be called before the French Courts for obligations contracted by him in a foreign country towards French persons.

Art. 15. A Frenchman may be called before a French Court for obligations contracted by him in a foreign country, even towards an alien.

ILLUSTRATIONS [1]

(1) *D* is a manufacturing corporation organized in Delaware and having its principal office in New York City. In the past, *D* has never engaged in any business or owned any property outside of the United States; but at present the management of the corporation is planning to build a factory in The Netherlands. *D* is about to acquire some land in The Netherlands for this purpose.

About a year ago, *D* negotiated with *P*, an individual then domiciled in New York City, with a view to hiring *P* as chief engineer for *D*'s plant in Omaha, Nebraska. The negotiations, conducted in New York City, resulted in a letter written by *D* to *P*. This letter, somewhat

4. This rule prevails, for instance, in Italy. See M. Cappelletti and J. M. Perillo, Civil Procedure in Italy 85 (1965).

5. See supra pp. 400–402.

* The reader will recall (see supra pp. 396–397) that these provisions of the French Code are modified by the European Judgments Convention. Under the terms of that Convention, Art. 14 can no longer be invoked against a domiciliary of another Common Market country. But both Art. 14 and Art. 15 are still in effect as against parties domiciled outside the Common Market area.

1. For detailed discussion of the problems raised by these illustrations, and fur-

ther references, see P. Herzog, Civil Procedure in France §§ 4.03–4.10 (1967); H. P. deVries and A. F. Lowenfeld, Jurisdiction in Personal Actions—A Comparison of Civil Law Views, 44 Iowa L.Rev. 306, 316–30 (1959); 2 G. R. Delaume, Transnational Contracts: Applicable Law and Settlement of Disputes, §§ 8.02 to 8.07 (Updated ed., 1986); T. E. Carbonneau, The French *Exequatur* Proceeding: The Exorbitant Jurisdictional Rules of Articles 14 and 15 (Code Civil) As Obstacles to the Enforcement of Foreign Judgments in France, 2 Hastings Int. & Comp.L.Rev. 307 (1979).

inartistically worded, immediately led to a dispute. *P* claimed that the letter evidenced and confirmed a binding contract, by which he was hired for a period of three years at an annual salary of $43,000, while *D* (meanwhile having received unfavorable reports on *P*'s skills as an engineer) refused to employ *P* and denied the existence of a contract, taking the position that the letter merely outlined some of the terms on the basis of which further negotiations were to take place. *P* thereupon demanded payment of damages, but his demand was ignored by *D*.

A few days ago, *D* received the summons and complaint in an action which *P* has instituted against *D* before a court in Marseille, France, where *P* presently resides. The complaint, based on the above-mentioned letter, alleges that *P* is a French citizen. *D* had never inquired about *P*'s citizenship, and since *P* presented himself as a graduate of an American engineering college, and spoke English without a noticeable accent, it never occurred to *D*'s officers during the negotiations with *P* that the latter might be a Frenchman.

Assuming that *P*'s allegation concerning his French citizenship is true, will you advise *D* to defend the Marseille action, or to default?

It is clear that Art. 14 of the French Civil Code by its terms covers our case. The French courts have consistently declined to read any exceptions or limitations into the language of that provision.

It seems equally clear that if a default judgment were entered against *D* by the Marseille court, such a judgment would not be enforceable anywhere in the United States.[2] But would the French judgment not constitute a danger to the property which *D* is about to acquire in The Netherlands? [3]

If *D* had known that *P* was a Frenchman, it might have protected itself by obtaining from *P* a waiver of his right to sue in France. It has long been recognized by the French courts that the right to invoke Arts. 14 and 15 of the French Civil Code can be waived, even in advance.[4] An advance waiver usually—but not necessarily—takes the form of an arbitration or prorogation clause.

2. This kind of a French judgment has been called a "common example" of a judgment that would not be recognized or enforced here. See Somportex Ltd. v. Philadelphia Chewing Gum Corp., 318 F.Supp. 161, at 165 (E.D.Pa. 1970), aff'd 453 F.2d 435 (3d Cir. 1971), cert. den. 405 U.S. 1017, 92 S.Ct. 1294 (1972).

More difficult questions would present themselves if *P*'s action had arisen out of some activity conducted by *D* in France. In that event it could be argued that the French court, even though *actually* it based its jurisdiction on *P*'s nationality, *might have* availed itself of a jurisdictional basis which our long-arm statutes now seem to recognize. Whether this argument would lead to recognition and enforcement of the French judgment, is unsettled. *Compare* Schibsby v. Westenholz, L.R. 6 Q.B. 155 (1870) and Mackender v. Feldia A. G., (1967) 2 Q.B. 590, at 599, *with* Cherun v. Frishman, 236 F.Supp. 292 (D.D.C. 1964).

For a helpful discussion of this difficult question, see P. Hay, International Versus Interstate Conflicts Law in the United States: A Survey of the Case Law, 35 Rabels Z. 429, at 449–50 (1971).

3. See supra pp. 400–402.

4. The right to sue under Art. 14 can be waived by the French plaintiff. Jurisdiction based on Art. 15, on the other hand, is effectively waived only if both parties consent to the waiver. See 1 Dalloz, Répertoire de Droit International (ed. by Ph. Francescakis) 430 (1968). For a collection of authorities supporting the proposition that the right to invoke arts. 14 and 15 can be waived by an agreement to arbitrate, see T. E. Carbonneau, The Elaboration of a French Court Doctrine on International Commercial Arbitration: A Study in Liberal Civilian Creativity, 55 Tul.L.Rev. 1, 19–21, 24–25 (1980).

The draftsman of a contract clause by which jurisdiction based on Arts. 14 and 15 is waived, should be careful to use unequivocal language. If the pertinent language of the contract is unclear, French courts often refuse to construe it as a waiver.

(2) *X*, a vacationing American law student, drove his Volkswagen through Yugoslavia. Near Zagreb, he had a collision with another car, a Volvo owned and operated by *Y* who turned out to be a citizen and domiciliary of Sweden. Both vehicles were damaged and *Z*, a young lady who was a passenger in the Volvo, suffered a whiplash injury.

If *Z* happens to be a French citizen, she can sue *X* in France. The French courts have held that the meaning of "obligations" in Art. 14 is not limited to contractual obligations. Consequently, Art. 14 can be invoked in any kind of action, including a tort action, even though the cause of action, apart from plaintiff's nationality, has no connection whatever with France.[5]

We may assume that at the present time *X* has no property in France. Nevertheless, *X* and his insurer will have to think twice before they decide to default in *Z*'s French action. The French default judgment may be enforceable, and probably will remain enforceable for a very long time, not only throughout the territory of the Common Market but also in all other countries which by virtue of a treaty or otherwise recognize the validity of French judgments rendered on the basis of Art. 14.

If Yugoslav law authorizes a direct action against a liability insurer, in that event *X*'s insurance company, also, may find itself summoned before a French court.

Even if none of the individuals involved in the accident were of French nationality, Art. 14 may come into play. Suppose *Y*'s car was collision-insured, and the insurer, a French company, has paid for the damage to the car. The French insurance company, as subrogee, could then sue *X* in France.[6] The Cour de Cassation has explicitly upheld the jurisdiction of the French courts in subrogation cases of this kind.[7]

(3) *A* is a columnist and *B* a middle-weight boxing champion. Both are, and for a long time have been, domiciled in New York City. Soon

---

5. The rule stated in the text is subject only to minor exceptions. The principal exception is to the effect that Art. 14 does not apply if the action involves immovable property situated outside of France.

Surprisingly, however, the Paris Court of Appeals held in a recent case that since article 15 (as well as article 14) speaks of "obligations contracted" with other parties, it was inapplicable in a divorce case. P. contre son épouse, Cour d'appel Paris, December 20, 1985, 113 Clunet 366 (1986). Will this be the prelude to a less expansive interpretation of articles 14 and 15? Not infrequently, the French Cour de Cassation has, after some hesitation, accepted novel views of the Paris Cour d'Appel. It is noteworthy in this connection that the Cour de Cassation itself has recently stated, in a case involving an American defendant, that article 14 is "subsidiary only". It may not be used if another jurisdictional basis is available. This means that if the defendant has an establishment in France and thus can be sued there under normal French jurisdictional rules, he must be sued where his establishment is and may not be sued before any other court in France, on the supposed ground that when article 14 is applicable the plaintiff can choose where in France he will sue. Société Cognacs and Brandies from France v. Sté. Orliac, Cass.civ., November 19, 1985, 113 Clunet 719 (1986).

6. In automobile collision cases, this may not happen very frequently; but in cases of maritime collisions the possibility of the involvement of a French insurance company, and of a French action brought by that company as subrogee, is a very real one, as experience has shown.

7. See deVries and Lowenfeld, supra n. 1, at 320–21.

after *A* in his column had made an uncomplimentary reference to *B*, the latter happened to spot the columnist at a New York night club and proceeded to beat him. *A*, having suffered a broken nose and other injuries, sued *B* in the New York Supreme Court. Summons and complaint were personally served on *B* at his apartment in New York. *B* objected to the jurisdiction of the court on the ground that he was a French citizen. The court, while recognizing that in fact *B* was a French citizen, dismissed the jurisdictional objection as frivolous. The case was then litigated on the merits. The jury brought in a verdict for *A* in the amount of $85,000, and judgment was entered on the verdict. There was no appeal. Attempts to secure satisfaction of the judgment in New York were unsuccessful, as *B* was out of work and had no assets in New York (or anywhere else in the United States).

A's lawyer has obtained information to the effect that *B* owns an apartment building in Paris, reputed to be worth half a million dollars. Will the New York judgment be enforced in France?

The answer is No. Under Art. 15 of the French Civil Code, the French courts would have had jurisdiction to entertain *A*'s tort action against *B*. In the French view, this jurisdiction is *exclusive*,[8] with the result that from the French standpoint the New York court lacked jurisdiction unless *B* waived his rights under Art. 15. If *B* had defended the New York action on the merits, without raising any jurisdictional objection, this might be regarded as a waiver. But since his lawyer shrewdly raised an objection (although no doubt he knew that under New York law it was a hopeless one), a French court probably would say that *B* did not voluntarily litigate the matter in New York, and hence did not waive his rights under Art. 15.[9] In all probability, therefore, the New York judgment will be refused enforcement in France.[10]

8. Until now this has been regarded as well settled, in spite of the fact that on its face the language of Art. 15 seems to be permissive rather than mandatory. See Carbonneau, supra n. 1, at 319–26. But see, for some interesting speculations as to a possible change in future case law, Ph. Franceskakis, Le contrôle de la compétence du juge étranger après l'arrêt Simitch de la Cour de Cassation, 74 Rev.cr.d.i.p. 243 (1985).

9. If *B* had defaulted in the New York action, and *A* had obtained a default judgment in New York, such judgment would be equally unenforceable in France. The French courts have held that a French defendant's default in a foreign action does not constitute a waiver of his jurisdictional objections under Art. 15.

10. When a French individual or corporation is sued in an American court, Art. 15 ordinarily makes it very doubtful whether a judgment for the plaintiff, should such a judgment be entered, will be enforced in France. This danger of non-enforcement may be a factor tending to persuade the American court to dismiss the action on forum-non-conveniens grounds. See Olympic Corp. v. Société Générale, 462 F.2d 376, 379 (2d Cir. 1972).

B. THE IMPACT OF "ORDRE PUBLIC" ON CONTINGENT FEE AGREEMENTS

GERMAN CIVIL CODE (INTRODUCTORY LAW) ARTICLE 6 [a]

Public Policy (ordre public) [b]

A legal rule of another country is not to be applied if its application would lead to a result that is manifestly incompatible with basic principles of German law. In particular, such a rule is not to be applied if its application is incompatible with fundamental [constitutional] rights.[c]

OPINION OF THE GERMAN BUNDESGERICHTSHOF IN THE MATTER OF DR. G. E. R., PLAINTIFF–RESPONDENT v. FREE STATE OF BAVARIA, DEFENDANT–APPELLANT

Seventh Civil Division, November 15, 1956, BGHZ 22, 162.

[The plaintiff is a member of the Bar of Washington, D.C. In 1949 he was retained by the defendant, the Bavarian Government, in the following matter:

Until June, 1948, the Reichsmark (RM) was legal tender in Germany. By Military Government Law #63, the so-called Monetary Conversion Law issued on June 27, 1948 (13 Fed.Reg. 4965), a new currency, the Deutschmark (DM), was substituted for the former RM. All RM banknotes were invalidated and withdrawn from circulation. Concerning the conversion of former RM credits into DM credits, the Law contained complicated provisions. Some RM credits were wiped out. Others, especially bank accounts, were converted at the ratio of 6½ DM for 100 RM. "Claims" (other than bank accounts) were converted "into

a. Text of article as enacted by the Law of July 25, 1986, supra page 847 n. 11. (Translated by P.H.) The corresponding Article 30 of the original Introductory Law, involved in the principal case, infra, read as follows: "A foreign law shall not be applied if its application would be contra bonos mores or would violate the purpose of a German law." The change appears to have been due in part to decisions of the German Constitutional Court to the effect that provisions of foreign law that contravene fundamental rights rules based on the German Constitution may not be applied by a German court. See F. K. Juenger, The German Constitutional Court and the Conflict of Laws, 20 Am.J.Comp.L. 1, 290 (1972); F. K. Juenger, Trends in European Conflicts Law, 60 Cornell L.Rev.

969, 977–83 (1975). What are the consequences of the change in wording likely to be?

b. The French expression *ordre public* appears as such in the original German text.

c. This provision is, of course, the counterpart of art. 31 of the Preliminary Dispositions of the Italian Civil Code, translated at p. 845 above. Again, note the difference in wording. Countries having different social systems may use further variants in wording. The new Yugoslav statute on private international law, supra p. 847, n. 19, art. 4 states that a foreign law may not be applied if it is contrary to Yugoslav principles of social organization.

DM so that the debtor shall be obligated to pay to the creditor one DM for every 10 RM due" (Article 16, par. 1 of Law #63), except that certain specified types of RM obligations (listed in Article 18), such as claims for personal injuries and other types of damage claims, were converted into DM at the rate of one DM for every RM. At the time of the currency reform, defendant owned credits of approximately RM 80,000,000 which were derived from the former government's management of concentration camps during the Nazi era. In order to utilize these funds for the benefit of concentration camp victims, defendant desired that these credits should not be wiped out, but should be converted into DM at the most favorable rate possible. Jurisdiction to determine this question was vested in the Bavarian Supreme Audit Court,[d] a quasi-judicial, independent body long antedating the Allied occupation at the end of World War II, and ordinarily functioning under German law. Defendant, nevertheless, considered it advisable to obtain the services of an American attorney, probably for the reason that the Monetary Conversion Law had been drafted and promulgated by the occupation authorities and that these authorities had the power, in effect, to nullify decisions of the Supreme Audit Court in matters of currency reform.

The parties entered into a written retainer agreement, pursuant to which the plaintiff was to receive, as his only fee, 1½% of the DM amount which would become available to the defendant by way of conversion into DM of the RM credits in question. It was expressly stipulated that this fee should become payable immediately upon occurrence of the hoped-for contingency, regardless of whether or not the success attained could be shown to be the result of plaintiff's efforts.

Subsequently, the Supreme Audit Court permitted conversion of defendant's RM credits into a substantial DM amount. The Allied authorities did not interfere with the decision, and the DM amount authorized by the Supreme Audit Court became actually available to the defendant. Plaintiff sued for 1½% of that amount, voluntary payment of his contingent fee having been refused. The court of first instance and the intermediate appellate court of Munich rendered judgment in favor of the plaintiff. Defendant appealed to the highest court.

In its opinion, the highest court first discusses the question what law governs the agreement between the parties. Relying on prior decisions (RGZ 151, 193; 149, 121, especially at 127) and other authorities, the court holds that a retainer agreement between attorney and client normally is intended to be governed by the law of the place

---

d. The German title of this body is Oberster Rechnungshof. There is a federal audit court, in addition to the audit courts of the various Laender. The functions of these audit courts, which are roughly comparable to those of the U.S. General Accounting Office, are lucidly described by Hillhouse and Lang, The German Federal Audit Court, 27 Accounting Review 530 (1952). For a brief account, see Hillhouse, Budget Management, in Litchfield, Governing Postwar Germany 307, 314–5 (1953).

where the attorney's office is located. In the present case, therefore, the law of the District of Columbia is controlling.

The lower courts had found that under the law of the District of Columbia the contingent fee agreement was valid and enforceable. The highest court held that this finding as to a point of foreign law is binding on the court of last resort.]

. . . Appellant's counsel argues that the lower courts committed error by failing to apply Article 30 of the Introductory Law to the Civil Code. He raises the question whether a percentage fee does not always violate the principles of boni mores or the purpose of the German laws. In his opinion, such violation is undeniable in a case in which the fee is payable regardless of whether or not the contingency has been brought about by the activity of the attorney. An agreement, it is argued, which enables the attorney to earn the fee without any effort of his own, is improperly oppressive and patently inconsistent with fundamental principles of German law.

This argument of the appellant is not valid.

(a) The defendant assumes that the terms of the agreement would have entitled the plaintiff to his fee even if the plaintiff had done nothing. This assumption is not in accordance with the factual findings of the intermediate appellate court, which are binding on this court. According to the letter of confirmation of October 28, 1949, to which the intermediate appellate court refers, the fee was payable *for work to be done by the plaintiff.* Immediately thereafter, the plaintiff in fact began his efforts. . . . The agreement in the case at bar did not contain any provision permitting the plaintiff to remain idle without endangering his right to compensation. It is, therefore, unnecessary to comment on the legal consequences which such a contractual provision might have.

(b) The effectiveness of the agreement, as construed by the lower courts, is not affected by Article 30 of the Introductory Law to the Civil Code.

According to that provision, a foreign law should not be applied if it is contra bonos mores, or if it contravenes the purpose of a German law. Neither is the case here.

(aa) In determining the question of immorality, we must consider not only the terms of the foreign law, but also the consequences which follow from its application in the individual case (RGZ 150, 283). This criterion makes it necessary to take into consideration all factors which affect the special color or flavor of the operative facts (RGZ 150, 1, especially at 5). Among these factors, we cannot disregard opinions held elsewhere within the orbit of our civilization, within the orbit, that is, which is linked together by common notions of morality. If it should turn out, for instance, that concerning the propriety of a certain type of contract, the views held in different countries are divided, we shall have to be particularly cautious in determining the question of immorality, even if the question is to be answered according to our own law. Examination of the issue at hand in accordance with these principles leads to the following:

In Germany, the written law formerly was silent concerning the question whether an attorney may accept from his client the promise of a percentage fee. Several decisions of the Reichsgericht had held that ordinarily such an agreement is professionally *unethical,* and that it is *immoral* within the meaning of Section 138 of the Civil Code if there are additional aggravating circumstances, such as ruthless exploitation of the client, guaranty of a minimum, lack of any limitation in point of time or waiver of causality [e] (RGZ 83, 111; 115, 141). In spite of many voices which criticized these holdings [citations], the highest court continued to adhere to the same view (RGZ 142, 70).[f] Finally, the legislator settled the issue; by Decree of April 21, 1944, Section 93 of the Law Concerning Attorneys' Fees was amended to provide that any contingent fee agreement between attorney and client is invalid.[g]

In foreign jurisdictions, there is no uniformity of views. In some countries the percentage fee is considered improper; for instance, quite decidedly, in England, Austria and France [citations, including references to Kalsbach, Standesrecht der Rechtsanwaelte (1956)]. [h] In other . . . countries an agreement providing for such a fee is proper and sometimes expressly recognized as lawful [citations]. By far the larger part of the United States of America subscribes to the latter view; the contingent fee is prohibited, probably under the influence of English practice, in a small minority of states,[i] but the minority group includes neither New York nor the District of Columbia. See Williston, A Treatise on the Law of Contracts, Vol. 6, page 4835 (1938). It is true that even in the United States there is some agitation for abolition, or at least limitation, of the contingent fees which frequently amount to 50% or more [citations]. This agitation, however, has had no success.

In Canon 13 [of the Canons of Professional Ethics] of the American Bar Association it is expressly provided:

> "A contract for a contingent fee, where sanctioned by law, should be reasonable under all the circumstances of the case, including the risk and uncertainty of the compensation, but should always be subject to the supervision of a court, as to its reasonableness."

e. "Waiver of causality" means a clause under which the attorney is entitled to the contingent fee regardless of whether or not the client's recovery is the *result* of the attorney's efforts.

f. RGZ 142, 70 is the decision reprinted supra page 702.

g. On July 26, 1957, the Law Concerning Attorneys' Fees was reenacted in revised form (BGBl 1957 I 907). Old Section 93 became new Section 3; but the provision expressly outlawing contingent fees was omitted. As to the significance of this omission, see supra p. 708.

h. This monograph on The Professional Law of Attorneys contains a great deal of useful comparative material.

i. Note that the German court's opinion was written in 1956. Since then, the minority jurisdictions mentioned in the opinion have, at least in principle, adopted the majority view, which thus has become the unanimous American position. See supra pp. 709–710.

Finally it might be mentioned that the so-called Monaco Conference [of the International Bar Association] in 1954, which considered the draft of an international code of professional ethics, failed to reach universal agreement on this point. Paragraph 17 of the draft essentially follows the above-quoted Canon 13 of the American Bar Association; it should be noted, however, that pursuant to paragraph 1 [of the draft] the attorney must obey, also, the ethical precepts prevailing in those countries in which his activity is intended to take effect [citations].[j]

It follows from the foregoing that there is no uniformity of views concerning the propriety of the contingent fee. Even in Germany the opinion has been expressed that there may be individual cases in which a percentage fee would not be unethical from a professional point of view. Immorality, and hence nullity pursuant to Section 138 of the Civil Code, generally is thought to exist only if there are additional special circumstances. Of course, these circumstances need not be so grave as to render the agreement itself immoral. The decisive point is that a German lawyer is an organ of the administration of justice and hence occupies a position which cannot be judged exclusively from a business point of view. Therefore, such an agreement has to come up to a higher standard than a contract among businessmen (RGZ 142, 70).

This higher standard, however, can be applied only in the case of a lawyer who actually occupies the position of an organ of the administration of German justice and who, *for this reason*, enjoys the special confidence of the public. A *foreign* attorney is not in the same category. Therefore, if he enters into an agreement concerning his compensation, the morality or immorality of such agreement must be determined according to the same criteria which would be applicable to the agreement of a private businessman. This especially for the reason that, as pointed out above, there is not only a lack of any uniform transnational regulation of attorneys' professional ethics, but also a great diversity of views on the subject.

Taking these principles into account, one cannot say that in the case at hand the result derived from the applicable foreign law is contra bonos mores. The percentage of the recovery accorded to the plaintiff is not excessively high. Contrary to the contention of the appellant, it is clear that under the terms of the agreement the plaintiff was entitled to the fee only after he used his best efforts, in accordance with his express promise, to help in prosecuting his client's claim. In addition, as plaintiff emphasized in his letter of confirmation, he believed that the agreement in question would serve the interests of the defendant as well; in that letter he stated expressly that he was willing to take into account the financial situation in which the Government of the defendant Free State then found itself, and that he would for this

j. At its 1956 meeting in Oslo, the International Bar Association approved the proposed International Code of Ethics for the Legal Profession; but by its terms the Code, formulated as a statement of principles for the guidance of lawyers handling cases of international character, is "in no way intended to supersede existing national or local rules of legal ethics. . . ." See Note, 5 Am.J.Comp.L. 707 (1956).

reason refrain from insisting upon any advance payment and would be satisfied with a contingent fee. It was clear, therefore, that his potentially extensive efforts might remain uncompensated, in case no recovery could be obtained.

Nor can any objection be made to the clause waiving causality [i.e., the clause in the retainer agreement providing that plaintiff is entitled to the contingent fee regardless of whether or not the defendant's recovery can be shown to be the result of plaintiff's efforts]. The plaintiff, not without some justification, pointed out in his letter of October 28, 1949, that he would have to do much of his work in the United States, while the final decision would be announced in Germany, and that under these circumstances it might well be impossible subsequently to determine whether the success achieved actually was produced by his work. The events which followed indeed proved that these apprehensions of the plaintiff were not baseless. [The court then discusses the complex relationship between German and Allied authorities which had jurisdiction in the matter of the conversion into DM of the RM accounts in question, and the steps which plaintiff took, or advised defendant to take, in order to prevent an adverse decision by the Allied authorities. In the end, the Allied authorities remained passive in the matter, and did not prevent the Bavarian Supreme Audit Court from determining the conversion case in defendant's favor. The court points out that under these circumstances it would indeed be exceedingly difficult, or even impossible, to prove or disprove that the favorable result finally achieved was the "result" of plaintiff's endeavors].

Considering these facts, no immoral overreaching can be found in the clause providing that plaintiff should be entitled to his fee regardless of whether or not the success achieved is the result of his work.

(bb) Nor can it be said that application of the foreign substantive rule contravenes the purpose of a German law.

It is true that the German rule (Sec. 93, 2nd paragraph, last sentence of the Law Concerning Attorneys' Fees) invalidates every agreement providing for a contingent fee of any kind. But this difference between our law and the law of the District of Columbia is not a sufficient reason for resorting to Art. 30 of the Introductory Law to the Civil Code. That would be justified only if the difference of political or social views [reflected in the German rule, on the one hand, and in the contrary rule of the District of Columbia, on the other] were so essential that application of the foreign rule would affect the very fundaments of our political or economic life (RGZ 119, 259, especially at 263.) This is not the case.

As has been pointed out above, the said provision of Sec. 93 has its foundation in the special status of a German attorney as an organ of the administration of justice under our system. These considerations are not pertinent to a foreign lawyer. He is not subject to any restrictions other than those flowing from the general laws, especially from Sec. 138 of the Civil Code. . . .

Affirmed.

NOTES AND QUESTIONS

(1) The German courts, in contrast to the courts of some other civil-law countries,[1] have been traditionally cautious in their use of the sharp weapon of "ordre public". One of the techniques employed in order to prevent overly frequent reliance on "ordre public" is the so-called doctrine of local contacts: the weaker the local contacts of the transaction, the more objectionable will the foreign solution have to be in order to be rejected.[2] In its opinion in the principal case, the court hinted at this point; but since the transaction had local as well as foreign contacts of considerable strength, the point was not decisive.

(2) Is the applicable standard of morality and public policy to be derived exclusively from the *national* legal system? Or should the court, in trying to determine that standard, look beyond its national frontiers?[3] Should the court enforce the local policy of the forum by invoking "ordre public", if it finds that even among nations sharing the forum country's cultural traditions there is disagreement on the point in question?[4]

As far as German law is concerned, has the recent reformulation of the Code's "public policy" provisions brought about a change in this respect? Article 6, as will be recalled, states that foreign law is not to be applied if it is incompatible with basic principles of German law, in particular with fundamental rights. When speaking of "fundamental rights", the legislator clearly refers to the those fundamental rights that are recognized by the German Constitution. But does the use of the words "in particular" imply that in the majority of cases—i.e., where no constitutionally protected rights are involved—, the focus should be on a transnational rather than a purely German standard, and that, consequently, the principal case is not overruled by the recent change in the wording of the pertinent Code provisions?

(3) The *Supreme Court of Austria in its decision of April 4, 1951* (SZ XXIV/93) dealt with a case in which plaintiff, a New York attorney who was a former Austrian lawyer, had been retained to recover some immovable property in Austria for his client. It was agreed that as

1. French and Italian cases reflect a tendency to invoke "ordre public" more readily. For a discussion of the interesting historical and doctrinal reasons explaining this difference in attitude see G. Husserl, Public Policy and Ordre Public, 25 Va.L. Rev. 37 (1938); W. Müller-Freienfels, Book Review, 22 Rabels Z. 735, 737–39 (1957).

2. Interestingly, in Schultz v. Boy Scouts of America, Inc., supra p. 849, n. 30, the New York Court of Appeals similarly noted a direct relationship between the applicability of the public policy doctrine and the strength of the ties connecting the case with the forum.

3. The principal case clearly supports a standard based on views and values shared by more than one nation—views and values to be ascertained by the comparative method. The lead of the principal case has been followed in other, more recent decisions. See J. Kropholler, Die vergleichende Methode und das internationale Privatrecht, 77 Z. für die vergleichende Rechtswissenschaft 1, at 10–11 (1978).

4. Cf. 1 Schlesinger, Formation of Contracts—A Study of the Common Core of Legal Systems, Introduction at 39–40 (1968); P. H. Neuhaus, Die Grundbegriffe des internationalen Privatrechts 372 (2d ed., 1976); Kropholler, supra n. 3.

compensation the attorney should receive a 20% interest in the property to be recovered. At the time when this agreement was made, both attorney and client were domiciled in New York. The client, who meanwhile had moved to Austria, eventually recovered the property as a result of plaintiff's services, but refused to convey the 20% interest to plaintiff. The latter thereupon sued the client for specific enforcement of the agreement. The court held for defendant, on the ground that defendant's obligation to convey an interest relating to immovable property situated in Austria was governed by Austrian law, and that under Austrian law the agreement was void as a *pactum de quota litis*. But the court strongly emphasized that if the 20% fee had been payable in money rather than in kind, the law of New York (where the attorney had his office) would have governed the agreement, and that in that event Austria's "ordre public" would *not* have prevented recovery of the fee in an Austrian court.[5] The decision, at least by way of dictum, thus exhibits a liberal attitude similar to that of the principal case.

(4) *Decision of the German Bundesgerichtshof of October 18, 1965,* BGHZ 44, 184, reported also in 19 NJW 296 (1966): Plaintiff was admitted to practice law in New York and Georgia. In 1945, he came to Germany as an American officer, and he remained a member of the American Occupation Forces until 1955. In 1950 he received permission from U.S. Headquarters to practice law in Germany as an American attorney (i.e., in matters involving either American law or the manifold decrees and regulations of the Occupation authorities). He then opened an office in West Berlin.

Defendants (apparently domiciled in Germany) are the widow and son of *L.B.*, a well-known conductor who was killed in a tragic accident on August 23, 1945. On that day, *L.B.* was riding in a British military vehicle, together with a British officer and the latter's driver. When the vehicle came to the border of the American sector of Berlin, an American guard requested the driver to stop. The driver, however, failed to stop, whereupon the American guard opened fire at the vehicle, killing *L.B.*

In 1952, defendants retained plaintiff to prosecute their claims arising from the accident, and agreed in writing to pay plaintiff 35% of the amounts to be recovered. By filing timely and properly documented claims, and by negotiations with the British Occupation authorities,[6] plaintiff succeeded in obtaining a payment of over $20,000 for the period until 1955, and an award of periodic payments of approximately $250 per month payable to defendants for the period after 1955.[7]

In this action, plaintiff seeks to recover a 35% contingent fee. The court of first instance limited plaintiff's recovery to 20% of the amount the defendants had received for the period up to 1955. The intermedi-

---

5. See L. Scheucher, Der ordre public im österreichischen Recht, 1 ZfRV 15, 33 (1960).

6. In these negotiations, plaintiff presumably stressed the negligence of the driver of the British military vehicle.

7. Sec. 844, subs. 2, of the German Civil Code provides that one who is responsible for the death of a person, must make periodic payments to the victim's dependents so as to compensate the dependents for the support they would have received from the victim had he remained alive. It is further provided that these periodic payments are to continue for the whole period of the victim's normal life expectancy. The award made by the Occupation authorities in the instant case probably was based on these German provisions, which are similar to the Mexican provisions involved in the famous case of Slater v. Mexican Nat. R. Co., 194 U.S. 120, 24 S.Ct. 581 (1904).

ate appellate court permitted plaintiff to recover the full 35% fee. The Bundesgerichtshof reversed and reinstated the judgment of the court of first instance.

Turning first to the "ordinary" choice-of-law rule, the court indicated that since plaintiff had an office in Berlin, a strong argument could be made for the application of German law; but in view of certain directives of the Occupation authorities which were in force in 1952, and of the findings made below regarding the intention of the parties, the court concluded that the contingent fee agreement was governed by the law of New York or Georgia. Under the law of these states the agreement was valid, according to expert opinions received by the courts below.

The only remaining issue involved the impact of the *ordre public* provision then embodied in Art. 30 of the Civil Code's Introductory Law. While expressing no doubt concerning the soundness of BGHZ 22, 162 (the 1956 decision reproduced supra), the court distinguished that decision on the ground that in the present case the enforcement of the contingent fee agreement would fundamentally subvert the strong and clearly expressed purpose of a German law. The court referred to § 844 of the German Civil Code [8] and other provisions which make it clear that the amounts recovered in a wrongful death case should serve to assure the livelihood of the dependents. This clear and strong policy would be thwarted if the relatively modest amounts received by the defendants were in effect reduced by 35%.

Although the court thus held Art. 30 to be applicable, the plaintiff's claim was not completely rejected; nor was it reduced to the rather low figure recoverable under the German statutory tariff.[9] The court pointed out that resort to Art. 30 is always exceptional, and that even where it applies, the impact of that provision upon the outcome of the case should be kept as minimal as possible. In the present case, therefore, plaintiff's claim should be reduced to the highest amount that appears "tolerable" in the light of all the circumstances of the case. On the basis of this reasoning, the Bundesgerichtshof approved the decision of the court of first instance, awarding the plaintiff less than he would have received under the terms of the agreement, but still considerably more than the German statutory tariff would allow him.

Does this case mark a retrogression from the liberal and cosmopolitan position taken by the court in its 1956 decision? Or can the two cases be validly distinguished? [10] Would an American court approve a 35% contingent fee in a comparable case?

(5) Suppose a client domiciled in civil-law country X retains L, a New York lawyer, to handle some legal matter in the United States. A 30 per cent contingent fee is agreed upon in writing. As a result of L's

8. See supra n. 7.

9. Reflecting a strong policy aimed at protection of dependents, German law provides for a relatively low *Gegenstandswert* (value of the matter in controversy) in wrongful death actions, with the result that the attorney's fee, if computed in accordance with the statutory tariff, is quite modest in such cases.

10. For an affirmative answer to this question, see G. Kegel, Internationales Privatrecht 64 (4th ed., 1977), on the ground that in the later case the fee was held to be excessive. Professor Kegel's thought seems to be that an "*ordre public*" objection to an excessive fee (assuming it is valid under the law selected by the ordinary choice-of-law rule) is different from, and stronger than, an objection based merely on the contingent nature of the fee. Cf. Ackermann v. Levine, infra n. 18.

activities, the client recovers one million Dollars; but when L demands 30 per cent of that amount, the client refuses to comply with the demand. L thereupon sues the client in a New York court, invoking long-arm jurisdiction. Although the client contests the claim, the New York court upholds the validity of the contingent fee agreement and enters summary judgment in the amount of $300,000 against the client. Will a court in X enforce that judgment?

The answer, of course, depends on the relevant conflict of laws rules of X,[11] with some of which the reader is familiar. As we have previously seen, we can assume that X will not enforce the judgment unless New York has jurisdiction in accordance with X's jurisdictional principles.[12] In the present case, this hurdle can probably be overcome by L if he can show that the client's obligation was to be performed in New York.[13] Some civil-law countries, moreover, will enforce foreign judgments only on condition of reciprocity; but this will not be a serious hurdle in the present situation, in view of New York's liberal provision for the enforcement of foreign judgments.[14]

The principal argument that is apt to be raised against X's enforcement of the New York judgment, is based on "public policy". Civil-law countries generally refuse recognition and enforcement to a foreign judgment if it violates local public policy.[15] For purposes of this rule, "public policy" usually is defined in the same way as for choice-of-law purposes.[16] According to some civil-law authorities, however, a "public policy" attack on a foreign judgment should be even more difficult than an attack on a foreign rule of substantive law.[17] In any event, it is clear that if X (in accordance with views such as those expressed in the principal case) would treat L's *claim* for a contingent fee as not violative of X's public policy, it will follow a fortiori that a foreign *judgment* based on such a claim will not be denied enforcement on public policy grounds.[18]

---

11. In many countries, foreign judgments can be enforced locally by way of a special proceeding that is simpler than a regular action. In France, this proceeding is known as an *exequatur* proceeding. Countries differ as to whether a foreign judgment may be given a res judicata effect before it has undergone such a procedure.

12. See supra p. 380.

13. See supra p. 393.

14. See N.Y.C.P.L.R. §§ 5301 ff., the New York version of the Uniform Foreign Country Money-Judgments Recognition Act. But note that a few countries require that reciprocity must exist by treaty, or that its existence must have been recognized by official decree.

15. Even the EEC Convention on Jurisdiction and the Recognition and Enforcement of Judgments, which otherwise greatly facilitates the enforcement of the Member States' judgments in other Member States (see supra pp. 404–405), makes it possible to refuse such enforcement on grounds of public policy. By way of contrast, our own Full Faith and Credit Clause

does not permit F-2 to deny full faith and credit to an F-1 judgment on the ground of F-2's public policy. Fauntleroy v. Lum, 210 U.S. 230, 28 S.Ct. 641 (1908). But see Restatement, Second, Conflict of Laws § 103 (1971 and 1986 proposed revisions). In this respect, full faith and credit is thus stronger under the United States Constitution than under the EEC Convention. The reader will remember, however, that in some other respects the reverse is true. See supra pp. 404–405.

In the hypothetical case discussed in the text, supra, the EEC Convention is, of course, inapplicable even if X is a member of the EEC, because the judgment to be enforced was rendered in a non-member country.

16. For an interesting German case discussing this matter in detail, see BGH, June 22, 1983, 4 I.Prax. 202 (1984).

17. See, e.g., R. Zöller, Zivilprozessordnung, § 328, Anno. 177 (14th ed., 1984); 1 R. Geimer & R. A. Schütze, Internationale Urteilsanerkennung 1058–59 (1983).

18. In *interstate* cases in the United States, the enforcement of an F-1 judgment cannot be successfully opposed on the ground of F–2's public policy. But if F–1 is a *foreign country*, such a public policy defense is possible under our law as well. For a case in which such a public policy defense was interposed in an action on a German judgment for a lawyer's fee computed under the German statutory tariff, see Ackermann v. Levine, 788 F.2d 830 (2d Cir. 1986).

*111 S.Ct. 1489   Eastern v. Floyd
(1991)*

D. CAVEAT: THE SPECIAL HAZARDS OF COMPARATIVE LAW

I. LANGUAGE DIFFICULTIES

American translation vi original text what does a American ct do

FRITZ MOSES, INTERNATIONAL LEGAL PRACTICE
4 Fordham L.Rev. 244, 248–51 (1935).

[Original footnotes omitted.]

"Words are very rascals," says Shakespeare's Clown in "Twelfth Night." . . . The flavor of a sentence is apt to change or disappear in a translation; and just this flavor may change the aspect of the case; . . .

The consequences of these difficulties can be seen in many instances. . . .

The German, French and Italian texts of the most carefully prepared Swiss Civil Code are equally authoritative. Yet various discrepancies between the three texts have crept in and courts have had to decide for the one or the other version. . . .

The discrepancies between the English and French texts of the Treaty of Versailles, both "authentic" according to a provision of the Treaty, have become the subject of numerous court decisions. [As an example, Dr. Moses mentions a provision of the Treaty which in the English version speaks of "*debts*", while the French text refers to "*dettes*." Though linguistically of the same origin, the two terms do not have the same meaning. Debt denotes an obligation to pay a sum certain. The French term is much broader and includes any kind of obligation, whether liquidated or not. In interpreting the Treaty, English judges apparently were not even aware of the different meaning of the French text, and limited the term "debt" to claims for a sum certain. French and Belgian judges, equally without recognizing the problem, treated unliquidated claims as "dettes".] [a]

While the limelight of international court proceedings brings into strong relief the linguistic mistakes in international treaties, the errors

---

a. Multilingual texts of national laws as well as international treaties (and "uniform laws" adopted by several nations speaking different languages) frequently engender such difficulties. Many examples are discussed by H. Dölle, Eine Vor-Studie zur Erörterung der Problematik mehrsprachiger Gesetzes- und Vertrags- texte, in the volume XXth Century Comparative and Conflicts Law—Legal Essays in Honor of Hessel E. Yntema 277 (1961), and by K. Lipstein, Some Practical Comparative Law: The Interpretation of Multi-Lingual Treaties with Special Regard to the EEC Treaties, 48 Tul.L.Rev. 907, 913–14 (1974).

made and misunderstandings arising in the daily intercourse of citizens of different nations are, of course, much more frequent.

There are treacherous words which sound almost alike in two different languages, but have a different meaning. The German word *eventuell*, for instance, does not mean *eventually*, but *perhaps*. The French *transaction* [may mean] *compromise*, while the French *compromis* means *arbitration clause*.[b] Interesting are the terms for *divorce* and *separation* in the various languages. The Romans used the term *divortium* in the sense of the American term *divorce*, but in Spain and the Latin-American countries the canonical law, opposed to a dissolution of the marriage bond, was applied directly or indirectly to matters relating to marriages, and therefore the word *divorcio* was used in the sense of separation. However, reforms of the family laws have been widespread, and the meaning of the word *divorcio* now differs among these countries, in some cases even within the countries before and after the reform. In some countries it means both divorce and separation. [In a number of countries it means only separation, and in others again it refers only to divorce.] In Germany divorce is *Scheidung* and separation *Trennung*; but in Austria these same German words have just the contrary meaning: *Trennung* corresponds to divorce or *Scheidung* in Germany and *Scheidung* to separation or *Trennung* in Germany;[c] and recently it happened here that, due to the translation of an Austrian decree as if it had been a German decree, an Austrian, although only separated from his wife, received a marriage license in New York.

NOTES

Translation difficulties are a prolific source of confusion in comparative law.

(1) Perhaps the most important terms in legal parlance are the words "law" and "right"; but a search for equivalents of these terms in foreign languages and foreign legal systems discloses considerable difficulties. In many languages, such as Latin, French, Italian, Spanish and German, there is only one word for "law" and "right" (ius, droit, diritto, derecho, Recht). To avoid ambiguity, legal writers sometimes use this one word solely in the sense of "right", and employ the term denoting a code or statute (loi, legge, Gesetz) as synonymous with "law." In a code jurisdiction this usage is on the whole satisfactory for the everyday work of the lawyer; but it may lead the uninitiated to the

b. Another slippery word, which in the languages and under the legal systems of the civil-law orbit sometimes has a meaning unsuspected by an English-speaking lawyer, is "director". In a foreign country, a person whose title sounds like "director", often is more nearly comparable to an officer than to a director of an American corporation. See Moses, loc. cit. supra, at 268–9; Société Internationale v. Clark, 8 F.R.D. 565 (D.C. 1948).

c. In 1938, after Dr. Moses' article was written, Austria adopted the German terminology. See 2A Bergmann, Internationales Ehe- und Kindschaftsrecht, pp. (Oesterreich) 32–49 (1966). But the point raised in the text still has practical significance with respect to pre-1938 decrees.

inaccurate conclusion that statutory law is the only kind of law known in those countries.[1]

Other legal writers and courts on the continent distinguish between "subjective" ius (right) and "objective" ius (law); but in the everyday use of the word ius, or of its modern equivalents, civilian lawyers do not always spell out whether they have the subjective or the objective ius in mind. Ye comparative lawyers beware!

In dealing with languages and legal systems of non-European origin it is even more important to take nothing for granted.[2] It seems, for instance, that in China and Japan the notion of "right" was totally unknown before the introduction of Western jurisprudence. The oriental languages, consequently, have no word expressing the notion of "right". There seems to have been the notion of duty and obligation, but the correlativity of right and duty is something that only Westerners take for granted.[3]

Similar observations have been made by Professor Macneil with respect to East African law:

> "The essence of customary law may be that even litigation is essentially a negotiating process, the goal of which is the wise pacifying of both parties rather than the effectuating of 'rights' of an injured party. The aim would therefore be to provide a satisfactory framework for future relations whether or not the 'command' of the judge conforms to prior notions (if any) of general rules. And it may follow that there is a large and essential element of 'unknowability' about customary law and that an attempt to make it known in the sense that non-customary law is known, is to change its character quite radically." [4]

To speak of "law" and "rights" in reference to such a system of customs, surely involves the danger of inaccuracy; yet, to explain the substance of the customary "law" without ever using those words, may

1. In order to negative this conclusion, the German Civil Code (Art. 2 of the Introductory Law) expressly provides that throughout the Code the term "Gesetz" means "any legal norm."

2. See J. Frank, Civil Law Influences on the Common Law, 104 U.Pa.L.Rev. 887, 918–19 (1956).

3. See Hozumi Nobushige, The New Japanese Civil Code as Material for the Study of Comparative Jurisprudence (Tokyo, 1912), quoted in Blakemore, Post-War Developments in Japanese Law, [1947] Wis.L.Rev. 631, 649; F. A. Narcisi, Special Considerations in Advising and Dealing with Foreign Businessmen and Attorneys, in D. M. Evans et al. (Eds.), Current Legal Aspects of Foreign Investment in the United States 4, 10–11 (1976).

In a recent study by Hyung I. Kim, Fundamental Legal Concepts of China and the West 91–96, 118–121 (1981), an attempt is made to show that the notion of "right" was not totally absent from traditional Chinese thinking, even though there was no single word expressing the notion. But the author admits that "right" is not a primary and independent concept for the Chinese; to the extent that it is possible at all to speak of an individual's entitlements, they must be thought of as flowing, in complex and somewhat artificial ways, from the socially conditioned duties of others. Thus the primary concept always remains that of duty, and there is no correlativity, in the Western sense, between "right" and "duty" as two independent and equally fundamental notions.

4. I. R. Macneil, Research in East African Law, 3 EALJ 47, 67 (1967). See also R. E. S. Tanner, The Codification of Customary Law in Tanzania, 2 EALJ 105 (1966). This point is, of course, connected with some of the observations previously made in that part of the course in which we attempted to classify and survey legal systems.

be difficult for one trained primarily in the common law or the civil law.

(2) The use of translations, especially Code translations, without resort to the original text, will not always lead to accurate and reliable results. There is one instance in which a reputable translator reversed the meaning of a Code provision by substituting the word "less" for the word "more".[4a] Other illustrations of the maxim of caveat lector exist, unfortunately, in abundant numbers.[5] The following example is taken from the Translation of the Swiss Civil Code by Robert P. Shick (Boston 1915), a translation which according to its title page was "corrected and revised" by Professor Eugen Huber, the famous draftsman of the Swiss Code, and which was published as an "Official Publication of the Comparative Law Bureau of the American Bar Association."

ORIGINAL GERMAN TEXT	ORIGINAL FRENCH TEXT	TRANSLATION BY SHICK (Italics added)	CORRECT TRANS- LATION
Artikel 11	**Article 11**	**Article 11**	**Article 11**
Rechtsfaehig ist jedermann. Fuer alle Menschen besteht demgemaess in den Schranken der Rechtsordnung die gleiche Faehigkeit, Rechte und Pflichten zu haben.	Toute personne jouit des droits civils. En conséquence, chacun a, dans les limites de la loi, une aptitude égale de devenir sujet de droits et d'obligations.	Every man is capable of rights. For all men, therefore, within the bounds of the law's regulation, the same capacity exists to have rights and duties.	Every person is capable of having rights. For all persons, therefore, within the bounds of the law's regulation, the same capacity exists to have rights and duties.
Artikel 12	**Article 12**	**Article 12**	**Article 12**
Wer handlungsfaehig ist, hat die Faehigkeit, durch seine Handlungen Rechte und Pflichten zu begruenden.	Quiconque a l'exercice des droits civils, est capable d'acquérir et de s'obliger.	He who has *commercial capacity* has the capacity by his acts to establish rights and duties.	Whoever is *capable of exercising rights*, is capable by his acts to create rights and duties.
Artikel 13	**Article 13**	**Article 13**	**Article 13**
Die Handlungsfaehigkeit besitzt, wer muendig und urteilsfaehig ist.	Toute personne majeure et capable de discernement a l'exercice des droits civils.	He possesses *commercial capacity* who is of age and capable of judgment.	Every person who is of age and capable of jugment is *capable of exercising rights*.

The Swiss Code, like most civil-law codes, distinguishes between the capacity to have rights (Art. 11) and the capacity to exercise rights (Arts. 12, 13). "Handlungsfaehigkeit", i.e. the capacity to exercise rights, is a term of art. It is defined in Art. 12. The next-following Article establishes the two legal requirements which a person must meet in order to be regarded as "handlungsfaehig."

The German noun "Handlung" means "act". The German word "Handel" means "commerce". Literally, therefore, Handlungsfaehigkeit is capacity to act, and Handelsfaehigkeit (a word which is not

---

4a. See the third edition of this book, at p. 399.

5. See e.g., Capistrano, Mistakes and Inaccuracies in Fisher's Translation of the

Spanish Civil Code, 9 Philippine L.J. 89 et seq., 141 et seq. (1929).

actually in use) would be commercial capacity. In the 1915 translation the two were confused, although the French text should make it clear even to one not too familiar with the German language that Arts. 12 and 13 have nothing whatever to do with commerce, conmercial law or "commercial capacity".[6]

In choosing the foregoing example, the authors of this book did not intend to be critical of Mr. Shick and his associates, who showed vision and skill in tackling a task of supreme difficulty. What the student should constantly keep in mind is that *every* translation (including those by the authors of this book) is at best a second-rate tool.[7]

A translation may be good enough for one purpose, and not sufficiently accurate for another. Where the decision of a case hinges on the precise meaning of language used in a foreign statute or code, it may be necessary for the translator to go through at least two stages of reasoning, by first establishing the literal, non-technical meaning of each term, and then showing a different technical meaning as evidenced by cases, commentaries, textbooks or any other embodiments of foreign law. Most of the older bilingual law dictionaries do not go much beyond the first stage. Among those published during the last few decades, however, there are several which not only *translate* but *explain* legal terms, and thus constitute more useful tools.[8]

II. DIFFERENCES IN CLASSIFICATION

INTRODUCTORY NOTE

The difficult problem of "classification", "qualification" or "characterization" in conflict of laws situations must be left to the books and courses on Conflict of Laws.[1] In this book, "classification" will not be viewed in the technical (Conflict of Laws) sense of the word. The term is here used more generally to denote situations, constantly arising in international legal practice, where danger of misunderstanding and absurdity arises from the fact that courts and legislators, when they formulate rules in terms of their own legal language, fail to indicate whether and how these terms can be applied to foreign institutions and phenomena.

---

6. According to Art. 116 of the Swiss Federal Constitution, the "national languages" are German, French, Italian and Romansch. The first three of these are also "official languages" (Amtssprachen) of the Confederation. It follows that the French (or Italian) text of the Civil Code is as "official" as the German text, even though Professor Huber's original draft was in German. 1 Egger, Kommentar zum Schweizerischen Zivilgesetzbuch, pp. 29–30 (1930).

7. See P. W. Schroth, Legal Translation, in J. N. Hazard & W. J. Wagner (Eds.), Law in the U.S.A. Faces Social and Scientific Change, 34 Am.J.Comp.L. (Supplement) 47 (1986).

8. For a listing of dictionaries, see Szladits, Bibliography on Foreign and Comparative Law 30–33 (1953 and Supps.). See also infra pp. 895–896.

1. See, e.g., 1 E. Rabel, The Conflict of Laws—A Comparative Study 52–72 (2d ed. prepared by U. Drobnig, 1958); Restatement, Second, Conflict of Laws § 7, and Reporter's Note (1971), where further references will be found.

THE TERM "NOTARY": NOTES AND QUESTIONS

(1) We have observed the striking differences in education and status between a continental notary and a notary in this country (see *supra* pp. 18–20). These differences have given rise to a problem of classification. Professor Nussbaum, in his book on German Private International Law (1932), page 95, long ago stated the problem as follows: "Insofar as German provisions require the embodiment of a jural act in a notarial record . . ., it may become doubtful to what extent a foreign recorder is to be regarded as a 'notary.' This is so especially with respect to Anglo-American 'notaries'. . . ."

In struggling with this problem, German courts and legal writers usually start with the observation that under German Law there are two kinds of documents executed with the help of a notary: (a) "Notarially authenticated" documents. These are ordinary signed writings, with respect to which the notary does no more than to authenticate the signature of one or several parties. (b) "Notarial Documents", i.e., protocols of what the parties declared and transacted in the notary's presence. A document of this latter kind is necessarily prepared and issued by the notary; as the reader knows, the notary retains the original of such a document, and issues only certified copies to the parties.

Where German law requires merely a notarially authenticated document (as, e.g., in the case of communications addressed to the Commercial Register and providing information concerning registrable facts),[1] it is generally recognized that such authentication can be provided by an American notary public.[2] To perform the authenticating function, does not require any legal learning, and thus it would seem that the differences between a civil-law notary and an American notary public are irrelevant so long as nothing but mere authentication of a signature is involved.

[margin note: where U.S. & German notaries are similar]

Where a true notarial document is required, however (as in the cases, among many others, of most real estate transactions and of promises to make a gift), it is the prevailing view among German courts and legal authors that a document drawn up by an American notary public does not meet this form requirement.[3] The reason is that such a document, because of the low status of the American notary public, simply is not a "notarial document", as that term is understood in Germany and other civil-law countries.[4]

(2) The question discussed in the preceding paragraphs is of considerable interest to international practitioners. Their clients, owning interests in German corporations or other German assets, often have to execute documents which under German law require notarial form. As the fees of a German notary, especially in matters involving large amounts, can be very substantial,[5] international practitioners often

---

1. See German Commercial Code, § 12.

2. See U. Drobnig, American-German Private International Law 381 (2d ed., 1972), and authorities there cited.

3. See ibid.

4. Another reason sometimes adduced is that an American notary public *under his own law* lacks power to prepare and

execute "notarial documents" within the German meaning of the term. See ibid. *Quaere*, however, whether statutes such as § 135 of the N.Y. Executive Law (see supra p. 780) do not supply such power.

5. In many cases, this is still true today, even though a statute of August 20, 1975 (BGB*l* I 2189) has had the effect of reduc-

explore the possibility of having the transaction recorded by a non-German notary.

Example: Suppose your client X Corp., a New York corporation, owns shares of Deutsche Luftverwertungs—G.m.b.H., a German limited responsibility company. X desires to assign these shares to its subsidiary, Y Corp., in such manner that the assignment will be recognized as valid in Germany. As the reader knows (supra p. 831), German law requires a notarial document for such assignment. In what form, if at all, can such assignment be effectively executed in New York? Proper analysis discloses that this question is a composite of two sub-questions:

(a) Would a German court, pursuant to German choice-of-law rules, consider the form of the assignment governed by New York law, and on that basis dispense with the requirement of a notarial protocol? [6]

(b) If the requirement is not dispensed with, can it be met by notarization in New York? Is a New York notary a "Notar" within the meaning of the German statute?

Even though New York law purports to give a New York notary public all the powers of a German "Notar",[7] a German court most probably would answer these questions in the negative, and would invalidate the assignment notarized in New York. Pursuant to § 17 of the Beurkundungsgesetz (Law Concerning Public Documents), a "Notar" is under a duty to advise the parties concerning the legal significance and consequences of the proposed transaction. Only a law-trained person can furnish such advice, and a New York notary public thus is unable to fill the shoes of a German "Notar".[8]

Some German intermediate appellate courts went further and held that even a Swiss notary, whose qualifications are similar to those of his German confreres, cannot perform the functions of a German "Notar" with respect to transactions governed by German law. The reason given for these holdings was that a Swiss notary, although he is law-trained, cannot properly advise the parties on matters of German law.[9] These holdings of intermediate appellate courts have been overruled by a recent decision of the court of last resort, wherein it was held that a document properly executed before a Swiss notary is a "notarial document" within the meaning of a German statute requiring such form for a transaction governed by German law.[10] The highest court emphasized, however, that it reached this result only on the ground

---

ing the "amount involved" in a number of instances.

In contrast to attorneys' fees, the statutory fees of a notary are not subject to agreement.

6. A negative answer to this controversial choice-of-law question, which was left open in BGHZ 80, 76 (1981), is suggested by some leading authors. See Baumbach-Hueck, GmbH Gesetz, § 2, Anno. 9 (14th ed., 1985); G. Kegel, Internationales Privatrecht 280–81 (4th ed., 1977). Thus, a German court probably would hold that the formal validity of the assignment is governed by German law rather than by New York law, even though the assignment is executed in New York.

7. See N.Y. Executive Law § 135, reproduced supra p. 780.

8. See supra n. 3.

9. For critical discussions of these holdings see J. Kropholler, Auslandsbeurkundungen im Gesellschaftsrecht, 140 Zeitschrift für Handelsrecht 394 (1976); H. Bernstein, Erwerb und Rückerwerb von GmbH-Anteilen im deutsch-amerikanischen Rechtsverkehr, id. at 414.

10. Decision of February 16, 1981, BGHZ 80, 76, discussed by Baumbach-Hueck, supra n. 6.

that in training and status a Swiss notary is on a par with his German colleagues. The court thus confirmed the above-stated conclusion that an American notary public, who lacks equivalent training and status, is not a "Notar" within the meaning of German statutes requiring a notarial document.

NOTE ON FOREIGN-DIRECTED STATUTES

The draftsmen of the German statute requiring "notarial" form for the transfer of a GmbH share in all probability focused their exclusive attention on the German institution of notaries, and gave little thought to the possibility that some parties might desire to execute such transfers before non-German notaries. Most statutes—in every legal system—are similarly written in local terms, with the result that doubts and difficulties are apt to arise when these terms have to be applied to foreign institutions.

Occasionally, however, one encounters other statutes—and their number seems to be increasing both here and abroad—which are specifically directed at foreign institutions, seeking in some way to control the domestic impact of such institutions. Even these foreign-directed statutes often pose problems (a) of interpreting the statutory language, and (b) of determining and correctly understanding the foreign institution to which the statute is sought to be applied in a particular case.

Limitations of space make it impossible to offer more than one example. Because of its great practical importance, a provision of the U.S. income tax law has been chosen to serve as such example.

Citizen taxpayers and domestic corporations have the right, within certain limits, to use the amount of foreign taxes paid or accrued during the taxable year as a credit against their United States income tax; but this privilege exists only if the foreign tax in question is an "income, war profits or excess profits tax", or "a tax paid in lieu of a tax upon income, war profits or excess profits." [1]

The question whether or not a particular foreign tax, which has no precise counterpart in our own tax system, is an "income tax" or a tax "in lieu of a tax on income", and thus entitles the taxpayer to a foreign tax credit, has produced a great deal of litigation.[2] The case which follows illustrates the type of questions arising in such litigation.

---

1. See 26 U.S.C.A. §§ 901(b)(1) and 903 (as of 1986). These provisions, which were not substantially changed by the Tax Reform Act of 1986, received their present form in the Internal Revenue Code of 1954. The corresponding provisions of the earlier Code are quoted in the opinion of the Tax Court, infra.

2. Many rulings and decisions on the point are collected in 8 Mertens, The Law of Federal Income Taxation, §§ 33.04–33.06 (Rev. Ed., 1980, and 1987 Supp.); P. F. Postlewaite, International Corporate Taxation, § 5.02 (1980); P. R. McDaniel & H. J. Ault, Introduction to United States International Taxation, § 6.02, especially subs. 6.2.3.1.2 (2nd ed., 1981); R. Hellawell & R. C. Pugh, The Study of Federal Tax Law—Transnational Transactions 75–145 (1981).

[Handwritten margin notes at top: "Characterization important? A tort suit or K suit — may determine choice of law."]

[Handwritten note: "How to classify a particular tax?"]

[Handwritten left margin note: "Interpreting U.S. tax statute not Columbia's laws"]

LANMAN & KEMP–BARCLAY & CO. OF COLOMBIA, PETITIONER v. COMMISSIONER OF INTERNAL REVENUE, RESPONDENT

Tax Court of the United States, 1956. 26 T.C. 582.

KERN, Judge. The sole issue for decision is whether the Colombian patrimony tax * of $3,257.67 (and the 35 per cent surcharge thereon of $1,120.22), accrued by the petitioner in 1947, is an income tax or a tax in lieu of a tax on income within the meaning of section 131 ** of the Internal Revenue Code of 1939 so as to qualify these amounts as foreign tax credits.

The petitioner bases its principal argument for the allowance of the credit on the contention that under the laws of the Republic of Colombia, the tax paid to that country was "a single tax, not divisible into separate parts," that it was "predominantly an income tax," and hence the entire amount paid qualifies for the credit under section 131(a). It points to the following indicia as support for its position on the classification of the tax: Article 64 of the Colombian tax law imposing the patrimony tax states that the income, patrimony, and excess profits taxes "shall be considered one and indivisible"; the judicial and administrative interpretations of the statute have construed the three levies as an indivisible whole, as only modalities or variations of the income tax; all information for the computation of the three-part tax and the surcharges thereon is submitted in a single report; the three levies are combined into one total which is reduced by the amount of an exemption before the surcharges are computed; and references in the Colombian law are to a single tax resulting from the combination of the three levies and the surcharges and not to separate taxes.

It is clear that under the law of the Republic of Colombia the patrimony tax is deemed to be a supplement to and indivisible from the income tax. It appears from the opinions of the Supreme Court of Justice that this characterization results not from mere administrative convenience in handling three taxes through one return, but from a fiscal policy based on the theory that the income tax, in order to be an equitable revenue system, requires a tax on capital to more fairly

---

* The court's Findings of Fact show that the Colombia tax law defines "taxable patrimony" as the value of the taxpayer's immovable and movable property, minus debts and certain other deductions. In effect, therefore, the patrimony tax is measured by the taxpayer's net worth.

** Sec. 131. Taxes of Foreign Countries and Possessions of United States.

(a) Allowance of Credit.—If the taxpayer chooses to have the benefits of this section the tax imposed by this chapter . . . shall be credited with:

(1) *Citizens and Domestic Corporations.* In the case of a citizen of the United States and of a domestic corporation, the amount of any income, war-profits, and excess-profits taxes paid or accrued during the taxable year to any foreign country or to any possession of the United States; . . . .

(h) *Credit for Taxes in Lieu of Income, etc., Taxes.* For the purposes of this section . . . the term "income, war-profits, and excess-profits taxes" shall include a tax paid in lieu of a tax upon income, war-profits, or excess-profits otherwise generally imposed by any foreign country or by any possession of the United States. [Footnote by the court.]

distribute the burdens among the nation's taxpayers and to prevent the state from being penalized if a property owner, through negligence or for some other reason, fails to realize the inherent productive potential of his property.*

However, it is well settled that the determination of whether or not a foreign levy qualifies as an income tax within the meaning of section 131(a) is to be made not upon the characterization of the foreign law, but under the criteria established by the internal revenue laws of the United States. Biddle v. Commissioner, 302 U.S. 573, 58 S.Ct. 379; ** Keasbey & Mattison Co. v. Rothensies, (C.A.3, 1943) 133 F.2d 894, certiorari denied 320 U.S. 739, 64 S.Ct. 39; L. Helena Wilson, 7 T.C. 1469. In other words, "the determinative question is whether the foreign tax is the substantial equivalent of an income tax as the term is understood in the United States." Commissioner v. American Metal Co., (C.A.2, 1955) 221 F.2d 134.

The doctrine that only those increases in value of property which are actually realized by the owner constitute taxable income is basic to the income tax system of the United States. See Commissioner v. Glenshaw Glass Co., 348 U.S. 426, 75 S.Ct. 473; United States v. Kirby Lumber Co., 284 U.S. 1, 52 S.Ct. 4; and Keasbey & Mattison Co. v. Rothensies, supra, in which the court said: "The defined concept of income has been uniformly restricted to a gain realized or a profit derived from capital, labor, or both." The Colombian income tax separately considered provides for the taxation of net income and its substantial equivalence to our own income tax has been recognized by the respondent in the instant case. The patrimony tax separately considered is really a tax on property and results in a levy upon the net value of the taxpayer's assets which will include any unrealized appreciation of such value. It is computed separately from the income tax

---

* The court's Findings of Fact contain the following:

"On October 7, 1938, the Supreme Court of Justice of the Republic of Colombia held in two cases, respectively, involving the Colombian Petroleum Company and the South American Gulf Oil Company, both Delaware corporations, that provisions in their contracts with the Government of Colombia, whereby they were exempt from all taxes except the national stamp taxes and the income tax, did not prevent the imposition of the subsequently enacted patrimony tax which was determined to be merely a supplement and addition to the income tax. The patrimony tax, the excess profits tax, and the income tax were held to be an indivisible whole.

"The Colombian income tax was already in effect when it was supplemented in 1935 by the patrimony tax and the excess profits tax. The purpose in enacting the latter two taxes was to round out the income tax and to make the Colombian tax system more fair and equitable by imposing a greater tax on those who had a greater ability to pay as represented both by income above a certain amount and by capital, whether or not such capital was then being productively employed. The patrimony tax is based upon the presumption that every piece of property has a certain productive ability, and the failure of the owner to achieve a return therefrom cannot deprive the state of its right to receive a revenue from this potential. Thus, the state is deemed entitled to a tax on the increment in value of unproductive property appreciating in value because of its location in a developing urban area. The patrimony tax and excess profits tax are, therefore, considered under Colombia law as merely modalities or variations of the income tax."

** See, especially, 302 U.S. at 578–9, 58 S.Ct. 379, at 381 (1938).

from information respecting the taxpayer's assets and liabilities and does not give effect to items of income and expense. The petitioner's own expert witness testified that it is possible for a taxpayer to be liable for a patrimony tax in a year when the taxpayer has no revenue and is not liable for the income tax, and such testimony is in accord with the language of Article 64. The computation of the patrimony tax and the computation of the surcharge thereon are not so integrated with the income tax itself as to create any problem of allocating the total tax paid to Colombia. We are not bound by the classification of the patrimony tax under Colombian law as part of the income tax. L. Helena Wilson, supra. After careful consideration of the Colombian tax law, it is our conclusion that there is no substantial equivalent to the patrimony tax under our income tax system, and that this part of the Colombian tax is not an income tax within the meaning of section 131(a).

The petitioner cites Helvering v. Campbell, (C.A.4, 1944) 139 F.2d 865, and Rev.Rul. 56–51 1956–1 C.B. 320, for the proposition that for the purpose of section 131 the classification of a single tax will be governed by its predominant character and argues that the tax in issue herein was predominantly an income tax. The authorities cited by the petitioner do not involve the allowance of a credit for a separately computed tax not based on income and are clearly distinguishable. Furthermore, the petitioner's classification of the Colombian tax as a single tax predominantly income in character depends on the characterization of the Colombian law which we have held above is not controlling.

The petitioner's final argument is that the patrimony tax is at least a tax in lieu of a tax on income within the meaning of section 131(h). The legislative purpose in enacting this subsection in 1942 is expressed in the report of the Senate Committee on Finance, S.Rept. No. 1631, 77th Cong., 2d Sess., pp. 131–132, as follows:

> "Your committee believes further amendments should be made in section 131. Under that section as it now stands, a credit is allowed against United States tax for income, war profits or excess profits taxes paid or accrued to any foreign country or to any possession of the United States. In the interpretation of the term income tax, the Commissioner, the Board, and the courts have consistently adhered to a concept of income tax rather closely related to our own, and if such foreign tax was not imposed upon a basis corresponding approximately to net income it was not recognized as a basis for such credit. Thus if a foreign country in imposing income taxation authorized, for reasons growing out of the administrative difficulties of determining net income or taxable basis within that country, a United States domestic corporation doing business in such country to pay a tax in lieu of such income tax but measured, for example, by gross income, gross

sales or a number of units produced within the country, such tax has not heretofore been recognized as a basis for a credit. Your committee has deemed it desirable to extend the scope of this section. Accordingly, subsection (f) of section 160 provides that the term 'income, war profits and excess profits taxes' shall, for the purposes of sections 131 and 23(c)(1), include a tax paid by a domestic taxpayer in lieu of the tax upon income, war profits and excess profits taxes which would otherwise be imposed upon such taxpayer by any foreign country or by any possession of the United States. . . ."

. . . The Committee Report and the regulations indicate that the substituted tax must be related to income or to the taxpayer's productive output. There is nothing in either to indicate that a property tax that has no relation to the taxpayer's income or production was to be deemed such a substitute. The petitioner was subject to and paid the Colombian income tax in 1947, and has been granted a credit under section 131(a) for the amount of such tax. The patrimony tax, which we have construed to be a property tax, was imposed not as a substitute for but as a supplement to the Colombian income tax and no deduction is allowable for the amount of such tax against the Colombian income tax. Therefore, the patrimony tax does not qualify as a tax in lieu of a tax on income within the meaning of section 131(h). See Compania Embotelladora Coca-Cola v. United States, 134 Ct.Cl. 723, 139 F.Supp. 953.*

NOTE

The method used by the courts in cases of this kind can be analogized to an attempt to find out whether a given peg fits into a particular hole. The peg in this case was the Colombian patrimony tax. The shape of that peg was of course determined by the law of Colombia. But the hole into which the taxpayer unsuccessfully sought to fit the peg, was the notion of "income tax", as that term is used in the U.S. Internal Revenue Code. Thus the shape of the hole was determined by U.S. law.

After careful consideration of the shape both of the peg and of the hole, the Court concluded, in effect, that the taxpayer was trying to fit a square peg into a round hole.*

* Accord: Abbot Laboratories International Co. v. United States, 160 F.Supp. 321 (N.D.Ill.E.D., 1958), aff'd per curiam 267 F.2d 940 (7 Cir. 1959).

* The "peg and hole" analogy can be used also in other (perhaps more complex) situations raising the issue whether a particular foreign institution has certain characteristics specified by our law. An example is presented by the Wood & Selick case, supra p. 188. The peg in that case was a French prescription statute. Under the forum's conflicts rule, there existed two different holes (extinguishment of remedy and extinguishment of right), and the question was how, and by what criteria, one could determine into which of the two holes the peg could be fitted more easily and more appropriately.

III. THE CONTRAST BETWEEN THE PRINTED WORD AND ACTUAL PRACTICE

[handwritten: → compare at this level]

[handwritten: U.S. publication of laws far superior to others]

NOTE ON THE SUBJECT OF "CORRUPTION"

(1) If we speak of a legal system as "corrupt", we usually mean that a substantial portion of governmental and especially of judicial business is disposed of in a manner which is not in accordance with the substantive and procedural rules announced in the law books.[1] To some extent, as the "realist" school of jurisprudence has taught us, such divergence between the printed word and actual practice can be observed in every legal system.[1a] But there are important differences of degree, differences ranging all the way from the stifling atmosphere of a Gestapo-ridden dictatorship[1b] to the subconscious bias or occasional indiscretion of a judge or other official from which even a decent system is not entirely safe.

(2) There are two principal channels through which, singly or in combination, corruption enters the machinery of the law: political influence and graft. The materials which follow these Notes, will deal with the more insidious forms of political corruption of legal systems.

The subject of graft might be equally interesting, but it is somewhat less susceptible of academic study. Those who are in the best position to observe this form of corruption are not inclined to publish the results of their research, and there exists as yet no Map of the World in which the various countries and areas are shaded or colored according to the degree of judicial honesty prevailing therein. Sociolo-

---

1. By widespread practices of evading and avoiding legal commands, the governed as well as the governing often contribute to the emasculation of the law as a regulating force in society. See, e.g., B. Kozolchyk, Law and the Credit Structure in Latin America, 7 Va.J.Int.L., No. 2, p. 1, at 33–35 (1967). Although these practices may become deeply ingrained, it would seem that in most instances they have initially come into existence as a reaction of the average citizen to official abuses. It may be defensible, therefore, in exploring the root causes of "corruption" of a legal system, to place more emphasis on the conduct of the governing than on that of the governed (though the ways in which they interact, may be manifold and complex).

1a. In studying the divergence between law in "the books" and law in action, one must keep in mind that "the books", especially when they offer reports of actual cases, often reveal important features of the law in action. But the extent to which "the books" thus reflect reality, differs from country to country, because the types of "books" available under one system may be much more revealing than those to be found in another. See K. H. Neumayer, Fremdes Recht aus Büchern, fremde Rechtswirklichkeit und die funktionelle Dimension in den Methoden der Rechtsvergleichung, 34 Rabels Z. 411, 414–17 (1970). A student of the law in action will find that his task is relatively easier when he focuses his attention on countries where there is a great wealth of reported judicial and administrative decisions, and where the published reports of such decisions thoroughly recite the underlying facts. Ibid. The reader will recall that in this respect there are significant differences not only between common-law and civil-law countries, but also among the latter. See supra pp. 649–650.

1b. Human rights violations usually involve governmental deviations from the "law" stated in the local law books. For an enlightening world-wide survey of such violations and deviations, see the European Parliament's Resolutions of May 17, 1983, entitled "Human Rights in the World" and "Human Rights in the Soviet Union", and accompanying Reports, all conveniently reproduced in 4 Human Rights Law Journal 1–127 (1983).

gists and anthropologists, however, have attempted to throw some light on the causes and patterns of graft in various parts of the world,[2] and occasionally one can find relevant nuggets of information in legal writings, as shown by the following quotation from a recent law review article:

> A recent empirical study of Rio de Janeiro lawyers found that 80% of those interviewed customarily made grease payments to the clerks. . . . In some states, payment of both "speed money" and "delay money" is common. Payments to make the entire file disappear are not infrequent in some areas.[2a]

International practitioners have a fairly accurate notion, based on experience and gossip, in what countries they can expect an impartial determination of litigated issues. They will try to avoid litigation in the courts of certain geographic areas, because they are almost intuitively aware of conditions such as these:

> . . . judges, police chiefs, and other local officials in Latin America are notoriously underpaid and provided with inadequate working facilities; judges in smaller cities are usually isolated from each other for months or years at a time—there are no annual conferences or conventions; and finally, their tenure may well depend on maintaining their local political contacts and friendships. Not surprisingly, then, while adequate social and economic legislation (such as labor and water laws) is not difficult to find in Latin America, in many cases it is ignored, inefficiently enforced, or implemented in a manner that unduly favors a given element of society.[3]

Experienced practitioners are aware, also, of the complexity of the "corruption" issue, especially in reference to developing countries. "Of course in many traditional societies the use of public office or authority for private advantage and gain was often expected and in part sanctioned. The officials of the traditional Chinese bureaucracy were permitted to retain a portion of the taxes they collected, and clerks and runners were permitted numerous 'customary' fees."[4] When modern Western political and legal institutions and standards are imposed on traditional peasant and pre-literate societies, such traditional customs turn into "corruption".[5]

As the reader will recall (see supra p. 30), the U.S. Congress has attempted to deal with this world-wide phenomenon by enacting the

2. See, e.g., the interesting study by S. Ottenberg, Local Government and Law in Southern Nigeria, in D. C. Buxbaum (Ed.), Traditional and Modern Legal Institutions in Asia and Africa 26 ff. (1967), where further references, not limited to African law, can be found.

2a. K. S. Rosenn, Civil Procedure in Brazil, 34 Am.J.Comp.L. 487, at 518 (n. 205) (1986). See also the same author's prior article, Brazil's Legal Culture: The Jeito Revisited, 1 Fla.Int.L.J. 1, 36 (1984).

3. J. R. Thome, The Process of Land Reform in Latin America, 1968 Wis.L.Rev. 9, at 20–21.

4. D. C. Buxbaum, Introduction, op. cit. supra n. 2, at 3. See also F. G. Dawson & I. L. Head, International Tribunals, National Courts and the Rights of Aliens 106 (1971) (referring to Spanish colonial policy "whereby minor officials, after purchasing their offices, were to receive their remuneration in fees from the public they were serving").

5. See Buxbaum, supra n. 4. For another interesting and ambitious attempt to explain the prevalence of "corruption" in developing countries, see C. Clapham, Third World Politics—An Introduction 50–54 (1985).

Foreign Corrupt Practices Act of 1977.[6] In unilaterally mounting this indiscriminate, global attack on "corruption", our lawmakers were too provincial to realize that in countries where (either de jure or de facto) governmental powers can be arbitrarily exercised, the "questionable payment" may be the only remedy by which a victim threatened with arbitrary government action can protect his interests.[7] In certain legal systems, such payments thus may serve purposes functionally comparable to what in our system might be accomplished by judicial and other legal remedies.[8]

With its undertone of moral reprobation, "corruption" is an emotive word. We should be cautious in its use when we discuss the—to us—strange conditions of traditional societies in the early stages of modernization.[9] There may be less need, however, to be restrained in making value judgments when we turn—as we now do—to the problem of political perversion of highly developed legal systems.

CARL ZEISS STIFTUNG v. V. E. B. CARL ZEISS, JENA

United States District Court, Southern District of New York, 1968.
293 F.Supp. 892.

[The parties' dispute relates primarily to the ownership of certain exceedingly valuable U.S. trademarks, which originally belonged to the Abbe Foundation in Jena, Germany. The plaintiff, a foundation existing under German law and having its corporate domicile in West Germany, claims to be the successor, and thus to have acquired all the trademark rights, of the Abbe Foundation. The defendant, a "people-owned enterprise" incorporated in 1951 under the law of Soviet-occu-

6. 91 Stat. 1494. See N. H. Jacoby, P. Nehemekis & R. Eells, Bribery and Extortion in World Business (1978); T. Atkeson, The Foreign Corrupt Practices Act of 1977, 12 Int. Lawyer 703 (1978); Note, Questionable Payments by Foreign Subsidiaries: The Extraterritorial Jurisdictional Effect of the Foreign Corrupt Practices Act of 1977, 3 Hastings Int. & Comp.L.Rev. 151 (1979).

It is interesting to compare the Foreign Corrupt Practices Act with the more intelligent European approaches to the problem. See, e.g., R. J. Goebel, Professional Responsibility Issues in International Law Practice, 29 Am.J.Comp.L. 1, 28 ff. (1981); M. Bogdan, International Trade and the New Swedish Provisions on Corruption, 27 Am.J.Comp.L. 665 (1979); W. Fikentscher & K. Waibl, Ersatz im Ausland gezahlter Bestechungsgelder, 7 IPRax 86 (1987).

7. See G. T. McLaughlin, The Criminalization of Questionable Foreign Payments by Corporations: A Comparative Legal Systems Analysis, 46 Ford.L.Rev. 1071, especially at 1095 (1978).

8. See ibid.

9. Legal institutions transplanted from a Western legal system to a non-Western environment often function in ways that appear anomalous to the Western observer. In instances of this kind it is important not to use the word "corruption" when in reality we deal with a transformation caused by cultural differences. The institution of the jury furnishes an apt illustration. In our view, that institution can function only if the jurors are able to exercise independent judgment, basing their decisions exclusively (or at least principally) on the evidence and on the court's instructions. If in a given culture the tribal or family ties of the jurors are so strong as to make the exercise of such independent judgment impossible, then trial by jury "would be impractical and anomalous." King v. Morton, 520 F.2d 1140 (D.C.Cir. 1975) (holding that factual findings on cultural conditions are necessary before it can be determined whether jury trials in American Samoa are feasible). See also the same case upon remand to the District Court, King v. Andrus, 452 F.Supp. 11 (D.D.C. 1977). See also supra pp. 332–335.

pied East Germany, contends that it (the defendant) is the true successor of the Abbe Foundation.

The parties' conflicting claims had given rise to litigation in many countries, including West Germany and East Germany. Some of these cases had been decided prior to the trial of the present action. The defendant relied heavily on some decisions in its favor rendered by East German courts, including a 1961 opinion of the Supreme Court of East Germany.[a]]

MANSFIELD, District Judge. . . . The opinions of the courts of East Germany prove to be of little assistance in resolving the issues before us . . . [The court points to the fact that the East German proceeding, which culminated in the 1961 opinion of the Supreme Court of East Germany, was conducted *ex parte*, and that the East German courts did not have before them much of the essential proof relied upon by the court in the present case.]

Quite aside from the fact that the decisions of the courts of East Germany were based on different factual premises, however, it must be recognized in weighing these decisions that East German courts do not speak as an independent judiciary of the type found in the United States or even in West Germany, but orient their judgment according to the wishes of the leaders of the socialist state, which are expressed through two coordinated administrative organs, the Ministry of Justice and the Office of the Attorney General. See "The Administration of Justice and the Concept of Legality in East Germany," 68 Yale L.J. 705, 707 (1959).[b] In short, even the East German Supreme Court is made responsible to the highest authorities of the state as a means of insuring "that the content of socialist law and its implementation through the courts are in harmony with the overall state administrative activity during the period of the comprehensive construction of socialism".[c] Law and Legislation in the German Democratic Republic (Comments on 1963 Decree as to Fundamental Tasks and Methods of Work of the Judiciary Organs (East Germany)). Nevertheless, to the extent that they may shed light on the legal issues before this Court, they have been considered.

Such consideration reveals the decisions of the Supreme Court of East Germany to be so completely lacking in any objectivity of approach and so thoroughly saturated with a combination of communist propaganda, diatribes against the "capitalist oriented" decisions of the

a. The East German decisions, having been rendered in a proceeding in which plaintiff received no notice and no opportunity to be heard, clearly did not have any collateral estoppel effect. It seems that defendant relied on those decisions primarily as evidence of the applicable German law.

b. The article cited in the text was by Professor Otto Kirchheimer, who was the author, also, of the comprehensive and in-

structive monograph Political Justice—The Use of Legal Procedure for Political Ends (1961).

c. Toward this purpose East German judges after being selected by the Ministry of Justice are "instructed" by it and are removable for inefficiency or unreliability arising out of policy differences. The "judge remains a simple party servant", 68 Yale L.J. 707–12, 749 (1959). [Footnote by the Court.]

West German courts, and absence of judicial restraint, that any logical analysis is obfuscated by their obvious political mission. [The court then quoted some choice morsels of propagandistic invective from the East German decisions in the Zeiss matter[d] and turned to other, more reliable evidence of the applicable German law. On the basis of that evidence, plaintiff was held to be the owner of the trademarks in question.[e]]

NOTES ON LAW IN ACTION

(1) *Ascertainment of Actual Practice.* In the principal case the court based its conclusions regarding the realities of the East German judicial system on a well-documented, thorough study by a leading scholar, which had appeared in the Yale Law Journal. Published materials of this kind are becoming more widely available; [*] their use is clearly authorized by FRCP Rule 44.1. Where no such materials are available, it may become necessary for the parties formally or informally to introduce expert evidence on the actual practices as well as the book law of the foreign country in question. Experience has shown, however, that evidence of law in action can be effectively presented only if the proponent keeps two important points in mind:

> (a) The actual working of a legal and political system can be understood only if the system is viewed as a whole. Even though the case at hand seemingly may involve no more than a narrow issue of foreign substantive law, a proper evaluation of the relevant foreign sources always requires an awareness of the actualities of the legislative and judicial process in the particular country. In the many situations, moreover, in which a case turns on the validity and effect of a judicial or other official act of a foreign government (e.g., a criminal conviction [1]), the true significance of

---

d. In Zschernig v. Miller, 389 U.S. 429, 88 S.Ct. 664, at 669–71 (1968), the United States Supreme Court took certain American state court judges to task for having displayed, in some of their opinions, foreign policy attitudes relating to the cold war, and for having engaged in "judicial criticism of nations established on a more authoritarian basis than our own". By our standards, some of the state court opinions castigated by the Supreme Court were indeed somewhat intemperate; but they were mild and judicious compared to the venomous attacks against "capitalist" courts that were contained in the Zeiss decisions of the East German courts.

e. This decision of the District Court was modified (on a point not relevant here) and as modified affirmed, 433 F.2d 686 (2 Cir., 1970), cert. den. 403 U.S. 905, 91 S.Ct. 2205 (1971). The District Court's findings concerning the attitudes and approach of the East German courts were left undisturbed (433 F.2d at 700–02).

For discussions tracing the history of the world-wide litigious struggle between Zeiss-

West and Zeiss-East, see I. Shapiro, Zeiss v. Zeiss—The Cold War in a Microcosm, 7 Int. Lawyer 235 (1973), and H. L. Bernstein, Corporate Identity in International Business: The Zeiss Controversy, 20 Am.J. Comp.L. 299 (1972). The latter article, at 305–06, points out that as to the relative merits of the East German and West German Supreme Court decisions the House of Lords in a 1967 decision (i.e., a decision antedating the principal case) had taken a view sharply at variance with that expressed by the American courts in the principal case. For comments on the House of Lords decision, see the opinion of the U.S. Court of Appeals, 433 F.2d at 700–02.

[*] A recent book on Soviet law in its very title emphasizes the dichotomy between the printed word and what actually happens. See O. S. Ioffe & P. B. Maggs, Soviet Law in Theory and Practice (1983). The same theme is sounded in the title of an even more recent book by Professor Ioffe: Soviet law and Soviet Reality (1985).

1. For further examples see infra.

the particular act to be evaluated may well escape a person who is not familiar with the over-all functioning of the system.

(b) Law in the books and law in action are not neatly separated compartments. A knowledgeable expert frequently will be able to find, in the law books themselves, striking indications of the actual corruption of a legal system. For example, Professor Kirchheimer's findings—relied upon by the court in the principal case—concerning the absence of judicial independence in East Germany were based, in large part, on statutory provisions and official pronouncements of communist functionaries in East Germany.[2]

Occasionally, special evidentiary difficulties may be encountered in instances where country X has deliberately attempted to conceal the realities of its law in action.[2a] The most reprehensible techniques of totalitarian governments, especially torture and other methods of terror, usually are practiced in secret. Some of the policies of such governments, moreover, may be so complex and shifting that even experts are unable to find tell-tale traces in published materials. In such a case, some courts may be willing, by way of judicial notice, to draw broad inferences from what is known of the general governmental system of X.[3] That failing, it becomes necessary to present evidence, or at least materials for judicial notice, concerning the specific practices in question. This may call for testimony by expert witnesses who have lived in X in the not-too-distant past, or otherwise have the requisite knowledge of actual conditions there.[4]

(2) *Limitations on the Courts' Power to Consider a Foreign Country's Law in Action.* Actual practices, as distinguished from book law, of foreign nations have been considered by American courts with particular frequency in cases arising under state statutes which regulate or limit the inheritance of property by non-resident aliens.[5] Some

2. The techniques which at the time in question were used in East Germany for the abrogation of judicial independence, were not fundamentally different from those applied by the predecessor (Nazi) regime. Concerning the latter, see Estate of Leefers, 127 Cal.App.2d 550, 274 P.2d 239 (1954); In re Krachler's Estate, 199 Or. 448, 263 P.2d 769 (1953); N. S. Marsh, Some Aspects of the German Legal System under National Socialism, 62 L.Q.Rev. 366 (1946). On the general problem of corruption of the legal order by fascist regimes, see A. H. Campbell, Fascism and Legality, 62 L.Q.Rev. 141 (1946).

2a. Even "laws" in the formal sense of the word sometimes are kept secret in communist countries. See H. J. Berman and P. B. Maggs, Disarmament Inspection Under Soviet Law 12–13 (1967).

3. See In re Volencki's Estate, 35 N.J. Super. 351, 114 A.2d 26 (1955), and other cases cited by Heyman, The Nonresident Alien's Right to Succession Under the "Iron Curtain Rule", 52 N.W.U.L.Rev. 221, 233–4 (1957).

Problems of this kind arise very often in deportation proceedings. By statute, the Attorney General is directed not to deport or return an alien to a particular country "if the Attorney General determines that such alien's life or freedom would be threatened in such country on account of race, religion, nationality, membership in a particular social group, or political opinion". 8 U.S.C.A. § 1253(h), as amended. The exceedingly numerous cases in which this provision has been invoked, are discussed in 1A Gordon & Rosenfield, Immigration Law and Procedure, § 5.16b (Rev. Ed., 1986, and Cum. Supp.).

4. See Canadian Overseas Ores Ltd. v. Compania de Acero del Pacifico S.A., 528 F.Supp. 1337, 1342–43 (S.D.N.Y. 1982), aff'd 727 F.2d 274 (2d Cir. 1984); In re Wells' Estate, 204 Misc. 975, 126 N.Y.S.2d 441 (Surr.Ct.N.Y.Co., 1953). See also Gordon & Rosenfield, supra n. 3.

5. For surveys of such statutes, see R. Solkin, United States, in the comparative study by D. Campbell (Ed.), Legal Aspects of Alien Acquisition of Real Property 153,

of these statutes are intended to be protective; they direct that so long as the non-resident alien heir, under the law of his own country, could not freely receive and enjoy the proceeds of his inheritance, such proceeds be kept for him in official custody here;[6] should he come to this country at a later time, his share will be paid over to him. Other statutes, in force in a dwindling number of states, provide for escheat of the non-resident alien's inheritance unless his country grants reciprocal inheritance rights to U.S. citizens. In order to determine the reciprocity issue arising under statutes of the latter type, state courts in many decisions explored the question whether *as a matter of law in action as well as book law* U.S. citizens would be able to inherit, and as heirs to receive, property situated in a particular foreign country. In Zschernig v. Miller, 389 U.S. 429, 88 S.Ct. 664 (1968), the U.S. Supreme Court disapproved these decisions. The Court reaffirmed an earlier holding[7] to the effect that such a reciprocity statute, on its face, is not necessarily unconstitutional; but the majority of the Court laid down the novel rule that in applying the reciprocity test, a state court may engage in *"no more than a routine reading"* of the foreign inheritance statutes. According to the majority opinion written by Mr. Justice Douglas, a state court intrudes into the area of foreign relations reserved to the national Government if it finds *on the basis of a study of actual practice* that the foreign country does not grant reciprocal rights to U.S. citizens. A state court's inquiry into a foreign country's *law in action* would, according to Mr. Justice Douglas, embarrass the United States Government in the conduct of its foreign policy.[8]

It is to be hoped that this unsound doctrine, which in effect puts blindfolds over the eyes of state court judges,[8a] soon will be reconsidered, and that in any event it will not be expanded beyond the area of aliens' inheritance rights.[9]

---

at 167–85 (1980); W. C. Snouffer, Nonresident Alien Inheritance Statutes and Foreign Policy—A Conflict?, 47 Or.L.Rev. 390, at 400 (1968). See also Comment, 13 Vill. L.Rev. 148 (1967); Note, 25 Syr.L.Rev. 597 (1974).

6. See ibid.

7. Clark v. Allen, 331 U.S. 503, 67 S.Ct. 1431 (1947).

8. This assertion by Mr. Justice Douglas was pure fancy. The Solicitor General of the United States, appearing as amicus curiae in the *Zschernig* case, after consultation with the U.S. State Department emphatically stated that as a matter of experience the implementation of state reciprocity statutes (of the kind involved in that case) has had no substantial impact on the foreign relations of this country. See the opinions of Justices Douglas, Stewart and Harlan in the *Zschernig* case.

8a. Cf. Estate of Hajridin, 33 N.Y.2d 955, 353 N.Y.S.2d 731, 309 N.E.2d 131 (1974), where in a brief memorandum opinion the New York Court of Appeals politely underscored the senselessness of the *Zschernig* limitation on the judicial power of state courts.

9. Prompted, at least in part, by the U.S. Supreme Court's *Zschernig* holding, the California Legislature in 1974 repealed the California reciprocity statute (Probate Code Section 259). See Note, Trust & Estate Planning: The Effect of Soviet Policies on Legacies from Abroad, 1 Hastings Int. & Comp.L.Rev. 195, 200–01 (1977).

Concerning the impact of the *Zschernig* holding on the *protective* type of "Iron Curtain" statutes (see supra, text at n. 6), the reader is referred to the discussion in the Note, 25 Syr.L.Rev. 597, at 616–21 (1974), where further references can be found.

Quaere whether the *Zschernig* doctrine applies in a case where an express provision of the testator's Will (rather than a state statute) conditions a legacy upon the foreign legatee's ability to obtain use, enjoyment and control of the property left to him. The question was raised (and discussed by the lower court), but ultimately left undecided in the interesting case of Will of Danilchenko, 64 Misc.2d 665, 315 N.Y.S.2d 153 (Surr. Ct., Dutchess Co., 1970), aff'd by a divided court, 37 A.D.2d 587, 323 N.Y.S.2d 150 (1971), aff'd without op., 30 N.Y.2d 504, 329 N.Y.S.2d 820, 280 N.E.2d 650 (1972). Cf. Matter of Kosek, 31

(3) *The Reasons for Studying Law In Action.*

(a) For the practicing lawyer, exploration of the law-in-action aspects of a foreign legal system becomes necessary in a variety of contexts. The litigator is not the only type of legal practitioner facing the task of such exploration. Knowledge of the actual practices as well as the book law of a foreign nation may be required, for instance, in order to determine the feasibility and reliability of treaty arrangements with that nation.[9a] Similarly, a study of the "investment climate" in a given country will have to include a thorough look at the social and institutional elements conditioning the certainty and enforceability of legal rights.

When we turn to litigated matters, we find that the outcome of innumerable cases has been influenced by proof of foreign law in action. The principal case furnishes an illustration. Only a few further examples can be given here:

(aa) Suppose the government of Graustark is interested in an action pending here. Witness *W*, a resident (and perhaps an official) of Graustark, testifies by deposition or in response to letters rogatory. His testimony is favorable to the government of Graustark. In evaluating the credibility of *W*, the court must examine whether under the conditions actually prevailing in Graustark, the witness, had he testified differently, would have had to fear arbitrary reprisals.[10] The same is true if *W* comes here and testifies in open court, but thereafter intends to return to Graustark.[11]

(bb) A motion for dismissal on grounds of *forum non conveniens* should be denied if the forum to which the motion seeks to relegate the plaintiff "is lacking in due process".[12]

In a recent case in which the allegedly more convenient forum was Iran, a federal District Court rejected defendant's *forum non conveniens* motion, saying:

N.Y.2d 475, 341 N.Y.S.2d 593, 294 N.E.2d 188 (1973). See also Note, 1 Hastings Int. & Comp.L.Rev. 195, at 208–12 (1977).

9a. Thorough and searching studies of foreign law have been undertaken for this exceedingly practical purpose. See, e.g., H. J. Berman & P. B. Maggs, Disarmament Inspection Under Soviet Law (1967); Z. L. Zile, R. Sharlet & L. C. Love, The Soviet Legal System and Arms Inspection: A Case Study in Policy Implementation (1972), reviewed by J.N. Hazard in 72 Colum.L.Rev. 1448 (1972) and by G. Ginsburgs in 21 Am.J.Comp.L. 188 (1973).

10. Cf. Zwack, v. Kraus Bros. & Co., 133 F.Supp. 929, 936–7 (S.D.N.Y. 1955), mod. on another point, and otherwise aff'd 237 F.2d 255 (2d Cir. 1956).

It has been suggested that *W*'s deposition should not even be taken, and that to do so would be a waste of time, if conditions in Graustark are such that the testimony of the witness is likely to be influenced by fear. The courts, however, have granted motions for the taking of depositions and the issuance of letters rogatory regardless of possible pressure upon the witness, saying that "the evaluation of evidence must wait until it is formally produced" at the trial. In re De Lowe's Estate, 143 N.Y.S.2d 270 (Surr.Ct.N.Y.Co., 1955). To the same effect see Bator v. Hungarian Commercial Bank of Pest, 275 App.Div. 826, 90 N.Y.S.2d 35 (1st Dept. 1949); Ecco High Frequency Corp. v. Amtorg Trading Corp., 196 Misc. 405, 94 N.Y.S.2d 400 (S.Ct.N.Y. Co., 1949), aff'd 276 App.Div. 827, 93 N.Y.S.2d 178 (1st Dept.; Van Voorhis, J., dissenting).

11. See Matter of Draganoff, 46 Misc.2d 167, 173, 259 N.Y.S.2d 20 (Surr.Ct.Westch. Co., 1965).

12. Gantuz v. Dominican S.S. Line, 22 Misc.2d 567, 198 N.Y.S.2d 421 (Sup.Ct. Bronx Co., 1960). To the same effect see Constructora Ordaz, N.V. v. Orinoco Mining Co., 262 F.Supp. 90 (D.Del. 1966); Flota Maritima Browning v. The Ciudad de la Habana, 181 F.Supp. 301 (D.Md. 1960).

". . . I have no confidence whatsoever in the plaintiff's ability to obtain justice at the hands of the courts administered by Iranian mullahs. On the contrary, I consider that if the plaintiffs returned to Iran to prosecute this claim, they would probably be shot." [12a]

In another recent case decided by the same court,[12b] a Bermuda corporation (CANOVER) sued a government-owned Chilean corporation (CAP) for payment of goods sold and delivered, and for repayment of a loan. CAP moved to dismiss on *forum non conveniens* grounds, arguing that the action could more conveniently be tried in Chile. In denying the motion, the court stated (at 1342–43):

. . . CANOVER has raised serious questions about the independence of the Chilean judiciary vis a vis the military junta currently in power. Having carefully considered the views of eminent experts on both sides, a significant doubt remains whether [CANOVER] could be assured of a fair trial in the Chilean courts in view of the fact that CAP is a state owned corporation. Specifically, the expressed power of the junta to amend or rescind constitutional provisions by decree impugns the continuing independence of the judiciary regardless of the fact that it appears that the constitutional provisions relating to the independence of the judiciary are currently in force. Affidavit of Henry P. DeVries, Professor of Latin American Law at Columbia University School of Law, ¶5, *citing* Executive Decree of September 11, 1973; Executive Decree No. 128 of November 12, 1973; Executive Decree No. 527 of June 17, 1974; Executive Decree No. 788 of December 2, 1974. There is some suggestion that the junta has in fact interceded in a pending case to request reversal of an interlocutory decision where the government was not a party. *Id.* at n. 6. While we do not hold as a matter of fact that the Chilean judiciary is not independent of the junta or that CANOVER could not possibly receive a fair trial there, the doubts raised are sufficiently serious to put the burden on CAP, the party asserting the appropriateness of the Chilean forum, to demonstrate its adequacy. Since we are unable to conclude from the differing views expressed by the experts that Chile would be an adequate forum, CAP has failed to carry its burden of persuasion that CANOVER's choice of forum should be disturbed. Accordingly, its motion to dismiss the complaint under the doctrine of *forum non conveniens* is denied.

By the same token, a contractual forum-selection clause purporting to confer exclusive jurisdiction on the courts of country X will not prevent an action in an American court if it can be shown that under the actual conditions prevailing in X the parties could not obtain a fair trial in the courts of X. It was so held, with

---

12a. Rasoulzadeh v. Associated Press, 574 F.Supp. 854, at 860–61 (S.D.N.Y. 1983), aff'd 767 F.2d 908 (2d Cir. 1985). See also Continental Grain Export Corp. v. Ministry of War—ETKA Co., 603 F.Supp. 724, 729 (S.D.N.Y. 1984), where it is pointed out that Iranian attorneys are unwilling to be retained by U.S. clients because of fear of persecution.

12b. Canadian Overseas Ores Ltd. v. Compania de Acero del Pacifico S.A., 528 F.Supp. 1337 (S.D.N.Y. 1982), aff'd 727 F.2d 274 (2d Cir. 1984).

specific reference to the post-revolutionary "Islamic courts" in Iran, in a number of recent cases.[12c]

(cc) The judgment of a foreign court will not be recognized or enforced here unless it was rendered "upon regular proceedings, after due citation or voluntary appearance . . ., and under a system of jurisprudence likely to secure an impartial administration of justice. . . ." [13] Whether the foreign court was "impartial", and whether its proceedings were "regular", can be determined only after examining the realities as well as the rules of its procedure.[14] This should be kept in mind, in particular, when the question arises whether effect should be given to foreign criminal judgments. Suppose D, a refugee from Graustark, was convicted of some offenses by a Graustark court.[15] Is this a "conviction" which under our immigration laws forever bars D from entering the United States? [16] Is it a "conviction" within the meaning of our recidivist statutes? [17] Is it a "conviction" even though there is no judicial independence in Graustark, and everybody knows that the Graustark Ministry of Justice often gives telephonic instructions to criminal courts, suggesting conviction of the accused, and specifying the expected sentence? [18] Would it be necessary to prove that

---

12c. See, e.g., McDonnell Douglas Corp. v. Islamic Republic of Iran, 757 F.2d 341, at 345–46 (8th Cir. 1985), where numerous other cases to the same effect are cited. See also supra n. 12a. But note that where an exclusive forum-selection clause is involved, the burden of proof may be on the party contending that the contractually chosen forum is inadequate.

13. Hilton v. Guyot, 159 U.S. 113, 202, 16 S.Ct. 139, 158 (1895). This dictum is good law even in those jurisdictions which reject the reciprocity doctrine announced in the same case. See Restatement, Second, Conflict of Laws § 98, Comment c (1971); W. L. M. Reese, The Status in This Country of Judgments Rendered Abroad, 50 Colum.L.Rev. 783, 795–96 (1950); C. H. Peterson, Foreign Country Judgments and the Second Restatement of Conflict of Laws, 72 Colum.L.Rev. 220, 249–51 (1972).

14. Provided the foreign judgment is regular on its face, it would seem that the burden of alleging and proving any defect of the foreign proceedings is on the party opposing recognition or enforcement of such judgment. See Peterson, ibid.

15. Perhaps the conviction was for an "economic crime"; perhaps it was for "tax evasion", the tax law being administered discriminatorily and as an instrument of the "class struggle". See the instructive German cases reported by M. M. Schoch in 55 Am.J.Int.L. 944–97 (1961).

16. See R. B. Schlesinger, Comment, 2 Am.J.Comp.L. 392, 397–99 (1953), and supra p. 29.

17. Under recidivist statutes, a former felony "conviction" in a foreign country often may lead to enhanced punishment. See, e.g., California Penal Code Section 668. Of course, if the former conviction is invalid, it may not be used in sentencing. United States v. Tucker, 404 U.S. 443, 92 S.Ct. 589 (1972). But what criteria should be employed in order to determine whether a foreign-country conviction (assuming it is valid under the law of the foreign country in question) must be treated as invalid by a court in the United States? It has been held that a foreign conviction is not necessarily invalidated by the foreign court's failure to grant the defendant a specific right (right to counsel) to which he would have been entitled in an American court. See Houle v. United States, 493 F.2d 915 (5th Cir. 1974). The opinion in that case, however, implicitly recognizes that the foreign conviction would have to be treated as invalid if the foreign system "has failed to provide a fair trial" (id. at 916). See also supra p. 29. In determining whether the foreign conviction was based on a fair trial, the sentencing court will have to look at the foreign country's entire criminal process as it affected the defendant; actual practice as well as the law in the books will have to be considered.

18. See the principal case, and the article by Professor Kirchheimer cited by the court. Cf. Marsh, supra n. 2, at 374; International Commission of Jurists, "Justice Enslaved", A Collection of Documents on the Abuse of Justice for Political Ends, pp. 126 ff. (1955).

such instructions were given in D's case, or would it suffice to prove the general practice?

(b) The comparatist, even if he is not a practicing lawyer faced with questions such as those suggested above, cannot afford to ignore the realities of the world in which he lives. Whatever his purpose in studying foreign institutions, he deceives himself if he limits his task to what Dean Wigmore called "the barren dissection of verbal texts".[19] This danger of self-deception is acute. Like many of the other pitfalls in comparative law, it stems from the indiscriminate use of domestic experience in dealing with foreign problems. In his own habitat, every experienced lawyer is a "practicing anthropologist", to use an expression coined by the late Jerome Frank. By living and practicing in his community, he becomes intuitively aware of the way in which legal institutions actually work;[20] but when he tries to penetrate into a foreign system, he has no such intuition or experience to guide him.

Once a student of comparative law recognizes this handicap, he is well on his way to overcome it. In the light of such recognition, he will be able more realistically to define his projects, to ask more searching questions and to become more critical in evaluating the sources from which valid answers can be obtained. Healthy skepticism thus may help to forge a sharpened tool for inquiry, a tool which in a limited area of human endeavor may be of some value in reducing man's ignorance of man.

19. Wigmore, More Jottings on Comparative Legal Ideas and Institutions, 6 Tulane L.Rev. 244, 263 (1932).

20. For example, in those American jurisdictions which still adhere to the contributory negligence rule, no local lawyer will be misled by the book-learning concerning that rule. He knows that juries do not always take such learning seriously.

APPENDIX

A BRIEF EXCURSUS ON COMPARATIVE AND FOREIGN LAW RESEARCH: HOW TO FIND THE RELEVANT MATERIALS

The main body of this book contains many hints as to the types of sources and authorities that should be consulted by a researcher facing legal problems arising under the law of a foreign country, especially a civil-law country. The purpose of this brief Appendix is to supplement and round out the previous discussions of the techniques of "where to look" in comparative and foreign law research.[1]

I. English-Language Materials

1. *Basic Tools*

Even a researcher who has to limit himself to works written in English, has an amazing wealth of materials available to him. The problem is to find them. The most useful first step ordinarily will be to consult that paragon of bibliographies, Professor C. Szladits' "Bibliography on Foreign and Comparative Law". The first volume of the Szladits bibliography, published in 1955, covers the period up to 1953; later periods are covered in subsequent volumes, and updating supplements have appeared annually in the American Journal of Comparative Law.[1a] Broken down by subjects (and, in an ingenious way, also by countries), the Szladits bibliography lists articles as well as books. It covers all relevant English-language writings, whether of broad or narrow scope, whether comparative or dealing with a single foreign system.[2]

In addition to the Szladits bibliography, the Index of Legal Periodicals as well as the Index of Foreign Legal Periodicals is available as a basic research tool. Even experienced scholars never cease to be

1. For more elaborate essays on the techniques of comparative and foreign law research, see M. P. Goderich and J. Stepan, Foreign and Comparative Law, in M. L. Cohen & R. C. Berring, How to Find the Law 609–637 (8th ed. 1983); S. A. Bayitch, Common Law and Civil Law: A Bibliographical Essay, 4 Inter-Am.L.Rev. 349 (1962). A helpful recent introduction to some major comparative law materials in English is K. Schwerin, Comparative Law Reflections, A Bibliographical Survey, 79 Nw.U.L.Rev. 1315 (1985).

1a. Prof. C. Szladits died in 1986. Nevertheless, a bound supplement volume of his bibliography covering the period 1978–1983 is still scheduled for publication. His latest annual bibliography for the American Journal of Comparative Law appeared in 1986.

2. There are also other, more specialized, bibliographies that focus on a specific subject, or on a particular country or group of countries. E.g. E. Weisbaum, Pacific Rim Legal Bibliography: A Guide to Legal Information Sources, 20 Int'l Law. 1401 (1986). For a selected bibliography limited to business law, see E. E. Murphy, Jr., A Guide to Foreign Law Source Material and Foreign Counsel, 19 Int'l Law. 39 (1985). (Bibliographic materials frequently appear in The International Lawyer). The Szladits Bibliography lists many other specialized bibliographies.

amazed at the incredible wealth of English-language articles on foreign and comparative law which over the years have appeared in American law reviews as well as in legal periodicals published in the British Commonwealth and elsewhere. Most of the law reviews in question can be found on the shelves of every medium-sized law library. The skillful researcher, who makes thorough use of the Index, thus can dig up a good deal of information on foreign and comparative law even in a library that does not specialize in foreign law materials.

Another basic tool with which the researcher should become familiar, is the International Encyclopedia of Comparative Law.[3] Planned as a seventeen-volume work, the Encyclopedia is not yet completed. Only volume XI/1 (1983) and volume XI/2 (1986), both covering torts, have been completed and are available in bound form. Many individual chapters of other volumes have been published separately. Some volumes, in particular volume I (National Reports),[4] appear to be nearing completion.[5] Each chapter contains a selected bibliography both of comparative and of single-country writings on the subject. In the areas of substantive private law and of civil procedure the Encyclopedia is becoming a valuable—although as yet not wholly comprehensive—tool for the initial stages of research. It should be kept in mind, however, that the bulk of public-law subjects and the areas of criminal law and criminal procedure are not intended to be covered by the Encyclopedia.

2. *Directions of Research*

In employing the basic tools mentioned above, and the further materials discovered by their use, the researcher should realize that when he deals with problems of foreign or comparative law, he usually has available to him both a *geographic approach* and a *subject-matter approach*, and that the two approaches complement each other. This affects the very mechanics of research. In using the Index of Legal Periodicals, for example, it is often advisable to look not only under the subject-matter headings, but also under the appropriate geographic heading that points to the country or region in question.

Even apart from such matters of mere mechanics, it is always important to keep in mind that in approaching a problem of foreign or comparative law, one can emphasize either the specific subject-matter or the fact that one deals with the legal system of a particular country or region. Suppose, for instance, that a reader of this book wishes to study the German land register, and to acquire more detailed information about that institution than is offered on pp. 684–696 supra. This research may take a geographic direction or a subject-matter direction (or both).

3. Professor K. Zweigert is the Responsible Editor and Professor U. Drobnig the Executive Secretary of the Encyclopedia.

4. See infra, text preceding n. 6.

5. For a list of the chapters published until 1980, see A. Sprudzs, The International Encyclopedia of Comparative Law: A Bibliographical Status Report, 28 Am.J. Comp.L. 93 (1980).

a. *The Geographic Direction.* A legal rule or institution can be correctly comprehended only in the context of the legal system of which it is a part. To come back to our example, it is clear that the rules concerning the land register which have been developed in German law, are apt to be misunderstood by a researcher who is unfamiliar with the general features of the German legal system. For such a researcher it might be advisable, therefore, to begin his work by seeking to learn something about the systematic and structural aspects of German law. A number of works which can be used for this purpose—including the National Reports in the first volume of the International Encyclopedia of Comparative Law—are mentioned and discussed supra at pp. 311–315.[6]

In addition, the researcher should know that many of the important national legal systems have been described in more comprehensive book-length introductory surveys. Some of these surveys have been repeatedly cited on the preceding pages: E.g., the two-volume work by E. J. Cohn et al., Manual of German Law (2nd Ed., 1968–71); N. Horn, H. Kötz & G. Leser, German Private and Commercial Law, An Introduction (T. Weir, tr. 1982); Amos and Walton's Introduction to French Law (3rd Ed. by F. H. Lawson, A. E. Anton and L. N. Brown, 1967); and The Italian Legal System—an Introduction, by M. Cappelletti, J. H. Merryman and J. M. Perillo (1967).[7]

To come back once more to our land register example: a researcher using Cohn's Manual of German Law would find in the first volume of that work not only a general introduction to the structure of the German Civil Code, but also (on pp. 186–202) a concise discussion of the very topic he is interested in, i.e., the German system of land registration. Moreover, the same book (on pp. 303–307) also contains samples of actual entries in a German land register.

By perusing the relevant parts of Cohn's Manual of German Law, our researcher also will have found, among other leads for further inquiry, several references to the relevant provisions of the German Civil Code. If his linguistic abilities are limited to English, he will then look for an English translation of that Code. A number of such translations are available, one of them of fairly recent vintage.[8] Many of the basic codes of important civil-law countries have been similarly translated; a listing of such translations can be found in the above-mentioned Szladits bibliography.

6. Some first-glance information on the law of a given foreign country may be obtained also from the Law Digests in Vol. VII of the Martindale-Hubbell Law Directory.

7. See also, G. L. Certoma, The Italian Legal System (1985). Similar works, surveying the legal systems of other countries or groups of countries, are listed in the Szladits bibliography. See also Goderich & Stepan, and K. Schwerin, supra n. 1. For some purposes, especially when the topic to be investigated has conflict of laws aspects, the researcher should consult, also, the relevant volume in the series "Bilateral Studies in Private International Law", published under the auspices of Columbia University's Parker School of Foreign and Comparative Law. E.g.: U. Drobnig, American-German Private International Law (2d ed., 1972).

8. See supra p. 533.

The researcher working in the business and commercial law area has particularly numerous sources of information at her or his disposal. There is a steadily increasing number of works on "business transactions" or "doing business" in certain countries or regions. See, e.g., the four volume loose-leaf work by B. Rüster (Ed.), Business Transactions in Germany (FRG) (1983–84). More summary, but reasonably up-to-date information on a number of countries is available in the "Doing Business in Europe" volume of the CCH Common Market Reporter.

b. *The Subject-Matter Direction.* A researcher working on a specific topic of foreign or comparative law will consult bibliographies (see supra), library catalogues and the indexes of legal periodicals in order to find a book or article dealing with his topic. If he is lucky, he will find a book or article which treats the topic comparatively, i.e. from the standpoint of several legal systems, including the one in which the researcher is primarily interested. Let us come back, once again, to our land register example. By making proper use of the Szladits bibliography, one is led to the English translation of the two-volume comparative treatise by V. Kruse (cited supra p. 685) which deals with the land registration systems of a number of countries, including Germany.[9]

If he fails to find a comparative treatment of his topic, or if the comparative treatments he has found do not answer all of his questions, the researcher will try to find a relevant single-country discussion. Lacking other starting points, he will again have to turn to the above-mentioned bibliographical and other reference tools in order to find English-language discussions of this kind.

II. Materials in Other Languages

1. *Research Tools Used in Foreign Countries*

A researcher who desires to study some aspect of the law of a particular foreign country, and who is familiar with that country's language, of course has an enormous wealth of sources and authorities available to him.[9a] But if his previous research experience has been limited to domestic law, he faces considerable difficulties. Even if he obtains access to a library that has a sufficiently large foreign law collection, he will soon find that the research tools to be used are quite different from those to which he is accustomed. Before he can dig into law books enshrining an alien system, he must first acquaint himself with the sources, authorities and research tools that are commonly consulted by lawyers practicing under that system. If he has studied

9. Eventually, a comparative treatment of land registration systems will appear also in the form of Chs. 4 and 14 of Vol. VI of the International Encyclopedia of Comparative Law; but these chapters have not yet been published. Some brief and rather general comparative observations on land registration can be found in a chapter (of the same volume) that is available now,

i.e., Ch. 2, Structural Variations in Property Law, at 6–7 (1975).

9a. For a list of bibliographies covering the legal literature of a particular country or region, or pertaining to a specific subject, see Goderich & Stepan, supra n. 1, at 615–20.

the materials presented in the earlier parts of this book, he will have acquired a measure of familiarity with the types of sources and authorities used by lawyers in civil-law countries. More extensive information of the same kind, collected for the specific purpose of aiding those engaged in foreign law research, is to be found in the series of volumes entitled "Guides to Foreign Legal Materials" which have been published under the auspices of Columbia University's Parker School of Foreign and Comparative Law. One of these volumes is the valuable "Guide to Foreign Legal Materials: French-German-Swiss" by Professor C. Szladits (1959).[9b] A brief but useful survey of comparative and foreign legal literature can be found also in R. David and J. E. C. Brierly, Major Legal Systems in the World Today, at 577–613 (3d Ed. 1985).

In dealing with a civil-law system, the researcher often will find that his starting point is a code provision, or a set of such provisions. Thus an up-to-date edition of the applicable code or codes is indispensable. An annotated code edition,[10] or—even better—a systematic commentary,[11] will furnish further references to relevant cases and legal writings.[12] In some civil-law countries, such as Germany, there are also collections of judicial decisions (reported in full or in summary form) that are arranged in the order of the relevant code sections.

Auxiliary statutes, as distinguished from provisions of the systematically arranged basic codes, are notoriously hard to find and are often overlooked by the novice. To guard against this danger, it is wise never to rely exclusively on the bare text of the code, but to treat code provisions as mere starting points for further research; the code provisions will point to the relevant sections of commentaries and treatises, and in works of the latter kind the reader normally will find references, not only to cases and scholarly writings, but to related auxiliary statutes as well.

2. Linguistic Aids and Shortcuts

The researcher who uses foreign-language materials but is not completely familiar with every nuance of foreign legal terminology, will tend to turn to a bilingual or multilingual dictionary. Many such dictionaries are available; they are listed in the Szladits bibliography. Although they must be used with caution (see supra pp. 871–72) such

---

9b. A revised edition was published as: C. Szladits & C. M. Germain, Guide to Foreign Legal Materials: French (2d rev. ed. 1985).

Cf. F. Dessomontet & T. Ansay (Eds.), Introduction to Swiss Law (1983). The 14 page bibliography contained in this book, which is limited to materials available in English, shows that there is an amazing wealth of English-language treatments of Swiss law.

10. E.g., The Petits Codes Dalloz in France.

11. See supra p. 224.

12. References to many of the leading commentaries and treatises can be found in Vol. 5, No. 45 (Foreign Law) of the valuable work entitled "Law Books Recommended for Libraries", published by the Association of American Law Schools under the editorship of Professor H. Bitner (1968). See also Vol. 1, No. 11 (Comparative Law) of the same work (1968, with 1974 Supp.). Both the "Foreign Law" and the "Comparative Law" parts of this work were prepared by Professor C. Szladits.

translation tools can be helpful. In recent years, the authors of an increasing number of such dictionaries have come to realize that it is not always possible to translate a term developed in one legal system into an exactly equivalent term belonging to another language and another legal system. Modern dictionaries, therefore, exhibit a growing tendency to substitute explanations for mere translations, thus becoming more sophisticated and more reliable tools.[12a]

Quite often, the linguistic barriers to one's research can be overcome by the use of a third language, i.e. of a language that is neither the researcher's mother tongue nor the language of the legal system under investigation. Suppose, for instance, the researcher is interested in the Penal Code of Ruritania, but is unfamiliar with the Ruritanian language. He should not give up his search when he discovers that there is no English translation of that Code. Many codes, and especially penal codes, have been translated into German or French. Thus, a researcher having a reading knowledge of either of these languages may well be capable of immersing himself into the translated text of the Ruritanian Code, even though there is no English translation. Quite generally, a wealth of materials and legal literature, dealing with the laws of every corner of the world, becomes available to those who have a reading knowledge of German, French, Italian or Spanish. Many examples of such a "third language" shortcut could be given. Even Soviet-Russian textbooks can be studied by a researcher who has no knowledge of any Slavic language, provided he knows German; the reason is that a number of such books have been translated into German for the benefit of East German lawyers and law students.

3. *Tools Which Do Not Exist*

There are several types of research tools that are part of the lifeblood of an American lawyer but do not exist in civil-law countries. There is no Shepard or similar citator for any civil-law jurisdiction except Louisiana,[13] and most civil-law countries have nothing comparable to our Digests and Encyclopedias.[14] The relevant cases are usually found through citations in commentaries and textbooks.[15] The most important judicial decisions, whether or not officially reported, are frequently printed or reprinted in full by legal periodicals, together

---

12a. T. Reynolds, Comparative Legal Dictionaries, 34 Am.J.Comp.L. 551 (1986) usefully surveys both bilingual and multilingual law dictionaries mediating between English and languages of the European continent.

13. In some countries, e.g., in Germany, there are loose-leaf services intended to make it easier to find pertinent cases; but, like the commentaries, they are keyed to sections of codes or statutes. Therefore, they can be used only by one familiar with the structure of the codes and auxiliary statutes. See also infra n. 15.

14. In France, there are alphabetically arranged encyclopedias, which in effect constitute treatises of encyclopedic coverage. For references, see Goderich & Stepan, supra n. 1, at 631.

15. For updating purposes one may have to use the annual or cumulative indexes of case reports or periodicals. But in a few countries one can find special publications containing combined annual indexes of judicial decisions and legal writings, such as the West German *Fundhefte* or the recently initiated French *Bibliographie juridique générale*.

with annotations by practitioners or scholars who are known as experts in the particular field. These annotations may be a source of further, amplifying case citations.[15a]

III. International Treaties

The practicing lawyer dealing with transnational legal problems has to keep in mind that a client's cause may be affected not only by the municipal laws of foreign nations, but also by treaties and other international agreements. Such agreements "may govern the inheritance of property and the withdrawal of its proceeds across international boundaries, may direct the channels of international trade, may dictate the choice and manner of making investments abroad, may facilitate the use of commercial arbitration in private international disputes, and may protect the procedural and substantive rights of foreign residents," [16] whether they be individuals or corporations. Applicable treaty provisions, and cases construing them, are not always easy to find. Even more difficult is the problem of obtaining up-to-date information as to what nations have ratified a multilateral treaty, and whether a given treaty has been amended, suspended, or abrogated. But for those who cannot find their way through the minefields and boobytraps of treaty research, some expert guidance is available.[17]

IV. Computer-Assisted Legal Research

To an increasing extent, it is possible to obtain access to foreign legal materials through computers or terminals located in the United States.[18] On LEXIS, for instance, French materials from about 1970 on may be retrieved, as well as materials on European Community and British law. United Kingdom and European Community law, and some other materials, are similarly available on WESTLAW. Some data bases not specializing in legal materials, such as Compuserve, also provide a variety of foreign legal materials.[19] It is even possible, by making appropriate arrangements, to get access from the United States

---

15a. In addition to general periodicals, in many countries there is a wealth of more specialized periodic publications dealing with specific topics. They are intended not only as outlets for scholarly views, but as research tools as well. Thus they contain, in addition to articles, also reprints of cases, sometimes with annotations, references to pertinent new statutes and regulations, and perhaps to other quasi-legislative or administrative materials, and bibliographies.

16. Hynning, Treaty Law for the Private Practitioner, 23 U.Chi.L.Rev. 36 (1955).

17. See M. O. Price, H. Bitner & S. R. Bysiewicz, Effective Legal Research 80–95, 420–23 (4th ed. 1979); V. Mostecky, International Law, in M. L. Cohen & R. C. Berring, How To Find the Law 638, at 644–56 (8th ed., 1983); J. M. Jacobstein & R. M. Mersky, Fundamentals of Legal Research 386–410 (3d ed. 1985).

18. Developments in this area are rapid, so that descriptions become quickly outdated. For recent comments, see J. C. Goedan, Legal Comparativists and Computerized Legal Information Systems: General Problems and the Present German Status of Computerized Legal Information, 14 Int. J. of Legal Information 1 (1986); M. P. Goderich & J. Stepan, supra note 1, at 635–36.

19. Available materials change rapidly. Detailed information can be obtained from Compuserve and similar organizations.

to CELEX, the European Communities' own data base for Community legal materials.[20]

20. For details see E. Hardt, On Line to Europe, in the October 1987 issue of *Europe*, p. 21.

INDEX

[**Note:** In using the Index, the reader should keep in mind that most parts of this book center on legal systems of the civil law orbit, and that specific illustrations and references often point to the law of a particular civil law country (most frequently France, Germany or Switzerland). Therefore, specific subject headings may appear in this Index, not as main headings, but as sub-headings under main headings such as Civil Law, Codes, France, Germany, etc.]

GERMANY—Cont'd
General principles of tort liability, 553–554.
Liability, 552ff.
  For judicial negligence, 609, 610.
  Of public officials, 510, 608ff.
Liability of state, 501ff, 609.
  Jurisdiction, 502ff.
Meaning of "fault," 553, 720.
Negligence, 553, 554.
Products liability, 560–561, 566.
Road Traffic Act, 553, 558.

GESTAPO, 725–728

GIFTS
Immoral causa, 747.

GLOSSATORS, 270ff

G.M.B.H.
See Limited Liability Company.

GOVERNMENT CONTRACTS, 512ff

GRAFT, 880–882

GREAT DICHOTOMIES, 293ff

GREECE
Civil Code, 546–547, 737, 756–757.
  Abuse of rights, 756–757.
  Rebus sic stantibus, 737.
Influence of Corpus Juris Civilis, 255–256.
Judicial review, 516.

GROTIUS, 280

GUARANTY
Form requirement, 589ff.

GUIANA
See Guyana.

GUYANA
  See also Roman-Dutch Law.
History, 247.
Legal system, 245ff, 290, 311.
  Common law influence, 320.

HAGUE CONFERENCE ON PRIVATE INTERNATIONAL LAW, 34, 402, 530
Convention Abolishing the Requirement of Legalization for Foreign Public Documents, 137.
United States membership, 409.

HAMMURABI, 9

HANDLUNGSFAEHIGKEIT, 871–872

HARMONIZATION
See Unification.

HINDU LAW, 317

HISTORY
See Civil Law, History; Codes, History; Universities.

HOLMES
(Mr. Justice Holmes), 54, 98, 101.

HUBER, EUGEN
See Switzerland, Codes, Civil Code.

HUMAN RIGHTS
See European Court of Human Rights; European Commission on Human Rights.

HUNGARY
Conflict of laws, 847.
Legal system, 290, 328.

I.G. FARBEN, 817

IMMIGRATION LAWS
References to foreign institutions, 29, 889–890.

IN PARI TURPITUDINE, 713

INCOME TAX
Meaning of term, 875ff.

INDIA
Legal system, 318.

INDONESIA
Adat law, 326.
Dualist system, 326.
Legal system, 326–327.
Marriage and divorce, 335.
Religious courts, 326.

INSTITUTES OF COMPARATIVE LAW, 225–226, 441

INTERLOCUTORY ORDER
See Civil Law, Procedure.

INTERNATIONAL COURT OF JUSTICE
General principles of law recognized by civilized nations, 35, 89ff.
Statute of, 35.

INTERNATIONAL JUDICIAL COOPERATION
  See also Conventions.
Consular conventions, 410–412.
Convention on Recognition and Enforcement of Foreign Arbitral Awards, 472–473.
Convention on Service Abroad of Judicial and Extra-judicial Documents in Civil and Commercial Matters, 412–413.
Convention on Settlement of Investment Disputes between States and Nationals of other States, 473.
Letters rogatory, 406–408.

†

Jurisdiction

Personal Jurisdiction
- Domicile (corp seat) of △
- consent
  a) general appearance
  b) consent in advance

     i) choice of law
     ii) choice of forum

- Long Arm
  a) tort -
  b) contract
     i) where made
     ii) where to be performed ✱ (majority states look here)
- Other basis of jurisdiction (improper or EXORBITANT)
  x) transient jurisdiction - American
  b) Nationality of 𝚷 - civil law country
  - △ has property in the forum